BaseBall america®

2009 PROSPECT
HANDBOOK

BASEBALL AMERICA INC. · DURHAM, N.C.

FOR GREAT PROSPECTS COVERAGE
ALL YEAR, VISIT ...

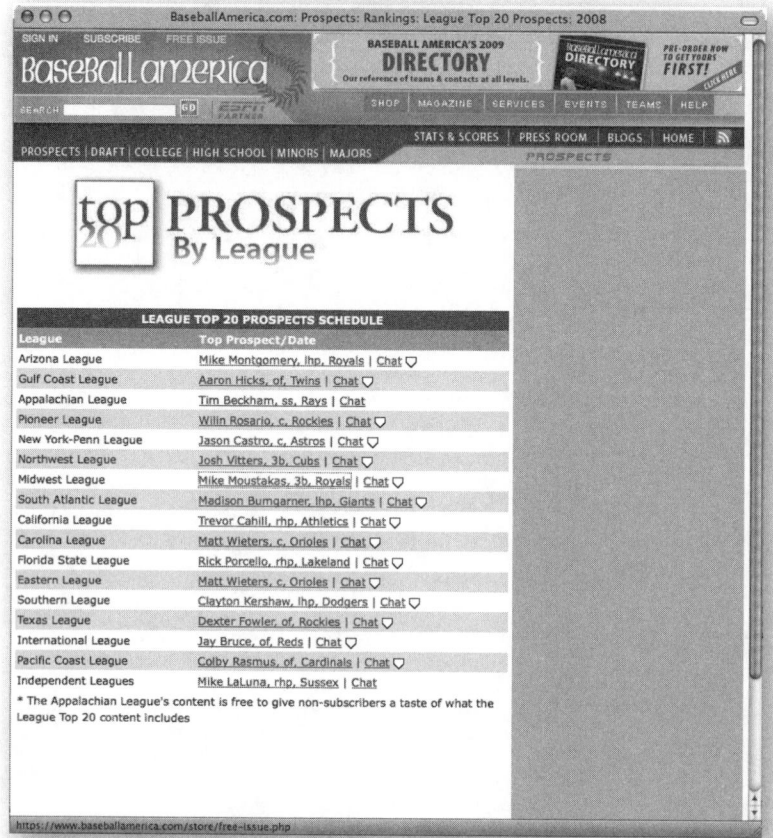

www.BaseballAmerica.com

BaseBall america
2009 PROSPECT
HANDBOOK

Editors
JIM CALLIS, WILL LINGO, JOHN MANUEL

Assistant Editors
BEN BADLER, KARY BOOHER, J.J. COOPER, MATT EDDY, AARON FITT,
JOSH LEVENTHAL, NATHAN RODE, JIM SHONERD

Contributing Writers
ANDY BAGGARLY, BILL BALLEW, MIKE BERARDINO, DERRICK GOOLD,
TOM HAUDRICOURT, JON PAUL MOROSI, JOHN PERROTTO, ED PRICE,
TRACY RINGOLSBY, ADAM RUBIN, PHIL ROGERS

Photo Editor
NATHAN RODE

Editorial Assistants
JESSE BURKHART, BRIAN CHMIELEWSKI, CONOR GLASSEY

Design & Production
SARA HIATT, LINWOOD WEBB

Jacket Photos
NEFTALI FELIZ BY BRIAN BISSELL; DAVID PRICE BY RICK BATTLE; TRAVIS SNIDER BY
MIKE JANES; MATT WIETERS BY SPORTS ON FILM; TIM LINCECUM BY BILL MITCHELL;
EVAN LONGORIA BY RODGER WOOD

BaseBall america

PRESIDENT/PUBLISHER: LEE FOLGER
EDITORS IN CHIEF: WILL LINGO, JOHN MANUEL
EXECUTIVE EDITOR: JIM CALLIS
DESIGN & PRODUCTION DIRECTOR: SARA HIATT

DISTRIBUTED BY SIMON & SCHUSTER
ISBN-13: 978-1-932391-24-4

STATISTICS COMPILED AND PROVIDED BY MAJOR LEAGUE BASEBALL ADVANCED MEDIA.

BaseballAmerica.com

TABLE OF CONTENTS

398

TOM PRIDDY

The Giants have their highest farm system ranking in BA history, led by lefthander Madison Bumgarner (above), catcher Buster Posey and infielder Angel Villalona

FOREWORD

Walking through our clubhouse after Game Seven of the American League Championship Series, I was struck by how many of our players, now drenched in champagne, were signed by Rays scouts and developed in our minor league system. Now they were days away from being introduced to the entire nation on the biggest stage in baseball, most of them for the first time.

But to readers of Baseball America's Prospect Handbook, they were already familiar faces. BA lets you know about their tools, their makeup and what role they might play on our club long before they played their first big league games.

There is a copy of this book in every front office in baseball. That's because in our industry, information is king, and nothing you will find in any newsstand or bookstore has more information on future major leaguers than Baseball America. Just as we can supplement the work of our scouts and analysts, with this book you'll gain an insider's detailed perspective on the young talent in each organization.

Our player development staff will sometimes refer to "back field guys"—insider jargon for those young players who have promising futures but are still under the radar, honing their skills on the back fields of our minor league complex in anonymity. But if you have this book, they won't be back field guys for you. Baseball America identifies those players and brings them to the forefront almost as quickly as our scouts are able to sign them.

Our minor league system is our lifeline, and the success we enjoyed in 2008 was built on a foundation of scouting and player development, both at home and abroad in countries such as the Dominican Republic and Venezuela. For most fans that foundation remains hidden from view, but here in our offices, it is our primary focus and something we cannot live without.

Baseball America's Prospect Handbook takes you inside the foundation of every major league club, with a level of detail and insight essential to a complete understanding of today's game.

ANDREW FRIEDMAN
EXECUTIVE VICE PRESIDENT, BASEBALL OPERATIONS
TAMPA BAY RAYS

In the midst of another long deadline week in advance of the Prospect Handbook being sent out, the Baseball America office was abuzz with activity. We were juggling a thousand things, trying to make sure it all came together as usual, and the stress level was high.

And then John Manuel, my fellow editor in chief and partner in crime for more than 10 years now, looked across the corridor of power (the doorway between our offices) and just said: "Man, doing this book is so much fun."

I had noticed it the week before at the Winter Meetings, not in regard to the Prospect Handbook in particular, but about baseball in general. Most people who work in this business have a pretty high level of job satisfaction. At Baseball America you certainly won't find many people dragging themselves into the office with dread each day. Sure, we take our jobs seriously and enjoy getting paid. But what makes it easy to work the long hours and to produce a good product is that we actually enjoy it.

This year is no exception. We're working into the wee hours a week before Christmas, still debating the relative merits of prospects at the back of an organization list and trading war stories about deadlines gone by. And we couldn't be happier.

Baseball America has been ranking prospects almost since the magazine began publishing in 1981. People have a natural affinity for lists, and baseball fans in particular love to stack players up against one another. The first BA prospect lists were top 10s, of course, because that's just the natural order of things. Eventually we got the idea to do a book of prospect lists, and we settled on 30 as a good way to go deep in an organization without getting into any real chaff. The first Prospect Handbook came out before the 2001 season, and while we tweak the format of the book each year, the basic format has remained unchanged.

Our rankings and the accompanying scouting reports make up the backbone of the book, and that will always be true. They're the product of a year's worth of information-gathering and the culmination of everything Baseball America does. The people who write up each organization talk to scouts, managers and coaches, instructors and coordinators, farm directors, scouting directors and anyone else with an educated opinion about the players in each organization. We want as many viewpoints as we can find, particularly those from outside an organization.

We rely on Jim Callis to coordinate all the information in the book, so that it all fits together and so every list is of the quality you expect. Jim discusses every list with each writer, and he and John in particular debate the rankings and help line the players up. There are a lot of reasons why this book is so good, and one is that we actually care where Mike Carp slotted into the Mariners prospect list when he came over in a trade with the Mets.

The three of us get our names on the top line of the book, but we're just part of a huge team of people who help make this massive collection of information come together into an attractive package. Big thanks to Sara Hiatt and Linwood Webb for their great work in the production and design of the book this year, yeoman work when they were shorthanded. Greg Levine and Brent Lewis have made the stats, which used to be one of the most trying parts of the book, a relative breeze. We salute our correspondents and full-time writers and editors for their incredible hard work. And of course the biggest thanks to you for continuing to buy this book. We think it's great, but that wouldn't matter unless you kept reading it.

A few housekeeping notes: Transactions for this book go through Dec. 14, so the last major deals included here are moves involving Rule 5 draftees and non-tenders. As always, you can find players even if they change organizations by using the handy index in the back. We also have a scouting report for unsigned first-rounder Joshua Fields on Page 494. And for the purposes of this book, a prospect is anyone who has no more than 50 innings pitched or 130 at-bats in the big leagues, regardless of service time. Finally, the grades you'll find for each team's drafts are based solely on the quality of the players signed, with no consideration for who players were traded for or how many picks a team might have lost.

We had a lot of fun doing it. We hope you have as much fun reading it.

WILL LINGO
EDITOR IN CHIEF
BASEBALL AMERICA

Among all the scouting lingo you'll come across in this book, perhaps no terms are more telling and prevalent than "profile" and "projection."

When scouts evaluate a player, their main objective is to identify—or project—what the player's future role will be in the major leagues. Each organization has its own philosophy when it comes to grading players, so we talked to scouts from several teams to provide general guidelines.

The first thing to know is what scouts are looking for. In short, tools. These refer to the physical skills a player needs to be successful in the major leagues. For a position player, the five basic tools are hitting, hitting for power, fielding, arm strength and speed. For a pitcher, the tools are based on the pitches he throws. Each pitch is graded, as well as a pitcher's control, delivery and durability.

The profiling system continues to evolve. Baseball is coming out of an era of historic offensive proportions, but the first year of the post-Mitchell Report era featured Miguel Cabrera leading the American League with 37 home runs—the first time since 1992 that a league leader didn't hit at least 40. While the emphasis in recent years has tilted profiles more and more towards offense, speed and defense may begin to creep higher up the list of priorities in coming years.

While more emphasis has been placed on hitting—which also covers getting on base—fielding and speed remain at a premium up the middle. As teams have sacrificed defense at the corner outfield slots, they continue to seek speedy center fielders to make up ground in the alleys. Most scouts prefer at least a 55 runner (on the 20-80 scouting scale; see chart) at short and center field, but as power increases at those two positions, running comes down.

Shortstops need range and at least average arm strength, and second basemen need to be quick on the pivot. Teams are more willing to put up with an immobile corner infielder if he can mash.

Arm strength is the one tool moving way down preference lists. For a catcher, it was always the No. 1 tool, though in today's game, scouts are looking for more offensive production from the position. Receiving skills, including game-calling, blocking pitches and release times, can make up for the lack of a plus arm.

On the mound, it doesn't just come down to pure stuff. While a true No. 1 starter on a first-division team should have a couple of 70 or 80 pitches in his repertoire, like Johan Santana and Tim Lincecum, they also need to produce 200-plus innings, 30 starts and 15-plus wins.

A player's overall future potential is also graded on the 20-80 scale, though some teams use a letter grade. This number is not just the sum of his tools, but rather a profiling system and a scout's ultimate opinion of the player.

70-80 (A): This category is reserved for the elite players in baseball. This player will be a perennial all-star, the best player at his position, one of the top five starters in the game or a frontline closer. Alex Rodriguez, Albert Pujols and Santana reside here.

60-69 (B): You'll find all-star-caliber players here: No. 2 starters on a championship club and first-division players. See Jon Lester, Torii Hunter and Carl Crawford.

55-59 (C+): The majority of first-division starters are found in this range, including quality No. 2 and 3 starters, frontline set-up men and second-tier closers.

50-54 (C): Solid-average everyday major leaguers. Most are not first-division regulars. This group also includes No. 4 and 5 starters.

45-49 (D+): Fringe everyday players, backups, some No. 5 starters, middle relievers, pinch-hitters and one-tool players.

40-44 (D): Up-and-down roster fillers, situational relievers and 25th players.

38-39 (O): Organizational players who provide depth for the minor leagues but are not considered future major leaguers.

20-37 (NP): Not a prospect.

THE SCOUTING SCALE

When grading a player's tools, scouts use a standard 20-80 scale. When you read that a pitcher throws an above-average slider, it can be interpreted as a 60 pitch, or a plus pitch. Plus-plus is 70, or well-above-average, and so on. Scouts don't throw 80s around very freely. Here's what each grade means:

80	OUTSTANDING
70	WELL-ABOVE-AVERAGE
60	ABOVE-AVERAGE
50	MAJOR LEAGUE AVERAGE
40	BELOW-AVERAGE
30	WELL-BELOW-AVERAGE
20	POOR

An Overview

Another feature of the Prospect Handbook is a depth chart of every organization's minor league talent. This shows you at a glance what kind of talent a system has and provides even more prospects beyond the top 30.

Players are usually listed on the depth charts where we think they'll ultimately end up. To help you better understand why players are slotted at particular positions, we show you here what scouts look for in the ideal candidate at each spot, with individual tools ranked in descending order.

LF
Power
Hitting
Fielding
Arm Strength
Speed

CF
Fielding
Hitting
Speed
Power
Arm Strength

RF
Hitting
Power
Arm Strength
Fielding
Speed

3B
Hitting
Power
Fielding
Arm Strength
Speed

SS
Fielding
Arm Strength
Hitting
Speed
Power

2B
Hitting
Fielding
Power
Speed
Arm Strength

1B
Power
Hitting
Fielding
Arm Strength
Speed

C
Fielding
Arm Strength
Hitting
Power
Speed

STARTING PITCHERS

No. 1 starter	No. 2 starter	No. 3 starter	No. 4-5 starters
• Two plus pitches	• Two plus pitches	• One plus pitch	• Command of two major league pitches
• Average third pitch	• Average third pitch	• Two average pitches	• Average velocity
• Plus-plus command	• Average command	• Average command	• Consistent breaking ball
• Plus makeup	• Average makeup	• Average makeup	• Decent changeup

CLOSER

- One dominant pitch
- Second plus pitch
- Plus command
- Plus-plus makeup

When Baseball America ranks prospects, there's almost always a byline attributing who finally put the players in order, who decided, "OK, this guy's 6 and this guy's 7." But all our rankings are more than one person's opinion. They are most often a reflection of the consensus of sources on the subject—managers, coaches, scouts, front-office personnel, the whole spectrum.

Except here, really. In this section of the Handbook, we get personal. Sifting through all the information we've gathered to this point, three of our editors give their own personal takes on the game's Top 50 prospects. This helps form the basis of the arguments that shape Baseball America's Top 100 Prospects. That list comes out during spring training, and we consider it the definitive guide to the best talent in the minor leagues.

The rules for these lists are the same for any prospect who appears in the Handbook: rookie standards of no more than 130 at-bats or 50 innings in the major leagues. We do not consider service time in our eligibility requirements.

As with any prospect list, these rankings represent how each person regarded the top minor league talent in the game at a moment in time. Ask us again in a few months—or even tomorrow—how these prospects stack up, and you'll get a different answer.

BILL MITCHELL

Athletics lefthander Brett Anderson is part of a bumper crop of talent entering 2009

JIM CALLIS

1.	David Price, lhp, Rays	26.	Matt LaPorta, of, Indians
2.	Matt Wieters, c, Orioles	27.	Alcides Escobar, ss, Brewers
3.	Pedro Alvarez, 3b, Pirates	28.	Derek Holland, lhp, Rangers
4.	Madison Bumgarner, lhp, Giants	29.	Carlos Santana, c, Indians
5.	Colby Rasmus, of, Cardinals	30.	Rick Porcello, rhp, Tigers
6.	Buster Posey, c, Giants	31.	Chris Tillman, rhp, Orioles
7.	Brett Anderson, lhp, Athletics	32.	Angel Villalona, 1b, Giants
8.	Trevor Cahill, rhp, Athletics	33.	Jordan Schafer, of, Braves
9.	Neftali Feliz, rhp, Rangers	34.	Andrew McCutchen, of, Pirates
10.	Tommy Hanson, rhp, Braves	35.	Jordan Zimmermann, rhp, Nationals
11.	Tim Beckham, ss, Rays	36.	Tim Alderson, rhp, Giants
12.	Eric Hosmer, 1b, Royals	37.	Josh Vitters, 3b, Cubs
13.	Lars Anderson, 1b, Red Sox	38.	Mat Gamel, 3b, Brewers
14.	Logan Morrison, 1b, Marlins	39.	Yonder Alonso, 1b, Reds
15.	Jason Heyward, of, Braves	40.	Fernando Martinez, of, Mets
16.	Travis Snider, of, Blue Jays	41.	Wade Davis, rhp, Rays
17.	Dexter Fowler, of, Rockies	42.	Brett Lawrie, c/3b, Brewers
18.	Mike Moustakas, 3b, Royals	43.	Matt Dominguez, 3b, Marlins
19.	Justin Smoak, 1b, Rangers	44.	Aaron Hicks, of, Twins
20.	Cameron Maybin, of, Marlins	45.	Jesus Montero, c, Yankees
21.	Mike Stanton, of, Marlins	46.	J.P. Arencibia, c, Blue Jays
22.	Brian Matusz, lhp, Orioles	47.	Dominic Brown, of, Phillies
23.	Gordon Beckham, ss, White Sox	48.	Jhoulys Chacin, rhp, Rockies
24.	Brett Wallace, 3b, Cardinals	49.	Wilmer Flores, ss, Mets
25.	Jarrod Parker, rhp, Diamondbacks	50.	Michael Inoa, rhp, Athletics

First-round pick Buster Posey should move through the Giants system quickly

Braves righthander Tommy Hanson dominated in the minors in 2008

WILL LINGO

1. Matt Wieters, c, Orioles
2. David Price, lhp, Rays
3. Colby Rasmus, of, Cardinals
4. Cameron Maybin, of, Marlins
5. Alcides Escobar, ss, Brewers
6. Trevor Cahill, rhp, Athletics
7. Madison Bumgarner, lhp, Giants
8. Neftali Feliz, rhp, Rangers
9. Tommy Hanson, rhp, Braves
10. Travis Snider, of, Blue Jays
11. Dexter Fowler, of, Rockies
12. Mike Stanton, of, Marlins
13. Logan Morrison, 1b, Marlins
14. Brett Anderson, lhp, Athletics
15. Jarrod Parker, rhp, Diamondbacks
16. Jason Heyward, of, Braves
17. Mike Moustakas, 3b, Royals
18. Carlos Santana, c, Indians
19. Gordon Beckham, ss, White Sox
20. Matt LaPorta, of, Indians
21. Derek Holland, lhp, Rangers
22. Pedro Alvarez, 3b, Pirates
23. Rick Porcello, rhp, Tigers
24. Brian Matusz, lhp, Orioles
25. Buster Posey, c, Giants
26. Eric Hosmer, 1b, Royals
27. Lars Anderson, 1b, Red Sox
28. Fernando Martinez, of, Mets
29. Austin Jackson, of, Yankees
30. Tim Beckham, ss, Rays
31. Jordan Zimmermann, rhp, Nationals
32. Elvis Andrus, ss, Rangers
33. Dayan Viciedo, 3b/of, White Sox
34. Taylor Teagarden, c, Rangers
35. J.P. Arencibia, c, Blue Jays
36. Wade Davis, rhp, Rays
37. Chris Tillman, rhp, Orioles
38. Jesus Montero, c, Yankees
39. Angel Villalona, 1b, Giants
40. Andrew McCutchen, of, Pirates
41. Greg Halman, of, Mariners
42. Dominic Brown, of, Phillies
43. Jason Castro, c, Astros
44. Nick Adenhart, rhp, Angels
45. Jhoulys Chacin, rhp, Rockies
46. Josh Vitters, 3b, Cubs
47. Gerardo Parra, of, Diamondbacks
48. Jake Arrieta, rhp, Orioles
49. Yonder Alonso, 1b, Reds
50. Aaron Hicks, of, Twins

Outfielder Jason Heyward is rocketing his way through the Braves farm system

Outfielder Mike Stanton solidifies a deep pool of prospects for the Marlins

JOHN MANUEL

1. Matt Wieters, c, Orioles
2. David Price, lhp, Rays
3. Neftali Feliz, rhp, Rangers
4. Tommy Hanson, rhp, Braves
5. Jason Heyward, of, Braves
6. Madison Bumgarner, lhp, Giants
7. Travis Snider, of, Blue Jays
8. Cameron Maybin, of, Marlins
9. Pedro Alvarez, 3b, Pirates
10. Mike Stanton, of, Marlins
11. Dexter Fowler, of, Rockies
12. Colby Rasmus, of, Cardinals
13. Brett Anderson, lhp, Athletics
14. Mike Moustakas, 3b, Royals
15. Buster Posey, c, Giants
16. Chris Tillman, rhp, Orioles
17. Trevor Cahill, rhp, Athletics
18. Gordon Beckham, ss, White Sox
19. Brian Matusz, lhp, Orioles
20. Alcides Escobar, ss, Brewers
21. Lars Anderson, 1b, Red Sox
22. Justin Smoak, 1b, Rangers
23. Logan Morrison, 1b, Marlins
24. Carlos Santana, c, Indians
25. Derek Holland, lhp, Rangers
26. Mat Gamel, 3b, Brewers
27. Matt LaPorta, of, Indians
28. J.P. Arencibia, c, Blue Jays
29. Austin Jackson, of, Yankees
30. Fernando Martinez, of, Mets
31. Wade Davis, rhp, Rays
32. Jesus Montero, c, Yankees
33. Rick Porcello, rhp, Tigers
34. Eric Hosmer, 1b, Royals
35. Angel Villalona, 1b, Giants
36. Tim Beckham, ss, Rays
37. Elvis Andrus, ss, Rangers
38. Dominic Brown, of, Phillies
39. Jordan Zimmermann, rhp, Nationals
40. Yonder Alonso, 1b, Reds
41. Aaron Hicks, of, Twins
42. Josh Vitters, 3b, Cubs
43. Jarrod Parker, rhp, Diamondbacks
44. Carlos Carrasco, rhp, Phillies
45. Jhoulys Chacin, rhp, Rockies
46. Tim Alderson, rhp, Giants
47. Jason Castro, c, Astros
48. Jordan Schafer, of, Braves
49. Chris Carter, 1b/3b/of, Athletics
50. Daniel Bard, rhp, Red Sox

	2008	2007	2006	2005	2004
1 Texas Rangers	4	28	16	16	16

Through aggressive trades, the draft and international signings, the Rangers rapidly have ascended from near the bottom of our farm system rankings to the top. From power arms such as Neftali Feliz to impact bats like Justin Smoak to middle-of-the-diamond talents, Texas has it all.

	2008	2007	2006	2005	2004
2 Florida Marlins	14	15	3	14	14

No organization can match the Marlins for having impact bats in full-season leagues. Cameron Maybin and Mike Stanton are a ridiculous 1-2 punch of five-tool talents, while Logan Morrison, Matt Dominguez, Chris Coghlan and Gaby Sanchez head a group of future big league regulars.

	2008	2007	2006	2005	2004
3 Oakland Athletics	27	27	26	8	17

Between last year's book and this year's publication, the Athletics move up a record-tying 24 spots. Oakland acquired a raft of prospects through all avenues. Only Texas can rival Oakland's depth of both pitchers and hitters who should be regulars.

	2008	2007	2006	2005	2004
4 Tampa Bay Rays	1	1	10	9	9

Tampa Bay will gladly trade its back-to-back No. 1 rankings for a move down of three spots—with an American League pennant thrown into the deal. David Price gives the Rays the game's top pitching prospect, but they'll have to get used to drafting at the back of the first round for a while.

	2008	2007	2006	2005	2004
5 San Francisco Giants	23	20	18	17	24

In a dramatic reversal of form, the Giants have become one of the game's strongest farm systems, with their highest talent ranking in BA history. San Francisco has spent its way to the top, handing out the five largest bonuses in club history in the last three years.

	2008	2007	2006	2005	2004
6 Atlanta Braves	8	16	7	5	4

One season outside the top 10 in the nine-year history of the Handbook makes Atlanta the game's most consistent scouting and player-development organization. Tommy Hanson and Jason Heyward are as good a combination of pitcher and hitter as any organization in the game has.

	2008	2007	2006	2005	2004
7 Cleveland Indians	19	10	9	7	6

With its most aggressive draft in years, Cleveland rocks back up our talent rankings. Yet despite spending liberally last June, the Indians' top two prospects came via trades in Carlos Santana (for Casey Blake) and Matt LaPorta (for C.C. Sabathia).

	2008	2007	2006	2005	2004
8 St. Louis Cardinals	13	23	21	30	28

This is the first top-10 ranking for the Cardinals since 1999, and the system's highest ranking since 1995. Scouting and farm director Jeff Luhnow operates differently from most, and right now he's assembling talent better than St. Louis has in more than a decade.

	2008	2007	2006	2005	2004
9 Baltimore Orioles	16	17	12	25	18

Orioles fans should go to bed every night thanking Dave Littlefield and the Pirates for passing on Matt Wieters in 2007. Obtaining Wieters, then trading Erik Bedard to the Mariners, kick-started the Orioles system. It's still a long climb in the majors, but Baltimore has reason for hope.

	2008	2007	2006	2005	2004
10 Milwaukee Brewers	21	5	5	3	1

The Brewers climb back into the top 10 after falling out last year, and that's after trading four minor leaguers for three months of C.C. Sabathia. The trick now is for Milwaukee to maintain its player-development mojo after the brain drain in its scouting department.

	2008	2007	2006	2005	2004
11 Kansas City Royals	24	11	23	28	19

Talk about buying your way up the list . . . The Royals have spent $37.1 million on their last six drafts, including $10 million on their last two first-rounders alone. The system lacks depth despite that, but Mike Moustakas and Eric Hosmer head a nice group of potential impact players.

	2008	2007	2006	2005	2004
12 Philadelphia Phillies	22	21	22	20	21

Not only did Philadelphia win the World Series with homegrown stars such as Ryan Howard, Cole Hamels, Chase Utley and Jimmy Rollins, but they also used extra picks to have their best draft in years. Philly fans will have to just boo the Eagles, because the Phils should be good for a while.

	2008	2007	2006	2005	2004
13 Boston Red Sox	2	9	8	21	23

Graduation and attrition have sapped the Red Sox system of talent. Justin Masterson, Jed Lowrie, Jacoby Ellsbury and Clay Buchholz—four of Boston's top five prospects a year ago—lost prospect status while contributing to the 2008 wild-card winners.

	2008	2007	2006	2005	2004
14 Cincinnati Reds	3	12	30	23	26

The quartet of Homer Bailey, Jay Bruce, Johnny Cueto and Joey Votto that powered the Reds up the charts has graduated. Cincinnati reloaded aggressively with a Latin American spending spree to supplement recent college draftees such as Yonder Alonso, Todd Frazier and Drew Stubbs.

	2008	2007	2006	2005	2004
15 New York Yankees	5	7	17	24	27

Yankees farm teams won but it was a down year in terms of prospects, as injuries, trades and poor performances plagued many of the system's top prospects. The signings of C.C. Sabathia and A.J. Burnett makes New York's recent emphasis of homegrown pitching seem like a thing of the past.

	2008	2007	2006	2005	2004
16 Chicago White Sox	28	26	14	12	20

16 Chicago White Sox

No GM in the game today is as bold as Kenny Williams, who gets more daring every year since winning the 2005 World Series. The White Sox added plenty of talent in '08, with top-10 pick Gordon Beckham, trade acquisitions like Tyler Flowers and Cuban signee Dayan Viciedo.

	2008	2007	2006	2005	2004
17 New York Mets	17	13	28	19	10

17 New York Mets

The Mets don't go over slot in the draft, and they aren't shy about trading minor leaguers for big league talent. Yet New York also has gotten contributions from homegrown players and has retained a modicum of depth thanks to draft finds like Brad Holt and international signings.

	2008	2007	2006	2005	2004
18 Pittsburgh Pirates	26	19	19	18	11

18 Pittsburgh Pirates

With 16 straight losing seasons, you'd think the Pirates would have put together a boffo farm system once or twice in that span. It hasn't happened, despite constant rebuilding. Let's see if Pedro Alvarez can finally get things turned around in the Steel City. No pressure, Pedro.

	2008	2007	2006	2005	2004
19 Toronto Blue Jays	25	25	25	15	8

19 Toronto Blue Jays

The Jays still don't like to draft high school pitchers, but by dipping their toe into the high school and international hitter pool, they've deepened their talent base. It also helps that they've drafted well when sticking to their college guns, adding impact bats like J.P. Arencibia and David Cooper.

	2008	2007	2006	2005	2004
20 Colorado Rockies	7	2	11	6	15

20 Colorado Rockies

The Rockies got no breaks this year in the majors or in the minors. Aside from Dexter Fowler's and Jhoulys Chacin's breakthrough seasons, Colorado experienced setbacks on the farm, including injuries to players such as Hector Gomez and Casey Weathers.

	2008	2007	2006	2005	2004
21 Washington Nationals	9	30	24	26	30

21 Washington Nationals

The Nats seemed to be making strides before a disastrous 2008, plagued by injuries and a botched negotiation with first-round pick Aaron Crow. Blaming a fallow system on MLB ownership in the Expos years is an excuse that's starting to lose potency with the passage of time.

	2008	2007	2006	2005	2004
22 Minnesota Twins	18	8	6	4	5

22 Minnesota Twins

Last year's ranking didn't reflect the Johan Santana trade, but that hasn't worked out too well for the Twins anyway. Minnesota's forte the last three years has been homegrown pitching; now Joe Mauer and Justin Morneau need a power bat to help them.

	2008	2007	2006	2005	2004
23 Los Angeles Dodgers	6	6	2	2	2

23 Los Angeles Dodgers

Decimated by trades, the Dodgers are about to hit a rut after a stunning run of impact talent through its system that produced the likes of Russell Martin, Matt Kemp and Clayton Kershaw. The next wave, led by Andrew Lambo and James McDonald, doesn't look as fruitful.

	2008	2007	2006	2005	2004
24 Seattle Mariners	11	24	27	11	12

24 Seattle Mariners

The Mariners take a major hit thanks to the Erik Bedard trade, which sapped them of three prospects; graduations of players who got big league auditions during a disastrous season in Seattle; and a failure to sign first-round pick Joshua Fields, the 2008 draft's longest holdout.

	2008	2007	2006	2005	2004
25 Los Angeles Angels	10	4	4	1	3

25 Los Angeles Angels

The Angels have dominated the American League West in recent seasons, but that could change soon. Oakland and Texas have two of the game's best farm systems, while Los Angeles has given away more draft picks in the last five years than any club. It shows in the system's talent dropoff.

	2008	2007	2006	2005	2004
26 Arizona Diamondbacks	15	3	1	13	13

26 Arizona Diamondbacks

The Diamondbacks have created a roadmap of how to tumble from the top ranking to near the bottom in near record time. Arizona has drafted conservatively, leading to a lack of power arms and bats, and traded prospects aggressively to supplement a young, talented big league team.

	2008	2007	2006	2005	2004
27 Chicago Cubs	20	18	15	10	7

27 Chicago Cubs

Every ounce of the Cubs' effort in recent years has gone into ending the game's longest World Series championship drought. Still, the Cubs haven't drafted well for several years, and the system just isn't positioned to help the big league club with rookies or trades anymore.

	2008	2007	2006	2005	2004
28 Detroit Tigers	29	14	13	29	22

28 Detroit Tigers

Hey, moving up one spot is a start for the Tigers, who have a bloated big league payroll and keep giving up minor leaguers for veterans in an effort to win now. Detroit's last three drafts haven't produced much besides Rick Porcello's promise.

	2008	2007	2006	2005	2004
29 San Diego Padres	12	29	29	27	25

29 San Diego Padres

The Padres made a huge leap up the rankings last year but fall right back down after a year of setbacks and graduations. With the big league team in turmoil and up for sale, San Diego looks like it's in for another long rebuilding stretch.

	2008	2007	2006	2005	2004
30 Houston Astros	30	22	20	22	29

30 Houston Astros

Back-to-back last-place finishes for the Astros, and it really isn't too close. At least first-year scouting director Bobby Heck produced a solid draft, led by No. 1 prospect Jason Castro. Now the Astros need two or three straight drafts like that to undo the damage of its recent poor run.

Arizona Diamondbacks

BY WILL LINGO

The Diamondbacks are moving into the next phase of their evolution. No longer young upstarts, they'll come to spring training with established players at most positions and the expectation of contending for the National League West title.

Arizona brought lots of young talent through its farm system in recent years, culminating in a 90-win season, NL West title and Division Series vic-

tory in 2007. The front office then bolstered the big league team with the acquisition of veterans like Dan Haren—who came over before the 2008 season in a trade that sent six prospects to the Athletics—as well as Adam Dunn, Jon Rauch and David Eckstein, who were acquired during the year.

The 2008 squad ultimately fell short of the playoffs, however, after spending most of the season in first place in the West. With the Rockies taking a big step back, Arizona spent May and June in first place, then battled with the Dodgers in the second half before relinquishing the division lead for good on Sept. 5.

A mediocre offense was to blame, as the Diamondbacks finished fifth in the NL in runs allowed (706) but 10th in runs scored (720). At least they scored more runs than they allowed, after making the playoffs despite a -20 run differential in 2007.

The Diamondbacks will depend on the continued improvement of young players like Stephen Drew and Justin Upton to remain in contention. They'll have to, because the farm system is dramatically thinner in talent than just a few years ago, when Arizona sat at the top of our minor league talent rankings.

That's the result of players like Drew and Upton moving quickly through the system to the big leagues, as well as the wholesale trading of prospects for big leaguers in the last couple of years. From last year's Top 30 list, eight of the top 17 prospects have been traded away. Off the 2007 list, 19 of the 30 players either have been traded or have graduated to the majors. The highest player from the 2007 Top 30 still in the farm system is outfielder Gerardo Parra, who has moved from No. 14 to No. 2 in our rankings.

Arizona also will rely on its young core because it doesn't have the money to plug holes Yankees-style. The Diamondbacks made news as one of the first professional sports franchises to announce layoffs during the recession, firing 31 people after the season ended.

The baseball-operations budget reportedly will be around $75 million for 2009, a total that includes

Arizona has traded away prospects for veteran reinforcements like Dan Haren

BILL MITCHELL

TOP 30 PROSPECTS

1. Jarrod Parker, rhp	16. Evan Frey, of
2. Gerardo Parra, of	17. Bryan Shaw, rhp
3. Daniel Schlereth, lhp	18. Ryne White, 1b
4. Mark Hallberg, ss/2b	19. Josh Whitesell, 1b
5. Wade Miley, lhp	20. Tony Barnette, rhp
6. Kevin Eichhorn, rhp	21. Wes Roemer, rhp
7. Cesar Valdez, rhp	22. Cyle Hankerd, of
8. Billy Buckner, rhp	23. Clay Zavada, lhp
9. Collin Cowgill, of	24. Isaias Asencio, of
10. Reynaldo Navarro, ss	25. Kyler Newby, rhp
11. Barry Enright, rhp	26. Leyson Septimo, lhp
12. Daniel Stange, rhp	27. James Skelton, c
13. Trevor Harden, rhp	28. Brooks Brown, rhp
14. Pedro Ciriaco, ss/2b	29. Ed Easley, c
15. Rossmel Perez, c	30. Tyrell Worthington, of

the major league payroll as well as the draft budget, among other things. Arizona was left to shop for stopgaps like Felipe Lopez and Scott Schoenweis over the winter. What flexibility the team did have resulted from Randy Johnson's $10 million salary coming off the books, as well as another $11 million from players like Orlando Hudson and Brandon Lyon.

Any help coming soon will be on the pitching side, where their draft efforts have focused in the last two years. It wouldn't be shocking to see 2007 first-rounder Jarrod Parker or 2008 first-rounder Daniel Schlereth in the big leagues at some point this year.

General Manager: Josh Byrnes. **Farm Director:** A.J. Hinch. **Scouting Director:** Tom Allison.

Class	Team	League	W	L	PCT	Finish*	Manager	Affiliated
Majors	Arizona	National	82	80	.506	9th (16)	Bob Melvin	—
Triple-A	Tucson Sidewinders	Pacific Coast	60	82	.423	15th (16)	Bill Plummer	1998
Double-A	Mobile BayBears	Southern	58	79	.423	10th (10)	Hector de la Cruz	2007
High A	Visalia Oaks	California	67	72	.482	7th (10)	Mike Bell	2007
Low A	South Bend Silver Hawks	Midwest	76	63	.547	2nd (14)	Mark Haley	1997
Short-season	Yakima Bears	Northwest	28	48	.368	8th (8)	Bob Didier	2001
Rookie	Missoula Osprey	Pioneer	21	54	.280	8th (8)	Audo Vicente	1999
Overall 2008 Minor League Record			310	398	.438	28th		

* Finish in overall standings (No. of teams in league). ^League champion.

LAST YEAR'S TOP 30

Rank	Player, Pos.	Status
1.	Carlos Gonzalez, of	(Rockies)
2.	Jarrod Parker, rhp	No. 1
3.	Brett Anderson, lhp	(Athletics)
4.	Max Scherzer, rhp	Majors
5.	Gerardo Parra, of	No. 2
6.	Emilio Bonifacio, 2b/ss	(Nationals)
7.	Aaron Cunningham, of	(Athletics)
8.	Chris Carter, 1b	(Athletics)
9.	Reynaldo Navarro, ss	No. 10
10.	Barry Enright, rhp	No. 11
11.	Wes Roemer, rhp	No. 21
12.	Brooks Brown, rhp	No. 28
13.	Greg Smith, lhp	(Rockies)
14.	Wilkin Castillo, c/inf	(Reds)
15.	Daniel Stange, rhp	No. 12
16.	Esmerling Vasquez, rhp	Dropped out
17.	Dallas Buck, rhp	(Reds)
18.	Doug Slaten, lhp	Majors
19.	Ed Easley, c	No. 29
20.	Tyrell Worthington, of	No. 30
21.	Matt Green, rhp	Dropped out
22.	Sean Morgan, rhp	Dropped out
23.	Emiliano Fruto, rhp	(Free agent)
24.	Clayton Conner, 3b	Dropped out
25.	Cyle Hankerd, of	No. 22
26.	Javier Brito, 1b	(Free agent)
27.	Hector Ambriz, rhp	Dropped out
28.	Alex Romero, of	Majors
29.	Pedro Ciriaco, ss	No. 14
30.	Leyson Septimo, lhp	No. 26

BEST TOOLS

Best Hitter for Average	Gerardo Parra
Best Power Hitter	Josh Whitesell
Best Strike-Zone Discipline	Mark Hallberg
Fastest Baserunner	Ollie Linton
Best Athlete	Tyrell Worthington
Best Fastball	Jarrod Parker
Best Curveball	Daniel Schlereth
Best Slider	Jarrod Parker
Best Changeup	Cesar Valdez
Best Control	Trevor Harden
Best Defensive Catcher	Ryan Babineau
Best Defensive Infielder	Pedro Ciriaco
Best Infield Arm	Pedro Ciriaco
Best Defensive Outfielder	Gerardo Parra
Best Outfield Arm	Gerardo Parra

PROJECTED 2012 LINEUP

Catcher	Chris Snyder
First Base	Conor Jackson
Second Base	Mark Hallberg
Third Base	Mark Reynolds
Shortstop	Stephen Drew
Left Field	Gerardo Parra
Center Field	Chris Young
Right Field	Justin Upton
No. 1 Starter	Brandon Webb
No. 2 Starter	Jarrod Parker
No. 3 Starter	Max Scherzer
No. 4 Starter	Dan Haren
No. 5 Starter	Wade Miley
Closer	Daniel Schlereth

TOP PROSPECTS OF THE DECADE

Year	Player, Pos.	2008 Org.
1999	Brad Penny, rhp	Dodgers
2000	John Patterson, rhp	Rangers
2001	Alex Cintron, ss	Orioles
2002	Luis Terrero, of	Orioles
2003	Scott Hairston, 2b	Padres
2004	Scott Hairston, 2b	Padres
2005	Carlos Quentin, of	White Sox
2006	Stephen Drew, ss	Diamondbacks
2007	Justin Upton, of	Diamondbacks
2008	Carlos Gonzalez, of	Athletics

TOP DRAFT PICKS OF THE DECADE

Year	Player, Pos.	2008 Org.
1999	Corey Myers, ss	Out of baseball
2000	Mike Schultz, rhp (2nd)	Hiroshima (Japan)
2001	Jason Bulger, rhp	Angels
2002	Sergio Santos, ss	Twins
2003	Conor Jackson, of	Diamondbacks
2004	Stephen Drew, ss	Diamondbacks
2005	Justin Upton, of	Diamondbacks
2006	Max Scherzer, rhp	Diamondbacks
2007	Jarrod Parker, rhp	Diamondbacks
2008	Daniel Schlereth, lhp	Diamondbacks

LARGEST BONUSES IN CLUB HISTORY

Travis Lee, 1996	$10,000,000
Justin Upton, 2005	$6,100,000
John Patterson, 1996	$6,075,000
Stephen Drew, 2004	$4,000,000
Max Scherzer, 2006	$3,000,000

ARIZONA DIAMONDBACKS

TOP 2009 ROOKIE: Gerardo Parra, of. The system has been cleared of most of its major league-ready talent, but its top hitter might force his way into the outfield.

BREAKOUT PROSPECT: Rossmel Perez, c. He has the tools to be an offensive catcher, and his arm is above average as well.

SLEEPER: Ollie Linton, of. The 13th-round pick from 2008 is already the fastest player in the system and just needs to get on base more.

SOURCE OF TOP 30 TALENT

Homegrown	26	Acquired	4
College	14	Trades	1
Junior college	1	Rule 5 draft	1
High school	4	Independent leagues	1
Draft-and-follow	1	Free agents/waivers	1
Nondrafted free agents	0		
International	6		

Numbers in parentheses indicate prospect rankings.

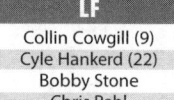

LF
Collin Cowgill (9)
Cyle Hankerd (22)
Bobby Stone
Chris Rahl

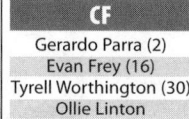

CF
Gerardo Parra (2)
Evan Frey (16)
Tyrell Worthington (30)
Ollie Linton

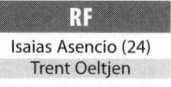

RF
Isaias Asencio (24)
Trent Oeltjen

3B
Clayton Conner
Brandon Burgess

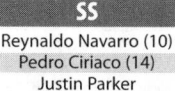

SS
Reynaldo Navarro (10)
Pedro Ciriaco (14)
Justin Parker

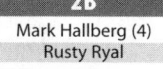

2B
Mark Hallberg (4)
Rusty Ryal

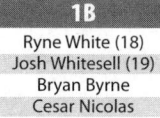

1B
Ryne White (18)
Josh Whitesell (19)
Bryan Byrne
Cesar Nicolas

C
Rossmel Perez (15)
James Skelton (27)
Ed Easley (29)
Ryan Babineau
Frank Curreri
Richard Mercado

RHP

Starters	Relievers
Jarrod Parker (1)	Daniel Stange (12)
Kevin Eichhorn (6)	Bryan Shaw (17)
Cesar Valdez (7)	Tony Barnette (20)
Billy Buckner (8)	Kyler Newby (25)
Barry Enright (11)	Brooks Brown (28)
Trevor Harden (13)	Jose Marte
Wes Roemer (21)	Reid Mahon
Esmerling Vasquez	Jailen Peguero
Miles Reagan	Leo Rosales
Brett Moorhouse	
Sean Morgan	
Matt Torra	
Hector Ambriz	
Matt Green	

LHP

Starters	Relievers
Wade Miley (5)	Daniel Schlereth (3)
Pat McAnaney	Clay Zavada (23)
Scott Maine	Leyson Septimo (26)
	Evan MacLane
	Jon Coutlangus

2008   BONUSES: $4.5 MILLION

Best Pure Hitter: 1B Ryne White (4) is a grinder who keeps his hands back and has the bat speed to catch up to good fastballs. He has excellent hand-eye coordination and an advanced, patient approach.

Best Power Hitter: The good thing about being 5-foot-9 for OF Colin Cowgill (5) is he's short to ball, with a compact swing and high finish that produces loft power.

Fastest Runner: At 5-foot-8 and 160 pounds, OF Ollie Linton (13) plays the little man's game with the best speed in the system. He's also an outstanding drag bunter.

Best Defensive Player: Linton is a ballhawk and above-average defender in center field. C Ryan Babineau (17) is an advanced receiver with a plus arm and threw out 40 percent of basestealers in the short-season Northwest League.

Best Fastball: LHP Daniel Schlereth (1) sits in the mid-90s and touches the high 90s with his heater. Fellow former college closer RHP Bryan Shaw (2) is a tick or two behind Schlereth.

Best Secondary Pitch: Schlereth pitched his way from eighth-rounder in 2007 to first-rounder in 2008 by improving the command of his fastball and devastating power curveball. LHP Wade Miley (1s) has a plus slider with 2-to-8 break.

Best Pro Debut: Cowgill led the NWL with 11 home runs in just 20 games there, then led the low Class A Midwest League playoffs with nine hits, including two homers. RHP Trevor Harden (14) moved from the bullpen to the rotation and struck out 64 in 42 innings with Rookie-level Missoula.

Best Athlete: A Santa Clara recruit, RHP Kevin Eichhorn (3) was a legit two-way prospect as a switch-hitting shortstop and pitcher, and he's ambidextrous.

Most Intriguing Background: Schlereth's father Mark is an actor and NFL analyst who was a Super Bowl-winning offensive lineman for the Redskins and Broncos. Eichhorn's father Mark finished third in the American League Rookie of the Year voting in 1986, part of an 11-year big league career. SS Justin Parker (6) is the older brother of 2007 Diamondbacks first-rounder RHP Jarrod Parker. RHP Jesse Orosco (38) is the son of the ex-big league pitcher of the same name who owns the major league record with 1,252 appearances.

Closest To The Majors: Schlereth will move quickly in relief. LHP Pat McAnaney (8) has a plus changeup and polished three-pitch mix, and he profiles as a fourth starter.

Best Late-Round Pick: Harden showed more presence and firmer stuff as a starter than expected and already has shown one of the best arms in the organization.

The One Who Got Away: RHP Daniel Webb (12) has big raw stuff (having hit 96 mph in the past) and will be one of the nation's top juco prospects at Northwest Florida State (Fla.) JC. LHP Danny Hultzen (10), who flashed an 88-92 mph fastball in the spring, ended up at Virginia.

Assessment: After focusing on pitchability with its 2007 draft class, Arizona got more power arms in 2008, headed by Schlereth and Shaw. However, the Diamondbacks' last few drafts remain short on impact, middle-of-the-diamond athletes and premium bats.

2007   BONUSES: $5.1 MILLION

RHP Jarrod Parker (1) needed just one year to become the franchise's top prospect, and he might need just one more to reach Arizona. SS Reynaldo Navarro (3) is raw but has one of the highest ceilings among the system's position players.

GRADE: B

2006   BONUSES: $6.6 MILLION

The Diamondbacks corralled two impact arms in RHP Max Scherzer (1) and LHP Brett Anderson (2), and used Anderson as a key component in the Dan Haren trade.

GRADE: B+

2005   BONUSES: $9.5 MILLION*

Until it was surpassed by four clubs in 2008, this was the most expensive draft ever. Arizona has no regrets about shelling out a then-record $6.1 million for OF Justin Upton (1). RHP Micah Owings (3) was used in a deal for Adam Dunn, while LHP Greg Smith (6) was part of the Haren package.

GRADE: A

2004   BONUSES: $5.7 MILLION*

The Diamondbacks found the left side of their infield in SS Stephen Drew (1) and 3B Mark Reynolds (16). RHP Ross Ohlendorf (4) factored into a trade for Randy Johnson.

GRADE: B+

*Draft analysis by John Manuel (2008) and Jim Callis (2004-07). Numbers in parentheses indicate draft rounds. *Bonuses for 2004-05 are first 10 rounds only.*

BILL MITCHELL

PROSPECT

JARROD PARKER, RHP

Born: Nov. 24, 1988.
Ht.: 6-0. **Wt.:** 180.
Bats: R. **Throws:** R.
Signed:
HS—Norwell, Ind., 2007
(1st round).
Signed by:
Mike Daughtry.

Parker overpowered weak competition in the Indiana high school ranks as an amateur, and when he returned to the state last season to pitch for low Class A South Bend, he was nearly as dominant while ranking as the Midwest League's No. 3 prospect. He was about two hours from home, where he had emerged from obscurity to become the ninth overall pick in the 2007 draft. Parker earned his first widespread attention pitching for USA Baseball's junior national team in 2006, shocking scouts with his easy velocity from a relatively small frame. He didn't pitch for the Diamondbacks in 2007 after signing for $2.1 million, then piled up 129 innings between the regular season and playoffs in 2008. Arizona closely monitored his workload, keeping him on very limited pitch counts early in the season, and he worked into the seventh inning just once all season. He seemed to tire at midseason but rebounded to go 3-0, 1.91 in his final six regular-season starts. He also was one of the most impressive pitchers in Arizona's instructional league camp.

From the first time scouts saw him, they have been impressed with the easy, high-90s velocity Parker generates from such a smooth arm action. He sits at 94 mph and touches 98 and looks like he could do it all day, drawing comparisons to Tim Lincecum. The Diamondbacks were also impressed with his feel for pitching and his aptitude in quickly improving his other three pitches. He developed better definition between his slider and curveball, with the slider the better pitch in Arizona's eyes. It's a true power breaker in the upper 80s. He seems more confident in the curveball, which also can be a plus pitch and is valuable for changing hitters' eye level. He never had to throw a changeup in high school but showed good feel for it. He was throwing it in hitter's counts and getting swings and misses by the end of the year. Parker is athletic and able to repeat his delivery, and he shows strong command of all four of his pitches. He's athletic and able to overcome his lack of height to get a good downhill plane on his pitches.

Parker needs to be diligent about working to the bottom of the zone, because while young hitters will chase his fastball up, better hitters won't. His fastball command is good for his experience level, but he's still working on locating the ball to both sides of the plate with precision. He's also learning how to work through a game efficiently without piling up huge pitch counts.

Arizona expected a great arm with the ninth overall pick, but Parker's polish has been a bonus, particularly with his limited amateur experience. His four legitimate pitches, command and polished delivery are a recipe for stability and success. He'll open 2009 at either high Class A Visalia or Double-A Mobile, depending on his spring, but either way he'll pitch at multiple levels this season--and one of those levels could be the big leagues.

Year	Club (League)	Class	W	L	ERA	G	GS	CG	SV	IP	H	R	ER	HR	BB	SO	AVG
2008	South Bend (MWL)	LoA	12	5	3.44	24	24	0	0	118	113	56	45	8	33	117	.251
MINOR LEAGUE TOTALS			12	5	3.44	24	24	0	0	118	113	56	45	8	33	117	.251

2 GERARDO PARRA, OF

BORN: May 6, 1987. **B-T:** L-L. **HT.:** 6-1. **WT.:** 186. **SIGNED:** Venezuela, 2004. **SIGNED BY:** Miguel Nava.

After winning the Midwest League batting title with a .320 average in 2007, Parra split 2008 between Visalia and Mobile but made his strongest impression after the regular season. Starting in center field for Zulia in his native Venezuela, he was hitting .333/.412/.522 in mid-December and ranked among the Venezuelan League leaders in several offensive categories. While the individual grades on Parra's tools aren't overwhelming, the sum of what he brings to every game adds up. His best attribute is a smooth batting stroke that generates bat speed. He also has a good approach at the plate and a feel for putting together quality at-bats. He's not a spectacular center fielder but is smooth, can run and makes all the plays. He has plenty of arm for center field, with good accuracy. Parra won't ever hit for great power, with a top end of 12-15 home runs a year, so if he has to move to an outfield corner he starts to look like a tweener. He can improve his plate discipline and learn to pull the ball more to get the most out of his swing. Parra will return to Double-A to open the season but should move up at some point and earn a September callup. As long as he can stay in center field, he should be a productive big leaguer.

Year	Club (League)	Class	AVG	G	AB	R	H	2B	3B	HR	RBI	BB	SO	SB	OBP	SLG
2005	Diamondbacks (DSL)	R	.384	64	237	53	91	14	5	6	45	22	25	26	.444	.561
2006	Missoula (PIO)	R	.328	69	271	46	89	18	4	4	43	25	30	23	.386	.469
2007	South Bend (MWL)	LoA	.320	110	444	64	142	25	4	6	57	30	51	24	.370	.435
	Visalia (CAL)	HiA	.284	24	102	11	29	2	1	2	14	4	17	2	.303	.382
2008	Visalia (CAL)	HiA	.301	50	196	26	59	8	4	2	19	23	31	12	.381	.413
	Mobile (SL)	AA	.275	73	265	35	73	14	6	4	33	24	34	16	.341	.419
MINOR LEAGUE TOTALS			.319	390	1515	235	483	81	24	24	211	128	188	103	.377	.451

3 DANIEL SCHLERETH, LHP

BORN: May 9, 1986. **B-T:** L-L. **HT.:** 6-0. **WT.:** 210. **DRAFTED:** Arizona, 2008 (1st round). **SIGNED BY:** Rodney Davis.

As a local product who attended nearby Arizona, Schlereth was well known to the Diamondbacks. So when he bounced back from Tommy John surgery in 2006 to show his power stuff again last spring, Arizona jumped on him with the 26th overall pick and signed him for $1.33 million. The son of former NFL offensive lineman and ESPN commentator Mark Schlereth, he dominated in the Midwest League playoffs after a late promotion. Schlereth is perfectly suited to a role at the back of a bullpen. He has an explosive fastball that sits in the mid-90s and a power curveball that's also a plus pitch, not to mention the adrenaline and makeup for the role. He showed good control of both pitches last spring and summer. Staying healthy and learning how to absorb a full season's worth of work, along with sharpening his command, are about the only things standing between Schlereth and a major league job. He worked on a change-up in instructional league to give him an occasional third option. Though he worked just 12 regular-season innings after signing, Schlereth probably will jump to Double-A to open 2009. The Diamondbacks won't hold him back if he shows he can handle more advanced hitters. He has the arm to be a closer someday.

Year	Club (League)	Class	W	L	ERA	G	GS	CG	SV	IP	H	R	ER	HR	BB	SO	AVG
2008	Missoula (PIO)	R	0	0	0.00	3	0	0	0	3	3	1	0	0	2	6	.250
	South Bend (MWL)	LoA	1	0	2.00	7	0	0	0	9	3	2	2	0	4	14	.103
MINOR LEAGUE TOTALS			1	0	1.50	10	0	0	0	12	6	3	2	0	6	20	.146

4 MARK HALLBERG, SS/2B

BORN: Dec. 9, 1985. **B-T:** R-R. **HT.:** 5-11. **WT.:** 170. **DRAFTED:** Florida State, 2007 (9th round). **SIGNED BY:** Luke Wrenn.

Hallberg jumped to high Class A for his first full season, but he tore a ligament in his left thumb on a tag play in his second game. He had surgery in mid-April and returned two months later. He made up for lost time by batting .362 and earning league MVP honors in Hawaii Winter Baseball. Hallberg is an organization favorite because he's polished and has few holes in his game. He understands his game and carries out a plan every day, and one team official calls him "Tommy Textbook." His only plus tool is his bat, and he should always be productive because he has the best strike-zone judgement in the system and never gives away at-bats. He should have average power. Most of Hallberg's pure tools are fringy. While he's a fundamentally sound shortstop he doesn't have the athletic ability or speed to play there every day. He played mostly second base in Hawaii and eventually should settle in there, with the ability to fill in at short and third base. The most apt comparison is Mark Loretta, a heady player who ends up as an offensive second baseman but can play all over the field. Hallberg is the kind of player who managers want on the field and batting second every day. He'll advance to Double-A in 2009.

Year	Club (League)	Class	AVG	G	AB	R	H	2B	3B	HR	RBI	BB	SO	SB	OBP	SLG
2007	Yakima (NWL)	SS	.313	58	233	44	73	15	1	6	32	22	21	12	.384	.464
2008	Visalia (CAL)	HiA	.283	69	272	42	77	10	2	3	29	30	28	5	.357	.368
MINOR LEAGUE TOTALS			.297	127	505	86	150	25	3	9	61	52	49	17	.370	.412

5 WADE MILEY, LHP

BILL MITCHELL

BORN: Nov. 13, 1986. **B-T:** L-L. **HT.:** 6-2. **WT.:** 190. **DRAFTED:** Southeastern Louisiana, 2008 (1st round supplemental). **SIGNED BY:** Trip Couch.

Miley was part of a banner crop of Louisiana high school lefties in 2005, as he, Jeremy Bleich (Yankees), Beau Jones (Braves) and Sean West (Marlins) all became supplemental first-round picks. Miley spent three years at Southeastern Louisiana before signing for $877,000 in 2008. His 119 strikeouts last spring trailed only big league alumni Kirk Bullinger and Jeff Williams (125 each) as the most in Southeastern Louisiana history. At his best, Miley offers three above-average pitches. His slider is his calling card and allows him to neutralize righthanders. His fastball ranges from 89-92 mph and can touch the mid-90s, though he's better off at lower velocity with more movement. His changeup shows flashes, and he threw a curveball in college as well. He's athletic and played center field in high school. Miley endured a heavy workload last spring, pitching 102 innings, so the Diamondbacks took it easy with him. He threw just 11 innings at short-season Yakima and mostly worked on the side during instructional league. His main focus for the coming year will be improving his fastball command and getting his delivery under control. Assuming he can tighten up his command, Miley has the well-rounded arsenal and durability to become a No. 3 starter in the big leagues. He'll crank up his pro career at one of Arizona's Class A affiliates this year.

Year	Club (League)	Class	W	L	ERA	G	GS	CG	SV	IP	H	R	ER	HR	BB	SO	AVG
2008	Yakima (NWL)	SS	1	1	4.91	7	0	0	0	11	11	6	6	0	5	11	.250
MINOR LEAGUE TOTALS			1	1	4.91	7	0	0	0	11	11	6	6	0	5	11	.250

6 KEVIN EICHHORN, RHP

BORN: Feb. 6, 1990. **B-T:** B-R. **HT.:** 6-0. **WT.:** 170. **DRAFTED:** HS—Aptos, Calif., 2008 (3rd round). **SIGNED BY:** Darold Brown.

Eichhorn was the best high school prospect in Northern California for the 2008 draft, but teams weren't sure where to draft him because he's still filling out and had a strong commitment to Santa Clara. Arizona took him in the third round and signed him for an above-slot $500,000. His father Mark pitched 11 seasons in the big leagues and helped coach Kevin's team to the 2002 Little League World Series. It's still not clear what kind of pitcher Eichhorn might grow into, but he has a nice foundation in place. He's a quality athlete who also would have played shortstop had he gone to college, and he has good balance in his delivery. He complements an 87-91 mph fastball with a curveball and changeup, and Arizona thinks his already-solid stuff has lots of room for improvement. He has good makeup and intelligence as well. Arizona gave Eichhorn just a brief taste of pro ball and limited work in instructional league, with improving his changeup the biggest focus. In addition to experience and innings, he needs to get more physical in his lower half and learn how to repeat his delivery. His most advanced skill is his ability to fill the zone, but he needs to learn the difference between strikes and quality strikes. With his background and ability, Eichhorn should be able to hit the ground running, so the Diamondbacks will start him off in low Class A this year.

Year	Club (League)	Class	W	L	ERA	G	GS	CG	SV	IP	H	R	ER	HR	BB	SO	AVG
2008	Missoula (PIO)	R	0	0	6.75	2	0	0	0	3	2	2	2	0	1	2	.222
MINOR LEAGUE TOTALS			0	0	6.75	2	0	0	0	3	2	2	2	0	1	2	.222

7 CESAR VALDEZ, RHP

BORN: March 17, 1985. **B-T:** R-R. **HT.:** 6-2. **WT.:** 200. **SIGNED:** Dominican Republic, 2005. **SIGNED BY:** Junior Noboa.

The Diamondbacks signed Valdez at the relatively old age of 20 in 2005, but he has moved quickly since. He broke out in 2008, going 13-8, 3.14 between two levels to win Arizona's minor league pitcher of the year award and a spot on the 40-man roster. Valdez's changeup is a legitimate plus pitch, with splitter action that generates swings and misses. He backs it with a sinker/slider combination, sitting around 90 mph and touching 92 with good movement on his fastball. He always has been a strike-thrower, and he has improved his fastball command and his ability to repeat his delivery. He has a knack for pitching and knows how to attack hitters, particularly by adding and subtracting velocity. Valdez has the repertoire of a pitcher who's reliable more than overpowering. His results in Double-A weren't nearly as good as in high Class A—though he had 10-strikeout games at both levels—indicating he needs to sharpen his command further. While he doesn't have top-end stuff, Valdez has enough weapons to get through a major league lineup as a back-of-the-rotation starter. He'll return to Mobile to start the season but will move up quickly if he handles Double-A hitters.

Year	Club (League)	Class	W	L	ERA	G	GS	CG	SV	IP	H	R	ER	HR	BB	SO	AVG
2005	Diamondbacks (DSL)	R	3	4	2.59	20	0	0	2	31	25	10	9	1	3	45	.208
2006	Yakima (NWL)	SS	7	5	3.15	16	16	2	0	97	97	43	34	5	20	81	.257
2007	South Bend (MWL)	LoA	7	10	3.41	25	25	2	0	148	130	63	56	11	32	106	.235
2008	Visalia (CAL)	HiA	10	3	2.53	15	15	1	0	96	88	36	27	5	16	80	.238
	Mobile (SL)	AA	3	5	4.06	12	12	0	0	64	63	30	29	2	23	60	.261
MINOR LEAGUE TOTALS			30	27	3.19	88	68	5	2	437	403	182	155	24	94	372	.243

8 BILLY BUCKNER, RHP

BORN: Aug. 27, 1983. **B-T:** R-R. **HT.:** 6-2. **WT.:** 215. **DRAFTED:** South Carolina, 2004 (2nd round). **SIGNED BY:** Spencer Graham (Royals).

Buckner came over from the Royals in a trade for Alberto Callaspo after the 2007 season, and his Diamondbacks career got off to a horrendous beginning. He allowed 24 earned runs in his first five starts at Triple-A Tucson and took a 7.94 ERA into May, but was much better the rest of the way, holding his own in spite of bouncing all season between Tucson, where he started, and Arizona, where he worked out of the bullpen. Buckner has the weapons to pitch in the middle of a rotation, with a lively, low-90s sinker and a curveball that's his favorite pitch. He can get batters to swing and miss with both of those pitches. His changeup is a notch behind, and he has used it much more often in the minors than in the majors. He also can throw a knuckle-curve. Buckner's strikeouts were down and walks were up last year, reflecting that he wasn't aggressive enough and didn't have confidence in all his pitches. He also needs to improve his command, which showed progress in 2007 but took a step back in 2008. Buckner has a resilient arm and his velocity goes up a tick out of the bullpen, so Arizona could easily use him in that role. But he holds his stuff well during games and has three good pitches when he's on, suggesting a starting role would be best. He'll compete for Arizona's fifth starter's job in spring training and could occupy a swingman role in 2008 as he sorts out his long-term future.

Year	Club (League)	Class	W	L	ERA	G	GS	CG	SV	IP	H	R	ER	HR	BB	SO	AVG
2004	Idaho Falls (PIO)	R	2	1	3.30	7	5	0	0	30	36	14	11	4	4	37	.303
2005	Burlington (MWL)	LoA	3	7	3.88	11	11	0	0	60	66	36	26	9	17	60	.268
	High Desert (CAL)	HiA	5	6	5.36	17	17	0	0	94	105	65	56	10	46	92	.285
2006	High Desert (CAL)	HiA	7	1	3.90	16	16	0	0	90	92	44	39	6	47	85	.271
	Wichita (TEX)	AA	5	3	4.64	13	13	0	0	76	78	40	39	7	39	63	.265
2007	Wichita (TEX)	AA	1	3	4.66	4	3	0	0	19	20	10	10	4	6	13	.253
	Omaha (PCL)	AAA	9	7	3.78	27	15	0	0	105	108	49	44	11	26	83	.271
	Kansas City (AL)	MAJ	1	2	5.29	7	5	0	0	34	37	20	20	5	16	17	.294
2008	Tucson (PCL)	AAA	5	10	4.95	21	20	0	0	116	136	74	64	9	43	69	.296
	Arizona (NL)	MAJ	1	0	3.21	10	0	0	0	14	16	5	5	3	4	11	.296
MINOR LEAGUE TOTALS			37	38	4.41	116	100	0	0	590	641	332	289	60	228	502	.278
MAJOR LEAGUE TOTALS			2	2	4.69	17	5	0	0	48	53	25	25	8	20	28	.294

9 COLLIN COWGILL, OF

BORN: May 22, 1986. **B-T:** R-L. **HT.:** 5-9. **WT.:** 195. **DRAFTED:** Kentucky, 2008 (5th round). **SIGNED BY:** Matt Haas.

After sitting out the 2007 college season with a broken hamate bone in his left hand, Cowgill hit .290 in the Cape Cod League that summer but declined to sign with the Athletics as a 29th-round pick. Arizona took him 24 rounds higher last year and signed him for $155,000. He again showed aptitude with wood bats, as he led the short-season Northwest League with 11 homers in just 20 games there before getting promoted. One team official calls Cowgill "hitterish." He combines a good approach at the plate with great bat speed, allowing him to consistently put a charge in the ball. He's a confident hitter who will wait on his pitch and crush mistakes. He's also an adept outfielder, with instincts and enough speed under way to play center field, though ultimately he'll probably be better suited to a corner. His arm is average. Cowgill has a couple of things working against him. For one he's already 22, and for another he's just 5-foot-9 and bats righthanded. Arizona brought him to instructional league to focus on cutting down his strike-outs because they'd like for him to hit first or second in the order. The main focus was improving his two-strike approach. The Diamondbacks compare him to Cody Ross for his ability to swing the bat and play anywhere in the outfield. With his age and what he has shown so far, Cowgill will get the chance to jump to Double-A out of spring training.

Year	Club (League)	Class	AVG	G	AB	R	H	2B	3B	HR	RBI	BB	SO	SB	OBP	SLG
2008	Yakima (NWL)	SS	.304	20	79	21	24	3	1	11	28	12	17	5	.415	.785
	South Bend (MWL)	LoA	.249	50	201	31	50	13	3	1	17	25	61	1	.346	.358
MINOR LEAGUE TOTALS			.264	70	280	52	74	16	4	12	45	37	78	6	.366	.479

10 REYNALDO NAVARRO, SS

BORN: Dec. 22, 1989. **B-T:** B-R. **HT.:** 5-10. **WT.:** 175. **DRAFTED:** HS—Gunabo, P.R., 2007 (3rd round). **SIGNED BY:** Ray Blanco.

Because the Diamondbacks lack a complex-based affiliate, Navarro has spent his first two pro seasons in the Rookie-level Pioneer League, where he was probably over his head. He played the entire 2008 season at 18 years old. Navarro has the tools to become an ideal No. 2 hitter. Scouts saw him playing around with switch-hitting as a high schooler in Puerto Rico, and he took it on full-time in instructional league after the 2007 season. He has shown enough progress that the Diamondbacks now like his lefthanded swing better than his natural righty stroke. He has a better swing from the left side, as it's more repeatable and has fewer holes. He does show more power as a righty, but his game always will be about moving the ball around rather than driving it. He also has above-average speed. Shortstop has been a struggle so far for Navarro, who made 28 errors in 2007 and 38 in 2008 to lead the Pioneer League both years. There's some question as to whether he has the arm or actions to stay there, and he may have to move to second base. Arizona says otherwise, arguing that his mistakes are sins of aggression and his first-step quickness and athleticism make him a legitimate shortstop. While the numbers don't show progress, the Diamondbacks were happy with Navarro's year, noting that he improved his body and his quickness and showed a much better idea at the plate. He'll move up to low Class A at age 19 and try to prove he can stay at short.

Year	Club (League)	Class	AVG	G	AB	R	H	2B	3B	HR	RBI	BB	SO	SB	OBP	SLG
2007	Missoula (PIO)	R	.250	60	212	21	53	4	0	1	17	6	41	6	.274	.283
2008	Missoula (PIO)	R	.258	72	291	42	75	17	7	2	31	25	77	17	.323	.385
MINOR LEAGUE TOTALS			.254	132	503	63	128	21	7	3	48	31	118	23	.303	.342

11 BARRY ENRIGHT, RHP

BORN: March 30, 1986. **B-T:** R-R. **HT.:** 6-2. **WT.:** 200. **DRAFTED:** Pepperdine, 2007 (2nd round). **SIGNED BY:** Hal Kurtzman.

In his first full season, Enright did the expected in making 29 starts and piling up 164 innings, which led the high Class A California League. His 143 strikeouts topped the league as well. His ERA wasn't what Arizona would have hoped for, but he was much better in the second half of the season, with a 5.11 ERA in the first half and 3.69 ERA in the second. Enright succeeds by throwing strikes and eating innings, and with his solid frame and clean arm action he has already shown he can be a workhorse. His fastball works around 90 mph, touching 92, and he tightened up his slider and showed progress with his changeup last season. He also showed an occasional curveball to give hitters a different look. His early struggles taught Enright the importance of fastball command as well as pitch efficiency. Early in the season he worked up in the zone way too often, and he also threw too many pitches. He doesn't throw anything overpowering so has to be able to spot his pitches. Enright's ceiling is as a back-of-the-rotation starter, and the key to reaching that will be how he handles lefthanders, who batted .320 against him last year (compared to .239 for righties), as he moves up. He'll move up to Double-A for 2009.

Year	Club (League)	Class	W	L	ERA	G	GS	CG	SV	IP	H	R	ER	HR	BB	SO	AVG
2007	Yakima (NWL)	SS	0	0	0.00	5	0	0	0	8	4	0	0	0	3	12	.148
	South Bend (MWL)	LoA	0	0	0.00	1	0	0	1	2	1	0	0	0	0	1	.167
	Visalia (CAL)	HiA	0	0	0.00	4	0	0	1	5	3	1	0	0	2	4	.167
2008	Visalia (CAL)	HiA	12	8	4.44	29	29	0	0	164	185	88	81	17	35	143	.281
MINOR LEAGUE TOTALS			12	8	4.07	39	29	0	2	179	193	89	81	17	40	160	.272

12 DANIEL STANGE, RHP

BORN: Dec. 22, 1985. **B-T:** R-R. **HT.:** 6-3. **WT.:** 185. **DRAFTED:** UC Riverside, 2006 (7th round). **SIGNED BY:** Mark Baca.

In a system that has been thinned out by graduation and trades, Stange provides the kind of power tools that have become fewer and farther between. He was drafted by the Braves out of high school in 2003 but headed to UC Riverside instead and became the closer there, and Arizona kept him in the role after drafting him in 2006. He was on the fast track but got derailed by Tommy John surgery in August 2007. Stange has the power arm and mentality to pitch at the back of a major league bullpen, with a fastball that can touch 99 but usually sits in the mid-90s as well as a slider that's a swing-and-miss pitch. He returned to action last June, dominating low Class A batters, and by the end of the summer he was touching 93 again. It was Stange's violent delivery that got him sent to the bullpen in the first place, so the Diamondbacks are working with him to tone it down enough to keep him healthy without costing him any life on his pitches. He'll have to sharpen his command as he moves up and returns to full strength. Arizona says Stange is getting close to where he was before he was hurt, and he had reached Double-A at that point, so he should head back there if he still looks good in spring training. If he's healthy and effective, he could move up quickly.

Year	Club (League)	Class	W	L	ERA	G	GS	CG	SV	IP	H	R	ER	HR	BB	SO	AVG
2006	Missoula (PIO)	R	5	2	4.25	27	0	0	13	36	39	19	17	2	17	48	.267
2007	Visalia (CAL)	HiA	4	5	3.19	38	0	0	16	42	37	26	15	3	18	53	.230
	Mobile (SL)	AA	1	0	5.40	5	0	0	1	7	9	4	4	1	2	5	.321
2008	South Bend (MWL)	LoA	1	0	1.59	11	0	0	1	17	11	3	3	0	1	17	.183
	Visalia (CAL)	HiA	1	2	3.95	11	0	0	0	14	10	6	6	2	6	14	.204
MINOR LEAGUE TOTALS			12	9	3.50	92	0	0	31	116	106	58	45	8	44	137	.239

13 TREVOR HARDEN, RHP

BORN: Sept. 1, 1987. **B-T:** B-R. **HT.:** 6-2. **WT.:** 215. **DRAFTED:** New Mexico JC, 2008 (14th round). **SIGNED BY:** Rodney Davis.

Harden made as strong an impression as any of the players in Arizona's 2008 draft class, dominating both out of the bullpen and as a starter at Missoula. He was an important recruit for Miami and would have been a closer candidate for the Hurricanes—the same role he had at New Mexico JC—but the Diamondbacks were able to sign him for $75,000. He missed six weeks of action before the draft with hamstring problems but was healthy at Rookie-level Missoula, showing a low-90s fastball that touched 94 with sink. His slider also can be a plus pitch though it's inconsistent, and he also already has a decent changeup. He's an adrenaline-rush pitcher who seems well suited for the back of the bullpen, but Arizona tried him as a starter because of his three-pitch mix and liked the results. He struck out 10 in each of his first two starts, showing his tremendous feel for how to attack hitters. He has a strong frame and clean delivery that suggest he'll be durable, and the Diamondbacks love his mound demeanor. It's a little early to get too excited, but Harden has a lot of ingredients for success. Team officials are interested to see what he'll do in the South Bend rotation.

Year	Club (League)	Class	W	L	ERA	G	GS	CG	SV	IP	H	R	ER	HR	BB	SO	AVG
2008	Missoula (PIO)	R	1	3	1.91	12	6	0	2	42	34	14	9	2	11	64	.224
MINOR LEAGUE TOTALS			1	3	1.91	12	6	0	2	42	34	14	9	2	11	64	.224

14 PEDRO CIRIACO, SS/2B

BORN: Sept. 27, 1985. **B-T:** R-R. **HT.:** 6-0. **WT.:** 160. **SIGNED:** Dominican Republic, 2003. **SIGNED BY:** Junior Noboa.

Ciriaco had always been much more about potential than performance in his five previous seasons in the organization, but a chance to repeat high Class A allowed him to put himself back into the Diamondbacks' plans. He was a California League all-star after putting together by far his best offensive season, then got added to the 40-man roster. Ciriaco could always run and play shortstop, but he tended to get the bat knocked out of his hands. He made adjustments with his approach and his hands, creating less movement in his swing, and started to hit the ball with some authority. He also greatly improved his basestealing efficiency, leading the organization with 40 steals and getting caught just nine times. The game also slowed down for him on defense, and his error total dropped for the second straight season, to 23. With continued improvements in his consistency he can be an above-average shortstop, with plenty of range and arm for the position. More important, he looks like he can hold his own with the bat as well. He worked out in the Diamondbacks' Dominican instructional camp over the winter and will be Mobile's starting shortstop to open 2009.

Year	Club (League)	Class	AVG	G	AB	R	H	2B	3B	HR	RBI	BB	SO	SB	OBP	SLG
2003	Diamondbacks (DSL)	R	.231	57	221	40	51	10	2	0	16	16	34	14	.290	.294
2004	Diamondbacks (DSL)	R	.349	67	252	45	88	11	4	1	18	19	33	29	.401	.437
2005	Missoula (PIO)	R	.240	69	254	28	61	9	4	2	31	7	50	7	.264	.331
2006	South Bend (MWL)	LoA	.264	128	550	77	145	15	5	2	32	32	96	19	.308	.320
2007	Visalia (CAL)	HiA	.251	119	463	61	116	14	5	3	39	20	81	20	.286	.322
2008	Visalia (CAL)	HiA	.310	124	520	85	161	26	5	5	61	18	89	40	.333	.408
MINOR LEAGUE TOTALS			.275	564	2260	336	622	85	25	13	197	112	383	129	.313	.352

15 ROSSMEL PEREZ, C

BORN: Aug. 26, 1989. **B-T:** B-R. **HT.:** 5-10. **WT.:** 180. **SIGNED:** Venezuela, 2006. **SIGNED BY:** Miguel Nava.

Perez remains a diamond in the rough for now, but he has the tools and has shown enough flashes of his ability that he could be on the verge of a breakout season. He spent his first domestic season at Missoula and was one of three Diamondbacks players on BA's Pioneer League Top 20 Prospects list (along with pitchers Bryan Shaw and Trevor Harden) despite uneven performance at the plate. Arizona signed him for $150,000 in 2006 as a switch-hitting catcher with good defensive tools. He has a solid approach at the plate with a smooth, line-drive swing and plenty of bat speed. He already walks more than he strikes out. His swing from the left is better at this point, and he's still growing into his body and tapping into his power, though he'll probably never have more than average power. He shows good quickness behind the plate and moves well, with soft hands and an above-average arm. With his quick release, he threw out 40 percent of basestealers last year. He's learning English to help him work with pitchers and is working on his game management. Perez is ready for full-season ball and should be South Bend's starting catcher in 2009.

Year	Club (League)	Class	AVG	G	AB	R	H	2B	3B	HR	RBI	BB	SO	SB	OBP	SLG
2006	Diamondbacks (DSL)	R	.155	32	71	7	11	2	0	0	5	10	12	0	.307	.183
2007	Diamondbacks (DSL)	R	.306	39	111	8	34	4	1	0	5	28	19	2	.469	.360
2008	Missoula (PIO)	R	.243	43	144	15	35	8	0	0	11	16	13	0	.323	.299
MINOR LEAGUE TOTALS			.245	114	326	30	80	14	1	0	21	54	44	2	.373	.294

16 EVAN FREY, OF

BORN: June 7, 1986. **B-T:** L-L. **HT.:** 6-0. **WT.:** 170. **DRAFTED:** Missouri, 2007 (10th round). **SIGNED BY:** Joe Robinson.

Few players understand their strengths and weaknesses as well as Frey, and he put all his skills on display last year. In his first full season, he earned a midseason promotion and finished the year with a .400 on-base percentage. He also impressed the organization with his performance in the Arizona Fall League, where he hit .288 with three triples. Frey occupied a center fielder/tablesetter role in college at Missouri and stepped right into the same role in pro ball. He's a mighty mite, with lots of fast twitch in a small package. He's an old-school, gritty player who understands that small ball is his game, so he puts the ball on the ground, moves it around the field and tries to use his above-average speed. He controls the strike zone and shows occasional gap power. Frey is a good center fielder with a playable throwing arm. In addition to speed he has good instincts and takes good routes, so his defense plays up, and he has the ability to play all three outfield positions. Still, while Frey gets the most out of his ability, he doesn't have a true plus tool, and without power or overwhelming speed he probably profiles as a fourth outfielder. Just don't try telling him that. He'll keep trying to overcome the doubters in Double-A this year.

Year	Club (League)	Class	AVG	G	AB	R	H	2B	3B	HR	RBI	BB	SO	SB	OBP	SLG
2007	Yakima (NWL)	SS	.309	58	246	48	76	8	6	0	21	27	42	13	.384	.390
2008	South Bend (MWL)	LoA	.327	75	309	54	101	16	6	0	29	39	38	20	.401	.417
	Visalia (CAL)	HiA	.297	56	229	44	68	5	5	3	18	37	46	17	.399	.402
MINOR LEAGUE TOTALS			.313	189	784	146	245	29	17	3	68	103	126	50	.395	.404

17 BRYAN SHAW, RHP

BORN: Nov. 8, 1987. **B-T:** B-R. **HT.:** 6-1. **WT.:** 210. **DRAFTED:** Long Beach State, 2008 (2nd round). **SIGNED BY:** Jim Dedrick.

Shaw hails from Livermore, Calif., where there must be something in the water. Both future Hall of Famer Randy Johnson and former Giants reliever Erick Threets are also from the city, and both have thrown 100 mph. Shaw sits more comfortably in the mid-90s, and as a 6-foot-1 righthander isn't quite as intimidating on the mound. He was Long Beach State's closer last spring, signing with Arizona as a second-round pick for $553,000, then worked out of the bullpen at Missoula and South Bend but didn't have as much success. His pure stuff is impressive, though, as he sits at 92-94 mph and touches 96 with his fastball, and has a power slider that could develop into a plus pitch. He also throws a splitter and a changeup, though both pitches need more development. Dialing in his command will be key for Shaw, particularly with his fastball, as will working the ball down in the strike zone. Shaw is young for a college junior, and will play the 2009 season at 21, so the Diamondbacks will be patient with him. In fact, they'll probably watch him through the spring and into the summer to see whether he'll be a starter or reliever. His stuff might be a bit short for the back of the bullpen, while he would take more time to develop as a starter. He should open his first full pro season in low Class A.

Year	Club (League)	Class	W	L	ERA	G	GS	CG	SV	IP	H	R	ER	HR	BB	SO	AVG
2008	Missoula (PIO)	R	0	1	6.75	10	0	0	2	17	24	19	13	2	7	17	.316
	South Bend (MWL)	LoA	0	1	4.03	11	0	0	0	22	18	12	10	0	6	16	.217
MINOR LEAGUE TOTALS			0	2	5.22	21	0	0	2	40	42	31	23	2	13	33	.264

18 RYNE WHITE, 1B

BORN: Oct. 17, 1986. **B-T:** L-L. **HT.:** 5-11. **WT.:** 205. **DRAFTED:** Purdue, 2008 (4th round). **SIGNED BY:** Mike Daughtry.

The Diamondbacks found a couple of polished college hitters who could move quickly through the organization with their fourth and fifth selections in the 2008 draft, White and Collin Cowgill. White finished third in batting in NCAA Division I in 2007 at .452, and while his average dropped more than 100 points in his draft year, he showed more power and the Diamondbacks signed him for $213,000. He hit seven home runs in Missoula to earn a promotion to South Bend, and then showed he has legitimate power to all fields by homering to left at Chase Field in the final game of instructional league when the Diamondbacks give their prospects a chance to play in a big league park. He also is a strong all-around hitter, and actually handled lefthanders better than righthanders last year. White immediately became the best defensive first baseman in the organization, with good footwork around the bag, and he's athletic enough to play in the outfield as well. He played there as a college freshman and has an average arm. White is a well-rounded player who gets the most out of his ability. He doesn't look like a star, with a slightly more powerful Sean Casey as his most optimistic comparison, but has a good probability of reaching the big leagues. He'll probably move up to high Class A to open 2009.

Year	Club (League)	Class	AVG	G	AB	R	H	2B	3B	HR	RBI	BB	SO	SB	OBP	SLG
2008	Missoula (PIO)	R	.274	58	234	40	64	13	1	7	38	26	41	1	.348	.427
	South Bend (MWL)	LoA	.358	12	53	6	19	6	0	0	13	4	10	0	.404	.472
MINOR LEAGUE TOTALS			.289	70	287	46	83	19	1	7	51	30	51	1	.358	.436

19 JOSH WHITESELL, 1B

BORN: April 14, 1982. **B-T:** L-L. **HT.:** 6-1. **WT.:** 225. **DRAFTED:** Loyola Marymount, 2003 (6th round). **SIGNED BY:** Anthony Arango (Expos).

Signed as a minor league free agent after five seasons in the Expos/Nationals organization, Whitesell was a revelation in his first experience above Double-A. He mashed at Tucson to earn a September callup, and a pinch-hit home run against the Rockies gave the Diamondbacks a glimpse of his value to a major league team. Whitesell's consistency was the most impressive aspect of his performance in Tucson, as he finished among the Pacific Coast League leaders in several offensive categories and set a career high for home runs. He has pure controlled violence in his lefthanded swing, and he's also able to take walks and knows how to put an at-bat together. He has some athletic ability but below-average speed, and he's a hard worker. He's an average first baseman and could be adequate as a fill-in in left field as well. He strikes out a lot, which is an acceptable tradeoff if he shows plus power, and some in the organization expect him to cut down on the strikeouts as he matures. Whitesell doesn't profile as an everyday player in the big leagues, but his lefty power is a nice luxury on the bench, and might be able to handle a platoon role. Arizona will give him every chance to earn a spot on the big league roster in spring training.

Year	Club (League)	Class	AVG	G	AB	R	H	2B	3B	HR	RBI	BB	SO	SB	OBP	SLG
2003	Vermont (NYP)	SS	.246	49	167	13	41	10	1	5	19	28	53	0	.365	.407
2004	Savannah (SAL)	LoA	.250	113	380	56	95	29	0	16	54	58	91	0	.351	.453
2005	Potomac (CAR)	HiA	.293	113	389	59	114	32	2	18	66	74	125	1	.416	.524
2006	Harrisburg (EL)	AA	.264	127	402	47	106	11	0	19	56	53	125	2	.354	.433
2007	Harrisburg (EL)	AA	.284	119	387	78	110	23	1	21	74	87	107	6	.425	.512
2008	Tucson (PCL)	AAA	.328	127	475	86	156	36	0	26	110	74	136	1	.425	.568
	Arizona (NL)	MAJ	.286	7	7	1	2	0	0	1	1	1	2	0	.444	.714
MINOR LEAGUE TOTALS			.283	648	2200	339	622	141	4	105	379	374	637	10	.394	.494
MAJOR LEAGUE TOTALS			.286	7	7	1	2	0	0	1	1	1	2	0	.444	.714

20 TONY BARNETTE, RHP

BORN: Nov. 9, 1983. **B-T:** R-R. **HT.:** 6-1. **WT.:** 192. **DRAFTED:** Arizona State, 2006 (10th round). **SIGNED BY:** Steve Kmetko.

Barnette had some success in his first two seasons in the organization, even making the Midwest League all-star team in 2007, but didn't really mark himself as a legitimate prospect until he skipped a level and seemingly improved from start to start in Double-A last season. He led the Southern League in strikeouts (133 in 154 innings) and ranked second in wins (11) and ninth in ERA (3.87). He always has thrown strikes with a fastball that ranges from 88-92 mph, but the Diamondbacks like to emphasize throwing quality strikes, and that's what Barnette did more of in 2008. His slider and changeup should be average pitches as well, with the slider occasionally a plus offering, and he commands those pitches well too. He can move the ball to all four quadrants of the strike zone and repeats his delivery, which has made him durable as a pro. Still, none of his pitches overpowers, he doesn't miss a lot of bats, and when he leaves the ball up he's prone to giving up home runs. So some think he will ultimately end up in the bullpen, where he spent most of his two years at Arizona State. As a senior draft in 2006, he's already 25, though skipping to Mobile and succeeding helped him speed up his timetable. He'll move up to Arizona's new Triple-A Reno affiliate and will be a candidate to fill big league openings if he pitches well.

Year	Club (League)	Class	W	L	ERA	G	GS	CG	SV	IP	H	R	ER	HR	BB	SO	AVG
2006	Missoula (PIO)	R	6	4	3.89	15	15	0	0	76	81	41	33	9	20	74	.265
2007	South Bend (MWL)	LoA	8	8	3.60	26	25	1	1	160	160	74	64	11	28	108	.262
2008	Mobile (SL)	AA	11	7	3.87	27	27	0	0	154	143	70	66	17	42	133	.246
MINOR LEAGUE TOTALS			25	19	3.76	68	67	1	1	390	384	185	163	37	90	315	.256

21 WES ROEMER, RHP

BORN: Oct. 7, 1986. **B-T:** R-R. **HT.:** 6-0. **WT.:** 200. **DRAFTED:** Cal State Fullerton, 2007 (1st round supplemental). **SIGNED BY:** Mark Baca.

On the plus side, Roemer took every turn in the rotation in his first full season and finished with 163 innings, second in the California League to rotation-mate Barry Enright. On the other hand, he tied for the league lead with 12 losses and was alone at the top with 25 homers allowed. The Diamondbacks prefer to focus on the big picture, noting that Roemer was 21 and learning how to apply his stuff against professional hitters, as well as how to work through the aches and pains of a long pro season. He's a bulldog and has always been a strike-thrower, so now he needs to learn that it's about the quality of the strikes, not the quantity. He piled up strikeouts in college, when he was a first-team All-American as a sophomore, but he needs to be a sinker/slider guy for whom strikeouts are only a by-product, and must be more efficient with his pitches. Similarly, while he can touch the mid-90s if he puts everything into a fastball, he is best off dialing it down to around 90 with good sink. His slider can be a plus pitch, but he falls in love with it at times. His changeup still isn't ready for prime time. Roemer showed flashes of his ability last year, giving up three runs or fewer in 17 starts, so Arizona hopes he can apply his ability more consistently in Double-A this season.

Year	Club (League)	Class	W	L	ERA	G	GS	CG	SV	IP	H	R	ER	HR	BB	SO	AVG
2007	Yakima (NWL)	SS	1	0	4.50	8	0	0	0	12	11	6	6	1	2	18	.234
2008	Visalia (CAL)	HiA	7	12	4.59	28	28	1	0	163	199	95	83	25	33	122	.308
MINOR LEAGUE TOTALS			8	12	4.59	36	28	1	0	175	210	101	89	26	35	140	.303

22 CYLE HANKERD, OF

BORN: Jan. 24, 1985. **B-T:** R-R. **HT.:** 6-3. **WT.:** 180. **DRAFTED:** Southern California, 2006 (3rd round). **SIGNED BY:** Hal Kurtzman.

After a standout college career at Southern California and impressive debut in 2006, when he won the Northwest League MVP award and batting title (.384), Hankerd stagnated a bit over his first two full seasons. A wrist injury held him back in 2007 at Visalia, but he was simply inconsistent at Mobile in 2008. The Diamondbacks sent him to Hawaii Winter Baseball to try to get his swing and confidence back, and he batted .318 and led the league with 30 RBIs. While he was playing against less experienced pitching, Hankerd did show a better swing and again hit to all fields, as he does when he's dialed in. He also showed some leverage in his swing, allowing him to tap into what should be above-average power. But for most of the last two seasons, he was a 6-foot-3 player who hit like a middle infielder. Hankerd is a below-average runner with an average arm, but he has become a slightly above-average corner outfielder with good positioning, routes and jumps. He played both left and right field last season. Hankerd will try to earn a Triple-A roster spot and put himself into Arizona's big league plans by continuing the success he had last fall.

Year	Club (League)	Class	AVG	G	AB	R	H	2B	3B	HR	RBI	BB	SO	SB	OBP	SLG
2006	Yakima (NWL)	SS	.384	54	216	24	83	17	0	4	38	13	54	0	.424	.519
	Lancaster (CAL)	HiA	.369	18	65	15	24	4	0	8	23	8	9	0	.474	.800
2007	Visalia (CAL)	HiA	.285	103	386	55	110	27	1	8	54	35	60	2	.368	.422
2008	Mobile (SL)	AA	.245	125	436	35	107	17	3	5	52	21	67	2	.291	.333
MINOR LEAGUE TOTALS			.294	300	1103	129	324	65	4	25	167	77	190	4	.356	.428

23 CLAY ZAVADA, LHP

BORN: June 28, 1984. **B-T:** L-L. **HT.:** 6-1. **WT.:** 195. **DRAFTED:** Southern Illinois-Edwardsville, 2006 (30th round). **SIGNED BY:** Mike Daughtry.

Zavada's story is the stuff movies are made from. The Diamondbacks took him late in the 2006 draft and his career got off to a decent start, but he asked for his release after the 2006 season when his father died, so he could help out his family. After a year away from the game, he was interested in getting back into baseball, so Arizona helped him hook on with Southern Illinois of the independent Frontier League. He posted a 1.72 ERA in 12 appearances, so Arizona brought him back, doing so by means of an unofficial trade with the Miners. Trades with independent clubs aren't allowed by Major League Baseball, so the Diamondbacks released first baseman Brad Miller to sign with Southern Illinois and re-signed Zavada. And he wasn't just a heartwarming story—Zavada dominated in South Bend. He was old for the league but he gave up just one hit to a lefthander in 35 innings. He has a fastball that sits in the low 90s that hitters have trouble picking up, as well as a changeup that can be a plus pitch, and his breaking ball is developing into enough of a weapon to allow him to dominate out of the pen. He's not overpowering but throws strikes and knows how to miss bats. He's very aggressive and controls both sides of the plate. Zavada is back on the radar and was added to the 40-man roster after the season. Now he'll try to make up for lost time, possibly jumping to the Mobile bullpen to start the season. He should at least be able to reach the big leagues as a lefty specialist and could be a little bit better than that.

Year	Club (League)	Class	W	L	ERA	G	GS	CG	SV	IP	H	R	ER	HR	BB	SO	AVG
2006	Missoula (PIO)	R	2	3	3.10	22	0	0	2	49	41	29	17	3	15	51	.225
2007	Did Not Play																
2008	Southern Illinois (FRN)	IND	2	1	1.72	12	0	0	4	16	7	3	3	0	4	22	.137
	South Bend (MWL)	LoA	3	1	0.51	24	0	0	8	35	6	2	2	1	5	54	.056
MINOR LEAGUE TOTALS			5	4	2.02	46	0	0	10	85	47	31	19	4	20	105	.162

24 ISAIAS ASENCIO, OF

BORN: Dec. 31, 1987. **B-T:** R-R. **HT.:** 6-0. **WT.:** 169. **SIGNED:** Dominican Republic, 2006. **SIGNED BY:** Junior Noboa.

Asencio spent two seasons in the Rookie-level Dominican Summer League before making his domestic debut with Missoula last year. He got off to a horrendous start, hitting .194 in his first month, but three multihit games won him player-of-the-week honors in the Pioneer League and seemed to get his swing dialed in, and he raised his average by 100 points over the rest of the season. Asencio is a collection of intriguing tools at this point, and the Diamondbacks are trying to harness and polish them. His baseball experience has been limited, so they're just excited that he has responded well to the challenges they've thrown at him. He has drawn comparisons to Juan Encarnacion not just for his build, but for his set-up at the plate, the power potential in his bat and his plus throwing arm. He has wiry strength and shows a knack for manipulating the barrel of the bat and generating good bat speed. Plate discipline is a foreign concept to him at this point, but if he gets to a pitch he can drive it. It's too early to say exactly what Asencio will be, but he's an interesting athlete with several potential plus tools. He'll be a project and could spend some more time in extended spring training before reporting to Yakima in June.

Year	Club (League)	Class	AVG	G	AB	R	H	2B	3B	HR	RBI	BB	SO	SB	OBP	SLG
2006	Diamondbacks (DSL)	R	.228	58	189	34	43	18	2	2	26	21	44	1	.324	.376
2007	Diamondbacks (DSL)	R	.091	8	22	1	2	2	0	0	1	4	4	2	.276	.182
2008	Missoula (PIO)	R	.293	58	215	34	63	10	5	9	36	6	53	3	.325	.512
MINOR LEAGUE TOTALS			.254	124	426	69	108	30	7	11	63	31	101	6	.321	.434

25 KYLER NEWBY, RHP

BORN: Feb. 22, 1985. **B-T:** R-R. **HT.:** 6-4. **WT.:** 225. **DRAFTED:** Mesa (Ariz.) CC, D/F 2004 (50th round). **SIGNED BY:** Steve Kmetko.

Newby was one of the final selections of the 2004 draft, signing with the Diamondbacks the next spring as a draft-and-follow. They sent him straight to the bullpen and he had great success in his first two seasons in the organization, earning a trip to Hawaii Winter Baseball after the 2006 season. He pitched well there, too, but he also strained a ligament in his elbow, essentially making 2007 a lost season for him. He was fully healthy in 2008 and put himself back on the organization radar, getting added to the 40-man roster at the end of the season. Newby has three quality pitches, allowing him to succeed without dominant velocity. His fastball peaks in the low-90s, but it's heavy and he commands it well, and his slider and splitter can also generate swings and misses. Newby also benefits from a deceptive delivery, and all his pitches come from the same arm slot, so batters have a hard time identifying them. He's never going to be more than a middle reliever, but his success against lefthanders (.165 opponent average, vs. .232 against righties) last season suggests he can be used for multiple-inning stretches. Despite his previous injury, his build also means he should be durable. If he pitches well in Double-A, Newby could be good bullpen insurance for the Diamondbacks as the year goes on.

ARIZONA DIAMONDBACKS

Year	Club (League)	Class	W	L	ERA	G	GS	CG	SV	IP	H	R	ER	HR	BB	SO	AVG
2005	Yakima (NWL)	SS	1	0	2.18	24	0	0	2	41	25	12	10	1	14	66	.172
2006	South Bend (MWL)	LoA	6	1	2.05	28	0	0	11	44	22	10	10	0	19	64	.151
2007	Visalia (CAL)	HiA	1	0	1.50	9	0	0	2	12	7	3	2	0	2	10	.156
2008	Visalia (CAL)	HiA	4	3	2.69	46	0	0	16	67	49	23	20	4	30	86	.199
MINOR LEAGUE TOTALS			12	4	2.30	107	0	0	31	164	103	48	42	5	65	226	.177

26 LEYSON SEPTIMO, LHP

BORN: July 7, 1985. **B-T:** L-L. **HT.:** 6-0. **WT.:** 150. **SIGNED:** Dominican Republic, 2003. **SIGNED BY:** Junior Noboa.

Septimo created a stir after the 2007 season, when news came out that he had been converted to the mound and was throwing in the high 90s. The Diamondbacks gambled (correctly) that no one would take him in the major league Rule 5 draft that year with such a thin record as a pitcher, but they didn't leave anything to chance after 2008, adding Septimo to the 40-man roster despite a modest first season on the mound. The reason is that everyone got a look at Septimo's powerful left arm, a rare commodity even if it's still in need of considerable polish. Septimo spent his first five years in the organization as an outfielder, and while his throws from the outfield were sometimes clocked in triple digits, he never had much success at the plate. His first season on the mound showed much more potential, though he's not a natural pitcher and still has a lot of work to do on the basics of his delivery and control. But a lefthander who can throw consistently in the mid-90s will get plenty of opportunity to work through the kinks. He uses a slider as his second pitch, and that's probably all he'll need in his short relief stints. Septimo is still relatively young at 23, and the Diamondbacks think when it clicks for him, he'll get to the big leagues quickly.

Year	Club (League)	Class	W	L	ERA	G	GS	CG	SV	IP	H	R	ER	HR	BB	SO	AVG
2008	Visalia (CAL)	HiA	0	2	5.49	27	0	0	1	41	42	27	25	4	33	44	.263
MINOR LEAGUE TOTALS			0	2	5.49	27	0	0	1	41	42	27	25	4	33	44	.263

27 JAMES SKELTON, C

BORN: Oct. 28, 1985. **B-T:** L-R. **HT.:** 5-11. **WT.:** 165. **DRAFTED:** HS—West Covina, Calif., 2004 (14th round). **SIGNED BY:** Rob Wilfong (Tigers).

The Diamondbacks aren't exactly looking for catchers in the big leagues, but they liked Skelton's package of skills so much that they took him in the major league Rule 5 draft from the Tigers. Skelton has been a productive offensive player in the Tigers system, and his on-base skills are off the charts. He hit .302 overall in 2008, the third straight season he has batted .300 or better, and he has good plate discipline and a patient approach. He's a singles hitter who offers little power. Skelton wasn't a bigger priority for the Tigers because it's not clear he will end up as a big league catcher. He has a small, slender body and isn't a great receiver. He has a strong arm and threw out 38 percent of basestealers last season, and he also showed improvement in handling pitchers last season. Arizona likes him as an offensive, athletic catcher, though he probably doesn't profile as an everyday player. He'll get a look at other positions in spring training, and the Diamondbacks will try to carry him as a third catcher who can play all over the field and get on base as a pinch-hitter. If they don't keep him, Skelton will have to be placed on waivers and offered back to the Tigers for half his $50,000 draft price.

Year	Club (League)	Class	AVG	G	AB	R	H	2B	3B	HR	RBI	BB	SO	SB	OBP	SLG
2004	Tigers (GCL)	R	.140	23	43	3	6	1	0	0	2	7	11	0	.260	.163
2005	Lakeland (FSL)	HiA	.000	1	1	0	0	0	0	0	0	0	1	0	.000	.000
	Tigers (GCL)	R	.182	17	33	6	6	1	0	0	1	13	9	0	.413	.212
2006	Oneonta (NYP)	SS	.300	42	130	20	39	8	1	1	22	21	29	1	.403	.400
2007	West Michigan (MWL)	LoA	.309	101	353	60	109	24	2	7	52	55	53	18	.402	.448
2008	Lakeland (FSL)	HiA	.307	63	212	43	65	8	2	3	23	64	50	14	.408	.406
	Erie (EL)	AA	.294	24	85	22	25	2	0	2	11	19	23	1	.425	.388
MINOR LEAGUE TOTALS			.292	271	857	154	250	44	5	13	111	179	176	34	.415	.400

28 BROOKS BROWN, RHP

BORN: June 20, 1985. **B-T:** L-R. **HT.:** 6-3. **WT.:** 205. **DRAFTED:** Georgia, 2006 (1st round supplemental). **SIGNED BY:** Howard McCullough.

Stuck on the worst team in the Southern League, Brown persevered and was Mobile's most reliable starter throughout 2008, taking a 3.63 ERA into the final month of the season. But the wheels came off after that, as his 0-5, 6.75 August made for an ugly season line. He followed it with a 5.61 ERA in 26 Arizona Fall League innings. Most think he simply wore down, as he showed no sign of injury. Brown is a sinker/slider pitcher who shows a good feel for pitching and comes right at hitters, and some managers in the Southern League called his sinker one of the league's best. He throws it at 88-92 mph and must keep it down in the zone to be effective. His slider has two-plane break and can also be a plus pitch when he commands it effectively. His changeup is a fringe-average pitch and hasn't developed as hoped, leading some to suggest Brown take his two good pitches and go to the bullpen. His big frame and durability say starter, but his results at the end of 2008 suggest otherwise. The Diamondbacks will give him a shot in the Reno rotation, where sharpening his command and keeping his stuff down will be even more important. But he's likely to earn his first big league opportunity as a reliever.

Year	Club (League)	Class	W	L	ERA	G	GS	CG	SV	IP	H	R	ER	HR	BB	SO	AVG
2006	Yakima (NWL)	SS	0	2	3.42	13	1	0	0	24	23	11	9	2	12	30	.250
2007	Visalia (CAL)	HiA	6	3	2.81	14	14	0	0	80	66	30	25	2	23	74	.224
	Mobile (SL)	AA	4	4	3.66	12	12	0	0	66	64	30	27	2	36	54	.261
2008	Mobile (SL)	AA	6	15	4.18	26	26	0	0	144	152	69	67	8	67	112	.278
MINOR LEAGUE TOTALS			16	24	3.66	65	53	0	0	314	305	140	128	14	138	270	.259

29 ED EASLEY, C

BORN: Dec. 21, 1985. **B-T:** R-R. **HT.:** 6-0. **WT.:** 192. **DRAFTED:** Mississippi State, 2007 (1st round supplemental). **SIGNED BY:** Mike Valarezo.

Easley won the Johnny Bench award as college baseball's best catcher in 2007, but he didn't look like it in 2008, struggling at the plate and behind it in his first full pro season. He has the tools to be a good catcher, with an average arm, but he threw out just 28 percent of basestealers in the California League and had 23 passed balls, so the Diamondbacks brought him to instructional league to work on his receiving. He also worked with former big league catchers Mike Macfarlane and Jason Phillips in the offseason. He played a little first base and third base in instructional league, but he needs to stay at catcher if he wants to be an everyday player. Easley is a battler at the plate, but he chases too many pitches and needs to improve his knowledge of the strike zone. He should have average power, but a hip slide in his swing sapped his power last year. He needs better body control both hitting and catching. Arizona still likes Easley's desire and baseball IQ and thinks he just struggled in dealing with failure for the first time. He'll move up to Double-A and is a candidate for a bounceback season.

Year	Club (League)	Class	AVG	G	AB	R	H	2B	3B	HR	RBI	BB	SO	SB	OBP	SLG
2007	Yakima (NWL)	SS	.250	33	124	21	31	1	1	6	20	9	30	1	.319	.419
2008	Visalia (CAL)	HiA	.247	118	453	52	112	20	1	6	53	42	106	1	.313	.336
MINOR LEAGUE TOTALS			.248	151	577	73	143	21	2	12	73	51	136	2	.314	.354

30 TYRELL WORTHINGTON, OF

BORN: Aug. 2, 1988. **B-T:** R-R. **HT.:** 6-0. **WT.:** 190. **DRAFTED:** HS—Winterville, N.C., 2007 (5th round). **SIGNED BY:** Howard McCullough.

Worthington was a football-first athlete in high school, and the Diamondbacks swayed him from an East Carolina football commitment by signing him to a $220,000 bonus. They knew he would be a project, but it has turned out to be a bigger undertaking than they expected because he has Graves' disease. It's a chronic hyperthyroid disorder that caused Worthington to lose weight and strength; doctors diagnosed the problem after the 2007 season and began treating it with medication. He remained in extended spring training for much of the season, working to get back into playing shape, and finally showed the same body and athleticism as his high school days by the end of the summer. Worthington is a driven player who worked hard to get back into shape and has the same drive to get to the big leagues. He has good hands, though he'll need lots of at-bats and instruction to put his raw strength into full use at the plate. He's an above-average runner with an average arm, so he should be able to handle center field. Worthington shows flashes, and now that he's healthy he'll get the opportunity to put together some at-bats with a full-season club.

Year	Club (League)	Class	AVG	G	AB	R	H	2B	3B	HR	RBI	BB	SO	SB	OBP	SLG
2007	Missoula (PIO)	R	.135	13	37	6	5	0	1	0	2	5	11	1	.238	.189
2008	Missoula (PIO)	R	.143	39	126	12	18	3	1	0	6	18	67	4	.255	.183
MINOR LEAGUE TOTALS			.141	52	163	18	23	3	2	0	8	23	78	5	.251	.184

Atlanta Braves

BY BILL BALLEW

No club in baseball, particularly one that has established itself as a perennial contender, ever wants to use the "R" word. And while the Braves may not be in a complete rebuilding mode after posting their worst record since 1990 and failing to reach the playoffs for the third straight year, they're doing some serious retooling.

Major changes began in earnest at the conclusion of the 2007 season, when John Schuerholz became the club's president and passed the general manager reins to right-hand man Frank Wren. Since then, Edgar Renteria and Mark Teixeira have been traded, Andruw Jones has left as a free agent and Tom Glavine and John Smoltz have hit the free agent market. Undaunted by giving up five prospects for Teixeira in a 2007 trade that will turn out to be one of Schuerolz's most regrettable moves, Atlanta sent four youngsters (most notably catcher Tyler Flowers) to the White Sox for Javier Vazquez and Boone Logan this winter.

For the most part, however, the Braves have been trying to get younger. Dealing Renteria and Teixeira yielded building blocks such as Jair Jurrjens, Casey Kotchman and outfield prospect Gorkys Hernandez. Atlanta put together its run of 14 consecutive playoff trips from 1991-2005 by constantly replenishing the big league roster with fresh, homegrown talent, and that blueprint for success remains intact.

Six of the Braves' eight lineup regulars in 2009 were drafted and developed by the club, and the farm system features as much depth as ever. Scouting director Roy Clark and his staff have filled the organization with several high-profile prospects with productive drafts throughout the current decade.

Outfielder Jason Heyward, the system's top position prospect, was selected 14th overall in 2007, but Atlanta has excelled in finding prospects outside of the first round. Righthander Tommy Hanson was a 22nd-rounder in 2005 and part of the now-defunct draft-and-follow process that also netted the Braves lefthander Cole Rohrbough (22nd round in 2006), Flowers (33rd in 2005) and outfielder Brandon Jones (24th in 2003). They also grabbed outfielder Jordan Schaefer (third round in 2005) and righthander Kris Medlen (10th round in 2006) far lower in the draft than their talents would merit today.

Atlanta also has reasserted itself on the worldwide front, starting with the hiring of Johnny Almaraz as director of international scouting and operations in late 2006. He oversaw the construction of a state-

Atlanta helped rebuild its system by dealing veterans for prospects like Jair Jurrjens

TONY FARLOW

TOP 30 PROSPECTS

1. Tommy Hanson, rhp	16. Tyler Stovall, lhp
2. Jason Heyward, of	17. Edgar Osuna, lhp
3. Jordan Schafer, of	18. Braeden Schlehuber, c
4. Gorkys Hernandez, of	19. Eric Campbell, 3b
5. Freddie Freeman, 1b	20. Matt Kennelly, c
6. Cole Rohrbough, lhp	21. Luis Sumoza, of
7. Jeff Locke, lhp	22. Stephen Marek, rhp
8. Julio Teheran, rhp	23. Paul Clemens, rhp
9. Kris Medlen, rhp	24. J.J. Hoover, rhp
10. Craig Kimbrel, rhp	25. Chad Rodgers, lhp
11. Brandon Hicks, ss	26. Scott Diamond, lhp
12. Cody Johnson, of	27. Jacob Thompson, rhp
13. Randall Delgado, rhp	28. James Parr, rhp
14. Brett DeVall, lhp	29. Todd Redmond, rhp
15. Zeke Spruill, rhp	30. Christian Bethancourt, c

of-the-art facility in the Dominican Republic that opened in 2007, and he and his scouting network are making inroads elsewhere in Latin America as well.

In the last two years, the Braves have signed such talents as righthander Julio Teheran (Colombia), righty Randall Delgado and catcher Christian Bethancourt (Panama), and lefties Santos Rodriguez (part of the Vazquez deal) and Carlos Perez (Dominican). Teheran, who cost $850,000, was the top pitcher on the international market in 2007. They also have intensified their efforts in Taiwan, landing righty Wei Cheng Huang and catcher Meng Hsiu Tsai.

General Manager: Frank Wren. **Farm Director:** Kurt Kemp. **Scouting Director:** Roy Clark.

Class	Team	League	W	L	PCT	Finish*	Manager	Affiliated
Majors	Atlanta	National	72	90	.444	12th (16)	Bobby Cox	—
Triple-A	Richmond Braves	International	63	78	.447	13th (14)	Dave Brundage	1966
Double-A	Mississippi Braves	Southern	73	66	.525	^3rd (10)	Phillip Wellman	2005
High A	Myrtle Beach Pelicans	Carolina	89	51	.636	1st (8)	Rocket Wheeler	1999
Low A	Rome Braves	South Atlantic	56	81	.409	14th (16)	Randy Ingle	2003
Rookie	Danville Braves	Appalachian	35	32	.522	5th (10)	Paul Runge	1993
Rookie	GCL Braves	Gulf Coast	29	29	.500	9th (16)	Jesus Alfaro	1998
Overall 2008 Minor League Record			345	337	.506	13th		

* Finish in overall standings (No. of teams in league). ^League champion.

LAST YEAR'S TOP 30

Rank	Player, Pos.	Status
1.	Jordan Schafer, of	No. 3
2.	Jason Heyward, of	No. 2
3.	Jair Jurrjens, rhp	Majors
4.	Brandon Jones, of	Majors
5.	Gorkys Hernandez, of	No. 4
6.	Brent Lillibridge, ss	(White Sox)
7.	Cole Rohrbough, lhp	No. 6
8.	Jeff Locke, lhp	No. 7
9.	Tommy Hanson, rhp	No. 1
10.	Julio Teheran, rhp	No. 8
11.	Cody Johnson, of	No. 12
12.	Tyler Flowers, 1b/c	(White Sox)
13.	Jon Gilmore, 3b	(White Sox)
14.	Brandon Hicks, ss	No. 11
15.	Steve Evarts, lhp	Dropped out
16.	Chad Rodgers, lhp	No. 25
17.	Joey Devine, rhp	(Athletics)
18.	Josh Anderson, of	Majors
19.	Freddie Freeman, 1b	No. 5
20.	Eric Campbell, 3b	No. 19
21.	Van Pope, 3b	Dropped out
22.	Erik Cordier, rhp	Dropped out
23.	Cory Rasmus, rhp	Dropped out
24.	Kris Medlen, rhp	No. 9
25.	Kala Ka'aihue, 1b	Dropped out
26.	Clint Sammons, c	Dropped out
27.	Jairo Cuevas, rhp	(Royals)
28.	Eric Barrett, lhp	Dropped out
29.	Diory Hernandez, ss/2b	Dropped out
30.	Phillip Britton, c	Dropped out

BEST TOOLS

Best Hitter for Average	Jason Heyward
Best Power Hitter	Cody Johnson
Best Strike-Zone Discipline	Jason Heyward
Fastest Baserunner	Gorkys Hernandez
Best Athlete	Jordan Schafer
Best Fastball	Craig Kimbrel
Best Curveball	Cole Rohrbough
Best Slider	Tommy Hanson
Best Changeup	Edgar Osuna
Best Control	Todd Redmond
Best Defensive Catcher	Clint Sammons
Best Defensive Infielder	Van Pope
Best Infield Arm	Brandon Hicks
Best Defensive Outfielder	Jordan Schafer
Best Outfield Arm	Jordan Schafer

PROJECTED 2012 LINEUP

Catcher	Brian McCann
First Base	Freddie Freeman
Second Base	Kelly Johnson
Third Base	Brandon Hicks
Shortstop	Yunel Escobar
Left Field	Gorkys Hernandez
Center Field	Jordan Schafer
Right Field	Jason Heyward
No. 1 Starter	Tommy Hanson
No. 2 Starter	Tim Hudson
No. 3 Starter	Jair Jurrjens
No. 4 Starter	Cole Rohrbough
No. 5 Starter	Charlie Morton
Closer	Craig Kimbrel

TOP PROSPECTS OF THE DECADE

Year	Player, Pos.	2008 Org.
1999	Bruce Chen, lhp	Out of baseball
2000	Rafael Furcal, ss	Dodgers
2001	Wilson Betemit, ss	Yankees
2002	Wilson Betemit, ss	Yankees
2003	Adam Wainwright, rhp	Cardinals
2004	Andy Marte, 3b	Indians
2005	Jeff Francoeur, of	Braves
2006	Jarrod Saltalamacchia, c	Rangers
2007	Jarrod Saltalamacchia, c	Rangers
2008	Jordan Schafer, of	Braves

TOP DRAFT PICKS OF THE DECADE

Year	Player, Pos.	2008 Org.
1999	Matt Butler, rhp (2nd round)	Out of baseball
2000	Adam Wainwright, rhp	Cardinals
2001	Macay McBride, lhp	Tigers
2002	Jeff Francoeur, of	Braves
2003	Luis Atilano, rhp (1st round supp.)	Nationals
2004	Eric Campbell, 3b (2nd round)	Braves
2005	Joey Devine, rhp	Athletics
2006	Cody Johnson, of	Braves
2007	Jason Heyward, of	Braves
2008	Brett DeVall, lhp (1st round supp.)	Braves

LARGEST BONUSES IN CLUB HISTORY

Jeff Francoeur, 2002	$2,200,000
Matt Belisle, 1998	$1,750,000
Jason Heyward, 2007	$1,700,000
Cody Johnson, 2006	$1,375,000
Macay McBride, 2001	$1,340,000

ATLANTA BRAVES

TOP 2009 ROOKIE: Tommy Hanson, rhp. He may not open the season with the Braves, but they won't be able to ignore his stuff for long.

BREAKOUT PROSPECT: Randall Delgado, rhp. He's skinny and only 19, but he already touches 94 mph with his fastball and has a pair of promising secondary pitches.

SLEEPER: Concepcion Rodriguez, of. His bat and power took significant steps forward in 2008.

SOURCE OF TOP 30 TALENT

Homegrown	26	Acquired	4
College	2	Trades	4
Junior college	5	Rule 5 draft	0
High school	11	Independent leagues	0
Draft-and-follow	2	Free agents/waivers	0
Nondrafted free agents	1		
International	5		

Numbers in parentheses indicate prospect rankings.

LF
Cody Johnson (12)
Willie Cabrera
Adam Milligan
Matt Young

CF
Jordan Schafer (3)
Gorkys Hernandez (4)
L.V. Ware

RF
Jason Heyward (2)
Luis Sumoza (21)
Concepcion Rodriguez
Jon-Mark Owings
Reid Gorecki

3B
Eric Campbell (19)
Van Pope
Jake Hanson

SS
Brandon Hicks (11)
Michael Fisher
Travis Adair

2B
Diory Hernandez
Travis Jones
J.C. Holt
Robert Brooks
Adam Coe

1B
Freddie Freeman (5)
Ernesto Mejia
Kala Ka'aihue
Barbaro Canizares
Gerardo Rodriguez

C
Braeden Schlehuber (18)
Matt Kennelly (20)
Christian Bethancourt (30)
Clint Sammons
Phillip Britton

RHP

Starters	Relievers
Tommy Hanson (1)	Craig Kimbrel (10)
Julio Teheran (8)	Stephen Marek (22)
Kris Medlen (9)	Cody Gearrin
Randall Delgado (13)	Luis Valdez
Zeke Spruill (15)	Deunte Heath
Paul Clemens (23)	Benino Pruneda
J.J. Hoover (24)	Jeff Lyman
Jacob Thompson (27)	Nick Fellman
James Parr (28)	Brett Butts
Todd Redmond (29)	Michael Nix
Anthony Lerew	Ferdin Tejeda
Erik Cordier	Sung Ki Jung
Ryne Reynoso	Cory Rasmus
David Francis	
Chris Vines	
Kyle Cofield	

LHP

Starters	Relievers
Cole Rohrbough (6)	Bryan Dumesnil
Jeff Locke (7)	Kevin Gunderson
Brett DeVall (14)	Steve Kent
Tyler Stovall (16)	Lee Hyde
Edgar Osuna (17)	
Chad Rodgers (25)	
Scott Diamond (26)	
Steve Evarts	
Jonny Venters	
Richard Sullivan	
Jose Ortegano	
Francisley Bueno	
Eric Barrett	

2008   BONUSES: $5.1 MILLION

BEST PURE HITTER: C Braeden Schlehuber (4) has good athletic ability for a catcher and repeats his solid swing. He has a feel for squaring up balls and should improve and hit for more power as he becomes more selective.

BEST POWER HITTER: The Braves long have coveted OF Adam Milligan (6) and his above-average lefthanded power, drafting him three times. They finally signed him away from a Vanderbilt commitment in 2008 for $350,000.

FASTEST RUNNER: SS Travis Adair (13) and 2B Robert Brooks (20) are above-average runners with good instincts, but the Braves didn't sign any burners.

BEST DEFENSIVE PLAYER: Schlehuber's athleticism helps make him a strong receiver and blocker, and he handled plenty of velocity at the CC of Southern Nevada. He has average arm strength.

BEST FASTBALL: RHP Craig Kimbrel (3) uses a lower arm angle, similar to that of 2005 first-rounder Joey Devine, to pump fastballs up to 98 mph. RHP Paul Clemens (7) has an electric arm and has touched 97 mph with his heater. RHP Zeke Spruill (2) has a low-90s fastball with excellent sink and plenty of projectability at 6-foot-4, 185 pounds.

BEST SECONDARY PITCH: LHP Tyler Stovall (2) and RHP Jacob Thompson (5) both feature above-average curveballs. Thompson, whose velocity was down all spring after an illness caused him to lose 25 pounds, also throws a solid slider and has a feel for a changeup.

BEST PRO DEBUT: RHP David Francis (12) went 5-3, 2.35 with 69 strikeouts in 54 innings, including a 16-strikeout effort in a six-inning no-hit outing July 22. Kimbrel, who finished the year in high Class A, picked up 10 saves and struck out 56 in 35 innings while giving up just two earned runs.

BEST ATHLETE: Brooks was a dual-threat quarterback in high school in Alabama and has fast-twitch athletic ability. He didn't play in 2008 after academics knocked him out of Auburn after he hit .281 with 36 RBIs.

MOST INTRIGUING BACKGROUND: Adair's father Rick has spent nearly three decades in professional baseball and is the Rangers' minor league pitching coordinator. Francis and Milligan roomed with the son of Braves scouting director Roy Clark at Walters State (Tenn.) CC.

CLOSEST TO THE MAJORS: Kimbrel will move quickly as a reliever. Thompson could rise as rapidly if he regains the low-90s velocity he showed in his first

two years at Virginia.

BEST LATE-ROUND PICK: Francis and Brooks both have upside comparable to the club's single-digit picks.

THE ONE WHO GOT AWAY: RHP Matthew Price (34), who threw 95 mph in workouts for the Braves, is attending Virginia Tech. Atlanta also made a strong run at RHP Michael Palazzone (18), now at Georgia.

ASSESSMENT: The Braves signed 10 juco players in the first 15 rounds, looking for upside as raw prep players become tougher to sign. That strategy will pay off if pitchers such as Kimbrel and Clemens follow in the footsteps of Atlanta's top prospect, juco product Tommy Hanson.

2007   BONUSES: $4.9 MILLION

OF Jason Heyward (1) and 1B Freddie Freeman (2) look like they'll form the heart of Atlanta's lineup of the future. SS Brandon Hicks (3) could give this draft a third everyday player. Unsigned RHP Joshua Fields (2) became a Mariners first-rounder a year later.

GRADE: A

2006   BONUSES: $8.1 MILLION

The Braves landed a pair of promising lefties in Jeff Locke (2) and Cole Rohrbough (22), as well as RHP Kris Medlen (10). OF Cody Johnson (1) has prodigious power, but the jury's still out as to whether he'll make consistent contact.

GRADE: B

2005   BONUSES: $4.2 MILLION*

SS Yunel Escobar (2) quickly won a job in Atlanta, and OF Jordan Schafer (3) will join him in the near future. RHP Joey Devine (1) recovered from being rushed to the majors to find success after a trade to Oakland. But the prize looks like RHP Tommy Hanson (22), while C Tyler Flowers (33), a fellow draft-and-follow, was the key component in the Javier Vazquez trade.

GRADE: A

2004   BONUSES: $1.8 MILLION*

The Braves didn't have a first-rounder and spent their top pick on 3B Eric Campbell (2), who has shown power when he hasn't been suspended. RHP James Parr (4) and C Clint Sammons (6) have had cups of coffee with the Braves.

GRADE: D

Draft analysis by John Manuel (2008) and Jim Callis (2004-07). Numbers in parentheses indicate draft rounds. *Bonuses for 2004-05 are first 10 rounds only.

PROSPECT

CARL KLINE

TOMMY HANSON, RHP

Born: Aug. 28, 1986.
Ht.: 6-6. **Wt.:** 210.
Bats: R. **Throws:** R.
Drafted: Riverside (Calif.) CC, D/F 2005 (22nd round).
Signed by: Tom Battista.

One of the team's big finds in the now-extinct draft-and-follow process, Hanson signed with the Braves for $325,000 in 2006 while turning down an opportunity to pitch at Arizona State. He made tremendous strides transforming from a thrower to a pitcher in 2007 under the tutelage of the late Bruce Dal Canton, his pitching coach at high Class A Myrtle Beach. Hanson broke out as one of the baseball's top pitching prospects in 2008. He dominated in a return to Myrtle Beach to start the season and easily handled a promotion to Double-A Mississippi, where he tossed a no-hitter with a career-best 14 strikeouts on June 25. He concluded the regular season leading the minors in opponent average (.175) and ranking second in strikeouts per nine innings (10.6) and fourth in strikeouts (163). Hanson capped his year by winning the pitching triple crown in the Arizona Fall League, going 5-0, 0.63 with 49 strikeouts in 29 innings. He also limited hitters in the offensive-oriented loop to a .105 average.

After displaying a tendency to rely on his fastball early in his minor league career, Hanson has developed four quality pitches that he throws for strikes. His moving fastball resides in the low to mid-90s and explodes in on the hands of righthanders. He added a hard slider in the upper 80s midway through last season, which brought about comparisons to John Smoltz's best offering while taking Hanson's considerable potential to a higher level. His overhand 12-to-6 curveball is a plus pitch that makes his slider even more difficult for hitters to diagnose. His changeup is at least major league average and has improved impressively over the past two years. Hanson mixes his pitches well, uses both sides of the plate and does an outstanding job of altering the eye level of hitters. He hides the ball well in his delivery, making him even tougher to hit. He displays impressive poise with a strong mound presence. He uses his height to his advantage by pitching on a steep downhill plane and challenges hitters throughout the lineup.

The key to Hanson's success is working ahead in the count. While his slider has become his best pitch, he must establish his fastball command and use all of his pitches. The few difficult outings he had in Double-A came when he issued too many walks and became too fine in the strike zone, giving hitters a chance to make more hard contact than usual.

The Braves believe Hanson is a future ace, which GM Frank Wren made clear early in the offseason when he refused to include the righthander in any trade talks, even those involving Jake Peavy. Though not a finished product, Hanson is getting close to joining the big league rotation. The trade for Javier Vazquez increased the odds that Hanson will open 2009 at the club's new Triple-A Gwinnett County affiliate, but he should make his major league debut before season's end.

Year	Club (League)	Class	W	L	ERA	G	GS	CG	SV	IP	H	R	ER	HR	BB	SO	AVG
2006	Danville (APP)	R	4	1	2.09	13	8	0	0	52	42	15	12	2	9	56	.218
2007	Rome (SAL)	LoA	2	6	2.59	15	14	0	0	73	51	28	21	6	26	90	.194
	Myrtle Beach (CAR)	HiA	3	3	4.20	11	11	0	0	60	53	33	28	10	32	64	.243
2008	Myrtle Beach (CAR)	HiA	3	1	0.90	7	7	0	0	40	15	6	4	0	11	49	.116
	Mississippi (SL)	AA	8	4	3.03	18	18	1	0	98	70	39	33	9	41	114	.197
MINOR LEAGUE TOTALS			20	15	2.73	64	58	1	0	323	231	121	98	27	119	373	.199

2 JASON HEYWARD, OF

RODGER WOOD

BORN: Aug. 9, 1989. **B-T:** L-L. **HT.:** 6-4. **WT.:** 220. **DRAFTED:** HS—McDonough, Ga., 2007 (1st round). **SIGNED BY:** Brian Bridges.

The 14th overall pick in the 2007 draft, Heyward continues to leave many observers wondering why 13 teams passed on the five-tool outfielder. Signed for $1.7 million, he ranked as the No. 2 prospect in the low Class A South Atlantic League in 2008. He finished third in hitting (.323) and fourth in on-base percentage (.388) as one of the SAL's youngest players at age 18. Heyward is a prototypical right fielder with impressive size, athleticism and makeup. He swings a big bat from the left side, drawing comparisons to the likes of Willie McCovey and Dave Parker. Heyward has outstanding plate discipline and pitch recognition for a teenager. He has average speed and is an intelligent baserunner. Defensively, he covers a lot of ground in right field and has a plus arm with excellent carry on his throws. While there is no question he has power in his bat, Heyward went deep only 11 times in 2008. The Braves believe he'll hit more homers once he learns to use his hands more efficiently and looks for pitches to pound. He's still working on getting better jumps on balls hit over his head and improving his routes on balls hit to his right. Heyward will return to high Class A, where he ended 2008, but his mature approach and ability to make rapid adjustments soon will put him on the fast track. Atlanta's No. 3 hitter of the future could make his big league debut in 2010.

Year	Club (League)	Class	AVG	G	AB	R	H	2B	3B	HR	RBI	BB	SO	SB	OBP	SLG
2007	Braves (GCL)	R	.296	8	27	1	8	4	0	1	5	2	4	1	.355	.556
	Danville (APP)	R	.313	4	16	3	5	1	0	0	1	1	5	0	.353	.375
2008	Rome (SAL)	LoA	.323	120	449	88	145	27	6	11	52	49	74	15	.388	.483
	Myrtle Beach (CAR)	HiA	.182	7	22	3	4	2	0	0	4	2	4	0	.240	.273
MINOR LEAGUE TOTALS			.315	139	514	95	162	34	6	12	62	54	87	16	.379	.475

3 JORDAN SCHAFER, OF

BORN: Sept. 4, 1986. **B-T:** L-L. **HT.:** 6-1. **WT.:** 190. **DRAFTED:** HS—Winter Haven, Fla., 2005 (3rd round). **SIGNED BY:** Greg Kilby.

The No. 1 prospect on this list a year ago, Schafer began 2008 with a 50-game suspension for alleged use of human growth hormone. He tried too hard to make up for lost time when he returned in May but salvaged his season with a hot August. Schafer has good hand-eye coordination with quick wrists and plus bat speed. He uses the entire field and has surprising power for his wiry frame. A premier defender in center field, he has excellent range and plus arm strength. He possesses above-average speed and has a knack for taking the right angle on hard-hit balls in the gaps. He's a supremely confident player with a tireless work ethic. Schafer hit just .196/.306/.299 against lefthanders last season, struggling to center the ball on the barrel of the bat. He's prone to streakiness and strikes out excessively during slumps, which often come from his tendency to put extreme pressure on himself. He runs well but isn't a standout basestealer. The suspension should have no long-term effect on his career. He'll probably open 2009 in Triple-A but could take over as Atlanta's center fielder by the end of the season.

Year	Club (League)	Class	AVG	G	AB	R	H	2B	3B	HR	RBI	BB	SO	SB	OBP	SLG
2005	Braves (GCL)	R	.203	49	182	18	37	12	3	3	19	13	49	13	.256	.352
2006	Rome (SAL)	LoA	.240	114	388	49	93	15	7	8	60	28	95	15	.293	.376
2007	Rome (SAL)	LoA	.372	30	129	16	48	15	2	5	20	16	31	4	.441	.636
	Myrtle Beach (CAR)	HiA	.294	106	436	70	128	34	8	10	43	40	95	19	.354	.477
2008	Mississippi (SL)	AA	.269	84	297	46	80	18	6	10	51	49	88	12	.378	.471
MINOR LEAGUE TOTALS			.270	383	1432	199	386	94	26	36	193	146	358	63	.339	.447

4 GORKYS HERNANDEZ, OF

BORN: Sept. 7, 1987. **B-T:** R-R. **HT.:** 6-0. **WT.:** 175. **SIGNED:** Venezuela, 2005. **SIGNED BY:** Ramon Pena (Tigers).

Hernandez won the Gulf Coast League batting title and Midwest League MVP award in his first two seasons in the United States, then was part of a one-sided trade with the Tigers that also delivered Jair Jurrjens in exchange for Edgar Renteria. Hernandez missed a month in 2008 with a hamstring injury, but recovered to earn accolades from managers as the Carolina League's most exciting player. Hernandez has all the tools to be a quintessential leadoff hitter and center fielder. He drives the ball from gap to gap with his line-drive swing and is a weapon on the bases with above-average speed. He covers tremendous ground in center with his quickness and precise routes, and he also has a strong, accurate arm. Hernandez still gives away too many at-bats despite cutting down on his swing, particularly with two strikes. He doesn't have much home run power yet swings for the fences on occasion. A more refined approach and improved strike-zone judgment will boost his modest walk totals and on-base percentage. With Jordan Schafer and Hernandez, the Braves have two of the premier center-field prospects in the game. Their skills are similar, and Schafer is only one rung higher on the organizational ladder. Hernandez will spend 2009 in Double-A.

Year	Club (League)	Class	AVG	G	AB	R	H	2B	3B	HR	RBI	BB	SO	SB	OBP	SLG
2005	Tigers (DSL)	R	.265	63	211	44	56	10	0	4	19	30	38	10	.377	.370
2006	Tigers (GCL)	R	.327	50	205	41	67	9	2	5	23	10	27	20	.356	.463
2007	West Michigan (MWL)	LoA	.293	124	481	84	141	25	5	4	50	36	69	54	.344	.391
2008	Myrtle Beach (CAR)	HiA	.264	100	406	75	107	23	6	5	42	48	79	20	.348	.387
MINOR LEAGUE TOTALS			.285	337	1303	244	371	67	13	18	134	124	213	104	.353	.398

5 FREDDIE FREEMAN, 1B

BORN: Sept. 12, 1989. **B-T:** L-R. **HT.:** 6-5. **WT.:** 210. **DRAFTED:** HS—Orange, Calif., 2007 (2nd round). **SIGNED BY:** Tom Battista

ROME BRAVES

Many scouts preferred Freeman as a power pitching prospect, but he wanted to swing the bat and the Braves were glad to oblige when they drafted him in the second round in 2007. The youngest player to sign out of the 2007 draft, he was named Braves minor league player of the year in 2008 after ranking second in the South Atlantic League in slugging (.521) and fourth in RBIs (95). Freeman is an RBI machine who relishes the opportunity to hit with runners on base. He's an aggressive hitter with a swing-first approach, yet he has good pitch recognition and doesn't chase pitches out of the zone. He drives the ball with authority with his sweet, smooth swing and should be able to produce significant home run totals at higher levels. His defense is well-above-average at first base, with some scouts comparing Freeman to Mark Grace but with more power. Freeman's approach doesn't lend itself to drawing a lot of walks. He has below-average speed, though he's by no means a baseclogger. The Braves could have moved Freeman to high Class A last season with relative ease, but they wanted to make certain he had a solid foundation of success as an 18-year-old. He'll move up to Myrtle Beach in 2009, and the Braves won't hold him back if he continues to produce.

Year	Club (League)	Class	AVG	G	AB	R	H	2B	3B	HR	RBI	BB	SO	SB	OBP	SLG
2007	Braves (GCL)	R	.268	59	224	24	60	7	0	6	30	7	33	1	.295	.379
2008	Rome (SAL)	LoA	.316	130	491	70	155	33	7	18	95	46	84	5	.378	.521
MINOR LEAGUE TOTALS			.301	189	715	94	215	40	7	24	125	53	117	6	.353	.477

6 COLE ROHRBOUGH, LHP

BORN: May 23, 1987. **B-T:** L-L. **HT.:** 6-3. **WT.:** 225. **DRAFTED:** Western Nevada CC, D/F 2006 (22nd round). **SIGNED BY:** Tim Moore.

The final draft-and-follow signed by the Braves before MLB eliminated the process, Rohrbough received a $675,000 bonus and ranked as the top prospect in the Appalachian League in his pro debut. An ankle injury suffered during offseason workouts and rotator-cuff tendinitis hampered his development last season. Rohrbough has electrifying stuff with three above-average pitches at times, including the best fastball/curveball combination in the system. His fastball has good movement while residing at 92-94 mph. His power curve borders on being unhittable when it is sharp with nasty late break. He has a tremendous feel for pitching and mixes his offerings well. Rohrbough tends to drop his arm slot on occasion, which decreases his fastball velocity and makes his curve flatter and hittable. He also needs to improve the consistency and fade of his changeup. Atlanta believes Rohrbough is a special talent and projects him as a possible No. 2 starter. He should be completely healthy in spring training and should advance to Double-A at some point in 2009, with a late-2010 big league ETA.

Year	Club (League)	Class	W	L	ERA	G	GS	CG	SV	IP	H	R	ER	HR	BB	SO	AVG
2007	Danville (APP)	R	3	2	1.08	8	7	0	0	33	20	8	4	1	8	58	.167
	Rome (SAL)	LoA	2	0	1.29	6	6	0	0	28	13	7	4	1	12	38	.138
2008	Rome (SAL)	LoA	3	4	4.94	13	12	0	0	55	55	37	32	3	31	76	.248
	Myrtle Beach (CAR)	HiA	2	2	3.41	5	5	1	0	32	27	16	12	0	8	28	.233
MINOR LEAGUE TOTALS			10	8	3.09	32	30	1	0	151	115	68	52	5	59	200	.208

7 JEFF LOCKE, LHP

BORN: Nov. 20, 1987. **B-T:** L-L. **HT.:** 6-2. **WT.:** 180. **DRAFTED:** HS—Conway, N.H., 2006 (2nd round). **SIGNED BY:** Lonnie Goldberg.

Locke ended 2007 on a seven-game winning streak, but last season was not as kind. He lacked run support and ranked third in the South Atlantic League with 12 losses. Nevertheless, he maintained his composure and showed three solid-average pitches. Locke's two best pitches are a 91-94 mph fastball with good movement and a hard curveball that borders on being a plus offering. He also throws a changeup that continues to show improvement with its depth. He does an excellent job of keeping the ball down in the zone, which helped limit opponents to six homers in 2008. His herky-jerky delivery creates deception and makes it difficult for hitters to pick up the ball. His mound presence and competitiveness are impressive for a young hurler. Locke tends to fall out of sync in his delivery and needs to repeat his mechanics with more consistency to achieve better command. He throws strikes but can locate his pitches better in the zone. He needs to fine-tune some of the nuances of his craft, such as fielding his position, holding runners and covering and backing up bases. The best pitching prospect from New Hampshire since Chris Carpenter, Locke could be a workhorse in the middle of a major league rotation. His next stop will be high Class A.

Year	Club (League)	Class	W	L	ERA	G	GS	CG	SV	IP	H	R	ER	HR	BB	SO	AVG
2006	Braves (GCL)	R	4	3	4.22	10	5	0	0	32	38	18	15	4	5	38	.299
2007	Danville (APP)	R	7	1	2.66	13	11	0	1	61	48	23	18	2	8	74	.213
2008	Rome (SAL)	LoA	5	12	4.06	25	24	1	0	140	150	75	63	6	38	113	.269
MINOR LEAGUE TOTALS			16	16	3.71	48	40	1	1	233	236	116	96	12	51	225	.259

8 JULIO TEHERAN, RHP

BORN: Jan. 27, 1991. **B-T:** R-R. **HT.:** 6-2. **WT.:** 165. **SIGNED:** Colombia, 2007. **SIGNED BY:** Miguel Teheran/Carlos Garcia.

The top amateur pitcher on the international market in 2007, Teheran signed for $850,000, thanks in part to his cousin Miguel, a Braves scout. Impressed by his maturity in spring training, Atlanta sent him to the Appalachian League, where he was the youngest pitcher at age 17. He developed a sore shoulder after two starts, and was used sparingly afterward. Teheran throws easy gas, displaying a 90-93 mph fastball with above-average life in instructional league. His changeup is also a plus pitch and he'll throw it any time in the count. His poise is remarkable, and he has a strong idea of what he needs to accomplish by working both sides of the plate as well as the top and bottom of the zone. Teheran needs to tighten the spin on his rolling curveball. He also must do a better job commanding his pitches in the zone. Though doctors found nothing wrong with his shoulder, he'll have to get stronger. He's still learning that he can't just overpower every hitter he faces. The Braves feel no need to rush Teheran and may keep him in extended spring before sending him back to Danville. He has top-of-the-rotation ability and will get all the time he needs to develop.

Year	Club (League)	Class	W	L	ERA	G	GS	CG	SV	IP	H	R	ER	HR	BB	SO	AVG
2008	Danville (APP)	R	1	2	6.60	6	6	0	0	15	18	12	11	2	4	17	.305
MINOR LEAGUE TOTALS			1	2	6.60	6	6	0	0	15	18	12	11	2	4	17	.305

9 KRIS MEDLEN, RHP

BORN: Oct. 7, 1985. **B-T:** B-R. **HT.:** 5-10. **WT.:** 175. **DRAFTED:** Santa Ana (Calif.) JC, 2006 (10th round). **SIGNED BY:** Tom Battista.

After dominating as a reliever and posting a 1.17 ERA in his first two years as a pro, Medlen faced adversity for the first time in the minors at Mississippi in the opening two months of the 2008 season. He moved into the rotation and proceeded to pitch as well as any Southern League starter, going 6-5, 3.11 in 17 starts before excelling in the playoffs. Medlen features a 92-94 mph fastball and a plus curveball in the upper 80s. He also has a solid changeup and a slider he'll throw to give hitters another pitch to think about. The additional innings as a starter allowed him to improve his command. A converted shortstop, he's athletic and helps his cause as a hitter and fielder. He's aggressive and tough on the mound. Medlen is undersized, which raises questions about his durability as a starter, though his stress-free delivery and ability to throw strikes works in his favor. His command isn't as sharp as his control, and the last step in his development will be to throw more quality strikes. A promotion to Triple-A is the most likely scenario for Medlen, though he could get a long look in spring training. He has the versatility to fit in as a starter, swingman or reliever depending on Atlanta's needs.

Year	Club (League)	Class	W	L	ERA	G	GS	CG	SV	IP	H	R	ER	HR	BB	SO	AVG
2006	Danville (APP)	R	1	0	0.41	20	0	0	10	22	14	2	1	0	2	36	.175
2007	Rome (SAL)	LoA	0	1	0.87	17	0	0	8	21	13	4	2	1	3	33	.169
	Myrtle Beach (CAR)	HiA	2	0	1.13	18	0	0	2	24	22	7	3	1	7	28	.239
	Mississippi (SL)	AA	0	0	11.57	3	0	0	1	2	4	3	3	0	2	2	.444
2008	Mississippi (SL)	AA	7	8	3.52	36	17	0	1	120	121	47	47	8	27	120	.268
MINOR LEAGUE TOTALS			10	9	2.66	94	17	0	22	189	174	63	56	10	41	219	.245

10 CRAIG KIMBREL, RHP

RODGER WOOD

BORN: May 28, 1988. **B-T:** R-R. **HT.:** 5-11. **WT.:** 205. **DRAFTED:** Wallace State (Ala.) CC, 2008 (3rd round). **SIGNED BY:** Brian Bridges.

The Braves drafted Kimbrel in the 33rd round in 2007, but he turned down a $125,000 bonus to return to Wallace State (Ala.) CC. He averaged 13.7 strikeouts per nine innings and limited batters to a .140 average as a sophomore, and the Braves signed him for $391,000 as a third-round pick. He was just as dominant in pro ball, concluding his debut with four scoreless innings in high Class A. Though he's somewhat undersized, Kimbrel has a strong frame and a lightning-quick arm. Throwing from a low three-quarters delivery, he has a fastball that resides at 92-95 mph and touches 98 with heavy sink. His heater tends to run in on righthanded hitters before exploding to the plate. He has a closer's mentality. Kimbrel needs more consistency with his control and two secondary pitches, both of which project to become average. His slider still gets slurvy and his changeup isn't reliable. Kimbrel made the best initial impression among members of Atlanta's 2008 draft class. He has the ingredients to become a major league closer. He'll stay on the fast track and could reach Double-A in his first full pro season.

Year	Club (League)	Class	W	L	ERA	G	GS	CG	SV	IP	H	R	ER	HR	BB	SO	AVG
2008	Danville (APP)	R	1	2	0.47	12	0	0	6	19	5	4	1	0	10	27	.076
	Rome (SAL)	LoA	2	0	0.71	10	0	0	4	13	6	1	1	0	4	26	.140
	Myrtle Beach (CAR)	HiA	0	0	0.00	2	0	0	0	4	5	0	0	0	1	3	.385
MINOR LEAGUE TOTALS			3	2	0.51	24	0	0	10	35	16	5	2	0	15	56	.131

11 BRANDON HICKS, SS

BORN: Sept. 14, 1985. **B-T:** R-R. **HT.:** 6-2. **WT.:** 200. **DRAFTED:** Texas A&M, 2007 (3rd round). **SIGNED BY:** John Barron.

Undrafted after leading San Jacinto (Texas) JC to the 2006 Junior College World Series, Hicks has risen rapidly since signing as a third-round pick in 2007. Featuring a tremendous work ethic and strong desire to win, he earned all-star honors in the Carolina League and managers rated him the circuit's best defensive shortstop last year. Hicks has a quick swing that generates above-average power, and he ranked fourth in the CL with 19 homers despite missing two weeks in April with a thigh bruise and spending part of August in Double-A. He does a good job using the entire field, but high strikeout totals have limited Hicks' batting average and overall production. He spread his stance out last June so he could see the ball better, but his numbers didn't noticeably improve. The Braves believe he'll become more consistent at the plate with additional experience. His speed is slightly above-average, and he's an excellent baserunner who can steal an occasional base. While not flashy at shortstop, Hicks combines solid defensive tools with great instincts. His range may be just fringe-average, but he charges balls well and has plus arm strength and a quick release. He's bigger than most shortstops, which leads some scouts to believe he might have to make a move to second or third base. With his power and defense, Hicks has a chance to be an everyday player in the majors. He'll spend 2009 in Double-A.

Year	Club (League)	Class	AVG	G	AB	R	H	2B	3B	HR	RBI	BB	SO	SB	OBP	SLG
2007	Danville (APP)	R	.224	18	58	14	13	3	1	3	13	12	18	1	.370	.466
	Rome (SAL)	LoA	.313	37	128	26	40	11	0	4	15	27	26	5	.433	.492
2008	Mississippi (SL)	AA	.241	16	54	9	13	3	1	1	7	7	17	0	.333	.389
	Myrtle Beach (CAR)	HiA	.234	93	342	68	80	23	2	19	56	45	122	14	.335	.480
MINOR LEAGUE TOTALS			.251	164	582	117	146	40	4	27	91	91	183	20	.361	.473

12 CODY JOHNSON, OF

BORN: Aug. 18, 1988. **B-T:** L-R. **HT.:** 6-4. **WT.:** 230. **DRAFTED:** HS—Lynn Haven, Fla., 2006 (1st round). **SIGNED BY:** Al Goetz.

The roller-coaster ride that is Johnson's career continued in 2008. One year after leading the Appalachian League in homers (17), extra-base hits (40) and slugging (.630), the 24th overall pick in 2006 did little more than air-condition ballparks during the first half of last season. He did make some adjustments, improving his selectivity, shortening his swing with two strikes and using the opposite field, and he ended up batting .296/.340/.578 in the second half. Signed for $1.375 million, Johnson possesses a classic slugger mentality and finished second in the South Atlantic League with 26 homers. He lives to record tape-measure shots and is capable of hitting the ball so hard that infielders don't have time to react. He has excellent bat speed and loves the ball up and out over the plate, which allows him to extend his long arms. The biggest question is whether he'll make enough consistent contact at higher levels. He ranked second in the minors with 177 strikeouts last year and has fanned 298 times in 222 pro games. Another concern is his defense in left field. Limited from an athletic standpoint, Johnson has shown some improvement but continues to struggle in taking the correct angles on balls. His arm strength rates as below-average. While several opposing SAL managers labeled him a designated hitter and questioned his attitude and approach to the game, Johnson did make strides with his maturity. The power is undeniable, but the rest of the package remains a work in progress. His next test will come in high Class A in 2009.

Year	Club (League)	Class	AVG	G	AB	R	H	2B	3B	HR	RBI	BB	SO	SB	OBP	SLG
2006	Braves (GCL)	R	.184	32	114	13	21	6	1	1	16	12	49	2	.260	.281
2007	Danville (APP)	R	.305	63	243	51	74	18	5	17	57	26	72	7	.374	.630
2008	Rome (SAL)	LoA	.252	127	468	62	118	26	1	26	89	40	177	8	.307	.479
MINOR LEAGUE TOTALS			.258	222	825	126	213	50	7	44	162	78	298	17	.321	.496

13 RANDALL DELGADO, RHP

BORN: Feb. 9, 1990. **B-T:** R-R. **HT.:** 6-3. **WT.:** 180. **SIGNED:** Panama, 2006. **SIGNED BY:** Luis Ortiz.

The Braves broke from their traditional pattern when they assigned Delgado to Danville instead of the Gulf Coast League in his first season in the United States in 2008. He continued his smooth progression since signing as a 16-year-old out of Panama, dominating in extended spring training and pitching well in the Appalachian League. The addition of strength and maturity to his tall, projectable frame has resulted in an increase in velocity over the past year. His fastball has improved from 89-91 mph to 90-93, topping out at 94. He shows a good feel for his changeup and curveball, both of which show above-average promise. He's still working on his secondary offerings and his control and command. He ranked second in the Appy League in both strikeouts (81 in 69 innings) and walks (30) last season. Delgado gets excellent leverage in his easy, repeatable delivery, throwing on a sharp downhill plane from a high three-quarters slot. He also hides the ball well, creating deception. Though still somewhat raw, Delgado quietly is developing into one of the premier pitching prospects in the system. He'll pitch in the low Class A Rome rotation in 2009.

Year	Club (League)	Class	W	L	ERA	G	GS	CG	SV	IP	H	R	ER	HR	BB	SO	AVG
2007	Braves (DSL)	R	1	2	2.00	11	10	0	0	45	34	12	10	2	12	50	.213
2008	Danville (APP)	R	3	8	3.13	14	14	0	0	69	63	32	24	5	30	81	.249
MINOR LEAGUE TOTALS			4	10	2.68	25	24	0	0	114	97	44	34	7	42	131	.235

14 BRETT DeVALL, LHP

BORN: Jan. 18, 1990. **B-T:** R-L. **HT.:** 6-4. **WT.:** 220. **DRAFTED:** HS—Niceville, Fla., 2008 (1st round supplemental). **SIGNED BY:** Brian Bridges.

DeVall was the first pick by the Braves and the second high school lefthander taken in the 2008 draft, going 40th overall and turning down a Georgia scholarship to sign for $1 million. He wound up pitching just 10 innings in his pro debut while battling forearm tenderness. Known for his pitchability, he put himself on the Braves' radar by pitching in the suburban Atlanta East Cobb League as well as for the U.S. national youth team. DeVall has excellent size, good mechanics and the ability to throw three pitches for strikes. His fastball resides at 88-91 mph and has good movement when he keeps it down. His curveball shows the promise of being a plus pitch but is still slurvy at this point. He entered pro ball with a well-developed changeup for a high school pitcher, and he should be able to develop it into a plus offering. DeVall doesn't have a true out pitch, but he has a strong foundation and a projectable body. His knowledge of how to set up hitters is advanced, which should make honing his secondary pitches somewhat easier. He'll get strong consideration for making the Rome rotation during spring training.

Year	Club (League)	Class	W	L	ERA	G	GS	CG	SV	IP	H	R	ER	HR	BB	SO	AVG
2008	Braves (GCL)	R	0	0	0.93	4	3	0	0	10	4	1	1	1	2	7	.125
MINOR LEAGUE TOTALS			0	0	0.93	4	3	0	0	10	4	1	1	1	2	7	.125

15 ZEKE SPRUILL, RHP

BORN: Sept. 11, 1989. **B-T:** B-R. **HT.:** 6-4. **WT.:** 185. **DRAFTED:** HS—Marietta, Ga., 2008 (2nd round). **SIGNED BY:** Brian Bridges.

The Braves are fond of drafting Atlanta-area players with strong makeup, and Spruill fit that description on both fronts. The 70th overall pick in the 2008 draft, he signed for $600,000 after attracting the team's interest while pitching in the East Cobb youth program. Possessing a tall, rangy frame with classic projectability, Spruill is a quality athlete. He had immediate success in pro ball, leading the Gulf Coast League with seven wins in as many decisions while displaying an impressive overall feel for pitching. His fastball sat in the low 90s with good life and solid sinking action during high school, but his velocity fell to the mid-80s during instructional league. The drop was common with Spruill when he went deep into games as an amateur, and the Braves believe it will be less of an issue once he adds strength. His mid-70s curveball has decent late bite, and his high-70s slider has potential. He's working on a changeup but hasn't developed feel for the pitch to throw it consistently. Prior to the draft, some scouts were concerned by Spruill's long arm action, but his ability to repeat his fluid delivery should allow him to stay healthy and throw strikes. While he's very much a work in progress, he possesses physical ability that can't be taught. He could earn a spot in low Class A this year.

Year	Club (League)	Class	W	L	ERA	G	GS	CG	SV	IP	H	R	ER	HR	BB	SO	AVG
2008	Braves (GCL)	R	7	0	2.93	10	3	0	0	40	42	16	13	1	8	32	.268
MINOR LEAGUE TOTALS			7	0	2.93	10	3	0	0	40	42	16	13	1	8	32	.268

16 TYLER STOVALL, LHP

BORN: Dec. 27, 1989. **B-T:** L-L. **HT.:** 6-1. **WT.:** 180. **DRAFTED:** HS—Hokes Bluff, Ala., 2008 (2nd round). **SIGNED BY:** Brian Bridges.

A multi-sport standout in high school, Stovall was part of five Alabama prep championship teams, one as a quarterback and four straight on the diamond. He established numerous state baseball records, including career wins (54) and strikeouts (683), and set a national mark with 95 career doubles. He also graduated at the top of his high school class with a 4.0 grade point average, and turned down Auburn to sign as a second-rounder for $750,000. Stovall's fastball resides in the low 90s, topping out at 94. His best pitch is his tight curveball, an offering he tends to rely on too often instead of working off his fastball. His changeup has some promise as well. He has good athleticism, though at 6-foot-1, he doesn't offer a lot of projection. He's one of several talented young arms in the mix for Rome's rotation in 2009.

Year	Club (League)	Class	W	L	ERA	G	GS	CG	SV	IP	H	R	ER	HR	BB	SO	AVG
2008	Braves (GCL)	R	1	1	6.30	7	3	0	0	20	20	15	14	1	14	29	.250
MINOR LEAGUE TOTALS			1	1	6.30	7	3	0	0	20	20	15	14	1	14	29	.250

17 EDGAR OSUNA, LHP

BORN: Nov. 25, 1987. **B-T:** L-L. **HT.:** 6-1. **WT.:** 170. **SIGNED:** Mexico, 2004. **SIGNED BY:** Julian Perez/Manuel Samaniego.

Osuna has flown under the radar since signing out of Mexico in 2004, but that's starting to change as he climbs through the lower minors. He ranked third in the Appalachian League with a 2.47 ERA in 2007, then was named Rome's pitcher of the year in 2008. He moved into the rotation in the second half and went 7-3, 3.32 with two complete games in 14 starts. He also has proven himself against more experienced hitters by pitching well in the Mexican Pacific League the last two winters. Osuna challenges hitters with an assortment of pitches that he mixes well. He spots his mid-80s fastball with precision and uses it to set up a plus curveball and the best changeup in the system. He has fine control and does a good job of locating his pitches. Osuna doesn't project off the charts physically, and his modest velocity makes him the quintessential crafty lefthander. But based on his ability and pitching knowledge, he has a strong chance of finding a role in the majors. A promotion to high Class A is in the immediate offing.

Year	Club (League)	Class	W	L	ERA	G	GS	CG	SV	IP	H	R	ER	HR	BB	SO	AVG
2005	Braves1 (DSL)	R	3	1	0.94	13	8	0	0	48	34	10	5	0	7	57	.202
2006	Braves (GCL)	R	0	1	0.92	6	2	0	2	20	15	4	2	0	1	18	.217
2007	Danville (APP)	R	5	3	2.47	13	6	0	2	55	55	19	15	4	11	66	.258
2008	Rome (SAL)	LoA	10	5	3.38	30	14	2	5	125	122	53	47	9	31	135	.253
MINOR LEAGUE TOTALS			18	10	2.51	62	30	2	9	247	226	86	69	13	50	276	.242

18 BRAEDEN SCHLEHUBER, C

BORN: Jan. 7, 1988. **B-T:** R-R. **HT.:** 6-3. **WT.:** 190. **DRAFTED:** CC of Southern Nevada, 2008 (4th round). **SIGNED BY:** Tom Battista.

Tyler Flowers' inclusion in the Javier Vazquez trade left Schlehuber as the best catching prospect in the system. A fourth-round pick last June, he gave up an Arkansas scholarship to sign for $240,000. He has the potential to stand out offensively and defensively. Schlehuber has excellent hand-eye coordination that allows him to center the ball on the barrel of the bat. He has good power that could develop into a plus tool as he adds strength to his 6-foot-3 frame. An aggressive hitter, he needs to hone his strike-zone discipline. He runs extremely well for a catcher, stealing a combined 23 bases between the CC of Southern Nevada and his pro debut in 2008. Schlehuber's athleticism gives him strong receiving and blocking skills. He has an average arm but threw out just 22 percent of basestealers in pro ball, in part because he tired by the end of the summer. He needs to get stronger and improve his game-calling skills. Schlehuber has impressed the Braves so much that they may send him to high Class A to open 2009.

Year	Club (League)	Class	AVG	G	AB	R	H	2B	3B	HR	RBI	BB	SO	SB	OBP	SLG
2008	Braves (GCL)	R	.268	41	123	18	33	4	0	0	11	10	27	7	.359	.301
MINOR LEAGUE TOTALS			.268	41	123	18	33	4	0	0	11	10	27	7	.359	.301

19 ERIC CAMPBELL, 3B

BORN: Aug. 6, 1985. **B-T:** R-R. **HT.:** 6-0. **WT.:** 205. **DRAFTED:** HS—Evansville, Ind., 2004 (2nd round). **SIGNED BY:** Sherard Clinkscales.

Campbell is the biggest enigma in the system. He was co-MVP in the Appalachian League in 2005 and led the South Atlantic League with 22 homers in 2006, but he has been suspended three times in the last three seasons. He missed the first two months of 2008 after the Braves sat him down for undisclosed reasons. On the positive side, he remained healthy after shoulder and thumb ailments slowed his development in 2007, and he posted impressive power numbers during his return to Myrtle Beach. He has attracted comparisons to Wilson Betemit, who ranked No. 1 on this list in 2001 and 2002 but failed to live up to his minor league billing before earning a reserve role in the majors. Campbell drives the ball to all fields with above-average power and continues to improve his plate discipline. He has below-average speed and athleticism, but he shows decent hands and a strong arm at third base. His makeup has been questioned by coaches and teammates, but he also has the tools to become a starting third baseman in the major leagues. He has left himself with little room for error as he advances to Double-A in 2009.

Year	Club (League)	Class	AVG	G	AB	R	H	2B	3B	HR	RBI	BB	SO	SB	OBP	SLG
2004	Braves (GCL)	R	.251	56	211	30	53	7	0	7	29	15	47	3	.306	.384
	Rome (SAL)	LoA	.136	7	22	0	3	0	0	0	1	2	7	0	.240	.136
2005	Danville (APP)	R	.313	66	262	77	82	26	2	18	64	28	64	15	.383	.634
2006	Rome (SAL)	LoA	.296	116	449	83	133	27	3	22	77	23	68	18	.335	.517
2007	Myrtle Beach (CAR)	HiA	.221	81	298	47	66	13	0	14	49	36	48	6	.312	.406
2008	Myrtle Beach (CAR)	HiA	.255	88	330	56	84	15	1	19	67	50	58	4	.362	.479
MINOR LEAGUE TOTALS			.268	414	1572	293	421	88	6	80	287	154	292	46	.339	.484

20 MATT KENNELLY, C

BORN: March 21, 1989. **B-T:** R-R. **HT.:** 6-2. **WT.:** 195. **SIGNED:** Australia, 2005. **SIGNED BY:** Phil Dale/Mark Petit.

A pitcher and corner infielder when he signed with the Braves as a 16-year-old from western Australia, Kennelly has started to make rapid progress in his development as a catcher with substantial offensive potential. The brother of Phillies minor league outfielder Tim Kennelly, Matt threw out 57 percent of basestealers last season, thanks to his strong and accurate arm. He also has strong receiving skills and leadership ability, and he's surprisingly sound fundamentally given his inexperience behind the plate. Kennelly already shows above-average pop when he pulls the ball and should develop more power as his body continues to mature. He has a smooth swing, though he struggles to recognize and handle breaking balls. He also could use some more patience at the plate. Kennelly has below-average speed, as expected from a catcher. He'll move up to low Class A in 2009.

Year	Club (League)	Class	AVG	G	AB	R	H	2B	3B	HR	RBI	BB	SO	SB	OBP	SLG
2007	Braves (GCL)	R	.215	39	107	10	23	4	0	2	10	5	19	0	.270	.308
2008	Rome (SAL)	LoA	.457	10	35	4	16	5	0	0	10	2	8	0	.475	.600
	Danville (APP)	R	.246	44	167	14	41	9	0	4	25	8	37	0	.278	.371
MINOR LEAGUE TOTALS			.259	93	309	28	80	18	0	6	45	15	64	0	.299	.375

21 LUIS SUMOZA, OF

BORN: July 15, 1988. **B-T:** R-R. **HT.:** 6-0. **WT.:** 170. **SIGNED:** Venezuela, 2004. **SIGNED BY:** German Robles (Red Sox).

The Braves believe they received considerably more than the usual return in a late-season trade that sent Mark Kotsay to the Red Sox. Atlanta had little use for Kotsay in September and received a young, toolsy outfielder whom it had scouted extensively in the past. Sumoza has a good feel for his swing and decent bat speed. His power currently rates as fringe-average, particularly for a corner outfielder, but he makes hard contact when he connects. He could produce more pop down the road if he can cut down on his strikeouts. He showed flashes in the Boston system, leading the Gulf Coast League with 24 extra-base hits in 2007. Sumoza had good all-around skills and has a chance to be a plus defender. Though he's a below-average runner, he's athletic, moves well in the outfield and has a strong arm with good carry. Most scouts project Sumoza as a decent regular or fourth outfielder at the major league level. After playing mostly left field for the Red Sox, he'll be the starting right fielder in Rome this season.

Year	Club (League)	Class	AVG	G	AB	R	H	2B	3B	HR	RBI	BB	SO	SB	OBP	SLG
2005	Red Sox/Padres (VSL)	R	.255	58	165	26	42	4	0	4	18	27	40	9	.364	.352
2006	Red Sox (GCL)	R	.205	38	117	13	24	5	1	1	14	10	38	7	.262	.291
2007	Red Sox (GCL)	R	.253	53	190	21	48	17	4	3	31	17	58	2	.316	.432
2008	Lowell (NYP)	SS	.301	51	193	31	58	15	0	11	38	21	59	9	.366	.549
	Rome (SAL)	LoA	.211	5	19	3	4	2	0	0	3	2	4	0	.286	.316
MINOR LEAGUE TOTALS			.257	205	684	94	176	43	5	19	104	77	199	27	.332	.418

22 STEPHEN MAREK, RHP

BORN: Sept. 3, 1983. **B-T:** L-R. **HT.:** 6-2. **WT.:** 200. **DRAFTED:** San Jacinto (Texas) JC, D/F 2004 (40th round). **SIGNED BY:** Chad McDonald (Angels).

Acquired with Casey Kotchman from the Angels in the Mark Teixeira deal last July, Marek was one of the top draft-and-follows on the market in the spring of 2005. He signed for $800,000 and made solid progress as a starter for three years in the Angels system before moving to the bullpen last April. Inconsistent command and mental focus led to that shift, and Marek still has work to do in both areas. Still, he has the stuff and makeup to be a set-up man in the big leagues. His fastball sits at 90-93 mph with good movement, and his 11-to-5 curveball may be a better pitch. His changeup lags behind his other two offerings but has the making of an average pitch. Marek has tried to refine his mechanics, particularly his release point, which tends to stray too high on occasion and hurts his fastball velocity and command. Added to Atlanta's 40-man roster in November, he'll enter spring training with an outside shot at earning a job in the bullpen. More likely, he'll open the campaign in Triple-A and make his big league debut later in the season.

Year	Club (League)	Class	W	L	ERA	G	GS	CG	SV	IP	H	R	ER	HR	BB	SO	AVG
2005	Orem (PIO)	R	1	3	4.50	15	14	0	0	66	74	37	33	7	25	55	.292
2006	Cedar Rapids (MWL)	LoA	10	2	1.96	19	19	1	0	119	95	27	26	8	24	100	.216
	R. Cucamonga (CAL)	HiA	2	3	3.94	6	6	0	0	32	26	14	14	4	13	33	.230
2007	R. Cucamonga (CAL)	HiA	8	10	4.30	25	25	1	0	134	133	78	64	17	49	106	.257
2008	Arkansas (TEX)	AA	2	6	3.66	34	0	0	3	47	39	20	19	2	21	57	.223
	Mississippi (SL)	AA	1	2	3.21	10	0	0	1	14	12	5	5	1	6	11	.261
MINOR LEAGUE TOTALS			24	26	3.52	109	64	2	4	412	379	181	161	39	138	362	.245

23 PAUL CLEMENS, RHP

BORN: Feb. 14, 1988. **B-T:** R-R. **HT.:** 6-4. **WT.:** 170. **DRAFTED:** Louisburg (N.C.) JC, 2008 (7th round). **SIGNED BY:** Billy Best.

One of 10 junior college products selected by the Braves in the first 15 rounds of the 2008 draft, Clemens had an ineffective sophomore season and dropped out of the rotation at Louisburg (N.C.) JC. Atlanta loved his electric arm and took him in the seventh round anyway, signing him for $150,000. Possessing a lean, athletic frame with plenty of projectability, Clemens uses whip-like arm action to produce a 91-94 mph fastball that touches 97. He spots his fastball well throughout the strike zone, and it dives inside on righthanded hitters. Clemens has flashed some promise with his curveball and changeup but both pitches remain inconsistent, as does his command. He throws strikes but gets hit more than someone with his fastball should. Atlanta believes Clemens has the arm to develop into a solid middle-of-the-rotation starter, though he'll need time to develop. Plans call for him to pitch in low Class A this season.

Year	Club (League)	Class	W	L	ERA	G	GS	CG	SV	IP	H	R	ER	HR	BB	SO	AVG
2008	Braves (GCL)	R	1	0	0.00	1	0	0	0	3	1	0	0	0	0	2	.111
	Danville (APP)	R	3	3	3.39	12	8	0	1	58	57	33	22	6	18	57	.252
	Rome (SAL)	LoA	0	1	9.00	1	1	0	0	4	7	5	4	0	2	0	.412
MINOR LEAGUE TOTALS			4	4	3.58	14	9	0	1	65	65	38	26	6	20	59	.258

24 J.J. HOOVER, RHP

BORN: Aug. 13, 1987. **B-T:** R-R. **HT.:** 6-3. **WT.:** 215. **DRAFTED:** Calhoun (Ala.) CC, 2008 (10th round). **SIGNED BY:** Brian Bridges.

The Braves convinced Hoover to bypass transferring to West Virginia by inking him for $400,000 at the signing deadline. His strong performance in the Cape Cod League, where he helped pitch Harwich to the league title, earned him an over-slot bonus. Hoover has a four-pitch arsenal, working off his low-90s fastball with good sink and some run. His curveball is a bit loopy and flashes good rotation, but it could be a plus pitch if he tightens it up. He also has a solid changeup and developed a hard slider during the spring at Calhoun (Ala.) CC. Hoover has a good overall feel for pitching and average command, so he should throw strikes at higher levels. He has a large, thick build with a pump delivery, and while he has a strong frame, he doesn't have much projectability remaining. He's still somewhat raw but has a solid foundation with four pitches and could be a potential workhorse in the middle of a rotation. He'll probably start his first full pro season in low Class A.

Year	Club (League)	Class	W	L	ERA	G	GS	CG	SV	IP	H	R	ER	HR	BB	SO	AVG
2008	Danville (APP)	R	1	0	0.00	2	0	0	0	5	4	0	0	0	1	6	.235
MINOR LEAGUE TOTALS			1	0	0.00	2	0	0	0	5	4	0	0	0	1	6	.235

25 CHAD RODGERS, LHP

BORN: Nov. 23, 1987. **B-T:** L-L. **HT.:** 6-3. **WT.:** 185. **DRAFTED:** HS—Walsh, Ohio, 2006 (3rd round). **SIGNED BY:** Nick Hostetler.

Rodgers joined fellow lefties Cole Rohrbough, Jeff Locke and Steve Evarts in a prospect-laden Rome rotation last spring. Like Locke, he received modest run support (which led to an eight-game losing streak), and like Rohrbough and Evarts, he experienced some physical problems. Rodgers pitched just 22 innings in the second half because of a strained shoulder, and he also had shoulder tendinitis in 2007. When healthy, Rodgers has above-average movement on his 89-91 mph fastball. His hard curveball features sharp bite, and his changeup continues to gain consistency after he altered his grip in 2007. He's a quality athlete and competitor who challenges hitters and throws strikes, but he must get stronger so he can pile up the innings he needs to develop. The Braves would like him to open 2009 in high Class A, but a return to Rome is possible if he's not at his best in spring training.

Year	Club (League)	Class	W	L	ERA	G	GS	CG	SV	IP	H	R	ER	HR	BB	SO	AVG
2006	Braves (GCL)	R	3	2	2.31	11	5	0	1	39	31	14	10	1	13	30	.217
2007	Danville (APP)	R	3	1	3.88	11	10	0	1	49	40	21	21	2	11	46	.220
2008	Rome (SAL)	LoA	2	10	4.53	20	16	0	0	91	96	54	46	5	28	77	.267
MINOR LEAGUE TOTALS			8	13	3.87	42	31	0	2	179	167	89	77	8	52	153	.244

26 SCOTT DIAMOND, LHP

BORN: July 30, 1986. **B-T:** L-L. **HT.:** 6-3. **WT.:** 190. **SIGNED:** Binghamton, NDFA 2007. **SIGNED BY:** Lonnie Goldberg.

In his introduction to pro ball, Diamond led Braves farmhands with 15 victories and ranked fourth in the Carolina League with a 2.89 ERA. Undrafted following his junior season at Binghamton in 2007, the Canadian signed with the Braves for $50,000 after twirling in the collegiate Coastal Plain League. He impressed during instructional league and spring training, so his debut wasn't a complete surprise. Diamond's success comes from mixing three pitches and working in the bottom third of the strike zone to produce groundouts. He has the ability to add and subtract velocity from all of his pitches. Diamond also excels at getting hitters to hit his pitch. He works ahead in the count and pounds the strike zone with an 89-91 mph fastball, a plus curveball and a changeup. He still needs to prove himself against quality hitters, but he's off to a good start. He'll face a strong test this season in Double-A.

Year	Club (League)	Class	W	L	ERA	G	GS	CG	SV	IP	H	R	ER	HR	BB	SO	AVG
2008	Rome (SAL)	LoA	3	1	3.08	9	9	0	0	53	47	20	18	2	11	38	.240
	Myrtle Beach (CAR)	HiA	12	2	2.79	17	15	1	0	100	95	42	31	6	28	85	.245
MINOR LEAGUE TOTALS			15	3	2.89	26	24	1	0	153	142	62	49	8	39	123	.244

27 JACOB THOMPSON, RHP

BORN: Nov. 19, 1986. **B-T:** R-R. **HT.:** 6-6. **WT.:** 215. **DRAFTED:** Virginia, 2008 (5th round).
SIGNED BY: Billy Best.

Thompson entered the spring of 2008 as a potential first-round pick after starring at Virginia and for the Team USA college national team. His junior season didn't unfold as planned, however. He struggled with an illness that caused him to lose 25 pounds, and also with his command and ability to pitch downhill, which caused his fastball to get hammered up in the strike zone. He dropped to the fifth round and signed in August for $190,000. After joining the Braves, Thompson showed an average 88-91 mph fastball after pitching at 90-93 in previous years. His plus curveball is his best pitch, and he also throws a slider that could become an above-average offering if it develops more consistent bite. His changeup is fringy and features some sink. Thompson has a large, lanky frame and a full windup that doesn't produce a lot of arm speed but does create deception. Repeating his delivery, trusting and improving his changeup, and maintaining a downhill plane will be the keys to Thompson's success in the pro ranks. Should he regain his previous form, Thompson has a chance to be a No. 3 starter. He'll begin his first full pro season in low Class A.

Year	Club (League)	Class	W	L	ERA	G	GS	CG	SV	IP	H	R	ER	HR	BB	SO	AVG
2008	Danville (APP)	R	0	0	1.93	2	1	0	0	5	4	1	1	0	1	5	.211
	Rome (SAL)	LoA	0	0	1.80	1	1	0	0	5	3	1	1	1	1	3	.158
MINOR LEAGUE TOTALS			0	0	1.86	3	2	0	0	10	7	2	2	1	2	8	.184

28 JAMES PARR, RHP

BORN: Feb. 27, 1986. **B-T:** R-R. **HT.:** 6-1. **WT.:** 185. **DRAFTED:** HS—Albuquerque, 2004 (4th round). **SIGNED BY:** Danny Bates.

For years Parr held promise, but he never really lived up to his potential after going 13-4, 3.41 in low Class A during his first full pro season. The light came on during 2008, as he solved Double-A, pitched even better in Triple-A and earned a big league callup. He won his major league debut on Sept. 4 with six shutout innings of two-hit ball in a 2-0 triumph against the Nationals. Parr has a classic sneaky-fast fastball. It rarely exits the high 80s, but it features boring, arm-side life. His ability to mix his pitches keeps hitters from teeing off. In addition, he throws a big-breaking curveball with tight spin and a changeup, both of which showed significant improvement last season. The keys to Parr's recent success were his ability to get ahead in the count by commanding his fastball and learning to trust his stuff. He has a cerebral approach and understands he must live in the bottom of the strike zone in order to get big leaguers out. He'll go to spring training with a chance to earn a spot in Atlanta's rotation, though the Javier Vazquez trade diminishes his chances.

Year	Club (League)	Class	W	L	ERA	G	GS	CG	SV	IP	H	R	ER	HR	BB	SO	AVG
2004	Braves (GCL)	R	3	2	4.24	10	10	0	0	40	39	19	19	2	12	40	.252
2005	Rome (SAL)	LoA	13	4	3.41	26	18	0	3	127	134	54	48	13	24	98	.269
2006	Myrtle Beach (CAR)	HiA	7	8	4.81	24	22	2	1	135	138	76	72	14	37	90	.269
2007	Myrtle Beach (CAR)	HiA	3	4	3.18	8	8	1	0	40	36	14	14	1	6	37	.252
	Mississippi (SL)	AA	4	5	4.59	18	16	0	0	98	111	51	50	8	25	75	.295
2008	Mississippi (SL)	AA	8	4	3.69	18	17	0	0	95	87	40	39	9	37	81	.246
	Richmond (IL)	AAA	5	3	3.23	10	9	0	0	56	49	20	20	4	14	44	.233
	Atlanta (NL)	MAJ	1	0	4.84	5	5	0	0	22	29	13	12	4	9	14	.315
MINOR LEAGUE TOTALS			43	30	4.00	114	100	3	4	590	594	274	262	51	155	465	.264
MAJOR LEAGUE TOTALS			1	0	4.84	5	5	0	0	22	29	13	12	4	9	14	.315

29 TODD REDMOND, RHP

BORN: May 17, 1985. **B-T:** R-R. **HT.:** 6-3. **WT.:** 210. **DRAFTED:** St. Petersburg (Fla.) JC, D/F 2004 (39th round). **SIGNED BY:** Rob Sidwell (Pirates).

Redmond joined the Braves prior to the 2008 season when they shipped spare reliever Tyler Yates to Pittsburgh. He regressed in his final season in the Pirates system, but made adjustments and emerged as the Southern League pitcher of the year in his first year as a Brave. He led the SL in wins (13) and strikeouts (133 in 166 innings) and helped Mississippi win the league title. Redmond works off his fastball and pitches to contact while allowing his defense to do its job. He pounds the strike zone with three pitches and fine overall command. He's not overpowering, working with a 90 mph fastball with a little sink, a solid curveball and a changeup. Redmond works on a good downhill plane, but sometimes drops his arm slot, gets under his pitches and leaves them up in the zone. He has to locate his pitches well to succeed and at times he runs into trouble if he tries to be too precise. Some scouts believe his future will be as a situational reliever rather than a starter, but the Braves plan to keep him in the rotation for now. He'll open 2009 in Triple-A after Atlanta protected him on its 40-man roster.

Year	Club (League)	Class	W	L	ERA	G	GS	CG	SV	IP	H	R	ER	HR	BB	SO	AVG
2005	Williamsport (NYP)	SS	1	2	1.98	15	14	0	0	73	62	22	16	2	21	63	.232
2006	Hickory (SAL)	LoA	13	6	2.75	27	27	0	0	160	137	64	49	13	33	148	.227
2007	Altoona (EL)	AA	1	1	3.12	3	3	0	0	17	15	6	6	2	3	12	.227
	Lynchburg (CAR)	HiA	7	12	4.54	25	25	0	0	143	151	82	72	13	32	95	.275
2008	Mississippi (SL)	AA	13	5	3.52	28	27	0	0	166	164	72	65	17	33	133	.257
MINOR LEAGUE TOTALS			35	26	3.35	98	96	0	0	559	529	246	208	47	122	451	.249

30 CHRISTIAN BETHANCOURT, C

BORN: Sept. 2, 1991. **B-T:** R-R. **HT.:** 6-0. **WT.:** 160. **SIGNED:** Panama, 2008. **SIGNED BY:** Roberto Aquino.

The Braves' increased efforts in Latin America continued with the signing of Bethancourt for $600,000 last March. Deemed the top catching prospect from the international ranks last year, he initially appeared on the radar when he played for Panama at the 2004 Little League World Series. He showed some bat speed and a decent feel for the strike zone as a 16-year-old in the Dominican Summer League, but the overall lack of strength in his swing shows his need for added development. While he doesn't have a big league body at this point, his potential behind the plate is obvious. A quality athlete for a catcher, he has a plus arm with true carry on his throws. He erased 43 percent of basestealers in his debut. He also has soft, quick hands and agility behind the plate. He'll be only 17 this season, so he'll probably make his U.S. debut in the Gulf Coast League.

Year	Club (League)	Class	AVG	G	AB	R	H	2B	3B	HR	RBI	BB	SO	SB	OBP	SLG
2008	Braves (DSL)	R	.267	34	116	12	31	6	3	0	17	11	25	1	.328	.371
MINOR LEAGUE TOTALS			.267	34	116	12	31	6	3	0	17	11	25	1	.328	.371

Baltimore Orioles

BY WILL LINGO

The Orioles must feel like they're running to stand still.

There are signs of hope. Catcher Matt Wieters was Baseball America's Minor League Player of the Year and may be the best prospect in baseball. The trade of Erik Bedard to the Mariners was a steal, giving Baltimore not only its closer (George Sherrill) and center fielder (Adam Jones) but also its best

pitching prospect (Chris Tillman) and a couple of other young prospects who could contribute. Aubrey Huff had a bounceback year, and Nick Markakis looks like he'll occupy right field in Camden Yards for years.

But there was at least as much bad news. The young pitchers the Orioles were counting on either weren't ready for prime time or got hurt. Radhames Liz and Garrett Olson took their lumps in Baltimore. Troy Patton, a key part of the Miguel Tejada trade with the Astros, went down with a torn labrum during spring training. Adam Loewen, who signed for a $3.2 million bonus as the No. 4 overall pick in 2002, officially washed out as a pitcher after continued elbow problems. The Orioles decided to try Loewen as a position player, and then lost him altogether when he signed with the Blue Jays after the season.

And in fact, the Orioles aren't even standing still. They're dropping back, falling into the cellar in the American League East for the first time since 1988. Baltimore's 68-93 record left it 17½ games out of fourth place and marked its 11th straight losing season.

Things aren't going to get any easier in the AL East. The Rays look like they'll be good for at least the next several years, and the Red Sox and Yankees will continue to be the Red Sox and Yankees. Even the Blue Jays finished 10 games above .500 and have a farm system that's showing improvement.

The Orioles are making progress in player development as well, with an influx of top-end talent in the last few years. Wieters is a legitimate cornerstone player, and the system's top three arms (Tillman, 2008 first-rounder Brian Matusz and Jake Arrieta) all look like legitimate big league starters. If it's to make a significant jump in the big league standings, Baltimore particularly needs its young pitchers to come through. The Orioles ranked 13th in the AL in ERA (5.13) in 2008 and head into 2009 with no proven big league starters behind Jeremy Guthrie, who's better suited for the middle or back of a rotation than the front.

At least with team president Andy MacPhail now

Dynamic players like Adam Jones provide the Orioles some hope for the future

TOP 30 PROSPECTS

1. Matt Wieters, c	16. David Hernandez, rhp
2. Chris Tillman, rhp	17. Jason Berken, rhp
3. Brian Matusz, lhp	18. Brad Bergesen, rhp
4. Jake Arrieta, rhp	19. Tyler Henson, 3b
5. Nolan Reimold, of	20. Matt Angle, of
6. Brandon Erbe, rhp	21. Pedro Beato, rhp
7. Billy Rowell, 3b	22. Bob McCrory, rhp
8. Troy Patton, lhp	23. Greg Miclat, ss
9. Brandon Snyder, 1b	24. Tony Butler, lhp
10. Kam Mickolio, rhp	25. Brandon Cooney, rhp
11. Chorye Spoone, rhp	26. Brandon Waring, 3b
12. Zach Britton, lhp	27. Justin Turner, 2b
13. Xavier Avery, of	28. Ryan Adams, 2b
14. L.J. Hoes, 2b	29. Lou Montanez, of
15. Bobby Bundy, rhp	30. Caleb Joseph, c

at the helm of the baseball operations, there's a feeling the franchise has a direction and someone with the patience to execute a plan. Spending $10.6 million to get Wieters, Arrieta and Matusz in the last two drafts should pay big dividends, and the trade with Seattle gave the rebuilding effort a huge boost. And owner Peter Angelos has been out of the headlines.

MacPhail recognizes the Orioles don't have the depth of talent to compete in the East, but he has assembled several pieces that could help them take a step forward. Getting back in the playoffs remains a mountain that seems too high to climb right now.

General Manager: Andy MacPhail. **Farm Director:** David Stockstill. **Scouting Director:** Joe Jordan.

Class	Team	League	W	L	PCT	Finish*	Manager	Affiliated
Majors	Baltimore	American	68	93	.422	13th (14)	Dave Trembley	—
Triple-A	Norfolk Tides	International	64	78	.451	11th (14)	Gary Allenson	2007
Double-A	Bowie Baysox	Eastern	84	58	.592	2nd (12)	Brad Komminsk	1993
High A	Frederick Keys	Carolina	63	76	.453	6th (8)	T. Thompson/R. Hebner	1989
Low A	Delmarva Shorebirds	South Atlantic	78	61	.561	5th (16)	Ramon Sambo	1997
Short-season	Aberdeen IronBirds	New York-Penn	36	39	.480	9th (14)	Gary Kendall	2002
Rookie	Bluefield Orioles	Appalachian	29	36	.446	8th (10)	Orlando Gomez	1958
Rookie	GCL Orioles	Gulf Coast	14	41	.255	16th (16)	Jesus Alfaro	2008

Overall 2008 Minor League Record 368 389 .486 20th
* Finish in overall standings (No. of teams in league). ^League champion.

LAST YEAR'S TOP 30

Rank	Player, Pos.	Status
1.	Matt Wieters, c	No. 1
2.	Radhames Liz, rhp	Majors
3.	Troy Patton, lhp	No. 8
4.	Nolan Reimold, of	No. 5
5.	Billy Rowell, 3b	No. 7
6.	Brandon Snyder, 1b/3b	No. 9
7.	Jake Arrieta, rhp	No. 4
8.	Chorye Spoone, rhp	No. 11
9.	Pedro Beato, rhp	No. 21
10.	Brandon Erbe, rhp	No. 6
11.	Mike Costanzo, 3b	Dropped out
12.	Garrett Olson, lhp	Majors
13.	Tim Bascom, rhp	Dropped out
14.	Scott Moore, 3b/of	Dropped out
15.	David Hernandez, rhp	No. 16
16.	Bob McCrory, rhp	No. 22
17.	Brandon Tripp, of	Dropped out
18.	Randor Bierd, rhp	Dropped out
19.	James Hoey, rhp	Dropped out
20.	Dennis Sarfate, rhp	Majors
21.	Zach Britton, lhp	No. 12
22.	Tyler Henson, ss	No. 19
23.	Jeff Fiorentino, of	Dropped out
24.	Matt Angle, of	No. 20
25.	Chris Vinyard, 1b	Dropped out
26.	Brad Bergesen, rhp	No. 18
27.	Tyler Kolodny, 3b	Dropped out
28.	Luis Lebron, rhp	Dropped out
29.	Jim Johnson, rhp	Majors
30.	Kieron Pope, of	Dropped out

BEST TOOLS

Best Hitter for Average	Matt Wieters
Best Power Hitter	Matt Wieters
Best Strike-Zone Discipline	Matt Wieters
Fastest Baserunner	Xavier Avery
Best Athlete	Tyler Henson
Best Fastball	Kam Mickolio
Best Curveball	Brian Matusz
Best Slider	David Hernandez
Best Changeup	Brian Matusz
Best Control	Brad Bergesen
Best Defensive Catcher	Matt Wieters
Best Defensive Infielder	Blake Davis
Best Infield Arm	Billy Rowell
Best Defensive Outfielder	Matt Angle
Best Outfield Arm	Nolan Reimold

PROJECTED 2012 LINEUP

Catcher	Matt Wieters
First Base	Brandon Snyder
Second Base	Brian Roberts
Third Base	Billy Rowell
Shortstop	Cesar Izturis
Left Field	Nolan Reimold
Center Field	Adam Jones
Right Field	Nick Markakis
Designated Hitter	Aubrey Huff
No. 1 Starter	Chris Tillman
No. 2 Starter	Brian Matusz
No. 3 Starter	Jake Arrieta
No. 4 Starter	Jeremy Guthrie
No. 5 Starter	Radhames Liz
Closer	George Sherrill

TOP PROSPECTS OF THE DECADE

Year	Player, Pos.	2008 Org.
1999	Matt Riley, lhp	Dodgers
2000	Matt Riley, lhp	Dodgers
2001	Keith Reed, of	Newark (Atlantic)
2002	Richard Stahl, lhp	Out of baseball
2003	Erik Bedard, lhp	Mariners
2004	Adam Loewen, lhp	Orioles
2005	Nick Markakis, of	Orioles
2006	Nick Markakis, of	Orioles
2007	Billy Rowell, 3b	Orioles
2008	Matt Wieters, c	Orioles

TOP DRAFT PICKS OF THE DECADE

Year	Player, Pos.	2008 Org.
1999	Mike Paradis, rhp	Out of baseball
2000	Beau Hale, rhp	Out of baseball
2001	Chris Smith, lhp	Out of baseball
2002	Adam Loewen, lhp	Orioles
2003	Nick Markakis, of	Orioles
2004	*Wade Townsend, rhp	Rays
2005	Brandon Snyder, c	Orioles
2006	Billy Rowell, 3b	Orioles
2007	Matt Wieters, c	Orioles
2008	Brian Matusz, lhp	Orioles

*Did not sign.

LARGEST BONUSES IN CLUB HISTORY

Matt Wieters, 2007	$6,000,000
Adam Loewen, 2002	$3,200,000
Brian Matusz, 2008	$3,200,000
Beau Hale, 2000	$2,250,000
Chris Smith, 2001	$2,175,000

BALTIMORE ORIOLES

TOP 2009 ROOKIE: Matt Wieters, c. Even if he doesn't break camp with the major league team, he'll be up quickly and has the talent to perform right away.

BREAKOUT PROSPECT: Bobby Bundy, rhp. A top draft prospect until he hurt his knee playing basketball, he signed for $600,000 in the eighth round last summer and could be the Orioles' next premium pitching prospect.

SOURCE OF TOP 30 TALENT			
Homegrown	23	Acquired	7
College	10	Trades	6
Junior college	3	Rule 5 draft	0
High school	10	Independent leagues	0
Draft-and-follow	0	Free agents/waivers	1
Nondrafted free agents	0		
International	0		

SLEEPER: Jesse Beal, rhp. A 14th-round pick out of a Virginia high school, Beal is 6-foot-7 with a smooth delivery and a fastball that already touches 92 mph with plenty of room for projection.

Numbers in parentheses indicate prospect rankings.

LF
Lou Montanez (29)
Kieron Pope
Ronnie Welty

CF
Xavier Avery (13)
Matt Angle (20)
Kyle Hudson
Danny Figueroa

RF
Nolan Reimold (5)
Brandon Tripp
Robbie Widlansky

3B
Billy Rowell (7)
Brandon Waring (26)
Tyler Kolodny
Mike Costanzo
Scott Moore
Corey Thomas

SS
Tyler Henson (19)
Greg Miclat (23)
Blake Davis
Garabez Rosa

2B
L.J. Hoes (14)
Justin Turner (27)
Ryan Adams (28)
Paco Figueroa
Carlos Rojas

1B
Brandon Snyder (9)
Chris Vinyard
Elvin Polanco
Joe Mahoney

C
Matt Wieters (1)
Caleb Joseph (30)
Luis Bernardo
Jordan Wolf
Dashenko Ricardo
Adam Donachie

RHP

Starters	Relievers
Chris Tillman (2)	Kam Mickolio (10)
Jake Arrieta (4)	David Hernandez (16)
Brandon Erbe (6)	Bob McCrory (22)
Chorye Spoone (11)	Brandon Cooney (25)
Bobby Bundy (15)	Jim Hoey
Jason Berken (17)	Pat Egan
Brad Bergesen (18)	Jim Miller
Pedro Beato (21)	Randor Bierd
Jesse Beal	Oliver Drake
Tim Bascom	
Jake Renshaw	
William Princivil	
Justin Moore	
Sean Gleason	
Luis Noel	

LHP

Starters	Relievers
Brian Matusz (3)	Tony Butler (24)
Troy Patton (8)	Wilfrido Perez
Zach Britton (12)	Rick Zagone
Cole McCurry	Tony Butler
	Nathan Nery

2008   BONUSES: $6.9 MILLION

BEST PURE HITTER: L.J. Hoes (3) batted .308 and walked more (30) than he struck out (22) in the Rookie-level Gulf Coast League, while making the transition from the outfield to second base. He still needs to smooth out his footwork, but the Orioles think he can remain at second.

BEST POWER HITTER: 3B Corey Thomas (13) has the best raw power in Baltimore's draft, though he barely played this summer after tweaking a knee in a postdraft minicamp. C Caleb Joseph (8) hit eight homers and can drive balls out to the opposite field.

FASTEST RUNNER: OFs Xavier Avery (2) and Kyle Hudson (4) are both 8 runners on the 2-8 scouting scale, with Hudson perhaps quicker out of the box. Hudson played in just 11 games before breaking his right hand on a headfirst slide.

BEST DEFENSIVE PLAYER: SS Greg Miclat (5) started his summer in the Cape Cod League and didn't sign until August. He has plus range and instincts to go with a solid arm.

BEST FASTBALL: LHP Brian Matusz (1) sits at 90-92 mph and touches 94—yet his fastball may be his third-best pitch. RHP Bobby Bundy (8), who signed for $600,000, hit 94 in a May workout for the Orioles when he pitched without a knee brace. He spent the spring pitching with the brace after tearing the anterior cruciate ligament in his right knee in December.

BEST SECONDARY PITCH: Matusz' curveball and changeup are so effective that sometimes he doesn't establish his fastball as much as he should.

BEST PRO DEBUT: LHP Rick Zagone (6) went 7-1, 2.89 with 79 strikeouts in 65 innings at short-season Aberdeen. He operates at 85-88 mph as a starter, relying on the life and command of his pitches.

BEST ATHLETE: Avery's power-speed combination has earned him comparisons to Carl Crawford. He was a blue-chip running back recruit ticketed for Georgia, while Hudson played wide receiver at Illinois.

MOST INTRIGUING BACKGROUND: RHP Oliver Drake (43) was drafted out of the Naval Academy and was able to withdraw and sign for $100,000 because he had yet to make his military commitment. He owns an 89-93 mph fastball and an interesting slider.

CLOSEST TO THE MAJORS: Matusz should reach Double-A in 2009 and could crack Baltimore's rotation by Opening Day 2010.

BEST LATE-ROUND PICK: RHP Jesse Beal (14) has the most upside, with size (6-foot-7), a sound delivery

and the chance for three solid pitches. OF Ronnie Welty (20), a Rookie-level Appalachian League all-star, is a lanky athlete in the mold of Hunter Pence.

THE ONE WHO GOT AWAY: Projectable RHP Kevin Brady (44) flashed a 95 mph fastball by the end of the summer, but a $450,000 offer couldn't dissuade him from attending Clemson.

ASSESSMENT: The Orioles not only landed the best pitcher in the draft (Matusz) with the No. 4 overall pick, but they also got him for a favorable $3,472,500 major league deal. After that, Baltimore loaded up on athletes with Avery, Hoes, Hudson and Welty.

2007   BONUSES: $8.0 MILLION

C Matt Wieters (1) won Baseball America's Minor League Player of the Year award in his pro debut and looks like a superstar. RHP Jake Arrieta (5) is also on his way to justifying a well above-slot bonus.

GRADE: A

2006   BONUSES: $5.4 MILLION

This crop has developed far more slowly than Baltimore hoped. 3B Billy Rowell's (1) bat isn't living up to the ninth overall pick, and RHP Pedro Beato (1s) lost his fastball last season.

GRADE: D

2005   BONUSES: $4.2 MILLION*

None of them looks like a star at this point, but the Orioles did land a big leaguer in LHP Garrett Olson (1s) and several of their best prospects: 1B Brandon Snyder (1), OF Nolan Reimold (2) and RHPs Brandon Erbe (3), Chorye Spoone (8) and David Hernandez (16).

GRADE: C

2004   BONUSES: $1.3 MILLION*

Baltimore botched this draft by antagonizing RHP Wade Townsend (1) to the point where he wouldn't sign. OF Jeff Fiorentino (3) rushed to the big leagues, then was discarded just as quickly. The highlight of this draft was RHP Kevin Hart (11), who was given away to the Cubs.

GRADE: D

*Draft analysis by Jim Callis. Numbers in parentheses indicate draft rounds. *Bonuses for 2004-05 are first 10 rounds only.*

PROSPECT

MIKE JANES

MATT WIETERS, C

Born: May 21, 1986.
Ht.: 6-5. **Wt.:** 230.
Bats: B. **Throws:** R.
Drafted: Georgia Tech,
2007 (1st round).
Signed by:
Dave Jennings.

L ots of prospects get hyped, but few deliver on their advance billing as dramatically as Wieters did in 2008, his debut season. He posted dominant performances both at the plate and behind it. He batted .355 (fifth in the minors) with a .454 on-base percentage (third) and .600 slugging percentage (10th), and his 1.054 OPS was surpassed only by two players who spent all or part of the year in the hitter-friendly Pacific Coast League. Wieters was an easy choice as BA's Minor League Player of the Year, not to mention the top prospect in the high Class A Carolina and Double-A Eastern leagues. He also ranked No. 1 in Hawaii Winter Baseball in the fall of 2007. Baltimore was hoping for a cornerstone player when it paid him a then-record $6 million up-front bonus as the fifth overall pick in the 2007 draft. Wieters enjoyed an All-America career at Georgia Tech, initially starring as a two-way player before his pitching duties dwindled as he showed his prowess as a catcher. After his first pro season, the Orioles couldn't be happier with their investment.

Wieters is an above-average hitter with above-average power, combining patience with the bat speed to drive pitches out of any part of the park. He's an amazingly polished offensive player with great pitch recognition and a knack for getting himself into favorable counts. And don't forget he's a switch-hitter. Behind the plate, he shows agility, soft hands and the strong arm that made him a quality pitcher. He threw out 46 percent of basestealers in the Carolina League, and 32 percent in the Eastern League. He also earned high marks for his handling of pitchers and his game-calling skills. And yet people still tend to mention Wieters' intangibles first when they give their rave reviews: his quiet leadership, his ideal combination of being confident yet humble, his feel for the nuances of the game. Orioles officials note, for example, how quickly he adapted to professional breaking pitches, making adjustments not only within games but within individual at-bats.

Wieters is a below-average runner, but he's athletic enough not to be a baseclogger, and he's plenty agile behind the plate. If you really want to look for negatives, you could wonder how long he'll stay behind the plate because he's so big. He clearly can handle the position, but if physical problems were to push him to first base, then his value would dip. But there's no reason at this point to think he won't spend at least the first five years of his big league career as a catcher.

The Orioles have done all they can to keep Wieters under wraps, eschewing a September callup for example, but Baltimore fans are well aware of him and anxious to pin their hopes for the future on his broad shoulders. With the trade of Ramon Hernandez there's nothing standing in his way, though the Orioles may sign a veteran so Wieters can open 2009 at Triple-A Norfolk. He'll reach the majors at some point during the season, though, and it's hard to see him going back down after that.

Year	Club (League)	Class	AVG	G	AB	R	H	2B	3B	HR	RBI	BB	SO	SB	OBP	SLG
2008	Frederick (CAR)	HiA	.345	69	229	48	79	8	0	15	40	44	47	1	.448	.576
	Bowie (EL)	AA	.365	61	208	41	76	14	2	12	51	38	29	1	.460	.625
MINOR LEAGUE TOTALS			.355	130	437	89	155	22	2	27	91	82	76	2	.454	.600

2 CHRIS TILLMAN, RHP

BORN: April 15, 1988. **B-T:** R-R. **HT.:** 6-5. **WT.:** 195. **DRAFTED:** HS—Fountain Valley, Calif., 2006 (2ND ROUND). **SIGNED BY:** Tim Reynolds (Mariners).

By just about any measure, the deal that brought four prospects and George Sherrill from Seattle for Erik Bedard was a steal for the Orioles, and Tillman could be the biggest prize of all. As the youngest pitcher in Double-A to start the season, he not only succeeded but at times dominated, and he ranked as the Eastern League's top pitching prospect. Tillman fits the pitching prototype, with a long, lean body, a smooth delivery, mound presence and three good pitches. He throws consistently in the low 90s, peaking at 94 mph, and showed an improved ability to keep his fastball down this season, though he has the stuff to pitch up in the zone at times. His curveball is also an above-average pitch. While Tillman shows the ability to throw strikes consistently with all his pitches, he still needs to sharpen his command. And while his changeup has become a usable pitch, it's still clearly No. 3 on his list and he needs to go to it more. Tillman's overall package and early success at a high level make him the best bet among the Orioles' three prized pitching prospects. He should at least pitch in the middle of the Baltimore rotation and has the potential to lead it. He'll open 2009 in Triple-A with an eye toward moving to the big leagues in 2010.

Year	Club (League)	Class	W	L	ERA	G	GS	CG	SV	IP	H	R	ER	HR	BB	SO	AVG
2006	Mariners (AZL)	R	2	0	0.82	5	0	0	1	11	9	4	1	0	5	16	.214
	Everett (NWL)	SS	1	3	7.78	5	5	0	0	20	25	17	17	4	15	29	.325
2007	Wisconsin (MWL)	LoA	1	4	3.55	8	8	0	0	33	31	21	13	1	13	34	.238
	High Desert (CAL)	HiA	6	7	5.26	20	20	0	0	103	107	79	60	12	48	105	.266
2008	Bowie (EL)	AA	11	4	3.18	28	28	0	0	136	115	53	48	10	65	154	.227
MINOR LEAGUE TOTALS			21	18	4.14	66	61	0	1	302	287	174	139	27	146	338	.248

3 BRIAN MATUSZ, LHP

BORN: Feb. 11, 1987. **B-T:** L-L. **HT.:** 6-5. **WT.:** 200. **DRAFTED:** San Diego, 2008 (1st round). **SIGNED BY:** Mark Ralston.

An unsigned Angels fourth-round pick out of an Arizona high school in 2005, Matusz went on to star at San Diego for three years. He went 12-2, 1.71 as a junior to earn first-team All-America honors, establishing himself as the top pitcher available in the 2008 draft. The Orioles got him with the fourth overall pick and signed him at the deadline for a major league contract worth $3,472,500, a relative bargain. Few pitchers come into professional baseball with better secondary stuff than Matusz's. His best pitch is probably his curveball, a plus pitch that he commands to both sides of the plate. His changeup is also an above-average pitch, and he leans on both pitches almost to the detriment of his fastball, which sits in the low 90s and touches 94 mph. Matusz also has an average slider, and he spots all his pitches well. Matusz will have to rely on his fastball more as a pro pitcher. His mechanics also could use some cleaning up, as he lands on a straight front leg sometimes. For the second straight year, the Orioles appear to have hit paydirt with their first-round pick. Matusz should move quickly and profiles as a middle-of-the-rotation starter who could be a No. 2 if he can dominate with his fastball as a pro. He performed well in the Arizona Fall League, so he could open his career at Double-A Bowie, though high Class A Frederick would be a safer bet.

Year	Club (League)	Class	W	L	ERA	G	GS	CG	SV	IP	H	R	ER	HR	BB	SO	AVG
2008	Did Not Play—Signed Late																

4 JAKE ARRIETA, RHP

BORN: March 6, 1986. **B-T:** R-R. **HT.:** 6-4. **WT.:** 225. **DRAFTED:** Texas Christian, 2007 (5th round). **SIGNED BY:** Jim Richardson.

Though he didn't perform well as a college junior, Arrieta had shown first-round stuff during his amateur career, so the Orioles gave him $1.1 million as a fifth-round pick in the 2007 draft. He looked well worth it in his 2008 pro debut, finishing as the Carolina League's ERA leader, pitcher of the year and top pitching prospect despite dealing with an oblique injury in June and departing early to pitch for the U.S. Olympic team. He made one start in Beijing, pitching six shutout innings with seven strikeouts against China. The Orioles thought Arrieta could get his velocity back with minor mechanical adjustments, and they were right. His fastball peaked at 96-97 mph in 2008 and showed explosive late movement, and he got stronger with more work. He shows good fastball command and isn't afraid to pitch inside, and his big frame should allow him to eat innings. Arrieta could have as many as three plus pitches to go with his fastball, but they all need work. His slider has the most potential, but his changeup should also be a good pitch as he uses it more. His curveball is a slow, big breaker that he'll need to tighten up. Some observers believe Arrieta will be better than both Chris Tillman and Brian Matusz, and the Orioles will be happy if they can build their future rotation around the trio. Arrieta will move up to Bowie to open 2009 and should be ready for a big league opportunity the following year.

Year	Club (League)	Class	W	L	ERA	G	GS	CG	SV	IP	H	R	ER	HR	BB	SO	AVG
2008	Frederick (CAR)	HiA	6	5	2.87	20	20	0	0	113	80	44	36	7	51	120	.199
MINOR LEAGUE TOTALS			6	5	2.87	20	20	0	0	113	80	44	36	7	51	120	.199

5 NOLAN REIMOLD, OF

BORN: Oct. 12, 1983. **B-T:** R-R. **HT.:** 6-4. **WT.:** 207. **DRAFTED:** Bowling Green State, 2005 (2nd round). **SIGNED BY:** Marc Ziegler.

After two injury-marred seasons, Reimold went back to Double-A Bowie, stayed healthy and got himself back on track. His 25 home runs tied for second in the Eastern League, and he was among the league leaders in slugging (.501) and OPS (.868) as well. Reimold has the raw power to compare with just about anyone's in the minors, rating a 70 on the 20-80 scouting scale. He crushes mistakes and should be an average overall hitter if he continues to make adjustments and shows the ability to consistently handle secondary pitches. He's athletic and has average speed and a plus arm. He's a big guy with long levers and an unconventional setup who is starting to figure out his swing, though Reimold realistically is a one-zone hitter who always will strike out a lot. He can be too patient at times and wants to do too much at others. He's not an instinctive defender and doesn't always take great routes, so he fits best in left field, especially with Nick Markakis ahead of him. Reimold's strong season earned him a spot on the Orioles' 40-man roster and a look in left field in spring training. The Orioles could use his power, but they have seen that rushing players to the big leagues has not served them well in recent years, so some Triple-A at-bats probably would be a better idea.

Year	Club (League)	Class	AVG	G	AB	R	H	2B	3B	HR	RBI	BB	SO	SB	OBP	SLG
2005	Aberdeen (NYP)	SS	.294	50	180	33	53	15	2	9	30	29	44	2	.392	.550
	Frederick (CAR)	HiA	.265	23	83	17	22	6	0	6	11	12	27	3	.371	.554
2006	Frederick (CAR)	HiA	.255	119	415	73	106	26	0	19	75	76	107	14	.379	.455
2007	Orioles (GCL)	R	.233	9	30	4	7	4	1	0	8	6	4	0	.410	.433
	Bowie (EL)	AA	.306	50	186	30	57	15	0	11	34	17	47	2	.365	.565
2008	Bowie (EL)	AA	.284	139	507	87	144	29	3	25	84	63	82	7	.367	.501
MINOR LEAGUE TOTALS			.278	390	1401	244	389	95	6	70	242	203	311	28	.375	.504

6 BRANDON ERBE, RHP

BORN: Dec. 25, 1987. **B-T:** R-R. **HT.:** 6-4. **WT.:** 180. **DRAFTED:** HS—Baltimore, 2005 (3rd round). **SIGNED BY:** Ty Brown.

Erbe went back to high Class A after making mechanical adjustments in instructional league following a rough 2007 season. He cut two runs off his ERA and led the Carolina League in strikeouts (151) and baserunners per inning (1.2), though he also topped the league by giving up 21 home runs. Erbe showed progress in just about every aspect of pitching and became more consistent with his smoothed-out windup. His fastball still touches the mid-90s, though he usually works in the low 90s, and his slider was more consistently a plus pitch. His two-seamer showed better sink and life and allowed him to work down in the zone more. He finished second in the CL in innings and learned how to pace himself better. While Erbe has improved his command, it's still not where it needs to be, and he too frequently leaves the ball up, as his home run total and 0.8 groundout/airout ratio show. His changeup has improved but still is a fringe-average pitch, and he needs to use it more. He still has some effort in his delivery and can be stubborn in taking instruction. Erbe will have two plus pitches if he continues along his development path. If he can bring his changeup along with them and improve his command, he's a big league starter. If not, he should be a late-inning reliever. He'll get every chance to remain in the rotation, moving to Double-A to open 2009.

Year	Club (League)	Class	W	L	ERA	G	GS	CG	SV	IP	H	R	ER	HR	BB	SO	AVG
2005	Bluefield (APP)	R	1	1	3.09	11	3	0	1	23	8	10	8	1	10	48	.103
	Aberdeen (NYP)	SS	1	1	7.71	3	1	0	0	7	6	6	6	0	4	9	.261
2006	Delmarva (SAL)	LoA	5	9	3.22	28	27	0	0	115	88	47	41	2	47	133	.217
2007	Frederick (CAR)	HiA	6	8	6.26	25	25	0	0	119	127	95	83	14	62	111	.273
2008	Frederick (CAR)	HiA	10	12	4.30	28	28	2	0	151	120	82	72	21	50	151	.216
MINOR LEAGUE TOTALS			23	31	4.55	95	84	2	1	415	349	240	210	38	173	452	.229

7 BILLY ROWELL, 3B

BORN: Sept. 10, 1988. **B-T:** L-R. **HT.:** 6-5. **WT.:** 205. **DRAFTED:** HS—Pennsauken, N.J., 2006 (1st round). **SIGNED BY:** Dean Albany.

Rowell had an inconsistent season as the youngest regular in the Carolina League, injuring his ankle in the first game and missing most of April. He struggled for long stretches, bottoming out at .213 in early July, but bounced back by batting .297 in August. The first high school hitter selected in the 2006 draft, he signed for $2.1 million. Rowell has the highest ceiling of any hitting prospect in the organization, though he still has a lot of work to do to develop his bat. His smooth swing and bat speed should allow him to hit for average and give him the power to drive the ball, and he can generate easy pop even when he shortens his swing—which he needs to do more often. His arm is his best defensive tool. Put simply, Rowell needs to grow up. He still has his own hitting coach, meaning he and the Orioles often are working at cross-purposes. He's still helpless against lefthanders, batting .187 against them in 2008. He has lost a lot of his speed as his body has matured, and his hands and feet don't work together well, raising questions about his ability to stay at third base. Rowell could answer a lot of the questions about whether he'll realize his potential by returning to the Carolina League and outworking everyone else. Otherwise, he'll be an erratic hitter with no defensive position.

Year	Club (League)	Class	AVG	G	AB	R	H	2B	3B	HR	RBI	BB	SO	SB	OBP	SLG
2006	Bluefield (APP)	R	.329	42	152	38	50	15	3	2	26	25	47	3	.422	.507
	Aberdeen (NYP)	SS	.326	11	43	8	14	4	0	1	6	4	12	0	.388	.488
2007	Delmarva (SAL)	LoA	.273	91	352	47	96	21	3	9	57	31	104	3	.335	.426
2008	Frederick (CAR)	HiA	.248	111	375	39	93	24	0	7	50	36	104	1	.315	.368
MINOR LEAGUE TOTALS			.274	255	922	132	253	64	6	19	139	96	267	7	.345	.419

8 TROY PATTON, LHP

BORN: Sept. 3, 1985. **B-T:** B-L. **HT.:** 6-1. **WT.:** 185. **DRAFTED:** HS—Magnolia, Texas, 2004 (9th round). **SIGNED BY:** Rusty Pendergrass (Astros).

Patton was a key part of the five-player package the Astros traded for Miguel Tejada in December 2007. Patton tried to rehab a sore shoulder during the offseason but got shut down with shoulder pain early in spring training, opting for surgery to repair a small labrum tear in March. When healthy, Patton offers solid stuff and strong command from the left side. He throws a four-seam fastball in the low 90s, touching 94 mph, and a two-seamer in the high 80s, complementing them with a slider and changeup. He has little margin for error, but his command and moxie allow his stuff to play up. Shoulder surgery is always worrisome for a pitcher, but Patton wasn't a power pitcher and the reports from his rehabilitation have been positive. He threw off flat ground in the late summer and was back on the mound in September, first throwing bullpens and then simulated games during instructional league. Patton's arm strength is back and Orioles officials say he looks free and easy, so he'll pitch without restrictions in spring training after taking the winter off. A successful return would be a boost for the major league rotation, though he may need some time in Triple-A first.

Year	Club (League)	Class	W	L	ERA	G	GS	CG	SV	IP	H	R	ER	HR	BB	SO	AVG
2004	Greeneville (APP)	R	2	2	1.93	6	6	0	0	28	23	8	6	1	5	32	.225
2005	Lexington (SAL)	LoA	5	2	1.94	15	15	0	0	79	59	24	17	3	20	94	.211
	Salem (CAR)	HiA	1	4	2.63	10	9	0	0	41	34	12	12	2	8	38	.227
2006	Salem (CAR)	HiA	7	7	2.93	19	19	1	0	101	92	49	33	4	37	102	.240
	Corpus Christi (TEX)	AA	2	5	4.37	8	8	0	0	45	48	26	22	6	13	37	.271
2007	Corpus Christi (TEX)	AA	6	6	2.99	16	16	0	0	102	96	38	34	10	33	69	.247
	Round Rock (PCL)	AAA	4	2	4.59	8	8	0	0	49	44	26	25	5	11	25	.247
	Houston (NL)	MAJ	0	2	3.55	3	2	0	0	13	10	6	5	3	4	8	.213
2008	Did Not Play—Injured																
MINOR LEAGUE TOTALS			27	28	3.01	82	81	1	0	446	396	183	149	31	127	397	.239
MAJOR LEAGUE TOTALS			0	2	3.55	3	2	0	0	13	10	6	5	3	4	8	.213

9 BRANDON SNYDER, 1B

BORN: Nov. 23, 1986. **B-T:** R-R. **HT.:** 6-2. **WT.:** 210. **DRAFTED:** HS—Centreville, Va., 2005 (1st round). **SIGNED BY:** Ty Brown.

Snyder has proven that if he's healthy, he'll hit. After a bounce-back season in 2007, the 13th overall pick in the 2005 draft built on it in his first exposure to high Class A ball, finishing second in the Carolina League in batting (.315) and in the top five in several other offensive categories, including slugging (.490) and OPS (.848). Snyder raised his average by about 50 points after former big leaguer and longtime hitting coach Richie Hebner took over as Frederick's manager at the end of May. Hebner took Snyder under his wing and improved his approach at the plate, helping him stay on offspeed pitches, work counts and drive the ball better. He always has shown the ability to hit for average, but 2008 was the first year he hit the ball hard consistently. All of Snyder's value lies in his bat. The idea to put him behind the plate never got off the ground because he couldn't stay healthy, and he's a below-average first baseman because of poor range and footwork—though he's an average runner. Some think he should get a longer look at third base, while others think he'll wind up in the outfield. Snyder has put in the work to become a better hitter, and he'll need to do the same on defense to avoid being a man without a position. He'll move up to Double-A and try to show he can do more than hit.

Year	Club (League)	Class	AVG	G	AB	R	H	2B	3B	HR	RBI	BB	SO	SB	OBP	SLG
2005	Bluefield (APP)	R	.271	44	144	26	39	8	0	8	35	28	36	7	.380	.493
	Aberdeen (NYP)	SS	.393	8	28	4	11	2	0	0	6	2	7	0	.419	.464
2006	Delmarva (SAL)	LoA	.194	38	144	12	28	12	0	3	20	9	55	0	.237	.340
	Aberdeen (NYP)	SS	.234	34	124	14	29	8	1	1	11	5	43	2	.267	.339
2007	Delmarva (SAL)	LoA	.283	118	448	63	127	23	3	11	58	44	107	0	.354	.422
2008	Frederick (CAR)	HiA	.315	116	435	70	137	33	2	13	80	29	83	3	.358	.490
MINOR LEAGUE TOTALS			.280	358	1323	189	371	86	6	36	210	117	331	12	.340	.436

10 KAM MICKOLIO, RHP

RODGER WOOD

BORN: May 10, 1984. **B-T:** R-R. **HT.:** 6-9. **WT.:** 255. **DRAFTED:** Utah Valley State, 2006 (18th round). **SIGNED BY:** Phil Geisler (Mariners).

Mickolio grew up in Montana, which has no high school baseball, and didn't play the sport until American Legion ball before his senior year. He rocketed through the minors in two seasons, having come to the Orioles in the Erik Bedard deal. He made his big league debut in August. Think Bobby Jenks, a big guy who came out of the wilderness with pure power stuff, only bigger. Mickolio is not subtle, reaching 96-97 mph with his fastball from an unorthodox crossfire delivery, and complementing it with a slider that's a well above-average pitch when it's on. Mickolio's delivery is all over the place, and the Orioles have worked on several tweaks to give him something more balanced and repeatable. They won't try a major overhaul because they don't want him to lose his arm speed or risk injury. His slider is at its best about one out of three outings, and his changeup and slurve aren't effective yet. If Baltimore is patient with Mickolio and gives him time to develop, he has the stuff to set up or close in the big leagues. He could use more seasoning in Triple-A, but his arm will be mighty tempting to the big league staff.

Year	Club (League)	Class	W	L	ERA	G	GS	CG	SV	IP	H	R	ER	HR	BB	SO	AVG
2006	Everett (NWL)	SS	1	0	2.78	21	0	0	4	32	34	14	10	1	7	26	.264
2007	West Tenn (SL)	AA	3	1	1.82	18	0	0	2	30	24	9	6	0	12	27	.224
	Tacoma (PCL)	AAA	3	3	3.75	14	0	0	1	24	19	12	10	3	10	28	.213
2008	Bowie (EL)	AA	2	1	4.70	28	0	0	1	38	39	21	20	2	22	40	.262
	Norfolk (IL)	AAA	1	0	1.80	17	0	0	2	20	13	7	4	0	9	23	.173
	Baltimore (AL)	MAJ	0	1	5.87	9	0	0	0	8	8	5	5	0	4	8	.267
MINOR LEAGUE TOTALS			10	5	3.12	98	0	0	10	144	129	63	50	6	60	144	.235
MAJOR LEAGUE TOTALS			0	1	5.87	9	0	0	0	8	8	5	5	0	4	8	.267

11 CHORYE SPOONE, RHP

BORN: Sept. 16, 1985. **B-T:** R-R. **HT.:** 6-1. **WT.:** 215. **DRAFTED:** Catonsville (Md.) CC, 2005 (8th round). **SIGNED BY:** Ty Brown.

Spoone went from a diamond in the rough to a legitimate starter prospect in his first 2½ years in pro ball after Orioles scouts found him at a nearby junior college. He pitched 152 innings in 2007, followed by a playoff MVP award as Frederick won the Carolina League title. But he came up with a sore shoulder last spring and was never right in 2008. Baltimore tried shutting him down for six weeks after his first four starts, but after five more starts he went out again, this time for good. Doctors found a small tear in his labrum that required surgery, and Spoone isn't expected to return to action until May or June. The Orioles considered the surgery minor and still added him to the 40-man roster in the offseason. When healthy, Spoone offers a lively 93-95 mph fastball, a power curveball and an improved changeup. Control and command were never his strong suits, however. He has matured a lot since he first entered the organization, and his injury will be a big test of his ability to handle adversity. The focus for 2009 will be just getting Spoone healthy, so he'll likely spend time at lower-level affiliates when he returns to action.

Year	Club (League)	Class	W	L	ERA	G	GS	CG	SV	IP	H	R	ER	HR	BB	SO	AVG
2005	Bluefield (APP)	R	2	5	8.03	15	3	0	0	25	27	25	22	3	13	27	.273
2006	Delmarva (SAL)	LoA	7	9	3.56	26	25	0	0	129	118	72	51	5	80	90	.241
2007	Frederick (CAR)	HiA	10	9	3.26	26	25	3	0	152	108	65	55	8	67	133	.200
2008	Bowie (EL)	AA	3	3	4.57	9	9	0	0	41	40	23	21	4	27	32	.252
MINOR LEAGUE TOTALS			22	26	3.86	76	62	3	0	347	293	185	149	20	187	282	.227

12 ZACH BRITTON, LHP

BORN: Dec. 22, 1987. **B-T:** L-L. **HT.:** 6-2. **WT.:** 180. **DRAFTED:** HS—Weatherford, Texas, 2006 (3rd round). **SIGNED BY:** Jim Richardson.

For a third-round pick who has experienced a lot of success so far as a pro, Britton gets surprisingly little attention. He came out of high school with a good fastball for a lefthander, touching the low 90s but more comfortably pitching at 88-90 mph. His heater has good sinking life and generates a lot of groundballs. He learned a slider during instructional league after the 2007 season, and his sinker/slider combination allowed him to dominate low Class A hitters at times in 2008. His changeup improved as well, but it's still inconsistent and he has trouble locating it. Overall command is Britton's biggest question mark, as he doesn't throw enough strikes. Those who don't like him see him as a good stuff/bad pitchability prospect and wonder how much he can improve in that area. Britton needs to get stronger, and if he does he could add a tick to his velocity. He'll step up to high Class A in 2009 and profiles as a middle-of-the-rotation starter if his command comes along.

Year	Club (League)	Class	W	L	ERA	G	GS	CG	SV	IP	H	R	ER	HR	BB	SO	AVG
2006	Bluefield (APP)	R	0	4	5.29	11	11	0	0	34	35	22	20	4	20	21	.271
2007	Aberdeen (NYP)	SS	6	4	3.68	15	15	0	0	64	64	33	26	1	22	45	.256
2008	Delmarva (SAL)	LoA	12	7	3.12	27	27	1	0	147	118	68	51	9	49	114	.219
MINOR LEAGUE TOTALS			18	15	3.56	53	53	1	0	245	217	123	97	14	91	180	.236

13 XAVIER AVERY, OF

BORN: Jan. 1, 1990. **B-T:** L-L. **HT.:** 5-11. **WT.:** 180. **DRAFTED:** HS—Ellenwood, Ga., 2008 (2nd round). **SIGNED BY:** Dave Jennings.

Baltimore focused heavily on athleticism in the 2008 draft, and Avery was the best pure athlete of the bunch. He committed to Georgia as a football player—viewed primarily as a running back though he also played cornerback in high school—but signed with the Orioles for $900,000 as a second-round pick. His best pure tool is speed, which rates a legitimate 80 on the 20-80 scouting scale. Pretty much everything beyond that is open to interpretation because Avery is so raw as a baseball player. He not only split his time between baseball and football but also faced inferior competition in high school, so while he has a feel for the game, the application of his skills isn't quite there yet. Avery held his own in the Rookie-level Gulf Coast League and worked on the basics of his batting stance in instructional league, standing taller and focusing on bunting and taking the ball the other way. He has a knack for putting the bat on the ball and shows explosive hands, which could lead to some power. With his tools, he should be an above-average defender in center field with an average arm. The Orioles have lauded his aptitude and eagerness for instruction, and while he has a long way to go, he's often compared to Carl Crawford. Avery will take a slower path than Crawford, though, and could open the year in extended spring training before heading to short-season Aberdeen.

Year	Club (League)	Class	AVG	G	AB	R	H	2B	3B	HR	RBI	BB	SO	SB	OBP	SLG
2008	Orioles (GCL)	R	.280	47	175	27	49	8	1	0	7	10	51	13	.333	.337
MINOR LEAGUE TOTALS			.280	47	175	27	49	8	1	0	7	10	51	13	.333	.337

14 L.J. HOES, 2B

BORN: March 5, 1990. **B-T:** R-R. **HT.:** 6-1. **WT.:** 181. **DRAFTED:** HS—Washington D.C., 2008 (3rd round). **SIGNED BY:** Dean Albany.

Hoes was thought to be a tough sign going into the 2008 draft because of questions about which position he would play as a pro and a strong commitment to North Carolina. Baltimore took him in the third round with the 81st overall pick, and while his bonus was over MLB's slot recommendation, it wasn't a bank-breaker at $490,000. He made a quick impression, batting .308 in the Gulf Coast League, then earning praise in instructional league for his feel for the game as well as his tools. Hoes has an advanced offensive approach and already shows an ability to use the whole field, with good power to right field. He also has patience and a good idea of the strike zone, walking more than he struck out in his pro debut. The work will come on the defensive side. Hoes was an outfielder (as well as a pitcher) in high school, but lacks the power for a corner or the speed to play center, so the Orioles moved him to second base. He made 15 errors in 42 games and has a long way to go as an infielder, but Baltimore is confident he'll adjust because he works hard and likes being on the field. He worked on his throws and his footwork around the bag in instructional league. Because of his advanced bat, Hoes will probably jump to low Class A Delmarva for his first full pro season.

Year	Club (League)	Class	AVG	G	AB	R	H	2B	3B	HR	RBI	BB	SO	SB	OBP	SLG
2008	Orioles (GCL)	R	.308	48	159	36	49	4	3	1	18	30	22	10	.416	.390
MINOR LEAGUE TOTALS			.308	48	159	36	49	4	3	1	18	30	22	10	.416	.390

15 BOBBY BUNDY, RHP

BORN: Jan. 13, 1990. **B-T:** R-R. **HT.:** 6-2. **WT.:** 215. **DRAFTED:** HS—Sperry, Okla., 2008 (8th round). **SIGNED BY:** Jim Richardson.

Baltimore went over MLB's slot recommendations to sign several players in the 2008 draft, and Bundy was the biggest outlier of them all at $600,000, the largest bonus handed out in the eighth round. The Orioles regarded him as a top-three-rounds talent and paid him that way, expecting him to recover the form he showed as a high school junior, when he was regarded as one of the best pitchers in the 2008 high school class. Between baseball seasons, however, he tore the anterior cruciate ligament in his right knee in a basketball game. He got back on the mound ahead of schedule and pitched with a knee brace last spring, leading Sperry (Okla.) High to a state title. Bundy's fastball velocity was down from its normal 92-95 mph to 88-91, and clubs worried about his signability because he had committed to Arkansas. Baltimore likes what it has seen from Bundy in limited action. He touched 93 mph in instructional league and should continue to regain his previous fastball. He also showed a big-breaking curveball, though he'll need to be more consistent with it. He has a lot to work on, from his changeup to his command, and could remain in extended spring training before joining Aberdeen next season.

Year	Club (League)	Class	W	L	ERA	G	GS	CG	SV	IP	H	R	ER	HR	BB	SO	AVG
2008	Orioles (GCL)	R	0	0	9.00	2	0	0	0	2	5	2	2	1	0	4	.455
MINOR LEAGUE TOTALS			0	0	9.00	2	0	0	0	2	5	2	2	1	0	4	.455

16 DAVID HERNANDEZ, RHP

BORN: May 13, 1985. **B-T:** R-R. **HT.:** 6-2. **WT.:** 180. **DRAFTED:** Cosumnes River (Calif.) JC, 2005 (16th round). **SIGNED BY:** James Keller.

Hernandez has piled up more than 140 innings in each of the last three seasons, and he took a leap forward as a prospect in 2008 by shaving more than two runs off his ERA from 2007. He topped the Eastern League with 166 strikeouts in 141 innings, the second straight year he led his league in whiffs, and ranked fourth with a 2.68 ERA. Hernandez's fastball sits in the low 90s and can touch 94 mph, and he gets a lot of strikeouts with it because his delivery is so deceptive and hitters struggle to pick up the ball before it's on top on them. His slider is a good pitch when it's on, with two-plane break at times, but he's not consistent enough with it. His changeup is even less reliable, though it did improve in 2008. Because he isn't entirely comfortable with his complementary pitches and likes to go after strikeouts, Hernandez tends to pile up big pitch counts with two- and four-seam fastballs and can wear down late in starts. Those factors, as well as the fact he succeeds more with deception than pure stuff, lead most scouts to project him as a reliever rather than a starter. For now, he'll continue to get the chance to pitch out of the rotation in Triple-A, but his first big league opportunity probably will come in the bullpen.

Year	Club (League)	Class	W	L	ERA	G	GS	CG	SV	IP	H	R	ER	HR	BB	SO	AVG
2005	Aberdeen (NYP)	SS	1	2	3.89	12	8	0	0	42	41	21	18	2	17	47	.255
2006	Delmarva (SAL)	LoA	7	8	4.15	28	28	0	0	145	134	83	67	13	71	154	.244
2007	Frederick (CAR)	HiA	7	11	4.95	28	27	0	0	145	139	86	80	16	47	168	.249
2008	Bowie (EL)	AA	10	4	2.68	27	27	0	0	141	112	53	42	10	71	166	.217
MINOR LEAGUE TOTALS			25	25	3.94	95	90	0	0	473	426	243	207	41	206	535	.239

17 JASON BERKEN, RHP

BORN: Nov. 27, 1983. **B-T:** R-R. **HT.:** 6-0. **WT.:** 195. **DRAFTED:** Clemson, 2006 (6th round). **SIGNED BY:** Dominic Viola.

Berken has made a habit of going through high peaks and low valleys. He was Clemson's top pitcher as a sophomore in 2004, then had Tommy John surgery in 2005 before bouncing back to help the Tigers reach the College World Series in 2006. He looked good after the Orioles drafted him that June, but then had a subpar 2007 as his velocity dipped, a problem that has bothered him ever since his elbow reconstruction. Berken put himself back on the radar in 2008 as part of a strong Bowie staff, showing more consistent velocity and a sharper slider. More important, he displayed much better fastball command and an ability to work the pitch down in the zone. He's a bulldog on the mound who can throw strikes with four pitches. His main two offerings are his fastball and slider, and he also owns a changeup and hard curveball that he's willing to throw in any count. None of his pitches is overpowering but when all four are working, he can be quite effective. He has good control but will have to sharpen his command in the zone because he doesn't have swing-and-miss stuff. His velocity can still waver at times, from 88-90 to 91-93 mph, but he maintained it in games much better in 2008. If Berken can pitch consistently as he did last July, when he went 3-0, 1.53 in five starts, he could be a nice back-of-the-rotation starter. He'll pitch in the Triple-A rotation this season.

Year	Club (League)	Class	W	L	ERA	G	GS	CG	SV	IP	H	R	ER	HR	BB	SO	AVG
2006	Aberdeen (NYP)	SS	1	4	2.80	9	8	0	0	45	39	20	14	4	5	46	.234
2007	Frederick (CAR)	HiA	9	9	4.53	27	26	2	0	151	160	90	76	12	49	124	.274
2008	Bowie (EL)	AA	12	4	3.58	26	25	2	0	146	141	69	58	9	38	125	.255
MINOR LEAGUE TOTALS			22	17	3.90	62	59	4	0	342	340	179	148	25	92	295	.260

18 BRAD BERGESEN, RHP

BORN: Sept. 25, 1985. **B-T:** L-R. **HT.:** 6-2. **WT.:** 205. **DRAFTED:** HS—Foothill, Calif., 2004 (4th round). **SIGNED BY:** Ed Sprague.

Bergesen has moved slowly through the system, going through everything from mononucleosis in 2006 to getting hit in the head by a batting-practice liner in 2007. Because he struggled in high Class A after getting drilled, the Orioles returned him there to open last season. He quickly earned a promotion after four strong outings, and ended up winning Eastern League pitcher-of-the-year honors. Bergesen doesn't earn more accolades as a prospect because his stuff is nothing special and gives him a ceiling no higher than that of a back-end starter. He's a strike-thrower who has a good delivery, repeats his pitches and keeps everything down, succeeding with command and a talent for mixing his offerings. Bergesen's best pitch is his sinker, which peaks in the low 90s, followed by a changeup that can induce swings and misses. Improved depth on his slider probably made the biggest difference for him last season, giving him three legitimate weapons. He wore down at the end of last season, compiling a 5.28 ERA in six August starts, but he still showed enough to get a shot at the Norfolk rotation to open 2009.

Year	Club (League)	Class	W	L	ERA	G	GS	CG	SV	IP	H	R	ER	HR	BB	SO	AVG
2004	Bluefield (APP)	R	0	0	7.94	5	0	0	0	6	7	5	5	1	3	6	.292
2005	Aberdeen (NYP)	SS	1	3	4.82	15	15	0	0	71	89	45	38	5	14	54	.308
2006	Delmarva (SAL)	LoA	5	4	4.27	18	14	1	0	86	97	44	41	6	10	49	.280
2007	Delmarva (SAL)	LoA	7	3	2.19	15	15	1	0	94	75	30	23	3	17	73	.214
	Frederick (CAR)	HiA	3	6	5.75	10	10	1	0	56	78	38	36	4	9	35	.332
2008	Frederick (CAR)	HiA	1	1	2.08	4	3	0	0	17	15	6	4	2	6	15	.227
	Bowie (EL)	AA	15	6	3.22	24	23	3	0	148	143	59	53	11	27	72	.253
MINOR LEAGUE TOTALS			32	23	3.76	91	80	6	0	479	504	227	200	32	86	304	.269

19 TYLER HENSON, 3B

BORN: Dec. 15, 1987. **B-T:** L-L. **HT.:** 6-2. **WT.:** 205. **DRAFTED:** HS—Tuttle, Okla., 2006 (5th round). **SIGNED BY:** Jim Richardson.

Henson's package of tools is as intriguing as any Orioles farmhand, but so far he has been a tease, looking great one week and lost the next. He was a three-sport star in high school, meriting NCAA Division I recruiting interest as a quarterback, and is the best athlete in the organization. The problem is putting those tools to use. Henson has the swing to hit for average and the bat speed to produce power, but his approach is undisciplined and leads to wild swings and lots of strikeouts. Some think if he could find a defensive home those problems would go away. Henson was drafted as a shortstop but moved to third base last year. While he has the arm for the hot corner, his throws were inconsistent and he piled up 29 errors—along with nine more in Hawaii Winter Baseball. The Orioles also have looked at him at second base but didn't like the results there, and some would like to see him back at shortstop or even center field. He could probably handle left field without a problem, but his value is greater in the infield so he'll get every chance to stay there. Henson has proven to be an adept basestealer, succeeding on 41 of his 47 attempts as a pro and further illustrating his athleticism and potential. He'll probably move up to high Class A and stay at third base for now, and he needs to put together a consistent season at the plate and in the field.

Year	Club (League)	Class	AVG	G	AB	R	H	2B	3B	HR	RBI	BB	SO	SB	OBP	SLG
2006	Bluefield (APP)	R	.230	43	148	21	34	5	2	0	13	18	49	1	.314	.291
2007	Aberdeen (NYP)	SS	.289	67	256	44	74	18	4	5	31	22	68	20	.353	.449
	Frederick (CAR)	HiA	.059	6	17	0	1	0	0	0	1	1	8	0	.105	.059
2008	Delmarva (SAL)	LoA	.265	127	502	71	133	25	3	11	62	25	121	20	.310	.392
MINOR LEAGUE TOTALS			.262	243	923	136	242	48	9	16	107	66	246	41	.319	.386

20 MATT ANGLE, OF

BORN: Sept. 10, 1985. **B-T:** L-R. **HT.:** 5-10. **WT.:** 175. **DRAFTED:** Ohio State, 2007 (7th round). **SIGNED BY:** Rich Morales.

Orioles scouts viewed Angle as a legitimate center fielder and leadoff hitter coming out of the 2007 draft, and he has done nothing in pro ball to change that impression. He's a little man who embraces all that means on the diamond and knows how to play the game. He's a natural baseball player whose best tool is his plus speed, and he has the instincts to put it to use on the basepaths. A smart hitter, he has a knack for bunting and uses a short stroke to spray the ball all over the field. He even has a solid arm for a center fielder. At the same time, though, there are significant questions about Angle. His average and on-base percentage both dropped from his pro debut to his first full season. He also got caught stealing 11 times in 48 attempts in 2008, compared to just four times in 38 tries in 2007. He has to excel at getting on base and using his speed because he offers little power. Some scouts wonder if he runs well enough to be an everyday big league center fielder, which would be a problem because he's not going to be enough of a run producer to play left. Angle will move up to high Class A in 2009 and try to show he can be a legitimate leadoff man.

Year	Club (League)	Class	AVG	G	AB	R	H	2B	3B	HR	RBI	BB	SO	SB	OBP	SLG
2007	Aberdeen (NYP)	SS	.301	66	236	60	71	4	4	0	14	47	40	34	.421	.352
2008	Delmarva (SAL)	LoA	.287	126	478	82	137	22	5	4	35	71	86	37	.385	.379
MINOR LEAGUE TOTALS			.291	192	714	142	208	26	9	4	49	118	126	71	.397	.370

21 PEDRO BEATO, RHP

BORN: Oct. 27, 1986. **B-T:** R-R. **HT.:** 6-5. **WT.:** 210. **DRAFTED:** St. Petersburg (Fla.) JC, 2006 (1st round supplemental). **SIGNED BY:** Nick Presto.

Signed for $1 million as a sandwich pick in 2006 after the Mets failed to sign him as a draft-and-follow, Beato is the biggest enigma in the system. He made steady progress in his first season and a half as he tried to work with a narrowed repertoire of pitches and improve his feel for pitching. But coming out of spring training last year, he lacked his usual mid-90s velocity and never found it. Baltimore shut him down for five weeks in mid-May and had his arm checked out a couple of times during the season, but found no physical problems. His difficulties may have resulted from his lower half getting out of whack in his delivery. He worked on his mechanics in instructional league and showed renewed pop on his fastball. He went to the Orioles' Dominican complex during the offseason to get a little more work and should be 100 percent for spring training. Beato mainly backs up his fastball with a curveball and changeup that have their moments but still need refinement. He's sharpening his slider to give him another breaking pitch. He could return to high Class A to open the season, and team officials hope he'll reassert himself as one of the organization's best prospects.

Year	Club (League)	Class	W	L	ERA	G	GS	CG	SV	IP	H	R	ER	HR	BB	SO	AVG
2006	Aberdeen (NYP)	SS	3	2	3.63	14	10	0	0	57	47	31	23	6	23	52	.222
2007	Delmarva (SAL)	LoA	7	8	4.05	27	27	0	0	142	139	75	64	10	59	106	.256
2008	Orioles (GCL)	R	0	0	2.53	2	2	0	0	11	10	3	3	1	1	3	.244
	Frederick (CAR)	HiA	4	10	5.85	19	19	0	0	97	119	74	63	11	33	51	.306
MINOR LEAGUE TOTALS			14	20	4.49	62	58	0	0	307	315	183	153	28	116	212	.266

22 BOB McCRORY, RHP

BORN: May 3, 1982. **B-T:** R-R. **HT.:** 6-1. **WT.:** 205. **DRAFTED:** Southern Mississippi, 2003 (4th round). **SIGNED BY:** Mike Tullier.

McCrory overcame Tommy John surgery in 2005, but ever since then he has battled nagging injuries as the Orioles try to get his body and arm used to everyday work. He was dominant last spring, with scouts issuing glowing reports on his performance, and continued that run in April in Triple-A. Baltimore called him up at the end of the month, but he got knocked around in his debut and then was used sparingly, sitting idle for nine days before getting sent back down. His arm bothered him after that, including in the Arizona Fall League, but he should be healthy for spring training. The reason McCrory remains on the 40-man roster is his pure closer stuff, highlighted by a lively fastball that can range from 92-97 mph and touch 99 at times. It's heavy and batters beat it into the ground. McCrory also shows a plus slider and plus changeup at times, and he'll even mix in a curveball once in a while. He throws across his body a little bit, but there are really no other factors to suggest long-term health problems and he might just have to learn to battle through occasional aches and pains. While he can overpower hitters, he also gets himself into trouble with walks. With a good spring, McCrory easily could win a big league bullpen job, but the most important thing is for him to consistently take the ball when called upon.

Year	Club (League)	Class	W	L	ERA	G	GS	CG	SV	IP	H	R	ER	HR	BB	SO	AVG
2003	Did Not Play—Injured																
2004	Delmarva (SAL)	LoA	0	1	7.59	8	0	0	0	11	13	16	9	3	15	11	.295
	Bluefield (APP)	R	4	3	1.92	11	11	0	0	52	42	21	11	3	32	51	.226
	Aberdeen (NYP)	SS	0	1	27.00	1	1	0	0	1	3	3	3	1	2	1	.500
2005	Aberdeen (NYP)	SS	2	1	3.28	5	5	0	0	25	21	9	9	2	8	21	.233
2006	Aberdeen (NYP)	SS	2	2	2.33	20	1	0	2	39	32	12	10	2	16	57	.230
2007	Frederick (CAR)	HiA	0	0	1.23	22	0	0	14	22	16	4	3	1	12	22	.205
	Bowie (EL)	AA	1	2	3.91	22	0	0	13	23	23	17	10	0	16	22	.247
2008	Aberdeen (NYP)	SS	0	0	18.00	1	0	0	0	1	1	2	2	0	2	2	.250
	Norfolk (IL)	AAA	2	3	3.80	35	1	0	5	45	41	22	19	1	24	35	.250
	Baltimore (AL)	MAJ	0	0	15.63	8	0	0	0	6	10	12	11	0	8	5	.370
MINOR LEAGUE TOTALS			11	13	3.14	125	19	0	34	218	192	106	76	13	127	222	.239
MAJOR LEAGUE TOTALS			0	0	15.63	8	0	0	0	6	10	12	11	0	8	5	.370

23 GREG MICLAT, SS

BORN: July 23, 1987. **B-T:** B-R. **HT.:** 5-9. **WT.:** 180. **DRAFTED:** Virginia, 2008 (5th round). **SIGNED BY:** Dean Albany.

In Miclat, the Orioles got an unheralded player who they believe is a legitimate shortstop—just what the organization sorely needs. He had a sore shoulder for most of last spring at Virginia after having surgery following the 2007 season, and his performance suffered on offense and defense. Baltimore still drafted him in the fifth round and signed him for an above-slot $225,000 bonus after he spent the summer in the Cape Cod League. He got his feet wet after signing and really made an impression during instructional league, where a small change in his approach at the plate made a big difference in his ability to drive the ball. He already shows good plate discipline, has quality at-bats and plays to his strengths by getting on base as a switch-hitter. Some already regard him as the best infield defender in the system, a legitimate shortstop with good range, hands and footwork. The big question is whether his arm will come all the way back after shoulder surgery, but the Orioles are encouraged by what they've seen so far. Miclat has a tremendous feel for the game with enough speed to steal bases, so if his shoulder recovers fully and he shows a little more pop in his bat, he could move in a hurry.

Year	Club (League)	Class	AVG	G	AB	R	H	2B	3B	HR	RBI	BB	SO	SB	OBP	SLG
2008	Orioles (GCL)	R	.500	1	4	1	2	1	0	0	1	0	2	0	.500	.750
	Aberdeen (NYP)	SS	.291	16	55	9	16	2	0	0	6	8	13	3	.391	.327
MINOR LEAGUE TOTALS			.305	17	59	10	18	3	0	0	7	8	15	3	.397	.356

24 TONY BUTLER, LHP

BORN: Nov. 18, 1987. **B-T:** L-L. **HT.:** 6-7. **WT.:** 205. **DRAFTED:** HS—Oak Creek, Wis., 2006 (3rd round). **SIGNED BY:** Joe Bohringer (Mariners).

The Orioles got plenty from the Mariners in the Erik Bedard trade—Adam Jones, Chris Tillman, George Sherrill and Kam Mickolio—so if Butler pans out, that would just be icing on the cake. His performance was all over the map in his year and a half in the Mariners system, but it's hard to deny the intrigue of a 6-foot-7 lefthander whose fastball touches 92 mph. He battled a dead arm and wasn't always in top shape with Seattle, and the same problems bothered him after the trade. He had a sore shoulder and pitched just 55 innings, getting shut down for most of May and then for the rest of the season in mid-June. No structural problems were discovered and he didn't require surgery, so Butler is expected to be healthy for spring training. At his best, he shows an 88-92 mph fastball with late life and natural sink, a curveball that's a plus pitch at times and a changeup that should be effective as well. Because of his limited experience and big frame, repeating his mechanics and commanding all his pitches are Butler's biggest issues. Staying healthy and getting in innings would allow him to work those problems out. A full season of steady performance in 2009 could rocket Butler up this list.

Year	Club (League)	Class	W	L	ERA	G	GS	CG	SV	IP	H	R	ER	HR	BB	SO	AVG
2006	Mariners (AZL)	R	2	0	2.57	5	3	0	0	14	5	4	4	0	9	25	.116
	Everett (NWL)	SS	1	2	2.76	9	9	0	0	42	23	16	13	2	25	52	.160
2007	Wisconsin (MWL)	LoA	4	7	4.75	20	18	1	0	85	78	52	45	10	46	73	.247
2008	Delmarva (SAL)	LoA	3	4	4.42	12	11	0	0	55	59	31	27	7	11	44	.273
MINOR LEAGUE TOTALS			10	13	4.07	46	41	1	0	197	165	103	89	19	91	194	.229

25 BRANDON COONEY, RHP

BORN: Aug. 2, 1985. **B-T:** R-R. **HT.:** 6-6. **WT.:** 263. **DRAFTED:** Florida Atlantic, 2007 (30th round). **SIGNED BY:** John Martin.

If you're looking for an Orioles breakout prospect for 2009, Cooney could be your man. He was drafted by the White Sox in 2004 (33rd round) out of Broward (Fla.) CC, then again by the Cardinals in 2006 (20th round) after he had moved on to Florida Atlantic. He again decided not to sign, hoping to better his position as a senior, but his ERA ballooned to 7.36 in 2007 and he fell to the 30th round. After he signed, he eventually was diagnosed with a shoulder problem that didn't require surgery. Rehab and a summer in the bullpen seem to have done the trick. Cooney showed a mid-90s fastball and touched 97 in 2008, and he also flashed a promising slider. He was on a tight leash, as Baltimore monitored his innings and didn't allow him to pitch on consecutive days. The results were so good that he'll stay in the bullpen. Cooney will pitch without restrictions in 2009 and probably will open the season in low Class A. He could move quickly if he continues to perform well.

Year	Club (League)	Class	W	L	ERA	G	GS	CG	SV	IP	H	R	ER	HR	BB	SO	AVG
2007	Bluefield (APP)	R	4	2	4.58	11	10	0	0	53	63	33	27	4	14	36	.301
2008	Aberdeen (NYP)	SS	1	3	3.81	28	0	0	10	26	24	13	11	3	9	38	.242
MINOR LEAGUE TOTALS			5	5	4.33	39	10	0	10	79	87	46	38	7	23	74	.282

26 BRANDON WARING, 3B

BORN: Jan. 2, 1986. **B-T:** R-R. **HT.:** 6-4. **WT.:** 195. **DRAFTED:** Wofford, 2007 (7th round). **SIGNED BY:** Steve Kring (Reds).

When the Orioles decided to clear Matt Wieters' path to the big leagues by trading Ramon Hernandez in December, they received Waring and second baseman Justin Turner from the Reds. Waring has established himself as a good power prospect by hitting 40 home runs in his first season and a half since being drafted. He was the South Carolina 4-A high school player of the year in 2004 and then headed to Wofford, where he finished second in NCAA Division I with 27 homers as a junior in 2007. He then led the Rookie-level Pioneer League with 20 bombs in his pro debut. Waring has a long swing but generates a lot of bat speed and shows power to all fields. He could add even more pop as he fills out his big frame. He tends to get pull-happy and chase pitches out of the zone, leading to big strikeout numbers. Waring started off as a skinny second baseman in high school, but as he has grown and filled out, he moved first to shortstop and then to third base. He also played some first base and may move there or to an outfield corner down the road because of concerns about his footwork and range at third. His arm is slightly above average, while his speed is a tick below. Waring will start off in high Class A with his new organization. His power potential is a needed commodity in the organization.

Year	Club (League)	Class	AVG	G	AB	R	H	2B	3B	HR	RBI	BB	SO	SB	OBP	SLG
2007	Billings (PIO)	R	.311	68	267	63	83	17	2	20	61	21	83	1	.369	.614
	Dayton (MWL)	LoA	1.000	1	1	0	1	0	0	0	2	0	0	0	1.000	1.000
2008	Dayton (MWL)	LoA	.270	119	441	63	119	23	2	20	71	43	156	1	.346	.467
MINOR LEAGUE TOTALS			.286	188	709	126	203	40	4	40	134	64	239	2	.355	.523

27 JUSTIN TURNER, 2B

BORN: Nov. 23, 1984. **B-T:** R-R. **HT.:** 5-11. **WT.:** 180. **DRAFTED:** Cal State Fullerton, 2006 (7th round). **SIGNED BY:** Mike Misuraca (Reds).

Part of December's Ramon Hernandez trade with the Reds, Turner played with Blake Davis on Cal State Fullerton's 2004 national championship team and could team with him again to form the double-play combination in Norfolk this year. Turner is a baseball rat who has a feel for the game and a competitive drive that ensures he gets the most out of his limited tools. He has a line-drive swing with gap power that has allowed him to hit .310 with a .377 on-base percentage during his minor league career. But there are some concerns as to how well his swing will play in the big leagues. His stroke could be more direct to the plate, and he employs an inside-out approach instead of using the entire field. Turner is a solid second baseman with excellent instincts that make up for his adequate range. He's a tick below-average runner. He'll never be a star, and his lack of arm strength may make it tough for him to fill a utility role in the big leagues, but his ability to hit for average and get on base will get him there.

Year	Club (League)	Class	AVG	G	AB	R	H	2B	3B	HR	RBI	BB	SO	SB	OBP	SLG
2006	Billings (PIO)	R	.338	60	231	53	78	16	3	6	41	23	38	12	.411	.511
2007	Dayton (MWL)	LoA	.311	117	466	70	145	25	4	10	59	39	72	12	.374	.446
	Sarasota (FSL)	HiA	.200	6	20	2	4	0	0	0	0	1	2	0	.238	.200
2008	Sarasota (FSL)	HiA	.316	33	136	23	43	8	1	0	11	12	19	3	.384	.390
	Chattanooga (SL)	AA	.289	78	280	45	81	14	1	8	42	33	54	2	.359	.432
MINOR LEAGUE TOTALS			.310	294	1133	193	351	63	9	24	153	108	185	29	.377	.445

28 RYAN ADAMS, 2B

BORN: April 21, 1987. **B-T:** R-R. **HT.:** 6-0. **WT.:** 195. **DRAFTED:** HS—New Orleans, 2006 (2nd round). **SIGNED BY:** Mike Tullier.

The Orioles drafted Adams as an offense-first middle infielder, but until 2008, he hadn't put up the numbers to back up that projection. In his first taste of full-season ball, he delivered by far the best offensive performance of his career. He showed good bat control and a knack for making solid contact, the ability to put a charge into the ball at times and even the speed to steal the occasional base. The problem has been defense. Adams made an astounding 52 errors last season, including 46 at second base. That gives him 70 in 187 career games there, so it might be time to try another position. The problem is that he hasn't shown much aptitude at shortstop or third base either, and he doesn't profile for an outfield corner with the bat. His arm is strong enough for short or third, but his footwork is lacking and his throws are erratic. Adams also has drawn criticism for an inconsistent mental approach and stubbornness in taking instruction in the past, but Baltimore was impressed with his makeup in 2008, as he continued to hit in spite of his defensive struggles. He'll move up to high Class A to open 2009, and the Orioles will continue to experiment with his position in spring training.

Year	Club (League)	Class	AVG	G	AB	R	H	2B	3B	HR	RBI	BB	SO	SB	OBP	SLG
2006	Bluefield (APP)	R	.256	34	133	24	34	8	1	2	7	19	32	2	.361	.376
	Aberdeen (NYP)	SS	.316	6	19	2	6	3	0	1	5	4	7	0	.458	.632
2007	Aberdeen (NYP)	SS	.236	67	246	29	58	10	2	3	22	18	63	8	.296	.329
2008	Delmarva (SAL)	LoA	.308	119	448	68	138	26	5	11	57	36	109	12	.367	.462
MINOR LEAGUE TOTALS			.279	226	846	123	236	47	8	17	91	77	211	22	.348	.414

29 LOU MONTANEZ, OF

BORN: Dec. 15, 1981. **B-T:** R-R. **HT.:** 6-2. **WT.:** 180. **DRAFTED:** HS—Miami, 2000 (1st round). **SIGNED BY:** Mike Soper (Cubs).

The Orioles were just looking for extra hitters to bolster the top of their system when they signed Montanez after the 2006 season, but he has shown enough that he now might be able to find a major league role. He won the Eastern League triple crown and MVP award in 2008, made his major league debut in August and homered off Nick Blackburn, Ervin Santana and James Shields. Baltimore kept him on its 40-man roster after the season. Montanez (then known as Luis) was the third overall pick in the 2000 draft coming out of high school, as a shortstop, but he never put it together with the Cubs. He struggled in the infield and didn't enjoy the defensive demands of playing there, so he moved to the outfield in 2004. He loves to hit and has shown the ability to hit for average and use the entire field against advanced pitching. He added power to his game last season, too. While he has the physical skills to play any outfield position, not to mention the infield, he's essentially limited to left field. He's a useful extra bat as an outfielder, but to be a big league regular he would have to move back to the infield, something that isn't happening. He should earn a spot as the fourth or fifth outfielder in Baltimore in spring training.

Year	Club (League)	Class	AVG	G	AB	R	H	2B	3B	HR	RBI	BB	SO	SB	OBP	SLG
2000	Cubs (AZL)	R	.344	50	192	50	66	16	7	2	37	25	42	11	.438	.531
	Lansing (MWL)	LoA	.138	8	29	2	4	1	0	0	0	3	6	0	.219	.172
2001	Lansing (MWL)	LoA	.255	124	499	70	127	33	6	5	54	34	121	20	.316	.375
2002	Daytona (FSL)	HiA	.265	124	487	69	129	21	5	4	59	44	89	14	.333	.353
2003	Daytona (FSL)	HiA	.253	126	486	51	123	18	3	5	38	33	89	11	.305	.333
2004	Daytona (FSL)	HiA	.215	21	79	8	17	4	2	1	7	7	16	2	.292	.354
	Boise (NWL)	SS	.297	72	266	47	79	15	7	8	48	35	53	5	.381	.496
2005	Peoria (MWL)	LoA	.305	82	315	54	96	28	2	12	48	32	46	10	.384	.521
	West Tenn (SL)	AA	.268	45	153	20	41	9	1	2	14	12	21	0	.325	.379
2006	West Tenn (SL)	AA	.369	38	141	24	52	11	0	2	25	15	26	5	.438	.489
	Iowa (PCL)	AAA	.224	82	245	23	55	12	0	8	31	17	44	0	.281	.371
2007	Norfolk (IL)	AAA	.259	69	212	27	55	11	0	7	26	22	35	1	.332	.410
	Bowie (EL)	AA	.339	31	121	24	41	2	0	3	11	10	16	3	.398	.430
2008	Bowie (EL)	AA	.335	116	451	90	151	32	5	26	97	36	63	4	.385	.601
	Baltimore (AL)	MAJ	.295	38	112	18	33	6	1	3	14	4	20	0	.316	.446
MINOR LEAGUE TOTALS			.282	988	3676	559	1036	213	38	85	495	325	667	86	.348	.430
MAJOR LEAGUE TOTALS			.295	38	112	18	33	6	1	3	14	4	20	0	.316	.446

30 CALEB JOSEPH, C

BORN: June 18, 1986. **B-T:** R-R. **HT.:** 6-3. **WT.:** 180. **DRAFTED:** Lipscomb, 2008 (7th round). **SIGNED BY:** Rich Morales.

Joseph had a standout career at Lipscomb. He earned all-Atlantic Sun Conference recognition in both his sophomore and junior seasons, as well as A-Sun tournament MVP honors in 2008 as Lipscomb won the title and reached NCAA regional play for the first time. He also got scouts' attention as a fill-in player in the Cape Cod League in 2007, eventually earning a spot in the league's all-star game. A seventh-round pick last June, he signed for $125,000. Joseph always has performed with the bat, showing good hands and the potential for above-average power. He can drive fastballs to all fields but still is learning to handle breaking stuff. Joseph is athletic and wiry and surprisingly strong, but he'll have to bulk up a bit to handle the rigors of a full pro season behind the plate. The Orioles would like for him to stay at catcher because he moves well and has good hands, and he's also bilingual and has a knack for working with pitchers. His arm is average and he erased 43 percent of basestealers in his pro debut. If he has to find a new position, he's athletic enough to handle second base, third base or left field. He impressed club officials in instructional league not only with his performance but also his work ethic. He'll open the season as the starting catcher in Delmarva.

Year	Club (League)	Class	AVG	G	AB	R	H	2B	3B	HR	RBI	BB	SO	SB	OBP	SLG
2008	Aberdeen (NYP)	SS	.261	63	238	34	62	19	0	8	34	15	56	2	.303	.441
MINOR LEAGUE TOTALS			.261	63	238	34	62	19	0	8	34	15	56	2	.303	.441

Boston Red Sox

BY JIM CALLIS

The Red Sox weren't able to repeat as World Series champions, but that's about the only way in which their 2008 season couldn't be described as a success.

At the major league level, Boston won 95 games and went to the playoffs for the fifth time in six years in spite of significant injuries and the Manny Ramirez soap opera. The Red Sox nearly pulled off their third huge comeback in the last five American League Championship Series before falling to the Rays 3-1 in Game Seven.

The core of the big league club is homegrown. Dustin Pedroia won the American League MVP award, while Kevin Youkilis finished third in the voting, Jon Lester tossed a no-hitter and blossomed into one of the game's top starters and Jonathan Papelbon maintained his status as an elite closer. Youngsters Clay Buchholz, Jacoby Ellsbury, Jed Lowrie and Justin Masterson all experienced growing pains, but also showed why they'll be a major part of the Red Sox's future.

Down on the farm, all six of Boston's U.S.-based affiliates finished with winning records and four advanced to the playoffs. The six clubs combined for a .541 winning percentage, the system's best in 32 years. More important, quality prospects drove that success.

Despite graduating four of their top five prospects from a year ago to the majors, the Red Sox have more talent on the way. First baseman Lars Anderson tore up Double-A at age 20 and could force his way into the big league lineup in short order. Righthander Michael Bowden, who's just a year older, has little left to prove in the minors and won his first major league start in August. Hard-throwing righty Daniel Bard found his niche as a reliever and could push for a bullpen spot by mid-2009. Further down, Boston has an enviable group of high-ceiling players, particularly at shortstop (starting with Yamaico Navarro) and in the outfield (led by Josh Reddick). The Red Sox continue to be aggressive in player acquisition, spending $10.5 million on draft bonuses in 2008.

One of the few negatives for the Red Sox came in August, when they fired Dominican Republic scouting supervisor Pablo Lantigua after he was implicated in baseball's bonus-skimming scandal. Lantigua's signees included third baseman Michael Almanzar, who made an impressive pro debut after signing for $1.5 million in 2007, and Navarro, a bargain at $20,000.

Boston's recent international scouting has mirrored its domestic production. Their Dominican finds also include righthander Stolmy Pimentel and shortstop

Homegrown players like Dustin Pedroia make up the core of the major league team

TOP 30 PROSPECTS

1. Lars Anderson, 1b	16. Kris Johnson, lhp
2. Michael Bowden, rhp	17. Argenis Diaz, ss
3. Nick Hagadone, lhp	18. Will Middlebrooks, 3b
4. Daniel Bard, rhp	19. Pete Hissey, of
5. Josh Reddick, of	20. Bryan Price, rhp
6. Casey Kelly, rhp/ss	21. Derrik Gibson, inf
7. Junichi Tazawa, rhp	22. Anthony Rizzo, 1b
8. Ryan Westmoreland, of	23. Kyle Weiland, of
9. Michael Almanzar, 3b	24. Zach Daeges, of
10. Yamaico Navarro, inf	25. Mitch Dening, of
11. Stolmy Pimentel, rhp	26. Richie Lentz, rhp
12. Oscar Tejeda, ss/3b	27. Felix Doubront, lhp
13. Ryan Kalish, of	28. Stephen Fife, rhp
14. Che-Hsuan Lin, of	29. Brock Huntzinger, rhp
15. Luis Exposito, c	30. Mark Wagner, c

Oscar Tejeda. Argenis Diaz (Venezuela) is the system's slickest-fielding shortstop prospect in years. In the Far East, they've found outfielders Che-Hsuan Lin (Taiwan), the 2008 Futures Game MVP, and Mitch Dening (Australia), not to mention Japanese big leaguers Daisuke Matsuzaka and Hideki Okajima. And they broke new ground in December by signing Japanese amateur Junichi Tazawa.

The Red Sox are hitting on all cylinders. They may not have won another World Series in 2008, but they'll continue to contend for championships on an annual basis.

General Manager: Theo Epstein. **Farm Director:** Mike Hazen. **Scouting Director:** Jason McLeod.

Class	Team	League	W	L	PCT	Finish*	Manager	Affiliated
Majors	Boston	American	95	67	.586	3rd (14)	Terry Francona	—
Triple-A	Pawtucket Red Sox	International	85	58	.594	3rd (14)	Ron Johnson	1973
Double-A	Portland Sea Dogs	Eastern	74	66	.529	4th (12)	Arnie Beyeler	2003
High A	Lancaster JetHawks	California	76	64	.543	2nd (10)	Chad Epperson	2007
Low A	Greenville Drive	South Atlantic	70	69	.504	8th (16)	Kevin Boles	2005
Short-season	Lowell Spinners	New York-Penn	40	33	.548	5th (14)	Gary DiSarcina	1996
Rookie	GCL Red Sox	Gulf Coast	28	27	.509	8th (16)	Dave Tomlin	1993
Overall 2008 Minor League Record			373	317	.541	5th		

* Finish in overall standings (No. of teams in league). ^League champion.

LAST YEAR'S TOP 30

Rank	Player, Pos.	Status
1.	Clay Buchholz, rhp	Majors
2.	Jacoby Ellsbury, of	Majors
3.	Lars Anderson, 1b	No. 1
4.	Justin Masterson, rhp	Majors
5.	Jed Lowrie, ss	Majors
6.	Ryan Kalish, of	No. 13
7.	Michael Bowden, rhp	No. 2
8.	Nick Hagadone, lhp	No. 3
9.	Oscar Tejeda, ss	No. 12
10.	Josh Reddick, of	No. 5
11.	Brandon Moss, of	(Pirates)
12.	Argenis Diaz, ss	No. 17
13.	Kris Johnson, lhp	No. 16
14.	Will Middlebrooks, ss	No. 18
15.	Ryan Dent, 2b/ss	Dropped out
16.	Michael Almanzar, 3b	No. 9
17.	Anthony Rizzo, 1b	No. 22
18.	Craig Hansen, rhp	(Pirates)
19.	Daniel Bard, rhp	No. 4
20.	Mark Wagner, c	No. 30
21.	Aaron Bates, 1b	Dropped out
22.	Dustin Richardson, lhp	Dropped out
23.	Jason Place, of	Dropped out
24.	Che-Hsuan Lin, of	No. 14
25.	Bubba Bell, of	Dropped out
26.	Chris Carter, 1b/of	Dropped out
27.	Hunter Jones, lhp	Dropped out
28.	Reid Engel, of	Dropped out
29.	Yamaico Navarro, ss/3b	No. 10
30.	Bryce Cox, rhp	Dropped out

BEST TOOLS

Best Hitter for Average	Lars Anderson
Best Power Hitter	Lars Anderson
Best Strike-Zone Discipline	Zach Daeges
Fastest Baserunner	Derrik Gibson
Best Athlete	Ryan Westmoreland
Best Fastball	Daniel Bard
Best Curveball	Casey Kelly
Best Slider	Nick Hagadone
Best Changeup	Stolmy Pimentel
Best Control	Michael Bowden
Best Defensive Catcher	Mark Wagner
Best Defensive Infielder	Argenis Diaz
Best Infield Arm	Will Middlebrooks
Best Defensive Outfielder	Che-Hsuan Lin
Best Outfield Arm	Josh Reddick

PROJECTED 2012 LINEUP

Catcher	Luis Exposito
First Base	Lars Anderson
Second Base	Dustin Pedroia
Third Base	Kevin Youkilis
Shortstop	Jed Lowrie
Left Field	Jason Bay
Center Field	Jacoby Ellsbury
Right Field	Josh Reddick
Designated Hitter	David Ortiz
No. 1 Starter	Jon Lester
No. 2 Starter	Josh Beckett
No. 3 Starter	Clay Buchholz
No. 4 Starter	Daisuke Matsuzaka
No. 5 Starter	Michael Bowden
Closer	Jonathan Papelbon

TOP PROSPECTS OF THE DECADE

Year	Player, Pos.	2008 Org.
1999	Dernell Stenson, of	Deceased
2000	Steve Lomasney, c	Out of baseball
2001	Dernell Stenson, of/1b	Deceased
2002	Seung Song, rhp	Lotte (Korea)
2003	Hanley Ramirez, ss	Marlins
2004	Hanley Ramirez, ss	Marlins
2005	Hanley Ramirez, ss	Marlins
2006	Andy Marte, 3b	Indians
2007	Daisuke Matsuzaka, rhp	Red Sox
2008	Clay Buchholz, rhp	Red Sox

TOP DRAFT PICKS OF THE DECADE

Year	Player, Pos.	2008 Org.
1999	Rick Asadoorian, of	Somerset (Atlantic)
2000	Phil Dumatrait, lhp	Pirates
2001	Kelly Shoppach, c (2nd round)	Indians
2002	Jon Lester, lhp (2nd round)	Red Sox
2003	David Murphy, of	Rangers
2004	Dustin Pedroia, ss (2nd round)	Red Sox
2005	Jacoby Ellsbury, of	Red Sox
2006	Jason Place, of	Red Sox
2007	Nick Hagadone, lhp (1st supp.)	Red Sox
2008	Casey Kelly, rhp/ss	Red Sox

LARGEST BONUSES IN CLUB HISTORY

Casey Kelly, 2008	$3,000,000
Daisuke Matsuzaka, 2006	$2,000,000
Ryan Westmoreland, 2008	$2,000,000
Junichi Tazawa, 2008	$1,800,000
Rick Asadoorian, 1999	$1,725,500

BOSTON RED SOX

TOP 2009 ROOKIE: Michael Bowden, rhp. A steady three-pitch starter, he's ready to contribute but may not get much of an opportunity.

BREAKOUT PROSPECT: Anthony Rizzo, 1b. He was hitting .373 before he was diagnosed with cancer, and he's healthy and should be at full strength in 2009.

SLEEPER: Dustin Richardson, lhp. He gets swings and misses with his fastball but struggles with his secondary stuff, so he could take off if he moves to the bullpen.

SOURCE OF TOP 30 TALENT			
Homegrown	30	Acquired	0
College	9	Trades	0
Junior college	1	Rule 5 draft	0
High school	10	Independent leagues	0
Draft-and-follow	1	Free agents/waivers	0
Nondrafted free agents	0		
International	9		

Numbers in parentheses indicate prospect rankings.

LF
Zach Daeges (24)
David Mailman
Chris Carter
Jeff Corsaletti
Chih-Hsien Chiang
Reid Engel

CF
Ryan Westmoreland (8)
Che-Hsuan Lin (14)
Bubba Bell
Jonathan Van Every
Jason Place

RF
Josh Reddick (5)
Ryan Kalish (13)
Pete Hissey (19)
Mitch Dening (25)
Bryan Peterson
Daniel Nava

3B
Michael Almanzar (9)
Will Middlebrooks (18)
Jorge Jimenez
Carson Blair

SS
Yamaico Navarro (10)
Oscar Tejeda (12)
Argenis Diaz (17)
Derrik Gibson (21)
Juan Ugas

2B
Ryan Dent
Kris Negron

1B
Lars Anderson (1)
Anthony Rizzo (22)
Aaron Bates
Jeff Bailey
Jon Still
Michael Jones
Eddie Lora

C
Luis Exposito (15)
Mark Wagner (30)
Dusty Brown
George Kottaras
Tim Federowicz
Ty Weeden
Ryan Lavarnaway
Oscar Perez

RHP

Starters	Relievers
Michael Bowden (2)	Daniel Bard (4)
Casey Kelly (6)	Bryan Price (20)
Junichi Tazawa (7)	Richie Lentz (26)
Stolmy Pimentel (11)	Miguel Gonzalez
Kyle Weiland (23)	Chris Province
Stephen Fife (28)	Bryce Cox
Brock Huntzinger (29)	T.J. Large
Charlie Zink	
David Pauley	
Ryne Lawson	
Caleb Clay	
Austin Bailey	
Tyler Wilson	
Hunter Strickland	
Roman Mendez	

LHP

Starters	Relievers
Nick Hagadone (3)	Hunter Jones
Kris Johnson (16)	Dustin Richardson
Felix Doubront (27)	Hunter Cervenka
Drake Britton	Mitch Herold
Manuel Rivera	

2008   BONUSES: $10.5 MILLION

BEST PURE HITTER: OF Pete Hissey (4), who signed for $1 million, has an easy, lefthanded stroke and a knack for pitch recognition. His swing and approach are more geared to line drives for now, but the Red Sox believe he can grow into 18-20 home run power.

BEST POWER HITTER: OF Ryan Westmoreland, whose $2 million bonus set a fifth-round record, has plus power among his many tools. OF Tyler Yockey (14) may have more raw power than anyone in Boston's draft, though he has to translate it into game production.

FASTEST RUNNER: Westmoreland can get from the left side of the plate to first base in less than 4.0 seconds. Once Westmoreland fills out, INF Derrik Gibson (2), a plus-plus runner, probably will be faster.

BEST DEFENSIVE PLAYER: SS/RHP Casey Kelly (1), who set a club record with his $3 million bonus, is a slick defender with plenty of arm strength.

BEST FASTBALL: Kelly offers power potential to go with his defense, but the Red Sox believe he has a brighter future on the mound and will play him both ways in 2009. They grade his fastball as a plus-plus pitch because he gets excellent command and late life at 90-91 mph. Among pitchers who have taken the mound, RHP Kyle Weiland (3) has the best combination of velocity (91-92 mph up to 95), life and command with his heater.

BEST SECONDARY PITCH: Kelly's power curveball, though RHP Stephen Fife's (3) curve isn't far behind. RHP Bryan Price (1s) has an impressive slider when he keeps his delivery under control.

BEST PRO DEBUT: A reliever at Notre Dame, Weiland went 3-3, 1.50 with a 68-10 K-BB ratio and a .166 opponent average as a starter at short-season Lowell.

BEST ATHLETE: Westmoreland has the tools to do everything on the diamond and was an all-state soccer player and basketball star in Rhode Island. In addition to his two-way potential, Kelly also had a scholarship to play quarterback at Tennessee. Gibson is another fast-twitch athlete.

MOST INTRIGUING BACKGROUND: Kelly's father Pat played in the majors and manages in the Reds system, while unsigned 3B Travis Shaw's (32, now at Kent State) dad Jeff was an all-star closer. 2B Tom DiBenedetto's (37) father Thomas is a part-owner of the Red Sox.

CLOSEST TO THE MAJORS: Weiland, especially if he returns to the bullpen. Fife's ability to throw strikes and get ground balls with solid stuff will allow him to move fast.

BEST LATE-ROUND PICK: OF Bryan Peterson (11), a star high school quarterback, has good power and athleticism. RHP Tyler Wilson (13) is a projectable 6-foot-6, 205-pounder.

THE ONE WHO GOT AWAY: Boston offered RHP Alex Meyer (20), a first-round talent, $2 million but it wasn't enough to lure him from a Kentucky scholarship.

ASSESSMENT: The Red Sox and Royals became the first clubs to spend $10 million on a draft. All that money bought Boston an impressive group of high school athletes (Kelly, Gibson, Hissey, Westmoreland) and solid college pitchers (Price, Fife, Weiland).

2007   BONUSES: $4.8 MILLION

Many of the Red Sox's top investments—LHPs Nick Hagadone (1s) and Drake Britton (23), 1B Anthony Rizzo (6), RHP Austin Bailey (16)—became ill or injured in 2008. But Hagadone is making a quick recovery and 3B Will Middlebrooks (5) may be on the verge of a breakout.

GRADE: C

2006   BONUSES: $8.6 MILLION

RHP Justin Masterson (2) already has made an impact in Boston. The Red Sox also found the two best hitting prospects in the system, 1B Lars Anderson (18) and OF Josh Reddick (17), in late rounds, and they have high hopes for RHP Daniel Bard (1) and OF Ryan Kalish (9).

GRADE: A

2005   BONUSES: $6.2 MILLION*

OF Jacoby Ellsbury (1) starred in the 2007 World Series. The next four picks—RHPs Craig Hansen (1), Clay Buchholz (1s) and Michael Bowden (1s), SS Jed Lowrie (1s)—all have reached the majors. Boston failed to sign three players who became first-rounders in 2008: 3B Pedro Alvarez (14), 1B Allan Dykstra (34) and C Jason Castro (43).

GRADE: A

2004   BONUSES: $1.8 MILLION*

The Red Sox didn't have a first-round pick, but their top choice, 2B Dustin Pedroia (2) is the reigning American League MVP. RHP Mike Rozier (12) has been a $1.575 million bust.

GRADE: B+

---

*Draft analysis by Jim Callis. Numbers in parentheses indicate draft rounds. *Bonuses for 2004-05 are first 10 rounds only.*

BILL MITCHELL

PROSPECT

LARS ANDERSON, 1B

Born: Sept. 25, 1987.
Ht.: 6-5. **Wt.:** 195.
Bats: L. **Throws:** L.
Drafted: HS—
Carmichael, Calif., 2006
(18th round).
Signed by: Blair Henry.

Anderson starred with the Team USA juniors in 2005, batting .464 with a team-high 11 RBIs at the Pan Am Championship in Mexico, and he led California high schoolers with 15 homers the following spring. Teams viewed him as a potential supplemental first-round pick, but Anderson had an inexperienced agent who didn't understand baseball's slotting system, and his $1 million price tag caused him to drop all the way to the 18th round. The Red Sox scouted him all summer and signed him in August for $825,000. He has justified that investment, establishing himself as the biggest offensive force in the Boston system while batting .304/.404/.480 in two pro seasons. Anderson began 2008 slowly, hitting just .277 with seven homers in the first two months at high Class A Lancaster, a hitter's haven. After missing the last two weeks in May with a minor wrist injury, he batted .361 with six homers over the next six weeks to earn a promotion to Double-A Portland at age 20, where he hit even better. Boston named him its minor league offensive player of the year.

Anderson has all the ingredients to hit for a high average with a lot of power. He has an advanced approach, as he recognizes pitches and identifies strikes better than most players his age. His quick hands and wrists allow him to let balls travel deep before he unleashes big raw power. There's little effort in his smooth lefthanded stroke, and he keeps the barrel of the bat in the hitting zone for a long time. The loft in his swing and the leverage in his 6-foot-5 frame bode well for his home run potential. He draws plenty of walks and doesn't strike out excessively. When the Red Sox signed Anderson, they had concerns about his defense, but he has answered them. He has improved his footwork and glovework at first base, where he does a nice job of scooping throws out of the dirt. He's a diligent worker who has impressed the organization with his intelligence and maturity.

Anderson can be too disciplined at the plate. His mindset is to work deep counts and drive balls on the outer half to the opposite field. He can do a better job of attacking hittable pitches early in the count, and once he starts turning on more inside pitches, he'll have plus power to all fields. Anderson isn't the quickest player, but he's not a baseclogger and has decent range at first.

One scout who saw Anderson in Double-A opined that he could hit major league pitching in 2009 if needed. All-star Kevin Youkilis could shift from first to third base if Mike Lowell is slow to recover from hip surgery, and the feeble production the Red Sox got from first base when Youkilis moved to third was a contributing factor in their American League Championship Series loss to the Rays. But it's also easy to forget that Anderson will just be 21, and Boston's preference would be for him to spend at least the bulk of the season at Triple-A Pawtucket and push for a big league job in 2010.

Year	Club (League)	Class	AVG	G	AB	R	H	2B	3B	HR	RBI	BB	SO	SB	OBP	SLG
2007	Greenville (SAL)	LoA	.288	124	458	69	132	35	3	10	69	71	112	2	.385	.443
	Lancaster (CAL)	HiA	.343	10	35	13	12	2	0	1	9	11	9	0	.489	.486
2008	Lancaster (CAL)	HiA	.317	77	306	58	97	19	1	13	50	46	64	0	.408	.513
	Portland (EL)	AA	.316	41	133	27	42	13	0	5	30	29	43	1	.436	.526
MINOR LEAGUE TOTALS			.304	252	932	167	283	69	4	29	158	157	228	3	.404	.480

2 MICHAEL BOWDEN, RHP

RODGER WOOD

BORN: Sept. 9, 1986. **B-T:** R-R. **HT.:** 6-3. **WT.:** 215. **DRAFTED:** HS—Aurora, Ill., 2005 (1st round supplemental). **SIGNED BY:** Danny Haas.

Bowden has moved quickly since the Red Sox took him 47th overall in a banner 2005 draft. He finished the season with three straight quality starts in the Triple-A International League and a win over the White Sox in his big league debut, at age 21. Bowden's fastball, curveball and changeup all drew votes as the best in the system. His 89-93 mph fastball plays better than its velocity because of its heavy life and the angle and deception he creates from a high three-quarters slot. His command was good to begin with and improved in 2008. He's fearless and works as hard as anyone in the system. Scouts have quibbled with Bowden's delivery, which was long in the back and short out front. He made nice adjustments in 2008, achieving a straighter line toward the plate and more extension. He could stand to tighten up his curveball, which was more of a power pitch when he was in high school. Bowden has a lower ceiling than the other players on this list, but he's a safe bet with a good chance to become a No. 3 starter. He'll do some fine-tuning in Triple-A until the Red Sox need him.

Year	Club (League)	Class	W	L	ERA	G	GS	CG	SV	IP	H	R	ER	HR	BB	SO	AVG
2005	Red Sox (GCL)	R	1	0	0.00	4	2	0	0	6	4	0	0	0	4	10	.190
2006	Greenville (SAL)	LoA	9	6	3.51	24	24	0	0	108	91	50	42	9	31	118	.224
	Wilmington (CAR)	HiA	0	0	9.00	1	1	0	0	5	9	5	5	0	1	3	.391
2007	Lancaster (CAL)	HiA	2	0	1.37	8	8	0	0	46	35	10	7	1	8	46	.212
	Portland (EL)	AA	8	6	4.28	19	19	1	0	97	105	51	46	9	33	82	.279
2008	Portland (EL)	AA	9	4	2.33	19	19	0	0	104	72	31	27	5	24	101	.192
	Pawtucket (IL)	AAA	0	3	3.38	7	6	0	0	40	40	16	15	5	5	29	.261
	Boston (AL)	MAJ	1	0	3.60	1	1	0	0	5	7	2	2	0	1	3	.333
MINOR LEAGUE TOTALS			29	19	3.15	82	79	1	0	406	356	163	142	29	106	389	.234
MAJOR LEAGUE TOTALS			1	0	3.60	1	1	0	0	5	7	2	2	0	1	3	.333

3 NICK HAGADONE, LHP

BORN: Jan. 1, 1986. **B-T:** L-L. **HT.:** 6-5. **WT.:** 230. **DRAFTED:** Washington, 2007 (1st round supplemental). **SIGNED BY:** John Booher.

Boston's top pick in the 2007 draft (55th overall), Hagadone allowed five earned runs in his pro debut and none since. The bad news is that he blew out his elbow on an awkward delivery in his third start of 2008, leading to Tommy John surgery in May. Hagadone's stuff took off after the Red Sox got him to make his delivery more compact and stop rushing toward the plate. His fastball sat at 95-97 mph the day he got hurt, and his slider showed more power and depth. He quickly picked up a changeup that he throws with good arm speed, fade and sink. His work ethic leaves the Red Sox with no doubt that he'll regain his stuff. Hagadone's health is obviously the biggest concern, but he was throwing four months after the surgery and progressing so quickly that Boston had to slow him down. His command wasn't as advanced as his stuff, and command is often the last thing to come back after Tommy John surgery. Hagadone is on target to open 2009 with one of the Red Sox's Class A affiliates. He projects as either a frontline starter or a dynamic reliever, and Boston's needs will dictate his future. He might have earned a big league cameo at the end of 2008 had he not gotten hurt.

Year	Club (League)	Class	W	L	ERA	G	GS	CG	SV	IP	H	R	ER	HR	BB	SO	AVG
2007	Lowell (NYP)	SS	0	1	1.85	10	10	0	0	24	14	5	5	1	8	33	.163
2008	Greenville (SAL)	LoA	1	1	0.00	3	3	0	0	10	5	3	0	0	6	12	.135
MINOR LEAGUE TOTALS			1	2	1.31	13	13	0	0	34	19	8	5	1	14	45	.154

4 DANIEL BARD, RHP

BORN: June 25, 1985. **B-T:** R-R. **HT.:** 6-4. **WT.:** 195. **DRAFTED:** North Carolina, 2006 (1st round). **SIGNED BY:** Jeff Zona.

After losing his command and confidence as a starter in his 2007 pro debut, Bard altered his mechanics and seemed more comfortable as a reliever in Hawaii Winter Baseball. Kept in that role in 2008, he was Boston's minor league pitcher of the year after ranking among the minor league bullpen leaders in strikeouts per nine innings (12.4) and opponent average (.158). Bard can overmatch hitters with his fastball, throwing 97-100 mph four-seamers and low-90s power sinkers with little effort. After struggling with a curveball and a slurve in the past, he finally found a second pitch in a solid mid-80s slider. It's not especially sharp, but the slider breaks enough to eat up hitters geared for his fastball. While Bard is doing a much better job repeating his delivery, he still gets around his pitches at times, causing them to flatten out. He cut his walk rate from 9.4 per nine innings in 2007 to 3.5 in 2008, but he still needs better control. He lacks deception, though it's not easy to catch up to his stuff. Bard has come a long way in a year, though he may project better as a set-up man than as a closer. He'll probably open 2009 in Triple-A and break into the Boston bullpen in a low-pressure role later in the year.

Year	Club (League)	Class	W	L	ERA	G	GS	CG	SV	IP	H	R	ER	HR	BB	SO	AVG
2007	Lancaster (CAL)	HiA	0	2	10.13	5	5	0	0	13	21	23	15	2	22	9	.350
	Greenville (SAL)	LoA	3	5	6.42	17	17	0	0	62	55	49	44	3	56	38	.250
2008	Greenville (SAL)	LoA	1	0	0.64	15	0	0	0	28	12	2	2	1	4	43	.129
	Portland (EL)	AA	4	1	1.99	31	0	0	7	50	30	14	11	3	26	64	.173
MINOR LEAGUE TOTALS			8	8	4.24	68	22	0	7	153	118	88	72	9	108	154	.216

5 JOSH REDDICK, OF

BORN: Feb. 19, 1987. **B-T:** L-R. **HT.:** 6-2. **WT.:** 180. **DRAFTED:** Middle Georgia JC, 2006 (17th round). **SIGNED BY:** Rob English.

Originally selected as a draft-and-follow candidate in 2006, Reddick homered that summer off Team USA's Ross Detwiler (who became the No. 6 overall pick in the 2007 draft), spurring the Red Sox to sign him immediately for $140,000. He has exceeded expectations by hitting .309/.354/.538 in two pro seasons, though he struggled in Double-A at the end of 2008. Reddick has a chance to become a five-tool player. While he's a free swinger, he doesn't chase pitches and has tremendous feel for making hard contact. He has solid-average speed and is capable of playing center field, and he has arguably the best outfield arm in the minors. With plus arm strength, a quick release and sniper accuracy, he has 41 assists in 209 pro games. Double-A pitchers exploited Reddick's aggressive nature, which keeps him from drawing many walks. He'll need to be more selective, but his problem is more a matter of not putting tough pitches in play than chasing balls out of the zone. Reddick will try to redeem himself against Double-A pitching in 2009. If the Red Sox don't sign Jason Bay to an extension, he could compete for a big league starting job in 2010.

Year	Club (League)	Class	AVG	G	AB	R	H	2B	3B	HR	RBI	BB	SO	SB	OBP	SLG
2007	Greenville (SAL)	LoA	.306	94	369	60	113	17	6	18	72	26	51	8	.352	.531
	Portland (EL)	AA	.000	1	1	0	0	0	0	0	0	0	0	0	.000	.000
2008	Greenville (SAL)	LoA	.340	14	53	7	18	4	2	0	9	5	8	2	.397	.491
	Lancaster (CAL)	HiA	.343	76	312	60	107	11	8	17	57	17	49	9	.375	.593
	Portland (EL)	AA	.214	34	117	22	25	4	2	6	25	12	25	3	.290	.436
MINOR LEAGUE TOTALS			.309	219	852	149	263	36	18	41	163	60	133	22	.354	.538

6 CASEY KELLY, RHP/SS

BORN: Oct. 4, 1989. **B-T:** R-R. **HT.:** 6-3. **WT.:** 194. **DRAFTED:** HS—Sarasota, Fla., 2008 (1st round). **SIGNED BY:** Anthony Turco.

One of the top two-way players and two-sport athletes in the 2008 draft, Kelly had the added leverage of a scholarship to play quarterback at Tennessee. After signing for a club-record $3 million as the 30th overall pick, he played only shortstop and didn't pitch in his pro debut. The Red Sox thought Kelly was the most advanced high school pitcher in the draft. His command and late life make his 90-91 mph fastball close to a plus-plus pitch, and his lean body and power spin on his curveball are promising signs for increased velocity in the future. He has tremendous feel, no surprise for someone whose father (Pat) played in the majors. As a shortstop, Kelly has fluid actions, a strong arm and projectable power. Kelly is still raw at the plate and struggled to make contact in his first taste of pro ball. Unless he squares up balls more consistently and solves breaking pitches, he won't hit for a high average or make the most of his raw power. Boston would like to see Kelly on the mound, while he prefers to play shortstop. He may do some of both at short-season Lowell or low Class A Greenville in 2009.

Year	Club (League)	Class	AVG	G	AB	R	H	2B	3B	HR	RBI	BB	SO	SB	OBP	SLG
2008	Red Sox (GCL)	R	.173	27	98	10	17	5	0	1	9	6	34	1	.229	.255
	Lowell (NYP)	SS	.344	9	32	5	11	5	1	0	4	0	8	0	.344	.563
MINOR LEAGUE TOTALS			.215	36	130	15	28	10	1	1	13	6	42	1	.255	.331

7 JUNICHI TAZAWA, RHP

BORN: June 6, 1986. **B-T:** R-R. **HT.:** 6-0. **WT.:** 175. **SIGNED:** Japan, 2008.
SIGNED BY: Jon Deeble/Craig Shipley.

After graduating from high school, Tazawa played for Nippon Oil ENEOS in a Japanese industrial league but did not sign with a Japanese professional team. He caught the attention of U.S. teams at the World Cup in Taiwan in November 2007, and he made waves by asking Japanese clubs not to select him in their 2008 draft. Tazawa, who likely would have been the top pick in that draft, wanted to immediately begin his career in the United States. Nippon Professional Baseball was not happy with the decision, and though it allowed him to leave, it also passed a rule where any amateur who spurns the Japanese draft to play overseas is banned from returning to play for a Japanese team for two years (three if he left as a high schooler). The pursuit of Tazawa heated up this fall, when he won MVP honors after carrying Nippon Oil to its first championship in the 32-team Intercity Baseball Tournament since 1995, then led the ENEOS to the semifinals of the industrial league's corporate championship. In his final outing at the latter event, he struck out 10 in a complete-game shutout. The Red Sox signed Tazawa in December to a three-year, $3.3 million major league contract that included a $1.8 million bonus. The Braves, Mariners and Rangers also made offers, with Texas reportedly dangling a four-year, $7 million deal. Boston won out because international scouts Jon Deeble and Craig Shipley showed interest early and because Tazawa wanted to play with Daisuke Matsuzaka. The consensus among several international scouts is that Tazawa's talent is equivalent to that of a late or supplemental first-round pick. Using the slightly smaller Japanese baseball, he showed good command of a low-90s fastball, a splitter that ranks as his best pitch and a pair of breaking balls (his slider is better than his curveball). He's a bit undersized at 6 feet and 175 pounds, but his clean delivery and strong shoulders and legs lend themselves to durability. He also has some deception that makes him tougher to hit. Tazawa likely will begin his career in Double-A. While he could reach Boston quickly as a reliever, his potential for two or three plus pitches and his advanced command make him intriguing as a possible starter.

Year	Club (League)	Class	W	L	ERA	G	GS	CG	SV	IP	H	R	ER	HR	BB	SO	AVG
2008	Did Not Play—Signed 2009 Contract																

8 RYAN WESTMORELAND, OF

BORN: April 27, 1990. **B-T:** L-R. **HT.:** 6-2. **WT.:** 195. **DRAFTED:** HS—Portsmouth, R.I., 2008 (5th round). **SIGNED BY:** Ray Fagnant.

The best position player to come out of Rhode Island since Rocco Baldelli, Westmoreland appeared to be strongly committed to Vanderbilt. The Red Sox drafted him in the fifth round and courted all him summer before signing him for $2 million. A shoulder injury prevented him from playing in the minors or instructional league. Also an all-state soccer player and basketball star, Westmoreland is the top athlete in the system. With his strength and easy plus-plus speed, he could be a 30-30 player in time. Thanks to his quick bat and good hand-eye coordination, he should be able to hit for average as well. He has the range to play center field and solid arm strength. Scouts who saw Westmoreland play in high school thought he needed to do a better job of incorporating his lower half into his swing. He's as much a baseball player as he is a pure athlete, so missing time this summer and fall shouldn't be a huge setback. Westmoreland had minor surgery to clean up his shoulder in November, which will knock him out of spring training and probably means that he'll make his pro debut at Lowell in June. He's not the center-field defender that Jacoby Ellsbury is, but Westmoreland has the potential for a more dynamic bat.

Year	Club (League)	Class	AVG	G	AB	R	H	2B	3B	HR	RBI	BB	SO	SB	OBP	SLG
2008	Did Not Play—Injured															

9 MICHAEL ALMANZAR, 3B

BORN: Dec. 2, 1990. **B-T:** R-R. **HT.:** 6-3. **WT.:** 190. **SIGNED:** Dominican Republic, 2007. **SIGNED BY:** Pablo Lantigua.

The son of former big league pitcher Carlos Almanzar, Michael signed in 2007 for $1.5 million, a club record for a Latin American amateur. He was advanced enough offensively that the Red Sox let him make his U.S. debut and even promoted him to low Class A at age 17. Almanzar has the swing, bat speed and leverage to hit for huge power once he matures physically. Given his bloodlines, it's no surprise he has better instincts and strike-zone awareness than most players his age. He's athletic for his size and shows a plus arm at third base. Almanzar is so young and raw that he'll require time to add strength and refine his tools. His struggles in the South Atlantic League were no surprise. He's a below-average runner and doesn't have a quick first step, so he may need to move from third to first base down the road. He needs more consistency with his approach and his defense, particularly on throws. Once again in 2009, Almanzar will be one of the youngest players in the SAL. Will Middlebrooks also is ready for Greenville, so Almanzar may have to share third base and see some time at DH.

Year	Club (League)	Class	AVG	G	AB	R	H	2B	3B	HR	RBI	BB	SO	SB	OBP	SLG
2008	Red Sox (GCL)	R	.348	23	89	16	31	6	1	1	11	8	15	3	.414	.472
	Greenville (SAL)	LoA	.207	35	140	12	29	5	2	2	11	5	39	0	.238	.314
MINOR LEAGUE TOTALS			.262	58	229	28	60	11	3	3	22	13	54	3	.309	.376

10 YAMAICO NAVARRO, INF

BORN: Oct. 31, 1987. **B-T:** R-R. **HT.:** 5-11. **WT.:** 180. **SIGNED:** Dominican Republic, 2005. **SIGNED BY:** Pablo Lantigua.

Navarro was one of the biggest surprises in the system in 2008. Signed for just $20,000 three years earlier, he jumped to the top of the Red Sox's crowded depth chart at shortstop by hitting for average and power and playing improved defense. Navarro whips the bat quickly through the hitting zone and barrels balls consistently, giving him power to all fields and the potential for 15-20 homers per season. He has solid speed but isn't a big basestealing threat. He has a plus arm and average range at shortstop, and he has seen time at second and third base to help ease Boston's shortstop logjam. Navarro can get out of control at the plate, taking vicious hacks, chasing wild pitches and missing hittable ones. He has a reasonably sound two-strike approach that he should incorporate earlier in counts. At times, he'll let an offensive slump affect his baserunning and defense. After looking like a utilityman in 2007, Navarro now projects as a regular shortstop. Where the Red Sox decide to deploy Argenis Diaz in 2009 will determine whether Navarro opens in Double-A, but he should get there at some point during the season.

Year	Club (League)	Class	AVG	G	AB	R	H	2B	3B	HR	RBI	BB	SO	SB	OBP	SLG
2006	Red Sox (DSL)	R	.279	53	201	29	56	13	5	3	37	21	29	5	.344	.438
2007	Lowell (NYP)	SS	.289	62	225	36	65	10	1	5	37	22	52	12	.357	.409
2008	Greenville (SAL)	LoA	.280	83	325	46	91	14	4	7	54	29	73	3	.341	.412
	Lancaster (CAL)	HiA	.348	42	181	33	63	13	2	4	23	12	30	3	.393	.508
MINOR LEAGUE TOTALS			.295	240	932	144	275	50	12	19	151	84	184	23	.355	.436

11 STOLMY PIMENTEL, RHP

BORN: Feb. 1, 1990. **B-T:** R-R. **HT.:** 6-3. **WT.:** 186. **SIGNED:** Dominican Republic, 2006. **SIGNED BY:** Luis Scheker.

Signed for only $25,000 in 2006, Pimentel was Boston's Latin program pitcher of the year in his 2007 pro debut. Determined to avoid the Rookie-level Gulf Coast League, he showed enough polish last spring to earn an assignment to the New York-Penn League. At 18, he was the short-season circuit's youngest rotation regular. Pimentel is an exceedingly projectable pitcher with already intriguing stuff. He has fine command of an 88-92 mph fastball that could add another 2-3 mph, and his advanced changeup is the best in the system. Both should be plus pitches with more consistency, while his curveball projects as an average offering. He has a loose arm, sound delivery and maturity beyond his years. He wasn't fazed when he drew the start in Lowell's annual game at Fenway Park. Pimentel's fastball is more notable for his command of it than its life, and his pitches flatten out when he doesn't stay on top of them. He needs to tighten his curveball, which will be a point of emphasis in 2009. Even if the Red Sox move him just one level per year, Pimentel will be ready for the majors at age 23. He has the arsenal, savvy and makeup to speed up that timetable, too. He'll pitch in low Class A in 2009.

Year	Club (League)	Class	W	L	ERA	G	GS	CG	SV	IP	H	R	ER	HR	BB	SO	AVG
2007	Red Sox (DSL)	R	3	1	2.90	14	13	0	0	62	44	20	20	2	22	60	.202
2008	Lowell (NYP)	SS	5	2	3.14	13	11	0	0	63	51	25	22	7	17	61	.224
MINOR LEAGUE TOTALS			8	3	3.02	27	24	0	0	125	95	45	42	9	39	121	.213

12 OSCAR TEJEDA, SS/3B

BORN: Dec. 26, 1989. **B-T:** R-R. **HT.:** 6-1. **WT.:** 177. **SIGNED:** Dominican Republic, 2006. **SIGNED BY:** Luis Scheker.

The Red Sox have pushed Tejeda aggressively since signing him for $525,000 in 2006. He made a strong U.S. debut as a 17-year-old in 2007, and while his numbers weren't as impressive last year, there were mitigating circumstances. Tejeda had surgery to repair a tiny hole in his heart during the offseason, and also came down with a staph infection in his forearm. The infection relegated him to extended spring training at the start of 2008, and recurred after he reported to Greenville. Tejeda hit just .231 with three extra-base hits and two walks in the first two months before finding his stride as one of the youngest regulars in low Class A. A rival international scouting director compared him to Alfonso Soriano when Boston signed him, and Tejeda could have interesting power once he strengthens his wiry frame and plate discipline. His hands generate plenty of bat speed and he has a fluid swing, so he should hit for average as well. A slightly below-average runner with good instincts on the bases, Tejeda could move to third base once he fills out. For now, he's a legitimate shortstop with solid range, reliable hands and a plus-plus arm that first attracted scouts when he was 14. Like most young infielders, he's still inconsistent defensively, having committed 44 errors in 139 pro games at shortstop. The Red Sox may send him back to low Class A to build his confidence at the start of 2009, but he should reach their new high Class A Salem affiliate by the end of the season.

Year	Club (League)	Class	AVG	G	AB	R	H	2B	3B	HR	RBI	BB	SO	SB	OBP	SLG
2007	Red Sox (GCL)	R	.295	45	173	23	51	13	1	1	21	15	27	6	.344	.399
	Lowell (NYP)	SS	.298	22	94	14	28	5	2	0	12	6	26	4	.347	.394
2008	Greenville (SAL)	LoA	.261	97	372	44	97	18	1	4	38	20	76	11	.301	.347
MINOR LEAGUE TOTALS			.275	164	639	81	176	36	4	5	71	41	129	21	.319	.368

13 RYAN KALISH, OF

BORN: March 28, 1988. **B-T:** L-L. **HT.:** 6-1. **WT.:** 205. **DRAFTED:** HS—Red Bank, N.J., 2006 (9th round). **SIGNED BY:** Ray Fagnant.

Though he had yet to reach full-season ball, Kalish's name surfaced prominently in trade rumors last offseason when the Red Sox were linked to the Twins and Johan Santana. After signing late for $600,000 as a ninth-round pick in 2006 and being brought along slowly before breaking the hamate bone in his right hand in 2007, Kalish finally got in a full season last year. He did spend most of April in extended spring training while completing his recovery from hamate surgery, and he seemed cautious with his swing once he returned. Kalish didn't turn the bat loose like he had in the past, which had a pronounced affect on his power. Boston hopes he'll trust his hands again in 2009 and envisions that he could develop the power for 15-20 homers annually, perhaps more if he adds some loft to his line drive swing. The rest of Kalish's game was solid as usual in 2008. He has a sweet lefty stroke and a good sense of the strike zone, so he should hit for average. Legend has it that he didn't swing and miss at a single pitch as a high school senior. While Kalish has slowed slightly as he has gained some strength, he's a 55 runner on the 20-80 scouting scale and possesses some basestealing savvy. A fundamentally sound defender who split time between center and right field last year, he fits better in right, though his arm is fringe-average. Kalish is a hard-nosed player who brings energy to the ballpark every day. He'll probably open 2009 in high Class A and has a chance to reach Double-A as a 21-year-old. He's sandwiched between Josh Reddick and Pete Hissey in the race to be Boston's right fielder of the future.

Year	Club (League)	Class	AVG	G	AB	R	H	2B	3B	HR	RBI	BB	SO	SB	OBP	SLG
2006	Red Sox (GCL)	R	.300	6	20	6	6	2	0	1	2	1	2	0	.333	.550
	Lowell (NYP)	SS	.200	11	35	8	7	0	1	0	4	2	14	2	.275	.257
2007	Lowell (NYP)	SS	.368	23	87	27	32	4	1	3	13	16	12	18	.471	.540
2008	Greenville (SAL)	LoA	.281	96	360	51	101	16	1	3	32	53	76	18	.376	.356
	Lancaster (CAL)	HiA	.233	18	73	6	17	6	0	2	14	8	23	1	.305	.397
MINOR LEAGUE TOTALS			.283	154	575	98	163	28	3	9	65	80	127	39	.375	.390

14 CHE-HSUAN LIN, OF

BORN: Sept. 21, 1988. **B-T:** R-R. **HT.:** 6-0. **WT.:** 180. **SIGNED:** Taiwan, 2007. **SIGNED BY:** Jon Deeble/Louie Lin.

The Red Sox have fortified their big league pitching staff with Japanese big leaguers Daisuke Matsuzaka and Hideki Okajima, and they've also worked the Far East for prospects as well. One of five Taiwanese players in the system, Lin missed the end of the minor league season to play in the Beijing Olympics, where he tied fellow Boston farmhand Chih-Hsien Chiang for his team lead with four RBIs. A national 100-meter and high jump champion in high school, Lin signed for $400,000 in 2007 and came straight to the United States. The Red Sox's 2008 defensive player of the year, he's one of the best center fielders in the minors. He has uncanny instincts, a quick first step and plus speed, allowing him to glide to balls with ease. He also has plus-plus arm strength, rare for a center fielder. Lin has yet to produce big numbers at the plate, but he handled low Class A as a 19-year-old and the offensive potential is there. He has bat speed and shows raw power in batting practice, but it hasn't translated into games yet. He did homer off a 94-mph fastball from the Rockies' Ryan Mattheus, helping him earn MVP honors at the 2008 Futures Game. He incorporates a big leg kick into his swing, and Boston is trying to improve his timing. Lin controls the strike zone well for his age, and he'll be valuable if he can develop on-base ability and occasional power to go with his defense and basestealing ability. Headed to high Class A, he's similar to but not quite as explosive as the Red Sox's incumbent center fielder, Jacoby Ellsbury.

Year	Club (League)	Class	AVG	G	AB	R	H	2B	3B	HR	RBI	BB	SO	SB	OBP	SLG
2007	Red Sox (GCL)	R	.263	43	175	33	46	10	6	4	22	17	42	14	.330	.457
	Lowell (NYP)	SS	.163	11	43	7	7	2	0	0	3	5	10	3	.265	.209
2008	Greenville (SAL)	LoA	.249	91	362	60	90	13	6	5	37	43	62	33	.342	.359
MINOR LEAGUE TOTALS			.247	145	580	100	143	25	12	9	62	65	114	50	.333	.378

15 LUIS EXPOSITO, C

BORN: Jan. 20, 1987. **B-T:** R-R. **HT.:** 6-3. **WT.:** 210. **DRAFTED:** St. Petersburg (Fla.) JC, D/F 2005 (31st round). **SIGNED BY:** Jon Lukens.

Suspended for virtually the entire 2007 for what club officials deemed a lack of maturity, Exposito did some growing up and responded with a breakout 2008, batting .293 with 21 homers. Signed as a draft-and-follow for $150,000 in 2006, he originally attracted the Red Sox with his defensive ability. They didn't envision him growing into plus power potential, but that's exactly what he has done, especially to his pull side. Exposito is very strong but sometimes lacks finesse at the plate. His approach can get primitive—see ball, try to crush ball—and he can give away at-bats. He doesn't have the softest hands, but he has worked diligently to improve his receiving. He has a strong arm, though his throws sometimes lack accuracy and he erased just 28 percent of basestealers last season. He blocks balls well and has developed his game-calling and leadership skills. Like most catchers, Exposito doesn't offer much speed on the bases. With his big frame, he'll have to continue to maintain his conditioning. He's the best in-house option to become a regular major league catcher, but Exposito isn't nearly ready to take over for a declining Jason Varitek yet. If Mark Wagner repeats Double-A, Exposito could start 2009 by returning to high Class A.

Year	Club (League)	Class	AVG	G	AB	R	H	2B	3B	HR	RBI	BB	SO	SB	OBP	SLG
2006	Lowell (NYP)	SS	.250	57	208	18	52	13	0	1	23	13	44	1	.301	.327
2007	Greenville (SAL)	LoA	.233	9	30	3	7	0	0	0	2	2	5	0	.281	.233
2008	Greenville (SAL)	LoA	.283	49	191	34	54	8	1	11	31	12	42	1	.328	.508
	Lancaster (CAL)	HiA	.301	55	226	31	68	13	2	10	37	9	47	0	.331	.509
MINOR LEAGUE TOTALS			.276	170	655	86	181	34	3	22	93	36	138	2	.318	.438

16 KRIS JOHNSON, LHP

BORN: Oct. 14, 1984. **B-T:** L-L. **HT.:** 6-4. **WT.:** 170. **DRAFTED:** Wichita State, 2006 (1st round supplemental). **SIGNED BY:** Ernie Jacobs.

Johnson still hasn't regained the curveball and control he had before he underwent Tommy John surgery at Wichita State in 2005, yet he has moved swiftly through the system. He skipped low Class A in 2007 and spent the entire 2008 season in Double-A. Johnson has a good fastball for a lefthander, sitting at 90-92 mph with little effort and life down in the zone. He had the lowest home run rate (0.3 per nine innings) in the Eastern League last year. Johnson's fastball and changeup both project as future 55 pitches on the 20-80 scouting scale, and his ability to refine his curveball ultimately will determine if he becomes a back-of-the-rotation starter or a reliever. His curve had the makings of a plus pitch with power and depth before he blew out his elbow, but now it's more slurvy. While Johnson can hit both sides of the plate, at time he just loses the strike zone. He has a very lean frame as a 24-year-old, so he doesn't project as a workhorse, and if he can't keep his pitch counts down, he'll struggle to last past five innings. The Red Sox have several veterans and youngsters Clay Buchholz, Justin Masterson and Michael Bowden ahead of him, so they can give Johnson all the time he needs to develop.

Year	Club (League)	Class	W	L	ERA	G	GS	CG	SV	IP	H	R	ER	HR	BB	SO	AVG
2006	Lowell (NYP)	SS	0	2	0.88	14	13	0	0	31	25	7	3	0	7	27	.229
2007	Lancaster (CAL)	HiA	9	7	5.56	27	27	0	0	136	148	91	84	20	57	100	.279
2008	Portland (EL)	AA	8	9	3.63	27	27	0	0	136	147	70	55	5	56	108	.277
MINOR LEAGUE TOTALS			17	18	4.22	68	67	0	0	303	320	168	142	25	120	235	.274

17 ARGENIS DIAZ, SS

BORN: Feb. 12, 1987. **B-T:** R-R. **HT.:** 5-11. **WT.:** 175. **SIGNED:** Venezuela, 2003. **SIGNED BY:** German Robles/Miguel Garcia.

Only one Red Sox shortstop (Rick Burleson, 1979) has been honored in the 51-year history of the Gold Glove awards, but Diaz could double that number one day. He has dazzled club officials with his defensive wizardry since arriving in the United States in 2006. His instincts are so outstanding and his actions so smooth that he has terrific range to both sides despite owning slightly below-average speed. He also has soft hands, and managers rated his arm the strongest among Eastern League infielders last season. The only thing he needs to work on defensively is a tendency to rush plays at times. Diaz has set career highs for batting average in each of the last two seasons, sandwiched around a .358 performance in Hawaii Winter Baseball, but he still has a ways to go offensively. He has some strength but lacks leverage in his swing and gets impatient, so he doesn't drive the ball consistently. He's not fast or aggressive on the bases, limiting his ability to steal or take extra bases. He needs to focus on making contact and getting on base, and he probably won't merit batting near the top of a lineup. Nevertheless, his defense is so special that he could become a big league regular in the mold of former Boston shortstop Alex Gonzales, sans the same pop. Diaz is the most advanced shortstop prospect in the system, though Yamaico Navarro, a superior hitter, is close to catching him. Diaz may return to Double-A to open the 2009 season.

Year	Club (League)	Class	AVG	G	AB	R	H	2B	3B	HR	RBI	BB	SO	SB	OBP	SLG
2004	Ciudad Alianza (VSL)	R	.236	50	165	28	39	12	0	0	22	20	29	7	.333	.309
2005	Red Sox/Padres (VSL)	R	.266	58	203	37	54	10	2	2	26	38	25	14	.390	.365
2006	Red Sox (GCL)	R	.263	37	133	16	35	2	1	0	11	6	23	3	.300	.293
2007	Greenville (SAL)	LoA	.279	99	405	62	113	25	5	2	40	36	92	5	.342	.380
2008	Lancaster (CAL)	HiA	.281	71	256	31	72	9	6	0	29	20	60	3	.330	.363
	Portland (EL)	AA	.288	39	139	20	40	8	2	2	23	10	30	0	.336	.417
MINOR LEAGUE TOTALS			.271	354	1301	194	353	66	16	6	151	130	259	32	.342	.360

18 WILL MIDDLEBROOKS, 3B

BORN: Sept. 9, 1988. **B-T:** R-R. **HT.:** 6-4. **WT.:** 200. **DRAFTED:** HS—Texarkana, Texas, 2007 (5th round). **SIGNED BY:** Jim Robinson.

A consensus sandwich-round talent in the 2007 draft, Middlebrooks had a seven-figure asking price that caused him to slide to the fifth round. He signed for $925,000, easily their highest bonus among Red Sox draftees that year. He signed late and had shoulder tendinitis, so he didn't make his debut until last June. In his first month at Lowell, Middlebrooks hit just .187/.227/.231. He chased pitches out of the zone, didn't attack balls he should crush and found himself constantly behind in the count. Club officials challenged him to change his approach and snap out of it, and he did. After he started looking for fastballs in specific locations and worked more counts, he batted .305/.352/.475 over the final seven weeks. He capped off his year with an impressive performance in instructional league, where he was the talk of Boston's camp. Middlebrooks still has more work to do offensively. His strike-zone discipline is just rudimentary at this point, and he has yet to turn his strength and leverage into power. He hit just one homer in 59 regular-season games, though he did go deep against Batavia flamethrower Adam Riefer in the New York-Penn League playoffs. He shows off his power in batting practice but uses more of a line-drive swing in games. Middlebrooks is extremely athletic for his size, drawing college football interest as a quarterback and exhibiting NFL potential as a punter. The Red Sox considered playing him at shortstop, but their logjam at that position led them to move him to third base. He looked very comfortable at the hot corner, with good body control and range and the best infield arm in the system. As a high schooler, he also created pro interest as a pitcher with a low-90s fastball and a promising curveball. He has average speed and stole 10 bases without being caught in 2008. Middlebrooks is ready for low Class A but Michael Almanzar also is headed for Greenville, so they'll have to share third base. Almanzar is more advanced offensively at this point, while Middlebrooks has more athleticism and strength and projects as a better defender.

Year	Club (League)	Class	AVG	G	AB	R	H	2B	3B	HR	RBI	BB	SO	SB	OBP	SLG
2008	Lowell (NYP)	SS	.254	59	209	21	53	17	2	1	21	12	73	10	.298	.368
MINOR LEAGUE TOTALS			.254	59	209	21	53	17	2	1	21	12	73	10	.298	.368

19 PETE HISSEY, OF

BORN: Jan. 17, 1990. **B-T:** L-L. **HT.:** 6-1. **WT.:** 180. **DRAFTED:** HS—Unionville, Pa., 2008 (4th round). **SIGNED BY:** Chris Calciano.

Hissey was part of Boston's aggressive draft spending in 2008, signing for $1 million in the fourth round. There are a lot of similarities between him and Ryan Kalish. Both are polished high school hitters from the Northeast who turned down Virginia scholarships to accept well above-slot bonuses. Hissey recognizes pitches and stays back on breaking balls better than most teenagers. He's also extremely disciplined in a way that's reminiscent of Lars Anderson when he began his pro career. Hissey's easy, compact swing and his approach are designed to hit line drives for now, but he's just starting to add strength and should eventually hit 18-20 homers per season. A shooting guard who could have played for a mid-major college basketball program, he's a good athlete with plus speed and a solid arm. He played mostly center field in his brief pro debut but projects more as a right fielder in the mold of former batting champ Paul O'Neill. Hissey is advanced enough to handle a jump to low Class A in his first full pro season.

Year	Club (League)	Class	AVG	G	AB	R	H	2B	3B	HR	RBI	BB	SO	SB	OBP	SLG
2008	Red Sox (GCL)	R	.238	6	21	6	5	1	0	0	3	4	4	3	.385	.286
	Lowell (NYP)	SS	.265	9	34	3	9	0	0	0	2	5	11	6	.359	.265
MINOR LEAGUE TOTALS			.255	15	55	9	14	1	0	0	5	9	15	9	.369	.273

20 BRYAN PRICE, RHP

BORN: Nov. 13, 1986. **B-T:** R-R. **HT.:** 6-4. **WT.:** 220. **DRAFTED:** Rice, 2008 (1st round supplemental). **SIGNED BY:** John Booher.

Despite his imposing size and fastball, Price barely got on the mound in his first two years at Rice, pitching just 17 innings because he lacked secondary pitches, command and confidence. He blossomed as a setup man last spring, however, pitching his way into the supplemental first round and earning an $849,000 bonus. He made nine starts in his pro debut—four more than he had in his college career—and the Red Sox will develop him as a rotation candidate. When he maintains a consistent delivery, Price can overmatch hitters with his fastball and slider. His heater ranges from 90-95 mph with sink and armside run. His slider can reach 87 mph with good tilt. He also has some feel for a changeup, though he's still learning to trust it in games. He's still in the process of harnessing his stuff. He doesn't always repeat his mechanics, costing him velocity, life and control of his pitches. Boston is trying to get him to stay more under control and develop more extension out front. Worn out at the end of the summer, Price focused on strength and conditioning during instructional league. He should open 2009 in Greenville's rotation, though he could move quickly as a reliever.

Year	Club (League)	Class	W	L	ERA	G	GS	CG	SV	IP	H	R	ER	HR	BB	SO	AVG
2008	Lowell (NYP)	SS	1	3	3.83	12	9	0	0	40	47	22	17	2	10	43	.281
MINOR LEAGUE TOTALS			1	3	3.83	12	9	0	0	40	47	22	17	2	10	43	.281

21 DERRIK GIBSON, INF

BORN: Dec. 5, 1989. **B-T:** R-R. **HT.:** 6-1. **WT.:** 170. **DRAFTED:** HS—Seaford, Del., 2008 (2nd round). **SIGNED BY:** Chris Calciano.

The highest position player drafted out of Delaware since the Expos made Delino DeShields a first-rounder in 1989, Gibson has a very similar game. Like DeShields, he's a fast-twitch athlete with plus-plus speed, an eye for drawing walks and the ability to sting the ball on occasion. A second-round pick who declined a North Carolina shortstop to sign for $600,000, Gibson helped his cause by going 5-for-6 with a walk and six steals when the Red Sox brought several of their 2008 draftees to Fenway Park for a July workout. He has the bat speed and patience to hit for average, and he could have average power once he fills out. He supplements his speed with good instincts on the bases, enabling him to go 16-for-16 stealing bases in his debut. Gibson has the hands, range and arm strength to play shortstop, though he moved around the GCL Red Sox infield in deference to Casey Kelly. Gibson also could handle center field if needed. He needs to cut down his long arm action and eliminate a hitch, though it hasn't led to throwing errors. His speed and versatility remind the Red Sox of a righthanded Chone Figgins. Gibson likely will play at Lowell in 2009, enabling him to spend most of his time at shortstop. He could make a run at Greenville with a strong spring, though that probably would mean shuttling around the infield again.

Year	Club (League)	Class	AVG	G	AB	R	H	2B	3B	HR	RBI	BB	SO	SB	OBP	SLG
2008	Red Sox (GCL)	R	.309	27	94	15	29	6	1	0	9	14	18	14	.411	.394
	Lowell (NYP)	SS	.086	14	35	4	3	0	0	0	3	6	11	2	.233	.086
MINOR LEAGUE TOTALS			.248	41	129	19	32	6	1	0	12	20	29	16	.361	.310

22 ANTHONY RIZZO, 1B

BORN: Aug. 8, 1989. **B-T:** L-L. **HT.:** 6-3. **WT.:** 220. **DRAFTED:** HS—Parkland, Fla., 2007 (6th round). **SIGNED BY:** Laz Gutierrez.

Rizzo was hitting .373 as an 18-year-old in low Class A when he was sidelined by what was thought to be a kidney infection in late April. Instead, he learned that he had limited stage classical Hodgkin's lymphoma, one of the more treatable forms of cancer. He missed the rest of season to get treatment, though he was able to hit in instructional league between chemotherapy sessions, which were scheduled to end in November. His cancer is in remission and he's expected to be able to fully participate in spring training. After signing for an above-slot $325,000 as a sixth-rounder in 2007, Rizzo enthused the Red Sox with his advanced approach at the plate. He continued to draw raves in 2008 before he became ill. His swing is geared more toward left-center at this point, and as he learns to turn on more pitches, he could hit 20 or more homers per season. Though he's a below-average runner, Rizzo shows agility and soft hands at first base. Also a pitcher in high school, he has a stronger arm than most first basemen. Rizzo's makeup and work ethic are also assets and should aid in his recovery. Boston won't push him but cautiously hopes he'll be able to open the season back in Greenville.

Year	Club (League)	Class	AVG	G	AB	R	H	2B	3B	HR	RBI	BB	SO	SB	OBP	SLG
2007	Red Sox (GCL)	R	.286	6	21	6	6	0	0	1	3	1	2	0	.375	.429
2008	Greenville (SAL)	LoA	.373	21	83	9	31	6	0	0	11	3	15	0	.402	.446
MINOR LEAGUE TOTALS			.356	27	104	15	37	6	0	1	14	4	17	0	.396	.442

23 KYLE WEILAND, OF

BORN: Sept. 12, 1986. **B-T:** L-R. **HT.:** 6-4. **WT.:** 195. **DRAFTED:** Notre Dame, 2008 (3rd round). **SIGNED BY:** Chris Mears.

Weiland spent most of his Notre Dame career as a reliever and struggled down the stretch before the 2008 draft, yet he thrived immediately and as a starter in pro ball after signing for $322,000 as a third-rounder. Had he not fallen one inning shy of qualifying, he would have led the New York-Penn League in ERA (1.50), K-BB ratio (68-10) and opponent batting average (.166). Weiland's long legs and loose arm have elicited physical comparisons to Jered Weaver, but Weiland has better pure stuff and throws from a more traditional arm slot. His fastball sits at 91-92 mph and tops out at 95, with late life down and in to righthanders. His low-80s breaking ball, which is closer to a curveball than a slider, has the potential to be a plus pitch. He also has feel for a changeup, giving him the chance to have three solid-or-better pitches. In college, Weiland sometimes fell in love with his breaking ball and struggled to locate his pitches effectively in the zone, but those weren't issues in his pro debut. His arm action is long in the back, which led to some of those command woes and may eventually lead him back to the bullpen. However, the Red Sox plan on developing the Fighting Irish's single-season (16) and career (25) saves leader as a starter for now. Weiland could be the first player from Boston's 2008 draft to reach the majors, and he's the best equipped to make the jump to high Class A if needed in 2009.

Year	Club (League)	Class	W	L	ERA	G	GS	CG	SV	IP	H	R	ER	HR	BB	SO	AVG
2008	Lowell (NYP)	SS	3	3	1.50	15	10	0	0	60	36	17	10	1	10	68	.166
MINOR LEAGUE TOTALS			3	3	1.50	15	10	0	0	60	36	17	10	1	10	68	.166

24 ZACH DAEGES, OF

BORN: Nov. 16, 1983. **B-T:** L-R. **HT.:** 6-4. **WT.:** 225. **DRAFTED:** Creighton, 2006 (6th round). **SIGNED BY:** Ernie Jacobs.

Benefiting from the launching pad at Lancaster, where he hit .396 with 13 homers in 65 games, Daeges led the high Class A California League in runs (124), hits (170), doubles (55, a league record), extra-base hits (81), RBIs (113), total bases (298) and walks (82) in 2007. He proved that he wasn't just a creation of Clear Channel Stadium last year, when he was one of the best hitters in the Eastern League. Daeges has the best plate discipline in the system and is reminiscent of Kevin Youkilis at the same stage of his career. Both had very discerning eyes at the plate and were line-drive hitters with doubles power, though Youkilis since has sacrificed some patience for home runs. Daeges has the strength to eventually follow the same path. Though he has played first and third base as well as all three outfield positions in the minors, he lacks Youkilis' defensive value. Daeges has below-average speed and fringy arm strength, so he's best suited for left field. Ticketed for Triple-A in 2009, he projects as a platoon outfielder and good lefty bat off the bench in the majors.

Year	Club (League)	Class	AVG	G	AB	R	H	2B	3B	HR	RBI	BB	SO	SB	OBP	SLG
2006	Lowell (NYP)	SS	.288	55	198	24	57	10	1	4	32	35	40	3	.402	.409
2007	Lancaster (CAL)	HiA	.330	127	515	124	170	55	5	21	113	82	97	4	.423	.579
2008	Portland (EL)	AA	.307	108	394	63	121	34	3	6	63	72	72	3	.412	.454
MINOR LEAGUE TOTALS			.314	290	1107	211	348	99	9	31	208	189	209	10	.415	.504

25 MITCH DENING, OF

BORN: Aug. 17, 1988. **B-T:** L-R. **HT.:** 6-1. **WT.:** 175. **SIGNED:** Australia, 2005. **SIGNED BY:** Jon Deeble.

Dening played for Red Sox Pacific Rim scouting coordinator Jon Deeble at MLB's Australian academy in 2005 before signing that September. After spending another year at the academy, he came to the United States in 2007 and has topped .300 in each of his first two pro seasons. He has quick hands and a short, sweet lefthanded swing. He stays inside the ball well and sprays line drives to all fields. He imparts good backspin on the ball, and once he adds more strength, turns on more pitches and learns the strike zone better, he could produce 30 doubles and 15 homers on an annual basis. The rest of Dening's tools—speed, outfield defense, arm strength—are average across the board. He played all three outfield positions last year and should settle in right field in long run. He's just beginning to develop, but the Red Sox are excited by what they've seen so far. They'll send him to low Class A in 2009.

Year	Club (League)	Class	AVG	G	AB	R	H	2B	3B	HR	RBI	BB	SO	SB	OBP	SLG
2007	Red Sox (GCL)	R	.301	47	176	21	53	8	1	1	18	19	26	11	.372	.375
2008	Lowell (NYP)	SS	.321	62	240	35	77	13	7	3	20	18	50	9	.375	.471
MINOR LEAGUE TOTALS			.313	109	416	56	130	21	8	4	38	37	76	20	.374	.430

26 RICHIE LENTZ, RHP

BORN: Aug. 6, 1984. **B-T:** R-R. **HT.:** 6-2. **WT.:** 200. **DRAFTED:** Washington, 2006 (19th round). **SIGNED BY:** John Booher.

Rarely has a team mined the middle rounds of a draft as well as the Red Sox did in 2006. They found Lars Anderson and Josh Reddick, now the system's top two position prospects, in the 17th and 18th rounds. With their next pick, they chose Lentz, who had worked only nine innings at Washington that spring while recovering from Tommy John surgery. After he pitching in front of Boston scouts in the New England Collegiate Baseball League—where he ranked as the No. 1 prospect after his freshman season in 2004—Lentz signed for $150,000. The son of Mike Lentz, the No. 2 overall pick in the June 1975 draft, Richie struggled to find the strike zone in his 2007 pro debut. He still battled his command at times last year, but he shot to Double-A while ranking eighth among minor league relievers by averaging 13.0 strikeouts per nine innings. The Red Sox got him to stay over the rubber more and added more downhill leverage in his delivery, and Lentz got more comfortable with his mechanics. They helped his fastball pick up, as it sat at 93-95 and topped out at 97 with nice armside run. He also regained his faith in his hard slider, which he had shied away from after blowing his elbow out throwing one in 2005. He even flashes a good changeup, though he doesn't need it much as a reliever. Lentz still has several items on his to-do list—throw more strikes, command the left side of the plate, tighten slider—but he has legitimate swing-and-miss stuff. If he progresses as much this year as he did in 2008, Lentz will finish the season in Boston.

Year	Club (League)	Class	W	L	ERA	G	GS	CG	SV	IP	H	R	ER	HR	BB	SO	AVG
2007	Greenville (SAL)	LoA	0	1	4.04	31	0	0	1	49	45	22	22	3	42	52	.249
2008	Lancaster (CAL)	HiA	4	3	2.87	28	0	0	1	53	32	20	17	3	30	77	.174
	Portland (EL)	AA	1	2	3.75	16	0	0	1	24	22	12	10	2	13	35	.237
MINOR LEAGUE TOTALS			5	6	3.49	75	0	0	3	126	99	54	49	8	85	164	.216

27 FELIX DOUBRONT, LHP

BORN: Oct. 23, 1987. **B-T:** L-L. **HT.:** 6-2. **WT.:** 190. **SIGNED:** Venezuela, 2004. **SIGNED BY:** Miguel Garcia.

Doubront went 11-4, 1.95 in his first two pro seasons before hitting the wall hard in 2007. He had hernia surgery in the offseason, preventing him from doing much conditioning, and developed a staph infection in his leg in spring training. He got shelled at Greenville until straining his elbow, and didn't fare much better in Lowell after returning. For all the luster he lost in 2007, Doubront regained it last season. He pushed himself hard to add strength to his frame, and the results showed. His fastball returned to 88-91 mph with good sink and finish, and he confidently threw inside against righthanders. He also showed improvement with his changeup, control and command. His changeup is his best secondary pitch, and it enabled him to be more effective against righties (.671 opponent OPS) than lefties (.746) last year. Doubront's changeup still can get better, but his curveball needs the most work. It will require some tightening to be more than just a get-me-over pitch. He has clean mechanics and his arm works easily. Back on track, Doubront will open 2009 in high Class A, where he made an impressive three-game cameo at the end of last season.

Year	Club (League)	Class	W	L	ERA	G	GS	CG	SV	IP	H	R	ER	HR	BB	SO	AVG
2005	Red Sox/Padres (VSL)	R	7	1	0.97	13	13	0	0	65	32	11	7	0	29	58	.152
2006	Red Sox (GCL)	R	2	3	2.52	11	11	0	0	54	41	17	15	6	13	36	.212
	Lowell (NYP)	SS	2	0	4.91	2	2	0	0	11	7	6	6	1	3	7	.179
2007	Greenville (SAL)	LoA	3	7	8.93	11	11	0	0	42	63	49	42	8	17	22	.337
	Lowell (NYP)	SS	1	3	5.66	8	8	0	0	35	41	24	22	2	11	25	.283
2008	Greenville (SAL)	LoA	12	8	3.67	23	23	0	0	115	115	53	47	9	24	118	.260
	Lancaster (CAL)	HiA	1	1	3.86	3	3	0	0	14	15	6	6	1	4	20	.278
MINOR LEAGUE TOTALS			28	23	3.88	71	71	0	0	336	314	166	145	27	101	286	.247

28 STEPHEN FIFE, RHP

BORN: Oct. 4, 1986. **B-T:** R-R. **HT.:** 6-3. **WT.:** 210. **DRAFTED:** Utah, 2008 (3rd round). **SIGNED BY:** Matt Mahoney.

Though he played on a Boise team that advanced to the 1999 Little League World Series, Fife didn't start pitching regularly until he turned 17. His mound career was slow to build momentum, as he wasn't drafted out of high school or Everett (Wash.) CC, and he couldn't crack the weekend rotation in his first year at Utah. He blossomed rapidly last spring, went in the third round of the draft and signed for $464,000. Fife was worn down after pitching 92 innings for the Utes, so the Red Sox kept him in relief in his pro debut. Because he has a strong build and easily generates groundballs, keeping his pitch counts down, he should develop into a workhorse. Fife's main pitches are an 89-93 mph fastball that touches 95 and keeps its velocity late in games, and a curveball that he can throw for strikes or get hitters to chase out of the zone. He also has a slider he'll use as a get-me-over pitch early in counts, and a changeup with sink. Those latter two pitches still need work, as his slider is slurvy and he features spotty arm speed and command with the changeup. As a college pitcher who features solid stuff down in the strike zone, Fife could move fast. It's not out of the question that he'll reach high Class A in 2009.

Year	Club (League)	Class	W	L	ERA	G	GS	CG	SV	IP	H	R	ER	HR	BB	SO	AVG
2008	Lowell (NYP)	SS	1	1	2.33	14	0	0	2	39	28	14	10	1	11	41	.196
MINOR LEAGUE TOTALS			1	1	2.33	14	0	0	2	39	28	14	10	1	11	41	.196

29 BROCK HUNTZINGER, RHP

BORN: June 2, 1988. **B-T:** R-R. **HT.:** 6-3. **WT.:** 200. **DRAFTED:** HS—Pendleton, Ind., 2007 (3rd round). **SIGNED BY:** Josh Loggins.

The Red Sox gave significant bonuses to three high school pitchers in the 2007 draft: Huntzinger ($225,000 in the third round), Austin Bailey ($285,000 in the 16th) and Drake Britton ($700,000 in the 23rd). While Bailey partially tore his labrum in April and Britton blew out his elbow in August, Huntzinger tore up the New York-Penn League. Facing hitters generally two or three years older than he was, he went 5-0 and was leading the NY-P with a 0.64 ERA before he was promoted to low Class A. Huntzinger lost his command in Greenville and surrendered a stunning 12 homers in 27 innings, but Boston was pleased with his first full pro season. Like Michael Bowden, he's a Midwestern high school product who pitches well with his fastball and has a strong build and work ethic. Huntzinger pounds both sides of the plate with a lively fastball that sits in the low 90s. His secondary pitches aren't as advanced as Bowden's were at the same stage of his career, but Huntzinger has a solid if inconsistent slider and a promising changeup with some fade. He has good athleticism and works from a three-quarters arm slot. While Huntzinger threw strikes in low Class A, he left his pitches up in the strike zone too often, something the Red Sox attribute to late-season fatigue. He's still ahead of most pitchers his age, and he has the feel to make the necessary adjustments when he returns to Greenville in 2009.

Year	Club (League)	Class	W	L	ERA	G	GS	CG	SV	IP	H	R	ER	HR	BB	SO	AVG
2007	Red Sox (GCL)	R	0	1	2.57	4	3	0	0	7	5	3	2	0	0	8	.192
2008	Lowell (NYP)	SS	5	0	0.64	8	8	1	0	42	25	3	3	1	7	32	.168
	Greenville (SAL)	LoA	2	3	7.09	6	6	0	0	27	34	23	21	12	6	11	.304
MINOR LEAGUE TOTALS			7	4	3.09	18	17	1	0	76	64	29	26	13	13	51	.223

30 MARK WAGNER, C

BORN: June 11, 1984. **B-T:** R-R. **HT.:** 6-1. **WT.:** 205. **DRAFTED:** UC Irvine, 2005 (9th round). **SIGNED BY:** James Orr.

Though he endured the worst full season of his pro career and Luis Exposito passed him as the system's best catching prospect, the Red Sox still think Wagner will become at least a big league backup. He's the best defensive catcher in the system, even if his pure tools are no better than average. He enhances his arm strength with a quick release, which enabled him to throw out 41 percent of basestealers in Double-A. He has worked very hard to improved his blocking and receiving, and he calls a good game. How much Wagner develops with the bat will determine how much he eventually plays in the majors. He has an unusual approach, stepping in the bucket and trying to serve balls to the opposite field with a flat stroke. While he'll always be more of a gap hitter than a home run threat, Wagner needs to get stronger so he can turn some of his harmless fly balls into doubles. After walking nearly as much as he struck out in his first three pro seasons, he didn't maintain the same plate discipline in 2008. Boston may send him back to Double-A for at least the start of 2009 so he can get his bat going, and he could surface in the majors at some point in 2010.

Year	Club (League)	Class	AVG	G	AB	R	H	2B	3B	HR	RBI	BB	SO	SB	OBP	SLG
2005	Lowell (NYP)	SS	.203	24	69	10	14	2	1	0	6	9	7	1	.309	.261
2006	Greenville (SAL)	LoA	.301	96	355	49	107	32	1	7	45	42	52	1	.386	.456
	Wilmington (CAR)	HiA	.169	17	65	8	11	4	0	1	5	7	9	0	.243	.277
2007	Lancaster (CAL)	HiA	.318	95	368	71	117	35	1	14	82	55	46	0	.406	.533
2008	Portland (EL)	AA	.219	94	342	44	75	19	0	10	48	38	78	0	.304	.363
MINOR LEAGUE TOTALS			.270	326	1199	182	324	92	3	32	186	151	192	2	.357	.432

Chicago Cubs

BY JIM CALLIS

Getting swept in the Division Series for the second straight year was a bitter fate for the Cubs, but it shouldn't obscure the job general manager Jim Hendry and his front office have done.

They may have fizzled in the playoffs, but the Cubs were the National League's best team during the regular season. A club that lost 96 games in 2006 won 97 in 2008—the most for Chicago since it made its last trip to the World Series 63 years earlier. The Cubs led the NL in runs scored—fueled in part by the league's best on-base percentage, a stunning development for a team that had been consistently allergic to walks—and ranked second in runs allowed.

Chicago's 182 wins in 2007-08 are its most in consecutive years since 1937-38. The Cubs' back-to-back playoff berths are their first since 1906-08, which concluded with the last World Series triumph in franchise history.

While Chicago's championship drought may be at 100 seasons and counting, there's reason to believe it could end in the near future. Hendry and his lieutenants have built a balanced club that is the class of a weakened NL Central. Trades (Derrek Lee, Aramis Ramirez) and free agents (Ryan Dempster, Mark DeRosa, Alfonso Soriano) have provided the foundation for the Cubs, but their farm system has pulled its weight as well.

Geovany Soto was a near-unanimous pick as NL rookie of the year in 2008, ending the team's long search for a catcher. Jeff Samardzija energized the bullpen when he came up at midseason. Carlos Marmol will take over as closer in 2009, Ryan Theriot has put an end to a revolving door at shortstop and swingman Sean Marshall has been steady in a variety of roles.

Focusing on winning now and worrying less about the future, the Cubs have used several of their best prospects in trades. They gave up righthander Sean Gallagher and catcher Josh Donaldson as part of a four-player package for Rich Harden last summer, and swapped flamethrower Jose Ceda for Kevin Gregg in November. Hendry then turned his attention to former Cy Young Award winner Jake Peavy and reportedly was willing to give up third baseman Josh Vitters—the top player on this list and the No. 3 overall pick in the 2007 draft—but couldn't agree to a deal with the Padres.

Promotions and trades have contributed to thinning out the system, and so have a series of uninspiring drafts. Chicago hasn't gotten long-term produc-

Jim Hendry built the NL's top team only to see the Cubs suffer a postseason collapse

BILL MITCHELL

TOP 30 PROSPECTS

1. Josh Vitters, 3b	16. Tyler Colvin, of
2. Jeff Samardzija, rhp	17. Marcos Mateo, rhp
3. Andrew Cashner, rhp	18. Chris Carpenter, rhp
4. Dae-Eun Rhee, rhp	19. Darwin Barney, ss
5. Welington Castillo, c	20. Marquez Smith, 3b/2b
6. Kevin Hart, rhp	21. Mitch Atkins, rhp
7. Starlin Castro, ss/2b	22. Esmailin Caridad, rhp
8. Ryan Flaherty, ss	23. Tony Thomas, 2b
9. Jay Jackson, rhp	24. Jake Fox, 1b/of
10. Hak-Ju Lee, ss	25. Ty Wright, of
11. Steve Clevenger, c/1b	26. Blake Parker, rhp
12. Micah Hoffpauir, 1b/of	27. Matt Cerda, c
13. Brandon Guyer, of	28. Logan Watkins, 2b
14. Junior Lake, ss	29. Alex Maestri, rhp
15. Jovan Rosa, 3b/1b	30. Su-Min Jung, rhp

tion out of a first-round pick since Kerry Wood in 1995. Soto, an 11th-round pick in 2001, was the first position player it signed and developed into an all-star since it drafted Joe Girardi in 1986.

The Cubs aren't expected to be affected by the bankruptcy filing of the Tribune Co., which bought the club in 1981. The Cubs and Wrigley Field aren't part of the bankruptcy proceeding. The Tribune Co. hopes to complete the sale of the team and the ballpark by Opening Day, though it has been trying to divest itself of both since Sam Zell bought the company out in April 2007.

General Manager: Jim Hendry. **Farm Director:** Oneri Fleita. **Scouting Director:** Tim Wilken.

Class	Team	League	W	L	PCT	Finish*	Manager	Affiliated
Majors	Chicago	National	97	64	.602	1st (16)	Lou Piniella	—
Triple-A	Iowa Cubs	Pacific Coast	83	59	.585	1st (16)	Pat Listach	1981
Double-A	Tennessee Smokies	Southern	62	77	.446	9th (10)	Buddy Bailey	2007
High A	Daytona Cubs	Florida State	73	59	.553	^3rd (12)	Jody Davis	1993
Low A	Peoria Chiefs	Midwest	60	78	.435	12th (14)	Ryne Sandberg	2005
Short-season	Boise Hawks	Northwest	43	33	.566	2nd (8)	Tom Beyers	2001
Rookie	AZL Cubs	Arizona	31	24	.564	5th (9)	Franklin Font	1997
Overall 2008 Minor League Record			352	330	.516	11th		

* Finish in overall standings (No. of teams in league). ^League champion.

LAST YEAR'S TOP 30

Rank	Player, Pos.	Status
1.	Josh Vitters, 3b	No. 1
2.	Geovany Soto, c/1b	Majors
3.	Tyler Colvin, of	No. 16
4.	Jose Ceda, rhp	(Marlins)
5.	Sean Gallagher, rhp	(Athletics)
6.	Donald Veal, lhp	(Pirates)
7.	Josh Donaldson, c	(Athletics)
8.	Jeff Samardzija, rhp	No. 2
9.	Tony Thomas, 2b	No. 23
10.	Kevin Hart, rhp	No. 6
11.	Billy Petrick, rhp	(Free agent)
12.	Eric Patterson, 2b/of	(Athletics)
13.	Kyler Burke, of	Dropped out
14.	Chris Huseby, rhp	Dropped out
15.	Welington Castillo, c	No. 5
16.	Dae-Eun Rhee, rhp	No. 4
17.	Robert Hernandez, rhp	Dropped out
18.	Sam Fuld, of	Dropped out
19.	Jake Fox, of/1b/c	No. 24
20.	Larry Suarez, rhp	Dropped out
21.	Ryan Acosta, rhp	Dropped out
22.	James Russell, lhp	Dropped out
23.	Alex Maestri, rhp	No. 29
24.	Darwin Barney, ss	No. 19
25.	Jose Ascanio, rhp	Dropped out
26.	Rocky Roquet, rhp	Dropped out
27.	Mark Holliman, rhp	(Brewers)
28.	Josh Lansford, 3b	Dropped out
29.	Steve Clevenger, c/1b	No. 11
30.	Tim Lahey, rhp	(Twins)

BEST TOOLS

Best Hitter for Average	Josh Vitters
Best Power Hitter	Josh Vitters
Best Strike-Zone Discipline	Sam Fuld
Fastest Baserunner	Tony Campana
Best Athlete	Brandon Guyer
Best Fastball	Jeff Samardzija
Best Curveball	Casey Lambert
Best Slider	Andrew Cashner
Best Changeup	Dae-Eun Rhee
Best Control	Esmailin Caridad
Best Defensive Catcher	Luis Flores
Best Defensive Infielder	Darwin Barney
Best Infield Arm	Junior Lake
Best Defensive Outfielder	Sam Fuld
Best Outfield Arm	Kyle Burke

PROJECTED 2012 LINEUP

Catcher	Geovany Soto
First Base	Aramis Ramirez
Second Base	Ryan Flaherty
Third Base	Josh Vitters
Shortstop	Starlin Castro
Left Field	Alfonso Soriano
Center Field	Brandon Guyer
Right Field	Tyler Colvin
No. 1 Starter	Carlos Zambrano
No. 2 Starter	Jeff Samardzija
No. 3 Starter	Andrew Cashner
No. 4 Starter	Rich Harden
No. 5 Starter	Ryan Dempster
Closer	Carlos Marmol

TOP PROSPECTS OF THE DECADE

Year	Player, Pos.	2008 Org.
1999	Corey Patterson, of	Reds
2000	Corey Patterson, of	Reds
2001	Corey Patterson, of	Reds
2002	Mark Prior, rhp	Padres
2003	Hee Seop Choi, 1b	Kia (Korea)
2004	Angel Guzman, rhp	Cubs
2005	Brian Dopirak, 1b	Blue Jays
2006	Felix Pie, of	Cubs
2007	Felix Pie, of	Cubs
2008	Josh Vitters, 3b	Cubs

TOP DRAFT PICKS OF THE DECADE

Year	Player, Pos.	2008 Org.
1999	Ben Christensen, rhp	Out of baseball
2000	Luis Montanez, ss	Orioles
2001	Mark Prior, rhp	Padres
2002	Bobby Brownlie, rhp	Nationals
2003	Ryan Harvey, of	Cubs
2004	Grant Johnson, rhp (2nd round)	Cubs
2005	Mark Pawelek, lhp	Cubs
2006	Tyler Colvin, of	Cubs
2007	Josh Vitters, 3b	Cubs
2008	Andrew Cashner, rhp	Cubs

LARGEST BONUSES IN CLUB HISTORY

Mark Prior, 2001	$4,000,000
Kosuke Fukudome, 2007	$4,000,000
Corey Patterson, 1998	$3,700,000
Josh Vitters, 2007	$3,200,000
Luis Montanez, 2000	$2,750,000

CHICAGO CUBS

TOP 2009 ROOKIE: Jeff Samardzija, rhp. He contributed to the 2008 pennant drive as a reliever, and this time around he could be a starter.

BREAKOUT PROSPECT: Brandon Guyer, of. The system's best athlete has the power and speed to move quickly if he can stay healthy.

SLEEPER: Dan McDaniel, rhp. The 2008 14th-rounder used his plus fastball/curve combo to dominate in his pro debut.

SOURCE OF TOP 30 TALENT

Homegrown	28	**Acquired**	2
College	14	Trades	2
Junior college	1	Rule 5 draft	0
High school	4	Independent leagues	0
Draft-and-follow	1	Free agents/waivers	0
Nondrafted free agents	0		
International	8		

Numbers in parentheses indicate prospect rankings.

LF
Drew Rundle

CF
Brandon Guyer (13)
Ty Wright (25)
Sam Fuld

RF
Tyler Colvin (16)
Nelson Perez
Kyler Burke
Brad Snyder
Dylan Johnston

3B
Josh Vitters (1)
Ryan Flaherty (8)
Jovan Rosa (15)
Marquez Smith (20)
Jonathan Mota

SS
Starlin Castro (7)
Hak-Ju Lee (10)
Junior Lake (14)
Darwin Barney (19)
Nate Samson

2B
Tony Thomas (23)
Logan Watkins (28)
Nate Spears
Josh Harrison
Marwin Gonzalez

1B
Micah Hoffpauir (12)
Jake Fox (24)
Russ Canzler
Rebel Ridling
Ryan Keedy

C
Welington Castillo (5)
Steve Clevenger (11)
Matt Cerda (27)
Carlos Perez
Luis Flores

RHP

Starters	Relievers
Jeff Samardzija (2)	Kevin Hart (6)
Andrew Cashner (3)	Marcos Mateo (17)
Dae-Eun Rhee (4)	Blake Parker (26)
Jay Jackson (9)	Alex Maestri (29)
Chris Carpenter (18)	David Patton
Mitch Atkins (21)	Dan McDaniel
Esmailin Caridad (22)	Jesse Estrada
Su-Min Jung (30)	Jose Ascanio
Aaron Shafer	Rocky Roquet
Larry Suarez	Justin Berg
Casey Coleman	Jordan Latham
Hung-Wen Chen	Alberto Cabrera
Ryan Searle	Randy Wells
	Julio Pena

LHP

Starters	Relievers
Jeffry Antigua	Casey Lambert
Jeff Beliveau	James Leverton
James Russell	Ed Campusano
Cody Hams	Jeremy Papelbon
	Luke Sommer

2008
BONUSES: $5.5 MILLION

BEST PURE HITTER: SS Ryan Flaherty (1s) or C Matt Cerda (4). Flaherty earned short-season Northwest League all-star honors by hitting .297 in his debut. Cerda hit .253 in Rookie ball, where his focus was on making the transition from shortstop to behind the plate.

BEST POWER HITTER: 1B Rebel Ridling (25) slugged 14 homers and reached low Class A. He's the strongest hitter Chicago drafted, though Flaherty may have more usable power in the long run.

FASTEST RUNNER: OF Tony Campana (13) can run the 60-yard dash in 6.3 seconds. He set the single-game (six), season (60) and career (104) stolen-base records at Cincinnati, and swiped 22 bags in 25 pro games.

BEST DEFENSIVE PLAYER: C Luis Flores (7) threw out 49 percent of basestealers in his debut. Campana's speed gives him exceptional range in center field.

BEST FASTBALL: Though RHP Andrew Cashner (1) struggled this summer, he did reach 99 mph and was unhittable in the high Class A Florida State League playoffs. He gets good run on his fastball, which sat at 96-98 when he relieved at Texas Christian. RHP Chris Carpenter (3), a Tommy John surgery alumnus, pitches at 92-95 mph and can touch 97.

BEST SECONDARY PITCH: Cashner's mid-80s slider has so much break that it looks like a power curveball at times.

BEST PRO DEBUT: RHP Jay Jackson (9) went 4-2, 2.88 with a 72-13 K-BB ratio in 50 innings, capping his season with a playoff victory to help Daytona win the FSL title. He throws a low-90s fastball, a hard slider and an average curveball, plus he has feel for a changeup.

BEST ATHLETE: 2B Logan Watkins (21) swings the bat well, runs a 6.6-second 60-yard dash and can play second base, shortstop or center field. He also was an all-state quarterback and defensive back in Kansas.

MOST INTRIGUING BACKGROUND: C Michael Brenly (36) is the son of Cubs broadcaster Bob, a former big league all-star and manager. RHP Casey Coleman's (15) grandfather and father (both named Joe) were both all-star pitchers. 2B Josh Harrison's (6) uncle John Shelby, 1B Ryan Keedy's father (16) Pat and unsigned RHP Dylan Moseley's (48, back at Louisiana Tech) brother Dustin all played in the majors. Flaherty's dad Ed has won two NCAA Division III national championships as the head coach at Southern Maine.

CLOSEST TO THE MAJORS: Cashner would be the obvious candidate if the Cubs weren't going to develop him as a starter. Don't be surprised if it's RHP David Cales (24), who has a plus slider and moxie.

BEST LATE-ROUND PICK: Watkins, who signed for $500,000.

THE ONE WHO GOT AWAY: RHPs Alex Wilson (10) and Sonny Gray (27) had first-round potential but injury questions and seven-figure price tags. Wilson missed the spring at Texas A&M while recovering from Tommy John surgery, while Gray broke his ankle in mid-April and was intent on attending Vanderbilt anyway.

ASSESSMENT: The Cubs believe Cashner will develop as a starter. In RHP Aaron Shafer (2) and Carpenter, they added two more arms who projected as first-rounders before having elbow problems. Flaherty and Cerda have the potential for premium bats at premium positions.

2007
BONUSES: $6.1 MILLION

3B Josh Vitters (1) should hit for plenty of power and average, which is why the Padres wanted him during the Jake Peavy trade talks. Chicago already used C Josh Donaldson (1s) in a deal for Rich Harden.

GRADE: C+

2006
BONUSES: $5.0 MILLION

RHP Jeff Samardzija (5) is becoming everything the Cubs thought he would when they ponied up a $10 million major league contract to keep him away from the NFL. A $1.3 million investment in RHP Chris Huseby (11) looks a lot less prudent. OF Tyler Colvin (1) struggled last season but still has upside.

GRADE: C

2005
BONUSES: $3.8 MILLION*

LHPs Mark Pawelek (1) and Donald Veal (2) once held considerable promise, but those days have passed.

GRADE: F

2004
BONUSES: $2.8 MILLION*

Chicago didn't have a first-round pick and wasted $1.26 million on RHP Grant Johnson (2). But RHP Sean Gallagher (12) was the key to the Harden trade, which also included 2B/OF Eric Patterson (8). The Cubs found two more big leaguers in OF Sam Fuld (10) and since-traded RHP Jerry Blevins (17).

GRADE: C+

---

*Draft analysis by Jim Callis. Numbers in parentheses indicate draft rounds. *Bonuses for 2004-05 are first 10 rounds only.*

BILL MITCHELL

JOSH VITTERS, 3B

Born: Aug. 27, 1989.
Ht.: 6-2. **Wt.:** 190.
Bats: R. **Throws:** R.
Drafted:
HS—Cypress, Calif., 2007
(1st round).
Signed by: Denny
Henderson/Tim Wilken.

Vitters starred on the showcase circuit in the summer of 2006, and his strong performance as a high school senior the following spring ensured that he'd go near the top of the first round. Picking third overall, the Cubs went to bed the night before the draft thinking the Royals would take him at No. 2, which would have left Chicago with righthander Jarrod Parker. But when Kansas City decided slugger Mike Moustakas wouldn't be too expensive, that left Vitters for the Cubs. Signed for $3.2 million minutes before the Aug. 15 deadline, Vitters needed time to start raking again. He was rusty at the end of the 2007 season and developed tendinitis in his left hand during minor league camp last spring. He missed the first two weeks of the season, then reinjured his hand while hitting three doubles in his first game at low Class A Peoria. He tried to play through the pain and went 0-for-10 in three games before Chicago shut him down for two months. Vitters went to short-season Boise when he was healthy. The Northwest League's youngest regular, he ranked as its No. 1 prospect, led the circuit with 25 doubles and fashioned a 26-game hitting streak. Vitters' brother Christian is an infielder in the Athletics system.

Though he has just 14 at-bats in full-season ball, Vitters is unquestionably the top position prospect in the system. With his exceptional bat speed, hand-eye coordination and ability to put the barrel on the ball, the only real question is whether he'll be more productive hitting for average than power. Using one of the smoothest righthanded strokes you'll ever see, he'll offer plenty of both. He made strides in terms of adding strength and using the whole field in 2008. The Cubs knew Vitters would hit, but they're also excited by the progress he has made at third base. He won't be a Gold Glover, but they're confident he can become an average defender. Infield instructor Bobby Dickerson improved Vitters' agility and footwork through drills, and he showed the ability to make throws from a variety of angles. He has the soft hands and strong arm for the position. His makeup is an asset, as he's extremely coachable and fits in well with teammates.

Once he physically matures, Vitters' fringy speed will become below-average. He's not a finished product at third base, though he has plenty of time to develop and will put in the work needed to improve. He's so geared up to make hard contact that he hasn't drawn many walks, and it may border on heresy to ask him to tone down his approach. He's still growing into his home run power, but his 28 doubles in 65 games last year are a strong indicator that he will.

Vitters got in additional work by attending the Cubs' Arizona and Dominican instructional league programs. He probably could handle an assignment to high Class A Daytona, but he may first spend a couple of months in Peoria. He could develop rapidly and push for a spot in the middle of the big league lineup by late 2010.

Year	Club (League)	Class	AVG	G	AB	R	H	2B	3B	HR	RBI	BB	SO	SB	OBP	SLG
2007	Cubs (AZL)	R	.067	7	30	0	2	0	0	0	2	1	9	0	.094	.067
	Boise (NWL)	SS	.190	7	21	2	4	0	0	0	1	2	5	1	.261	.190
2008	Peoria (MWL)	LoA	.214	4	14	1	3	3	0	0	1	0	5	0	.214	.429
	Boise (NWL)	SS	.328	61	259	38	85	25	2	5	37	13	45	1	.365	.498
MINOR LEAGUE TOTALS			.290	79	324	41	94	28	2	5	41	16	64	2	.327	.435

2 JEFF SAMARDZIJA, RHP

BORN: Jan. 23, 1985. **B-T:** R-R. **HT.:** 6-5. **WT.:** 220. **DRAFTED:** Notre Dame, 2006 (5th round). **SIGNED BY:** Stan Zielinski.

Samardzija had an NFL future after setting every significant receiving record at Notre Dame. The Cubs initially signed him for $250,000 as a fifth-round pick in 2006, then gave him a five-year, $10 million big league contract to keep him away from football. His development was painfully slow until he got to Triple-A Iowa in late June, but a month later he was pitching vital innings out of Chicago's bullpen. Samardzija took off after he absorbed changes to his delivery and started turning his stuff loose. He gets good run on a fastball that touches 96 mph when he starts and 98 when he relieves. His splitter can be a devastating swing-and-miss pitch, and his slider is a plus offering at times. He's an intense competitor who thrives on pressure and big crowds. Samardzija is still a work in progress, and hitters solved him more easily his second time around the National League. He lacks consistency with his control and secondary pitches, which include a changeup. His fastball gets more groundouts than strikeouts despite its velocity and life. Slowing down his delivery has enabled him to pitch more under control, but it also has cost him deception and one scout said it puts more stress on his shoulder. The Cubs would like to continue developing Samardzija as a starter and will do so in Triple-A if they have enough other bullpen arms this spring. They think he can become a frontline starter, though outside observers believe it's more likely that he'll be a top set-up man or closer.

Year	Club (League)	Class	W	L	ERA	G	GS	CG	SV	IP	H	R	ER	HR	BB	SO	AVG
2006	Boise (NWL)	SS	1	1	2.37	5	5	0	0	19	18	5	5	1	6	13	.247
	Peoria (MWL)	LoA	0	1	3.27	2	2	0	0	11	6	5	4	1	6	4	.167
2007	Daytona (FSL)	HiA	3	8	4.95	24	20	1	0	107	142	69	59	8	35	45	.323
	Tennessee (SL)	AA	3	3	3.41	6	6	0	0	34	33	15	13	8	9	20	.250
2008	Tennessee (SL)	AA	3	5	4.86	16	15	0	0	76	71	43	41	6	42	44	.252
	Iowa (PCL)	AAA	4	1	3.13	6	6	1	0	37	32	13	13	5	16	40	.241
	Chicago (NL)	MAJ	1	0	2.28	26	0	0	1	28	24	12	7	0	15	25	.226
MINOR LEAGUE TOTALS			14	19	4.26	59	54	2	0	285	302	150	135	29	114	166	.276
MAJOR LEAGUE TOTALS			1	0	2.28	26	0	0	1	28	24	12	7	0	15	25	.226

3 ANDREW CASHNER, RHP

BORN: Sept. 11, 1986. **B-T:** R-R. **HT.:** 6-5. **WT.:** 185. **DRAFTED:** Texas Christian, 2008 (1st round). **SIGNED BY:** Trey Forkerway.

Cashner could have signed with the Rockies as a draft-and-follow or the Cubs as a 29th-rounder in 2007, but opted to transfer to Texas Christian instead. The move paid off as he became a closer and pitched his way into the first round, signing for $1.54 million as the 19th overall pick. He struggled for much of his pro debut but came on in the high Class A Florida State League playoffs, hitting 99 mph and winning the championship clincher. Getting outstanding whip from his long, lean frame, Cashner pitched at 96-98 mph as a reliever at TCU. His mid-80s slider can be just as electric, breaking so much that it looks like a power curveball at times. Chicago believes in his changeup too and will try to develop him as a starter. To stay in the rotation, Cashner will have to improve his command. It deserted him for much of his debut, and his velocity also was down, problems the Cubs attribute to getting rusty during a long layoff and having to reacclimate to starting. He'll also have to refine his changeup and rely on it more often. Like Jeff Samardzija, Cashner has the raw ability to pitch in the front half of a big league rotation and can always fall back on being a late-inning reliever. He'll start for now, opening his first full season at one of Chicago's Class A affiliates.

Year	Club (League)	Class	W	L	ERA	G	GS	CG	SV	IP	H	R	ER	HR	BB	SO	AVG
2008	Cubs (AZL)	R	0	0	0.00	1	1	0	0	1	1	1	0	0	0	2	.333
	Boise (NWL)	SS	1	1	4.96	6	4	0	0	16	19	12	9	1	19	16	.302
	Daytona (FSL)	HiA	0	1	13.50	1	1	0	0	3	4	4	4	0	4	1	.364
MINOR LEAGUE TOTALS			1	2	5.85	8	6	0	0	20	24	17	13	1	23	19	.312

4 DAE-EUN RHEE, RHP

BORN: March 23, 1989. **B-T:** L-R. **HT.:** 6-2. **WT.:** 190. **SIGNED:** Korea, 2007. **SIGNED BY:** Steve Wilson.

The Cubs have had a significant presence in Korea for the last decade, starting with handing out seven-figure bonuses to Hee-Seop Choi and Jae-Kuk Ryu. Signed for $525,000 in July 2007, Rhee allowed just one run over his first three pro starts last April. Then he hurt his elbow in his fourth outing, leading to Tommy John surgery. He has a clean and balanced delivery, so overuse in Korea may have been the culprit. Rhee wowed scouts before he got hurt. Pitching in the April chill of the Midwest League, he showed precocious feel for three pitches. His changeup is the best in system, and it dives at the plate with splitter action. His fastball sat at 90-92 mph and touched 94, while his curveball was a solid-average pitch. He fearlessly threw all of his pitches for strikes, and they all could develop into plus pitches once he's healthy. He has put his downtime to use by improving his English and his conditioning. Rhee won't see game action until midseason at the earliest. The good news is that he's so young that he'll still be ahead of the development curve when he returns. Once he does and builds his arm back up, he won't need much beyond more experience. If he can stay healthy and regain his feel and stuff, Rhee may have a more realistic chance of becoming a quality starter than Jeff Samardzija or Andrew Cashner. Rhee won't be at full strength and effectiveness in 2009, so the Cubs will be patient.

Year	Club (League)	Class	W	L	ERA	G	GS	CG	SV	IP	H	R	ER	HR	BB	SO	AVG
2008	Peoria (MWL)	LoA	4	1	1.80	10	10	0	0	40	28	13	8	0	16	33	.194
MINOR LEAGUE TOTALS			4	1	1.80	10	10	0	0	40	28	13	8	0	16	33	.194

5 WELINGTON CASTILLO, C

JOHN SPEAR

BORN: April 24, 1987. **B-T:** R-R. **HT.:** 6-0. **WT.:** 200. **SIGNED:** Dominican Republic, 2004. **SIGNED BY:** Jose Serra.

After finally developing an all-star catcher in Geovany Soto, the Cubs have another possible regular on the way. Castillo was the Double-A Southern League's youngest catcher in 2008, when he also appeared in the Futures Game. He has drawn Yadier Molina comparisons since arriving in the United States in 2006. He has the ingredients to become Molina's equal behind the plate—and a more dangerous hitter. Castillo handles the bat well and has the strength to hit at least 10-15 homers annually in the majors. His plus arm is his standout tool, and he threw out 36 percent of basestealers last year. Castillo is still raw in many phases of the game. He doesn't control the strike zone yet and has yet to decipher breaking pitches, which is why righthanders manhandled him to the tune of .228/.283/.293 in 2008. His receiving skills are good but he loses focus too often, resulting in 23 errors and 34 passed balls over the last two years. He sits back too far from the plate and gets too flashy at times. He's a well-below-average runner. With Soto in Chicago, there's no need to rush Castillo. He'd benefit from a full season in Double-A to make several adjustments offensively and defensively.

Year	Club (League)	Class	AVG	G	AB	R	H	2B	3B	HR	RBI	BB	SO	SB	OBP	SLG
2005	Cubs (DSL)	R	.289	60	204	29	59	14	0	1	28	19	28	1	.370	.373
2006	Boise (NWL)	SS	.167	3	6	1	1	0	0	0	0	1	0	0	.286	.167
	Cubs (AZL)	R	.192	7	26	4	5	0	0	0	0	1	6	0	.250	.192
2007	Peoria (MWL)	LoA	.271	98	317	41	86	11	2	11	44	23	77	1	.334	.423
2008	Daytona (FSL)	HiA	.273	33	121	15	33	8	0	0	12	4	23	1	.299	.339
	Tennessee (SL)	AA	.298	57	198	25	59	11	0	4	24	14	50	0	.362	.414
	Iowa (PCL)	AAA	.200	1	5	0	1	0	0	0	1	0	1	0	.200	.200
MINOR LEAGUE TOTALS			.278	259	877	115	244	44	2	16	109	62	185	3	.341	.388

6 KEVIN HART, RHP

BORN: Dec. 29, 1982. **B-T:** R-R. **HT.:** 6-4. **WT.:** 220. **DRAFTED:** Maryland, 2004 (11th round). **SIGNED BY:** Ty Brown (Orioles).

Hart floundered in the Orioles system before joining the Cubs in a December 2006 trade for Freddie Bynum. Once Double-A Tennessee pitching coach Dennis Lewellyn taught Hart a cut fastball, he shot to the majors and finished 2007 on Chicago's playoff roster. He wasn't as effective in the big leagues last season. Though the Cubs used Hart in a variety of roles in Triple-A, he's just plain nasty as a reliever. Coming out of the bullpen, he can blow hitters away with 94-96 mph fastballs and chew up their bats with cutters. He's tough to hit when he has his confidence and goes after batters. His arm is resilient, allowing him to pitch multiple innings at a time or on consecutive days. When major leaguers got the better of Hart last April, he started nibbling instead of challenging them. His control deteriorated, as did manager Lou Piniella's trust in him. Hart's curveball and changeup can throw hitters off balance but grade as fringe average. The Cubs have determined that Hart's future is as a reliever. He can make the big league bullpen with a good spring, and doing so would make it easier for Chicago to develop Jeff Samardzija as a starter. The Padres asked for Hart during the Jake Peavy trade talks in December.

Year	Club (League)	Class	W	L	ERA	G	GS	CG	SV	IP	H	R	ER	HR	BB	SO	AVG
2004	Aberdeen (NYP)	SS	3	0	3.77	9	0	0	1	14	10	7	6	0	7	16	.189
	Delmarva (SAL)	LoA	2	0	3.77	4	2	0	0	14	13	6	6	0	5	16	.232
2005	Delmarva (SAL)	LoA	9	8	4.55	28	28	0	0	152	170	101	77	9	54	164	.278
2006	Frederick (CAR)	HiA	6	11	4.61	28	27	0	0	148	149	97	76	18	65	122	.258
2007	Iowa (PCL)	AAA	4	1	3.54	9	8	1	0	56	56	23	22	6	23	39	.271
	Tennessee (SL)	AA	8	5	4.24	18	17	0	0	102	100	59	48	13	27	92	.255
	Chicago (NL)	MAJ	0	0	0.82	8	0	0	0	11	7	1	1	0	4	13	.189

Year	Club (League)	Class	W	L	ERA	G	GS	CG	SV	IP	H	R	ER	HR	BB	SO	AVG
2008	Tennessee (SL)	AA	0	0	3.00	1	1	0	0	3	2	1	1	0	2	3	.200
	Iowa (PCL)	AAA	4	2	2.81	26	10	0	5	58	38	19	18	3	20	63	.187
	Chicago (NL)	MAJ	2	2	6.51	21	0	0	0	28	39	24	20	2	18	23	.325
MINOR LEAGUE TOTALS			36	27	4.17	123	93	1	6	548	538	313	254	49	203	515	.255
MAJOR LEAGUE TOTALS			2	2	4.89	29	0	0	0	39	46	25	21	2	22	36	.293

7 STARLIN CASTRO, SS/2B

BORN: March 24, 1990. **B-T:** R-R. **HT.:** 6-1. **WT.:** 160. **SIGNED:** Dominican Republic, 2006. **SIGNED BY:** Jose Serra.

The Rookie-level Arizona League Cubs had three legitimate shortstop prospects last summer in Castro, fellow Dominican Junior Lake and $500,000 bonus baby Logan Watkins. Castro and Lake shared shortstop and moved around the infield, while Watkins played second base and left field. Castro flashes an interesting package of tools. He has a good approach at the plate and isn't overmatched by breaking balls. His hands and wrists work well, giving him some power. He has average speed with the potential for more. At shortstop, he has plus range, steady hands and a solid arm with good accuracy. He displays fine instincts at the plate and in the field. Carrying just 160 pounds on his 6-foot-1 frame, Castro needs to get stronger. Once he does, he could have close to average power and plus speed. He's still learning how to steal bases after getting caught five times in 11 tries last season. If everything comes together for Castro, the Cubs think he can become their first all-star shortstop since Shawon Dunston in 1990. Figuring out how to get time at shortstop for Castro, Lake, Watkins and 2008 supplemental first-rounder Ryan Flaherty poses a dilemma. Chicago will make sure Castro plays regularly there in 2009, most likely at Boise.

Year	Club (League)	Class	AVG	G	AB	R	H	2B	3B	HR	RBI	BB	SO	SB	OBP	SLG
2007	Cubs (DSL)	R	.299	60	221	47	66	6	2	2	31	23	24	13	.371	.371
2008	Cubs (AZL)	R	.311	51	196	33	61	11	5	3	22	14	33	6	.364	.464
MINOR LEAGUE TOTALS			.305	111	417	80	127	17	7	5	53	37	57	19	.368	.415

8 RYAN FLAHERTY, SS

BORN: July 27, 1986. **B-T:** L-R. **HT.:** 6-3. **WT.:** 200. **DRAFTED:** Vanderbilt, 2008 (1st round supplemental). **SIGNED BY:** Antonio Grissom.

Flaherty batted cleanup behind No. 2 overall pick Pedro Alvarez (Pirates) at Vanderbilt, where he set a school record with a 38-game hitting streak. Drafted 39 picks after Alvarez in June, Flaherty signed for $1.5 million and earned Northwest League all-star honors in his debut. His father Ed has won two national championships as the head coach at NCAA Division III Southern Maine. Flaherty's sweet lefthanded swing and his hand-eye coordination make him a consistent hitter, and he should develop at least average power as he fills out his lanky frame. He's a solid athlete, featuring average speed and a strong arm. His makeup and instincts are top notch. Scouts don't believe Flaherty has the range to play shortstop in the majors, though the Cubs caution not to bet against his desire. Usually a dependable fielder, he made 16 errors in 52 pro games. He profiles well at third base, though Aramis Ramirez and Josh Vitters would loom as two huge obstacles should Flaherty move there. He can get pull-conscious and expand his strike zone when he's thinking of home runs, and he's better off just letting his power come naturally. Chicago has a glut of shortstop prospects at the lower levels of the system, but remains committed to playing Flaherty there for now. As the oldest and most advanced hitter of that group, he could jump to high Class A to help lessen the logjam.

Year	Club (League)	Class	AVG	G	AB	R	H	2B	3B	HR	RBI	BB	SO	SB	OBP	SLG
2008	Boise (NWL)	SS	.297	56	219	39	65	19	2	8	26	24	51	4	.369	.511
MINOR LEAGUE TOTALS			.297	56	219	39	65	19	2	8	26	24	51	4	.369	.511

9 JAY JACKSON, RHP

BORN: Oct. 27, 1987. **B-T:** R-R. **HT.:** 6-1. **WT.:** 195. **DRAFTED:** Furman, 2008 (9th round). **SIGNED BY:** Antonio Grissom.

The Cubs sought athletic pitchers in the 2008 draft, and Jackson, a two-way star at Furman, fit the bill. He already has blown away expectations for a ninth-round pick since signing for $90,000. He finished his first pro summer in high Class A, where he allowed three runs in five outings, including a victorious playoff start as Daytona won the Florida State League title. Jackson has the chance to have four average-or-better pitches. His two best weapons are a 90-93 mph fastball that reaches 95, and a mid-80s slider with hard bite. He also has an average 75-78 mph curveball and a feel for a changeup. He works quickly and confidently, challenging hitters by pounding the strike zone. Jackson's control is ahead of his command, and his next step will be to refine his ability to locate his pitches within the strike zone. He's not especially tall, so he has to stay on top of his pitches to work in the bottom of the zone. He may not have much projection remaining, but he's not lacking for stuff. In a system short on legitimate starting pitchers, Jackson already has moved near the top of the depth chart. He'll begin 2009 no lower than high Class A and could advance to Double-A before season's end.

Year	Club (League)	Class	W	L	ERA	G	GS	CG	SV	IP	H	R	ER	HR	BB	SO	AVG
2008	Boise (NWL)	SS	0	0	5.00	3	1	0	0	9	7	5	5	1	1	14	.212
	Peoria (MWL)	LoA	2	2	3.00	6	1	0	0	24	22	8	8	3	5	37	.253
	Daytona (FSL)	HiA	2	0	1.59	4	3	0	0	17	11	4	3	0	7	21	.183
MINOR LEAGUE TOTALS			4	2	2.88	13	5	0	0	50	40	17	16	4	13	72	.222

10 HAK-JU LEE, SS

BORN: Nov. 4, 1990. **B-T:** L-R. **HT.:** 6-2. **WT.:** 175. **SIGNED:** Korea, 2008. **SIGNED BY:** Paul Weaver/Steve Wilson.

Background: Lee was the prize among the Cubs' 2008 international signees, agreeing to a $725,000 bonus in June. Chicago landed two more Koreans late in the summer, righthander Su-Min Jung ($510,000) and catcher Jae-Hoon Ha ($225,000). Lee reported to MLB's Australian Baseball Academy to prepare for coming to the United States. He injured his elbow, requiring Tommy John surgery. With his array of tools, Lee has a chance to be a special shortstop. He's a lefthanded hitter who stays inside the ball well and uses the whole field. He may even have some power once he fills out his exceedingly skinny frame. He has the plus-plus speed to create havoc once he reaches base. He had a strong arm before he got hurt, and he exhibits fluid actions at shortstop. The Tommy John surgery actually isn't a major setback, because he's still just 18 and the Cubs expect him to be ready for spring training. Bigger concerns are his need to add strength and adapt to a new culture. He has a reputation for being a bit of a hot dog. One international scout who wasn't a huge fan thought he was a slap hitter whose hands and arm were questionable for a shortstop. Lee could be the first Korean middle infielder to reach the big leagues. Because he has no pro experience and the Cubs have several lower-level shortstop prospects, he'll head to the Arizona League in June.

Year	Club (League)	Class	AVG	G	AB	R	H	2B	3B	HR	RBI	BB	SO	SB	OBP	SLG
2008	Did Not Play—Injured															

11 STEVE CLEVENGER, C/1B

BORN: April 5, 1986. **B-T:** L-R. **HT.:** 6-0. **WT.:** 195. **DRAFTED:** Chipola (Fla.) JC, 2006 (7th round). **SIGNED BY:** Keith Stohr.

Clevenger hoped to transfer to Texas after hitting .347 as a freshman at Southeastern Louisiana, but a problem with his credits landed him at Chipola (Fla.) JC instead—and made him draft-eligible a year earlier than planned. The Cubs liked his bat and signed him for $150,000 as a seventh-rounder in 2006. A shortstop in college, he lacked the speed for the middle infield, so Chicago exposed him to catching during instructional league in the fall of 2006. He got a little time behind the plate in 2007 before catcher became his primary position last season. Clevenger has the tools necessary to become a big league regular. He has a gift for making contact, spraying line drives to all fields. The Cubs believe his offense will pick up once his body gets accustomed to catching. Once he strengthens his legs so they can contribute more to his swing, some scouts think he could hit 30 doubles and 10-15 homers annually as an everyday player. Clevenger made a lot of progress with his defense in 2008. He has an above-average arm and threw out 30 percent of basestealers last year. Technically, he's a better receiver right now than Welington Castillo, who has concentration lapses. Clevenger still needs to develop more defensively, but he's definitely on the right track. His speed, while below-average, isn't bad for a catcher. With all-star Geovany Soto in Chicago, the Cubs aren't in need of a regular backstop. Clevenger may be better suited than Castillo to complement Soto because he hits lefthanded and has the versatility to play first base and other positions in a pinch. He's ready to catch regularly in Double-A this year, but Castillo may be headed back to Tennessee as well.

Year	Club (League)	Class	AVG	G	AB	R	H	2B	3B	HR	RBI	BB	SO	SB	OBP	SLG
2006	Boise (NWL)	SS	.286	63	220	35	63	8	1	2	21	26	28	5	.363	.359
2007	Boise (NWL)	SS	.373	22	83	10	31	9	0	0	18	4	6	0	.398	.482
	Daytona (FSL)	HiA	.323	43	164	21	53	8	1	2	24	13	5	0	.368	.421
2008	Tennessee (SL)	AA	.247	29	89	5	22	5	1	1	15	10	10	0	.314	.360
	Daytona (FSL)	HiA	.313	84	284	36	89	20	0	2	39	39	41	7	.393	.405
MINOR LEAGUE TOTALS			.307	241	840	107	258	50	3	7	117	92	90	12	.372	.399

12 MICAH HOFFPAUIR, 1B/OF

BORN: March 1, 1980. **B-T:** L-L. **HT.:** 6-3. **WT.:** 215. **DRAFTED:** Lamar, 2002 (13th round). **SIGNED BY:** Steve Riha.

After missing the last three weeks of 2006 with a left knee injury, Hoffpauir had been selected to play in the

Triple-A all-star game and was on the verge of his first big league callup in 2007 when he tore cartilage in his right knee. He recovered from surgery to correct that problem, only to strain his left oblique in big league camp last spring. Once he got back on the diamond in May, Hoffpauir took out his frustration on pitchers. The Cubs 2008 minor league player of the year, he became the fifth player in modern PCL history to hit four homers in one game, finishing with 25 homers and 100 RBIs in just 71 Triple-A contests. He also hit well in four trips to Chicago, putting himself in the team's plans for 2009. Hoffpauir has power to all fields and looks to hit mistakes early in the count before toning his swing down if he gets two strikes. He did a better job of using the opposite field last season than he had in the past. He could put up Lyle Overbay-type numbers if he got the chance to play every day. Managers rated Hoffpauir the best defensive first baseman in the PCL, and he shows soft hands and a solid arm for the position. He also saw time on the outfield corners in 2008, and the consensus is that his speed, range and arm are below-average but he could fill in there for short stints. He's not going to displace Derrek Lee as the Cubs' first baseman, but he could fill Daryle Ward's role as a lefty bat off the bench while offering much more defensive ability than Ward. Chicago spent the offseason looking for a lefthanded-hitting right fielder, and Hoffpauir is a dark horse in that competition.

Year	Club (League)	Class	AVG	G	AB	R	H	2B	3B	HR	RBI	BB	SO	SB	OBP	SLG
2002	Boise (NWL)	SS	.301	60	216	35	65	10	3	10	41	7	35	2	.330	.514
2003	Daytona (FSL)	HiA	.254	124	477	59	121	33	2	8	58	44	96	2	.323	.382
2004	West Tenn (SL)	AA	.306	94	340	58	104	20	6	11	75	27	61	1	.347	.497
	Iowa (PCL)	AAA	.333	1	3	0	1	1	0	0	1	1	0	0	.500	.667
2005	West Tenn (SL)	AA	.160	7	25	1	4	0	0	1	2	0	6	0	.160	.280
	Iowa (PCL)	AAA	.268	119	392	48	105	14	3	3	47	38	59	2	.334	.342
2006	West Tenn (SL)	AA	.268	40	138	28	37	11	2	10	31	20	29	0	.362	.594
	Iowa (PCL)	AAA	.267	77	255	34	68	9	1	12	49	33	59	1	.345	.451
2007	Iowa (PCL)	AAA	.319	82	310	56	99	24	0	16	73	24	34	2	.365	.552
2008	Iowa (PCL)	AAA	.362	71	290	63	105	34	2	25	100	17	46	2	.393	.752
	Chicago (NL)	MAJ	.342	33	73	14	25	8	0	2	8	6	24	1	.400	.534
MINOR LEAGUE TOTALS			.290	675	2446	382	709	156	19	96	477	211	425	12	.346	.487
MAJOR LEAGUE TOTALS			.342	33	73	14	25	8	0	2	8	6	24	1	.400	.534

13 BRANDON GUYER, OF

BORN: Jan. 28, 1986. **B-T:** R-R. **HT.:** 6-1. **WT.:** 216. **DRAFTED:** Virginia, 2007 (5th round). **SIGNED BY:** Billy Swoope.

The best athlete in the system, Guyer needed some time before he was able to truly show off his tools in pro ball. He dislocated his left shoulder in a home-plate collision during an NCAA regional game shortly before the Cubs made him a fifth-round pick in 2007. Doctors recommended rehab rather than surgery, and he played in pain during his pro debut before having an operation in the offseason. While working his way back into shape during spring training, he came down with a stress fracture in his right elbow. Guyer finally joined Peoria in mid-May, and he showed what he can do once he was 100 percent in mid-June. Guyer has plus-plus speed and raw power. He homered and fell a double shy of hitting for the cycle when Peoria hosted a Midwest League game at Wrigley Field on July 29. Guyer will need to make some adjustments at the plate, such as improving his pitch recognition, plate discipline and ability to handle breaking balls. He brings a football mentality to the ballpark, a remnant of his days as an all-state running back and linebacker for his Virginia high school. That aggressiveness helps him on the basepaths, where he has the quickness to steal bases in the big leagues. Though Guyer played mostly left field last year to reduce the strain on his shoulder and elbow, he has the range to play center and an adequate arm for the position. If everything comes together for him, he could be a stronger version of Aaron Rowand. The Cubs won't be surprised if Guyer has a breakout year and pushes his way to Double-A in 2009, and it's possible that he could begin the season there.

Year	Club (League)	Class	AVG	G	AB	R	H	2B	3B	HR	RBI	BB	SO	SB	OBP	SLG
2007	Cubs (AZL)	R	.222	17	72	10	16	4	1	1	5	5	16	6	.309	.347
	Boise (NWL)	SS	.268	19	71	9	19	1	0	0	14	6	9	5	.346	.282
2008	Peoria (MWL)	LoA	.269	88	327	55	88	27	3	14	38	19	63	22	.331	.498
MINOR LEAGUE TOTALS			.262	124	470	74	123	32	4	15	57	30	88	33	.330	.443

14 JUNIOR LAKE, SS

BORN: March 27, 1990. **B-T:** R-R. **HT.:** 6-3. **WT.:** 175. **SIGNED:** Dominican Republic, 2007. **SIGNED BY:** Jose Serra/Marino Encarnacion.

Part of a shortstop timeshare with Starlin Castro in the Arizona League last summer, Lake lacks Castro's instincts and polish but owns the strongest infield arm in the system. While he spent more time at short than Castro did, the consensus is that Lake is the more likely of the two to switch positions in the future. That won't come for a while, however, because Lake has the ability to stay there. He eats up a lot of ground with his long legs and his arm rates a 65 on the 20-80 scouting scale. The rest of Lake's game is intriguing, too. The ball comes off his bat well and he has a lot of room to add strength to his skinny 6-foot-3 frame, so he could develop plus power. Like many young hitters, he'll have to tighten his strike zone and learn to cope with offspeed pitches. Lake's speed is average out of the box but he's better underway, as evidenced by his six triples and 12 steals in 14 tries last year. The Cubs would like both Castro and Lake to play regularly at shortstop in 2009, though they've yet to figure out how they're going to pull that off. If he has to move to a less challenging position, Lake should have enough bat for second or third base.

Year	Club (League)	Class	AVG	G	AB	R	H	2B	3B	HR	RBI	BB	SO	SB	OBP	SLG
2007	Cubs (DSL)	R	.274	62	223	41	61	16	2	3	30	16	53	9	.341	.404
2008	Cubs (AZL)	R	.286	47	168	24	48	4	6	2	23	13	42	12	.335	.417
MINOR LEAGUE TOTALS			.279	109	391	65	109	20	8	5	53	29	95	21	.339	.409

15 JOVAN ROSA, 3B/1B

BORN: Oct. 26, 1987. **B-T:** R-R. **HT.:** 6-3. **WT.:** 210. **DRAFTED:** Lake City (Fla.) CC, D/F 2006 (22nd round). **SIGNED BY:** Keith Stohr.

The Cubs not only have a logjam at shortstop at the lower levels of the system, but they also have a similar situation at third base. Josh Vitters, Rosa and Marquez Smith all were ready to start 2008 in low Class A, and the problem solved itself when Vitters went down with a hand injury and Rosa shifted over to first base until Smith got promoted in July. Signed for $180,000 as part of the final class of draft-and-follows in May 2007, Rosa showed improved bat speed and strength in his first full pro season. His Midwest League-leading 42 doubles hint at his power potential, with expectations that some of them will turn into homers down the road. Rosa's future will be brighter if he can stick at third base, though that remains to be seen. He has below-average speed and awkward footwork at the hot corner, where he committed 21 errors in just 71 games last year. His arm is strong, but his range and hands are a little shaky. Rosa does have some athleticism, so he has the potential to improve through hard work. He'll be the everyday third baseman at Daytona this year.

Year	Club (League)	Class	AVG	G	AB	R	H	2B	3B	HR	RBI	BB	SO	SB	OBP	SLG
2007	Cubs (AZL)	R	.340	39	144	25	49	7	1	3	26	10	34	0	.389	.465
	Boise (NWL)	SS	.250	14	48	3	12	0	0	0	5	3	12	0	.321	.250
2008	Peoria (MWL)	LoA	.293	128	481	58	141	43	4	7	81	40	127	3	.353	.443
MINOR LEAGUE TOTALS			.300	181	673	86	202	50	5	10	112	53	173	3	.358	.434

16 TYLER COLVIN, OF

BORN: Sept. 5, 1985. **B-T:** L-L. **HT.:** 6-3. **WT.:** 190. **DRAFTED:** Clemson, 2006 (1st round). **SIGNED BY:** Antonio Grissom.

The first draft pick of scouting director Tim Wilken's tenure with the Cubs, Colvin signed for $1.475 million as the 13th overall choice in 2006. Chicago saw him as a budding Steve Finley or Shawn Green in his first two pro seasons, but Colvin hit the wall hard in Double-A last season. A bum elbow may have been partially to blame, as he played in pain but without complaint before having Tommy John surgery in the offseason. Scouts with others clubs think his problems go beyond his elbow, as he cuts himself off in his swing and employs a dead-pull approach that results in too many rolled-over grounders. Colvin does have the bat speed, loft and strength to hit 20 or more homers on an annual basis. He boosted his walk total from 15 in 2007 to 44 last year, though more discipline is needed. He showed average or better tools across the board in previous seasons, but they were more fringy in 2008. His speed was down a bit, and that can't be attributed to his elbow. The Cubs now concede that he'll play on an outfield corner rather than in center, and if his arm bounces back he should be able to handle right field. Colvin was bothered by shoulder problems at the end of 2007, and he'll probably miss the first month of the 2009 season before returning to Double-A. Chicago would love for him to stay healthy and start making more progress, because it's looking for a lefty-hitting right fielder.

Year	Club (League)	Class	AVG	G	AB	R	H	2B	3B	HR	RBI	BB	SO	SB	OBP	SLG
2006	Boise (NWL)	SS	.268	64	265	50	71	12	6	11	53	17	55	12	.313	.483
2007	Daytona (FSL)	HiA	.306	63	245	38	75	24	3	7	50	10	47	10	.336	.514
	Tennessee (SL)	AA	.291	62	247	34	72	11	2	9	31	5	54	7	.313	.462
2008	Tennessee (SL)	AA	.256	137	540	68	138	27	11	14	80	44	101	7	.312	.424
MINOR LEAGUE TOTALS			.274	326	1297	190	356	74	22	41	214	76	257	36	.316	.460

17 MARCOS MATEO, RHP

BORN: April 18, 1984. **B-T:** R-R. **HT.:** 6-1. **WT.:** 160. **SIGNED:** Dominican Republic, 2004. **SIGNED BY:** Johnny Almaraz (Reds).

The Cubs have done a fine job of acquiring promising arms in minor trades, grabbing Jose Ceda (for Todd Walker), Kevin Hart (for Freddie Bynum), Jose Ascanio (for Will Ohman and Omar Infante) and Justin Berg (for Matt Lawton) in recent years. When Chicago designated Buck Coats for assignment in August 2007, it spun him off to the Reds for Mateo, whose cousin Juan used to pitch for the Cubs. Chicago used Mateo mostly as a starter in his first full season in the organization to give him innings to develop. Pitching coordinator Mark

Riggins and Daytona pitching coach David Rosario worked diligently to smooth out what had been a herky-jerky delivery. Mateo is destined for the bullpen and is far from consistent, but he does have one of the most electric arms in the system. When he's fresh, his fastball ranges from 92-97 mph yet isn't necessarily his best pitch. At the time of the trade, Mateo had just started to flash an average breaking ball, and now he can run his hard slider up to 91 mph with unhittable tilt at times. He only dabbles with a changeup and employs a full-speed-ahead approach, but that'll be less of an issue when he eventually becomes a full-time reliever. Added to the 40-man roster in November, Mateo will advance to Double-A and may continue to work as a starter to give him more time on the mound.

Year	Club (League)	Class	W	L	ERA	G	GS	CG	SV	IP	H	R	ER	HR	BB	SO	AVG
2004	Reds (DSL)	R	4	2	2.61	15	8	1	0	69	62	25	20	2	17	57	.238
2005	Reds (GCL)	R	2	3	4.30	13	4	0	0	44	54	26	21	2	10	23	.309
2006	Billings (PIO)	R	5	1	3.20	18	0	0	1	45	43	17	16	2	20	30	.262
2007	Dayton (MWL)	LoA	2	4	3.50	41	0	0	6	72	68	29	28	2	24	63	.260
2008	Peoria (MWL)	LoA	1	0	1.20	8	0	0	1	15	4	3	2	1	7	20	.085
	Daytona (FSL)	HiA	4	3	3.57	25	16	0	0	88	87	42	35	6	29	65	.257
MINOR LEAGUE TOTALS			18	13	3.29	120	28	1	8	333	318	142	122	15	107	258	.255

18 CHRIS CARPENTER, RHP

BORN: Dec. 26, 1985. **B-T:** R-R. **HT.:** 6-4. **WT.:** 215. **DRAFTED:** Kent State, 2008 (3rd round). **SIGNED BY:** Lucas McKnight.

Carpenter was the highest-drafted high school pitcher in the 2004 draft to opt for college, turning down the Tigers out of the seventh round. He blew out his elbow throwing a 93 mph fastball as a freshman at Kent State, leading to Tommy John surgery in 2005 and a second operation to clean out scar tissue in 2006. As a draft-eligible sophomore in 2007, he made a run at the first round before fading late and dropping to the Yankees in the 18th round. When he left the Cape Cod League with a tired arm, New York lost interest in signing him. The Cubs got him with a third-round pick and a $385,000 bonus in 2008, and Carpenter could be a bargain if he can stay on the mound. He consistently works at 92-95 mph and touches 97 with his fastball, and he has tightened up his hard curveball over the last year. His changeup has shown improvement as well, though it's not reliable as his two main pitches. Carpenter struggled to harness his stuff at times in college, and he did so in his pro debut. He has a big, strong frame that enables him to throw downhill and should help in terms of durability. The Cubs may send him to Daytona to keep him in warm weather at the start of the 2009 season. If he can stay healthy, Carpenter will shoot up this list and through the minor leagues.

Year	Club (League)	Class	W	L	ERA	G	GS	CG	SV	IP	H	R	ER	HR	BB	SO	AVG
2008	Cubs (AZL)	R	0	0	18.00	1	1	0	0	1	2	2	2	0	1	1	.500
	Boise (NWL)	SS	4	2	4.22	10	6	0	0	32	32	21	15	2	22	24	.258
MINOR LEAGUE TOTALS			4	2	4.64	11	7	0	0	33	34	23	17	2	23	25	.266

19 DARWIN BARNEY, SS

BORN: Nov. 8, 1985. **B-T:** R-R. **HT.:** 5-10. **WT.:** 170. **DRAFTED:** Oregon State, 2007 (4th round). **SIGNED BY:** John Bartsch.

Winning follows Barney, who was a catalyst for back-to-back College World Series titles at Oregon State in 2006-07 and a key part of a Florida State League championship in his first full pro season. His constant energy and his knack for making things happen are more impressive than any of his individual tools. Though his arm and range are just average, he's the best defensive infielder in the system, thanks to his instincts, ability to read balls off the bat, fast hands and quick release. When they signed him, the Cubs thought Barney undercut too many pitches at the plate. They solved that problem when Daytona hitting coach Richie Zisk handed him a 35-ounce bat last June. The change didn't transform him into Derek Jeter, but Barney did start hitting more liners and hard grounders and using the opposite field more. He batted .287 over the final two months, .407 in the FSL playoffs and .302 in the Arizona Fall League. He still offers only modest power, and while he handles the bat well, he's going to bat in the bottom of a big league order unless he starts drawing more walks. Barney is somewhat reminiscent of Ryan Theriot, another former CWS champion made good, but he doesn't have Theriot's speed. Barney will advance to Double-A this season.

Year	Club (League)	Class	AVG	G	AB	R	H	2B	3B	HR	RBI	BB	SO	SB	OBP	SLG
2007	Cubs (AZL)	R	.444	5	18	6	8	3	0	0	2	4	0	0	.545	.611
	Peoria (MWL)	LoA	.273	44	176	27	48	9	3	2	21	11	22	5	.323	.392
2008	Daytona (FSL)	HiA	.262	123	409	46	107	22	4	3	51	38	58	8	.325	.357
MINOR LEAGUE TOTALS			.270	172	603	79	163	34	7	5	74	53	80	13	.332	.375

20 MARQUEZ SMITH, 3B/2B

BORN: March 20, 1985. **B-T:** R-R. **HT.:** 5-10. **WT.:** 200. **DRAFTED:** Clemson, 2007 (8th round). **SIGNED BY:** Antonio Grissom.

A teammate of Tyler Colvin's at Clemson, Smith turned down the Cubs as a 35th-round pick in 2006. He signed for $30,000 when Chicago drafted him in the eighth round the following year. Smith turned in a solid first full pro season in 2008 despite being nagged by hamstring and finger injuries much of the time. He has quick wrists and a reasonably disciplined approach, allowing him to hit for a decent average with some power. There's more life and athleticism in his squatty frame than might be apparent at first glance. Though Smith is a slightly below-average runner, he's a surprisingly versatile defender with a strong arm. Hawaii Winter Baseball named him its defensive player of the year for his work at third base for the league champion Waikiki BeachBoys, and he also gets the job done at second base. Shortstop would be a stretch because Smith wouldn't haven enough range, but there's no reason he couldn't play the outfield corners. With his build, bat and arm, he'd be an intriguing candidate for a catching conversion. Smith will move up to Double-A in 2009. There may not be a big league starting job in his future, but he could provide value as a utilityman with pop.

Year	Club (League)	Class	AVG	G	AB	R	H	2B	3B	HR	RBI	BB	SO	SB	OBP	SLG
2007	Boise (NWL)	SS	.275	54	193	37	53	11	1	5	41	37	40	1	.381	.420
	Peoria (MWL)	LoA	.297	18	64	13	19	3	0	3	14	7	8	0	.375	.484
2008	Peoria (MWL)	LoA	.295	84	315	55	93	17	4	14	49	35	65	1	.370	.508
	Daytona (FSL)	HiA	.237	38	131	16	31	10	1	3	17	12	29	0	.315	.397
MINOR LEAGUE TOTALS			.279	194	703	121	196	41	6	25	121	91	142	2	.364	.461

21 MITCH ATKINS, RHP

BORN: Oct. 1, 1985. **B-T:** R-R. **HT.:** 6-3. **WT.:** 225. **DRAFTED:** HS—McLeansville, N.C., 2004 (7th round). **SIGNED BY:** Billy Swoope.

Atkins' makeup is more impressive than his arsenal, but that didn't stop him from winning 17 games—one off the minor league lead—and the Cubs' minor league pitcher of the year award in 2008. His best pitch is an 89-92 mph fastball with average sink; the fastball is most notable for Atkins' ability to locate it. Atkins commands his entire repertoire, which also consists of a cutter, curveball and changeup. His curve has a chance to develop into a solid-average pitch. Atkins has an innate feel for pitching and isn't afraid to let hitters put the ball in play. He has little margin for error and gave up 25 homers last season, but he doesn't let anything faze him. A case in point came Aug. 3 against Salt Lake. Three of the first four batters hit rockets off Atkins, who then adjusted so well that he retired the final 16 batters he faced, 11 via strikeouts. Strong and durable, he has yet to miss a minor league start. Chicago added him to its 40-man roster over the winter and Atkins will audition for a middle-relief job in big league camp. It wouldn't surprise the Cubs if he eventually carved out a larger role for himself.

Year	Club (League)	Class	W	L	ERA	G	GS	CG	SV	IP	H	R	ER	HR	BB	SO	AVG
2004	Cubs (AZL)	R	2	2	7.89	10	8	0	0	30	42	33	26	0	14	20	.333
2005	Boise (NWL)	SS	3	6	5.03	15	15	0	0	73	85	45	41	8	30	59	.291
2006	Peoria (MWL)	LoA	13	4	2.41	25	25	0	0	138	110	47	37	10	53	127	.217
2007	Daytona (FSL)	HiA	8	7	3.13	20	20	1	0	115	99	51	40	14	31	88	.235
	Tennessee (SL)	AA	1	1	5.54	7	4	0	0	26	30	18	16	5	11	18	.288
2008	Tennessee (SL)	AA	9	6	3.76	18	18	0	0	110	107	58	46	14	27	88	.250
	Iowa (PCL)	AAA	8	1	4.47	10	10	0	0	54	48	29	27	11	23	44	.236
MINOR LEAGUE TOTALS			44	27	3.84	105	100	1	0	547	521	281	233	62	189	444	.250

22 ESMAILIN CARIDAD, RHP

BORN: Oct. 28, 1985. **B-T:** R-R. **HT.:** 5-10. **WT.:** 193. **SIGNED:** Dominican Republic, 2007. **SIGNED BY:** Jose Serra.

Caridad originally turned pro with Japan's Hiroshima Carp. He made two brief appearances in the Japanese majors in 2007 and spent most of that year at the Carp's academy in the Dominican, where Cubs scout Jose Serra spotted him. A technicality made Caridad a free agent, and Chicago won him over with a $175,000 bonus, an invitation to big league camp and a visit from Jim Hendry during the general manager's trip to the Cubs' Dominican base. Caridad has a quick arm and one of the better fastballs in the system, a low-90s heater that tops out at 96 mph. It induces more groundouts than strikeouts because it flattens out at times and he lacks deception in his delivery. On the other hand, his smooth mechanics give him terrific control. The rest of Caridad's arsenal is ordinary: an average three-quarters breaking ball and a fringy changeup with some splitter action. Some club officials project Caridad as a starter, but it's more likely that his ultimate role will be as a reliever or swingman. After a strong performance in the Arizona Fall League, he's ready for Triple-A and could get his first taste of the big leagues in 2009.

Year	Club (League)	Class	W	L	ERA	G	GS	CG	SV	IP	H	R	ER	HR	BB	SO	AVG
2008	Daytona (FSL)	HiA	6	4	4.41	14	13	0	0	69	64	35	34	3	17	38	.252
	Tennessee (SL)	AA	7	3	3.16	14	14	0	0	83	67	31	29	15	21	50	.218
MINOR LEAGUE TOTALS			13	7	3.73	28	27	0	0	152	131	66	63	18	38	88	.234

23 TONY THOMAS, 2B

BORN: July 10, 1986. **B-T:** R-R. **HT.:** 5-10. **WT.:** 185. **DRAFTED:** Florida State, 2007 (3rd round). **SIGNED BY:** Rolando Pino.

The Cubs made Thomas a third-round pick in 2007 after he batted .430 at Florida State and led NCAA Division I in runs (91), doubles (33) and total bases (189). He entered pro ball with a good-hit, no-field reputation and lived up to it in his debut. Some club officials considered him a better pure hitter than No. 3 overall pick Josh Vitters. But after skipping a level and jumping to high Class A in 2008, Thomas did an about-face. He got off to a good start when pitchers busted him inside and he started to turn on balls, but he didn't adjust well when they started pitching him on the outer half. On the other hand, he worked hard on his defense, showed improved range and arm strength and led Florida State League second basemen with a .989 fielding percentage. The Cubs wonder whether he focused so much on his glove that it took away from his bat. Thomas righted himself in the postseason, batting a league-best .483 to win MVP honors as Daytona won the FSL title. He has quick hands, good strength for his size and an aggressive swing. If he can tighten his strike zone and use the opposite field more, he can get back to hitting for a high average with a healthy amount of doubles. He's an average runner who can steal bases thanks to his savvy. His hands and footwork still leave something to be desired at second base, and he doesn't have natural defensive instincts. Chicago wants to promote Thomas and double-play partner Darwin Barney as a tandem, so they'll move up to Double-A together this year.

Year	Club (League)	Class	AVG	G	AB	R	H	2B	3B	HR	RBI	BB	SO	SB	OBP	SLG
2007	Cubs (AZL)	R	.176	5	17	7	3	0	2	0	6	2	5	0	.286	.412
	Boise (NWL)	SS	.308	46	182	44	56	12	8	5	33	25	41	28	.404	.544
2008	Daytona (FSL)	HiA	.266	113	443	62	118	30	4	7	43	34	113	22	.320	.400
MINOR LEAGUE TOTALS			.276	164	642	113	177	42	14	12	82	61	159	50	.344	.441

24 JAKE FOX, 1B/OF

BORN: July 20, 1982. **B-T:** R-R. **HT.:** 6-0. **WT.:** 210. **DRAFTED:** Michigan, 2003 (3rd round). **SIGNED BY:** Stan Zielinski.

There are scouts who swear that Fox's plus power would produce 25 homers if he got the chance to play every day in the majors. The problem is that those longballs would come with a low batting average, plenty of strikeouts and absolutely no defensive ability. Fox has accumulated 14 big league at-bats in his six seasons in the organization, and he hurt his cause by not performing in Triple-A to start 2008. That led to a demotion in early May, after which he led the Southern League in slugging (.580). Fox can crush any fastball out of any park, in part because he sits on fastballs and sells out for power every time. He can't handle breaking balls, won't work counts and rarely listens to batting coaches. Power is Fox's only tool, and one scout described his defense as "a notch above horrific." Drafted as a catcher, he's now a first baseman/corner outfielder with substandard speed, range, hands and arm strength. The best-case scenario is for Fox to have a career similar to that of Ryan Garko, another former college catcher who's dangerous with both a bat and a glove. Coming off a big winter in the Dominican League, Fox will take another crack at Triple-A in 2009. The Cubs already have a righthanded-hitting first baseman in Derrek Lee, so Fox really needs a trade to an American League club.

Year	Club (League)	Class	AVG	G	AB	R	H	2B	3B	HR	RBI	BB	SO	SB	OBP	SLG
2003	Cubs (AZL)	R	.240	15	50	4	12	5	0	1	6	5	14	0	.321	.400
	Lansing (MWL)	LoA	.260	29	100	13	26	8	0	5	12	8	19	0	.330	.490
2004	Lansing (MWL)	LoA	.287	97	366	49	105	19	3	14	55	17	75	2	.331	.470
2005	Daytona (FSL)	HiA	.281	83	270	37	76	20	0	9	40	26	48	5	.357	.456
2006	Daytona (FSL)	HiA	.313	66	249	45	78	15	1	16	61	27	49	4	.383	.574
	West Tenn (SL)	AA	.269	55	193	20	52	17	0	5	25	9	44	0	.304	.435
2007	Tennessee (SL)	AA	.284	91	359	60	102	23	1	18	60	17	72	6	.327	.504
	Chicago (NL)	MAJ	.143	7	14	3	2	2	0	0	1	1	2	0	.200	.286
	Iowa (PCL)	AAA	.283	25	99	18	28	7	0	6	19	5	23	2	.343	.535
2008	Iowa (PCL)	AAA	.222	29	117	17	26	10	1	6	26	2	31	3	.242	.479
	Tennessee (SL)	AA	.307	105	388	76	119	29	1	25	79	46	73	4	.397	.580
MINOR LEAGUE TOTALS			.285	595	2191	339	624	153	7	105	383	162	448	26	.346	.505
MAJOR LEAGUE TOTALS			.143	7	14	3	2	2	0	0	1	1	2	0	.200	.286

25 TY WRIGHT, OF

BORN: Feb. 26, 1985. **B-T:** R-R. **HT.:** 6-0. **WT.:** 185. **DRAFTED:** Oklahoma State, 2007 (7th round). **SIGNED BY:** Brian Milner.

A four-year starter at Oklahoma State, Wright led the Big 12 Conference in hitting (.405) and set a league record with a 35-game hitting streak as a senior in 2007. Signed for $42,000 as a seventh-round pick, he draws comparisons to Reed Johnson, a fellow gamer who solidified the Cubs' outfield last year. Wright showed his grit by playing through a sports hernia for the final two months of the 2008 season. He has a gift for putting the barrel on the ball, making steady line-drive contact. He has gap power and slightly above-average speed, a package that could deliver 25-30 doubles, 12-15 homers and 20 steals per year. Wright has good instincts on the bases and in the outfield, and he's capable of playing all three spots. He stuck mostly to left field last year while slowed by the hernia. Wright's arm strength merits only a 35 on the 20-80 scouting scale, but he gets rid of the ball quickly and runners challenge him at their own risk. He racked up 13 assists in just 90 games last season. One of the most mentally tough players in the system, Wright refuses to let himself fail. He'll continue to get chances to prove himself, and the next step will be Double-A.

Year	Club (League)	Class	AVG	G	AB	R	H	2B	3B	HR	RBI	BB	SO	SB	OBP	SLG
2007	Boise (NWL)	SS	.317	52	189	40	60	12	2	8	44	23	22	6	.408	.529
	Peoria (MWL)	LoA	.284	19	74	5	21	1	0	2	5	5	15	5	.329	.378
2008	Daytona (FSL)	HiA	.300	113	426	60	128	21	1	8	72	41	71	7	.370	.411
MINOR LEAGUE TOTALS			.303	184	689	105	209	34	3	18	121	69	108	18	.377	.440

26 BLAKE PARKER, RHP

BORN: June 19, 1985. **B-T:** R-R. **HT.:** 6-3. **WT.:** 235. **DRAFTED:** Arkansas, 2006 (16th round). **SIGNED BY:** Brian Milner.

Parker played several positions and never hit much as a three-year starter at Arkansas, but the one tool he showed constantly was a strong arm. The Cubs signed him for $30,000 as a 16th-round pick in 2006, and after he hit .224/.325/.367 in his first pro summer, they took his bat away. In two years on the mound, Parker has posted a 2.20 ERA, conquered high Class A and put together a nice three-pitch mix. He has a low-90s sinker that touches 95 mph and often seems to disappear at the plate. He picked up a changeup from Dae-Eun Rhee, who owns the best in the system, when they were Peoria teammates at the beginning of 2008. Parker's changeup shows the makings of becoming a reliable pitch, and his slider is improving as well. Chicago has deployed Parker from the bullpen, where his confidence and mound presence fit nicely. His main needs are to improve his control, command and consistency, and he got extra work in with an assignment to Hawaii Winter Baseball. Parker has developed rapidly and might get a big league look at the end of 2009, which he'll begin in Double-A.

Year	Club (League)	Class	W	L	ERA	G	GS	CG	SV	IP	H	R	ER	HR	BB	SO	AVG
2007	Cubs (AZL)	R	1	0	1.80	11	0	0	2	15	10	6	3	0	3	14	.185
	Boise (NWL)	SS	1	0	3.18	8	0	0	0	11	15	5	4	0	7	10	.319
2008	Peoria (MWL)	LoA	3	0	1.33	23	0	0	3	47	32	8	7	2	18	51	.193
	Iowa (PCL)	AAA	0	0	6.00	2	0	0	0	3	1	2	2	1	2	3	.091
	Daytona (FSL)	HiA	1	2	3.38	20	0	0	9	21	17	8	8	0	10	21	.221
MINOR LEAGUE TOTALS			6	2	2.20	64	0	0	14	98	75	29	24	3	40	99	.211

27 MATT CERDA, C

BORN: June 20, 1990. **B-T:** L-R. **HT.:** 5-9. **WT.:** 165. **DRAFTED:** HS—Oceanside, Calif., 2008 (4th round). **SIGNED BY:** Denny Henderson.

Cerda's hitting ability has been evident since he starred at the 2001 Little League World Series as an 11-year-old. Hall of Famer Tony Gwynn watched him in action on television and said, "That's the sweetest swing I've ever seen from a kid that age." Though Cerda continued to produce at the plate in high school and at showcases, his future defensive home was less obvious because of his below-average size and speed. The Cubs found a solution after signing him for $500,000 as a fourth-rounder last summer—they made him a catcher. Cerda gave up seven passed balls and 16 steals in 13 pro games, but Chicago was pleased with the progress he made in a short time behind the plate. He has the arm, hands and agililty to develop good catch-and-throw skills, though that will take some time. Focusing on his catching responsibilities took away from his hitting in his pro debut, but he did rip a double off Giants prospect Tim Alderson during instructional league. Cerda has quick hands, a discerning eye and a short swing geared for line drives, though he probably won't hit for much power. There are a lot of similarities between him and Steve Clevenger, another pure hitter who made the infielder-to-catcher move. The Cubs believe Cerda is strong enough mentally and as a hitter to possibly handle a jump to low Class A for his first full season. They may also give him some time at second base when he's not behind the plate.

Year	Club (League)	Class	AVG	G	AB	R	H	2B	3B	HR	RBI	BB	SO	SB	OBP	SLG
2008	Cubs (AZL)	R	.253	42	154	29	39	5	1	2	15	21	25	2	.341	.338
MINOR LEAGUE TOTALS			.253	42	154	29	39	5	1	2	15	21	25	2	.341	.338

28 LOGAN WATKINS, 2B

BORN: Aug. 29, 1989. **B-T:** L-R. **HT.:** 5-11. **WT.:** 170. **DRAFTED:** HS—Goddard, Kan., 2008 (21st round). **SIGNED BY:** Brandon Mozley.

The biggest surprise the Cubs pulled in the 2008 draft came when they gave Watkins, a 21st-rounder, a $500,000 bonus. He received some predraft buzz, but not nearly enough to indicate that a team would spend third-round money to lure him away from a Wichita State scholarship. A gifted athlete, he was an all-state quarterback and defensive back for his Kansas high school football team. He swings the bat well and has a disciplined, contact-oriented approach, though he'll need to get much stronger to hit with any authority. Speed is Watkins' most obvious tool, and he might cover more ground at shortstop than Arizona League teammates Starlin Castro and Junior Lake. He played second base and left field, however, while they shared shortstop. Watkins has the range for center field and has a solid arm. The Cubs still haven't figured out what to do with all their young shortstops and where to play Watkins. They may use him at several different positions in Boise this season.

Year	Club (League)	Class	AVG	G	AB	R	H	2B	3B	HR	RBI	BB	SO	SB	OBP	SLG
2008	Cubs (AZL)	R	.325	27	80	15	26	3	0	0	14	20	19	2	.462	.363
MINOR LEAGUE TOTALS			.325	27	80	15	26	3	0	0	14	20	19	2	.462	.363

29 ALEX MAESTRI, RHP

BORN: June 1, 1985. **B-T:** R-R. **HT.:** 6-0. **WT.:** 185. **SIGNED:** Italy, 2006. **SIGNED BY:** Bill Holmberg.

The Cubs spotted Maestri at MLB's inaugural European Baseball Academy in Tirrenia, Italy, in the summer of 2005 and made him the first Italian pitcher ever signed by a major league club. He's a legitimate prospect, not just a curiosity, with surprising stuff and pitchability given his background. Maestri showed a lot of promise as a reliever in 2007, but didn't fare as well when he moved to the rotation in 2008. The Cubs made the move because he has a deep enough repertoire, but the result was diminished stuff, not to mention a tender shoulder that caused him to be shut down in July. His fastball went from 87-90 mph when he signed to 90-94 when he came out of the bullpen in 2007, but it dropped back down to the upper 80s last year. His slider, which is one of the best in the system and devastates righthanders, also wasn't as sharp. Maestri has the potential for an average changeup, and he needs an offspeed pitch to keep hitters honest. He's athletic and repeats his delivery well, allowing him to throw strikes. Chicago will return Maestri to the bullpen in 2009, and it's not inconceivable that he could climb from Double-A to the majors this year.

Year	Club (League)	Class	W	L	ERA	G	GS	CG	SV	IP	H	R	ER	HR	BB	SO	AVG
2006	Boise (NWL)	SS	4	3	3.80	22	0	0	1	43	36	20	18	4	13	35	.232
2007	Peoria (MWL)	LoA	6	3	2.26	48	4	0	12	84	57	24	21	7	15	83	.186
2008	Daytona (FSL)	HiA	5	3	3.69	15	14	0	0	78	72	39	32	5	27	66	.248
	Tennessee (SL)	AA	0	1	6.55	2	2	0	0	11	14	8	8	2	3	10	.318
MINOR LEAGUE TOTALS			15	10	3.30	87	20	0	13	215	179	91	79	18	58	194	.225

30 SU-MIN JUNG, RHP

BORN: April 1, 1990. **B-T:** R-R. **HT.:** 6-2. **WT.:** 190. **SIGNED:** Korea, 2008. **SIGNED BY:** Paul Weaver/Steve Wilson.

Remaining active in Korea, the Cubs signed two more players late last summer, Jung for $510,000 and catcher Jae-Hoon Ha for $225,000. Jung is a product of Busan High, which also spawned big leaguers Shin-Soo Choo and Cha Seung Baek. Jung opened 2008 as Busan's No. 3 pitcher, with Tae Kyeong Ahn (who signed with the Rangers) the ace. While Ahn outperformed him, Jung surpassed him as a prospect. He was pitching at 82-84 mph in March but boosted his fastball to the upper 80s and touched the low 90s by the end of the summer. He has a clean arm action and the room to add strength, so he may have more velocity in him. Jung spins the ball better than most international pitchers and has the makings of a power curveball. He also started to make some progress with a changeup during instructional league. Other clubs considered Jung the equivalent of a late second-rounder or early third-rounder, and the Cubs paid him like one. They'll unveil him in the Arizona League in June.

Year	Club (League)	Class	W	L	ERA	G	GS	CG	SV	IP	H	R	ER	HR	BB	SO	AVG
2008	Did Not Play—Signed 2009 Contract																

Chicago White Sox

BY PHIL ROGERS

In the end, after his big league team had survived three elimination games in three days against three different opponents, Kenny Williams was left with good memories of 2008. But the pendulum generally swings wildly for the White Sox and their general manager, and that remains as true as ever.

While Chicago won its third American League Central title in Williams' eight seasons in charge, 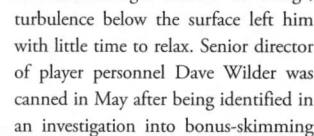 turbulence below the surface left him with little time to relax. Senior director of player personnel Dave Wilder was canned in May after being identified in an investigation into bonus-skimming from players signed in the Dominican Republic, and in the aftermath, Buddy Bell replaced Alan Regier as farm director. It was the second year in a row that Williams made a major in-season change, as longtime scouting director Duane Shaffer was sacked in June 2007.

Williams' characteristic aggressiveness has rewarded the White Sox handsomely in many cases. They wouldn't have made the playoffs in 2008 without signing Cuban free agent Alexei Ramirez or trading first-base prospect Chris Carter to Arizona for Carlos Quentin, who might have won the AL MVP award had he not broken his hand in September. Acquiring John Danks and Gavin Floyd in the 2006-07 offseason has put their rotation in good shape for years to come, a credit to Williams' deal-making ability.

Nick Swisher did turn in a disappointing season after the White Sox sent their top two prospects (lefthander Gio Gonzalez, righthander Fautino de los Santos) and best position prospect (outfielder Ryan Sweeney) to Oakland for him last January. And that move seemed to spark a change in Williams' habit of using his farm system to acquire veterans.

The White Sox began the offseason by doing the reverse. Williams sent Swisher (and righty prospect Kanekoa Texeira) to the Yankees for a pair of young righthanders, Jhonny Nunez and Jeff Marquez. Then he pulled off a six-player deal with the Braves, giving up Javier Vazquez and Boone Logan for catcher Tyler Flowers, infielder Brent Lillibridge, lefthander Santos Rodriguez and third baseman Jon Gilmore.

Chicago rarely has developed its own impact players under Williams, and in recent years has done an especially poor job of advancing hitters. But now the White Sox are talking about going into spring training with Chris Getz in the second-base mix, Josh Fields as the frontrunner at third base and Brian Anderson and Jerry Owens battling for the center-field job.

Further away but more promising is a group of

CHRIS PROCTOR

Trade acquisition Carlos Quentin helped power the White Sox back to the playoffs

TOP 30 PROSPECTS

1. Gordon Beckham, ss	16. Jhonny Nunez, rhp
2. Dayan Viciedo, 3b/of	17. Brent Morel, 3b
3. Aaron Poreda, lhp	18. Santos Rodriguez, lhp
4. Tyler Flowers, c	19. Brian Omogrosso, rhp
5. Clayton Richard, lhp	20. Jeff Marquez, rhp
6. Brandon Allen, 1b	21. Jon Gilmore, 3b
7. Jordan Danks, of	22. Jon Link, rhp
8. Brent Lillibridge, ss	23. Dexter Carter, rhp
9. Chris Getz, 2b/ss/of	24. Dan Hudson, rhp
10. John Shelby, of	25. Carlos Torres, rhp
11. John Ely, rhp	26. Jayson Nix, 2b
12. Cole Armstrong, c	27. Adam Russell, rhp
13. Eduardo Escobar, ss/2b	28. Lance Broadway, rhp
14. Clevelan Santeliz, rhp	29. C.J. Retherford, 3b
15. Jose Martinez, of	30. Gregory Infante, rhp

2008 draftees—shortstop Gordon Beckham, third baseman Brent Morel and center fielder Jordan Danks—who have replenished the system's inventory of position players. First baseman Brandon Allen also took a huge step forward in 2008 and could emerge as an eventual replacement for Paul Konerko as Chicago looks to get younger and more athletic.

The system's pitching depth took a hit with the first Swisher trade, though lefties Aaron Poreda and Clayton Richard are close to assuming prominent roles. Richard was their most impressive pitcher in the AL Division Series against the Rays.

General Manager: Kenny Williams. **Farm Director:** Buddy Bell. **Scouting Director:** Doug Laumann.

Class	Team	League	W	L	PCT	Finish*	Manager	Affiliated
Majors	Chicago	American	89	74	.546	5th (14)	Ozzie Guillen	—
Triple-A	Charlotte Knights	International	63	78	.447	12th (14)	Marc Bombard	1999
Double-A	Birmingham Barons	Southern	74	63	.540	2nd (10)	Carlos Subero	1986
High A	Winston-Salem Warthogs	Carolina	71	68	.511	4th (8)	Tim Blackwell	1997
Low A	Kannapolis Intimidators	South Atlantic	67	68	.496	9th (16)	Chris Jones	2001
Rookie	Great Falls Voyagers	Pioneer	39	37	.513	^4th (8)	Chris Cron	2003
Rookie	Bristol White Sox	Appalachian	34	30	.531	4th (10)	Bobby Thigpen	1995
Overall 2008 Minor League Record			348	344	.503	16th		

* Finish in overall standings (No. of teams in league). ^League champion.

LAST YEAR'S TOP 30

Rank	Player, Pos.	Status
1.	Gio Gonzalez, lhp	(Athletics)
2.	Fautino de los Santos, rhp	(Athletics)
3.	Aaron Poreda, lhp	No. 3
4.	Lance Broadway, rhp	No. 28
5.	Jack Egbert, rhp	Dropped out
6.	Ryan Sweeney, of	(Athletics)
7.	Jose Martinez, of	No. 15
8.	Chris Getz, 2b	No. 9
9.	John Ely, rhp	No. 11
10.	Juan Silverio, ss	Dropped out
11.	John Shelby, of	No. 10
12.	Adam Russell, rhp	No. 27
13.	Kyle McCulloch, rhp	Dropped out
14.	Nevin Griffith, rhp	Dropped out
15.	Lucas Harrell, rhp	Dropped out
16.	Charlie Haeger, rhp	(Free agent)
17.	Christian Marrero, 1b	Dropped out
18.	Sergio Morales, of	Dropped out
19.	Justin Cassel, rhp	Dropped out
20.	Sergio Miranda, ss	Dropped out
21.	Francisco Hernandez, c	Dropped out
22.	Ehren Wasserman, rhp	Dropped out
23.	Donny Lucy, c	Dropped out
24.	Oneli Perez, rhp	(Free agent)
25.	Brian Omogrosso, rhp	No. 19
26.	Dewon Day, rhp	(Red Sox)
27.	Brandon Allen, 1b	No. 6
28.	Sal Sanchez, of	Dropped out
29.	Robert Valido, ss	Dropped out
30.	Lyndon Estill, of	Dropped out

BEST TOOLS

Best Hitter for Average	Chris Getz
Best Power Hitter	Dayan Viciedo
Best Strike-Zone Discipline	Chris Getz
Fastest Baserunner	Justin Greene
Best Athlete	Jordan Danks
Best Fastball	Aaron Poreda
Best Curveball	Nate Jones
Best Slider	Jon Link
Best Changeup	John Ely
Best Control	Levi Maxwell
Best Defensive Catcher	Cole Armstrong
Best Defensive Infielder	Eduardo Escobar
Best Infield Arm	Brent Morel
Best Defensive Outfielder	Jordan Danks
Best Outfield Arm	Sal Sanchez

PROJECTED 2012 LINEUP

Catcher	Tyler Flowers
First Base	Brandon Allen
Second Base	Gordon Beckham
Third Base	Josh Fields
Shortstop	Alexei Ramirez
Left Field	Dayan Viciedo
Center Field	Jordan Danks
Right Field	Carlos Quentin
Designated Hitter	Paul Konerko
No. 1 Starter	John Danks
No. 2 Starter	Aaron Poreda
No. 3 Starter	Gavin Floyd
No. 4 Starter	Mark Buehrle
No. 5 Starter	Clayton Richard
Closer	Bobby Jenks

TOP PROSPECTS OF THE DECADE

Year	Player, Pos.	2008 Org.
1999	Carlos Lee, 3b	Astros
2000	Kip Wells, rhp	Royals
2001	Jon Rauch, rhp	Diamondbacks
2002	Joe Borchard, of	Braves
2003	Joe Borchard, of	Braves
2004	Joe Borchard, of	Braves
2005	Brian Anderson, of	White Sox
2006	Bobby Jenks, rhp	White Sox
2007	Ryan Sweeney, of	Athletics
2008	Aaron Poreda, lhp	White Sox

TOP DRAFT PICKS OF THE DECADE

Year	Player, Pos.	2008 Org.
1999	Jason Stumm, rhp	Out of baseball
2000	Joe Borchard, of	Braves
2001	Kris Honel, rhp	Cardinals
2002	Royce Ring, lhp	Braves
2003	Brian Anderson, of	White Sox
2004	Josh Fields, 3b	White Sox
2005	Lance Broadway, rhp	White Sox
2006	Kyle McCulloch, rhp	White Sox
2007	Aaron Poreda, lhp	White Sox
2008	Gordon Beckham, ss	White Sox

LARGEST BONUSES IN CLUB HISTORY

Joe Borchard, 2003	$5,300,000
Dayan Viciedo, 2008	$4,000,000
Gordon Beckham, 2008	$2,600,000
Jason Stumm, 1999	$1,750,000
Royce Ring, 2002	$1,600,000

CHICAGO WHITE SOX

TOP 2009 ROOKIE: Dayan Viciedo, 3b/of. He's not as major league-ready as fellow Cuban defector Alexei Ramirez was, but he's not far away either.

BREAKOUT PROSPECT: Brent Morel, 3b. The White Sox were ecstatic to get him in the third round of the 2008 draft, and they think he'll hit for average and power while providing solid defense.

SLEEPER: Jordan Kendall, of. One of the system's top athletes, he had offers to play defensive back from top college football programs.

SOURCE OF TOP 30 TALENT			
Homegrown	21	Acquired	9
College	14	Trades	7
Junior college	0	Rule 5 draft	1
High school	1	Independent leagues	0
Draft-and-follow	0	Free agents/waivers	1
Nondrafted free agents	1		
International	5		

Numbers in parentheses indicate prospect rankings.

LF
Stefan Gartrell
Miguel Negron
Kenny Gilbert
Johny Celis
Jimmy Gallagher

CF
Jordan Danks (7)
John Shelby (10)
Sergio Morales
Kent Gerst
Kenny Williams Jr.
Justin Greene

RF
Jose Martinez (15)
Jordan Kendall
David Cook
Sal Sanchez

3B
Dayan Viciedo (2)
Brent Morel (17)
Jon Gilmore (21)
C.J. Retherford (29)
Javier Castillo

SS
Gordon Beckham (1)
Brent Lillibridge (8)
Eduardo Escobar (13)
Juan Silverio
Tyler Kuhn
Sergio Miranda

2B
Chris Getz (9)
Jayson Nix (26)
Greg Paiml
Dale Mollenhauer
Drew Garcia

1B
Brandon Allen (6)
Christian Marrero
Jorge Castillo
Mark Fleisher

C
Tyler Flowers (4)
Cole Armstrong (12)
Donny Lucy
Francisco Hernandez
Matt Inouye
Mike Grace
Orlando Santos
Kevin Dubler

RHP

Starters	Relievers
John Ely (11)	Brian Omogrosso (19)
Clevelan Santeliz (14)	Jon Link (22)
Jhonny Nunez (16)	Carlos Torres (25)
Jeff Marquez (20)	Adam Russell (27)
Dexter Carter (23)	Nathan Jones
Dan Hudson (24)	Drew O'Neil
Lance Broadway (28)	Henry Mabee
Gregory Infante (30)	Santo Luis
Jack Egbert	Leroy Hunt
Lucas Harrell	Stephen Sauer
Justin Cassel	Matt Zaleski
Levi Maxwell	
Matt Long	
Charlie Shirek	
Steven Upchurch	
Johnnie Lowe	
Anthony Carter	
Jacob Rasner	
Kyle McCulloch	

LHP

Starters	Relievers
Aaron Poreda (3)	Garrett Johnson
Clayton Richard (5)	Ronald Morales
Santos Rodriguez (18)	
Kevin Skogley	
Wes Whisler	
Justin Edwards	

2008   BONUSES: $4.7 MILLION

BEST PURE HITTER: Two low-round picks, SS Tyler Kuhn (15) and 1B Jorge Castillo (26). Kuhn batted .424 as a West Virginia senior and .375 as a Rookie-level Pioneer League all-star. Castillo, who tried catching in instructional league, batted .373 and reached low Class A in his debut.

BEST POWER HITTER: SS Gordon Beckham (1), who tied for the NCAA Division I lead with 28 homers. 3B Brent Morel (3) should develop at least average power as well.

FASTEST RUNNER: OF Justin Greene (20) has plus-plus speed, and while he's raw, he led the Rookie-level Appalachian League with 26 steals.

BEST DEFENSIVE PLAYER: OF Jordan Danks (7) has good instincts and covers the gaps well in center field.

BEST FASTBALL: Former Old Dominion teammates Dexter Carter (13) and Dan Hudson (5). Carter throws harder at 92-93 mph and a peak of 96, while Hudson has more life. RHP Drew O'Neil (4) reminds Chicago of Pat Neshek and gets late, heavy sink on his 89-93 mph fastball.

BEST SECONDARY PITCH: The White Sox drafted RHP Steven Upchurch (12) for his plus-plus changeup. His fastball dipped to 87-90 mph this year but was at 90-93 the previous summer. Hudson's slider is the best breaking pitch in Chicago's draft.

BEST PRO DEBUT: Carter led the Pioneer League in ERA (2.23) and went 6-1 with 89 strikeouts in 68 innings. Hudson went 5-4, 3.36 and topped the league in strikeouts (90 in 70 innings), and he fanned 12 in the championship clincher.

BEST ATHLETE: Danks was the best college all-around athlete in the 2008 draft, and he'll be a steal for $525,000 if he can deliver on more of his power potential. OF Kenny Williams Jr. (6) didn't get to show off his athleticism while battling a shoulder injury.

MOST INTRIGUING BACKGROUND: Williams' father is a former big leaguer and Chicago's general manager, whom the club insists wasn't involved in the decision to draft Kenny Jr. Danks' brother John led the White Sox with a 3.32 ERA this year. Unsigned LHP Kyle Long (23, now at Florida State) is the son of NFL Hall of Famer Howie Long. Unsigned 1B Travis Otto's (49, now at Illinois Wesleyan) father Dave pitched in the majors, while 2B Drew Garcia's (21) grandfather Dave managed in the big leagues.

CLOSEST TO THE MAJORS: Beckham. The White Sox plan on keeping him at shortstop, though he could slide over to second base if Alexei Ramirez seizes their big league job.

BEST LATE-ROUND PICK: Carter or Kuhn. Carter dropped in the draft after posting an 8.76 ERA as an Old Dominion junior, while Kuhn just slipped through the cracks.

THE ONE WHO GOT AWAY: OF Randall Thorpe (29), who opted to attend Texas A&M, is a quality athlete with plus-plus speed.

ASSESSMENT: The White Sox were delighted to get Beckham with the No. 8 overall pick after believing he'd get picked ahead of them. Morel has flown under the radar but Chicago thinks he might move just as quickly, and Danks is now the best athlete in the system.

2007   BONUSES: $2.8 MILLION

LHP Aaron Poreda (1) is the best pitching prospect in the system, while RHP Jon Ely (3) is the top right-hander. They're also the only members of this crop to crack our White Sox Top 30.

GRADE: C

2006   BONUSES: $2.9 MILLION

RHP Kyle McCulloch (1) wasn't going to light up radar guns, but he was supposed to get to the majors quickly. That hasn't happened. OF John Shelby (5) is the highlight of this draft.

GRADE: D

2005   BONUSES: $2.7 MILLION*

The White Sox have traded away their best draftees—OFs Aaron Cunningham (6), RHP Daniel Cortes (7) and 1B/3B Chris Carter (15)—though Carter did net them Carlos Quentin. 2B Chris Getz (4) and LHP Clayton Richard (8) are ready to help the big league club, but RHP Lance Broadway (1) isn't a big part of Chicago's plans.

GRADE: C+

2004   BONUSES: $6.3 MILLION*

3B Josh Fields (1) and 1B Brandon Allen (5) are Chicago's corner infielders of the future. The White Sox traded LHP Gio Gonzalez (1s) twice, first to get Jim Thome and then to land Nick Swisher.

GRADE: B+

*Draft analysis by Jim Callis. Numbers in parentheses indicate draft rounds. *Bonuses for 2004-05 are first 10 rounds only.*

PROSPECT

GORDON BECKHAM, SS

Born: Sept. 16, 1986.
Ht.: 6-0. **Wt.:** 190.
Bats: R. **Throws:** R.
Drafted: Georgia, 2008
(1st round).
Signed by:
Nick Hostetler/
Kevin Burrell.

With the No. 8 overall pick in the 2008 draft, the White Sox picked in the top 10 for the first time since they landed Alex Fernandez with the fourth choice in 1990. Last year, the choice came at a time when Chicago had few impact position players in its system, and taking Beckham filled two needs—a power bat and a middle infielder. Signed for $2.6 million two days before the Aug. 15 deadline, he was the top college shortstop and one of the most polished players in the draft. The son of a former South Carolina quarterback, Beckham starred in both football and baseball at the Westminster School in Atlanta but went undrafted as a senior. He turned down a chance to play quarterback at the Air Force Academy in favor of focusing on baseball at Georgia. He led the Bulldogs to a second-place finish at the 2008 College World Series, hitting .474 with five homers and 20 RBIs in 14 NCAA tournament games. His 28 homers set a school record and tied for the Division I lead, while his .411 average was Georgia's best since 1982. His 53 career homers established another Bulldogs mark. Beckham hit the ground running as a pro, playing well in 14 games at low Class A Kannapolis before an impressive tour of duty in the Arizona Fall League.

Hitting will be Beckham's ticket to the big leagues. He doesn't have a classic stroke but has strong forearms and quick wrists, generating impressive bat speed. Though he isn't built like a power hitter, he centers the ball well and the ball jumps off his bat. He led the Cape Cod League with nine homers in 2007, suggesting that his power comes from more than a metal bat. He's willing to use the entire field and was well coached at Georgia, developing a strong knowledge of the strike zone and a willingness to walk. He has unusual pitch recognition for a young hitter. A good athlete, Beckham has average speed and the arm and instincts to stick at shortstop. His game has drawn comparisons to Michael Young's. He also has strong makeup and says his goal is "to lead the White Sox one day the way Derek Jeter leads the Yankees."

The biggest question with Beckham is whether he'll remain at shortstop. Before the draft, scouts were split on his defensive ability, but the White Sox believe he can stay there. His hands aren't the softest, and he'll have to work to get smoother at fielding grounders. Though he moves well, he doesn't project as much of a basestealer.

Beckham's chance to become Chicago's first homegrown shortstop since Bucky Dent hinges on how well Alexei Ramirez takes to a planned move from second base to short in 2009. If Ramirez establishes himself at shortstop, Beckham likely will move to second or third base in the near future. He has enough bat to carry him at either position. Beckham probably will open the season at high Class A Winston-Salem and finish it at Double-A Birmingham. He could be in Chicago by 2010.

Year	Club (League)	Class	AVG	G	AB	R	H	2B	3B	HR	RBI	BB	SO	SB	OBP	SLG
2008	Kannapolis (SAL)	LoA	.310	14	58	11	18	2	0	3	8	5	7	0	.365	.500
MINOR LEAGUE TOTALS			.310	14	58	11	18	2	0	3	8	5	7	0	.365	.500

2 DAYAN VICIEDO, 3B/OF

BORN: March 10, 1989. **B-T:** R-R. **HT.:** 6-1. **WT.:** 248. **SIGNED:** Cuba, 2008. **SIGNED BY:** Doug Laumann/Jose Ortega.

After the success of Alexei Ramirez, the White Sox in December gave Viciedo a four-year major league contract with a $4 million bonus and a $10 million total guarantee. He was the top player on Cuba's junior national team in 2005 and 2006. He played three seasons for Villa Clara in Cuba's Serie Nacional, hitting .337 with 14 homers as a rookie in 2005-06, and nearly made the inaugural World Baseball Classic that spring—at age 16. He defected by taking a boat to Mexico in May 2008, and he established residency in the Dominican Republic so he could become a free agent. Viciedo has the power to hit 40-plus homers in a season, thanks to a quick swing that's triggered by strong wrists. He has power to all fields and hits moonshots to left field when pitchers make mistakes inside. He also pitched for Cuba's junior national team and has enough arm to play anywhere on the field. His soft hands are an asset at third base. Conditioning and motivation were major question marks for Viciedo in recent years, however. He reportedly weighed more than 260 pounds when teams first scouted him in the Dominican but was working to get in shape. The White Sox asked him to drop at least 10 pounds before spring training. His size limits his mobility, which could be a problem at third base or in the outfield. He doesn't run well. He's an aggressive hitter who will chase bad pitches. Viciedo will compete against Josh Fields for Chicago's third-base job in spring training, but that's not his only possible route to the majors. He also has been told to get in shape to possibly play the outfield. He would benefit from time in the minors, but the White Sox will want him to be around fellow Cubans Ramirez and Jose Contreras, easing his transition. Viciedo has a high ceiling but brings a bigger risk than the more experienced and athletic Ramirez.

Year	Club (League)	Class	AVG	G	AB	R	H	2B	3B	HR	RBI	BB	SO	SB	OBP	SLG
05-06	Villa Clara (Cuba)	—	.337	86	323	54	109	16	4	14	58	21	44	3	—	.542
06-07	Villa Clara (Cuba)	—	.252	90	301	39	76	14	3	8	35	49	52	12	—	.399
07-08	Villa Clara (Cuba)	—	.294	57	177	41	52	5	1	10	38	28	27	2	—	.503
SERIE NACIONAL TOTALS			.296	233	801	134	237	35	8	32	131	98	123	17	—	.479

3 AARON POREDA, LHP

BORN: Oct. 1, 1986. **B-T:** L-L. **HT.:** 6-6. **WT.:** 240. **DRAFTED:** San Francisco, 2007 (1st round). **SIGNED BY:** Joe Butler/Adam Virchis.

The 25th overall pick in the 2007 draft, Poreda caught Ozzie Guillen's eye in spring training, when the Chicago manager called him "a real No. 1 guy." Poreda finished his first full season in Double-A and then displayed one of the most impressive arms in the Arizona Fall League. General manager Kenny Williams refused to give him up when the Rockies wanted him in a proposed Brian Fuentes trade—a high compliment given Williams' willingness to deal prospects. Poreda's calling card is his fastball, which generally parks in the mid-90s and has touched 100 mph. White Sox coaches have helped him develop a power slider, and while it isn't a plus pitch, it does keep hitters from sitting on his fastball. He throws strikes easily and is built for durability. Poreda still is refining his slider, and he doesn't have a lot of trust in his rudimentary changeup. His fastball straightens out at times, making him hittable. To succeed against big leaguers, he'll have to learn how to change speeds and possibly develop a cut fastball, a weapon favored by White Sox pitching coach Don Cooper. Poreda's AFL performance was so good that he forced himself into consideration for Chicago's 2009 staff. He'll probably open the season at Triple-A Charlotte. Some scouts see Poreda as a dominating reliever, but he will remain a starter for the time being.

Year	Club (League)	Class	W	L	ERA	G	GS	CG	SV	IP	H	R	ER	HR	BB	SO	AVG
2007	Great Falls (PIO)	R	4	0	1.17	12	8	0	0	46	29	7	6	1	10	48	.181
2008	Winston-Salem (CAR)	HiA	5	5	3.31	12	12	1	0	73	67	31	27	1	18	46	.238
	Birmingham (SL)	AA	3	4	2.98	15	15	1	0	88	81	34	29	5	22	72	.249
MINOR LEAGUE TOTALS			12	9	2.69	39	35	2	0	207	177	72	62	7	50	166	.231

4 TYLER FLOWERS, C

BORN: Jan. 24, 1986. **B-T:** R-R. **HT.:** 6-4. **WT.:** 220. **DRAFTED:** Chipola (Fla.) JC, D/F 2005 (33rd round). **SIGNED BY:** Al Goetz (Braves).

Flowers signed with the Braves as a draft-and-follow out of Chipola (Fla.) JC, where he played with rising prospects such as Brewers third baseman Mat Gamel and Cubs catcher Steve Clevenger. He tested positive for performance-enhancing drugs shortly after turning pro, drawing a 50-game suspension. He spent most of his first full pro season in 2007 at first base while recovering from knee surgery that March, but he moved back behind the plate in 2008. He started terrorizing pitchers with his prodigious power in big league camp and continued all the way through the Arizona Fall League, which he led with 12 homers and a .973 slugging percentage. White Sox GM Kenny Williams saw him play several times in the AFL and made him the centerpiece of the deal that sent Javier Vazquez and Boone Logan to Atlanta in December. Flowers has a potent bat with plus power that continues to improve. He excels at working deep counts—he led the high Class A Carolina League with 98 walks—and forcing pitchers to throw him pitches he can mash to all fields. Some scouts wonder if Flowers is more of a mistake hitter than a true power threat, but the big question is whether he can stay behind the plate. There are mixed reports on his arm, receiving skills and footwork, though his backers believe he just needs more experience. He threw out only 28 percent of basestealers in 2008, giving up 112 steals and committing 11 passed balls in 86 games. He's still learning to call a game and master many of the mechanics of catching, such as making accurate throws and blocking balls. Williams says he's confident Flowers will develop into an all-star catcher. He runs well for his size but is still a below-average runner. Flowers was blocked by Brian McCann with the Braves, but Chicago expects him to be able to take over when A.J. Pierzynski's contract expires after the 2010 season, if not before. Flowers likely will start 2009 in Double-A.

Year	Club (League)	Class	AVG	G	AB	R	H	2B	3B	HR	RBI	BB	SO	SB	OBP	SLG
2006	Danville (APP)	R	.279	34	129	24	36	9	0	5	16	16	30	0	.373	.465
2007	Rome (SAL)	LoA	.298	106	389	65	116	34	2	12	70	49	74	3	.378	.488
2008	Myrtle Beach (CAR)	HiA	.288	122	413	72	119	32	1	17	88	98	102	8	.427	.494
MINOR LEAGUE TOTALS			.291	262	931	161	271	75	3	34	174	163	206	11	.400	.488

5 CLAYTON RICHARD, LHP

BORN: Sept. 12, 1983. **B-T:** L-L. **HT.:** 6-5. **WT.:** 240. **DRAFTED:** Michigan, 2005 (8th round). **SIGNED BY:** Nathan Durst/Mike Shirley.

A backup quarterback at Michigan, Richard rarely was considered more than a fringe prospect before 2008. He went from not earning an invitation to big league camp to pitching quality innings in the Division Series, with plenty of highlights along the way. He started in the Futures Game, was offered a spot on the U.S. Olympic team before Chicago called him up and took a shutout into the seventh inning at Yankee Stadium in a September start. At 6-foot-5, Richard is a taller version of Mark Buehrle. He works quickly and throws strikes with three pitches, including an 88-92 mph fastball with natural sink that induces lots of groundballs. He has exceptional command and mound presence. Richard lacks a put-away pitch and had trouble missing bats for much of his big league stint. His changeup is average at best and his slurvy breaking ball lacks consistency. He may be better off working as a reliever who can focus on his sinker. Richard could be consistent enough to have a long career as a starter, if not quite the second coming of Buehrle. The trade of Javier Vazquez gives Richard a clear path to make the White Sox's 2009 rotation, and he also has shown the ability to bounce back quickly out of the bullpen if he's needed there.

Year	Club (League)	Class	W	L	ERA	G	GS	CG	SV	IP	H	R	ER	HR	BB	SO	AVG
2005	Great Falls (PIO)	R	2	1	2.85	10	9	0	0	41	37	19	13	2	12	39	.240
	Kannapolis (SAL)	LoA	0	1	5.23	3	2	0	0	10	14	7	6	1	1	8	.326
2006	KaNnapolis (SAL)	LoA	6	6	3.67	18	17	0	0	96	117	47	39	0	28	54	.310
	Winston-Salem (CAR)	HiA	1	3	4.56	4	4	1	0	24	29	18	12	2	6	12	.315
2007	Winston-Salem (CAR)	HiA	8	12	3.63	28	27	1	0	161	159	86	65	11	59	99	.262
2008	Birmingham (SL)	AA	6	6	2.47	13	13	1	0	84	66	29	23	2	16	53	.217
	Charlotte (IL)	AAA	6	0	2.45	7	7	1	0	44	33	12	12	3	4	33	.204
	Chicago (AL)	MAJ	2	5	6.04	13	8	0	0	48	61	37	32	5	13	29	.303
MINOR LEAGUE TOTALS			29	29	3.33	83	79	4	0	460	455	218	170	21	126	298	.262
MAJOR LEAGUE TOTALS			2	5	6.04	13	8	0	0	48	61	37	32	5	13	29	.303

6 BRANDON ALLEN, 1B

BORN: Feb. 12, 1986. **B-T:** L-R. **HT.:** 6-2. **WT.:** 235. **DRAFTED:** HS—Montgomery, Texas, 2004 (5th round). **SIGNED BY:** Paul Provas/Keith Staab.

Allen had a difficult transition to pro ball, batting .248 with 379 strikeouts in 362 games over his first four seasons. A commitment to nutrition and conditioning turned him into a physical specimen and made all the difference in 2008. He led the Carolina League in slugging (.527) and homered twice off David Price in his first Double-A game. Power had been Allen's only real strong suit, but he also showed the ability to hit for average in 2008. A former football prospect as a linebacker, he improved his speed as well and nearly matched his previous career total with 17 steals. He also showed much better agility at first base. Allen no longer looks like a DH but must continue to work on his fielding. His hands are suspect and he's not comfortable making quick throws. He swings and misses a lot, especially against lefthanders, and might whiff 150 times a year in the big leagues. With Jim Thome in the final year of his contract and Paul Konerko signed only through 2010, Allen is emerging at an opportune pace. The last hitter to show this much power at Birmingham was Chris Young, who hit 32 homers for the Diamondbacks two years later. Allen could return to Double-A to start 2009 but should finish in Triple-A.

Year	Club (League)	Class	AVG	G	AB	R	H	2B	3B	HR	RBI	BB	SO	SB	OBP	SLG
2004	Bristol (APP)	R	.205	58	185	17	38	9	1	3	23	16	60	2	.280	.314
2005	Great Falls (PIO)	R	.264	66	231	41	61	11	2	11	42	32	69	7	.366	.472
2006	Kannapolis (SAL)	LoA	.213	109	395	36	84	17	2	15	68	22	126	6	.257	.380
2007	Kannapolis (SAL)	LoA	.283	129	516	84	146	39	5	18	93	39	124	7	.337	.483
2008	Winston-Salem (CAR)	HiA	.279	89	319	57	89	26	4	15	44	41	83	14	.372	.527
	Birmingham (SL)	AA	.275	41	153	30	42	6	2	14	31	19	41	3	.358	.614
MINOR LEAGUE TOTALS			.256	492	1799	265	460	108	16	76	301	169	503	39	.326	.460

7 JORDAN DANKS, OF

SPORTS ON FILM

BORN: Aug. 7, 1986. **B-T:** L-R. **HT.:** 6-4. **WT.:** 210. **DRAFTED:** Texas, 2008 (7th round). **SIGNED BY:** Keith Staab/Derek Valenzuela.

The younger brother of White Sox lefty John, Danks was the first member of his family on the club's radar. Chicago drafted Jordan out of high school in 2005, 22 months before trading for John. Jordan's stock slid somewhat when he didn't show much power during his college career, but the White Sox had to give him an above-slot $525,000 bonus to sign him as a seventh-rounder. Danks is an excellent athlete with a big frame and keen instincts. He has good bat speed and gap power, and he should hit for average and have an on-base percentage worthy of the top of the order. He's a plus runner, which helps him on the bases and in center field, where he has the skills to develop into a Gold Glove fielder. He has excellent range and a plus arm. His work ethic is strong. Danks hit just 13 homers in three years at Texas. Some scouts believe his power will come once he adds strength to his lanky frame, while others think his swing mechanics and timing are lacking. He needs to improve his pitch recognition and cut down his swing when he's behind in the count. It's easy to see Danks as a big league center fielder even if he doesn't hit for power. It's his goal to play behind his older brother, and that could happen as early as the end of 2010. He'll open his first full pro season in high Class A.

Year	Club (League)	Class	AVG	G	AB	R	H	2B	3B	HR	RBI	BB	SO	SB	OBP	SLG
2008	Kannapolis (SAL)	LoA	.325	10	40	10	13	4	1	2	7	4	14	1	.400	.625
MINOR LEAGUE TOTALS			.325	10	40	10	13	4	1	2	7	4	14	1	.400	.625

8 BRENT LILLIBRIDGE, SS

BORN: Sept. 18, 1983. **B-T:** R-R. **HT.:** 5-11. **WT.:** 192. **DRAFTED:** Washington, 2005 (4th round). **SIGNED BY:** Greg Hopkins (Pirates).

Lillibridge has been traded twice in the last three offseasons. Though he quickly established himself as one of the few position prospects in the Pirates system, Pittsburgh dealt him to the Braves in a deal for Adam LaRoche after the 2006 season. He spent two years as Atlanta property, making his major league debut last April, before coming to the White Sox in December in a four-player package for Javier Vazquez and Boone Logan. Lillibridge is coming off easily his worst year as a pro, as he didn't get his average above the Mendoza Line for good until mid-June. One of the major knocks against him is his inability to handle failure, a problem that reared its head again when he let his offensive woes carry over to his defense. Despite last season's difficulties, Lillibridge has good hands at the plate with above-average pop for his size and the ability to drive the ball to all fields. He also has plus speed and the instincts to read pitchers well, making him a solid stolen-base threat. He needs to become a better bunter and play more of a small-ball game while continuing to reduce his strikeouts. Defensively, his range and arm strength both rate above average, and he has the overall skill set to play shortstop in the big leagues. The White Sox plan on moving Alexei Ramirez to shortstop in 2009, so Lillibridge will compete with Chris Getz and Jayson Nix for the second-base job. Chicago GM Kenny Williams said he envisions Lillibridge eventually filling the super-utility role that Pablo Ozuna held for much of the last four seasons.

Year	Club (League)	Class	AVG	G	AB	R	H	2B	3B	HR	RBI	BB	SO	SB	OBP	SLG
2005	Williamsport (NYP)	SS	.243	42	169	19	41	12	4	4	18	14	35	10	.305	.432
2006	Hickory (SAL)	LoA	.299	74	274	59	82	18	5	11	43	51	61	29	.414	.522
	Lynchburg (CAR)	HiA	.313	54	201	47	63	10	3	2	28	36	43	24	.426	.423
2007	Mississippi (SL)	AA	.275	52	204	31	56	8	3	3	17	20	60	14	.355	.387
	Richmond (IL)	AAA	.287	87	321	47	92	14	2	10	41	20	59	28	.331	.436
2008	Richmond (IL)	AAA	.220	90	355	46	78	18	7	4	39	33	90	23	.294	.344
	Atlanta (NL)	MAJ	.200	29	80	9	16	6	1	1	8	3	23	2	.238	.338
MINOR LEAGUE TOTALS			.270	399	1524	249	412	80	24	34	186	174	348	128	.352	.421
MAJOR LEAGUE TOTALS			.200	29	80	9	16	6	1	1	8	3	23	2	.238	.338

9 CHRIS GETZ, 2B/SS/OF

BORN: Aug. 30, 1983. **B-T:** L-R. **HT.:** 6-0. **WT.:** 185. **DRAFTED:** Michigan, 2005 (4th round). **SIGNED BY:** Mike Shirley.

The most advanced hitter in the system, Getz recovered from a 2007 stress fracture in his left leg to add to his resume. He hit .302 and continued to control the strike zone while showing newfound power. He played in the Futures Game and might have made Chicago's postseason roster if a pitch hadn't broken his left wrist in late August. Getz gets on base by working counts and making consistent line-drive contact to all fields. He uses his first-step quickness to get more than his share of infield hits and to steal a few bases. A versatile defender, he saw time at second base, shortstop, third base and left field in 2008. He's not flashy anywhere but makes the routine play. Getz never had hit more than three homers in a season before getting 11 in 2008, when he was based in a hitter's park. While he occasionally pitched in relief at Michigan, some scouts question his arm, which limits him on the left side of the infield and on the double-play pivot. With Alexei Ramirez moving to shortstop, Getz was the White Sox's best in-house option for second base until they signed free agent Jayson Nix and traded for Brent Lillibridge. Getz will need a fully healthy wrist to win the job in spring training. Long term, he projects as more of a utilityman than a regular.

Year	Club (League)	Class	AVG	G	AB	R	H	2B	3B	HR	RBI	BB	SO	SB	OBP	SLG
2005	Great Falls (PIO)	R	.333	6	24	3	8	1	0	0	4	1	2	2	.346	.375
	Kannapolis (SAL)	LoA	.304	55	214	38	65	13	2	1	28	35	10	11	.407	.397
2006	Birmingham (SL)	AA	.256	130	508	67	130	15	6	2	36	52	47	19	.326	.321
2007	Birmingham (SL)	AA	.299	72	278	40	83	10	2	3	29	36	30	13	.382	.381
2008	Charlotte (IL)	AAA	.302	111	404	60	122	24	1	11	52	41	53	11	.366	.448
	Chicago (AL)	MAJ	.286	10	7	2	2	0	0	0	1	0	1	1	.286	.286
MINOR LEAGUE TOTALS			.286	374	1428	208	408	63	11	17	149	165	142	56	.361	.381
MAJOR LEAGUE TOTALS			.286	10	7	2	2	0	0	0	1	0	1	1	.286	.286

10 JOHN SHELBY, OF

BORN: Aug. 6, 1985. **B-T:** L-R. **HT.:** 5-10. **WT.:** 190. **DRAFTED:** Kentucky, 2006 (5th round). **SIGNED BY:** Mike Shirley.

The son of former big leaguer John "T-Bone" Shelby, "Treybone" is one of the best athletes in the system. A second baseman in college, he moved to the outfield in mid-2007. A Carolina League all-star in 2008, he led White Sox farmhands with 33 steals while playing through hamstring problems. He went on to finish with 80 RBIs, and was second in the league with a .515 slugging percentage and 37 doubles. Shelby has the best combination of power and speed in the system. Though he's only 5-foot-10, he's strong for his size. He adds to his plus speed with good baserunning instincts and could develop into an even bigger stolen-base threat. He's improving in center field and has an average arm. Shelby's strike-zone judgment is lacking. He often gets himself out swinging at bad pitches early in the count and rarely walks. He'll have to improve his on-base percentage if he's going to use his speed at the top of the order. He has the tools for center field but still needs better jumps and routes. Shelby will be tested in 2009 at Birmingham, a notoriously tough park for hitters with a lot of ground to cover in center. He and Jordan Danks will battle to be the long-term center fielder for a team that has tried 11 different players there since trading Aaron Rowand following the 2005 season.

Year	Club (League)	Class	AVG	G	AB	R	H	2B	3B	HR	RBI	BB	SO	SB	OBP	SLG
2006	Great Falls (PIO)	R	.272	66	250	37	68	12	3	8	36	18	55	8	.332	.440
2007	Kannapolis (SAL)	LoA	.301	122	488	83	147	35	9	16	79	35	77	19	.352	.508
2008	Winston-Salem (CAR)	HiA	.295	114	447	81	132	37	7	15	80	22	98	33	.331	.510
MINOR LEAGUE TOTALS			.293	302	1185	201	347	84	19	39	195	75	230	60	.340	.495

11 JOHN ELY, RHP

BORN: May 17, 1986. **B-T:** R-R. **HT.:** 6-1. **WT.:** 190. **DRAFTED:** Miami (Ohio), 2007 (3rd round). **SIGNED BY:** Mike Shirley/Keith Staab.

In his first full season as a pro, Ely skipped low Class A and struggled initially, going 3-11, 5.51 through mid-July. But he rallied to go 7-1, 2.86 in his last eight starts, helping Winston-Salem reach the playoffs. He has a history of winning, going 69-25 dating to his days as a star at Homewood-Flossmoor High in the Chicago suburbs. Ely's best pitch is a plus-plus changeup, and he does a nice job of setting it up with an 88-94 mph fastball with good movement. His 12-to-6 curveball can be an out pitch at times, too. Ely works fast, throws strikes and has never missed a start. He's a fierce competitor and fields his position well. Ely's curveball remains inconsistent and gets hit a long way when he hangs it. He sometimes seems reluctant to work inside, minimizing his advantage against righthanders. He lacks a big frame and a traditional delivery, and there's a lot of effort in his delivery. With a solid rotation and prospects such as Aaron Poreda and Clayton Richard ahead of him, there's no reason to rush Ely. He'll move to Double-A Birmingham and could figure in midseason trade speculation, especially if the pitchers ahead of him continue to progress.

Year	Club (League)	Class	W	L	ERA	G	GS	CG	SV	IP	H	R	ER	HR	BB	SO	AVG
2007	Great Falls (PIO)	R	6	1	3.86	13	12	0	0	56	55	26	24	6	14	56	.259
2008	Winston-Salem (CAR)	HiA	10	12	4.71	27	27	0	0	145	142	83	76	18	46	134	.259
MINOR LEAGUE TOTALS			16	13	4.47	40	39	0	0	201	197	109	100	24	60	190	.259

12 COLE ARMSTRONG, C

BORN: Aug. 24, 1983. **B-T:** L-R. **HT.:** 6-3. **WT.:** 210. **DRAFTED:** Chipola (Fla.) JC, 2003 (16th round). **SIGNED BY:** Al Goetz (Braves).

Armstrong was coming off a .228 season in low Class A when the White Sox plucked him from the Braves system in the Triple-A phase of the 2005 Rule 5 draft. He made big strides as a hitter in 2007, earning a spot on the 40-man roster, and has continued that development. In the Arizona Fall League, he emerged as a middle-of-the-order bat for the hitter-heavy Peoria Saguaros. Armstrong has solid power and has worked hard to improve his ability to hit for average, use all fields and work counts. Managers rated him the best defensive catcher in the Double-A Southern League. He has an average arm and threw out 36 percent of basestealers in 2008, and he's a good receiver who works well with pitchers. Armstrong is prone to extended slumps at the plate. He overthinks at times and falls into funks. He's not patient, looking to put the ball in play early in the count and drawing few walks. He runs like a catcher. His value is enhanced by being a lefthanded-hitting catcher, but the White Sox already have one in A.J. Pierzynski, so Armstrong may spend much of 2009 in Triple-A. He looked like Chicago's catcher of the future until the trade for Tyler Flowers, but he might fit well as Flowers' backup, providing quality defense and a lefty bat.

Year	Club (League)	Class	AVG	G	AB	R	H	2B	3B	HR	RBI	BB	SO	SB	OBP	SLG
2003	Braves (GCL)	R	.118	9	17	0	2	0	0	0	0	1	2	0	.167	.118
2004	Danville (APP)	R	.316	49	174	30	55	9	0	6	46	29	17	0	.411	.471
2005	Rome (SAL)	LoA	.228	105	378	34	86	26	1	7	42	32	71	0	.283	.357
2006	Birmingham (SL)	AA	.120	8	25	3	3	0	0	0	0	2	2	0	.185	.120
	Winston-Salem (CAR)	HiA	.237	42	131	9	31	5	0	2	14	17	30	0	.322	.321
2007	Winston-Salem (CAR)	HiA	.288	80	285	35	82	17	0	12	39	23	69	1	.342	.474
	Birmingham (SL)	AA	.239	22	71	2	17	6	0	1	12	3	20	0	.273	.366
2008	Birmingham (SL)	AA	.252	64	218	27	55	17	0	6	31	10	31	0	.293	.413
	Charlotte (IL)	AAA	.275	35	138	12	38	12	0	2	17	5	27	0	.310	.406
MINOR LEAGUE TOTALS			.257	414	1437	152	369	92	1	36	201	122	269	1	.315	.397

13 EDUARDO ESCOBAR, SS/2B

BORN: Jan. 5, 1989. **B-T:** B-R. **HT.:** 5-10. **WT.:** 150. **SIGNED:** Venezuela, 2006. **SIGNED BY:** Amador Arias.

The diminutive Escobar didn't arrive until April but still made the most of his first season with a U.S. visa. He opened eyes in extended spring training and did so well in his first week at Rookie-level Great Falls that he was promoted to low Class A. He slid over to second base when first-round pick Gordon Beckham arrived at Kannapolis in August. Escobar is a fluid fielder in the mold of Ozzie Guillen and Omar Vizquel, with good range, excellent hands and a solid arm. A switch-hitter, he has some pop when he centers the ball. He's an adept bunter who's comfortable with a small-ball approach. His plus speed allows him to get infield hits. Escobar often seems defensive at the plate, slapping the ball around. He has limited power and rarely drives the ball into the gaps. He also lacks basestealing instincts, so his offensive value might be limited to his batting average. With college shortstops like Beckham, Sergio Miranda and Tyler Kuhn also in the lower levels, the White Sox face a challenge developing Escobar, who's behind those three as a hitter. He'll likely stay in low Class A and possibly force a position change for Kuhn. Escobar is a better defender, and he'll advance as quickly as his bat allows.

Year	Club (League)	Class	AVG	G	AB	R	H	2B	3B	HR	RBI	BB	SO	SB	OBP	SLG
2006	Orioles/White Sox (VSL)	R	.236	46	123	21	29	3	1	0	17	14	25	7	.317	.276
2007	White Sox2 (DSL)	R	.291	64	247	56	72	5	4	0	18	22	45	19	.359	.344
2008	Great Falls (PIO)	R	.417	6	24	6	10	2	1	1	4	2	3	1	.464	.708
	Kannapolis (SAL)	LoA	.267	60	243	37	65	6	1	0	22	13	65	4	.302	.300
MINOR LEAGUE TOTALS			.276	176	637	120	176	16	7	1	61	51	138	31	.334	.328

14 CLEVELAN SANTELIZ, RHP

BORN: Sept. 1, 1986. **B-T:** R-R. **HT.:** 6-0. **WT.:** 190. **SIGNED:** Venezuela, 2004. **SIGNED BY:** Roberto Espinoza.

Santeliz has gone 7-22, 5.28 in three years in the United States, yet the White Sox didn't have to think long about whether he was worth protecting on their 40-man roster this offseason. Some club officials believe he has the strongest arm in the system. Outside of a disastrous stint at Great Falls in 2006, Santeliz had been a reliever throughout his pro career. But after Buddy Bell replaced Alan Regier as farm director, he moved Santeliz from the bullpen in Double-A to the rotation in high Class A. Santeliz's fastball has gained velocity as his body has matured the last two years, and he now works from 90-96 mph. He also shows the makings of a plus slider, though the pitch needs much more consistency. There are mixed reports on his changeup, though Chicago thinks it can become an effective pitch for him. While Santeliz has a live arm, he throws with effort, doesn't repeat his delivery well and has erratic control and command. He can get too emotional at times. Shoulder soreness knocked him out for all of May, but he had no further issues after reporting to Winston-Salem. Santeliz still has a way to go with his development, but when he's on, he flashes front-of-the-rotation stuff. He'll return to Double-A in 2009, this time as a starter.

Year	Club (League)	Class	W	L	ERA	G	GS	CG	SV	IP	H	R	ER	HR	BB	SO	AVG
2004	DSL White Sox (DSL)	R	0	1	7.71	13	1	0	0	16	19	16	14	1	13	19	.283
2005	DSL White Sox (DSL)	R	2	3	3.03	15	1	0	2	33	27	18	11	0	13	34	.223
2006	Kannapolis (SAL)	LoA	0	2	6.85	16	0	0	0	24	30	19	18	4	15	21	.319
	Great Falls (PIO)	R	1	8	4.77	14	14	0	0	66	62	41	35	9	32	61	.248
2007	Kannapolis (SAL)	LoA	1	4	6.69	27	0	0	0	38	40	35	28	4	27	37	.274
	Winston-Salem (CAR)	HiA	2	1	4.30	14	0	0	0	15	10	7	7	3	9	18	.192
2008	Birmingham (SL)	AA	0	1	4.41	10	0	0	0	16	14	8	8	2	8	6	.246
	Winston-Salem (CAR)	HiA	3	6	4.90	15	15	0	0	68	55	47	37	8	48	60	.224
MINOR LEAGUE TOTALS			9	26	5.16	124	31	0	2	275	257	191	158	31	165	256	.249

15 JOSE MARTINEZ, OF

BORN: July 25, 1988. **B-T:** R-R. **HT.:** 6-5. **WT.:** 170. **SIGNED:** Venezuela, 2006. **SIGNED BY:** Amador Arias/Dave Wilder.

A classic toolsy prospect with a high ceiling, Martinez has spent about half his short pro career in extended spring training and in the training room, playing only 104 games in his first two full years as a pro. He had found his stride in low Class A, raising his average from .180 to .306 over the course of a month, when he tore the anterior cruciate ligament in his knee. Surgery ended his season but he's expected to be ready for the start of the 2009 season. Martinez's body hasn't matured yet, but he looks like a Juan Gonzalez starter kit. He can put on a show in batting practice with power to all fields, and his quick bat also should give him the ability to hit for some average. He's a free swinger and will have to show more discipline as he moves up the ladder, however. Martinez is raw in other phases of the game as well. While he has plus speed, he's still refining his basestealing ability. He has the range for center field but has spent most of his career in right field, and he has the arm for that position. Martinez has impressed the White Sox with his makeup and work ethic, which should help him in his recovery. He's the son of former Sox infielder Carlos Martinez, and the brother of outfielder Teodoro Martinez, who signed with the Rangers in August.

Year	Club (League)	Class	AVG	G	AB	R	H	2B	3B	HR	RBI	BB	SO	SB	OBP	SLG
2006	Orioles/White Sox (VSL)	R	.278	54	158	26	44	8	0	4	30	25	29	5	.384	.405
2007	Bristol (APP)	R	.282	65	245	34	69	11	3	7	37	22	53	12	.348	.437
2008	Kannapolis (SAL)	LoA	.306	39	144	19	44	5	0	2	18	12	26	7	.359	.382
MINOR LEAGUE TOTALS			.287	158	547	79	157	24	3	13	85	59	108	24	.362	.413

16 JHONNY NUNEZ, RHP

BORN: Nov. 26, 1985. **B-T:** R-R. **HT.:** 6-3. **WT.:** 185. **SIGNED:** Dominican Republic, 2003. **SIGNED BY:** Andres Lopez (Dodgers).

Nunez has the best arm and upside of the three pitching prospects in the trade that sent Nick Swisher to the Yankees in November. The White Sox also acquired Wilson Betemit and swapped one righty prospect (Kanekoa Texeira) for another (Jeff Marquez) in the deal. New York had picked up Nunez just four months earlier, getting him from the Nationals for Alberto Gonzalez. Double-A Eastern League managers were stunned that Washington gave up such a live arm for a middling middle infielder. Nunez originally signed with the Dodgers and went to the Nationals in a 2006 trade for Marlon Anderson. They worked Nunez as a starter in high Class A during the first half of 2008, but he featured sharper stuff after a promotion and a move to the bullpen. Nunez shows two plus pitches at times: a fastball that sits at 92-94 mph and touches 95, and a slider with some power and inconsistent tilt. He throws from a low arm slot and was outstanding after the Yankees helped him achieve better balance in his delivery. He dominated in the EL playoffs and pitched well in instructional league. Nunez doesn't have a feel for an offspeed pitch and struggles against lefthanders when he doesn't command his fastball. The White Sox have yet to determine Nunez's role for 2009, but he has a good chance to open the season in Triple-A.

Year	Club (League)	Class	W	L	ERA	G	GS	CG	SV	IP	H	R	ER	HR	BB	SO	AVG
2004	Dodgers1 (DSL)	R	2	1	1.73	7	7	0	0	36	30	8	7	1	6	23	.229
	Dodgers2 (DSL)	R	2	0	4.60	4	3	0	0	16	17	9	8	0	4	12	.262
2005	Dodgers (DSL)	R	4	3	1.92	15	8	1	0	52	29	13	11	0	13	40	.153
2006	Dodgers (GCL)	R	6	0	1.58	10	7	0	0	57	35	12	10	0	19	56	.177

Year	Club (League)	Class	W	L	ERA	G	GS	CG	SV	IP	H	R	ER	HR	BB	SO	AVG
2007	Hagerstown (SAL)	LoA	4	6	4.05	23	22	0	0	107	97	59	48	10	48	86	.239
2008	Potomac (CAR)	HiA	2	8	5.22	21	17	0	0	81	88	51	47	11	21	82	.276
	Harrisburg (EL)	AA	0	0	1.13	5	0	0	0	8	9	1	1	0	6	8	.300
	Trenton (EL)	AA	1	0	1.86	8	0	0	0	19	16	5	4	2	6	26	.229
MINOR LEAGUE TOTALS			21	18	3.26	93	64	1	0	376	321	158	136	24	123	333	.228

17 BRENT MOREL, 3B

BORN: April 21, 1987. **B-T:** R-R. **HT.:** 6-1. **WT.:** 220. **DRAFTED:** Cal Poly, 2008 (3rd round). **SIGNED BY:** Gary Woods/Derek Valenzuela.

Having lost their second-round pick as compensation for signing free agent Scott Linebrink, the White Sox had to sit out 77 picks after taking Gordon Beckham with the eighth overall choice last June. They rated Morel as a solid second-round talent and were delighted to get him in the third round, where they signed him for $440,000. He signed quickly enough to play 60 games, including 45 in low Class A, and to establish himself as one of the better hitters in the system. Morel has a solid approach at the plate, looks to jump on fastballs and drives the ball from gap to gap. Chicago thinks he'll develop at least average power. He has good pitch recognition, which should help him against advanced pitching. Morel is athletic and runs better than most third basemen. He has good range and a plus arm at the hot corner. The White Sox won't be afraid to push Morel, who should open his first full pro season in high Class A.

Year	Club (League)	Class	AVG	G	AB	R	H	2B	3B	HR	RBI	BB	SO	SB	OBP	SLG
2008	Great Falls (PIO)	R	.375	15	64	11	24	0	2	0	3	6	7	7	.437	.438
	Kannapolis (SAL)	LoA	.297	45	172	26	51	6	2	6	24	16	28	5	.359	.459
MINOR LEAGUE TOTALS			.318	60	236	37	75	6	4	6	27	22	35	12	.380	.453

18 SANTOS RODRIGUEZ, LHP

BORN: Jan. 2, 1988. **B-T:** L-L. **HT.:** 6-6. **WT.:** 185. **DRAFTED:** Dominican Republic, 2006. **SIGNED BY:** Roberto Aquino (Braves).

The most anonymous of the four prospects the White Sox acquired when they shipped Javier Vazquez and Boone Logan to the Braves in December, Rodriguez shouldn't stay that way for long. He's an ultra-projectable lefthander who already tops out at 97 mph with his fastball, and he led Rookie-level Gulf Coast League relievers in opponent batting average (.155) and strikeouts per nine innings (14.0) last season. The ball appears to jump out of his hand, producing a fastball that sits at 91-93 mph with above-average sinking action. He also has the makings of a plus pitch with a flat slider that has some late bite. His changeup has a ways to go and will be a point of emphasis when Chicago makes him a starter in 2009. Though not overly athletic, Rodriguez is capable of putting his delivery together and is hard to hit when everything falls into place. He does struggle on occasion to repeat his delivery and to throw strikes, which isn't uncommon for a pitcher who's so tall and so young. After spending the last two years in the GCL, he should be ready for a jump to low Class A.

Year	Club (League)	Class	W	L	ERA	G	GS	CG	SV	IP	H	R	ER	HR	BB	SO	AVG
2007	Braves (GCL)	R	0	1	6.67	12	2	0	2	28	29	25	21	3	21	35	.248
2008	Braves (GCL)	R	1	2	2.79	14	0	0	5	29	16	12	9	0	13	45	.155
MINOR LEAGUE TOTALS			1	3	4.71	26	2	0	7	57	45	37	30	3	34	80	.205

19 BRIAN OMOGROSSO, RHP

BORN: April 24, 1984. **B-T:** R-R. **HT.:** 6-4. **WT.:** 230. **DRAFTED:** Indiana State, 2006 (6th round). **SIGNED BY:** Nathan Durst/Keith Staab/Mike Shirley.

The White Sox thought Omogrosso might be on the verge of breaking out in 2008, but he instead spent three stints on the disabled list with blister problems and worked only 39 innings. A similar scenario played out three years earlier, when Omogrosso was on course to be a top pick in the 2005 draft, only to have Tommy John surgery. When healthy, he's a power pitcher whose low three-quarters delivery makes him tough on righthanders. Omogrosso can ride his 91-93 mph two-seam fastball in on the hands of righties or blow them away with a four-seamer that touches 96. He flashed a plus slider before his elbow required reconstruction, but it hasn't had the same tilt since. He lost valuable development time last year, as he needs innings to refine his slider and his control. He does a good job of keeping the ball down but sometimes struggles to find the strike zone. Some club officials believe Omogrosso would have earned a big league promotion in 2008 if not for his blister problems and expect him to get to Chicago in 2009.

Year	Club (League)	Class	W	L	ERA	G	GS	CG	SV	IP	H	R	ER	HR	BB	SO	AVG
2006	Kannapolis (SAL)	LoA	1	2	3.19	22	0	0	2	37	27	14	13	2	13	23	.209
2007	Winston-Salem (CAR)	HiA	8	8	3.74	40	14	1	5	120	94	60	50	7	57	108	.211
2008	Birmingham (SL)	AA	2	3	3.69	17	5	0	1	39	32	19	16	2	25	26	.230
MINOR LEAGUE TOTALS			11	13	3.63	79	19	1	8	196	153	93	79	11	95	157	.214

20 JEFF MARQUEZ, RHP

BORN: Aug. 10, 1984. **B-T:** R-R. **HT.:** 6-2. **WT.:** 190. **DRAFTED:** Sacramento CC, 2004 (1st round supplemental). **SIGNED BY:** Jeff Patterson (Yankees).

The White Sox have made a habit of turning premium draft picks who have stalled with other teams into effective big league starters—see John Danks and Gavin Floyd—and will try to do the same with Marquez. He came to Chicago in the Nick Swisher trade, and the Yankees sold low. The 2004 supplemental first-rounder had his best year in 2007, improving his curveball and changeup and garnering Ramiro Mendoza comparisons for his sinker. Last season, he missed two months with a tired arm and didn't trust his secondary pitches. Marquez still has a hard sinker, though he hit 94 mph less frequently in 2008 and more often sat at 88-90 mph. He was too predictable because hitters knew to look for his fastball when he needed a strike. His curveball and changeup regressed but were still average pitches. The Yankees had him incorporate his slider more frequently after he was demoted to Double-A, and his velocity also improved. He finished strong in the Eastern League playoffs and earned a trip to the Arizona Fall League. Marquez competes well and can get a ground ball when he needs it. He might fit better in middle relief, but if he throws four pitches for strikes, he still should fit at the back of a rotation. When the White Sox traded Javier Vazquez in December, they created an opening in their rotation and will let Marquez compete for the chance to fill it during spring training.

Year	Club (League)	Class	W	L	ERA	G	GS	CG	SV	IP	H	R	ER	HR	BB	SO	AVG
2004	Yankees (GCL)	R	2	0	0.63	4	2	0	0	14	10	1	1	0	4	18	.189
	Staten Island (NYP)	SS	2	4	3.02	11	11	0	0	51	51	26	17	2	20	36	.267
2005	Charelston, SC (SAL)	LoA	9	13	3.42	27	27	1	0	140	138	64	53	4	61	107	.257
2006	Yankees (GCL)	R	0	1	3.18	2	2	0	0	6	7	2	2	1	1	8	.304
	Tampa (FSL)	HiA	7	5	3.61	18	17	0	0	92	102	56	37	4	29	82	.279
2007	Trenton (EL)	AA	15	9	3.65	27	27	2	0	155	166	80	63	11	44	94	.270
2008	Scranton/W-B (IL)	AAA	6	7	4.69	14	14	1	0	81	93	51	42	12	24	33	.300
	Yankees (GCL)	R	1	0	5.40	2	1	0	0	7	10	4	4	0	1	6	.333
	Trenton (EL)	AA	1	1	2.93	3	3	0	0	15	12	5	5	0	7	12	.218
MINOR LEAGUE TOTALS			43	40	3.60	108	104	4	0	561	589	289	224	34	191	396	.270

21 JON GILMORE, 3B

BORN: Aug. 23, 1988. **B-T:** R-R. **HT.:** 6-3. **WT.:** 195. **DRAFTED:** HS—Iowa City, Iowa, 2007 (1st round supplemental). **SIGNED BY:** Terry Tripp (Braves).

The White Sox significantly upgraded their third-base depth in 2008 by signing Cuban defector Dayan Viciedo, drafting Brent Morel and trading for Gilmore. Part of the Javier Vazquez deal with the Braves, Gilmore signed for $900,000 as a supplemental first-round pick in 2007. He went 33rd overall, the highest an Iowa high school player ever has gone in the draft. The brother-in-law of Ben Zobrist, Gilmore produced mixed results in his first full pro season. An opening assignment to low Class A proved to be too much for him, though he recovered nicely in the Appalachian League. Gilmore has an unorthodox approach at the plate but generates good power to all fields. He's raw but in the early stages of developing into a professional hitter. When he has his confidence, he swings the bat with authority and makes solid contact. He'll need to improve his patience at the plate and his ability to handle breaking balls. Gilmore moves well for a big man and drew some interest from college football programs as a quarterback. He made progress defensively in 2008, displaying improved footwork at third base. He has a strong arm, but he needs to shorten his arm action to throw the ball quicker and straighter. He remains somewhat stiff in his actions at the hot corner, though he has good hands and above-average reactions. Gilmore will give low Class A another try in 2009.

Year	Club (League)	Class	AVG	G	AB	R	H	2B	3B	HR	RBI	BB	SO	SB	OBP	SLG
2007	Braves (GCL)	R	.284	43	162	11	46	5	1	1	29	4	28	0	.296	.346
2008	Danville (APP)	R	.337	67	258	27	87	23	0	4	31	13	41	0	.365	.473
	Rome (SAL)	LoA	.186	27	102	6	19	1	0	0	4	2	20	1	.202	.196
MINOR LEAGUE TOTALS			.291	137	522	44	152	29	1	5	64	19	89	1	.313	.379

22 JON LINK, RHP

BORN: March 23, 1984. **B-T:** R-R. **HT.:** 6-1. **WT.:** 175. **DRAFTED:** Bluefield (Va.), 2005 (26th round). **SIGNED BY:** Ash Lawson (Padres).

Credit Joe Butler for doing a thorough job scouting the high Class A California League. It was Butler's recommendation that prompted GM Kenny Williams to ask for Link when the Padres approached the White Sox about Rob Mackowiak at the trade deadline in 2007. In his first full season in the Chicago system, Link led the minor leagues with 35 saves and earned himself a spot on Chicago's 40-man roster. Unlike most relievers, he can attack hitters with three pitches. His hard slider is his strikeout pitch, but he also has a low-90s fastball with sink and movement and an effective changeup. Link's lone negative in 2008 was that he had more trouble finding the strike zone than he had in the past. If he can control his pitches better, he'll be ready for the majors. Link has excellent mound presence and is a student of the game. He wore out pitching coach J.R. Perdew's ear at

Birmingham, often sitting next to him in the dugout for the first seven innings, always talking baseball. Because he has three pitches, some believe Link could make an easy transition into the starting rotation. But he enjoys closing, which suits his personality, and will remain in that role this year in Triple-A.

Year	Club (League)	Class	W	L	ERA	G	GS	CG	SV	IP	H	R	ER	HR	BB	SO	AVG
2005	Eugene (NWL)	SS	3	3	4.42	25	7	0	0	59	67	33	29	5	8	44	.285
2006	Fort Wayne (MWL)	LoA	5	5	4.91	53	0	0	3	62	72	45	34	3	24	57	.283
2007	Lake Elsinore (CAL)	HiA	2	1	3.07	41	0	0	13	41	32	16	14	5	11	45	.209
	Winston-Salem (CAR)	HiA	1	0	2.55	14	0	0	3	18	16	5	5	1	4	19	.246
2008	Birmingham (SL)	AA	5	4	3.02	56	0	0	35	57	48	21	19	3	27	66	.223
MINOR LEAGUE TOTALS			16	13	3.84	189	7	0	54	237	235	120	101	17	74	231	.255

23 DEXTER CARTER, RHP

BORN: Feb. 5, 1987. **B-T:** R-R. **HT.:** 6-6. **WT.:** 195. **DRAFTED:** Old Dominion, 2008 (13th round). **SIGNED BY:** Chuck Fox.

After playing with Justin Upton at Greenbrier Christian Academy in Chesapeake, Va., Carter was a 12th-round pick of the Rangers out of high school in 2005. He opted to go the college route but then got somewhat lost. He posted an 8.76 ERA and walked nearly a batter per inning in 2008, but the White Sox saw enough potential to draft him it the 13th round. Now he looks like a $32,500 bargain after he led the Pioneer League with a 2.23 ERA and combined with former Old Dominion teammate Dan Hudson to pitch Great Falls to the league title. Carter posted eye-popping numbers in the hitter-friendly circuit, thanks to two plus pitches: a lively 92-93 mph fastball that peaks at 96, and a swing-and-miss curveball. Both his breaking ball and his control were much more consistent than they were in college, the result of working with White Sox coaches to refine his delivery. Carter got on a straighter line to the plate and developed a more consistent landing point. His changeup lags behind his other two pitches but has some potential. He's athletic and his big frame allows him to work on a good downward plane. Carter must show he can repeat his success in a full-season league but projects as a possible middle-of-the-rotation starter or more. He could reach high Class A in 2009 if he continues to thrive.

Year	Club (League)	Class	W	L	ERA	G	GS	CG	SV	IP	H	R	ER	HR	BB	SO	AVG
2008	Great Falls (PIO)	R	6	1	2.23	15	12	0	0	69	44	23	17	3	25	89	.179
MINOR LEAGUE TOTALS			6	1	2.23	15	12	0	0	69	44	23	17	3	25	89	.179

24 DAN HUDSON, RHP

BORN: March 9, 1987. **B-T:** R-R. **HT.:** 6-4 **WT.:** 220. **DRAFTED:** Old Dominion, 2008 (5th round). **SIGNED BY:** Chuck Fox/Nick Hostetler.

Hudson didn't slump as badly as Dexter Carter did in 2008 at Old Dominion, but he did have the worst season of his three-year career with the Monarchs and dropped to the fifth round of the draft. Reunited with Carter in Great Falls after signing for $180,000, he led the Pioneer League with 90 strikeouts in 70 innings and fanned 12 over six innings in the championship-clinching playoff victory. Working from a three-quarters arm slot, Hudson throws an 88-92 mph fastball that explodes at the plate, riding in on righthanders and tailing away from lefthanders. He has an average slider and gets strikeouts by throwing it down in the zone. He's gaining confidence in his changeup. Hudson should be durable, as he has a strong frame and keeps his pitch counts down by throwing strikes and getting groundouts. If he performs well in spring training, he could skip a level and start 2009 in high Class A.

Year	Club (League)	Class	W	L	ERA	G	GS	CG	SV	IP	H	R	ER	HR	BB	SO	AVG
2008	Great Falls (PIO)	R	5	4	3.36	14	14	0	0	70	52	30	26	6	22	90	.202
MINOR LEAGUE TOTALS			5	4	3.36	14	14	0	0	70	52	30	26	6	22	90	.202

25 CARLOS TORRES, RHP

BORN: Oct. 22, 1982. **B-T:** R-R. **HT.:** 6-1. **WT.:** 185. **DRAFTED:** Kansas State, 2004 (15th round). **SIGNED BY:** Paul Provas/Keith Staab.

Torres had a circuitous college career, playing at four schools—Allan Hancock (Calif.) JC, Grossmont (Calif.) JC, San Jose State and Kansas State—in four years. Torres wasn't drafted until after his senior season with the Wildcats, and even then he went in the 15th round. He had the best season of his five-year pro career in 2008, matching his previous total with nine wins, which led the Southern League at the time of his promotion to Triple-A. Torres has a strong, durable arm that has proved resilient as he has shuttled between starting and relieving. He has a low-90s fastball that can hit 94 at times to go with a plus cutter. He does a good job of pitching down in the strike zone. Torres' biggest need is to improve his feel for his changeup, which he needs to help him against lefthanders after they torched him in the Arizona Fall League. He projects as a workhorse reliever in the majors and his first opportunity with Chicago could come in 2009.

Year	Club (League)	Class	W	L	ERA	G	GS	CG	SV	IP	H	R	ER	HR	BB	SO	AVG
2004	Bristol (APP)	R	2	2	4.74	19	0	0	1	38	43	30	20	2	12	28	.281
2005	Great Falls (PIO)	R	1	1	2.88	5	5	0	0	25	18	8	8	1	8	26	.205
	Kannapolis (SAL)	LoA	1	3	3.53	8	8	0	0	43	28	20	17	4	23	54	.179
2006	Winston-Salem (CAR)	HiA	3	8	4.69	25	20	0	1	94	116	66	49	7	55	76	.304
2007	Winston-Salem (CAR)	HiA	0	2	3.72	19	0	0	3	36	33	16	15	0	10	41	.248
	Birmingham (SL)	AA	2	2	3.70	36	0	0	1	56	57	26	23	3	22	59	.269
2008	Birmingham (SL)	AA	9	5	3.20	21	17	0	0	101	86	40	36	4	29	93	.234
	Charlotte (IL)	AAA	0	0	4.58	8	1	0	0	20	23	10	10	2	11	19	.295
MINOR LEAGUE TOTALS			18	23	3.87	141	51	0	6	414	404	216	178	23	170	396	.257

26 JAYSON NIX, 2B

BORN: Aug. 26, 1982. **B-T:** R-R. **HT.:** 5-11. **WT.:** 185. **DRAFTED:** HS—Midland, Texas, 2001 (1st round supplemental). **SIGNED BY:** Dar Cox (Rockies).

A Rockies' supplemental first-round pick in 2001, Nix becomes a project for White Sox hitting coach Greg Walker after Chicago signed him as a minor league free agent in October. Nix has long shown Gold Glove skills —Carney Lansford once called him the best defensive second baseman he ever has seen—but his bat stalled once he got to Double-A in 2004. He did have the best offensive season of his career in 2008—but that came in his third year in Triple-A and after he botched a chance to seize Colorado's second-base job by hitting .111 in the majors in April. The brother of Reds outfielder Laynce Nix, Jayson tries too hard at times, grinding the bat handle rather than relaxing and trusting the talent that made him the 44th player drafted in 2001. He has shown power in the minors and with Team USA, both at the 2007 World Cup and the 2008 Olympics, but sometimes gets too homer-happy and he showed little punch in his big league stint. He has good speed and instincts on the basepaths and in the field. He also has sure hands and a stronger arm than most second basemen. Nix will compete with Chris Getz and Brent Lillibridge for the White Sox' second-base job in spring training. It might be his last chance to show he can play on an everyday basis in the majors.

Year	Club (League)	Class	AVG	G	AB	R	H	2B	3B	HR	RBI	BB	SO	SB	OBP	SLG
2001	Casper (PIO)	R	.294	42	153	28	45	10	1	5	24	21	43	1	.385	.471
2002	Asheville (SAL)	LoA	.246	132	487	73	120	29	2	14	79	62	105	14	.340	.400
2003	Visalia (CAL)	HiA	.281	137	562	107	158	46	0	21	86	54	131	24	.351	.475
2004	Tulsa (TEX)	AA	.213	123	456	58	97	17	1	14	58	40	101	14	.292	.346
2005	Tulsa (TEX)	AA	.236	131	501	68	118	27	0	11	47	29	92	10	.289	.355
2006	Colorado Springs (PCL)	AAA	.251	103	358	39	90	14	1	2	26	32	61	15	.317	.313
2007	Colorado Springs (PCL)	AAA	.292	124	439	80	128	33	2	11	58	31	79	24	.342	.451
2008	Colorado (NL)	MAJ	.125	22	56	2	7	2	0	0	2	7	17	1	.234	.161
	Colorado Springs (PCL)	AAA	.303	67	264	63	80	21	2	17	51	27	64	11	.373	.549
MINOR LEAGUE TOTALS			.260	859	3220	516	836	197	9	95	429	296	676	113	.330	.415
MAJOR LEAGUE TOTALS			.125	22	56	2	7	2	0	0	2	7	17	1	.234	.161

27 ADAM RUSSELL, RHP

BORN: April 14, 1983. **B-T:** R-R. **HT.:** 6-4. **WT.:** 250. **DRAFTED:** Ohio, 2004 (6th round). **SIGNED BY:** Nathan Durst/Larry Grefer.

There's nothing subtle about Russell, a big man who challenges hitters with a fastball that parks in the low 90s and occasionally reaches 95. He was used exclusively as a reliever for the first time in 2008 and made a smooth transition, spending almost as much time in the big league bullpen as in Triple-A. If hitters try to sit on Russell's fastball, he can get outs with a curveball that rates as a plus pitch at times. He varies his arm slot, sometimes dropping down to a low three-quarters angle, and has a high-maintenance delivery that easily gets out of whack. As a result, he has inconsistent control and command. He also seemed a little reluctant to challenge hitters on the inner half once he got to Chicago, though that's not uncommon for a pitcher getting his first taste of the major leagues. He never has been able to develop much of a changeup, though it's less important now that he's coming out of the bullpen. The White Sox have several veteran righthanders in their bullpen, so Russell will need a strong spring training in order to break camp with the club.

Year	Club (League)	Class	W	L	ERA	G	GS	CG	SV	IP	H	R	ER	HR	BB	SO	AVG
2004	Great Falls (PIO)	R	4	0	2.37	15	4	0	0	38	31	11	10	2	18	33	.228
	Kannapolis (SAL)	LoA	0	2	9.00	2	2	0	0	10	18	11	10	3	7	3	.409
2005	Kannapolis (SAL)	LoA	9	7	3.78	24	24	0	0	126	116	61	53	10	55	82	.246
2006	Winston-Salem (CAR)	HiA	7	3	2.66	17	17	0	0	95	80	35	28	5	39	61	.235
	Birmingham (SL)	AA	3	3	4.75	10	10	0	0	55	59	33	29	5	19	47	.269
2007	Birmingham (SL)	AA	9	11	4.80	38	20	0	1	139	159	81	74	8	58	95	.290
2008	Charlotte (IL)	AAA	3	2	2.89	25	0	0	0	37	28	13	12	3	19	28	.203
	Chicago (AL)	MAJ	4	0	5.19	22	0	0	0	26	30	15	15	1	10	22	.291
MINOR LEAGUE TOTALS			35	28	3.89	131	77	0	1	500	491	245	216	36	215	349	.259
MAJOR LEAGUE TOTALS			4	0	5.19	22	0	0	0	26	30	15	15	1	10	22	.291

28 LANCE BROADWAY, RHP

BORN: Aug. 20, 1983. **B-T:** R-R. **HT.:** 6-2. **WT.:** 210. **DRAFTED:** Texas Christian, 2005 (1st round).
SIGNED BY: Keith Staab.

Seeing apparently isn't believing when it comes to the White Sox and Broadway. He has made two big league starts and beat the Royals in both of them, allowing two runs in 11⅓ innings. Chicago paid him $1.57 million as the 15th overall pick in the 2005 draft—taking him ahead of such players as Jacoby Ellsbury and Matt Garza—but seems more likely to use Broadway as trade bait than to give him a chance at making the big league rotation. Broadway hasn't pitched nearly as well as a Triple-A starter (19-16, 4.55) or big league reliever (6.92 ERA in 13 innings), and he regressed after a fast start at Charlotte last year. He's a conditioning freak with a good feel for pitching, if not overwhelming stuff. He has to locate his fastball because it arrives at 88-91 mph, and he sometimes overthrows and loses his command. His curveball and changeup are his best pitches, and he also mixes in a cutter/slider. He doesn't appear to be in Chicago's 2009 plans, which means he'll spend a third season in Triple-A unless he gets traded.

Year	Club (League)	Class	W	L	ERA	G	GS	CG	SV	IP	H	R	ER	HR	BB	SO	AVG
2005	Winston-Salem (CAR)	HiA	1	3	4.58	11	11	0	0	55	68	31	28	4	20	58	.306
2006	Birmingham (SL)	AA	8	8	2.74	25	25	2	0	154	160	59	47	10	40	111	.269
	Charlotte (IL)	AAA	0	0	3.00	1	1	0	0	6	5	2	2	0	1	6	.217
2007	Charlotte (IL)	AAA	8	9	4.65	26	26	2	0	155	155	86	80	17	78	108	.264
	Chicago (AL)	MAJ	1	1	0.87	4	1	0	0	10	5	2	1	0	5	14	.143
2008	Charlotte (IL)	AAA	11	7	4.66	24	23	1	0	145	166	87	75	24	44	101	.292
	Chicago (AL)	MAJ	1	0	7.07	7	1	0	0	14	20	11	11	4	5	7	.328
MINOR LEAGUE TOTALS			28	27	4.05	87	86	5	0	515	554	265	232	55	183	384	.278
MAJOR LEAGUE TOTALS			2	1	4.44	11	2	0	0	24	25	13	12	4	10	21	.260

29 C.J. RETHERFORD, 3B

BORN: Aug. 14, 1985. **B-T:** R-R. **HT.:** 5-11. **WT.:** 190. **SIGNED:** Arizona State, NDFA 2007.
SIGNED BY: Alan Regier.

Retherford was draft-eligible for five straight years from 2003-07, but he never drew a nibble out of high school or at South Mountain (Ariz.) CC or Arizona State. He already has exceeded expectations since signing as a nondrafted free agent. He led the Pioneer League with 30 doubles and 47 extra-base hits in his 2007 pro debut, then followed up by skipping a level and earning Carolina League all-star honors. He also led both of his minor league clubs in homers. Retherford has a good approach at the plate, plus the ability to make consistent contact and drive the ball to all fields. He has fringe-average speed but good baserunning instincts. His arm is his best defensive tool, and he has worked hard to soften his hands at third base. Still, he's not a standout defender at the hot corner. He played several positions and even pitched at Arizona State, and his best path to the big leagues may be as an offensive-minded utilityman. Retherford should continue to hit for average with at least gap power in Double-A this season.

Year	Club (League)	Class	AVG	G	AB	R	H	2B	3B	HR	RBI	BB	SO	SB	OBP	SLG
2007	Great Falls (PIO)	R	.318	61	261	53	83	30	4	13	48	24	45	2	.389	.613
2008	Winston-Salem (CAR)	HiA	.295	130	461	66	136	28	1	16	71	37	78	11	.350	.464
MINOR LEAGUE TOTALS			.303	191	722	119	219	58	5	29	119	61	123	13	.364	.518

30 GREGORY INFANTE, RHP

BORN: July 10, 1987. **B-T:** R-R. **HT.:** 6-2. **WT.:** 185. **SIGNED:** Venezuela, 2006. **SIGNED BY:** Amador Arias.

Infante didn't sign out of Venezuela until he was 18 years old, and his career moved slowly until he started putting things together when he repeated the Rookie-level Appalachian League last season. He had control problems at every stop, including an assignment to low Class A at the start of 2008, but he suddenly started throwing strikes when he returned to Bristol in the summer. Infante's biggest problem was overthrowing, something he doesn't need to do. His arm strength and clean delivery allow him to range from 89-95 with his fastball, and he usually sits at 91-93. He maintains his velocity deep into starts. His 74-79 mph downer curveball is a solid second offering but he has yet to show much mastery of his changeup. Now Infante must build on his breakthough when he gets a second chance at Kannapolis in 2009. He could be a No. 3 starter if he maximizes his potential, though he's a long way off.

Year	Club (League)	Class	W	L	ERA	G	GS	CG	SV	IP	H	R	ER	HR	BB	SO	AVG
2006	Orioles/White Sox (VSL)	R	0	0	8.61	10	2	0	0	23	25	28	22	2	26	17	.291
2007	Bristol (APP)	R	2	3	4.01	10	8	0	0	34	25	17	15	1	23	33	.207
2008	Kannapolis (SAL)	LoA	1	2	6.59	4	3	0	0	14	16	12	10	0	12	11	.286
	Bristol (APP)	R	4	3	2.66	13	12	0	0	74	63	26	22	4	19	57	.232
MINOR LEAGUE TOTALS			7	8	4.29	37	25	0	0	145	129	83	69	7	80	118	.242

Cincinnati Reds

BY J.J. COOPER

The minute Walt Jocketty was added as a special adviser to Reds president and CEO Bob Castellini in early 2008, the running assumption was that the former Cardinals general manager eventually would take over the same job in Cincinnati.

What was surprising was how quickly that happened.

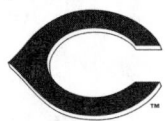

Just 21 games into the season, Castellini pulled the trigger, firing Wayne Krivsky and turning the franchise over to Jocketty, who had won six division titles, two National League pennants and a World Series title in St. Louis. Krivsky could argue that he got dumped just when some of his handiwork was starting to pay off.

The Reds were a disappointing 9-12, but rookie Johnny Cueto had turned in three quality starts in four outings, an auspicious beginning for a team that had spent nearly a decade trying to produce a home-grown starting pitcher. Edinson Volquez, acquired by Krivsky in an offseason trade for Josh Hamilton, had allowed three runs in four starts. He finished the season with a 3.21 ERA—the best by a Cincinnati starter since Elmer Dessens in 2002. Joey Votto had taken over at first base and Jay Bruce could have done the same in right field but had to wait until late May for a callup.

The Reds finished the year at 74-88, a two-win improvement over 2007 but their eighth consecutive losing season. Jocketty traded away pending free agents Adam Dunn and Ken Griffey Jr. The youth movement continued with center fielder Chris Dickerson and catcher Ryan Hanigan making cases for everyday jobs.

For a club that spent the early part of the decade getting little or no help from the farm, it was an encouraging sign. Partly in recognition of the system's success, Jocketty retained Krivsky's farm director, Terry Reynolds, and scouting director, Chris Buckley.

Cincinnati is in limbo as it prepares for 2009. On one hand, the development of Bruce, Cueto, Volquez and Votto gives the Reds a solid young nucleus to build around. But on the other hand, their offense ranked 12th and their pitching staff 13th in the National League last year. Any significant improvements will have to come from within than from player acquisitions.

One thing that would help is if righthander Homer Bailey made good on his potential. The seventh overall

The Reds trade with Texas cost them Josh Hamilton, but netted ace Edinson Volquez

GEORGE GOJKOVICH

TOP 30 PROSPECTS

1. Yonder Alonso, 1b	16. Ryan Hanigan, c
2. Todd Frazier, ss/3b/1b	17. Ramon Ramirez, rhp
3. Drew Stubbs, of	18. Matt Maloney, lhp
4. Chris Valaika, ss	19. Zach Cozart, ss
5. Yorman Rodriguez, of	20. Juan Carlos Sulbaran, rhp
6. Kyle Lotzkar, rhp	21. Dallas Buck, rhp
7. Neftali Soto, 3b	22. Chris Heisey, of
8. Juan Francisco, 3b	23. Danny Dorn, of
9. Juan Duran, of	24. Carlos Fisher, rhp
10. Devin Mesoraco, c	25. Pedro Viola, lhp
11. Daryl Thompson, rhp	26. Sean Watson, rhp
12. Chris Dickerson, of	27. Robert Manuel, rhp
13. Jordan Smith, rhp	28. Craig Tatum, c
14. Josh Roenicke, rhp	29. Adam Rosales, inf
15. Zach Stewart, rhp	30. Alex Buchholz, 2b

pick in 2004 has been bombed in five big league stints over the past two years, and his stuff, command and confidence all went backward last season. The Reds reportedly have shopped him to other clubs, something that would have been unthinkable a year ago.

The farm system won't be able to produce as much quality in 2009 as it did last year, when Bruce, Bailey, Votto and Cueto graduated to the majors from the first four spots on this list. But their Triple-A Louisville and Double-A Carolina affiliates should be stocked with potential big league contributors, giving the Reds improved depth if injuries crop up.

General Manager: Walt Jocketty . **Farm Director:** Terry Reynolds. **Scouting Director:** Chris Buckley.

Class	Team	League	W	L	PCT	Finish*	Manager	Affiliate
Majors	Cincinnati	National	74	88	.457	10th (16)	Dusty Baker	—
Triple-A	Louisville Bats	International	88	56	.611	1st (14)	Rick Sweet	2000
Double-A	Chattanooga Lookouts	Southern	67	72	.482	8th (10)	M. Goff/J. Dismuke	1988
High A	Sarasota Reds	Florida State	60	78	.435	10th (12)	Joe Ayrault	2005
Low A	Dayton Dragons	Midwest	66	72	.478	11th (14)	Donnie Scott	2000
Rookie	Billings Mustangs	Pioneer	42	32	.568	2nd (8)	Julio Garcia	1974
Rookie	GCL Reds	Gulf Coast	25	31	.446	14th (16)	Pat Kelly	1999
Overall 2008 Minor League Record			348	341	.505	15th		

* Finish in overall standings (No. of teams in league). ^League champion.

LAST YEAR'S TOP 30

Rank	Player, Pos.	Status
1.	Jay Bruce, of	Majors
2.	Homer Bailey, rhp	Majors
3.	Joey Votto, 1b/of	Majors
4.	Johnny Cueto	Majors
5.	Drew Stubbs, of	No. 3
6.	Devin Mesoraco, c	No. 10
7.	Todd Frazier, ss	No. 2
8.	Juan Francisco, 3b	No. 8
9.	Josh Roenicke, rhp	No. 14
10.	Matt Maloney, lhp	No. 18
11.	Kyle Lotzkar, rhp	No. 6
12.	Jared Burton, rhp	Majors
13.	Chris Valaika, ss	No. 4
14.	Neftali Soto, ss	No. 7
15.	Pedro Viola, lhp	No. 25
16.	Sean Watson, rhp	No. 26
17.	Craig Tatum, c	No. 28
18.	Zach Cozart, ss	No. 19
19.	Paul Janish, ss/2b	Dropped out
20.	Carlos Fisher, rhp	No. 24
21.	Travis Wood, lhp	Dropped out
22.	Adam Rosales, 1b/3b	No. 29
23.	Brandon Waring, 3b	(Orioles)
24.	Sam LeCure, rhp	Dropped out
25.	Jose Castro, ss	Dropped out
26.	Tyler Pelland, lhp	Dropped out
27.	Chris Dickerson, of	No. 12
28.	Danny Dorn, of	No. 23
29.	Justin Turner, 2b/ss	(Orioles)
30.	Sergio Valenzuela, rhp	(Mexican League)

BEST TOOLS

Best Hitter for Average	Yonder Alonso
Best Power Hitter	Juan Francisco
Best Strike-Zone Discipline	Yonder Alonso
Fastest Baserunner	Theodis Bowe
Best Athlete	Yorman Rodriguez
Best Fastball	Josh Roenicke
Best Curveball	Kyle Lotzkar
Best Slider	Jordan Smith
Best Changeup	Ramon Ramirez
Best Control	Robert Manuel
Best Defensive Catcher	Ryan Hanigan
Best Defensive Infielder	Zach Cozart
Best Infield Arm	Juan Francisco
Best Defensive Outfielder	Drew Stubbs
Best Outfield Arm	Yorman Rodriguez

PROJECTED 2012 LINEUP

Catcher	Devin Mesoraco
First Base	Yonder Alonso
Second Base	Brandon Phillips
Third Base	Todd Frazier
Shortstop	Chris Valaika
Left Field	Joey Votto
Center Field	Drew Stubbs
Right Field	Jay Bruce
No. 1 Starter	Edinson Volquez
No. 2 Starter	Johnny Cueto
No. 3 Starter	Aaron Harang
No. 4 Starter	Bronson Arroyo
No. 5 Starter	Homer Bailey
Closer	Francisco Cordero

TOP PROSPECTS OF THE DECADE

Year	Player, Pos.	2008 Org.
1999	Rob Bell, rhp	White Sox
2000	Gookie Dawkins, ss	Royals
2001	Austin Kearns, of	Nationals
2002	Austin Kearns, of	Nationals
2003	Chris Gruler, rhp	Out of baseball
2004	Ryan Wagner, rhp	Nationals
2005	Homer Bailey, rhp	Reds
2006	Homer Bailey, rhp	Reds
2007	Homer Bailey, rhp	Reds
2008	Jay Bruce, of	Reds

TOP DRAFT PICKS OF THE DECADE

Year	Player, Pos.	2008 Org.
1999	Ty Howington, lhp	Out of baseball
2000	David Espinosa, ss	Camden (Atlantic)
2001	*Jeremy Sowers, lhp	Indians
2002	Chris Gruler, rhp	Out of baseball
2003	Ryan Wagner, rhp	Nationals
2004	Homer Bailey, rhp	Reds
2005	Jay Bruce, of	Reds
2006	Drew Stubbs, of	Reds
2007	Devin Mesoraco, c	Reds
2008	Yonder Alonso, 1b	Reds

*Did not sign.

LARGEST BONUSES IN CLUB HISTORY

Chris Gruler, 2002	$2,500,000
Yorman Rodriguez, 2008	$2,500,000
Homer Bailey, 2004	$2,300,000
Drew Stubbs, 2006	$2,000,000
Juan Duran, 2008	$2,000,000
Yonder Alonso, 2008	$2,000,000

CINCINNATI REDS

TOP 2009 ROOKIE: Josh Roenicke, rhp. As a flamethrowing reliever, the former UCLA wide receiver has an easy path to making an immediate impact.

BREAKOUT PROSPECT: Dallas Buck, rhp. Four years ago, the Reds traded for an injured Daryl Thompson, then patiently waited for him to regain his stuff. The same thing could happen with Buck, part of the Adam Dunn deal with the Diamondbacks.

SOURCE OF TOP 30 TALENT			
Homegrown	25	Acquired	5
College	15	Trades	4
Junior college	1	Rule 5 draft	0
High school	4	Independent leagues	0
Draft-and-follow	0	Free agents/waivers	1
Nondrafted free agents	1		
International	4		

SLEEPER: Byron Wiley, of. Wiley slipped in the draft because of a poor junior year at Kansas State, but he has the tools to quickly become one of the system's top outfield prospects.

Numbers in parentheses indicate prospect rankings.

LF
Danny Dorn (23)

CF
Drew Stubbs (3)
Yorman Rodriguez (5)
Chris Dickerson (12)
Chris Heisey (22)
Sean Henry
David Sappelt
Justin Reed
Andrew Means

RF
Juan Duran (9)
Byron Wiley
Denis Phipps

3B
Todd Frazier (2)
Neftali Soto (7)
Adam Rosales (29)

SS
Chris Valaika (4)
Zach Cozart (19)
Paul Janish

2B
Alex Buchholz (30)
Cody Puckett
Jose Castro
Michael Griffin

1B
Yonder Alonso (1)
Juan Francisco (8)
Logan Parker
Tonys Gutierrez

C
Devin Mesoraco (10)
Ryan Hanigan (16)
Craig Tatum (28)
Alvin Colina
Kevin Coddington

RHP

Starters	Relievers
Kyle Lotzkar (6)	Josh Roenicke (14)
Daryl Thompson (11)	Zach Stewart (15)
Jordan Smith (13)	Carlos Fisher (24)
Ramon Ramirez (17)	Sean Watson (26)
Juan Carlos Sulbaran (20)	Robert Manuel (27)
Dallas Buck (21)	Ramon Geronimo
Evan Hildenbrandt	Tyler Cline
Sam LeCure	Clayton Shunick
Josh Ravin	Derrik Lutz
Curtis Partch	
Matt Klinker	

LHP

Starters	Relievers
Matt Maloney (18)	Pedro Viola (25)
Ismael Guillon	Philippe Valiquette
Matt Fairel	Danny Ray Herrera
Travis Wood	Alexander Smit
Ben Jukich	
Jeremy Horst	

2008
BONUSES: $4.8 MILLION

BEST PURE HITTER: 1B Yonder Alonso (1) had the best combination of a short swing, plate discipline and strength in the draft. His polished approach led to 140 walks against just 66 strikeouts in his final two seasons at Miami.

BEST POWER HITTER: Alonso overpowers balls to all fields and slugged better than .700 in each of his last two college seasons.

FASTEST RUNNER: OF Theodis Bowe (21), a 5-foot-9 Delaware prep product, has been timed to first base in 3.9 seconds from the left side, even quicker on bunts. OF Andrew Means (11), a wide receiver at Indiana, gets to first in 4.0 seconds from the right side.

BEST DEFENSIVE PLAYER: OF David Sappelt (9) has the speed and arm strength to play an above-average center field.

BEST FASTBALL: RHP Zach Stewart (3) brings 93-96 mph heat out of the bullpen, with excellent sink. RHP Juan Carlos Sulbaran (30) sits at 91-94 mph at times as a starter, while RHP Tyler Cline (4) was touching 94 mph before a pair of freak injuries sidelined him in instructional league.

BEST SECONDARY PITCH: LHP Matt Fairel (35), who signed late for $250,000, throws his above-average curveball and solid changeup for strikes. Stewart regained the bite on his slider when Cincinnati moved him back to the bullpen. Sulbaran's curveball is at least average with the potential to get better. RHP Clayton Schunick (5) had a terrible debut but has shown a plus splitter.

BEST PRO DEBUT: 2B Alex Buchholz (6) dominated the Rookie-level Pioneer League, batting .396/.471/.604 while missing a month with a broken bone in his left hand. OF Byron Wiley (22) hit .227 in the spring for Kansas State but bounced back to bat .328/.427/.635 at Billings.

BEST ATHLETE: Wiley wins among position players, while Stewart has uncommon agility and speed for a pitcher. He fields his position and repeats his delivery well.

MOST INTRIGUING BACKGROUND: Sulbaran pitched for the Netherlands Antilles during Haarlem Honkbal Week last summer, giving up only one hit against Cuba in six innings and earning a spot on the Dutch Olympic team. Means led Indiana's football team in receiving yards in 2008. Unsigned OF Patrick White (49) set the NCAA Division I-A record for career rushing yards by a quarterback. The West Virginia star was a fourth-round pick of the Angels out of high school in 2004 and has been drafted three times since.

CLOSEST TO THE MAJORS: Alonso signed a major league contract and might be ready by the end of 2009. Stewart also should move fast.

BEST LATE-ROUND PICK: Sulbaran, the best starting pitcher the Reds drafted, signed for $500,000.

THE ONE WHO GOT AWAY: LHP Eric Pfisterer (15) should be an impact two-way talent for Duke. The Reds liked his three-pitch mix on the mound.

ASSESSMENT: The Reds decided they couldn't pass on Alonso's bat, even with Joey Votto enjoying an excellent rookie season. Spending a little extra helped land two needed, intriguing arms in Sulbaran and Fairel, whose success could determine the strength of this class.

2007
BONUSES: $4.9 MILLION

C Devin Mesoraco's (1) development has been a bit rocky so far, but nothing has slowed INF Todd Frazier (1s) and RHP Kyle Lotzkar (1s) is the system's top pitching prospect. SS Zach Cozart (2) and 3B Neftali Soto (3) have been impressive, too.

GRADE: B

2006
BONUSES: $4.8 MILLION

The Reds' patience with OF Drew Stubbs (1) is on the verge of paying off. SS Chris Valaika's (3) bat has been a revelation, as has RHP Josh Roenicke's (10) power arm.

GRADE: C+

2005
BONUSES: $3.8 MILLION*

OF Jay Bruce (1) is the cornerstone of this franchise. Since-traded RHP Jeff Stevens (6) and INF Adam Rosales (12) are two sleepers who have gotten time in the majors.

GRADE: B+

2004
BONUSES: $4.7 MILLION*

RHP Homer Bailey (1) once looked like a future ace but has failed in five big league stints. There's still hope, because he's only 22. SS Paul Janish (5) is the only other hope for this draft crop.

GRADE: C

*Draft analysis by John Manuel (2008) and Jim Callis (2004-07). Numbers in parentheses indicate draft rounds. *Bonuses for 2004-05 are first 10 rounds only.*

PROSPECT

YONDER ALONSO, 1B

Born: April 8, 1987.
Ht.: 6-2. **Wt.:** 215.
Bats: L. **Throws:** R.
Drafted:
Miami, 2008 (1st round).
Signed by: Tony Arias.

DAVID STONER

A lonso's father Luis played and coached for the Havana Industriales of Cuba's Serie Nacional. When Luis brought his family to the United States in 1995, it was baseball that helped Alonso learn English as he played in pickup games with friends around the neighborhood. He established himself as a prospect as a four-year starter at Coral Gables (Fla.) High, the same school that produced Mike Lowell. A 16th-round pick of the Twins out of high school, Alonso opted to head to Miami instead. He showed his ability to hit with wood bats by batting .338 with a .468 on-base percentage in the Cape Cod League in 2007. He followed up by finishing second in the Atlantic Coast Conference in homers (24), slugging percentage (.777) and OPS (1.311) as a junior, trailing only College Player of the Year Buster Posey. The Reds drafted Alonso seventh overall in June and the negotiations went down to the wire. He wanted a $7 million bonus, and friend Alex Rodriguez offered to let him stay in A-Rod's New York apartment while playing independent ball to prepare for the 2009 draft. In the end, Alonso agreed to a five-year, $4.55 million big league contact that included a $2 million bonus. He made a brief cameo in the high Class A Florida State League before heading to Hawaii Winter Baseball for his first extensive pro experience. He batted .308/.419/.510 with the Waikiki Beach Boys to earn HWB all-star honors.

Alonso is the rare hitter who has both plus power and the swing and pitch awareness to hit for a high average as well. He has good balance and a loose, short stroke that allows him to drive the ball to all fields. His best power is to the alleys, which fits perfectly with Cincinnati's Great American Ballpark. Unlike most sluggers, Alonso is allergic to strikeouts. He drew 172 walks while fanning just 103 times in his college career. The Reds also are excited by his workaholic makeup.

Offensively, Alonso has yet to prove that he can recognize and hit a quality breaking ball, though Cincinnati thinks he'll be able to do just that. The bigger question is how the Reds eventually will fit him and Joey Votto into the same lineup. They had flirted with the idea of letting Alonso play some third base, his high school position, but they have decided to leave him at first. He's a below-average athlete and runner whose range lack of range would have made him a liability at the hot corner. He's no Gold Glover at first base either, though his soft hands and adequate arm should allow him to develop into at least an average defender.

Though Cincinnati already had Votto, Alonso's polished bat was too good to pass up. He was one of the most big league-ready hitters in the 2008 draft and could start 2009 at the Reds' new Double-A Carolina affiliate. Because he's already on the 40-man roster, it's not inconceivable that he'll play in the majors by September. He could battle for an everyday job in Cincinnati in 2010, with Votto possibly moving to left field.

Year	Club (League)	Class	AVG	G	AB	R	H	2B	3B	HR	RBI	BB	SO	SB	OBP	SLG
2008	Sarasota (FSL)	HiA	.316	6	19	1	6	1	0	0	2	5	5	0	.440	.368
MINOR LEAGUE TOTALS			.316	6	19	1	6	1	0	0	2	5	5	0	.440	.368

2 TODD FRAZIER, SS/1B/3B

BORN: Feb. 12, 1986. **B-T:** R-R. **HT.:** 6-3. **WT.:** 215. **DRAFTED:** Rutgers, 2007 (1st round supplemental). **SIGNED BY:** Jeff Brookens.

The third brother in his family to get drafted, Frazier first hit the national stage when he led Toms River, N.J., to the 1998 Little League World Series title. A 2007 supplemental first-round pick who signed for $875,000, he played four positions and hit well at two Class A stops in his first full season, which he concluded by leading Hawaii Winter Baseball in slugging (.547). Frazier has above-average raw power and translates it well into games. While he has an unconventional swing, he clearly understands it and knows how to make adjustments. Since turning pro, he has learned to quicken his stride, enabling him to get his left foot down quicker and handle fastballs that previously gave him trouble. Though his future defensive home remains in doubt, his soft hands and strong arm should fit at third base and he has looked solid in limited time in left field. He has average speed and is a good athlete for his size. The Reds have been impressed by how he's both a team leader and one of the guys in the clubhouse. Frazier extends his front arm early in his swing, and though he has shortened the arm bar as a pro, it still leads some scouts to wonder if he'll be able to handle inside fastballs in the big leagues. His range is substandard at shortstop, and his versatility has meant that he's competent at many positions but a master at none. Frazier likely will continue to play several positions in Double-A and could get his first big league exposure late in 2009. He profiles best at third base but the Reds have more holes in the outfield, so he could wind up in left.

Year	Club (League)	Class	AVG	G	AB	R	H	2B	3B	HR	RBI	BB	SO	SB	OBP	SLG
2007	Billings (PIO)	R	.319	41	160	29	51	6	5	5	25	18	22	3	.409	.513
	Dayton (MWL)	LoA	.318	6	22	4	7	3	0	2	5	2	4	0	.375	.727
2008	Dayton (MWL)	LoA	.321	30	112	25	36	10	0	7	20	15	28	4	.402	.598
	Sarasota (FSL)	HiA	.281	100	366	62	103	20	3	12	54	41	84	8	.357	.451
MINOR LEAGUE TOTALS			.298	177	660	120	197	39	8	26	104	76	138	15	.378	.500

3 DREW STUBBS, OF

BORN: Oct. 4, 1984. **B-T:** R-R. **HT.:** 6-4. **WT.:** 200. **DRAFTED:** Texas, 2006 (1st round). **SIGNED BY:** Brian Wilson.

When the Reds signed Stubbs for $2 million as the eighth overall pick in 2006, they knew he was a stellar athlete but would need some time to adjust to pro ball. Things started to click for him last season, when he regained his speed after having surgery for a turf-toe injury. He climbed to Triple-A Louisville and had his best season as a pro. Stubbs has excellent bat speed, above-average raw power, a plus arm and plus-plus speed that allows him to steal bases and run down everything in center field. He made significant strides at the plate by widening his stance, cutting down his swing a little bit and improving his already solid selectivity. His home run production diminished as a result, but scouts believe it was a wise tradeoff, as his power will re-emerge as he continues to make solid contact. The biggest concern with Stubbs always has been strikeouts, and he probably never will hit for a high average. He could help his cause if he were a better bunter, but he hasn't mastered the skill. While he's very good in the outfield, he seems uncomfortable going back to the wall on balls. The Reds have an opening in center field that Stubbs may be able to fill in the second half of the season. First, he'll head to Triple-A for some final tuneups.

Year	Club (League)	Class	AVG	G	AB	R	H	2B	3B	HR	RBI	BB	SO	SB	OBP	SLG
2006	Billings (PIO)	R	.252	56	210	39	53	7	3	6	24	32	64	19	.368	.400
2007	Dayton (MWL)	LoA	.270	129	497	93	134	29	5	12	43	69	142	23	.364	.421
2008	Sarasota (FSL)	HiA	.261	86	303	49	79	21	4	5	38	50	82	27	.366	.406
	Chattanooga (SL)	AA	.315	26	92	12	29	8	0	0	9	11	21	3	.400	.402
	Louisville (IL)	AAA	.293	19	75	14	22	4	2	2	10	6	20	3	.354	.480
MINOR LEAGUE TOTALS			.269	316	1177	207	317	69	14	25	124	168	329	75	.367	.415

4 CHRIS VALAIKA, SS

BORN: Aug. 14, 1985. **B-T:** R-R. **HT.:** 6-1. **WT.:** 180. **DRAFTED:** UC Santa Barbara, 2006 (3rd round). **SIGNED BY:** Rex de la Nuez.

Valaika broke into pro ball by fashioning a 32-game hitting streak and winning the MVP award in the Rookie-level Pioneer League, and he hasn't stopped hitting. He led Cincinnati farmhands with a .317 average and ranked second with 81 RBIs in 2008, earning him the team's minor league player of the year award. The Reds love Valaika's instincts and his desire to outwork everyone else, which help explain why he's an above-average hitter despite tools that don't blow scouts away. His swing is easily maintainable and he's comfortable hitting to the opposite field. He has a tick above-average bat speed, which should allow him to slug 15 homers annually in the big leagues. He's an average runner. Valaika continues to survive at shortstop and has the bat to profile at second base if he needs to move. Valaika doesn't have the quick feet clubs want in a shortstop, though his quick release and strong arm help make up for his lack of range. When he first made it to Double-A, he chased fastballs up and out of the zone, though he quickly adjusted. His aggressiveness leads to strikeouts. His swing isn't picture-perfect, as he sometimes drops his shoulder and collapses on his backside. Valaika has exceeded expectations and has proven he can be a solid-hitting regular in the middle infield. Second base seems like his best fit, but that's occupied by Brandon Phillips. Cincinnati has a greater need at shortstop, and Valaika might get the chance to fill it by the end of 2009.

Year	Club (League)	Class	AVG	G	AB	R	H	2B	3B	HR	RBI	BB	SO	SB	OBP	SLG
2006	Billings (PIO)	R	.324	70	275	58	89	22	4	8	60	24	61	2	.387	.520
2007	Dayton (MWL)	LoA	.307	79	300	38	92	20	3	10	56	17	72	1	.353	.493
	Sarasota (FSL)	HiA	.253	57	217	26	55	9	1	2	23	13	42	0	.310	.332
2008	Sarasota (FSL)	HiA	.363	32	135	20	49	9	0	7	31	7	28	2	.393	.585
	Chattanooga (SL)	AA	.301	97	379	58	114	19	1	11	50	28	74	7	.352	.443
MINOR LEAGUE TOTALS			.306	335	1306	200	399	79	9	38	220	89	277	12	.357	.467

5 YORMAN RODRIGUEZ, OF

BORN: Aug. 15, 1992. **B-T:** R-R. **HT.:** 6-3. **WT.:** 175. **SIGNED:** Venezuela, 2008. **SIGNED BY:** Tony Arias.

The Reds scouted Rodriguez for three years before signing him in August for $2.5 million, the largest bonus ever for a Venezuelan prospect. His first pro experience came in instructional league. His first at-bat was against Orioles lefthander Brian Matusz, the No. 4 pick in the 2008 draft. In Rodriguez and Dominican outfielder Juan Duran, Cincinnati believes it got the equivalent of two extra first-round picks in 2008. No one doubts Rodriguez's athleticism. He projects to hit for above-average power, already has gained 10 pounds during his short time in the United States and should continue to get stronger as he matures. He has plus-plus speed and uses it well in center field, where he's an above-average defender. He showed off the best outfield arm in the system during instructional league. Multiple scouts from other teams say that Rodriguez is helpless against breaking balls right now because he gets caught lunging for the ball instead of staying back and trusting his hands. He also has next to no experience against pro-caliber pitching, so his bat could take time to develop. Several scouts also were worried about how he carried himself, saying he has a cockiness that could prove to be a problem. Rodriguez didn't look lost against older pitchers in instructional league. He'll open 2009 in extended spring training before seeing his first game action in the Rookie-level Gulf Coast League.

Year	Club (League)	Class	AVG	G	AB	R	H	2B	3B	HR	RBI	BB	SO	SB	OBP	SLG
2008	Did Not Play—Signed 2009 Contract															

6 KYLE LOTZKAR, RHP

BORN: Oct. 24, 1989. **B-T:** L-R. **HT.:** 6-4. **WT.:** 200. **DRAFTED:** HS—Delta, B.C., 2007 (1st round supplemental). **SIGNED BY:** Bill Bychowski.

Lotzkar set the stage for going 53rd overall in the 2007 draft when he touched 96 mph with Team Canada in the World Junior Championships the previous fall. His 2008 season ended when he came down with a small stress fracture in his elbow in August. However, he was back throwing on the side a month later and showed no ill effects when he participated in instructional league. Before he got hurt, Lotzkar confirmed his status as the Reds' most promising young pitcher. He has the potential to have three plus pitches. His fastball sits at 91-93 mph with excellent life, and his free-and-easy delivery allows it to jump on hitters. Unlike many young pitchers, he trusts his secondary pitches, a power curveball that gets strikeouts and a changeup. Health is the biggest concern with Lotzkar, who also was held back in extended spring training until June because he had a sore neck. His control and command need refinement, and his curveball and changeup lack consistency. If he can stay healthy and add polish, Lotzkar could end up becoming a No. 2 starter. At age 19, he'll still be on track if he returns to low Class A Dayton in 2009.

Year	Club (League)	Class	W	L	ERA	G	GS	CG	SV	IP	H	R	ER	HR	BB	SO	AVG
2007	Reds (GCL)	R	0	2	3.86	7	7	0	0	21	21	10	9	2	7	24	.263
	Billings (PIO)	R	0	0	1.13	2	2	0	0	8	1	1	1	1	3	12	.040
2008	Dayton (MWL)	LoA	2	3	3.58	10	10	0	0	38	29	19	15	2	24	50	.215
MINOR LEAGUE TOTALS			2	5	3.38	19	19	0	0	67	51	30	25	5	34	86	.213

7 NEFTALI SOTO, 3B

BORN: Feb. 28, 1989. **B-T:** R-R. **HT.:** 6-2. **WT.:** 180. **DRAFTED:** HS—Manati, P.R., 2007 (3rd round). **SIGNED BY:** Tony Arias.

Soto was supposed to spend 2008, his first full pro season, at Rookie-level Billings. But when Dayton third

baseman Brandon Waring fractured his thumb in early July, Soto moved up to low Class A and never left. His .500 slugging percentage would have ranked second in the Midwest League if he had enough at-bats to qualify. Soto broke Juan Gonzalez's youth home run records in Puerto Rico. His raw strength and bat speed give him 60-65 power on the 20-80 scouting scale. Though he has a long, vicious swing, he has hit for average and made contact thanks to his excellent hand-eye coordination. He has a strong arm at third base. Soto's speed is well-below-average and his athleticism isn't much better. He moved from shortstop to third base last year, and he may need a less challenging position in the future. He struggles to charge bunts and slow rollers, his range is limited, his footwork is rough and his throws sometimes lack accuracy. He has a solid gameplan at the plate but needs to show he can take a walk when pitchers work around him. Soto was held back in Billings because of the Reds' logjam at third base, which also could mean that he starts 2009 back in low Class A. His bat is ready for a bigger challenge, but Cincinnati wants to keep him at the hot corner as long as possible.

Year	Club (League)	Class	AVG	G	AB	R	H	2B	3B	HR	RBI	BB	SO	SB	OBP	SLG
2007	Reds (GCL)	R	.303	40	152	18	46	7	5	2	28	11	31	2	.355	.454
2008	Billings (PIO)	R	.388	15	67	12	26	10	1	4	11	4	10	1	.423	.746
	Dayton (MWL)	LoA	.326	52	218	26	71	15	1	7	36	7	36	1	.343	.500
MINOR LEAGUE TOTALS			.327	107	437	56	143	32	7	13	75	22	77	4	.360	.522

8 JUAN FRANCISCO, 3B

BORN: June 24, 1987. **B-T:** L-R. **HT.:** 6-2. **WT.:** 210. **SIGNED:** Dominican Republic, 2004. **SIGNED BY:** Juan Peralta.

Johnny Cueto's emergence was the Reds' first significant Latin American success story since Mario Soto starred in the early 1980s. Next in line is Francisco, who led the Midwest League with 25 homers in 2007 and Cincinnati farmhands with 23 in 2008. He appeared in the Futures Game last year, wowing observers with his power during batting practice. Francisco's game is all about power, and he can drive the ball out of any part of any park. He has a quick bat and his long arms give him tremendous leverage. He also owns a strong arm that rates as a 70 on the 20-80 scouting scale. Though he's expected to outgrow third base, he does have a solid first step and decent speed. Francisco has a long stroke that isn't conducive to consistent contact. His plate discipline is poor and he gives away too many at-bats by being overly aggressive. Scouts are worried that he could grow to Dmitri Young proportions if he doesn't stay on top of his conditioning. His range already is below average at third base, and he'll probably wind up at first base rather than the outfield. The Reds eventually will have to sort through all their third-base candidates, but for now, Francisco appears headed to Double-A to man the hot corner. They're worried less about his defense and more with him learning to lay off pitches out of the strike zone.

Year	Club (League)	Class	AVG	G	AB	R	H	2B	3B	HR	RBI	BB	SO	SB	OBP	SLG
2005	DSL Reds (DSL)	R	.228	49	158	7	36	10	1	4	20	14	26	2	.293	.380
2006	Reds (GCL)	R	.280	45	182	24	51	14	0	3	30	6	35	2	.305	.407
	Billings (PIO)	R	.333	9	36	6	12	3	0	2	0	2	8	0	.333	.417
2007	Dayton (MWL)	LoA	.268	135	534	69	143	21	4	25	90	23	161	12	.301	.463
2008	Sarasota (FSL)	HiA	.277	127	516	71	143	34	5	23	92	19	123	1	.303	.496
MINOR LEAGUE TOTALS			.275	316	1268	170	349	72	9	51	214	48	327	17	.303	.467

9 JUAN DURAN, OF

BORN: Sept. 2, 1991. **B-T:** R-R. **HT.:** 6-6. **WT.:** 190. **SIGNED:** Dominican Republic, 2007. **SIGNED BY:** Tony Arias.

The Reds exploited a little-noticed loophole to sign Duran six months before other teams realized he was eligible. He didn't reach the minimum age of 16 until two days after the international signing period ended in 2007, but Cincinnati assistant GM Bob Miller knew of a rule that permitted a player to sign if he'd turn 17 before the end of his first season. The Reds landed Duran in February for $2 million and assigned him to the Pioneer League, where the season ended Sept. 5. He didn't play for Billings, instead spending the summer in the Rookie-level Dominican Summer League. Duran already has the best raw power in the system. His swing has natural loft and the ball carries off his bat to all fields. His massive frame has room for another 40-50 pounds of strength, so he could be a beast in a few years. He has a balanced approach and a fluid swing. He has plus speed, though he'll slow down as he fills out. That likely will mean he'll move from center field to right, and he has the arm for the latter position. Duran grew six inches in the span of a year, and he's still getting adjusted to his newfound height. He's more gawky than fluid at this point and sometimes looks awkward on the bases and in the outfield. He has a balky elbow, possibly related to his growth spurt, but it should clear up. Duran's rough performance in the DSL shows that he's still raw and needs time to develop. He's still just 17 and will be well ahead of the development curve in the Gulf Coast League this summer.

Year	Club (League)	Class	AVG	G	AB	R	H	2B	3B	HR	RBI	BB	SO	SB	OBP	SLG
2008	Reds (DSL)	R	.215		135	15	29	3	4	1	14	24	47	8	.340	.319
MINOR LEAGUE TOTALS			.215		135	15	29	3	4	1	14	24	47	8	.340	.319

10 DEVIN MESORACO, C

BORN: June 19, 1988. **B-T:** R-R. **HT.:** 6-1. **WT.:** 200. **DRAFTED:** HS—Punxsutawney, Pa., 2007 (1st round). **SIGNED BY:** Lee Seras.

Mesoraco blew out his elbow pitching as a sophomore in high school, but recovered from Tommy John surgery to become a first-round pick two years later as a catcher. The first backstop drafted in the first round by the Reds since Dan Wilson in 1990, he signed for $1.4 million. Injuries to both his thumbs have nagged him in pro ball, the result of diving head-first into bases. Mesoraco has the tools to be an all-star catcher. He has natural strength and a strong arm, and he's a better runner and athlete than most backstops. Once his thumbs healed, he was Cincinnati's best player in instructional league. The Reds believe his desire to succeed will help him work through the adjustments he has to make. Several scouts said that Mesoraco was one of the more disappointing players in the Midwest League last year. They felt he had gained some bad weight and showed bad body language on the field. He has yet to produce much at the plate and his bat seemed to slow as the season went along, though his thumb injuries contributed. He got too mechanical in his throwing and erased just 17 percent of basestealers. He also has problems blocking balls in the dirt. Mesoraco might benefit from repeating low Class A. He's young enough that it wouldn't put his development behind, and catchers generally have a slower path to the majors anyway.

Year	Club (League)	Class	AVG	G	AB	R	H	2B	3B	HR	RBI	BB	SO	SB	OBP	SLG
2007	Reds (GCL)	R	.219	40	137	16	30	4	0	1	8	15	26	2	.310	.270
2008	Dayton (MWL)	LoA	.261	83	306	29	80	13	1	9	42	20	64	2	.311	.399
MINOR LEAGUE TOTALS			.248	123	443	45	110	17	1	10	50	35	90	4	.311	.359

11 DARYL THOMPSON, RHP

BORN: Nov. 2, 1985. **B-T:** R-R. **HT.:** 6-0. **WT.:** 180. **DRAFTED:** HS—La Plata, Md., 2003 (8th round). **SIGNED BY:** Alex Smith (Expos).

It may seem like Thompson has been around forever—he was drafted by the Montreal Expos, after all—but he's actually right on schedule and will play the entire 2009 season as a 23-year-old. The Reds' last hope to get something significant out of the 2006 Austin Kearns/Felipe Lopez trade with Washington, Thompson needed more than two years to fully recover from labrum surgery. He regained 3-4 mph on his fastball in 2008 and can spot his 92-94 mph heater to both sides of the plate. He also throws an inconsistent changeup, an improving 78-82 mph slider and a slow curveball. His changeup has the potential to be his second-best pitch, with fade and sink when he has a feel for it. Thompson did a good job early in the season of getting ahead of hitters, which allowed him to use his full assortment of pitches. He's willing to throw all four at any point in the count. His curve is best used sparingly, when hitters aren't looking for it, because it isn't a swing-and-miss pitch, and his slider lacks the velocity to be a true out pitch. Thompson's fastball is major league-ready, so if his offspeed offerings catch up he can be a solid No. 3 or 4 starter, but concerns about his durability persist. His fastball lost some of its zip as the season progressed, and he seemed to wear down after his big league callup. Thompson will compete for the Reds' fifth-starter job in spring training, and his command and steadiness give him a solid shot at winning it.

Year	Club (League)	Class	W	L	ERA	G	GS	CG	SV	IP	H	R	ER	HR	BB	SO	AVG
2003	Expos (GCL)	R	1	2	2.15	12	10	0	0	46	49	16	11	1	11	18	.288
2004	Savannah (SAL)	LoA	4	9	5.08	25	21	0	0	103	117	66	58	13	30	79	.296
2005	Savannah (SAL)	LoA	2	3	3.35	11	11	0	0	54	46	23	20	3	24	48	.232
2006	Vermont (NYP)	SS	0	1	6.75	4	4	0	0	7	5	5	5	0	5	8	.200
	Reds (GCL)	R	0	0	2.57	5	4	0	0	14	10	4	4	1	4	16	.222
2007	Dayton (MWL)	LoA	5	0	0.96	5	5	0	0	28	16	3	3	1	2	24	.165
	Sarasota (FSL)	HiA	9	5	3.77	22	22	0	0	105	106	51	44	19	31	97	.262
2008	Chattanooga (SL)	AA	3	2	1.76	10	10	0	0	61	44	19	12	2	14	56	.208
	Louisville (IL)	AAA	5	0	2.76	7	7	0	0	46	39	15	14	4	9	33	.232
	Cincinnati (NL)	MAJ	0	2	6.91	3	3	0	0	14	20	11	11	3	7	6	.328
	Reds (GCL)	R	0	0	0.00	1	0	0	0	4	2	1	0	0	0	3	.133
	Sarasota (FSL)	HiA	0	2	6.89	3	3	0	0	16	20	12	12	2	7	7	.339
MINOR LEAGUE TOTALS			29	24	3.41	105	97	0	0	483	454	215	183	46	137	389	.254
MAJOR LEAGUE TOTALS			0	2	6.91	3	3	0	0	14	20	11	11	3	7	6	.328

12 CHRIS DICKERSON, OF

BORN: April 10, 1982. B-T: L-L. **HT.:** 6-3. **WT.:** 225. **DRAFTED:** Nevada-Las Vegas, 2003 (16th round). **SIGNED BY:** Keith Chapman.

For years, the scouting report on Dickerson was the same. He was the organization's best athlete, but no one was sure whether he ever would turn his impressive tools into production because he would mix hot weeks with monthlong slumps. But in 2008 he showed an improved ability to recognize sliders, his nemesis in previous years, which paid off in his most productive season and an outstanding major league debut that ended early because of a stress fracture in his heel. Dickerson still struck out once every 3.2 at-bats last year, but that was an improvement over 2007. He did a better job of recognizing which pitches to lay off, got himself into more fastball counts and better tapped into his impressive raw power. A cousin of NFL Hall of Famer Eric Dickerson, he's an outstanding center fielder, with the speed to run down balls in the gaps and an average arm. He could steal 25-30 bases a year if he gets 500 at-bats. But that might never happen because he struggles to hit lefties. Last year 16 of his 17 homers and 44 of his 53 extra-base hits came against righthanders. His other goal for 2009 is to stay healthy. The stress fracture is the latest in a litany of injuries that includes elbow problems (2004) and a sore shoulder (2006). Some scouts question whether Dickerson can sustain the progress he made last year, but his strong debut should at least give him a shot to be a platoon center fielder.

Year	Club (League)	Class	AVG	G	AB	R	H	2B	3B	HR	RBI	BB	SO	SB	OBP	SLG
2003	Billings (PIO)	R	.244	58	201	36	49	6	4	6	38	39	66	9	.376	.403
2004	Dayton (MWL)	LoA	.303	84	314	50	95	15	3	4	34	51	92	27	.410	.408
	Potomac (CAR)	HiA	.200	15	45	5	9	2	0	0	5	7	14	3	.321	.244
2005	Sarasota (FSL)	HiA	.236	119	436	68	103	17	7	11	43	53	124	19	.325	.383
2006	Chattanooga (SL)	AA	.242	115	389	65	94	21	7	12	48	65	129	21	.355	.424
2007	Chattanooga (SL)	AA	.272	30	114	11	31	4	1	1	11	7	31	7	.325	.351
	Louisville (IL)	AAA	.260	104	354	58	92	11	6	13	44	52	131	23	.361	.435
2008	Louisville (IL)	AAA	.287	97	349	65	100	16	9	11	53	54	102	26	.384	.479
	Cincinnati (NL)	MAJ	.304	31	102	20	31	9	2	6	15	17	35	5	.413	.608
MINOR LEAGUE TOTALS			.260	622	2202	358	573	92	37	58	276	328	689	135	.363	.415
MAJOR LEAGUE TOTALS			.304	31	102	20	31	9	2	6	15	17	35	5	.413	.608

13 JORDAN SMITH, RHP

BORN: Feb. 4, 1986. **B-T:** R-R. **HT.:** 6-3. **WT.:** 206. **DRAFTED:** CC of Southern Nevada, 2006 (6th round). **SIGNED BY:** Jeff Morris.

Smith's 2008 season started strong and finished poorly, but he provided reason for optimism. He opened 2008 at high Class A Sarasota and quickly earned a promotion to Double-A, after which he failed to make it out of the sixth inning in seven of his 11 starts. Finally in late July, Smith told Chattanooga's trainer that his knee had been bothering him for a while. An exam showed he had torn cartilage, which required surgery and shut him down for the rest of the season. The injury was a relief of sorts because it explained why his season had gone south. When healthy, Smith has a heavy 91-94 mph fastball with excellent sink. He also throws a plus slider that induces weak contact rather than strikeouts and a fringy changeup. Smith doesn't miss a lot of bats, but everything he throws is heavy and he induces lots of grounders. Even while scuffling in Double-A, he recorded twice as many groundouts as flyouts. He also lives in the strike zone and likes to pitch inside, busting hitters on the hands with pitches that can sting. Smith's knee has recovered, and he'll return to Double-A to start the season.

Year	Club (League)	Class	W	L	ERA	G	GS	CG	SV	IP	H	R	ER	HR	BB	SO	AVG
2006	Billings (PIO)	R	6	3	3.01	14	14	0	0	69	58	29	23	3	20	49	.227
2007	Dayton (MWL)	LoA	10	8	3.84	26	26	0	0	134	133	74	57	8	40	96	.258
2008	Sarasota (FSL)	HiA	7	2	2.55	10	10	0	0	67	61	23	19	2	7	44	.241
	Chattanooga (SL)	AA	2	6	5.40	11	11	0	0	55	72	42	33	6	17	42	.316
MINOR LEAGUE TOTALS			25	19	3.66	61	61	0	0	324	324	168	132	19	84	231	.259

14 JOSH ROENICKE, RHP

BORN: Aug. 4, 1982. **B-T:** R-R. **HT.:** 6-3. **WT.:** 200. **DRAFTED:** UCLA, 2006 (10th round). **SIGNED BY:** Rex de la Nuez.

At spring training last year, Roenicke made a big impression by coming into manager Dusty Baker's office and introducing himself. He also impressed on the mound, where Roenicke quickly showed he had the organization's best arm. His fastball is a plus-plus pitch with natural life, sitting at 94-95 mph and touching 99. He has the natural athleticism expected from a former college quarterback/wide receiver. He walked on to UCLA's baseball team after coming to school on a football scholarship. Besides his fastball, Roenicke also throws an 88-89 mph cutter and an inconsistent slider. He also has an adequate changeup, but he rarely uses it as a short reliever. When he's on, Roenicke can strike out the side, as he did in his final big league outing of the season, but he can get too enamored with velocity and focus on firing fastballs rather than setting up hitters. He'll come to spring training with a chance to earn a job in the Cincinnati bullpen and has the stuff to eventually pitch at the back end of it. The son of former outfielder Gary Roenicke and the nephew of Ron Roenicke, Josh became the family's third big leaguer when he earned a September callup. He also has two brothers, Jarrett and Jason, who are minor leaguers.

CINCINNATI REDS

Year	Club (League)	Class	W	L	ERA	G	GS	CG	SV	IP	H	R	ER	HR	BB	SO	AVG
2006	Reds (GCL)	R	1	0	1.17	7	0	0	0	8	8	2	1	0	3	9	.258
	Billings (PIO)	R	1	0	6.32	14	0	0	6	16	10	11	11	1	12	24	.179
2007	Sarasota (FSL)	HiA	2	1	3.25	27	0	0	16	28	23	10	10	1	15	41	.225
	Chattanooga (SL)	AA	1	1	0.95	19	0	0	8	19	12	3	2	0	6	15	.185
2008	Chattanooga (SL)	AA	4	2	3.27	22	0	0	10	22	21	10	8	2	12	28	.253
	Louisville (IL)	AAA	2	0	2.54	35	0	0	3	39	34	11	11	2	14	43	.234
	Cincinnati (NL)	MAJ	0	0	9.00	5	0	0	0	3	6	3	3	0	2	6	.400
MINOR LEAGUE TOTALS			11	4	2.95	124	0	0	43	131	108	47	43	6	62	160	.224
MAJOR LEAGUE TOTALS			0	0	9.00	5	0	0	0	3	6	3	3	0	2	6	.400

15 ZACH STEWART, RHP

BORN: Sept. 28, 1986. **B-T:** R-R. **HT.:** 6-2. **WT.:** 205. **DRAFTED:** Texas Tech, 2008 (3rd round). **SIGNED BY:** Jerry Flowers.

Though he was just drafted last June, Stewart could find a role in the big league bullpen quickly. He started his college career at Angelo State (Texas) and North Central Texas CC before spending the 2008 season at Texas Tech. He earned attention as a possible first-round pick early in the spring but slid to the third round, in part because the Red Raiders used him in different roles as their pitching staff fell apart. He spent most of the season as the closer but ended up as the Friday starter at the end of the year, putting together a 130-pitch effort against Baylor in his last start of the season. After signing him for $450,000, the Reds were happy to move him back to the bullpen, where his 93-96 mph fastball and biting 82-85 mph slider give him a pair of potential out pitches. His fastball has lots of natural sink, which makes it hard for hitters to drive. His slider became sweepier as a starter, but it tightened back up once he joined the Reds. He threw a somewhat promising changeup as a starter, but will have little need for it now that he's back in the bullpen. His command and delivery are polished for a late-inning reliever, and he should spend most of his first full pro season in Double-A.

Year	Club (League)	Class	W	L	ERA	G	GS	CG	SV	IP	H	R	ER	HR	BB	SO	AVG
2008	Dayton (MWL)	LoA	1	2	0.55	11	0	0	3	16	10	2	1	0	3	13	.175
	Sarasota (FSL)	HiA	0	2	1.62	13	0	0	2	17	16	5	3	0	11	23	.262
MINOR LEAGUE TOTALS			1	4	1.09	24	0	0	5	33	26	7	4	0	14	36	.220

16 RYAN HANIGAN, C

BORN: Aug. 16, 1980. **B-T:** R-R. **HT.:** 6-0. **WT.:** 195. **SIGNED:** Rollins (Fla.), NDFA 2002. **SIGNED BY:** John Brickley.

Hanigan made it to the big leagues the hard way. He signed as a nondrafted free agent after impressing the Reds in the Cape Cod League in 2002, then made a steady six-year climb through the system. Injuries earned him an emergency callup in September 2007, and his steady hitting and defense forced the Reds to take notice last season. They waived David Ross in August to give Hanigan a shot. He's a line-drive hitter who hits from an exaggerated closed stance. He has solid plate coverage and draws plenty of walks, while his strikeout rate was among the best in the system. And while he doesn't have a lot of power—he never has hit more than six homers in a season—his ability to get on base means he won't be a liability in the lineup. Hanigan doesn't have any tool that grades out better than average, but he has solid catch-and-throw skills and pitchers like working with him. He threw out 37 percent of basestealers in 2008. Hanigan is 28, so there's no projection left to him, but his package is interesting. He should win the Reds' backup catching job after the December trade for Ramon Hernandez provided a veteran starter.

Year	Club (League)	Class	AVG	G	AB	R	H	2B	3B	HR	RBI	BB	SO	SB	OBP	SLG
2002	Dayton (MWL)	LoA	.273	6	11	1	3	1	0	0	1	2	0	.333	.364
2003	Dayton (MWL)	LoA	.277	92	311	43	86	12	0	1	31	40	44	3	.363	.325
	Louisville (IL)	AAA	.333	1	3	1	1	0	0	0	0	0	1	0	.500	.333
2004	Potomac (CAR)	HiA	.296	119	429	58	127	21	0	5	56	49	51	6	.369	.380
2005	Chattanooga (SL)	AA	.321	100	333	45	107	14	1	4	29	50	41	4	.418	.405
2006	Chattanooga (SL)	AA	.246	56	126	17	31	2	0	0	14	19	23	0	.347	.262
	Louisville (IL)	AAA	.154	8	13	2	2	0	0	0	1	6	2	0	.421	.154
2007	Chattanooga (SL)	AA	.299	60	197	30	59	14	1	3	27	41	30	0	.420	.426
	Louisville (IL)	AAA	.252	41	127	16	32	5	0	1	9	14	15	0	.333	.315
	Cincinnati (NL)	MAJ	.300	5	10	3	3	1	0	0	2	1	2	0	.364	.400
2008	Louisville (IL)	AAA	.324	75	272	37	88	14	0	4	35	25	39	1	.392	.419
	Cincinnati (NL)	MAJ	.271	31	85	9	23	2	0	2	9	10	9	0	.367	.365
MINOR LEAGUE TOTALS			.294	558	1822	250	536	83	2	18	202	245	248	14	.383	.372
MAJOR LEAGUE TOTALS			.274	36	95	12	26	3	0	2	11	11	11	0	.367	.368

17 RAMON RAMIREZ, RHP

BORN: Sept. 16, 1982. **B-T:** R-R. **HT.:** 5-10. **WT.:** 170. **SIGNED:** Venezuela, 2000. **SIGNED BY:** Ronquito Garcia (Padres).

For a team that struggled for years to develop international talent, the Reds now have several interesting prospects coming out of their Latin American program. They picked up Ramirez in 2003 after he was released by the Padres, and the only real attention he drew came from a 50-game steroid suspension in 2006. A midseason promotion to Triple-A last season seemed to give him a new boost of confidence. His outstanding changeup got even sharper and some scouts rate it as an 80 on the 20-80 scouting scale. He maintains his arm speed with the pitch, commands it, keeps it down in the zone and has the confidence to throw it at any time. It also has the fade to generate swings and misses. The rest of Ramirez's pitches are pretty average, though his changeup makes them play up. He throws an 89-92 mph fastball, a 79-82 mph slider and an inconsistent curveball, and his command of those pitches doesn't match that of his changeup. Some question whether his reliance on the changeup will work as a starter over the long term—he threw nearly 50 percent changeups in the big leagues—but it was quite effective in his big league audition late in the season. Ramirez will be in the thick of the race to be Cincinnati's fifth starter, and if he doesn't win that job, his fastball/changeup combo also would be effective out of the bullpen.

Year	Club (League)	Class	W	L	ERA	G	GS	CG	SV	IP	H	R	ER	HR	BB	SO	AVG
2000	Padres (DSL)	R	4	3	2.96	10	9	0	0	52	43	19	17	2	14	60	.225
2001	Padres (DSL)	R	0	0	21.60	2	0	0	0	2	2	5	4	0	3	2	.286
2002	Did not pitch																
2003	Cagua (VSL)	R	1	5	3.79	19	4	0	4	40	43	24	17	0	10	49	.277
2004	Billings (PIO)	R	3	6	3.39	17	12	0	1	74	63	36	28	7	36	60	.250
2005	Dayton (MWL)	LoA	5	7	4.50	30	19	0	0	114	114	69	57	8	50	90	.265
2006	Sarasota (FSL)	HiA	4	5	4.29	15	11	1	0	65	66	33	31	11	21	53	.261
2007	Sarasota (FSL)	HiA	5	2	4.05	15	12	0	1	73	64	37	33	5	25	86	.232
	Chattanooga (SL)	AA	5	1	4.60	16	0	0	1	31	30	16	16	3	12	35	.254
	Louisville (IL)	AAA	1	0	0.00	5	2	0	0	15	7	0	0	0	6	16	.149
2008	Chattanooga (SL)	AA	2	3	4.70	11	9	0	0	46	41	29	24	6	15	52	.237
	Louisville (IL)	AAA	4	5	3.08	19	15	0	1	99	76	37	34	8	42	93	.215
	Cincinnati (NL)	MAJ	1	1	2.67	5	4	0	0	27	17	8	8	3	11	21	.183
MINOR LEAGUE TOTALS			34	37	3.84	159	93	1	8	612	549	305	261	50	234	596	.243
MAJOR LEAGUE TOTALS			1	1	2.67	5	4	0	0	27	17	8	8	3	11	21	.183

18 MATT MALONEY, LHP

BORN: Jan. 16, 1984. **B-T:** L-L. **HT.:** 6-4. **WT.:** 220. **DRAFTED:** Mississippi, 2005 (3rd round). **SIGNED BY:** Mike Stauffer (Phillies).

Picked up in the Kyle Lohse trade with the Phillies in July 2007, Maloney ranked third in the minors with 177 strikeouts that season and fourth in the Triple-A International League with 132 last year. His whiffs come not from overpowering hitters, but from his ability to mix four pitches and move them around the zone. Maloney throws an 88-91 mph fastball with natural sink, a plus changeup and an average slider and curveball. He commands all four pitches and can throw them all at any point in the count. Like any pitcher who has less than overwhelming stuff and is always around the plate, Maloney always has to walk a tightrope. He gives up a lot of fly balls and homers. His overall 2008 numbers would have looked better if he hadn't given up 19 runs in his final three starts. Maloney is close to big league-ready, with a ceiling as a fourth or fifth starter or a useful arm out of the bullpen. With the Reds suddenly flush with starting candidates, he's an underdog in the competition to become their No. 5 starter.

Year	Club (League)	Class	W	L	ERA	G	GS	CG	SV	IP	H	R	ER	HR	BB	SO	AVG
2005	Batavia (NYP)	SS	2	1	3.89	8	8	0	0	37	38	20	16	2	15	36	.277
2006	Lakewood (SAL)	LoA	16	9	2.03	27	27	2	0	169	120	54	38	5	73	180	.194
2007	Reading (EL)	AA	9	7	3.94	21	21	1	0	126	117	70	55	13	45	115	.246
	Chattanooga (SL)	AA	2	2	2.57	4	4	0	0	28	17	9	8	4	3	39	.175
	Louisville (IL)	AAA	2	1	3.18	3	3	0	0	17	10	6	6	2	6	23	.169
2008	Louisville (IL)	AAA	11	5	4.68	25	25	2	0	140	143	75	73	18	39	132	.264
Reds (GCL)		R	1	0	0.00	1	0	0	0	6	1	0	0	0	0	9	.056
MINOR LEAGUE TOTALS			43	25	3.38	89	88	5	0	522	446	234	196	44	181	534	.229

19 ZACH COZART, SS

BORN: Aug. 12, 1985. **B-T:** R-R. **HT.:** 6-1. **WT.:** 185. **DRAFTED:** Mississippi, 2007 (2nd round). **SIGNED BY:** Jerry Flowers.

When the Reds drafted Cozart in the second round in 2007, some scouts thought they might be wasting $407,250 on a no-hit, good-glove shortstop. But while he still has some holes in his swing, he showed solid pop during his first full pro season while continuing to play slick defense. Managers rated him the best defensive shortstop in the Midwest League. Cozart has soft hands, fluid actions, a quick first step, a knack for positioning and solid range. His arm is a touch short for a shortstop, but his quick release and accuracy allow it to grade out as average. His excellent defense is all the more surprising considering he's a slightly below-average runner, timed at 4.3 seconds from home to first. At the plate, Cozart is still not a sure thing, but he showed some power and a knack for putting the bat on the ball last season. He still struggles to recognize breaking balls, and his swing is more inside-out than is ideal. He also could stand to draw more walks. Because of the shortstops ahead of him in the system, Cozart was stuck in low Class A all year despite being ready to move up. He'll take that step to Sarasota in 2009.

Year	Club (League)	Class	AVG	G	AB	R	H	2B	3B	HR	RBI	BB	SO	SB	OBP	SLG
2007	Dayton (MWL)	LoA	.239	53	184	28	44	7	2	2	18	11	36	3	.288	.332
2008	Dayton (MWL)	LoA	.280	109	418	57	117	20	6	14	49	24	77	3	.330	.457
MINOR LEAGUE TOTALS			.267	162	602	85	161	27	8	16	67	35	113	6	.317	.419

20 JUAN CARLOS SULBARAN, RHP

BORN: Nov. 9, 1989. **B-T:** R-R. **HT.:** 6-2. **WT.:** 198. **DRAFTED:** HS—Plantation, Fla., 2008 (30th round). **SIGNED BY:** Tony Arias.

On most high school teams, Sulbaran would have been the star. But last spring at American Heritage High in Plantation, Fla., he was overshadowed by teammates Eric Hosmer (No. 3 overall pick, Royals) and Adrian Nieto (fifth round, Nationals). The Reds were intrigued by Sulbaran's three-pitch mix and bought him out of his scholarship to Florida for $500,000 after taking a flier on him in the 30th round. A native of Curacao, Sulbaran made a convincing case for his bonus by holding Cuba's national team to one run in six innings while pitching for the Dutch team at the Haarlem Honkbal tournament. After turning pro, he got a rematch against Cuba in the Olympics, allowing two earned runs in 4⅔ innings. In that game, he struggled with his command but showed an ability to work out of jams against experienced hitters. He'll also pitch for the Dutch at this spring's World Baseball Classic. For a teenager, Sulbaran has an advanced approach and good control. He throws a 91-94 mph fastball and a promising curveball and changeup. At 6-foot-2, he gets a good downhill plane on his pitches. The Reds got their first up-close look at him in instructional league and think that his international experience will allow him to make his pro debut in low Class A.

Year	Club (League)	Class	W	L	ERA	G	GS	CG	SV	IP	H	R	ER	HR	BB	SO	AVG
2008	Did Not Play—Signed Late																

21 DALLAS BUCK, RHP

BORN: Nov. 11, 1984. **B-T:** R-R. **HT.:** 6-2. **WT.:** 195. **DRAFTED:** Oregon State, 2006 (3rd round). **SIGNED BY:** Ed Gustafson (Diamondbacks).

When the Reds finally decided to trade Adam Dunn, they acquired Buck along with Micah Owings and catching prospect Wilkin Castillo from the Diamondbacks. Buck showed first-round talent as an Oregon State sophomore in 2005, but his arm came up sore the next year. He pitched through pain and managed to succeed despite diminished velocity, playing a key role in the Beavers' 2006 College World Series championship. Buck had a partial ligament tear in his elbow, which dropped him to the third round of the draft, and he signed for a cut-rate $250,000. He tried to recover through rest and rehab before having Tommy John surgery midway through the 2007 season. He returned in mid-2008, though his fastball didn't climb back above 90 mph until after the trade. He showed 90-92 mph velocity in three starts with Sarasota, but he has yet to show the same power sink he had before the injury. He also throws a slider and a changeup, and he's still regaining the feel for them as well. Buck's ability to throw strikes and compete hasn't changed. If he can get back to what he was before the injury, he has legitimate front-of-the-rotation stuff. If not, his competitiveness and guile may allow him to survive anyway. It's too early to know if he left his best stuff in Corvallis.

Year	Club (League)	Class	W	L	ERA	G	GS	CG	SV	IP	H	R	ER	HR	BB	SO	AVG
2007	Visalia (CAL)	HiA	4	4	3.41	16	16	0	0	98	84	49	37	10	31	88	.231
2008	South Bend (MWL)	LoA	1	4	3.94	9	8	1	0	46	44	20	20	5	10	24	.250
	Visalia (CAL)	HiA	0	1	0.00	1	1	0	0	5	3	3	0	1	1	4	.167
	Sarasota (FSL)	HiA	0	1	4.15	3	3	0	0	13	9	6	6	0	4	9	.191
MINOR LEAGUE TOTALS			5	10	3.51	29	28	1	0	161	140	78	63	16	46	125	.231

22 CHRIS HEISEY, OF

BORN: Dec. 14, 1984. **B-T:** R-R. **HT.:** 6-0. **WT.:** 200. **DRAFTED:** Messiah (Pa.), 2006 (17th round). **SIGNED BY:** Jeff Brookens.

Heisey doesn't grab attention at first glance. He doesn't have any tools that stand out, he's undersized and he has no pedigree. That explains why he didn't have any NCAA Division I offers coming out of high school, and why he figured he was heading to tiny Messiah (Pa.) College to become a teacher. But as people see him over a longer stretch, his appeal grows. Heisey is an excellent defensive outfielder with a strong arm who can play all three spots. Thanks to his ability to read pitchers, he's a threat on the basepaths (he stole 32 bases in 34 tries last season). He knows how to work counts to draw walks. He plays the game with a chip on his shoulder, thanks to how hard he has had to work to get noticed. Heisey is effective against lefthanders (he hit .378/.468/.538 against them in 2008) but will have to prove he can handle righties (.265/.346/.419) with solid stuff as he moves up the ladder. Heisey may not profile as a big league regular, but his versatility, defensive prowess and speed give him the chance to develop into a valuable role player. And that may be selling him short, something he has fought for years.

Year	Club (League)	Class	AVG	G	AB	R	H	2B	3B	HR	RBI	BB	SO	SB	OBP	SLG
2006	Billings (PIO)	R	.286	70	245	46	70	10	0	6	37	28	33	11	.362	.400

2007	Dayton (MWL)	LoA	.289	104	374	60	108	24	2	9	46	25	57	19	.350	.436
	Sarasota (FSL)	HiA	.349	12	43	6	15	1	0	1	5	4	6	3	.396	.442
2008	Sarasota (FSL)	HiA	.287	117	436	77	125	31	7	7	51	57	69	27	.381	.438
	Chattanooga (SL)	AA	.316	19	79	11	25	6	1	2	10	3	15	5	.341	.494
MINOR LEAGUE TOTALS			.291	322	1177	200	343	72	10	25	149	117	180	65	.365	.433

23 DANNY DORN, OF/1B

BORN: July 20, 1984. **B-T:** L-L. **HT.:** 6-2. **WT.:** 190. **DRAFTED:** Cal State Fullerton, 2006 (32nd round). **SIGNED BY:** Mike Misuraca.

Dorn struggles to hit lefthanders, has had trouble staying healthy in pro ball and isn't a good defensive outfielder. But he has two valuable gifts: Nolan Ryan would have trouble getting a fastball by him, and he feasts on righthanders. When he's healthy, Dorn has a short swing and can drive the ball to the opposite field. Scouts projected him to hit for gap power coming out of college, but he has been better than that, delivering a homer every 20 at-bats as a pro. Dorn's bat will have to carry him because he's a tick below-average runner and is only adequate in left field or at first base. Dorn has a bad shoulder that will occasionally pop out, and he required 15 stitches and a month on the sidelines after cutting his leg open making a sliding catch last April. Dorn has hit at every level, so he'll move up to Triple-A this year. Thanks to his bat he should end up as a valuable bench player or platoon outfielder. He already has proven to be a bargain after signing as a college senior for only $1,000.

Year	Club (League)	Class	AVG	G	AB	R	H	2B	3B	HR	RBI	BB	SO	SB	OBP	SLG
2006	Billings (PIO)	R	.354	60	206	48	73	17	2	8	40	36	36	3	.457	.573
2007	Sarasota (FSL)	HiA	.281	92	338	49	95	21	1	12	66	32	69	3	.359	.456
	Chattanooga (SL)	AA	.311	26	90	20	28	6	1	8	21	15	23	1	.422	.667
2008	Chattanooga (SL)	AA	.277	98	336	64	93	21	2	21	60	42	84	1	.367	.539
	Sarasota (FSL)	HiA	.250	5	20	3	5	2	0	1	3	1	8	0	.286	.500
MINOR LEAGUE TOTALS			.297	281	990	184	294	67	6	50	190	126	220	8	.387	.528

24 CARLOS FISHER, RHP

BORN: Feb. 22, 1983. **B-T:** R-R. **HT.:** 6-3. **WT.:** 210. **DRAFTED:** Lewis-Clark State (Idaho), 2005 (11th round). **SIGNED BY:** Howard Bowens.

A converted outfielder who moved to the mound while playing at Citrus (Calif.) JC and later added polish at NAIA power Lewis-Clark State (Idaho), Fisher may prove to be another bullpen find for the Reds. He had success as a starter in his first two full seasons, but wore down after a mid-2007 promotion to Double-A. That worked out fine for his long-term development because his arm action and maximum-effort delivery always have been more suited to a bullpen role. Working in relief for the first time as a pro, Fisher could focus on throwing his fastball, cutter and slider, and he scrapped his changeup. His fastball sits at 91-93 mph and will touch 95. It's effective because it has heavy sink, which helps induce groundouts. He had a rough ending to his Arizona Fall League campaign, allowing one run in his first six outings and 11 in his final four stints. Fisher should return to Triple-A with a chance to help out the major league bullpen at some point during 2009 if he can improve his control and consistency.

Year	Club (League)	Class	W	L	ERA	G	GS	CG	SV	IP	H	R	ER	HR	BB	SO	AVG
2005	Billings (PIO)	R	4	4	4.19	15	8	0	1	54	56	30	25	3	19	45	.268
2006	Dayton (MWL)	LoA	12	5	2.76	27	27	0	0	150	133	53	46	5	38	122	.237
2007	Sarasota (FSL)	HiA	4	1	2.20	7	7	0	0	41	34	12	10	1	7	41	.221
	Chattanooga (SL)	AA	5	9	4.29	21	21	0	0	113	127	61	54	11	42	94	.291
2008	Chattanooga (SL)	AA	1	5	3.73	36	0	0	8	51	52	28	21	3	20	46	.259
	Louisville (IL)	AAA	5	0	1.04	14	0	0	0	17	14	2	2	0	9	21	.215
MINOR LEAGUE TOTALS			31	24	3.34	120	63	0	9	426	416	186	158	23	135	369	.256

25 PEDRO VIOLA, LHP

BORN: June 29, 1983. **B-T:** L-L. **HT.:** 6-1. **WT.:** 185. **SIGNED:** Dominican Republic, 2005. **SIGNED BY:** Luis Baez/Maximo Rombley.

The Giants originally signed Viola for $20,000 as an outfielder, but they voided the deal when they learned he forged a birth certificate to make himself appear three years younger. The Reds later picked him up as a 22-year-old pitcher for $1,000. He has been inconsistent and hasn't gotten past Double-A at age 25, though he has spent just two full seasons in the United States. At his best, Viola has a 92-95 mph fastball, a slider with bite and a changeup that has a chance to be an average pitch. At his worst, he throws an 89-91 mph heater and a sloppy breaking ball while struggling with his command. Some club officials think his problems may have been tied to him still getting acclimated to life in the States, and he did post a 2.25 ERA after the all-star break. He also pitched better after moving to the rotation, going 3-1, 2.45, and the Reds now say he could be a No. 3 or 4 starter down the road. As a reliever, Viola doesn't really fit as a lefty specialist because lefthanders actually have hit him better than righties. He'll compete for a rotation spot in Triple-A during the spring.

Year	Club (League)	Class	W	L	ERA	G	GS	CG	SV	IP	H	R	ER	HR	BB	SO	AVG
2006	Reds (DSL)	R	3	5	2.04	15	12	0	0	62	50	25	14	0	20	77	.214
2007	Dayton (MWL)	LoA	3	1	1.87	22	0	0	2	43	29	14	9	3	17	49	.190
	Sarasota (FSL)	HiA	0	1	0.90	10	0	0	2	20	14	2	2	0	7	28	.187
	Chattanooga (SL)	AA	0	0	0.95	14	0	0	2	19	12	3	2	2	6	17	.176
2008	Chattanooga (SL)	AA	4	7	4.48	52	7	0	2	82	88	50	41	6	36	84	.278
MINOR LEAGUE TOTALS			10	14	2.70	113	19	0	8	226	193	94	68	11	86	255	.228

26 SEAN WATSON, RHP

BORN: July 24, 1985. **B-T:** R-R. **HT.:** 6-2. **WT.:** 215. **DRAFTED:** Tennessee, 2006 (2nd round). **SIGNED BY:** Perry Smith.

The Reds may have drafted a future closer during the 2006 draft, though it was supposed to be Watson, not 10th-rounder Josh Roenicke. Watson has had a much bumpier path in pro ball. He has struggled with his command and his weight, but there are still times when he shows flashes of the talent that made him a second-round pick. Command is his big problem, as he too often falls behind in the count, and his 92-94 mph fastball is relatively straight, which makes it hittable if batters can sit on it. He has a tendency to fly open early in his delivery, which leads to pitches missing up in the zone. His conditioning always has been a problem, though he did get into better shape as the 2008 season went on. Watson's knuckle-curve is an out pitch when he gets ahead of hitters, but when his fingers get sweaty, he loses the feel for the pitch. He throws it sparingly and has been forced to rely more on his slider. This will be a big year for Watson, who needs to show that he can develop the consistency that has been lacking.

Year	Club (League)	Class	W	L	ERA	G	GS	CG	SV	IP	H	R	ER	HR	BB	SO	AVG
2006	Billings (PIO)	R	0	0	1.52	7	4	0	1	24	16	7	4	0	5	19	.190
	Dayton (MWL)	LoA	1	2	8.59	10	0	0	0	15	22	14	14	2	5	16	.349
2007	Dayton (MWL)	LoA	5	2	1.88	13	13	0	0	72	58	20	15	7	13	85	.226
	Sarasota (FSL)	HiA	4	4	5.43	14	10	0	0	55	54	34	33	8	21	50	.257
2008	Sarasota (FSL)	HiA	0	1	4.50	22	0	0	10	20	19	10	10	4	14	30	.247
	Chattanooga (SL)	AA	1	2	4.37	31	0	0	3	35	27	18	17	1	28	45	.214
MINOR LEAGUE TOTALS			11	11	3.81	97	27	0	14	220	196	103	93	22	86	245	.240

27 ROBERT MANUEL, RHP

BORN: July 9, 1983. **B-T:** R-R. **HT.:** 6-3. **WT.:** 190. **SIGNED:** Sam Houston State, NDFA 2005. **SIGNED BY:** Doug Gassaway (Mets).

When scouts watch Manuel pitch, they just shake their heads. He rears back and throws 88-90 mph fastballs at hitters who are looking for fastballs. Yet time after time, they walk back to the dugout disappointed. Scouts can't explain it, but they can't quibble with the results. Manuel was a high school and junior college shortstop who didn't take up pitching until he got to Sam Houston State. He went undrafted but signed with the Mets as a free agent, and the Reds picked him up less than a year later in a swap for Dave Williams. Manuel's delivery is compact and he manages to hide the ball for a long time. Most important, his fastball seems to have a little hop to it at the plate, even if he lacks above-average velocity. Because he can spot it to all four quadrants of the plate, Manuel gets away with throwing fastball after fastball, mixing in a fringy slider or changeup infrequently. In the past, Manuel struggled because he spent time miscast as a starter. Once the Reds put him in the bullpen for good in 2008, he took off, having success in high Class A, Double-A and in the Arizona Fall League. The Reds added him to the 40-man roster after the season, fearing someone would take him in the Rule 5 draft if they didn't. Manuel will head to Triple-A needing to prove that he can continue to thrive with pedestrian stuff.

Year	Club (League)	Class	W	L	ERA	G	GS	CG	SV	IP	H	R	ER	HR	BB	SO	AVG
2005	Mets (GCL)	R	8	1	2.06	12	5	0	0	57	55	19	13	2	4	49	.250
	Brooklyn (NYP)	SS	0	0	1.80	2	0	0	0	5	5	1	1	1	0	5	.250
2006	Dayton (MWL)	LoA	0	3	4.31	13	7	0	1	48	58	27	23	5	4	36	.294
	Sarasota (FSL)	HiA	0	0	4.50	6	0	0	0	8	10	7	4	3	2	4	.313
2007	Sarasota (FSL)	HiA	6	5	4.03	33	11	0	1	98	100	47	44	3	22	93	.265
2008	Sarasota (FSL)	HiA	1	0	0.00	4	0	0	0	8	5	1	0	0	3	11	.172
	Chattanooga (SL)	AA	5	3	1.40	47	0	0	3	77	47	16	12	2	15	92	.172
	Louisville (IL)	AAA	0	0	0.00	1	0	0	0	2	2	0	0	0	0	0	.250
MINOR LEAGUE TOTALS			20	12	2.88	118	23	0	5	303	282	118	97	16	50	290	.244

28 CRAIG TATUM, C

BORN: March 18, 1983. **B-T:** R-R. **HT.:** 6-0. **WT.:** 225. **DRAFTED:** Mississippi State, 2004 (3rd round). **SIGNED BY:** Jerry Flowers.

Tatum was the Mississippi high school player of the year in 2001 as a senior at Hattiesburg High, and his family has a farm not far from Jets quarterback Brett Favre's property. He went to Mississippi State to add polish, and three years later the Reds took him in the third round as a redshirt sophomore and signed him for $450,000.

He quickly became one of the best defensive catchers in the system. Tatum missed most of 2005 with an elbow injury that required Tommy John surgery, but showed few ill effects upon his return. He has above-average arm strength and threw out 38 percent of basestealers last season. He's a solid receiver who frames pitches, blocks balls well and calls a good game. At the plate, Tatum uses the whole field with power to the gaps that allows him to occasionally leave the yard. He's a well below-average runner. He probably won't hit enough to be a big league regular, and he looked overmatched in his short exposure to Triple-A last year, but his defensive skills make him a useful emergency option in 2009. If Tatum can continue to improve his hitting, he has a chance to be a major league backup down the road.

Year	Club (League)	Class	AVG	G	AB	R	H	2B	3B	HR	RBI	BB	SO	SB	OBP	SLG
2004	Billings (PIO)	R	.221	42	149	19	33	8	3	2	21	21	36	2	.322	.356
2005	Dayton (MWL)	LoA	.188	37	128	16	24	7	1	1	12	21	30	0	.311	.281
2006	Dayton (MWL)	LoA	.277	98	343	41	95	21	0	8	37	32	70	3	.344	.408
2007	Sarasota (FSL)	HiA	.320	58	219	29	70	15	0	10	39	9	41	0	.348	.525
	Chattanooga (SL)	AA	.231	46	173	21	40	10	1	2	22	17	49	0	.299	.335
2008	Chattanooga (SL)	AA	.253	86	293	31	74	18	1	8	57	26	59	1	.312	.403
	Louisville (IL)	AAA	.179	10	39	1	7	0	0	0	4	0	16	0	.175	.179
MINOR LEAGUE TOTALS			.255	377	1344	158	343	79	6	31	192	126	301	6	.321	.392

29 ADAM ROSALES, INF

BORN: May 20, 1983. **B-T:** R-R. **HT.:** 6-1. **WT.:** 195. **DRAFTED:** Western Michigan, 2005 (12th round). **SIGNED BY:** Rick Sellers.

Rosales starred but went undrafted out of high school or as a junior at Western Michigan. After an outstanding senior season, scout Rick Sellers persuaded Cincinnati to take him as an inexpensive senior sign. The knock on Rosales was that he had an aluminum-bat swing, but he has performed well enough with wood to join Jay Bruce as the only members of the Reds' 2005 draft to make it to the big leagues. Rosales' swing can get loopy, but he has hit for average with adequate power. He doesn't profile as a platoon player, but he should be a good utilityman. Rosales can play all four infield positions and the outfield corners if needed, though he doesn't have the range to be an everyday shortstop. His best position is third base, where his slightly above-average arm displays good accuracy and he gets to show off his soft hands. He's a below-average runner. Rosales will head to spring training with a chance to stick with Cincinnati as a backup.

Year	Club (League)	Class	AVG	G	AB	R	H	2B	3B	HR	RBI	BB	SO	SB	OBP	SLG
2005	Billings (PIO)	R	.321	34	140	29	45	14	0	5	25	13	37	2	.396	.529
	Dayton (MWL)	LoA	.328	32	134	24	44	8	0	9	21	10	24	3	.378	.590
2006	Sarasota (FSL)	HiA	.213	34	122	15	26	8	2	2	14	20	27	3	.329	.361
	Dayton (MWL)	LoA	.270	55	222	36	60	9	3	6	29	15	40	5	.328	.419
2007	Sarasota (FSL)	HiA	.294	69	248	47	73	23	5	5	48	31	46	9	.393	.488
	Chattanooga (SL)	AA	.278	67	255	51	71	18	6	13	31	37	66	4	.377	.549
2008	Louisville (IL)	AAA	.287	117	432	70	124	29	7	11	58	22	82	7	.339	.463
	Cincinnati (NL)	MAJ	.207	18	29	0	6	1	0	0	2	1	4	1	.233	.241
MINOR LEAGUE TOTALS			.285	408	1553	272	443	109	23	51	226	148	322	33	.360	.484
MAJOR LEAGUE TOTALS			.207	18	29	0	6	1	0	0	2	1	4	1	.233	.241

30 ALEX BUCHHOLZ, 2B

BORN: Sept. 30, 1987. **B-T:** R-R. **HT.:** 6-0. **WT.:** 185. **DRAFTED:** Delaware, 2008 (6th round). **SIGNED BY:** Jeff Brookens.

The Reds have kept a close eye on the Hens, partly because pro scout Jeff Taylor is a Delaware alum. In 2007, the Reds drafted a pair of Blue Hens, outfielder Brandon Menchaca (who signed in the 15th round) and right-hander Mike McGuire (who opted to return to school after going in the 46th). But while scouting them, Jeff Brookens also took note of Buchholz, then a sophomore, and pressed the Reds to take him in 2008. Cincinnati scouting director Chris Buckley always has emphasized drafting middle infielders with solid baseball instincts, and Buchholz definitely fits that bill. Signed for $125,000 as a sixth-rounder, Buchholz played third base at Delaware, but projects better offensively at second. His hitting ability and power are solid average to a tick above, thanks to his impressive bat speed. Buchholz has a solid arm, reliable hands and good instincts, but his speed and range are below average. As with Chris Valaika, his bat will be his path to the big leagues. Buchholz had an outstanding pro debut despite missing five weeks when an errant pitch broke the hamate bone in his left hand, and he actually raised his average from .366 to .396 after returning to the lineup. The Reds are curious to see how he looks at shortstop and will play him on both sides of the second-base bag in low Class A this year.

Year	Club (League)	Class	AVG	G	AB	R	H	2B	3B	HR	RBI	BB	SO	SB	OBP	SLG
2008	Billings (PIO)	R	.396	34	134	31	53	15	2	3	26	16	25	3	.471	.604
MINOR LEAGUE TOTALS			.396	34	134	31	53	15	2	3	26	16	25	3	.471	.604

Cleveland Indians

BY BEN BADLER

Grady Sizemore's superlative season wasn't enough to push the Indians past .500

After the Indians nearly reached the 2007 World Series, forecasts had them contending for another American League Central title in 2008. Yet despite outscoring their opponents by 44 runs, the Indians finished 81-81. They languished in last place for much of the season until mid-August, precipitating the trade of C.C. Sabathia to the Brewers on July 7, though their 40-28 record after the all-star break was the sixth-best in baseball.

Sabathia is the only star the Indians have drafted since they made him the 20th overall selection in 1998. The club has gotten little return on its first-round and supplemental first-round choices since. The Tribe had 12 such picks from 2000-03, and only Jeremy Guthrie has found any big league success—and that came after the Orioles claimed him on waivers.

Sabathia's departure left Ben Francisco, Ryan Garko, Aaron Laffey and Jensen Lewis as the only homegrown draftees to make much of an impact for 2008 Indians. Former Tribe draft picks Ryan Church, Guthrie, Kevin Kouzmanoff and Luke Scott have enjoyed various degrees of success with other clubs.

Nevertheless, the Indians have found other ways to build a perennial contender. Asdrubal Cabrera, Franklin Gutierrez, Travis Hafner, Cliff Lee, Kelly Shoppach and Grady Sizemore all came to Cleveland as minor leaguers through trades, while Shin-Soo Choo had only two big league hits before the Tribe acquired him. Victor Martinez signed out of Venezuela, while Fausto Carmona, Jhonny Peralta and Rafael Perez were found in the Dominican Republic.

By dealing Sabathia and Casey Blake, Cleveland continued its history of bolstering its farm system with other organizations' prospects. Catcher Carlos Santana, the prize of the Blake trade, and outfielder Matt LaPorta, the key to the Sabathia deal, became the Tribe's two best prospects. Two more players in those transactions, outfielder/first baseman Michael Brantley and righthander Jon Meloan, also should help the big league club in the near future.

For the first time in five years, righthander Adam Miller doesn't rank No. 1 on this prospect list, but he still has as much star potential as any Indians draftee in the system. Miller could join Meloan in immediately upgrading a bullpen that posted the second-worst relief ERA (5.13) in the majors last season.

Another homegrown arm, lefty David Huff, could upgrade the 2009 rotation, while outfielder Nick

TOP 30 PROSPECTS

1. Carlos Santana, c	16. Abner Abreu, 3b/of
2. Matt LaPorta, of	17. Tony Sipp, lhp
3. Nick Weglarz, of	18. Jon Meloan, rhp
4. Adam Miller, rhp	19. Jeff Stevens, rhp
5. Beau Mills, 1b	20. Trey Haley, rhp
6. Lonnie Chisenhall, ss	21. Scott Lewis, lhp
7. Kelvin de la Cruz, lhp	22. Zach Putnam, rhp
8. David Huff, lhp	23. Tim Fedroff, of
9. Michael Brantley, of/1b	24. Cord Phelps. 2b
10. Luis Valbuena, 2b	25. Jordan Brown, 1b
11. Carlos Rivero, ss	26. Delvi Cid, of
12. Wes Hodges, 3b	27. Bryce Stowell, rhp
13. Hector Rondon, rhp	28. Josh Tomlin, rhp
14. T.J. House, lhp	29. John Gaub, lhp
15. Trevor Crowe, of	30. Jose Ozoria, ss

Weglarz and first baseman Beau Mills, both Tribe draftees, could crack the lineup by the end of 2010.

In an effort to reap more from the draft, Cleveland spent $7 million on its 2008 crop—up from $3.6 million the year before. The Indians doled out $1.1 million to Lonnie Chisenhall in the first round and far exceeded MLB's slot recommendations to land righties Trey Haley, Zach Putnam and Bryce Stowell, lefty T.J. House and outfielder Tim Fedroff. They also maintained a strong international presence, paying $715,000 for Venezuelan catcher Alex Monsalve and $575,000 for Dominican shortstop Jose Ozoria.

General Manager: Mark Shapiro. **Farm Director:** Ross Atkins. **Scouting Director:** Brad Grant.

Class	Team	League	W	L	PCT	Finish*	Manager	Affiliated
Majors	Cleveland	American	81	81	.500	8th (14)	Eric Wedge	—
Triple-A	Buffalo Bisons	International	66	77	.462	10th (14)	Torey Lovullo	1995
Double-A	Akron Aeros	Eastern	80	62	.563	3rd (12)	Mike Sarbaugh	1997
High A	Kinston Indians	Carolina	72	66	.522	3rd (8)	Chris Tremie	1987
Low A	Lake County Captains	South Atlantic	75	65	.536	7th (16)	Aaron Holbert	2003
Short-season	Mahoning Valley Scrappers	New York-Penn	31	44	.413	12th (14)	Travis Fryman	1999
Rookie	GCL Indians	Gulf Coast	27	29	.482	11th (16)	Rouglas Odor	2006
Overall 2008 Minor League Record			351	343	.506	14th		

* Finish in overall standings (No. of teams in league). ^League champion.

LAST YEAR'S TOP 30

Rank	Player, Pos.	Status
1.	Adam Miller, rhp	No. 4
2.	Chuck Lofgren, lhp	Dropped out
3.	Beau Mills, 1b	No. 5
4.	Wes Hodges, 3b	No. 12
5.	Aaron Laffey, lhp	Majors
6.	Nick Weglarz, of	No. 3
7.	Jordan Brown, 1b/of	No. 25
8.	David Huff, lhp	No. 8
9.	Ben Francisco, of	Majors
10.	Jensen Lewis, rhp	Majors
11.	Masahide Kobayashi, rhp	Majors
12.	Tony Sipp, lhp	No. 17
13.	Matt McBride, c	Dropped out
14.	Trevor Crowe, of	No. 15
15.	Chris Jones, lhp	Dropped out
16.	Scott Lewis, lhp	No. 21
17.	Sung-Wei Tseng, rhp	Dropped out
18.	Carlos Rivero, ss	No. 11
19.	Jeff Stevens, rhp	No. 19
20.	Josh Rodriguez, ss	Dropped out
21.	Ryan Miller, lhp	Dropped out
22.	Michael Aubrey, 1b	Dropped out
23.	John Drennen, of	Dropped out
24.	Wyatt Toregas, c	Dropped out
25.	Brad Snyder, of	(Cubs)
26.	Frank Herrmann, rhp	Dropped out
27.	Chris Nash, 1b	Dropped out
28.	Hector Rondon, rhp	No. 13
29.	Reid Santos, lhp	(Blue Jays)
30.	Joey Mahalic, lhp	Dropped out

BEST TOOLS

Best Hitter for Average	Michael Brantley
Best Power Hitter	Matt LaPorta
Best Strike-Zone Discipline	Nick Weglarz
Fastest Baserunner	Delvi Cid
Best Athlete	Michael Brantley
Best Fastball	Adam Miller
Best Curveball	Kelvin de la Cruz
Best Slider	Adam Miller
Best Changeup	David Huff
Best Control	David Huff
Best Defensive Catcher	Wyatt Toregas
Best Defensive Infielder	Mark Thompson
Best Infield Arm	Carlos Rivero
Best Defensive Outfielder	Delvi Cid
Best Outfield Arm	Matt Brown

PROJECTED 2012 LINEUP

Catcher	Carlos Santana
First Base	Matt LaPorta
Second Base	Luis Valbuena
Third Base	Lonnie Chisenhall
Shortstop	Jhonny Peralta
Left Field	Nick Weglarz
Center Field	Grady Sizemore
Right Field	Shin-Soo Choo
Designated Hitter	Beau Mills
No. 1 Starter	Cliff Lee
No. 2 Starter	Fausto Carmona
No. 3 Starter	Kelvin de la Cruz
No. 4 Starter	David Huff
No. 5 Starter	T.J. House
Closer	Adam Miller

TOP PROSPECTS OF THE DECADE

Year	Player, Pos.	2008 Org.
1999	Russell Branyan, 3b	Brewers
2000	C.C Sabathia, lhp	Brewers
2001	C.C. Sabathia, lhp	Brewers
2002	Corey Smith, 3b	Angels
2003	Brandon Phillips, ss/2b	Reds
2004	Grady Sizemore, of	Indians
2005	Adam Miller, rhp	Indians
2006	Adam Miller, rhp	Indians
2007	Adam Miller, rhp	Indians
2008	Adam Miller, rhp	Indians

TOP DRAFT PICKS OF THE DECADE

Year	Player, Pos.	2008 Org.
1999	Will Hartley, c (2nd round)	Out of baseball
2000	Corey Smith, 3b	Angels
2001	Dan Denham, rhp	Angels
2002	Jeremy Guthrie, rhp	Orioles
2003	Michael Aubrey, 1b	Indians
2004	Jeremy Sowers, lhp	Indians
2005	Trevor Crowe, of	Indians
2006	David Huff, lhp (1st round supp.)	Indians
2007	Beau Mills, 3b/1b	Indians
2008	Lonnie Chisenhall, ss	Indians

LARGEST BONUSES IN CLUB HISTORY

Danys Baez, 1999	$4,500,000
Jeremy Guthrie, 2002	$3,000,000
Jeremy Sowers, 2004	$2,475,000
Michael Aubrey, 2003	$2,010,000
Dan Denham, 2001	$1,860,000

CLEVELAND INDIANS

TOP 2009 ROOKIE: Adam Miller, rhp. A move to the bullpen could keep him healthy and allow him to dominate.

BREAKOUT PROSPECT: T.J. House, lhp. The Indians are eager to see what the athletic southpaw with a lively low-90s fastball can do after paying him $750,000 as a 16th-round pick.

SLEEPER: Elvis Araujo, lhp. A 6-foot-6, 215-pound Venezuelan, he touched the low 90s with his fastball as a 17-year-old.

SOURCE OF TOP 30 TALENT			
Homegrown	24	Acquired	6
College	13	Trades	6
Junior college	1	Rule 5 draft	0
High school	4	Independent leagues	0
Draft-and-follow	0	Free agents/waivers	0
Nondrafted free agents	0		
International	6		

Numbers in parentheses indicate prospect rankings.

LF
Matt LaPorta (2)
Nick Weglarz (3)
Michael Brantley (9)
Trevor Crowe (15)
John Drennen

CF
Tim Fedroff (23)
Delvi Cid (26)
Jason Denham

RF
Abner Abreu (16)
Roman Pena
Matt Brown
Tim Palinscar

3B
Lonnie Chisenhall (6)
Wes Hodges (12)
Jeremie Tice
Jared Goedert

SS
Carlos Rivero (11)
Jose Ozoria (30)
Ronald Rivas
Kevin Fontanez

2B
Luis Valbuena (10)
Cord Phelps (24)
Karexon Sanchez
Josh Rodriguez

1B
Beau Mills (5)
Jordan Brown (25)
Michael Aubrey
Stephen Head
Nate Recknagel

C
Carlos Santana (1)
Alex Monsalve
Wyatt Toregas
Chris Gimenez
Matt McBride

RHP

Starters	Relievers
Hector Rondon (13)	Adam Miller (4)
Trey Haley (20)	Jon Meloan (18)
Zach Putnam (22)	Jeff Stevens (19)
Bryce Stowell (27)	Mike Pontius
Josh Tomlin (28)	Robert Bryson
Chris Archer	David Roberts
Jeanmar Gomez	Carlos Moncrief
Chen-Chang Lee	Mike McGuire
Clayton Cook	Erik Stiller
Frank Herrmann	Neil Wagner
Kevin Dixon	Jonathan Holt
Steven Wright	Josh Judy
	Sung-Wei Tseng

LHP

Starters	Relievers
Kelvin de la Cruz (7)	Tony Sipp (17)
David Huff (8)	John Gaub (29)
T.J. House (14)	Ryan Edell
Scott Lewis (21)	Shawn Nottingham
Chuck Lofgren	
Eric Berger	
Ryan Miller	
Elvis Araujo	
Chris Jones	

2008　　　　　　　　　　　　　　BONUSES: $7.0 MILLION

BEST PURE HITTER: SS Lonnie Chisenhall's (1) fluid swing and ability to make consistent line-drive contact made him one of the most attractive hitters in the 2008 draft. OF Tim Fedroff (7), who signed for $725,000, and 2B Cord Phelps (3) aren't far behind.

BEST POWER HITTER: 1B Nate Recknagel (19) set a Michigan record with 23 homers in the spring but got just four pro at-bats after breaking the hamate bone in his left hand during the NCAA playoffs. He might get a look at catcher in the future. 3B Jeremie Tice (6), who slammed 25 homers in his lone season at the College of Charleston, also has intriguing power.

FASTEST RUNNER: OF Donnie Webb (10) has plus speed.

BEST DEFENSIVE PLAYER: SS/2B Kevin Fontanez (24) is a pure defender with tremendous actions and a strong arm.

BEST FASTBALL: RHP Carlos Moncrief (14) can hit 96 mph, while RHP Zach Putnam (5) can reach 95, and both should throw harder now that they're focusing on pitching after being two-way players in college. Putnam, who signed for $600,000, gets nasty sink on his two-seamer. RHPs Trey Haley (2), David Roberts (4) and Mike McGuire (43) all can touch 94 mph.

BEST SECONDARY PITCH: LHP T.J. House (16) throws a power slurve in the mid-80s. He also has a low-90s fastball, and the combo earned him a $750,000 bonus. Moncrief's slider and Putnam's splitter are plus pitches at times.

BEST PRO DEBUT: LHP Eric Berger (8) reached low Class A while going 2-0, 2.11 with a 45-11 K-BB ratio in 38 innings. He's regaining his stuff after Tommy John surgery in 2007, currently working at 89-91 mph and flashing a 12-to-6 curveball.

BEST ATHLETE: Fedroff is more athletic than his 5-foot-11, 220-pound frame would indicate. He has the best combination of power and speed in Cleveland's draft, and he can play center field.

MOST INTRIGUING BACKGROUND: 1B/3B Adam Abraham (13) played two seasons of major junior hockey before opting for baseball during the NHL lockout.

CLOSEST TO THE MAJORS: Putnam projects better as a reliever and could reach Double-A in that role during his first full pro season. Phelps and Berger also will be on the fast track.

BEST LATE-ROUND PICK: The Indians spent heavily to sign House and polished RHP Bryce Stowell (22), who got $725,000 after an all-star summer in the Cape Cod League. Among the less-costly players, athletic OF Tim Palinscar (40) and McGuire stick out. Plagued by injuries and inconsistency at Delaware, McGuire struck out 47 in 40 innings in his first taste of pro ball.

THE ONE WHO GOT AWAY: Cleveland made a run at projectable RHPs Otto Roberts (23) and Michael Goodnight (27). Roberts decided to attend Creighton, while Goodnight headed to Houston.

ASSESSMENT: Chisenhall and Phelps could inject offense into the Tribe's infield. But the story of this draft was Cleveland's aggressiveness in signing Haley (whose $1.25 million bonus exceeded Chisenhall's $1.1 million), Putnam, Fedroff, House and Stowell.

2007　　　　　　　　　　　　　　BONUSES: $3.6 MILLION

The Indians drafted 1B Beau Mills (1) for his power, and he led the system with 21 homers in his first full season. He has to carry the flag for this draft because Cleveland gave up its second- and third-rounders as free-agent compensation.

GRADE: C

2006　　　　　　　　　　　　　　BONUSES: $6.5 MILLION

The Tribe didn't have a first-rounder, but both LHP David Huff (1s) and 3B Wes Hodges (2) could start in the majors at some point this season.

GRADE: C+

2005　　　　　　　　　　　　　　BONUSES: $4.9 MILLION*

RHP Jensen Lewis (3) took over as Cleveland's closer last August. OF Nick Weglarz (3) is the system's best truly homegrown prospect, making up for slow-developing OFs Trevor Crowe (1) and John Drennen (1s).

GRADE: C+

2004　　　　　　　　　　　　　　BONUSES: $4.9 MILLION*

This crop is all about lefthanders. Jeremy Sowers (1) and Chuck Lofgren (4) have regressed terribly, but Scott Lewis (3) won all four of his big league starts in September and there's still hope for Tony Sipp (45).

GRADE: C

*Draft analysis by Jim Callis. Numbers in parentheses indicate draft rounds. *Bonuses for 2004-05 are first 10 rounds only.*

BILL MITCHELL

PROSPECT

CARLOS SANTANA, C

Born: April 8, 1986.
Ht.: 5-11. **Wt.:** 188.
Bats: B. **Throws:** R.
Signed:
Dominican Republic,
2004.
Signed by:
Andres Lopez (Dodgers).

The Dodgers signed Santana out of the Dominican Republic for $75,000 in 2004, and he split time between third base and the outfield in his first two pro seasons. Los Angeles has had success converting position players into catchers, most notably Russell Martin, and they had Santana make the transition during instructional league following the 2006 season. In his first season catching, Santana hit just .223/.318/.370 at low Class A Great Lakes, though he had nearly as many walks (40) as strikeouts (45). In 2008 he led the high Class A California League with a .994 OPS and won league MVP honors despite getting traded on July 26. The Dodgers wanted Casey Blake to fill a hole at third base, but they also didn't want to pick up any of the roughly $2 million remaining on his contract. In return for paying Blake's remaining salary, the Indians were able to increase their return, getting Santana along with righthander Jon Meloan. Santana didn't slow down after switching organizations, destroying high Class A pitching for a month with Kinston. He received a late-season promotion for Double-A Akron's playoff run, though a minor groin strain kept him mostly on the bench.

Santana has shown good strike-zone discipline ever since signing with the Dodgers. He swings aggressively at strikes and routinely squares up balls with authority, using his lower half well and getting good extension. He has a good two-strike approach and doesn't chase pitches outside the strike zone. He should hit for a high average and OBP with average power. He's more athletic than most catchers. Though he still has work to do behind the plate, Santana has good defensive tools. He moves well and has a strong arm.

Most of Santana's improvement must come behind the plate, and he's still learning the nuances of catching. He sometimes lacks accuracy with his throws and erased 27 percent of basestealers. After committing 20 passed balls in 67 games in 2007, he cut that number to 14 in 106 contests last season, but he still needs to get better. He also led Cal League catchers with 16 errors in 80 games. Balls down and in to his glove side can give him trouble and he must get smoother receiving balls on the outer half, as he tends to get stiff-wristed at times. He's making progress blocking balls but that's another skill he's still working on. He understands English well but doesn't yet speak the language comfortably. Santana usually has a good stroke at the plate, but he can get too long with his swing and too wild with his feet at times. He's a below-average runner, though an occasional threat to steal.

Kelly Shoppach's big year means that the Indians won't have to rush Santana, who will begin 2009 on a prospect-laden Akron club. He has all the ingredients to become an all-star catcher and could reach Cleveland by the end of 2010.

Year	Club (League)	Class	AVG	G	AB	R	H	2B	3B	HR	RBI	BB	SO	SB	OBP	SLG
2005	Dodgers (GCL)	R	.295	32	78	14	23	4	1	1	14	16	8	0	.412	.410
2006	Vero Beach (FSL)	HiA	.268	54	198	16	53	10	2	3	18	23	43	0	.345	.384
	Ogden (PIO)	R	.303	37	132	31	40	5	1	7	27	30	19	4	.423	.515
2007	Great Lakes (MWL)	LoA	.223	86	292	32	65	20	1	7	36	40	45	5	.318	.370
2008	Inland Empire (CAL)	HiA	.323	99	350	88	113	34	4	14	96	69	59	7	.431	.563
	Kinston (CAR)	HiA	.352	29	105	34	37	5	1	6	19	20	24	3	.452	.590
	Akron (EL)	AA	.125	2	8	3	1	0	0	1	2	0	2	0	.125	.500
MINOR LEAGUE TOTALS			.285	339	1163	218	332	78	10	39	212	198	200	19	.388	.470

2 MATT LaPORTA, OF

RODGER WOOD

BORN: Jan. 8, 1985. **B-T:** R-R. **HT.:** 6-2. **WT.:** 210. **DRAFTED:** Florida, 2007 (1st round). **SIGNED BY:** Charlie Aliano (Brewers).

After signing for $2 million as the seventh overall pick in the 2007 draft, LaPorta opened his first full pro season in Double-A and was named to the Futures Game before the Brewers made him the key chip they used to acquire C.C. Sabathia. Shortly afterward, he left for the Beijing Olympics. LaPorta's physical frame, strength and load in his swing help him generate well above-average power. He has the patience to take walks, and he also aggressively punishes mistakes. He can drive the ball out of the park to all fields when he gets his arms extended. Though he played first base at Florida, scouts have been impressed with his outfield instincts. Like a lot of power hitters, LaPorta still has some holes in his swing—in his case, high and inside, and against offspeed pitches low and away. He struggled after the trade and again in Venezuelan winter ball when pitchers fed him soft stuff in hitter's counts. Though he has some feel for the outfield, he has below-average speed and range with fringy arm strength. Though the Indians could use his power now, LaPorta likely will begin 2009 at their new Triple-A Columbus affiliate. Depending on the needs of the club, he could play either first base or left field, and he'll have an above-average bat at any position.

Year	Club (League)	Class	AVG	G	AB	R	H	2B	3B	HR	RBI	BB	SO	SB	OBP	SLG
2007	Helena (PIO)	R	.259	7	27	4	7	1	0	2	4	1	8	0	.286	.519
	West Virginia (SAL)	LoA	.318	23	88	18	28	8	0	10	27	7	22	0	.392	.750
2008	Huntsville (SL)	AA	.288	84	302	56	87	23	2	20	66	45	63	2	.402	.576
	Akron (EL)	AA	.233	17	60	6	14	1	0	2	8	4	12	0	.299	.350
MINOR LEAGUE TOTALS			.285	131	477	84	136	33	2	34	105	57	105	2	.382	.577

3 NICK WEGLARZ, OF

CARL KLINE

BORN: Dec. 16, 1987. **B-T:** L-L. **HT.:** 6-3. **WT.:** 245. **DRAFTED:** HS—Stevensville, Ont., 2005 (3rd round). **SIGNED BY:** Les Pajari.

After missing nearly the entire 2006 season with a broken hamate bone in his right hand, Weglarz has had two successful years in Class A ball. He was one of the Carolina League's youngest players before he joined Canada's Olympic team in August. Weglarz belted two home runs in a loss against Cuba and was Canada's best hitter despite being its second-youngest player. Weglarz has uncanny discipline for a player his age and size, rarely offering at pitches outside of the strike zone and showing the potential to draw 100 walks in a season. He generates excellent loft, bat speed and leverage with his swing and shows plus-plus power potential, giving him an outstanding combination of power and patience. Weglarz reduced some of his extraneous hand movement in his trigger, but his hand setup is still a work in progress. His legs help him generate his power, but he needs to consistently get the back half of his body through the ball. With his enormous size, he'll have to work to maintain his already below-average speed and to stay in left field. His range and arm are both fringy at best. Weglarz is on the same track as Matt LaPorta, one level behind him. Weglarz will open 2009 with Double-A Akron and he could crack the major league roster by mid-2010.

Year	Club (League)	Class	AVG	G	AB	R	H	2B	3B	HR	RBI	BB	SO	SB	OBP	SLG
2005	Burlington (APP)	R	.231	41	147	22	34	11	0	2	13	17	42	2	.313	.347
2006	Indians (GCL)	R	.000	1	2	0	0	0	0	0	0	0	2	0	.000	.000
2007	Lake County (SAL)	LoA	.276	125	439	75	121	28	0	23	82	82	129	1	.395	.497
	Kinston (CAR)	HiA	.143	2	7	1	1	0	0	1	1	1	2	0	.250	.571
2008	Kinston (CAR)	HiA	.272	106	375	68	102	20	5	10	41	71	78	9	.396	.432
MINOR LEAGUE TOTALS			.266	275	970	166	258	59	5	36	137	171	253	12	.382	.448

4 ADAM MILLER, RHP

BORN: Nov. 26, 1984. **B-T:** R-R. **HT.:** 6-4. **WT.:** 200. **DRAFTED:** HS—McKinney, Texas, 2003 (1st round supplemental). **SIGNED BY:** Matt Ruebel.

The No. 1 prospect on this list the previous four years, Miller continues to show great promise and an inability to stay healthy. His 2008 season ended in May when he had surgery on his right middle finger, and he went to the Dominican League to make up for lost time. Miller's fastball is the best in the organization, a lively 93-95 mph heater that regularly touched 97 mph in his early winter-ball outings. When he's at his best, his slider is a plus-plus 86-88 mph pitch with late break, and it too looked good in the Dominican. He also uses a two-seam fastball to get groundballs. He has a relatively stress-free delivery and good command. The only thing that has kept Miller from the majors so far is his health. He strained his elbow in 2005 and had elbow and finger issues in 2007 before missing most of the 2008 season. Some scouts feel that his arm action may continue to cause him elbow problems, as he has a high back elbow. He needs to leverage his lower half more frequently in his delivery. A starter throughout his minor league career, Miller may have to move to the bullpen for health reasons. He should compete for a big league relief role in 2009 and soon could become the dominant closer the Indians have sorely lacked in recent years.

Year	Club (League)	Class	W	L	ERA	G	GS	CG	SV	IP	H	R	ER	HR	BB	SO	AVG
2003	Burlington (APP)	R	0	4	4.96	10	10	0	0	33	30	20	18	2	9	23	.250
2004	Lake County (SAL)	LoA	7	4	3.36	19	19	1	0	91	79	39	34	7	28	106	.240
	Kinston (CAR)	HiA	3	2	2.08	8	8	0	0	43	29	17	10	1	12	46	.193
2005	Mahoning Valley (NYP)	SS	0	0	5.06	3	3	0	0	11	17	6	6	0	4	6	.405
	Kinston (CAR)	HiA	2	4	4.83	12	12	0	0	60	76	43	32	5	17	45	.318
2006	Buffalo (IL)	AAA	0	0	5.79	1	1	0	0	5	4	3	3	0	3	4	.235
	Akron (EL)	AA	15	6	2.75	26	24	1	0	154	129	56	47	9	43	157	.226
2007	Buffalo (IL)	AAA	5	4	4.82	19	11	1	0	65	68	39	35	4	21	68	.265
2008	Buffalo (IL)	AAA	0	1	1.88	6	6	0	0	29	26	9	6	0	12	20	.239
MINOR LEAGUE TOTALS			32	25	3.51	104	94	3	0	490	458	232	191	28	149	475	.250

5 BEAU MILLS, 1B

BORN: Aug. 15, 1986. **B-T:** L-R. **HT.:** 6-2. **WT.:** 220. **DRAFTED:** Lewis-Clark State (Idaho), 2007 (1st round). **SIGNED BY:** Greg Smith.

After being suspended at Fresno State for academic shortcomings after his sophmore year, Mills transferred to Lewis-Clark State (Idaho). He led the Warriors to their 15th national championship in 2007, hitting an NAIA-record 38 homers, and signed for $1.575 million as the 13th overall pick in the draft. The son of former big leaguer and Red Sox bench coach Brad Mills, he led the system with 21 homers in his first full pro season. Mills generates plus power to all fields with good leverage and strength. He stays balanced at the plate, has a pure swing and possesses the patience to draw walks. His arm strength improved after the Indians put him on an extensive throwing program following a shoulder impingement in 2006 that didn't require surgery. While Mills does have a good feel for hitting and for the strike zone, he's susceptible to chasing both breaking balls in the dirt and high fastballs. He needs to adjust his two-strike approach. He moved from third base to first base in 2008, but his footwork isn't clean and his actions around the bag aren't the smoothest. Mills is a below-average runner. Mills will start 2009 in Double-A. He could compete for a big league job in 2010, though the system is heavy with sluggers who profile best at first base.

Year	Club (League)	Class	AVG	G	AB	R	H	2B	3B	HR	RBI	BB	SO	SB	OBP	SLG
2007	Mahoning Valley (NYP)	SS	.179	8	28	5	5	2	0	0	1	3	7	0	.303	.250
	Lake County (SAL)	LoA	.271	44	177	32	48	12	1	5	36	14	38	0	.333	.435
	Kinston (CAR)	HiA	.275	10	40	7	11	6	0	1	5	4	8	0	.375	.500
2008	Kinston (CAR)	HiA	.293	125	482	78	141	34	3	21	90	54	105	2	.373	.506
MINOR LEAGUE TOTALS			.282	187	727	122	205	54	4	27	132	75	158	2	.361	.479

6 LONNIE CHISENHALL, SS

BORN: Oct. 4, 1988. **B-T:** L-R. **HT.:** 6-1. **WT.:** 200. **DRAFTED:** Pitt (N.C.) CC, 2008 (1st round). **SIGNED BY:** Bob Mayer .

Rated the nation's No. 1 freshman before the 2007 season, Chisenhall looked as good as advertised until South Carolina dismissed him from the team following his arrest on charges of larceny. Chisenhall transferred to Pitt (N.C.) CC for 2008 and batted .410/.528/.765 with just eight strikeouts in 218 plate appearances before the Indians made him the 29th overall pick in June. He signed with the Indians for $1.1 million. Chisenhall combines an excellent feel for hitting with nice balance and a pure swing that's short and quick to the ball. His frame and stroke are geared more for line drives, but he projects to hit for average power. He has a strong arm and surprised Cleveland with how well he handled shortstop in his pro debut. Chisenhall uses the entire field well, but he could do a better job of keeping his hands inside the ball at times. His speed, range and hands don't stand out, so he likely faces a move to third base in the near future. With better defensive tools, he would profile nicely at second base, but that's probably a stretch. He should have enough bat for the hot corner, and Chisenhall could move there in 2009. His bat is advanced enough that he could skip a level and open 2009 in high Class A, putting him on pace to reach the majors as early as 2011.

Year	Club (League)	Class	AVG	G	AB	R	H	2B	3B	HR	RBI	BB	SO	SB	OBP	SLG
2008	Mahoning Valley (NYP)	SS	.290	68	276	38	80	20	3	5	45	24	32	7	.355	.438
MINOR LEAGUE TOTALS			.290	68	276	38	80	20	3	5	45	24	32	7	.355	.438

7 KELVIN DE LA CRUZ, LHP

CARL KLINE

BORN: Aug. 1, 1988. **B-T:** L-L. **HT.:** 6-5. **WT.:** 187. **SIGNED:** Dominican Republic, 2004. **SIGNED BY:** Johnny Martinez.

When the Indians signed de la Cruz in 2004, the lanky lefty pitched at 83-84 mph and topped out at 86. His velocity has climbed steadily each year, and he finally reached full-season ball in 2008. De la Cruz now sits at 89-92 mph and touches 93-94 with his four-seam fastball. He's still growing and getting stronger, so he could add more velocity. His best pitch is his 75-77 mph curveball, which has two-plane depth and neutralizes lefties and righties. He also mixes in a two-seam fastball with good sink and a changeup that shows promise. De la Cruz struggles to maintain his mid- to high three-quarters arm slot, which impedes his ability to throw strikes. Better balance and separation over the rubber will allow him to repeat his release point out front. Scouts have differing opinions about his athleticism, though that may be because he's still growing into his body and coordination. He needs to throw his changeup more often and it has taken a back seat in developmental priority to fastball command. De la Cruz again will be one of the high Class A Carolina League's youngest pitchers in 2009. How quickly he can make the necessary mechanical adjustments will dictate the speed of his ascent.

Year	Club (League)	Class	W	L	ERA	G	GS	CG	SV	IP	H	R	ER	HR	BB	SO	AVG
2005	Indians1 (DSL)	R	3	3	2.36	13	12	0	1	53	49	23	14	3	16	39	.234
2006	Indians (GCL)	R	1	2	10.98	9	4	0	0	20	32	29	24	2	13	15	.360
2007	Indians (GCL)	R	3	0	0.50	3	3	0	0	18	7	1	1	1	2	20	.117
	Mahoning Valley (NYP)	SS	2	4	3.98	12	12	0	0	54	41	27	24	5	34	53	.216
2008	Akron (EL)	AA	1	0	7.20	1	1	0	0	5	4	4	4	1	3	4	.222
	Lake County (SAL)	LoA	8	4	1.69	18	18	1	0	96	71	23	18	2	34	96	.207
	Kinston (CAR)	HiA	3	2	6.44	8	8	0	0	29	35	22	21	1	25	36	.292
MINOR LEAGUE TOTALS			21	15	3.46	64	58	1	1	275	239	129	106	15	127	263	.232

8 DAVID HUFF, LHP

RODGER WOOD

BORN: Aug. 22, 1984. **B-T:** L-L. **HT.:** 6-2. **WT.:** 190. **DRAFTED:** UCLA, 2006 (1st round supplemental). **SIGNED BY:** Vince Sagisi.

After signing for $950,000 as a supplemental first-rounder in 2006, Huff appeared poised to rise rapidly through the system. Instead, elbow soreness shut him down in May 2007, though he was able to avoid surgery. He bounced back in 2008, breezing through the upper levels of the minors. Huff is athletic and repeats his excellent delivery to pound the zone with each of his pitches, the best of which is a plus changeup. He commands both sides of the plate with his 87-92 mph fastball. He improved his slider in 2008, and it's now a reliable third pitch. Huff also has a curveball, but it's more of a show-me pitch. He won't overpower anyone with velocity, though he has more on his fastball than fellow Indians lefthanders Aaron Laffey and Jeremy Sowers. After his elbow woes, the Indians kept him on a short leash in 2008, so he still has to prove he can pitch effectively the third time through the lineup against big league hitters. Huff will compete for a role in Cleveland's rotation during spring training. He has the potential to develop into a No. 3 or 4 starter.

Year	Club (League)	Class	W	L	ERA	G	GS	CG	SV	IP	H	R	ER	HR	BB	SO	AVG
2006	Mahoning Valley (NYP)	SS	0	1	5.87	4	4	0	0	8	9	5	5	0	7	8	.300
2007	Kinston (CAR)	HiA	4	2	2.72	11	11	0	0	60	57	23	18	4	15	46	.251
2008	Akron (EL)	AA	5	1	1.92	11	10	1	0	66	44	17	14	5	14	62	.189
	Buffalo (IL)	AAA	6	4	3.01	16	16	0	0	81	68	31	27	8	15	81	.224
MINOR LEAGUE TOTALS			15	8	2.70	42	41	1	0	214	178	76	64	17	51	197	.224

9 MICHAEL BRANTLEY, OF/1B

BILL MITCHELL

BORN: May 15, 1987. **B-T:** L-L. **HT.:** 6-2. **WT.:** 180. **DRAFTED:** HS—Fort Pierce, Fla., 2005 (7th round). **SIGNED BY:** Larry Pardo (Brewers).

The son of former big leaguer Mickey Brantley, Michael ranked second in the minors in plate appearances per strikeout (17.7) in 2008. At the end of the season, the Indians selected him over infielder Taylor Green as the player to be named in the C.C. Sabathia trade. Brantley has outstanding barrel control and contact-hitting ability, spraying the ball to all fields. He has walked more than he has struck out in each of his four pro seasons. He has a quick bat and a fundamentally sound swing, and he was able to generate more loft in his swing in 2008 than he had shown in previous years. A good athlete, he has plus speed and good instincts on the bases. Brantley has shown very little power in his career, though at 6-foot-2 and with broad shoulders he has the potential to develop some pop. Despite his speed and feel for other aspects of the game, he has received mixed reviews in center field, where he doesn't get the best reads off the bat. His lack of power doesn't play as well in left field or at first base. His arm strength is below average. Brantley has proven himself everywhere but Triple-A. He'll need to start driving the ball with more authority to find a regular role in the big leagues, however.

Year	Club (League)	Class	AVG	G	AB	R	H	2B	3B	HR	RBI	BB	SO	SB	OBP	SLG
2005	Brewers (AZL)	R	.347	44	173	34	60	3	1	0	19	22	13	14	.426	.376
	Helena (PIO)	R	.324	10	34	8	11	2	0	0	3	6	4	2	.425	.382
2006	West Virginia (SAL)	LoA	.300	108	360	47	108	10	2	0	42	61	51	24	.402	.339
2007	West Virginia (SAL)	LoA	.335	56	218	41	73	15	1	2	32	31	22	18	.413	.440
	Huntsville (SL)	AA	.251	59	187	28	47	6	1	0	21	29	25	17	.353	.294
2008	Huntsville (SL)	AA	.319	106	420	80	134	17	2	4	40	50	27	28	.395	.398
MINOR LEAGUE TOTALS			.311	383	1392	238	433	53	7	6	157	199	142	103	.399	.372

10 LUIS VALBUENA, 2B

BORN: Nov. 30, 1985. **B-T:** L-R. **HT.:** 5-10. **WT.:** 200. **SIGNED:** Venezuela, 2002. **SIGNED BY:** Emilio Carrasquel (Mariners).

The Indians played a small part in a three-team, 12-player trade at the Winter Meetings, sending Franklin Gutierrez to the Mariners and receiving Joe Smith from the Mets and Valbuena from Seattle. Valbuena made strides after a difficult 2007 season in Double-A by returning there, raising his OBP by 70 points and increasing his power output. He earned a promotion to Triple-A at the end of June, and then played regularly for the Mariners in September, pushing Jose Lopez to first base. With a line-drive stroke and a knack for making contact, Valbuena is geared to hit for average with occasional power to the gaps. On the flip side, he has just enough juice to get himself in trouble when he gets pull-happy. He stands out with his bat speed, contact-hitting skills and ability to work the count. Valbuena always has handled the bat well and shown a good eye at the plate, but his recent defensive improvement has raised his chances of playing regularly in the majors. While his speed is average at best, he shows good range to both sides and has a strong arm at second base. He turns the double-play pivot quickly and efficiently. Valbuena is ready for an expanded big league role and has a higher offensive ceiling than Cleveland's 2008 starter, Asdrubal Cabrera.

Year	Club (League)	Class	AVG	G	AB	R	H	2B	3B	HR	RBI	BB	SO	SB	OBP	SLG
2003	Aguirre (VSL)	R	.228	50	167	26	38	11	4	1	22	20	25	3	.323	.359
2004	Aguirre (VSL)	R	.361	61	216	44	78	24	6	2	34	27	15	11	.444	.556
2005	Tacoma (PCL)	AAA	.000	3	4	0	0	0	0	0	0	1	2	0	.200	.000
	Everett (NWL)	SS	.261	74	287	47	75	10	3	12	51	31	37	14	.333	.443
2006	Wisconsin (MWL)	LoA	.286	89	325	45	93	16	6	3	38	44	44	21	.371	.400
	Inland Empire (CAL)	HiA	.252	43	163	18	41	10	1	2	10	14	26	1	.315	.362
2007	West Tenn (SL)	AA	.239	122	444	55	106	23	3	11	44	48	83	10	.311	.378
2008	West Tenn (SL)	AA	.304	70	240	43	73	12	2	9	40	31	37	8	.381	.483
	Tacoma (PCL)	AAA	.302	58	212	41	64	9	0	2	20	28	32	10	.383	.373
	Seattle (AL)	MAJ	.245	18	49	6	12	5	0	0	1	4	11	0	.315	.347
MINOR LEAGUE TOTALS			.276	570	2058	319	568	115	25	42	259	244	301	78	.355	.417
MAJOR LEAGUE TOTALS			.245	18	49	6	12	5	0	0	1	4	11	0	.315	.347

11 CARLOS RIVERO, SS

BORN: May 20, 1988. **B-T:** R-R. **HT.:** 6-3. **WT.:** 210. **SIGNED:** Venezuela, 2005. **SIGNED BY:** Stewart Ruiz.

Rivero signed for $100,000 as a 16-year-old in 2005, and he's still just tapping into his potential. The second-youngest regular in the Carolina League in 2008, he exploded in the final month, batting .358/.413/.587 with five of his eight homers in the season's final 28 games. Rivero has plus power that's evident in batting practice, though that power has yet to manifest itself in games with much frequency. As his frame continues to fill out, his power should continue to grow. He has a sound swing that generates plenty of bat speed, and he is a good athlete. Defensively, he offers soft hands and a strong arm. While Rivero has tools, the gap between his potential and his present ability is still significant. He struggles to recognize breaking pitches, and he needs to get his hands into a better load position. He has the arm for shortstop, but 16 of his 24 errors last season came on throws. He's a below-average runner with below-average lateral range, and scouts from other clubs think a move to third base might be a better fit. If he puts everything together, some club officials believe he could become another Jhonny Peralta. Rivero will reach Double-A before he turns 21 and could join the Indians at some point in 2010.

Year	Club (League)	Class	AVG	G	AB	R	H	2B	3B	HR	RBI	BB	SO	SB	OBP	SLG
2005	Indians1 (DSL)	R	.257	66	237	21	61	6	0	0	31	12	26	7	.295	.283
2006	Indians (GCL)	R	.284	37	134	17	38	6	0	2	22	10	20	0	.338	.373
	Burlington (APP)	R	.212	16	66	3	14	3	0	1	7	5	11	0	.264	.303
2007	Lake County (SAL)	LoA	.261	115	436	59	114	26	0	7	62	47	84	1	.332	.369
2008	Kinston (CAR)	HiA	.282	108	411	46	116	27	1	8	64	36	84	1	.342	.411
MINOR LEAGUE TOTALS			.267	342	1284	146	343	68	1	18	186	110	225	9	.326	.364

12 WES HODGES, 3B

BORN: Sept. 14, 1984. **B-T:** R-R. **HT.:** 6-2. **WT.:** 206. **DRAFTED:** Georgia Tech, 2006 (2nd round). **SIGNED BY:** Jerry Jordan.

After battling injuries the previous two years—a stress fracture in his leg in his draft year in 2006, then a broken toe and a strained hamstring during his pro debut in 2007—Hodges came into last season in better physical condition and put together a strong first half in Double-A, earning a spot in the Futures Game and the Eastern League all-star game. He has good barrel awareness, spraying the ball and hitting for power to all fields. He has a natural feel for hitting, so much so that he taught himself to hit lefthanded after breaking a bone in his hand during his senior year of high school—and batted .430. Hodges' hands work well at the plate, and he maximizes his strength by getting good leverage in his swing. Most of his value is tied up in his bat, as he's a below-average runner and scouts question whether he can remain at third base. His hands are decent, but he lacks first-step quickness and agility and his footwork gets him into trouble. He committed 28 errors in 125 games at third base with Akron, then eight more in 22 Arizona Fall League games. Hodges has average arm strength, but he doesn't get his body into his throws and doesn't use his legs properly. The Indians have had a revolving door at third base in recent years, and Hodges may be able to put an end to that after spending some time in Triple-A.

Year	Club (League)	Class	AVG	G	AB	R	H	2B	3B	HR	RBI	BB	SO	SB	OBP	SLG
2007	Kinston (CAR)	HiA	.288	104	393	60	113	22	3	15	71	44	90	0	.367	.473
2008	Akron (EL)	AA	.290	133	504	70	146	29	3	18	97	52	105	3	.354	.466
MINOR LEAGUE TOTALS			.289	237	897	130	259	51	6	33	168	96	195	3	.360	.469

13 HECTOR RONDON, RHP

BORN: Feb. 26, 1988. **B-T:** R-R. **HT.:** 6-3. **WT.:** 180. **SIGNED:** Venezuela, 2004. **SIGNED BY:** Stewart Ruiz.

Despite being one of the youngest pitchers in the Carolina League last year, Rondon was also one of its best. He pitched in the Futures Game and led all Indians farmhands with 145 strikeouts. He works mostly off a lively fastball that he commands well to both sides of the plate. His heater ranges from 89-94 mph with running life, occasionally touching 95. His changeup is an average to plus pitch that could be consistently above average with more work. His breaking ball improved during the season but is still a work in progress. The pitch went from a high-70s slurve to a low-80s true slider more often as he learned to stay behind the ball more rather than getting around on it. Working from a low- to mid-three-quarters arm slot with a loose, easy delivery, Rondon improved his ability to locate his pitches down in the zone as the season progressed. After being added to the 40-man roster in November, he should continue his ascent in Double-A this year.

Year	Club (League)	Class	W	L	ERA	G	GS	CG	SV	IP	H	R	ER	HR	BB	SO	AVG
2005	Indians1 (DSL)	R	3	3	1.65	15	12	1	1	65	60	24	12	2	8	55	.230
2006	Indians (GCL)	R	3	4	5.13	11	11	0	0	53	62	34	30	6	3	32	.286
2007	Lake County (SAL)	LoA	7	10	4.37	27	27	0	0	136	143	78	66	13	27	113	.269
2008	Kinston (CAR)	HiA	11	6	3.60	27	27	0	0	145	130	63	58	12	42	145	.239
MINOR LEAGUE TOTALS			24	23	3.74	80	77	1	1	399	395	199	166	33	80	345	.254

14 T.J. HOUSE, LHP

BORN: Sept. 29, 1989. **B-T:** L-L. **HT.:** 6-2. **WT.:** 215. **DRAFTED:** HS—Picayune, Miss., 2008 (16th round). **SIGNED BY:** Chuck Bartlett.

House struck out 20 batters in a game as a high school junior and carried over that success into a dominant senior season in 2008. Most teams viewed House as a likely candidate to attend Tulane, and his high price tag dropped him all the way to the 16th round. The Indians, who were as aggressive as any team in the draft, signed him for $750,000, the equivalent of second-round money. A good athlete who was a member of his high school's state champion swim team in 2006, he has a smooth, fluid delivery and draws physical comparisons to Mike Hampton. House throws a lively low-90s fastball with sink and a mid-80s power breaking ball. He also throws a changeup, but it needs more work. Despite his youth, House already has a good feel for pitching. Though he has yet to make his pro debut, Cleveland might be tempted to expose him to low Class A at some point in 2009.

Year	Club (League)	Class	W	L	ERA	G	GS	CG	SV	IP	H	R	ER	HR	BB	SO	AVG
2008	Did Not Play—Signed Late																

15 TREVOR CROWE, OF

BORN: Nov. 17, 1983. **B-T:** B-R. **HT.:** 6-0. **WT.:** 190. **DRAFTED:** Arizona, 2005 (1st round).
SIGNED BY: Joe Graham.

Crowe was the first college outfielder drafted in 2004, but his career hasn't progressed as well as those of former Pacific-10 Conference rivals Jacoby Ellsbury and Travis Buck, who were taken after him. Selected 14th overall, Crowe hit a wall after getting promoted to Akron and being asked to try to become a second baseman in late 2006. He finally put his offensive game back together in 2008, succeeding in his third try at Double-A and making his way to Triple-A despite battling nagging injuries that affected his swing. He earned a spot on the 40-man roster with his performance. Crowe is an excellent athlete with good strike-zone discipline, but scouts question whether he'll ever hit for enough average or power to become a big league starter. While he has above-average speed, he's not the most instinctive center fielder and has a fringy arm. That makes him more of a left fielder—especially with Grady Sizemore in Cleveland—but his power is less than ideal for that position. The Indians have an uncertain left field situation, so Crowe could get an opportunity in the near future after opening 2009 in Triple-A.

Year	Club (League)	Class	AVG	G	AB	R	H	2B	3B	HR	RBI	BB	SO	SB	OBP	SLG
2005	Mahoning Valley (NYP)	SS	.255	12	51	9	13	2	1	1	6	6	8	4	.345	.392
	Lake County (SAL)	LoA	.258	44	178	18	46	8	2	0	23	18	25	7	.327	.326
	Akron (EL)	AA	.100	3	10	1	1	0	0	0	0	0	3	0	.100	.100
2006	Kinston (CAR)	HiA	.329	60	219	51	72	15	2	4	31	48	46	29	.449	.470
	Lake County (SAL)	LoA	.000	2	5	0	0	0	0	0	0	0	1	0	.000	.000
	Akron (EL)	AA	.234	39	154	20	36	7	2	1	13	20	24	16	.318	.325
2007	Akron (EL)	AA	.259	133	518	87	134	26	4	5	50	62	71	28	.341	.353
2008	Akron (EL)	AA	.323	49	198	45	64	16	2	4	28	27	29	13	.404	.485
	Buffalo (IL)	AAA	.274	35	146	25	40	12	2	5	13	15	43	5	.350	.486
MINOR LEAGUE TOTALS			.275	377	1479	256	406	86	15	20	164	196	250	102	.361	.394

16 ABNER ABREU, 3B/OF

BORN: Oct. 24, 1989. **B-T:** R-R. **HT.:** 6-3. **WT.:** 180. **SIGNED:** Dominican Republic, 2006. **SIGNED BY:** Junior Betances.

The Indians signed Abreu in October 2006 for $75,000, a fraction of the $550,000 that his brother, outfielder Esdras Abreu, received from the Rangers last summer. Abner began his pro career shuttling around the infield in the Rookie-level Dominican Summer League in 2007, then focused on third base last year. He led the Rookie-level Gulf Coast League in homers (11), extra-base hits (31) and slugging (.538). A good athlete, Abreu uses his legs well in his swing and generates easy power to all fields with plus bat speed and strong hands. He's still growing into his frame and could develop even more pop as he matures physically. Abreu's strike-zone discipline and pitch recognition are rudimentary. He's prone to chasing breaking balls outside the zone and doesn't show much patience. Abreu's defense at third base is rough. His hands and actions aren't ideal for the hot corner, and 12 of his 18 errors in 49 games last year came on misplays rather than throws. He does have a strong arm and his future could be in right field. The Indians tried him in the outfield during instructional league. They won't give up on him as a third baseman in 2009, when he could push for a shot at low Class A.

Year	Club (League)	Class	AVG	G	AB	R	H	2B	3B	HR	RBI	BB	SO	SB	OBP	SLG
2007	Indians (DSL)	R	.303	56	228	34	69	13	7	4	41	18	46	5	.353	.474
2008	Indians (GCL)	R	.251	51	199	32	50	16	4	11	37	9	52	4	.289	.538
MINOR LEAGUE TOTALS			.279	107	427	66	119	29	11	15	78	27	98	9	.324	.504

17 TONY SIPP, LHP

BORN: July 12, 1983. **B-T:** L-L. **HT.:** 6-0. **WT.:** 190. **DRAFTED:** Clemson, 2004 (45th round).
SIGNED BY: Tim Moore.

A two-way player for Meridian (Miss.) CC and Clemson, Sipp slipped to the 45th round of the 2004 draft after a lackluster junior season. He rebounded with a promising summer in the Cape Cod League, and Cleveland signed him for $130,000. He moved to the bullpen midway through his first full pro season and was in line for a shot at the big league bullpen in 2007, but instead he hurt his elbow and succumbed to Tommy John surgery. Despite the injury, the Indians protected Sipp on the 40-man roster, and his comeback has been promising. Sipp returned to game action last June and was at his strongest in the season's final month, allowing one run in his final 16 innings. His fastball velocity returned to 89-93 mph, and batters continued to have trouble picking up the ball out of his hand thanks to the deception in his delivery. His slider and changeup are both above-average pitches at times. Like most players returning from Tommy John surgery, Sipp wasn't at his sharpest with his command in his first year back, particularly with his secondary pitches. He'll open 2009 in Triple-A and should get an opportunity to pitch in Cleveland this year if he can stay healthy.

Year	Club (League)	Class	W	L	ERA	G	GS	CG	SV	IP	H	R	ER	HR	BB	SO	AVG
2004	Mahoning Valley (NYP)	SS	3	1	3.16	10	10	0	0	43	33	23	15	5	13	74	.212
2005	Lake County (SAL)	LoA	4	1	2.22	13	12	0	0	69	47	19	17	5	19	71	.196
	Kinston (CAR)	HiA	2	2	2.66	22	5	0	2	47	34	19	14	4	23	59	.205
2006	Akron (EL)	AA	4	2	3.13	29	4	0	3	60	44	23	21	2	21	80	.201
2007	Did Not Play—Injured																
2008	Indians (GCL)	R	0	0	0.00	3	1	0	0	4	0	0	0	0	1	4	.000
	Kinston (CAR)	HiA	0	0	1.13	5	0	0	0	8	4	2	1	0	3	10	.148
	Akron (EL)	AA	0	3	3.74	16	0	0	1	22	19	12	9	4	7	32	.235
MINOR LEAGUE TOTALS			13	9	2.74	98	32	0	6	253	181	98	77	20	87	330	.201

18 JON MELOAN, RHP

BORN: July 11, 1984. **B-T:** R-R. **HT.:** 6-3. **WT.:** 225. **DRAFTED:** Arizona, 2005 (5th round). **SIGNED BY:** Brian Stephenson (Dodgers).

Meloan went 27-2 as a starter in his last two seasons at Arizona, then spent most of his pro career as a reliever as he climbed quickly through the Dodgers system. Los Angeles put him back in the rotation last year at Triple-A, but he struggled and his control suffered. The Dodgers dealt him with catcher Carlos Santana to acquire Casey Blake in July, after which the Indians moved Meloan back to the bullpen. He's more ideally suited for relief because of his repertoire and the effort in his delivery. His fastball sat at 88-91 mph when he was a starter and jumped back to 92-95 when he returned to the bullpen. His heater flashes armside run and sink. His out pitch is a hard breaking ball. He also has a changeup and a cutter, but he works primarily with two pitches in relief. Meloan aggressively goes after hitters and has the makeup to pitch in the late innings. The Indians had one of the worst bullpens in the majors in 2008, and he has the stuff and opportunity to help upgrade the unit.

Year	Club (League)	Class	W	L	ERA	G	GS	CG	SV	IP	H	R	ER	HR	BB	SO	AVG
2005	Ogden (PIO)	R	0	2	3.69	16	6	0	1	39	30	16	16	4	18	54	.210
2006	Columbus (SAL)	LoA	1	1	1.54	12	0	0	1	23	9	5	4	2	7	41	.118
	Vero Beach (FSL)	HiA	1	0	2.50	4	3	0	0	18	15	6	5	2	4	27	.221
	Jacksonville (SL)	AA	1	0	1.69	5	0	0	0	11	3	2	2	1	5	23	.086
2007	Jacksonville (SL)	AA	5	2	2.18	35	0	0	19	45	24	13	11	3	18	70	.155
	Las Vegas (PCL)	AAA	1	0	1.69	14	0	0	1	21	12	5	4	2	9	21	.158
	Los Angeles (NL)	MAJ	0	0	11.05	5	0	0	0	7	8	9	9	1	8	7	.286
2008	Las Vegas (PCL)	AAA	5	10	4.97	21	20	0	0	105	119	72	58	7	60	99	.289
	Buffalo (IL)	AAA	0	1	4.30	12	0	0	0	15	12	8	7	1	9	12	.235
	Cleveland (AL)	MAJ	0	0	0.00	2	0	0	0	2	0	0	0	0	1	2	.000
MINOR LEAGUE TOTALS			15	16	3.47	119	29	0	22	277	224	127	107	22	130	347	.220
MAJOR LEAGUE TOTALS			0	0	8.68	7	0	0	0	9	8	9	9	1	9	9	.242

19 JEFF STEVENS, RHP

BORN: Sept. 5, 1983. **B-T:** R-R. **HT.:** 6-2. **WT.:** 205. **DRAFTED:** Loyola Maramount, 2005 (6th round). **SIGNED BY:** Mike Misuraca (Reds).

One year after drafting Stevens, the Reds shipped him to the Indians as the player to be named in the Brandon Phillips trade in 2006. Stevens began his tenure with the Indians as a starter before moving to the bullpen in 2007. The new role agreed with him, as he has averaged 11.6 strikeouts per nine innings during the last two seasons and pitched for Team USA at the World Cup in 2007 and the Olympics in 2008. He earned the save in the gold-medal game at the World Cup. Stevens has a high back elbow in his delivery, which creates deception. His four-seam fastball usually ranges from 90-94 mph and touches 95. He's aggressive with his fastball and uses it frequently, mixing in a mid-70s curveball and a cutter as well. His control wasn't as sharp last season, and once he irons it out he should get the opportunity to work out of the Cleveland bullpen. He profiles as a setup man in the big leagues and claimed a spot on the 40-man roster in November.

Year	Club (League)	Class	W	L	ERA	G	GS	CG	SV	IP	H	R	ER	HR	BB	SO	AVG
2005	Billings (PIO)	R	4	4	2.98	13	8	0	0	54	44	20	18	4	15	58	.220
2006	Dayton (MWL)	LoA	2	4	4.43	14	6	0	0	43	42	22	21	6	16	43	.261
	Lake County (SAL)	LoA	7	3	4.42	16	15	0	0	73	65	40	36	4	23	60	.232
2007	Kinston (CAR)	HiA	3	2	2.31	15	0	0	0	35	18	13	9	2	9	37	.150
	Akron (EL)	AA	3	1	3.17	34	0	0	2	48	40	17	17	4	16	65	.223
2008	Akron (EL)	AA	5	1	2.51	17	0	0	1	29	19	8	8	2	11	37	.188
	Buffalo (IL)	AAA	0	3	3.94	19	0	0	5	30	19	14	13	3	16	44	.181
MINOR LEAGUE TOTALS			24	18	3.52	128	29	0	8	312	247	134	122	25	106	344	.216

20 TREY HALEY, RHP

BORN: June 21, 1990. **B-T:** R-R. **HT.:** 6-3. **WT.:** 180. **DRAFTED:** HS—Nacogdoches, Texas, 2008 (2nd round). **SIGNED BY:** Kevin Cullen.

Haley was the Texas Class 2A 2008 player of the year after starring as a pitcher and an outfielder. The Indians made him the first high schooler drafted from the state in June, nabbing him in the second round and 76th overall. They lured him away from a strong commitment to Rice with a $1.25 million bonus, more money than they gave to first-rounder Lonnie Chisenhall. Haley generated buzz early in the spring by touching 94 mph, but when crosscheckers and scouts flocked to see him, he usually worked at 91-92 in the first inning before dropping down to 88-89 later in games. He flashes a power curveball with two-plane break that's a plus pitch at times but is inconsistent. His changeup also shows promise as well. Haley has an athletic, projectable frame, and with his size he gets good downward angle toward home plate. He struggles to repeat his mechanics, which impedes his command. He also has a tendency to overthrow with effort and a head-jerk in his delivery. Of the players that the Indians went over slot recommendations to sign in 2008, Haley offers the highest upside.

Year	Club (League)	Class	W	L	ERA	G	GS	CG	SV	IP	H	R	ER	HR	BB	SO	AVG
2008	Indians (GCL)	R	0	0	0.00	1	1	0	0	1	0	0	0	0	1	1	.000
	Mahoning Valley (NYP)	SS	0	1	54.00	2	1	0	0	1	4	8	8	0	6	1	.571
MINOR LEAGUE TOTALS			0	1	30.86	3	2	0	0	2	4	8	8	0	7	2	.364

21 SCOTT LEWIS, LHP

BORN: Sept. 26, 1983. **B-T:** B-L. **HT.:** 6-0. **WT.:** 195. **DRAFTED:** Ohio State, 2004 (3rd round). **SIGNED BY:** Bob Mayer.

The Indians have taken things slowly with Lewis, who had Tommy John surgery as an Ohio State sophomore and battled biceps tendinitis in his first two pro seasons. He didn't reach Double-A until his fourth year in pro ball and started 2008 in extended spring training recovering from a strained left lat muscle. He returned to Akron in June, then received a promotion to Triple-A in August after not allowing more than one earned run in seven consecutive starts. Lewis made his major league debut on Sept. 10, throwing eight shutout innings of three-hit ball against the Orioles. He blanked the Twins for six innings in his next outing and wound up winning all four of his big league starts. Lewis succeeds with his secondary pitches and his refusal to issue walks. His curveball is an above-average pitch that comes in anywhere from 72-78 mph, while his 75-78 mph changeup is a solid-average to plus offering. His fastball velocity is below average, sitting at 85-88 mph and touching 89. The deception in Lewis' delivery and his ability to mix his pitch sequences keeps hitters off balance. The Indians sent him to the Dominican Winter League to give him more innings and will let him challenge for a spot in the big league rotation during spring training.

Year	Club (League)	Class	W	L	ERA	G	GS	CG	SV	IP	H	R	ER	HR	BB	SO	AVG
2004	Mahoning Valley (NYP)	SS	0	2	5.06	3	3	0	0	5	5	3	3	0	1	13	.250
2005	Mahoning Valley (NYP)	SS	0	1	4.60	7	6	0	0	16	13	8	8	2	6	24	.224
2006	Kinston (CAR)	HiA	3	3	1.48	27	26	0	0	116	84	24	19	3	28	123	.203
2007	Akron (EL)	AA	7	9	3.68	27	25	0	0	135	135	58	55	13	34	121	.262
2008	Akron (EL)	AA	6	2	2.33	13	13	0	0	73	62	22	19	2	9	61	.224
	Buffalo (IL)	AAA	2	2	2.63	4	4	1	0	24	19	8	7	2	4	21	.221
	Cleveland (AL)	MAJ	4	0	2.63	4	4	0	0	24	20	9	7	4	6	15	.222
MINOR LEAGUE TOTALS			18	19	2.71	81	77	1	0	369	318	123	111	22	82	363	.232
MAJOR LEAGUE TOTALS			4	0	2.63	4	4	0	0	24	20	9	7	4	6	15	.222

22 ZACH PUTNAM, RHP

BORN: July 3, 1987. **B-T:** R-R. **HT.:** 6-2. **WT.:** 225. **DRAFTED:** Michigan, 2008 (5th round). **SIGNED BY:** Derrick Ross.

Another of Cleveland's over-slot signees from the 2008 draft, Putnam received $600,000 as a fifth-rounder. He flashed a first-round arm at times at Michigan, but he was inconsistent with his secondary pitches and sent out mixed vibes about his signability, which is why he was available with the 171st overall pick. Putnam throws a 91-92 mph fastball with heavy sink, and the pitch peaks at 95 with riding life. His splitter is a plus pitch at times and his slider can reach the mid-80s. He also has a changeup and a curveball, though the curve is mostly a show-me pitch. He pulled double duty as a DH for the Wolverines, and it's possible that his stuff could improve and get more consistent now that he's a full-time pitcher. Despite his deep repertoire, Putnam may wind up as a reliever. His secondary pitches aren't always reliable, and the consensus among scouts is that he'd be most effective pitching primarily with his sinker. A thick, full-bodied pitcher, Putnam doesn't use his legs enough in his mechanics and tends to power through his delivery. If the Indians use him out of the bullpen, he could move quickly and get a taste of Double-A in his first full pro season.

Year	Club (League)	Class	W	L	ERA	G	GS	CG	SV	IP	H	R	ER	HR	BB	SO	AVG
2008	Mahoning Valley (NYP)	SS	0	1	3.72	3	3	0	0	10	7	5	4	0	5	8	.206
MINOR LEAGUE TOTALS			0	1	3.72	3	3	0	0	10	7	5	4	0	5	8	.206

23 TIM FEDROFF, OF

BORN: Feb. 4, 1987. **B-T:** L-R. **HT.:** 5-11. **WT.:** 220. **DRAFTED:** North Carolina, 2008 (7th round).
SIGNED BY: Bob Mayer.

Fedroff became North Carolina's starting right fielder as a freshman and helped the Tar Heels reach the College World Series twice in two years. He batted .404 and led the Heels with 12 homers and a .642 slugging percentage as a draft-eligible sophomore in 2008, then signed for $725,000 (the second-highest bonus in the seventh round last year) shortly before the Aug. 15 deadline. Fedroff isn't imposing physically, but he has good strength, particularly in his forearms and wrists. He drives balls to the gaps with occasional home run power. His plate discipline is solid and he has a nice, compact lefty swing, but he needs to quiet his approach, stay on the ball longer and use his legs better. Despite his stocky build, Fedroff is a good athlete with above-average speed. He broke into pro ball as a center fielder, though his defense elicits mixed reviews and his arm strength is fringy. He might be better suited to play on a corner, though he'd have to develop more power to be a regular there. Fedroff should reach high Class A at some point during his first full pro season.

Year	Club (League)	Class	AVG	G	AB	R	H	2B	3B	HR	RBI	BB	SO	SB	OBP	SLG
2008	Mahoning Valley (NYP)	SS	.319	23	91	12	29	6	1	0	12	10	20	1	.382	.407
MINOR LEAGUE TOTALS			.319	23	91	12	29	6	1	0	12	10	20	1	.382	.407

24 CORD PHELPS, 2B

BORN: Jan. 23, 1987. **B-T:** B-R. **HT.:** 6-2. **WT.:** 200. **DRAFTED:** Stanford, 2008 (3rd round).
SIGNED BY: Don Lyle.

Phelps was a late bloomer at Stanford, where he played sparingly as a freshman and didn't hit a homer until his junior year in 2008, when he clocked 13. The power surge elevated his prospect status, and he signed for $327,000 as a third-round pick. Phelps doesn't have flashy tools, but he's a savvy player who approaches each at-bat with a good plan at the plate. He has a strong frame, an upright stance and a line-drive swing, though he needs to reduce the load with his hands. He's a switch-hitter whose stroke tends to get a little longer from the right side. He has fringe-average speed but runs the bases well. At second base, Phelps' arm strength, range, hands and ability to turn the double play are all solid. He's big for a second baseman, but he's a steady fielder with the athleticism to stay in the middle infield. He has good instincts in almost all phases of the game, which help his tools play up. The Indians aren't afraid to challenge Phelps, who could start his first full season in high Class A.

Year	Club (League)	Class	AVG	G	AB	R	H	2B	3B	HR	RBI	BB	SO	SB	OBP	SLG
2008	Indians (GCL)	R	.000	1	3	0	0	0	0	0	1	0	2	0	.000	.000
	Mahoning Valley (NYP)	SS	.312	35	141	24	44	10	2	2	21	15	22	4	.376	.454
MINOR LEAGUE TOTALS			.306	36	144	24	44	10	2	2	22	15	24	4	.366	.444

25 JORDAN BROWN, 1B

BORN: Dec. 18, 1983. **B-T:** L-L. **HT.:** 6-0. **WT.:** 205. **DRAFTED:** Arizona, 2005 (4th round). **SIGNED BY:** Joe Graham.

After winning MVP awards in the Carolina and Eastern leagues during his first two full pro seasons, Brown couldn't replicate that success in Triple-A in 2008. The Indians think he might have been pressing because he was so close to the majors, and he deviated from his normally disciplined approach and chased more pitches outside of the strike zone. Brown is at his best when he uses a short swing, works counts and sprays line drives to all fields. His average bat speed isn't conducive to hitting for power and he has less pop than most big league first basemen. He may have been trying too hard to hit homers so he could earn his first callup to Cleveland. He still made consistent contact, but he didn't square up as many balls and his stroke got long at times. Brown is a below-average runner, and an attempt to play him in left field in 2006 didn't work out well. His defense at first base did improve last year, as he continued to show good hands and reactions while improving his footwork. Brown needs to get back to his patient approach in Triple-A this year.

Year	Club (League)	Class	AVG	G	AB	R	H	2B	3B	HR	RBI	BB	SO	SB	OBP	SLG
2005	Mahoning Valley (NYP)	SS	.253	19	75	15	19	1	0	3	7	3	7	2	.291	.387
2006	Kinston (CAR)	HiA	.290	125	473	71	137	26	7	15	87	51	59	4	.362	.469
2007	Akron (EL)	AA	.333	127	483	85	161	36	2	11	76	63	56	11	.421	.484
2008	Buffalo (IL)	AAA	.281	109	420	52	118	30	3	7	51	35	67	3	.337	.417
MINOR LEAGUE TOTALS			.300	380	1451	223	435	93	12	36	221	152	189	20	.372	.455

26 DELVI CID, OF

BORN: July 19, 1989. **B-T:** R-R. **HT.:** 6-2. **WT.:** 170. **SIGNED:** Dominican Republic, 2006. **SIGNED BY:** Cesar Geronimo.

Abner Abreu wasn't the only promising prospect to make his pro debut on the Indians' 2007 Dominican Summer League club. Cid, a fellow Dominican, showed the ability to hit for average and get on base, and continued to demonstrate those skills when he came Stateside in 2008. A lanky, wiry athlete, Cid is the fastest runner in the organization. He has the plus-plus speed to be a quality basestealer and center fielder, but he's still raw in those phases of the game. Though he slugged just .323 last season, he has good bat speed and some projectable power. Cid is an aggressive player in all aspects of the game, though he does show some discipline at the plate. He crashed into a wall in August, injuring the Lisfranc joint in his right foot and requiring surgery. He should be healthy for spring training, but he's still years away from being big league ready.

Year	Club (League)	Class	AVG	G	AB	R	H	2B	3B	HR	RBI	BB	SO	SB	OBP	SLG
2007	Indians (DSL)	R	.302	65	262	37	79	8	2	1	24	28	49	21	.378	.359
2008	Indians (GCL)	R	.299	35	127	17	38	3	0	0	11	17	28	14	.384	.323
MINOR LEAGUE TOTALS			.301	100	389	54	117	11	2	1	35	45	77	35	.380	.347

27 BRYCE STOWELL, RHP

BORN: Sept. 23, 1986. **B-T:** R-R. **HT.:** 6-2. **WT.:** 205. **DRAFTED:** UC Irvine, 2008 (22nd round). **SIGNED BY:** Jason Smith.

Undrafted out of high school, where he also played water polo, Stowell began his college career at Pepperdine. He pitched sparingly as a freshman before ranking as the No. 1 prospect in the Central Illinois Collegiate League that summer. Stowell opted to transfer to UC Irvine, but had to sit out a year because the Waves wouldn't grant him his release. Despite a solid 2008 season, he lasted 22 rounds in the draft because teams worried about his signability as a draft-eligible sophomore. After he earned all-star honors in the Cape Cod League, the Indians signed him just before the Aug. 15 deadline for $725,000. Stowell has a relatively fluid delivery and throws a fastball that sits at 89-91 mph and peaks at 93 mph. His hard slider is his No. 2 pitch, and he also throws a changeup. He showed improved command of both secondary pitches last summer, and Cape observers also thought he exuded more confidence in his second stint in the league. Stowell will need to continue to develop his changeup to remain a starter. He'll make his pro debut with one of Cleveland's Class A affiliates in 2009.

Year	Club (League)	Class	W	L	ERA	G	GS	CG	SV	IP	H	R	ER	HR	BB	SO	AVG
2008	Did Not Play—Signed Late																

28 JOSH TOMLIN, RHP

BORN: Oct. 19, 1984. **B-T:** R-R. **HT.:** 6-1. **WT.:** 195. **DRAFTED:** Texas Tech, 2006 (18th round). **SIGNED BY:** Mike Daly.

Tomlin was a two-way player at Angelina (Texas) JC in 2005—as was Clay Buchholz—when the Padres drafted him in the 11th round, but he transferred to Texas Tech rather than turning pro. He has had success as both a starter and reliever and served in both roles in 2008. Tomlin doesn't overpower hitters, but he pounds the strike zone and had the best K-BB ratio (109-16) among Carolina Leaguers with 100 innings last season. He mixes his pitches and his locations, keeping hitters off balance with four useable offerings. He locates his 88-91 mph fastball to both sides of the plate. He has two breaking balls, the best of which is a 12-to-6 curveball. He also throws a slider that doesn't have much depth but has cutter-like action. He'll throw his 75-78 mph changeup in any count. Tomlin is a good athlete who repeats his delivery well. At times he shortens his stride, which leads him to pitch more uphill and flattens out his stuff. Ticketed for Double-A, Tomlin can become a No. 4 or 5 starter if everything clicks.

Year	Club (League)	Class	W	L	ERA	G	GS	CG	SV	IP	H	R	ER	HR	BB	SO	AVG
2006	Mahoning Valley (NYP)	SS	8	2	2.09	15	15	0	0	77	56	24	18	5	15	69	.196
2007	Lake County (SAL)	LoA	10	3	3.30	26	15	0	0	104	103	44	38	10	19	89	.255
	Kinston (CAR)	HiA	1	1	3.58	6	5	0	0	28	24	13	11	0	12	20	.231
2008	Buffalo (IL)	AAA	1	0	3.86	1	1	0	0	7	6	3	3	2	1	3	.250
	Kinston (CAR)	HiA	9	5	2.98	40	9	1	3	103	82	40	34	10	16	109	.222
MINOR LEAGUE TOTALS			29	11	2.94	88	45	1	3	318	271	124	104	27	63	290	.228

29 JOHN GAUB, LHP

BORN: April 28, 1985. **B-T:** R-L. **HT.:** 6-2. **WT.:** 200. **DRAFTED:** Minnesota, 2006 (21st round). **SIGNED BY:** Byron Ewing.

After touching 96 mph and striking out 65 in 39 innings as a sophomore reliever at Minnesota, Gaub entered 2006 as the top draft prospect in the Upper Midwest. His stock dropped, however, when he had trouble bouncing back from arthroscopic shoulder surgery. Gaub's fastball dropped to 81-84 mph and his curveball lost its bite, so he plummeted to the 21st round. After the Indians invested $155,000 in him, he had more shoulder surgery and pitched just four innings in 2007 before breaking out last season. He ranked second among low Class A South Atlantic League relievers by averaging 14.1 strikeouts per nine innings. Gaub did touch 94 mph, but his fastball sat around 90 and he got swings and misses thanks to the deception in his delivery. He threw from a more overhand arm slot with the Golden Gophers, but he has since lowered his arm angle and ditched his curve in favor of a slider, which improved throughout the season. Gaub needs to repeat his new delivery more frequently and issue fewer walks. He'll advance to high Class A and try to prove he can sustain his success without the high-octane stuff he showed in college.

Year	Club (League)	Class	W	L	ERA	G	GS	CG	SV	IP	H	R	ER	HR	BB	SO	AVG
2007	Indians (GCL)	R	0	0	2.25	4	0	0	0	4	4	1	1	0	4	4	.308
2008	Lake County (SAL)	LoA	1	1	3.38	34	0	0	2	64	44	30	24	3	32	100	.195
MINOR LEAGUE TOTALS			1	1	3.31	38	0	0	2	68	48	31	25	3	36	104	.201

30 JOSE OZORIA, SS

BORN: Feb. 17, 1992. **B-T:** R-R. **HT.:** 6-0. **WT.:** 170. **SIGNED:** Dominican Republic, 2008. **SIGNED BY:** Omar Rodgers.

The Indians were aggressive not only in the draft but also on the international market in 2008. Cleveland signed two of the top Latin American 16-year-olds during the international signing period, nabbing Ozoria for $575,000 and Venezuelan catcher Alex Monsalve for $715,000. Though Monsalve received more money, Ozoria's bat speed and feel for hitting make him a better prospect at this point. He isn't very physical, which will limit his power projection, and he has a stiff arm bar at times in his swing. He currently has below-average speed, though with his youth, athleticism and light body type, he could develop into an average to plus runner. Ozoria's defense at shortstop draws good reviews from scouts, who praised his solid actions, quick lateral movement and hands. He's far away from the big leagues, but with the lack of quality middle infielders in the system, Ozoria already is one of the Indians' best shortstop prospects.

Year	Club (League)	Class	AVG	G	AB	R	H	2B	3B	HR	RBI	BB	SO	SB	OBP	SLG
2008	Did Not Play															

Colorado Rockies

BY TRACY RINGOLSBY

After a dream season the year before, 2008 was a bit of a nightmare for the Rockies.

Colorado was Baseball America's Organization of the Year in 2007, winning a franchise-record 90 games with a largely homegrown team that blazed into the postseason with wins in 14 of its final 15 games. The Rockies then blew through the playoffs and reached the World Series for the first time ever before getting swept by the Red Sox.

With a young core of players who all seemed to still be on the way up, along with a farm system that BA rated as the game's seventh-best entering the year,

 Colorado had high expectations heading into the season. The front office made few moves and was willing to rely on its farm system to fill any holes that appeared.

The major league team never got it together, however, limping along on the fringes of contention all season in the mediocre National League West. The Rockies finally fell out of the running in September and finished 74-88, a decline of 16 wins from 2007.

Troy Tulowitzki, depended on as a franchise cornerstone, was hurt much of the year and batted a lackluster .263/.332/.401 when he did play. Several other young players took steps back as the offense scored 113 fewer runs than it had the year before. On the pitching front, Jeff Francis saw his ERA balloon to 5.01. Former No. 1 prospect Franklin Morales, who looked like a future ace at the end of 2007, went 1-2, 6.39 in five starts and found himself back in Triple-A.

Reflecting the disappointment of the season, the front office made wholesale changes to the big league staff after the season, keeping manager Clint Hurdle but getting rid of just about everyone else. The Rockies also traded their best player, Matt Holliday, to the Athletics ahead of his impending free agency.

The news wasn't any better on the farm, where Morales' performance was reflective of a system where most of the top prospects regressed. Ian Stewart and Greg Reynolds did graduate to the big leagues, though neither marked himself as a surefire regular going forward. Shortstop Hector Gomez and righthander Casey Weathers both had Tommy John surgery.

One bright spot for the organization was the continued development of outfielder Dexter Fowler, who becomes the Rockies' top prospect after playing for Team USA in the Olympics. He'll be expected to step in at center field after the Rockies cleared the way by nontendering Willy Taveras after last season.

Matt Holliday's November departure ended a disappointing 2008 season in Colorado

TOP 30 PROSPECTS

1. Dexter Fowler, of	16. Aneury Rodriguez, rhp
2. Jhoulys Chacin, rhp	17. Shane Lindsay, rhp
3. Christian Friedrich, lhp	18. Eric Young Jr., 2b/of
4. Wilin Rosario, c	19. Ryan Mattheus, rhp
5. Hector Gomez, ss	20. Darin Holcomb, 3b
6. Casey Weathers, rhp	21. Aaron Weatherford, rhp
7. Esmil Rogers, rhp	22. Brandon Hynick, rhp
8. Seth Smith, of	23. Juan Morillo, rhp
9. Michael McKenry, c	24. Cory Riordan, rhp
10. Charlie Blackmon, of	25. Chaz Roe, rhp
11. Delta Cleary, of	26. Cory Wimberly, 2b
12. Connor Graham, rhp	27. Jonathan Herrera, 2b
13. Chris Nelson, ss	28. Christian Colonel, of/inf
14. Tyler Massey, of	29. Joe Koshansky, 1b
15. Parker Frazier, rhp	30. Carlos Martinez, ss

Fowler is a great example of Colorado's aggressive nature in recent drafts. In August 2004, the Rockies saved $2 million when they traded Larry Walker to the Cardinals. They used a chunk of that money to sign Fowler, days before he planned to enroll at Miami.

The Rockies' increased presence in Latin America continues to pay dividends. Venezuelan righthander Jhoulys Chacin and Dominican catcher Wilin Rosario were two of their few prospects who significantly boosted their stock in 2008. Chacin led all minor leaguers with 18 wins, while Rosario ranked as the No. 1 prospect in the Rookie-level Pioneer League.

General Manager: Dan O'Dowd. **Farm Director:** Marc Gustafson. **Scouting Director:** Bill Schmidt.

Class	Team	League	W	L	PCT	Finish*	Manager	Affiliated
Majors	Colorado	National	74	88	.457	11th (16)	Clint Hurdle	—
Triple-A	Colorado Springs Sky Sox	Pacific Coast	71	72	.497	8th (16)	Tom Runnells	1993
Double-A	Tulsa Drillers	Texas	58	82	.414	7th (8)	Stu Cole	2003
High A	Modesto Nuts	California	70	69	.504	5th (10)	Jerry Weinstein	2005
Low A	Asheville Tourists	South Atlantic	83	56	.597	2nd (16)	Joe Mikulik	1994
Short-season	Tri-City Dust Devils	Northwest	36	40	.474	5th (8)	Fred Ocasio	2001
Rookie	Casper Ghosts	Pioneer	36	37	.493	5th (8)	Tony Diaz	2001
Overall 2008 Minor League Record			354	356	.499	18th		

* Finish in overall standings (No. of teams in league). ^League champion.

LAST YEAR'S TOP 30

Rank	Player, Pos.	Status
1.	Franklin Morales, lhp	Majors
2.	Ian Stewart, 3b	Majors
3.	Dexter Fowler, of	No. 1
4.	Hector Gomez, ss	No. 5
5.	Greg Reynolds, rhp	Majors
6.	Casey Weathers, rhp	No. 6
7.	Chris Nelson, ss	No. 13
8.	Brandon Hynick, rhp	No. 22
9.	Pedro Strop, rhp	(Rangers)
10.	Chaz Roe, rhp	No. 25
11.	Juan Morillo, rhp	No. 23
12.	Seth Smith, of	No. 8
13.	Esmil Rogers, rhp	No. 7
14.	Brian Rike, of	Dropped out
15.	Jayson Nix, 2b	(White Sox)
16.	Michael McKenry, c	No. 9
17.	Joe Koshansky, 1b	No. 29
18.	Jhoulys Chacin, rhp	No. 2
19.	Ryan Speier, rhp	Majors
20.	Daniel Mayora, 2b	Dropped out
21.	Darren Clarke, rhp	Dropped out
22.	Eric Young Jr., 2b	No. 18
23.	Helder Velasquez, ss/2b	Dropped out
24.	Corey Wimberly, 2b	No. 26
25.	Jonathan Herrera, ss	No. 27
26.	Lars Davis, c	Dropped out
27.	Keith Weiser, lhp	Dropped out
28.	Aneury Rodriguez, rhp	No. 16
29.	Connor Graham, rhp	No. 12
30.	Cory Riordan, rhp	No. 24

BEST TOOLS

Best Hitter for Average	Seth Smith
Best Power Hitter	Joe Koshansky
Best Strike-Zone Discipline	Matt Miller
Fastest Baserunner	Cory Wimberly
Best Athlete	Dexter Fowler
Best Fastball	Juan Morillo
Best Curveball	Christian Friedrich
Best Slider	Parker Frazier
Best Changeup	Jhoulys Chacin
Best Control	Parker Frazier
Best Defensive Catcher	Michael McKenry
Best Defensive Infielder	Helder Velasquez
Best Infield Arm	Helder Velasquez
Best Defensive Outfielder	Dexter Fowler
Best Outfield Arm	Brian Rike

PROJECTED 2012 LINEUP

Catcher	Chris Iannetta
First Base	Brad Hawpe
Second Base	Hector Gomez
Third Base	Ian Stewart
Shortstop	Troy Tulowitzki
Left Field	Seth Smith
Center Field	Dexter Fowler
Right Field	Tyler Massey
No. 1 Starter	Ubaldo Jimenez
No. 2 Starter	Aaron Cook
No. 3 Starter	Jhouyls Chacin
No. 4 Starter	Jeff Francis
No. 5 Starter	Christian Friedrich
Closer	Manny Corpas

TOP PROSPECTS OF THE DECADE

Year	Player, Pos.	2008 Org.
1999	Choo Freeman, of	Out of baseball
2000	Choo Freeman, of	Out of baseball
2001	Chin-Hui Tsao, rhp	Royals
2002	Chin-Hui Tsao, rhp	Royals
2003	Aaron Cook, rhp	Rockies
2004	Chin-Hui Tsao, rhp	Royals
2005	Ian Stewart, 3b	Rockies
2006	Ian Stewart, 3b	Rockies
2007	Troy Tulowitzki, ss	Rockies
2008	Franklin Morales, lhp	Rockies

TOP DRAFT PICKS OF THE DECADE

Year	Player, Pos.	2008 Org.
1999	Jason Jennings, rhp	Rangers
2000	*Matt Harrington, rhp	Out of baseball
2001	Jayson Nix, 2b	Rockies
2002	Jeff Francis, lhp	Rockies
2003	Ian Stewart, 3b	Rockies
2004	Chris Nelson, ss	Rockies
2005	Troy Tulowitzki, ss	Rockies
2006	Greg Reynolds, rhp	Rockies
2007	Casey Weathers, rhp	Rockies
2008	Christian Friedrich, lhp	Rockies

*Did not sign.

LARGEST BONUSES IN CLUB HISTORY

Greg Reynolds, 2006	$3,250,000
Jason Young, 2000	$2,750,000
Troy Tulowitzki, 2005	$2,300,000
Chin-Hui Tsao, 1999	$2,200,000
Chris Nelson, 2004	$2,150,000

COLORADO ROCKIES

TOP 2009 ROOKIE: Seth Smith, of. He has the purest swing of any hitter in the system and will get the chance to replace Matt Holliday.

BREAKOUT PROSPECT: Parker Frazier, rhp. He pounds the strike zone and is adding velocity as his body starts to fill out.

SLEEPER: Brian Rike, of. He has power potential and a true right-field arm.

SOURCE OF TOP 30 TALENT			
Homegrown	30	Acquired	0
College	13	Trades	0
Junior College	1	Rule 5 draft	0
High school	5	Indpendents	0
Draft-and-follow	2	Free agents/waivers	0
Nondrafted free agents	0		
International	9		

Numbers in parentheses indicate prospect rankings.

LF
Seth Smith (8)
Tyler Massey (14)
Cole Garner

CF
Dexter Fowler (1)
Charlie Blackmon (10)
Delta Cleary (11)
Anthony Jackson
Michael Mitchell

RF
Matt Miler
Brian Rike
Daniel Carte
Kevin Clarke
David Christiansen

3B
Darin Holcomb (20)
Christian Colonel (28)

SS
Hector Gomez (5)
Chris Nelson (13)
Carlos Martinez (30)
Helder Velazquez

2B
Eric Young Jr. (18)
Cory Wimberly (26)
Jonathan Herrera (27)
Daniel Mayora

1B
Joe Koshansky (29)
Mike Pavlik
Jeff Kindel
Kiel Roling

C
Wilin Rosario (4)
Michael McKenry (9)
Lars Davis
Jordan Pacheco

RHP		LHP	
Starters	**Relievers**	**Starters**	**Relievers**
Jhouyls Chacin (2)	Casey Weathers (6)	Chrisitan Friedrich (3)	Adam Bright
Esmil Rogers (7)	Ryan Mattheus (19)	Xavier Cedeno	Brandon Durden
Conor Graham (12)	Aaron Weatherford (21)	Keith Weiser	Craig Rodriguez
Parker Frazier (15)	Juan Morillo (23)	Kenneth Durst	
Aneury Rodriguez (16)	Andrew Johnston		
Shane Lindsay (17)	Steven Register		
Brandon Hynick (22)			
Cory Riordan (24)			
Chaz Roe (25)			
Samuel Deduno			
Johnathan Aristil			
Bruce Billings			

2008 BONUSES: $4.2 MILLION

BEST PURE HITTER: OF Charlie Blackmon (2) can do it all, using the entire field, bunting for hits and showing surprising line-drive power. OF Tyler Massey (14) got a $525,000 bonus out of a Tennessee high school thanks to his excellent makeup and natural hitting ability.

BEST POWER HITTER: C Kiel Roling (6) is a physical beast with strength and leverage in his swing, producing above-average raw power. Knee surgery in November 2007 caused him to get too big and slowed his bat in 2008, when he hit just eight homers for Arizona State, but his bat quickened as he got in better shape as a pro.

FASTEST RUNNER: Blackmon's plus-plus speed stands out in the class.

BEST DEFENSIVE PLAYER: SS Thomas Field (24) has a Jason Bartlett build and similar defensive skills, with arm strength and excellent range.

BEST FASTBALL: RHP Aaron Weatherford (3) sits at 91-94 mph and has thrown harder from a high slot and maximum-effort delivery. Fellow Southeastern Conference product Stephen Dodson (10) still has projection and sits in the low 90s with his four-seamer.

BEST SECONDARY PITCH: LHP Christian Friedrich (1) has a solid-average fastball, but his above-average breaking balls—a slider and true 12-to-6 curveball—are his trademarks. RHP Kurt Yacko (8), a two-way player at NCAA Division III Chapman (Calif.), has a plus slider and is learning to pitch now that he's given up hitting.

BEST PRO DEBUT: Blackmon ranked second in the short-season Northwest League in batting at .338/.390/.466. Friedrich struck out 50 in just 36 innings while going 2-1, 3.35 as Blackmon's Tri-City teammate.

BEST ATHLETE: Blackmon edges OF Delta Cleary (37), a former high school quarterback and plus runner.

MOST INTRIGUING BACKGROUND: Cleary is an explosive dunker in basketball, hinting at his family background—he's a cousin of NBA star Shawn Marion. Blackmon was primarily a pitcher at Young Harris (Ga.) JC and in his first year at Georgia Tech before getting a chance to hit in 2008. RHP Rod Scurry's (31) father Rod Sr. spent parts of eight seasons in the majors.

CLOSEST TO THE MAJORS: Friedrich's polish and four-pitch mix puts him on the fast track. Weatherford also could move quickly as a reliever.

BEST LATE-ROUND PICK: The Rockies went above slot for Massey and Cleary ($250,000) and are happy with the early results.

THE ONE WHO GOT AWAY: The Rockies wanted 2B/3B Andy Burns (25), the best Colorado prep hitter in years, and followed him this summer in the Northwoods League, but he followed through on his commitment to Kentucky. Redshirt sophomore 3B Chris Dominguez (5) took his above-average power and raw skills back to Louisville.

ASSESSMENT: The Rockies were pleasantly surprised to get Friedrich 25th and may have a true find in Blackmon. Massey (the only high school player the Rockies signed) and Cleary provide a needed infusion of high-upside young talent to another college-heavy class.

2007 BONUSES: $3.7 MILLION

RHP Casey Weathers (1) isn't on the fast track any longer after having Tommy John surgery. RHP Parker Frazier (8) and 3B Darin Holcomb (12) are intriguing sleepers.

GRADE: C

2006 BONUSES: $6.2 MILLION

RHP Greg Reynolds (2) is looking more and more like a reach as the No. 2 overall selection, though he has reached the majors already. C Michael McKenry (7) is advancing thanks to his power and arm strength.

GRADE: C

2005 BONUSES: $6.0 MILLION*

SS Troy Tulowitzki (1) may have followed a terrific rookie season with a disappointing encore, but he's still a keeper. Unsigned SS Reese Havens (29) developed into a first-rounder three years later.

GRADE: B+

2004 BONUSES: $4.0 MILLION*

The Rockies may get three starters out of this draft in OF Seth Smith (2), C Chris Iannetta (4) and OF Dexter Fowler (14), and Fowler is the top prospect in the system. There's still hope for SS Chris Nelson (1) too, and seven players (including Smith and Iannetta) already have reached the majors.

GRADE: B+

*Draft analysis by John Manuel (2008) and Jim Callis (2004-07). Numbers in parentheses indicate draft rounds. *Bonuses for 2004-05 are first 10 rounds only.*

JOHN WILLIAMSON

AMERICAN LEAGUE EAST

1 PROSPECT

DEXTER FOWLER, OF
Born: March 12, 1986.
Ht.: 6-4. **Wt.:** 186.
Bats: B. **Throws:** R.
Drafted:
HS—Milton, Ga., 2004
(14th round).
Signed by:
Damon Iannelli.

F owler had a breakthrough season in 2008 after injuries limited him to 164 games the two previous seasons. A Double-A Texas League all-star for Tulsa, he was selected to play in the Futures Game at Yankee Stadium, played for the U.S. Olympic team, and made his big league debut in September. A 14th-rounder in 2004, Fowler didn't debut until the following season because the Rockies didn't sign him until August, after a trade of Larry Walker provided payroll savings that were used for his $925,000 bonus. Fowler scared teams off because he had offers to play baseball at Miami, where he was headed before signing with the Rockies, and basketball at Harvard. A High School All-American, he was ranked by Baseball America as the 10th-best high school position player available in the 2004 draft. He played in summer league programs with Chris Nelson, the Rockies' first-round draft choice in 2004.

There are few players with as complete a package of tools as Fowler, from physical ability to his personality. Constantly smiling, he plays center field and runs the bases with a flair that conjures up memories of a young Garry Maddox and Willie Wilson. His feet don't seem to ever leave the ground with his effortless stride. He is a plus runner who gets good breaks on balls defensively and has a plus arm for a center fielder. He continues to make strides offensively and started to show an ability to drive the ball in 2008. Having not begun to switch-hit until he got into pro ball, Fowler is stronger from the right side of the plate, batting .405 in 84 at-bats against lefthanders last season, but has good technique from the left side, even though he does use a split grip. He said it gives him a feeling of bat control, and the organization has taken a hands-off approach to that situation.

Fowler has no glaring holes. It's a matter of how quickly he'll make adjustments. Fowler has a sleek, athletic build that figures to steadily get stronger, although he will never be bulky, and with that strength will come run-production power. However, that is still a projection at this point. At each level he has had to adjust to the command of pitchers, and learn not to be in a hurry to chase pitches out of the zone. He has too much speed to give away at-bats and needs to make more contact with two strikes. He has excellent speed, but needs to learn how to use it as an offensive weapon in terms of stealing bases and bunting.

Fowler is expected to be a key part of the Rockies' long-term foundation with his ability to play center field in spacious Coors Field. He might hit leadoff but could develop enough power to move lower in the order, perhaps as a No. 3 or No. 5 hitter. Natural progression will have him open this season with Triple-A Colorado Springs, but with his raw abilities, Fowler has the ability to push up the development plan. The quick adjustment he made at Tulsa last year has moved Fowler onto the fast track.

Year	Club (League)	Class	AVG	G	AB	R	H	2B	3B	HR	RBI	BB	SO	SB	OBP	SLG
2005	Casper (PIO)	R	.273	62	220	43	60	10	4	4	23	27	73	18	.357	.409
2006	Asheville (SAL)	LoA	.296	99	405	92	120	31	6	8	46	43	79	43	.373	.462
2007	Modesto (CAL)	HiA	.273	65	245	43	67	7	5	2	23	44	64	20	.397	.367
2008	Tulsa (TEX)	AA	.335	108	421	92	141	31	9	9	64	65	89	20	.431	.515
	Colorado (NL)	MAJ	.154	13	26	3	4	0	0	0	0	0	5	0	.185	.154
MINOR LEAGUE TOTALS			.301	334	1291	270	388	79	24	23	156	179	305	101	.394	.452
MAJOR LEAGUE TOTALS			.154	13	26	3	4	0	0	0	0	0	5	0	.185	.154

2 JHOUYLS CHACIN, RHP

BORN: Jan. 7, 1988. **B-T:** R-R. **HT.:** 6-1. **WT.:** 179. **SIGNED:** Venezuela, 2004.
SIGNED BY: Francisco Cartaya.

In his first full season, Chacin shot up the Rockies' charts, splitting time with their two full-season Class A affiliates. He led the minor leagues with 18 wins, ranking third overall in innings and sixth in ERA and strikeouts. He boasts a 23-5 record in his last 37 professional starts. Chacin has mastered his fastball and changeup, capable of throwing either pitch in any situation. The fastball has picked up velocity and now sits around 92 mph, touching 94, with heavy sinking action. He uses the same arm action for his change, which has become an out pitch, particularly against lefthanded hitters. He's a strong athlete with the ability to repeat his mechanics. His curveball doesn't have the sharpness that Chacin will need to be a big league starter. He can throw the pitch for strikes, and it has some power at 78-80 mph, but right now it's below average. Chacin will step into the middle of a big league rotation, and if his curveball develops into a plus pitch, he can be a top-of-the-rotation starter. After reaching high Class A in his first full season, he should be challenged again in 2009 and could even reach Colorado at some point.

Year	Club (League)	Class	W	L	ERA	G	GS	CG	SV	IP	H	R	ER	HR	BB	SO	AVG
2005	Rockies (DSL)	R	3	1	4.32	16	4	0	0	50	43	32	24	5	16	48	.219
2006	Rockies (DSL)	R	4	1	1.49	12	11	1	0	73	60	20	12	4	18	67	.226
2007	Casper (PIO)	R	6	5	3.13	16	16	0	0	92	85	45	32	5	26	77	.248
2008	Asheville (SAL)	LoA	10	1	1.86	16	16	2	0	111	82	30	23	3	30	98	.205
	Modesto (CAL)	HiA	8	2	2.31	12	12	0	0	66	61	20	17	3	12	62	.247
MINOR LEAGUE TOTALS			31	10	2.48	72	59	3	0	392	331	147	108	20	102	352	.228

3 CHRISTIAN FRIEDRICH, LHP

BORN: July 8, 1987. **B-T:** R-L. **HT.:** 6-4. **WT.:** 218. **DRAFTED:** Eastern Kentucky, 2008 (1st round). **SIGNED BY:** Scott Corman.

Undrafted out of high school, Friedrich bloomed at Eastern Kentucky into one of the best lefthanded pitchers at the college level in 2008. The son of a dentist whose client list includes several Cubs execs such as GM Jim Hendry, Friedrich was 20-7, 1.83 in his three years at Eastern Kentucky, and caught the attention of scouts by dominating the wood-bat New England Collegiate and Cape Cod leagues. Friedrich has a feel for pitching, with a solid-average fastball ranging from 89-92 mph. He complements his fastball with two good breaking balls: a big-time curveball that has a 12-to-6 movement and a slider. His changeup is evolving, as it's not a pitch he has needed at the amateur level. It should develop into an average pitch down the line with his feel for pitching. At times Friedrich's fastball command can be spotty, an important area for improvement as he lacks overpowering velocity. Friedrich figures to be a solid big league starter and could find his way to Coors Field at some point in the 2010 season. He could move quickly, akin to Jeff Francis' rapid rise, and while this year figures to begin at high Class A Modesto, it's not out of the question he could earn a midseason promotion.

Year	Club (League)	Class	W	L	ERA	G	GS	CG	SV	IP	H	R	ER	HR	BB	SO	AVG
2008	Tri-City (NWL)	SS	2	1	3.25	8	8	0	0	36	31	16	13	2	8	50	.228
	Asheville (SAL)	LoA	0	1	7.50	3	3	0	0	12	14	10	10	2	7	15	.269
MINOR LEAGUE TOTALS			2	2	4.31	11	11	0	0	48	45	26	23	4	15	65	.239

4 WILIN ROSARIO, C

BORN: Feb. 23, 1989. **B-T:** R-R. **HT.:** 5-11. **WT.:** 195. **SIGNED:** Dominican Republic, 2006. **SIGNED BY:** Felix Feliz.

Rosario seeks to join in the growing number of impact Latin American players the Rockies have produced under the guidance of director of Latin operations Rolando Fernandez. He impressed the organization with his maturity level, considering he was one of the youngest players in the Pioneer League, and he was the league's No. 1 prospect. Rosario showed the bat speed to handle good fastballs, promising run production ability at a position where offense is a luxury. He is athletic and moves well behind the plate. The fact he threw out 46 percent of basestealers in a league where pitchers are more focused on throwing strikes than holding runners underscores his arm strength. The physical skills are there, but Rosario is still young and honing those skills. Catching requires a mental maturity, learning to isolate personal struggles or successes so they don't affect the handling of a pitcher. It takes time to learn the nuances of pitch selection. Rosario will make the move to a full-season team this year, and the low Class A South Atlantic League should prove a good test of his endurance. With Chris Iannetta in the big leagues there is no reason to rush Rosario, so he will be given a chance to prove himself at each step in the minor leagues.

Year	Club (League)	Class	AVG	G	AB	R	H	2B	3B	HR	RBI	BB	SO	SB	OBP	SLG
2006	Rockies (DSL)	R	.249	62	213	28	53	7	0	3	25	16	56	5	.309	.324
2007	Casper (PIO)	R	.209	34	115	11	24	4	0	2	9	11	38	2	.283	.296
2008	Casper (PIO)	R	.316	66	263	48	83	15	3	12	49	24	57	4	.371	.532
MINOR LEAGUE TOTALS			.271	162	591	87	160	26	3	17	83	51	151	11	.332	.411

5 HECTOR GOMEZ, SS

BORN: March 5, 1988. **B-T:** R-R. **HT.:** 6-1. **WT.:** 164. **SIGNED:** Dominican Republic, 2004. **SIGNED BY:** Felix Feliz.

After earning all-star honors in the South Atlantic League in 2007, Gomez' career hit a roadblock in 2009. In the season opening game for Modesto, he fouled a ball off his left shin, causing a stress fracture. During his rehab he injured his right elbow, requiring Tommy John surgery on July 1. The hope is he can be ready by Opening Day. Gomez excels defensively. He has excellent range, and before the troubles of a year ago had the strongest arm of any player in the organization. He has a quick bat and can't be overpowered. As he fills out he should add the strength to collect extra-base hits. His arm strength will be watched carefully as he returns from surgery, but most players return with as much—if not more—arm strength. Plate discipline has been a problem, marginalizing what little power he has. With Troy Tulowitzki entrenched at Coors Field there is no need to rush shortstops through the system, which benefits Gomez. After losing the 2008 season to injuries, Gomez will be watched carefully during the spring to make sure his elbow has healed fully before he is sent out. Then he figures to return to Modesto for a second shot. With youth on his side, Gomez has plenty of time to regain his stature as a premier shortstop prospect.

Year	Club (League)	Class	AVG	G	AB	R	H	2B	3B	HR	RBI	BB	SO	SB	OBP	SLG
2005	Rockies (DSL)	R	.335	67	242	49	81	16	1	6	43	24	38	15	.423	.483
2006	Casper (PIO)	R	.327	50	202	24	66	9	4	5	35	11	26	5	.364	.485
	Tri-City (NWL)	SS	.244	12	45	4	11	3	0	0	6	0	14	0	.255	.311
2007	Asheville (SAL)	LoA	.266	124	534	89	142	34	8	11	61	29	120	20	.309	.421
2008	Modesto (CAL)	HiA	.333	1	3	0	1	0	0	0	0	0	0	0	.333	.333
MINOR LEAGUE TOTALS			.293	254	1026	166	301	62	13	22	145	64	198	40	.346	.443

6 CASEY WEATHERS, RHP

BORN: June 10, 1985. **B-T:** R-R. **HT.:** 6-1. **WT.:** 200. **DRAFTED:** Vanderbilt, 2007 (1st round). **SIGNED BY:** Scott Corman.

Converted from outfielder to pitcher in junior college, Weathers was on a fast track to the big leagues until he threw a pitch in the Arizona Fall League and felt something pop. He tore the ulnar collateral ligament in his right forearm, requiring ligament transplant surgery that will knock him out of the 2009 season. He was coming off a solid season at Double-A Tulsa that included an Olympic bronze medal with Team USA. His fastball can hit the mid-90s but loses movement when the velocity rises. In the low 90s he has late life that makes hitters jump. He complements the fastball with a late-breaking slider that will sit in the mid-80s. The combination provides swing-and-miss opportunities for Weathers, who has a late-inning mentality. Command and health are Weathers' two biggest challenges. He has to not only throw strikes, but also quality strikes. He can be timid at times against lefthanded hitters, who batted .319 against him (as opposed to .165 for righthanded hitters). Weathers will get a chance to get stronger while rehabbing in 2009. He should return in 2010 without any problems and will be in the big leagues as soon as he shows there are no lingering concerns from the injury.

Year	Club (League)	Class	W	L	ERA	G	GS	CG	SV	IP	H	R	ER	HR	BB	SO	AVG
2007	Asheville (SAL)	LoA	0	1	4.61	13	0	0	2	14	6	7	7	2	7	19	.130
	Modesto (CAL)	HiA	0	0	0.00	1	0	0	0	1	0	0	0	0	2	2	.000
2008	Tulsa (TEX)	AA	2	1	3.05	44	0	0	2	44	34	18	15	1	28	54	.210
MINOR LEAGUE TOTALS			2	2	3.36	58	0	0	4	59	40	25	22	3	37	75	.190

7 ESMIL ROGERS, RHP

BORN: Aug. 14, 1985. **B-T:** R-R. **HT.:** 6-1. **WT.:** 176. **SIGNED:** Dominican Republic, 2003. **SIGNED BY:** Felix Feliz.

Signed as a shortstop, Rogers struggled with the bat. After hitting .209 in three years in the Rookie-level Dominican Summer League, he agreed to give up hitting in 2006 and has made a solid adjustment to the mound. For a converted player, Rogers has adapted well to the craft of pitching. He has a solid delivery and good arm action, producing a 92-94 mph fastball with late life. The curveball came quickly. It has a hard break and can be a strikeout pitch. He has shown solid control. Rogers' inexperience with pitching shows in nuances such as defense and holding runners. The only below-average pitch in his arsenal is a changeup, which lacks consistency. Rogers was protected in his workload the first two years he pitched, but last season he took his regular turn all year in the California League. He is ready for the move to Double-A, and the Rockies believe he can be in their rotation by 2010. If his changeup doesn't make progress, his two-pitch arsenal and live arm should allow him to be an effective reliever quickly.

Year	Club (League)	Class	W	L	ERA	G	GS	CG	SV	IP	H	R	ER	HR	BB	SO	AVG
2006	Casper (PIO)	R	3	6	6.96	15	15	1	0	63	78	53	49	8	24	40	.306
2007	Asheville (SAL)	LoA	7	4	3.75	19	18	1	0	118	125	60	49	6	42	90	.272
2008	Modesto (CAL)	HiA	9	7	3.95	25	25	0	0	144	146	73	63	9	45	116	.264
MINOR LEAGUE TOTALS			19	17	4.46	59	58	2	0	325	349	186	161	23	111	246	.275

8 SETH SMITH, OF

BORN: Sept. 30, 1982. **B-T:** L-L. **HT.:** 6-3. **WT.:** 225. **DRAFTED:** Mississippi, 2004 (2nd round). **SIGNED BY:** Damon Iannelli.

Smith is a quality athlete who went to Mississippi as a quarterback, but got stuck behind Eli Manning and never took a snap in three years as the backup. A 48th-round pick of Arizona out of high school, he was a member of Team USA when it won a silver medal in the 2003 Pan American Games. Smith has the best swing of any player in the organization. He is a prototypical lefthanded bat, a low-ball hitter who has shown the ability to drive balls into the gaps. He has an excellent feel for the strike zone, and while his home run totals have been modest, he has given the Rockies reason to believe his power is coming on by hitting opposite-field homers in Washington and San Francisco last year. Smith has the ability to play any of the three outfield positions and has a strong, accurate arm, but still hasn't shown the ability to stay focused defensively. He will get himself out of rhythm at the plate when he exaggerates the leg kick he uses as a timing mechanism. Smith is ready to stay in the big leagues. He already has shown the awareness to handle the challenge of coming off the bench (14-for-42 as a big league pinch-hitter), and with the departure of Matt Holliday he'll get his shot to lay claim to an everyday job.

Year	Club (League)	Class	AVG	G	AB	R	H	2B	3B	HR	RBI	BB	SO	SB	OBP	SLG
2004	Casper (PIO)	R	.369	56	233	46	86	21	3	9	61	25	47	9	.427	.601
	Tri-City (NWL)	SS	.259	9	27	6	7	1	1	2	5	1	3	0	.276	.593
2005	Modesto (CAL)	HiA	.300	129	533	87	160	45	6	9	72	44	115	4	.353	.458
2006	Tulsa (TEX)	AA	.294	130	524	79	154	46	4	15	71	51	74	4	.361	.483
2007	Colorado Springs (PCL)	AAA	.317	129	451	68	143	34	6	17	82	39	73	7	.381	.528
	Colorado (NL)	MAJ	.625	7	8	4	5	0	1	0	0	0	1	0	.625	.875
2008	Colorado Springs (PCL)	AAA	.323	68	248	55	80	16	2	10	53	46	46	11	.426	.524
	Colorado (NL)	MAJ	.259	67	108	13	28	7	0	4	15	15	23	1	.350	.435
MINOR LEAGUE TOTALS			.313	521	2016	341	630	161	22	62	344	206	358	36	.379	.506
MAJOR LEAGUE TOTALS			.284	74	116	17	33	7	1	4	15	15	24	1	.366	.466

9 MICHAEL McKENRY, C

BORN: March 4, 1985. **B-T:** R-R. **HT.:** 5-10. **WT.:** 200. **DRAFTED:** Middle Tennessee State, 2006 (7th round). **SIGNED BY:** Scott Corman.

McKenry has shown steady improvement in his three pro seasons, and capped off his rise into legitimate prospect status when he was one of the stronger offensive players in the Arizona Fall League. He followed up a team-high 18 home runs at high Class A Modesto by finishing second in the AFL with nine homers. McKenry has been a quality defensive catcher since his youth, and has only added to that reputation, throwing out 46 percent of opposing basestealers in 2008. He moves well behind the plate, likes to work a pitcher through a game and has a plus arm, augmented by a quick release. Now the offense is starting to come, too. In two years in full-season leagues he has shown legitimate power. He quickly gets into hitting position and plants his front leg firmly. McKenry can get in a hurry at the plate and will chase pitches. He needs to make more consistent contact to turn into an everyday catcher in the big leagues. Some scouts question his athleticism and consider him a bad-body player. McKenry is moving a step at a time, and that means Tulsa for 2009. He has the defensive ability and mental toughness to ensure at least a backup job in the big leagues. If he becomes more disciplined at the plate, he has the potential to handle starting duties on a contender.

Year	Club (League)	Class	AVG	G	AB	R	H	2B	3B	HR	RBI	BB	SO	SB	OBP	SLG
2006	Tri-City (NWL)	SS	.216	66	245	28	53	16	1	4	23	22	49	3	.303	.339
2007	Asheville (SAL)	LoA	.287	113	408	79	117	35	1	22	90	66	84	8	.392	.539
2008	Modesto (CAL)	HiA	.258	111	400	59	103	28	1	18	75	55	101	2	.360	.468
MINOR LEAGUE TOTALS			.259	290	1053	166	273	79	3	44	188	143	234	13	.359	.465

10 CHARLIE BLACKMON, OF

RODGER WOOD

BORN: July 1, 1986. **B-T:** L-L. **HT.:** 6-3. **WT.:** 200. **DRAFTED:** Georgia Tech, 2008 (2nd round). **SIGNED BY:** Alan Matthews.

A pitcher at Young Harris (Ga.) JC, Blackmon moved to the outfield during the 2007 summer in the Texas Collegiate League. He was drafted out of high school (2004, 28th round, Marlins) and again out of Young Harris (2005, 20th round, Red Sox) before opting to transfer to Georgia Tech, where he ranked fourth in the Atlantic Coast Conference in batting in 2008. Blackmon shows five-tool potential. He runs well enough to play any of the three outfield positions, primarily playing right field in college and moving to center field in his pro debut. He has a picture-book lefthanded swing and has shown line-drive power into the alleys. He has plus-plus speed and the arm strength that would be expected from a converted pitcher. Blackmon's inexperience as a hitter shows, however. He makes contact but will chase pitches out of the strike zone. With his speed he has to realize that walks are of value. He has quick hands but tends to get started too soon in his swing. Signed as a college senior, Blackmon needs to be challenged in the minor leagues, with a jump to Modesto likely. With his defensive ability, he has what it takes to be a fourth outfielder, but with continued maturation offensively he could be an everyday center fielder.

Year	Club (League)	Class	AVG	G	AB	R	H	2B	3B	HR	RBI	BB	SO	SB	OBP	SLG
2008	Tri-City (NWL)	SS	.338	68	290	42	98	21	5	2	33	16	37	13	.390	.466
MINOR LEAGUE TOTALS			.338	68	290	42	98	21	5	2	33	16	37	13	.390	.466

11 DELTA CLEARY, OF

BORN: Aug. 14, 1989. **B-T:** B-R. **HT.:** 6-3. **WT.:** 175. **DRAFTED:** Louisiana State-Eunice JC, 2008 (37th round). **SIGNED BY:** Damon Iannelli.

A quarterback on his high school football team in Jonesboro, Ark., and a guard who averaged 13 points per game for the Arkansas Class 6-A state championship basketball team, Cleary is a pure athlete. He had opportunities to play basketball and football at the Division I level but opted to play baseball, going the junior college route. After hitting .411 and helping Louisiana State-Eunice win its second Division II national juco title his freshman year, Cleary signed with the Rockies, who gave him a $250,000 bonus. The cousin of Miami Heat forward Shawn Marion, Cleary shows power potential to all fields but does get caught off-balance on his front foot when he gets too anxious. He is a plus runner but can get bogged down getting out of the box by a big swing. Cleary's athleticism is most apparent when he is in center field. He gets good breaks on balls, covers plenty of ground and has a slightly above-average arm. As he focuses on baseball and refines his game, Cleary has the ability to become an impact center fielder. He could put up big numbers in 2009 at low Class A Asheville.

Year	Club (League)	Class	AVG	G	AB	R	H	2B	3B	HR	RBI	BB	SO	SB	OBP	SLG
2008	Casper (PIO)	R	.276	27	105	22	29	2	1	3	9	6	19	4	.321	.400
MINOR LEAGUE TOTALS			.276	27	105	22	29	2	1	3	9	6	19	4	.321	.400

12 CONNOR GRAHAM, RHP

BORN: Dec. 30, 1985. **B-T:** R-R. **HT.:** 6-7. **WT.:** 235. **DRAFTED:** Miami (Ohio), 2007 (5th round). **SIGNED BY:** Ed Santa.

Primarily a reliever his first two years in college, Graham moved into a rotation role with the Rockies because the team simply wanted him to log innings. After spending his pro debut getting in shape at the short-season level, Graham started to change the thinking about his future. He flourished in the role of a starter at Asheville, ranking second in the South Atlantic League (to Giants top prospect Madison Bumgarner) in ERA despite the hitter-friendly environment. His two plus pitches are a mid-90s fastball with movement and a hard slider, which he sometimes struggles to command. He ranked second in the SAL in walks. He messes with a curveball and has the makings of a changeup, and will have to refine one of those pitches to make the move to the big leagues as a power starter. If he can't add an offspeed pitch, he still has the ability to be an impact late-inning reliever. Given his age and his success in the SAL, Graham should move to Tulsa in 2009.

Year	Club (League)	Class	W	L	ERA	G	GS	CG	SV	IP	H	R	ER	HR	BB	SO	AVG
2007	Tri-City (NWL)	SS	1	0	2.37	6	4	0	0	19	23	7	5	2	6	18	.303
2008	Asheville (SAL)	LoA	12	6	2.26	26	26	2	0	147	99	50	37	3	83	138	.189
MINOR LEAGUE TOTALS			13	6	2.27	32	30	2	0	166	122	57	42	5	89	156	.204

13 CHRIS NELSON, SS

BORN: Sept. 3, 1985. **B-T:** R-R. **HT.:** 5-11. **WT.:** 195. **DRAFTED:** HS—Decatur, Ga., 2004 (1st round). **SIGNED BY:** Damon Iannelli.

After a second half in 2007 that had Rockies officials thinking that Nelson was ready to live up to expectations of being a first-round pick, he took a step backward last season. He struggled early at Tulsa, and then was sidelined with a broken hamate bone. Nelson returned in the Arizona Fall League, and his offensive performance started to trend upward again. Considered the best high school prospect in the 2004 draft, Nelson—a summer league teammate of Dexter Fowler in high school—still has exceptional bat speed that evokes Gary Sheffield. He lacks the plate discipline to take advantage of his fast hands, however. He will chase breaking pitches, a problem that was exposed when he moved up a level. He has a laser arm, but never looks comfortable at shortstop (24 errors in 72 games at Tulsa). He projects as a second baseman and would have been moved last year, but coming off that strong second half in 2007 the Rockies did not want to disrupt his offensive development. With a return to Tulsa this year, he'll move to second.

Year	Club (League)	Class	AVG	G	AB	R	H	2B	3B	HR	RBI	BB	SO	SB	OBP	SLG
2004	Casper (PIO)	R	.347	38	147	36	51	6	3	4	20	20	42	6	.432	.510
2005	Asheville (SAL)	LoA	.241	79	315	51	76	13	3	3	38	25	88	7	.304	.330
2006	Asheville (SAL)	LoA	.260	118	466	69	121	38	1	11	76	32	101	14	.313	.416
2007	Modesto (CAL)	HiA	.289	133	529	97	153	42	7	19	99	55	92	27	.358	.503
2008	Modesto (CAL)	HiA	.167	8	30	2	5	1	0	1	5	2	8	0	.219	.300
	Tulsa (TEX)	AA	.237	73	283	38	67	18	2	3	42	35	69	6	.324	.346
MINOR LEAGUE TOTALS			.267	449	1770	293	473	118	16	41	280	169	400	60	.335	.421

14 TYLER MASSEY, OF

BORN: July 21, 1989. **B-T:** L-L. **HT.:** 6-0. **WT.:** 205. **DRAFTED:** HS—Chattanooga, Tenn., 2008 (14th round). **SIGNED BY:** Scott Corman.

Massey was a mid-round find for the Rockies in 2008. Teams shied away from him because he had a baseball ride to Virginia, but by the 14th round, Rockies scouting director Bill Schmidt couldn't resist and opted to select Massey, whose father is the football coach at the Baylor School in Chattanooga. Massey's season was cut short when he ran into a wall at Rookie-level Casper in late August, leading to surgery to repair a torn left anterior cruciate ligament. He is expected to be ready by the start of spring training. Given a $525,000 signing bonus spread over four years, Massey shows the mentality of a player who also had Division I football options. He has raw power and a feel for hitting. With a short lefthanded stroke and good balance, he uses the whole field. A pitcher and first baseman in high school, Massey is an average runner best suited for first base or a corner outfield spot.

Year	Club (League)	Class	AVG	G	AB	R	H	2B	3B	HR	RBI	BB	SO	SB	OBP	SLG
2008	Casper (PIO)	R	.257	19	70	7	18	4	0	1	5	1	18	5	.278	.357
MINOR LEAGUE TOTALS			.257	19	70	7	18	4	0	1	5	1	18	5	.278	.357

15 PARKER FRAZIER, RHP

BORN: Nov. 11, 1988. **B-T:** R-R. **HT.:** 6-5. **WT.:** 180. **DRAFTED:** HS—Tulsa, 2007 (8th round). **SIGNED BY:** Dar Cox.

The son of former big league pitcher and current Rockies television analyst George Frazier, Parker had a lot of interest from colleges when he came out of high school. But his focus has always been on professional baseball and he never gave schools such as Arkansas and Oral Roberts serious consideration. Early indications are it was a wise decision. He has started to get stronger and fill out, and as a result his late-sinking fastball has clicked from the upper 80s to a consistent 92-93 mph. That helped him have success last year after an ugly pro debut at Casper. He has a hard slider and quality changeup to go with the heat. Most important, Frazier throws quality strikes. He has walked just 38 batters in 132 professional innings. He doesn't get many strikeouts but makes up for it with ground balls, posting a 2.0 groundout/airout ratio at short-season Tri-City. The Rockies have been cautious with Frazier, who has yet to pitch in a full-season league. Now he is ready to move quicker, and could jump up to Modesto.

Year	Club (League)	Class	W	L	ERA	G	GS	CG	SV	IP	H	R	ER	HR	BB	SO	AVG
2007	Casper (PIO)	R	3	5	10.07	16	10	0	0	45	78	54	50	8	18	22	.386
2008	Tri-City (NWL)	SS	5	5	3.83	15	15	0	0	87	94	41	37	3	20	47	.281
MINOR LEAGUE TOTALS			8	10	5.95	31	25	0	0	132	172	95	87	11	38	69	.321

16 ANEURY RODRIGUEZ, RHP

BORN: Dec. 13, 1987. **B-T:** R-R. **HT.:** 6-3. **WT.:** 180. **SIGNED:** Dominican Republic, 2005. **SIGNED BY:** Felix Feliz.

Rodriguez just turned 21 in December, but he's already moving up to Double-A. Having come to the United States at the age of 17, Rodriguez has a feel for pitching beyond his years, but when he gets into a jam he will overthrow and add to his problems. He has walked only 144 batters in 446 professional innings. He has a fastball that is a solid 91-92 mph with late movement, and his curveball is a good complementary offering, with out-pitch potential. He already has a feel for a changeup and is quite pitch-efficient for his age. He led the Cal League with two complete-game shutouts. The Rockies are still looking for him grow into his body, feeling not only that he could bulk up but he could still add an inch or two of height given the size of his hands. Even with a second-half stumble at Modesto last year, Rodriguez remains on the fast track and will take on the challenge of the hitter-friendly Texas League.

Year	Club (League)	Class	W	L	ERA	G	GS	CG	SV	IP	H	R	ER	HR	BB	SO	AVG
2005	Casper (PIO)	R	3	4	7.55	15	15	0	0	62	77	54	52	7	26	47	.309
2006	Tri-City (NWL)	SS	4	4	4.14	15	15	1	0	76	78	42	35	2	30	69	.261
2007	Asheville (SAL)	LoA	9	9	5.15	28	28	1	0	152	182	105	87	19	48	160	.298
2008	Modesto (CAL)	HiA	9	10	3.74	27	27	2	0	156	148	78	65	12	40	139	.251
MINOR LEAGUE TOTALS			25	27	4.82	85	85	4	0	446	485	279	239	40	144	415	.277

17 SHANE LINDSAY, RHP

BORN: Jan. 25, 1985. **B-T:** R-R. **HT.:** 6-1. **WT.:** 205. **SIGNED:** Australia, 2003. **SIGNED BY:** Phil Allen.

Lindsay's injury-plagued career got a major boost during the Arizona Fall League. Healthy for the first time in three years, Lindsay got his fastball back to hitting the upper 90s again, forcing the Rockies to put him on the 40-man roster so they would avoid losing him in the Rule 5 draft. The 2005 Northwest League pitcher of the year, Lindsay was bothered by a torn labrum that cut short his 2006 season and forced him to miss all of 2007. He was making his comeback in 2008 before a barroom brawl resulted in a broken hand. He returned in time to pitch for Asheville in the Sally League playoffs, striking out 10 in six innings in a loss to league champion Augusta. Lindsay, who has thrown just 222 innings in five pro seasons, needs to put together a full season and show that his dominance can be sustained. He will pitch in the 92-94 range but can hit 98, and he has a knucklecurve that he can consistently throw for strikes. He needs to refine his changeup to give him something offspeed that would allow him to be a factor in a big league rotation.

Year	Club (League)	Class	W	L	ERA	G	GS	CG	SV	IP	H	R	ER	HR	BB	SO	AVG
2004	Casper (PIO)	R	1	1	6.75	17	0	0	0	21	22	24	16	1	19	31	.256
2005	Tri-City (NWL)	SS	6	1	1.89	13	13	0	0	67	37	21	14	1	34	107	.163
2006	Tri-City (NWL)	SS	2	2	2.79	6	5	0	0	29	18	10	9	0	17	48	.176
	Asheville (SAL)	LoA	2	1	2.67	7	7	0	0	34	26	15	10	2	27	43	.211
2007	Did Not Play—Injured																
2008	Modesto (CAL)	HiA	2	3	3.99	10	10	0	0	47	33	29	21	1	34	56	.194
	Asheville (SAL)	LoA	1	2	5.55	6	6	0	0	24	30	16	15	1	12	26	.306
MINOR LEAGUE TOTALS			14	10	3.44	59	41	0	0	222	166	115	85	6	143	311	.206

18 ERIC YOUNG JR., 2B/OF

BORN: May 25, 1985. **B-T:** B-R. **HT.:** 5-10. **WT.:** 180. **DRAFTED:** Chandler-Gilbert (Ariz.) CC, D/F 2003 (30th round). **SIGNED BY:** Mike Garlatti.

The son of original Rockies second baseman and current ESPN analyst Eric Young Sr., the younger Young is strikingly similar to the player his dad was, albeit with more strength. His game is built on speed, as he led the minor leagues in stolen bases in 2006 while playing for Asheville and still turns in big steals totals at higher levels. Even though Young missed a month at Tulsa with a broken hamate bone in his left hand last year, he stole 46 bases for the Drillers, and then exploded offensively in the AFL, where he led the league with a .430 average, .504 on-base percentage, 37 runs and 20 stolen bases. Young has embraced the small-ball approach, but needs to become more consistent with his strike zone to take advantage of the speed he possesses. The biggest challenge for Young is defense. He is a stiff-fielding infielder, which led the Rockies to give him a look in center field in the AFL. He adapted quickly to tracking balls, but arm strength became an issue. He's on the 40-man roster and headed to Triple-A for 2009, where he will continue to work on center field as well as second base.

Year	Club (League)	Class	AVG	G	AB	R	H	2B	3B	HR	RBI	BB	SO	SB	OBP	SLG
2004	Casper (PIO)	R	.264	23	87	20	23	5	1	0	7	20	13	14	.407	.345
2005	Casper (PIO)	R	.301	63	219	48	66	7	7	3	25	35	52	25	.404	.438
2006	Asheville (SAL)	LoA	.295	128	482	92	142	28	6	5	49	67	75	87	.391	.409
2007	Modesto (CAL)	HiA	.291	130	540	113	157	29	11	8	63	46	105	73	.359	.430
2008	Tulsa (TEX)	AA	.290	105	403	74	117	24	4	3	33	61	77	46	.391	.392
MINOR LEAGUE TOTALS			.292	449	1731	347	505	93	29	19	177	229	322	245	.384	.412

19 RYAN MATTHEUS, RHP

BORN: Nov. 10. **1983. B-T:** R-R. **HT.:** 6-3. **WT.:** 215. **DRAFTED:** Sacramento CC, D/F 2003 (19th round). **SIGNED BY:** Gary Wilson.

Brought over to big league camp during spring training when the Rockies needed an extra arm as insurance, Mattheus caught the attention of manager Clint Hurdle with his ability to consistently throw strikes. It led to the decision to move Mattheus from the rotation to the bullpen at Tulsa last year, and it worked. For the first time in four full professional seasons, he had an ERA below 5.00 and he showed the necessary resiliency to work late innings. His control also improved significantly, perhaps because he no longer needed to worry about an offspeed pitch. He has a hard sinking fastball, a four-seamer that can reach 94 mph and a plus slider. His inability to develop a changeup or split-finger pitch has left him vulnerable to lefthanded hitters, who tagged him for a .318 average last year (compared to .210 for righthanders). Added to the 40-man roster, Mattheus will get a long look in the spring, but first he will have to prove he has overcome shoulder tendinitis that forced him to come home early from the Arizona Fall League.

Year	Club (League)	Class	W	L	ERA	G	GS	CG	SV	IP	H	R	ER	HR	BB	SO	AVG
2004	Casper (PIO)	R	3	3	4.94	7	7	0	0	27	27	16	15	2	14	16	.262
2005	Asheville (SAL)	LoA	7	6	5.82	23	23	0	0	128	142	90	83	16	52	102	.278
2006	Modesto (CAL)	HiA	7	12	5.19	28	28	1	0	156	198	103	90	5	65	131	.313
2007	Tulsa (TEX)	AA	9	11	5.56	26	26	1	0	159	182	100	98	13	55	102	.294
2008	Tulsa (TEX)	AA	2	5	3.28	58	0	0	17	58	50	27	21	5	27	56	.245
MINOR LEAGUE TOTALS			28	37	5.23	142	84	2	17	528	599	336	307	41	213	407	.290

20 DARIN HOLCOMB, 3B

BORN: Dec. 7, 1985. **B-T:** R-R. **HT.:** 5-11. **WT.:** 205. **DRAFTED:** Gonzaga, 2007 (12th round). **SIGNED BY:** Gary Wilson.

Holcomb doesn't open eyes when he walks onto the field, but so far he has put up the kind of results that force scouts to pay attention. He has a bit of Ron Cey in him, with a small, stout build, and modest athleticism but a toughness and determination to succeed. Consider the fact that he was the MVP in the South Atlantic League last year, but still ranked just 17th on Baseball America's Sally League prospect list. A grinder who can hit, he led the league in doubles and RBIs, finished second in on-base percentage and batting average and showed the plate discipline to draw more walks than strikeouts. He stays back on the ball and has good pitch recognition. He has extra-base power, but isn't the home run hitter teams usually look at from the corner infield spots. He doesn't have the quick reflexes at third base, and isn't built like a player who would seem fit to move to second base, which could result in an eventual move to left field. Holcomb wore down late and didn't perform with the bat—a first—in Hawaii Winter Baseball, batting .163. He could push for a jump to Tulsa with a strong spring or take it one step at a time and report to Modesto.

Year	Club (League)	Class	AVG	G	AB	R	H	2B	3B	HR	RBI	BB	SO	SB	OBP	SLG
2007	Tri-City (NWL)	SS	.303	74	277	46	84	23	1	12	51	31	30	7	.391	.523
2008	Asheville (SAL)	LoA	.318	137	509	89	162	46	0	14	102	65	60	6	.400	.491
MINOR LEAGUE TOTALS			.313	211	786	135	246	69	1	26	153	96	90	13	.397	.503

21 AARON WEATHERFORD, RHP

BORN: Dec. 19, 1986. **B-T:** R-R. **HT.:** 6-1. **WT.:** 189. **DRAFTED:** Mississippi State, 2008 (3rd round). **SIGNED BY:** Damon Iannelli.

Shoulder tendinitis forced Weatherford to miss the month of March at Mississippi State and wound up costing him his entire first pro season, after the Rockies signed for $350,000. The Rockies are confident that the problems are minimal, but there are concerns in some circles that he will battle arm problems throughout his career because of a max-effort delivery and slight frame. The Rockies see him as a legitimate late-inning relief candidate, which will allow him to be monitored on pitch counts and innings. He can dominate hitters. He allowed only 20 baserunners—10 walks and 10 hits—and struck out 62 in 32 innings of relief for Mississippi State last spring. He struck out 177 batters in 169 career innings at Mississippi State, helping lead an upstart Bulldogs team to the College World Series in Ron Polk's penultimate season in 2007. Weatherford has an over-the-top arm slot with a fastball that will sit in the 91-94 mph range. He has shown command of both sides of the plate with the fastball. His second pitch is a split-finger fastball. A swing-and-miss pitch that is rarely a strike, the splitter becomes an out pitch when he commands his fastball and can get ahead in the count. Weatherford also throws a hard curveball. He could wind up as a closer long-term as his splitter gives him a weapon to neutralize lefthanded hitters, which Casey Weathers lacks.

Year	Club (League)	Class	W	L	ERA	G	GS	CG	SV	IP	H	R	ER	HR	BB	SO	AVG
2008	Did Not Play—Injured																

22 BRANDON HYNICK, RHP

BORN: March 7, 1985. **B-T:** R-R. **HT.:** 6-3. **WT.:** 205. **DRAFTED:** Birmingham-Southern, 2006 (8th round). **SIGNED BY:** Damon Iannelli.

After winning league pitcher of the year honors in his first two professional seasons, Hynick faced his first real challenge at Double-A in 2008. He got knocked around in two of his first three starts, lasting past the fifth inning only once. Then he adjusted, going at least six innings in 23 of his last 24 starts, and he finished the season strong, capped off by a 1.56 ERA in August. He is a control pitcher in the Brad Radke mold, with durability as his best attribute. He ranked ninth in the minors in innings in '08 after leading the minors in that category the year before. He throws quality strikes with his two-seam fastball, which has good sink. Hynick doesn't produce exceptional ground-ball numbers and can be susceptible to home runs if he doesn't command his stuff. He has issued just 71 walks in 426 professional innings. He complements a high 80s fastball with a splitter, quality changeup and curveball. His curveball remains inconsistent, but the split-finger is a swing-and-miss out pitch. Hynick has little margin for error, and hitters know he's going to be around the strike zone. If he misses his spots he will get hit hard. He profiles as a durable innings-eater but strictly as a back-of-the-rotation option. He's headed to Triple-A to try to prove himself again.

Year	Club (League)	Class	W	L	ERA	G	GS	CG	SV	IP	H	R	ER	HR	BB	SO	AVG
2006	Casper (PIO)	R	4	3	2.39	12	12	0	0	64	55	23	17	3	8	70	.227
	Tri-City (NWL)	SS	0	0	2.57	2	1	0	0	7	5	2	2	0	1	9	.208
2007	Modesto (CAL)	HiA	16	5	2.52	28	28	3	0	182	170	64	51	13	31	136	.243
2008	Tulsa (TEX)	AA	10	7	4.44	27	27	0	0	172	183	93	85	27	31	97	.270
MINOR LEAGUE TOTALS			30	15	3.28	69	68	3	0	426	413	182	155	43	71	312	.251

23 JUAN MORILLO, RHP

BORN: Nov. 5, 1983. **B-T:** R-R. **HT.:** 6-3. **WT.:** 190. **SIGNED:** Dominican Republic, 2001. **SIGNED BY:** Rolando Fernandez.

It is now or never time for Morillo, who has made three brief trips to the majors. He is out of options, so either the Rockies will keep him in their bullpen out of spring training, or they'll have to run him through waivers to send him to the minors. Teams would be tempted to put in a claim on Morillo because of his raw arm strength. He has hit 100 mph in the past according to scouts from other organizations, though the Rockies say he pitches best at 95. The problem is throwing strikes. His slider can be an out pitch, but is too inconsistent for Morillo to count on. He dabbled with a split-finger pitch, but that led to a sore arm, so he is back to using a changeup, which hasn't come easily to him. Converted to a reliever two years ago with the hope it would help him be more aggressive and throw more strikes, he responded well in 2007, his best statistical season, but gave back that progress last year. Given his roster situation, Morillo figures to be in the big leagues this year, but it's a question of which team will find roster space.

Year	Club (League)	Class	W	L	ERA	G	GS	CG	SV	IP	H	R	ER	HR	BB	SO	AVG
2001	Rockies (DSL)	R	2	4	6.81	14	7	0	0	36	35	31	27	1	38	20	.248
2002	Rockies (DSL)	R	1	5	4.75	14	11	0	0	55	49	44	29	1	33	43	.230
2003	Casper (PIO)	R	1	6	5.91	15	15	0	0	64	85	73	42	6	40	44	.318
2004	Tri-City (NWL)	SS	3	2	2.98	14	14	0	0	66	56	34	22	0	41	73	.226
2005	Asheville (SAL)	LoA	1	3	4.54	7	7	0	0	34	40	24	17	2	13	43	.290
	Modesto (CAL)	HiA	6	5	4.41	20	20	0	0	112	107	69	55	10	65	101	.258
2006	Tulsa (TEX)	AA	12	8	4.62	27	27	1	0	140	128	82	72	13	80	132	.248
	Colorado (NL)	MAJ	0	0	15.75	1	1	0	0	4	8	7	7	3	3	4	.421
2007	Tulsa (TEX)	AA	6	4	2.35	46	0	0	0	57	44	19	15	2	27	59	.210
	Colorado Springs (PCL)	AAA	0	1	3.72	7	0	0	0	10	7	4	4	0	4	12	.200
	Colorado (NL)	MAJ	0	0	9.82	4	0	0	0	4	3	4	4	1	1	3	.214
2008	Colorado (NL)	MAJ	0	0	0.00	1	0	0	0	1	1	0	0	0	0	0	.250
	Colorado Springs (PCL)	AAA	1	0	5.28	52	0	0	0	60	53	38	35	3	56	55	.244
MINOR LEAGUE TOTALS			33	38	4.51	216	101	1	0	634	604	418	318	38	397	582	.252
MAJOR LEAGUE TOTALS			0	0	11.42	6	1	0	0	9	12	11	11	4	4	7	.324

24 CORY RIORDAN, RHP

BORN: May 25, 1986. **B-T:** R-R. **HT.:** 6-4. **WT.:** 200. **DRAFTED:** Fordham, 2007 (6th round). **SIGNED BY:** Mike Garlatti.

Riordan doesn't grab a scout's attention when he is warming up. He is an acquired taste. The Atlantic-10 Conference rookie of the year in 2005, he attracted his most attention as an amateur when he was one of the top starters in the Cape Cod League in 2006. Riordan has a knack for making the right pitch at the right time. He isn't afraid to pitch backward and catch a hitter off balance. He isn't going to overpower hitters with a fastball ranging from 87-92 mph, but it does tail away from lefthanded hitters. There's a bit of bend in his slider, which currently grades as below-average, but he has a good feel for changing speeds and has a solid curveball that is in the mid-70s. The key is he throws strikes. He walked 29 batters in 168 innings at Asheville and ranked second in the league in strikeouts, behind only Giants stud prospect Madison Bumgarner. He could pick up some velocity if he would use his lower body better and lengthen the stride in his delivery. If the slider continues to elude him, he could become a dependable, durable bullpen workhorse.

Year	Club (League)	Class	W	L	ERA	G	GS	CG	SV	IP	H	R	ER	HR	BB	SO	AVG
2007	Tri-City (NWL)	SS	2	3	4.25	14	11	0	1	66	69	34	31	5	17	65	.265
2008	Asheville (SAL)	LoA	8	9	3.65	26	25	2	0	168	185	91	68	18	29	160	.274
MINOR LEAGUE TOTALS			10	12	3.82	40	36	2	1	233	254	125	99	23	46	225	.272

25 CHAZ ROE, RHP

BORN: Oct. 9, 1986. **B-T:** R-R. **HT.:** 6-5. **WT.:** 180. **DRAFTED:** HS—Lexington, Ky., 2005 (1st round supplemental). **SIGNED BY:** Scott Corman.

Roe had arthroscopic surgery on his left knee during spring training, which delayed the start of his 2008 season to May 22. Roe, however, was able to add innings at the end by pitching in the Arizona Fall League. He is 22, but still has a body with projection that hasn't filled out. A quality athlete who had the option of following in his father's footsteps and playing quarterback at Kentucky but opted for pro baseball instead, Roe is reaching a turning point in his career. A decision has to be made on whether he would be better served in the bullpen. He has a quality fastball that sits in the low 90s, and a big-time curveball that is a definite swing and miss pitch. Roe's changeup, however, remains mediocre, and without a third pitch it's tough turning over a lineup enough times to start. He also hangs too many curves and leaves his fastball up in the zone, making him homer-prone. Roe needs to either improve his changeup or significantly improve his fastball command, which is made more difficult by his long, not-yet-mature frame.

Year	Club (League)	Class	W	L	ERA	G	GS	CG	SV	IP	H	R	ER	HR	BB	SO	AVG
2005	Casper (PIO)	R	5	2	4.17	12	12	0	0	50	31	25	23	2	36	55	.175
2006	Asheville (SAL)	LoA	7	4	4.06	19	19	0	0	100	105	54	45	4	47	80	.273
2007	Modesto (CAL)	HiA	7	11	4.33	29	29	2	0	170	148	93	82	17	73	131	.235
2008	Modesto (CAL)	HiA	2	1	5.49	3	3	0	0	20	24	17	12	1	3	16	.279
	Tulsa (TEX)	AA	5	4	4.27	16	16	1	0	105	98	57	50	15	34	70	.248
MINOR LEAGUE TOTALS			26	22	4.29	79	79	3	0	445	406	246	212	39	193	352	.243

26 CORY WIMBERLY, 2B

BORN: Oct. 26, 1983. **B-T:** B-R. **HT.:** 5-8. **WT.:** 180. **DRAFTED:** Alcorn State, 2005 (6th round). **SIGNED BY:** Damon Iannelli.

The Rockies dodged a bullet during the Winter Meetings when Wimberly slid through the Rule 5 draft. He's an Eric Yelding/Bip Roberts type, with plus makeup in addition to tremendous speed. Wimberly understands that he is a speed player and his success depends upon getting on base and creating turmoil. He is a small-ball guy. In three full minor league seasons he has only 51 extra-base hits, but he also has 145 stolen bases. He has been hampered by leg muscle pulls, limiting him to 287 games the last three years. He will bunt and slap at the ball but strikes out more than a speed-oriented hitter should. The Rockies want Wimberly to focus more on making contact. A good fastball will overmatch him. Defensively he provides value in that he can fill in at second, shortstop, third base and center field, but he doesn't have the hands to take advantage of his range, and will drop his arm angle, keeping him from finishing his throws. Wimberly is ready to move up to Triple-A after consecutive seasons at Tulsa.

Year	Club (League)	Class	AVG	G	AB	R	H	2B	3B	HR	RBI	BB	SO	SB	OBP	SLG
2005	Casper (PIO)	R	.381	67	281	58	107	10	0	1	22	18	27	36	.427	.427
2006	Modesto (CAL)	HiA	.325	87	342	72	111	6	4	2	24	30	42	50	.404	.383
2007	Tulsa (TEX)	AA	.268	92	365	63	98	15	1	4	33	19	52	36	.323	.348
2008	Tulsa (TEX)	AA	.291	108	388	65	113	17	2	0	26	41	45	59	.370	.345
MINOR LEAGUE TOTALS			.312	354	1376	258	429	48	7	7	105	108	166	181	.378	.372

27 JONATHAN HERRERA, 2B

BORN: Nov. 3, 1984. **B-T:** B-R. **HT.:** 5-9. **WT.:** 165. **SIGNED:** Venezuela, 2002. **SIGNED BY:** Francisco Cartaya.

Herrera made his big league debut last year, yet was removed from the 40-man roster in November. The Rockies say that was more a statement on the organization's middle infield depth than Herrera's abilities. The club did immediately re-sign him to a minor league deal and invited him to big league spring training. A natural righthanded hitter, Herrera has worked on switch-hitting hard enough that he is actually more in sync from the left side of the plate now. He is a contact hitter, but after stealing 34 bases in Modesto in 2006, he has a combined total of 34 thefts over the last two years. He was originally a shortstop, which gives him utility infielder potential, and he worked in the outfield last season to add to his versatility. Herrera has little power to speak of, limiting his offensive upside and preventing him from being a big league regular.

Year	Club (League)	Class	AVG	G	AB	R	H	2B	3B	HR	RBI	BB	SO	SB	OBP	SLG
2002	Rockies (DSL)	R	.300	61	230	39	69	10	2	0	22	25	27	23	.371	.361
2003	Casper (PIO)	R	.308	39	159	27	49	7	1	1	25	10	25	12	.355	.384
2004	Asheville (SAL)	LoA	.279	95	380	71	106	20	2	6	35	26	80	21	.335	.389
2005	Asheville (SAL)	LoA	.310	19	87	17	27	2	0	0	5	8	11	6	.384	.333
	Modesto (CAL)	HiA	.258	73	310	48	80	9	4	2	30	23	52	9	.315	.332
2006	Modesto (CAL)	HiA	.310	127	487	87	151	20	8	7	77	58	67	34	.382	.427
2007	Tulsa (TEX)	AA	.257	131	509	65	131	24	4	3	40	36	69	18	.315	.338
2008	Colorado (NL)	MAJ	.230	28	61	5	14	1	1	0	3	4	10	1	.277	.279
	Colorado Springs (PCL)	AAA	.310	66	226	40	70	7	0	3	31	19	30	15	.367	.381
MINOR LEAGUE TOTALS			.286	611	2388	394	683	99	21	22	265	205	361	138	.348	.373
MAJOR LEAGUE TOTALS			.230	28	61	5	14	1	1	0	3	4	10	1	.277	.279

28 CHRISTIAN COLONEL, OF/3B/1B

BORN: Dec. 25, 1981. **B-T:** R-R. **HT.:** 6-2. **WT.:** 210. **DRAFTED:** Texas Tech, 2003 (5th round). **SIGNED BY:** Dar Cox.

Colonel has versatility that creates value at the big league level. Primarily a corner infielder, he also played second base, left field and right field for Colorado Springs in 2008, and was the emergency catcher for the SkySox. He is not a home run hitter, so given his positions, the ability to move around will allow him to get some at-bats. Colonel can provide offensive help, even while lacking the kind of power that would profile him as a regular at a corner spot. His career-best for home runs, 17, came in his second try at the Double-A Texas League, but he's hit .300 or better in three of the last four seasons, makes consistent contact with gap power and doesn't strike out much. A league all-star selection each of the last two seasons, Colonel has decent speed, particularly once he is on the bases. He has an accurate arm and soft hands, which allows him to move around defensively without concerns. He isn't on the 40-man roster at age 27, meaning time is running out even for a versatile player like Colonel. He will have to earn a reserve spot on Colorado's roster to avoid a return to Triple-A.

Year	Club (League)	Class	AVG	G	AB	R	H	2B	3B	HR	RBI	BB	SO	SB	OBP	SLG
2003	Tri-City (NWL)	SS	.245	56	208	21	51	8	1	1	21	19	31	9	.331	.308
2004	Asheville (SAL)	LoA	.249	119	429	62	107	23	0	9	65	49	73	35	.343	.366
2005	Modesto (CAL)	HiA	.310	96	364	73	113	32	3	7	60	47	66	1	.396	.473
2006	Tulsa (TEX)	AA	.271	115	387	47	105	24	0	10	43	35	64	11	.335	.411
2007	Tulsa (TEX)	AA	.309	134	527	78	163	47	0	17	84	46	80	6	.362	.495
2008	Colorado Springs (PCL)	AAA	.308	117	429	72	132	33	2	12	65	34	65	7	.360	.478
MINOR LEAGUE TOTALS			.286	637	2344	353	671	167	6	56	338	230	379	69	.356	.434

29 JOE KOSHANSKY, 1B

BORN: May 26, 1982. **B-T:** L-L. **HT.:** 6-4. **WT.:** 225. **DRAFTED:** Virginia, 2004 (6th round). **SIGNED BY:** Jay Matthews.

Koshansky is trapped, with Todd Helton and Garrett Atkins both standing between him and the big leagues. An all-star in each of his five minor league seasons, Koshansky has legitimate big league power. He has hit at least 31 home runs in three of the last four years, and has driven in at least 99 runs in each of those four seasons with a full-season minor league team. With the power, however, comes an aggressiveness at home plate that works against him. He has struck out 663 times (and walked just 280 times) in 2,242 professional at-bats, including 22 strikeouts in 50 big league at-bats the last two years. Koshansky has a long, sweeping swing that produces raw power but is grooved, with plenty of holes for advanced pitchers to exploit. Defensively he is adequate at first and has a strong arm for a first baseman, owing to his background in college, when he pitched as well as hit. However, Koshansky's baseclogging below-average speed and limited athleticism preclude a move to the outfield that would possibly give him a shot at playing time. Unless Helton and Atkins are unable to play, Koshansky—who is on the 40-man roster—will return to Colorado Springs for a third season.

Year	Club (League)	Class	AVG	G	AB	R	H	2B	3B	HR	RBI	BB	SO	SB	OBP	SLG
2004	Tri-City (NWL)	SS	.234	66	239	41	56	18	0	12	43	31	84	1	.330	.460
2005	Asheville (SAL)	LoA	.291	120	453	92	132	31	1	36	103	53	122	6	.373	.603
	Tulsa (TEX)	AA	.267	12	45	5	12	3	0	2	12	2	15	0	.292	.467
2006	Tulsa (TEX)	AA	.284	132	500	84	142	28	0	31	109	64	134	3	.371	.526
2007	Colorado Springs (PCL)	AAA	.295	136	498	79	147	30	2	21	99	67	128	4	.380	.490
	Colorado (NL)	MAJ	.083	17	12	0	1	1	0	0	2	2	5	0	.200	.167
2008	Colorado Springs (PCL)	AAA	.300	122	457	90	137	36	4	31	121	60	158	1	.380	.600
	Colorado (NL)	MAJ	.211	18	38	5	8	3	0	3	8	1	17	0	.250	.526
MINOR LEAGUE TOTALS			.286	588	2192	391	626	146	7	133	487	277	641	15	.369	.541
MAJOR LEAGUE TOTALS			.180	35	50	5	9	4	0	3	10	3	22	0	.236	.440

30 CARLOS MARTINEZ, SS

BORN: Sept. 22, 1988. **B-T:** R-R. **HT.:** 5-11. **WT.:** 175. **SIGNED:** Dominican Republic, 2005. **SIGNED BY:** Felix Feliz.

The Rockies signed Martinez as a 16-year-old to a $650,000 bonus in July 2005, the biggest bonus they ever gave a Latin player. As much as they wanted to land Martinez, the idea behind the bonus was to send a message throughout the Caribbean that the Rockies were ready to be a player in the market. Martinez spent 2006 in the Rookie-level Dominican Summer League and played part-time with Casper in 2007 before finally getting everyday duty with the Ghosts last year. He has surprising line-drive power despite his size, but gets anxious at the plate and gets caught out front when facing soft stuff. He has agility in the field and a strong arm, but carelessness, particularly with his throws, causes errors. He made 25 of them in just 65 games last year. He's a good runner who tied for second in the Pioneer League in stolen bases, though his baserunning needs polishing. After two years in Casper, Martinez needs to make a significant move, which should mean earning a spot in Asheville instead of staying back in extended spring for a third season.

Year	Club (League)	Class	AVG	G	AB	R	H	2B	3B	HR	RBI	BB	SO	SB	OBP	SLG
2006	Rockies (DSL)	R	.221	57	213	22	47	11	1	1	29	13	38	13	.295	.296
2007	Casper (PIO)	R	.200	45	140	15	28	2	1	1	10	3	37	2	.242	.250
2008	Casper (PIO)	R	.284	65	250	41	71	14	3	2	27	21	54	21	.350	.388
MINOR LEAGUE TOTALS			.242	167	603	78	146	27	5	4	66	37	129	36	.306	.323

Detroit Tigers

BY JON PAUL MOROSI

Any analysis of the Tigers' 2008 season begins with what transpired at the Winter Meetings over two days in December 2007. Detroit stunned many by acquiring Miguel Cabrera and Dontrelle Willis from the Marlins for a package of six prospects, with the previously untouchable Cameron Maybin and Andrew Miller among them. The message was clear: After winning the American League pennant in 2006, then missing the postseason in 2007, the Tigers would settle for nothing less than a World Series championship in 2008.

Instead, they finished last in the American League

Central. Their $139 million Opening Day player payroll, the second-highest in baseball, was the most ever for any team to finish with a losing record.

"I thought we had a club that would compete to win a championship, and it's apparent we were significantly off on that, which is my responsibility," club president and general manager Dave Dombrowski said. "I'm embarrassed that you have a very large payroll and you don't do well. Now what we need to do is go out and try to fix it."

The disappointment was wrenching because of how much of Detroit's future had been mortgaged on the lost season. In addition to giving up Maybin and Miller, they also dealt standout prospects Jair Jurrjens and Gorkys Hernandez to the Braves for shortstop Edgar Renteria. While Jurrjens led National League rookies with 13 victories and Hernandez continued to progress through the minors, Renteria played poorly in the field and had one of his worst years at the plate.

In terms of wins and losses, the farm system didn't have a banner year, either. Righthander Rick Porcello was the lone Tiger to make Baseball America's preseason Top 100 Prospects list, or one of BA's minor league Top 10 Prospects lists after the season. Only low Class A West Michigan reached the postseason.

One year after signing Porcello, lefthander Casey Crosby and shortstop Cale Iorg to well-above-slot bonuses, Detroit was more conservative in the 2008 draft. The Tigers spent $3.7 million on signing bonuses—down from $7.9 million in 2007—and didn't exceed Major League Baseball's slot recommendations for any pick.

Despite all the bad news, Detroit officials were encouraged by the development of many prospects during the 2008 season, particularly some of their pitchers.

After arriving in Detroit in a blockbuster trade, Dontrelle Willis bombed in 2008

MORRIS FOSTOFF

TOP 30 PROSPECTS

1. Rick Porcello, rhp	16. Alfredo Figaro, rhp
2. Ryan Perry, rhp	17. Luis Marte, rhp
3. Cale Iorg, ss	18. Scott Green, rhp
4. Casey Crosby, lhp	19. Jonathan Kibler, lhp
5. Jeff Larish, 1b/3b	20. Alex Avila, c
6. Wilkin Ramirez, of	21. Clete Thomas, of
7. Scott Sizemore, 2b	22. Robbie Weinhardt, rhp
8. Cody Satterwhite, rhp	23. Brandon Douglas, ss
9. Dusty Ryan, c	24. Mauricio Robles, lhp
10. Brett Jacobson, rhp	25. Michael Hollimon, 2b/ss
11. Casey Fien, rhp	26. Brandon Hamilton, rhp
12. Ryan Strieby, 1b	27. Danny Worth, ss
13. Casper Wells, of	28. Zach Simons, rhp
14. Rudy Darrow, rhp	29. Kyle Bloom, lhp
15. Freddy Dolsi, rhp	30. Will Rhymes, 2b/ss

Porcello reinforced his status as one of the top arms minor league baseball. Though he was much younger than many hitters he faced, he led the high Class A Florida State League with a 2.66 ERA in his pro debut. The Lakeland bullpen behind him boasted several intriguing arms, including 2008 draft picks Ryan Perry, Cody Satterwhite and Robbie Weinhardt. Strike-throwing righthander Casey Fien and sidearmer Rudy Darrow have a chance to make the Tigers' Opening Day roster in 2009. Crosby made a rapid return from Tommy John surgery and was very impressive in instructional league.

General Manager: Dave Dombrowski. **Farm Director:** Dan Lunetta. **Scouting Director:** David Chadd.

Class	Team	League	W	L	PCT	Finish*	Manager	Affiliated
Majors	Detroit	American	74	88	.457	12th (14)	Jim Leyland	—
Triple-A	Toledo Mud Hens	International	75	69	.521	4th (14)	Larry Parrish	1987
Double-A	Erie SeaWolves	Eastern	68	74	.479	8th (12)	Tom Brookens	2001
High A	Lakeland Tigers	Florida State	67	70	.489	7th (12)	Andy Barkett	1967
Low A	West Michigan Whitecaps	Midwest	72	65	.526	5th (14)	Joe DePastino	1997
Short-season	Oneonta Tigers	New York-Penn	33	31	.446	10th (14)	Ryan Newman	1999
Rookie	GCL Tigers	Gulf Coast	27	31	.466	12th (16)	Basilio Cabrera	1995
Overall 2008 Minor League Record			342	350	.494	19th		

* Finish in overall standings (No. of teams in league). ^League champion.

LAST YEAR'S TOP 30

Rank	Player, Pos.	Status
1.	Rick Porcello, rhp	No. 1
2.	Cale Iorg, ss	No. 3
3.	Scott Sizemore, 2b	No. 7
4.	Michael Hollimon, 2b/ss	No. 25
5.	Yorman Bazardo, rhp	(Free agent)
6.	Jeff Larish, 1b	No. 5
7.	Matt Joyce, of	(Rays)
8.	Danny Worth, ss	No. 27
9.	Francisco Cruceta, rhp	(Free agent)
10.	Brandon Hamilton, rhp	No. 26
11.	Jordan Tata, rhp	Dropped out
12.	Clete Thomas, of	No. 21
13.	Casey Crosby, lhp	No. 4
14.	Wilkin Ramirez, of	No. 6
15.	Freddy Guzman, of	(Mariners)
16.	Brent Clevlen, of	Dropped out
17.	Jeff Gerbe, rhp	Dropped out
18.	Virgil Vasquez, rhp	(Red Sox)
19.	Tony Giarratano, ss	Out of baseball
20.	Brent Dlugach, ss	Dropped out
21.	Charlie Furbush, lhp	Dropped out
22.	Jonah Nickerson, rhp	Dropped out
23.	Jeramy Laster, of	Dropped out
24.	Brennan Boesch, of	Dropped out
25.	Clay Rapada, lhp	Dropped out
26.	Duane Below, lhp	Dropped out
27.	James Skelton, c	(Diamondbacks)
28.	Ryan Strieby, 1b	No. 12
29.	Freddy Dolsi, rhp	No. 15
30.	Preston Larrison, rhp	(Nationals)

BEST TOOLS

Best Hitter for Average	Scott Sizemore
Best Power Hitter	Ryan Strieby
Best Strike-Zone Discipline	James Skelton
Fastest Baserunner	Kyle Peter
Best Athlete	Cale Iorg
Best Fastball	Ryan Perry
Best Curveball	Rick Porcello
Best Slider	Ryan Perry
Best Changeup	Rick Porcello
Best Control	Jonathan Kibler
Best Defensive Catcher	Jeff Kunkel
Best Defensive Infielder	Brent Dlugach
Best Infield Arm	Cale Iorg
Best Defensive Outfielder	Clete Thomas
Best Outfield Arm	Clete Thomas

PROJECTED 2012 LINEUP

Catcher	Gerald Laird
First Base	Miguel Cabrera
Second Base	Scott Sizemore
Third Base	Jeff Larish
Shortstop	Cale Iorg
Left Field	Wilkin Ramirez
Center Field	Curtis Granderson
Right Field	Casper Wells
Designated Hitter	Magglio Ordonez
No. 1 Starter	Justin Verlander
No. 2 Starter	Rick Porcello
No. 3 Starter	Jeremy Bonderman
No. 4 Starter	Casey Crosby
No. 5 Starter	Armando Galarraga
Closer	Ryan Perry

TOP PROSPECTS OF THE DECADE

Year	Player, Pos.	2008 Org.
1999	Gabe Kapler, of	Brewers
2000	Eric Munson, 1b/c	Brewers
2001	Brandon Inge, c	Tigers
2002	Nate Cornejo, rhp	Out of baseball
2003	Jeremy Bonderman, rhp	Tigers
2004	Kyle Sleeth, rhp	Out of baseball
2005	Curtis Granderson, of	Tigers
2006	Justin Verlander, rhp	Tigers
2007	Cameron Maybin, of	Marlins
2008	Rick Porcello, rhp	Tigers

TOP DRAFT PICKS OF THE DECADE

Year	Player, Pos.	2008 Org.
1999	Eric Munson, 1b/c	Brewers
2000	Matt Wheatland, rhp	Out of baseball
2001	Kenny Baugh, rhp	Marlins
2002	Scott Moore, ss	Orioles
2003	Kyle Sleeth, rhp	Out of baseball
2004	Justin Verlander, rhp	Tigers
2005	Cameron Maybin, rhp	Marlins
2006	Andrew Miller, lhp	Marlins
2007	Rick Porcello, rhp	Tigers
2008	Ryan Perry, rhp	Tigers

LARGEST BONUSES IN CLUB HISTORY

Rick Porcello, 2007	$3,580,000
Andrew Miller, 2006	$3,550,000
Eric Munson, 1999	$3,500,000
Kyle Sleeth, 2003	$3,350,000
Justin Verlander, 2004	$3,120,000

DETROIT TIGERS

TOP 2009 ROOKIE: Jeff Larish, 1b/3b. He could ake over at the hot corner if Brandon Inge can't get his bat going.

BREAKOUT PROSPECT: Casey Fien, rhp. His strike-throwing approach and fine performance in the Arizona Fall League could earn him a spot in the Opening Day bullpen.

SLEEPER: Jared Gayhart, rhp. Primarily an outfielder at Rice, Gayhart has moved to the mound full-time and has a fastball that sits at 92-94 mph.

SOURCE OF TOP 30 TALENT			
Homegrown	27	Acquired	3
College	19	Trades	1
Junior college	0	Rule 5 draft	1
High school	3	Independent leagues	0
Draft-and-follow	1	Free agents/waivers	1
Nondrafted free agents	0		
International	4		

Numbers in parentheses indicate prospect rankings.

LF
Wilkin Ramirez (6)
Clete Thomas (21)
Londell Taylor
Brent Wyatt

CF
Casper Wells (13)
Andy Dirks
Kyle Peter
Luis Salas

RF
Brent Clevlen
Avisail Garcia
Alexis Espinoza
Brennan Boesch
Deik Scram

3B
Jeff Larish (5)
Santo DeLeon
Francisco Martinez
Michael Bertram
Roger Tomas

SS
Cale Iorg (3)
Brandon Douglas (23)
Danny Worth (27)
Brent Dlugach
Audy Ciriaco

2B
Scott Sizemore (7)
Michael Hollimon (25)
Will Rhymes (30)
Justin Henry
Gustavo Nunez

1B
Ryan Strieby (12)
Ryan Roberson
Chris Carlson

C
Dusty Ryan (9)
Alex Avila (20)

RHP

Starters	Relievers
Rick Porcello (1)	Ryan Perry (2)
Luis Marte (17)	Cody Satterwhite (8)
Brandon Hamilton (26)	Brett Jacobson (10)
Jonah Nickerson	Casey Fien (11)
Thad Weber	Rudy Darrow (14)
Andrew Hess	Freddy Dolsi (15)
Jeff Gerbe	Alfredo Figaro (16)
Chris Lambert	Scott Green (18)
Luis Sanz	Robbie Weinhardt (22)
Luke Putkonen	Zach Simons (28)
Josh Rainwater	Jared Gayhart
Eddie Bonine	Tyler Stohr
	Jay Sborz
	Anthony Shawler
	Brett Jensen
	Noah Krol

LHP

Starters	Relievers
Casey Crosby (4)	Kyle Bloom (29)
Jonathan Kibler (19)	Clay Rapada
Mauricio Robles (24)	Kris Regas
Jade Todd	Josh Kite
Matt Hoffman	
Charlie Furbush	
Lucas French	
Duane Below	

BEST PURE HITTER: C Alex Avila (5) uses the whole field and batted .305 in low Class A. Whether he can stay behind the plate remains to be seen, but he works hard and the Tigers say he has shown improvement.

BEST POWER HITTER: Avila or SS Brandon Douglas (11). After drilling 17 homers at Alabama in the spring, Avila went just deep once as a pro, partly the result of West Michigan's ballpark. Douglas is more of a doubles hitter than a home run threat.

FASTEST RUNNER: OF Andy Dirks (8) and Douglas have plus speed.

BEST DEFENSIVE PLAYER: Dirks or Douglas. Dirks is a legitimate center fielder, though there are some questions as to whether Douglas will stick at shortstop with his average range and arm strength. He's versatile enough to play anywhere in the infield or outfield.

BEST FASTBALL: The Tigers spent their first four picks on righthanders who can light up a radar gun. Ryan Perry (1) cracked 100 mph seven times in one instructional league outing. Cody Satterwhite (2) and Scott Green (3) hit 97 after turning pro, while Brett Jacobson (4) maxed out at 95. RHP Jared Gayhart (12), who was primarily an outfielder at Rice, has a 92-94 mph fastball and should add velocity as he concentrates on pitching.

BEST SECONDARY PITCH: Perry's slider is more consistent than Satterwhite's, and Detroit likes Perry's changeup enough to consider developing him as a starter.

BEST PRO DEBUT: RHP Robbie Weinhardt (10) reached high Class A while going 3-1, 1.76 with four saves and 48 strikeouts in 41 innings. He pitches to both sides of the plate with a 92 mph fastball with good life and a hard breaking ball. Jacobson went 2-2, 1.52 with a 31-5 K-BB ratio in 30 innings in low Class A.

BEST ATHLETE: Douglas rates an edge over Dirks because he has a little more pop.

MOST INTRIGUING BACKGROUND: The Tigers drafted both of assistant GM Al Avila's sons, Alex and 2B Alan (47), who now attends Nova Southeastern (Fla.). RHP Mark Sorensen's (32) father Lary was an all-star pitcher, while unsigned C Eric Roof's (46, back at Michigan State) father Gene and uncle Phil both played in the majors.

CLOSEST TO THE MAJORS: Perry, Satterwhite, Weinhardt and Jacobson all could progress quickly in relief roles. The Tigers may develop Perry like the Mariners handled Brandon Morrow, speeding him to the majors as a reliever and later turning him into a starter.

BEST LATE-ROUND PICK: Weinhardt or Douglas, who finished the year playing in Double-A.

THE ONE WHO GOT AWAY: Detroit signed its first 17 picks before failing to land RHP Scott Weismann (18), who took his 88-91 mph fastball and good curve to Clemson.

ASSESSMENT: After paying big money to sign Justin Verlander, Cameron Maybin, Andrew Miller and Rick Porcello with their last four first-rounders, the Tigers adhered to MLB's slot recommendations in 2008. They loaded up on power arms, led by Perry, though they all could wind up as relievers.

2007   BONUSES: $8.0 MILLION

MLB lambasted the Tigers for ignoring slot recommendations, but they don't regret spending $7 million on RHP Rick Porcello (1), $1,497,500 on SS Cale Iorg (6) or $748,500 on LHP Casey Crosby (5).

GRADE: B+

2006   BONUSES: $6.0 MILLION

Detroit landed the draft's top prospect, LHP Andrew Miller (1), with the No. 6 pick and sent him to the Marlins a year later in the Miguel Cabrera/Dontrelle Willis trade. 1B Ryan Strieby (4) and 2B Scott Sizemore (5) could crack the big league lineup in the next couple of years.

GRADE: C+

2005   BONUSES: $3.8 MILLION*

OF Cameron Maybin (1) was a steal at No. 10 overall, but he too was packaged in the Cabrera/Willis deal. OF Matt Joyce (12) was a revelation as a rookie last year and shipped to Tampa for Edwin Jackson, while 1B/3B Jeff Larish (5) soon could find a starting job in Detroit.

GRADE: A

2004   BONUSES: $5.4 MILLION*

RHP Justin Verlander (1) may be all the Tigers get out of this crop, but he's not a bad draft class all by himself.

GRADE: B+

*Draft analysis by Jim Callis. Numbers in parentheses indicate draft rounds. *Bonuses for 2004-05 are first 10 rounds only.*

CLIFF WELCH

PROSPECT

RICK PORCELLO, RHP

Born: Dec. 27, 1988.
Ht.: 6-5. **Wt.:** 195.
Bats: R. **Throws:** R.
Drafted: HS—West Orange, N.J., 2007 (1st round).
Signed by: Bill Buck.

Universally regarded as the top high school pitcher in the 2007 draft, Porcello slid to the Tigers at No. 27 overall because of signability concerns. A strong student, Porcello committed to North Carolina but agreed to terms with Detroit shortly before the Aug. 15 deadline. He signed a $7 million major league contract, matching Josh Beckett's record for guaranteed money for a high school pitcher and including a club-record $3.58 million bonus. Porcello is rapidly justifying the investment. Just one year removed from a decorated career at Seton Hall Prep in West Orange, N.J., he led the high Class A Florida State League with a 2.66 ERA in his 2008 pro debut. The only hitch came in August, when he missed two weeks with tonsillitis. His grandfather Sam Dente played for the Indians in the 1954 World Series.

Porcello has all the stuff to be a frontline pitcher in the major leagues. His four-seam fastball has reached 97 mph, but his best pitch is a heavy two-seamer that averages 92 mph and ranges up to 95, with boring action in on the fists of righthanders. With his sinker and tall, athletic body, Porcello is reminiscent of Roy Halladay. Like the Blue Jays ace, Porcello often keeps the ball on the edges of the plate and down in the zone, and he gets a lot of groundouts. Though he has little pro experience, his fastball command is already better than average. He also has shown good feel for his changeup and can throw it in any count. At the Tigers' suggestion, he shelved his slider last season in order to focus on his curveball, and the results were encouraging. Detroit placed him on a 75-pitch limit for each start, and Porcello easily adapted by enticing more swings early in the count. He had an impressive stay in instructional league, a tribute to his strength and endurance. Porcello has earned consistent praise from club officials and teammates alike for his work ethic, humility and ability to assimilate instruction. He's poised beyond his years and has strong, competitive makeup.

Porcello overthrew his 12-to-6 curve at times and therefore struggled to command it. During instructional league, though, he demonstrated an ability to throw his curve for strikes. He should strike out more hitters once the curve is fully developed, but it's difficult to argue with the success he had while pitching to contact. He got nearly 2.5 groundball outs for every air out, an impressive ratio.

At the time Porcello was drafted, many said he was the best high school pitcher since Josh Beckett. After one full season, it's hard to argue with that opinion. Porcello should start 2009 at Double-A Erie, and it's possible—like Beckett in 2001—that he'll reach the majors before the end of his second full pro season. The Tigers rotation was a major weakness in 2008, and their emphasis on winning now could push Porcello to Detroit by midseason. By all indications, he'll have an important role with the big league staff by 2010 at the latest.

Year	Club (League)	Class	W	L	ERA	G	GS	CG	SV	IP	H	R	ER	HR	BB	SO	AVG
2008	Lakeland (FSL)	HiA	8	6	2.66	24	24	0	0	125	116	51	37	7	33	72	.244
MINOR LEAGUE TOTALS			8	6	2.66	24	24	0	0	125	116	51	37	7	33	72	.244

2 RYAN PERRY, RHP

CHRIS PROCTOR

BORN: Feb. 13, 1987. **B-T:** R-R. **HT.:** 6-4. **WT.:** 200. **DRAFTED:** Arizona, 2008 (1st round). **SIGNED BY:** Brian Reid.

Perry was a shortstop when he enrolled at Arizona, but left as one of the hardest throwers in the amateur ranks. He has relatively little experience as a pitcher—and missed half his sophomore season because of injuries sustained in a motorcycle accident—but his electrifying arm sets him apart. He reached 100 mph on radar guns before and after signing with the Tigers for $1.48 million as the 21st overall pick in the 2008 draft. Perry is a tall, imposing figure on the mound, with tremendous arm strength and dominant stuff. His four-seam fastball sits at 97-98 mph. He recently has developed a mid-90s two-seamer with sink and can put hitters away with a power slider in the high-80s. Loose, easy arm action adds to his appeal. He has strong makeup and wants the ball. Inconsistent command prevented Perry from succeeding as a starter at Arizona, and in his pro debut he tended to throw the ball over the heart of the plate when he fell behind in the count. His delivery is clean, but his front shoulder opens early on occasion. He has a changeup in his repertoire, though it's not fully developed. The Tigers plan to let Perry continue developing as a reliever, and he projects as a possible closer. Given the inconsistency of the Detroit bullpen last season, he could reach the majors in 2009.

Year	Club (League)	Class	W	L	ERA	G	GS	CG	SV	IP	H	R	ER	HR	BB	SO	AVG
2008	Tigers (GCL)	R	0	0	0.00	2	0	0	0	2	0	0	0	0	0	4	.000
	Lakeland (FSL)	HiA	1	2	3.86	12	0	0	4	12	15	6	5	0	7	12	.300
MINOR LEAGUE TOTALS			1	2	3.29	14	0	0	4	14	15	6	5	0	7	16	.268

3 CALE IORG, SS

CLIFF WELCH

BORN: Sept. 6, 1985. **B-T:** R-R. **HT.:** 6-2. **WT.:** 175. **DRAFTED:** Alabama, 2007 (6th round). **SIGNED BY:** David Chadd.

One of Detroit's above-slot signings in the 2007 draft, Iorg missed two college seasons while serving on a Mormon mission to Portugal. Iorg's tools and pedigree—his father Garth and uncle Dane played in the big leagues—made the Tigers comfortable signing him out of the sixth round for $1,497,500. Scouts like Iorg's physicality and explosiveness. His batting stance has been compared to that of a young Nomar Garciaparra, and he has the raw power to hit 15-20 homers annually. His range and arm strength are average or a tick above, and they play up because of his good instincts. His speed is solid-average. At times, the two-year layoff is evident in Iorg's play. Despite a relatively compact swing, Iorg had 111 strikeouts at high Class A Lakeland, a sign that his pitch recognition must improve. His intense makeup sometimes works against him. Iorg lost developmental time with a strained throwing shoulder in 2008 but made up at-bats in instructional league. Tigers GM Dave Dombrowski already has predicted that Iorg will become an all-star, and he looks like the club's best homegrown infielder since Travis Fryman. Iorg will move up to Double-A and needs more minor league seasoning, though his raw ability could push him to Detroit by season's end.

Year	Club (League)	Class	AVG	G	AB	R	H	2B	3B	HR	RBI	BB	SO	SB	OBP	SLG
2007	Tigers (GCL)	R	.182	3	11	1	2	0	0	0	0	1	6	0	.308	.182
	Lakeland (FSL)	HiA	.278	5	18	0	5	2	0	0	5	1	5	0	.316	.389
2008	Lakeland (FSL)	HiA	.251	99	383	61	96	15	7	10	47	35	111	22	.329	.405
MINOR LEAGUE TOTALS			.250	107	412	62	103	17	7	10	52	37	122	22	.328	.398

4 CASEY CROSBY, LHP

BORN: Sept. 17, 1988. **B-T:** R-L. **HT.:** 6-5. **WT.:** 200. **DRAFTED:** HS—Maple Park, Ill., 2007 (5th round). **SIGNED BY:** Marty Miller.

An all-state pitcher and wide receiver at his suburban Chicago high school, Crosby has seen his pro career start slowly. It took the commissioner's office two weeks to grant final approval for his above-slot $748,500 bonus in the 2007 draft. Then he hurt his elbow in instructional league and missed virtually all of 2008 while rehabilitating from the Tommy John surgery. When he appeared in the Rookie-level Gulf Coast League less than nine months after the operation, he displayed first-round stuff. Crosby has a strong, lean body and electric left arm. His fastball averages 94 mph and climbs as high as 97 mph with late life. At this point, he has better command of his four-seamer than his two-seamer. He has improved the arm action on his 84-85 mph circle changeup. His delivery offers some deception. The mere fact that he pitched at all in 2008 speaks to his athleticism. Crosby lacks polish because he has so little pro experience. He throws a curveball and sweepy, hard slider that at times he throws as hard as 87 mph, but they're mediocre, and the distinction between them is blurred. He must learn to repeat his pitches more consistently. The Tigers love Crosby's competitive fire and believe he could develop into a quality big league starter. He'll open with one of their Class A affiliates in 2009.

Year	Club (League)	Class	W	L	ERA	G	GS	CG	SV	IP	H	R	ER	HR	BB	SO	AVG
2008	Tigers (GCL)	R	0	0	0.00	3	3	0	0	5	4	1	0	0	3	2	.211
MINOR LEAGUE TOTALS			0	0	0.00	3	3	0	0	5	4	1	0	0	3	2	.211

5 JEFF LARISH, 1B/3B

STEVE MOORE

BORN: Oct. 11, 1982. **B-T:** L-R. **HT.:** 6-2. **WT.:** 200. **DRAFTED:** Arizona State, 2005 (5th round). **SIGNED BY:** Brian Reid.

Larish is a polarizing player among scouts. He has made steady progress through the system, hitting 67 homers in his three full minor league seasons, and acquitted himself well in his big league debut. Larish's greatest asset is raw power to the pull field. Though there's virtually no load with his hands, he can crush fastballs over the inner half of the plate. He's not a threat to steal but has decent speed and good awareness on the bases. He's already an average defender at first base and he could become a plus defender in time. Larish tends to wait for a perfect pitch to hit, which can work against him. He finds himself in a lot of 0-2 counts, and better pitchers were able to exploit his passivity. His detractors don't like his unorthodox batting stance, in which he turns his head to face the pitcher and keeps his hands still prior to the pitch. He has yet to show that he can hit quality strikes over the outside corner, and he struggles with breaking pitches. With Miguel Cabrera entrenched as their long-term first baseman, the Tigers had Larish play third base (which he played as a freshman at Arizona State) in the Arizona Fall League. His rust showed, but his work ethic gives him the chance to become decent at the spot. Barring an injury or trade, Larish likely will start 2009 in Triple-A.

Year	Club (League)	Class	AVG	G	AB	R	H	2B	3B	HR	RBI	BB	SO	SB	OBP	SLG
2005	Tigers (GCL)	R	.222	6	18	1	4	1	0	0	4	4	5	0	.375	.278
	Oneonta (NYP)	SS	.297	18	64	16	19	3	0	6	13	13	6	0	.430	.625
2006	Lakeland (FSL)	HiA	.258	135	457	76	118	34	2	18	65	81	101	9	.379	.460
2007	Erie (EL)	AA	.267	132	454	71	121	25	2	28	101	87	108	6	.390	.515
2008	Toledo (IL)	AAA	.250	103	384	49	96	20	2	21	64	50	109	0	.341	.477
	Detroit (AL)	MAJ	.260	42	104	12	27	6	0	2	16	7	34	2	.306	.375
MINOR LEAGUE TOTALS			.260	394	1377	213	358	83	6	73	247	235	329	15	.375	.488
MAJOR LEAGUE TOTALS			.260	42	104	12	27	6	0	2	16	7	34	2	.306	.375

6 WILKIN RAMIREZ, OF

RODGER WOOD

BORN: Oct. 25, 1985. **B-T:** R-R. **HT.:** 6-2. **WT.:** 190. **SIGNED:** Dominican Republic, 2003. **SIGNED BY:** Ramon Pena.

Originally signed as a third baseman, Ramirez struggled with his defense and his health before moving to left field in 2007. His intriguing tools finally translated into consistent success in 2008, as he enjoyed the best season of his career. Ramirez has a strong, muscular frame. His calling card is his combination of extra-base power and above-average speed, rare for a corner outfielder his size. He has a relatively upright batting stance, with a controlled stride and smooth righthanded swing. His arm strength is a plus tool. He's a confident player who carries himself well on the field. For all Ramirez's offensive ability, his inability to recognize breaking pitches has slowed his progress and explained a poor showing in his brief stay at Triple-A Toledo. His play in left field has improved, though he's still a subpar and, at times, disinterested defender. He doesn't have the instincts of a natural outfielder and probably won't be able to play center or right field. If he learns how to hit breaking balls, Ramirez could be an everyday player and possibly a 20-20 man in the big leagues. But if he does not make more regular contact, it will be difficult for the Tigers to overlook his defensive limitations.

Year	Club (League)	Class	AVG	G	AB	R	H	2B	3B	HR	RBI	BB	SO	SB	OBP	SLG
2003	Tigers (GCL)	R	.275	54	200	34	55	6	7	5	35	13	51	6	.321	.450
2004	Did Not Play—Injured															
2005	West Michigan (MWL)	LoA	.262	131	493	69	129	21	2	16	65	35	143	21	.317	.410
2006	Lakeland (FSL)	HiA	.225	66	249	31	56	10	4	8	33	10	69	8	.259	.394
2007	Lakeland (FSL)	HiA	.273	88	319	48	87	7	4	10	41	20	86	28	.315	.414
	Erie (EL)	AA	.215	34	121	15	26	3	1	2	14	8	38	6	.273	.306
2008	Toledo (IL)	AAA	.083	11	36	2	3	1	0	0	0	1	11	1	.132	.111
	Erie (EL)	AA	.303	110	433	74	131	24	7	19	73	43	138	26	.371	.522
MINOR LEAGUE TOTALS			.263	494	1851	273	487	72	25	60	261	130	536	96	.316	.426

7 SCOTT SIZEMORE, 2B

CLIFF WELCH

BORN: Jan. 4, 1985. **B-T:** R-R. **HT.:** 6-0. **WT.:** 185. **DRAFTED:** Virginia Commonwealth, 2006 (5th round). **SIGNED BY:** Bill Buck.

Sizemore's strong performance in the 2007 Arizona Fall League, where he batted .356 and played solidly at shortstop, seemingly put him in line for a breakthrough season in 2008. However, he played in just 53 games before breaking the hamate bone in his left hand in early June. Sizemore has a short, compact swing that enables him to hit singles and doubles and avoid strikeouts. He's a grinder who draws comparisons to Placido Polanco, whom he ultimately may succeed as Detroit's second baseman. Much like Polanco, he has a knack for getting the barrel of his bat on the ball. He recognizes pitches well and rarely has bad at-bats. He's an average runner who has shown the instincts for stealing bases in the lower minors. Moved to second base in 2007, Sizemore is still just a so-so defender. His arm is adequate and his range is nothing special. He's willing to work and is making progress, however. Near the end of spring training last year, the Tigers started him on a program to improve his lateral movement and first-step quickness. His line-drive stroke isn't conducive to hitting home runs. Sizemore should be ready for spring training, but lingering tenderness in the wrist has been a concern. As long as he does not suffer any more setbacks, he should begin 2009 in Double-A.

Year	Club (League)	Class	AVG	G	AB	R	H	2B	3B	HR	RBI	BB	SO	SB	OBP	SLG
2006	Oneonta (NYP)	SS	.327	70	294	49	96	15	4	3	37	32	47	7	.394	.435
2007	West Michigan (MWL)	LoA	.265	125	438	78	116	33	5	4	48	73	60	16	.376	.390
2008	Lakeland (FSL)	HiA	.286	53	203	32	58	11	1	4	20	24	44	14	.365	.409
MINOR LEAGUE TOTALS			.289	248	935	159	270	59	10	11	105	129	151	37	.379	.409

8 CODY SATTERWHITE, RHP

CHRIS PROCTOR

BORN: Jan. 27, 1987. **B-T:** R-R. **HT.:** 6-4. **WT.:** 205. **DRAFTED:** Mississippi, 2008 (2nd round). **SIGNED BY:** Jim Rough.

Satterwhite had first-round ability but dropped to the second round of the 2008 draft when he struggled as a starter at Ole Miss. The Tigers, who signed him for $606,000, like his power arm better out of the bullpen anyway. He has had more success in that role and closed for Team USA in the summer of 2007. Satterwhite's four-seam fastball is regularly clocked at 94-97 mph and has good movement. His arms and legs are so long that it seems as if he's on top of the hitter by the time he releases the ball. There's deception in his high three-quarters delivery. He has a lean, athletic build. Satterwhite's secondary pitches currently rate as below-average. His slider climbs up to 84-86 mph and has downward tilt, but he doesn't command it well. He doesn't locate his changeup well either. An inability to repeat his delivery is the main reason for his inconsistency, but he made improvements in that regard during instructional league. Satterwhite has the stuff to set up or close and seems likely to continue developing as a reliever. He'll probably start his first full season at Double-A. If he makes progress with his consistency, he could end the year in Detroit.

Year	Club (League)	Class	W	L	ERA	G	GS	CG	SV	IP	H	R	ER	HR	BB	SO	AVG
2008	Tigers (GCL)	R	0	0	0.00	3	0	0	1	2	4	0	0	0	1	2	.400
	Lakeland (FSL)	HiA	0	0	4.42	17	0	0	2	18	16	10	9	0	12	22	.232
MINOR LEAGUE TOTALS			0	0	3.92	20	0	0	3	21	20	10	9	0	13	24	.253

9 DUSTY RYAN, C

BORN: Sept. 2, 1984. **B-T:** R-R. **HT.:** 6-4. **WT.:** 220. **DRAFTED:** Merced (Calif.) JC, D/F 2003 (48th round). **SIGNED BY:** Tom Hinkle.

A torn meniscus in his right knee cost Ryan three months in 2007, and he batted .182 in Hawaii Winter Baseball. His big arm and questionable bat prompted a meeting with team officials last spring, when they discussed the possibility of moving him to the mound. He decided to stick with catching, had his best season as a pro and impressed during a September callup. Incorporating a toe tap as a timing mechanism and repositioning his hands resulted in a smoother, more direct swing that unleashed Ryan's prodigious raw power. He's still known for his plus-plus arm and threw out 46 percent of big league basestealers. As a tall catcher, Ryan has trouble blocking some balls in the dirt. In his 15 games in the majors, Detroit pitchers threw 14 wild pitches. His transfer on throws is also a little slower than it could be. Offensively, he looked vulnerable to the sharper breaking balls he saw in the big leagues. The Tigers gave up promising young righthanders Guillermo Moscoso and Carlos Melo to acquire Gerald Laird from the Rangers, ending Ryan's chances of starting for Detroit in 2009. He could serve as Laird's backup or return to Triple-A to work on improving his receiving skills.

DETROIT TIGERS

Year	Club (League)	Class	AVG	G	AB	R	H	2B	3B	HR	RBI	BB	SO	SB	OBP	SLG
2004	Oneonta (NYP)	SS	.274	54	157	20	43	11	1	4	26	24	52	6	.369	.433
2005	West Michigan (MWL)	LoA	.183	75	241	21	44	11	0	4	21	22	70	3	.255	.278
2006	West Michigan (MWL)	LoA	.245	98	322	49	79	13	2	6	35	44	102	3	.344	.354
2007	Tigers (GCL)	R	.063	6	16	1	1	0	0	0	1	4	5	0	.250	.063
	Lakeland (FSL)	HiA	.214	46	145	17	31	0	0	7	22	18	52	0	.310	.359
2008	Erie (EL)	AA	.253	82	296	46	75	17	2	15	50	38	95	2	.340	.476
	Toldeo (IL)	AAA	.315	20	73	12	23	7	2	2	13	6	27	0	.370	.548
	Detroit (AL)	MAJ	.318	15	44	6	14	2	0	2	7	5	13	0	.380	.500
MINOR LEAGUE TOTALS			.237	381	1250	166	296	59	7	38	168	156	403	14	.326	.386
MAJOR LEAGUE TOTALS			.318	15	44	6	14	2	0	2	7	5	13	0	.380	.500

10 BRETT JACOBSON, RHP

BORN: Nov. 9, 1986. **B-T:** R-R. **HT.:** 6-6. **WT.:** 205. **DRAFTED:** Vanderbilt, 2008 (4th round). **SIGNED BY:** Harold Zonder.

Jacobson has a tremendous arm and great pitcher's body, but he fell to the fourth round of the 2008 draft because of his uneven performance in college. He started games in each of his three seasons at Vanderbilt but finished each year in the bullpen. Signed for $230,000, Jacobson has had his greatest success as a reliever and his mentality is best suited for that role. His best pitch is his fastball, which sat at 88-91 mph when he started but jumps to 92-95 mph when he works out of the bullpen. He did a better job of commanding his heater in his pro debut than he had in college, which led to a successful summer. Jacobson's over-the-top release point creates good downward action on his fastball, and hitters have difficulty elevating it. An exaggerated leg kick and herky-jerky delivery add some deception. He had thrown a slider but had trouble locating it in the strike zone, so Tigers pitching coordinator Jon Matlack helped him install a curveball during instructional league. Jacobson came up with a hard, 12-to-6 breaker that fits his high arm slot better. His changeup is promising but still has a ways to go, and he probably won't use it much as a reliever. He has the power stuff to profile as setup man. Jacobson will move up to high Class A in 2009 and could move quickly.

Year	Club (League)	Class	W	L	ERA	G	GS	CG	SV	IP	H	R	ER	HR	BB	SO	AVG
2008	West Michigan (MWL)	LoA	2	2	1.52	21	0	0	1	30	26	7	5	0	5	31	.236
MINOR LEAGUE TOTALS			2	2	1.52	21	0	0	1	30	26	7	5	0	5	31	.236

11 CASEY FIEN, RHP

BORN: Oct. 21, 1983. **B-T:** R-R. **HT.:** 6-2. **WT.:** 195. **DRAFTED:** Cal Poly, 2006 (20th round). **SIGNED BY:** Tim McWilliam.

Fien is on the cusp of the big leagues, and he has taken an uncommon route to get there. In 2003, he was in the starting rotation at William Penn, an NAIA university in Oskaloosa, Iowa. Then he returned to his native California, pitched for Golden West JC as a sophomore, and transferred to Cal Poly for his junior and senior seasons. The Tigers made him a 20th-round draft pick in 2006, and he has pounded the strike zone ever since. Fien rarely walks batters and is fearless on the mound. He made two scoreless appearances in big league spring-training games last year, though he hadn't pitched above low Class A at the time. Fien's signature pitch is a sinker that he throws at 91-92 mph. He uses the sinker both to get ahead of hitters and as an out pitch. As long as he gets good movement with it down in the zone, he's fine. The rest of his repertoire doesn't worry hitters, as he has a slurvy 82-84 mph breaking ball and a below-average changeup. Fien began 2008 as the closer at Double-A, earned a promotion to Triple-A and finished with a strong performance in the Arizona Fall League. This spring, he'll compete for a spot in Detroit's bullpen.

Year	Club (League)	Class	W	L	ERA	G	GS	CG	SV	IP	H	R	ER	HR	BB	SO	AVG
2006	Oneonta (NYP)	SS	1	1	2.74	20	0	0	1	43	39	17	13	1	8	37	.248
2007	West Michigan (MWL)	LoA	6	1	3.10	39	0	0	6	61	55	28	21	4	10	77	.233
2008	Erie (EL)	AA	3	3	2.96	40	0	0	12	46	38	16	15	5	12	42	.226
	Toledo (IL)	AAA	2	0	2.40	12	0	0	1	15	14	4	4	2	4	17	.246
MINOR LEAGUE TOTALS			12	5	2.90	111	0	0	20	164	146	65	53	12	34	173	.236

12 RYAN STRIEBY, 1B

BORN: Aug. 9, 1985. **B-T:** R-R. **HT.:** 6-5. **WT.:** 235. **DRAFTED:** Kentucky, 2006 (4th round). **SIGNED BY:** Harold Zonder.

In a span of three years, Strieby has leaped from Edmonds (Wash.) CC to status as one of the top position players in the Detroit system. The 2006 Southeastern Conference player of the year in his lone season at Kentucky, he blossomed at high Class A in 2008. He led the pitcher-friendly Florida State League with 29 homers and 94 RBIs despite missing the final 19 games because of a broken hamate bone in his left hand. The Tigers have been impressed with Strieby's ability to absorb information, and his breakthrough year illustrated why. He made some in-season adjustments to his hitting approach, including a more open stance that improved his pitch recognition. He also learned how to drive with his legs and leverage the ball. The result was a 19-homer barrage in 39 games after July 1. Strieby has a tall frame and strong build, with as much raw power to all fields as any player in the system. His swing is more fluid than that of most power hitters, though he still struggles with some breaking pitches. His value lies mostly in his bat, as he's just an adequate defender at first base and a below-average runner. Strieby should be healthy in time to participate in spring training, though hamate injuries have been known to sap a hitter's power for a while. He'll open the season in Double-A.

Year	Club (League)	Class	AVG	G	AB	R	H	2B	3B	HR	RBI	BB	SO	SB	OBP	SLG
2006	Oneonta (NYP)	SS	.241	61	224	26	54	9	0	4	25	25	58	1	.319	.335
2007	West Michigan (MWL)	LoA	.253	123	443	65	112	23	2	16	76	63	78	6	.347	.422
2008	Lakeland (FSL)	HiA	.278	112	421	65	117	19	7	29	94	46	101	0	.352	.563
MINOR LEAGUE TOTALS			.260	296	1088	156	283	51	9	49	195	134	237	7	.343	.459

13 CASPER WELLS, OF

BORN: Nov. 23, 1984. **B-T:** R-R. **HT.:** 6-2. **WT.:** 210. **DRAFTED:** Towson, 2005 (14th round). **SIGNED BY:** Bill Buck.

The Colonial Athletic Association player of the year in 2005, when the Tigers drafted him in the 14th round, Wells spent nearly all of his first three pro seasons playing for Rookie-level or short-season affiliates. But he blossomed into a legitimate prospect last year, thanks to his above-average tools and blue-collar work ethic. He and Mariners outfielder Greg Halman were the only players to amass at least 25 homers and steals in the minors, and Detroit rewarded Wells with a spot on its 40-man roster in November. If he's able to shorten his swing in two-strike situations, he could be a five-tool player. Wells has tremendous raw power, which he showed off in the regular season and in the Arizona Fall League afterward. He has a strong, stocky build and deceptively good speed. As a pitcher at Towson, he displayed a low-90s fastball, and he has a well above-average throwing arm for an outfielder. Wells has very good outfield instincts and can play all three positions well. He also played some first base in the AFL, which should expand his opportunities to reach the majors. Wells crushes lefthanded pitching, which should enable him to reach the majors as a platoon outfielder at the very least. If he can find a way to put the ball in play against the toughest righthanders, the Tigers may have an everyday player on their hands. He's ready for a move to Triple-A.

Year	Club (League)	Class	AVG	G	AB	R	H	2B	3B	HR	RBI	BB	SO	SB	OBP	SLG
2005	Tigers (GCL)	R	.220	45	141	25	31	9	5	5	20	18	59	6	.341	.461
2006	Lakeland (FSL)	HiA	.152	11	33	4	5	1	0	1	4	4	9	1	.300	.273
	Oneonta (NYP)	SS	.229	35	105	19	24	8	0	1	14	9	27	1	.305	.333
2007	Lakeland (FSL)	HiA	.500	2	2	0	1	1	0	0	0	0	1	0	.500	1.000
	Oneonta (NYP)	SS	.265	67	260	46	69	18	11	9	47	18	64	8	.323	.523
2008	West Michigan (MWL)	LoA	.240	50	179	30	43	7	0	10	26	22	39	17	.351	.447
	Erie (EL)	AA	.289	75	270	60	78	18	6	17	53	30	66	8	.376	.589
MINOR LEAGUE TOTALS			.254	285	990	184	251	62	22	43	164	101	265	41	.343	.491

14 RUDY DARROW, RHP

BORN: Feb. 11, 1984. **B-T:** R-R. **HT.:** 5-10. **WT.:** 180. **DRAFTED:** Nicholls State, 2006 (32nd round). **SIGNED BY:** Mike Gambino.

Darrow has one of the most intriguing personal stories of any player in the system, in addition to one of the best fastballs. He began his collegiate athletic career as a wrestler—in the 125-pound weight class—at Labette (Kan.) CC. He separated a growth plate in his throwing elbow as a freshman, which halted his wrestling season but didn't prevent him from playing baseball that spring. Darrow ultimately gave up wrestling, and head baseball coach Aaron Keal moved him from the outfield to the mound. He adopted a sidearm style after undergoing Tommy John surgery in 2004 and blossomed as a prospect last year. He jumped from low Class A to Double-A without missing a beat, and he ended 2008 by pitching well in the Arizona Fall League. Darrow's low arm slot has made his short stature almost irrelevant, especially because his fastball reaches 94 mph with plus sink. Righthanders struggle to lift his pitches and he allowed only one home run in 62 innings last year. His sweeping slider has promise as an out pitch, though he needs to command it better. He throws an occasional changeup, but it's not a big part of his repertoire and he needs a better one to combat lefties. He has good control and a resilient arm. He has a lively personality, aggressive makeup and loves to compete. Darrow could arrive in the majors as a middle reliever sometime this year.

Year	Club (League)	Class	W	L	ERA	G	GS	CG	SV	IP	H	R	ER	HR	BB	SO	AVG
2006	Tigers (GCL)	R	0	0	11.25	5	0	0	1	4	3	5	5	0	4	5	.200
2007	Oneonta (NYP)	SS	4	3	2.41	26	0	0	1	37	30	11	10	0	10	39	.222
2008	West Michigan (MWL)	LoA	4	2	1.85	33	0	0	4	49	39	13	10	1	15	43	.213
	Erie (EL)	AA	1	1	2.63	14	0	0	6	14	13	7	4	0	8	14	.241
MINOR LEAGUE TOTALS			9	6	2.52	78	0	0	12	104	85	36	29	1	37	101	.220

15 FREDDY DOLSI, RHP

BORN: Jan. 9, 1983. **B-T:** R-R. **HT.:** 6-0. **WT.:** 160. **SIGNED:** Dominican Republic, 2003. **SIGNED BY:** Ramon Pena.

Prior to last season, Dolsi was a hard-throwing 25-year-old who had one inning of experience above Class A. He pitched well in big league camp and earned his first callup in early May, after injuries and inconsistencies created an opening in Detroit's bullpen. He adapted to the majors quickly, and Tigers manager Jim Leyland called upon him to protect leads in the seventh and eighth innings. But then Dolsi struggled in late June and through most of July, precipitating a return to the minors. He experienced some fatigue in his throwing shoulder but was never placed on the disabled list. Dolsi throws a lively, four-seam fastball that maintained plus velocity (94-96 mph) and movement throughout the season. He also has a two-seamer that averages 87-89 mph and rides in on the hands of righthanders. The downside with his fastball is that his command of the pitch is average at best. He's confident enough in his slider to throw it in almost any count, but it's inconsistent. Dolsi is small and generates his velocity with a lot of effort in his quick delivery, which hampers his control. He spins off the mound, which leaves him in an awkward fielding position. Dolsi probably could use some more development in the minors, but it wouldn't be a surprise if he made the Opening Day roster.

Year	Club (League)	Class	W	L	ERA	G	GS	CG	SV	IP	H	R	ER	HR	BB	SO	AVG
2003	Tigers (GCL)	R	1	1	4.70	8	2	0	0	23	27	20	12	1	12	19	.281
	Tigers (DSL)	R	3	1	1.96	4	4	0	0	23	18	10	5	0	5	21	.202
2004	Tigers (DSL)	R	6	7	2.39	14	14	0	0	83	60	40	22	2	31	97	.199
2005	West Michigan (MWL)	LoA	1	0	2.43	23	0	0	0	37	36	16	10	5	14	27	.247
2006	Lakeland (FSL)	HiA	4	4	4.01	30	0	0	1	43	47	25	19	5	17	29	.278
2007	Lakeland (FSL)	HiA	5	3	3.48	48	0	0	23	52	52	24	20	3	17	44	.267
	Erie (EL)	AA	0	0	0.00	1	0	0	0	1	1	0	0	0	1	0	.250
2008	Lakeland (FSL)	HiA	0	1	6.14	9	0	0	5	7	7	5	5	1	3	11	.241
	Erie (EL)	AA	0	0	0.00	3	0	0	2	3	1	0	0	0	1	1	.111
	Toledo (IL)	AAA	0	0	1.00	4	0	0	1	9	5	1	1	0	3	7	.167
	Detroit (AL)	MAJ	1	5	3.97	42	0	0	2	48	50	21	21	3	28	29	.267
MINOR LEAGUE TOTALS			20	17	3.01	144	20	0	32	281	254	141	94	17	104	256	.238
MAJOR LEAGUE TOTALS			1	5	3.97	42	0	0	2	48	50	21	21	3	28	29	.267

16 ALFREDO FIGARO, RHP

BORN: July 7, 1984. **B-T:** R-R. **HT.:** 6-0. **WT.:** 173. **SIGNED:** Dominican Republic, 2004. **SIGNED BY:** Angel Santana (Dodgers).

Figaro originally signed with the Dodgers, but when Los Angeles released him after his first pro season, Detroit grabbed him the following spring. He has been a starter but seems destined to move to the bullpen—the same career path traveled by his cousin, Tigers reliever Fernando Rodney. Figaro has a strong, wiry body and an arm that works well. He's capable of whipping fastballs at 93-96 mph and has touched 98. He seems to have his best velocity when he focuses on throwing strikes rather than lighting up radar guns. Figaro is animated on the mound, which makes it difficult to predict how he'll perform over the course of each start. Shorter relief stints would give him a better chance to repeat his delivery. His effective changeup bears a slight resemblance to Rodney's signature pitch, though it doesn't have the same devastating movement. Figaro has a pair of hard breaking balls but struggles to throw either his curveball or slider for strikes. In many respects, he has a similar profile to Freddy Dolsi. Figaro had a strong showing in instructional league last year, which could allow him to open 2009 in Double-A. Detroit added him to its 40-man roster in November.

Year	Club (League)	Class	W	L	ERA	G	GS	CG	SV	IP	H	R	ER	HR	BB	SO	AVG
2004	Dodgers1 (DSL)	R	0	0	9.82	5	0	0	0	7	10	10	8	0	7	6	.303
2005	Tigers (DSL)	R	8	2	1.87	14	13	0	1	77	51	29	16	0	31	100	.181
2006	Tigers (GCL)	R	3	1	0.70	14	4	0	1	38	29	7	3	0	12	31	.210
2007	Lakeland (FSL)	HiA	0	2	4.76	5	4	0	0	23	26	15	12	0	6	6	.292
	Oneonta (NYP)	SS	4	2	3.38	11	11	0	0	53	56	23	20	1	16	40	.269
2008	West Michigan (MWL)	LoA	12	2	2.05	19	19	2	0	123	99	35	28	0	30	96	.218
	Lakeland (FSL)	HiA	0	5	4.91	6	5	1	0	29	37	22	16	2	12	23	.311
MINOR LEAGUE TOTALS			27	14	2.64	74	56	3	2	351	308	141	103	3	114	302	.233

17 LUIS MARTE, RHP

BORN: Aug. 26, 1986. **B-T:** R-R. **HT.:** 5-11. **WT.:** 170. **SIGNED:** Dominican Republic, 2005. **SIGNED BY:** Ramon Pena.

Marte had been an off-the-radar prospect prior to his up-and-down 2008 season. In early May, based on a series of strong performances at high Class A, he was regarded as one of the best pitchers in the system. He was regularly reaching 93-94 mph with his four-seam fastball and showing good secondary stuff. Then he came down with a sprained right elbow after a slider-heavy start at Double-A. He missed two months, returned in late July and wasn't as consistent over the remainder of the season. Marte ended his year in the Arizona Fall

League, where his fastball velocity was down in his first two starts there before spiking to an average of 92 mph and peak of 95 in his third. At the very least, it appears that his arm strength has returned. When healthy, Marte has a well-developed repertoire, with a low-90s fastball, an 81-84 mph power slider and a changeup. He throws more four-seam fastballs than running two-seamers, but he's at his best when he mixes the two. He has good command and is eager to challenge hitters. He also has shown an ability to make adjustments. Marte's injury history and short stature lead to concerns about a lack of durability that could prevent him from reaching his considerable ceiling. But he's only 22 and has time on his side. He'll likely start this season back in Double-A.

Year	Club (League)	Class	W	L	ERA	G	GS	CG	SV	IP	H	R	ER	HR	BB	SO	AVG
2006	Tigers (DSL)	R	8	0	1.38	11	11	2	0	65	41	12	10	0	15	90	.176
2007	Tigers (GCL)	R	2	0	0.75	2	2	1	0	12	8	1	1	0	1	12	.186
	West Michigan (MWL)	LoA	1	2	2.83	15	2	0	3	35	28	13	11	2	11	36	.220
2008	Lakeland (FSL)	HiA	3	2	1.98	7	7	0	0	41	29	11	9	1	11	41	.196
	Tigers (GCL)	R	0	1	3.60	1	0	0	0	5	5	2	2	0	0	5	.238
	Erie (EL)	AA	4	4	5.05	10	10	0	0	57	57	35	32	8	26	32	.264
MINOR LEAGUE TOTALS			18	9	2.72	46	32	3	3	215	168	74	65	11	64	216	.213

18 SCOTT GREEN, RHP

BORN: Aug. 10, 1985. **B-T:** R-R. **HT.:** 6-7. **WT.:** 240. **DRAFTED:** Kentucky, 2008 (3rd round). **SIGNED BY:** Harold Zonder.

Green gambled and lost when he turned down an $800,000 offer from the Red Sox in the summer of 2007. He had missed all of 2006 after Tommy John surgery and pitched just 18 innings at Kentucky in 2007 before Boston drafted him in the 15th round. He pitched well in the Cape Cod League, piquing the Red Sox's interest, but opted to return to school in hopes of becoming a first-round pick. Instead, he had had a disappointing spring, lost his job in Kentucky's rotation and dropped to the third round, where he signed for $373,000. After turning pro, Green showed quality stuff as a reliever. He sat at 94-95 mph and touched 97 mph with his fastball, and he hit 87-88 mph with his slider. His 6-foot-7 frame and high arm slot allow him to drive his pitches down in the strike zone. However, he has significant effort in his delivery, costing him life and command on his pitches. His slider is inconsistent and his changeup is less reliable. The Tigers are considering returning him to the rotation, but that may be a stretch because he has yet to show much durability. Besides blowing out his elbow, he had a series of minor injuries in college and he missed two weeks in August with a right forearm strain. One scout who saw him in the Midwest League described Green's upside as becoming another Mike Timlin. Green figures to open 2009 in high Class A.

Year	Club (League)	Class	W	L	ERA	G	GS	CG	SV	IP	H	R	ER	HR	BB	SO	AVG
2008	West Michigan (MWL)	LoA	1	2	3.57	15	0	0	2	18	14	9	7	1	5	15	.219
MINOR LEAGUE TOTALS			1	2	3.57	15	0	0	2	18	14	9	7	1	5	15	.219

19 JONATHAN KIBLER, LHP

BORN: Aug. 10, 1986. **B-T:** L-L. **HT.:** 6-4. **WT.:** 215. **DRAFTED:** Michigan State, 2007 (30th round). **SIGNED BY:** Tom Osowski.

In each of the past three seasons, the Tigers' minor league pitcher of the year has been a late-round pick from a Midwestern college: Burke Badenhop in 2006, Duane Below in 2007 and Kibler in 2008. Kibler, who pitched at Western Carolina and Dundalk (Md.) CC before transferring to Michigan State, has the highest ceiling of the group. He led the low Class A Midwest League in wins (14) and ERA (1.75). Kibler has an easy, repeatable, straight-ahead delivery and spots his fastball to both sides of the plate. His trademark is a sinker that averages 89 mph and tops out at 92. It jumps on hitters because of deception in his delivery. He doesn't have plus velocity but he can get outs up in the strike zone because of his superior command. His secondary pitches are an effective 77-81 mph slurve and a usable 76-79 mph changeup. Kibler's stuff is just average at best, raising some concern about his long-term projection. Though his strong frame should enable him to be a workhorse, shoulder fatigue forced him to the disabled list late in August. The injury isn't serious, and he went to instructional league to address his fielding deficiencies. Kibler was the unquestioned ace at West Michigan in 2008, but he's not likely to have that role in the majors. He should get there, very possibly as a steady No. 4 or 5 starter. This year, high Class A awaits.

Year	Club (League)	Class	W	L	ERA	G	GS	CG	SV	IP	H	R	ER	HR	BB	SO	AVG
2007	Tigers (GCL)	R	3	2	2.43	7	5	0	0	30	26	10	8	0	6	23	.241
	Oneonta (NYP)	SS	0	0	2.38	2	2	0	0	11	8	3	3	0	3	11	.200
2008	West Michigan (MWL)	LoA	14	5	1.75	23	23	2	0	154	103	39	30	4	32	126	.190
MINOR LEAGUE TOTALS			17	7	1.89	32	30	2	0	195	137	52	41	4	41	160	.198

20 ALEX AVILA, C

BORN: Jan. 29, 1987. **B-T:** L-R. **HT.:** 5-11. **WT.:** 210. **DRAFTED:** Alabama, 2008 (5th round).
SIGNED BY: Jim Rough.

Alabama head coach Jim Wells made Avila a full-time catcher prior to the 2008 season, and his draft stock improved greatly as a result. Avila batted .343 with a team-leading 17 home runs, numbers that looked even better considering he was a lefthanded hitter playing a premium position. When Detroit took him in the fifth round of last year's draft, it was Avila's father—Tigers assistant GM Al—who called to tell him the news. Detroit also drafted Avila's other son, second baseman Alan in the 47th round, though he opted to attend Nova Southeastern (Fla.). Alex signed quickly to low Class A and reported directly to low Class A, where he gained valuable experience behind the plate. He's a natural hitter who should contribute enough offensively to profile as an everyday catcher. He has below-average running speed but will get his share of doubles thanks to his line-drive stroke. A .305 average in his pro debut showed that he had little trouble adjusting to wood bats. Avila is a very intuitive player, thanks in part to his bloodlines, and his feel for the game should help him develop into a big league catcher. Though he needs to refine his receiving skills, he made strides in that department during instructional league. His throwing arm has a chance to be average, and he threw out 33 percent of basestealers in his debut. He handles a pitching staff well. Avila will open 2009 in high Class A.

Year	Club (League)	Class	AVG	G	AB	R	H	2B	3B	HR	RBI	BB	SO	SB	OBP	SLG
2008	West Michigan (MWL)	LoA	.305	58	213	21	65	14	0	1	22	27	41	0	.383	.385
MINOR LEAGUE TOTALS			.305	58	213	21	65	14	0	1	22	27	41	0	.383	.385

21 CLETE THOMAS, OF

BORN: Nov. 14, 1983. **B-T:** L-R. **HT.:** 5-11. **WT.:** 195. **DRAFTED:** Auburn, 2005 (6th round).
SIGNED BY: Jerome Cochran.

Thomas hadn't played above Double-A prior to 2008 but caught the eye of Tigers manager Jim Leyland in spring training. Soon after the team learned Curtis Granderson would begin the regular season on the disabled list, Thomas was plucked from minor league camp and placed on the 25-man roster. His first big league at-bat was an 11th-inning double on Opening Day, which reflected his quick bat and competitive calm. He uses the whole field and has gap power, but he strikes out too much because he has trouble with breaking pitches. Thomas runs well and is an above-average defender. Capable of playing all three outfield positions, he takes good routes on flyballs and throws well. He had two stints with Detroit in the first half then slumped at Triple-A after the all-star break, for a reason that became clear only after the season was over. Thomas tore a ligament in his throwing elbow prior to a June 21 game in San Diego but played through the injury for more than two months. He underwent Tommy John surgery in September, and it's likely that he'll begin this season on the disabled list. The injury will cost him development time and hurt his chances to contribute in the majors this year. His tools and grit should make him a big leaguer in the long run, perhaps as a platoon outfielder.

Year	Club (League)	Class	AVG	G	AB	R	H	2B	3B	HR	RBI	BB	SO	SB	OBP	SLG
2005	Oneonta (NYP)	SS	.386	18	70	19	27	5	1	1	14	12	11	9	.488	.529
	West Michigan (MWL)	LoA	.284	51	194	39	55	8	5	0	11	21	37	11	.356	.376
2006	Lakeland (FSL)	HiA	.257	132	529	67	136	30	5	6	40	56	127	34	.333	.367
2007	Erie (EL)	AA	.280	137	528	97	148	30	6	8	53	59	110	18	.359	.405
2008	Detroit (AL)	MAJ	.284	40	116	7	33	9	1	1	9	14	26	2	.366	.405
	Toledo (IL)	AAA	.247	76	291	44	72	18	2	9	45	37	88	29	.333	.416
MINOR LEAGUE TOTALS			.272	414	1612	266	438	91	19	24	163	185	373	101	.352	.396
MAJOR LEAGUE TOTALS			.284	40	116	7	33	9	1	1	9	14	26	2	.366	.405

22 ROBBIE WEINHARDT, RHP

BORN: Dec. 8, 1985. **B-T:** R-R. **HT.:** 6-2. **WT.:** 205. **DRAFTED:** Oklahoma State, 2008 (10th round). **SIGNED BY:** Chris Wimmer.

In Weinhardt, the Tigers got a steal for $15,000 in the 10th round of the 2008 draft. While he can't match the pure velocity of the pitchers Detroit took at the top of the draft, he throws plenty hard and has the pitchability to reach the big leagues quickly. His fastball ranges from 90-93 mph and has touched 94. More important, he can throw it to both sides of the plate and it has great movement, boring in on the hands of righthanders. He baffled hitters in his pro debut and didn't allow an earned run in his first 28 innings. Batters simply do not get good swings against Weinhardt because of the late life on his fastball and some deception in his delivery. He throws mostly two- and four-seam fastballs, and he has a good understanding of when to use each of them. He also commands a circle changeup that has some sink. His hard slider has a chance to be average but looked flat at the end of last year. His strong frame gives the Tigers reason to believe Weinhardt can develop into a resilient middle reliever. He could spend his first full pro season in Double-A.

Year	Club (League)	Class	W	L	ERA	G	GS	CG	SV	IP	H	R	ER	HR	BB	SO	AVG
2008	Tigers (GCL)	R	0	0	0.00	3	0	0	0	6	6	3	0	0	2	4	.261
	Lakeland (FSL)	HiA	3	1	2.04	21	0	0	4	35	19	11	8	1	11	44	.162
MINOR LEAGUE TOTALS			3	1	1.76	24	0	0	4	41	25	14	8	1	13	48	.179

23 BRANDON DOUGLAS, SS

BORN: Aug. 27, 1985. **B-T:** R-R. **HT.:** 6-0. **WT.:** 185. **DRAFTED:** Northern Iowa, 2008 (11th round). **SIGNED BY:** Marty Miller.

If last summer was an indication of things to come, Douglas might have been among the best late-round picks in the 2008 draft. A natural hitter who has been compared to fellow Iowan Casey Blake, Douglas made four stops in the system, performing well at each level and finishing in Double-A. Not bad for an 11th-round pick who signed for $65,000. A good athlete, Douglas uses a compact swing to pull a lot of base hits into left field. He can be a free swinger but still has a knack for putting the bat on the ball. Once he becomes more selective, he could hit 25-30 doubles and 10-15 homers over a full season. His speed is a tick above average and he has the instincts to steal bases. Douglas spent most of last summer as a shortstop, but average range and arm strength may make him a better fit at second base. He'll need to become a more sure-handed fielder in order to stay in the middle of the diamond. A super-utility role could also be in his future. The Tigers won't be afraid to challenge Douglas with an assignment to high Class A or perhaps Double-A in 2009.

Year	Club (League)	Class	AVG	G	AB	R	H	2B	3B	HR	RBI	BB	SO	SB	OBP	SLG
2008	Tigers (GCL)	R	.333	7	27	9	9	2	0	1	5	3	2	3	.387	.519
	West Michigan (MWL)	LoA	.436	9	39	5	17	3	0	1	8	1	2	0	.463	.590
	Erie (EL)	AA	.263	5	19	2	5	0	0	1	2	0	2	1	.263	.421
	Oneonta (NYP)	SS	.312	47	189	33	59	5	5	1	12	10	19	13	.350	.407
MINOR LEAGUE TOTALS			.328	68	274	47	90	10	5	4	27	14	25	17	.364	.445

24 MAURICIO ROBLES, LHP

BORN: March 5, 1989. **B-T:** L-L. **HT.:** 5-10. **WT.:** 160. **SIGNED:** Venezuela, 2006. **SIGNED BY:** German Robles.

The Tigers fielded their own Rookie-level Venezuelan Summer League team for the first time in 2007, and Robles became the first player from that roster to reach a full-season affiliate. He was among the youngest starters in the low Class A Midwest League last year, when he had a remarkable run of success at pitcher-friendly Fifth Third Ballpark. He allowed only one earned run in 51 innings—for a 0.18 ERA. Inconsistent command and fastball velocity was an issue on the road, where he had a 5.80 ERA with 39 walks in 40 innings. Reports vary on Robles' fastball. When he's on his game, he has a 91-94 mph heater with tailing life. When he's not, it sits at 88-91 mph with less movement. His velocity has been known to fluctuate even from inning to inning, though he peaked at 95 during instructional league. Short but athletic, Robles was an outfielder before signing in 2006. His inability to repeat his delivery is a significant concern. His curveball averages 82-83 mph and has some depth but lacks a consistent shape. He throws the curve with a noticeably slower arm speed. He has below-average command across the board, and his changeup isn't well developed. Robles remains very raw but he could rise through the system once he learns to harness and trust his stuff. First-pitch strikes will be vital to his development this year in Class A.

Year	Club (League)	Class	W	L	ERA	G	GS	CG	SV	IP	H	R	ER	HR	BB	SO	AVG
2006	Tigers/Marlins (VSL)	R	0	1	3.38	14	0	0	0	16	17	7	6	0	16	20	.279
2007	Tigers (VSL)	R	3	6	3.26	14	14	0	0	69	60	33	25	4	27	83	.237
2008	West Michigan (MWL)	LoA	5	3	2.66	23	16	0	0	91	54	27	27	2	54	79	.176
MINOR LEAGUE TOTALS			8	10	2.96	51	30	0	0	176	131	67	58	6	97	182	.211

25 MICHAEL HOLLIMON, 2B/SS

BORN: June 14, 1982. **B-T:** B-R. **HT.:** 6-1. **WT.:** 185. **DRAFTED:** Oral Roberts, 2005 (16th round). **SIGNED BY:** Steve Taylor.

After an uneven college career, Hollimon has exceeded expectations as a 16th-round pick in the 2005 draft. He has made a steady climb through the farm system, earning high marks for his offensive tools and makeup. An injury to Ramon Santiago brought Hollimon to the majors last year, and he homered off Mark Lowe during his brief stint with the Tigers. But issues with his left shoulder, which he dislocated in spring training, sidetracked Hollimon after that. The pain returned in June and was so severe that he had to change his batting stance. He slumped badly at Triple-A in the second half and underwent surgery in September to repair a torn labrum. He's expected to miss roughly half of the 2009 season. That will make it challenging for him to return to the majors in 2009, but there's little doubt that Hollimon has big league talent. His body is strong and compact, and he offers raw power and average speed. His swing can get long, however, leaving him vulnerable to inside fastballs and resulting in an abnormally high number of strikeouts for a switch-hitter. Hollimon has seen time at second base, third base and shortstop, and he fits best at second with his average range and fringy arm. He's already 26 and unlikely to get much better, but he could provide value as a super-utility player capable of moving around the infield and outfield.

Year	Club (League)	Class	AVG	G	AB	R	H	2B	3B	HR	RBI	BB	SO	SB	OBP	SLG
2005	Oneonta (NYP)	SS	.275	72	255	66	70	13	10	13	53	50	76	8	.391	.557
2006	West Michigan (MWL)	LoA	.278	128	449	69	125	29	13	15	54	77	124	19	.386	.501
2007	Erie (EL)	AA	.282	127	471	91	133	34	8	14	76	64	121	17	.371	.478
	Toledo (IL)	AAA	.211	5	19	2	4	1	1	0	2	1	4	0	.250	.368
2008	Detroit (AL)	MAJ	.261	11	23	4	6	2	1	1	2	1	6	0	.280	.565
	Toledo (IL)	AAA	.211	91	331	56	70	16	4	15	33	45	109	7	.306	.420
MINOR LEAGUE TOTALS			.264	423	1525	284	402	93	36	57	218	237	434	51	.364	.484
MAJOR LEAGUE TOTALS			.261	11	23	4	6	2	1	1	2	1	6	0	.280	.565

26 BRANDON HAMILTON, RHP

BORN: Dec. 25, 1988. **B-T:** R-R. **HT.:** 6-2. **WT.:** 205. **DRAFTED:** HS—Millbrook, Ala., 2007 (1st round supplemental). **SIGNED BY:** Jim Rough.

The Tigers love Hamilton's power stuff and high ceiling, even if he struggled during his first full season as a pro. They gave the 2007 supplemental first-rounder the chance to start at low Class A in mid-May after he opened the year in extended spring training, but he overthrew and struggled with his control. He regained his footing after a demotion to the Gulf Coast League, and by the end of instructional league, Hamilton had made progress with his secondary pitches. At this point, he has better command of his plus power curveball (82-83 mph) and changeup (79-80 mph) than his fastball. He has developed confidence in his changeup, which has sinking movement. Hamilton's four-seam fastball averages 91-92 mph and peaked at 96 in his final outing of instructional league. He also has learned to blend in some two-seamers. His fastball command will have to improve in order for him to succeed at upper levels. He also needs to work on repeating his delivery, which has a lot of effort and moving parts. Hamilton has the raw ability to pitch in the major leagues and will get a second chance at low Class A this year.

Year	Club (League)	Class	W	L	ERA	G	GS	CG	SV	IP	H	R	ER	HR	BB	SO	AVG
2007	Tigers (GCL)	R	1	1	3.10	7	5	0	0	20	12	9	7	2	12	23	.171
2008	West Michigan (MWL)	LoA	0	5	5.01	8	6	0	0	32	34	25	18	2	28	22	.286
	Tigers (GCL)	R	5	1	1.86	9	7	0	0	39	27	12	8	1	13	42	.186
MINOR LEAGUE TOTALS			6	7	3.25	24	18	0	0	91	73	46	33	5	53	87	.219

27 DANNY WORTH, SS

BORN: Sept. 30, 1985. **B-T:** R-R. **HT.:** 6-1. **WT.:** 180. **DRAFTED:** Pepperdine, 2007 (2nd round). **SIGNED BY:** Tim McWilliam.

After reaching Double-A within months of signing in 2007, Worth had a somewhat disappointing first full season of pro ball. He has been billed as a plus defender but committed 18 errors in 80 games. Bursitis behind his throwing shoulder limited him to just six games in the final two months. The bursitis, which affected his shoulder and back, likely explains why his offensive production dropped late in the season. It also raised concerns about Worth's overall durability. He's slightly built and wore down in the second half. He entered the offseason knowing that he must add more strength in order to make it as an everyday player. Worth has limited ceiling at the plate. He doesn't have great bat speed or much power, so while he may hit for a decent average with his share of walks and a few doubles, that's about it. He has below-average speed, though he does show good instincts on the bases. Defense is where Worth stands out. He has good range, reliable hands and a smooth transfer. Though his arm strength is just average, he enhances it with a quick release. With a solid spring, Worth could break camp as the Tigers' everyday shortstop at Triple-A. He needs to have a strong 2009 season in order to remain one level ahead of Cale Iorg.

Year	Club (League)	Class	AVG	G	AB	R	H	2B	3B	HR	RBI	BB	SO	SB	OBP	SLG
2007	Lakeland (FSL)	HiA	.251	51	171	22	43	9	2	2	21	18	39	6	.325	.363
	Erie (EL)	AA	.429	5	14	4	6	2	1	0	4	1	1	1	.438	.714
2008	Erie (EL)	AA	.254	79	295	44	75	18	3	5	33	32	59	8	.331	.386
	Toledo (IL)	AAA	.500	1	2	0	1	0	0	0	0	0	0	0	.500	.500
MINOR LEAGUE TOTALS			.259	136	482	70	125	29	6	7	58	51	99	15	.333	.388

28 ZACH SIMONS, RHP

BORN: May 23, 1985. **B-T:** L-R. **HT.:** 6-3. **WT.:** 200. **DRAFTED:** Everett (Wash.) CC, 2005 (2nd round). **SIGNED BY:** Gary Wilson (Rockies).

Despite being a former second-round pick, Simons wasn't among the Rockies' top relief prospects at the start of last season. On April 30, Colorado sent him to Detroit in a trade for Jason Grilli. Simons embraced the fresh start and pitched impressively in high Class A. After initially struggling with his command, he allowed only 20 hits over his final 44 innings. Simons throws a four-seam fastball that sits in the low-90s, tops out at 95 mph and seems to have a burst of life as it nears the batter. His heater's explosiveness causes hitters to jam themselves, resulting in a lot of weak flyouts. His out pitch is a power curveball with good depth. When he commands it well, it's a plus pitch. His changeup pales in comparison to his other two pitches, but it could become an adequate third offering. He tends to struggle when he speeds up his delivery, resulting in more effort and less control. The Tigers are pleased with the manner in which he has absorbed instruction during the short time he's been with the organization. As long as he can locate his fastball and curve, Simons should reach the big leagues as a middle reliever. He'll advance to Double-A in 2009.

Year	Club (League)	Class	W	L	ERA	G	GS	CG	SV	IP	H	R	ER	HR	BB	SO	AVG
2005	Tri-City (NWL)	SS	6	5	3.81	15	15	0	0	83	75	39	35	8	23	40	.240
2006	Asheville (SAL)	LoA	6	9	6.29	26	21	1	0	112	134	91	78	14	49	60	.295
2007	Asheville (SAL)	LoA	8	2	4.52	42	0	0	1	70	69	37	35	6	31	62	.261
2008	Modesto (CAL)	HiA	1	0	2.70	7	0	0	0	13	12	5	4	1	9	14	.255
	Lakeland (FSL)	HiA	5	2	2.36	39	0	0	2	53	29	15	14	2	30	61	.166
MINOR LEAGUE TOTALS			26	18	4.52	129	36	1	3	331	319	187	166	31	142	237	.255

29 KYLE BLOOM, LHP

BORN: Feb. 21, 1983. **B-T:** R-L. **HT.:** 6-4. **WT.:** 186. **DRAFTED:** Illinois State, 2004 (5th round).
SIGNED BY: Duane Gustavson (Pirates).

Bloom has yet to pitch above Double-A in five pro seasons, but he intrigued the Tigers enough that they took him in the major league Rule 5 draft at the Winter Meetings. Now he has to stick on their big league roster in 2009, or else they have to put him on waivers and offer him back to the Pirates for half of the $50,000 draft price. Bloom's strengths are that he's lefthanded and has learned how to command his 88-91 mph fastball to all four quadrants of the strike zone with decent movement. He throws his changeup with good arm action, making it hard to distinguish from his fastball, and also has a serviceable slider. Though he commands his fastball, he often gets himself into trouble with walks. Bloom primarily has been a starter during his career, though he did see some relief action last season and seems better suited to that role at the major league level.

Year	Club (League)	Class	W	L	ERA	G	GS	CG	SV	IP	H	R	ER	HR	BB	SO	AVG
2004	Williamsport (NYP)	SS	4	3	2.60	12	12	0	0	45	34	19	13	2	13	46	.209
2005	Hickory (SAL)	LoA	4	1	1.87	12	12	0	0	63	38	15	13	3	33	58	.176
	Lynchburg (CAR)	HiA	3	5	5.86	12	12	0	0	63	61	45	41	12	43	34	.255
2006	Lynchburg (CAR)	HiA	7	8	4.30	25	25	0	0	128	122	63	61	15	61	108	.261
2007	Lynchburg (CAR)	HiA	9	12	5.51	25	25	1	0	129	144	83	79	14	57	90	.282
	Altoona (EL)	AA	1	1	0.90	2	2	0	0	10	5	3	1	1	6	10	.147
2008	Altoona (EL)	AA	5	8	4.19	28	22	1	0	110	103	57	51	9	55	93	.244
MINOR LEAGUE TOTALS			33	38	4.26	116	110	2	0	547	507	285	259	56	268	439	.247

30 WILL RHYMES, 2B/SS

BORN: April 1, 1983. **B-T:** L-R. **HT.:** 5-9. **WT.:** 155. **DRAFTED:** William & Mary, 2005 (27th round).
SIGNED BY: Bill Buck.

Often overlooked because of his small stature, Rhymes has nonetheless made himself into a prospect. He'll never be mistaken for a toolsy middle infielder, but his peskiness has earned him praise as a lefthanded-hitting version of David Eckstein. Rhymes brings one element—speed—that the Tigers have sorely lacked on their big league roster. His plus speed and instincts have allowed him to steal bases at an 81 percent clip in the minors. Though he'll need to be a contact hitter to stick in the majors, he has been known to take huge swings and will chase pitches outside the strike zone. His superb hand-eye coordination allows him to overcome those shortcomings much of the time. Rhymes should develop into a solid defender at second base, his most natural position, though his footwork around the bag needs to improve. He has good hands and solid range at second base. He doesn't have enough arm to be a regular shortstop, but he could fill in there for a few days if needed. Rhymes offers enough on both sides of the ball that he profiles as an Aaron Miles-type utility player. He helped his cause by hitting .287 in the Arizona Fall League and will open 2009 as Detroit's starting second baseman in Triple-A.

Year	Club (League)	Class	AVG	G	AB	R	H	2B	3B	HR	RBI	BB	SO	SB	OBP	SLG
2005	Oneonta (NYP)	SS	.328	61	250	49	82	11	3	2	27	25	15	14	.391	.420
2006	West Michigan (MWL)	LoA	.261	126	506	80	132	19	2	3	39	53	53	23	.332	.324
2007	Lakeland (FSL)	HiA	.304	88	326	43	99	12	2	4	35	44	38	24	.389	.390
	Erie (EL)	AA	.265	39	155	21	41	6	0	1	21	6	20	5	.297	.323
2008	Erie (EL)	AA	.306	131	516	76	158	21	7	3	60	44	66	17	.362	.391
	Toledo (IL)	AAA	.320	6	25	5	8	0	1	0	2	2	4	0	.370	.400
MINOR LEAGUE TOTALS			.292	451	1778	274	520	69	15	13	184	174	196	83	.357	.370

Florida Marlins

BY MIKE BERARDINO

Trading off franchise stalwarts Miguel Cabrera and Dontrelle Willis for a package of kids was supposed to send the Marlins into another freefall as they retooled for the future. Instead, it set them up for a surprising 84-win season while adding to a rapidly growing stash of prospects in a well-balanced system.

Saddled with the sport's lowest Opening Day payroll ($22 million, roughly half of what the second-lowest club, the Rays, spent) and widely predicted to lose 90-plus games, Florida rallied under second-year manager Fredi Gonzalez to post the third-highest victory total (84) in its existence. The Marlins finished third in the rugged National League East, 7½ games behind the eventual World Series champion Phillies. Despite a flawed blueprint that relied too heavily on home runs and included a shaky defense, they missed the wild card by just 5½ games.

In mid-May, the Marlins signed Hanley Ramirez to a six-year, $70 million extension. It was the largest contract ever awarded by a Jeffrey Loria-owned team.

But in the offseason, they once again sought to keep payroll down while also adding speed and defense. Florida traded Kevin Gregg, Mike Jacobs, Scott Olsen and Josh Willingham before they could go to arbitration, getting Emilio Bonifacio and Leo Nunez for the big league roster and righthanders Jose Ceda and P.J. Dean plus infielder Jake Smolinski for their farm system.

As for last winter's blockbuster, Andrew Miller, the big lefty who highlighted the six-player haul the Marlins received from the Tigers for Cabrera and Willis, had an uneven first season in South Florida. He finished up in the bullpen after missing more than a month in the second half with patellar tendinitis, though he did show enough to convince management to trade Olsen.

The other megaprospect in the Cabrera-Willis deal was electric center fielder Cameron Maybin. He was an eye-popping revelation once he was recalled for the season's final 10 days and ranks No. 1 on this prospect list for the second straight year.

In the minors, Florida affiliates won at a combined .530 clip—their best record since 2001—while receiving a number of outstanding performances, particularly from a growing crop of position prospects. Gaby Sanchez was named MVP of the Double-A Southern

Fredi Gonzalez guided unheralded Florida to its third-highest win total in team history

MORRIS FOSTOFF

TOP 30 PROSPECTS

1. Cameron Maybin, of	16. Chris Leroux, rhp
2. Mike Stanton, of	17. Tim Wood, rhp
3. Logan Morrison, 1b	18. Brad Hand, lhp
4. Sean West, lhp	19. Bryan Petersen, of
5. Ryan Tucker, rhp	20. P.J. Dean, rhp
6. Matt Dominguez, 3b	21. Jesus Delgado, rhp
7. Kyle Skipworth, c	22. Hector Correa, rhp
8. Gaby Sanchez, 1b/3b	23. Eulogio de la Cruz, rhp
9. Chris Coghlan, 2b	24. Edgar Olmos, lhp
10. Jose Ceda, rhp	25. Jake Smolinski, 2b
11. John Raynor, of	26. Brett Hayes, c
12. Brett Sinkbeil, rhp	27. Dan Meyer, lhp
13. Aaron Thompson, lhp	28. Greg Burns, of
14. Scott Cousins, of	29. Kyle Winters, rhp
15. Isaac Galloway, of	30. Graham Taylor, lhp

League, while fellow first baseman Logan Morrison earned the same honor in the high Class A Florida State League and easily won the batting title with a .332 average. Outfielder Mike Stanton, 18, blasted 39 homers for low Class A Greensboro.

Picking sixth in the June draft, the Marlins selected high school catcher Kyle Skipworth. Skipworth immediately became the best catching prospect in a system that had lacked one. However, the Marlins continued to sit on the sidelines of the international market, where they were one of just six clubs not to hand out a single six-figure bonus in 2008.

General Manager: Michael Hill. **Farm Director:** Brian Chattin. **Scouting Director:** Stan Meek.

Class	Team	League	W	L	PCT	Finish*	Manager	Affiliated
Majors	Florida	National	84	77	.522	7th (16)	Fredi Gonzalez	—
Triple-A	Albuquerque Isotopes	Pacific Coast	68	75	.476	10th (16)	Dean Treanor	2003
Double-A	Carolina Mudcats	Southern	80	60	.571	1st (10)	Matt Raleigh	2003
High A	Jupiter Hammerheads	Florida State	74	64	.536	5th (12)	Brandon Hyde	2002
Low A	Greensboro Grasshoppers	South Atlantic	66	72	.478	11th (16)	Edwin Rodriguez	2002
Short-season	Jamestown Jammers	New York-Penn	47	29	.618	3rd (14)	Darin Everson	2002
Rookie	GCL Marlins	Gulf Coast	30	24	.556	5th (16)	Steve Watson	1992
Overall 2008 Minor League Record			365	324	.530	7th		

* Finish in overall standings (No. of teams in league). ^League champion.

LAST YEAR'S TOP 30

Rank	Player, Pos.	Status
1.	Cameron Maybin, of	No. 1
2.	Chris Volstad, rhp	Majors
3.	Brett Sinkbeil, rhp	No. 12
4.	Ryan Tucker, rhp	No. 5
5.	Sean West, lhp	No. 4
6.	Gaby Hernandez, rhp	(Mariners)
7.	Chris Coghlan, 2b	No. 9
8.	Matt Dominguez, 3b	No. 6
9.	Aaron Thompson, lhp	No. 13
10.	Dallas Trahern, rhp	Dropped out
11.	Mike Stanton, of	No. 2
12.	Gaby Sanchez, 1b	No. 8
13.	Hector Correa, rhp	No. 22
14.	John Raynor, of	No. 11
15.	Scott Cousins, of	No. 14
16.	Logan Morrison, 1b	No. 3
17.	Henry Owens, rhp	Dropped out
18.	Eulogio de la Cruz, rhp	No. 23
19.	Chris Leroux, rhp	No. 16
20.	Brett Hayes, c	No. 26
21.	Kyle Winters, rhp	No. 29
22.	Greg Burns, of	No. 28
23.	Brett Carroll, of	Dropped out
24.	Harvey Garcia, rhp	Dropped out
25.	Scott Nestor, rhp	Dropped out
26.	Jacob Marceaux, rhp	Dropped out
27.	Jesus Delgado, rhp	No. 21
28.	Tom Hickman, of	Dropped out
29.	Graham Taylor, lhp	No. 30
30.	Jai Miller, of	Dropped out

BEST TOOLS

Best Hitter for Average	Logan Morrison
Best Power Hitter	Mike Stanton
Best Strike-Zone Discipline	Chris Coghlan
Fastest Baserunner	John Raynor
Best Athlete	Mike Stanton
Best Fastball	Jose Ceda
Best Curveball	Brad Hand
Best Slider	Sean West
Best Changeup	Aaron Thompson
Best Control	Graham Taylor
Best Defensive Catcher	Brett Hayes
Best Defensive Infielder	Matt Dominguez
Best Infield Arm	Matt Dominguez
Best Defensive Outfielder	Cameron Maybin
Best Outfield Arm	Brett Carroll

PROJECTED 2012 LINEUP

Catcher	Kyle Skipworth
First Base	Gaby Sanchez
Second Base	Dan Uggla
Third Base	Matt Dominguez
Shortstop	Hanley Ramirez
Left Field	Logan Morrison
Center Field	Cameron Maybin
Right Field	Mike Stanton
No. 1 Starter	Josh Johnson
No. 2 Starter	Ricky Nolasco
No. 3 Starter	Chris Volstad
No. 4 Starter	Andrew Miller
No. 5 Starter	Sean West
Closer	Ryan Tucker

TOP PROSPECTS OF THE DECADE

Year	Player, Pos.	2008 Org.
1999	A.J. Burnett, rhp	Blue Jays
2000	A.J. Burnett, rhp	Blue Jays
2001	Josh Beckett, rhp	Red Sox
2002	Josh Beckett, rhp	Red Sox
2003	Miguel Cabrera, 3b	Tigers
2004	Jeremy Hermida, of	Marlins
2005	Jeremy Hermida, of	Marlins
2006	Jeremy Hermida, of	Marlins
2007	Chris Volstad, rhp	Marlins
2008	Cameron Maybin, of	Marlins

TOP DRAFT PICKS OF THE DECADE

Year	Player, Pos.	2008 Org.
1999	Josh Beckett, rhp	Red Sox
2000	Adrian Gonzalez, 1b	Padres
2001	Garrett Berger, rhp (2nd)	Bridgeport (Atlantic)
2002	Jeremy Hermida, of	Marlins
2003	Jeff Allison, rhp	Marlins
2004	Taylor Tankersley, lhp	Marlins
2005	Chris Volstad, rhp	Marlins
2006	Brett Sinkbeil, rhp	Marlins
2007	Matt Dominguez, 3b	Marlins
2008	Kyle Skipworth, c	Marlins

LARGEST BONUSES IN CLUB HISTORY

Josh Beckett, 1999	$3,625,000
Adrian Gonzalez, 2000	$3,000,000
Livan Hernandez, 1996	$2,500,000
Kyle Skipworth, 2008	$2,300,000
Jason Stokes, 2000	$2,027,000

FLORIDA MARLINS

TOP 2009 ROOKIE: Cameron Maybin, of. Barring a huge spring flop, the center-field job belongs to the prize of the Miguel Cabrera/Dontrelle Willis trade.

BREAKOUT PROSPECT: Tim Wood, rhp. Strong showings in the Southern League playoffs and the Arizona Fall League put him on the 40-man roster.

SLEEPER: Todd Doolittle, rhp. His size and stuff may not blow anyone away, but he keeps getting outs.

SOURCE OF TOP 30 TALENT			
Homegrown	23	Acquired	7
College	9	Trades	6
Junior college	0	Rule 5 draft	0
High school	12	Independent leagues	0
Draft-and-follow	2	Free agents/waivers	1
Nondrafted free agents	0		
International	0		

Numbers in parentheses indicate prospect rankings.

LF
John Raynor (11)
Tom Hickman
Lorenzo Scott
Kevin Mattison

CF
Cameron Maybin (1)
Scott Cousins (14)
Isaac Galloway (15)
Greg Burns (28)
Jai Miller

RF
Mike Stanton (2)
Bryan Petersen (19)
Brett Carroll

3B
Matt Dominguez (6)
Lee Mitchell
Paul Gran
Joel Staples

SS
Jose Torres
Ozzie Martinez
Augustin Septimo

2B
Chris Coghlan (9)
Jake Smolinski (25)
Danny Pertusati
Brandon Turner

1B
Logan Morrison (3)
Gaby Sanchez (8)
Ernie Banks

C
Kyle Skipworth (7)
Brett Hayes (26)

RHP

Starters	Relievers
Ryan Tucker (5)	Jose Ceda (10)
Brett Sinkbeil (12)	Chris Leroux (16)
P.J. Dean (20)	Tim Wood (17)
Hector Correa (22)	Jesus Delgado (21)
Kyle Winters (29)	Eulogio de la Cruz (23)
Burke Badenhop	Todd Doolittle
Dallas Trahern	Pete Andrelczyk
Jeff Allison	Eli Villanueva
Blake Brewer	Henry Owens
Kyle Kaminska	Jared Yecker
	Kris Harvey
	Corey Madden
	Andrew Battisto

LHP

Starters	Relievers
Sean West (4)	Dan Meyer (27)
Aaron Thompson (13)	Jeff Gogal
Brad Hand (18)	Dan Jennings
Edgar Olmos (24)	Matt Yourkin
Graham Taylor (30)	Ricardo Hernandez
	Kelvin Ferreira

2008

BEST PURE HITTER: The Marlins believe in Kyle Skipworth (1) as a catcher but were comforted that his lefthanded bat profiles elsewhere if he doesn't remain behind the plate. He showed the ability to make adjustments by adding a slight crouch to his stance that helped him get to low pitches.

BEST POWER HITTER: Skipworth has the fast bat, feel for the barrel and hand-eye coordination to produce excellent power.

FASTEST RUNNER: The Marlins were shocked to get five-tool OF Isaac Galloway (8) so low, despite his poor spring. He's a 7 runner on the 2-8 scouting scale and also has good baserunning instincts.

BEST DEFENSIVE PLAYER: 3B Paul Gran (7) made only one error as a senior at Washington State and has excellent range to go with good hands and an average arm. He's good enough to fill in at shortstop, and add in his lefthanded bat and he fits the utility profile perfectly.

BEST FASTBALL: RHP Blake Brewer (11) reached 94 mph, sits in the low 90s and has projection to spare at 6-foot-5 and 180 pounds. LHP Brad Hand (2) has heavy life down in the zone and reaches 93 mph.

BEST SECONDARY PITCH: Hand's hard curveball with downer action. Brewer also has a good, hard curve. LHP Edgar Olmos (3) has an intriguing changeup that he turns over, giving it screwball action.

BEST PRO DEBUT: After missing all but eight games with Mississippi State last spring with hamstring problems, 2B Brandon Turner (12) hit .331/.372/.417 for short-season Jamestown. Hand showed enough polish in his Rookie-level Gulf Coast League stint to earn a promotion to Jamestown, going 3-2, 2.64 with 46 strikeouts in 48 innings overall. Athletic 2B Danny Pertusati (13) hit .295/.348/.392 while adjusting to playing infield after a prep career in the outfield and as a football quarterback.

BEST ATHLETE: Galloway is a cut above most baseball players with speed, strength and fast-twitch muscles.

MOST INTRIGUING BACKGROUND: RHP Drew Clothier (37) struck out 24 in 20 innings at Jamestown before the Army changed its policy on allowing West Point graduates to play professional sports, forcing Clothier to report for active duty. Brewer's older brother Brent was a second-round pick of the Brewers in 2006.

CLOSEST TO THE MAJORS: LHP Dan Jennings' (9) fastball runs up to 93 mph in shorter stints, and

his slider plays up out of the bullpen as well. That's likely his future role, as his changeup is underdeveloped.

BEST LATE-ROUND PICK: Brewer could be the best pitcher the Marlins drafted after Hand.

THE ONE WHO GOT AWAY: Georgia persuaded RHP Trevor Holder (10), the No. 1 starter on its College World Series runner-up club, to return for his senior season.

ASSESSMENT: After two hitter-heavy drafts, the Marlins went after projectable pitchers with five of their first six picks. Yet the two top talents were up-the-middle prep hitters in Skipworth and Galloway, and their fortunes likely will determine the success of this draft class.

2007

3B Matt Dominguez (1) and OF Mike Stanton (2) had stunning first full seasons in the minors and are a major part of the Marlins' future. OF Bryan Petersen (4) is a sleeper.

GRADE: A

2006

RHP Brett Sinkbeil's (1) health and stuff have been mildly disappointing, but 2B Chris Coghlan (1s) has lived up to expectations and OF John Raynor (9) has exceeded them.

GRADE: C+

2005

Florida famously spent five picks before the second round on pitchers, but the best choice of all may be 1B Logan Morrison (22), a draft-and-follow. Another 1B, Gaby Sanchez (4), is on the verge of starting in the majors. Among the highly drafted arms, RHPs Chris Volstad (1) and Ryan Tucker (1s) and LHP Sean West (1s) are keepers.

GRADE: A

2004

This draft already has sent four players to Florida, but they're all marginal contributors. The best of them, LHP Taylor Tankersley (1), regressed mightily in 2008.

GRADE: D

*Draft analysis by John Manuel (2008) and Jim Callis (2004-07). Numbers in parentheses indicate draft rounds. *Bonuses for 2004-05 are first 10 rounds only.*

ROBERT GURGANUS

PROSPECT

CAMERON MAYBIN, OF

Born: April 4, 1987.
Ht.: 6-4. **Wt.:** 205.
Bats: R. **Throws:** R.
Drafted:
HS—Asheville, N.C., 2005
(1st round).
Signed by:
Bill Buck (Tigers).

Once considered untouchable and the jewel of the Tigers system, Maybin was pried away in December 2007 as part of an eight-player blockbuster that cost the Marlins franchise stalwarts Miguel Cabrera and Dontrelle Willis. Lefty Andrew Miller also came south along with four lesser prospects, and though Miller broke camp with Florida last season, it's Maybin who will determine the eventual success or failure of the deal. The 10th overall pick in the 2005 draft, he signed for $2.65 million. Widely considered among the best athletes in that draft, the main reason for his modest slide was a perception that his bat would need more time to develop. He shot holes in that theory by reaching the majors at age 20 in 2007, his second pro season. His first two big league hits came off Roger Clemens, a single and homer, but overall he struggled at the plate in a brief cameo with the contending Tigers. Nagging injuries have slowed his progress the past two seasons. In 2007, he partially dislocated his right shoulder and strained his left shoulder. In 2008, he missed three weeks in July with a pulled ribcage muscle and a few days in August with a staph infection. He still managed to bounce back in time to lead Double-A Carolina within one win of a Southern League championship before dazzling onlookers during an eight-game audition with the Marlins in late September. He ranked as the top position prospect in the SL.

Maybin has five-tool ability. His quick hands give him lightning bat speed, which combined with his raw strength should allow him to hit for plus power as he fills out and makes more consistent contact. He also has the plus-plus speed to beat out infield hits and steal bases. While his plate discipline still has a ways to go, it has improved notably and he draws walks. Defensively, he has tremendous closing speed and strong instincts that enable him to read the ball off the bat and make highlight-reel plays in center field. He also brandishes a strong throwing arm that evokes memories of a young Andre Dawson. Maybin also draws praise for his makeup.

Strikeouts remain the biggest concern for Maybin, who was fanned in 31 percent of his pro at-bats. He's still learning to recognize the spin on offspeed pitches and to lay off fastballs up in the zone. He has a late hitch in his swing that counteracts some of his bat speed. He batted leadoff after his callup and delivered four-hit games in his first two starts, but he currently fits better a bit lower in the lineup. Florida believes he'll become a more aggressive and effective basestealer and a major threat once he learns how to read pitchers and lengthen his leads.

Maybin will get every opportunity to seize the center-field job for good in spring training. Only a disastrous showing would send him back to the minors. He should develop into the best center fielder in Marlins history.

Year	Club (League)	Class	AVG	G	AB	R	H	2B	3B	HR	RBI	BB	SO	SB	OBP	SLG
2006	West Michigan (MWL)	LoA	.304	101	385	59	117	20	6	9	69	50	116	27	.387	.457
2007	Tigers (GCL)	R	.571	2	7	1	4	0	0	0	1	2	2	0	.667	.571
	Lakeland (FSL)	HiA	.304	83	296	58	90	14	5	10	44	43	83	25	.393	.486
	Erie (EL)	AA	.400	6	20	9	8	1	0	4	8	6	6	0	.538	1.050
	Detroit (AL)	MAJ	.143	24	49	8	7	3	0	1	2	3	21	5	.208	.265
2008	Carolina (SL)	AA	.277	108	390	73	108	15	8	13	49	60	124	21	.375	.456
	Florida (NL)	MAJ	.500	8	32	9	16	2	0	0	2	3	8	4	.543	.563
MINOR LEAGUE TOTALS			.298	300	1098	200	327	50	19	36	171	161	331	73	.389	.476
MAJOR LEAGUE TOTALS			.284	32	81	17	23	5	0	1	4	6	29	9	.341	.383

2 MIKE STANTON, OF

RODGER WOOD

BORN: Nov. 8, 1989. **B-T:** R-R. **HT.:** 6-5. **WT.:** 205. **DRAFTED:** HS—Sherman Oaks, Calif., 2007 (2nd round). **SIGNED BY:** Tim McDonnell.

Southern California offered Stanton a baseball scholarship and a walk-on opportunity as a receiver/defensive back at Southern California, while Nevada-Las Vegas wanted him to play football and walk-on in baseball. Instead, the Marlins stole him in the second round of the 2007 draft for $475,000. In his first full pro season, he ranked second in the minors in homers (39) and total bases (286) and fourth in slugging (.611). While low Class A Greensboro's NewBridge Bank Park is a bandbox, Stanton's homers weren't flukes. He hit 18 on the road and showed regular light-tower power, prompting comparisons to a young Dave Winfield. He has plus speed and runs out every ball, never letting opponents or the score get him off his game. He has a solid-average arm and played well in both center and right field in 2008. Stanton's strikeout totals remain high, but Florida insists he has no problem with pitch recognition. He has yet to develop basesteal-ing instincts. He worked with Greensboro pitching coach John Duffy to improve his throwing mechanics and get more out of his arm strength. Even when he could have helped them acquire Manny Ramirez for the stretch drive, the Marlins deemed Stanton strictly off limits. They're already daydreaming about an outfield that includes Cameron Maybin in center and Stanton in right, but the latter probably won't arrive until 2010 at the earliest.

Year	Club (League)	Class	AVG	G	AB	R	H	2B	3B	HR	RBI	BB	SO	SB	OBP	SLG
2007	Marlins (GCL)	R	.269	8	26	6	7	2	0	0	1	1	6	0	.321	.346
	Jamestown (NYP)	SS	.067	9	30	2	2	1	0	1	2	3	15	0	.147	.200
2008	Greensboro (SAL)	LoA	.293	125	468	89	137	26	3	39	97	58	153	4	.381	.611
MINOR LEAGUE TOTALS			.279	142	524	97	146	29	3	40	100	62	174	4	.365	.574

3 LOGAN MORRISON, 1B

MORRIS FOSTOFF

BORN: Aug. 25, 1987. **B-T:** L-L. **HT.:** 6-2. **WT.:** 215. **DRAFTED:** Maple Woods (Mo.) CC, D/F 2005 (22nd round). **SIGNED BY:** Ryan Wardinsky.

Morrison turned down $95,000 as a 22nd-round pick out of high school so he could attend Maple Woods (Mo.) CC, the same school that produced Albert Pujols. While there, he grew two inches and added 20 pounds of muscle, prompting the Marlins to sign him for $225,000 as a draft-and-follow. He exploded last season to claim MVP honors in the high Class A Florida State League, which he led in batting (.332), hits (162), doubles (38) and on-base percentage (.402). Morrison has a flat swing that stays in the zone for an exception-ally long time. He has plus power and blasted several memorable shots last season, but he does a nice job of ignoring that temptation and working the gaps. His plate discipline keeps improving and he refrains from chasing pitches out of the zone. He projects as a .300 hitter with 30-homer potential. He keeps getting better defensively, too, flashing a strong arm and a willingness to nail lead runners. Morrison's range at first base is still fairly limited. He's a below-average runner, though not bad once he gets going. Offensively, however, there's not much not to like. After batting .404/.444/.667 in the Arizona Fall League, Morrison will head to Florida's new Double-A Jacksonville affiliate. He could get to the majors at some point in 2009 and battle Gaby Sanchez for a starting job. The Marlins also could move Morrison to left field after he showed decent aptitude there in the AFL.

Year	Club (League)	Class	AVG	G	AB	R	H	2B	3B	HR	RBI	BB	SO	SB	OBP	SLG
2006	Marlins (GCL)	R	.270	26	89	10	24	4	0	1	7	10	12	1	.343	.348
	Jamestown (NYP)	SS	.203	23	74	6	15	3	0	1	11	11	17	0	.295	.284
2007	Greensboro (SAL)	LoA	.267	128	453	71	121	22	2	24	86	48	96	2	.343	.483
2008	Jupiter (FSL)	HiA	.332	130	488	71	162	38	1	13	74	57	80	9	.402	.494
MINOR LEAGUE TOTALS			.292	307	1104	158	322	67	3	39	178	126	205	12	.366	.464

4 SEAN WEST, LHP

STEVE MOORE

BORN: June 15, 1986. **B-T:** L-L. **HT.:** 6-8. **WT.:** 200. **DRAFTED:** HS—Shreveport, La., 2005 (1st round supplemental). **SIGNED BY:** Ryan Fox.

Signed for $775,000 out of high school, West continues to tantalize with what might be the highest ceiling of the five pitchers the Marlins drafted before the second round in 2005. He missed the entire 2007 season following surgery to repair a torn labrum, and he pitched only three times in the first two months last season because of blisters. He got better each month afterward and then greatly impressed scouts in the Arizona Fall League. His big frame and three-quarters arm slot have earned him comparisons to a young Randy Johnson. West owns a big fastball, which sits at 92-94 mph and touches 96. He features two different sliders, one tighter than the other, and his changeup has shown potential. He continues to mature on and off the mound, battling through outings when he lacks his best stuff. Not surprisingly for such a big man, West struggles at times with his delivery. He tends to shorten his stride, which causes his front side to become too stiff and leaves his arm to drag behind his body, negatively affecting his control. He needs to trust his changeup more. West has yet to pitch above Class A, but his strong work in Arizona has put him on the fast track to the majors. The Marlins will continue to be very careful with him, properly viewing him as a future rotation topper. He figures to open the year at Double-A Jacksonville, but a call to the majors isn't far away.

Year	Club (League)	Class	W	L	ERA	G	GS	CG	SV	IP	H	R	ER	HR	BB	SO	AVG
2005	Marlins (GCL)	R	2	3	2.35	9	8	0	0	38	33	12	10	2	7	40	.229
	Jamestown (NYP)	SS	0	2	5.73	3	3	0	0	11	17	7	7	1	5	14	.362
2006	Greensboro (SAL)	LoA	8	5	3.74	21	21	0	0	120	115	55	50	13	40	102	.255
2007	Did Not Play—Injured																
2008	Jupiter (FSL)	HiA	6	5	2.41	21	20	0	0	101	79	33	27	3	60	92	.224
MINOR LEAGUE TOTALS			16	15	3.13	54	52	0	0	270	244	107	94	19	112	248	.245

5 RYAN TUCKER, RHP

BORN: Dec. 6, 1986. **B-T:** R-R. **HT.:** 6-2. **WT.:** 190. **DRAFTED:** HS—Temple City, Calif., 2005 (1st round supplemental). **SIGNED BY:** John Cole.

A 2005 compensation pick for the loss of former closer Armando Benitez, Tucker signed for $975,000 and reached the majors midway through his third full pro season. However, he was back in Double-A three weeks after taking his lumps. Blessed with an overpowering fastball that continues to rank among the best in the system, Tucker pitches at 92-95 mph and touches 97. When his slider is on, it's tight and features late break. He continued to use his changeup upon a return to Carolina where he pitched out of the bullpen. His mound presence is a plus and Marlins owner Jeffrey Loria raves about his bulldog mentality. Tucker has a tendency to rely too heavily on his fastball, a failing big leaguers readily exploited. His slider command is inconsistent, causing him to lose confidence with the pitch. Previous attempts at mastering a curveball and cutter were scrapped. He can be hard on himself, growing too emotional when things go against him. He drew a 2007 suspension for twice having words with high Class A Jupiter pitching coach Reid Cornelius, but there have been no further problems. With the big league rotation seemingly over-booked, Tucker is wisely angling for a future in short relief. If he doesn't make the Florida bullpen out of spring training, he'll likely head to the club's new Triple-A New Orleans affiliate and return to starting.

Year	Club (League)	Class	W	L	ERA	G	GS	CG	SV	IP	H	R	ER	HR	BB	SO	AVG
2005	Marlins (GCL)	R	3	3	3.69	8	7	0	0	32	35	13	13	0	16	23	.315
	Jamestown (NYP)	SS	1	1	8.36	4	4	0	0	14	21	14	13	3	8	18	.323
2006	Greensboro (SAL)	LoA	7	13	5.00	25	25	2	0	131	123	86	73	14	67	133	.246
2007	Jupiter (FSL)	HiA	5	8	3.71	24	24	1	0	138	142	64	57	6	46	104	.264
2008	Carolina (SL)	AA	5	3	1.58	25	12	0	0	91	64	17	16	2	37	74	.195
	Florida (NL)	MAJ	2	3	8.27	13	6	0	0	37	46	34	34	8	23	28	.305
MINOR LEAGUE TOTALS			21	28	3.81	86	72	3	0	406	385	194	172	25	174	352	.250
MAJOR LEAGUE TOTALS			2	3	8.27	13	6	0	0	37	46	34	34	8	23	28	.305

6 MATT DOMINGUEZ, 3B

BORN: Aug. 28, 1989. **B-T:** R-R. **HT.:** 6-2. **WT.:** 180. **DRAFTED:** HS—Chatsworth, Calif., 2007 (1st round). **SIGNED BY:** Tim McDonnell.

Despite his all-around excellence, Dominguez is used to being overshadowed. He shared the left side of the Chatsworth (Calif.) High infield with Mike Moustakas, who went second overall in the 2007 draft—10 picks ahead of Dominguez. He had a lacklus-ter pro debut after signing for $1.8 million but recovered nicely in 2008 at Greensboro, though Mike Stanton generated more headlines. Dominguez's defense is the first thing everyone notices. He has exceptionally smooth hands and actions in the field, along with a strong arm and quick release that have drawn comparisons to Mike Lowell's. Dominguez could play third base in the big leagues right now. His bat really came around last season, as he showed a quicker bat and more fluid swing than he had in his debut. Adding strength remains a must, especially after a bout with mononucleosis cost Dominguez the first six weeks of last season and caused him to drop 15 pounds. He has a tendency to lunge at times at the plate and can get tied up with hard stuff on the inner half. He's a below-average runner whose quickness and range have been called into question. Next season will be key for Dominguez as he makes the transition from hitter-friendly Greensboro to the larger parks of the Florida State League. He remains the top third baseman in the system and should reach the majors in 2011.

Year	Club (League)	Class	AVG	G	AB	R	H	2B	3B	HR	RBI	BB	SO	SB	OBP	SLG
2007	Marlins (GCL)	R	.100	5	20	0	2	0	0	0	2	1	2	0	.136	.100
	Jamestown (NYP)	SS	.189	10	37	3	7	2	0	1	4	1	12	0	.211	.324
2008	Greensboro (SAL)	LoA	.296	88	345	59	102	16	0	18	70	28	68	0	.354	.499
MINOR LEAGUE TOTALS			.276	103	402	62	111	18	0	19	76	30	82	0	.331	.463

7 KYLE SKIPWORTH, C

BORN: March 1, 1990. **B-T:** L-R. **HT.:** 6-3. **WT.:** 195. **DRAFTED:** HS—Rubidoux, Calif., 2008 (1st round). **SIGNED BY:** Robby Corsaro.

Skipworth didn't become a full-time catcher until he was a junior in high school, after the incumbent catcher (the head coach's brother) graduated. As a senior, he drew comparisons to Joe Mauer, the only other prep catcher taken in the top 10 picks in the past 13 drafts, and set a California state record with hits in 18 consecutive plate appearances. Drafted sixth overall, Skipworth signed quickly for $2.3 million. Though he struggled in his pro debut, the Mauer comparisons extend to his hitting. Skipworth has the bat speed and strength to hit for average and power as he matures. A first-rate receiver with excellent hands and footwork, he required little tweaking from roving catching instructor Tim Cossins. He quickly took on game-calling responsibilities and showed a knack for handling pitchers. He has a strong, accurate throwing arm and a quick release, which helped him lead the Rookie-level Gulf Coast League by nailing 36 percent of basestealers. Skipworth piled up too many strikeouts in the GCL, but he isn't the first high pick to struggle in his first pro summer. He needs to add strength and bulk to his lanky frame. His arm action can get long at times. He never had called pitches until he reached pro ball, so that has been an adjustment. The Marlins haven't had a catcher this promising since Charles Johnson in the early 1990s. Skipworth will start 2009 in low Class A, and his bat will dictate how fast he climbs.

Year	Club (League)	Class	AVG	G	AB	R	H	2B	3B	HR	RBI	BB	SO	SB	OBP	SLG
2008	Marlins (GCL)	R	.208	43	159	22	33	6	0	5	21	13	46	2	.263	.340
MINOR LEAGUE TOTALS			.208	43	159	22	33	6	0	5	21	13	46	2	.263	.340

8 GABY SANCHEZ, 1B/3B

BORN: Sept. 2, 1983. **B-T:** R-R. **HT.:** 6-2. **WT.:** 225. **DRAFTED:** Miami, 2005 (4th round). **SIGNED BY:** John Martin.

Suspended under a cloud of mystery his entire junior year at Miami, Sanchez was a fourth-round steal for the Marlins. He signed for $250,000, largely on the recommendation of East Coast scouting supervisor Mike Cadahia, who had known him for years. Sanchez won the short-season New York-Penn League batting title at .355 in his pro debut and the Southern League MVP award last summer. His plate discipline ranks right with Chris Coghlan's as the best in the system. Sanchez makes excellent adjustments from pitch to pitch and has learned to use the whole field. He shows outstanding gap power and could hit almost anywhere in the lineup besides leadoff. After trying catcher and third base, he has worked hard to become a plus defender at first base, with managers rating him the best in the SL. Big-time power isn't in Sanchez's toolbox, as his 17 homers last season were a career high. He tends to dive for balls and can struggle against top pitching, with some scouts questioning his bat speed. He'll have to keep a close watch on his conditioning. He has below-average speed, though his lateral quickness has improved. Having reached the majors for a brief look last September, Sanchez heads to spring training with an excellent shot at winning the starting first-base job. The Marlins dealt incumbent Mike Jacobs to the Royals in a salary-related move, but they also did so knowing Sanchez was ready to break through.

Year	Club (League)	Class	AVG	G	AB	R	H	2B	3B	HR	RBI	BB	SO	SB	OBP	SLG
2005	Jamestown (NYP)	SS	.355	62	234	34	83	16	0	5	42	16	24	11	.401	.487
2006	Greensboro (SAL)	LoA	.317	55	189	43	60	12	0	14	40	39	20	6	.447	.603
	Marlins (GCL)	R	.333	3	6	1	2	1	0	0	3	5	0	0	.636	.500
	Jupiter (FSL)	HiA	.182	16	55	13	10	3	1	1	7	12	12	1	.324	.327
2007	Jupiter (FSL)	HiA	.279	133	473	89	132	40	3	9	70	64	74	6	.369	.433
2008	Carolina (SL)	AA	.314	133	478	70	150	42	1	17	92	69	70	17	.404	.513
	Florida (NL)	MAJ	.375	5	8	0	3	2	0	0	1	0	2	0	.375	.625
MINOR LEAGUE TOTALS			.305	402	1435	250	437	114	5	46	254	205	200	41	.397	.487
MAJOR LEAGUE TOTALS			.375	5	8	0	3	2	0	0	1	0	2	0	.375	.625

9 CHRIS COGHLAN, 2B

BORN: June 18, 1985. **B-T:** L-R. **HT.:** 6-1. **WT.:** 195. **DRAFTED:** Mississippi, 2006 (1st round supplemental). **SIGNED BY:** Mark Willoughby.

Winning the Cape Cod League batting title put Coghlan on the map the summer before his draft year in 2006. Selected 36th overall and signed for $950,000, he represented the Marlins at the Futures Game in his first full season and was MVP of the Southern League all-star game in 2008. Coghlan has an innate ability to put the barrel of the bat on the ball. He also shows strong plate discipline, and Marlins owner Jeffrey Loria proudly calls him a professional hitter. A solid-average runner, Coghlan has made himself into a legitimate basestealing threat by studying pitchers. Predominantly a third baseman in college, he has made himself into a solid second baseman. His baseball smarts and work ethic bode well for him. Coghlan's hands aren't the softest, and he remains a work in progress around the bag at second. He probably won't hit for much power, though he does tend to find the gaps. It was a surprise when the Marlins acquired slick-fielding second baseman Emilio Bonifacio from the Nationals in November. Coghlan is a superior hitter and could bounce back to third base if needed, but his fast track to the majors as Dan Uggla's eventual replacement has gained a potential roadblock.

Year	Club (League)	Class	AVG	G	AB	R	H	2B	3B	HR	RBI	BB	SO	SB	OBP	SLG
2006	Marlins (GCL)	R	.286	2	7	2	2	0	0	0	3	0	1	0	.286	.286
	Jamestown (NYP)	SS	.298	28	94	14	28	5	1	0	12	13	9	5	.373	.372
2007	Greensboro (SAL)	LoA	.325	81	305	60	99	26	4	10	64	47	43	19	.419	.534
	Jupiter (FSL)	HiA	.200	34	130	17	26	5	3	2	18	15	19	5	.277	.331
2008	Carolina (SL)	AA	.298	132	483	83	144	32	5	7	74	67	65	34	.396	.429
MINOR LEAGUE TOTALS			.293	277	1019	176	299	68	13	19	171	142	137	63	.386	.442

10 JOSE CEDA, RHP

STEVE MOORE

BORN: Jan. 28, 1987. **B-T:** R-R. **HT.:** 6-4. **WT.:** 275. **SIGNED:** Dominican Republic, 2004. **SIGNED BY:** Felix Francisco/Randy Smith (Padres).

It's rare for a young power arm like Ceda to get traded twice in two years, but that was the case when the Marlins somehow acquired him for Kevin Gregg in November. Chicago had stolen him from the Padres in a mid-2006 deal for Todd Walker. His hulking frame and power repertoire have earned him comparisons to Lee Smith and Armando Benitez. Ceda's fastball sits at 95-97 mph and touches 100, and he also flashes a hard slider that can be overpowering. He moved to the bullpen for good in June, and he has a 2.12 ERA, .149 opponent average and 14.1 strikeouts per nine innings in that role over the last two years. Ceda's command and control are inconsistent because he doesn't always repeat his delivery well. Escogido dropped him in the Dominican League this winter after he walked two batters and threw a wild pitch without recording an out in his lone outing. His changeup was a weak third pitch, though he doesn't need it now as a reliever. Durability has been an issue, though more when he was a starter. He missed two months with a stiff shoulder in 2007. His weight remains a concern and likely always will for such a large man. He'll get every opportunity to break camp with the Marlins in 2009. He likely would start out by setting up young closer Matt Lindstrom, but some believe it's only a matter of time before the job is Ceda's.

Year	Club (League)	Class	W	L	ERA	G	GS	CG	SV	IP	H	R	ER	HR	BB	SO	AVG
2005	Padres (DSL)	R	4	2	1.50	13	9	2	2	60	38	18	10	2	29	83	.174
2006	Padres (AZL)	R	2	0	5.09	8	4	0	0	23	20	14	13	1	13	31	.235
	Cubs (AZL)	R	0	0	0.75	5	3	0	0	12	6	2	1	0	7	21	.154
	Boise (NWL)	SS	1	0	3.27	3	3	0	0	11	5	4	4	1	2	11	.139
2007	Cubs (AZL)	R	0	0	2.45	2	1	0	0	4	2	1	1	0	3	3	.182
	Peoria (MWL)	LoA	2	2	3.11	21	6	0	0	46	14	18	16	1	31	66	.093
2008	Daytona (FSL)	HiA	2	2	4.80	15	12	0	0	54	41	29	29	4	28	53	.212
	Tennessee (SL)	AA	2	1	2.08	22	0	0	9	30	26	8	7	2	14	42	.234
MINOR LEAGUE TOTALS			13	7	3.03	89	38	2	11	241	152	94	81	11	127	310	.180

11 JOHN RAYNOR, OF

BORN: Jan. 4, 1984. **B-T:** R-R. **HT.:** 6-2. **WT.:** 185. **DRAFTED:** UNC Wilmington, 2006 (9th round). **SIGNED BY:** Joel Matthews.

After the Marlins named him their minor league player of the year and the low Class A South Atlantic League tabbed him as its MVP in 2007, Raynor skipped a level and had no trouble adapting to Double-A. Florida stole him for $17,500 as a college senior in the 12th round in 2006, a year after he had turned down the Orioles as a 12th-rounder. A career .316 hitter in pro ball, Raynor has an inside-out swing that produces good gap power. His on-base ability and his speed make him a leadoff candidate, though ideally he'd make more consistent contact if he batted atop a lineup. The fastest runner in the system, Raynor regularly gets from the right side of the plate to first base in 4.1 seconds. Once on base, he puts tremendous pressure on opponents, having stolen 123 bases (at an 85 percent success rate) in 296 pro games. While he's quick enough to play center field, he has spent more time in left field because his arm is below-average. Raynor hit for the cycle in his third game in the Arizona Fall League this offseason, but 10 days later he was shut down for the year after an errant pitch left him with a hairline fracture in his left hand. If he's healthy, he could challenge for a big league starting job by the end of 2009.

Year	Club (League)	Class	AVG	G	AB	R	H	2B	3B	HR	RBI	BB	SO	SB	OBP	SLG
2006	Jamestown (NYP)	SS	.286	54	199	36	57	8	4	4	21	17	51	21	.356	.427
2007	Greensboro (SAL)	LoA	.333	116	445	110	148	28	8	13	57	66	98	54	.429	.519
2008	Carolina (SL)	AA	.312	126	452	104	141	29	6	13	51	62	122	48	.402	.489
MINOR LEAGUE TOTALS			.316	296	1096	250	346	65	18	30	129	145	271	123	.405	.490

12 BRETT SINKBEIL, RHP

BORN: Dec. 26, 1984. **B-T:** R-R. **HT.:** 6-3. **WT.:** 190. **DRAFTED:** Missouri State, 2006 (1st round). **SIGNED BY:** Ryan Wardinsky.

Signed for $1.525 million after going 19th overall in the 2006 draft, Sinkbeil has had a hard time staying healthy. A strained oblique caused him to drop slightly in the draft, and he missed time in his first full pro season with an elbow issue and a herniated disc in his back. He managed to make all of his starts in 2008, but his performance in Double-A was disappointing. His fastball velocity dropped a tick, though he still has a 90-93 mph heater with good late life. His hard slider is the best in the system, and he throws it at 84-87 mph. No one questions his work ethic, and his changeup has shown signs of improvement. For someone with his stuff, Sinkbeil doesn't miss a lot of bats, which puts a premium on having quality defenders behind him. If he's not getting his slider over, his fastball can be hittable, and he works up in the strike zone too much. Scouts aren't enamored with his pendulum-like arm action. Sinkbeil must re-establish himself in 2009, and some believe a move to the bullpen could do just that. His sinker-slider repertoire profiles well in a set-up role, though the Marlins figure to keep him in the rotation for now.

Year	Club (League)	Class	W	L	ERA	G	GS	CG	SV	IP	H	R	ER	HR	BB	SO	AVG
2006	Jamestown (NYP)	SS	2	0	1.23	5	5	0	0	22	14	4	3	1	8	22	.192
	Greensboro (SAL)	LoA	1	1	4.99	8	8	0	0	40	45	22	22	5	14	32	.290
2007	Jupiter (FSL)	HiA	6	4	3.42	14	14	1	0	79	82	41	30	8	14	49	.268
2008	Carolina (SL)	AA	5	9	5.02	26	26	1	0	143	172	84	80	12	51	66	.306
MINOR LEAGUE TOTALS			14	14	4.28	53	53	2	0	284	313	151	135	26	87	169	.285

13 AARON THOMPSON, LHP

BORN: Feb. 28, 1987. **B-T:** L-L. **HT.:** 6-3. **WT.:** 195. **DRAFTED:** HS—Houston, 2005 (1st round). **SIGNED BY:** Dennis Cardoza.

The Marlins selected Thompson 22nd overall in 2005, one pick ahead of Jacoby Ellsbury and three before Matt Garza. Thompson had been committed to Texas A&M, but when the Aggies changed coaching staffs, he opted to sign for $1.225 million. He has yet to justify that investment, though he has made steady progress. Thompson's changeup has been his best pitch for a while, though he lost his feel for it early last season. His fastball velocity has improved to the point where he pitches at 88-91 mph and touches 93. He has a solid curveball as well but must do a better job of maintaining his arm slot when he throws it. Though he's slow to the plate, he holds runners well and might have the best pickoff move in the system. He also does a good job of varying how long he waits to start his delivery to control the running game. A minor shoulder problem cost Thompson two months in 2008, and when the Marlins sent him to the Arizona Fall League for extra work, he tried relieving in hopes of getting to the majors sooner. He pitched well early in the AFL before tiring and getting hit hard late. Florida figures to send him back to Double-A as a starter this year.

Year	Club (League)	Class	W	L	ERA	G	GS	CG	SV	IP	H	R	ER	HR	BB	SO	AVG
2005	Marlins (GCL)	R	2	4	4.50	8	8	0	0	32	42	20	16	1	10	41	.316
	Jamestown (NYP)	SS	1	2	3.10	5	5	0	0	20	25	13	7	1	10	17	.301
2006	Greensboro (SAL)	LoA	8	8	3.63	24	24	0	0	134	139	68	54	12	35	114	.270
2007	Jupiter (FSL)	HiA	4	6	3.37	20	19	0	0	115	121	64	43	2	35	84	.266
2008	Marlins (GCL)	R	0	0	2.00	2	2	0	0	9	8	2	2	0	1	9	.242
	Carolina (SL)	AA	2	5	5.62	16	16	0	0	82	111	61	51	9	40	53	.331
MINOR LEAGUE TOTALS			17	25	3.97	75	74	0	0	392	446	228	173	25	131	318	.287

14 SCOTT COUSINS, OF

BORN: Jan. 22, 1985. **B-T:** L-L. **HT.:** 6-2. **WT.:** 190. **DRAFTED:** San Francisco, 2006 (3rd round). **SIGNED BY:** John Hughes.

No one can accuse Cousins of holding back. In mid-April, he went after a foul ball and went sliding into a low concrete wall at Jupiter. Though he sustained a deep bone bruise in his knee that had trouble healing, he pronounced himself ready to go after three weeks. The Marlins kept holding him out until the bruising stopped clouding his MRI exams. Finally, after two months, Cousins returned to action in a summer also complicated by the loss of a beloved uncle. By August he had been promoted to Double-A, where he played a key role in Carolina's run to the Southern League championship series. He later went to the Arizona Fall League, where he more than held his own while initially sharing center-field duties with fellow Marlins prospect John Raynor. Cousins was a two-way player in college, and some clubs liked his potential more as a pitcher. Florida zeroed in on his athleticism and never has regretted its decision. He's a potential five-tool player with bat speed and strength, though he can get too aggressive at times. He has plus speed but is still learning to use it to steal bases. He's capable of playing all three outfield positions, with the range for center field and the arm strength and accuracy for right. Cousins will return to Double-A to open 2009 and soon could bid for a spot in the Marlins outfield.

Year	Club (League)	Class	AVG	G	AB	R	H	2B	3B	HR	RBI	BB	SO	SB	OBP	SLG
2006	Jamestown (NYP)	SS	.211	21	90	11	19	1	0	1	6	4	17	3	.253	.256
2007	Greensboro (SAL)	LoA	.292	110	421	69	123	25	0	18	74	38	92	16	.358	.480
2008	Marlins (GCL)	R	.000	2	6	0	0	0	0	0	0	0	5	0	.000	.000
	Jupiter (FSL)	HiA	.304	49	191	35	58	9	2	9	29	20	47	11	.370	.513
	Carolina (SL)	AA	.264	27	91	15	24	7	1	1	9	10	28	4	.350	.396
MINOR LEAGUE TOTALS			.280	209	799	130	224	42	3	29	118	72	189	34	.346	.449

15 ISAAC GALLOWAY, OF

BORN: Oct. 10, 1989. **B-T:** R-R. **HT.:** 6-2. **WT.:** 190. **DRAFTED:** HS—Rancho Cucamonga, Calif., 2008 (8th round). **SIGNED BY:** Robbie Corsaro.

As a sophomore in high school, Galloway established himself as a likely first-round pick in the 2008 draft. But he pressed as a senior and slumped, causing him to plummet before the Marlins finally took him in the eighth round with the 238th overall pick. After turning down a San Diego State scholarship to sign quickly for $245,000, Galloway promptly set about proving his doubters wrong. Strikeouts were an initial concern, but some early adjustments by roving hitting coordinator John Mallee got Galloway to stay inside the ball better and use his hips more efficiently. The ball began jumping off his bat from that point forward. Tools-wise, there's much to like about Galloway's package, with future power perhaps the only missing piece. He doesn't have much of a load in his swing, which restricts his ability to drive the ball and catch up to fastballs at times. A true center fielder, he has drawn comparisons to a young Torii Hunter for his tall, lanky frame and a gliding stride that enables him to cover tons of ground. His plus arm would also make him a nice fit in right field. He has plus-plus speed and good instincts on the bases. Galloway should open his first full season in low Class A.

Year	Club (League)	Class	AVG	G	AB	R	H	2B	3B	HR	RBI	BB	SO	SB	OBP	SLG
2008	Marlins (GCL)	R	.286	48	199	29	57	13	5	1	23	4	33	4	.303	.417
MINOR LEAGUE TOTALS			.286	48	199	29	57	13	5	1	23	4	33	4	.303	.417

16 CHRIS LEROUX, RHP

BORN: April 14, 1984. **B-T:** L-R. **HT.:** 6-6. **WT.:** 210. **DRAFTED:** Winthrop, 2005 (7th round). **SIGNED BY:** Joel Matthews.

A former catcher with a strong frame, Leroux converted to the mound at Winthrop and terrorized college hitters with a big-breaking curveball. Unfortunately, he threw it so much that some blame it for him blowing out his elbow and requiring Tommy John surgery two months before the 2005 draft. The Marlins weren't deterred, selecting him in the seventh round, signing him for $152,000 and letting him focus on his rehab. He didn't make his pro debut until mid-2006, and he has held up well since. Florida didn't let Leroux pitch on consecutive days at all in 2007, but there were no such restrictions last year. The Marlins have taken away his curveball and given him a slider instead, and he throws a tight one at 87-88 mph. He also boasts a fastball that ranges from 92-96 mph. He shows good mound presence and makeup, and he profiles as a possible closer. A member of Canada's World Cup team in 2007, Leroux should move up to Double-A in 2009 after being added to the 40-man roster in November.

Year	Club (League)	Class	W	L	ERA	G	GS	CG	SV	IP	H	R	ER	HR	BB	SO	AVG
2006	Greensboro (SAL)	LoA	0	3	6.10	3	3	0	0	10	13	7	7	2	6	9	.325
	Marlins (GCL)	R	0	0	4.09	4	4	0	0	11	10	9	5	0	1	9	.250
	Jamestown (NYP)	SS	0	1	7.94	4	4	0	0	11	13	13	10	0	12	4	.283
2007	Greensboro (SAL)	LoA	2	3	4.14	46	0	0	0	72	72	38	33	6	29	76	.261
2008	Jupiter (FSL)	HiA	6	7	3.65	57	0	0	1	74	60	37	30	6	26	78	.225
MINOR LEAGUE TOTALS			8	14	4.29	114	11	0	1	178	168	104	85	14	74	176	.251

17 TIM WOOD, RHP

BORN: Nov. 16, 1982. **B-T:** R-R. **HT.:** 6-1. **WT.:** 185. **DRAFTED:** Pima (Ariz.) CC, 2002, D/F (44th round). **SIGNED BY:** Scott Stanley.

A former draft-and-follow pick, Wood succumbed to Tommy John surgery in 2005, midway through his third pro season. He had a breakthrough season despite a minor shoulder issue that cost him some time in 2008. He held Florida State League hitters to a .182 average and while he initially found the going rough in Double-A, he didn't give up an earned run in seven appearances in the Southern League playoffs. He continued to pitch well in the Arizona Fall League, which earned him a spot on the 40-man roster. Working as many as three innings at a time during the regular season, Wood surprised those who might have made assumptions about him based on his unassuming, freckled appearance. His fastball sits in the mid-90s and touches 97 mph. When he gets on top of it, his heater features some natural sink. He also flashes a sharp power slider that has the making of an out pitch, and a hard changeup with plus action down in the zone. He throws strikes and keeps the ball down, surrendering just three homers in 60 innings last season. He figures to open 2009 back in Double-A, but he could bid for a shot at the Marlins' bullpen by midseason.

Year	Club (League)	Class	W	L	ERA	G	GS	CG	SV	IP	H	R	ER	HR	BB	SO	AVG
2003	Jamestown (NYP)	SS	0	2	5.35	16	4	0	2	39	44	33	23	2	28	32	.289
2004	Greensboro (SAL)	LoA	2	3	4.22	24	8	0	1	70	73	47	33	12	22	70	.263
2005	Greensboro (SAL)	LoA	1	2	9.28	5	5	0	0	21	29	23	22	2	15	10	.312
2006	Jupiter (FSL)	HiA	2	7	5.83	16	16	0	0	63	65	43	41	4	25	52	.273
2007	Jupiter (FSL)	HiA	0	2	3.81	17	0	0	0	26	24	14	11	1	8	26	.245
2008	Jupiter (FSL)	HiA	5	2	1.80	27	1	0	1	40	25	10	8	1	15	22	.182
	Carolina (SL)	AA	2	1	5.75	12	0	0	0	20	20	14	13	2	6	15	.250
MINOR LEAGUE TOTALS			12	19	4.85	117	34	0	4	280	280	184	151	24	119	227	.260

18 BRAD HAND, LHP

BORN: March 20, 1990. **B-T:** L-L. **HT.:** 6-2. **WT.:** 185. **DRAFTED:** HS—Chaska, Minn., 2008 (2nd round). **SIGNED BY:** Bob Oldis.

The best Minnesota high school prospect since Joe Mauer, Hand is a classic cold-weather pitcher with a physical, country-strong frame. He walked away from an Arizona State scholarship to sign for $760,000 after going early in the second round last June. He also played football and hockey in high school, where he doubled as a power-hitting first baseman. Marlins pitching coordinator Wayne Rosenthal worked with Hand to smooth out a violent delivery in which he would land with a stiff front leg and fly open with his front shoulder. Those adjustments have cost him velocity in the short term, but he still works at 88-91 mph and tops out at 93 with heavy life. His command improved markedly, too, allowing him to get a quick taste of short-season Jamestown at the end of his pro debut. Hand also owns the best curveball in the system, a hard downer, and his changeup gives him the chance to have three plus pitches. He throws from a mid three-quarters arm slot and must be careful not to drop his arm, lest his pitches begin to sail. He'll start his first full pro season in low Class A.

Year	Club (League)	Class	W	L	ERA	G	GS	CG	SV	IP	H	R	ER	HR	BB	SO	AVG
2008	Marlins (GCL)	R	2	0	2.48	9	7	0	0	33	25	16	9	0	11	34	.212
	Jamestown (NYP)	SS	1	2	3.00	3	3	0	0	15	11	6	5	0	10	12	.208
MINOR LEAGUE TOTALS			3	2	2.64	12	10	0	0	48	36	22	14	0	21	46	.211

19 BRYAN PETERSEN, OF

BORN: April 9, 1986. **B-T:** L-R. **HT.:** 6-0. **WT.:** 200. **DRAFTED:** UC Irvine, 2007 (4th round). **SIGNED BY:** Tim McDonnell.

In an organization suddenly teeming with center-field prospects, Petersen shouldn't be overlooked. A fourth-round pick in 2007, when he led UC Irvine to the College World Series, he spent part of his first full season in Double-A. He hit .351 in a two-week stint at Carolina, and with all the terrific athletes in the system, it was Petersen who was the lone 20-20 player in 2008. The knock on him always had been his tendency to pile up strikeouts on breaking balls out of the zone, but he cut his whiffs way down in the second half last year. With the help of hitting coordinator John Mallee, he was able to flatten his swing and start spraying line drives into the gaps. He shows power to the pull side but will have more success once he puts aside thoughts of 30-homer seasons. He stays in well against lefties, is proficient at bunting and has a knack for stealing bases with good speed and savvy. Defensively, he isn't at the level of Cameron Maybin or Greg Burns, but Petersen shows solid range and strong instincts. A former college pitcher, he has a strong, accurate arm and a knowledge of how to use it. He has a good chance to begin 2009 in Double-A.

Year	Club (League)	Class	AVG	G	AB	R	H	2B	3B	HR	RBI	BB	SO	SB	OBP	SLG
2007	Jamestown (NYP)	SS	.250	57	216	27	54	13	1	5	24	18	53	11	.318	.389
2008	Greensboro (SAL)	LoA	.301	79	296	60	89	10	2	19	58	38	74	15	.381	.541
	Carolina (SL)	AA	.351	12	37	5	13	2	0	1	10	5	6	1	.409	.486
	Jupiter (FSL)	HiA	.265	40	155	23	41	5	0	3	12	15	29	7	.339	.355
MINOR LEAGUE TOTALS			.280	188	704	115	197	30	3	28	104	76	162	34	.355	.450

20 P.J. DEAN, RHP

BORN: Oct. 27, 1988. **B-T:** R-R. **HT.:** 6-3. **WT.:** 175. **DRAFTED:** HS—New Caney, Texas, 2007 (7th round). **SIGNED BY:** Tyler Wilt (Nationals).

An Oklahoma signee, Dean was all but packed for Norman when the Nationals swooped in with a $120,000 bonus for the seventh-rounder in 2007. That aggressiveness paid off 17 months later, when Washington sent him with second basemen Emilio Bonifacio and Jake Smolinski to get arbitration-eligible Scott Olsen and Josh Willingham from the Marlins. Dean has a lean, projectable frame, and he already has added strength and velocity after just one full pro season. He dominated more experienced competition in the New York-Penn League in 2008, permitting opponents to bat just .169. His fastball, which sat at 88-91 mph during his first pro summer, parked at 91-92 mph and topped out at 94 last year. His heater features plus life and could add still more velocity as he fills out. Dean also features a hard curve and an improved changeup he uses against both lefties and righties. Fastball command remains a bit of an issue, but he has excellent feel for pitching. He should start 2009 in low

Class A, where he'll be tested by the tight confines of Greensboro's NewBridge Bank Park.

Year	Club (League)	Class	W	L	ERA	G	GS	CG	SV	IP	H	R	ER	HR	BB	SO	AVG
2007	Nationals (GCL)	R	3	1	4.06	9	5	0	0	31	27	16	14	1	11	26	.225
2008	Vermont (NYP)	SS	4	1	1.57	10	10	0	0	46	26	10	8	2	16	34	.169
MINOR LEAGUE TOTALS			7	2	2.57	19	15	0	0	77	53	26	22	3	27	60	.193

21 JESUS DELGADO, RHP

BORN: April 19, 1984. **B-T:** R-R. **HT.:** 6-1. **WT.:** 200. **SIGNED:** Venezuela, 2001. **SIGNED BY:** Ben Cherington (Red Sox).

Delgado made great strides in 2008. He served as the Marlins' sole representative at the Futures Game, where he hit 98 mph on the Yankee Stadium radar gun. "Maybe my arm got excited," said Delgado, who later earned a September callup to the majors. Originally signed by the Red Sox in 2001, he missed his first two full pro seasons following Tommy John surgery. Part of the Josh Beckett/Mike Lowell trade after the 2005 season, he also spent time on the disabled list in his first two years in the Florida system, with a pulled muscle under his armpit in 2006 and a strained shoulder in 2007. Pitching exclusively out of the bullpen, he managed to stay healthy and pumped 94-96 mph fastballs throughout the 2008 season. He backs up his heat with a hard curveball and a tight slider, the latter a more recent addition to his arsenal. He also has a potential plus pitch in his changeup, though he needs to throw it more often. A former outfielder who moved to the mound shortly after Boston signed him, Delgado has good athleticism. His makeup and work ethic are solid, but he can get down on himself at times. He's in the mix for a major league bullpen role in 2009.

Year	Club (League)	Class	W	L	ERA	G	GS	CG	SV	IP	H	R	ER	HR	BB	SO	AVG
2001	Red Sox (DSL)	R	0	2	5.34	10	8	0	0	32	31	25	19	1	14	19	.240
2002	Did Not Play—Injured																
2003	Did Not Play—Injured																
2004	Red Sox (GCL)	R	0	0	10.80	1	0	0	0	2	4	2	2	0	0	2	.500
	Augusta (SAL)	LoA	1	5	5.22	21	16	0	0	59	61	40	34	10	26	34	.275
2005	Greenville (SAL)	LoA	7	3	3.50	33	0	0	2	72	57	30	28	3	39	69	.215
2006	Jupiter (FSL)	HiA	2	4	2.58	28	0	0	0	38	33	19	11	0	18	40	.231
2007	Carolina (SL)	AA	5	7	4.80	31	16	0	1	94	97	59	50	6	45	75	.266
2008	Albuquerque (PCL)	AAA	0	0	11.81	6	0	0	0	11	17	14	14	2	4	6	.362
	Carolina (SL)	AA	5	2	3.45	42	0	0	1	57	46	27	22	2	31	52	.229
	Florida (NL)	MAJ	0	0	4.50	2	0	0	0	2	1	1	1	0	3	0	.167
MINOR LEAGUE TOTALS			20	23	4.45	172	40	0	4	364	346	216	180	24	177	297	.251
MAJOR LEAGUE TOTALS			0	0	4.50	2	0	0	0	2	1	1	1	0	3	0	.167

22 HECTOR CORREA, RHP

BORN: March 18, 1988. **B-T:** R-R. **HT.:** 6-3. **WT.:** 165. **DRAFTED:** HS—Hatillo, P.R., 2006 (4th round). **SIGNED BY:** Carlos Berroa.

Correa ranked right behind Mike Stanton and Gaby Sanchez at No. 13 on this list a year ago, but he mistakenly tried to extend that momentum by pitching through a shoulder problem that wound up costing him four months of mound time in 2008. His rehab path was bumpy at times, though for the most part he showed the necessary discipline. Team officials believe he learned his lesson after trying to conceal an injury. Correa managed to return for a fall minicamp and showed only slightly diminished velocity. Instead of humming fastballs at 91-94 mph and touching 95 mph like he had in 2007, he worked mostly at 90-92. He has a low-80s slider that shows good bite, but he remains more comfortable using a changeup that shows excellent action. The shoulder problems came as a surprise because he has a loose arm and smooth, easily repeatable delivery, which allows him to throw strikes. His frame is lean and projectable. He's a good athlete with plus makeup. Correa will open his third straight season in low Class A, with hopes of finally advancing in 2009.

Year	Club (League)	Class	W	L	ERA	G	GS	CG	SV	IP	H	R	ER	HR	BB	SO	AVG
2006	Marlins (GCL)	R	1	2	1.76	10	5	0	0	41	38	13	8	1	15	38	.244
2007	Greensboro (SAL)	LoA	1	5	9.29	8	8	0	0	31	55	40	32	7	16	20	.401
	Jamestown (NYP)	SS	6	3	3.22	11	11	0	0	59	61	25	21	5	13	83	.261
2008	Greensboro (SAL)	LoA	0	1	6.30	4	4	0	0	10	15	8	7	1	1	9	.326
	Marlins (GCL)	R	0	0	13.50	1	1	0	0	3	5	4	4	0	2	2	.357
MINOR LEAGUE TOTALS			8	10	4.52	34	29	0	0	143	174	90	72	14	47	152	.296

23 EULOGIO DE LA CRUZ, RHP

BORN: March 12, 1984. **B-T:** R-R. **HT.:** 5-11. **WT.:** 175. **SIGNED:** Dominican Republic, 2001. **SIGNED BY:** Ramon Pena (Tigers).

Acquired from the Tigers as part of the haul from the Miguel Cabrera/Dontrelle Willis trade, de la Cruz made it to the majors for a spot start in late May but flopped badly when he returned as a reliever. He spent the bulk of 2008 in the Triple-A rotation but still profiles as a reliever. De la Cruz's fastball clocks in at 94-96 mph and tops out at 98, but it tends to straighten out when he overthrows. His plus changeup has outstanding sink that makes it a swing-and-miss pitch, but hitters tended to avoid it during his brief exposure to the majors. Once de la Cruz finds a reliable breaking ball he could become a useful part of the big league bullpen, but that remains a work in progress. Last year, he didn't show much feel for a hard curveball that had shown the makings of a plus pitch in the past. The Marlins tried to tighten it up into a slider but he resisted their requests to use it in games. De la Cruz has a wonderful personality and solid work ethic, but it's unclear whether he'll get the most out of his big fastball. Incidentally, he prefers his given name but teammates and coaches have come to call him "Frankie," a tradition that began in Tigers camp with manager Jim Leyland.

Year	Club (League)	Class	W	L	ERA	G	GS	CG	SV	IP	H	R	ER	HR	BB	SO	AVG
2002	Tigers (GCL)	R	1	1	2.63	20	0	0	1	38	40	24	11	0	21	46	.260
	Oneonta (NYP)	SS	0	0	23.14	2	0	0	0	2	7	8	6	0	4	4	.500
2003	Tigers (GCL)	R	2	2	2.59	22	0	0	7	24	18	10	7	0	15	30	.205
	Oneonta (NYP)	SS	0	0	10.80	2	0	0	0	3	6	4	4	0	1	4	.400
2004	West Michigan (MWL)	LoA	2	4	3.83	54	0	0	17	54	51	30	23	2	33	44	.239
2005	Erie (EL)	AA	0	1	16.20	1	0	0	0	2	3	3	3	0	4	0	.286
	Lakeland (FSL)	HiA	4	3	3.39	40	10	0	5	96	66	46	36	5	36	97	.191
2006	Erie (EL)	AA	5	6	3.43	38	12	0	2	105	103	46	40	3	45	87	.258
	Toledo (IL)	AAA	0	0	11.57	1	1	0	0	2	4	3	3	1	2	3	.333
2007	Detroit (AL)	MAJ	0	0	6.75	6	0	0	0	7	10	8	5	1	4	5	.357
	Erie (EL)	AA	4	5	3.41	11	11	2	0	66	54	31	25	5	19	57	.224
	Toledo (IL)	AAA	3	6	3.52	22	1	0	0	38	41	17	15	0	18	25	.289
2008	Albuquerque (PCL)	AAA	13	8	4.34	25	25	0	0	147	139	85	71	13	60	118	.253
	Florida (NL)	MAJ	0	0	18.00	6	1	0	0	9	15	20	18	2	11	4	.375
MINOR LEAGUE TOTALS			34	30	3.80	238	60	2	32	578	531	307	244	29	258	515	.243
MAJOR LEAGUE TOTALS			0	0	13.21	12	1	0	0	16	25	28	23	3	15	9	.368

24 EDGAR OLMOS, LHP

BORN: April 12, 1990. **B-T:** L-L. **HT.:** 6-5. **WT.:** 180. **DRAFTED:** HS—Van Nuys, Calif., 2008 (3rd round). **SIGNED BY:** Tim McDonnell.

The Marlins took high school lefthanders with their second- and third-round picks in the 2008 draft, with Olmos following Brad Hand. Olmos, who had committed to Arizona, signed for $478,000 in the third round. He carries tremendous projection with his live, loose arm and a tall, skinny frame. When he first showed up at Florida's training base in Jupiter, his arm slot was all over the place, depending on what type of pitch he was throwing. With the help of roving pitching coordinator Wayne Rosenthal, he settled on a high three-quarters delivery. Olmos had a bout of shoulder tendinitis that caused him to be shut down after one start in the Gulf Coast League, but his fastball was back up to 91 mph with tremendous life after he returned for a fall minicamp. His changeup needs significant improvement for him to take it from the bullpen to the game, but it has screwball action when it's on. His slow 70-72 mph curveball and his 73-76 mph slider are solid breaking pitches for which he has a good feel. His mechanics are sound and he does a nice job of keeping his front side closed. Olmos has a pleasant personality and a willingness to work. Because he has limited pro experience, he'll probably open 2009 in extended spring training before heading to Jamestown in June.

Year	Club (League)	Class	W	L	ERA	G	GS	CG	SV	IP	H	R	ER	HR	BB	SO	AVG
2008	Marlins (GCL)	R	0	0	0.00	1	1	0	0	2	2	0	0	0	0	5	.250
MINOR LEAGUE TOTALS			0	0	0.00	1	1	0	0	2	2	0	0	0	0	5	.250

25 JAKE SMOLINSKI, 2B

BORN: Feb. 9, 1989. **B-T:** R-R. **HT.:** 5-11. **WT.:** 185. **DRAFTED:** HS—Rockford, Ill., 2007 (2nd round). **SIGNED BY:** Steve Arnieri (Nationals).

Part of the Scott Olsen/Josh Willingham trade with the Nationals in November, Smolinski must get healthy before he can play for his new organization. His first pro season in 2007 ended when he broke his foot by fouling a ball off of it, and he missed two months last summer with a broken thumb. His worst injury yet came in instructional league, when he got streamrolled while turning a double play and blew out his left knee. Smolinski will miss at least a couple months of the 2009 season following reconstructive surgery, but the Marlins still liked him enough to trade for him. A good athlete who played shortstop and quarterback in high school, he projects as a possible Chris Coghlan type with a bit more pop. Smolinski already has good gap power and should hit more homers as he improves his pitch recognition and adds some loft to his line-drive stroke. He has solid plate discipline. Finding a position for Smolinski could be challenging, as his arm is average and his speed was fringy before his knee injury. Washington played him in left field in 2007 and at second base in 2008. He'll probably start back at second base when he's ready to go at midseason.

FLORIDA MARLINS

Year	Club (League)	Class	AVG	G	AB	R	H	2B	3B	HR	RBI	BB	SO	SB	OBP	SLG
2007	Nationals (GCL)	R	.305	28	105	18	32	8	0	1	16	13	24	7	.387	.410
2008	Hagerstown (SAL)	LoA	.261	50	184	28	48	12	1	4	22	19	33	1	.338	.402
	Nationals (GCL)	R	.111	3	9	0	1	0	0	0	2	1	1	0	.200	.111
	Vermont (NYP)	SS	.306	24	98	17	30	8	1	0	9	9	17	4	.370	.408
MINOR LEAGUE TOTALS			.280	105	396	63	111	28	2	5	49	42	75	12	.356	.399

26 BRETT HAYES, C

BORN: Feb. 13, 1984. **B-T:** R-R. **HT.:** 6-1. **WT.:** 200. **DRAFTED:** Nevada, 2005 (2nd round supplemental). **SIGNED BY:** John Hughes.

As hoped, a catcher emerged from the Marlins system in 2008 and took over starting duties. However, it was John Baker who did so, not Hayes, who entered the year as Florida's best catching prospect. Now he must hustle to re-establish himself, but time could be running out with first-rounder Kyle Skipworth now in the pipeline. Hayes' continued problems with strike-zone judgment have frustrated some club officials who wonder if he'll ever be more than another Matt Treanor with strong defense but low production. A career .252 hitter in pro ball, Hayes offers decent gap power. No one questions his intelligence or desire to improve. A fiery leader who isn't afraid to push pitchers, he calls a strong game but struggles at times with blocking balls in the dirt. He has worked tirelessly with catching coordinator Tim Cossins on his footwork and throwing mechanics, improving his success rate against basestealers to 35 percent last year. Hayes has below-average speed but isn't bad for a catcher. A product of the same high school (Notre Dame High in Sherman Oaks, Calif.) as Marlins No. 2 prospect Mike Stanton, he was added to the 40-man roster in November. He'll go to big league camp as a longshot to make the club.

Year	Club (League)	Class	AVG	G	AB	R	H	2B	3B	HR	RBI	BB	SO	SB	OBP	SLG
2005	Marlins (GCL)	R	.417	3	12	2	5	1	0	0	2	0	2	0	.417	.500
	Jamestown (NYP)	SS	.239	36	117	11	28	6	1	1	12	12	21	3	.313	.333
2006	Greensboro (SAL)	LoA	.245	82	278	39	68	13	1	9	38	29	61	4	.321	.396
2007	Jupiter (FSL)	HiA	.338	17	65	10	22	3	1	1	11	9	10	2	.413	.462
	Carolina (SL)	AA	.234	74	273	22	64	16	0	3	31	18	51	2	.280	.326
2008	Carolina (SL)	AA	.232	54	181	19	42	8	0	6	18	10	43	1	.275	.376
	Albuquerque (PCL)	AAA	.293	37	116	21	34	3	1	5	17	4	23	1	.331	.466
MINOR LEAGUE TOTALS			.252	303	1042	124	263	50	4	25	129	82	211	13	.310	.380

27 DAN MEYER, LHP

BORN: July 3, 1981. **B-T:** R-L. **HT.:** 6-3. **WT.:** 220. **DRAFTED:** James Madison, 2002 (1st round supplemental). **SIGNED BY:** J.J. Picollo (Braves).

The Marlins have liked Meyer ever since the Braves drafted him 34th overall in 2002. Six years later they finally had a chance to acquire him—after his stock had dropped so much that they were able to claim him off waivers from the Athletics. He ranked as the top lefthanded pitching prospect in the upper minors when he was the key piece in the trade that sent Tim Hudson to Atlanta in 2004, but Meyer has been stymied by injuries and ineffectiveness ever since. That lends further credence to the belief that the Braves don't make many mistakes when trading their own pitching prospects. Meyer's struggles with Oakland were both physical and mental. He had surgery in 2006 to remove a small piece of bone from his throwing shoulder, and his confidence and his mechanics fell apart. Though his performance last year wasn't particularly inspiring, Florida believes he could be on the verge of a breakthrough. His fastball velocity has returned to the low 90s, and his slider could yet become a plus pitch. Regaining the feel for his changeup has proven more difficult, and it was never considered more than average at best in the past. After spending most of the last four years in Triple-A, Meyer will get a chance to break camp with the Marlins as a situational lefty or middle reliever.

Year	Club (League)	Class	W	L	ERA	G	GS	CG	SV	IP	H	R	ER	HR	BB	SO	AVG
2002	Danville (APP)	R	3	3	2.74	13	13	1	0	66	47	22	20	4	18	77	.198
2003	Rome (SAL)	LoA	4	4	2.87	15	15	0	0	82	76	35	26	6	15	95	.248
	Myrtle Beach (CAR)	HiA	3	6	2.87	13	13	0	0	78	69	29	25	7	17	63	.236
2004	Greenville (SL)	AA	6	3	2.22	14	13	0	0	65	50	17	16	1	12	86	.216
	Richmond (IL)	AAA	3	3	2.79	12	11	0	0	61	62	23	19	6	25	60	.270
	Atlanta (NL)	MAJ	0	0	0.00	2	0	0	0	2	2	0	0	0	1	1	.286
2005	Sacramento (PCL)	AAA	2	8	5.36	19	17	0	0	89	101	64	53	15	43	63	.286
2006	Sacramento (PCL)	AAA	3	3	5.07	10	10	0	0	50	63	32	28	10	20	29	.315
2007	Midland (TEX)	AA	0	0	6.75	1	1	0	0	4	5	3	3	2	4	2	.357
	Sacramento (PCL)	AAA	8	2	3.28	21	21	0	0	115	103	44	42	12	51	105	.243
	Oakland (AL)	MAJ	0	2	8.82	6	3	0	0	16	20	19	16	2	9	11	.294
2008	Sacramento (PCL)	AAA	10	5	4.48	22	20	0	0	123	113	65	61	10	52	109	.245
	Oakland (AL)	MAJ	0	4	7.48	11	4	0	0	28	35	28	23	6	14	20	.304
MINOR LEAGUE TOTALS			42	37	3.60	140	134	1	0	733	689	334	293	73	257	689	.251
MAJOR LEAGUE TOTALS			0	6	7.63	19	7	0	0	46	57	47	39	8	24	32	.300

28 GREG BURNS, OF

BORN: Nov. 7, 1986. **B-T:** L-L. **HT.:** 6-2. **WT.:** 185. **DRAFTED:** HS—West Covina, Calif., 2004 (3rd round). **SIGNED BY:** Robby Corsaro.

Strikeouts are becoming even more of an issue with Burns, whose game must be predicated on speed and contact. As a result, he spent the full year in high Class A as fellow outfielders John Raynor, Scott Cousins and Bryan Petersen moved ahead of him and two more (Isaac Galloway, Bryan Petersen) passed him on this list. Burns has made himself more of a threat against lefties and his body continues to fill out with muscle, but he's still not putting up offensive numbers. He regressed in 2008 as his strikeout rate rose to a career-high 38 percent of his at-bats. He's at his best when he uses his strong hands and flat swing to put the ball in play, the better to take advantage of his blazing speed. Burns has yet to master bunting, and while he's a solid basestealer, he could do better considering his natural gifts. A plus defender with tremendous range and closing speed, he isn't afraid to throw his body into walls. His arm is average. Burns turned his back on a scholarship to play receiver at Hawaii, which made him an object of local curiosity when he was assigned to Hawaii Winter Baseball after last season. His athleticism, strong work ethic and outstanding makeup make him still worth watching as he tackles Double-A in 2009.

Year	Club (League)	Class	AVG	G	AB	R	H	2B	3B	HR	RBI	BB	SO	SB	OBP	SLG
2004	Marlins (GCL)	R	.243	42	136	28	33	5	4	0	7	26	48	7	.372	.338
2005	Jamestown (NYP)	SS	.257	65	241	43	62	5	2	1	11	39	84	17	.366	.307
2006	Greensboro (SAL)	LoA	.231	105	342	44	79	13	8	2	23	38	109	20	.307	.333
2007	Greensboro (SAL)	LoA	.280	120	414	70	116	21	4	7	54	40	122	39	.347	.401
2008	Jupiter (FSL)	HiA	.244	121	377	55	92	12	5	3	28	61	143	34	.351	.326
MINOR LEAGUE TOTALS			.253	453	1510	240	382	56	23	13	123	204	506	117	.345	.346

29 KYLE WINTERS, RHP

BORN: April 22, 1987. **B-T:** R-R. **HT.:** 6-4. **WT.:** 190. **DRAFTED:** HS—Arvada, Colo., 2005 (5th round). **SIGNED BY:** Scott Stanley.

Winters' supporters keep waiting for him to take off, but it truly hasn't happened yet. The main culprit is nagging injuries, such as the groin problem that cost him a few starts in 2008, and the minor elbow issue that caused him to be shut down near the end of the previous season. Raised in Colorado, he came into the system somewhat raw and projectable, reminding some of fellow Coloradans Roy Halladay and Brandon McCarthy. Winters pitches at 88-91 mph with natural cut action on his fastball. He uses two breaking balls, with his 84-85 mph slider more effective than his curveball. His changeup has the potential to be a solid third pitch. Winters is smart and coachable but he also tries to be too perfect at times. He had a pair of seven-walk games last year in high Class A when he refused to adjust to tight strike zones. He'll advance to Double-A in 2009.

Year	Club (League)	Class	W	L	ERA	G	GS	CG	SV	IP	H	R	ER	HR	BB	SO	AVG
2005	Marlins (GCL)	R	0	4	3.64	11	10	0	0	42	37	26	17	4	12	33	.237
2006	Jamestown (NYP)	SS	6	6	2.45	15	15	0	0	88	63	31	24	2	15	60	.194
2007	Greensboro (SAL)	LoA	8	4	3.95	19	19	1	0	112	105	55	49	13	20	68	.245
2008	Jupiter (FSL)	HiA	6	4	3.68	22	21	0	0	110	100	52	45	6	50	65	.242
MINOR LEAGUE TOTALS			20	18	3.45	67	65	1	0	352	305	164	135	25	97	226	.231

30 GRAHAM TAYLOR, LHP

BORN: May 25, 1984. **B-T:** L-L. **HT.:** 6-3. **WT.:** 225. **DRAFTED:** Miami (Ohio), 2006 (10th round). **SIGNED BY:** Matt Anderson.

Taylor won't wow anyone with his raw repertoire, as evidenced by his $10,000 signing bonus out of Miami (Ohio), but it's hard to argue with his results. He has gone 28-16, 3.07 while pitching his way to Double-A by the end of his third pro season, posting a career 4.9-1 strikeout-walk ratio. If the commissioner's office hadn't blocked the Cubs from including significant cash in a proposed trade that would have sent Jacque Jones to the Marlins in mid-2007, Taylor reportedly would have been sent to Chicago. He succeeds by mixing his pitches and pounding the strike zone. He has a sneaky 85-89 mph fastball with plus life, a big-breaking slurve and a changeup with good tailing action. When he gets on a roll, he's a groundball machine. Deception is part of his delivery, as Taylor hides the ball well and confuses hitters. He works fast, follows the gameplan and has strong mound presence. Conditioning has been an issue in the past, but he has worked hard to lose the bad-body tag. Taylor battled his command a bit after a late callup to Double-A in 2008, but he'll return there this season and the Marlins will keep pushing him up the ladder until he fails.

Year	Club (League)	Class	W	L	ERA	G	GS	CG	SV	IP	H	R	ER	HR	BB	SO	AVG
2006	Jamestown (NYP)	SS	3	5	2.47	13	13	0	0	66	59	26	18	2	4	48	.243
2007	Greensboro (SAL)	LoA	11	3	2.68	25	25	3	0	164	135	59	49	16	18	135	.222
	Jupiter (FSL)	HiA	1	1	8.10	2	2	0	0	10	16	9	9	0	5	3	.356
2008	Jupiter (FSL)	HiA	11	6	3.46	23	22	1	0	140	147	59	54	7	25	95	.268
	Carolina (SL)	AA	2	1	3.04	5	5	0	0	24	29	11	8	4	8	15	.312
MINOR LEAGUE TOTALS			28	16	3.07	68	67	4	0	404	386	164	138	29	60	296	.251

Houston Astros

BY KARY BOOHER

When the Astros wheeled across the finish line in 2008, team officials said they had two reasons to be optimistic. The big league club improved by 13½ games over the year before, and the June draft launched what Houston hopes is the rebirth of a depleted farm system.

If that sounds as if it's grasping at straws, well, it is. The Astros have traveled a bumpy and unsettling road since their 2005 World Series loss to the White Sox, so they'll take anything they can get to combat the painful reality that they have fallen from power in the National League Central.

While the Astros finished 86-76 and leapfrogged the Cardinals for a third-place finish, they had to hoof it to get there. Talk of wild-card contention briefly bubbled up in August but quickly faded despite a 42-24 second half. Nevertheless, it provided first-year general manager Ed Wade with some comfort after attempting to clean up the mess he inherited.

The immediate future hardly looks encouraging, however. Between the majors and the recent draft class, the farm system has been gutted in recent years by trades, the loss of draft picks and the unwillingness of owner Drayton McLane to pony up signing bonus money that might have cushioned the fall.

In 2007, for example, Houston gave up its first- and second-round picks as free-agent compensation, then failed to sign its third- and fourth-rounders. A year later, only one player from the first six rounds of that draft, outfielder Collin DeLome, remains in the organization. The aftermath has been tough to stomach. Astros minor league affiliates combined for a .397 winning percentage in 2008, easily the worst mark in baseball. Scouts from other organizations say they have to search far and wide to find Houston prospects who might be big league contributors.

The Astros say the reconstruction has begun. They spent $6.5 million on the 2008 draft, their first under scouting director Bobby Heck. Heck showed that he wasn't afraid to take chances, spending the 10th and 38th choices on catcher Jason Castro and righthander Jordan Lyles though neither was considered a consensus talent for those slots. Initial returns on both players were positive. After the season, Houston handed out contract extensions through 2010 to Heck, farm director Ricky Bennett and assistant GM David Gottfried.

At the same time, however, the Astros continued their penurious ways by announcing they would pull

ANDREW WOOLEY

Lance Berkman's outstanding season helped Houston contend in 2008

TOP 30 PROSPECTS

1. Jason Castro, c	16. Josh Flores, of
2. Bud Norris, rhp	17. David Duncan, lhp
3. Ross Seaton, rhp	18. Chris Hicks, rhp
4. Brian Bogusevic, of	19. Samuel Gervacio, rhp
5. Chris Johnson, 3b	20. Federico Hernandez, c
6. Jordan Lyles, rhp	21. Gilbert de la Vara, lhp
7. Felipe Paulino, rhp	22. T.J. Steele, of
8. Drew Sutton, 2b/ss	23. Eli Iorg, of
9. Collin DeLome, of	24. Polin Trinidad, lhp
10. Jay Austin, of	25. Chris Blazek, lhp
11. Tommy Manzella, ss	26. Jerrod Holloway, lhp
12. Chia-Jen Lo, rhp	27. Phil Disher, 1b
13. Sergio Perez, rhp	28. Leandro Cespedes, rhp
14. Brad Dydalewicz, lhp	29. Lou Palmisano, c
15. Brad James, rhp	30. Luis Cruz, lhp

out of Venezuela. Thanks to the efforts of Andres Reiner, who left to join the Rays three years ago, they had been scouting pioneers in the nation, signing such players as Bobby Abreu, Freddy Garcia, Carlos Guillen, Melvin Mora and Johan Santana.

The organization also experienced several changes. Longtime field coordinator Tom Wiendenbauer was reassigned to the scouting department, with administrative coach Al Pedrique taking his place. Triple-A Round Rock manager Dave Clark moved up to become the big league third-base coach, replacing Jackie Moore, who joined the Rangers.

General Manager: Ed Wade. **Farm Director:** Ricky Bennett. **Scouting Director:** Bobby Heck.

Class	Team	League	W	L	PCT	Finish*	Manager	Affiliated
Majors	Houston	National	86	76	.534	5th (16)	Cecil Cooper	—
Triple-A	Round Rock Express	Pacific Coast	64	79	.448	13th (16)	Dave Clark	2005
Double-A	Corpus Christi Hooks	Texas	55	85	.393	8th (8)	Luis Pujols	2005
High A	Salem Avalanche	Carolina	56	84	.400	8th (8)	Jim Pankovits	2003
Low A	Lexington Legends	South Atlantic	45	93	.326	16th (16)	Gregg Langbehn	2001
Short-season	Tri-City Valley Cats	New York-Penn	28	45	.384	13th (14)	Pete Rancont	2001
Rookie	Greeneville Astros	Appalachian	30	36	.455	7th (10)	Rodney Linares	2004
Overall 2008 Minor League Record			278	422	.397	30th		

* Finish in overall standings (No. of teams in league). ^League champion.

LAST YEAR'S TOP 30

Rank	Player, Pos.	Status
1.	J.R. Towles, c	Majors
2.	Felipe Paulino, rhp	No. 7
3.	Juan Gutierrez, rhp	(Diamondbacks)
4.	Michael Bourn, of	Majors
5.	Bud Norris, rhp	No. 2
6.	Brad James, rhp	No. 15
7.	Chad Reinke, rhp	(Padres)
8.	Eli Iorg, of	No. 23
9.	Josh Flores, of	No. 16
10.	Mitch Einerston, of	Droppped out
11.	Collin DeLome, of	No. 9
12.	Sergio Perez, rhp	No. 13
13.	Chris Johnson, 3b/1b	No. 5
14.	Samuel Gervacio, rhp	No. 19
15.	Tommy Manzella, ss	No. 11
16.	Paul Estrada, rhp	Dropped out
17.	Max Sapp, c	Dropped out
18.	Jordan Parraz, of	(Royals)
19.	Brian Bogusevic, lhp	No. 4
20.	Yordany Ramirez, of	Dropped out
21.	Wesley Wright, lhp	Majors
22.	Devon Torrence, of	Dropped out
23.	Lou Santangelo, c	Dropped out
24.	Mark McLemore, lhp	(Free agent)
25.	Robert Bono, rhp	Dropped out
26.	Koby Clemens, 3b	Dropped out
27.	Josh Muecke, lhp	Dropped out
28.	Johnny Ash, 2b	(Brewers)
29.	Matt Cusick, 2b	(Yankees)
30.	Jimmy Van Ostrand, of/1b	Dropped out

BEST TOOLS

Best Hitter for Average	Jason Castro
Best Power Hitter	Chris Johnson
Best Strike-Zone Discipline	Drew Sutton
Fastest Baserunner	Jay Austin
Best Athlete	Jay Austin
Best Fastball	Felipe Paulino
Best Curveball	Ross Seaton
Best Slider	Samuel Gervacio
Best Changeup	Brad Dydalewicz
Best Control	Polin Trinidad
Best Defensive Catcher	Jason Castro
Best Defensive Infielder	Tommy Manzella
Best Infield Arm	Chris Johnson
Best Defensive Outfielder	Josh Flores
Best Outfield Arm	Yordany Ramirez

PROJECTED 2012 LINEUP

Catcher	Jason Castro
First Base	Lance Berkman
Second Base	Drew Sutton
Third Base	Chris Johnson
Shortstop	Tommy Manzella
Left Field	Carlos Lee
Center Field	Michael Bourn
Right Field	Hunter Pence
No. 1 Starter	Roy Oswalt
No. 2 Starter	Bud Norris
No. 3 Starter	Ross Seaton
No. 4 Starter	Jordan Lyles
No. 5 Starter	Wandy Rodriguez
Closer	Jose Valverde

TOP PROSPECTS OF THE DECADE

Year	Player, Pos.	2008 Org.
1999	Lance Berkman, of	Astros
2000	Wilfredo Rodriguez, lhp	Out of baseball
2001	Roy Oswalt, rhp	Astros
2002	Carlos Hernandez, lhp	Dodgers
2003	John Buck, c	Royals
2004	Taylor Buchholz, rhp	Rockies
2005	Chris Burke, 2b	Diamondbacks
2006	Jason Hirsh, rhp	Rockies
2007	Hunter Pence, of	Astros
2008	Jason Castro, c	Astros

TOP DRAFT PICKS OF THE DECADE

Year	Player, Pos.	2008 Org.
1999	Mike Rosamond, of	Out of baseball
2000	Robert Stiehl, rhp	Out of baseball
2001	Chris Burke, ss	Diamondbacks
2002	Derick Grigsby, rhp	Out of baseball
2003	Jason Hirsh, rhp (2nd round)	Rockies
2004	Hunter Pence, of	Astros
2005	Brian Bogusevic, lhp	Astros
2006	Max Sapp, c	Astros
2007	*Derek Dietrich, 3b (3rd round)	Georgia Tech
2008	Jason Castro, c	Astros

*Did not sign.

LARGEST BONUSES IN CLUB HISTORY

Chris Burke, 2001	$2,125,000
Jason Castro, 2008	$2,070,000
Max Sapp, 2006	$1,400,000
Brian Bogusevic, 2005	$1,375,000
Robert Stiehl, 2000	$1,125,000

HOUSTON ASTROS

TOP 2009 ROOKIE: Bud Norris, rhp. After shining in the Arizona Fall League, he could crack the rotation or serve as a key reliever.

BREAKOUT PROSPECT: Samuel Gervacio, rhp. His slider is a legitimate strikeout pitch.

SLEEPER: J.B. Shuck, of. The 2008 sixth-round pick has bricklayer hands, Popeye forearms and plenty of speed.

SOURCE OF TOP 30 TALENT

Homegrown	28	Acquired	2
College	14	Trades	0
Junior college	3	Rule 5 draft	2
High school	5	Independent leagues	0
Draft-and-follow	0	Free agents/waivers	0
Nondrafted free agents	0		
International	6		

Numbers in parentheses indicate prospect rankings.

LF
Collin DeLome (9)
Mitch Einerston
Jon Gaston

CF
Brian Bogusevic (4)
Jay Austin (10)
Josh Flores (16)
T.J. Steele (22)
Jacob Priday

RF
Eli Iorg (23)
J.B. Shuck
Danny Meier

3B
Chris Johnson (5)
Mark Saccomanno
David Flores

SS
Tommy Manzella (11)
Wladimir Sutil

2B
Drew Sutton (8)
Edwin Maysonet

1B
Phil Disher (27)
Mark Ori

C
Jason Castro (1)
Federico Hernandez (20)
Lou Palmisano (29)
Max Sapp
Lou Santangelo
Koby Clemens

RHP

Starters	Relievers
Bud Norris (2)	Felipe Paulino (7)
Ross Seaton (3)	Chris Hicks (18)
Jordan Lyles (6)	Samuel Gervacio (19)
Chia-Jen Lo (12)	Phil Rummel
Sergio Perez (13)	Dan Mescaros
Brad James (15)	Jack Tilghman
Leandro Cespedes (28)	Arcenio Leon
Kyle Greenwalt	
Robert Bono	
Jose Trinidad	
Henry Villar	

LHP

Starters	Relievers
Brad Dydalewicz (14)	Gilbert de la Vara (21)
David Duncan (17)	Chris Blazek (25)
Polin Trinidad (24)	Josh Muecke
Jerrod Holloway (26)	Pat Urckfitz
Luis Cruz (30)	
Colton Pitkin	
Tyler Lumsden	

2008   BONUSES: $6.5 MILLION

BEST PURE HITTER: C Jason Castro (1) hit .341 with wood bats in the Cape Cod League in 2007, showing the excellent balance that is his hallmark. He keeps his bat in the strike zone a long time.

BEST POWER HITTER: 1B Phil Disher (15) has raw power to rival former South Carolina teammate Justin Smoak, the 11th overall pick. Disher has a sound swing from the right side and tremendous strength.

FASTEST RUNNER: OF Jay Austin (2) has excellent athleticism and plus-plus speed on the field, and he has been clocked even faster in workouts, earning 80 grades on the 20-80 scouting scale.

BEST DEFENSIVE PLAYER: Athletic enough to play in the outfield in the Cape, Castro is a strong receiver with an average, accurate arm and excellent intangibles such as work ethic and intelligence. Austin could be a premium defender in center field once he gains experience.

BEST FASTBALL: RHPs Jordan Lyles (1s) and Chris Hicks (14) both hit 95-96 mph this summer, which RHP Ross Seaton (3) did prior to the draft. Lyles has the best present command.

BEST SECONDARY PITCH: Five-foot-9 LHP Luis Cruz (9) has shown a plus changeup with sink and fade, and it could get even better. Fellow LHPs David Duncan (5, splitter) and Jarred Holloway (10, power curveball) also have strong secondary pitches.

BEST PRO DEBUT: Disher ranked second in the short-season New-York Penn League in homers (13), hits (85) and doubles (20) while batting .304/.381/.536. Tri-City teammate OF J.B. Schuck (6) batted .300/.385/.430 and walked (35) more than he struck out (34). Lyles struck out 64 and walked just 10 in 50 innings at Rookie-level Greeneville while going 3-3, 3.99.

BEST ATHLETE: Austin is more athlete than baseball player right now, but that's mostly because of his elite athletic ability and inexperience. OF T.J. Steele (4) also has all-around tools but is a notch or two behind Austin.

MOST INTRIGUING BACKGROUND: SS Jeff Hulett (12) is the second son of ex-big leaguer Tim Hulett to play pro ball, joining older brother Tug.

CLOSEST TO THE MAJORS: Castro's polish stands out in a draft that leaned toward raw talent.

BEST LATE-ROUND PICK: Disher doesn't have a true position, but he has improved at first base and may have an impact bat. The Astros also have high hopes for nondrafted free agent LHP Pat Urckfitz of Monroe (N.Y.) CC, who showed three average pitches.

THE ONE WHO GOT AWAY: 1B Chase Davidson (3) wanted second-round money, and while the Astros budged it wasn't enough to keep him from becoming part of a deep recruiting class at Georgia.

ASSESSMENT: In his first season as scouting director, Bobby Heck made bold calls on Castro and Lyles, who weren't consensus choices at picks 10 and 38 but have looked good so far. The Astros gauged signability well, avoiding the embarrassment of their 2007 draft.

2007   BONUSES: $1.6 MILLION

The Astros didn't have picks in the first two rounds, went cheap and misgauged signability, a deadly combination. A year later, OF Collin DeLome (5) was the only viable prospect—and the only choice left from the first six rounds in the system.

GRADE: F

2006   BONUSES: $3.6 MILLION

C Max Sapp (1) hasn't panned out, but 3B Chris Norris (4) and RHP Bud Norris (6) are two of the system's best and most advanced prospects.

GRADE: C

2005   BONUSES: $4.1 MILLION*

LHP Brian Bogusevic (1) failed on the mound, though he made encouraging progress after moving to the outfield last season. OF Eli Iorg (1s) has never gotten going, leaving Bogusevic as this crop's only hope. 3B Koby Clemens (8) did get his dad to spend an extra year with the Astros.

GRADE: D

2004   BONUSES: $2.2 MILLION*

The Astros made up for not having a first-rounder by grabbing OF Hunter Pence (2) with their top pick. There's still hope for C Justin Towles (20) despite his disappointing rookie season. INF/OF Ben Zobrist (6), LHP Troy Patton (9) and RHP Chad Reineke (13) would be useful—if they hadn't been traded.

GRADE: B+

*Draft analysis by John Manuel (2008) and Jim Callis (2004-07). Numbers in parentheses indicate draft rounds. *Bonuses for 2004-05 are first 10 rounds only.*

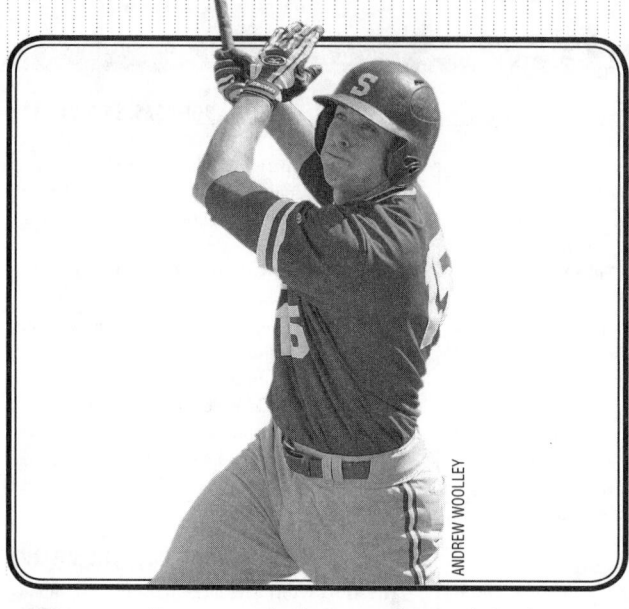

ANDREW WOOLLEY

AMERICAN LEAGUE EAST

PROSPECT

JASON CASTRO, C

Born: June 18, 1987.
Ht.: 6-3. **Wt.:** 210.
Bats: L. **Throws:** R.
Drafted:
Stanford, 2008
(1st round).
Signed by:
Joe Graham/Bobby Heck.

Castro was a known commodity before attending Stanford, as he was one of the top high school catchers in Northern California at Castro Valley High. The Red Sox drafted him in the 43rd round in 2005, though he would have gone higher if not for his college commitment. It wasn't until his breakout summer of 2007 in the Cape Cod League when he truly stamped himself as a premium pro prospect, however. Castro hit .263 in his first two college seasons, and then he posted the Cape's second-best average (.341). He would have pulled more catching duty had he not deferred to Buster Posey, the Florida State All-American and eventual Giants 2008 first-rounder, so he also played first base and even the outfield. By last June, he found himself as the Astros' first-round pick and centerpiece of the organization's push for a farm system turnaround. Drafted 10th overall, he signed for $2.07 million, the second-largest bonus in Astros history. That came after Castro paced Stanford to the College World Series, leading the Cardinal in both average (.376) and total bases (171) while finishing with 14 home runs and 73 RBIs.

Castro has all the tools to be a legitimate offensive catcher. He's got a loose swing, yet it has loft and scouts have rated his raw power at 55-60 on the 20-80 scouting scale. His success comes from staying inside the ball and he should be able to hit for average. A lefthanded hitter, most of his power is up the middle, and scouts say as he gets stronger he could develop power the other way. Castro spent most of his first two years at Stanford as a reserve, mostly at first base and DH. Scouts warmed up to him after his Cape performance, then saw him as a first-rounder when he smoothly handled catching duties as a junior. As a pro, he showed good leadership and seemed to enjoy calling games. He has soft hands and blocks balls well. His arm strength and accuracy also are solid, and scouts like his footwork and quick release. He threw out 33 percent of basestealers in his professional debut.

While one scout thought he had the best swing on the West Coast, Castro can get too loose at the plate. That could spell trouble, particularly against lefthanders. He showed in Hawaii Winter Baseball he could stay in against them, but advanced lefthanders will try to get Castro to chase. He also sometimes has trouble against sliders from righthanders. In his debut, he would connect with those pitches but roll over and hit weak grounders to first base. Because he didn't call games in college, he'll have to hone that skill in the minors.

Because the Astros left the Carolina League and signed a new high Class A affiliation agreement with Lancaster, they can shepherd Castro into his first full season by keeping him on the West Coast in the California League. He played briefly last season, with additional time in Hawaii Winter Baseball. He seems a safe bet to at least be a solid major league catcher, with the potential to be quite a bit more.

Year	Club (League)	Class	AVG	G	AB	R	H	2B	3B	HR	RBI	BB	SO	SB	OBP	SLG
2008	Tri-City (NYP)	SS	.275	39	138	10	38	9	0	2	12	22	32	0	.383	.384
MINOR LEAGUE TOTALS			.275	39	138	10	38	9	0	2	12	22	32	0	.383	.384

2 BUD NORRIS, RHP

BORN: March 2, 1985. **B-T:** R-R. **HT.:** 6-0. **WT.:** 195. **DRAFTED:** Cal Poly, 2006 (6th round). **SIGNED BY:** Dennis Twombley.

It was an up and down season for Norris, but the Astros were encouraged by how it closed. An elbow strain kept him out from mid-May to early July at Double-A Corpus Christi, but he came back and responded with a terrific second half (3.85 ERA in 43 innings) despite being on 75-pitch limits. Overall, he struck out 9.45 per nine innings. Norris seems clear of health issues and proved it in the Arizona Fall League. Thanks to a stocky build and strong legs, he pounds the zone with his fastball and shows a hard, short slider. The fastball was clocked at 98 mph in the AFL, but he works better when it's 93-95 and he spots it. Thanks to an adjustment in his delivery, he created better angles to attack hitters. The slider benefited the most, breaking down and away from righthanders now, rather than only horizontally. Norris is generously listed at 6 feet, so he doesn't get great downward plane on his pitches, and his fastball can flatten out if he tries to simply blow it by people. He'll need to maintain his improved delivery after a slight drift had kept him from getting good life on his pitches. He also needs to fully integrate his changeup. He shows a feel for it but didn't throw it often in the fall. Many believe Norris could challenge for a big league role in spring training. At the least he could be the club's No. 6 starter, biding his time at Triple-A Round Rock and waiting for a need. Long-term, he'll have to develop a true third pitch if he's to remain a starter.

Year	Club (League)	Class	W	L	ERA	G	GS	CG	SV	IP	H	R	ER	HR	BB	SO	AVG
2006	Tri-City (NYP)	SS	2	0	3.79	15	3	0	2	38	28	20	16	1	13	46	.200
2007	Lexington (SAL)	LoA	2	8	4.75	22	22	0	0	97	85	58	51	8	41	117	.233
	Salem (CAR)	HiA	1	0	1.50	1	1	0	0	6	4	1	1	0	1	2	.190
2008	Corpus Christi (TEX)	AA	3	8	4.05	19	19	0	0	80	89	42	36	8	31	84	.286
MINOR LEAGUE TOTALS			8	16	4.24	57	45	0	2	221	206	121	104	17	86	249	.246

3 ROSS SEATON, RHP

BORN: Sept. 18, 1989. **B-T:** L-R. **HT.:** 6-4. **WT.:** 215. **DRAFTED:** HS—Houston, 2008 (3rd round supplemental). **SIGNED BY:** Rusty Pendergrass/Mike Burns.

Seaton was relatively unheralded at the beginning of his senior year. But then he touched 96 mph in the spring, rocketing up draft boards, and landed as the top prep pitcher in the Texas prep ranks. He graduated as his high school's valedictorian and signed for $700,000 as a third-round supplemental pick. He didn't sign until late July and made just three starts in his pro debut. Scouts love Seaton's big frame, feel and command of three pitches, even out of a quarterback-like release. He has a smooth and easy delivery that's repeatable, allowing his fastball to sit consistently at 90-94 mph. His slider can be devastating to young hitters, and his changeup is a nice weapon. The Astros liked the way he pitched to contact in instructional league and that he enjoys talking pitching. He has a businesslike approach. Seaton tends to get jumpy off his back side, resulting in hurried, off-target throws. One scout said Seaton needed to use his legs more out of his delivery because, like many young pitchers, he tries to generate most of his velocity from his upper body. An adjustment there would help sharpen the slider, turning it into more of a late breaker. Given his drive, frame and maturity, Seaton projects to be a No. 2 starter in the majors with a shot to be a top-of-the-rotation figure. He'll likely open at low Class A Lexington, in the same rotation with Jordan Lyles, Houston's supplemental first-round pick in the same draft.

Year	Club (League)	Class	W	L	ERA	G	GS	CG	SV	IP	H	R	ER	HR	BB	SO	AVG
2008	Greeneville (APP)	R	0	0	13.50	3	3	0	0	4	8	7	6	1	2	4	.381
MINOR LEAGUE TOTALS			0	0	13.50	3	3	0	0	4	8	7	6	1	2	4	.381

4 BRIAN BOGUSEVIC, OF

BORN: Feb. 18, 1984. **B-T:** L-L. **HT.:** 6-3. **WT.:** 215. **DRAFTED:** Tulane, 2005 (1st round). **SIGNED BY:** Mike Rosamond.

Bogusevic rated No. 19 on this list a year ago, but that was when he was a lefthander trying to solve command issues that had plagued him ever since he signed for a $1.375 million as a first-rounder in 2005. But in July he and the Astros agreed it was time to ditch pitching. Bogusevic, a two-way star at Tulane, got a quick refresher course at Salem and then returned to the Texas League. He was great in Corpus Christi, then fared well in the Arizona Fall League, landing a spot on the Astros' 40-man roster. Bogusevic quickly made the conversion as a hitter and played center field well. He has a good approach at the plate and lets the ball get deep in the zone, allowing him to stay inside the ball well. It's a controlled approach, and his hits typically travel up the middle and to the opposite field. He covers a lot of ground in center and naturally has an above-average arm. Unlike Rick Ankiel, the last lefty to make a similar conversion, Bogusevic has trouble pulling inside pitches. His wrists aren't as quick as Ankiel's, who in the year he made the switch hit 21 home runs largely because he could turn around hard fastballs. Pitchers can get aggressive with Bogusevic and run it inside on him as a result. After a half-season of bashing in the Texas League and a good performance in the Arizona Fall League, Bogusevic will get pushed to Round Rock. His athleticism will get him to the majors, and his bat could leapfrog him over Michael Bourn.

Year	Club (League)	Class	AVG	G	AB	R	H	2B	3B	HR	RBI	BB	SO	SB	OBP	SLG
2007	Corpus Christi (TEX)	AA	.500	2	2	0	1	0	0	0	0	0	0	0	.500	.500
2008	Salem (CAR)	HiA	.217	8	23	4	5	2	0	1	6	4	1	1	.357	.435
	Corpus Christi (TEX)	AA	.371	42	124	21	46	10	2	3	20	16	24	8	.447	.556
MINOR LEAGUE TOTALS			.349	52	149	25	52	12	2	4	26	20	25	9	.433	.537

5 CHRIS JOHNSON, 3B

BORN: Oct. 1, 1984. **B-T:** R-R. **HT.:** 6-3. **WT.:** 220. **DRAFTED:** Stetson, 2006 (4th round). **SIGNED BY:** Jon Bunnell.

Johnson, the son of former big leaguer Ron Johnson, is the Astros' best power prospect in the high minors and could be an answer to the parent club's uncertain third base situation. He made a successful jump to Double-A in 2008, anchoring the Corpus Christi lineup before getting a late July promotion to Round Rock. Power is Johnson's best attribute. At the plate, he typically drives balls to left field and up the middle as he uses a wide stance and strong arms to get the bat head through the zone. Defensively, he has a plus arm at the hot corner, and when he gets to balls his throws whiz through the air. Even though Johnson saw his on-base and slugging percentages increase from previous seasons, he still has a habit of getting too aggressive and selling out for the longball. He can get fooled by breaking pitches. And because of a thick lower half, his range is just decent at third base. Johnson seems like he's at least a half-season away from contributing in the big leagues, but he could reach the majors sooner if the Astros struggle to replace Ty Wigginton, whom they non-tendered.

Year	Club (League)	Class	AVG	G	AB	R	H	2B	3B	HR	RBI	BB	SO	SB	OBP	SLG
2006	Tri-City (NYP)	SS	.212	60	222	18	47	7	1	1	29	11	35	7	.251	.266
2007	Lexington (SAL)	LoA	.259	64	255	37	66	14	0	8	44	17	38	3	.304	.408
	Salem (CAR)	HiA	.263	60	224	24	59	11	0	6	38	8	41	1	.292	.393
2008	Corpus Christi (TEX)	AA	.324	84	330	43	107	24	0	12	58	20	61	5	.364	.506
	Round Rock (PCL)	AAA	.218	30	101	10	22	2	1	1	9	5	25	0	.252	.287
MINOR LEAGUE TOTALS			.266	298	1132	132	301	58	2	28	178	61	200	16	.304	.395

6 JORDAN LYLES, RHP

RODGER WOOD

BORN: Oct. 19, 1990. **B-T:** R-R. **HT.:** 6-4. **WT.:** 185. **DRAFTED:** HS—Hartsville, S.C, 2008 (1st round supplemental). **SIGNED BY:** J.D. Alleva/Clarence Johns.

After his strong workout for club officials, the Astros pushed Lyles up their draft board, bucking consensus when they took him with the 38th overall pick in the 2008 draft. Lyles was not in BA's predraft Top 200, nor a top three rounds consideration for all but a handful of teams, even though he was the top prep prospect in South Carolina. He signed for $930,000 on the night of his high school graduation, spurning a University of South Carolina scholarship. He had also toyed with the idea of playing wide receiver for Steve Spurrier's Gamecocks. Lyles has a free and easy, classic delivery that the Astros say needs little tweaking. He shelved his cutter once in pro ball, and saw an immediate improvement in his fastball as it jumped from 86-88 mph in the spring to 90-96 all summer. He had good command of it even with the added velocity. His curveball has rotation and shape to it, and he has shown a feel for a changeup. Consistency will be paramount as Lyles advances through the system. He has trouble repeating his secondary stuff, especially the curveball. It flattens out at times. He has a tendency to elevate his fastball, and that will get him knocked around higher up in the minors. Lyles projects to be a solid No. 3 starter at this point, with a shot to be a No. 2. The Astros have plenty of time to nurture him and will tag-team him with Ross Seaton at Lexington to open 2008.

Year	Club (League)	Class	W	L	ERA	G	GS	CG	SV	IP	H	R	ER	HR	BB	SO	AVG
2008	Greeneville (APP)	R	3	3	3.99	13	13	0	0	50	44	26	22	4	10	64	.228
	Tri-City (NYP)	SS	0	0	6.35	2	2	0	0	6	7	5	4	2	7	4	.292
MINOR LEAGUE TOTALS			3	3	4.23	15	15	0	0	55	51	31	26	6	17	68	.235

7 FELIPE PAULINO, RHP

BORN: Oct. 5, 1983. **B-T:** R-R. **HT.:** 6-3. **WT.:** 245. **SIGNED:** Dominican Republic, 2001. **SIGNED BY:** Andres Reiner/Omar Lopez.

Just as excitement built around Paulino in spring training 2008, the Astros shut him down because of a pinched nerve in his throwing shoulder. With his return maddeningly pushed back time and again, he made only an August appearance at Round Rock before bursitis in his shoulder forced him back to the disabled list. He got some winter work in the Dominican League, with the Astros optimistic he would be ready in spring training. Paulino, who converted from shortstop early in his career, is an absolute flamethrower once clocked at 102 mph. Even if there is a slight dip in his velocity, he has enough to dominate and attack hitters because he showed an ability to locate his fastball before the injury. And if it's on, watch out for his hammer 80-85 mph curve. Like most hard throwers, Paulino needs an effective third pitch to maintain a rotation slot. The curve and changeup are not consistent enough, and his eagerness to attack leads to flying open in his delivery. He probably profiles better as a reliever. The Astros have few arms with as much upside as Paulino's and they'll give him every opportunity to work his way to the big leagues. He could be best eased in as a set-up man with eyes on the closer's job. That is, if he can stay healthy.

Year	Club (League)	Class	W	L	ERA	G	GS	CG	SV	IP	H	R	ER	HR	BB	SO	AVG
2002	Venoco (VSL)	R	0	0	1.29	4	0	0	0	7	4	1	1	1	6	4	.182
2003	Venoco (VSL)	R	1	0	5.59	5	0	0	0	10	6	6	6	0	12	13	.194
	Martinsville (APP)	R	2	2	5.61	16	0	0	1	26	23	20	16	0	19	27	.235
2004	Greeneville (APP)	R	1	3	7.59	10	10	0	0	32	30	30	27	4	22	37	.246
2005	Tri-City (NYP)	SS	2	2	3.82	13	2	0	1	31	21	15	13	2	11	34	.189
	Lexington (SAL)	LoA	1	1	1.85	7	5	0	0	24	21	8	5	2	6	30	.233
2006	Salem (CAR)	HiA	9	7	4.35	27	26	0	0	126	119	67	61	13	59	91	.250
2007	Corpus Christi (TEX)	AA	6	9	3.62	22	21	0	0	112	103	55	45	6	49	110	.238
	Houston (NL)	MAJ	2	1	7.11	5	3	0	0	19	22	15	15	5	7	11	.289
2008	Round Rock (PCL)	AAA	0	0	0.00	1	0	0	0	1	1	0	0	0	1	1	.333
MINOR LEAGUE TOTALS			22	24	4.25	105	64	0	2	368	328	202	174	28	185	347	.237
MAJOR LEAGUE TOTALS			2	1	7.11	5	3	0	0	19	22	15	15	5	7	11	.289

8 DREW SUTTON, 2B/SS

BORN: June 30, 1983. **B-T:** B-R. **HT.:** 6-3. **WT.:** 190. **DRAFTED:** Baylor, 2004 (15th round). **SIGNED BY:** Pat Murphy.

With his career in danger of stagnating, the switch-hitting Sutton returned to Corpus Christi for a second full season, blistered the Texas League and won a spot on the 40-man roster after the season. He led the TL in hits, doubles and runs, while finishing second in OBP and third in slugging. For a lanky middle infielder, Sutton shows surprising power, as he tracks the ball into the zone before typically making solid contact. That's on top of being a potential high OBP guy. He also looks slightly better and more comfortable from the left side. Prior to the season, he smoothed his swing by working with Jaime Cevallos, a former golf pro who uses computer models as a learning tool. The biggest question facing Sutton is whether he will hit against advanced pitching. He must continue to do a better job of taking strike one and working the count rather than fishtailing through an at-bat by being overly aggressive. He isn't a true shortstop, though he has enough arm for the position and could fill in there. He's better at second, showing poise in making the pivot. He also has played third base and center field. Sutton will head to Round Rock this year, with a shot to become a midseason callup. Because he can play several positions, he ideally fits as a utility player.

Year	Club (League)	Class	AVG	G	AB	R	H	2B	3B	HR	RBI	BB	SO	SB	OBP	SLG
2004	Tri-City (NYP)	SS	.280	63	250	43	70	10	0	1	16	39	50	2	.379	.332
2005	Salem (CAR)	HiA	.257	43	148	22	38	5	1	3	12	29	34	4	.382	.365
	Lexington (SAL)	LoA	.286	62	231	46	66	19	2	13	42	36	51	4	.394	.554
2006	Salem (CAR)	HiA	.263	125	456	65	120	27	2	15	48	69	84	20	.360	.430
2007	Corpus Christi (TEX)	AA	.269	128	480	81	129	28	1	9	53	57	86	24	.351	.388
2008	Corpus Christi (TEX)	AA	.317	133	520	102	165	39	4	20	69	76	98	20	.408	.523
MINOR LEAGUE TOTALS			.282	554	2085	359	588	128	10	61	240	306	403	74	.378	.441

9 COLLIN DeLOME, OF

BORN: Dec. 18, 1985. **B-T:** L-R. **HT.:** 6-2. **WT.:** 195. **DRAFTED:** Lamar, 2007 (5th round). **SIGNED BY:** Rusty Pendergrass.

DeLome was the highest-drafted Astro to sign in 2007, a dubious honor considering Houston didn't own first- or second-round picks and compounded that by failing to sign their third- and fourth-rounders. Signed for $135,000, he entered pro ball fairly raw but had an encouraging debut in the New York-Penn League, followed by 22 home runs in Class A ball last year. DeLome is a toolshed and has a great body that's lean and athletic. He shows good power from the left side and generates great bat speed. He also has great foot speed as well as good arm strength for a center fielder. In instructional league, he got down the line in 4.01 seconds on drag bunts. DeLome struggled to make enough contact in his first full season, and to tame his penchant for strikeouts he'll need to shorten an extremely long swing. He starts out with a twitch in his back elbow and then has difficulty checking his swing because he is so aggressive. If he quiets it down, he could start to go up the middle, but right now he's another in a long line of pull-happy young hitters. Scouts envision DeLome as a corner outfielder with legitimate power if he can tone down his swing and develop a better approach. He'll open back in high Class A and take the next step to Corpus Christi by midseason if he performs well in an extremely hitter-friendly environment.

Year	Club (League)	Class	AVG	G	AB	R	H	2B	3B	HR	RBI	BB	SO	SB	OBP	SLG
2007	Tri-City (NYP)	SS	.300	65	243	31	73	17	6	6	28	23	65	9	.374	.494
2008	Lexington (SAL)	LoA	.261	61	226	41	59	9	6	12	36	18	71	7	.329	.513
	Salem (CAR)	HiA	.232	68	237	40	55	14	3	10	35	17	57	7	.305	.443
MINOR LEAGUE TOTALS			.265	194	706	112	187	40	15	28	99	58	193	23	.336	.483

10 JAY AUSTIN, OF

BORN: Aug. 10, 1990. **B-T:** L-L. **HT.:** 5-11. **WT.:** 170. **DRAFTED:** HS— Atlanta, 2008 (2nd round). **SIGNED BY:** Lincoln Martin/Clarence Johns.

Austin was one of the youngest players in the Rookie-level Appalachian League last year, which is why the Astros aren't fretting too much about the meager offensive production in his pro debut. He hit 50 home runs in his prep career and committed to Southern California before choosing instead to sign for a $715,000 bonus. While Houston has a few toolsy outfielders in its system, none have the same all-around potential as Austin. A lefthanded hitter and center fielder, he has the range to patrol the middle garden, the bat to handle leadoff and speed that could make him a major basestealing threat. His swing is fluid and quick and he shows good hand-eye coordination. His tendency for now is to hit line drives with some power to the gaps. He's a plus runner out of the box with 4.1-second times down the line and seems to skate, grading out as a 70 runner underway. Austin tried carrying over his home run hitting from high school and racked up the strikeouts. He just needs to trust his tools and not worry about swinging for the fences. Scouts found that he tends to cheat in his approach as he leans forward with his body, although it's not exactly a lunge. A good curveball can wipe him out. In the outfield, he's learning to track fly balls and to take better routes. He has a below-average arm, but a weight and conditioning program could add some power to his throws. One scout compared Austin to Michael Bourn, not as fast but with a better bat. The Astros plan to station Austin with the Lexington workout group in spring training. Because he is so young and raw, they acknowledge he could benefit from a stay in extended spring training before returning to short-season ball, however.

Year	Club (League)	Class	AVG	G	AB	R	H	2B	3B	HR	RBI	BB	SO	SB	OBP	SLG
2008	Greeneville (APP)	R	.198	55	212	31	42	4	2	0	14	19	69	14	.277	.236
MINOR LEAGUE TOTALS			.198	55	212	31	42	4	2	0	14	19	69	14	.277	.236

11 TOMMY MANZELLA, SS

BORN: April 16, 1983. **B-T:** R-R. **HT.:** 6-2. **WT.:** 190. **DRAFTED:** Tulane, 2005 (3rd round). **SIGNED BY:** Mike Rosamond.

Manzella endured an emotional 2008 season, during which his mother died from ovarian cancer. That came just as Manzella received a promotion to Round Rock after he earned Texas League midseason all-star honors at Corpus Christi. His performance dropped off significantly in the Pacific Coast League, raising concerns about his future profile. Tall, lean and athletic, Manzella has a good swing and covers the strike zone fairly well, but he doesn't show enough strength in his lower half to generate much leverage or power. At times, he can drop the bat head on mistake pitches. But the key with Manzella will be whether he can hit for enough average to be an everyday player. Defensively, he's a slick fielder in the mold of former Astro Adam Everett, with good feet and balance and good range going both ways. He makes strong throws across the diamond. His defense isn't quite as good as Everett's, though his offense should be better. How much better will determine his long-term role. The

Astros saw enough to add Manzella to the 40-man roster after the season, and they'll give him a chance to break camp as a backup infielder. If not, he will return to Round Rock.

Year	Club (League)	Class	AVG	G	AB	R	H	2B	3B	HR	RBI	BB	SO	SB	OBP	SLG
2005	Tri-City (NYP)	SS	.232	53	220	24	51	6	4	0	18	9	39	5	.260	.295
2006	Lexington (SAL)	LoA	.275	99	338	50	93	22	1	7	43	33	80	16	.340	.408
2007	Salem (CAR)	HiA	.238	57	223	28	53	13	0	0	24	19	30	5	.305	.296
	Corpus Christi (TEX)	AA	.289	64	228	35	66	12	3	1	15	19	40	10	.343	.382
2008	Corpus Christi (TEX)	AA	.299	54	224	27	67	11	5	4	34	17	35	4	.346	.446
	Round Rock (PCL)	AAA	.219	61	228	19	50	15	1	0	15	17	39	0	.273	.294
MINOR LEAGUE TOTALS			.260	388	1461	183	380	79	14	12	149	114	263	40	.314	.358

12 CHIA-JEN LO, RHP

BORN: April 7, 1986. **B-T:** R-R. **HT.:** 6-1. **WT.:** 190. **SIGNED:** Taiwan, 2008. **SIGNED BY:** Glen Barker.

Houston sought to raise its profile in the Pacific Rim two years ago and dispatched Glen Barker to scout the region. His first major signing came in November with Lo, who received a $250,000 bonus and became the first Taiwanese pitcher in the Astros system. He shouldn't be overwhelmed by his new surroundings, having pitched for his national team in the Beijing Olympics, allowing one run in two relief innings, as well as several other major events since 2004. Lo has primarily worked in relief in the past, but a potential four-pitch arsenal with a clean delivery have the Astros willing to give him a shot as a starter. He showed a 91-92 mph fastball after signing and has reached as high as 96. He also throws a splitter, slider and change. The splitter isn't overpowering, but Lo gets it to bottom out. The slider comes in at 79-81 and has late life, but needs more sharpness to be an out pitch. His changeup is just OK at this point. The Astros find a lot to like about his delivery and build. Unlike Japanese pitchers who often have a pause, or Korean pitchers who can be herky-jerky, Lo is fluid and balanced. After finishing his college education, Lo will join the Astros in spring training and could open as high as high Class A.

Year	Club (League)	Class	W	L	ERA	G	GS	CG	SV	IP	H	R	ER	HR	BB	SO	AVG
2008	Did Not Play—Signed Late																

13 SERGIO PEREZ, RHP

BORN: Dec. 5, 1984. **B-T:** R-R. **HT.:** 6-3. **WT.:** 230. **DRAFTED:** Tampa, 2006 (2nd round). **SIGNED BY:** Jon Bunnell.

Perez missed most of the 2008 season because of a groin injury followed by a freak broken hand injury that occurred while he was trying to bunt. He rediscovered his fire in the Arizona Fall League, continuing his ascent from NCAA Division II Tampa, where he led the team to a national title in 2006 with a win in the semifinals and a save in the championship. As he did in college, Perez attacks hitters with a 90-94 mph fastball, sitting most often at 91. Another weapon is his major league average slider, which has good depth and tilt at around 85 mph. His changeup is solid but would be more effective if he would pace himself better out of his delivery. Perez tries to combat sometimes so-so command by throwing from a high three-quarters arm slot, though he tends to lower it at times. He's already got an arm wrap, so that slows down his delivery as well. Despite an encouraging effort in the AFL, look for Perez to return to Corpus Christi, with a shot to reach Round Rock before the all-star break if he pitches well. He has the pitches to remain a starter for now, though most believe he'll eventually be better in the bullpen.

Year	Club (League)	Class	W	L	ERA	G	GS	CG	SV	IP	H	R	ER	HR	BB	SO	AVG
2006	Lexington (SAL)	LoA	3	0	2.20	11	0	0	0	16	9	6	4	0	8	21	.153
2007	Salem (CAR)	HiA	7	10	4.00	25	25	0	0	128	129	67	57	9	43	84	.265
2008	Corpus Christi (TEX)	AA	2	3	2.30	7	5	0	0	27	30	8	7	3	8	18	.283
MINOR LEAGUE TOTALS			12	13	3.56	43	30	0	0	172	168	81	68	12	59	123	.258

14 BRAD DYDALEWICZ, LHP

BORN: March 24, 1990. **B-T:** L-L. **HT.:** 6-1. **WT.:** 180. **DRAFTED:** HS—Austin, 2008 (8th round). **SIGNED BY:** Rusty Pendergrass/Bobby Heck.

Houston signed Dydalewicz just before the Aug. 15 deadline last year for an above-slot, $425,000 bonus, after failing to sign Georgia high school first baseman and third-round pick Chase Davidson. Dydalewicz instantly became their most exciting lefthanded starter prospect, even though he sneaked in just 10 late-season innings after signing and will play the 2009 season at 19 years old. He throws a live fastball and plus curveball, with enough arm strength to suggest his heater will consistently sit in the low 90s as he advances. He was 90-94 mph in the spring, an encouraging sign considering he tore his ACL in 2007 while playing football. The curveball has 1-7 shape, and it's difficult for hitters to pick up. Dydalewicz creates deception out of a delivery that has a lot of moving parts. At times, his front shoulder flies open, and his elbow gets underneath the ball, resulting in pitches left up in the zone. At least one scout sees Dydalewicz as a future Billy Wagner type, but the Astros want him to start, if only to get as many innings as possible in order to enhance all of his pitches, including a changeup that he rarely threw last year. They could push him to Lexington if he has a good spring, but it's more likely that Dydalewicz stays back in extended spring training before joining a short-season club.

Year	Club (League)	Class	W	L	ERA	G	GS	CG	SV	IP	H	R	ER	HR	BB	SO	AVG
2008	Greeneville (APP)	R	0	0	2.70	4	4	0	0	10	7	3	3	1	3	6	.206
MINOR LEAGUE TOTALS			0	0	2.70	4	4	0	0	10	7	3	3	1	3	6	.206

15 BRAD JAMES, RHP

BORN: June 19, 1984. **B-T:** R-R. **HT.:** 6-2. **WT.:** 200. **DRAFTED:** North Central Texas JC, 2004 (29th round). **SIGNED BY:** Pat Murphy.

James, obtained from the same school in the same draft that produced J.R. Towles, rated No. 6 on this list a year ago but regressed during a frustrating season in which he battled back problems that limited him to 18 starts at Corpus Christi and led to a seven-week absence in the second half. The Astros point to James breaking a bone in his right foot after the 2007 season, and then trying to overcompensate on the mound as his downfall. A screw was inserted in his foot during surgery and led James to push off the rubber more carefully. Inadvertently, he fell into bad habits, throwing across his body, and saw his low 90s sinker become less effective as it flattened out. There was hope he would get himself straightened out in the Arizona Fall League, but he ended up reverting to the problems that forced him to the DL during the regular season. When on, his sinker dominates low in the zone, and he still had a 2.0 groundout/airout ratio last year. But he has a tendency to fall in love with the sinker too much, so he has tried to incorporate his slider more frequently. His changeup still lags far behind. Long term, James projects as a reliever, but for now he'll go back to Corpus Christi, where a rotation slot will allow him to make up for lost innings.

Year	Club (League)	Class	W	L	ERA	G	GS	CG	SV	IP	H	R	ER	HR	BB	SO	AVG
2004	Greeneville (APP)	R	2	6	4.44	13	10	0	0	53	49	36	26	1	26	38	.245
2005	Greeneville (APP)	R	3	3	4.97	13	13	0	0	63	65	42	35	2	24	48	.265
2006	Lexington (SAL)	LoA	6	2	1.36	17	14	1	0	92	75	24	14	3	28	51	.220
2007	Salem (CAR)	HiA	9	2	1.98	16	16	0	0	96	72	27	21	5	33	55	.207
	Corpus Christi (TEX)	AA	1	5	5.17	9	9	0	0	47	53	27	27	2	20	22	.294
2008	Corpus Christi (TEX)	AA	6	6	4.45	18	18	0	0	93	107	52	46	9	35	45	.300
MINOR LEAGUE TOTALS			27	24	3.43	86	80	1	0	444	421	208	169	22	166	259	.252

16 JOSH FLORES, OF

BORN: Nov. 18, 1985. **B-T:** R-R. **HT.:** 6-0. **WT.:** 195. **DRAFTED:** Triton (Ill.) JC, 2005 (4th round). **SIGNED BY:** Kevin Stein.

Flores is one of the toolsiest outfielders in the organization, but it has been hard for the Astros to get a clear read on his ability because of injuries and inconsistency. After batting .219 there in 2007, he was set to return to Corpus Christi in 2008 but slipped on a curb outside a restaurant in the offseason, blew out his left knee and had surgery to repair two ligaments. That wiped out regular season for him. However, a return in instructional league to shake off the rust had the Astros optimistic about his ability to bounce back from the injury. Timid at first upon his return, Flores finished strong and did not appear bothered by the knee when jumping out of the box. Refining his hitting approach remains the biggest point of emphasis for Flores, as his game is (or should be) based on speed and putting the ball in play. In instructs last fall, he struggled with balls on the outer half of the plate. He needs better plate discipline to bat at the top of the order, and unfortunately has shown little interest in bunting. He has the speed to play center field, though he's still learning the nuances of the position, and an average arm. The key to Flores' success will be his legs, and he'll return to Corpus Christi and try to get back on track.

Year	Club (League)	Class	AVG	G	AB	R	H	2B	3B	HR	RBI	BB	SO	SB	OBP	SLG
2005	Greeneville (APP)	R	.335	59	248	49	83	12	5	8	25	16	57	20	.384	.520
	Lexington (SAL)	LoA	.278	5	18	1	5	2	0	0	1	1	4	4	.316	.389
2006	Lexington (SAL)	LoA	.253	125	475	81	120	19	2	11	35	33	107	28	.313	.371
2007	Salem (CAR)	HiA	.325	63	246	49	80	16	6	5	30	23	47	25	.392	.500
	Corpus Christi (TEX)	AA	.219	60	192	29	42	8	3	2	12	18	40	14	.284	.323
2008	Did Not Play—Injured															
MINOR LEAGUE TOTALS			.280	312	1179	209	330	57	16	26	103	91	255	91	.340	.422

17 DAVID DUNCAN, LHP

BORN: June 1, 1986. **B-T:** L-L. **HT.:** 6-9. **WT.:** 230. **DRAFTED:** Georgia Tech, 2008 (5th round). **SIGNED BY:** Lincoln Martin.

Duncan has been a frequent favorite on teams' draft boards, with the Twins taking him in the 14th round in 2005 out of high school—when he was rated the top prep prospect in Ohio—and the Nationals taking him in the 23rd round in 2007 as a draft-eligible sophomore. The Astros took him in the fifth round last year and signed him for $185,000, and it's understandable why they would dream on him as well. He's a big lefty who held down Georgia Tech's Friday night starter role the past two seasons, leading the Yellow Jackets in strikeouts and innings last year. Because of his size, he has the natural downward plane on his pitches and three legitimate weapons in his fastball, curve and splitter. The split is his out pitch and could be a plus pitch if he consistently commands it as a pro. His fastball sits around 88-92 mph, and he showed great command of it in his debut. The curve remains rudimentary, as it looks loopy and does not yet have the desired spin. Some people view Duncan as a potential set-up reliever, but the Astros will give him every chance to stick in a starter's role. He'll open 2009 at low Class A Lexington.

Year	Club (League)	Class	W	L	ERA	G	GS	CG	SV	IP	H	R	ER	HR	BB	SO	AVG
2008	Tri-City (NYP)	SS	3	4	4.88	14	14	0	0	55	60	37	30	5	9	45	.269
MINOR LEAGUE TOTALS			3	4	4.88	14	14	0	0	55	60	37	30	5	9	45	.269

18 CHRIS HICKS, RHP

BORN: Feb. 17, 1987. **B-T:** R-R. **HT.:** 6-3. **WT.:** 207. **DRAFTED:** Georgia Tech, 2008 (14th round). **SIGNED BY:** Lincoln Martin.

Hicks' family moved from St. Louis to suburban Atlanta after his high school junior year, and he stayed local by attending college at Georgia Tech. He spent the last two seasons as a set-up man and closer, and signed for $150,000 despite his 8.67 ERA in 27 appearances last season. The Astros were intrigued by his frame and power stuff, however, and will give him a shot at starting. After seeing Hicks take batting practice at short-season Tri-City last summer, they noted his strength and athletic frame, with broad shoulders and strong legs. Hicks does have the potential for several weapons. His fastball was sitting 92-95 mph in the spring and then touched 96 in Hawaii Winter Baseball. He also showed a knuckle-curve and a power slider, though both need a lot of refinement. The knuckle-curve tends to flatten out. He used a split-finger in college but is working on developing a changeup. The big key will be command, however, which is what kept him from being more effective in college. The Astros think his arm could handle 200 innings a year eventually, so they'll slot him into Lexington's rotation and see if he has the command for it.

Year	Club (League)	Class	W	L	ERA	G	GS	CG	SV	IP	H	R	ER	HR	BB	SO	AVG
2008	Tri-City (NYP)	SS	0	0	3.38	6	0	0	0	8	3	3	3	1	3	13	.111
MINOR LEAGUE TOTALS			0	0	3.38	6	0	0	0	8	3	3	3	1	3	13	.111

19 SAMUEL GERVACIO, RHP

BORN: Jan. 10, 1985. **B-T:** R-R. **HT.:** 6-0. **WT.:** 170. **SIGNED:** Dominican Republic, 2002. **SIGNED BY:** Julio Linares.

The Astros added Gervacio to the 40-man roster after the 2007 season, and while he hasn't reached the majors yet he did open eyes in a late-season promotion from Corpus Christi to Round Rock. In his final two appearances he mowed down 13 in six innings, and he has consistently averaged better than a strikeout per inning. Throwing from a three-quarters delivery and at times sidearm, Gervacio creates deception and can run his fastball up to 94 mph, even touching 95 late in the season. He throws two versions of his slider, and both are effective. One breaks sharply down and away, a big emphasis in the Astros system, and he also throws a backdoor slider that starts in and dives back over the plate. His changeup can be a plus pitch, but he goes to it only on occasion. To get major league hitters out he'll have to sharpen his fastball command and reduce his reliance on the slider, which can get him into trouble. He always falls back on it in key situations, rather than leaning on a fastball that would cross up hitters in breaking ball counts. Because he varies his delivery, his release point gets inconsistent, and he complicates the situation by being out of position as he falls off to the first-base side of the mound. He'll return to Round Rock to start the season but could pitch his way into the big league bullpen at some point.

Year	Club (League)	Class	W	L	ERA	G	GS	CG	SV	IP	H	R	ER	HR	BB	SO	AVG
2003	Astros (DSL)	R	4	0	2.01	24	0	0	6	45	34	13	10	3	14	50	.206
2004	Astros (DSL)	R	1	4	1.92	29	0	0	13	52	30	18	11	2	29	81	.160
2005	Greeneville (APP)	R	3	2	2.67	21	0	0	8	34	24	10	10	1	6	53	.190
	Lexington (SAL)	LoA	1	0	0.96	5	0	0	0	9	4	1	1	0	1	11	.125
2006	Lexington (SAL)	LoA	7	5	2.58	47	0	0	10	84	58	28	24	8	28	89	.197
2007	Salem (CAR)	HiA	1	3	2.44	39	0	0	18	55	42	16	15	1	15	80	.204
	Corpus Christi (TEX)	AA	3	2	1.99	13	0	0	0	23	15	7	5	1	11	24	.197
2008	Corpus Christi (TEX)	AA	2	5	4.13	47	0	0	5	65	69	36	30	8	26	82	.275
	Round Rock (PCL)	AAA	1	0	2.25	3	0	0	0	8	6	2	2	0	3	14	.207
MINOR LEAGUE TOTALS			23	21	2.60	228	0	0	60	374	282	131	108	24	133	484	.206

20 FEDERICO HERNANDEZ, C

BORN: Feb. 9, 1988. **B-T:** B-R. **HT.:** 6-0. **WT.:** 170. **SIGNED:** Venezuela, 2006. **SIGNED BY:** Pablo Torrealba/Adriano Rodriguez.

The Astros have long tapped into the talent pool in Venezuela and discovered Hernandez as an 18-year-old in Caracas. A cousin of Reds catcher Ramon Hernandez, he was regarded by Rookie-level Appalachian League managers as the top defensive catcher in the league last year. That's an impressive feat, considering he did not take up the position until signing. He has a good arm and good accuracy, and he showed 1.95-second pop times consistently in instructional league. His receiving skills, feet, soft hands and ability to call a game also get high marks. Hernandez also blocks balls well, with good range behind the plate, and always shows good hustle. At the plate, he has started switch-hitting and projects as an average hitter who isn't expected to have much power. He is undisciplined at this point, with a tendency to chase pitches. He looks better from his natural right side now, showing good balance in instructional league. From the left side, he has timing issues and shows more hand movement trying to set up. Like most catchers, he is a below-average runner. Even if Hernandez develops only fringe-average hitting ability, he would project as a starting backstop based on his defensive potential. He is expected to open 2009 at Lexington.

Year	Club (League)	Class	AVG	G	AB	R	H	2B	3B	HR	RBI	BB	SO	SB	OBP	SLG
2006	Astros (VSL)	R	.274	39	117	22	32	2	0	2	9	12	22	0	.346	.342
2007	Astros (VSL)	R	.299	48	167	24	50	10	2	1	23	11	20	2	.344	.401
2008	Greeneville (APP)	R	.298	36	114	14	34	8	0	3	17	8	19	0	.347	.447
MINOR LEAGUE TOTALS			.291	123	398	60	116	20	2	6	49	31	61	2	.346	.397

21 GILBERT DE LA VARA, LHP

BORN: Oct. 4, 1984. **B-T:** L-L. **HT.:** 5-11. **WT.:** 160. **DRAFTED:** Pima (Ariz.) CC, D/F 2004 (15th round). **SIGNED BY:** Mike Brown (Royals).

As they did last offseason, the Astros dipped into the major league Rule 5 draft at the Winter Meetings in December to try to strengthen their bullpen from the left side. Last year it was Dodgers farmhand Wesley Wright, who made 71 appearances in Houston and stuck with the team. This time it was de la Vara, a former Royals farmhand who split last season between high Class A Wilmington and Double-A Northwest Arkansas. De la Vara can touch 91 mph but generally pitches at 87-89. His curveball is a big bender with enough depth that many righthanded hitters just take the pitch and hope for the best. His changeup improved quite a bit last season, but they key to his chances for sticking in the big leagues will be improving his command. De la Vara has shown enough stuff to get righthanded hitters out, though his long-term role remains as a lefty specialist. Scouts long have questioned his durability due to his slight frame, and he's had trouble maintaining the quality of his stuff in back-to-back outings. If he doesn't stick on the 25-man roster he'll have to clear waivers and be offered back to the Royals for half the $50,000 draft price.

Year	Club (League)	Class	W	L	ERA	G	GS	CG	SV	IP	H	R	ER	HR	BB	SO	AVG
2005	Royals (AZL)	R	4	1	2.33	16	1	0	3	39	31	10	10	2	13	43	.226
2006	Burlington (MWL)	LoA	4	4	3.38	27	1	0	9	51	35	21	19	3	12	64	.196
	High Desert (CAL)	HiA	0	5	5.61	16	3	0	4	34	43	30	21	3	14	36	.316
2007	Wilmington (CAR)	HiA	2	1	0.82	22	0	0	7	33	20	4	3	1	12	26	.180
	Wichita (TEX)	AA	3	2	5.74	19	0	0	1	27	33	19	17	3	10	16	.306
2008	Wilmington (CAR)	HiA	3	3	3.65	24	0	0	2	44	33	18	18	1	12	31	.217
	NW Arkansas (TEX)	AA	3	0	2.76	21	0	0	2	33	23	12	10	0	15	21	.205
MINOR LEAGUE TOTALS			19	16	3.40	145	6	0	28	260	218	114	98	13	88	237	.233

22 T.J. STEELE, OF

BORN: Sept. 21, 1986. **B-T:** R-R. **HT.:** 6-3. **WT.:** 215. **DRAFTED:** Arizona, 2008 (4th round). **SIGNED BY:** Mark Ross.

Scouts are mixed when it comes to Steele, though everyone agrees the Astros will have something if his hitting emerges from a cupboard of tools. The Astros are gambling that it will, having signed him to a $267,000 bonus as their fourth-round pick last year. They've actually been on his trail since he was at Canyon del Oro High, a Tucson powerhouse that also produced Ian Kinsler and Shelley and Chris Duncan. He was Houston's 22nd-round pick in 2005 but headed to Arizona, so the Astros finally got their man. Steele comes packaged in a big frame but with the speed and athleticism to play center field. He covers a lot of ground thanks to plus speed and instincts, and his arm is playable. He's a plus runner who swiped 28 of 30 bags for the Wildcats last year, and at times he provides pop. He has big holes in his swing, however, particularly against breaking balls. He has trouble recognizing the spin on offspeed pitches. The Astros are emphasizing that he recognize fastball counts better, which would make him more selective, and not worry about offspeed stuff all the time. The Astros had to shut him down in mid-August after he injured his thumb diving for a ball in the outfield, but they'll still expect him to win a job with their Lancaster club in the spring.

Year	Club (League)	Class	AVG	G	AB	R	H	2B	3B	HR	RBI	BB	SO	SB	OBP	SLG
2008	Tri-City (NYP)	SS	.283	40	159	18	45	8	1	3	21	6	51	6	.320	.403
MINOR LEAGUE TOTALS			.283	40	159	18	45	8	1	3	21	6	51	6	.320	.403

23 ELI IORG, OF

BORN: March 14, 1983. **B-T:** R-R. **HT.:** 6-3. **WT.:** 200. **DRAFTED:** Tennessee, 2005 (1st round supplemental). **SIGNED BY:** Mike Rosamond.

Three years after he signed for $900,000, Iorg put up the worst offensive numbers of his career at Corpus Christi. But it would be premature to throw the former Tennessee standout on the scrap heap just yet. The son of former big leaguer Garth Iorg, Eli was coming off Tommy John surgery on his right elbow in 2007, and it appeared to affect his timing. Though he did show occasional home run power, he showed a penchant for strikeouts and his slugging percentage was a career low. Pitchers rarely felt threatened and went on the offensive, knowing he struggled to stay on breaking pitches. Iorg can get passive at the plate, taking pitches when it would be wiser to jump on something he can drive. Iorg was also hard on himself during his struggles and didn't handle adversity well. Defensively, he is at least average across the board but needs work on little things like getting his feet set. He had shown an above-average arm before the surgery. He profiles as a corner outfielder but needs to make big strides with the bat. He'll likely move up to Round Rock and try to sway scouts who have doubts about his ability to produce at the plate in spite of his family's baseball lineage.

Year	Club (League)	Class	AVG	G	AB	R	H	2B	3B	HR	RBI	BB	SO	SB	OBP	SLG
2005	Greeneville (APP)	R	.333	35	138	36	46	7	2	7	34	9	27	12	.391	.565
2006	Lexington (SAL)	LoA	.256	125	469	68	120	32	4	15	85	33	119	42	.313	.437
2007	Salem (CAR)	HiA	.296	44	162	35	48	12	4	5	24	14	36	14	.350	.512
2008	Corpus Christi (TEX)	AA	.268	127	459	53	123	21	5	11	59	23	112	21	.308	.407
MINOR LEAGUE TOTALS			.274	331	1228	192	337	72	15	38	202	79	294	89	.325	.450

24 POLIN TRINIDAD, LHP

BORN: Nov. 19, 1984. **B-T:** L-L. **HT.:** 6-3. **WT.:** 170. **SIGNED:** Dominican Republic, 2002. **SIGNED BY:** Julio Linares/Rick Aponte.

The Astros swapped out righthander Paul Estrada with Trinidad on the 40-man roster after the 2008 season, protecting Trinidad from the Rule 5 draft in spite of his slow path through the system. He spent three years in the Rookie-level Dominican Summer League before making his U.S. debut in 2005, and then meandered his way to Corpus Christi last May. Trinidad looks like an average lefty at first glance, but his stuff is sneaky good. His 88-90 mph fastball plays up with good command to both sides of the plate, and he works in a changeup to keep hitters off balance. Best of all, he isn't afraid to pitch to contact. He throws from a three-quarters delivery, muddling his curveball. The breaker is slurvy and needs more depth and sharpness to it if he wants it to be an effective pitch in the big leagues. He also has a tendency to fall into deep counts and struggles with holding runners. The Astros, whom he represented in the Futures Game in Yankee Stadium last summer, will send him to Round Rock in 2009, and he would likely be suitable for an emergency spot start in the big leagues.

Year	Club (League)	Class	W	L	ERA	G	GS	CG	SV	IP	H	R	ER	HR	BB	SO	AVG
2002	Astros (DSL)	R	2	1	4.74	17	7	0	0	49	59	32	26	1	6	49	.286
2003	Astros (DSL)	R	0	1	2.57	2	2	0	0	7	7	5	2	0	2	6	.219
2004	Astros (DSL)	R	1	0	1.38	5	1	0	0	13	9	4	2	0	3	12	.184
2005	Greeneville (APP)	R	1	2	4.89	14	8	0	2	50	65	34	27	5	11	47	.308
2006	Greeneville (APP)	R	4	4	2.39	13	13	0	0	75	59	24	20	2	10	66	.208
	Tri-City (NYP)	SS	0	0	4.50	2	1	0	0	8	14	4	4	0	3	5	.389
2007	Lexington (SAL)	LoA	6	8	4.18	23	23	1	0	131	118	62	61	16	35	120	.242
	Salem (CAR)	HiA	2	1	2.81	4	4	0	0	26	23	9	8	4	3	23	.237
2008	Salem (CAR)	HiA	4	2	2.32	10	10	0	0	62	46	18	16	2	11	34	.202
	Corpus Christi (TEX)	AA	6	5	3.61	18	18	0	0	107	109	47	43	13	21	75	.263
MINOR LEAGUE TOTALS			26	24	3.56	108	87	1	2	529	509	239	209	43	105	437	.249

25 CHRIS BLAZEK, LHP

BORN: March 2, 1984. **B-T:** L-L. **HT.:** 6-0. **WT.:** 195. **DRAFTED:** Vermont, 2005 (23rd round). **SIGNED BY:** Mike Maggart.

The unheralded Blazek made enough of an impression in the minors last season to earn a trip to the Arizona Fall League, but he was shut down before he pitched there because of elbow tendinitis. It was a disappointing finish to his most encouraging season. Having pitched in Connecticut in high school and in the America East Conference at Vermont, Blazek has always been under the radar and a bit slower in his development as a cold-weather product. But he has made himself into a reliable reliever. He was setting up Samuel Gervacio most of the year at Corpus Christi, where he showed more confidence and buzzed his fastball in at 90-92 mph with late life. He also has a decent slider. Scouts liked the way he was unafraid to bust batters inside. Blazek's to-do list includes getting a better handle on his delivery. He tends to jump off the back side and get out too fast in an attempt to generate more velocity, but it tends to affect his command, which has otherwise improved since he signed. Some think it would also be helpful for him to incorporate a changeup into his repertoire. His AFL absence helped the Astros sneak him through the Rule 5 draft, as he wasn't protected on the 40-man roster. For now, he projects as a situational lefty and will head to the Round Rock bullpen in 2009.

Year	Club (League)	Class	W	L	ERA	G	GS	CG	SV	IP	H	R	ER	HR	BB	SO	AVG
2005	Tri-City (NYP)	SS	0	0	0.00	3	0	0	1	6	1	0	0	0	2	9	.059
	Lexington (SAL)	LoA	1	0	6.18	18	0	0	0	28	27	20	19	7	16	20	.252
2006	Lexington (SAL)	LoA	2	1	3.82	41	0	0	4	71	66	35	30	6	42	66	.248
2007	Salem (CAR)	HiA	4	2	4.07	50	0	0	8	66	61	33	30	5	28	62	.243
2008	Corpus Christi (TEX)	AA	4	4	4.52	47	0	0	2	70	67	38	35	8	28	84	.253
MINOR LEAGUE TOTALS			11	7	4.27	159	0	0	15	240	222	126	114	26	116	241	.245

26 JARROD HOLLOWAY, LHP

BORN: Aug. 28, 1988. **B-T:** R-L. **HT.:** 6-3. **WT.:** 218. **DRAFTED:** St. Petersburg (Fla.) JC, 2008 (10th round). **SIGNED BY:** Jon Bunnell.

Holloway took a somewhat circuitous route to pro ball. An Arkansas native, he spent his freshman year at Mississippi State, then transferred to St. Petersburg JC and signed for $150,000 after one season. His fastball and curve both rate as plus pitches, with his heater ranging from 90-95 mph. A downer curveball from his 6-foot-3 frame has the Astros just as excited, and he also shows a slider at times. Holloway has long struggled with command, which kept him from getting consistent innings at Mississippi State. Holloway's problems come because he gets rushed and tries to do too much. In his debut at Tri-City, he issued almost as many walks as strikeouts and uncorked 12 wild pitches. Because he is a big-bodied lefty, the Astros put him on an offseason conditioning program that will help him with his durability. The drills would also have the added benefit of further disciplining Holloway on the mound so that he quiets down his delivery. He'll move up to full-season ball at Lexington this season.

Year	Club (League)	Class	W	L	ERA	G	GS	CG	SV	IP	H	R	ER	HR	BB	SO	AVG
2008	Tri-City (NYP)	SS	0	5	4.07	13	13	0	0	49	48	31	22	2	27	37	.270
MINOR LEAGUE TOTALS			0	5	4.07	13	13	0	0	49	48	31	22	2	27	37	.270

27 PHIL DISHER, 1B

BORN: June 17, 1985. **B-T:** R-R. **HT.:** 6-2. **WT.:** 215. **DRAFTED:** South Carolina, 2008 (15th round). **SIGNED BY:** J.D. Alleva.

While South Carolina's potent infield trio of Justin Smoak, Reese Havens and James Darnell (who all went among the first 69 picks in the draft) soaked up almost all of the attention from scouts last year, Houston thinks Disher could be a diamond in the rough. As the Gamecocks' senior catcher last year, he provided depth to the lineup two years after he moved onto the radar with a three-homer series that pushed South Carolina to an NCAA super-regional. He put on a power display in the New York-Penn League after signing, though scouts aren't sure yet if it will play as he moves up. Disher is pull-happy, and his approach needs work because he leads with his front side and doesn't have good balance. Breaking balls also are a problem area because he doesn't recognize them well. He's a slow runner, but the Astros are focused on his bat. They immediately moved him to first base, putting him through intense drills to improve his first-step quickness and fielding. He needs to stay down on grounders as well as maintain balance. They may also try him in left field. The Astros will push him to Lancaster, a big jump but considering his age a logical one.

Year	Club (League)	Class	AVG	G	AB	R	H	2B	3B	HR	RBI	BB	SO	SB	OBP	SLG
2008	Tri-City (NYP)	SS	.304	71	280	40	85	20	3	13	56	33	71	1	.381	.536
MINOR LEAGUE TOTALS			.304	71	280	40	85	20	3	13	56	33	71	1	.381	.536

28 LEANDRO CESPEDES, RHP

BORN: April 19, 1987. **B-T:** R-R. **HT.:** 5-11. **WT.:** 160. **SIGNED:** Dominican Republic, 2005. **SIGNED BY:** Julio Linares/Sergio Beltre.

Trying to gauge Cespedes after his emergence last year is like trying to size up the new kid in school: Should the guys dig in to protect their turf, or will he just be lost in the shuffle? Cespedes was the best pitcher on a lackluster Lexington staff in 2008, building on his reputation as a strikeout machine by ranking fifth in the South Atlantic League in K's. He's not a big guy, with comparisons to Ramon Ortiz for his body type, and his fastball sits around 87-91 mph. He also throws a slider and splitter, with the splitter the better pitch right now. The splitter shows occasional sweep and decent bite, while the slider flattens out too often. Cespedes doesn't have great downward plane on his pitches, and out of a three-quarters delivery has a bad habit of throwing across his body. But he shows no fear and attacks hitters, sometimes too much. The Astros like his growing confidence, though, and point to his second-half numbers last year when his ERA dropped by more than three runs and he struck out 82 in 70 innings. He will move on to Lancaster in 2009.

Year	Club (League)	Class	W	L	ERA	G	GS	CG	SV	IP	H	R	ER	HR	BB	SO	AVG
2005	Astros (DSL)	R	1	0	1.88	14	1	0	2	29	25	16	6	0	11	30	.229
2006	Astros (DSL)	R	2	3	2.39	11	8	0	0	49	35	14	13	2	11	54	.200
2007	Greeneville (APP)	R	4	5	3.15	11	10	0	0	54	48	23	19	2	12	52	.234
	Lexington (SAL)	LoA	0	1	4.38	3	2	0	0	12	10	6	6	1	5	12	.213
2008	Lexington (SAL)	LoA	4	6	4.02	28	27	0	0	130	138	73	58	19	45	137	.267
MINOR LEAGUE TOTALS			11	15	3.35	67	48	0	2	274	256	132	102	24	84	285	.243

29 LOU PALMISANO, C

BORN: Sept. 16, 1982. **B-T:** R-R. **HT.:** 6-1. **WT.:** 205. **DRAFTED:** Broward (Fla.) CC, 2003 (3rd round). **SIGNED BY:** Larry Pardo (Brewers).

Palmisano topped a thin crop of Brewers catching prospects a few years ago, but he fell back because of injuries and poor offensive performance since then, and Houston was able to get him out of the major league Rule 5 draft, via a cash trade with the Orioles. The Astros want J.R. Towles to get everyday time in Triple-A, and 2006 first-round pick Max Sapp has ballooned out of shape, so they added to their catching depth in acquiring Palmisano. He should be a serviceable catch-and-throw backstop behind Humberto Quintero and is known for calling a good game. If he provides any offense, it will be a bonus. Palmisano was the MVP of the Rookie-level Pioneer League in 2003 and showed power and strike-zone discipline when he was at his best. However, his performance has tailed off since then, and he missed most of last season after surgery on his left knee to repair a meniscus tear he sustained in spring training. The Astros are confident he is healthy after scouting him in the Arizona Fall League, where he hit .405 with two home runs in 50 at-bats. He remains subject to Rule 5 draft requirements and will have to clear waivers and be offered back to the Brewers if he doesn't stick in the big leagues.

Year	Club (League)	Class	AVG	G	AB	R	H	2B	3B	HR	RBI	BB	SO	SB	OBP	SLG
2003	Helena (PIO)	R	.391	47	174	32	68	13	2	6	43	18	29	13	.458	.592
2004	Beloit (MWL)	LoA	.293	113	409	59	120	22	3	7	65	43	93	3	.371	.413
2005	Brevard County (FSL)	HiA	.255	118	432	47	110	16	7	5	49	34	65	3	.314	.359
2006	Huntsville (SL)	AA	.241	99	332	39	80	17	1	4	37	48	65	2	.338	.334
2007	Huntsville (SL)	AA	.256	103	351	49	90	22	1	11	63	57	80	8	.368	.419
2008	Brewers (AZL)	R	.276	8	29	4	8	2	1	0	1	5	4	1	.382	.414
	Brevard County (FSL)	HiA	.306	19	72	8	22	2	0	2	8	5	11	0	.367	.417
MINOR LEAGUE TOTALS			.277	507	1799	238	498	94	15	35	266	210	347	30	.360	.404

30 LUIS CRUZ, LHP

BORN: Sept. 10, 1990. **B-T:** L-L. **HT.:** 5-9. **WT.:** 170. **DRAFTED:** HS—San Juan, P.R., 2008 (9th round). **SIGNED BY:** Joey Sola.

Astros scouts flew to Puerto Rico last year to drop in on Cruz at the recommendation of part-time scout Joey Sola. A center fielder in high school, he had experimented on the mound and then pitched in a tournament, showing only a high 80s fastball. But Sola knew that Cruz was fatigued from the season and had more life on his fastball than he showed. Sure enough, the Astros saw it not long after drafting him and signing him for $150,000. Despite having a small frame along the lines of J.C. Romero, Cruz is deceptive. He can buzz his fastball up to 93 mph, and it jumps on hitters. He uses a changeup that has good sink and fade as an out pitch. Though his curveball is still rudimentary, it has some tightness and good rotation. He missed the final six weeks due to a sore elbow, and because he's a crossfire delivery guy, will spend the spring making some corrections to his delivery. He will be a project but could shoot up this list if his pitches come together.

Year	Club (League)	Class	W	L	ERA	G	GS	CG	SV	IP	H	R	ER	HR	BB	SO	AVG
2008	Greeneville (APP)	R	1	1	2.28	7	7	0	0	24	20	7	6	2	7	19	.227
MINOR LEAGUE TOTALS			1	1	2.28	7	7	0	0	24	20	7	6	2	7	19	.227

Kansas City Royals

BY J.J. COOPER

L ike the Athletics before them, the Rays have become the hope for the hopeless. While the disparities between large- and small-revenue clubs stack the deck in favor of the Yankees, Red Sox and others, Tampa Bay proved again in 2008 that a less-advantaged club can succeed if it drafts well, develops its own players and makes wise trades.

That's good news for the Royals. But it also leads to the question: If the Rays can do it, why hasn't Kansas City been able to break through?

It doesn't take long to find the answer. Over the past decade, the Royals have struggled to produce big leaguers and have lost more trades than they have won. Add it all up and you have a team that has finished below .500 in 14 of the last 15 seasons and has the worst record in baseball over the last 10 years (671-948, .414). It's not for a lack of opportunities. Like Tampa Bay, Kansas City has consistently drafted high. In the past 10 drafts, the Royals have had the No. 1 pick once, three more choices in the top three and nine top-10 selections.

With that bounty, it would be fair to expect a team largely built from within. Yet only four of the 14 hitters who recorded 100 at-bats and three of the 16 pitchers who threw 25 innings for the Royals in 2008 were originally signed by the club.

Kansas City has been willing to spend money on the draft, as the $37.1 million it has invested in the first 10 rounds of the last six drafts is more than any other club. But the Royals haven't gotten a lot of bang for their buck. Whiffing on first-round draft picks early in the decade (Mike Stodolka, Colt Griffin, Chris Lubanski) proved costly. They're also still waiting for recent first-rounders Billy Butler, Alex Gordon and Luke Hochevar to fully pay off.

A bigger problem has been Kansas City's inability to find talent after the first round. Though the Royals have spent heavily, $24.1 million of that $37.1 million went to first-rounders. Mike Aviles (seventh round, 2003) was a $1,000 bargain, and first baseman Kila Ka'aihue (15th round, 2002) has a chance to become a big league regular. But they're the only non-first-rounders from the 2001-03 to have any success, and the 2004-06 drafts have yet to show much more promise.

As a result, Kansas City dismissed scouting director Deric Ladnier and handed his duties to farm director J.J. Picollo, who now has the title of assistant general manager for scouting and player development.

ED WOLFSTEIN

Rookie shortstop Mike Aviles was a pleasant surprise for the Royals

TOP 30 PROSPECTS

1. Mike Moustakas, 3b	16. Derrick Robinson, of
2. Eric Hosmer, 1b	17. Jason Taylor, 3b/1b
3. Daniel Cortes, rhp	18. Julio Pimentel, rhp
4. Mike Montgomery, lhp	19. Salvador Perez, c
5. Tim Melville, rhp	20. Carlos Fortuna, rhp
6. Danny Duffy, lhp	21. Matt Mitchell, rhp
7. Danny Gutierrez, rhp	22. Adrian Ortiz, of
8. Carlos Rosa, rhp	23. Mitch Maier, of
9. Kila Ka'aihue, 1b	24. Joe Dickerson, of
10. Blake Wood, rhp	25. Juan Abreu, rhp
11. Johnny Giavotella, 2b	26. Jose Bonilla, c
12. Kelvin Herrera, rhp	27. Kyle Martin, ss/3b
13. Henry Barrera, rhp	28. Sam Runion, rhp
14. Tyler Sample, rhp	29. Yowill Espinal, ss
15. David Lough, of	30. Keaton Hayenga, rhp

Before he left, Ladnier put together what should be his best draft. The Royals set a record by spending $11.1 million on bonuses and landed three players considered to be first-round talents: first baseman Eric Hosmer, lefthander Mike Montgomery and righty Tim Melville.

The Royals bolstered their braintrust by hiring Mike Arbuckle as senior advisor for scouting and player development. Arbuckle had spent 16 years with the Phillies, rising to assistant GM after finding many of the key players for Philadelphia's World Series championship club during his tenure as scouting director.

General Manager: Dayton Moore. **Farm and Scouting Director:** J.J. Picollo.

Class	Team	League	W	L	PCT	Finish*	Manager	Affiliated
Majors	Kansas City	American	75	87	.463	11th (14)	Trey Hillman	—
Triple-A	Omaha Royals	Pacific Coast	63	81	.438	14th (16)	Mike Jirschele	1969
Double-A	NW Arkansas Naturals	Texas	75	65	.536	4th (8)	Brian Poldberg	2008
High A	Wilmington Blue Rocks	Carolina	69	71	.493	5th (8)	Darryl Kennedy	2007
Low A	Burlington Bees	Midwest	73	65	.529	^4th (14)	Brian Rupp	2001
Rookie	Idaho Falls Chukars	Pioneer	33	43	.434	7th (8)	Jim Gabella	2001
Rookie	Burlington Royals	Appalachian	24	41	.369	10th (10)	Tony Tijerina	2007
Rookie	AZL Royals	Arizona	23	33	.411	6th (9)	Julio Bruno	2008

Overall 2008 Minor League Record 360 399 .474 24th
* Finish in overall standings (No. of teams in league). ^League champion.

LAST YEAR'S TOP 30

Rank	Player, Pos.	Status
1.	Mike Moustakas, ss	No. 1
2.	Daniel Cortes, rhp	No. 3
3.	Luke Hochevar, rhp	Majors
4.	Billy Buckner, rhp	(Diamondbacks)
5.	Blake Wood, rhp	No. 10
6.	Danny Duffy, lhp	No. 6
7.	Carlos Rosa, rhp	No. 8
8.	Julio Pimentel, rhp	No. 18
9.	Matt Mitchell, rhp	No. 21
10.	Yasuhiko Yabuta, rhp	Majors
11.	Derrick Robinson, of	No. 16
12.	Sam Runion, rhp	No. 28
13.	Tyler Lumsden, lhp	(Astros)
14.	Blake Johnson, rhp	Dropped out
15.	Ryan Braun, rhp	Dropped out
16.	Chris Lubanski, of	Dropped out
17.	Justin Huber, of/1b	(Free agent)
18.	Jeff Bianchi, ss	Dropped out
19.	Brett Fisher, lhp	Dropped out
20.	Neal Musser, lhp	Dropped out
21.	Fernando Cruz, 3b	Dropped out
22.	David Lough, of	No. 15
23.	Mitch Maier, of	No. 23
24.	Chris McConnell, ss	Dropped out
25.	Jose Duarte, of	Dropped out
26.	Joe Dickerson, of	No. 24
27.	Keaton Hayenga, rhp	No. 30
28.	Dusty Hughes, lhp	Dropped out
29.	Mike Aviles, inf	Majors
30.	Rowdy Hardy, lhp	Dropped out

BEST TOOLS

Best Hitter for Average	Eric Hosmer
Best Power Hitter	Mike Moustakas
Best Strike-Zone Discipline	Kila Ka'aihue
Fastest Baserunner	Adrian Ortiz
Best Athlete	Derrick Robinson
Best Fastball	Carlos Rosa
Best Curveball	Danny Gutierrez
Best Slider	Henry Barrera
Best Changeup	Blake Wood
Best Control	Danny Gutierrez
Best Defensive Catcher	Salvador Perez
Best Defensive Infielder	Mario Lisson
Best Infield Arm	Mike Moustakas
Best Defensive Outfielder	Jose Duarte
Best Outfield Arm	Jose Duarte

PROJECTED 2012 LINEUP

Catcher	John Buck
First Base	Eric Hosmer
Second Base	Johnny Giavotella
Third Base	Alex Gordon
Shortstop	Mike Aviles
Left Field	David DeJesus
Center Field	Coco Crisp
Right Field	Mike Moustakas
Designated Hitter	Billy Butler
No. 1 Starter	Zack Greinke
No. 2 Starter	Gil Meche
No. 3 Starter	Daniel Cortes
No. 4 Starter	Luke Hochevar
No. 5 Starter	Mike Montgomery
Closer	Joakim Soria

TOP PROSPECTS OF THE DECADE

Year	Player, Pos.	2008 Org.
1999	Carlos Beltran, of	Mets
2000	Dee Brown, of	Angels
2001	Chris George, lhp	Blue Jays
2002	Angel Berroa, ss	Dodgers
2003	Zack Greinke, rhp	Royals
2004	Zack Greinke, rhp	Royals
2005	Billy Butler, of	Royals
2006	Alex Gordon, 3b	Royals
2007	Alex Gordon, 3b	Royals
2008	Mike Moustakas, ss	Royals

TOP DRAFT PICKS OF THE DECADE

Year	Player, Pos.	2008 Org.
1999	Kyle Snyder, rhp	Red Sox
2000	Mike Stodolka, lhp	Royals
2001	Colt Griffin, rhp	Out of baseball
2002	Zack Greinke, rhp	Royals
2003	Chris Lubanski, of	Royals
2004	Billy Butler, of	Royals
2005	Alex Gordon, 3b	Royals
2006	Luke Hochevar, rhp	Royals
2007	Mike Moustakas, ss	Royals
2008	Eric Hosmer, 1b	Royals

LARGEST BONUSES IN CLUB HISTORY

Eric Hosmer, 2008	$6,000,000
Alex Gordon, 2005	$4,000,000
Mike Moustakas, 2007	$4,000,000
Luke Hochevar, 2006	$3,500,000
Jeff Austin, 1998	$2,700,000

KANSAS CITY ROYALS

TOP 2009 ROOKIE: Kila Kaaihue, 1b. The Mike Jacobs trade makes his path tougher, but the Texas League MVP's power and patience deserve a chance.

BREAKOUT PROSPECT: Kelvin Herrera, rhp. The little righthander with a big fastball and good feel for pitching is on the verge of making a name for himself.

SLEEPER: John Lamb, lhp. He fractured his elbow in a car accident four months before the 2008 draft, but he could prove to be a steal as a fifth-rounder.

SOURCE OF TOP 30 TALENT			
Homegrown	28	Acquired	2
College	6	Trades	2
Junior college	0	Rule 5 draft	0
High school	14	Independent leagues	0
Draft-and-follow	1	Free agents/waivers	0
Nondrafted free agents	0		
International	7		

Numbers in parentheses indicate prospect rankings.

LF
Jason Taylor (17)
Chris Lubanski

CF
David Lough (15)
Derrick Robinson (16)
Adrian Ortiz (22)
Mitch Maier (23)
Paulo Orlando
Jose Duarte
Patrick Norris
Hilton Richardson
Alex Llanos

RF
Joe Dickerson (24)
Jordan Parraz
Nicholas Francis
Carlo Testa
Cody Strait

3B
Mike Moustakas (1)
Fernando Cruz
Mario Lisson
Jake Kuebler

SS
Guelin Beltre
J.D. Alfaro
Chris McConnell

2B
Johnny Giavotella (11)
Kyle Martin (27)
Yowill Espinal (29)
Kurt Mertins
Jeff Bianchi
Malcolm Culver

1B
Eric Hosmer (2)
Kila Kaaihue (9)
Clint Robinson

C
Salvador Perez (19)
Jose Bonilla (26)
Sean McCauley
Mauricio Matos
Travis Jones

RHP

Starters	Relievers
Daniel Cortes (3)	Henry Barrera (13)
Tim Melville (5)	Julio Pimentel (18)
Danny Gutierrez (7)	Juan Abreu (25)
Carlos Rosa (8)	Chris Nicoll
Blake Wood (10)	Frederico Castaneda
Kelvin Herrera (12)	Chris Hayes
Tyler Sample (14)	
Carlos Fortuna (20)	
Matt Mitchell (21)	
Sam Runion (28)	
Keaton Hayenga (30)	
Edward Cegarra	
Chase Hentges	
Blake Johnson	
Jairo Cuevas	
Alex Caldera	
Greg Billo	

LHP

Starters	Relievers
Mike Montgomery (4)	Ben Swaggerty
Danny Duffy (6)	Derrick Saito
John Lamb	Dusty Hughes
Brent Fisher	Brandon Sisk
	Rowdy Hardy

2008   BONUSES: $11.1 MILLION

BEST PURE HITTER: 1B Eric Hosmer (1) ultimately could be more productive than fellow Royals top-five picks Alex Gordon and Mike Moustakas. 2B Johnny Giavotella (2), who has uncanny bat control, hit .299 and was a catalyst in low Class A Burlington's Midwest League championship.

BEST POWER HITTER: Hosmer generates exceptional power with an easy flick of his wrists and already shows a knack for hitting homers to the opposite field. C Travis Jones (50) has plus power and bested Hosmer in a home run derby at the Connie Mack World Series.

FASTEST RUNNER: OF Alex Llanos (6) runs the 60-yard dash in 6.6 seconds.

BEST DEFENSIVE PLAYER: J.D. Alfaro (9) plays a solid shortstop and has a strong arm that delivered 91-92 mph fastballs when he closed games for Grayson County (Texas) CC.

BEST FASTBALL: RHP Tim Melville (4), a projected first-rounder who slid because of signability and received a $1.25 million bonus, has the most consistent velocity at 91-95 mph. RHP Tyler Sample (3) has the best high-end velo at 96 mph, while LHP Mike Montgomery (1s) has the best life. Montgomery usually pitches at 90-92 mph and can reach 95.

BEST SECONDARY PITCH: Sample's knuckle-curve has 12-to-6 break and is a true swing-and-miss pitch.

BEST PRO DEBUT: Montgomery ranked as the No. 1 prospect in the Rookie-level Arizona League after going 2-1, 1.69 with 34 strikeouts in 43 innings.

BEST ATHLETE: 2B/RHP Malcolm Culver (8) turned down a scholarship to play wide receiver at San Diego State. Kansas City drafted him as a pitcher, but he had a tender arm and thus made his debut as an infielder. Healthy again, he may try shortstop in 2009. Montgomery averaged 20 points a game for his high school basketball team as a senior.

MOST INTRIGUING BACKGROUND: Unsigned 1B Beau Brett's (29, now at Southern California) uncle George is the best player in Royals history and the club's vice president of baseball operations. Beau is also the nephew of former all-star Ken and the son of Spokane Indians owner Bobby. 3B Jake Kuebler (17), who has power and arm strength, is Gordon's cousin. Culver's brother Tyrone is a safety for the NFL's Miami Dolphins. Alfaro's brother Jason got a cup of coffee in the majors.

CLOSEST TO THE MAJORS: Hosmer should hit his

way to Kansas City in short order. If Giavotella can improve his range and first-step quickness, he won't need much seasoning.

BEST LATE-ROUND PICK: RHP Chase Hentges (14) has a clean delivery, a low-90s fastball and a hard breaking ball that he throws for strikes.

THE ONE WHO GOT AWAY: The Royals liked 3B Jason Esposito's (7) offensive potential enough to offer him a seven-figure bonus, but that couldn't sway him from Vanderbilt.

ASSESSMENT: The Royals spent a record $11,148,000 on this crop, including $8.2 million on Hosmer, Melville and Montgomery. Kansas City replaced scouting director Deric Ladnier in September, though his last draft likely will have been his best.

2007   BONUSES: $6.6 MILLION

3B Mike Moustakas' (1) bat is as good as advertised, and LHP Danny Duffy (3) quickly has become one of the system's best mound prospects

GRADE: B+

2006   BONUSES: $6.7 MILLION

RHP Luke Hochevar (1) hasn't missed many bats in the majors, and while it's too early to call him a bust, he may have a tough time living up to his No. 1 overall selection in the draft. When he's on, RHP Blake Wood (3) shows better stuff than Hochevar.

GRADE: C

2005   BONUSES: $6.0 MILLION*

3B Alex Gordon (1) also hasn't lived up to expectations as the No. 2 overall pick, yet his future looks brighter than Hochevar's. RHP Danny Gutierrez (33), a draft-and-follow, took a big step forward in 2008.

GRADE: B

2004   BONUSES: $5.8 MILLION*

1B Billy Butler (1) struggled at times last season but still looks like the Royals' cleanup hitter of the future. LHP J.P. Howell (1s) had a breakthrough season—two years after Kansas City traded him for Joey Gathright.

GRADE: B

*Draft analysis by Jim Callis. Numbers in parentheses indicate draft rounds. *Bonuses for 2004-05 are first 10 rounds only.*

PAUL GIERHART

PROSPECT

**MIKE
MOUSTAKAS,
3B**

Born: Sept. 11, 1988.
Ht: 6-0. **Wt:** 195.
Bats: L. **Throws:** R.
Drafted:
HS—Chatsworth, Calif.,
2007 (1st round).
Signed by: John Ramey.

For years, Moustakas was the strong second fiddle to Chatsworth (Calif.) High teammate Matt Dominguez. In 2007, Moustakas established himself as an even better prospect than his fellow first-round pick by slimming down and showing his power potential. He set the California state records for home runs in a season (24) and career (52). The No. 2 overall pick in the 2007 draft, he signed for $4 million right at the Aug. 15 deadline. Though he got just 41 at-bats at Rookie-level Idaho Falls that summer, his advanced approach left the Royals with no qualms about sending him to low Class A Burlington in 2008. Moustakas struggled to adapt to breaking balls and the cold weather during the first month, but he made adjustments and ranked as the Midwest League's No. 1 prospect by season's end. He was the league's first teenage home run champ since Steve Gibralter in 1992.

Moustakas punishes balls with quick wrists, exceptional bat speed and a vicious stroke. When he gets a fastball teed up where he's expecting it, he can easily drive it out of the park, and his power rates as a 70 on the 20-80 scouting scale. He also makes consistent contact and should hit for average. After his early problems with breaking balls, where he was getting out on his front foot and beating them into the ground, Moustakas learned to keep his weight back on his back leg and use his legs to drive them. Kansas City actually was happy to see him prove he could deal with an extended slump and make the necessary adjustments. Moustakas is a much better fit at third base than shortstop, where he played in high school and opened 2008. Clocked as high as 97 mph off the mound in high school, he has a strong arm that's a big asset at third base. He also played the outfield in high school, and some scouts believe his arm, frame and makeup would make him an outstanding catcher. The Royals will keep him at third base, however, to expedite getting his bat to the big leagues.

Moustakas has the bat speed to turn on most any fastball, but he gets pull-conscious and can do a better job of using the entire field. While he improved at hitting breaking balls as the season went along, he needs to recognize which ones he can drive and which he should lay off. Considering he made a midseason transition to third base, Moustakas handled it very well, but he still needs to work on reading the ball off the bat and charging bunts and choppers. He lacks elite athleticism, so he'll have to work to maintain his first-step quickness,

Though Kansas City tries to be conservative when it comes to moving players through the system, Moustakas has the talent to accelerate his timetable. He'll move up to high Class A Wilmington in 2009 and could reach the majors as early as the end of the 2010 season. With Alex Gordon at third base, Moustakas may have to change positions again down the line, but he moves well enough and definitely has enough arm to handle a corner-outfield assignment.

Year	Club (League)	Class	AVG	G	AB	R	H	2B	3B	HR	RBI	BB	SO	SB	OBP	SLG
2007	Idaho Falls (PIO)	R	.293	11	41	6	12	4	1	0	10	4	8	0	.383	.439
2008	Burlington (MWL)	LoA	.272	126	496	77	135	25	3	22	71	43	86	8	.337	.468
MINOR LEAGUE TOTALS			.274	137	537	83	147	29	4	22	81	47	94	8	.341	.466

2 ERIC HOSMER, 1B

JOHN SPEAR

BORN: Oct. 24, 1989. **B-T:** L-L. **HT.:** 6-5. **WT.:** 215. **DRAFTED:** HS—Plantation, Fla., 2008 (1st round). **SIGNED BY:** Alex Mesa.

As an eighth grader, Hosmer was a 5-foot-9, pudgy baseball rat. A growth spurt gave him a start on becoming a prospect, and he remade himself with an intense workout program. The most dangerous prep hitter in the 2008 draft, he went third overall and signed for a club-record $6 million. His pro debut was cut short when MLB ordered him to sit out after he got caught up in a grievance involving No. 2 overall pick Pedro Alvarez. Hosmer has the kind of bat speed and raw power that can't be taught. He and Mike Moustakas have comparable raw power, and the consensus is that Hosmer hits the ball a little bit harder. While most young power hitters are looking to yank and crank, he's very adept at sitting back and driving balls to the opposite field. He won't get to use it, but he has one of the best fastballs in the system, having been clocked as high as 97 mph. He has soft hands at first base and enough speed and athleticism to play in the outfield. Even with all his gifts as a hitter, Hosmer does need to develop a gameplan instead of just hitting whatever the pitcher throws. He'll wind up with below-average speed as he gets older. Like Moustakas before him, Hosmer is advanced enough to handle low Class A despite getting little previous exposure to pro ball. He should be the Royals' No. 3 hitter of the future.

Year	Club (League)	Class	AVG	G	AB	R	H	2B	3B	HR	RBI	BB	SO	SB	OBP	SLG
2008	Idaho Falls (PIO)	R	.364	3	11	2	4	2	0	0	2	3	2	0	.533	.545
MINOR LEAGUE TOTALS			.364	3	11	2	4	2	0	0	2	3	2	0	.533	.545

3 DANIEL CORTES, RHP

JOHN SPEAR

BORN: March 4, 1987. **B-T:** R-R. **HT.:** 6-6. **WT.:** 225. **DRAFTED:** HS—Pomona, Calif., 2005 (7th round). **SIGNED BY:** Dan Ontiveros (White Sox).

The throw-in in the Mike MacDougal deal with the White Sox has become the prize now that lefthander Tyler Lumsden has crashed and burned in Triple-A. The Royals got more than they bargained for in Cortes, who has added height, strength and velocity in the two years since he was traded. Cortes has a 91-93 mph fastball that touches 96 mph, but his out pitch is his plus 12-to-6 curveball. He used to throw a slider with the White Sox, but showed his aptitude by quickly picking up the curve with the Royals. Some believe he could move rapidly with a move to the bullpen, where his fastball could play up to 96-97 mph. He has the personality to handle the pressure of working as a setup man or closer. Cortes' changeup isn't very effective and he doesn't trust it much. He needs to improve it to handle lefties, who hit .285/.396/.455 against him in 2008. His command needs more polish. When he gets in trouble, he tends to speed up his delivery, which causes him to leave his pitches up in the zone. Cortes could pitch in Kansas City's bullpen right now, but he'll likely work out of Triple-A Omaha's rotation instead. He still has significant work to do but has the ingredients to become a frontline starter.

Year	Club (League)	Class	W	L	ERA	G	GS	CG	SV	IP	H	R	ER	HR	BB	SO	AVG
2005	Bristol (APP)	R	1	4	5.17	15	7	0	0	38	44	23	22	2	13	38	.289
2006	Kannapolis (SAL)	LoA	3	9	4.01	20	19	0	0	108	109	61	48	6	38	96	.260
	Burlington (MWL)	LoA	1	2	6.69	7	7	0	0	35	40	27	26	7	17	30	.284
2007	Wilmington (CAR)	HiA	8	8	3.07	24	24	0	0	123	102	50	42	7	45	120	.226
2008	NW Arkansas (TEX)	AA	10	4	3.78	23	23	0	0	117	103	51	49	13	55	109	.241
MINOR LEAGUE TOTALS			23	27	4.00	89	80	0	0	421	398	212	187	35	168	393	.250

4 MIKE MONTGOMERY, LHP

JOHN SPEAR

BORN: July 1, 1989. **B-T:** L-L. **HT.:** 6-5. **WT.:** 180. **DRAFTED:** HS—Newhall, Calif., 2008 (1st round supplemental). **SIGNED BY:** Dan Ontiveros.

Montgomery was leading his high school basketball team in scoring when his coach kicked him off the team in January for recording too many technical fouls. That gave him a chance to focus on pitching, which paid off as he showed improved velocity and an advanced approach. Signed for $988,000 as the 36th overall pick, he ranked as the No. 1 prospect in the Rookie-level Arizona League. Montgomery's long arms and athletic frame should allow him to continue to add 20-30 pounds and more velocity. He already sits at 90-92 mph and touches 95 with nice life on his fastball. He pairs it with a unique palm curveball that he developed because it puts little stress on his arm. His 80-mph changeup already rates as average and has the potential to be an out pitch. As his basketball career showed, he's an intense competitor. Montgomery can spin a breaking ball, but the Royals want him to find a more conventional grip and he has yet to find one that he's comfortable with. Other than that, he's very polished for his age and just needs more innings to develop. Montgomery is advanced enough to head to low Class A, though he may spend time in extended spring to avoid the April chill of the Midwest League. He has the potential to become the franchise's best lefthander since Danny Jackson.

Year	Club (League)	Class	W	L	ERA	G	GS	CG	SV	IP	H	R	ER	HR	BB	SO	AVG
2008	Royals (AZL)	R	2	1	1.69	12	9	0	0	43	31	12	8	2	12	34	.211
MINOR LEAGUE TOTALS			2	1	1.69	12	9	0	0	43	31	12	8	2	12	34	.211

5 TIM MELVILLE, RHP

BILL MITCHELL

BORN: Oct. 9, 1989. **B-T:** R-R. **HT.:** 6-5. **WT.:** 205. **DRAFTED:** HS—Wentzville, Mo., 2008 (4th round). **SIGNED BY:** Deric Ladnier.

Melville entered 2008 as the top prep pitching prospect in the draft, but concerns about his price tag and a senior season that didn't quite live up to expectations caused him to slide to the fourth round. The Royals snapped him up and signed him for $1.25 million—$960,000 above slot. He's the second Holt High (Wentzville, Mo.) product to figure prominently in the last two drafts, as Holt grad and Missouri State product Ross Detwiler went sixth overall in 2007. At his best, Melville has a 91-95 mph fastball, a plus curveball and an adequate changeup. He has plenty of athleticism and repeats his free and easy delivery, so he has no trouble throwing strikes. He also has the frame to add weight, so he could throw consistently in the mid-90s when he's fully matured. Melville has clean mechanics, but they may have gotten too polished early last spring, costing him deception and velocity. He abandoned some tweaks and reverted to his old delivery by the end of the high school season, and his stuff improved. He needs to find more consistency with his curveball and to refine his changeup. Melville didn't sign until the Aug. 15 deadline, so he'll be making his pro debut in 2009. Fronted by Mike Montgomery and Melville, Burlington's rotation could be one of the best in low Class A.

Year	Club (League)	Class	W	L	ERA	G	GS	CG	SV	IP	H	R	ER	HR	BB	SO	AVG
2008	Did Not Play—Signed Late																

6 DANNY DUFFY, LHP

PAUL GIERHART

BORN: Dec. 21, 1988. **B-T:** L-L. **HT.:** 6-2. **WT.:** 185. **DRAFTED:** HS—Lompoc, Calif., 2007 (3rd round). **SIGNED BY:** Rick Schroeder.

Duffy has come a long way since he was a 5-foot-4 high school freshman with a 70-mph fastball. He has dominated the lower levels of the minors, going 10-7, 1.97 with 165 strikeouts in 119 innings. The Royals shut him down in late August because of shoulder discomfort, but he could have pitched in the Midwest League playoffs if they hadn't played it safe. Duffy has a nice fastball for a lefty, sitting at 88-92 mph and touching 94. At times, his curveball is a plus pitch and his changeup rates as slightly above average. He has good mound presence and challenges hitters, throwing strikes and keeping the ball down in the zone. He has shortened his stride since turning pro, allowing him to throw on more of a downhill plane, and he also has fixed a tendency to throw across his body. Like many young pitchers, Duffy is prone to overthrowing when he gets into a jam, costing him command. He'll also get cute and lob up an 85-86 mph fastball at times. He rarely has feel for both of his secondary pitches on the same day, and his curve can get loopy. The Royals haven't had a pair of potential frontline lefties like Mike Montgomery and Duffy in years. With his three-pitch mix and maturity, there's no reason Duffy shouldn't continue to succeed in high Class A in 2009.

Year	Club (League)	Class	W	L	ERA	G	GS	CG	SV	IP	H	R	ER	HR	BB	SO	AVG
2007	Royals (AZL)	R	2	3	1.45	11	9	0	0	37	24	14	6	0	17	63	.178
2008	Burlington (MWL)	LoA	8	4	2.20	17	17	0	0	82	56	26	20	4	25	102	.193
MINOR LEAGUE TOTALS			10	7	1.97	28	26	0	0	119	80	40	26	4	42	165	.188

7 DANNY GUTIERREZ, RHP

JOHN SPEAR

BORN: March 8, 1987. **B-T:** R-R. **HT.:** 6-1. **WT.:** 180. **DRAFTED:** Riverside (Calif.) CC, D/F 2005 (33rd round). **SIGNED BY:** John Ramey.

Gutierrez has made great strides since signing as a draft-and-follow in 2006. His velocity jumped during instructional league in 2007 and he sustained the increase in 2008, which made him a different pitcher. He missed all of May with a hairline fracture in his pitching elbow, but he pitched well afterward. In the first game of the Midwest League finals, he outdueled South Bend ace Jarrod Parker with 11 strikeouts over six scoreless innings. Gutierrez pounds the lower part of the strike zone with his fastball, generating plenty of grounders. He pitched at 88-92 mph early in the season but was working at 90-95 with good life at the end of the year. He has power and 12-to-6 break on a curveball that buries itself just as it reaches the plate. He also shows some feel for a changeup. He can locate his pitches to all four quadrants of the strike zone. He limits the running game by varying his timing to the plate and his pickoff move. After the elbow scare, Gutierrez needs to show he can stay healthy and sustain his improved velocity over a full season. When he operates in the low 90s, his other pitches play up. If he can improve his changeup, the sky is the limit. There's some talk that Gutierrez could handle a jump to Double-A Northwest Arkansas, though the Royals usually aren't that aggressive. He'll probably open 2009 in high Class A Wilmington.

Year	Club (League)	Class	W	L	ERA	G	GS	CG	SV	IP	H	R	ER	HR	BB	SO	AVG
2006	Idaho Falls (PIO)	R	0	4	6.57	14	9	0	0	49	74	42	36	6	21	36	.359
2007	Royals (AZL)	R	0	0	0.00	1	1	0	0	3	1	0	0	0	1	3	.100
	Burlington (MWL)	LoA	1	2	4.88	7	7	0	0	31	32	18	17	2	12	27	.264
2008	Burlington (MWL)	LoA	4	4	2.70	19	18	0	0	90	83	38	27	7	25	104	.246
MINOR LEAGUE TOTALS			5	10	4.15	41	35	0	0	174	190	98	80	15	59	170	.281

8 CARLOS ROSA, RHP

BORN: Sept. 21, 1984. **B-T:** R-R. **HT.:** 6-1. **WT.:** 185. **SIGNED:** Dominican Republic, 2001. **SIGNED BY:** Luis Silverio/Pedro Silverio.

Royals third-base coach Luis Silverio spotted Rosa when he was the team's director of Dominican operations in 2001. At the time, Rosa was a skinny kid throwing 88-89 mph, but Silverio immediately realized his potential and signed him for $25,000. Rosa almost was included in the Mike Jacobs trade this offseason, but Florida backed off because of the forearm strain that ended his season in August. Rosa's four-seam fastball is one of the system's best. He sits between 92-94 mph as a starter and runs it up to 96-97 as a reliever. His slider gives him a second plus pitch. He already has good control and does a nice job of pitching down in the zone, leading to lots of groundballs. Staying healthy has been a concern for Rosa, who missed the entire 2005 season after Tommy John surgery, although the Royals say he's healthy now. If he's going to be a starter, he'll have to improve his fringy changeup. He still has nights where he lacks feel for his slider. While he throws strikes, he needs to sharpen his command. The Royals have to decide whether to bring him up now as a setup man or send him back to Triple-A to hone his skills as a starter.

Year	Club (League)	Class	W	L	ERA	G	GS	CG	SV	IP	H	R	ER	HR	BB	SO	AVG
2002	Royals (GCL)	R	0	4	6.19	10	9	0	0	32	52	32	22	3	12	11	.361
	Royals (DSL)	R	1	0	1.80	1	1	0	0	5	3	1	1	0	0	2	.167
2003	Royals (AZL)	R	5	3	3.63	15	11	0	0	69	79	36	28	4	18	54	.288
2004	Royals (AZL)	R	0	0	4.91	4	4	0	0	11	14	6	6	1	9	8	.326
	Burlington (MWL)	LoA	0	5	4.67	8	8	0	0	35	41	24	18	1	17	23	.297
2006	Burlington (MWL)	LoA	8	6	2.53	24	24	1	0	139	121	50	39	6	54	102	.239
	High Desert (CAL)	HiA	0	1	7.15	3	3	0	0	11	20	12	9	1	4	13	.392
2007	Wilmington (CAR)	HiA	2	1	0.39	4	4	0	0	23	18	2	1	0	3	15	.209
	Wichita (TEX)	AA	6	6	4.36	21	17	0	1	97	101	50	47	8	43	70	.272
2008	NW Arkansas (TEX)	AA	4	2	1.20	8	8	0	0	45	30	8	6	2	7	42	.189
	Kansas City (AL)	MAJ	0	0	2.70	2	0	0	0	3	3	1	1	0	0	3	.250
	Omaha (PCL)	AAA	4	3	4.09	11	11	0	0	51	51	24	23	3	12	44	.267
MINOR LEAGUE TOTALS			30	31	3.48	109	100	1	1	518	530	245	200	29	179	384	.267
MAJOR LEAGUE TOTALS			0	0	2.70	2	0	0	0	3	3	1	1	0	0	3	.250

9 KILA KA'AIHUE, 1B

BORN: March 29, 1985. **B-T:** L-R. **HT.:** 6-2. **WT.:** 230. **DRAFTED:** HS—Honolulu, 2002 (15th round). **SIGNED BY:** Eric Tokunaga.

Improving his conditioning and diet enabled Ka'aihue to overcome knee problems and take off in 2008, when he was the Texas League MVP. His father Kila Sr. played 11 years in the minors and his brother Kala is a first baseman in the Braves system. With healthy knees, Ka'aihue had much improved balance at the plate and used his legs and hips to turn on pitches. He always had outstanding plate discipline—he led the minors with 104 walks in 2008—and his newfound strength allowed him to finally take advantage of fastball counts. His bat speed also got better and he started catching up to plus fastballs that had blown him away in the past. Ka'aihue has to hit for power because he lacks athleticism and speed, making him a liability as a runner and defender. He needs to walk a fine line between being disciplined and too passive, as he sometimes lets hittable pitches go by. It's hard to know if Ka'aihue's 2008 breakout is a sign of things to come or a repeat of Craig Brazell's 2007, which led to a trip to Japan. The Royals didn't do him any favors by trading for Mike Jacobs, so Ka'aihue will have to make his own opportunity.

Year	Club (League)	Class	AVG	G	AB	R	H	2B	3B	HR	RBI	BB	SO	SB	OBP	SLG
2002	Royals (GCL)	R	.259	43	139	15	36	8	0	3	21	26	35	0	.381	.381
2003	Burlington (MWL)	LoA	.238	114	395	53	94	21	1	11	63	67	87	1	.355	.380
2004	Burlington (MWL)	LoA	.246	125	390	57	96	23	2	15	62	64	98	1	.361	.431
2005	High Desert (CAL)	HiA	.304	132	493	84	150	31	2	20	90	97	97	2	.428	.497

2006	Wichita (TEX)	AA	.199	103	327	40	65	15	0	6	45	49	73	0	.303	.300
2007	Wilmington (CAR)	HiA	.251	60	207	28	52	8	0	9	42	35	38	1	.360	.420
	Wichita (TEX)	AA	.246	70	244	37	60	13	0	12	40	41	40	0	.359	.447
2008	NW Arkansas (TEX)	AA	.314	91	287	64	90	11	0	26	79	80	41	3	.463	.624
	Omaha (PCL)	AAA	.316	33	114	27	36	4	0	11	21	24	26	0	.439	.640
	Kansas City (AL)	MAJ	.286	12	21	4	6	0	0	1	1	3	2	0	.375	.429
MINOR LEAGUE TOTALS			.262	771	2596	405	679	134	5	113	463	483	535	8	.382	.448
MAJOR LEAGUE TOTALS			.286	12	21	4	6	0	0	1	1	3	2	0	.375	.429

10 BLAKE WOOD, RHP

BORN: Aug. 8, 1985. **B-T:** R-R. **HT.:** 6-4. **WT.:** 225. **DRAFTED:** Georgia Tech, 2005 (3rd round). **SIGNED BY:** Spencer Graham.

Wood missed the first three months of the 2007 season after back surgery to repair a herniated disc. While recovering, he focused on improving his conditioning, lost 25 pounds and improved his athleticism. He stayed healthy in 2008, though he struggled once he reached Double-A. On the nights where everything is working, Wood looks like he's ready for the big leagues. He has a heavy fastball that sits between 92-94 mph and touches 97. He'll also flash a power curveball and a plus changeup. Some believe he's more likely to stick as a starter than Daniel Cortes or Carlos Rosa. There are still too many games where Wood can't locate his fastball, buries his curveball in the dirt and doesn't have feel for his changeup. He doesn't always repeat his delivery, which leads to command issues, and too often speeds up his tempo. When he drops his arm slot, he leaves his fastball up in the zone and his curve loses bite. He rarely has both his curve and changeup working in the same outing. Unless he wows the Royals in spring training, Wood will head back to Double-A. If he can improve his command, he has a chance to become a No. 2 or 3 starter in the majors.

Year	Club (League)	Class	W	L	ERA	G	GS	CG	SV	IP	H	R	ER	HR	BB	SO	AVG
2006	Idaho Falls (PIO)	R	3	1	4.50	12	12	0	0	52	50	28	26	1	15	46	.258
2007	Royals (AZL)	R	0	0	0.00	4	4	0	0	10	9	2	0	0	0	15	.250
	Burlington (MWL)	LoA	2	1	3.03	7	7	0	0	36	32	12	12	3	14	26	.239
	Wilmington (CAR)	HiA	0	1	4.66	2	2	0	0	10	9	5	5	1	3	11	.257
2008	Wilmington (CAR)	HiA	3	2	2.67	10	10	0	0	57	32	17	17	3	15	63	.168
	NW Arkansas (TEX)	AA	5	7	5.30	18	18	2	0	87	96	55	51	7	32	76	.283
MINOR LEAGUE TOTALS			13	12	3.98	53	53	2	0	251	228	119	111	15	79	237	.245

11 JOHNNY GIAVOTELLA, 2B

BORN: July 10, 1987. **B-T:** R-R. **HT.:** 5-8. **WT.:** 185. **DRAFTED:** New Orleans, 2008 (2nd round). **SIGNED BY:** Scott Nichols.

New Orleans' Tom Walter named Giavotella a team captain as a sophomore—the first time he'd done that in 11 years as a head coach. It was a reward for Giavotella's intensity and his leadership skills. He showed the same qualities when he helped spark Burlington to the Midwest League title after signing with the Royals for $787,000 as a second-round pick last summer. Giavotella was an all-state second baseman on New Orleans Jesuit High's state championship team, and even though he's only 5-foot-8, he was a standout linebacker on the football team as well. He's built like a fire hydrant with massive forearms and a barrel chest. Giavotella has a compact swing that allows him to turn on fastballs and wait on breaking balls and changeups, though he's currently vulnerable to being pitched on the outer half. He has a very good batting eye and should continue to rack up high on-base percentages thanks to advanced pitch-recognition skills. Giavotella will have to hit because his defense will never be a strength. He showed improvement on the double-play pivot after the Royals moved his hands up to quicken his exchange, but he doesn't have much range to his right and likely never will rate better than a 45 defensively on the 20-80 scouting scale. He has solid arm strength and average speed. On the basepaths, the Royals have worked to get him squared him up more so he can get a better first step on his jumps. Giavotella should head to high Class A for his first full pro season.

Year	Club (League)	Class	AVG	G	AB	R	H	2B	3B	HR	RBI	BB	SO	SB	OBP	SLG
2008	Burlington (MWL)	LoA	.299	68	278	50	83	18	2	4	26	25	34	10	.355	.421
MINOR LEAGUE TOTALS			.299	68	278	50	83	18	2	4	26	25	34	10	.355	.421

12 KELVIN HERRERA, RHP

BORN: Dec. 31, 1989. **B-T:** R-R. **HT.:** 5-10. **WT.:** 162. **SIGNED:** Dominican Republic, 2006. **SIGNED BY:** Daurys Nin/Rafael Vasquez.

When Danny Duffy and Matt Mitchell were shut down at Burlington in August, the Royals needed to find someone to step right into the Midwest League playoff race. Herrera proved up to the challenge, going 2-0, 2.13 in three outings and turning in a quality start in his lone postseason outing. He has yet to find a challenge in pro ball, as he dominated the Rookie-level Dominican Summer League in 2007 before blowing away the Rookie-level Appalachian League in 2008. There are few pitchers in the system with a higher ceiling than Herrera. Though he's just 5-foot-10, he has quality stuff, commands his fastball to both sides of the plate and shows an advanced feel for pitching. As an 18-year-old last season, he was sitting at 91-92 mph and touching 95. He's especially tough on righthanders because his fastball rides in on their hands and his slurvy curveball has some bite. He also throws a solid changeup and has precocious command of both of his offspeed pitches. He also has made a quick adjustment to life in the United States. Herrera will return to low Class A to start the season, but he may force Kansas City to give him an early promotion.

Year	Club (League)	Class	W	L	ERA	G	GS	CG	SV	IP	H	R	ER	HR	BB	SO	AVG
2007	Royals (DSL)	R	4	1	0.84	11	5	0	1	43	30	6	4	1	15	50	.197
2008	Burlington (APP)	R	2	2	1.42	11	8	0	0	51	48	17	8	0	5	45	.254
	Burlington (MWL)	LoA	2	0	2.13	3	1	0	0	13	13	4	3	0	2	7	.265
MINOR LEAGUE TOTALS			8	3	1.27	25	14	0	1	106	91	27	15	1	22	102	.233

13 HENRY BARRERA, RHP

BORN: Nov. 25, 1985. **B-T:** R-R. **HT.:** 6-0. **WT.:** 205. **DRAFTED:** HS—Rosemead, Calif, 2004 (5th round). **SIGNED BY:** Luis Cordoba.

Barrera has one of the best arms in the system, and befitting a dominating reliever, he's all about power. But it has been a very slow climb for the righthander with the mid-90s fastball, which explains why the Royals had to deliberate long and hard before protecting him on the 40-man roster in November. Barrera's problems have revolved around an awkward delivery that caused command problems. Coming out of high school, he crow-hopped on his right leg as he began his leg kick at the start of his delivery. His weight shift frequently was so far ahead of his arm that his right foot had left the rubber before he released the ball. He had to be sent back to extended spring in 2007 from low Class A Burlington to rework his motion because it clearly was illegal. Barrera's delivery still flirts with being illegal—it depends on the interpretation of the umpire on any given night—but he has toned it down and has reduced the effort involved. Barrera's secondary pitches have improved as a result. His mid-80s slider and splitter are now plus pitches at times when they had been average at best. The awkwardness of his delivery does create deception, which helps because his slider and splitter aren't that different. His split doesn't drop straight down but cuts like his slider, which has just a little more sweep to it. If Barrera can continue to refine his delivery, he has the stuff to be a late-innings reliever. After enjoying his first extended success in four pro seasons, he'll have to keep improving to handle a jump to Double-A this year.

Year	Club (League)	Class	W	L	ERA	G	GS	CG	SV	IP	H	R	ER	HR	BB	SO	AVG
2005	Royals (AZL)	R	1	1	4.73	19	0	0	6	27	33	15	14	1	9	23	.289
2006	Royals (AZL)	R	0	1	5.48	16	0	0	2	23	20	18	14	0	17	30	.225
2007	Burlington (MWL)	LoA	2	2	4.35	30	0	0	4	52	53	28	25	4	15	53	.261
2008	Wilmington (CAR)	HiA	0	3	2.81	42	0	0	4	58	47	21	18	2	24	78	.224
MINOR LEAGUE TOTALS			3	7	4.02	107	0	0	16	159	153	82	71	7	65	184	.248

14 TYLER SAMPLE, RHP

BORN: June 27, 1989. **B-T:** L-R. **HT.:** 6-7. **WT.:** 245. **DRAFTED:** HS—Denver, 2008 (3rd round). **SIGNED BY:** Ken Munoz.

Unlike with most high school pitching prospects, scouts don't have to do a lot of projecting to forecast how Sample will fill out as an adult. The 18-year-old already has a big league body at 6-foot-7 and 245 pounds. The Royals drafted him in the third round last June and their $500,000 bonus persuaded him to give up an Arkansas scholarship. Sample had Tommy John surgery as a high school sophomore, but his stuff has fully returned. His fastball sits at 92-94 mph and topped out at 96 with good life. He pairs it with a 12-to-6 knuckle-curve, a pitch popular in the Denver area thanks to the late Bus Campbell, a former Blue Jays scout who had a knack for teaching it. Roy Halladay was his prized pupil. Sample also throws a changeup, though it needs plenty of polish. He's very raw, as he needs to lengthen his stride to improve his command and must learn to repeat his delivery. His inability to locate his fastball led to a rocky pro debut, but the Royals believe his problems are easily correctable. If he can refine his mechanics and makes sure he doesn't gain too much weight, he could blossom into a frontline starter. Kansas City may take it slow with Sample and let him open 2009 in extended spring training.

Year	Club (League)	Class	W	L	ERA	G	GS	CG	SV	IP	H	R	ER	HR	BB	SO	AVG
2008	Royals (AZL)	R	0	5	9.00	10	8	0	0	27	30	36	27	0	29	39	.270
MINOR LEAGUE TOTALS			0	5	9.00	10	8	0	0	27	30	36	27	0	29	39	.270

15 DAVID LOUGH, OF

BORN: Jan. 20, 1986. **B-T:** L-L. **HT.:** 6-0. **WT.:** 180. **DRAFTED:** Mercyhurst (Pa.), 2007 (11th round). **SIGNED BY:** Jason Bryans.

Lough was a baseball, football and soccer star in high school. He decided to focus on football as a wide receiver and kick returner at Mercyhurst (Pa.) College, and also opted to walk-on to the baseball team as well. He was an instant starter in center field as a freshman and quickly realized that at his size, he had a much brighter future in baseball. It was a wise choice as the Royals made him the highest draft pick (11th round) ever from Mercyhurst, which also produced big leaguers John Costello and David Lee. Despite his lack of stature, Lough has some impressive physical tools. He has a very muscular frame and has impressive raw power thanks to a quick bat and solid swing that comes with an exaggerated high finish. He's still unrefined at the plate, which partly can be attributed to the fact that he has spent only two years as a full-time baseball player. He did show steady improvement in 2008, with 31 of his 48 extra-base hits coming during the second half. Lough has plus speed and is average defensively in center field and above-average in left. His arm is a tick below-average, which prevents him from playing in right. Despite his speed, Lough isn't a very good basestealer because he doesn't get good jumps and still is learning how to read pitchers. He'll move to high Class A in 2009, and may have to play a lot of left field on a Wilmington club with multiple center fielders. Lough has one of the highest ceilings in the system, though he has a long way to go to turn his potential into big league production.

Year	Club (League)	Class	AVG	G	AB	R	H	2B	3B	HR	RBI	BB	SO	SB	OBP	SLG
2007	Burlington (APP)	R	.337	24	86	15	29	6	0	2	12	4	13	6	.380	.477
2008	Burlington (MWL)	LoA	.268	126	488	76	131	21	11	16	62	35	70	12	.329	.455
MINOR LEAGUE TOTALS			.279	150	574	91	160	27	11	18	74	39	83	18	.337	.458

16 DERRICK ROBINSON, OF

BORN: Sept. 28, 1987. **B-T:** B-L. **HT.:** 5-11. **WT.:** 170. **DRAFTED:** HS—Gainesville, Fla., 2006 (4th round). **SIGNED BY:** Cliff Pastornicky.

Robinson could patrol center field in Kansas City right now, but he has a long way to go to prove that he can hit enough to make it to Kansas City. The Royals spent $850,000 to get Robinson to give up a football scholarship to Florida, and he has shown the athleticism and makeup they were hoping for. But at the plate, the switch-hitter's lefthanded swing still looks unnatural. He has shown improved pitch recognition and is using his hands better. Where he used to survive on bloop hits, he now has more line-drive singles and doubles, especially when he's hitting righthanded. But Robinson will have to make more strides with pitch recognition and develop the ability to take a walk if he's going to ever be anything more than a No. 9 hitter. He's also still honing his ability to bunt, which would immediately improve his batting average. He can fly down the line in 3.8-3.9 seconds from home to first from the left side, and steals bases largely with his pure speed. If he improved his leads and his ability to read pitchers' moves, he could steal even more than the 62 bags he nabbed last year. In the outfield, he has the speed to run down balls in the gaps, and through hard work he has improved his arm to where it's now just a tick below average. Kansas City has pushed Robinson aggressively, but after struggling for three seasons, he'd be best off returning to high Class A to try to help him develop some confidence at the plate.

Year	Club (League)	Class	AVG	G	AB	R	H	2B	3B	HR	RBI	BB	SO	SB	OBP	SLG
2006	Royals (AZL)	R	.233	54	176	25	41	6	3	1	24	24	55	20	.335	.318
2007	Burlington (MWL)	LoA	.243	102	407	42	99	11	3	2	26	32	100	34	.299	.300
	Wilmington (CAR)	HiA	.385	3	13	1	5	1	0	0	0	1	0	1	.429	.462
2008	Wilmington (CAR)	HiA	.245	124	497	69	122	22	8	0	34	51	97	62	.316	.322
MINOR LEAGUE TOTALS			.244	283	1093	137	267	40	14	3	84	108	252	117	.314	.315

17 JASON TAYLOR, 3B/1B

BORN: Jan. 14, 1988. **B-T:** R-R. **HT.:** 6-0. **WT.:** 210. **DRAFTED:** HS—Virginia Beach, 2006 (2nd round). **SIGNED BY:** Steve Connelly.

After missing the 2007 season when the Royals sent him home for undisclosed personal reasons, Taylor bounced back with a solid year in low Class A, leading the Midwest League in walks (81) and hitting more homers (17) than any player in the minors who stole at least 40 bases last year. A second-round pick in 2006, Taylor has a unique combination of strengths and weaknesses. His speed is a tick below average, yet he swiped 40 bases in 54 tries because he's aggressive on the basepaths and reads pitchers well. He strikes out frequently, which helps explain his subpar batting average, but he's an on-base machine thanks to his ability to draw walks. He hits for power, yet there are questions of whether he'll hit for enough to fit the profile of a first baseman, the position at which he ended 2008. A high school shortstop, Taylor became a third baseman when he turned pro. He lacked range at the hot corner, and when Mike Moustakas needed to move there, Taylor slid over to first base. It's possible that he could get an opportunity to try left field. His on-base ability stands out in an organization that has few players with that skill, but he still has a lot to prove as he advances up the ladder.

Year	Club (League)	Class	AVG	G	AB	R	H	2B	3B	HR	RBI	BB	SO	SB	OBP	SLG
2006	Royals (AZL)	R	.258	46	151	27	39	8	1	0	22	26	30	7	.374	.325
2007	Did Not Play—Suspended															
2008	Burlington (MWL)	LoA	.242	127	433	79	105	17	4	17	58	81	97	40	.372	.418
MINOR LEAGUE TOTALS			.247	173	584	106	144	25	5	17	80	107	127	47	.372	.394

18 JULIO PIMENTEL, RHP

BORN: Dec. 14, 1985. **B-T:** R-R. **HT.:** 6-1. **WT.:** 190. **SIGNED:** Dominican Republic, 2003. **SIGNED BY:** Pablo Peguero/Angel Santana (Dodgers).

For a righthander with quality stuff, Pimentel has climbed through the minors much slower than expected, which may partly explain why the Dodgers were willing to include him in a trade for Elmer Dessens in 2006. He needed three years to master high Class A, then ran into trouble again in his first exposure to Double-A last year. Despite his struggles, he was named to the Futures Game, where he showed off a lively 90-93 mph fastball. His changeup has late fade and at times gives him a second swing-and-miss pitch. He also does a good job of throwing strikes. But the sum of the parts never has added up for Pimentel. He struggles with rushing his delivery when he gets into jams, and he has a knack of cruising for several innings before suddenly and completely falling apart. Some scouts believe he'll be better off as a reliever, where his mechanical issues and his lack of a consistent curveball will be less of an issue. Kansas City will keep him a starter for now, but his role could change if he can't solve Double-A in his second chance.

Year	Club (League)	Class	W	L	ERA	G	GS	CG	SV	IP	H	R	ER	HR	BB	SO	AVG
2003	Dodgers N (DSL)	R	1	1	4.09	8	3	0	0	22	17	12	10	1	13	24	.221
2004	Columbus (SAL)	LoA	10	8	3.48	23	23	2	0	111	106	56	43	14	47	102	.260
2005	Vero Beach (FSL)	HiA	8	10	5.08	26	24	1	0	124	149	79	70	9	43	105	.305
2006	Vero Beach (FSL)	HiA	3	8	5.69	30	9	0	2	74	85	56	47	4	45	77	.290
	High Desert (CAL)	HiA	2	1	3.18	12	0	0	2	23	21	8	8	3	10	26	.244
2007	Wilmington (CAR)	HiA	12	4	2.65	27	22	0	0	153	145	56	45	8	43	73	.250
2008	NW Arkansas (TEX)	AA	7	13	5.38	28	28	0	0	157	193	103	94	17	52	115	.307
MINOR LEAGUE TOTALS			43	45	4.29	154	109	3	4	664	716	370	317	56	253	522	.280

19 SALVADOR PEREZ, C

BORN: May 10, 1990. **B-T:** R-R. **HT.:** 6-3. **WT.:** 175. **SIGNED:** Venezuela, 2006. **SIGNED BY:** Juan Indiago.

The Royals have a clear need for catching help, but their top catching prospects are years away from the majors. Perez is the best of the bunch, as the 18-year-old Venezuelan combines solid defensive skills with a potentially potent bat. A twisted ankle cost him nearly half of his 2008 season. At 6-foot-3, he doesn't have a typical backstop's build, but the Royals compare his body to Sandy Alomar Jr.'s. Perez sets a good target behind the plate, shows soft hands and does a decent job of blocking balls in the dirt. His arm rates a 55 on the 20-80 scouting scale, though it plays a tick better than that because of his quick exchange. He threw out 45 percent of basestealers last season. At the plate, Perez is slowly gaining strength, which is paying off in improved bat speed. He's still not a power hitter, but he caught up to fastballs last year that would have blown him away in 2007. His swing is still a little lengthy, and it likely always will be because of his long arms, but he showed an improved path to the ball in 2008. He should get his first taste of full-season ball with a move to low Class A in 2009.

Year	Club (League)	Class	AVG	G	AB	R	H	2B	3B	HR	RBI	BB	SO	SB	OBP	SLG
2007	Royals (AZL)	R	.244	30	86	10	21	3	0	0	10	5	10	1	.320	.279
2008	Burlington (APP)	R	.325	13	40	4	13	0	1	0	10	5	5	0	.404	.375
	Idaho Falls (PIO)	R	.395	12	43	7	17	3	1	1	6	2	5	0	.413	.581
MINOR LEAGUE TOTALS			.302	55	169	21	51	6	2	1	26	12	20	1	.363	.379

20 CARLOS FORTUNA, RHP

BORN: March 31, 1990. **B-T:** R-R. **HT.:** 6-2. **WT.:** 200. **SIGNED:** Dominican Republic. **SIGNED BY:** Daurys Nin.

Like Kelvin Herrera, Fortuna is a largely unpublicized Latin American prospect who could end up rocketing up this list a year from now. The live-armed teenager already can touch 95-96 mph with his fastball. Fortuna has a clean arm action and a solid delivery, but he still needs to refine nearly everything. He has shown the ability to spin a breaking ball which leads the Royals to believe he'll pick up the pitch, but his curveball is very fringy right now and he struggles to locate it. His changeup might be a tick ahead of the curveball at this point. Fortuna's command wavers and he doesn't always repeat his delivery, but Kansas City believes he just needs innings to fix most of the problems, and he has shown that he's a fast learner. He had adjusted very well to life in the United States and has picked up English. At worst, if Fortuna doesn't pick up a curveball, the Royals think he easily could add a slider to become a power arm out of the pen. With his fastball and delivery, he has a lot of potential as a starter and will get every opportunity to succeed in that role. He's not ready for full-season ball, so he'll begin 2009 in extended spring training.

Year	Club (League)	Class	W	L	ERA	G	GS	CG	SV	IP	H	R	ER	HR	BB	SO	AVG
2007	Royals (DSL)	R	1	2	3.94	10	3	0	0	32	26	14	14	2	12	28	.234
2008	Royals (AZL)	R	2	2	5.82	11	5	0	0	39	39	26	25	5	19	41	.267
MINOR LEAGUE TOTALS			3	4	4.97	21	8	0	0	71	65	40	39	7	31	69	.253

21 MATT MITCHELL, RHP

BORN: March 31, 1989. **B-T:** R-R. **HT.:** 6-2. **WT.:** 205. **DRAFTED:** HS—Barstow, Calif., 2007 (14th round). **SIGNED BY:** John Ramey.

After leading the Arizona League with a 1.80 ERA in his 2007 pro debut, Mitchell held his own after making the jump to low Class A last season. But his season ended on a down note, as he was shut down in late August with elbow discomfort and required Tommy John surgery that will sideline him for the entire 2009 season. There's a potential bright spot to the injury, however. Mitchell was throwing a fringe-average fastball that usually sat between 89-90 mph last summer while he was less than 100 percent. There's a good chance he'll come back throwing harder, which would allow his above-average changeup and improving curveball to play up. Mitchell uses a palmball grip for his changeup because of his small hands, and it works for him. Mitchell has excellent contol for a young pitcher, but unless he gains some velocity, he'll have to be very precise as he climbs the ladder because he doesn't have put-away stuff. If his rehab goes well, he should return at high Class A in 2010.

Year	Club (League)	Class	W	L	ERA	G	GS	CG	SV	IP	H	R	ER	HR	BB	SO	AVG
2007	Royals (AZL)	R	5	1	1.80	14	7	0	1	55	34	16	11	0	25	72	.183
2008	Burlington (MWL)	LoA	8	8	3.47	25	21	0	0	117	116	55	45	9	25	77	.260
MINOR LEAGUE TOTALS			13	9	2.94	39	28	0	1	172	150	71	56	9	50	149	.237

22 ADRIAN ORTIZ, OF

BORN: Jan. 14, 1987. **B-T:** L-R. **HT.:** 6-0. **WT.:** 180. **DRAFTED:** Pepperdine, 2007 (5th round). **SIGNED BY:** Johnny Ramos.

If Derrick Robinson is the Royals' toolsiest center-field candidate, Ortiz is their fastest. His entire game is built around his 80 speed on the 20-80 scouting scale. Against lefthanders, he sometimes takes a running start at the ball as he tries to slap it onto the ground, though he has the ability to stay back and drive the ball into the gap against righties. He can fly from home to first in 3.8 seconds, turns liners in the gaps into triples and choppers into base hits, which explains why he has batted .308 or better at each of his three pro stops. But to be a leadoff hitter, Ortiz needs to become more patient. He too often swings at the first or second pitch, and he drew only 24 walks last season, a concern for a player who has to be a tablesetter. His utter lack of power is also a problem, as upper-level pitchers won't be afraid to bust him inside. For all his speed, Ortiz must improve at picking his spots to run after getting caught 20 times in 54 steal attempts in 2008. He's an excellent center fielder with very good range and an above-average arm with a quick release and pinpoint accuracy. He led the Midwest League with 18 assists in just 99 games and finished 2008 with a total of 22. Ortiz will return to high Class A to start 2009, where he'll join David Lough, Paulo Orlando and Robinson in an extremely speedy outfield.

Year	Club (League)	Class	AVG	G	AB	R	H	2B	3B	HR	RBI	BB	SO	SB	OBP	SLG
2007	Idaho Falls (PIO)	R	.326	61	264	44	86	9	1	0	24	9	36	17	.348	.367
2008	Burlington (MWL)	LoA	.308	100	422	50	130	10	7	3	33	15	68	29	.334	.386
	Wilmington (CAR)	HiA	.311	28	103	10	32	5	2	0	12	9	11	5	.388	.398
MINOR LEAGUE TOTALS			.314	189	789	104	248	24	10	3	69	33	115	51	.346	.381

23 MITCH MAIER, OF

BORN: June 30, 1982. **B-T:** L-R. **HT.:** 6-2. **WT.:** 210. **DRAFTED:** Toledo, 2003 (1st round). **SIGNED BY:** Jason Bryans.

There's very little projection left in the 26-year-old Maier, but he has proven that he can be a useful contributor in the majors. The Royals made him the final pick in 2003's first round, in part because he was willing to sign for a below-slot $900,000 bonus. Maier does a lot of little things well. He can play a solid center field—he was the best defensive center fielder on the big league roster before Kansas City traded for Coco Crisp—and can play anywhere in the outfield and even serve as an emergency catcher. He has average speed with solid instincts that allow him to take an extra base and steal if he catches a pitcher napping. He also hits for solid average with a little bit of pop and has showed an improved approach and swing in recent years, but he still doesn't provide enough offense to be a big league regular. Maier dreamed of being a defensive back for Michigan as a kid, and he still carries that all-out mentality onto the baseball field. He missed only a couple of weeks after a Zach Jackson fastball broke three bones in his face in mid-August. Maier will likely never be more than a backup outfielder, but his attitude, versatility and decent bat should help him spend 2009 in Kansas City.

Year	Club (League)	Class	AVG	G	AB	R	H	2B	3B	HR	RBI	BB	SO	SB	OBP	SLG
2003	Royals (AZL)	R	.350	51	203	41	71	14	6	2	45	18	25	7	.403	.507
2004	Burlington (MWL)	LoA	.300	82	317	41	95	24	3	4	36	27	51	34	.354	.432
	Wilmington (CAR)	HiA	.264	51	174	25	46	9	2	3	17	15	29	9	.326	.391
2005	High Desert (CAL)	HiA	.336	50	211	42	71	26	1	8	32	12	43	6	.370	.583
	Wichita (TEX)	AA	.255	80	322	55	82	21	5	7	49	15	47	10	.289	.416
2006	Wichita (TEX)	AA	.306	138	543	95	166	35	7	14	92	41	96	13	.357	.473
	Kansas City (AL)	MAJ	.154	5	13	3	2	0	0	0	0	2	4	0	.267	.154
2007	Omaha (PCL)	AAA	.279	140	544	75	152	29	5	14	62	33	89	7	.320	.428
2008	Omaha (PCL)	AAA	.316	85	345	57	109	24	1	9	41	29	42	12	.366	.470
	Kansas City (AL)	MAJ	.286	34	91	9	26	1	1	0	9	2	18	0	.316	.319
MINOR LEAGUE TOTALS			.298	677	2659	431	792	182	30	61	374	190	422	98	.345	.458
MAJOR LEAGUE TOTALS			.269	39	104	12	28	1	1	0	9	4	22	0	.309	.298

24 JOE DICKERSON, OF

BORN: Oct. 3, 1986. **B-T:** L-L. **HT.:** 6-1. **WT.:** 190. **DRAFTED:** HS—Yorba Linda, Calif., 2005 (4th round). **SIGNED BY:** John Ramey.

Dickerson saw his 2008 season end early, as a fastball in on the hands broke his left index finger on July 13 and sidelined him until the Arizona Fall League. He's a classic tweener. If you're an optimist, you focus on his solid bat, his defense in right field and his ability to play center field in a pinch. If you're a pessimist, you fixate on his lack of a clear profile. He doesn't project to hit enough to be a big league corner outfielder, and he doesn't play defense well enough to be a big league center fielder. In any case, Dickerson has been one of the most consistent hitters in the system since the Royals made him a fourth-round pick in 2005. As he has climbed the ladder, he has showed diminishing power production, in part because he's learned how to use the whole field instead of employing the pull-happy approach he entered pro ball with. His bat control allows him to put the barrel on the ball consistently. He has a tick above-average speed, but that never has paid off in basestealing success. He can use that speed to take an extra base and to cover more ground that most right fielders. His arm is average. Dickerson has moved one level at a time though the system and will continue to do so in 2009, when he advances to Double-A.

Year	Club (League)	Class	AVG	G	AB	R	H	2B	3B	HR	RBI	BB	SO	SB	OBP	SLG
2005	Royals (AZL)	R	.294	56	214	27	63	12	9	4	40	27	46	9	.371	.491
2006	Idaho Falls (PIO)	R	.281	63	242	36	68	14	3	7	38	19	34	9	.338	.450
2007	Burlington (MWL)	LoA	.289	115	419	50	121	23	2	3	43	38	76	26	.354	.375
2008	Wilmington (CAR)	HiA	.297	87	310	39	92	10	10	5	45	31	48	24	.376	.442
MINOR LEAGUE TOTALS			.290	321	1185	152	344	59	24	19	166	115	204	68	.360	.429

25 JUAN ABREU, RHP

BORN: April 8, 1985. **B-T:** R-R. **HT.:** 6-0. **WT.:** 170. **SIGNED:** Dominican Republic, 2003. **SIGNED BY:** Pedro Silverio.

Abreu has shown a great arm, iffy command and rotten luck during his time with the Royals. He missed 2007 with an elbow injury, but bounced back with a strong season in low Class A. After combining with Danny Duffy on a no-hitter on Aug. 7, however, Abreu stepped on a baseball during a conditioning drill, twisted his ankle and missed the rest of the year. He has one of the best arms in the system with a 93-94 mph fastball that touches 97, and his 12.3 strikeouts per nine innings last year was the highest average among full-season Royals pitchers. On the downside, he always has struggled with his control and his health. His delivery has a little funkiness to it that makes it hard to pick up the ball but also makes it hard for him to find the strike zone. Abreu sets up on the far right side of the rubber and throws from a three-quarters arm slot that makes him especially tough on righthanders, who hit .209/.315/.314 against him last season. He also throws an 11-to-5 curveball that has depth. As a 24-year-old, Abreu will be old for high Class A in 2009, but if he can continue to improve his control he could be a useful power arm out of the bullpen.

Year	Club (League)	Class	W	L	ERA	G	GS	CG	SV	IP	H	R	ER	HR	BB	SO	AVG
2003	Royals (DSL)	R	0	2	2.25	5	2	0	0	16	16	12	4	0	7	10	.242
2004	Royals (DSL)	R	2	1	4.06	9	7	0	0	31	22	15	14	0	20	33	.198
2005	Royals (AZL)	R	2	5	6.88	14	13	0	0	52	72	49	40	4	27	52	.327
2006	Idaho Falls (PIO)	R	4	2	5.76	20	0	0	2	50	39	34	32	4	35	57	.223
2007	Did not play—Injured																
2008	Burlington (MWL)	LoA	4	4	3.66	22	4	0	7	76	59	40	31	6	42	104	.214
MINOR LEAGUE TOTALS			12	14	4.83	70	26	0	9	226	208	150	121	14	131	256	.245

26 JOSE BONILLA, C

BORN: Aug. 4, 1988. **B-T:** R-R. **HT.:** 5-10. **WT.:** 180. **SIGNED:** Dominican Republic, 2006. **SIGNED BY:** Ramon Martinez.

While Salvador Perez is lanky for a catcher, Bonilla has the more traditional squat, muscular build. His present tools may grade out a tick above Perez's, but Perez's better defense and long-term potential give him the edge on this list. Of the two, Bonilla has a better arm, as it grades as a 60 on the 20-80 scouting scale. He threw out 43 percent of basestealers in 2008. He showed improvement receiving the ball, but he still needs to become consistent behind the plate. Using a compact swing, Bonilla has shown some power and the ability to use the entire field. He runs very well for a catcher and actually has enough athleticism to potentially play second base or outfield, though the Royals have no intention of moving him. He's a long ways away but has all the tools to become a big league everyday catcher. With Perez and Sean McCauley ahead of him, Bonilla likely will move up to Idaho Falls in 2009.

Year	Club (League)	Class	AVG	G	AB	R	H	2B	3B	HR	RBI	BB	SO	SB	OBP	SLG
2007	Royals (AZL)	R	.000	3	5	0	0	0	0	0	0	0	2	0	.000	.000
2008	Royals (AZL)	R	.357	34	112	20	40	9	3	5	24	5	22	5	.405	.625
MINOR LEAGUE TOTALS			.342	37	117	20	40	9	3	5	24	5	24	5	.389	.598

27 KYLE MARTIN, SS/3B

BORN: Nov. 22, 1984. **B-T:** R-R. **HT.:** 6-0. **WT.:** 175. **DRAFTED:** Texas Tech, 2007 (29th round). **SIGNED BY:** Gerald Turner.

Martin earned all-Pacific Coast Conference honors in each of his two seasons at San Diego Mesa JC, then turned in two more solid years at Texas Tech. His modest size and tools helped him fall to the 29th round in 2007, but he has shown intriguing power since signing for $1,000. In his pro debut, he ranked second in the Appalachian League with 10 homers, and he followed up by hitting nine in only 190 at-bats as a utility infielder in low Class A in 2008. He was held back in extended spring until late May, and he struggled to get at-bats on a team that had Mike Moustakas, Johnny Giavotella and Jason Taylor in the infield. As a result, the Royals sent Martin to Hawaii Winter Baseball, where he emerged as a prospect. He tied former Texas Tech teammate Roger Kieschnick for the HWB lead with six homers, and he ranked second with 12 doubles and fourth with a .518 slugging percentage. Martin generates good bat speed and has a sound swing, and the ball jumps off his bat in surprising fashion for someone his size. He's too aggressive and will have to be more patient as he advances through the minors, and he has struggled to make consistent contact at times. Defensively, Martin's hands grade out as average, though his arm and range may be a tick short for shortstop. He fits better defensively at second or third base, but he's still a little raw at second because he's not accustomed to playing on that side of the bag. He has the power and defensive profile to be a big league utilityman and needs to be tested in 2009, either at high Class A or Double-A, as a 24-year-old.

Year	Club (League)	Class	AVG	G	AB	R	H	2B	3B	HR	RBI	BB	SO	SB	OBP	SLG
2007	Burlington (APP)	R	.242	58	215	33	52	17	0	10	35	13	46	3	.294	.460
	Idaho Falls (PIO)	R	.583	3	12	1	7	2	0	1	3	1	0	1	.615	1.000
2008	Burlington (MWL)	LoA	.316	56	190	26	60	13	1	9	28	17	40	2	.373	.537
MINOR LEAGUE TOTALS			.285	117	417	60	119	32	1	20	66	31	86	6	.339	.511

28 SAM RUNION, RHP

BORN: Nov. 9, 1988. **B-T:** R-R. **HT.:** 6-4. **WT.:** 220. **DRAFTED:** HS—Asheville, N.C., 2007 (2nd round). **SIGNED BY:** Steve Connelly.

Asheville, N.C., has been a hot destination for scouts in recent years, as Cameron Maybin, Justin Jackson and Runion have gone in the top two rounds of the last four drafts. As a senior in 2007, Runion outdueled Madison Bumgarner in an April start that helped cement his status as a premium prospect. The Royals knew when they drafted Runion that he was somewhat raw and would require patience, and that has been the case. He has a lively fastball that generally sits at 91-92 mph and touches 94. When he keeps his arm angle up, he gets good downward plane on his heater. His lack of a consistent breaking ball led to him getting shelled in low Class A last year, but he showed improvement after a demotion. Runion's curveball is best when he slows down and snaps it off with 11-to-5 break. In the Midwest League, he started dropping his arm and trying to throw his breaking ball with more velocity, and it became a slurvy slider with some sweep. Runion has a little bit of feel for a changeup, but he doesn't replicate his fastball arm speed when throwing it. Runion has the stuff to be a power reliever, but the Royals look at his body and fastball and see a reason to keep developing him as a starter. While he needs to refine his stuff, he has done a good job of finding the strike zone. He'll take a second crack at low Class A in 2009.

Year	Club (League)	Class	W	L	ERA	G	GS	CG	SV	IP	H	R	ER	HR	BB	SO	AVG
2007	Royals (AZL)	R	3	4	5.82	12	9	0	0	51	61	36	33	4	17	51	.310
2008	Burlington (MWL)	LoA	2	5	5.75	9	5	0	0	41	54	35	26	7	9	11	.327
	Burlington (APP)	R	3	4	3.35	10	10	0	0	48	47	25	18	4	10	30	.253
MINOR LEAGUE TOTALS			8	13	4.95	31	24	0	0	140	162	96	77	15	36	92	.296

29 YOWILL ESPINAL, 2B/SS

BORN: April 1, 1991. **B-T:** R-R. **HT.:** 6-0. **WT.:** 170. **SIGNED:** Dominican Republic, 2007. **SIGNED BY:** Fausto Morel.

Espinall is part of the Royals' renewed push to find talent in the Caribbean. He signed in 2007 for $250,000, while AZL Royals double-play partner Guelin Beltre signed for $230,000. The two likely will climb the ladder together for several years. Espinal makes the Top 30 ahead of Beltre on the basis of his superior physicality. Unlike many young Dominican signees, Espinal already has some stockiness and strength which should give him average power to go with his above-average speed. Like many young Dominican signees, he has to improve his plate discipline—he walked only twice in 204 at-bats in his pro debut last summer. He shows average range and a plus arm at shortstop, but he's not as flashy as Beltre and may outgrow the position and end up as an offense-first second baseman. Espinal broke the hamate bone in his hand, ending his season early and causing him to miss instructional league. He should be ready for spring training, however, and has an outside chance of earning a spot in low Class A.

Year	Club (League)	Class	AVG	G	AB	R	H	2B	3B	HR	RBI	BB	SO	SB	OBP	SLG
2008	Royals (AZL)	R	.240	50	204	21	49	4	3	4	19	2	42	13	.248	.348
MINOR LEAGUE TOTALS			.240	50	204	21	49	4	3	4	19	2	42	13	.248	.348

30 KEATON HAYENGA, RHP

BORN: July 10, 1988. **B-T:** R-R. **HT.:** 6-5. **WT.:** 180. **DRAFTED:** HS—Eastlake, Wash., 2007 (31st round). **SIGNED BY:** Scott Ramsay.

The Royals believed enough in Hayenga to give him a $300,000 bonus in 2007 despite the fact that he was recovering from a torn labrum. He suffered the shoulder injury when he dove into a base in high school and jammed his shoulder. He has yet to throw a pitch in an official game, but Kansas City got the first glimpse of what it paid for during instructional league when his fastball sat at 92-94 mph in his first outing. A prep basketball standout, Hayenga is an above-average athlete with a relatively clean and repeatable delivery. The Royals had him focus on throwing mainly fastballs and changeups in instructs, but he had a 12-to-6 curveball with depth before he got hurt. He showed solid command in his return to the mound in instructional league. Club officials have been impressed with Hayenga's dedication to rehabbing his shoulder and think they landed a steal in the 31st round. It's unlikely that Hayenga will break camp with a full-season club in 2009, though he could head to low Class A after a stint in extended spring training.

Year	Club (League)	Class	W	L	ERA	G	GS	CG	SV	IP	H	R	ER	HR	BB	SO	AVG
2007	Did Not Play—Injured																
2008	Did Not Play—Injured																

Los Angeles Angels

BY KARY BOOHER

The Angels seemed to have everything going their way when the 2008 playoffs opened. They owned the majors' best record at 100-62, and ran away with the American League West for their fourth division crown in five years. With the additions of Torii Hunter and Mark Teixeira, they had their most dangerous heart of the order since winning the 2002 World Series.

Unfortunately for Los Angeles, its 2008 season ended like so many others have recently. The Red Sox ushered them out of the AL playoffs for the third time in five years, and the Angels have  won just one of their past five postseason series. It was a sour ending, and key players such as Garrett Anderson, Jon Garland, record-setting closer Francisco Rodriguez and Teixeira became free agents after the season.

Still, the Angels remain in position to contend for the foreseeable future. Their 2008 Opening Day payroll of $119 million ranked sixth among the 30 teams, and owner Arte Moreno remains committed to winning through both free agency and player development. In his first season as general manager, former farm director Tony Reagins moved aggressively to bolster his team, signing Hunter as a free agent and swinging trades for Garland and Teixeira.

As usual, Los Angeles got a ton of mileage from homegrown talent. Garland was the only import in the rotation, as John Lackey, Ervin Santana, Joe Saunders and Jered Weaver combined for 56 wins. Rodriguez and Scot Shields continued to anchor the bullpen, with assistance from Jose Arredondo. Jeff Mathis and Mike Napoli ably shared catching duties, double-play partners Howie Kendrick and Erick Aybar continued to develop and Anderson extended his franchise career leadership in several offensive categories.

More new faces could be on the way. The Angels will try to re-sign Teixeira, but if they can't, that could mean the first extended opportunity for slugger Kendry Morales since he signed a $4.5 million major league contract after defecting from Cuba. The system's top prospect, righthander Nick Adenhart, could replace Garland in the rotation. Infielders Sean Rodriguez and Brandon Wood are ready for expanded roles after decimating Triple-A pitching, and reliever Kevin Jepsen could help offset the loss of Rodriguez.

Los Angeles' U.S.-based affiliates combined for a .542 winning percentage in 2008, the system's best performance since 1995. Triple-A Salt Lake opened 22-

Angels manager Mike Scioscia should have plenty of talent to make a World Series run

TOP 30 PROSPECTS

1. Nick Adenhart, rhp	16. Clay Fuller, of
2. Jordan Walden, rhp	17. Chris Pettit, of
3. Peter Bourjos, of	18. Matt Sweeney, 3b
4. Trevor Reckling, lhp	19. Manuarys Correa, rhp
5. Sean O'Sullivan, rhp	20. Robert Fish, lhp
6. Kevin Jepsen, rhp	21. Ryan Chaffee, rhp
7. Hank Conger, c	22. Andrew Romine, ss
8. Mark Trumbo, 1b	23. Rolando Gomez, ss
9. Anthony Ortega, rhp	24. Alex Torres, lhp
10. Mason Tobin, rhp	25. Matt Brown, 3b/1b
11. Tyler Chatwood, rhp	26. Luis Jimenez, 3b
12. Will Smith, lhp	27. Terrell Alliman, of/3b
13. Bobby Wilson, c	28. David Herndon, rhp
14. Ryan Mount, 2b	29. Nick Green, rhp
15. Rafael Rodriguez, rhp	30. Hainley Statia, ss

1, the best start ever by a minor league team and was one of three full-season affiliates to reach the playoffs. Double-A Arkansas won an improbable Texas League title after a 62-78 regular season, and low Class A Cedar Rapids reached the Midwest League finals.

While the franchise emphasizes scouting and development, its thirst for free agents presents a hurdle in the draft that has been difficult to overcome. The Angels have yielded their first-round pick as free agent compensation in three of the last four drafts, and no team spent less on the 2007-08 drafts than their $4.5 million.

General Manager: Tony Reagins. **Farm Director:** Abe Flores. **Scouting Director:** Eddie Bane.

Class	Team	League	W	L	PCT	Finish*	Manager	Affiliated
Majors	Los Angeles	American	100	62	.617	1st (14)	Mike Scioscia	—
Triple-A	Salt Lake Bees	Pacific Coast	84	60	.583	2nd (16)	Bobby Mitchell	2001
Double-A	Arkansas Travelers	Texas	62	78	.443	^6th (8)	Bobby Magallanes	2001
High A	R. Cucamonga Quakes	California	67	74	.475	8th (10)	Ever Magallanes	2001
Low A	Cedar Rapids Kernels	Midwest	72	66	.522	6th (14)	Keith Johnson	1993
Rookie	Orem Owlz	Pioneer	52	23	.693	1st (8)	Tom Kotchman	2001
Rookie	AZL Angels	Arizona	39	17	.696	1st (9)	Tyrone Boykin	2001
Overall 2008 Minor League Record			376	318	.542	4th		

* Finish in overall standings (No. of teams in league). ^League champion.

LAST YEAR'S TOP 30

Rank	Player, Pos.	Status
1.	Brandon Wood, 3b/ss	Majors
2.	Nick Adenhart, rhp	No. 1
3.	Jordan Walden, rhp	No. 2
4.	Hank Conger, c	No. 7
5.	Sean O'Sullivan, rhp	No. 5
6.	Stephen Marek, rhp	(Braves)
7.	Sean Rodriguez, ss/2b	Majors
8.	Nick Green, rhp	No. 29
9.	Peter Bourjos, of	No. 3
10.	Anel de los Santos, c	Dropped out
11.	Hainley Statia, ss	No. 30
12.	Jose Arredondo, rhp	Majors
13.	Young-Il Jung, rhp	Dropped out
14.	Ryan Mount, 2b	No. 14
15.	P.J. Phillips, ss	Dropped out
16.	Trevor Reckling, lhp	No. 4
17.	Matt Sweeney, 3b	No. 18
18.	Terry Evans, of	Dropped out
19.	Chris Pettit, of	No. 17
20.	Barret Browning, lhp	Dropped out
21.	Mason Tobin, rhp	No. 10
22.	Rich Thompson, rhp	Dropped out
23.	Jeremy Haynes, rhp	Dropped out
24.	Jon Bachanov, rhp	Dropped out
25.	Bobby Wilson, c	No. 13
26.	Jason Bulger, rhp	Dropped out
27.	Robert Fish, lhp	No. 20
28.	Andrew Romine, ss	No. 22
29.	Mark Trumbo, 1b	No. 8
30.	Clay Fuller, of	No. 16

BEST TOOLS

Best Hitter for Average	Hank Conger
Best Power Hitter	Mark Trumbo
Best Strike-Zone Discipline	Andrew Romine
Fastest Baserunner	Peter Bourjos
Best Athlete	P.J. Phillips
Best Fastball	Jordan Walden
Best Curveball	Kevin Jepsen
Best Slider	Rafael Rodriguez
Best Changeup	Nick Adenhart
Best Control	David Herndon
Best Defensive Catcher	Anel de los Santos
Best Defensive Infielder	Rolando Gomez
Best Infield Arm	Andrew Romine
Best Defensive Outfielder	Peter Bourjos
Best Outfield Arm	Julio Perez

PROJECTED 2012 LINEUP

Catcher	Mike Napoli
First Base	Mark Trumbo
Second Base	Howie Kendrick
Third Base	Brandon Wood
Shortstop	Erick Aybar
Left Field	Torii Hunter
Center Field	Peter Bourjos
Right Field	Vladimir Guerrero
Designated Hitter	Hank Conger
No. 1 Starter	John Lackey
No. 2 Starter	Ervin Santana
No. 3 Starter	Jered Weaver
No. 4 Starter	Joe Saunders
No. 5 Starter	Nick Adenhart
Closer	Jose Arredondo

TOP PROSPECTS OF THE DECADE

Year	Player, Pos.	2008 Org.
1999	Ramon Ortiz, rhp	Orix (Japan)
2000	Ramon Ortiz, rhp	Orix (Japan)
2001	Joe Torres, lhp	White Sox
2002	Casey Kotchman, 1b	Braves
2003	Francisco Rodriguez, rhp	Angels
2004	Casey Kotchman, 1b	Braves
2005	Casey Kotchman, 1b	Braves
2006	Brandon Wood, ss	Angels
2007	Brandon Wood, ss	Angels
2008	Brandon Wood, 3b/ss	Angels

TOP DRAFT PICKS OF THE DECADE

Year	Player, Pos.	2008 Org.
1999	John Lackey, rhp (2nd round)	Angels
2000	Joe Torres, lhp	White Sox
2001	Casey Kotchman, 1b	Braves
2002	Joe Saunders, lhp	Angels
2003	Brandon Wood, ss	Angels
2004	Jered Weaver, rhp	Angels
2005	Trevor Bell, rhp (1st round supp.)	Angels
2006	Hank Conger, c	Angels
2007	Jon Bachanov, rhp (1st round supp.)	Angels
2008	Tyler Chatwood, rhp (2nd round)	Angels

LARGEST BONUSES IN CLUB HISTORY

Jered Weaver, 2004	$4,000,000
Kendry Morales, 2004	$3,000,000
Troy Glaus, 1997	$2,250,000
Joe Torres, 2000	$2,080,000
Casey Kotchman, 2001	$2,075,000

LOS ANGELES ANGELS

TOP 2009 ROOKIE: Kevin Jepsen, rhp. A surprise addition to the playoff roster, he could play a key set-up role and possibly even pull closer duty.

BREAKOUT PROSPECT: Clay Fuller, of. He's a switch-hitter with plus speed and some power potential.

SLEEPER: Eddie McKiernan, rhp. A 17th-round pick out of high school in 2007, he misses bats with his fastball-curve combo.

SOURCE OF TOP 30 TALENT

Homegrown	30	Acquired	0
College	2	Trades	0
Junior college	5	Rule 5 draft	0
High school	15	Independent leagues	0
Draft-and-follow	3	Free agents/waivers	0
Nondrafted free agents	0		
International	5		

Numbers in parentheses indicate prospect rankings.

LF
Chris Pettit (17)
Terry Evans
Jeremy Moore
Anthony Norman
Marcel Champagnie

CF
Peter Bourjos (3)
Clay Fuller (16)
Bradley Coon

RF
Terrell Alliman (27)
Angel Castillo
Julio Perez

3B
Matt Brown (25)
Luis Jimenez (26)
Larry Infante
Kevin Ramos
Adam Younger

SS
Andrew Romine (22)
Rolando Gomez (23)
Hainley Statia (30)
P.J. Phillips
Darwin Perez
Jean Almanzar

2B
Ryan Mount (14)
Freddy Sandoval
Alexia Amarista
Nate Sutton
Hector Estrella
Ivan Contreras

1B
Mark Trumbo (8)
Matt Sweeney (18)
Gabe Jacobo
Nick Farnsworth
Roberto Lopez

C
Hank Conger (7)
Bobby Wilson (13)
Ben Johnson
Anel de los Santos
Franklin Lopez
Ikku Sumi

RHP

Starters	Relievers
Nick Adenhart (1)	Kevin Jepsen (6)
Jordan Walden (2)	Rafael Rodriguez (15)
Sean O'Sullivan (5)	David Herndon (28)
Anthony Ortega (9)	Eddie McKiernan
Mason Tobin (10)	Jason Bulger
Tyler Chatwood (11)	Marco Albano
Mauarys Correra (19)	Bobby Cassevah
Ryan Chaffee (21)	Trevor Bell
Nick Green (29)	Ryan Aldridge
Jose Perez	Ryan Brasier
Esmerilin Jimenez	Michael Kohn
Fabio Martinez	Kevin Nabors
Baudilio Lopez	Chris Scholl
Young-Il Jung	
Jon Bachanov	
Pil-Joon Jang	

LHP

Starters	Relievers
Trevor Reckling (4)	Barret Browning
Will Smith (12)	Leonard Calderon
Robert Fish (20)	Dan Davidson
Alex Torres (24)	Andrew Taylor
Michael Anton	
Manuel Flores	
Buddy Boshiers	
Josh Blanco	
Jayson Miller	

2008

BEST PURE HITTER: 1B Gabe Jacobo (10) reached low Class A and hit .324/.357/.556 with 10 homers in his first pro summer. He may not have enough power to profile at first base, so he'll need to work hard to play third base or the outfield. 1B/OF Roberto Lopez (25) also opened eyes with a stunning pro debut.

BEST POWER HITTER: Jacobo has the most current power, but 1B Nick Farnsworth (9) should pass him as he adds strength and experience.

FASTEST RUNNER: OF Matt Crawford (23) may have been old for the Rookie-level Arizona League, but he used his plus speed to win the batting title (.373) and steal 19 bases in 21 tries. OF Marcel Champagnie (15) also has above-average wheels.

BEST DEFENSIVE PLAYER: Rolando Gomez (11) is a cousin of former all-star and Gold Glover Tony Fernandez, and he has similar actions at shortstop. He signed for $450,000.

BEST FASTBALL: RHP Tyler Chatwood (2) is figuring out command, but velocity is no problem. He repeatedly hit 94 mph during his pro debut and can touch 97. RHP Michael Kohn (13) did the same, utilizing a short arm action that made his fastball seem to get on hitters even quicker. Both were two-way players as amateurs, Chatwood in high school and Kohn at the College of Charleston.

BEST SECONDARY PITCH: Chatwood's size (5-foot-11) and fastball/curveball combination have earned him comparisons to Roy Oswalt. RHP Kevin Nabors' (26) curveball may enable him to make it to the majors as a reliever. RHP Ryan Chaffee (3) has a plus changeup—and a low-90s fastball—though he has yet to make his pro debut after injuring his foot at the Junior College World Series.

BEST PRO DEBUT: Lopez was the Rookie-level Pioneer League's MVP, leading the league in batting (.400), runs (68), hits (108), RBIs (72), on-base percentage (.480) and slugging (.667). LHP Jayson Miller (30), a finesse pitcher, was PL pitcher of the year after going 8-2, 2.33 with a 68-7 K-BB ratio in 81 innings.

BEST ATHLETE: Chatwood was also a prospect as a multi-tooled outfielder.

MOST INTRIGUING BACKGROUND: Gomez. Unsigned OF Zach Cone's (3) father Ronnie was a Georgia Tech running back drafted by the New York Jets.

CLOSEST TO THE MAJORS: Los Angeles didn't sign a four-year college player until Jacobo in the 10th round, so it's unlikely anyone will make a quick impact. Kohn or Nabors could be the best candidate as a reliever.

BEST LATE-ROUND PICK: Lopez or Kohn.

THE ONE WHO GOT AWAY: The Angels failed to sign the two best athletes they drafted, Cone and OF Khiry Cooper (5). They met Cone's asking price twice only to be turned down so he could attend Georgia, while Cooper opted to play wide receiver at Nebraska.

ASSESSMENT: The Angels lacked a first-round pick for the third time in four years, and for the second straight draft, they ranked 29th among the 30 teams in bonus spending. Not signing two of their first five picks was another blow, so their draft again rests on late-round choices.

2007

The Angels gave up their first- and second-rounders as free agent compensation, and their top pick, RHP Jon Bachanov (1s), needed Tommy John surgery and has yet to throw a pro pitch. LHP Trevor Reckling (8) and RHP Mason Tobin (16) were nifty late-round finds.

GRADE: C

2006

C Hank Conger (1) has all-star potential but has to stay healthy. RHP Jordan Walden (12) blossomed as a draft-and-follow, earning a $1 million bonus.

GRADE: C+

2005

A draft-and-follow proved to be the top pick of this draft as well, as RHP Sean O'Sullivan (3) exudes pitchability. Los Angeles didn't have a first-rounder, spent its top choice on RHP Trevor Bell (1s) and failed to sign two of the top five selections in the 2008 draft, LHP Brian Matusz (4) and C Buster Posey (50).

GRADE: C

2004

The Angels have no regrets about blowing away slot recommendations to sign RHPs Jered Weaver (1) and Nick Adenhart (14) and 1B Mark Trumbo (18). Weaver has reached double digits in big league victories for three straight years, while Adenhart is the system's best prospect and Trumbo its best slugger.

GRADE: B

*Draft analysis by Jim Callis. Numbers in parentheses indicate draft rounds. *Bonuses for 2004-05 are first 10 rounds only.*

BILL MITCHELL

PROSPECT

NICK ADENHART, RHP

Born: Aug. 24, 1986.
Ht.: 6-3. **Wt.:** 185.
Bats: R. **Throws:** R.
Drafted:
HS—Williamsport, Md.,
2004 (14th round).
Signed by: Dan Radcliff.

Baseball America's Youth Player of the Year in 2003, Adenhart rivaled Homer Bailey as the top high school pitching prospect in the 2004 draft until he blew out his elbow that May and needed Tommy John surgery. Undaunted, the Angels drafted Adenhart in the 14th round and signed him for $710,000. Adenhart began 2008 by going 4-0, 0.87 in his first five starts at Triple-A Salt Lake before Los Angeles whisked him to the big leagues and asked him to pitch on three days' rest against the Athletics. The experiment bombed, as he lasted just two innings and gave up five earned runs. After he continued to struggle with his control in subsequent starts against the Royals and White Sox, the Angels returned him to Triple-A and he never found his April groove again. Adenhart won just one of his next 10 starts and went 5-13, 7.08 the rest of the way.

Despite his struggles, Adenhart continued to show quality stuff. He works off a 90-95 mph fastball that rides in on righthanders. He also has two promising secondary pitches, a hard curveball and a rapidly improving changeup. He has good arm speed, fade and sink on his changeup, which is more reliable than his curve. He uses his size to throw his pitches on a downward trajectory that makes it difficult to drive the ball against him. Adenhart has topped 150 innings in each of the last three seasons, burying any concerns about his health, with his only missed time coming with a minor sore shoulder in 2007. He's a good athlete, which allows him to repeat his delivery and should result in at least solid control and command.

An inability to execute his pitches hampered Adenhart in Triple-A. When he got into jams, he couldn't pitch his way out. He nibbled too much and became too predictable when he fell behind in the count. He had trouble throwing his curveball for strikes, and the pitch lacks consistent depth. That's part of the reason righthanders handled him more easily than lefties, batting .314 against him. Adenhart's command deserted him at times in 2007 as well, and Los Angeles has tried to get him to understand that he doesn't need to pitch away from contact. The Angels believe he might have gotten lost trying to please his coaches rather than pitch to his strengths.

The Angels still believe in Adenhart, but he needs to start putting things together from a mental standpoint. He could spend much of 2009 in Triple-A, as Los Angeles will have at most one opening in its rotation. If the Angels don't re-sign Jon Garland or import another veteran, Adenhart will compete with Nick Green, Dustin Moseley and Anthony Ortega in spring training. As stunning as his struggles were in 2008, Adenhart is still just 22 and has a chance to become a frontline starter if he does a better job using his quality stuff.

Year	Club (League)	Class	W	L	ERA	G	GS	CG	SV	IP	H	R	ER	HR	BB	SO	AVG
2005	Angels (AZL)	R	2	3	3.68	13	12	1	0	44	39	26	18	0	24	52	.245
	Orem (PIO)	R	1	0	0.00	1	1	0	0	6	3	1	0	0	0	7	.143
2006	Cedar Rapids (MWL)	LoA	10	2	1.95	16	16	1	0	106	84	33	23	2	26	99	.215
	R. Cucamonga (CAL)	HiA	5	2	3.78	9	9	0	0	52	51	23	22	1	16	46	.258
2007	Arkansas (TEX)	AA	10	8	3.65	26	26	0	0	153	158	72	62	7	65	116	.273
2008	Los Angeles (AL)	MAJ	1	0	9.00	3	3	0	0	12	18	12	12	0	13	4	.360
	Salt Lake (PCL)	AAA	9	13	5.76	26	26	0	0	145	173	99	93	15	75	110	.306
MINOR LEAGUE TOTALS			37	28	3.87	91	90	2	0	507	508	254	218	25	206	430	.266
MAJOR LEAGUE TOTALS			1	0	9.00	3	3	0	0	12	18	12	12	0	13	4	.360

2 JORDAN WALDEN, RHP

BORN: Nov. 16, 1987. **B-T:** R-R. **HT.:** 6-5. **WT.:** 220. **DRAFTED:** Grayson County (Texas) CC, D/F 2006 (12th round). **SIGNED BY:** Arnold Braithwaite.

Walden fell to the 12th round after entering 2006 as the top high school prospect in the draft, but he boosted his stock with a year at Grayson County (Texas) Community College and signed for $1 million as a draft-and-follow. He has justified the investment so far, reaching high Class A Rancho Cucamonga in his first full pro season as that team threatened to make the playoffs. He also showed the strongest arm in the system. Walden's calling card remains his fastball, which touched 101 and sat at 91-94 mph in 2008. He throws it on an impressive downward plane, and one observer said facing his heater was "like trying to hit a brick." His 86-87 mph slider has good tilt. He pitches to both sides of the plate and has the frame to be a workhorse. Against more advanced hitters, Walden will need to fine-tune his secondary pitches. He needs to dust off his changeup to better set up his fastball. His slider is inconsistent, at times losing velocity and shape. During instructional league, Los Angeles had him focus on repeating his delivery, which would help improve his command. Walden projects as a No. 2 or No. 3 starter with an ETA of mid-2010. If he doesn't open 2009 in Double-A Arkansas, he should get there by the end of the season.

Year	Club (League)	Class	W	L	ERA	G	GS	CG	SV	IP	H	R	ER	HR	BB	SO	AVG
2007	Orem (PIO)	R	1	1	3.08	15	15	0	0	64	49	27	22	3	17	63	.209
2008	Cedar Rapids (MWL)	LoA	4	6	2.18	18	18	1	0	107	80	32	26	3	32	91	.207
	R. Cucamonga (CAL)	HiA	5	2	4.04	9	9	0	0	49	42	30	22	4	24	50	.226
MINOR LEAGUE TOTALS			10	9	2.85	42	42	1	0	221	171	89	70	10	73	204	.212

3 PETER BOURJOS, OF

BORN: March 31, 1987. **B-T:** R-R. **HT.:** 6-1. **WT.:** 175. **DRAFTED:** HS—Scottsdale, Ariz., 2005 (10th round). **SIGNED BY:** John Gracio.

The son of former big leaguer and current Brewers scout Chris Bourjos, Peter signed for an above-slot $325,000 as a 10th-round pick in 2005. Hand injuries hampered his first taste of full-season ball in 2007, but they did not impact his impressive speed. He rebounded to lead the high Class A California League with 50 steals in 2008, and ranked fifth in the circuit with 150 hits. Bourjos is a legitimate center fielder with plus-plus speed, the ability to cover both gaps with ease and a solid arm. He improved as a basestealer in 2008, succeeding on 83 percent of his attempts, up from 70 percent previously in his career. He has good bat speed, drives balls to the gaps and could have at least average power. His arm is solid for center field. Despite his solid season, there are still questions about Bourjos' bat. He has a funky swing and though he showed some improvement, he still chases pitches out of the strike zone and rarely walks. He'll need to show a much more patient approach to realize his potential as a leadoff hitter. He struggles to make adjustments at times, leading to extended slumps. Bourjos was 21 last season, so he still has plenty of time to improve. The Angels don't need to rush him and will send him to Double-A in 2009.

Year	Club (League)	Class	AVG	G	AB	R	H	2B	3B	HR	RBI	BB	SO	SB	OBP	SLG
2006	Orem (PIO)	R	.292	65	250	42	73	16	7	5	28	22	67	13	.354	.472
2007	Angels (AZL)	R	.313	4	16	3	5	0	1	0	2	1	2	0	.353	.438
	Cedar Rapids (MWL)	LoA	.274	63	237	37	65	9	6	5	29	20	53	19	.335	.426
2008	R. Cucamonga (CAL)	HiA	.295	121	509	83	150	29	10	9	51	19	96	50	.326	.444
MINOR LEAGUE TOTALS			.290	253	1012	165	293	54	24	19	110	62	218	82	.335	.447

4 TREVOR RECKLING, LHP

BORN: May 22, 1989. **B-T:** L-L. **HT.:** 6-2. **WT.:** 205. **DRAFTED:** HS—Newark, N.J., 2007 (8th round). **SIGNED BY:** Greg Morhardt.

Overshadowed among New Jersey high schoolers by Rick Porcello in 2007 and on low Class A Cedar Rapids' staff by Jordan Walden in 2008, Reckling is starting to make a name for himself. The Midwest League's youngest regular starting pitcher last season—he didn't turn 19 until late May—led the Kernels with 10 wins and spun a 29-inning score-less streak. Reckling could have three pitches that grade better than average. His drop-off-the-table curveball has the most upside. He spots his 87-91 mph fastball to both sides of the plate and down in the strike zone. His changeup may be his most dependable pitch, which is unusual for a teenager. He's a good athlete with a smooth delivery, and he does a nice job of staying on top of his pitches with a high-three-quarters arm slot. Reckling's curveball has so much movement that he's still working to command it consistently, and he can fall in love with it at times. He tired late in the season, going 3-5, 5.72 in his final nine starts, so he'll need to get stronger. He had a difficult time settling in at the start of games, as his 6.23 ERA and .324 opponent average in the first inning were easily his highest in any frame. The

LOS ANGELES ANGELS

Angels tend to play it conservatively with high school draft picks, so Reckling probably will spend all of 2009 in high Class A. He has a ceiling of a No. 3 starter.

Year	Club (League)	Class	W	L	ERA	G	GS	CG	SV	IP	H	R	ER	HR	BB	SO	AVG
2007	Angels (AZL)	R	3	1	2.75	9	5	0	2	36	33	13	11	2	7	55	.236
2008	Cedar Rapids (MWL)	LoA	10	7	3.37	26	26	1	0	152	137	64	57	8	59	128	.246
MINOR LEAGUE TOTALS			13	8	3.25	35	31	1	2	188	170	77	68	10	66	183	.244

5 SEAN O'SULLIVAN, RHP

BORN: Sept. 1, 1987. **B-T:** R-R. **HT.:** 6-1. **WT.:** 220. **DRAFTED:** Grossmont (Calif.) JC, D/F 2005 (3rd round). **SIGNED BY:** Tim Corcoran.

Like Jordan Walden, O'Sullivan entered his senior year as the top prep pitching prospect in the nation, saw his velocity and his stock drop and signed the following spring as a draft-and-follow. While O'Sullivan never regained his power stuff, he has made the transformation into a crafty pitcher who can toy with hitters. That he knows how to win understandably has the Angels excited. He won ERA titles in each of his first two pro seasons and led the California League with 16 victories in his third. O'Sullivan no longer overpowers hitters, but he gets them out by commanding three pitches that rate as average or slightly above. His fastball tops out at 92 mph, so he changes speeds and keeps it down with decent life, generating groundouts. He also throws a curveball and changeup. He's aggressive in the strike zone and extremely poised. It remains to be seen how well O'Sullivan will fare against advanced hitters without a true out pitch. His fastball could use more movement, and his curve could use tighter spin. His stuff tends to drop off after five innings, which means he might be better as a middle reliever than as a workhorse starter. Double-A will be a good test for O'Sullivan in 2009. If his secondary stuff comes around, he could be a No. 4 starter on a big league contender.

Year	Club (League)	Class	W	L	ERA	G	GS	CG	SV	IP	H	R	ER	HR	BB	SO	AVG
2006	Orem (PIO)	R	4	0	2.14	14	14	0	0	71	65	23	17	2	7	55	.239
2007	Cedar Rapids (MWL)	LoA	10	7	2.22	25	25	0	0	158	136	58	39	6	40	125	.227
2008	R. Cucamonga (CAL)	HiA	16	8	4.73	28	25	1	0	158	167	94	83	8	50	111	.268
MINOR LEAGUE TOTALS			30	15	3.23	67	64	1	0	388	368	175	139	16	97	291	.246

6 KEVIN JEPSEN, RHP

BORN: July 26, 1984. **B-T:** R-R. **HT.:** 6-3. **WT.:** 215. **DRAFTED:** HS—Sparks, Nev., 2002 (2nd round). **SIGNED BY:** Todd Blyleven.

Jepsen labored for five seasons in Class A, partly because he had to overcome a torn labrum in 2004 and then moved to a bullpen role in 2006. Not only did the Angels not protect him on their 40-man roster after the 2007 season, but they also didn't invite him to big league camp. Yet he ended last season with an Olympic bronze medal—he didn't allow a run in six innings for Team USA in Beijing—and a spot on Los Angeles' playoff roster. Jepsen's fastball buzzes in the mid-90s and seems to have late jump that makes it tougher to hit. His true 12-to-6 curveball gives hitters fits and changes their eye level. He works down in the zone and his pitches are tough to lift, as evidenced by his 2.3 groundout/airout ratio in 2008. Jepsen can get erratic at times with his fastball and gets into jams when he doesn't throw strikes. He relied on overmatching minor league hitters and will have to learn how to set up big leaguers. Free agent Francisco Rodriguez's departure now opens a full-time role in the Angels bullpen for Jepsen. Jose Arredondo and Scot Shields will get the first shot to replace Rodriguez as closer, but Jepsen could contend for the job in the future.

Year	Club (League)	Class	W	L	ERA	G	GS	CG	SV	IP	H	R	ER	HR	BB	SO	AVG
2002	Angels (AZL)	R	1	3	6.84	8	5	0	0	26	29	22	20	3	12	19	.274
2003	Cedar Rapids (MWL)	LoA	6	3	2.65	10	10	0	0	51	32	24	15	2	28	42	.180
2004	Cedar Rapids (MWL)	LoA	8	10	3.43	27	27	1	0	144	122	68	55	6	77	136	.232
2005	Angels (AZL)	R	0	1	5.52	7	7	0	0	15	8	10	9	1	11	17	.151
	R. Cucamonga (CAL)	HiA	0	1	10.66	4	4	0	0	13	19	18	15	2	10	11	.333
2006	R. Cucamonga (CAL)	HiA	4	4	3.58	47	0	0	16	50	51	26	20	2	34	46	.270
2007	R. Cucamonga (CAL)	HiA	1	5	4.19	44	0	0	3	54	61	29	25	2	38	50	.292
2008	Arkansas (TEX)	AA	2	1	1.42	25	0	0	11	32	22	5	5	0	18	35	.198
	Salt Lake (PCL)	AAA	1	3	2.35	15	0	0	2	23	17	9	6	3	12	21	.213
	Los Angeles (AL)	MAJ	0	1	4.32	9	0	0	0	8	8	5	4	0	4	7	.250
MINOR LEAGUE TOTALS			23	31	3.75	187	53	1	32	408	361	211	170	21	240	377	.239
MAJOR LEAGUE TOTALS			0	1	4.32	9	0	0	0	8	8	5	4	0	4	7	.250

7 HANK CONGER, C

BORN: Jan. 29, 1988. **B-T:** B-R. **HT.:** 6-0. **WT.:** 205. **DRAFTED:** HS—Huntington Beach, Calif., 2006 (1st round). **SIGNED BY:** Bobby DeJardin.

A second-generation Korean-American, Conger got his nickname from his grandfather's favorite player, Hank Aaron. Since signing for $1.35 million, Conger has been limited from showing off his own power by a string of hand, back, hamstring and shoulder injuries. He didn't begin the 2008 season until May 31 and caught only 10 games. But he was a postseason hero, with 13 RBIs in eight games as Arkansas won an improbable Texas League championship. Conger has prodigious power from both sides of the plate, making him a bigger offensive threat than most catchers. He can let balls travel deep before turning his quick bat loose and driving them a long way. Above-average arm strength is his biggest asset on defense. Because he has caught just 91 games in three pro seasons, Conger has yet to prove he can stay behind the plate. He's a well-below-average runner who lacks agility and quick footwork, which in turn hampers his release on throws. He can get too aggressive as a hitter, and he's much more effective hitting lefthanded than righthanded. The Angels didn't want Conger to risk re-injuring his shoulder, so they didn't have him throw in instructional league. He'll resume catching in Double-A in 2009 and has all-star potential if he can stay healthy and improve defensively.

Year	Club (League)	Class	AVG	G	AB	R	H	2B	3B	HR	RBI	BB	SO	SB	OBP	SLG
2006	Angels (AZL)	R	.319	19	69	11	22	3	4	1	11	7	11	1	.382	.522
2007	Angels (AZL)	R	.267	3	15	2	4	1	0	0	3	0	3	0	.267	.333
	Cedar Rapids (MWL)	LoA	.290	84	290	33	84	20	0	11	48	21	48	9	.336	.472
2008	R. Cucamonga (CAL)	HiA	.303	73	294	47	89	20	2	13	75	14	55	2	.333	.517
MINOR LEAGUE TOTALS			.298	179	668	93	199	44	6	25	137	42	117	12	.338	.494

8 MARK TRUMBO, 1B

BORN: Jan. 16, 1986. **B-T:** R-R. **HT.:** 6-4. **WT.:** 220. **DRAFTED:** HS—Villa Park, Calif., 2004 (18th round). **SIGNED BY:** Tim Corcoran.

The Angels intercepted Trumbo before he began classes at Southern California in 2004, signing him for an 18th-round-record $1.425 million. Though most teams liked him more as a pitcher, Los Angeles was more intrigued with his power potential. He made slow but steady improvement before exploding in 2008, leading Angels farmhands with 32 homers and 93 RBIs. Trumbo has plus power, and when he gets his arms extended he can crush the ball. He has made a conscious effort to be less pull-conscious. He doesn't strike out excessively for a slugger. He has a strong arm, especially for a first baseman. Trumbo will need to hone his plate discipline to handle more advanced pitchers with better command. His value lies almost totally in his bat, as he's not much of an athlete, runner or defender. He has put in time to improve his footwork at first base, yet he still made 22 errors in 124 games there last season. Scouts are curious to see how Trumbo will handle better breaking balls in the upper minors. He'll start 2009 in Double-A and if all goes well, he could challenge for a big league job by mid-2010.

Year	Club (League)	Class	AVG	G	AB	R	H	2B	3B	HR	RBI	BB	SO	SB	OBP	SLG
2005	Orem (PIO)	R	.274	71	299	45	82	23	1	10	45	21	67	2	.322	.458
2006	Cedar Rapids (MWL)	LoA	.220	118	428	43	94	19	0	13	59	44	99	5	.293	.355
2007	Cedar Rapids (MWL)	LoA	.272	128	471	57	128	27	2	14	76	34	98	10	.326	.427
2008	R. Cucamonga (CAL)	HiA	.283	103	407	70	115	28	2	26	68	26	67	7	.329	.553
	Arkansas (TEX)	AA	.276	32	123	13	34	7	1	6	25	7	29	1	.311	.496
MINOR LEAGUE TOTALS			.262	452	1728	228	453	104	6	69	273	132	360	25	.316	.449

9 ANTHONY ORTEGA, RHP

BORN: Aug. 24, 1985. **B-T:** R-R. **HT.:** 6-0. **WT.:** 170. **SIGNED:** Venezuela, 2003. **SIGNED BY:** Carlos Porte.

Ortega won just 18 games in his first four pro seasons before earning 14 victories in 2008, when the Angels named him their minor league pitcher of the year. He cemented his breakthrough season by winning five of his six Triple-A starts. Ortega took off once he started doing a better job of pitching down in the zone and generating more groundouts. His best pitch is his fastball, which ranges from 90-95 mph. He has enhanced his fastball with improved feel for his changeup. His curveball is an average pitch. He does a good job of throwing strikes and keeping his pitch counts down, which allowed him to work at least six innings in 20 of his 28 starts last season. Ortega doesn't have an out pitch, so he has to be pinpoint with his location. He doesn't beat himself with walks but he's hittable because he's always around the zone. Like many young pitchers, he can do a better job of repeating his pitches. He must work on his focus and avoid the mental lapses that plague him at times. While he doesn't have a high ceiling, Ortega could become a No. 4 starter in the majors. If the Angels don't re-sign Jon Garland or add a veteran to replace him, Ortega will compete for the final spot in the rotation during spring training.

Year	Club (League)	Class	W	L	ERA	G	GS	CG	SV	IP	H	R	ER	HR	BB	SO	AVG
2004	Angels (DSL)	R	2	6	2.45	13	13	0	0	81	64	28	22	3	13	61	.215
2005	Angels (DSL)	R	7	4	0.86	14	14	2	0	94	62	20	9	2	21	100	.182
2006	R. Cucamonga (CAL)	HiA	0	1	2.08	5	1	0	1	9	9	6	2	0	5	5	.281
	Orem (PIO)	R	1	1	0.79	2	2	0	0	11	6	3	1	0	2	11	.162
	Cedar Rapids (MWL)	LoA	1	6	4.21	12	12	0	0	66	71	36	31	5	27	55	.280
2007	R. Cucamonga (CAL)	HiA	7	11	4.02	28	28	1	0	163	157	84	73	17	68	127	.254
2008	Arkansas (TEX)	AA	9	7	3.73	22	22	1	0	135	124	65	56	11	49	83	.247
	Salt Lake (PCL)	AAA	5	0	2.52	6	6	0	0	39	46	14	11	2	6	22	.282
MINOR LEAGUE TOTALS			32	36	3.08	102	98	4	1	599	539	256	205	40	191	464	.240

10 MASON TOBIN, RHP

BORN: July 8, 1987. **B-T:** R-R. **HT.:** 6-4. **WT.:** 220. **DRAFTED:** Everett (Wash.) CC, 2007 (16th round). **SIGNED BY:** Casey Harvie.

The Braves controlled Tobin's rights for two years as a draft-and-follow before Los Angeles signed him for $125,000 as a 16th-rounder in 2007. He didn't allow a run in his first three outings last season, but he strained his shoulder shortly afterward and didn't pitch after June 6. After showing average velocity in his pro debut, Tobin worked in the low 90s and touched 97 mph in low Class A before his shoulder acted up. He has heavy sink and nice armside run on his heater, which he delivers from a low three-quarters arm slot. He also flashes a hard slider. His size and less-than-fluid delivery combined to make him an intimidating presence on the mound. Tobin's slider gets slurvy at times and his changeup is just in its rudimentary stages, allowing hitters to sit on his fastball. He sometimes gets under his pitches, causing them to flatten out. His shoulder isn't a long-term worry, though it did cost him valuable development time. He pitches with some effort in his delivery, which causes more concern about his durability. The Angels expect Tobin to be healthy for spring training and probably will ease him back into pitching at high Class A. If he doesn't refine his secondary pitches, his fastball alone could make him a dynamic reliever.

Year	Club (League)	Class	W	L	ERA	G	GS	CG	SV	IP	H	R	ER	HR	BB	SO	AVG
2007	Angels (AZL)	R	2	0	0.95	8	7	0	0	28	17	5	3	1	7	32	.177
	Orem (PIO)	R	2	1	3.21	6	6	0	0	28	23	10	10	0	7	23	.230
2008	Cedar Rapids (MWL)	LoA	2	3	3.13	8	8	1	0	37	29	13	13	2	18	18	.225
MINOR LEAGUE TOTALS			6	4	2.50	22	21	1	0	94	69	28	26	3	32	73	.212

11 TYLER CHATWOOD, RHP

BORN: Dec. 16, 1989. **B-T:** R-R. **HT.:** 5-11. **WT.:** 175. **DRAFTED:** HS—East Valley, Calif., 2008 (2nd round). **SIGNED BY:** Tim Corcoran.

The Angels gave up their 2008 first-round pick as compensation for free agent Torii Hunter, making second-rounder Chatwood their top selection. He signed for $547,000, turning down the chance to play both ways at UCLA. Chatwood stands just 5-foot-11, short for a pitcher and not ideal for throwing on a downward plane. But there's no denying his arm strength, as he routinely touched 94 mph in his pro debut and hit 97 as an amateur. He also features a knee-buckling curveball, and his size and top two pitches have prompted comparisons to Roy Oswalt. Rookie-level Arizona League Angels pitching coach Trevor Wilson likened him to Jeff Brantley. To follow in Oswalt's and Brantley's footsteps and become an all-star, Chatwood will have to improve his changeup and command. He not only needs to harness his stuff but also needs to be more aggressive going after hitters. He has impressive athleticism and showed five-tool potential as an outfielder. Los Angeles has no plans to move him off the mound, however, though it may take things slow and let him spend 2009 at Rookie-level Orem.

Year	Club (League)	Class	W	L	ERA	G	GS	CG	SV	IP	H	R	ER	HR	BB	SO	AVG
2008	Angels (AZL)	R	1	2	3.08	11	11	0	0	38	25	15	13	1	36	48	.195
MINOR LEAGUE TOTALS			1	2	3.08	11	11	0	0	38	25	15	13	1	36	48	.195

12 WILL SMITH, LHP

BORN: July 10, 1988. **B-T:** R-L. **HT.:** 6-5. **WT.:** 230. **DRAFTED:** Gulf Coast (Fla.) CC, 2008 (7th round). **SIGNED BY:** Tom Kotchman.

Angels scout Tom Kotchman, who doubles as their Orem manager, has a knack for finding talent at small colleges and junior colleges. His most notable discoveries are Howie Kendrick (St. John's River, Fla., CC) and Scot Shields (Lincoln Memorial, Tenn.), and his most recent is Smith. He signed for $150,000 out of Gulf Coast (Fla.) CC, the same school where Kotchman grabbed David Herndon two years earlier. Smith showed tremendous feel for pitching at Orem in his pro debut. He threw all of his pitches for strikes—his 76-6 K-BB ratio was the best in the Pioneer League—worked both sides of the plate and changed speeds effectively. He also used his big frame to deliver his pitches on a steep downward plane. Smith works off a four-seam fastball that ranges from 87-93 mph. His curveball is a plus pitch and he can add and subtract velocity from it, reaching the low 80s. If he can get a better feel for a changeup, it could become an average pitch for him. Smith is more advanced than most 20-year-olds, which could tempt the Angels to challenge him in high Class A this year.

Year	Club (League)	Class	W	L	ERA	G	GS	CG	SV	IP	H	R	ER	HR	BB	SO	AVG
2008	Orem (PIO)	R	8	2	3.08	16	14	0	0	73	73	28	25	6	6	76	.253
MINOR LEAGUE TOTALS			8	2	3.08	16	14	0	0	73	73	28	25	6	6	76	.253

13 BOBBY WILSON, C

BORN: April 8, 1983. **B-T:** R-R. **HT.:** 6-0. **WT.:** 220. **DRAFTED:** St. Petersburg (Fla.) JC, D/F 2002 (48th round). **SIGNED BY:** Tom Kotchman.

Add Wilson to the growing list of players signed by Angels scout/Orem manager Tom Kotchman who have graduated to the major leagues. Wilson, who played with Kotchman's son Casey on Seminole (Fla.) High's national championship team in 2001, earned a September callup because he handles the bat and his duties behind the plate equally well. He doesn't have tremendous bat speed or power, but he makes consistent hard contact and is good for doubles if not home runs. He controls the strike zone well and is at his best when he uses the whole field. Wilson has spent the past two seasons in the high minors, so he has experience with many of the Angels' young pitchers. He draws praise for his game-calling ability, and his instincts and sound fundamentals allow his defensive tools to play up. He has average arm strength yet threw out 43 percent of basestealers last year, and he also showed his soft hands by committing just one passed ball in 62 Triple-A games. While he moves well behind the plate, he's a well-below-average runner. Though his ability to contribute offensively and defensively is just what Los Angeles manager Mike Scioscia (a former all-star catcher) wants, Wilson probably will return to Salt Lake unless the club trades Jeff Mathis or Mike Napoli.

Year	Club (League)	Class	AVG	G	AB	R	H	2B	3B	HR	RBI	BB	SO	SB	OBP	SLG
2003	Provo (PIO)	R	.284	57	236	36	67	12	0	6	62	18	31	0	.329	.411
2004	Cedar Rapids (MWL)	LoA	.268	105	396	45	106	23	0	8	64	30	55	5	.320	.386
2005	R. Cucamonga (CAL)	HiA	.290	115	466	66	135	32	1	14	77	30	61	2	.333	.453
2006	Arkansas (TEX)	AA	.286	103	374	45	107	26	0	9	53	33	47	1	.350	.428
2007	Arkansas (TEX)	AA	.271	50	181	24	49	9	0	6	27	22	26	5	.348	.420
	Salt Lake (PCL)	AAA	.295	40	132	15	39	13	1	3	22	8	18	1	.336	.477
2008	Salt Lake (PCL)	AAA	.312	72	260	33	81	20	0	4	45	29	45	0	.386	.435
	Los Angeles (AL)	MAJ	.167	7	6	0	1	0	0	0	1	1	3	0	.286	.167
MINOR LEAGUE TOTALS			.286	542	2045	264	584	135	2	50	350	170	283	14	.342	.427
MAJOR LEAGUE TOTALS			.167	7	6	0	1	0	0	0	1	1	3	0	.286	.167

14 RYAN MOUNT, 2B

BORN: Aug. 17, 1986. **B-T:** L-R. **HT.:** 6-0. **WT.:** 175. **DRAFTED:** HS—Chino Hills, Calif., 2005 (2nd round). **SIGNED BY:** Tim Corcoran.

The good news is that Mount started to show the offensive promise that made him a second-round pick, setting career highs across the board. The bad news is that he continued to fight injuries and appeared in just 82 games. He sprained a knee when Todd Linden barreled into him on a double-play attempt in spring training, sidelining Mount until May 31. In 2007, he played in just 88 games (which remains his career high) because of hamstring and quadriceps injuries. Mount has above-average power for a middle infielder and is capable of turning on pitches or driving them to the opposite field. He can get too aggressive however, lunging after offspeed pitches and drawing few walks. Mount's fringe-average speed prompted his move from shortstop to second base in 2007. He has solid range and arm strength, though he occasionally will rush his throws. He's stuck in an organization with no shortage of offensive middle infielders, but Mount can help his cause with a healthy 2009 season in Double-A.

Year	Club (League)	Class	AVG	G	AB	R	H	2B	3B	HR	RBI	BB	SO	SB	OBP	SLG
2005	Angels (AZL)	R	.216	29	102	15	22	7	1	1	17	17	31	4	.325	.333
2006	Orem (PIO)	R	.285	69	277	54	79	14	2	9	38	36	67	10	.370	.448
2007	Angels (AZL)	R	.333	3	12	0	4	0	0	0	0	1	1	0	.429	.333
	Cedar Rapids (MWL)	LoA	.251	85	303	47	76	11	3	7	36	29	70	19	.320	.376
2008	R. Cucamonga (CAL)	HiA	.290	82	338	68	98	17	5	16	49	23	67	10	.337	.512
MINOR LEAGUE TOTALS			.270	268	1032	184	279	49	11	33	140	106	236	43	.341	.435

15 RAFAEL RODRIGUEZ, RHP

BORN: Sept. 24, 1984. **B-T:** R-R. **HT.:** 6-1. **WT.:** 175. **SIGNED:** Dominican Republic, 2001. **SIGNED BY:** Leo Perez.

Signed for $780,000 out of the Dominican in 2001, Rodriguez had intermittent elbow problems while he remained a starter. After he stayed healthy but got shelled in Double-A in 2006, the Angels decided to make him a full-time reliever. He spent most of the last two seasons at Arkansas as well, making tremendous strides with his control in 2008. He did a nice job setting up Kevin Jepsen for the Travelers in the first half before taking over as closer once Jepsen advanced to Triple-A. Rodriguez's fastball showed improved velocity (92-95 mph) and sink last season, and he also did a better job of pounding the bottom of the strike zone. His heater might not even be his best pitch, as his slider ranks as the best in the system. He didn't have much luck developing a changeup as a starter and doesn't need it much as a reliever, but he nevertheless made strides with his change last year. Added to the 40-man roster in October, Rodriguez should open the season in Triple-A, where he had limited success in six appearances at the end of 2008.

Year	Club (League)	Class	W	L	ERA	G	GS	CG	SV	IP	H	R	ER	HR	BB	SO	AVG
2002	Angels (AZL)	R	2	1	3.99	8	8	0	0	38	37	19	17	4	20	50	.255
	Provo (PIO)	R	1	1	5.96	6	6	0	0	26	26	17	17	3	14	25	.268
2003	Cedar Rapids (MWL)	LoA	10	11	4.31	26	26	1	0	144	129	85	69	7	59	100	.236
2004	Angels (AZL)	R	0	2	6.46	4	4	0	0	15	18	12	11	1	5	13	.295
	Cedar Rapids (MWL)	LoA	1	5	6.48	7	7	0	0	33	36	27	24	5	19	35	.273
2005	Cedar Rapids (MWL)	LoA	5	2	2.78	13	13	0	0	74	61	24	23	5	27	74	.220
	R. Cucamonga (CAL)	HiA	4	4	6.75	14	14	0	0	72	84	58	54	11	33	44	.292
2006	R. Cucamonga (CAL)	HiA	3	0	0.53	3	3	0	0	17	15	1	1	0	2	20	.234
	Arkansas (TEX)	AA	5	10	6.63	24	24	0	0	133	175	111	98	28	55	83	.321
2007	Arkansas (TEX)	AA	0	6	4.16	46	1	0	0	71	79	36	33	6	30	42	.287
2008	Salt Lake (PCL)	AAA	2	0	6.28	9	0	0	0	14	20	12	10	2	6	8	.351
	Arkansas (TEX)	AA	2	4	1.86	42	0	0	11	53	46	11	11	3	11	48	.237
MINOR LEAGUE TOTALS			35	46	4.79	202	106	1	11	692	726	413	368	75	281	542	.271

16 CLAY FULLER, OF

BORN: June 17, 1987. **B-T:** B-R. **HT.:** 6-2. **WT.:** 190. **DRAFTED:** HS—Spring Branch, Texas, 2006 (4th round). **SIGNED BY:** Kevin Ham.

After spending two years in the Arizona League, Fuller made the jump to low Class A last season and showed more upside than any position player at Cedar Rapids. Athleticism runs in his family, as his father and two brothers played football at Texas Tech. One of those siblings, Cody, is also an outfielder in the Angels system. As soon as Clay turned pro, Los Angeles turned him into a switch-hitter. He has had limited success learning to hit lefthanded so far, batting just .244 with 95 strikeouts in 315 at-bats from that side in 2008. He has better balance and more confidence batting from his natural right side. However, he has shown the ability to draw walks and hit for gap power against both lefties and righties. He's still growing into his 6-foot-2 frame, and with more strength and experience could develop into a 15-homer threat. Fuller has plus speed to go with his pop, which allowed him to rank fourth in the minors with 13 triples last season. He has shown aptitude for stealing bases, succeeding on 78 percent of his career attempts. He covers a lot of ground in center field and has an average arm. He'll move up to high Class A in 2009.

Year	Club (League)	Class	AVG	G	AB	R	H	2B	3B	HR	RBI	BB	SO	SB	OBP	SLG
2006	Angels (AZL)	R	.268	45	157	28	42	3	5	0	10	25	47	14	.383	.350
	Orem (PIO)	R	.000	1	2	0	0	0	0	0	0	1	2	1	.333	.000
2007	Angels (AZL)	R	.301	45	183	55	55	10	4	5	30	24	52	21	.398	.481
2008	Cedar Rapids (MWL)	LoA	.260	125	438	77	114	19	13	9	47	68	122	36	.379	.425
MINOR LEAGUE TOTALS			.271	216	780	160	211	32	22	14	87	118	223	72	.384	.422

17 CHRIS PETTIT, OF

BORN: Aug. 15, 1984. **B-T:** R-R. **HT.:** 6-0. **WT.:** 190. **DRAFTED:** Loyola Marymount, 2006 (19th round). **SIGNED BY:** Bobby DeJardin.

Pettit went from a college senior drafted in the 19th round in 2006 to the Angels' minor league player of the year in 2007. But all the momentum he generated crashed to a halt when he broke his right foot chasing a fly ball on Opening Day. He missed nearly three months and once he returned, he didn't look like the same player who entered the year with a career .330 batting average in pro ball. He has been likened to a poor man's Jason Bay, though probably more of a fourth outfielder than a regular on a contender. Pettit doesn't have a plus tool except for his bat but he doesn't have a glaring weakness, either. He works counts well and has some pull power, though he tends to turn on more pitches than he should. He projects to hit for a solid average with perhaps 10-15 homers per season. Pettit's speed is fringy, though he has the instincts to steal some bases. Likewise, while his range is short for center field, he can handle the position in a pinch and throws well enough to play right field. Pettit's determination allows him to get the most out of his tools. He got back on track by hitting .359 in the Arizona Fall League, and he could push for a quick promotion if he has a hot start in Double-A in 2009.

Year	Club (League)	Class	AVG	G	AB	R	H	2B	3B	HR	RBI	BB	SO	SB	OBP	SLG
2006	Orem (PIO)	R	.336	68	226	41	76	25	3	7	54	31	48	5	.445	.566
2007	Cedar Rapids (MWL)	LoA	.346	64	228	47	79	24	1	9	41	23	41	17	.429	.579
	R. Cucamonga (CAL)	HiA	.309	69	265	54	82	20	2	9	54	36	48	13	.395	.502
2008	Angels (AZL)	R	.231	3	13	3	3	1	0	0	2	2	2	0	.333	.308
	Arkansas (TEX)	AA	.248	61	222	27	55	12	2	6	26	16	39	5	.320	.401
MINOR LEAGUE TOTALS			.309	265	954	172	295	82	8	31	177	108	178	40	.398	.509

18 MATT SWEENEY, 3B

BORN: April 14, 1988. **B-T:** L-R. **HT.:** 6-3. **WT.:** 212. **DRAFTED:** HS—Rockville, Md., 2006 (8th round). **SIGNED BY:** Dan Radcliff.

Sweeney established himself as one of the system's best power hitters in his first two pro seasons, but he missed all of 2008 with an ankle injury. He originally hurt the ankle when he was hit by a pitch at the end of 2007, and it bothered him throughout spring training. The Angels originally hoped he'd miss just a month, but he eventually had surgery to remove bone chips and repair ligament damage. When he was healthy, Sweeney's power rivaled that of Brandon Wood, Mark Trumbo and Hank Conger. He recognizes pitches well and swings aggressively, with good loft in his stroke. His size, thick forearms and well-balanced lower half are suited for driving the ball. He's not fooled too often, though he could stand to draw more walks and use the whole field more. Sweeney lacked agility and had below-average speed before he got hurt, and the injury could cost him on both counts. Though he has a solid arm, few scouts gave him a chance to remain at third base long term because of his substandard range and reliability. He had an .850 fielding percentage and 48 errors in 127 games at the hot corner. If Sweeney has lost even half a step, he could be moving to first base sooner rather than later. Los Angeles would like to push him to Double-A at some point in 2009, perhaps even out of spring training.

Year	Club (League)	Class	AVG	G	AB	R	H	2B	3B	HR	RBI	BB	SO	SB	OBP	SLG
2006	Angels (AZL)	R	.341	44	170	38	58	11	7	5	39	23	27	4	.431	.576
	Orem (Pio)	R	.167	2	6	0	1	0	0	0	0	0	2	0	.286	.167
2007	Cedar Rapids (MWL)	LoA	.260	119	439	64	114	29	2	18	72	38	88	7	.324	.458
2008	Did Not Play—Injured															
MINOR LEAGUE TOTALS			.281	165	615	102	173	40	9	23	111	61	117	11	.354	.488

19 MANUARYS CORREA, RHP

BORN: Jan. 5, 1989. **B-T:** R-R. **HT.:** 6-3. **WT.:** 170. **SIGNED:** Dominican Republic, 2006. **SIGNED BY:** Leo Perez.

Correa has been quite impressive in two years of Rookie ball, going 15-2, 2.82 overall and leading the Arizona League in strikeouts (67 in 58 innings) during his U.S. debut despite being promoted with two weeks left in the season. Extremely projectable at 6-foot-3 and 170 pounds, he already has quality stuff. His four-seam fastball sits at 92-93 mph and his two-seamer has nice armside run. His secondary pitches are a plus slider and an encouraging changeup. He already shows an advanced ability to repeat his delivery and throw strikes. Correa projects as a possible No. 2 starter, though he has yet to be tested by the grind of a full season. He could get that opportunity in 2009, when he could make the leap to low Class A.

Year	Club (League)	Class	W	L	ERA	G	GS	CG	SV	IP	H	R	ER	HR	BB	SO	AVG
2007	Angels (DSL)	R	8	1	2.16	14	14	0	0	88	71	27	21	3	27	68	.225
2008	Angels (AZL)	R	5	1	2.65	10	8	0	0	58	56	23	17	1	10	67	.249
	Orem (PIO)	R	2	0	6.20	5	4	0	0	20	32	16	14	3	5	17	.368
MINOR LEAGUE TOTALS			15	2	2.82	29	26	0	0	166	159	66	52	7	42	152	.253

20 ROBERT FISH, LHP

BORN: Jan. 19, 1988. **B-T:** L-L. **HT.:** 6-3. **WT.:** 225. **DRAFTED:** HS—Fontana, Calif., 2006 (6th round). **SIGNED BY:** Tim Corcoran.

Fish was relatively unheralded as a high schooler in baseball-rich southern California and hasn't gotten much hype despite striking out a batter per inning over three seasons as a pro. He ranked fifth in the Midwest League with 138 strikeouts in 143 innings last year in his first taste of full-season ball. His funky arm action—he wraps his wrist in the back of his delivery—didn't endear him to scouts as an amateur, but it works to deceive hitters. The Angels haven't tried to alter his mechanics and have just turned him loose. Fish works off a fastball that ranges from 88-94 mph, though he often loses velocity after 90 pitches. Both his curveball and changeup are average pitches but need more consistency. He's still learning the nuances of pitching, as he tends to try to finesse the final out of an inning, nibbling and throwing unnecessary additional pitches that shorten his starts. His mechanics often hamper his command, though he went 3-1, 2.31 over his final seven starts in 2008 while walking just 12 in 39 innings. He'll advance to high Class A this season.

Year	Club (League)	Class	W	L	ERA	G	GS	CG	SV	IP	H	R	ER	HR	BB	SO	AVG
2006	Angels (AZL)	R	1	0	3.21	10	1	0	0	14	13	5	5	0	12	16	.245
2007	R. Cucamonga (CAL)	HiA	0	1	6.00	1	1	0	0	3	3	2	2	1	4	4	.273
	Orem (PIO)	R	3	4	3.27	16	15	0	0	72	62	33	26	4	31	77	.239
2008	Cedar Rapids (MWL)	LoA	10	4	4.85	28	28	0	0	143	138	87	77	12	68	138	.254
MINOR LEAGUE TOTALS			14	9	4.27	55	45	0	0	232	216	127	110	17	115	235	.249

21 RYAN CHAFFEE, RHP

BORN: May 15, 1988. **B-T:** R-R. **HT.:** 6-1. **WT.:** 205. **DRAFTED:** Chipola (Fla.) JC, 2008 (3rd round). **SIGNED BY:** Tom Kotchman.

As a freshman, Chaffee pitched a complete-game five-hitter to shut down New Mexico in the final game of the 2007 Junior College World Series, giving Chipola (Fla.) its first national title. He got off to a slow start as a sophomore before breaking a bone in his foot last March, requiring surgery to insert a screw. Chaffee returned to pitch in the Florida state juco tournament, striking out 17 on two days' rest to beat Manatee in the finals. He reinjured his foot at the Juco World Series and never took the mound for the Angels after spurning a Louisiana State scholarship to sign for $338,000 as a third-rounder. When healthy, Chaffee attacks hitters with a variety of pitches and arm angles. He works with a low-90s fastball with late movement, three varieties of breaking balls (an over-the-top curve, a slurve from a three-quarters slot and a sweeping slider from down low). He also has a plus changeup. While changing his arm angle throws hitters off balance, it also hampers Chaffee's command at times. Los Angeles is anxious to see him on the mound and is optimistic that he'll be able to pitch in spring training. They may be cautious with him and have him open the season in extended spring training.

Year	Club (League)	Class	W	L	ERA	G	GS	CG	SV	IP	H	R	ER	HR	BB	SO	AVG
2008	Did Not Play—Injured																

22 ANDREW ROMINE, SS

BORN: Dec. 24, 1985. **B-T:** B-R. **HT.:** 6-1. **WT.:** 180. **DRAFTED:** Arizona State, 2007 (5th round). **SIGNED BY:** John Gracio.

Romine is part of a baseball family that includes his father Kevin, who played parts of seven seasons in the majors, and his brother Austin, who could be the Yankees' catcher of the future. The two brothers were both 2007 draft picks—Austin went in the second round, three rounds earlier than Andrew—and spent their first full pro seasons in low Class A. Andrew led the Midwest League with 62 stolen bases and ranked second with 79 runs, though there are still questions about his bat. He's a switch-hitter who offers little power and needs to improve from the right side. He makes good contact but doesn't draw an excessive amount of walks, as pitchers aren't afraid to challenge him. Though he has plus speed, he still must improve his basestealing technique after getting caught 18 times last year. Romine, who succeeded Dustin Pedroia as Arizona State's shortstop, is a fine defender. He has above-average actions, range, hands and arm strength, and he makes accurate throws. Romine will be 23 this season, so the Angels may try to get him to Double-A at some point.

Year	Club (League)	Class	AVG	G	AB	R	H	2B	3B	HR	RBI	BB	SO	SB	OBP	SLG
2007	Orem (PIO)	R	.286	56	231	38	66	6	6	5	35	16	38	12	.337	.429
2008	Cedar Rapids (MWL)	LoA	.260	126	461	79	120	21	4	2	34	55	76	62	.347	.336
MINOR LEAGUE TOTALS			.269	182	692	117	186	27	10	7	69	71	114	74	.344	.367

23 ROLANDO GOMEZ, SS

BORN: June 18, 1989. **B-T:** L-R. **HT.:** 5-9. **WT.:** 160. **DRAFTED:** HS—Pembroke Pines, Fla., 2008 (11th round). **SIGNED BY:** Demetrius Figgins.

No team has spent less on bonuses in the last two drafts than the Angels' $4.5 million, though Los Angeles did triple MLB's slot recommendation to sign Gomez for $450,000 as an 11th-rounder last summer. Gomez scared most clubs off with his asking price and his Miami scholarship, but Los Angeles valued his defensive ability. He's a cousin of former all-star and Gold Glove shortstop Tony Fernandez, and he shows similar actions at shortstop. He has soft hands and his good footwork puts himself in position to make plays. His fringe-average arm strength leads some scouts to predict he'll move to second base, but the Angels believe he can stay at short. Though he's small, he has plus speed and some pop, which have earned him comparisons to Rafael Furcal. Gomez can get into trouble when he tries to hit for power, and he's better off working counts and spraying balls into the gaps. He'll need to get stronger to cope with the rigors of pro ball, and he has the work ethic to make it happen. He got only 15 at-bats after signing, so Los Angeles may hold off assigning him to a full-season club to start 2009.

Year	Club (League)	Class	AVG	G	AB	R	H	2B	3B	HR	RBI	BB	SO	SB	OBP	SLG
2008	Angels (AZL)	R	.133	4	15	2	2	0	1	0	2	1	3	0	.188	.267
MINOR LEAGUE TOTALS			.133	4	15	2	2	0	1	0	2	1	3	0	.188	.267

24 ALEX TORRES, LHP

BORN: Dec. 8, 1987. **B-T:** L-L. **HT.:** 5-10. **WT.:** 160. **SIGNED:** Venezuela, 2005. **SIGNED BY:** Carlos Porte.

Torres opened 2008 with his third straight assignment to the Arizona League, but after he allowed a total of four runs in four starts, the Angels deemed him ready to jump to high Class A. He more than held his own, considering his age (20) and how hitter-friendly the California League is, recording a pair of double-digit strike-out performances in August. Torres is undersized, but he can keep hitters guessing by varying his arm angle. He also can crank his fastball up to the low 90s, though he's more effective when it buzzes in around 89-90 mph and generates tons of groundouts. Torres backs up his fastball with a curveball that features tight spin. He needs to do a better job of throwing his curve for strikes. He lacks a third pitch at this point, and Los Angeles had him focus on his changeup during instructional league. The change would give him a needed weapon against lefthanders, who hit .339/.435/.441 against him in the Cal League. It would make sense for Torres to open 2009 back in Rancho Cucamonga, but don't be surprised if he reaches Double-A later in the year. He has one of the best lefty arms in the system.

Year	Club (League)	Class	W	L	ERA	G	GS	CG	SV	IP	H	R	ER	HR	BB	SO	AVG
2005	Angels (DSL)	R	4	2	1.52	9	9	1	0	53	23	20	9	2	23	87	.122
2006	Angels (AZL)	R	2	5	4.29	14	9	0	1	50	42	28	24	1	36	47	.235
2007	Angels (AZL)	R	1	0	4.76	4	0	0	0	6	4	6	3	0	8	3	.190
2008	Angels (AZL)	R	4	0	1.54	4	4	0	0	23	11	4	4	1	10	24	.153
	R. Cucamonga (CAL)	HiA	3	2	3.91	10	10	0	0	53	52	26	23	1	29	62	.264
MINOR LEAGUE TOTALS			14	9	3.05	41	32	1	1	186	132	84	63	5	106	223	.201

25 MATT BROWN, 3B/1B

BORN: Aug. 8, 1982. **B-T:** R-R. **HT.:** 6-0. **WT.:** 200. **DRAFTED:** HS—Hayden, Idaho, 2001 (10th round). **SIGNED BY:** Jack Uhey.

Brown's eighth season in pro ball was his best. He hit .320/.373/.580 at Salt Lake, collected his first big league hit, earned Pacific Coast League MVP honors at the Triple-A all-star game and won an Olympic bronze medal. Brown was Team USA's most dangerous hitter in Beijing, leading the squad with two homers (including a key three-run shot in the bronze medal game) and 10 RBIs. Power is his calling card, and Team USA batting coach Reggie Smith thinks Brown could be a bigger threat if he did a better job of incorporating his lower half into his swing. He made more consistent contact in 2008, which could allow him to compete for the Angels' third-base job if they decide to deploy Chone Figgins elsewhere this season. If he gets that opportunity, Brown must fight a tendency to try to do too much, which has contributed to his 1-for-24 performance with 11 strikeouts in three brief big league stints. His bat is his ticket to the big leagues, as he's a below-average runner who's merely an adequate defender. Brown has played all four infield positions and both outfield corners during his pro career, and he fits best at first or third base. He has the arm for the hot corner but his range is just passable.

Year	Club (League)	Class	AVG	G	AB	R	H	2B	3B	HR	RBI	BB	SO	SB	OBP	SLG
2001	Angels (AZL)	R	.163	46	141	14	23	7	1	1	21	18	30	1	.275	.248
2002	Angels (AZL)	R	.361	28	97	16	35	7	0	2	22	15	14	3	.443	.495
	Provo (PIO)	R	.296	32	108	14	32	5	1	0	11	15	21	3	.406	.361
2003	Cedar Rapids (MWL)	LoA	.207	49	164	22	34	6	1	3	15	19	36	1	.307	.311
	Provo (PIO)	R	.292	65	233	58	68	19	0	11	52	42	56	2	.412	.515
2004	Cedar Rapids (MWL)	LoA	.233	122	437	67	102	20	4	23	82	33	126	6	.303	.455
2005	R. Cucamonga (CAL)	HiA	.262	125	488	68	128	39	4	12	65	40	125	4	.329	.432
2006	Arkansas (TEX)	AA	.293	134	515	77	151	41	3	19	79	47	108	7	.362	.495
2007	Anaheim (AL)	MAJ	.000	4	5	0	0	0	0	0	0	2	1	1	.286	.000
	Salt Lake (PCL)	AAA	.276	110	391	69	108	30	2	19	60	45	106	5	.358	.509
2008	Salt Lake (PCL)	AAA	.320	97	400	75	128	33	4	21	67	32	80	4	.373	.580
	Los Angeles (AL)	MAJ	.053	11	19	0	1	1	0	0	3	1	10	0	.100	.105
MINOR LEAGUE TOTALS			.272	808	2974	480	809	207	20	111	474	306	702	36	.351	.467
MAJOR LEAGUE TOTALS			.042	15	24	0	1	1	0	0	3	3	11	1	.148	.083

26 LUIS JIMENEZ, 3B

BORN: Jan. 18, 1988. **B-T:** R-R. **HT.:** 6-1. **WT.:** 170. **SIGNED:** Dominican Republic, 2005. **SIGNED BY:** Leo Perez.

Jimenez has won two home run titles in the last two years. He led the Rookie-level Dominican Summer League with 11 homers in 2007 and the Pioneer League with 15 in his U.S. debut last summer. He also topped the Pioneer League in doubles (28) and extra-base hits (49) as part of a core of Latin Americans who pushed Orem to the league finals. He generates power with bat speed and strength, and his frame easily has room for more muscle. While he has a quiet, balanced setup, he gets too aggressive and chases pitches out of the zone. He'll need more discipline at higher levels. Jimenez has decent athleticism and speed, and he shows a strong arm at third base. He injured his right shoulder diving back into a base on a pickoff play in early August, and spent the rest of the summer as a DH. He should be healthy for spring training and ready for an assignment to low Class A.

Year	Club (League)	Class	AVG	G	AB	R	H	2B	3B	HR	RBI	BB	SO	SB	OBP	SLG
2006	Angels (DSL)	R	.284	25	74	12	21	9	1	1	10	7	9	4	.341	.473
2007	Angels (DSL)	R	.313	67	256	49	80	19	2	11	55	10	27	16	.347	.531
2008	Orem (PIO)	R	.331	66	284	57	94	28	6	15	65	11	45	6	.361	.630
MINOR LEAGUE TOTALS			.318	158	614	118	195	56	9	27	130	28	81	26	.353	.570

27 TERRELL ALLIMAN, OF/3B

BORN: Oct. 15, 1988. **B-T:** R-R. **HT.:** 6-3. **WT.:** 185. **DRAFTED:** HS—Waterloo, Ont., 2007 (43rd round). **SIGNED BY:** Alex Messier.

After turning down the Brewers as a 28th-round pick in 2006, Alliman returned to the Bluevale Collegiate Institute (Waterloo, Ont.) and went in the 43rd round a year later. He wasn't a high priority for the Angels, though Midwest crosschecker Ron Marigny and Canadian area scout Alex Messier pushed all summer for the club to sign him. Alliman agreed to a $25,000 bonus at the Aug. 15 deadline, and that looks like money well spent after his 2008 pro debut. He led the Arizona League with 17 doubles while ranking third in hits (61), fourth in RBIs (39) and fifth in batting (.339). His bat speed lends itself to power, though he needs to tone down his tendency to uppercut and pull pitches. Los Angeles has worked with him on keeping his hands inside the ball, which would allow him to do a better job of using the opposite field. A good athlete, Alliman has good speed and solid arm strength. He struggled at third base last year, making 10 errors in just 18 games, and looked better in right field. He'll probably open 2009 in extended spring training before heading to Orem in June.

Year	Club (League)	Class	AVG	G	AB	R	H	2B	3B	HR	RBI	BB	SO	SB	OBP	SLG
2008	Angels (AZL)	R	.339	45	180	36	61	17	5	1	39	12	44	8	.383	.506
MINOR LEAGUE TOTALS			.339	45	180	36	61	17	5	1	39	12	44	8	.383	.506

28 DAVID HERNDON, RHP

BORN: Sept. 4, 1985. **B-T:** R-R. **HT.:** 6-3. **WT.:** 230. **DRAFTED:** Gulf Coast (Fla.) JC, 2006 (5th round). **SIGNED BY:** Tom Kotchman.

A 23rd-round pick of the Twins in 2005, Herndon emerged as a top draft-and-follow the next spring. When Minnesota heeded MLB's wishes to keep spending down and didn't meet Herndon's asking price, he re-entered the 2006 draft, went in the fifth round and quickly signed for $157,500. He made steady progress in his first two pro seasons but hit the wall last spring in high Class A, going 2-6, 5.94 in 12 starts. Moved to the bullpen, he immediately took to his new role, posting a 2.90 ERA and converting 17 of 19 save opportunities. He also performed well as a reliever in the Arizona Fall League. Herndon's top pitch is his fastball, a heavy sinker that usually sits in the low 90s and produces a slew of groundballs. His secondary pitches never were consistent when he pitched as a starter, and they aren't as crucial now that he's a reliever. His slider shows tilt at times and ranks ahead of his changeup. Herndon has little difficulty throwing strikes, so if he can just refine his slider into a reliable second option, he should move quickly. He'll step up to Double-A this season.

Year	Club (League)	Class	W	L	ERA	G	GS	CG	SV	IP	H	R	ER	HR	BB	SO	AVG
2006	Orem (PIO)	R	5	2	2.21	14	14	0	0	69	65	25	17	6	10	36	.242
2007	Cedar Rapids (MWL)	LoA	13	8	4.02	25	24	2	0	152	175	80	68	10	20	83	.290
2008	R. Cucamonga (CAL)	HiA	3	7	5.01	43	12	0	17	101	120	58	56	10	16	70	.301
MINOR LEAGUE TOTALS			21	17	3.94	82	50	2	17	322	360	163	141	26	46	189	.283

29 NICK GREEN, RHP

BORN: Aug. 20, 1984. **B-T:** R-R. **HT.:** 6-4. **WT.:** 200. **DRAFTED:** Darton (Ga.) JC, 2004 (35th round). **SIGNED BY:** Chris McAlpin.

Signed for a mere $1,500 out of Darton (Ga.) JC after turning down $80,000 from the Astros out of high school, Green could be about to pay big dividends. Angels GM Tony Reagins has declared that Green will be in the mix to fill a rotation opening if one exists in spring training. The organization still has faith in him after he got bombed in Triple-A in August and in the Arizona Fall League. Green has one of the best changeups in the system, with late sink and some screwball action, but he has little margin for error because he lacks a swing-and-miss pitch. His fastball sits at 88-91 mph and his curveball parks in the mid-70s. He throws strikes and can work both sides of the plate, but he's extremely vulnerable when he pitches up in the strike zone. He led the Pacific Coast League in homers surrendered last season with 31. Green doesn't have huge upside, projecting as a No. 4 starter at best, but he should make his big league debut in 2009 if he can improve his command.

Year	Club (League)	Class	W	L	ERA	G	GS	CG	SV	IP	H	R	ER	HR	BB	SO	AVG
2004	Provo (PIO)	R	4	3	4.03	17	10	0	0	51	56	28	23	4	20	44	.275
2005	Cedar Rapids (MWL)	LoA	3	3	3.58	26	8	1	2	101	95	47	40	11	14	74	.249
2006	R. Cucamonga (CAL)	HiA	5	3	4.15	11	11	1	0	65	77	31	30	9	19	57	.291
	Arkansas (TEX)	AA	8	5	4.41	17	17	0	0	112	115	64	55	23	21	77	.268
2007	Arkansas (TEX)	AA	10	8	3.68	28	28	2	0	178	164	80	73	17	32	107	.243
2008	Salt Lake (PCL)	AAA	8	8	5.32	28	28	0	0	159	186	101	94	31	44	112	.292
MINOR LEAGUE TOTALS			38	30	4.25	127	102	4	2	667	693	351	315	95	150	471	.268

30 HAINLEY STATIA, SS

BORN: Jan. 19, 1986. **B-T:** B-R. **HT.:** 5-10. **WT.:** 160. **DRAFTED:** HS—Lake Worth, Fla., 2004 (9th round). **SIGNED BY:** Mike Silvestri.

The injury bug bit several of the Angels' top position prospects in 2008, including catcher Hank Conger, outfielders Terry Evans and Chris Pettit, and third baseman Mike Sweeney. Statia joined that list when he strained his right hamstring in early June. He missed three weeks and played in only two more games before reinjuring the hamstring, costing him a trip to the Olympics with the Dutch national team. A native of Curacao, he starred for the Netherlands at the 2007 World Cup, earning recognition as the tournament's top defensive player. Before he got hurt, Statia was having his worst offensive season as a pro. While he's never going to hit home runs, he needs to get stronger so he can't be overpowered by good fastballs. His speed is fringy, so despite good instincts he won't be a stolen-base threat, which means he needs to focus on making contact and getting on base. Statia isn't spectacular at shortstop, though his ability to anticipate plays gives him solid range. He has exceptional hands and an accurate arm. Scouts still see him as a major league utilityman, and he's blocked by a proliferation of shortstop options in the organization. Statia will try to boost his stock when he returns to Double-A this season.

Year	Club (League)	Class	AVG	G	AB	R	H	2B	3B	HR	RBI	BB	SO	SB	OBP	SLG
2005	R. Cucamonga (CAL)	HiA	.245	23	106	12	26	2	0	1	8	5	13	6	.286	.292
	Orem (PIO)	R	.300	68	277	44	83	17	6	2	41	23	40	12	.360	.426
2006	Cedar Rapids (MWL)	LoA	.297	111	417	68	124	31	1	1	38	52	54	23	.379	.384
	R. Cucamonga (CAL)	HiA	.300	18	60	8	18	2	1	0	8	8	7	1	.386	.367
2007	R. Cucamonga (CAL)	HiA	.288	135	549	86	158	27	7	3	74	48	79	29	.344	.379
2008	Arkansas (TEX)	AA	.242	59	223	26	54	12	3	1	20	14	17	8	.288	.336
MINOR LEAGUE TOTALS			.284	414	1632	244	463	91	18	8	189	150	210	79	.346	.376

Los Angeles Dodgers

BY ED PRICE

Sure, Manny Ramirez got the headlines for helping the Dodgers reach the playoffs in 2008—and win a postseason series for the first time in 20 years. But the real impetus was all the young talent the club had assembled over the previous few years. Los Angeles may have won just 84 games, but that was enough to take the National League West by two games over the Diamondbacks.

Young veterans such as Chad Billingsley, Jonathan Broxton, Andre Ethier, Matt Kemp, James Loney and Russell Martin formed the heart of the team. Billingsley was the club's best starting pitcher, while Broxton took over as closer when Takashi Saito went down. Ethier and Kemp vastly outperformed Andruw Jones and Juan Pierre at a fraction of the price, while Loney led the team with 90 RBIs and Martin was its lone all-star.

Rookies such as Blake DeWitt, Clayton Kershaw and Cory Wade stepped in to make valuable contributions as well. DeWitt filled a hole at third base early in the year and took over for a banged-up Jeff Kent at the end, while Kershaw held down the fourth spot in the rotation and Wade provided quality middle relief.

The farm system also offered valuable trade fodder. With owner Frank McCourt unwilling (or unable) to take on additional payroll, the Dodgers gave up more in terms of prospects in order to avoid taking on more salary.

To get Casey Blake, Los Angeles parted with Carlos Santana, whom it had converted from an outfielder into one of baseball's top catching prospects, and righthander Jon Meloan. In the three-team deal that brought Ramirez from the Red Sox, the Dodgers sent third baseman Andy LaRoche, who had been their top position prospect, and righty Bryan Morris to the Pirates. They also got Greg Maddux late in the season for a pair of minor prospects, lefty Michael Watt and righty Eduardo Perez.

Manager Joe Torre, brought in after clubhouse rifts helped spell the end for Grady Little, had to manage this transition—and the pivotal addition of Ramirez. After sulking his way out of Boston, Ramirez spurred Los Angeles to a 19-8 finish. He hit .396 with 53 RBIs in as many regular-season games, then led the Dodgers to a Division Series upset of the Cubs.

Los Angeles' roster for the NL Championship Series against the Phillies included 10 homegrown players, including six of the 11 pitchers on the roster. The farm system could provide more reinforcements

The future of the Dodgers rests with young major leaguers like Clayton Kershaw

LARRY GOREN

TOP 30 PROSPECTS

1. Andrew Lambo, of	16. Xavier Paul, of
2. James McDonald, rhp	17. Kyle Russell, of
3. Ethan Martin, rhp	18. Jon Michael Redding, rhp
4. Josh Lindblom, rhp	19. Tony Delmonico, c/2b
5. Scott Elbert, lhp	20. Justin Miller, rhp
6. Ivan DeJesus Jr., ss/2b	21. Brent Leach, lhp
7. Devaris Gordon, ss	22. Jamie Hoffman, of
8. Josh Bell, 3b	23. Daigoro Rondon, rhp
9. Chris Withrow, rhp	24. Victor Garate, lhp
10. Nathan Eovaldi, rhp	25. Javy Guerra, rhp
11. Austin Gallagher, 3b	26. James Adkins, lhp
12. Ramon Troncoso, rhp	27. Alfredo Silverio, of
13. Pedro Baez, 3b	28. Lucas May, c
14. Travis Schlichting, rhp	29. Josh Wall, rhp
15. Steven Johnson, rhp	30. Jordan Pratt, rhp

in 2009. Ivan DeJesus Jr. or Chin-Hung Lu could get a look at shortstop if Rafael Furcal leaves as a free agent, while James McDonald could slide into the rotation if Derek Lowe departs.

With so many players reaching the majors or being traded, the Dodgers are thinner at the upper levels of the minors than they have been in recent years. They believe they're replenished their system with their last two drafts, which have included six of the top 10 prospects on this list: outfielder Andrew Lambo; righthanders Ethan Martin, Josh Lindblom, Chris Withrow and Nathan Eovaldi; and shortstop Devaris Gordon.

General Manager: Ned Colletti. **Farm Director:** DeJon Watson. **Scouting Director:** Tim Hallgren.

Class	Team	League	W	L	PCT	Finish*	Manager	Affiliated
Majors	Los Angeles	National	84	78	.519	8th (16)	Joe Torre	—
Triple-A	Las Vegas 51s	Pacific Coast	74	69	.517	7th (16)	Lorenzo Bundy	2001
Double-A	Jacksonville Suns	Southern	68	72	.486	7th (10)	John Shoemaker	2002
High A	Inland Empire 66ers	California	68	73	.482	6th (10)	John Valentin	2007
Low A	Great Lakes Loons	Midwest	54	85	.388	14th (14)	Juan Bustabad	2007
Rookie	Ogden Raptors	Pioneer	42	33	.560	3rd (8)	Mike Brumley	2003
Rookie	GCL Dodgers	Gulf Coast	30	26	.536	6th (16)	Jeff Carter	2001
Overall 2008 Minor League Record			336	358	.484	21st		

* Finish in overall standings (No. of teams in league). ^League champion.

LAST YEAR'S TOP 30

Rank	Player, Pos.	Status
1.	Clayton Kershaw, lhp	Majors
2.	Andy LaRoche, 3b	(Pirates)
3.	Chin-Lung Hu, ss	Majors
4.	Scott Elbert, lhp	No. 5
5.	Blake DeWitt, 2b	Majors
6.	Chris Withrow, rhp	No. 9
7.	James McDonald, rhp	No. 2
8.	Jon Meloan, rhp	(Indians)
9.	Delwyn Young, of	Majors
10.	Pedro Baez, 3b	No. 13
11.	Josh Bell, 3b	No. 8
12.	Bryan Morris, rhp	(Pirates)
13.	Ivan DeJesus Jr., ss	No. 6
14.	Andrew Lambo, of/1b	No. 1
15.	Josh Wall, rhp	No. 29
16.	Ramon Troncoso, rhp	No. 12
17.	Lucas May, c	No. 28
18.	Greg Miller, lhp	Dropped out
19.	James Adkins, lhp	No. 26
20.	Javy Guerra, rhp	No. 25
21.	Mario Alvarez, lhp	Dropped out
22.	Justin Miller, rhp	No. 20
23.	Xavier Paul, of	No. 16
24.	Tim Sexton, rhp	Dropped out
25.	Carlos Santana, c	(Indians)
26.	Cory Wade, rhp	Majors
27.	Justin Orenduff, rhp	Dropped out
28.	Preston Mattingly, 2b/of	Dropped out
29.	Alfredo Silverio, of	No. 27
30.	Geison Aguasviva, lhp	Dropped out

BEST TOOLS

Best Hitter for Average	Andrew Lambo
Best Power Hitter	Josh Bell
Best Strike-Zone Discipline	Ivan DeJesus
Fastest Baserunner	Devaris Gordon
Best Athlete	Devaris Gordon
Best Fastball	Josh Lindblom
Best Curveball	Scott Elbert
Best Slider	Travis Schlichting
Best Changeup	James McDonald
Best Control	James McDonald
Best Defensive Catcher	A.J. Ellis
Best Defensive Infielder	Devaris Gordon
Best Infield Arm	Pedro Baez
Best Defensive Outfielder	Jamie Hoffman
Best Outfield Arm	Xavier Paul

PROJECTED 2012 LINEUP

Catcher	Russell Martin
First Base	James Loney
Second Base	Blake DeWitt
Third Base	Josh Bell
Shortstop	Ivan DeJesus Jr.
Left Field	Andrew Lambo
Center Field	Matt Kemp
Right Field	Andre Ethier
No. 1 Starter	Clayton Kershaw
No. 2 Starter	Chad Billingsley
No. 3 Starter	Hiroki Kuroda
No. 4 Starter	James McDonald
No. 5 Starter	Josh Lindblom
Closer	Jonathan Broxton

TOP PROSPECTS OF THE DECADE

Year	Player, Pos.	2008 Org.
1999	Angel Pena, c	Out of baseball
2000	Chin-Feng Chen, of	La New (Taiwan)
2001	Ben Diggins, rhp	Out of baseball
2002	Ricardo Rodriguez, rhp	Edmonton (Golden)
2003	James Loney, 1b	Dodgers
2004	Edwin Jackson, rhp	Rays
2005	Joel Guzman, ss/of	Rays
2006	Chad Billingsley, rhp	Dodgers
2007	Andy LaRoche, 3b	Pirates
2008	Clayton Kershaw, lhp	Dodgers

TOP DRAFT PICKS OF THE DECADE

Year	Player, Pos.	2008 Org.
1999	Jason Repko, ss/of	Dodgers
2000	Ben Diggins, rhp	Out of baseball
2001	Brian Pilkington, rhp (2nd)	Out of baseball
2002	James Loney, 1b	Dodgers
2003	Chad Billingsley, rhp	Dodgers
2004	Scott Elbert, lhp	Dodgers
2005	*Luke Hochevar, rhp (1st supp.)	Royals
2006	Clayton Kershaw, lhp	Dodgers
2007	Chris Withrow, rhp	Dodgers
2008	Ethan Martin, rhp	Dodgers

*Did not sign.

LARGEST BONUSES IN CLUB HISTORY

Clayton Kershaw, 2006	$2,300,000
Joel Guzman, 2001	$2,255,000
Ben Diggins, 2000	$2,200,000
Hideo Nomo, 1995	$2,000,000
Ethan Martin, 2008	$1,730,000

LOS ANGELES DODGERS

TOP 2009 ROOKIE: James McDonald, rhp. His eye-opening performance in the NL Championship Series earned him a spot on the roster, either in the rotation or the bullpen.

BREAKOUT PROSPECT: Travis Schlichting, rhp. After learning to pitch in the independent Northern League, he could show up soon in the big league bullpen with his sinker/slider combination.

SLEEPER: Cole St. Clair, lhp. He looked like a lock first-round pick before he got hurt at Rice, enabling the Dodgers to grab him in the seventh round last June.

SOURCE OF TOP 30 TALENT			
Homegrown	28	Acquired	2
College	5	Trades	0
Junior college	3	Rule 5 draft	1
High school	14	Independent leagues	1
Draft-and-follow	1	Free agents/waivers	0
Nondrafted free agents	1		
International	4		

Numbers in parentheses indicate prospect rankings.

LF
Andrew Lambo (1)
Tommy Giles
James Tomlin
Preston Mattingly

CF
Xavier Paul (16)
Jovanny Rosario
Nick Buss
Trayvon Robinson

RF
Kyle Russell (17)
Jamie Hoffman (22)
Alfredo Silverio (27)

3B
Josh Bell (8)
Pedro Baez (13)

SS
Ivan DeJesus Jr. (6)
Devaris Gordon (7)
Adolfo Gonzalez

2B
Jaime Pedroza

1B
Austin Gallagher (11)
Russell Mitchell
Drew Locke

C
Tony Delmonico (19)
Lucas May (28)
A.J. Ellis
Kenley Jansen

RHP

Starters	Relievers
James McDonald (2)	Ramon Troncoso (12)
Ethan Martin (3)	Travis Schlichting (14)
Josh Lindblom (4)	Daigoro Rondon (23)
Chris Withrow (9)	Justin Orenduff
Nathan Eovaldi (10)	Luis Garcia
Steven Johnson (15)	Robert Blevins
Jon Michael Redding (18)	
Justin Miller (20)	
Javy Guerra (25)	
Josh Wall (29)	
Jordan Pratt (30)	
Timothy Sexton	
Mario Alvarez	
Jesus Castillo	

LHP

Starters	Relievers
Scott Elbert (5)	Brent Leach (21)
James Adkins (26)	Victor Garate (24)
Geison Aguasviva	Cole St. Clair
Cody White	Greg Miller

2008   BONUSES: $4.4 MILLION

BEST PURE HITTER: 2B Tony Delmonico's (6) polish showed when he batted .340/.443/.716 at Rookie-level Ogden. The Dodgers tried him at catcher in instructional league. SS Devaris Gordon (4) is much more raw, but he still managed to hit .331/.371/.430 at Ogden.

BEST POWER HITTER: OF Kyle Russell (3) led NCAA Division I with 28 homers in 2007 and set the Texas career mark with 57. He has a propensity for striking out, but he did go deep 11 times in his pro debut.

FASTEST RUNNER: Gordon has top-of-the-line speed and stole 18 bases in 60 pro games. He flew under the radar of many clubs because he was academically ineligible during the spring at Seminole (Fla.) CC.

BEST DEFENSIVE PLAYER: Gordon, who has tremendous actions and range at shortstop.

BEST FASTBALL: RHPs Ethan Martin (1), Josh Lindblom (2) and Nathan Eovaldi (11) all range from 90-96 mph. Lindblom has the best fastball life and command. Martin, the first high school pitcher taken in June, has yet to debut after tearing the meniscus in his right knee during a fielding drill in a postdraft minicamp.

BEST SECONDARY PITCH: Martin has a power curveball that arrives at 80-81 mph with good depth and tilt.

BEST PRO DEBUT: Lindblom gets the nod over Delmonico and Gordon for reaching Double-A in his first summer. He posted a 2.12 ERA and a 37-5 K-BB ratio in 34 innings.

BEST ATHLETE: Martin initially captured attention as an athletic, power-hitting third baseman. As a position player, he would have been drafted in the first two rounds.

MOST INTRIGUING BACKGROUND: Gordon is the son of Phillies reliever Tom Gordon. Other draftees with big league relatives include 3B Austin Yount (12), whose father Larry made one appearance and whose uncle Robin is a Hall of Famer; 2B/OF Brian Ruggiano (23), whose brother Justin is a Rays outfielder; and LHP Jonathan Runnels (29), whose grandfather Pete won two American League batting titles.

CLOSEST TO THE MAJORS: Though Lindblom had more success as a reliever at Purdue, the Dodgers plan on developing him as a starter. He'll still begin 2009 in Double-A and could reach the majors by the end of the season. LHP Cole St. Clair (7) hasn't regained the plus stuff he had before hurting his shoulder in 2007, but his still-solid arsenal and competitiveness could get him to the big league bullpen in a hurry.

BEST LATE-ROUND PICK: Eovaldi had Tommy John surgery in May 2007 but rushed back for his senior season. His signability was in question but the Dodgers got him for $250,000.

THE ONE WHO GOT AWAY: Power-hitting 3B Zack Cox (20) was a top-two-rounds talent who was intent on attending Arkansas.

ASSESSMENT: Healthy again by instructional league, Martin could take the same quick development path as former Dodgers high school first-rounders Chad Billingsley and Clayton Kershaw. Lindblom could pay off quickly, while Russell, Gordon and Delmonico are intriguing position players.

2007   BONUSES: $3.6 MILLION

OF Andrew Lambo's (4) emergence as the system's best hitter has taken the sting out of RHP Chris Withrow (1) having elbow problems and LHP James Adkins (1s) struggling in his first full pro season.

GRADE: C

2006   BONUSES: $5.7 MILLION

LHP Clayton Kershaw (1) shot to the majors and looks like a future star, while RHP Bryan Morris (1) was used in the Manny Ramirez trade. 2B Preston Mattingly (1s) has been a bust, however, and unsigned RHP Alex White (14) will be one of the first pitchers selected in the 2009 draft.

GRADE: B+

2005   BONUSES: $2.2 MILLION*

The Dodgers didn't have a true first-rounder and had a celebrated breakdown in negotiations with RHP Luke Hochevar (1s), who would go No. 1 overall in 2006. But they did land SS Ivan DeJesus Jr. (2), 3B Josh Bell (4) and RHP Jon Meloan (5).

GRADE: C

2004   BONUSES: $5.6 MILLION*

2B/3B Blake DeWitt (1s) and RHP Cory Wade (10) helped Los Angeles make the playoffs last year. LHP Scott Elbert (1) is on the mend after shoulder surgery, but RHP Justin Orenduff (1s) hasn't bounced back as well.

GRADE: B

*Draft analysis by Jim Callis. Numbers in parentheses indicate draft rounds. *Bonuses for 2004-05 are first 10 rounds only.*

PROSPECT

ANDREW LAMBO, OF

Born: Aug. 11, 1988.
Ht.: 6-3. **Wt.:** 190.
Bats: L. **Throws:** L.
Drafted: HS—Newbury Park, Calif., 2007 (4th round).
Signed by: Chuck Crim.

PAUL GIERHART

A preseason high school All-American in 2007, Lambo fell from a possible supplemental first-round pick to the fourth round because of makeup concerns. At Cleveland High in Reseda, Calif., he got suspended as a freshman for missing classes, then got caught smoking marijuana under the bleachers as a sophomore. Though there were no further incidents in his final two years after he transferred 35 miles north to Newbury Park (Calif.) High, scouts still thought he was immature. But Dodgers area scout Chuck Crim pushed for Lambo, and Los Angeles took him in the fourth round. He had grown up a Dodgers fan, and they signed him away from an Arizona State commitment for a slot bonus of $164,250. Lambo won the Guy Wellman Award as the Dodgers' best first-year player in 2007, when he ranked second in the Rookie-level Gulf Coast League in on-base percentage (.440) and third in hitting (.343). He played in the low Class A Midwest League all-star game in his first full season last year. As one of the few bright spots on a bad Great Lakes club, Lambo ranked among the MWL leaders in several categories when he was promoted to Double-A Jacksonville in late August, just two weeks after turning 20. Los Angeles made the move so he'd be eligible to play in the Arizona Fall League, but he handled the jump well, hitting safely in all eight games he played. Lambo capped his year by hitting .313 in the AFL, where he was the youngest player.

Lambo has plus raw power and bat speed, with an ideal swing path and mechanics. For a big player, he has a short and direct path to the ball, and he's very consistent with his stroke. He shows mainly gap power now, but he has the big frame to provide leverage for more homers in the future. He hangs in well against lefthanders, hitting .323 against them in 2008. Though he hasn't been a pro for long, Lambo has the confidence that makes him feel he can hit any pitcher. After playing right field and first base in his pro debut, he played a solid left field last season, about on par with Andre Ethier. If he returned to first base, his main position in high school, he'd be an above-average defender. Lambo has put his off-field problems behind him and has started to grow up.

Lambo's stroke is very level, and he may need to make some adjustments to add loft and produce more power in the future. Despite his textbook swing, he fanned 119 times in 2008 and will need to tighten up his strike zone. While he was a successful high school pitcher, his arm is just adequate, which prompted his move from right field to left. He's a well below-average runner, though he compensates on defense by reading balls well off the bat.

Lambo projects as a middle-of-the-order bat, someone who can hit .285-.300 with 25 or more homers in the big leagues. His AFL performance reinforced that he has advanced hitting ability and gives the Dodgers confidence that he can handle a full-time assignment to their new Double-A Chattanooga affiliate in 2009. He could make his big league debut toward the end of 2010.

Year	Club (League)	Class	AVG	G	AB	R	H	2B	3B	HR	RBI	BB	SO	SB	OBP	SLG
2007	Dodgers (GCL)	R	.343	54	181	38	62	15	1	5	32	29	34	1	.440	.519
2008	Great Lakes (MWL)	LoA	.288	123	472	58	136	33	2	15	79	41	110	5	.346	.462
	Jacksonville (SL)	AA	.389	8	36	7	14	2	1	3	12	2	9	0	.421	.750
MINOR LEAGUE TOTALS			.308	185	689	103	212	50	4	23	123	72	153	6	.376	.492

2 JAMES McDONALD, RHP

BORN: Oct. 19, 1984. **B-T:** L-R. **HT.:** 6-5. **WT.:** 195. **DRAFTED:** Golden West (Calif.) JC, D/F 2002 (11th round). **SIGNED BY:** Bobby Darwin.

McDonald's father James Sr. played college basketball at Southern California and then made the Los Angeles Rams as a tight end. James Jr. is also a cousin of former big leaguers Darnell and Donzell McDonald. He made a name for himself in last year's postseason, striking out seven Phillies in 5¹/₃ scoreless innings in the National League Championship Series. McDonald can add and subtract velocity from all three of his pitches—fastball, curveball and changeup—and has strong command. His best pitch is his 11-5 curve, which ranges from 69-77 mph, and his changeup is a plus offering with sink. When he pitched in relief in the majors, his fastball jumped up to 93-94 mph. He pitches from a high arm angle, using his height to deliver the ball on a downward plane to the hitter. He also shows great composure and feel for pitching. His first postseason pitch, with the bases loaded in the third inning of Game Two of the NLCS, was a changeup to Pat Burrell for a swinging strike. He's a terrific athlete who spent 2004-05 as an outfielder when he came down with a sore arm. McDonald's fastball is very straight, and when he pitches as a starter it has fringy velocity at 87-91 mph. However, his secondary pitches help compensate for his fastball's shortcomings. His curveball can be inconsistent at times. The Dodgers' 2009 rotation is unsettled thanks to free agency and Chad Billingsley's broken leg. McDonald will make the Opening Day roster in some capacity, with a good chance of earning a job as a starter. He projects as a No. 3 starter or late-inning reliever.

Year	Club (League)	Class	W	L	ERA	G	GS	CG	SV	IP	H	R	ER	HR	BB	SO	AVG
2003	Dodgers (GCL)	R	2	4	3.33	12	9	0	0	49	39	20	18	3	15	47	.220
2005	Ogden (PIO)	R	0	0	1.50	4	0	0	0	6	4	3	1	0	2	9	.174
2006	Columbus (SAL)	LoA	5	10	3.98	30	22	2	0	142	119	72	63	15	65	146	.229
2007	Inland Empire (CAL)	HiA	6	7	3.95	16	15	0	0	82	79	37	36	8	21	104	.253
	Jacksonville (SL)	AA	7	2	1.71	10	10	0	0	53	42	14	10	5	16	64	.218
2008	Jacksonville (SL)	AA	5	3	3.19	22	22	0	0	119	98	47	42	12	46	113	.227
	Las Vegas (PCL)	AAA	2	1	3.63	5	4	0	0	22	17	9	9	3	7	28	.200
	Los Angeles (NL)	MAJ	0	0	0.00	4	0	0	0	6	5	0	0	0	1	2	.227
MINOR LEAGUE TOTALS			27	27	3.41	99	82	2	0	473	398	202	179	46	172	511	.229
MAJOR LEAGUE TOTALS			0	0	0.00	4	0	0	0	6	5	0	0	0	1	2	.227

3 ETHAN MARTIN, RHP

BORN: June 6, 1989. **B-T:** R-R. **HT.:** 6-2. **WT.:** 195. **DRAFTED:** HS—Toccoa, Ga., 2008 (1st round). **SIGNED BY:** Lon Joyce.

As a high school quarterback and star third baseman/pitcher in high school, Martin never suffered a serious injury. He won BA's 2008 High School Player of the Year award, went 15th overall in the draft (he was the first prep pitcher taken) and signed for $1.73 million. Then at the Dodgers' postdraft minicamp, he tore the meniscus in his right knee when he slipped covering first base during a fielding drill. He returned in instructional league but has yet to make his official pro debut. A good athlete who could have been drafted in the second round as a slugging third baseman, Martin stands out most with his arm strength. His fastball ranges from 90-96 mph, sits at 92-94 and has bat-breaking run and sink. He has the makings of a power curveball with depth, tilt and hard rotation. Due to his past as a hitter, Martin remains raw as a pitcher and missed needed development time thanks to his knee injury. He must clean up his delivery and his changeup also needs a lot of work. Martin needs lots of innings to close the gap between his current ability and his potential as a frontline starter. He has a good chance to make his debut in low Class A and could advance quickly once things start coming together.

Year	Club (League)	Class	W	L	ERA	G	GS	CG	SV	IP	H	R	ER	HR	BB	SO	AVG
2008	Did Not Play—Injured																

4 JOSH LINDBLOM, RHP

BORN: June 15, 1987. **B-T:** R-R. **HT.:** 6-5. **WT.:** 220. **DRAFTED:** Purdue, 2008 (2nd round). **SIGNED BY:** Chet Sergo.

The Dodgers liked Lindblom out of high school in 2005, but the Astros picked him in the third round just as Los Angeles was ready to take him. Lindblom turned down Houston, went to Tennessee and then transferred to Purdue, where he became a closer. He worked just 41 innings as a junior, so scouts didn't see him much, and the Dodgers felt fortunate to get Lindblom with a second-round pick and $663,000 bonus. Lindblom touched 96 mph as a college reliever, and he still pitched with plus velocity (89-94) as a pro starter, with plenty of heavy life on his fastball. His heater bores in on righthanders, his slider has lateral tilt and his splitter is a swing-and-miss pitch. He has a durable body, clean delivery and good mound presence. Hitters can sometimes pick up Lindblom's pitches too easily out of his high arm slot. He tends to favor his splitter over his changeup, which the Dodgers want him to use more often. For now, the Dodgers will leave Lindblom as a starter, knowing he always can go back to relief. He finished his first pro summer in Double-A and will head back there to open 2009. He should be the first member of Los Angeles' 2008 draft class to reach the majors—perhaps sometime this year.

Year	Club (League)	Class	W	L	ERA	G	GS	CG	SV	IP	H	R	ER	HR	BB	SO	AVG
2008	Great Lakes (MWL)	LoA	0	0	1.86	8	8	0	0	29	14	6	6	2	4	33	.137
	Jacksonville (SL)	AA	0	0	3.60	1	1	0	0	5	5	2	2	0	1	4	.263
MINOR LEAGUE TOTALS			0	0	2.12	9	9	0	0	34	19	8	8	2	5	37	.157

5 SCOTT ELBERT, LHP

BORN: Aug. 13, 1985. **B-T:** L-L. **HT.:** 6-1. **WT.:** 210. **DRAFTED:** HS—Seneca, Mo., 2004 (1st round). **SIGNED BY:** Mitch Webster.

A 2004 first-round pick who signed for $1.575 million, Elbert had scar tissue removed from the labrum in his shoulder in 2007. The shoulder issues also forced him to spend much of the past three seasons in Double-A, but when he jumped to the majors last August, he struck out five of the first seven hitters he faced. He spent 2008 as a reliever because the Dodgers wanted him to work his way back more slowly. Elbert still has a live arm, and his fastball was back up to 90-94 mph in 2008. He has a hard, two-plane curveball at 83-86 mph and runs it under the hands of righthanders. His changeup is also a plus pitch at times. He usually operates in the bottom of the strike zone. A former all-state running back, Elbert has a football mentality on the mound, resulting in a high-effort delivery and a tendency for his front side to fly open when he rushes. Missing most of 2007 didn't help his mechanics, and there's some thought he may not be able to go back to starting because he can't repeat his delivery. He pitches away from contact, leading to erratic control and command. If Elbert makes the Dodgers out of spring training, it will be as a reliever. If not, he'll probably return to starting at their new Triple-A Albuquerque affiliate. If he can't reassert himself in that role, he'll still be valuable as a late-inning reliever, perhaps even a closer.

Year	Club (League)	Class	W	L	ERA	G	GS	CG	SV	IP	H	R	ER	HR	BB	SO	AVG
2004	Ogden (PIO)	R	2	3	5.26	12	12	0	0	50	47	33	29	5	30	45	.270
2005	Columbus (SAL)	LoA	8	5	2.66	25	24	1	0	115	83	37	34	8	57	128	.200
2006	Vero Beach (FSL)	HiA	5	5	2.37	17	15	0	0	84	57	27	22	4	41	97	.193
	Jacksonville (SL)	AA	6	4	3.61	11	11	0	0	62	40	26	25	11	44	76	.187
2007	Jacksonville (SL)	AA	0	1	3.86	3	3	0	0	14	6	6	6	0	10	24	.128
2008	Jacksonville (SL)	AA	4	1	2.40	25	1	0	0	41	22	14	11	2	20	46	.157
	Los Angeles (NL)	MAJ	0	1	12.00	10	0	0	0	6	9	8	8	2	4	8	.346
MINOR LEAGUE TOTALS			25	19	3.12	93	66	1	0	366	255	143	127	30	202	416	.198
MAJOR LEAGUE TOTALS			0	1	12.00	10	0	0	0	6	9	8	8	2	4	8	.346

6 IVAN DeJESUS JR., SS/2B

JON SOOHOO/LA DODGERS

BORN: May 1, 1987. **B-T:** R-R. **HT.:** 5-11. **WT.:** 189. **DRAFTED:** HS—Guaynabo, P.R., 2005 (2nd round). **SIGNED BY:** Manny Estrada.

The son of the former big league shortstop by the same name, DeJesus stood out much more with his defense than his offense before 2008. Then he led the Southern League in on-base percentage (.419) and ranked fifth in hitting (.324). He played in the Futures Game and finished the season with a 23-game hitting streak. DeJesus has an advanced approach, uses the whole field and shows good plate discipline. He has the ability to square up a fastball, and some power could come as he gets older, because he knows which pitches to pull. Defensively, he has solid range and arm strength to go with good actions and instincts. He's an average runner with savvy on the bases. His bilingualism, leadership skills and personality help make him a positive clubhouse presence. DeJesus has a tendency to be too flashy on defense, especially with his throws, and otherwise gets careless mentally. Some SL observers thought he looked more comfortable at second base. He won't be a big home run or stolen base threat. For now, DeJesus will stay at shortstop, where the Dodgers have a greater need. He could get a chance to replace free agent Rafael Furcal in the big league lineup, but more likely is headed to Triple-A.

Year	Club (League)	Class	AVG	G	AB	R	H	2B	3B	HR	RBI	BB	SO	SB	OBP	SLG
2005	Dodgers (GCL)	R	.339	33	121	18	41	5	0	0	11	10	22	8	.389	.380
	Ogden (PIO)	R	.208	20	72	4	15	1	0	0	3	6	18	3	.296	.222
2006	Columbus (SAL)	LoA	.277	126	483	65	134	17	2	1	44	63	85	16	.361	.327
2007	Inland Empire (CAL)	HiA	.287	121	428	69	123	22	3	4	52	57	64	11	.371	.381
2008	Jacksonville (SL)	AA	.324	128	463	91	150	21	2	7	58	76	81	16	.419	.423
MINOR LEAGUE TOTALS			.295	428	1567	247	463	66	7	12	168	212	270	54	.381	.369

7 DEVARIS GORDON, SS

JOHN SPEAR

BORN: April 22, 1988. **B-T:** L-R. **HT.:** 5-11. **WT.:** 150. **DRAFTED:** Seminole (Fla.) CC, 2008 (4th round). **SIGNED BY:** Scott Hennessey.

A son of big league reliever Tom Gordon, Devaris originally attended Southeastern (Fla.) before transferring to junior college to become eligible for the 2008 draft. He didn't play at Seminole (Fla.) CC because of a grade mixup, so scouts couldn't see him in game action last spring. As a Royals farmhand, Dodgers farm director DeJon Watson once roomed with Tom Gordon, who tipped off Watson about his son. Los Angeles liked what it saw in workouts and signed him for $250,000 in the fourth round. Gordon is a pure athlete who can cover 60 yards in 6.3 seconds and dunk a basketball despite standing 5-foot-11. He sprays the ball from gap to gap and showed little rust by ranking fourth in the Rookie-level Pioneer League batting race with a .331 average in his pro debut. He has plus range to both sides, a solid arm and the actions of a big league shortstop. Despite his big league bloodlines, Gordon is raw and the time off last spring didn't help. With his size, his power potential is limited. He must learn to play more under control so he can be a more consistent defender. Gordon will move as fast as he can mature, with his next test to come in low Class A. If all goes well, he could blossom into a leadoff hitter and plus defender.

Year	Club (League)	Class	AVG	G	AB	R	H	2B	3B	HR	RBI	BB	SO	SB	OBP	SLG
2008	Ogden (PIO)	R	.331	60	251	45	83	13	3	2	27	16	29	18	.371	.430
MINOR LEAGUE TOTALS			.331	60	251	45	83	13	3	2	27	16	29	18	.371	.430

8 JOSH BELL, 3B

JON SOOHOO/LA DODGERS

BORN: Nov. 13, 1986. **B-T:** B-R. **HT.:** 6-3. **WT.:** 235. **DRAFTED:** HS—Santaluces, Fla., 2005 (4th round). **SIGNED BY:** Manny Estrada.

Bell lost 30 pounds before the 2008 season and was playing well at high Class A Inland Empire until a knee problem shut him down in late May. Surgery revealed a small divot in the cartilage near his kneecap which, if left untreated, could have expanded and threatened his career. Bell has the most raw power in the system and combines it with good leverage in his swing. He has a good approach at the plate, swinging mostly at strikes and using the whole field. He has an above-average arm at third base. His noticeably improved dedication to his career does give Bell more of a chance to stay at the hot corner, but his lack of speed and range still may force a move. He has a thick lower half—earning the nickname "Baby Kemp" for his resemblance to Matt Kemp—and could wind up at first base or an outfield corner. Bell was scheduled to resume baseball activity in December and take part in a winter development program at Dodger Stadium in early January. He still has a high ceiling with the bat and should make his first trip to Double-A in 2009.

Year	Club (League)	Class	AVG	G	AB	R	H	2B	3B	HR	RBI	BB	SO	SB	OBP	SLG
2005	Dodgers (GCL)	R	.318	45	157	26	50	7	1	1	21	20	33	5	.399	.395
2006	Ogden (PIO)	R	.308	64	250	45	77	17	3	12	53	23	72	4	.367	.544
2007	Great Lakes (MWL)	LoA	.289	108	398	65	115	21	3	15	62	39	109	5	.354	.470
	Inland Empire (CAL)	HiA	.173	20	75	4	13	2	1	2	9	3	19	0	.203	.307
2008	Inland Empire (CAL)	HiA	.273	51	187	34	51	12	2	6	21	31	56	4	.373	.455
MINOR LEAGUE TOTALS			.287	288	1067	174	306	59	10	36	166	116	289	18	.357	.462

9 CHRIS WITHROW, RHP

JON SOOHOO/LA DODGERS

BORN: April 1, 1989. **B-T:** R-R. **HT.:** 6-3. **WT.:** 195. **DRAFTED:** HS—Midland, Texas, 2007 (1st round). **SIGNED BY:** Calvin Jones.

Withrow, whose father Mike pitched professionally and coached him in high school, signed for $1.35 million as the 20th overall pick in the 2007 draft. He has pitched just 13 innings since, however, missing most of 2008 with a tender elbow. He managed to get back on the mound for four innings in August and took part in instructional league. Withrow hit 98 mph with his fastball in the 2007 Gulf Coast League championship game and sat at 92-94 mph in 2008. He has a power curveball and a clean delivery. He's a solid athlete who would have been a two-way player at Baylor if he hadn't turned pro. Because he was away from pitching so long, Withrow needs to regain his command of the strike zone. While he has shown a feel for a changeup, it's not reliable yet. He hasn't had a serious injury, but his health has to be a concern. The Dodgers remain high on Withrow but also will continue to monitor his workload closely. They may have him open 2009 in Inland Empire so he can avoid the cold climate of the Midwest League. Getting in a full, healthy year would be a step in the right direction.

Year	Club (League)	Class	W	L	ERA	G	GS	CG	SV	IP	H	R	ER	HR	BB	SO	AVG
2007	Dodgers (GCL)	R	0	0	5.00	6	4	0	0	9	5	5	5	0	4	13	.167
2008	Inland Empire (CAL)	HiA	0	0	4.50	4	0	0	0	4	2	2	2	0	6	1	.182
MINOR LEAGUE TOTALS			0	0	4.85	10	4	0	0	13	7	7	7	0	10	14	.171

10 NATHAN EOVALDI, RHP

BORN: Feb. 13, 1990. **B-T:** R-R. **HT.:** 6-3. **WT.:** 195. **DRAFTED:** HS—Alvin, Texas, 2008 (11th round). **SIGNED BY:** Chris Smith.

After Tommy John surgery in May 2007, Eovaldi rushed back to pitch as a high school senior, returning to game action 11 months after surgery. Committed to Texas A&M, he scared clubs off with his signability. But area scout Chris Smith didn't give up, and the Dodgers signed Eovaldi in the 11th round for $250,000. Eovaldi projects as a classic Texas power pitcher. His fastball already had climbed back to 91-93 mph in the spring, and in his final outing of the summer, he didn't throw a pitch under 94 and hit 96 mph 20 times. He has a strong body, a decent delivery with good downhill plane and an aggressive approach on the mound. Eovaldi's hard breaking ball was inconsistent before he got hurt and he didn't try to throw it as a high school senior. The Dodgers helped him develop a tighter, sharper curveball in instructional league and think it can develop into a solid-average pitch in time. He has little experience using a changeup. While he will need innings to polish some rough edges, Eovaldi could move fast because of his live arm. He should open 2009 in the Great Lakes rotation, looking to grind through a full pro season. The development of his changeup will help determine if Eovaldi remains a starter long-term or moves to the bullpen.

Year	Club (League)	Class	W	L	ERA	G	GS	CG	SV	IP	H	R	ER	HR	BB	SO	AVG
2008	Dodgers (GCL)	R	0	1	1.13	6	0	0	1	8	6	1	1	0	3	9	.207
	Ogden (PIO)	R	0	0	0.00	1	0	0	0	3	1	0	0	0	0	2	.125
MINOR LEAGUE TOTALS			0	1	0.84	7	0	0	1	11	7	1	1	0	3	11	.189

11 AUSTIN GALLAGHER, 3B

BORN: Nov. 16, 1988. **B-T:** L-R. **HT.:** 6-5. **WT.:** 210. **DRAFTED:** HS—Manheim Township, Pa., 2007 (3rd round). **SIGNED BY:** Clair Rierson.

Taking his size, makeup and the fact he succeeded offensively in high Class A at 19 into account, Gallagher has established himself as a potential middle-of-the-order bat. He comes from athletic bloodlines; his father Glenn (Austin's actual first name is also Glenn) played football and baseball at Clemson and was the Blue Jays' third-round pick in 1981. He later became a Division II and Division III college baseball coach, and his son has some of the savvy that goes with growing up around the game. Gallagher began 2008 in extended spring training but went to Inland Empire after Josh Bell got shut down in May with a knee injury. Despite long arms and a big build, he stays inside the ball and can drive the ball to the opposite field as well as pull it. His plate coverage and discipline are impressive for a large-body hitter. He has plus bat speed and could develop from a line-drive hitter into a power threat thanks to the leverage in his swing. If the home-run power doesn't come, however, Gallagher may not fit the profile of an everyday major leaguer, since he isn't quick or agile and will probably have to move across the diamond when he grows too big to play third base. He's already played some first base and needs work at both infield corner spots to become an average defender. Despite his strong offensive season, he's likely headed back to high Class A at least to start 2009.

Year	Club (League)	Class	AVG	G	AB	R	H	2B	3B	HR	RBI	BB	SO	SB	OBP	SLG
2007	Ogden (PIO)	R	.284	55	197	28	56	11	0	4	17	19	33	1	.346	.401
2008	Inland Empire (CAL)	HiA	.293	78	307	36	90	33	1	5	55	29	73	1	.349	.456
MINOR LEAGUE TOTALS			.290	133	504	64	146	44	1	9	72	48	106	2	.348	.435

12 RAMON TRONCOSO, RHP

BORN: Feb. 16, 1983. **B-T:** R-R. **HT.:** 6-2. **WT.:** 200. **SIGNED:** Dominican Republic, 2002. **SIGNED BY:** Pablo Peguero.

After being added to the 40-man roster and going to big league camp for the first time, Troncoso made Los Angeles' Opening Day roster out of spring training. After six appearances in April he was sent down to Triple-A when Nomar Garciaparra came off the disabled list. Troncoso lost his mechanics and command for a while at Las Vegas but came back up in late June and stuck through the end of the season. With a funky arm action, Troncoso gets good sink on his 92-95 mph fastball (he induced six double plays in 38 big league innings) but his velocity wavers. He throws a slider that can be above-average when he doesn't get under it. Troncoso made three starts for Azucareros in his native Dominican Republic in November to work on throwing changeups to lefties and closing down his front side to get a consistent release point on his slider. He threw well, walking only one in 15 innings of those starts and limiting lefthanders to a .200 average. If he can throw his power sinker consistently for strikes he can be a very good big league reliever, and figures to be part of Los Angeles' bullpen again in 2009.

Year	Club (League)	Class	W	L	ERA	G	GS	CG	SV	IP	H	R	ER	HR	BB	SO	AVG
2002	Dodgers E (DSL)	R	2	4	2.27	11	7	0	0	40	47	23	10	0	14	29	.287
2003	Dodgers E (DSL)	R	2	2	2.47	11	7	0	0	47	39	23	13	1	13	38	.228
2004	Dodgers1 (DSL)	R	2	0	0.00	9	0	0	3	12	9	0	0	0	3	8	.220
	Dodgers2 (DSL)	R	0	3	5.73	8	0	0	2	22	27	17	14	0	9	21	.293
2005	Columbus (SAL)	LoA	2	3	6.69	13	6	0	1	38	58	33	28	2	13	27	.360
	Ogden (PIO)	R	6	2	3.68	29	0	0	13	37	40	19	15	0	12	30	.278
2006	Columbus (SAL)	LoA	4	0	2.41	23	0	0	15	34	28	11	9	1	7	22	.241
	Vero Beach (FSL)	HiA	1	3	6.75	18	0	0	0	29	43	27	22	1	14	31	.347
2007	Inland Empire (CAL)	HiA	3	1	1.04	16	0	0	7	26	18	6	3	0	3	30	.194
	Jacksonville (SL)	AA	7	3	3.12	35	0	0	7	52	52	19	18	3	18	39	.263
2008	Las Vegas (PCL)	AAA	4	0	4.99	22	0	0	0	31	43	24	17	1	16	18	.336
	Los Angeles (NL)	MAJ	1	1	4.26	32	0	0	0	38	37	19	18	2	12	38	.268
MINOR LEAGUE TOTALS			33	21	3.66	195	20	0	48	367	404	202	149	9	122	293	.282
MAJOR LEAGUE TOTALS			1	1	4.26	32	0	0	0	38	37	19	18	2	12	38	.268

13 PEDRO BAEZ, 3B

BORN: March 11, 1988. **B-T:** R-R. **HT.:** 6-2. **WT.:** 195. **SIGNED:** Dominican Republic, 2007. **SIGNED BY:** Elvio Jimenez.

The Dodgers had hoped the toolsy Baez could hold his own in the low Class A at 20 years old and in his first full pro season. But he started out 2-for-28 and the Dodgers decided the league was too fast for Baez, sending him down in mid-June. He wound up leading Ogden in homers and RBIs after being sent down, and ranked as the Rookie-level Pioneer League's No. 11 prospect. Lanky but strong, Baez has as many tools as anyone in the system, with power and a plus arm (clocked at 95 mph across the diamond), average hands and the ability to make dazzling plays at third, though his footwork can get sloppy. He can get pull-happy and out of rhythm at the plate at times, getting himself out on breaking balls, and the power will play in the majors if he learns to use the middle of the field. Having skipped straight to the U.S. after signing, he has to learn to handle the competition and daily grind; he tended to get down on himself during his struggles at Great Lakes and showed inconsistent focus. If third base doesn't work out, he can always try pitching, but the Dodgers intend to be patient with a hitter who shows such power. Baez will give low Class A another try in 2009.

Year	Club (League)	Class	AVG	G	AB	R	H	2B	3B	HR	RBI	BB	SO	SB	OBP	SLG
2007	Dodgers (GCL)	R	.274	53	201	35	55	14	2	3	39	17	40	3	.341	.408
2008	Great Lakes (MWL)	LoA	.178	59	185	23	33	10	1	1	16	17	45	3	.244	.259
	Ogden (PIO)	R	.267	61	247	37	66	20	1	12	50	18	69	2	.317	.502
MINOR LEAGUE TOTALS			.243	173	633	95	154	44	4	16	105	52	154	8	.303	.401

14 TRAVIS SCHLICHTING, RHP

BORN: Oct. 19, 1984. **B-T:** R-R. **HT.:** 6-4. **WT.:** 190. **DRAFTED:** HS—Round Rock, Texas, 2003 (4th round). **SIGNED BY:** Jonathan Bonifay (Rays).

Tampa Bay drafted Schlichting, a high school teammate of John Danks, with the first pick of the fourth round in 2003—as a lanky infielder. He played third base in the Rays and Angels systems (he was traded for Josh Paul) and eventually tried as a pitcher for five games in rookie ball 2006 before being released. He signed on with the independent Kansas City T-Bones as a pitcher and was spotted by the Dodgers. Scouting director Logan White remembered seeing Schlichting pitch once as a high schooler, and after Texas area scout Chris Smith worked out Schlichting, the Dodgers signed him in November 2007 to fill in at Double-A. There he established himself as a prospect, earning a spot on the 40-man roster this fall. Tall and strong, Schlichting throws 90-94 mph with heavy armside, bat-breaking sink from a three-quarters arm slot. He complements his fastball with an 84-86 mph slider that can have tilt and bite. His slider lacks consistency and his fastball lacks command, For a converted player, especially, he is aggressive and confident on the mound. He went to the Arizona Fall League to accelerate his development as a pitcher and work on adding depth to his slider and picked up the first three saves of his career. He's intriguing as a potential future closer though he most likely fits into a middle relief role.

Year	Club (League)	Class	W	L	ERA	G	GS	CG	SV	IP	H	R	ER	HR	BB	SO	AVG
2006	Angels (AZL)	R	0	0	0.00	5	0	0	0	8	4	0	0	0	2	13	.148
2007	Kansas City (NOR)	IND	1	2	5.29	41	0	0	0	51	72	33	30	4	29	47	.338
2008	Jacksonville (SL)	AA	6	4	3.77	33	0	0	0	60	58	31	25	4	18	49	.260
MINOR LEAGUE TOTALS			6	4	3.34	38	0	0	0	67	62	31	25	4	20	62	.248

15 STEVEN JOHNSON, RHP

BORN: Aug. 31, 1987. **B-T:** R-R. **HT.:** 6-1. **WT.:** 185. **DRAFTED:** HS—Brooklandville, Md., 2005 (13th round). **SIGNED BY:** Clair Rierson.

Johnson's father Dave pitched 77 games for Pittsburgh, Baltimore and Detroit in 1987-93 and is a broadcaster for the Orioles. After a solid Hawaii Winter Baseball performance in 2007, Johnson repeated low Class A and earned the start in the Midwest League all-star game. He was leading the league in wins when he was promoted to the California League in late June. Despite struggling there, he led the organization with 12 victories and ranked third with 112 strikeouts. Johnson has a high-effort, aggressive delivery and gets under the ball at times but shows smarts and desire on the mound, compensating for stuff that isn't eye-popping. His velocity bumped up at Inland Empire, to 90-93 mph at times, but command can be an issue. Johnson also throws a get-it-over, overhand curve, a slider with some depth and bite and an average changeup. He projects as a big league reliever or back-end starter. He'll head back to the Cal League for 2009.

Year	Club (League)	Class	W	L	ERA	G	GS	CG	SV	IP	H	R	ER	HR	BB	SO	AVG
2005	Dodgers (GCL)	R	0	2	9.53	6	3	0	0	11	18	12	12	1	4	14	.360
2006	Jacksonville (SL)	AA	0	0	0.00	2	0	0	0	5	2	0	0	0	2	3	.133
	Ogden (PIO)	R	5	5	3.89	14	14	0	0	79	79	37	34	4	25	86	.267
2007	Great Lakes (MWL)	LoA	3	6	4.85	18	16	0	0	82	90	57	44	2	40	65	.280
2008	Great Lakes (MWL)	LoA	9	2	2.34	13	13	0	0	73	59	21	19	4	25	57	.223
	Inland Empire (CAL)	HiA	3	6	7.10	11	11	0	0	52	68	47	41	9	21	55	.318
MINOR LEAGUE TOTALS			20	21	4.48	64	57	0	0	301	316	174	150	20	117	280	.272

16 XAVIER PAUL, OF

BORN: Feb. 25, 1985. **B-T:** L-R. **HT.:** 6-0. **WT.:** 200. **DRAFTED:** HS—Slidell, La., 2003 (4th round). **SIGNED BY:** Clarence Johns.

The youngest player in the Dodgers' big league camp last spring, Paul hit .347 in Triple-A after the all-star break and ended up having his best season since his 2003 pro debut. He was a high school infielder and pitcher but was moved to the outfield as a pro and to center field in 2007. Built like Jay Payton, Paul has improved his defense in center, although he still rates mediocre overall with a plus arm. Because he won't hit enough to play a corner, unless Paul's defense in center improves, he projects as a fourth outfielder and role player. Paul has some strength and can drive the ball from gap to gap, resulting in a solid-average hit tool. Although Paul shows above-average speed in the field, he needs to improve his basestealing, running more often and with a better success rate. He was gaining needed experience facing plenty of breaking stuff in the Mexican Pacific League, where he ranked among league leaders in batting and runs scored. While Paul is on the 40-man roster, he's ticketed to return to the Pacific Coast League thanks to Los Angeles' glut of outfielders.

Year	Club (League)	Class	AVG	G	AB	R	H	2B	3B	HR	RBI	BB	SO	SB	OBP	SLG
2003	Ogden (PIO)	R	.307	69	264	60	81	15	6	7	47	34	58	11	.384	.489
2004	Columbus (SAL)	LoA	.262	128	465	69	122	26	6	9	72	56	127	10	.341	.402
2005	Vero Beach (FSL)	HiA	.247	85	288	42	71	15	3	7	41	32	81	1	.328	.392
2006	Vero Beach (FSL)	HiA	.285	120	470	62	134	23	3	13	49	38	114	22	.343	.430
2007	Jacksonville (SL)	AA	.291	118	422	64	123	21	2	11	50	48	112	17	.366	.429
2008	Las Vegas (PCL)	AAA	.316	115	443	82	140	28	5	9	68	43	96	17	.378	.463
MINOR LEAGUE TOTALS			.285	635	2352	379	671	128	25	56	327	251	588	78	.356	.432

17 KYLE RUSSELL, OF

BORN: June 27, 1986. **B-T:** L-L. **HT.:** 6-5. **WT.:** 190. **DRAFTED:** Texas, 2008 (3rd round). **SIGNED BY:** Chris Smith.

Russell turned down a reported $800,000 offer from the Cardinals as a fourth-round pick in 2007, when he led NCAA Division I with 28 homers as a draft-eligible sophomore at Texas. He hit 19 homers as a junior, giving him the Longhorns career record of 57, and Los Angeles signed him for $410,000. Long, lean and athletic, Russell is a high-risk, high-reward pick. He has long levers and generates tremendous raw power but has many holes in his swing. He had significant struggles throughout his amateur career when using wood bats, from the Area Code Games in high school to summer college circuits such as the Cape Cod League (where he struck out in more than half his at-bats in 2006). He also gets pull-happy at times and will probably never hit for a high average. With a narrow build, he tends to use his quick hands and not his body, but more strength may come in the future. His swing is short despite his long arms and he hangs in well against lefty pitching. Russell is already a major league-caliber defender in right field and can play center if needed, with good instincts in the outfield, an above-average arm and average speed. Russell should begin 2009 in low Class A.

Year	Club (League)	Class	AVG	G	AB	R	H	2B	3B	HR	RBI	BB	SO	SB	OBP	SLG
2008	Ogden (PIO)	R	.279	61	219	46	61	13	5	11	46	27	82	4	.365	.534
MINOR LEAGUE TOTALS			.279	61	219	46	61	13	5	11	46	27	82	4	.365	.534

18 JON MICHAEL REDDING, RHP

BORN: Nov. 16, 1987. **B-T:** R-R. **HT.:** 6-1. **WT.:** 195. **DRAFTED:** Florida CC, 2008 (5th round). **SIGNED BY:** Scott Hennessey.

Redding attended Lowndes County High, the same south Georgia school that produced J.D. and Stephen Drew. Redding pitched two seasons at Florida CC, earning first-team all-state and conference pitcher of the year honors as a sophomore, going 8-5, 2.02. He had accepted an offer from Louisiana State, but he signed with Los Angeles as a fifth-round pick for $178,000 and went to the Pioneer League, where the Dodgers opted to limit his innings after a heavy juco workload (125 innings, including five complete games). His fastball sits at 90-92 mph with good movement and touches 94. The Dodgers like his slider, although he needs to get a consistent release point with that pitch. His curve is hard, 77-79 mph, and he has the beginnings of a changeup. Redding's greatest strength is that he repeats his delivery and his arm action is clean, allowing him to throw strikes consistently. Redding also shows competitiveness, strength and athleticism. Despite his excellent juco season, he wasn't a consensus fifth-round talent due to his college commitment and shorter frame. His command could enable him to move quickly through the system and top out as a No. 3 starter in the majors.

Year	Club (League)	Class	W	L	ERA	G	GS	CG	SV	IP	H	R	ER	HR	BB	SO	AVG
2008	Ogden (PIO)	R	0	4	5.17	13	9	0	0	31	39	26	18	4	11	36	.305
MINOR LEAGUE TOTALS			0	4	5.17	13	9	0	0	31	39	26	18	4	11	36	.305

19 TONY DELMONICO, C/2B

BORN: April 27, 1987. **B-T:** R-R. **HT.:** 6-0. **WT.:** 195. **DRAFTED:** Florida State, 2008 (6th round). **SIGNED BY:** Scott Hennessey.

The 2008 draft was the first time teams had a chance to select Delmonico, who enrolled at Tennessee as a freshman a semester early, graduating high school in December. That gave him a chance to play for his father Rod, who was the head coach of the Volunteers for 18 years, but he was fired after Tony's sophomore season. Father and son both headed to Florida State, Rod as a volunteer assistant coach and Tony as a shortstop—even though Tony had lost the shortstop job at Tennessee. Scouts long have sought to try Delmonico, an intelligent and scrappy player, at catcher for years. After signing him for $150,000 as a sixth-round pick, the Dodgers gave him a chance to stay in the infield at Ogden, but after 10 errors in 30 games at second base, Delmonico began the conversion to catching in instructional league and impressed the Dodgers with how well he handled it. He has the arm for the position and showed good hands, an ability to call a game and leadership skills in his first weeks behind the plate. But he has to work on his footwork, pitch-blocking skills, setup and exchange on throwing out runners. His offensive approach is sound—aggressive but with strike-zone judgment—as he uses the gaps and shows raw pull power. Delmonico's future and timetable all hinge on his ability to grasp his new position. He'll have to make defensive progress to earn a spot in low Class A this season.

Year	Club (League)	Class	AVG	G	AB	R	H	2B	3B	HR	RBI	BB	SO	SB	OBP	SLG
2008	Ogden (PIO)	R	.340	35	141	38	48	20	0	11	39	18	28	0	.443	.716
MINOR LEAGUE TOTALS			.340	35	141	38	48	20	0	11	39	18	28	0	.443	.716

20 JUSTIN MILLER, RHP

BORN: Aug. 2, 1987. **B-T:** R-R. **HT.:** 6-3. **WT.:** 190. **DRAFTED:** Johnson County (Kan.) CC, 2007 (6th round). **SIGNED BY:** Mitch Webster.

Also a right fielder in college, Miller caught the Dodgers' eyes just before the draft when he hit 93 mph in relief, and did it again with seven shutout innings in a start against they Yankees in the Gulf Coast League playoffs. He became Great Lakes' Opening Day starter last year. Miller came within two outs of a no-hitter in August, a game the Loons eventually lost 3-2—typical of Miller's season. Despite an awful record, he ranked fifth in the organization in ERA at 3.99. Miller's two-way background has left him somewhat raw an inexperienced as a pitcher—he threw just 18 innings in juco ball—yet he makes up for it by being a good athlete with tough makeup. He features a heavy 88-92 mph sinker and throws a groundball-inducing slider, and got 2.77 groundouts for every airout in 2008. He can be inconsistent with his arm slot as he continues to learn proper mechanics, and that inconsistency led to an ugly 74-82 walk-strikeout ratio. Miller's changeup has come a long way but is still a work in progress, although he has shown a feel for it at times. If it all comes together, he could be a middle-of-the-rotation starter, but because of his lack of experience on the mound he may not develop quickly.

Year	Club (League)	Class	W	L	ERA	G	GS	CG	SV	IP	H	R	ER	HR	BB	SO	AVG
2007	Dodgers (GCL)	R	2	1	3.57	7	4	0	1	18	22	10	7	0	2	12	.306
2008	Great Lakes (MWL)	LoA	4	11	3.99	27	25	0	0	140	132	76	62	6	74	82	.250
MINOR LEAGUE TOTALS			6	12	3.94	34	29	0	1	158	154	86	69	6	76	94	.257

21 BRENT LEACH, LHP

BORN: Nov. 18, 1982. **B-T:** L-L. **HT.:** 6-5. **WT.:** 213. **DRAFTED:** Delta State (Miss.), 2005 (6th round). **SIGNED BY:** Dennis Moeller.

Leach, who had Tommy John surgery in college before transferring from Southern Mississippi to NCAA Division II Delta State, also has to deal with hyperhidrosis, a medical condition in which a person sweats excessively and unpredictably. He gets treatment with mild electric shocks to his hands. He's overcome both maladies to earn a spot on the 40-man roster. Limited in 2007 by a torn lat (side) muscle, Leach—who led the Pioneer League with a 2.43 ERA in 2005—began last year by repeating high Class A, but he earned a promotion just a month into the season and took over as closer in Jacksonville. Leach throws a 90-92 mph fastball with an average curve and a changeup that improved last year to where it can be considered a plus pitch. He also has an excellent pickoff move. His weakness is command, which is the result of an inconsistent delivery, and it continued to be an issue in the Arizona Fall League. If Leach can improve his control, he has the stuff to reach the majors as soon as 2009.

Year	Club (League)	Class	W	L	ERA	G	GS	CG	SV	IP	H	R	ER	HR	BB	SO	AVG
2005	Ogden (PIO)	R	5	3	2.43	14	13	1	0	67	53	21	18	4	29	77	.227
2006	Columbus (SAL)	LoA	4	2	3.27	10	10	0	0	52	41	22	19	2	31	67	.230
	Vero Beach (FSL)	HiA	3	4	4.56	30	0	0	1	49	48	34	25	1	32	57	.265
2007	Inland Empire (CAL)	HiA	0	0	0.45	14	0	0	4	20	14	2	1	1	11	23	.203
2008	Inland Empire (CAL)	HiA	0	1	1.35	9	0	0	3	13	11	2	2	0	4	13	.239
	Jacksonville (SL)	AA	2	2	2.88	40	0	0	12	59	44	23	19	2	34	49	.215
MINOR LEAGUE TOTALS			14	12	2.90	117	23	1	20	261	211	104	84	10	141	286	.231

22 JAMIE HOFFMANN, OF

BORN: Aug. 20, 1984. **B-T:** R-R. **HT.:** 6-3. **WT.:** 221. **SIGNED:** HS—New Ulm, Minn., NDFA 2003. **SIGNED BY:** Jeff Schugel.

An eighth-round pick of the NHL's Carolina Hurricanes in 2003 with a linebacker's body, Hoffman nearly went to Colorado College to play hockey before signing with the Dodgers. He homered in his only at-bat in big league camp in the spring but started last year 2-for-22 with Jacksonville. He rallied and earned a spot in the Southern League all-star game. Hoffman can play all three outfield positions—center field capably—with a throwing arm and speed that grade out as average or a tick above, and he gets good jumps and runs good routes. He remains one of the Dodgers' best defensive outfielders. Mostly a gap hitter, he has some power but has an open stance and sometimes loses his timing in his swing. When he's out of rhythm, his swing gets long. An overachiever who does a lot of things well but not great, Hoffman went to the Arizona Fall League after the season and hit safely in 10 of the 11 games he played. If he learns to hit lefthanders with more authority—he has just 21 extra-base hits and three homers off lefthanders the last four full seasons—he could hit enough to be a regular. The Dodgers love his desire, drive and grinder mentality, likely earning him a trip to Triple-A for 2009.

Year	Club (League)	Class	AVG	G	AB	R	H	2B	3B	HR	RBI	BB	SO	SB	OBP	SLG
2005	Columbus (SAL)	LoA	.308	79	321	53	99	13	9	1	24	39	73	10	.383	.414
	Vero Beach (FSL)	HiA	.241	46	166	26	40	6	2	1	10	10	45	3	.287	.319
2006	Vero Beach (FSL)	HiA	.252	121	433	50	109	16	0	5	29	35	94	15	.309	.323
	Las Vegas (PCL)	AAA	.300	4	10	0	3	0	0	0	0	1	3	1	.417	.300
2007	Inland Empire (CAL)	HiA	.309	116	433	67	134	22	7	9	81	47	70	19	.378	.455
2008	Jacksonville (SL)	AA	.278	133	478	64	133	20	3	10	71	54	73	28	.350	.395
MINOR LEAGUE TOTALS			.281	499	1841	260	518	77	21	26	215	186	358	76	.348	.388

23 DAIGORO RONDON, RHP

BORN: Nov. 4, 1986. **B-T:** R-R. **HT.:** 6-2. **WT.:** 163. **SIGNED:** Dominican Republic, 2004. **SIGNED BY:** Ezequiel Sepulveda/Andres Lopez.

After Rondon spent three years in the Rookie-level Dominican Summer League and then excelled in 2007 in the Gulf Coast League, the Dodgers pushed him to a full-season league for the first time. Rondon opened in the Midwest League, but after getting knocked around and moved to the bullpen, he was sent down to Rookie-level Ogden for the final month to pitch in relief. There he held hitters to a .207 average, adding 4⅓ scoreless innings in the playoffs. Rondon has an electric arm, throwing 92-96 mph with good movement on his fastball and complementing it with a sound, power slider. He continued to improve in instructional league. Rondon stays around the plate but can be immature on the mound at times, getting stubborn about pitching up in the strike zone, making him easy to read at times for hitters. His progress will be a matter of getting innings in and maturing. He'll give low Class A another shot in 2009.

Year	Club (League)	Class	W	L	ERA	G	GS	CG	SV	IP	H	R	ER	HR	BB	SO	AVG
2004	Dodgers1 (DSL)	R	0	6	9.35	7	6	0	0	17	36	24	18	2	12	20	.409
2005	Dodgers (DSL)	R	4	3	3.04	13	12	0	0	56	47	22	19	3	19	56	.229
2006	Dodgers (DSL)	R	6	4	3.07	14	12	0	1	67	58	33	23	3	21	53	.226
2007	Dodgers (GCL)	R	7	2	2.77	12	7	1	1	65	68	22	20	1	4	59	.275
2008	Great Lakes (MWL)	LoA	4	11	6.96	21	11	0	0	74	113	64	57	7	28	82	.345
	Ogden (PIO)	R	1	0	1.17	5	0	0	0	8	6	1	1	0	2	11	.207
MINOR LEAGUE TOTALS			22	26	4.32	72	48	1	2	287	328	166	138	16	86	281	.284

24 VICTOR GARATE, LHP

BORN: Sept. 25, 1984. **B-T:** L-L. **HT.:** 6-2. **WT.:** 185. **SIGNED:** Venezuela, 2001. **SIGNED BY:** Andres Reiner/Pablo Torrealba (Astros).

After seven years with the Astros organization and just 26 appearances in full-season leagues, Garate finally experienced success in pro ball after switching organizations. The Dodgers acquired him in the Triple-A portion of the 2007 Rule 5 draft for $12,000. By mid-May he moved into the low Class A rotation, striking out 12 in one July start. He was promoted to the high Class A California League on July 22 and by the end of the season led Dodgers farmhands in ERA (2.79) and strikeouts (150). No full-season pitcher who threw more than 100 innings in 2008 exceeded Garate's average of 11.6 strikeouts per nine innings. Aggressive and competitive, he throws 89-92 mph, harder than he did with Houston, with good finish from a low-three-quarters delivery. His lack of athleticism leads in part to below-average command. The fastball moves in on lefthanders and his sweeping slider, while flat at times, can be effective against lefthanders. He also throws a changeup. The gutsy Garate, who spent the winter as a reliever in Venezuela, projects as a poor man's Brian Fuentes. He should move up to Double-A in 2009.

Year	Club (League)	Class	W	L	ERA	G	GS	CG	SV	IP	H	R	ER	HR	BB	SO	AVG
2002	Venoco (VSL)	R	1	3	1.98	13	0	0	2	27	22	8	6	0	10	22	.222
2003	Venoco (VSL)	R	3	1	1.39	12	12	0	0	71	39	14	11	3	18	65	.163
2004	Venoco 1 (VSL)	R	3	2	1.53	9	5	1	1	35	26	11	6	0	10	42	.215
2005	Greeneville (APP)	R	4	1	5.57	19	0	0	0	32	21	20	20	2	26	53	.189
2006	Tri-City (NYP)	SS	4	0	0.92	21	0	0	8	39	14	6	4	2	21	59	.112
2007	Lexington (SAL)	LoA	3	1	6.43	26	0	0	1	42	47	32	30	3	35	41	.292
	Tri-City (NYP)	SS	3	1	3.31	17	0	0	2	33	31	15	12	4	7	45	.242
2008	Great Lakes (MWL)	LoA	6	3	1.85	17	12	0	0	78	61	22	16	4	28	103	.215
	Inland Empire (CAL)	HiA	3	0	4.70	7	7	0	0	38	44	20	20	6	14	47	.289
MINOR LEAGUE TOTALS			30	12	2.84	141	36	1	14	396	305	148	125	24	169	477	.215

25 JAVY GUERRA, RHP

BORN: Oct. 31, 1985. **B-T:** R-R. **HT.:** 6-1. **WT.:** 196. **DRAFTED:** HS—Denton, Texas, 2004 (4th round). **SIGNED BY:** Mike Leuzinger.

During a second straight season in high Class A, Guerra made progress in 2008. Still rounding into form after 2005 Tommy John surgery, he moved to the bullpen, better suited for his aggressive power arsenal, and made a solid impression in Hawaii Winter Baseball, where he had one of the league's harder fastballs. A bit undersized, Guerra has a quick arm that produces a hard but straight fastball at 89-93 mph, occasionally hitting 96. His command was off last year as he had a delivery flaw with his lead leg, and his mechanics have been a work in progress since removing crow hop he had in his motion as an amateur. He has a slider, a changeup and a curveball that can be above-average at times, but he needs to improve his control of all his pitches, his feel for pitching and his maturity. At times in the past he hasn't taken the game as seriously as he needs to. Guerra passed through the Rule 5 draft unscathed and should head to Double-A in 2009.

Year	Club (League)	Class	W	L	ERA	G	GS	CG	SV	IP	H	R	ER	HR	BB	SO	AVG
2004	Dodgers (GCL)	R	4	1	3.38	11	9	0	0	40	31	18	15	3	19	36	.214
2005	Columbus (SAL)	LoA	2	5	4.96	11	11	0	0	53	51	35	29	3	23	40	.249
2006	Ogden (PIO)	R	1	3	4.82	7	7	0	0	28	37	18	15	1	20	22	.330
2007	Inland Empire (CAL)	HiA	6	9	6.27	27	24	0	1	118	139	98	82	10	80	121	.296
2008	Inland Empire (CAL)	HiA	5	4	4.07	31	3	0	2	66	68	34	30	0	44	63	.262
MINOR LEAGUE TOTALS			18	22	5.05	87	54	0	3	305	326	203	171	17	186	282	.273

26 JAMES ADKINS, LHP

BORN: Nov. 26, 1985. **B-T:** L-L. **HT.:** 6-5. **WT.:** 195. **DRAFTED:** Tennessee, 2007 (1st round supplemental). **SIGNED BY:** Marty Lamb.

Signed for $787,500 in 2007 after becoming Tennessee's all-time strikeout leader, Adkins actually pitched better after a late-July promotion to Double-A in his first full pro season last year. Limited to short outings in his first pro season because of his heavy workload in college, he shied away from using his below-average fastball and as a result didn't throw enough strikes. His big 11-to-5 curve and slider both have a chance to become plus pitches. But Adkins is tall, awkward and unathletic. Comparable to Brian Tallet, Adkins needs to work on using his fastball, even though it has below-average 87-89 mph velocity, and commanding it in the strike zone. He just hasn't thrown enough fastballs to learn to command the pitch yet. He does throw downhill and earns high marks for his improved work habits and good competitiveness. With improved strength and endurance, Adkins profiles as a back-end starter in the Doug Davis mold. If that fails, his pair of breaking balls makes him a potential relief specialist. He's headed back to Double-A in 2009.

Year	Club (League)	Class	W	L	ERA	G	GS	CG	SV	IP	H	R	ER	HR	BB	SO	AVG
2007	Great Lakes (MWL)	LoA	0	1	2.42	11	11	0	0	26	17	7	7	1	10	30	.181
2008	Inland Empire (CAL)	HiA	5	8	5.34	19	18	0	0	88	106	64	52	6	38	75	.295
	Jacksonville (SL)	AA	1	3	4.74	8	8	0	0	38	42	24	20	5	28	25	.269
MINOR LEAGUE TOTALS			6	12	4.69	38	37	0	0	152	165	95	79	12	76	130	.271

27 ALFREDO SILVERIO, OF

BORN: May 6, 1987. **B-T:** R-R. **HT.:** 6-2. **WT.:** 164. **SIGNED:** Dominican Republic, 2003. **SIGNED BY:** Angel Santana.

A year after leading the Gulf Coast League in average (.373), hits (72) and RBI (46) in 2007, Silverio seemed on the verge of a breakout season. He began 2008 in extended spring training due to a tender shoulder, as the Dodgers held him back from the cold of the Midwest League. He then joined Great Lakes in early May and found tougher sledding than he had in Rookie ball. He was at his best down the stretch, hitting .304 with 15 RBI over his final 25 games. As a free swinger who rarely walks (53 in 291 career games), he remains a project who is still a long way away from the majors. Silverio, who has drawn physical comparisons to George Bell, has a chance to hit for power if his approach improves. And while his arm is well above-average, the rest of his defense needs work. The Dodgers sent him to Hawaii Winter Baseball with an emphasis on quality at-bats—working the count and getting a good pitch to hit. He held up fairly well under the long grind. The Dodgers see Silverio as a strong, physical corner outfielder, and that projection depends mostly on his plate discipline. He's headed to high Class A in 2009.

Year	Club (League)	Class	AVG	G	AB	R	H	2B	3B	HR	RBI	BB	SO	SB	OBP	SLG
2004	Dodgers2 (DSL)	R	.240	59	192	18	46	6	2	1	16	7	36	5	.273	.307
2005	Dodgers (DSL)	R	.244	25	82	11	20	2	0	1	14	10	15	2	.316	.305
2006	Dodgers (DSL)	R	.276	61	225	36	62	12	6	6	48	18	44	6	.335	.462
2007	Dodgers (GCL)	R	.373	51	193	38	72	9	3	6	46	11	32	5	.406	.544
2008	Great Lakes (MWL)	LoA	.263	95	376	37	99	15	4	10	45	7	83	6	.279	.404
MINOR LEAGUE TOTALS			.280	291	1068	140	299	44	15	24	169	53	210	24	.316	.417

28 LUCAS MAY, C

BORN: Oct. 24, 1984. **B-T:** R-R. **HT.:** 6-0. **WT.:** 190. **DRAFTED:** HS—Ballwin, Mo., 2003 (8th round). **SIGNED BY:** Mitch Webster.

After moving from shortstop to outfield in 2005, May converted to catcher in 2007 and was added to the 40-man roster in 2008. After a big season in the California League he spent time in big league camp but surprised the organization when he struggled with Double-A pitching, offensively and defensively in 2008. May's inexperience shows behind the plate; he is still learning how to handle a pitching staff and how to call a game. Like a smaller version of Michael Barrett, he has the athleticism, arm strength and agility but his catching and throwing, while improving, still need sharpening. He committed 24 passed balls last year after 31 in 2007, and threw out just 29 percent of basestealers last season. His athletic ability has helped him make some adjustments, and while the Dodgers love May's makeup, he has lost weight and needs to work on maintaining his strength at his new position. May, who played against Blake DeWitt in their high-school days, has good bat speed and very good power potential but doesn't make adjustments at the plate and gets power-happy, chasing breaking balls away. He'll return to Double-A searching for more consistency in all phases of the game this season.

Year	Club (League)	Class	AVG	G	AB	R	H	2B	3B	HR	RBI	BB	SO	SB	OBP	SLG
2003	Dodgers (GCL)	R	.252	48	159	19	40	8	0	0	10	19	38	11	.350	.302
2004	Ogden (PIO)	R	.286	34	147	25	42	5	2	5	30	8	37	4	.329	.449
2005	Columbus (SAL)	LoA	.229	99	385	46	88	14	2	9	53	16	92	5	.267	.345
2006	Columbus (SAL)	LoA	.273	119	450	76	123	27	9	18	82	35	130	14	.332	.493
2007	Inland Empire (CAL)	HiA	.256	128	507	81	130	25	3	25	89	36	107	5	.313	.465
2008	Jacksonville (SL)	AA	.230	107	392	54	90	27	1	13	54	32	112	6	.294	.403
MINOR LEAGUE TOTALS			.251	535	2040	301	513	106	17	70	318	146	516	45	.309	.423

29 JOSH WALL, RHP

BORN: Jan. 21, 1987. **B-T:** R-R. **HT.:** 6-6. **WT.:** 192. **DRAFTED:** HS—Baker, La., 2005 (2nd round). **SIGNED BY:** Dennis Moeller.

Maturity has been an issue for Wall, who signed for $480,000 after he was drafted between Kevin Slowey and Yunel Escobar. Wall is tall and rangy, built like Aaron Sele, and while he can hit 95-96 mph with good arm action he sometimes sits at 88-91, just major league average. He has a curve that has some tilt and depth that long has been his best pitch, another facet that earns him comparisons to Sele. He also throws a slider and a changeup. Some days Wall is unhittable; some days everything is over the plate. He was pushed to high Class A at 19 last year and wasn't aggressive enough in the strike zone. Wall is still learning the nuances of being a professional, such as having a between-starts routine and how to study hitters. If Wall matures physically and mentally, he could be a middle-to-back-of-the-rotation starter, and to this point, his best asset has been durability, as he's thrown 258 innings the last two seasons combined. He's most likely headed back to Inland Empire for 2009.

Year	Club (League)	Class	W	L	ERA	G	GS	CG	SV	IP	H	R	ER	HR	BB	SO	AVG
2005	Dodgers (GCL)	R	1	3	3.86	5	4	0	0	14	13	8	6	2	8	5	.245
2006	Ogden (PIO)	R	3	5	5.86	14	14	0	0	66	80	56	43	5	33	41	.305
2007	Great Lakes (MWL)	LoA	6	10	4.18	26	24	1	1	129	136	71	60	8	48	103	.269
2008	Inland Empire (CAL)	HiA	9	6	6.28	27	25	0	0	129	152	92	90	12	63	101	.297
MINOR LEAGUE TOTALS			19	24	5.29	72	67	1	1	338	381	227	199	27	152	250	.286

30 JORDAN PRATT, RHP

BORN: May 17, 1985. **B-T:** R-R. **HT.:** 6-3. **WT.:** 195. **DRAFTED:** HS—Independence, Ore., 2003 (5th round). **SIGNED BY:** Hank Jones.

Pratt has yet to progress past Class A and passed through the Rule 5 draft unscathed, yet the Dodgers remain excited about his potential. He was the No. 2-ranked player in Oregon in the 2003 draft behind fellow prep righty Dallas Buck, who went on to star at Oregon State. Pratt signed out of high school and has made slow progress harnessing his electric arsenal. His fastball runs up to 94 mph, and it features natural cutting action that makes it a buzzsaw against lefthanders. They posted a .589 OPS against Pratt in the hitter-friendly California League with two extra-base hits, and he held them to a 2-for-35 mark in Hawaii Winter Baseball. Pratt also has a power curveball and short, sharp slider that grade out as average to above-average as well. The problem is command, as he ranked third in the Cal League in walks even while making only one start, and his 21 wild pitches led the league. Scouts who saw Pratt in Hawaii said he showed better control there by being more consistent keeping his front shoulder closed. He tends to over-analyze his mistakes rather than making quick adjustments. The Dodgers hope to push him to Double-A in 2009.

Year	Club (League)	Class	W	L	ERA	G	GS	CG	SV	IP	H	R	ER	HR	BB	SO	AVG
2003	Ogden (PIO)	R	0	9	7.69	16	8	0	0	46	65	54	39	4	18	31	.325
2004	Ogden (PIO)	R	2	6	9.50	12	12	0	0	48	74	60	51	7	36	46	.363
2005	Ogden (PIO)	R	2	2	3.25	14	0	0	0	28	24	12	10	0	14	35	.235
	Columbus (SAL)	LoA	0	1	6.06	6	1	0	0	16	13	13	11	1	11	14	.213
2006	Columbus (SAL)	LoA	8	4	4.85	34	1	0	0	78	76	46	42	1	58	83	.254
2007	Inland Empire (CAL)	HiA	3	5	6.72	44	0	0	0	83	77	69	62	2	75	94	.249
2008	Inland Empire (CAL)	HiA	4	3	4.83	42	1	0	2	69	49	38	37	2	67	80	.203
MINOR LEAGUE TOTALS			19	30	6.16	168	23	0	2	368	378	292	252	17	279	383	.267

Milwaukee Brewers

BY TOM HAUDRICOURT

The Brewers farm system already had provided the big league club with a homegrown infield (Prince Fielder, Rickie Weeks, J.J. Hardy, Bill Hall), a pair of slugging corner outfielders (Ryan Braun, Corey Hart) and an ace in the making (Yovani Gallardo). It kept on giving in 2008, providing the ammunition for Milwaukee to acquire C.C. Sabathia.

Not many clubs would trade their top prospect for a rental, but that's exactly what the Brewers did in early July. They included outfielder Matt LaPorta, their 2007 first-round pick who was tearing up Double-A, with lefty Zach Jackson, righty Rob Bryson

and a player to be named (outfielder Michael Brantley) to get Sabathia, a pending free agent.

The Brewers figured Sabathia was just the pitcher to get them over the top and into the post-season for the first time since 1982. He was everything Milwaukee hoped for and more, going 11-2, 1.65 and pitching a four-hitter against the Cubs on the final day of the season to clinch a wild-card berth.

Though Sabathia, BA's Major League Player of the Year, lost his lone playoff start as the Phillies eliminated the Brewers in the National League Division Series and later left for a $161 million contract from the Yankees, general manager Doug Melvin said he'd make the trade again.

"We have no regrets," Melvin said. "The fact that we were able to make the deal is a tribute to the depth of talent in our farm system."

Even with the trades and graduations to the majors, the system continues to churn out talent. Manny Parra won 10 games as a rookie, and in a preview of coming attractions, shortstop Alcides Escobar, third baseman Mat Gamel and catcher Angel Salome made their big league debuts in September. Milwaukee was able to restock through the draft, where compensation for the loss of free agents Francisco Cordero and Scott Linebrink gave the club six of the first 62 selections in June. After popping Canadian prep slugger Brett Lawrie in the first round, the Brewers focused on pitching. The Brewers may have a similar bonanza in 2009, when they'll get two early picks for Sabathia and as many as three more if both Ben Sheets and Brian Shouse also leave via free agency.

But for the first time in nine years, Jack Zduriencik won't be running their draft. The Mariners hired Zduriencik, the scouting director who was BA's 2007 Executive of the Year, as their GM in October. Zduriencik took two of his top lieutenants, assistant

Athletic slugger Ryan Braun helped the Brew Crew to its first playoff berth since 1982

TOP 30 PROSPECTS

1. Alcides Escobar, ss	16. Lee Haydel, of
2. Mat Gamel, 3b	17. Brent Brewer, ss
3. Brett Lawrie, c/3b	18. R.J. Seidel, rhp
4. Jeremy Jeffress, rhp	19. Eduardo Morlan, rhp
5. Angel Salome, c	20. Seth Lintz, rhp
6. Lorenzo Cain, of	21. Omar Aguilar, rhp
7. Cutter Dykstra, of	22. Wily Peralta, rhp
8. Taylor Green, 3b	23. Efrain Nieves, lhp
9. Cole Gillespie, of	24. Evan Frederickson, lhp
10. Jonathan Lucroy, c	25. Luis Pena, rhp
11. Jake Odorizzi, rhp	26. Amaury Rivas, rhp
12. Zach Braddock, lhp	27. Eric Farris, 2b
13. Alexandre Periard, rhp	28. Cody Adams, rhp
14. Caleb Gindl, of	29. Logan Schafer, of
15. Cody Scarpetta, rhp	30. Tim Dillard, rhp

scouting director Tony Blengino and East crosschecker Tom McNamara, with him to Seattle. The Brewers promoted West crosschecker Bruce Seid to replace Zduriencik and tabbed Midwest crosschecker Ray Montgomery as Seid's assistant.

Milwaukee will enter 2009 with a new manager as well. Owner Mark Attanasio made the decision to fire Ned Yost due to a September swoon, and interim manager Dale Sveum wasn't retained. The Brewers then turned to Ken Macha, who had a .568 winning percentage and captured two division titles in four years with the Athletics from 2003-06.

General Manager: Doug Melvin. **Farm Director:** Reid Nichols. **Scouting Director:** Bruce Seid.

Class	Team	League	W	L	PCT	Finish*	Manager	Affiliated
Majors	Milwaukee	National	90	72	.556	3rd (16)	N. Yost/D. Sveum	—
Triple-A	Nashville Sounds	Pacific Coast	59	81	.421	16th (16)	Frank Kremblas	2005
Double-A	Huntsville Stars	Southern	73	67	.521	4th (10)	Don Money	1999
High A	Brevard County Manatees	Florida State	66	72	.478	8th (12)	Mike Guerrero	2005
Low A	West Virginia Power	South Atlantic	77	62	.554	6th (16)	Jeff Isom	2003
Rookie	Helena Brewers	Pioneer	35	41	.461	6th (8)	Rene Gonzales	2003
Rookie	AZL Brewers	Arizona	13	42	.236	9th (9)	Tony Diggs	2001
Overall 2008 Minor League Record			323	365	.469	26th		

* Finish in overall standings (No. of teams in league). ^League champion.

LAST YEAR'S TOP 30

Rank	Player, Pos.	Status
1.	Matt LaPorta, of	(Indians)
2.	Manny Parra, lhp	Majors
3.	Alcides Escobar, ss	No. 1
4.	Jeremy Jeffress, rhp	No. 4
5.	Mat Gamel, 3b	No. 2
6.	Cole Gillespie, of	No. 9
7.	Brent Brewer, ss	No. 17
8.	Angel Salome, c	No. 5
9.	Lorenzo Cain, of	No. 6
10.	Caleb Gindl, of	No. 14
11.	Rob Bryson, rhp	(Indians)
12.	Mark Rogers, rhp	Dropped out
13.	Zach Braddock, lhp	No. 12
14.	Luis Pena, rhp	No. 25
15.	R.J. Seidel, rhp	No. 18
16.	Jonathan Lucroy, c	No. 10
17.	Taylor Green, 3b	No. 8
18.	Cody Scarpetta, rhp	No. 15
19.	Nick Tyson, rhp	Dropped out
20.	Alexandre Periard, rhp	No. 13
21.	Darren Ford, of	(Giants)
22.	Lee Haydel, of	No. 16
23.	Eric Farris, 2b	No. 27
24.	Michael Brantley, of/1b	(Indians)
25.	Stephen Chapman, of	Dropped out
26.	Hernan Iribarren, 2b	Dropped out
27.	Steve Hammond, lhp	(Giants)
28.	Charlie Fermaint, of	Dropped out
29.	Chris Errecart, 1b	Dropped out
30.	Brendan Katin, of	Dropped out

BEST TOOLS

Best Hitter for Average	Mat Gamel
Best Power Hitter	Brett Lawrie
Best Strike-Zone Discipline	Taylor Green
Fastest Baserunner	Lee Haydel
Best Athlete	Brent Brewer
Best Fastball	Jeremy Jeffress
Best Curveball	Cody Scarpetta
Best Slider	Zach Braddock
Best Changeup	Bobby Bramhall
Best Control	Chris Cody
Best Defensive Catcher	Carlos Corporan
Best Defensive Infielder	Alcides Escobar
Best Infield Arm	Alcides Escobar
Best Defensive Outfielder	Lorenzo Cain
Best Outfield Arm	Brendan Katin

PROJECTED 2012 LINEUP

Catcher	Brett Lawrie
First Base	Prince Fielder
Second Base	J.J. Hardy
Third Base	Mat Gamel
Shortstop	Alcides Escobar
Left Field	Ryan Braun
Center Field	Rickie Weeks
Right Field	Corey Hart
No. 1 Starter	Yovani Gallardo
No. 2 Starter	Manny Parra
No. 3 Starter	Jake Odorizzi
No. 4 Starter	Carlos Villanueva
No. 5 Starter	Zach Braddock
Closer	Jeremy Jeffress

TOP PROSPECTS OF THE DECADE

Year	Player, Pos.	2008 Org.
1999	Ron Belliard, 2b	Nationals
2000	Nick Neugebauer, rhp	Out of baseball
2001	Ben Sheets, rhp	Brewers
2002	Nick Neugebauer, rhp	Out of baseball
2003	Brad Nelson, 1b	Brewers
2004	Rickie Weeks, 2b	Brewers
2005	Rickie Weeks, 2b	Brewers
2006	Prince Fielder, 1b	Brewers
2007	Yovani Gallardo, rhp	Brewers
2008	Matt LaPorta, of	Indians

TOP DRAFT PICKS OF THE DECADE

Year	Player, Pos.	2008 Org.
1999	Ben Sheets, rhp	Brewers
2000	Dave Krynzel, of	Diamondbacks
2001	Mike Jones, rhp	Brewers
2002	Prince Fielder, 1b	Brewers
2003	Rickie Weeks, 2b	Brewers
2004	Mark Rogers, rhp	Brewers
2005	Ryan Braun, 3b	Brewers
2006	Jeremy Jeffress, rhp	Brewers
2007	Matt LaPorta, of	Indians
2008	Brett Lawrie, c/3b	Brewers

LARGEST BONUSES IN CLUB HISTORY

Rickie Weeks, 2003	$3,600,000
Ben Sheets, 1999	$2,450,000
Ryan Braun, 2005	$2,450,000
Prince Fielder, 2002	$2,400,000
Mark Rogers, 2004	$2,200,000

MILWAUKEE BREWERS

TOP 2009 ROOKIE: Alcides Escobar, ss. It's going to be difficult to keep him in the minors, especially now that his offense has started to catch up to his major league-ready defense.

BREAKOUT PROSPECT: Cody Scarpetta, rhp. Fully recovered from a finger injury that delayed his entrance into pro ball, he's an aggressive pitcher with the stuff to move quickly.

SLEEPER: Steffan Wilson, 1b. In a system not exactly overflowing with power, Wilson had 51 extra-base hits and 100 RBIs in low Class A last season.

SOURCE OF TOP 30 TALENT			
Homegrown	29	Acquired	1
College	6	Trades	0
Junior college	2	Rule 5 draft	1
High school	12	Independent leagues	0
Draft-and-follow	5	Free agents/waivers	0
Nondrafted free agents	0		
International	4		

Numbers in parentheses indicate prospect rankings.

LF
Cole Gillespie (9)
Caleb Gindl (14)
Chuckie Caufield
Eric Fryer

CF
Lorenzo Cain (6)
Cutter Dykstra (7)
Lee Haydel (16)
Logan Schafer (29)
Charlie Fermaint

RF
Erik Komatsu
Brendan Katin
Freddy Parejo

3B
Mat Gamel (2)
Taylor Green (8)
Adam Heether
Zelous Wheeler
John Delaney

SS
Alcides Escobar (1)
Brent Brewer (17)
Yohannis Perez
Matt Cline
Jose Duran
Michael Marseco
Carlos George

2B
Eric Farris (27)
Hernan Iribarren
Mike Bell
Kenny Holmberg
Jimmy Mojica

1B
Brad Nelson
Steffan Wilson
Chris Errecart
Stephen Chapman
Curt Rindal
Brock Kjeldgaard

C
Brett Lawrie (3)
Angel Salome (5)
Jonathan Lucroy (10)
Vinny Rottino
Carlos Corporan
Martin Maldonado
Andy Bouchie

RHP

Starters	Relievers
Jeremy Jeffress (4)	Eduardo Morlan (19)
Jake Odorizzi (11)	Omar Aguilar (21)
Alexandre Periard (13)	Wily Peralta (22)
Cody Scarpetta (15)	Luis Pena (25)
R.J. Seidel (18)	Tim Dillard (30)
Seth Lintz (20)	Joe Bateman
Amaury Rivas (26)	Steve Bray
Cody Adams (28)	Robert Hinton
Mark DiFelice	Dave Johnson
Donovan Hand	Jason Shiell
Josh Butler	Mike McClendon
Evan Anundsen	Nick Tyson
Trey Watten	Josh Wahpepah
Roque Mercedes	Rob Wooten

LHP

Starters	Relievers
Zach Braddock (12)	Mitch Stetter
Efrain Nieves (23)	Bobby Bramhall
Evan Frederickson (24)	Casey Baron
Josh Romanski	Rafael Lluberes
Sam Narron	Mike Ramlow
Lindsay Gulin	
David Welch	
Brae Wright	
Derek Miller	
Chris Cody	
Dan Merklinger	

2008
BONUSES: $8.4 MILLION

BEST PURE HITTER: C/3B Brett Lawrie (1), the best Canadian hitting prospect in a decade, has tremendous bat speed and a feel for hitting combined with extreme confidence. He'll need polish but most scouts believe he'll hit for average.

BEST POWER HITTER: Scouts have graded Lawrie with well above-average power. His fireworks on a spring tour of the Dominican Republic with Canada's junior national team—including five home runs in a doubleheader—have become legend among scouts who saw them.

FASTEST RUNNER: OF Cutter Dykstra grades as a 70 runner on the 20-80 scouting scale and has aggressiveness on the bases to go with his speed.

BEST DEFENSIVE PLAYER: OF Logan Schafer (8) has premium athletic ability and defensive ability in center field, shades of Steve Finley.

BEST FASTBALL: LHP Evan Frederickson (1s) sat at 91-93 mph this spring, then reached 97-98 in a predraft workout. He had a dead arm after signing, though. RHP Trey Watten (7) has shown mid-90s heat at times and has projection at 6-foot-4 and 190 pounds. He also could improve as he gives up hitting, as he played third base at Abilene Christian (Texas).

BEST SECONDARY PITCH: RHP Seth Lintz (2) has a quick arm and power breaking ball, while Watten has flashed a plus slider.

BEST PRO DEBUT: OF Erik Komatsu (8) ranked among Rookie-level Pioneer League leaders in several offensive categories while batting .321/.394/.538 with 11 homers. After reporting late following North Carolina's College World Series run, RHP Rob Wooten (13) posted a 38-5 K-BB ratio and didn't allow a homer while spending most of his time at low Class A West Virginia.

BEST ATHLETE: The Brewers got plenty of athleticism, with Dykstra and Lawrie edging RHP Jake Odorizzi (1s), a prep wide receiver with a chance for four solid-or-better pitches. Dykstra posted the best SPARQ score during the 2007 Area Code Games.

MOST INTRIGUING BACKGROUND: Dykstra's father Lenny had a 12-year career with the Mets and Phillies, leading both to pennants. Lawrie made the Canadian Olympic baseball team, while his sister Danielle pitched for Canada's Olympic softball team.

CLOSEST TO THE MAJORS: Schafer and Wooten have a leg up as collegians, but if Lawrie takes to catching, he'll rocket to the majors.

BEST LATE-ROUND PICK: SS Carlos George (46) has a live body and good infield actions, as well as speed and a plus arm. His bat is a bit raw, but his glove will buy him time.

THE ONE WHO GOT AWAY: RHP Kyle Winkler (37) has elicited comparisons to Brad Lincoln, the No. 4 overall pick in 2006, for his short but strong body and four-pitch mix, including a fastball that reaches 94 mph. He opted to attend Texas Christian.

ASSESSMENT: In his last draft for Milwaukee, scouting director Jack Zduriencik had extra selections for the first time and balanced high-risk picks such as Frederickson with solid choices such a LHP Josh Romanski (5). A solid class could become outstanding if Lawrie becomes an offensive force at catcher.

2007
BONUSES: $4.3 MILLION

OF Matt LaPorta (1) was a surprise selection at No. 7 overall, but he paid quick dividends as the key player in the C.C. Sabathia trade. C Jonathan Lucroy (3), 2B Eric Farris (4) and OF Caleb Gindl (5) were the next picks in an offensive-minded draft. RHP Cody Scarpetta (11), healthy again after a finger injury, bears watching.

GRADE: B+

2006
BONUSES: $5.5 MILLION

Few pitchers can match RHP Jeremy Jeffress' (1) triple-digit velocity, though he has been slowed by a suspension for smoking marijuana. OF Cole Gillespie (3) is making steady progress, while RHP R.J. Seidel (16) could be on the verge of a breakout.

GRADE: C+

2005
BONUSES: $3.8 MILLION*

As if OF Ryan Braun (1) weren't enough, the Brewers found a second masher in 3B Mat Gamel (5). 3B Taylor Green (25) was shrewdly picked up via the draft-and-follow process.

GRADE: A

2004
BONUSES: $4.3 MILLION*

If RHP Yovani Gallardo (2) can stay healthy, he'll be the ace Milwaukee thought it was getting in RHP Mark Rogers (1), who has struggled with injuries and poor command. C Angel Salome (5) and OF Lorenzo Cain (17), a draft-and-follow, could start for the Brewers in the near future.

GRADE: B+

*Draft analysis by John Manuel (2008) and Jim Callis (2004-07). Numbers in parentheses indicate draft rounds. *Bonuses for 2004-05 are first 10 rounds only.*

BRIAN BISSELL

PROSPECT

ALCIDES ESCOBAR, SS

Born: Dec. 16, 1986.
Ht.: 6-1. **Wt.:** 182.
Bats: R. **Throws:** R.
Signed:
Venezuela, 2003.
Signed by:
Epy Guerrero.

egendary scout Epy Guerrero's tenure with the Brewers wasn't as long or distinguished as his time with the Astros, Yankees and Blue Jays. But he may have added another all-star to his résumé when he signed Escobar for a mere $33,000 out of Venezuela in 2003. He quickly established himself as the best defensive infielder in the system, but it took Escobar a while to answer questions about his bat. He put those to rest when he hit a career-high .306 while reaching Double-A in 2007, and he had an even better season when he returned to Huntsville in 2008. He batted .328, led the Southern League with 179 hits and managers rated him the most exciting player, best defensive shortstop and strongest infield arm in the circuit. Summoned to Milwaukee in September to add depth for the stretch drive, he singled off Scott Schoeneweis in his first big league at-bat.

Escobar makes playing shortstop look easy. He gobbles up ground with long strides, getting to balls that other shortstops can't come close to reaching. He has a true shortstop's arm, making strong, accurate throws even while on the move. He has soft hands, a good feel for the position and long arms that allow him to scoop up balls that initially appear beyond his grasp. Escobar has made tremendous strides as a hitter in the last two seasons. He was noticeably stronger in 2008, and pitchers no longer can just knock the bat out of his hands. His eight homers exceeded his previous career total of seven over four seasons, and he projects to hit 10-15 longballs annually in the majors. He also did a better job of adapting to breaking pitches and understanding what pitchers were trying to do to him. Escobar improved on the bases as well, using his plus speed to steal 34 bases in 42 attempts—an 81 percent success rate that exceeded his previous career mark of 70 percent.

At times, Escobar is too aggressive at the plate. He doesn't draw many walks, which hurts his chances of batting near the top of the lineup. His focus should be on getting on base, though at 22 he still has plenty of time to mature as a hitter. At times he tries to make plays in the field that can't be made, resulting in needless errors. But it's difficult to tell Escobar to dial down his effort because he also pulls off plays that look impossible.

There's no question that Escobar could play defense in the big leagues right now. Whether he could handle the jump offensively is another matter. The Brewers already have a solid shortstop in J.J. Hardy, but he can't do the things at the position that Escobar can do. Hardy eventually will move to second or third base, or perhaps be used in a trade for some much-needed pitching. If management stands pat for now, Escobar probably will open 2009 at Triple-A Nashville so he can get regular time. It's going to be tough to hold him back much longer.

Year	Club (League)	Class	AVG	G	AB	R	H	2B	3B	HR	RBI	BB	SO	SB	OBP	SLG
2004	Helena (PIO)	R	.281	68	231	38	65	8	0	2	24	20	44	20	.348	.342
2005	West Virginia (SAL)	LoA	.271	127	520	80	141	25	8	2	36	20	90	30	.305	.362
2006	Brevard County (FSL)	HiA	.257	87	350	47	90	9	1	2	33	19	56	28	.296	.306
2007	Brevard County (FSL)	HiA	.325	63	268	37	87	8	3	0	25	7	35	18	.345	.377
	Huntsville (SL)	AA	.283	62	226	27	64	5	4	1	28	11	36	4	.314	.354
2008	Huntsville (SL)	AA	.328	131	546	95	179	24	5	8	76	31	82	34	.363	.434
	Milwaukee (NL)	MAJ	.500	9	4	2	2	0	0	0	0	0	1	0	.500	.500
MINOR LEAGUE TOTALS			.292	538	2141	324	626	79	21	15	222	108	343	134	.329	.370
MAJOR LEAGUE TOTALS			.500	9	4	2	2	0	0	0	0	0	1	0	.500	.500

2 MAT GAMEL, 3B

BORN: July 26, 1985. **B-T:** L-R. **HT.:** 6-0. **WT.:** 200. **DRAFTED:** Chipola (Fla.) JC, 2005 (4th round). **SIGNED BY:** Doug Reynolds.

Gamel was the best hitter in the minor leagues in the first half of the 2008 season, batting .375/.433/.612 in Double-A. His emergence as a legitimate force made it easier for the Brewers to include 2007 first-round pick Matt LaPorta in the C.C. Sabathia trade. Gamel's production plummeted dramatically in the second half, and he later revealed that his right elbow had been bothering much of the time. Gamel uses the entire field, drives balls to the gaps and has enough pop in his bat to hit for high average with at least 20 homers per year in the majors. He knows the strike zone—he reached base in 53 consecutive games last year—and has a quick, compact swing. He hangs in well against lefthanders because of his willingness to take the ball the other way. He's mentally tough and doesn't give away many at-bats. He's an average runner with solid arm strength. The Brewers insist Gamel will have to play his way off third base, and he just might do that. A year after leading the minors with 53 errors, he committed 32 in 131 games. Poor footwork still leads to some atrocious throws, and his errors often come in bunches when his mechanics fall apart. He has worked hard to improve but still is far short of being ready to play defense in the majors. Gamel's bat will get him to the big leagues but it's difficult to project where he'll fit defensively. He could take over at first base if the Brewers decide to trade Prince Fielder, while others think he should move to the outfield. Gamel will open 2009 at the hot corner, most likely in Triple-A.

Year	Club (League)	Class	AVG	G	AB	R	H	2B	3B	HR	RBI	BB	SO	SB	OBP	SLG
2005	West Virginia (SAL)	LoA	.174	8	23	2	4	0	0	1	1	5	9	0	.321	.304
	Helena (PIO)	R	.327	50	199	34	65	15	2	5	37	12	49	7	.375	.497
2006	West Virginia (SAL)	LoA	.288	129	493	65	142	28	5	17	88	52	81	9	.359	.469
2007	Brevard County (FSL)	HiA	.300	128	466	78	140	37	8	9	60	58	98	14	.378	.472
2008	Huntsville (SL)	AA	.329	127	508	96	167	35	7	19	96	55	111	6	.395	.537
	Nashville (PCL)	AAA	.238	5	21	3	5	0	0	1	3	2	10	0	.304	.381
	Milwaukee (NL)	MAJ	.500	2	2	0	1	1	0	0	0	0	1	0	.500	1.000
MINOR LEAGUE TOTALS			.306	447	1710	278	523	115	22	52	285	184	358	36	.375	.490
MAJOR LEAGUE TOTALS			.500	2	2	0	1	1	0	0	0	0	1	0	.500	1.000

3 BRETT LAWRIE, C/3B

BORN: Jan. 18, 1990. **B-T:** R-R. **HT.:** 5-11. **WT.:** 200. **DRAFTED:** HS—Langley, B.C., 2008 (1st round). **SIGNED BY:** Marty Lehn.

The Brewers made Lawrie the highest drafted position player ever out of Canada when they selected him 16th overall last June. He had committed to playing for his country at the World Junior Championships in July, then unexpectedly was added to the Olympic roster as well. Signed for $1.7 million, he has yet to make his pro debut. Lawrie is an exceptional hitter, especially for his age, with a quick bat, aggressive nature and burgeoning power. The fact that he used wood bats while touring with Canada's national teams made his offensive exploits all the more impressive. He has committed to the idea of catching, where his bat would stand out the most and he could take advantage of his arm strength. His agility and drive to succeed will help him behind the plate. His speed and athleticism are above-average. Lawrie has no clear position, having seen time at catcher, third base and the outfield. He had a reputation for being disinterested in the defensive side of the game as an amateur, but he has risen to the challenge of catching. Brewers scouts still talk about the day Lawrie belted five home runs in a doubleheader against Seattle's Dominican extended spring training team. His bat is advanced enough for him to make his debut at Milwaukee's new low Class A Wisconsin affiliate, but the progress he makes defensively will dictate how quickly he advances. He should hit enough to be a big league regular at any position.

Year	Club (League)	Class	AVG	G	AB	R	H	2B	3B	HR	RBI	BB	SO	SB	OBP	SLG
2008	Did Not Play															

4 JEREMY JEFFRESS, RHP

BORN: Sept. 21, 1987. **B-T:** R-R. **HT.:** 6-1. **WT.:** 185. **DRAFTED:** HS—South Boston, Va., 2006 (1st round). **SIGNED BY:** Tim McIlvaine.

A 2006 first-rounder who signed for $1.55 million, Jeffress began last season serving the remainder of a 50-game suspension for testing positive for marijuana near the end of 2007. He returned in mid-May and earned a second-half promotion to Double-A, a move made so he could qualify for extra work in the Arizona Fall League. With a fastball that often approaches 100 mph, Jeffress is one of the hardest throwers in the minors. His heater doesn't have much movement but he delivers it with a free and easy motion that makes the ball explode on hitters. He throws from a high three-quarters angle that makes his 11-to-5 curveball particularly tough to hit when he gets it over the plate. It's easy to see why, but Jeffress falls in love with the radar gun at times. When he's having trouble commanding his curve, he becomes a one-pitch pitcher. He has worked on his changeup but it's not consistent enough for hitters to worry about it. His control is shaky, leaving him prone to big innings when he can't find the plate. He failed multiple drug tests in the past but has promised the Brewers there will be no relapses. Some scouts think Jeffress would fit nicely as an overpowering closer, but the Brewers still hope he can add enough polish to remain a starter. He left the AFL early with a shoulder strain, but with a big spring, he could open the season in Triple-A.

Year	Club (League)	Class	W	L	ERA	G	GS	CG	SV	IP	H	R	ER	HR	BB	SO	AVG
2006	Brewers (AZL)	R	2	5	5.88	13	4	0	0	34	30	26	22	0	25	37	.227
2007	West Virginia (SAL)	LoA	9	5	3.13	18	18	0	0	86	62	43	30	8	44	95	.201
2008	Brevard County (FSL)	HiA	4	6	4.08	15	14	1	0	79	65	39	36	5	41	102	.226
	Huntsville (SL)	AA	2	1	5.52	4	4	0	0	15	17	9	9	2	11	13	.298
MINOR LEAGUE TOTALS			17	17	4.08	50	40	1	0	214	174	117	97	15	121	247	.222

5 ANGEL SALOME, C

BORN: Oct. 11, 1985. **B-T:** R-R. **HT.:** 5-7. **WT.:** 199. **DRAFTED:** HS—New York, 2004 (5th round). **SIGNED BY:** Tony Blengino.

Salome has hit at every level and took that to new heights in 2008, when he ran away with the Southern League batting title with a .360 average. After he made his big league debut in September, the Brewers sent him to the Arizona Fall League to hone his defense, but he played only one game before shoulder soreness shut him down. Salome often steps in the bucket and flies open with his swing, but his great hand-eye coordination and his upper-body strength make it work. He stays on the ball and drives it to all fields, and he can even handle pitches on the outer half despite his unorthodox style. His pure arm strength rates a 65 or 70 on the 20-80 scouting scale and he does a good job of blocking pitches. Salome often gets his footwork messed up behind the plate, resulting in inaccurate throws and stolen bases. He threw out 26 percent of basestealers while allowing 90 swipes in 78 games last year. He still needs to work on his game-calling. He's a well below-average runner. He was suspended for 50 games in 2007 after testing positive for performance-enhancing drugs, but the Brewers don't believe that will be an issue again. Whether Salome will improve enough behind the plate to become a big league starter remains to be seen. He certainly looks like he'll hit, but his short stature makes it difficult to project him playing anywhere but catcher. He'll open 2009 in Triple-A.

Year	Club (League)	Class	AVG	G	AB	R	H	2B	3B	HR	RBI	BB	SO	SB	OBP	SLG
2004	Brewers (AZL)	R	.235	20	81	7	19	7	0	0	8	4	14	2	.271	.321
2005	West Virginia (SAL)	LoA	.254	29	118	15	30	7	1	4	21	8	17	1	.302	.432
	Helena (PIO)	R	.415	37	159	34	66	17	0	8	50	15	16	6	.469	.673
2006	West Virginia (SAL)	LoA	.292	105	418	63	122	31	2	10	85	39	63	7	.349	.447
2007	Brevard County (FSL)	HiA	.318	68	258	33	82	20	0	6	53	12	32	1	.341	.465
2008	Huntsville (SL)	AA	.360	98	367	67	132	30	2	13	83	33	57	3	.415	.559
	Milwaukee (NL)	MAJ	.000	3	3	0	0	0	0	0	0	0	1	0	.000	.000
MINOR LEAGUE TOTALS			.322	357	1401	219	451	112	5	41	300	111	199	20	.370	.497
MAJOR LEAGUE TOTALS			.000	3	3	0	0	0	0	0	0	0	1	0	.000	.000

6 LORENZO CAIN, OF

BORN: April 13, 1986. **B-T:** R-R. **HT.:** 6-2. **WT.:** 180. **DRAFTED:** Tallahassee (Fla.) CC, D/F 2004 (17th round). **SIGNED BY:** Doug Reynolds.

After they included Matt LaPorta in the C.C. Sabathia trade in July, the Brewers promoted Cain to replace him in Huntsville. He performed so well that Milwaukee moved him on to Triple-A and the Arizona Fall League. They also committed to playing him in center field after he primarily played in right in the past. Cain is an impressive athlete. He runs well, giving him the range for center field and making him a threat on the basepaths. He has the potential to hit 20 homers per year, though most of his power comes to the gaps now. He owns solid arm strength as well. Cain's power wasn't ideal for a corner outfielder, but it's less of an issue in center field. He's still learning to be patient at the plate, though he's not terribly aggressive. He didn't start playing baseball until high school, so he's not the most instinctive player. Cain might have to go back to Huntsville to open 2009, but the Brewers hope he'll be ready for Triple-A at some point during the season. With Michael Brantley going to Cleveland as part of the Sabathia deal, Cain is easily the most advanced center-field prospect in the system.

Year	Club (League)	Class	AVG	G	AB	R	H	2B	3B	HR	RBI	BB	SO	SB	OBP	SLG
2005	Brewers (AZL)	R	.356	50	205	45	73	18	5	5	37	20	32	12	.418	.566
	Helena (PIO)	R	.208	6	24	4	5	0	0	0	1	1	6	0	.321	.208
2006	West Virginia (SAL)	LoA	.307	132	527	91	162	36	4	6	60	58	104	34	.384	.425
2007	Brevard County (FSL)	HiA	.276	126	482	67	133	21	3	2	44	37	97	24	.338	.344
2008	Nashville (PCL)	AAA	.158	6	19	0	3	0	0	0	2	3	6	0	.273	.158
	Brevard County (FSL)	HiA	.287	80	317	50	91	22	4	7	41	29	68	19	.358	.448
	Huntsville (SL)	AA	.277	40	148	21	41	9	5	4	17	19	41	6	.363	.486
MINOR LEAGUE TOTALS			.295	440	1722	278	508	106	21	24	202	167	354	95	.367	.423

7 CUTTER DYKSTRA, OF

JOHN SPEAR

BORN: June 29, 1989. **B-T:** R-R. **HT.:** 5-11. **WT.:** 180. **DRAFTED:** HS—Westlake Village, Calif., 2008 (2nd round). **SIGNED BY:** Corey Rodriguez.

Dykstra is a chip off the old block, the son of former all-star and agitator Lenny Dykstra. The major difference is that Cutter bats righthanded and played shortstop until moving to center field at the end of his high school career. He was slowed by a groin injury after signing for $737,000 as a second-rounder in June. A terrific athlete, Dykstra finished first in the SPARQ performance testing at the 2007 Area Code Games. He has excellent bat speed and some loft in his swing, giving him surprising power for his size. He has good balance and a compact stroke, hitting the ball mostly to left and center field. He has plus-plus speed and is very aggressive on the bases. Dykstra has fringy arm strength, which is why he couldn't have played shortstop in pro ball. His arm will be tested in center field, and he's still in the early stages of learning the position. He doesn't project to grow physically but can get by with his athleticism and aggressiveness, much like his father. His move to center is good for both him and the Brewers, who are a bit thin at that position after trading Brantley and Darren Ford last season. Dykstra could move through the system quickly and will start 2009 in low Class A.

Year	Club (League)	Class	AVG	G	AB	R	H	2B	3B	HR	RBI	BB	SO	SB	OBP	SLG
2008	Brewers (AZL)	R	.269	10	26	5	7	0	0	0	0	5	7	0	.406	.269
	Helena (PIO)	R	.271	38	144	24	39	9	0	5	17	21	30	4	.367	.438
MINOR LEAGUE TOTALS			.271	48	170	29	46	9	0	5	17	26	37	4	.374	.412

8 TAYLOR GREEN, 3B

BORN: Nov. 2, 1986. **B-T:** L-R. **HT.:** 5-10. **WT.:** 185. **DRAFTED:** Cypress (Calif.) CC, D/F 2005 (25th round). **SIGNED BY:** Bruce Seid.

The Brewers' 2007 minor league player of the year, Green spent the second half of last season wondering where he'd be in 2009. He was a potential player to be named in the C.C. Sabathia trade with the Indians, who ultimately opted to take outfielder/first baseman Michael Brantley. Green missed the last three weeks of the regular season after a pitch hit him on the left wrist, then had his nose broken by a bad-hop grounder in the AFL. His tools aren't overly impressive, but Green has good instincts and a feel for the game. As one scout put it, "He's just a baseball player." Though not big in stature, he has good balance and bat speed and generates decent power. He has a good eye at the plate and makes consistent contact. He draws high marks for his makeup and work ethic. Taylor doesn't have the power associated with third base. He'd profile better offensively at second base, but he may lack the quickness for the position. He's a below-average runner with decent range and a merely adequate arm at the hot corner. Green played second base earlier in his career, but the Brewers seem committed to keeping him at third. He has a better chance of sticking at third base than Gamel, and he'll move up to Double-A in 2009.

Year	Club (League)	Class	AVG	G	AB	R	H	2B	3B	HR	RBI	BB	SO	SB	OBP	SLG
2006	Helena (PIO)	R	.231	62	221	36	51	12	1	1	23	29	35	0	.328	.308
2007	West Virginia (SAL)	LoA	.327	111	397	68	130	29	2	14	86	51	65	0	.406	.516
2008	Brevard County (FSL)	HiA	.289	114	418	46	121	19	0	15	73	61	59	4	.382	.443
MINOR LEAGUE TOTALS			.292	287	1036	150	302	60	3	30	182	141	159	4	.380	.442

9 COLE GILLESPIE, OF

BORN: June 20, 1984. **B-T:** R-R. **HT.:** 6-1. **WT.:** 205. **DRAFTED:** Oregon State, 2006 (3rd round). **SIGNED BY:** Brandon Newell.

Gillespie has been an organization favorite since signing shortly after leading Oregon State to the 2006 College World Series title. Overshadowed by a roster full of top prospects at Huntsville last season and battling a toe injury that required surgery after the season, he nonetheless made the Southern League all-star team. Gillespie lived up to his reputation as a gap hitter by pounding out 38 doubles last season, second in the SL. He has just average power but shows a keen eye at the plate and knows how to lay off strikes he can't do much with. He moves well in left field and also has played in right, showing an accurate arm. His speed and athleticism are average, and he shows good instincts on the bases. While Gillespie doesn't have a glaring shortcoming, he also doesn't have a standout tool that will carry him to regular playing time in the majors. He's a solid hitter but not an offensive force. He's a decent defender but fits best in left field, which puts more pressure on his bat. It's difficult to project Gillespie supplanting corner outfielders Ryan Braun and Corey Hart in Milwaukee. He could be a valuable fourth outfielder after spending some time in Triple-A.

Year	Club (League)	Class	AVG	G	AB	R	H	2B	3B	HR	RBI	BB	SO	SB	OBP	SLG
2006	Helena (PIO)	R	.344	51	186	49	64	12	1	8	31	40	34	18	.464	.548
2007	Brevard County (FSL)	HiA	.267	129	438	75	117	25	3	12	62	72	95	16	.378	.420
2008	Huntsville (SL)	AA	.281	131	462	73	130	38	4	14	79	75	102	17	.386	.472
MINOR LEAGUE TOTALS			.286	311	1086	197	311	75	8	34	172	187	231	51	.397	.464

10 JONATHAN LUCROY, C

BORN: June 13, 1986. **B-T:** R-R. **HT.:** 6-1. **WT.:** 206. **DRAFTED:** Louisiana-Lafayette, 2007 (3rd round). **SIGNED BY:** Brian Sankey.

The Brewers were thrilled to get Lucroy in the third round of the 2007 draft after giving up their second-rounder as compensation for free agent Jeff Suppan. They knew Lucroy was more advanced offensively than defensively, and he has lived up to that reputation while advancing to high Class A in his first full pro season. Lucroy is an advanced hitter with a very good eye at the plate. He covers both sides of the dish, limiting his strikeouts. He has pop in his bat and proved it by hitting 20 homers to rank second in the system in 2008. He has quick hands and uses the whole field, which is why he hits for a high average. His quick release allowed him to throw out 45 percent of basestealers last season, and he's a leader behind the plate. While he gets rid of the ball in a hurry, Lucroy's arm strength is fringy. He still needs to work on the intricacies of catching, such as blocking balls, framing pitches and calling games. He has below-average speed but runs better than most catchers. The Brewers have yearned to develop a catcher who can both contribute offensively and handle himself behind the plate, and Lucroy just might prove to be their man. He'll open 2009 in Double-A and advance as his defensive progress dictates.

Year	Club (League)	Class	AVG	G	AB	R	H	2B	3B	HR	RBI	BB	SO	SB	OBP	SLG
2007	Helena (PIO)	R	.342	61	234	35	80	18	2	4	39	16	37	0	.383	.487
2008	West Virginia (SAL)	LoA	.310	65	239	45	74	16	1	10	33	30	39	8	.391	.510
	Brevard County (FSL)	HiA	.292	64	236	31	69	12	1	10	44	28	45	1	.364	.479
MINOR LEAGUE TOTALS			.315	190	709	111	223	46	4	24	116	74	121	9	.379	.492

11 JAKE ODORIZZI, RHP

BORN: March 27, 1990. **B-T:** R-R. **HT.:** 6-2. **WT.:** 175. **DRAFTED:** HS—Highland, Ill., 2008 (1st round supplemental). **SIGNED BY:** Harvey Kuenn Jr.

A fantastic athlete, Odorizzi also was a star shortstop for his high school team with a good bat, as well as an all-league wide receiver in football. Some teams rated him as the best prep pitcher in the 2008 draft, but the Brewers were able to get him with the No. 32 overall pick. They signed him away from a Louisville commitment for $1.06 million. Odorizzi pitched at 92-95 mph as a high school senior but didn't show that velocity in his pro debut. The Brewers attributed the dropoff to a dead-arm stage, and they limited him to 21 innings. He has a clean, repeatable delivery, which bodes well for his command going forward, and the ball seems to explode out of his hand, making his fastball even tougher to hit. Odorizzi's second pitch is a slider that still needs refinement. He also throws a curveball and has been working on his changeup. Concentrating solely on pitching should accelerate his progress, and he'll open his first full pro season in low Class A. His poise and drive may allow him to move quickly for a high school pitcher. With a plus fastball and potential for four solid pitches, he has the raw material to be a frontline starter.

Year	Club (League)	Class	W	L	ERA	G	GS	CG	SV	IP	H	R	ER	HR	BB	SO	AVG
2008	Brewers (AZL)	R	1	2	3.48	11	4	0	0	21	18	10	8	2	9	19	.220
MINOR LEAGUE TOTALS			1	2	3.48	11	4	0	0	21	18	10	8	2	9	19	.220

12 ZACH BRADDOCK, LHP

BORN: Aug. 23, 1987. **B-T:** L-L. **HT.:** 6-4. **WT.:** 230. **DRAFTED:** Burlington (N.J.) CC, D/F 2005 (18th round). **SIGNED BY:** Tony Blengino.

Braddock's ability makes him one of the most intriguing pitching prospects in the system. Now, if the Brewers could only keep him on the mound. Elbow tenderness limited him to 71 innings last season, and he worked only in short relief in August after sitting out more than three weeks. He had Tommy John surgery in high school, so the elbow problems last year were a source of concern. He also worked just 47 innings in 2007 because of shoulder soreness. When healthy, Braddock profiles as a starter with three quality pitches: a 90-93 mph fastball, a sharp slider and an improving changeup. Despite the elbow problems, he normally pitches with a fluid delivery that makes his fastball get on hitters quicker than they expect. His command wasn't as sharp last year as it had been in 2007, in part because of the elbow problems, yet he still missed a lot of bats. With the combination of the sore elbow and emotional issues that required medication in the past, Braddock's maturity and determination have been tested. He has moved up through the system even though he hasn't pitched much, and the Brewers believe if they can keep him on the mound for a full season, he'll blossom quickly. He'll get a chance to earn a job in Double-A during spring training.

Year	Club (League)	Class	W	L	ERA	G	GS	CG	SV	IP	H	R	ER	HR	BB	SO	AVG
2006	Helena (PIO)	R	2	2	5.49	14	8	0	0	39	32	26	24	3	31	30	.227
2007	West Virginia (SAL)	LoA	3	1	1.15	10	9	0	0	47	28	6	6	1	15	68	.168
2008	West Virginia (SAL)	LoA	0	0	0.00	2	2	0	0	6	2	1	0	0	3	13	.095
	Brevard County (FSL)	HiA	4	7	5.51	21	11	0	0	65	55	44	40	7	42	80	.226
MINOR LEAGUE TOTALS			9	10	4.00	47	30	0	0	158	117	77	70	11	91	191	.205

13 ALEXANDRE PERIARD, RHP

BORN: June 15, 1987. **B-T:** L-R. **HT.:** 6-1. **WT.:** 185. **DRAFTED:** HS—St. Eustache, Quebec, 2004 (16th round). **SIGNED BY:** Jay Lapp.

Periard is taking a slow, steady path through the system, which seemingly parallels his game. He's not a flashy strikeout pitcher, rather a dependable source of groundouts who touches 95 mph with his fastball at times. He pitches regularly at 91-92 mph with good sink. His slider is an out pitch and his changeup is average, though he needs to be more consistent with both. Periard also throws a curveball that needs work. He struggled after being promoted to Double-A in the second half of 2008, but he was just 21 and his performance didn't concern the Brewers. When he moved up, he learned that he'll have to pitch to both sides or the plate or he'll get hit. He has a strong lower half that allows him to drop and drive and keep the ball down. An aggressive, confident pitcher, he pounds the strike zone and lets his infield defense work for him, though it's clear he still needs to refine his command. The Brewers will send Periard back to Huntsville to start 2009 and hope he earns another midseason promotion.

Year	Club (League)	Class	W	L	ERA	G	GS	CG	SV	IP	H	R	ER	HR	BB	SO	AVG
2005	Brewers (AZL)	R	0	1	5.08	11	4	0	1	28	43	23	16	1	10	22	.358
2006	Brewers (AZL)	R	3	1	4.64	13	4	0	1	43	45	31	22	1	18	25	.266
2007	West Virginia (SAL)	LoA	7	7	3.55	23	18	0	2	109	115	49	43	8	21	55	.271
2008	Brevard County (FSL)	HiA	9	6	3.51	19	18	1	0	113	114	52	44	6	30	76	.256
	Huntsville (SL)	AA	2	4	5.68	8	8	0	0	38	42	25	24	3	16	20	.288
MINOR LEAGUE TOTALS			21	19	4.06	74	52	1	4	331	359	180	149	19	95	198	.275

14 CALEB GINDL, OF

BORN: Aug. 31, 1988. **B-T:** L-L. **HT.:** 5-9. **WT.:** 185. **DRAFTED:** HS—Milton, Fla., 2007 (5th round). **SIGNED BY:** Doug Reynolds.

A year after winning the batting title in the Rookie-level Pioneer League during his pro debut, Gindl finished among the leaders in several offensive categories in the low Class A South Atlantic League as a 19-year-old. He went to Hawaii Winter Baseball to get more work after the season and hit .281/.361/.438 in 96 at-bats. Gindl's individual tools don't grade out impressively, but he gets the job done, especially at the plate. Built a bit like Brian Giles, he's very aggressive at the plate, has good hand-eye coordination and can put a charge into the ball despite his short, stocky frame. He has mostly gap power and runs well enough to pile up doubles. The Brewers like his makeup and maturity, particularly for his age. He was also a lefthanded pitcher in high school, so he'll have plenty of arm for left field, where he'll likely end up because he's only an average defender at best. Gindl can get too aggressive at the plate and accumulated a lot of strikeouts last season, though his 63 walks and .388 on-base percentage show he does have an idea of the strike zone. He just needs to be more disciplined. Gindl's challenge going forward will be whether he'll hit for enough power to play left field in the majors. He'll continue his steady climb this year at high Class A Brevard County.

Year	Club (League)	Class	AVG	G	AB	R	H	2B	3B	HR	RBI	BB	SO	SB	OBP	SLG
2007	Helena (PIO)	R	.372	55	207	40	77	22	3	5	42	20	38	4	.420	.580
2008	West Virginia (SAL)	LoA	.307	137	508	86	156	38	4	13	81	63	144	14	.388	.474
MINOR LEAGUE TOTALS			.326	192	715	126	233	60	7	18	123	83	182	18	.397	.505

15 CODY SCARPETTA, RHP

BORN: Aug. 25, 1988. **B-T:** R-R. **HT.:** 6-3. **WT.:** 242. **DRAFTED:** HS—Guilford, Ill., 2007 (11th round). **SIGNED BY:** Harvey Kuenn Jr.

Milwaukee drafted Scarpetta's father Dan in the third round in 1982, and Cody would have factored in a similar area in the 2007 draft if he hadn't torn the flexor tendon at the base of his right index figure in late April. He had surgery in late May, and the Brewers knew he wouldn't pitch any more that year when they took him in the 11th round. They initially signed him away from a Creighton scholarship for $325,000, but when he needed a second surgery, the club voided that deal and swiftly re-signed him for $125,000. Scarpetta stayed in extended spring training last year before making his pro debut in June. Big and strong, he throws a heavy sinker in the low to mid-90s and backs it up with a 12-to-6 curveball that can also be a plus pitch. He's improving his changeup and also throws a decent slider. With a power arm, Scarpetta is aggressive on the mound, pounding strikes at hitters and seldom falling behind in the count. Now that he's past the finger injury, Scarpetta could move quickly through the system. With a thick build, he'll have to watch his conditioning, though that bulk helps produce his power. He's also working to clean up his delivery. Scarpetta was a late addition to Hawaii Winter Baseball but got knocked around, compiling an 8.03 ERA in 12 innings. He'll likely open 2009 in low Class A.

Year	Club (League)	Class	W	L	ERA	G	GS	CG	SV	IP	H	R	ER	HR	BB	SO	AVG
2008	Brewers (AZL)	R	1	0	0.57	6	5	0	0	16	8	1	1	0	8	27	.154
	Helena (PIO)	R	1	0	3.48	6	3	0	0	21	18	10	8	2	8	31	.237
MINOR LEAGUE TOTALS			2	0	2.23	12	8	0	0	36	26	11	9	2	16	58	.203

16 LEE HAYDEL, OF

BORN: July 15, 1987. **B-T:** L-R. **HT.:** 6-1. **WT.:** 190. **DRAFTED:** Delgado (La.) CC, D/F 2006 (19th round). **SIGNED BY:** Joe Mason.

The Brewers believe Haydel is just beginning to scratch the surface of his potential, and his production has already been pretty good for his experience level. Milwaukee signed him for $624,000 as one of the last draft-and-follows in 2007, after he had decided to attend Delgado (La.) CC instead of Louisiana State out of high school. Haydel has exceptional speed but hasn't been selective enough at the plate to take full advantage of his best tool. He has little power so he needs to bunt more, draw walks and get on base. With a .289 career average, all he has to do is boost his OBP. He also needs to work on getting better jumps and reading pitchers because he gets caught stealing too often. He has a ceiling as a legitimate leadoff hitter, which the Brewers lack at present. Haydel has good range in center and chases down balls in the gaps, and his arm is solid for the position. He'll need time to fully develop, but the potential is there to become a player comparable to Jacoby Ellsbury. Haydel will continue his step-by-step progress by moving up to high Class A in 2009.

Year	Club (League)	Class	AVG	G	AB	R	H	2B	3B	HR	RBI	BB	SO	SB	OBP	SLG
2007	Helena (PIO)	R	.276	62	254	42	70	12	5	0	20	12	44	12	.311	.362
2008	West Virginia (SAL)	LoA	.295	131	522	68	154	21	8	0	50	32	107	34	.337	.366
MINOR LEAGUE TOTALS			.289	193	776	110	224	33	13	0	70	44	151	46	.328	.365

17 BRENT BREWER, SS

BORN: Dec. 19, 1987. **B-T:** R-R. **HT.:** 6-2. **WT.:** 190. **DRAFTED:** HS—Tyrone, Ga., 2006 (2nd round). **SIGNED BY:** Doug Reynolds.

No one questions the athleticism of Brewer, who turned down a scholarship to play wide receiver and short-stop at Florida State after the Brewers gave him a $600,000 bonus in 2006. He has tremendous range at short, getting to balls that many players have no chance to field, and he has the strong arm a big league shortstop needs. He also runs well and has good strength, which should result in more homers as he gains experience. But here's the rub: Brewer just doesn't make contact often enough. In 449 at-bats at two Class A stops last season, he struck out 111 times. That's better than the 170 whiffs he accumulated the previous season, but Brewer still needs to improve his pitch recognition and stop swinging at pitches he can't hit. He also sacrificed power to make better contact, hitting nine fewer home runs. His defensive consistency has improved, with 35 errors in 2008, down from 48 the year before, but he still gets careless with his throws and must continue to work on the fundamentals. The Brewers actually were encouraged that he went from batting .213 at West Virginia to .251 at Brevard County, but he still has to prove that he can put his impressive tools to good use. Milwaukee hopes that will come as he gets more repetitions. He's a hard worker with strong leadership qualities, which will help, and he'll return to high Class A to improve on last year's performance.

Year	Club (League)	Class	AVG	G	AB	R	H	2B	3B	HR	RBI	BB	SO	SB	OBP	SLG
2006	Brewers (AZL)	R	.264	45	182	25	48	3	6	3	22	16	53	10	.328	.396
2007	West Virginia (SAL)	LoA	.251	127	518	86	130	25	7	11	49	46	170	42	.315	.390
2008	West Virginia (SAL)	LoA	.213	47	174	25	37	13	2	0	17	18	54	16	.294	.310
	Brevard County (FSL)	HiA	.251	76	275	36	69	17	2	2	25	25	57	15	.316	.349
MINOR LEAGUE TOTALS			.247	295	1149	172	284	58	17	16	113	105	334	83	.314	.369

18 R.J. SEIDEL, RHP

BORN: Sept. 3, 1987. **B-T:** R-R. **HT.:** 6-6. **WT.:** 190. **DRAFTED:** HS—LaCrosse, Wis., 2006 (16th round). **SIGNED BY:** Harvey Kuenn Jr.

Seidel is still young and developing, so the Brewers expect him to have ups and downs. That's exactly what happened last season in low Class A, where he slumped in the second half. Though he didn't get to pitch a lot as a high schooler in Wisconsin, Seidel has a good feel for pitching, in part because his father Dick pitched in the Yankees system in the early 1980s. He's not overpowering with an 89-92 mph fastball, but Seidel has allowed just 12 homers in 163 innings in hitter-friendly environments, reflecting his pitchability. His curveball continues to be inconsistent, but he has an advanced changeup for his experience level. After missing time with biceps tendinitis in 2007, Seidel stayed healthy and took a regular turn last year, which was encouraging, though he seemed a bit worn out by season's end. He has a great pitcher's frame and is still filling out, so he should get stronger and add velocity. With his stuff, savvy, frame and bloodlines, he has a ceiling as a middle-of-the-rotation starter.

Year	Club (League)	Class	W	L	ERA	G	GS	CG	SV	IP	H	R	ER	HR	BB	SO	AVG
2007	Helena (PIO)	R	4	0	3.07	12	8	0	0	41	30	20	14	2	16	36	.207
2008	West Virginia (SAL)	LoA	9	5	4.51	26	25	0	0	122	135	72	61	10	45	81	.284
MINOR LEAGUE TOTALS			13	5	4.15	38	33	0	0	163	165	92	75	12	61	117	.266

19 EDUARDO MORLAN, RHP

BORN: March 1, 1986. **B-T:** R-R. **HT.:** 6-2. **WT.:** 220. **DRAFTED:** HS—Miami, 2004 (3rd round). **SIGNED BY:** Hector Otero (Twins).

In his first season in the Rays organization after coming over from the Twins the Delmon Young/Matt Garza trade, Morlan wasn't as overpowering as he had been in the past. He did appear in the Futures Game, where he caught the eye of Brewers special assistant Dick Groch. That led to Milwaukee selecting Morlan in the major league Rule 5 draft at the Winter Meetings. He cost the club $50,000, and he has to stay on the big league roster throughout 2009 or else be placed on waivers and offered back to Tampa Bay for half the draft price. It's not that the Rays didn't him value as a prospect, but with a World Series club and a deep farm system, they didn't have room for him on their 40-man roster. Morlan regularly throws in the low 90s and touches 94 mph. His slider wasn't as crisp last season as it was in the past, but it's a strikeout pitch with two-plane depth when it's on. He does a good job of throwing strikes and his stuff was sharper in the Puerto Rican League this winter. That gives the Brewers hope that Morlan can fill the seventh- or eighth-inning role Guillermo Mota handled for them last season.

Year	Club (League)	Class	W	L	ERA	G	GS	CG	SV	IP	H	R	ER	HR	BB	SO	AVG
2004	Twins (GCL)	R	1	2	2.84	11	2	0	1	25	25	14	8	1	10	28	.245
2005	Elizabethton (APP)	R	2	0	0.82	4	4	0	0	22	6	2	2	0	6	30	.085
	Beloit (MWL)	LoA	4	4	4.38	10	10	0	0	51	39	25	25	5	31	55	.207
2006	Beloit (MWL)	LoA	5	5	2.29	28	18	1	2	106	78	31	27	6	38	125	.202
2007	Fort Myers (FSL)	HiA	4	3	3.15	41	0	0	18	66	55	25	23	7	17	92	.218
	New Britain (EL)	AA	1	0	2.25	2	0	0	0	4	3	1	1	0	3	7	.200
2008	Montgomery (SL)	AA	4	2	3.64	30	0	0	1	47	44	21	19	5	15	45	.242
MINOR LEAGUE TOTALS			21	16	2.94	126	34	1	22	322	250	119	105	24	120	382	.209

20 SETH LINTZ, RHP

BORN: Feb. 7, 1990. **B-T:** R-R. **HT.:** 6-2. **WT.:** 175. **DRAFTED:** HS—Lewisburg, Tenn., 2008 (2nd round). **SIGNED BY:** Joe Mason.

Lintz's draft stock shot up after a growth spurt and increased strength boosted his lively fastball from the high 80s into the low 90s last spring. He graduated second in his high school class and was committed to Kentucky, but the Brewers were able to sign him for an above-slot $900,000 in the second round. They limited Lintz to 18 innings in the Rookie-level Arizona League, in part because he's still growing into his body. He struggled with his command but still struck out 26 hitters. Lintz relies primarily on his fastball, which has touched 94 mph, and has a power 12-to-6 curveball that's very effective when he gets it over the plate. It could become a plus pitch. He also throws a slider and changeup, both of which are inconsistent. He shows good makeup and the Brewers like the way he competes, so he just needs to throw more strikes and get innings. Because of his age and the need to get bigger and stronger, Lintz will start on a slow track to the majors and might begin 2009 in extended spring training.

Year	Club (League)	Class	W	L	ERA	G	GS	CG	SV	IP	H	R	ER	HR	BB	SO	AVG
2008	Brewers (AZL)	R	0	3	6.87	9	6	0	0	18	22	20	14	3	16	26	.289
MINOR LEAGUE TOTALS			0	3	6.87	9	6	0	0	18	22	20	14	3	16	26	.289

21 OMAR AGUILAR, RHP

BORN: March 31, 1985. **B-T:** L-R. **HT.:** 5-11. **WT.:** 220. **DRAFTED:** Merced (Calif.) JC, 2005 (30th round). **SIGNED BY:** Justin McCray.

An eighth-round selection of the Giants in 2004, Aguilar was the highest pick in that draft to enroll at a junior college. He touched 98 mph that fall at Merced (Calif.) JC and seemed poised for a big payday in the spring. But he came down with a sore elbow and barely pitched before the draft, causing San Francisco to back off and Aguilar to drop to the Brewers in the 30th round. He had Tommy John surgery after signing, which meant that his career didn't really get going until 2007. He made big strides as a closer in 2008, earning a promotion to Huntsville. He has a power arm, with a 94-96 mph fastball and an 85-87 slider. Double-A hitters pounded him when he used his fastball too much, so Aguilar began using his secondary pitches more, including an improving changeup that he can throw for strikes. He also throws cutters, burying them in on the hands of lefthanders. His fastball doesn't have a lot of movement but it gets in on hitters fast. Command is a problem for Aguilar at times, but he made strides in that department last season. Though he has closed in the minors, Aguilar projects as a setup man in the majors. He has the temperament and stuff to handle the late innings, and could get his first big league callup at the end of 2009.

Year	Club (League)	Class	W	L	ERA	G	GS	CG	SV	IP	H	R	ER	HR	BB	SO	AVG
2006	Brewers (AZL)	R	0	1	6.00	6	6	0	0	9	5	6	6	0	9	10	.167
2007	West Virginia (SAL)	LoA	7	4	4.81	42	0	0	9	58	51	33	31	1	36	68	.241
2008	Brevard County (FSL)	HiA	3	0	0.35	19	0	0	13	26	13	2	1	0	10	25	.155
	Huntsville (SL)	AA	0	3	3.08	28	0	0	4	38	26	24	13	5	22	42	.191
MINOR LEAGUE TOTALS			10	8	3.51	95	6	0	26	131	95	65	51	6	77	145	.206

22 WILY PERALTA, RHP

BORN: May 8, 1989. **B-T:** R-R. **HT.:** 6-2. **WT.:** 225. **SIGNED:** Dominican Republic, 2005. **SIGNED BY:** Fausto Sosa Pena/Fernando Arango.

Peralta was a breakthrough international signing for the Brewers, who gave him $450,000 in 2005, but he had Tommy John surgery after debuting in 2006 and missed all of the next season. He bounced back in a big way in 2008, showing off what some scouts thought was the best arm in the Pioneer League. Peralta regularly threw his fastball in the mid-90s, sometimes reaching 97-98 mph, and mixed in an improved slider that could be a big pitch for him down the road. Used exclusively in relief to protect his elbow last year, he seldom threw his changeup. Peralta still fights command issues at times, and with a thick build he'll have to stay on top of his conditioning. He's still young and figures to be even better two years removed from surgery. He could sail through the system if his secondary pitches continue to improve. He has reestablished himself as one of the top power pitchers in the organization and could become a late-inning reliever or perhaps a closer.

Year	Club (League)	Class	W	L	ERA	G	GS	CG	SV	IP	H	R	ER	HR	BB	SO	AVG
2006	Brewers (AZL)	R	2	5	6.63	14	6	0	0	38	51	37	28	5	20	28	.319
2007	Did not play—Injured																
2008	Helena (PIO)	R	1	1	3.07	15	2	0	2	29	23	14	10	4	8	36	.209
	West Virginia (SAL)	LoA	0	1	10.80	2	2	0	0	5	6	6	6	0	3	3	.316
MINOR LEAGUE TOTALS			3	7	5.47	31	10	0	2	72	80	57	44	9	31	67	.277

23 EFRAIN NIEVES, LHP

BORN: Nov. 15, 1989. **B-T:** L-L. **HT.:** 6-0. **WT.:** 175. **DRAFTED:** HS—Gurabo, P.R., 2007 (7th round). **SIGNED BY:** Manolo Hernandez/Charlie Sullivan.

When the Brewers drafted Nieves as a 17-year-old out of the Puerto Rico Baseball Academy in 2007, his fastball topped out at 88 mph. Bigger and stronger last season, he added a couple of ticks to his fastball. An advanced pitcher for his age, Nieves should be able to add even more velocity as he matures. He already has an out pitch in his consistent changeup. He also throws a nice curve and has worked on improving his slider, which is tough on lefties. He pounds the strike zone, seldom issuing walks. Nieves has some deception in his delivery, which allows him to sneak his fastball in on righthanders. He'll give up hits because he's around the strike zone a lot, but it also works to his advantage when he gets ahead of hitters and leaves them susceptible to his breaking stuff. Showing great composure on the mound for a youngster, Nieves just needs innings to polish his repertoire. He'll move up to full-season ball at Wisconsin in 2009.

Year	Club (League)	Class	W	L	ERA	G	GS	CG	SV	IP	H	R	ER	HR	BB	SO	AVG
2007	Brewers (AZL)	R	2	4	5.31	13	7	0	0	41	38	29	24	3	25	45	.244
	Helena (PIO)	R	1	0	0.00	2	0	0	0	5	3	0	0	0	1	4	.188
2008	Helena (PIO)	R	6	3	4.48	16	11	0	0	76	78	40	38	9	10	66	.264
MINOR LEAGUE TOTALS			9	7	4.59	31	18	0	0	122	119	69	62	12	36	115	.254

24 EVAN FREDERICKSON, LHP

BORN: Sept. 23, 1986. **B-T:** L-L. **HT.:** 6-6. **WT.:** 238. **DRAFTED:** San Francisco, 2008 (1st round supplemental). **SIGNED BY:** Justin McCray.

Frederickson moved dramatically up the Brewers' draft board after he attended a workout in Milwaukee a few days before the draft and stunned the scouts on hand by throwing in the high 90s with regularity and ease. Figuring he might be a late bloomer, they grabbed him with the 35th overall pick and signed him for $1.01 million. After he got to low Class A, they soon were reminded why he wasn't rated as highly before that workout. He has a tendency to be wild—very wild, in fact. Frederickson went through a dead-arm period and totally lost the strike zone at times, walking 26 hitters and throwing 10 wild pitches in 20 innings. He struggled though similar issues at Virginia Tech for two years before transferring to San Francisco. The big-bodied Frederickson's mechanics elude him at times. He's at his best when commanding his breaking ball, a slurve thrown from a three-quarters arm angle in the low 80s. When he throws it for strikes, lefthanders have no chance. It's too early to determine a role for Frederickson, because everything depends on his control. He's the classic boom-or-bust pitcher. If he conquers his command issues, he'll move dramatically up this list.

Year	Club (League)	Class	W	L	ERA	G	GS	CG	SV	IP	H	R	ER	HR	BB	SO	AVG
2008	Helena (PIO)	R	0	0	3.09	3	3	0	0	12	13	7	4	1	5	16	.289
	West Virginia (SAL)	LoA	0	1	6.20	9	4	0	0	20	16	19	14	1	26	18	.229
MINOR LEAGUE TOTALS			0	1	5.06	12	7	0	0	32	29	26	18	2	31	34	.252

25 LUIS PENA, RHP

BORN: Jan. 10, 1983. **B-T:** R-R. **HT.:** 6-5. **WT.:** 200. **SIGNED:** Venezuela, 1999. **SIGNED BY:** Epy Guerrero.

Pena threw the ball so well in the first half of the 2008 season, that he seemed on the verge of getting a call to the big leagues at any time. But following a poor outing in the Triple-A all-star game, he started to lose his control and began walking hitters in bunches. He never got his act together, blowing any shot at even a September callup. It was a far cry from the previous season, when Pena made great strides and earned a spot on the 40-man roster after bouncing back from shoulder surgery that held him back in 2005 and '06. He not only lost command of his mid-90s fastball in 2008, but he also couldn't get his slider over the plate and his confidence waned. Focus was a problem as well, as he converted save opportunities but struggled in other situations. Pena still has a great pitcher's body and live arm, so he can return to good graces by showing up in spring training and throwing strikes. When he gets his fastball over the plate, his slider can be a devastating weapon and he has the stuff to pitch at the back of a bullpen.

Year	Club (League)	Class	W	L	ERA	G	GS	CG	SV	IP	H	R	ER	HR	BB	SO	AVG
2000	San Joaquin (VSL)	R	2	3	4.02	20	7	0	2	54	35	31	24	7	30	41	.190
2001	Brewers (AZL)	R	3	4	4.63	11	2	0	0	35	42	23	18	2	13	20	.300
2002	Brewers (AZL)	R	4	1	3.49	11	7	0	0	49	45	28	19	1	24	52	.239
2003	Beloit (MWL)	LoA	2	6	3.90	23	18	1	0	90	92	51	39	6	46	53	.267
2004	Beloit (MWL)	LoA	9	3	3.92	21	16	0	0	99	101	50	43	7	35	76	.268
2005	Brevard County (FSL)	HiA	2	6	4.26	15	12	0	0	76	72	39	36	6	28	51	.258
2006	Brevard County (FSL)	HiA	4	6	4.41	23	11	0	1	65	68	34	32	6	33	59	.274
2007	Brevard County (FSL)	HiA	5	0	2.08	16	0	0	6	22	14	5	5	1	7	27	.184
	Huntsville (SL)	AA	0	4	2.89	35	0	0	12	47	36	15	15	1	14	42	.211
2008	Nashville (PCL)	AAA	2	3	6.93	52	0	0	15	49	54	40	38	4	47	49	.284
MINOR LEAGUE TOTALS			33	36	4.14	227	73	1	36	585	559	316	269	41	277	470	.254

26 AMAURY RIVAS, RHP

BORN: Dec. 20, 1985. **B-T:** R-R. **HT.:** 6-2. **WT.:** 204. **SIGNED:** Dominican Republic, 2005. **SIGNED BY:** Fernando Arango/Fausto Sosa Pena.

Rivas had Tommy John surgery in December 2006 but quickly worked himself back to full strength last season, and it showed. After a solid showing in low Class A, the first real challenge of his career, he earned a late-season bump up to Brevard County. Rivas' fastball remains his best pitch, sitting regularly at 91-92 mph while reaching 95 at times. It also features good movement. Once just a thrower with a good arm, he has begun to develop his slider and changeup, becoming more of a pitcher. His slider shows plus potential, while his changeup is a work in progress. He shows confidence and a bulldog approach on the mound. Rivas needs to continue to work on command of his secondary pitches to remain a starting pitcher. Otherwise, he might project as a setup man down the road. He'll return to high Class A to start the season.

Year	Club (League)	Class	W	L	ERA	G	GS	CG	SV	IP	H	R	ER	HR	BB	SO	AVG
2005	Brewers (AZL)	R	2	3	6.91	14	6	0	0	42	56	36	32	1	16	34	.326
2006	Brewers (AZL)	R	1	0	6.43	4	2	0	0	14	17	12	10	1	3	12	.293
	Helena (PIO)	R	5	4	3.02	10	10	0	0	54	48	28	18	6	16	36	.236
2007	Brewers (AZL)	R	0	0	3.12	6	6	0	0	9	3	4	3	1	4	10	.107
2008	West Virginia (SAL)	LoA	8	3	3.50	19	15	0	0	90	83	41	35	11	32	70	.239
	Brevard County (FSL)	HiA	1	2	4.20	7	6	0	0	30	35	16	14	2	11	20	.294
MINOR LEAGUE TOTALS			17	12	4.24	60	45	0	0	238	242	137	112	22	82	182	.261

27 ERIC FARRIS, 2B

BORN: March 3, 1986. **B-T:** R-R. **HT.:** 5-10. **WT.:** 170. **DRAFTED:** Loyola Marymount, 2007 (4th round). **SIGNED BY:** Corey Rodriguez.

Farris grows on observers the more they watch him. Scouts first noticed him in the Cape Cod League after his sophomore season at Loyola Marymount, and he has been consistently productive wherever he has been. Farris has little pop in his bat and doesn't project to develop much, though he will drive the ball into the gaps on occasion. He excels at making contact but needs to draw more walks to boost his on-base percentage. Once he reaches base, Farris is a threat to steal. He's not a blazing runner but gets good breaks and reads pitchers well. He's very athletic and could probably play shortstop if needed. He has above-average defensive skills at second base, with range both to his left and right, good instincts, sure hands and a strong arm. Farris handles himself well on the field and could profile as a super utility player down the road, a la Chone Figgins—though without that much speed. For now, the Brewers want to keep Farris at second base and see how he develops.

Year	Club (League)	Class	AVG	G	AB	R	H	2B	3B	HR	RBI	BB	SO	SB	OBP	SLG
2007	Helena (PIO)	R	.326	63	239	34	78	16	2	1	34	16	22	21	.369	.423
2008	West Virginia (SAL)	LoA	.293	103	454	73	133	21	4	3	54	24	50	32	.332	.377
MINOR LEAGUE TOTALS			.304	166	693	107	211	37	6	4	88	40	72	53	.345	.392

28 CODY ADAMS, RHP

BORN: Nov. 26, 1986. **B-T:** R-R. **HT.:** 6-2. **WT.:** 180. **DRAFTED:** Southern Illinois, 2008 (2nd round). **SIGNED BY:** Harvey Kuenn Jr.

Adams pitched a lot at Southern Illinois last spring, having a disappointing spring and costing himself a chance to go in the first round. After winning 10 games in 2007 for the Salukis, he went just 6-4 and was much more hittable as a junior. The Brewers got him with their sixth selection and signed him for $653,000 as a second-rounder. Considering Adams' college workload, the Brewers weren't surprised when he got off to a slow start in pro ball. They took it easy with him, keeping him on a tight pitch limit. He's mostly a fastball/slider pitcher, throwing consistently in the low 90s and topping out at 95-96 mph. Used as both a starter and reliever at Helena, he was encouraged to throw his changeup more and made progress with the pitch. Prone at times to mechanical problems in college—he would overstride and get under his pitches—he showed better command as a pro. Adams is more of a pitch-to-contact pitcher than a strikeout guy, and he's an intelligent, tough competitor. He needs to continue to work on sharpening his slider to complement his fastball. When pitching in shorter bursts in relief, his velocity stayed at his top range, but he has enough in his arsenal to remain as a starter for now. Adams will open his first full pro season in low Class A.

Year	Club (League)	Class	W	L	ERA	G	GS	CG	SV	IP	H	R	ER	HR	BB	SO	AVG
2008	Helena (PIO)	R	5	4	3.48	14	5	0	0	54	56	30	21	3	16	37	.273
MINOR LEAGUE TOTALS			5	4	3.48	14	5	0	0	54	56	30	21	3	16	37	.273

29 LOGAN SCHAFER, OF

BORN: Sept. 8, 1986. **B-T:** L-L. **HT.:** 6-1. **WT.:** 170. **DRAFTED:** Cal Poly, 2008 (3rd round). **SIGNED BY:** Corey Rodriguez.

Schafer spent his freshman season at Cuesta (Calif.) JC before transferring to Cal Poly, where he led the team in homers as a junior. He played his way into the Brewers' plans with a strong predraft workout, so they took him the third round last June and signed him for $404,000. One of the better athletes in the Brewers' draft class, Schafer has average tools across the board and already is a solid defender in center, reminding some of Steve Finley at the same age. He also draws comparisons to Mark Kotsay for getting the most out of his ability. Promoted to low Class A soon after signing, Schafer impressed more in the field than at the plate. He also got in 86 at-bats in Hawaii Winter Baseball, batting .244/.347/.337. He has a good swing with raw power, but he'll have to improve his strike-zone discipline to tap into it. He's an average runner but must work on getting better jumps after he was caught on eight of his 12 steal attempts in his pro debut. Because he already can hold his own in center, Schafer could move steadily through the system if he can produce at the plate. Milwaukee considers him a real sleeper and will send him back to low Class A in 2009.

Year	Club (League)	Class	AVG	G	AB	R	H	2B	3B	HR	RBI	BB	SO	SB	OBP	SLG
2008	Helena (PIO)	R	.240	8	25	4	6	0	1	2	8	5	4	1	.355	.560
	West Virginia (SAL)	LoA	.276	43	181	25	50	13	2	0	20	8	42	3	.306	.370
MINOR LEAGUE TOTALS			.272	51	206	29	56	13	3	2	28	13	46	4	.313	.393

30 TIM DILLARD, RHP

BORN: July 19, 1983. **B-T:** B-R. **HT.:** 6-4. **WT.:** 205. **DRAFTED:** Itawamba (Miss.) CC, D/F 2002 (34th round). **SIGNED BY:** Doug Reynolds.

A former starter working his second season in relief in 2008, Dillard showed a better grasp of pitching in short spurts and earned his first taste of big league action. He's the second member of his family to reach the majors, following in the footsteps of his father Steve. Dillard isn't overpowering but has good command of a heavy 89-93 mph sinker. He mixes in sliders and changeups to give hitters something else to consider, but the sinker remains his bread-and-butter pitch. Dillard is a classic pitch-to-contact pitcher who relies on dependable infield defense. He lives in the strike zone, so he gives up his share of hits. Dillard is a smart, dedicated pitcher who's learning the nuances of setting up hitters. He profiles as a resilient middle reliever who can handle multiple innings in an outing. After making a decent impression with the Brewers last season, he'll get his chance to earn a spot in the bullpen in the spring.

Year	Club (League)	Class	W	L	ERA	G	GS	CG	SV	IP	H	R	ER	HR	BB	SO	AVG
2003	Brewers (AZL)	R	1	2	3.79	11	4	0	0	36	36	19	15	1	5	32	.261
	Helena (PIO)	R	0	0	0.00	3	0	0	0	5	5	0	0	0	2	6	.250
2004	Beloit (MWL)	LoA	2	5	3.94	43	1	0	10	78	89	46	34	4	22	61	.280
2005	Brevard County (FSL)	HiA	12	10	2.48	28	28	5	0	185	150	64	51	9	31	128	.219
2006	Huntsville (SL)	AA	10	7	3.15	29	25	1	0	163	167	76	57	10	36	108	.261
2007	Nashville (PCL)	AAA	8	4	4.74	34	16	1	0	133	167	72	70	13	37	62	.316
2008	Nashville (PCL)	AAA	6	1	1.99	37	0	0	2	63	57	21	14	5	28	55	.244
	Milwaukee (NL)	MAJ	0	0	4.40	13	0	0	0	14	17	12	7	2	6	5	.293
MINOR LEAGUE TOTALS			39	29	3.27	185	74	7	12	663	671	298	241	42	161	452	.262
MAJOR LEAGUE TOTALS			0	0	4.40	13	0	0	0	14	17	12	7	2	6	5	.293

Minnesota Twins

BY JOHN MANUEL

To improve by nine victories from 2007 to 2008, the Twins followed a simple formula: They traded arguably baseball's best pitcher for little immediate return, and dealt a defensive whiz at shortstop and a developing ace for a league-average outfielder, reserve infielder and Triple-A outfielder. They lost their perennial Gold Glove center fielder, who's also a consistent power threat, and signed a raft of low-level free agents who didn't pan out.

Longtime general manager Terry Ryan stepped down in September 2007 and admitted last fall that he was leaving successor Bill Smith a mess. Impending

free agent Johan Santana angled for a trade and Smith obliged, dealing him to the Mets for raw outfielder Carlos Gomez and three pitchers who didn't live up to expectations in 2008.

Smith was aggressive in his first season as GM, also pulling the trigger on the six-player deal that brought Delmon Young, Brendan Harris and Jason Pridie from the Rays but cost Jason Bartlett, Matt Garza and minor league righthander Eduardo Morlan. Tampa Bay writers voted Bartlett the Rays' MVP while Garza was MVP of the American League Championship Series.

Yet somehow it worked. Once again, the Twins turned to their farm system and it came through. Denard Span, a 2002 first-round pick who hit seven home runs in his minor league career entering 2008, hit six after his promotion to Minnesota and was the team's third-best offensive player, after MVP candidates Joe Mauer and Justin Morneau.

The system also allowed Minnesota to replace Santana, Garza and free agent Carlos Silva with rookies Nick Blackburn and Glen Perkins and Francisco Liriano, who returned from Tommy John surgery. Blackburn, No. 1 on this list last year, led the Twins in starts and innings while going 11-11, 4.05 and taking a tough 1-0 loss in the regular-season playoff with the White Sox. Perkins, No. 2 two years ago, tied Kevin Slowey (who was in his second year) for the team lead with 12 victories.

The success of the young, homegrown rotation— Scott Baker is the oldest member at 27—was a testament to the harmonious relationship between the Twins' scouting and player-development operations, and also to roving pitching coordinator Rick Knapp. After 13 years with Minnesota, Knapp left to become the Tigers' big league pitching coach, with 18-year organizational veteran Eric Rasmussen tabbed to replace him.

MORRIS FOSTOFF

Nick Blackburn emerged as a workhorse in 2008, leading the Twins in starts and innings

TOP 30 PROSPECTS

1. Aaron Hicks, of	16. Brian Duensing, lhp
2. Ben Revere, of	17. Luke Hughes, 3b/of
3. Wilson Ramos, c	18. Rene Tosoni, of
4. Jose Mijares, lhp	19. David Bromberg, rhp
5. Danny Valencia, 3b	20. Deolis Guerra, rhp
6. Anthony Swarzak, rhp	21. Deibinson Romero, 3b
7. Shooter Hunt, rhp	22. Matt Tolbert, ss/2b
8. Kevin Mulvey, rhp	23. Steven Tolleson, util
9. Carlos Gutierrez, rhp	24. Rob Delaney, rhp
10. Angel Morales, of	25. Anthony Slama, rhp
11. Jeff Manship, rhp	26. Philip Humber, rhp
12. Tyler Robertson, lhp	27. Michael McCardell, rhp
13. Trevor Plouffe, ss	28. David Winfree, of
14. Chris Parmelee, 1b/of	29. Loek Van Mil, rhp
15. Joe Benson, of	30. Michael Tonkin, rhp

The system keeps supplying cheap, complementary parts to allow BA's Manager of the Year, Ron Gardenhire, to fill out a competitive roster. Mike Radcliff, Minnesota's scouting director for 14 years, ascended to player personnel director in 2008, and former crosschecker Deron Johnson ran the Twins' draft for the first time, with Radcliff's input. Johnson's initial effort started with toolsy outfielder Aaron Hicks—a first-round talent as both a hitter and a pitcher—and a pair of college righthanders, Carlos Gutierrez and Shooter Hunt. All three made this Top 10 list.

General Manager: Bill Smith. **Farm Director:** Jim Rantz. **Scouting Director:** Deron Johnson.

Class	Team	League	W	L	PCT	Finish*	Manager	Affiliated
Majors	Minnesota	American	88	75	.540	6th (14)	Ron Gardenhire	—
Triple-A	Rochester Red Wings	International	74	70	.514	6th (14)	Stan Cliburn	2003
Double-A	New Britain Rock Cats	Eastern	64	77	.454	10th (12)	Bobby Cuellar	1995
High A	Fort Myers Miracle	Florida State	77	59	.566	2nd (12)	Jeff Smith	1993
Low A	Beloit Snappers	Midwest	71	67	.514	8th (14)	Nelson Prada	2005
Rookie	Elizabethton Twins	Appalachian	41	25	.621	^1st (10)	Ray Smith	1974
Rookie	GCL Twins	Gulf Coast	35	21	.625	2nd (16)	Jake Mauer	1989
Overall 2008 Minor League Record			362	319	.532	6th		

* Finish in overall standings (No. of teams in league). ^League champion.

LAST YEAR'S TOP 30

Rank	Player, Pos.	Status
1.	Nick Blackburn, rhp	Majors
2.	Joe Benson, of	No. 15
3.	Wilson Ramos, c	No. 3
4.	Tyler Robertson, lhp	No. 12
5.	Anthony Swarzak, rhp	No. 6
6.	Ben Revere, of	No. 2
7.	Jason Pridie, of	Dropped out
8.	Brian Duensing, lhp	No. 16
9.	Jeff Manship, rhp	No. 11
10.	Trevor Plouffe, ss	No. 13
11.	Jose Mijares, lhp	No. 4
12.	Chris Parmelee, of	No. 14
13.	Deibinson Romero, 3b	No. 21
14.	Glen Perkins, lhp	Majors
15.	David Bromberg, rhp	No. 19
16.	Ryan Mullins, lhp	Dropped out
17.	Estarlin de los Santos, ss	Dropped out
18.	Michael McCardell, rhp	No. 27
19.	Loek Van Mil, rhp	No. 29
20.	Denard Span, of	Majors
21.	Alex Burnett, rhp	Dropped out
22.	Danny Valencia, 3b	No. 5
23.	Oswaldo Sosa, rhp	Dropped out
24.	Rene Tosoni, of	No. 18
25.	Julio DePaula, rhp	(Free agent)
26.	Dan Berlind, rhp	Dropped out
27.	Erik Lis, of/1b	Dropped out
28.	Anthony Slama, rhp	No. 25
29.	Brian Bass, rhp	(Orioles)
30.	Bradley Tippett, rhp	Dropped out

BEST TOOLS

Best Hitter for Average	Ben Revere
Best Power Hitter	Chris Parmelee
Best Strike-Zone Discipline	Aaron Hicks
Fastest Baserunner	Ben Revere
Best Athlete	Aaron Hicks
Best Fastball	Carlos Gutierrez
Best Curveball	Shooter Hunt
Best Slider	Bobby Lanigan
Best Changeup	Deolis Guerra
Best Control	Bradley Tippett
Best Defensive Catcher	Wilson Ramos
Best Defensive Infielder	Matt Tolbert
Best Infield Arm	Yancarlos Ortiz
Best Defensive Outfielder	Aaron Hicks
Best Outfield Arm	Aaron Hicks

PROJECTED 2012 LINEUP

Catcher	Joe Mauer
First Base	Justin Morneau
Second Base	Alexi Casilla
Third Base	Danny Valencia
Shortstop	Trevor Plouffe
Left Field	Ben Revere
Center Field	Aaron Hicks
Right Field	Delmon Young
Designated Hitter	Jason Kubel
No. 1 Starter	Francisco Liriano
No. 2 Starter	Scott Baker
No. 3 Starter	Kevin Slowey
No. 4 Starter	Nick Blackburn
No. 5 Starter	Glen Perkins
Closer	Joe Nathan

TOP PROSPECTS OF THE DECADE

Year	Player, Pos.	2008 Org.
1999	Michael Cuddyer, 3b	Twins
2000	Michael Cuddyer, 3b	Twins
2001	Adam Johnson, rhp	So. Maryland (Atlantic)
2002	Joe Mauer, c	Twins
2003	Joe Mauer, c	Twins
2004	Joe Mauer, c	Twins
2005	Joe Mauer, c	Twins
2006	Francisco Liriano, lhp	Twins
2007	Matt Garza, rhp	Rays
2008	Nick Blackburn, rhp	Twins

TOP DRAFT PICKS OF THE DECADE

Year	Player, Pos.	2008 Org.
1999	B.J. Garbe, of	Out of baseball
2000	Adam Johnson, rhp	So. Maryland (Atlantic)
2001	Joe Mauer, c	Twins
2002	Denard Span, of	Twins
2003	Matt Moses, 3b	Twins
2004	Trevor Plouffe, ss	Twins
2005	Matt Garza, rhp	Rays
2006	Chris Parmelee, of/1b	Twins
2007	Ben Revere, of	Twins
2008	Aaron Hicks, of	Twins

LARGEST BONUSES IN CLUB HISTORY

Joe Mauer, 2001	$5,150,000
B.J. Garbe, 1999	$2,750,000
Adam Johnson, 2000	$2,500,000
Ryan Mills, 1998	$2,000,000
Michael Cuddyer, 1997	$1,850,000

MINNESOTA TWINS

TOP 2009 ROOKIE: Jose Mijares, lhp. After an impressive September callup, the hard-throwing southpaw should set up Joe Nathan.

BREAKOUT PROSPECT: Rene Tosoni, of. He has a sweet swing and just needs to stay healthy to put up numbers.

SLEEPER: Bobby Lanigan, rhp. His premium slider alone should allow him to dominate lower levels.

SOURCE OF TOP 30 TALENT

Homegrown	27	**Acquired**	**3**
College	8	Trades	3
Junior college	0	Rule 5 draft	0
High school	10	Independent leagues	0
Draft-and-follow	3	Free agents/waivers	0
Nondrafted free agents	1		
International	5		

Numbers in parentheses indicate prospect rankings.

LF
Luke Hughes (17)
Dustin Martin
Juan Portes
Danny Ortiz
Evan Bigley
Michael Harrington

CF
Aaron Hicks (1)
Ben Revere (2)
Joe Benson (15)
Jason Pridie

RF
Angel Morales (10)
Rene Tosoni (18)
David Winfree (28)

3B
Danny Valencia (5)
Deibinson Romero (21)
Matt Macri
Nick Romero
Reggie Williams

SS
Trevor Plouffe (13)
Estarlin de los Santos
Paul Kelly
Yancarlos Ortiz
Tyler Ladendorf
James Beresford

2B
Matt Tolbert (22)
Steven Tolleson (23)
Steve Singleton
Dominic de la Osa

1B
Chris Parmelee (14)
Erik Lis
Brock Peterson
Jon Waltenbury
Mike Gonzales

C
Wilson Ramos (3)
Drew Butera
Jose Morales
Alexander Soto
Danny Lehmann
Danny Rams

RHP

Starters	Relievers
Anthony Swarzak (6)	Carlos Gutierrez (9)
Shooter Hunt (7)	Rob Delaney (24)
Kevin Mulvey (8)	Anthony Slama (25)
Jeff Manship (11)	Loek Van Mil (29)
David Bromberg (19)	Armando Gabino
Deolis Guerra (20)	Charles Nolte
Philip Humber (26)	Tim Lahey
Michael McCardell (27)	Blair Erickson
Michael Tonkin (30)	Zachary Ward
Bobby Lanigan	
B.J. Hermsen	
Jason Jones	
Steven Hirschfield	
Bradley Tippett	
Matt Fox	
Miguel Munoz	
Angelo Sanchez	

LHP

Starters	Relievers
Tyler Robertson (12)	Jose Mijares (4)
Brian Duensing (16)	Kyle Aselton
Martire Garcia	Spencer Steedley
Ryan Mullins	Jean Mijares
Dan Osterbrock	

2008

BEST PURE HITTER: Some teams liked OF Aaron Hicks (1) better on the mound due to his 97-mph fastball, but the Twins always preferred him as a position player. They like his swing and bat speed, and he hit .318 in the Rookie-level Gulf Coast League. OF Danny Ortiz (4) has a short, sweet stroke thanks to quick hands and good strength for his size.

BEST POWER HITTER: 1B Mike Gonzales (9) has power to all fields and led California junior colleges with 18 homers last spring. Hicks also has surprising raw power.

FASTEST RUNNER: Hicks has turned in better times since the Twins signed him and rates as a plus-plus runner.

BEST DEFENSIVE PLAYER: The Twins like strong, athletic SS Tyler Ladendorf (3) for his hands, arm strength and actions, and he has plenty of offensive upside as well. Hicks has center-field tools and more than enough arm for right field if he outgrows center.

BEST FASTBALL: With Hicks not in the mix, RHP Carlos Gutierrez (1) gets the nod for his low-90s two-seamer with Derek Lowe sink. RHP B.J. Hermsen (6) has a low-90s four-seamer and plenty of projectability as an Iowan with a 6-foot-6, 230-pound frame.

BEST SECONDARY PITCH: RHP Shooter Hunt (1s) projected to go in the first 15 picks most of the spring thanks in part to his plus curveball. He slipped due to command issues and his lack of a true changeup, but the same was said of Scott Baker when he came out of college in 2003.

BEST PRO DEBUT: Hicks earned top prospect honors in the GCL, slugging .491 and stealing 12 bases in 14 attempts. LHP Dan Osterbrock (7) led the Rookie-level Appalachian League in strikeouts with 104 in 75 innings while going 7-2, 3.00 with just eight walks.

BEST ATHLETE: The Twins considered Hicks the draft's top athlete, and he has baseball instincts and savvy to go with his tools.

MOST INTRIGUING BACKGROUND: RHP Michael Tonkin (30), whom Minnesota signed away from Southern California for $230,000, is Jason Kubel's brother-in-law. Gonzales' father Pete was a fifth-round pick of the Red Sox in 1981 and had a brief minor league career.

CLOSEST TO THE MAJORS: Gutierrez will build innings and work on his command as a minor league starter but should move quickly as a reliever. Hunt also could hop on the fast track if he improves his command of his two plus pitches.

BEST LATE-ROUND PICK: Tonkin is projectable at 6-foot-7 and has shown velocity and usable secondary stuff, including a changeup with armside run and sink. He needs strength and consistency.

THE ONE WHO GOT AWAY: RHP Kyle Witten (22) has shown four pitches, including a two-plane slider. He should crack Cal State Fullerton's weekend rotation after transferring from Bakersfield (Calif.) JC.

ASSESSMENT: The Twins hoped Hicks would get to them, and he exceeded their expectations afterward. Hunt also could turn out to be a coup for first-year scouting director Deron Johnson, while Tonkin and Hermsen give the organization two more big, young arms.

2007

He may have been a shocker as a first-round pick, but OF Ben Revere led the minors in hitting last season. OF Angel Morales (3) has some of the best raw power in the system.

GRADE: B

2006

The top three choices—OFs Chris Parmelee (1) and Joe Benson (2) and LHP Tyler Robertson (3)—all have shown flashes but had injury problems in 2008. 3B Danny Valencia (19) has blown past them all.

GRADE: C

2005

The Twins found a pair of rotation anchors in RHPs Matt Garza (1) and Kevin Slowey (2), though they traded Garza away. 1B Henry Sanchez (1s) has disappointed, but RHP David Bromberg (32) and OF Rene Tosoni (36) were nice finds as draft-and-follows.

GRADE: A

2004

Minnesota had a bounty of picks before the second round, but only LHP Glen Perkins (1) has delivered as hoped. INF Trevor Plouffe (1) has grinded his way to Triple-A, but RHPs Kyle Waldrop (1), Matt Fox (1s) and Jay Rainville (1s) probably aren't going to make it.

GRADE: C

*Draft analysis by John Manuel (2008) and Jim Callis (2004-07). Numbers in parentheses indicate draft rounds. *Bonuses for 2004-05 are first 10 rounds only.*

PROSPECT

AARON HICKS, OF

Born: Oct. 2, 1989.
Ht.: 6-2. **Wt.:** 170.
Bats: B. **Throws:** R.
Drafted:
HS—Long Beach, 2008
(1st round).
Signed by:
John Leavitt.

JERRY HALE

Hicks is a Los Angeles kid who doesn't fit into preconceived stereotypes. He's an African-American who spent much of the last three years playing at Major League Baseball's Urban Youth Academy, becoming its highest-drafted alumnus when the Twins took him 14th overall in June. He's also a scratch golfer who won a slew of tournaments as a teenager and considered a golf career. When he learned that his father played baseball professionally—Joseph Hicks was a Padres 12th-round pick in 1975 and played four seasons in the minors—he decided to focus his prodigious athletic ability on the diamond, helping Wilson High win the No. 1 national ranking and its first California Interscholastic Federation title in 50 years in 2007. Minnesota considered Hicks the best athlete in the 2008 draft, and he was the Los Angeles area's best since Darryl Strawberry was the No. 1 overall choice in June 1980. While the Twins preferred Hicks as an outfielder, other clubs were prepared to take him in the first round as a pitcher after seeing his fastball range from 94-97 mph last spring. Minnesota has no reason to question its decision, as Hicks ranked as the No. 1 prospect in the Rookie-level Gulf Coast League after signing quickly for $1.78 million.

Sometimes it seems like there's nothing Hicks can't do. He's a premium athlete with growing skills and true five-tool ability. He's a switch-hitter who's a natural from the right side and improved from the left by lowering his hands and unleashing his bat speed. He was more polished and selective at the plate in his debut than the Twins thought he might be, and his eye allowed him to get to his above-average power potential earlier than expected. He projects to hit 20-25 homers annually as he matures. Hicks has plus-plus speed and good baserunning instincts that should improve with experience. He glides to balls in the outfield and has a top-of-the-scale throwing arm that would play in any outfield spot or on the mound if necessary. In the unlikely event he doesn't hit, he can try to make it as a pitcher.

Mostly, Hicks just needs experience facing quality breaking balls. His hands are good enough that he should be able to trust them and stay back on pitches that spin. The game comes so easily to him that at times he has concentration lapses. He's still learning to be a pro in terms of handling the grind of a long season, when to show he's having fun and when to have more of a game face. Some organizations had doubts about Hicks' bat and preferred him on the mound, and one GCL stint doesn't quite answer all those questions.

Hicks' tools resemble those of departed Twins center fielder Torii Hunter, though he should move more quickly through the minors than Hunter did and have better plate discipline. He's the rare combination of an athlete with a fairly polished hitting approach who also plays a premium position. Minnesota is deep in young outfielders in the majors and minors, but Hicks' combination of tools, skills and athletic ability stands out. He'll head to low Class A Beloit for his first full pro season and should make a steady climb to the majors, arriving in 2011.

Year	Club (League)	Class	AVG	G	AB	R	H	2B	3B	HR	RBI	BB	SO	SB	OBP	SLG
2008	Twins (GCL)	R	.318	45	173	32	55	10	4	4	27	28	32	12	.409	.491
MINOR LEAGUE TOTALS			.318	45	173	32	55	10	4	4	27	28	32	12	.409	.491

2 BEN REVERE, OF

PAUL GIERHART

BORN: May 3, 1988. **B-T:** L-R. **HT.:** 5-9. **WT.:** 166. **DRAFTED:** HS—Lexington, Ky., 2007 (1st round). **SIGNED BY:** Billy Corrigan.

Revere was far from a consensus first-round talent in 2007, but Minnesota special assistant Joe McIlvane got on him early as a potential first-round bat. The Twins took him 28th overall and signed him for a below-slot $750,000 bonus. He justified their faith by leading the minors in batting (.379) and winning low Class A Midwest League MVP honors in 2008. The Twins drafted Revere because of a strong conviction he would hit, and he's the system's best hitter. He has surprising gap power in his compact, muscular frame and lashes line drives to all fields. He has explosive speed and steals infield hits. While he has room for improvement at small ball, he's a solid bunter and improving basestealer. Revere started 2008 in extended spring training to work on his short game, which still needs polish. He also started on a throwing program that improved his arm strength, though it remains below average. He'll be an asset in center field but is still working on his reads and jumps. While he has fast-track hitting ability, Revere has work to do smoothing out some of his rough edges and the Twins like to preach patience. Fully recovered from arthroscopic knee surgery in August, he'll be part of a prospect-laden high Class A Fort Myers outfield in 2009, along with Joe Benson, Chris Parmelee and Rene Tosoni.

Year	Club (League)	Class	AVG	G	AB	R	H	2B	3B	HR	RBI	BB	SO	SB	OBP	SLG
2007	Twins (GCL)	R	.325	50	191	46	62	6	10	0	29	13	20	21	.388	.461
2008	Beloit (MWL)	LoA	.379	83	340	51	129	17	10	1	43	27	31	44	.433	.497
MINOR LEAGUE TOTALS			.360	133	531	97	191	23	20	1	72	40	51	65	.416	.484

3 WILSON RAMOS, C

CHRIS PROCTOR

BORN: Aug. 10, 1987. **B-T:** R-R. **HT.:** 6-0. **WT.:** 205. **SIGNED:** Venezuela, 2004. **SIGNED BY:** Jose Leon.

Ramos has acquired a reputation for being a slow starter. He didn't earn a spot on a full-season team to open 2007 and he batted .203 in April last season. He rallied to hit safely in his last 15 games and lead Fort Myers in homers (13) and RBIs (78) while earning Florida State League all-star honors. Ramos has learned to translate his raw power into games and projects to hit 20-25 homers annually down the line. With excellent size and strength in his compact, athletic frame, he's built to catch. He has a very strong arm and led the FSL by throwing out 43 percent of basestealers. He has improved to be an average receiver and blocker behind the plate. A free swinger, Ramos would hit for even more power if he became more selective. He's a slow runner who's prone to hitting into double plays. His poor starts have included playing with a lack of energy, which the Twins hope improves as he matures. He's getting better at learning English, which will help him lead pitching staffs more effectively. Added to the 40-man roster this fall, Ramos should jump to Double-A in 2009. With 25-year-old Joe Mauer ahead of him, however, he seems destined to be a backup or trade bait rather than a regular for Minnesota.

Year	Club (League)	Class	AVG	G	AB	R	H	2B	3B	HR	RBI	BB	SO	SB	OBP	SLG
2005	Twins (DSL)	R	.252	39	127	16	32	5	1	1	15	8	13	1	.295	.331
2006	Twins (GCL)	R	.286	46	154	18	44	12	1	3	26	12	14	4	.339	.435
2007	Beloit (MWL)	LoA	.291	73	292	40	85	17	1	8	42	19	61	1	.345	.438
2008	Fort Myers (FSL)	HiA	.288	126	452	50	130	23	2	13	78	37	103	0	.346	.434
MINOR LEAGUE TOTALS			.284	284	1025	124	291	57	5	25	161	76	191	6	.338	.422

4 JOSE MIJARES, LHP

BORN: Oct. 29, 1984. **B-T:** L-L. **HT.:** 6-0. **WT.:** 230. **SIGNED:** Venezuela, 2002. **SIGNED BY:** Jose Leon.

Held back by inconsistent commitment to the game and conditioning, Mijares was making progress on both fronts last winter in the Venezuelan League when he was involved in a one-car crash in January. He broke a bone in his elbow and injured his shoulder but recovered to pitch by the end of June. Called to the majors in September, he became the Twins' most reliable middle reliever down the stretch. Mijares has reached as high as 98 mph with his lively fastball in the past and sat at 92-94 mph in September. He backs his fastball with a low-80s slider and has flashed a power curveball as well. The mix has made him as effective against lefties and righties throughout his career. Mijares must continue to watch his weight carefully. If he's in shape, he'll improve both his command and durability, his two greatest liabilities. A mature, dependable Mijares should be the Twins' top setup man in 2009, filling a need made more acute by Pat Neshek's Tommy John surgery. He could succeed Joe Nathan as Minnesota's closer when Nathan's contract expires after 2011.

Year	Club (League)	Class	W	L	ERA	G	GS	CG	SV	IP	H	R	ER	HR	BB	SO	AVG
2002	Cagua (VSL)	R	2	5	3.91	13	9	0	0	53	51	29	23	2	27	42	.264
2003	Tronconero 1 (VSL)	R	2	4	1.05	11	7	0	0	52	28	17	6	1	15	58	.159
2004	Twins (GCL)	R	4	0	2.43	19	0	0	5	30	22	9	8	1	15	25	.208
2005	Beloit (MWL)	LoA	6	3	4.31	20	6	0	2	54	43	28	26	6	40	78	.219
	Fort Myers (FSL)	HiA	0	0	1.50	5	1	0	0	12	5	4	2	1	5	17	.116
2006	Fort Myers (FSL)	HiA	3	5	3.57	27	5	0	0	63	52	30	25	10	27	77	.226
2007	Rochester (IL)	AAA	0	1	6.23	5	0	0	0	9	9	7	6	3	5	6	.265
	New Britain (EL)	AA	5	3	3.54	46	0	0	9	61	40	26	24	7	48	75	.183
2008	Twins (GCL)	R	2	1	2.45	7	0	0	0	11	10	3	3	0	1	16	.238
	Fort Myers (FSL)	HiA	0	0	2.61	5	0	0	0	10	7	3	3	0	3	8	.194
	New Britain (EL)	AA	1	1	2.93	11	0	0	2	15	16	5	5	2	7	17	.258
	Minnesota (AL)	MAJ	0	1	0.87	10	0	0	0	10	3	1	1	0	0	5	.088
MINOR LEAGUE TOTALS			25	23	3.19	169	28	0	18	370	283	161	131	33	193	419	.212
MAJOR LEAGUE TOTALS			0	1	0.87	10	0	0	0	10	3	1	1	0	0	5	.088

5 DANNY VALENCIA, 3B

RODGER WOOD

BORN: Sept. 19, 1984. **B-T:** R-R. **HT.:** 6-2. **WT.:** 200. **DRAFTED:** Miami, 2006 (19th round). **SIGNED BY:** Hector Otero.

The Twins have been searching for an everyday third baseman since Corey Koskie left as a free agent after the 2004 season, and Valencia is the latest heir to the throne. He was a Florida State League all-star in 2008 and finished strongly at Double-A New Britain. Valencia's bat speed ranks among the best in the organization. He has good hand-eye coordination and can turn on good fastballs and drive them out of the park. He's strong enough to hit for power from pole to pole. He has improved his pitch recognition and can punish hanging breaking balls. He's a good athlete with first-step quickness and an above-average arm at third base. Consistency, in terms of concentration and execution, would propel Valencia from average to plus defensively. He'd also benefit from more patience at the plate. He rubs some teammates and club officials the wrong way with bouts of immaturity, including taking bad at-bats with him into the field and showing up umpires. He has below-average speed but isn't a liability on the bases. The Twins were looking outside—again—for a third baseman, but a more mature, focused Valencia could provide an internal answer. He's expected to get his first Triple-A test sometime in 2009.

Year	Club (League)	Class	AVG	G	AB	R	H	2B	3B	HR	RBI	BB	SO	SB	OBP	SLG
2006	Elizabethton (APP)	R	.311	48	190	30	59	13	0	8	29	15	34	0	.365	.505
2007	Beloit (MWL)	LoA	.302	66	242	44	73	15	0	11	35	28	54	3	.374	.500
	Fort Myers (FSL)	HiA	.291	61	230	28	67	8	2	6	31	16	48	1	.332	.422
2008	Fort Myers (FSL)	HiA	.336	60	220	35	74	19	3	5	44	27	43	2	.402	.518
	New Britain (EL)	AA	.289	69	266	40	77	18	2	10	32	18	70	2	.334	.485
MINOR LEAGUE TOTALS			.305	304	1148	177	350	73	7	40	171	104	249	8	.361	.485

6 ANTHONY SWARZAK, RHP

BORN: Sept. 10, 1985. **B-T:** R-R. **HT.:** 6-3. **WT.:** 195. **DRAFTED:** HS—Fort Lauderdale, Fla., 2004 (2nd round). **SIGNED BY:** Brad Weitzel.

The third prep pitcher Minnesota drafted in 2004, Swarzak has stayed healthy, unlike the two selected before him (Kyle Waldrop, Jay Rainville). Swarzak's career hit a bump when he drew a 50-game suspension after testing positive for a recreational drug in 2007. He struggled in Double-A in 2008 before finishing with a flourish after his first promotion to Triple-A. Swarzak has the best combination of stuff, youth and experience of any Twins starter in the minors. He has two plus pitches in his 91-93 mph fastball that touches 95 and his high-70s curveball with 12-to-6 break. He has become better at locating his curve. While he threw a solid changeup as an amateur, Swarzak has lost the feel for it as a pro. In Double-A, he struggled locating his fastball down in the zone, a mechanical issue tied to finishing off his pitches, and got hammered as a result. He has improved his mound demeanor but some scouts still question his competitiveness. Swarzak's fastball-curveball combo would make him a prime bullpen candidate, but club officials prefer him in a starting role. He responded positively to his exposure to Triple-A, where he'll return in 2009.

Year	Club (League)	Class	W	L	ERA	G	GS	CG	SV	IP	H	R	ER	HR	BB	SO	AVG
2004	Twins (GCL)	R	5	3	2.63	11	9	0	1	48	46	20	14	1	6	42	.251
2005	Beloit (MWL)	LoA	9	5	4.04	18	18	0	0	91	81	48	41	7	32	101	.238
	Fort Myers (FSL)	HiA	3	4	3.66	10	10	0	0	59	72	25	24	3	11	55	.300
2006	Fort Myers (FSL)	HiA	11	7	3.27	27	27	2	0	146	131	56	53	8	60	131	.242
2007	Fort Myers (FSL)	HiA	0	0	2.30	3	3	0	0	16	14	6	4	0	5	18	.241
	New Britain (EL)	AA	5	4	3.23	15	14	1	0	86	78	34	31	6	23	76	.241
2008	New Britain (EL)	AA	3	8	5.67	20	20	0	0	102	126	71	64	12	37	76	.304
	Rochester (IL)	AAA	5	0	1.80	7	7	0	0	45	41	14	9	4	14	26	.243
MINOR LEAGUE TOTALS			41	31	3.64	111	108	3	1	593	589	274	240	41	188	525	.259

7 SHOOTER HUNT, RHP

BORN: Aug. 16, 1986. **B-T:** R-R **HT.:** 6-3. **WT.:** 200. **DRAFTED:** Tulane, 2006 (1st round supplemental). **SIGNED BY:** Jack Powell.

As a New Jersey high schooler, Hunt played catcher and pitched on a scout team coached by Twins area scout John Wilson. After transferring from Virginia, he ranked among the NCAA Division I leaders in ERA and strikeouts in both his seasons at Tulane. He faded down the stretch and fell out of the first round in 2008, but Minnesota happily scooped him up with the first pick of the sandwich round and signed him for $1.08 million. Hunt has premium stuff and reminds Twins scouts of Scott Baker. His fastball sits at 91-94 mph, and his curveball already ranks as the best in the system. It's a two-plane breaker with depth and power that he throws with conviction. Command has vexed Hunt since he became a full-time pitcher as a high school senior. He improved his strike-throwing ability in instructional league by moving his feet closer together, which aided in maintaining his load in his delivery and providing better balance. He lacks confidence and consistency with his changeup, but it does have potential. To start 2009, Hunt will return to low Class A, where he struggled when he tired late in his pro debut. If his improvements from instructional league take hold, he could move rapidly and challenge for a big league rotation spot late in 2010.

Year	Club (League)	Class	W	L	ERA	G	GS	CG	SV	IP	H	R	ER	HR	BB	SO	AVG
2008	Elizabethton (APP)	R	0	0	0.47	4	4	0	0	19	4	3	1	0	6	34	.066
	Beloit (MWL)	LoA	1	4	5.46	7	7	0	0	31	26	21	19	2	27	34	.230
MINOR LEAGUE TOTALS			1	4	3.58	11	11	0	0	50	30	24	20	2	33	68	.172

8 KEVIN MULVEY, RHP

BORN: May 26, 1985. **B-T:** R-R. **HT.:** 6-2. **WT.:** 190. **DRAFTED:** Villanova, 2006 (2nd round). **SIGNED BY:** Scott Hunter (Mets).

The Mets' top draft pick (second round) in 2006, Mulvey outperformed the other two pitchers (Deolis Guerra, Philip Humber) who came to the Twins in the Johan Santana trade. He started and finished strong at Triple-A Rochester, though he won just once in a three-month span in between. At his best, Mulvey competes hard with pitchability and above-average stuff. His fastball can reach 94 mph, though it usually sits at 87-91 with sink. He can vary his plus slider, giving it more tilt and bite or shortening it up to almost a cutter. He throws his curveball and changeup for strikes and has good mound savvy. Mulvey rarely had his best velocity, life or command last season, and his pitches generally were less sharp than they had been when he was a Met. Twins officials theorize the pressure of the trade and a desire to get to the majors prompted him to go for strikeouts, leading to less efficiency, deeper pitch counts and some overthrowing that sapped his stuff. He's not as good fielding his position or holding runners as he needs to be. Mulvey and Humber will compete for a job as a middle reliever/spot starter during spring training. Mulvey projects as a No. 4 starter, but Minnesota needs him more in the bullpen in the short term.

Year	Club (League)	Class	W	L	ERA	G	GS	CG	SV	IP	H	R	ER	HR	BB	SO	AVG
2006	Mets (GCL)	R	0	0	0.00	1	1	0	0	2	1	0	0	0	0	1	.143
	Binghamton (EL)	AA	0	1	1.35	3	3	1	0	13	10	4	2	1	5	10	.217
2007	Binghamton (EL)	AA	11	10	3.32	26	26	0	0	152	145	74	56	4	43	110	.252
	New Orleans (PCL)	AAA	1	0	0.00	1	1	0	0	6	2	0	0	0	0	3	.095
2008	Rochester (IL)	AAA	7	9	3.77	27	27	1	0	148	152	80	62	16	48	121	.265
MINOR LEAGUE TOTALS			19	20	3.36	58	58	2	0	321	310	158	120	21	96	245	.253

9 CARLOS GUTIERREZ, RHP

BORN: Sept. 22, 1986. **B-T:** R-R. **HT.:** 6-3. **WT.:** 205. **DRAFTED:** Miami, 2008 (1st round). **SIGNED BY:** Hector Otero.

Gutierrez started 17 games as a sophomore at Miami before missing 2007 with Tommy John surgery. He returned as a closer and became one of three Hurricanes drafted in the first round last June, joining Yonder Alonso (Reds) and Jemile Weeks (Athletics). Gutierrez signed for $1.29 million. He has the best fastball in the system when velocity, command and especially movement are factored in. His low-90s sinker has drawn comparisons to Derek Lowe's, and he had a 2.6 groundout/airout ratio and didn't allow a homer in his pro debut. Gutierrez' delivery is so easy that his pitches seem to jump on hitters. He's excellent at holding runners, and despite making a costly error in the College World Series, he's an above-average fielder. At times, Gutierrez shows a plus slider in the mid-80s, but he lacks consistency with it. His changeup is in the rudimentary stages but has flashed some sink. The Twins intend to see if Gutierrez can emulate Lowe as a starter who works off his sinker almost exclusively. They also hope putting him in their high Class A rotation will help him hone his fastball command. If the need arises,

Minnesota could shift him back to the bullpen and put him on the fast track.

Year	Club (League)	Class	W	L	ERA	G	GS	CG	SV	IP	H	R	ER	HR	BB	SO	AVG
2008	Fort Myers (FSL)	HiA	3	1	2.10	16	0	0	1	26	23	7	6	0	7	19	.240
MINOR LEAGUE TOTALS			3	1	2.10	16	0	0	1	26	23	7	6	0	7	19	.240

10 ANGEL MORALES, OF

RODGER WOOD

BORN: Nov. 24, 1989. **B-T:** R-R. **HT.:** 6-1. **WT.:** 180. **DRAFTED:** HS—Caguas, P.R., 2007 (3rd round). **SIGNED BY:** Hector Otero.

Morales emerged as Puerto Rico's top prospect for the 2007 draft at a winter showcase, creating some first-round buzz, but he fell to the third round after an up-and-down spring. The Twins kept him in extended spring training to start 2008. Once he got on the diamond, he led the Rookie-level Appalachian League in homers (15) and slugging percentage (.623). Morales has wicked raw power, with plenty of leverage and strength in his swing. He's more than a one-dimensional slugger, as only Aaron Hicks and Joe Benson have more tools and raw ability in the system. Morales has plus speed and plays a quality center field, though he's expected to slow down some as he fills out and eventually wind up in right. His plus arm plays at either spot. Hicks and Benson are raw, but Morales is behind them in terms of his tools translating into games. He struck out in 39 percent of his at-bats last season because he doesn't recognize or handle breaking balls well. He employs a dead-pull approach despite having the strength to hit for power to all fields. Morales' upside is prodigious and the Twins will be extremely patient with him. He'll head to low Class A in 2009, part of an anticipated one-step-at-a-time climb to the majors.

Year	Club (League)	Class	AVG	G	AB	R	H	2B	3B	HR	RBI	BB	SO	SB	OBP	SLG
2007	Twins (GCL)	R	.256	38	121	18	31	6	3	2	15	12	44	11	.357	.405
2008	Elizabethton (APP)	R	.301	54	183	33	55	12	1	15	28	26	72	7	.413	.623
MINOR LEAGUE TOTALS			.283	92	304	51	86	18	4	17	43	38	116	18	.391	.536

11 JEFF MANSHIP, RHP

BORN: Jan. 16, 1985. **B-T:** R-R. **HT.:** 6-2. **WT.:** 202. **DRAFTED:** Notre Dame, 2006 (14th round). **SIGNED BY:** Billy Milos.

The Twins have several pitchers of similar ability at the upper levels of their system, and Manship could yet wind up being the best of a group that includes Brian Duensing, Philip Humber, Kevin Mulvey and Anthony Swarzak. Manship has physically matured as a pro, adding two inches and 35 pounds, and has the stuff to be a big league starter. He has become more comfortable pitching off his fastball to both sides of the plate and has good control of the pitch, which sits at 88-91 mph with solid sink. He touches 93 with his fastball but could stand to command it better, having sacrificed a bit of command for more power. To do that, he'll need to become more efficient in his delivery. His mid-70s curveball remains Manship's best pitch, and he has a feel for the strike zone with it. When he got his first taste of Double-A last year, he learned that his curve alone wasn't enough for him to dominate, and he was homer-prone when made mistakes with his offspeed stuff. His changeup and slider give him two more pitches he can throw for strikes, though neither stands out. Scouts commend Manship's ability to compete without his best stuff and adjust within games when his plan of attack isn't working. He has answered questions about his durability—which stem in part from Tommy John surgery he had in 2003—by surpassing 180 innings last year (including a successful stint in the Arizona Fall League). He'll return to Double-A to start 2009.

Year	Club (League)	Class	W	L	ERA	G	GS	CG	SV	IP	H	R	ER	HR	BB	SO	AVG
2006	Twins (GCL)	R	0	0	0.00	2	0	0	0	6	3	0	0	0	1	10	.150
	Fort Myers (FSL)	HiA	0	0	2.08	4	3	0	0	9	7	3	2	0	2	12	.212
2007	Beloit (MWL)	LoA	7	1	1.51	13	13	0	0	78	51	15	13	4	9	77	.185
	Fort Myers (FSL)	HiA	8	5	3.15	13	13	0	0	71	77	38	25	5	25	59	.270
2008	Fort Myers (FSL)	HiA	7	3	2.86	13	13	1	0	79	68	31	25	0	20	63	.231
	New Britain (EL)	AA	3	6	4.46	14	14	0	0	77	90	47	38	8	24	62	.292
MINOR LEAGUE TOTALS			25	15	2.91	59	56	1	0	319	296	134	103	17	81	283	.243

12 TYLER ROBERTSON, LHP

BORN: Dec. 23, 1987. **B-T:** L-L. **HT.:** 6-5. **WT.:** 225. **DRAFTED:** HS—Fair Oaks, Calif., 2006 (3rd round). **SIGNED BY:** Kevin Bootay.

Robertson thrived in low Class A in 2007, and the son of Rangers scout Jay Robertson seemed primed to break out further last season. Instead, his velocity dropped all spring, to the point where he was throwing in the low 80s. Diagnosed with shoulder tendinitis, he didn't pitch after July 7 and hadn't regained sufficient arm strength to get back on the mound in instructional league. At his best, Robertson throws four pitches for strikes, including an average 88-92 mph fastball, a plus slider, a solid-average curveball and an average changeup. He's a student of the game and hard worker who knows how to use his stuff better than most pitchers his age. Robertson's stiff arm action has concerned scouts since high school, and his tendinitis this summer won't quiet that chorus. Even the Twins admit his arm action limits his projection despite his big, physical body. At best, he has lost development time. At worst, there's no guarantee his arm strength will return to its previous peak. Eric Rasmussen was his pitching coach at Fort Myers in 2008, and now he's in charge of getting Robertson back up to speed as the organization's pitching coordinator. A healthy Robertson would be the Twins' top starting pitching prospect, and he could move to Double-A if he shows his old stuff.

Year	Club (League)	Class	W	L	ERA	G	GS	CG	SV	IP	H	R	ER	HR	BB	SO	AVG
2006	Twins (GCL)	R	4	2	4.25	11	10	0	0	49	54	23	23	2	15	54	.280
2007	Beloit (MWL)	LoA	9	5	2.29	18	16	2	1	102	87	33	26	3	33	123	.226
2008	Fort Myers (FSL)	HiA	5	3	2.72	15	15	0	0	83	78	36	25	3	31	73	.247
MINOR LEAGUE TOTALS			18	10	2.85	44	41	3	1	234	219	92	74	8	79	250	.245

13 TREVOR PLOUFFE, SS/3B

BORN: June 15, 1986. **B-T:** R-R. **HT.:** 6-1. **WT.:** 175. **DRAFTED:** HS—West Hills, Calif., 2004 (1st round). **SIGNED BY:** Bill Mele.

Scouts still remember Plouffe fondly as a prep pitching prospect, and he would have played both ways at Southern California had he not signed for $1.5 million as a first-round pick. He has grinded his way to the doorstep of the majors, reaching Triple-A for the first time in 2008. He played more third base there and added experience at second base in addition to playing shortstop. However, the Twins don't think of him as a utility-man, seeing him instead as a slugging middle infielder in the Khalil Greene mold. Plouffe's hands and throwing arm made him a first-round pick. He still has a cannon for an arm that plays well on the left side of the infield, and his hands work at the plate and in the field. He has the hand-eye coordination to get the barrel of the bat to the ball and has average power, especially to the gaps. Club officials project he could hit 15-20 homers annually in the majors once he learns which pitches to lay off and which to drive. As with Greene, poor pitch recognition continues to depress Plouffe's offensive production. He's an aggressive, early-count hitter who tries to hit the first fastball he sees, in part because he lacks confidence or a consistent approach when faced with offspeed pitches or two-strike counts. He's a fringe-average runner who's fast becoming below average. His power will determine whether Plouffe becomes a big league regular. He could fit sooner than later as a utility player in Minnesota but will have to play with energy to earn a spot on manager Ron Gardenhire's bench. More likely, he's headed back to Triple-A Rochester after being added to the 40-man roster in November.

Year	Club (League)	Class	AVG	G	AB	R	H	2B	3B	HR	RBI	BB	SO	SB	OBP	SLG
2004	Elizabethton (APP)	R	.283	60	237	29	67	7	2	4	28	19	34	2	.340	.380
2005	Beloit (MWL)	LoA	.223	127	466	58	104	18	0	13	60	50	78	8	.300	.345
2006	Fort Myers (FSL)	HiA	.246	125	455	60	112	26	4	4	45	58	93	8	.333	.347
2007	New Britain (EL)	AA	.274	126	497	75	136	37	2	9	50	38	89	12	.326	.410
2008	New Britain (EL)	AA	.269	58	227	32	61	17	3	3	21	16	43	4	.325	.410
	Rochester (IL)	AAA	.256	66	250	34	64	17	3	6	39	14	47	1	.292	.420
MINOR LEAGUE TOTALS			.255	562	2132	288	544	122	14	39	243	195	384	35	.319	.380

14 CHRIS PARMELEE, 1B/OF

BORN: Feb. 24, 1988. **B-T:** L-L. **HT.:** 6-1. **WT.:** 228. **DRAFTED:** HS—Chino Hills, Calif., 2006 (1st round). **SIGNED BY:** John Leavitt.

Parmelee and Joe Benson were Minnesota's top two picks in the 2006 draft—Parmelee went 20th overall and signed for $1.5 million—and they've played together ever since. Their ties include an unfortunate coincidence from 2008, when both played just 69 games at Beloit because of injuries. Parmelee got hurt playing first base, crashing into the wall in foul ground to make a catch and breaking his left wrist. Prior to the injury, he had continued his evolution into a power threat, more likely a first baseman in an organization loaded with outfielders with more well-rounded tools. Parmelee has more power, especially usable power, than any Twins farmhand, and he's also one of the system's more selective hitters. He significantly increased his walk rate in 2008, drawing more bases on balls in a half-season than he did in all of 2007. Putting himself in more good hitter's counts, he also unlocked his power more, falling one home run short of his '07 total. Parmelee has strength and a nice natural loft to his swing to produce power, though the Twins believe his numbers will fall next year while he recovers from his wrist injury and deals with more spacious ballparks in the Florida State League. With all those deep counts come strikeouts, and Parmelee will have to make more consistent contact at higher levels for his power to play. Some scouts question his bat speed and ability to catch up to good velocity. He still needs to improve at first base to avoid becoming a DH down the line, and he's a below-average runner. All of Parmelee's value is in his bat, a rarity among Twins prospects, but he has started to perform.

Year	Club (League)	Class	AVG	G	AB	R	H	2B	3B	HR	RBI	BB	SO	SB	OBP	SLG
2006	Twins (GCL)	R	.279	45	154	29	43	7	4	8	32	23	47	3	.369	.532
	Beloit (MWL)	LoA	.227	11	22	2	5	1	0	0	2	5	9	0	.370	.273

			AVG	G	AB	R	H	2B	3B	HR	RBI	BB	SO	SB	OBP	SLG
2007	Beloit (MWL)	LoA	.239	128	447	56	107	23	5	15	70	46	137	8	.313	.414
2008	Beloit (MWL)	LoA	.239	69	226	41	54	10	3	14	49	52	83	3	.385	.496
MINOR LEAGUE TOTALS			.246	253	849	128	209	41	12	37	153	126	276	14	.346	.453

15 JOE BENSON, OF

BORN: March 5, 1988. **B-T:** R-R. **HT.:** 6-2. **WT.:** 211. **DRAFTED:** HS—Joliet, Ill., 2006 (2nd round).
SIGNED BY: Billy Milos.

Benson could have played football and baseball at Purdue, a testament to his strength, athleticism and tools. He was making strong progress in 2008, but he tried to play through a back injury sustained in an offseason car accident. His performance suffered, and doctors eventually diagnosed a fractured vertebra. He finally shut it down in late June and wasn't healthy enough to play in instructional league. A healthy Benson has better raw tools than any player in the system save Aaron Hicks, with excellent bat speed, raw power and premium strength. He's fast (4.0 seconds to first base from the right side) and has true center-field range. Unlike many football players, he has an excellent throwing arm, and he ranked second in the Midwest League in outfield assists (14 in just 69 games) despite his injury. Despite his tools, hitting hasn't come easy to Benson, who seemed to be thinking more at the plate this year instead of reacting, especially in trying to combat breaking balls. He's going to need plenty of at-bats to improve his instincts, pitch recognition and hitting skills. Back injuries can be troublesome, but the Twins have had players return from them with tools intact, such as former all-star Chuck Knoblauch. Benson is in the right organization for a raw, toolsy prep player who will need to make up for lost time. Minnesota is patient and loaded with outfielders, and Benson could conceivably return to low Class A for a third season, though a promotion is likely.

Year	Club (League)	Class	AVG	G	AB	R	H	2B	3B	HR	RBI	BB	SO	SB	OBP	SLG
2006	Twins (GCL)	R	.260	52	196	30	51	11	5	5	28	21	41	9	.335	.444
	Beloit (MWL)	LoA	.263	8	19	2	5	0	0	0	1	0	6	1	.263	.263
2007	Beloit (MWL)	LoA	.255	122	432	73	110	18	8	5	38	49	124	18	.347	.368
2008	Beloit (MWL)	LoA	.248	69	254	39	63	16	3	4	27	24	73	17	.326	.382
MINOR LEAGUE TOTALS			.254	251	901	144	229	45	16	14	94	94	244	45	.337	.386

16 BRIAN DUENSING, LHP

BORN: Feb. 22, 1983. **B-T:** L-L. **HT.:** 5-11. **WT.:** 195. **DRAFTED:** Nebraska, 2005 (3rd round).
SIGNED BY: Mark Wilson.

Like Jeff Manship, Duensing had Tommy John surgery in college, and like Manship, he's an organization favorite because of his ability to throw four pitches for strikes. However, his command wasn't as sharp in 2008 as it had been previously, and he had his worst season as a pro. Duensing's best trait is his ability to manipulate his pitches. His fastball sits at 88-90 mph, but he can run it up to 94, particularly when working out of the bullpen, as he did for the bronze-medal U.S. Olympic team in Beijing. He also throws a slow curveball, a hard slider that he can shorten to a cutter or slow down into a slurve, and a changeup that remains his best pitch. The Twins don't pinpoint one reason for his lack of sharpness last season but he couldn't put opponents away when he was ahead in the count. His versatility and outstanding makeup could make Duensing more valuable as a middle reliever, and one club official sees him as a lefthanded version of Matt Guerrier. Middle-relief roles are readily available in Minnesota while the rotation looks less open. Duensing will compete for a bullpen job in spring training after getting added to the 40-man roster in November.

Year	Club (League)	Class	W	L	ERA	G	GS	CG	SV	IP	H	R	ER	HR	BB	SO	AVG
2005	Elizabethton (APP)	R	4	3	2.32	12	9	0	0	50	49	19	13	4	16	55	.249
2006	Beloit (MWL)	LoA	2	3	2.94	11	11	0	0	70	68	26	23	3	14	55	.257
	Fort Myers (FSL)	HiA	2	5	4.24	7	7	0	0	40	47	25	19	4	8	33	.296
	New Britain (EL)	AA	1	2	3.65	10	9	0	0	49	51	29	20	6	18	30	.277
2007	New Britain (EL)	AA	4	1	2.66	9	9	0	0	51	47	19	15	2	7	38	.240
	Rochester (IL)	AAA	11	5	3.24	19	19	3	0	117	115	54	42	13	30	86	.261
2008	Rochester (IL)	AAA	5	11	4.28	25	24	0	0	139	150	75	66	16	34	77	.278
MINOR LEAGUE TOTALS			29	30	3.45	93	88	3	0	516	527	247	198	48	127	374	.266

17 LUKE HUGHES, 3B/2B

BORN: Aug. 2, 1984. **B-T:** R-R. **HT.:** 6-0. **WT.:** 200. **SIGNED:** Australia, 2002. **SIGNED BY:** Howard Norsetter.

The Twins' international efforts are as wide-ranging as any team, with Hughes the latest Australian to make waves as a prospect. (Grant Balfour, who found success with the Rays in 2008, has been the best product of the Twins' efforts Down Under.) Protected on the 40-man roster in November, Hughes never has been considered a top prospect in the past because of a litany of minor injuries and an inability to garner consistent playing time. His 99 games and 391 at-bats in 2008 were both career highs, even though he missed time with a hamstring pull that kept him out of most of June. He was healthy enough to play in both the Double-A Eastern League all-star game and the Futures Game, where he put on a power display in batting practice on par with anyone on hand. Hughes has true plus power. He came to spring camp stronger and in better shape than ever before, and when he squares a ball up, it flies. He doesn't have a pure swing or approach—he's a front-foot hitter and lacks patience—but generates above-average bat speed and can kill good fastballs. Hughes came up as a middle infielder and hasn't found a position he can play regularly at an average level. He's not smooth defensively with stiff hands, and the Twins sent him to Venezuela for winter ball to get more reps at third base, but Aragua soon shifted him to left field. If Hughes can't play infield well, he likely won't be a regular and fits better as a utility player. He logged time at second base and played briefly at all three outfield spots in 2008. He's likely headed to Triple-A in 2009, where he may have to compete with Danny Valencia for playing time at third base.

Year	Club (League)	Class	AVG	G	AB	R	H	2B	3B	HR	RBI	BB	SO	SB	OBP	SLG
2003	Twins (GCL)	R	.305	54	190	22	58	9	4	2	25	15	22	5	.361	.426
2004	Elizabethton (APP)	R	.284	44	141	20	40	8	1	3	19	9	30	1	.338	.418
2005	Beloit (MWL)	LoA	.257	72	292	42	75	14	2	7	42	21	63	4	.319	.390
	Fort Myers (FSL)	HiA	.202	23	84	9	17	3	1	0	7	2	15	0	.222	.262
2006	Fort Myers (FSL)	HiA	.231	95	333	31	77	15	0	4	37	23	72	6	.287	.312
2007	New Britain (EL)	AA	.283	92	315	56	89	18	2	9	43	34	68	4	.356	.438
2008	New Britain (EL)	AA	.319	70	285	53	91	15	3	15	40	28	70	4	.385	.551
	Rochester (IL)	AAA	.283	29	106	17	30	7	1	3	21	7	30	2	.325	.453
MINOR LEAGUE TOTALS			.273	479	1746	250	477	89	14	43	234	139	370	26	.332	.414

18 RENE TOSONI, OF

BORN: July 2, 1986. **B-T:** L-R. **HT.:** 6-1. **WT.:** 194. **DRAFTED:** Chipola (Fla.) JC, D/F 2005 (36th round). **SIGNED BY:** Jim Ridley.

While Chris Parmelee and Joe Benson were early-round picks, Minnesota had them repeat the Midwest League in 2008 while sending Tosoni, a 36th-round draft-and-follow, to high Class A though he had just 11 at-bats above Rookie ball. Tosoni was batting .325 and making the Twins look smart when he fouled a pitch off his left foot on May 16. He broke a bone on the top of his foot and missed three months. He was rusty when he returned, with one hit in 14 at-bats. Tosoni has a sweet, short swing, and only Ben Revere projects to hit for a better average among Twins farmhands. Tosoni is patient, keeps the bat in the hitting zone for a long time and stings the ball to all fields. He's not one-dimensional, either. He's an average runner who's a capable center fielder, and his arm plays above-average with accuracy, strength and a quick release. Despite his lack of experience, Tosoni has added polish on the fundamentals, such as running the bases, hitting cutoff men and grinding through at-bats. Unlike Benson and Parmelee, he lacks the above-average raw power normally associated with a corner outfielder, which is probably what he'll be in the long run. Tosoni will return to the Florida State League, hardly a power-hitting haven, in hopes of staying healthy and having his first full season in 2009.

Year	Club (League)	Class	AVG	G	AB	R	H	2B	3B	HR	RBI	BB	SO	SB	OBP	SLG
2007	Elizabethton (APP)	R	.301	63	236	58	71	13	4	3	31	32	48	13	.407	.428
	Beloit (MWL)	LoA	.273	2	11	1	3	1	0	0	1	0	2	0	.273	.364
2008	Twins (GCL)	R	.667	2	6	3	4	0	0	1	3	0	1	0	.667	1.167
	Fort Myers (FSL)	HiA	.300	42	140	27	42	7	3	1	19	21	30	3	.408	.414
MINOR LEAGUE TOTALS			.305	109	393	89	120	21	7	5	54	53	81	16	.408	.433

19 DAVID BROMBERG, RHP

BORN: Sept. 14, 1987. **B-T:** L-R. **HT.:** 6-5. **WT.:** 241. **DRAFTED:** Santa Ana (Calif.) JC, D/F 2005 (32nd round). **SIGNED BY:** Dan Cox.

Several scouts liked Bromberg's power potential when he was a high schooler in Malibu, but he instead has found success as a pitcher since signing as a draft-and-follow for $40,000. He led the minor leagues with 177 strikeouts in 2008, thanks to a finishing kick that included 50 whiffs in 35 innings over his final six starts. Bromberg is still making adjustments to being a full-time pitcher and learned to pace himself through a full season in low Class A, holding the velocity on his 88-92 mph fastball all season. He touches 95 at times with his four-seamer but pitches off the two-seamer, more notable for its sink than its run. He varies the velocity and shape of his curveball, his strikeout pitch. It really came around in the second half as he got a better handle on his mechanics. Former pitching coordinator Rick Knapp used planter stands to rig a directional training drill that got Bromberg to stop over-rotating in his delivery. His changeup is solid average, and he improved in quickening his time to the plate and handling the running game. Better fastball command will be crucial for Bromberg to keep getting strikeouts at higher levels, and he'll have to work to maintain his body, as he's not particularly athletic. He led the Midwest League in hit batters (19) and wild pitches (16). He projects as an innings-eating mid-rotation starter as he learns to be more efficient and not go for swinging strikes on every pitch. He's ticketed for high Class A this year.

Year	Club (League)	Class	W	L	ERA	G	GS	CG	SV	IP	H	R	ER	HR	BB	SO	AVG
2006	Twins (GCL)	R	3	3	2.66	10	10	2	0	51	42	21	15	2	18	31	.230
2007	Elizabethton (APP)	R	9	0	2.78	13	11	0	0	58	45	19	18	4	32	81	.211
2008	Beloit (MWL)	LoA	9	10	4.44	27	27	0	0	150	149	81	74	10	54	177	.262
MINOR LEAGUE TOTALS			21	13	3.72	50	48	2	0	259	236	121	107	16	104	289	.245

20 DEOLIS GUERRA, RHP

BORN: April 17, 1989. **B-T:** R-R. **HT.:** 6-5. **WT.:** 200. **SIGNED:** Venezuela, 2005. **SIGNED BY:** Rafael Bournigal (Mets).

Guerra was the biggest pitching prospect (physically and in terms of reputation) to come from the Mets in the Johan Santana deal. Signed out of Venezuela in 2005 for $700,000, Guerra was on the fast-track with New York. In 2007, he hit 95 mph with his fastball and showed a plus changeup as an 18-year-old in high Class A. He even pitched in the Futures Game in San Francisco. But he was far from the same pitcher after the trade, enduring a difficult season with his new organization. Whether Twins coaches altered Guerra or he altered himself is a matter of debate in the organization, but something changed with Guerra, who lost any consistency in his delivery. He threw different pitches from different release points and showed a stiff, stabbing arm action that Minnesota scouts didn't see in 2007. He topped out at 90 mph and sat in the mid- to upper 80s for most of 2008. His changeup still showed signs of being a plus pitch, and club officials do believe he can spin a break-ing ball, which was a concern earlier in his career. Most distressing, one Twins official described him as having a "low-energy" body, and he'll have to get in better shape. Two things salvaged the year for Guerra. He threw a career-high 130 innings, and he made adjustments in instructional league that brought back most of his velocity. Minnesota will see which Guerra shows up in spring training, though he's expected to a make a fourth trip to high Class A in any case.

Year	Club (League)	Class	W	L	ERA	G	GS	CG	SV	IP	H	R	ER	HR	BB	SO	AVG
2006	Hagerstown (SAL)	LoA	6	7	2.20	17	17	0	0	82	59	22	20	3	37	64	.208
	St. Lucie (FSL)	HiA	1	1	6.14	2	2	0	0	7	9	6	5	1	6	5	.290
2007	St. Lucie (FSL)	HiA	2	6	4.01	21	20	0	0	90	80	44	40	9	25	66	.240
2008	Fort Myers (FSL)	HiA	11	9	5.47	26	25	1	0	130	138	85	79	12	71	71	.272
MINOR LEAGUE TOTALS			20	23	4.20	66	64	1	0	309	286	157	144	25	139	206	.247

21 DEIBINSON ROMERO, 3B

BORN: Sept. 24, 1986. **B-T:** R-R. **HT.:** 6-0. **WT.:** 193. **SIGNED:** Dominican Republic, 2004. **SIGNED BY:** Fred Guerrero.

The Twins had hoped Romero would begin to emerge as a third-base option for them last season after he made a run at the Appalachian League triple crown and a successful cameo at Beloit in 2007. He returned to the Snappers in 2008 but as with Joe Benson and Chris Parmelee, injuries short-circuited his season. Robinson needed minor left knee surgery in late April, sidelining him for nearly two months (and opening a roster spot for Ben Revere). When he returned in mid-June, Romero got hot, showing his bat speed, quick stroke and raw power. However, he went out for the season on July 18 when he broke his right leg falling into the dugout while making a running catch. He'll have to prove he can regain the agility to stay in the infield, and he wasn't scheduled to begin workouts until January 2009, an indication of the severity of injury. His hands can be a bit hard, but he has an above-average arm and all the tools to fit the profile of a regular third baseman—if he can stay healthy. Minnesota showed its faith in Romero by placing him on its 40-man roster, and he could earn a spot in high Class A with a strong spring.

Year	Club (League)	Class	AVG	G	AB	R	H	2B	3B	HR	RBI	BB	SO	SB	OBP	SLG
2005	Twins (DSL)	R	.206	49	175	21	36	4	0	1	12	12	36	7	.286	.246
2006	Twins (GCL)	R	.313	50	176	37	55	10	2	4	38	13	37	6	.365	.460
2007	Elizabethton (APP)	R	.316	66	247	60	78	16	2	9	52	34	47	9	.406	.506
	Beloit (MWL)	LoA	.300	2	10	2	3	1	0	0	3	1	4	0	.364	.400
2008	Beloit (MWL)	LoA	.268	40	149	21	40	8	1	3	18	7	38	1	.309	.396
MINOR LEAGUE TOTALS			.280	207	757	141	212	39	5	17	123	67	162	23	.350	.412

22 MATT TOLBERT, INF

BORN: May 4, 1982. **B-T:** B-R. **HT.:** 6-0. **WT.:** 177. **DRAFTED:** Mississippi, 2004 (16th round). **SIGNED BY:** Mark Quimuyog.

A four-year starter at Mississippi, Tolbert was known much more for his glove than his bat. He batted just .288 for the Rebels and rarely drove the ball. As a pro, however, he has retained his reputation for hard-nosed play and good defense while adding a respectable bat. Tolbert surprised the Twins by making the Opening Day roster last April and wound up spending most of 2008 in the majors, though he missed nearly four months with torn liga-ments in his left thumb. He doesn't hit enough to profile as a regular on a championship team, but Tolbert stays within himself offensively and does all the little things, such as making contact, hitting behind runners and bunting. He doesn't hit for any power but recognizes his limitations. His energy and defensive versatility make him a favorite of manager Ron Gardenhire, and his best tool—his speed—makes him an excellent late-inning option as a pinch-runner and defensive replacement. Mostly a second baseman coming up through the minors, he shuttled between second, third base and shortstop last season. He has reliable range, soft hands and a solid arm. Tolbert essentially is a younger, cheaper, bigger version of Nick Punto and could take Punto's utility role in 2009.

Year	Club (League)	Class	AVG	G	AB	R	H	2B	3B	HR	RBI	BB	SO	SB	OBP	SLG
2004	Elizabethton (APP)	R	.308	33	104	23	32	7	2	3	18	12	13	3	.376	.500
2005	Fort Myers (FSL)	HiA	.266	111	417	55	111	20	6	3	46	35	80	11	.326	.365
2006	Fort Myers (FSL)	HiA	.303	40	155	20	47	6	3	4	24	14	17	7	.360	.458
	New Britain (EL)	AA	.258	72	248	33	64	15	1	3	35	30	43	5	.341	.363
2007	Rochester (IL)	AAA	.293	121	417	65	122	24	7	6	53	37	56	11	.353	.427
2008	New Britain (EL)	AA	.250	14	56	6	14	3	0	0	6	1	6	3	.263	.304
	Minnesota (AL)	MAJ	.283	41	113	18	32	6	3	0	6	7	19	7	.322	.389
MINOR LEAGUE TOTALS			.279	391	1397	202	390	75	19	19	182	129	215	40	.342	.401
MAJOR LEAGUE TOTALS			.283	41	113	18	32	6	3	0	6	7	19	7	.322	.389

23 STEVEN TOLLESON, INF/OF

BORN: Nov. 1, 1983. **B-T:** R-R. **HT.:** 5-10. **WT.:** 172. **DRAFTED:** South Carolina, 2005 (5th round). **SIGNED BY:** Ricky Taylor.

Tolleson is the son of ex-big leaguer Wayne Tolleson, who spent parts of 10 seasons in the majors as a light-hitting utility infielder. Tolleson is more physical than his father and projects to be a better hitter, thriving in 2008 despite missing time with a broken index finger. His tools grade out as average across the board except for his power, which is below average. However, he can drive some balls into the gaps and stayed strong through the Arizona Fall League, where he ranked among the league batting leaders. Of more concern are Tolleson's range and hands at shortstop, as they both grade out a bit short to play everyday. He's a better fit at second base and also has seen time in center field. His best-case scenario would be a career akin to Ryan Freel's. Tolleson hits more than the typical Twins utility infielder (such as Nick Punto or Matt Tolbert), but defense and speed often garner more time in that role for Minnesota. Added to the 40-man roster during the offseason, Tolleson will work on his defense and try to keep his offensive momentum in Triple-A in 2009.

Year	Club (League)	Class	AVG	G	AB	R	H	2B	3B	HR	RBI	BB	SO	SB	OBP	SLG
2005	Elizabethton (APP)	R	.321	16	56	18	18	6	1	2	8	11	4	2	.457	.571
	Beloit (MWL)	LoA	.176	31	102	16	18	2	0	3	10	17	23	3	.311	.284
2006	Beloit (MWL)	LoA	.287	47	171	23	49	8	2	2	16	27	34	7	.390	.392
	Twins (GCL)	R	.250	2	8	1	2	0	0	0	1	0	0	0	.222	.250
	Fort Myers (FSL)	HiA	.268	49	157	23	42	8	1	4	23	22	24	3	.353	.408
2007	Fort Myers (FSL)	HiA	.285	132	487	75	139	24	4	5	35	79	97	27	.388	.382
2008	New Britain (EL)	AA	.300	93	343	54	103	28	1	9	50	44	74	12	.382	.466
MINOR LEAGUE TOTALS			.280	370	1324	210	371	76	9	25	143	200	256	54	.379	.408

24 ROB DELANEY, RHP

BORN: Sept. 8, 1984. **B-T:** L-R. **HT.:** 6-3. **WT.:** 225. **DRAFTED:** St. John's, NDFA 2006. **SIGNED BY:** John Wilson.

Delaney was the setup man for 2005 Red Sox first-rounder Craig Hansen for two seasons at St. John's and then started 15 games as a redshirt junior in 2006. After Delaney went undrafted that June, Twins area scout John Wilson snapped him up as a free agent for $500. Delaney has done nothing but pound the strike zone since, with great success. He formed an impressive bullpen tandem with Anthony Slama at Fort Myers in the first half of 2008, then moved up to Double-A. Delaney's fastball has average velocity, sitting at 90-91 mph and touching 92, and he throws a heavy ball with excellent sink and surprising armside run. He has above-average command of his fastball as well as pitches to both sides of the plate with it. His slider is his second-best offering, suiting his low three-quarters arm slot, and he added tilt to it. He has been death to righthanders, limiting them to a .150 average last season. Delaney tired a bit in the Arizona Fall League at the end of 2008, and he was trying too hard to throw hard, costing him movement. His lack of an effective changeup or splitter to combat lefthanders is his biggest weakness, but his fastball command may be enough to make him a capable middle reliever.

Year	Club (League)	Class	W	L	ERA	G	GS	CG	SV	IP	H	R	ER	HR	BB	SO	AVG
2006	Twins (GCL)	R	1	3	4.64	17	0	0	2	33	37	23	17	4	1	27	.278
	Fort Myers (FSL)	HiA	0	0	5.40	3	0	0	0	5	7	3	3	1	0	3	.333
2007	Beloit (MWL)	LoA	1	0	0.77	36	0	0	28	47	25	8	4	1	6	56	.152
	Fort Myers (FSL)	HiA	2	0	1.54	17	0	0	7	23	19	4	4	1	10	27	.221
2008	Fort Myers (FSL)	HiA	1	2	1.42	23	0	0	13	32	24	6	5	1	4	34	.207
	New Britain (EL)	AA	2	1	1.05	23	0	0	5	34	20	4	4	2	7	38	.171
MINOR LEAGUE TOTALS			7	6	1.91	119	0	0	55	174	132	48	37	10	28	185	.207

25 ANTHONY SLAMA, RHP

BORN: Jan . 6, 1984. **B-T:** R-R. **HT.:** 6-3. **WT.:** 207. **DRAFTED:** San Diego, D/F 2006 (39th round). **SIGNED BY:** John Leavitt.

The Twins drafted Slama in the 39th round in 2006 after his fourth year at San Diego. After he pitched as a fifth-year senior, they signed him before the 2007 draft for $4,000. He made a quick impact in his 2007 debut before tearing up high Class A last season, first as Rob Delaney's setup man, then as a closer after Delaney's promotion. Slama ranked third among minor league relievers with 13.9 strikeouts per nine innings. He lacks closer stuff but gets results with a low-90s fastball that tops out at 93 mph. It has solid sink, and he also gets groundballs with his average slider, which he throws for strikes. While he doesn't have Delaney's command, he has good control, rarely elevates his pitches and didn't give up his first home run as a pro until the Florida State League playoffs. Slama has plenty of deception, from a front arm that flashes out during his delivery to a lower arm slot and somewhat herky-jerky motion. The combination leaves scouts a bit skeptical, despite undeniable results. Slama will be 25 in 2009, and it's time to see if his deception and solid stuff can play above Class A. His spring performance will dictate his assignment, but he could jump a level or two.

Year	Club (League)	Class	W	L	ERA	G	GS	CG	SV	IP	H	R	ER	HR	BB	SO	AVG
2007	Elizabethton (APP)	R	0	0	2.45	6	0	0	4	7	2	2	2	0	1	10	.091
	Beloit (MWL)	LoA	1	1	1.48	21	0	0	10	24	15	4	4	0	9	39	.172
2008	Fort Myers (FSL)	HiA	4	1	1.01	51	0	0	25	71	43	12	8	0	24	110	.173
MINOR LEAGUE TOTALS			5	2	1.23	78	0	0	39	103	60	18	14	0	34	159	.168

26 PHILIP HUMBER, RHP

BORN: Dec. 21, 1982. **B-T:** R-R. **HT.:** 6-4. **WT.:** 225. **DRAFTED:** Rice, 2004 (1st round). **SIGNED BY:** Dave Lottsfeldt (Mets).

The third overall choice in the 2004 draft and recipient of a $3 million bonus, Humber had an opportunity after the Mets included him in the Johan Santana trade. He pitched well in spring training, striking out nine and giving up just two runs in 14 innings in big league camp. However, he didn't make Minnesota's staff and didn't pitch well at chilly Rochester. He was demoted to the bullpen twice but finally got hot in late July, winning six of his last seven decisions, and he pitched well in relief during a September callup. While he hasn't had No. 3 overall pick stuff since Tommy John surgery in 2005, Humber still runs his 88-91 mph fastball up to 93-94 in shorter stints, and when he's right, he drives the ball downhill. His curveball remains a plus pitch, thrown with power in the upper 80s. He throws a solid changeup with some sink, but his fastball and change flatten out when he elevates them, leaving him vulnerable to home runs. Humber is out of options, which could help his cause in trying to earn a long-relief role in Minnesota in 2009.

Year	Club (League)	Class	W	L	ERA	G	GS	CG	SV	IP	H	R	ER	HR	BB	SO	AVG
2005	St. Lucie (FSL)	HiA	2	6	4.99	14	14	0	0	70	74	41	39	6	18	65	.273
	Binghamton (EL)	AA	0	1	6.75	1	1	0	0	4	4	3	3	0	2	2	.250
2006	Mets (GCL)	R	0	0	6.75	1	1	0	0	4	7	3	3	0	1	7	.389
	St. Lucie (FSL)	HiA	3	1	2.37	7	7	0	0	38	24	12	10	4	9	36	.178
	Binghamton (EL)	AA	2	2	2.88	6	6	0	0	34	25	12	11	4	10	36	.195
	New York (NL)	MAJ	0	0	0.00	2	0	0	0	2	0	0	0	0	1	2	.000
2007	New Orleans (PCL)	AAA	11	9	4.27	25	25	0	0	139	129	70	66	21	44	120	.244
	New York (NL)	MAJ	0	0	7.71	3	1	0	0	7	9	6	6	1	2	2	.300
2008	Rochester (IL)	AAA	10	8	4.56	31	23	2	0	136	145	76	69	21	49	106	.273
	Minnesota (AL)	MAJ	0	0	4.63	5	0	0	0	12	11	6	6	4	5	6	.250
MINOR LEAGUE TOTALS			28	27	4.25	85	77	2	0	426	408	217	201	56	133	372	.250
MAJOR LEAGUE TOTALS			0	0	5.23	10	1	0	0	21	20	12	12	5	8	10	.250

27 MICHAEL McCARDELL, RHP

BORN: April 13, 1985. **B-T:** R-R. **HT.:** 6-5. **WT.:** 220. **DRAFTED:** Kutztown (Pa.), 2007 (5th round). **SIGNED BY:** John Wilson.

McCardell gives the Twins yet another pitchability righthander, and he has a plus offering in his curveball, one of the best in the system. He added another solid offspeed pitch by throwing his changeup a mandated 10 percent of the time last year, and it made significant progress to become a solid-average weapon. A college third baseman who also pitched for NCAA Division II power Kutztown (Pa.), McCardell offers projection despite being 23 due to a good frame and clean, easy arm action. He wore down in his first year as a full-time pitcher in a full-season league, missing time with bone spurs in his elbow in late April and early May. Fatigue caused him to occasionally fly open with his shoulder and drag his arm behind, causing his fastball velocity to dip. He touched 90 and sat in the upper 80s most of the season after reaching 93 in 2007. With his size, solid delivery and increased experience, the Twins expect his fastball to maintain average velocity in the future. More strength and stamina also would add power to his curve, which at times can get soft. A solid athlete, McCardell competes well and earns plaudits for his toughness. He'll head to high Class A and help David Bromberg anchor the Fort Myers rotation in 2009.

Year	Club (League)	Class	W	L	ERA	G	GS	CG	SV	IP	H	R	ER	HR	BB	SO	AVG
2007	Twins (GCL)	R	2	0	2.50	4	2	0	1	18	11	5	5	2	3	25	.177
	Elizabethton (APP)	R	5	1	2.00	8	8	0	0	45	29	12	10	3	5	70	.179
2008	Beloit (MWL)	LoA	9	4	2.86	22	21	1	0	135	110	51	43	10	25	139	.219
MINOR LEAGUE TOTALS			16	5	2.63	34	31	1	1	198	150	68	58	15	33	234	.206

28 DAVID WINFREE, OF

BORN: Aug. 5, 1985. **B-T:** R-R. **HT.:** 6-3. **WT.:** 215. **DRAFTED:** HS—Virginia Beach, Va., 2003 (13th round). **SIGNED BY:** John Wilson.

Righthanded power is getting harder to find, and the Twins have been patient with Winfree, who has as much as anyone in the system except for Angel Morales. They waited through his 2006 season, when he went home for a spell while questioning his commitment to the game. He has become a better competitor the last two seasons and slowly is unlocking his power. A solid run producer with a knack for situational hitting, Winfree finished third in the Eastern League in RBIs (87) and sixth in homers (19) last season. Never particularly selective, he cut down on his strikeouts while increasing his power numbers and walk rate while repeating Double-A. His power comes from his strength, especially in his forearms and hands. He generates leverage and bat speed and can drive the ball out to all fields. A solid athlete, Winfree seemed freed up by a move to right field, where his above-average arm strength played better than at third base. He's still learning some nuances of the outfield. He's passed through the Rule 5 draft twice now, but the Twins believe in his power. Winfree should get his first shot at Triple-A in 2009.

Year	Club (League)	Class	AVG	G	AB	R	H	2B	3B	HR	RBI	BB	SO	SB	OBP	SLG
2003	Twins (GCL)	R	.129	23	70	4	9	1	2	0	3	2	16	0	.164	.200
2004	Elizabethton (APP)	R	.286	59	217	31	62	8	0	8	37	18	51	1	.349	.433
2005	Beloit (MWL)	LoA	.294	135	562	80	165	31	5	16	101	22	93	3	.329	.452
2006	Twins (GCL)	R	.200	4	15	2	3	1	0	0	1	1	4	0	.250	.267
	Fort Myers (FSL)	HiA	.276	67	261	43	72	13	2	13	48	19	59	2	.328	.490
2007	New Britain (EL)	AA	.267	123	460	57	123	27	5	12	51	26	106	0	.308	.426
2008	New Britain (EL)	AA	.252	126	453	59	114	27	3	19	87	41	87	2	.319	.450
MINOR LEAGUE TOTALS			.269	537	2038	276	548	108	17	68	328	129	416	8	.318	.439

29 LOEK VAN MIL, RHP

BORN: Sept. 15, 1984. **B-T:** R-R. **HT.:** 7-1. **WT.:** 225. **SIGNED:** Netherlands, 2005. **SIGNED BY:** Howard Norsetter.

Scouts remain intrigued by Van Mil, who's atypical in just about every way. He signed when he was 20 years old after Twins scouts worked with him while he was a teen, trying to get a 7-footer to pitch like one. Van Mil threw almost sidearm as an amateur, and he has evolved into a overhand power pitcher with a chance to be a legitimate factor in a big league bullpen. Van Mil has shown a mid-90s fastball and a mid-80s slider, and both are plus pitches at times. He's coordinated and has a sound delivery with a clean arm action when all the parts work together. That's harder to do at his size, leading to periodic bouts of wildness. Van Mil left Beloit in July to pitch for the Dutch Olympic team, and when he arrived in Beijing he quickly emerged as a team leader. However, in a side session prior to the tournament, he overthrew and felt a pop in his elbow. Though he has a partial ligament tear, Minnesota opted against immediate Tommy John surgery in hopes rehabilitation would return him to full health. He appeared headed for surgery in December, though. Van Mil passed through the Rule 5 draft and may miss the entire 2009 season if he has surgery, further delaying his progress.

Year	Club (League)	Class	W	L	ERA	G	GS	CG	SV	IP	H	R	ER	HR	BB	SO	AVG
2006	Twins (GCL)	R	1	2	3.30	10	8	0	0	44	51	31	16	3	17	24	.290
2007	Elizabethton (APP)	R	2	2	2.63	13	0	0	0	24	14	10	7	0	17	23	.171
2008	Beloit (MWL)	LoA	2	2	3.22	28	0	0	3	45	36	21	16	5	25	42	.221
MINOR LEAGUE TOTALS			5	6	3.12	51	8	0	3	112	101	62	39	8	59	89	.240

30 MICHAEL TONKIN, RHP

BORN: Nov. 19, 1989. **B-T:** R-R. **HT.:** 6-7. **WT.:** 215. **DRAFTED:** HS—Palmdale, Calif., 2008 (30th round). **SIGNED BY:** Dan Cox.

Tonkin has ties to the Twins before they drafted him last June, as his sister is married to Jason Kubel. He dropped to the 30th round because teams thought it would be difficult to sign him away from a commitment to Southern California, but he spurned the Trojans for a $230,000 bonus. Tonkin gets good sinking life and armside run on his two-seam fastball from a low three-quarters arm slot, sitting at 89-91 mph and touching 94 consistently. He also has shown a feel for a changeup, which has above-average potential with good sinking movement that mirrors his fastball. Tonkin threw a curveball with tilt and some sweep as an amateur, but his slot lends itself more to a slider down the line. He'll need some time to develop, as he's still growing into his lanky 6-foot-6 frame. He could earn a rotation spot in low Class A this year, but but a numbers crunch could hold him back in extended spring training.

Year	Club (League)	Class	W	L	ERA	G	GS	CG	SV	IP	H	R	ER	HR	BB	SO	AVG
2008	Twins (GCL)	R	0	1	3.27	6	1	0	0	11	10	4	4	0	3	8	.244
MINOR LEAGUE TOTALS			0	1	3.27	6	1	0	0	11	10	4	4	0	3	8	.244

New York Mets

BY ADAM RUBIN

When Mets general manager Omar Minaya signed Pedro Martinez after the 2004 season, he justified the four-year, $53 million deal in part by suggesting Latin American teenagers would flock to sign with New York as a result.

An increased profile resulting from the Martinez signing, coupled with the opening of a state-of-the-art academy in the Dominican Republic, have been the cornerstones of the Mets' plans to retool their farm system.

New York believes it's starting to see dividends from its efforts in Latin America. Dominican outfielder Fernando Martinez and Venezuelan shortstop Wilmer  Flores rank as the Nos. 1 and 2 prospects in the organization. Two more Dominicans, third baseman Jefry Marte and righthander Jenrry Mejia, also cracked the organization's top 10, and Dominican righty Maikel Cleto would have joined them if he hadn't been included in a trade for J.J. Putz.

The Mets also included Venezuelan righty Deolis Guerra in the deal that brought Johan Santana to New York. While they'd make that move again and again, it further depleted a system that was already thin at the upper levels.

For the second straight year, the Mets collapsed in September and handed the National League East title to the Phillies. This time, New York lost 10 of its final 17 games and was once again eliminated with a loss to the also-ran Marlins on the final day of the season.

One of the bright spots down the stretch was the procession of several young players from the minors to Shea Stadium. Daniel Murphy and Nick Evans, both natural corner infielders who started 2008 in Double-A, ultimately platooned in left field for the Mets. Lefthander Jonathon Niese made three September starts at age 21. Eddie Kunz, a sandwich pick just a year earlier, and Bobby Parnell contributed out of the bullpen.

Though the Mets have been as conservative in the draft as they have been aggressive on the international market, they did have a bonanza last June. After forfeiting their 2006 and 2007 first-round picks as compensation for free agents Billy Wagner and Moises Alou, New York had three of the first 33 picks in 2008—the product of free agent Tom Glavine signing with the Braves.

Interestingly, the third of those three choices made the biggest impression. Righthander Brad Holt has the best fastball in the system and has jumped on the fast track to the majors. The Mets expect fiirst baseman Ike Davis and shortstop Reese Havens to fare better in 2009 after uninspiring pro debuts.

STEVE MOORE

Rookie Daniel Murphy hit well in September as the Mets stumbled and fell out of the race

TOP 30 PROSPECTS

1. Fernando Martinez, of	16. Ruben Tejada, ss
2. Wilmer Flores, ss	17. Dillon Gee, rhp
3. Jonathon Niese, lhp	18. Scott Shaw, rhp
4. Brad Holt, rhp	19. Tobi Stoner, rhp
5. Bobby Parnell, rhp	20. Lucas Duda, 1b
6. Jefry Marte, 3b	21. Francisco Pena, c
7. Jenrry Mejia, rhp	22. Greg Veloz, 2b
8. Reese Havens, ss	23. Josh Thole, c
9. Nick Evans, 1b/of	24. Brant Rustich, rhp
10. Eddie Kunz, rhp	25. Nathan Vineyard, lhp
11. Ike Davis, 1b	26. Elvin Ramirez, rhp
12. Cesar Puello, of	27. Darren O'Day, rhp
13. Scott Moviel, rhp	28. Dylan Owen, rhp
14. Zach Lutz, 3b	29. Javier Rodriguez, of
15. Mike Antonini, lhp	30. Aderlin Rodriguez, 3b

Because many of the top players in the system are still teenagers, there won't be many new faces making their debuts when New York unveils Citi Field this season. The lone player not already exposed to the majors who may have an impact is Martinez.

Murphy has made a good case for a regular job, which ideally would be at second base but more realistically would be in left, and Parnell has a shot at a bullpen role. Otherwise, the Mets will be a mostly veteran team, and they turned to proven commodities ($37 million free agent Francisco Rodriguez and Putz) to upgrade their relief corps during the offseason.

General Manager: Omar Minaya. **Farm Director:** Adam Wogan. **Scouting Director:** Rudy Terrasas.

Class	Team	League	W	L	PCT	Finish*	Manager(s)	Affiliated
Majors	New York	National	89	73	.549	4th (16)	W. Randolph/J. Manuel	—
Triple-A	New Orleans Zephyrs	Pacific Coast	66	75	.468	12th (16)	K. Oberkfell/M. Scott	2007
Double-A	Binghamton Mets	Eastern	73	69	.514	5th (12)	Mako Oliveras	1992
High A	St. Lucie Mets	Florida State	53	81	.396	12th (12)	Tim Teufel	1988
Low A	Savannah Sand Gnats	South Atlantic	61	76	.445	12th (16)	Donovan Mitchell	2007
Short-season	Brooklyn Cyclones	New York-Penn	45	30	.600	4th (14)	Edgar Alfonzo	2001
Rookie	Kingsport Mets	Appalachian	34	32	.515	6th (10)	Pedro Lopez	1980
Rookie	GCL Mets	Gulf Coast	27	27	.500	10th (16)	Juan Lopez	2004

Overall 2008 Minor League Record 359 390 .479 22nd
* Finish in overall standings (No. of teams in league). ^League champion.

LAST YEAR'S TOP 30

Rank	Player, Pos.	Status
1.	Fernando Martinez, of	No. 1
2.	Deolis Guerra, rhp	(Twins)
3.	Carlos Gomez, of	(Twins)
4.	Kevin Mulvey, of	(Twins)
5.	Eddie Kunz, rhp	No. 10
6.	Brant Rustich, rhp	No. 24
7.	Philip Humber, rhp	(Twins)
8.	Jonathon Niese, lhp	No. 3
9.	Nathan Vineyard, lhp	No. 25
10.	Bobby Parnell, rhp	No. 5
11.	Joe Smith, rhp	(Indians)
12.	Scott Moviel, rhp	No. 13
13.	Stephen Clyne, rhp	Dropped out
14.	Nick Carr, rhp	Dropped out
15.	Daniel Murphy, 3b	Majors
16.	Greg Veloz, 2b	No. 22
17.	Wilmer Flores, ss	No. 2
18.	Ruben Tejada, ss	No. 16
19.	Mike Carp, 1b	(Mariners)
20.	Nick Evans, 1b	No. 9
21.	Francisco Pena, c	No. 21
22.	Phillips Orta, rhp	Dropped out
23.	Adam Bostick, lhp	Dropped out
24.	Emmanuel Garcia, 2b	Dropped out
25.	Steven Register, rhp	(Rockies)
26.	Mike Antonini, lhp	No. 15
27.	Jefry Marte, 3b	No. 6
28.	Juan Lagares, ss	Dropped out
29.	Lucas Duda, 1b	No. 20
30.	Elvin Ramirez, rhp	No. 26

BEST TOOLS

Best Hitter for Average	Wilmer Flores
Best Power Hitter	Fernando Martinez
Best Strike-Zone Discipline	Reese Havens
Fastest Baserunner	Javier Rodriguez
Best Athlete	Greg Veloz
Best Fastball	Brad Holt
Best Curveball	Jonathon Niese
Best Slider	Brant Rustich
Best Changeup	Dillon Gee
Best Control	Dillon Gee
Best Defensive Catcher	Mike Nickeas
Best Defensive Infielder	Ruben Tejada
Best Infield Arm	Shawn Bowman
Best Defensive Outfielder	Kirk Nieuwenhuis
Best Outfield Arm	Javier Rodriguez

PROJECTED 2012 LINEUP

Catcher	Francisco Pena
First Base	Daniel Murphy
Second Base	Reese Havens
Third Base	David Wright
Shortstop	Jose Reyes
Left Field	Fernando Martinez
Center Field	Carlos Beltran
Right Field	Wilmer Flores
No. 1 Starter	Johan Santana
No. 2 Starter	Mike Pelfrey
No. 3 Starter	Jonathon Niese
No. 4 Starter	Brad Holt
No. 5 Starter	John Maine
Closer	Francisco Rodriguez

TOP PROSPECTS OF THE DECADE

Year	Player, Pos.	2008 Org.
1999	Alex Escobar, of	Nationals
2000	Alex Escobar, of	Nationals
2001	Alex Escobar, of	Nationals
2002	Aaron Heilman, rhp	Mets
2003	Jose Reyes, ss	Mets
2004	Kazuo Matsui, ss	Astros
2005	Lastings Milledge, of	Nationals
2006	Lastings Milledge, of	Nationals
2007	Mike Pelfrey, rhp	Mets
2008	Fernando Martinez, of	Mets

TOP DRAFT PICKS OF THE DECADE

Year	Player, Pos.	2008 Org.
1999	Neal Musser, lhp (2nd round)	Royals
2000	Billy Traber, lhp	Yankees
2001	Aaron Heilman, rhp	Mets
2002	Scott Kazmir, lhp	Rays
2003	Lastings Milledge, of	Nationals
2004	Philip Humber, rhp	Twins
2005	Mike Pelfrey, rhp	Mets
2006	Kevin Mulvey, rhp (2nd round)	Twins
2007	Eddie Kunz, rhp (1st round supp.)	Mets
2008	Ike Davis, 1b	Mets

LARGEST BONUSES IN CLUB HISTORY

Mike Pelfrey, 2005	$3,550,000
Philip Humber, 2004	$3,000,000
Scott Kazmir, 2002	$2,150,000
Lastings Milledge, 2003	$2,075,000
Geoff Goetz, 1997	$1,700,000

NEW YORK METS

TOP 2009 ROOKIE: Bobby Parnell, rhp. A starter throughout his minor league career, he could be a bullpen weapon with his explosive fastball.

BREAKOUT PROSPECT: Ruben Tejada, ss. Over his head in high Class A at 18 years old, he remained unfazed and held his own in Hawaii Winter Baseball.

SLEEPER: Sean Ratliff, of. Drafted in the fourth round last June out of Stanford, he needs to make more contact but has intriguing raw power.

SOURCE OF TOP 30 TALENT			
Homegrown	29	Acquired	1
College	13	Trades	0
Junior college	0	Rule 5 draft	1
High school	6	Independent leagues	0
Draft-and-follow	0	Free agents/waivers	0
Nondrafted free agents	0		
International	10		

Numbers in parentheses indicate prospect rankings.

LF
Fernando Martinez (1)
Sean Ratliff

CF
Javier Rodriguez (29)
Carl Loadenthal

RF
Cesar Puello (12)
Kirk Nieuwenhuis
Caleb Stewart

3B
Jefry Marte (6)
Zach Lutz (14)
Aderlin Rodriguez (30)
Stefan Welch
Shawn Bowman

SS
Wilmer Flores (2)
Reese Havens (8)
Ruben Tejada (16)
Juan Lagares
Jose Coronado

2B
Greg Veloz (22)
Emmanuel Garcia

1B
Nick Evans (9)
Ike Davis (11)
Lucas Duda (20)
Jeff Flagg

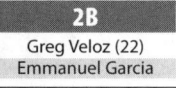

C
Francisco Pena (21)
Josh Thole (23)
Dock Doyle
Mike Nickeas
Jordan Abruzzo

RHP

Starters	Relievers
Brad Holt (4)	Bobby Parnell (5)
Jenrry Mejia (7)	Eddie Kunz (10)
Scott Moviel (13)	Brant Rustich (24)
Dillon Gee (17)	Darren O'Day (27)
Scott Shaw (18)	Rocky Cherry
Tobi Stoner (19)	Connor Robertson
Elvin Ramirez (26)	Carlos Muniz
Dylan Owen (28)	John Madden
John Holdzkom	Stephen Clyne
Oscar Melendez	Brandon Moore
Kyle Allen	

LHP

Starters	Relievers
Jonathon Niese (3)	Mike Antonini (15)
Nathan Vineyard (25)	Adam Bostick
Angel Calero	

2008

BEST PURE HITTER: The Mets' top two selections, 1B Ike Davis (1) and SS Reese Havens (1), went in the first 22 picks due to their offensive potential. Both have quick bats and hand-eye coordination that allow them to get the barrel to the ball consistently when they're going well.

BEST POWER HITTER: Davis didn't homer as a pro but showed above-average juice at Arizona State once he learned to incorporate his lower half more into his swing. OF Sean Ratliff (4) has contact issues but tremendous raw power due to quick hands and excellent strength. At 6-foot-6 and 250 pounds, 1B/DH Jeff Flagg (27) has huge strength and well-above-average raw power.

FASTEST RUNNER: OF Javier Rodriguez (2) has plus speed. Ratliff and OF Kirk Niewenhuis (3) both run a tick above average.

BEST DEFENSIVE PLAYER: Davis pitched and played some right field at Arizona State, but he excels at first base, with a strong arm and sound actions. Niewenhuis could be an average center fielder or above-average on the corners, featuring a strong throwing arm.

BEST FASTBALL: RHP Brad Holt (1s) had one of the draft's best heaters, sitting at 93-96 mph with good life on a downhill plane, and he throws it enough to have developed solid command.

BEST SECONDARY PITCH: While he relies heavily on his fastball, Holt has flashed a plus power slider. RHP Kyle Allen (24) has polish, including feel for an average changeup with plus potential.

BEST PRO DEBUT: Holt led the short-season New York-Penn League in ERA (1.87) and strikeouts (96) while giving up just 43 hits in 72 innings. And he did it throwing 90 percent fastballs. RHP Scott Shaw (16) gave the Cyclones a second consistent starter, going 6-3, 2.80 after posting a 6.78 ERA in three seasons at Illinois.

BEST ATHLETE: OF Javier Rodriguez (2) was the first player picked out of Puerto Rico this year due to his lean, athletic body, raw power and above-average speed.

MOST INTRIGUING BACKGROUND: Davis' father Ron is a former all-star reliever who pitched 11 seasons in the majors.

CLOSEST TO THE MAJORS: Holt's combination of fastball velocity and command will put him on the fast track.

BEST LATE-ROUND PICK: Allen has an average fastball and potential for an average slider to go with

his changeup and savvy. Shaw has excellent size at 6-foot-5, 225 pounds and solid-average stuff across the board, and his confidence grew with a taste of success.

THE ONE WHO GOT AWAY: OF Neil Medchill (33) returned to Oklahoma State after a strong summer in the California Collegiate League, showing right-field tools including raw power and a plus arm.

ASSESSMENT: Holt's blazing start offset disappointing debuts by Davis (no homers) and Havens (a sore arm precluded him from playing a position). The Mets didn't go over slot for a single player and will have to hit with some of their dark horses to produce depth behind their top picks.

2007

RHP Eddie Kunz (1s), the Mets' top pick reached the majors in 2008 but wasn't ready. RHP Scott Moviel (2) has one of the higher ceilings among pitchers in the system. LHP Nathan Vineyard (1s) already has succumbed to shoulder surgery.

GRADE: C

2006

Again without a first-rounder, New York spent its top choice on RHP Kevin Mulvey (2), who became part of the Johan Santana trade. RHP Joe Smith (3) opened the next year with the Mets and was included in the J.J. Putz deal this offseason. But the real find was OF/INF Daniel Murphy (13), who played a platoon role for New York last summer.

GRADE: C+

2005

RHP Mike Pelfrey (1) finally has started to show why the Mets gave him a $5.25 million major league contract. LHP Jonathon Niese (7), the system's top pitching prospect, and RHP Bobby Parnell (9) could join him on the big league staff this season.

GRADE: C+

2004

1B/OF Nick Evans (5) will be the only contributor in New York. The Mets have used RHPs Philip Humber (1) and Gaby Hernandez (3) and 1B Mike Carp (9) in trades for Santana, Putz and Paul LoDuca.

GRADE: C

*Draft analysis by John Manuel (2008) and Jim Callis (2004-07). Numbers in parentheses indicate draft rounds. *Bonuses for 2004-05 are first 10 rounds only.*

KEVIN PATAKY

PROSPECT

FERNANDO MARTINEZ, OF

Born: Oct. 10, 1988.
Ht.: 6-1. **Wt.:** 190.
Bats: L. **Throws:** R.
Signed: Dominican Republic, 2005.
Signed by: Rafael Bournigal/Sandy Johnson/Eddy Toledo.

Mets chief operating officer Jeff Wilpon once predicted Carlos Gomez and Martinez would flank Carlos Beltran as the outfielders when the team christened its new stadium, Citi Field, in 2009. Gomez since has joined the Twins as part of the Johan Santana trade, and the acclaim for Martinez has diminished a little. Signed out of the Dominican Republic for $1.3 million in 2005, he has been pushed aggressively by New York. Martinez was the youngest player in the Double-A Eastern League in each of the last two seasons, and the youngest player in the history of the Arizona Fall League in 2007. Because of his youth, Martinez hasn't dominated in the minors, but he had a solid return engagement with Binghamton last year, then got off to an excellent start in the Dominican League over the winter.

Martinez still has youth on his side. He turned 20 during the offseason, making him the equivalent of a college sophomore or junior, and he'd surely be a first-round pick if he were entering the 2009 draft coming out of a U.S. college. His bat speed helps him catch up to good fastballs, and he has power to all fields. He can hit some monster home runs when he connects. While he profiles to play an outfield corner in the future, Martinez is holding his own in center field. He has improved his defense and now shows average range and arm strength. He has solid-average speed once he gets going on the bases, ramping it up when he goes from first to third base or senses a triple. His attitude is top-notch. Binghamton manager Mako Oliveras noted that Martinez often was the first player at the ballpark so he could get extra work.

Martinez has been injury-prone. He missed time in 2006 with a bone bruise in his hand and a knee sprain; in 2007 with a broken hamate bone in his right hand; and in 2008 with recurring trouble with his right hamstring. The lost development time has stymied his efforts to improve his strike-zone discipline. Martinez's outfield routes also need work, though they did get better last season. He'll probably wind up in left field, where he played regularly in the Dominican this winter, though the Mets won't make that move until he reaches the majors. Martinez is slow out of the batter's box and isn't going to steal many bases.

When he signed, Martinez acquired the hype that goes with a big signing bonus and being a top prospect for a New York team. He's not going to be the next Beltran because he doesn't have the same package of all-around plus tools. Some scouts outside the organization see Martinez as a tweener, a left fielder who lacks impact power, while others see a gifted hitter with an improving approach who should develop average to plus power. General manager Omar Minaya has said he expects Martinez to begin the year at Triple-A Buffalo.

Year	Club(League)	Class	AVG	G	AB	R	H	2B	3B	HR	RBI	BB	SO	SB	OBP	SLG
2006	Mets (GCL)	R	.250	1	4	1	1	0	0	0	0	0	1	0	.250	.250
	Hagerstown (SAL)	LoA	.333	45	192	24	64	14	2	5	28	15	36	7	.389	.505
	St. Lucie (FSL)	HiA	.193	30	119	18	23	4	2	5	11	6	24	1	.254	.387
2007	Binghamton (EL)	AA	.271	60	236	32	64	11	1	4	21	20	51	3	.336	.377
	Mets (GCL)	R	.111	3	9	1	1	0	1	0	1	1	6	0	.200	.333
2008	Mets (GCL)	R	.429	4	14	2	6	1	1	0	0	0	2	0	.467	.643
	Binghamton (EL)	AA	.287	86	352	48	101	19	4	8	43	27	73	6	.340	.432
MINOR LEAGUE TOTALS			.281	229	926	126	260	49	11	22	104	69	193	17	.338	.429

2 WILMER FLORES, SS

BORN: Aug. 6, 1991. **B-T:** R-R. **HT.:** 6-3. **WT.:** 175. **SIGNED:** Venezuela, 2007. **SIGNED BY:** Robert Alfonzo/Ismael Cruz.

As a 14-year-old at the Agua Linda Academy in Valencia, Venezuela, Flores already stood out against players preparing to sign contracts as international free agents. He belted 90-mph fastballs to the opposite field over a 300-foot wall. Organizers at the academy, which also has produced Pablo Sandoval (Giants), Mario Martinez (Mariners) and Alex Monsalve (Indians), were so impressed with Flores' arm that they debated grooming him as a pitcher before opting for shortstop. He signed with the Mets in 2007 for $750,000 and became short-season Brooklyn's youngest player ever when he finished the 2008 season there. Flores quickly established himself as a dangerous hitter, and in a Rookie-level Appalachian League game last summer, Danville walked him intentionally with runners at first and second. He has premium bat speed and a knack for finding the ball with the barrel of the bat. His patience and selectivity improved even as he saw a steady stream of offspeed pitches. Flores has a plus arm at shortstop, though he doesn't flash it on routine plays. Flores lacks first-step quickness and is a below-average runner (4.6 seconds to first base), so he doesn't profile as a shortstop down the line. He showed a tendency to chase pitches up in the zone and can get pull-happy. He's so green that the Kingsport coaching staff had to teach Flores how to dive for balls. Flores already has started to draw some Miguel Cabrera comparisons. He'll open 2009 at low Class A Savannah as a 17-year-old, and with the way the Mets challenge their top prospects, he could find himself as high as Double-A by his 18th birthday in August. New York will keep him at shortstop until he shows he can't play there, with third base or an outfield corner his eventual destination.

Year	Club (League)	Class	AVG	G	AB	R	H	2B	3B	HR	RBI	BB	SO	SB	OBP	SLG
2008	Kingsport (APP)	R	.310	59	245	36	76	12	4	8	41	12	28	2	.352	.490
	Savannah (SAL)	LoA	.400	1	5	1	2	0	0	0	0	0	2	0	.400	.400
	Brooklyn (NYP)	SS	.267	8	30	3	8	1	0	0	1	1	7	0	.290	.300
MINOR LEAGUE TOTALS			.307	68	280	40	86	13	4	8	42	13	37	2	.347	.468

3 JONATHON NIESE, LHP

BORN: Oct. 27, 1986. **B-T:** L-L. **HT.:** 6-4. **WT.:** 215. **DRAFTED:** HS—Defiance, Ohio, 2005 (7th round). **SIGNED BY:** Erwin Bryant.

Born the day the Mets won their last World Series, Niese comes from the same Defiance (Ohio) High program as Chad Billingsley. Summoned to the big leagues ahead of schedule last September, he struggled in two of his three outings but tossed eight scoreless innings against the Braves in his second start. Niese's signature pitch is a 12-to-6 curveball. He also throws an 88-93 mph fastball with natural cutting action that allows him to combat righthanders, as does his solid changeup. He generally has good control, though like many young pitchers, he nibbled too much in his first taste of the majors. His mechanics create deception that's imperative for a pitcher with solid but not outstanding stuff. After he battled weight issues early in his pro career, improved eating habits have allowed him to shed 21 pounds. Niese needs to do a better job of throwing his curveball for strikes. His delivery, which features a pronounced arch in his back, may hinder his command. Given the team's history of awarding a young pitcher a rotation spot—including Mike Pelfrey, Brian Bannister and Tyler Yates in recent years— it's entirely possible that Niese will break camp with the Mets. He's the early favorite to be New York's No. 5 starter in 2009, and he profiles as a possible No. 3 starter down the line.

Year	Club (League)	Class	W	L	ERA	G	GS	CG	SV	IP	H	R	ER	HR	BB	SO	AVG
2005	Mets (GCL)	R	1	0	3.65	7	5	0	0	25	23	10	10	1	10	24	.245
2006	Hagerstown (SAL)	LoA	11	9	3.93	25	25	1	0	124	121	67	54	7	62	132	.256
	St. Lucie (FSL)	HiA	0	2	4.50	2	2	0	0	10	8	8	5	0	5	10	.216
2007	St. Lucie (FSL)	HiA	11	7	4.29	27	27	2	0	134	151	78	64	9	31	110	.285
2008	Binghamton (EL)	AA	6	7	3.04	22	22	2	0	124	118	53	42	5	44	112	.253
	New Orleans (PCL)	AAA	5	1	3.40	7	7	0	0	40	34	15	15	4	14	32	.231
	New York (NL)	MAJ	1	1	7.07	3	3	0	0	14	20	11	11	2	8	11	.333
MINOR LEAGUE TOTALS			34	26	3.74	90	88	5	0	457	455	231	190	26	166	420	.261
MAJOR LEAGUE TOTALS			1	1	7.07	3	3	0	0	14	20	11	11	2	8	11	.333

4 BRAD HOLT, RHP

BORN: Oct. 13, 1986. **B-T:** R-R. **HT.:** 6-4. **WT.:** 194. **DRAFTED:** UNC Wilmington, 2008 (1st round supplemental). **SIGNED BY:** Marlin McPhail.

Though he was their third choice in the 2008 draft at No. 33 overall, the Mets view Holt as their top pick in retrospect, ahead of first-rounders Ike Davis and Reese Havens. Signed for $1.04 million, he led the short-season New York Penn League in ERA (1.87), strikeouts (96), strikeouts per nine innings (11.9) and opponent average (.171). Holt's fastball typically ranges from 93-96 mph and registers as high as 98. He has good control of the pitch. He has a strong frame and solid mechanics, so durability shouldn't be an issue. He's mentally tough, with the makeup to get out of jams as a starter or finish games as a closer. Holt relies mainly on his fastball for success. He'll flash some average or plus sliders, but he usually holds on to it too long before releasing it. His changeup is even more raw. He has trouble throwing his secondary pitches for strikes and ranked second in the NY-P with 33 walks. Mets farm director Tony Bernazard compares Holt to Mike Pelfrey and considers him ahead of Pelfrey at a similar stage of their careers. Holt could open 2009 in the Binghamton rotation and appear in the majors by season's end. Some scouts think he's destined to be a reliever, but New York is grooming him as a starter for now.

Year	Club (League)	Class	W	L	ERA	G	GS	CG	SV	IP	H	R	ER	HR	BB	SO	AVG
2008	Brooklyn (NYP)	SS	5	3	1.87	14	14	0	0	72	43	18	15	3	33	96	.171
MINOR LEAGUE TOTALS			5	3	1.87	14	14	0	0	72	43	18	15	3	33	96	.171

5 BOBBY PARNELL, RHP

BORN: Sept. 8, 1984. **B-T:** R-R. **HT.:** 6-4. **WT.:** 200. **DRAFTED:** Charleston Southern, 2005 (9th round). **SIGNED BY:** Marlin McPhail.

After limited previous experience on the mound, Parnell began pitching regularly at Charleston Southern. He posted 6.82 and 8.86 ERAs in his final two college seasons but has surged ahead as a professional. He earned the trust of Mets manager Jerry Manuel and pitched some critical relief innings in September. Parnell throws a heavy fastball anywhere from 89-97 mph. When he's throwing strikes, he gets plenty of strikeouts and groundouts. His slider and changeup give him the chance to have three plus pitches. While he has a good fastball, Parnell doesn't show his top velocity consistently within games, either as a starter or as a reliever. He lacks a feel for pitching that made it hard to go through a lineup three or four times as a starter, but that won't be a problem if he's a reliever. His lack of confidence in his changeup is another obstacle to starting. Before the Mets signed Francisco Rodriguez, Parnell was a candidate to become their closer of the future. His best chance of breaking camp with the Mets in 2009 is out of the bullpen, though he continued to work as a starter in the Arizona Fall League.

Year	Club (League)	Class	W	L	ERA	G	GS	CG	SV	IP	H	R	ER	HR	BB	SO	AVG
2005	Brooklyn (NYP)	SS	2	3	1.73	15	14	0	0	73	48	20	14	1	29	67	.185
2006	Hagerstown (SAL)	LoA	5	10	4.04	18	18	1	0	94	84	50	42	7	40	84	.239
	St. Lucie (FSL)	HiA	0	1	9.26	3	3	0	0	12	16	13	12	3	9	13	.333
2007	St. Lucie (FSL)	HiA	3	3	3.25	12	12	0	0	55	56	22	20	0	22	62	.259
	Binghamton (EL)	AA	5	5	4.77	17	17	0	0	89	98	54	47	9	38	74	.276
2008	Binghamton (EL)	AA	10	6	4.30	24	24	0	0	128	126	66	61	14	57	91	.258
	New Orleans (PCL)	AAA	2	2	6.64	5	4	0	0	20	25	16	15	0	9	23	.298
	New York (NL)	MAJ	0	0	5.40	6	0	0	0	5	3	3	3	0	2	3	.176
MINOR LEAGUE TOTALS			27	30	4.04	94	92	1	0	470	453	241	211	34	204	414	.251
MAJOR LEAGUE TOTALS			0	0	5.40	6	0	0	0	5	3	3	3	0	2	3	.176

6 JEFRY MARTE, 3B

BORN: June 21, 1991. **B-T:** R-R. **HT.:** 6-1. **WT.:** 187. **SIGNED:** Dominican Republic, 2007. **SIGNED BY:** Ramon Pena/Ismael Cruz/Marciano Alvarez.

Signed by the Mets after turning 16 in 2007, Marte received a $550,000 bonus. International scouting director Ismael Cruz labeled Marte's bat the quickest in the 2007 international class. He ranked as the No. 3 prospect in the Rookie-level Gulf Coast League in his pro debut. An outstanding young hitter, Marte uses the whole field when he's at his best. Mets officials are confident he'll hit for average and draw his share of walks while developing solid-average power. The ball jumps off his bat differently than with most players, and he has good pitch-recognition skills for his age. He's a deceptively good runner, with baserunning knowledge and aggressiveness enhancing his average speed. He's also advanced in terms of maturity. His arm is solid-average. While he has the tools for third base, Marte is an erratic and raw defender, and there's no certainty that's his ultimate position. He gets in trouble at the plate when he wants to pull the ball.

He swings at some bad breaking pitches, though he should develop more discipline with experience. New York isn't shy about pushing its top prospects. Assuming Marte follows the path of comparable Mets international signings, he could begin the season in low Class A.

Year	Club (League)	Class	AVG	G	AB	R	H	2B	3B	HR	RBI	BB	SO	SB	OBP	SLG
2008	Mets (GCL)	R	.325	44	154	29	50	14	3	4	24	13	30	2	.398	.532
MINOR LEAGUE TOTALS			.325	44	154	29	50	14	3	4	24	13	30	2	.398	.532

7 JENRRY MEJIA, RHP

BRIAN BISSELL

BORN: Oct. 11, 1989. **B-T:** R-R. **HT.:** 6-2. **WT.:** 190. **SIGNED:** Dominican Republic, 2007. **SIGNED BY:** Ramon Pena/Ismael Cruz/Sandy Rosario/Juan Mercado.

The Mets are ecstatic about the bargain they received in signing Mejia for just $16,500. The second-youngest regular pitcher in the New York-Penn League last summer, he got knocked around in his first two outings before going 3-1, 2.40 the rest of the way. Mejia has a quality fastball, sitting in the mid-90s even while pitching out of the stretch and touching 98 mph at times. Some scouts believe he'll hit 100 mph once he matures. His changeup has such sink and depth with high-80s velocity that some scouts consider it a two-seam fastball, while some hitters think it's a curveball. He attacks hitters and competes well. He's also in top physical condition, so he should be durable. He attacks hitters and competes well. Mejia has difficulty repeating his delivery, hampering his command. His curveball is his third-best pitch and it's wildly inconsistent. Like many young power arms, he's overly reliant on his fastball. The Mets will continue to challenge Mejia and could jump him to high Class A in 2009. He'll continue to start to gain experience and work on his secondary pitches, but he could fit best as a late-inning relief option in the long run.

Year	Club (League)	Class	W	L	ERA	G	GS	CG	SV	IP	H	R	ER	HR	BB	SO	AVG
2007	Mets (DSL)	R	2	3	2.47	14	7	0	1	44	24	17	12	0	27	47	.160
2008	Mets (GCL)	R	2	0	0.60	3	3	1	0	15	9	1	1	0	3	15	.164
	Brooklyn (NYP)	SS	3	2	3.49	11	11	0	0	57	42	22	22	4	23	52	.209
MINOR LEAGUE TOTALS			7	5	2.73	28	21	1	1	115	75	40	35	4	53	114	.185

8 REESE HAVENS, SS

RODGER WOOD

BORN: Oct. 20, 1986. **B-T:** L-R. **HT.:** 6-1. **WT.:** 195. **DRAFTED:** South Carolina, 2008 (1st round). **SIGNED BY:** Marlin McPhail.

Drafted out of high school by the Rockies, Havens passed on seven-figure offers from teams that wanted him in the first round. After two disappointing years at South Carolina, he took off after shortening his swing while hitting .315 in the Cape Cod League. Havens batted .359/.486/.645 as a junior, went 22nd overall last June and signed for $1.419 million. An offensive-minded grinder, Havens has a good idea of the strike zone, gets into hitter's counts and consistently drives balls to the gaps. He has average power and strong offensive instincts. He's a savvy defender with good hands and arm strength, tools that had some clubs dreaming of him as a catcher. Some scouts wonder how Havens' new stance—he lowered his hands in the Cape—will translate to wood bats. He works a lot of deep counts and needs a better two-strike approach to cut down on his strikeouts. Elbow trouble and a groin pull limited him to DH duties in his pro debut, and the Mets need to find out where he fits defensively. He's a fringe-average runner and his range doesn't stand out at shortstop. Havens declined the chance to play in Hawaii Winter Baseball, preferring to rehab at home. He'll stick at shortstop for now, but projects as an offensive second baseman once he reaches the majors. He should begin 2009 at high Class A St. Lucie.

Year	Club (League)	Class	AVG	G	AB	R	H	2B	3B	HR	RBI	BB	SO	SB	OBP	SLG
2008	Brooklyn (NYP)	SS	.247	23	85	13	21	6	2	3	11	11	27	3	.340	.471
MINOR LEAGUE TOTALS			.247	23	85	13	21	6	2	3	11	11	27	3	.340	.471

9 NICK EVANS, 1B/OF

STEVE MOORE

BORN: Jan. 30, 1986. **B-T:** R-R. **HT.:** 6-3. **WT.:** 210. **DRAFTED:** HS—Phoenix, 2004 (5th round). **SIGNED BY:** Dave Birecki.

After Evans spent the 2007 season in high Class A, he headed home to Phoenix because a stress fracture in his right hand left him unable to play in Hawaii Winter Baseball. Healthy again last season, he surged all the way to New York, breaking into the majors with a three-double performance May 24 in Colorado. Primarily a first baseman in the minors, he ultimately platooned in left field with fellow rookie Daniel Murphy. Mets officials believe Evans ultimately will hit for more power than Murphy. While his swing can get long, he has above-average bat speed and can beat good fastballs. He mashed lefthanders throughout the minors and in the majors. He has a solid-average arm and has worked hard to catch up defensively in left field. Power is Evans' lone above-average tool, and he needs to be more selective to be more than a platoon player. Scouts question whether he'll produce enough to be an everyday first baseman and think he may be best suited as a utility corner bat. He needs to improve his physical strength and polish his defense. He's a fringy runner but not a baseclogger. Evans was rushed to the big leagues and should get more seasoning in Triple-A with Fernando Tatis re-signing with the Mets. With Carlos Delgado's contract up after the 2009 season, Evans could find himself in New York's first-base mix a year from now.

Year	Club (League)	Class	AVG	G	AB	R	H	2B	3B	HR	RBI	BB	SO	SB	OBP	SLG
2004	Mets (GCL)	R	.258	50	182	36	47	10	3	7	27	14	51	3	.311	.462
2005	Kingsport (APP)	R	.344	15	64	11	22	7	0	6	22	4	17	1	.382	.734
	Brooklyn (NYP)	SS	.252	57	226	30	57	11	3	6	33	17	34	0	.302	.407
2006	Hagerstown (SAL)	LoA	.254	137	511	55	130	33	3	15	67	45	99	2	.320	.419
2007	St. Lucie (FSL)	HiA	.286	103	378	65	108	25	1	15	54	53	64	3	.374	.476
2008	Binghamton (EL)	AA	.311	75	296	52	92	18	7	14	53	26	64	2	.365	.561
	New York (NL)	MAJ	.257	50	109	18	28	10	0	2	9	7	24	0	.303	.404
MINOR LEAGUE TOTALS			.275	437	1657	249	456	104	17	63	256	159	329	11	.340	.473
MAJOR LEAGUE TOTALS			.257	50	109	18	28	10	0	2	9	7	24	0	.303	.404

10 EDDIE KUNZ, RHP

STEVE MOORE

BORN: April 8, 1986. **B-T:** R-R. **HT.:** 6-5. **WT.:** 265. **DRAFTED:** Oregon State, 2007 (1st round supplemental). **SIGNED BY:** Jim Reeves.

For the second straight season, the Mets brought a reliever from the previous year's draft to the big leagues. Unlike Joe Smith, Kunz had little success and was demoted after just four appearances. Part of two College World Series championships at Oregon State, he signed for $720,000 as New York's top pick (sandwich round) in the 2007 draft. Kunz built up his arm strength through the 2008 season. He regularly threw 91-92 mph sinkers in April, then worked at 94-95 and touched 97 later in the season. His 3.6 groundout/airout ratio ranked first among Double-A relievers. When it's on, his slider parks in the mid-80s with good bite. Kunz gets himself into trouble with an inconsistent release point and varied arm slots. He'll fly open too soon in his delivery, causing his arm to drag and elevating pitches in the strike zone. He needs to continue to improve the command of his slider, which made some progress in 2008. Though he'll compete for a bullpen spot with the Mets in spring training, he's more likely to open the season as a closer in Triple-A. He projects as a seventh- or eighth-inning reliever in the majors, especially now that Francisco Rodriguez has come to New York.

Year	Club (League)	Class	W	L	ERA	G	GS	CG	SV	IP	H	R	ER	HR	BB	SO	AVG
2007	Brooklyn (NYP)	SS	0	1	6.75	12	0	0	5	12	8	9	9	0	8	9	.190
2008	Binghamton (EL)	AA	1	4	2.79	44	0	0	27	48	39	19	15	0	25	43	.222
	New York (NL)	MAJ	0	0	13.50	4	0	0	0	3	5	4	4	1	1	1	.455
	New Orleans (PCL)	AAA	0	1	7.94	6	0	0	0	6	9	5	5	1	2	4	.346
MINOR LEAGUE TOTALS			1	6	3.95	62	0	0	32	66	56	33	29	1	35	56	.230
MAJOR LEAGUE TOTALS			0	0	13.50	4	0	0	0	3	5	4	4	1	1	1	.455

11 IKE DAVIS, 1B

BORN: March 22, 1987. **B-T:** L-L. **HT.:** 6-5. **WT.:** 195. **DRAFTED:** Arizona State, 2008 (1st round). **SIGNED BY:** Mike Brown.

Davis shouldn't be intimidated when he ultimately arrives at Citi Field, the Mets' new home. The Mets' top pick in the 2008 draft already was taking batting practice off Hall of Famer Goose Gossage at Yankee Stadium at 14 years old. Davis' father Ron was a big league reliever for 11 seasons, including from 1978-81 as a Yankee. After flashing power in college, Davis was slow to recover from a strained oblique muscle and failed to homer in 215 at-bats at Brooklyn after signing for $1.575 million. Still, the Mets regard Davis as a future power hitter. Davis needs to mature physically—unlike Reese Havens, their other 2008 first-rounder, whom they feel will have a quicker route to the big leagues. He carried the pressure of being the Mets' top pick and pressed. He's considered a slick defensive first baseman—the type who could contend for a Gold Glove some day, which will help if his bat doesn't develop as hoped. Davis may eventually be asked to play right field because of his strong arm. Davis—a lefty thrower and hitter, unlike his father—pitched his freshman year at Arizona State, then played right field his sophomore year and first base and pitcher as a junior. He was capable of registering 92 mph on the mound. He has below-average speed. Davis appears ticketed for high Class A to begin 2009.

Year	Club (League)	Class	AVG	G	AB	R	H	2B	3B	HR	RBI	BB	SO	SB	OBP	SLG
2008	Brooklyn (NYP)	SS	.256	58	215	17	55	15	0	0	17	23	43	0	.326	.326
MINOR LEAGUE TOTALS			.256	58	215	17	55	15	0	0	17	23	43	0	.326	.326

12 CESAR PUELLO, OF

BORN: April 1, 1991. **B-T:** R-R. **HT.:** 6-2. **WT.:** 195. **SIGNED:** Dominican Republic, 2007. **SIGNED BY:** Ramon Pena/Ismael Cruz/Marciano Alvarez.

An athletic teenager who eventually should hit for average as he matures, Puello showed steady improvement during his first pro season, batting .242 in June, .271 in July and .357 in August in the Gulf Coast League. He cut down chasing breaking balls out of the zone and, as a result, lessened his strikeout tendency. Puello is considered a faster runner than fellow '07 international signee Jefry Marte and should be a proficient basestealer despite not being a burner. He needs to improve his jumps and learn the proper stealing situations. Puello covers ground well in the outfield. Projected to hit for some power, Puello still will need to concentrate on improving his on-base percentage. He hits a lot of balls in the air, so coaches are working to temper his uppercut swing. He walked five times and struck out 32 times in 151 at-bats in 2008 and still needs to resist swinging at breaking balls in the dirt, an area in which he actually showed progress. Puello, who signed with the Mets for $400,000, has a slightly above-average arm. While he should play center field in the lower minors, the Mets view him as a player whose value is tied to his bat and should wind up in left field. A pure projection at this point, Puello likely will begin 2009 at Kingsport.

Year	Club (League)	Class	AVG	G	AB	R	H	2B	3B	HR	RBI	BB	SO	SB	OBP	SLG
2008	Mets (GCL)	R	.305	40	151	24	46	6	0	1	17	5	32	13	.350	.364
MINOR LEAGUE TOTALS			.305	40	151	24	46	6	0	1	17	5	32	13	.350	.364

13 SCOTT MOVIEL, RHP

BORN: May 7, 1988. **B-T:** R-R. **HT.:** 6-11. **WT.:** 235. **DRAFTED:** HS—Berea, Ohio, 2007 (2nd round). **SIGNED BY:** Erwin Bryant.

The youngest of four brothers, Moviel comes from a baseball family. Sibling Greg, a lefthander, pitched in the Mariners organization. Paul, a fellow righthander and a 36th-round pick in 2003, pitched in the White Sox and Rays organizations. Moviel was prepared to follow the path of fellow Ohioan-turned-Yankees-first-rounder Andrew Brackman: pitch for North Carolina State, and compete for the Wolfpack basketball team—or at least try to as a 6-foot-11 walk-on. Then the Mets selected Moviel 77th overall in the 2007 draft and he bypassed college for the minors. Moviel sat at 90 mph with his fastball last year, tossed an 84-86 mph changeup and had a 75-79 mph curveball, with the more effective breaking pitches being the ones thrown with more power. Like many taller pitchers, Moviel needs time to grow into his body, though the former Michigan basketball recruit is not as awkward as might be expected for his size and is an above-average athlete. Moviel needs to develop a changeup as he rises in the Mets system. He's ticketed for high Class A to open 2009.

Year	Club (League)	Class	W	L	ERA	G	GS	CG	SV	IP	H	R	ER	HR	BB	SO	AVG
2007	Mets (GCL)	R	0	2	3.38	12	12	0	0	40	45	23	15	2	11	37	.281
2008	Savannah (SAL)	LoA	9	8	4.43	24	24	0	0	120	128	75	59	9	36	82	.271
	St. Lucie (FSL)	HiA	1	0	0.00	1	1	0	0	5	2	0	0	0	1	2	.133
MINOR LEAGUE TOTALS			10	10	4.04	37	37	0	0	165	175	98	74	11	48	121	.270

14 ZACH LUTZ, 3B

BORN: June 3, 1986. **B-T:** R-R. **HT.:** 6-1. **WT.:** 220. **DRAFTED:** Alvernia (Pa.), 2007 (5th round). **SIGNED BY:** Scott Hunter.

Lutz had been billed as the player to watch at Brooklyn in 2007, but in the first game of his pro debut, he suffered a season-ending injury. Fielding a backhand play down the line in the first inning of his Cyclones debut, Lutz rolled over his foot. He gutted through two at-bats, but spent the next six months on crutches with a fractured navicular bone at the top of the foot. Lutz, the first freshman first-team all-American in NCAA Division III history, and the D-III national player of the year his final collegiate season, finally returned to action as the Cyclones opened their 2008 season. He has a chance to be a special hitter if he can stay healthy. The ball has a different sound off of his bat. While Lutz has the ability to play third base, he also could land at first base or left field. He's considered an average fielder at best, with an unspectacular arm and fringy range. Mets officials, however, insist that some of that less-than-stellar range stemmed from gutting through a quadriceps injury last season. That leg issue resulted in Lutz's season prematurely ending July 18. The Mets hope Lutz says healthy for once as he heads for low Class A and club officials again are looking for a breakout season from him.

Year	Club (League)	Class	AVG	G	AB	R	H	2B	3B	HR	RBI	BB	SO	SB	OBP	SLG
2007	Brooklyn (NYP)	SS	.000	1	2	0	0	0	0	0	0	0	0	0	.000	.000
2008	Brooklyn (NYP)	SS	.333	24	72	9	24	4	0	3	12	14	12	0	.442	.514
MINOR LEAGUE TOTALS			.324	25	74	9	24	4	0	3	12	14	12	0	.432	.500

15 MIKE ANTONINI, LHP

BORN: Aug. 6, 1985. **B-T:** R-L. **HT.:** 6-0. **WT.:** 190. **DRAFTED:** Georgia College & State, 2007 (18th round). **SIGNED BY:** Marlin McPhail.

Antonini's baseball tutor was his stepfather John Fleming, now the head coach of NCAA Division III Neumann College in Aston, Pa. Fleming was Antonini's pitching coach through his junior year of high school, then served as interim head coach his senior year when Antonini's Cardinal O'Hara High (Springfield, Pa.) team won its first Catholic League championship in 20 years. Antonini's primary assets: He's lefthanded, he has a feel for a plus changeup and he is considered fearless and crafty with the ability to pitch inside. His fastball settles in the upper 80s and reaches 90 mph on occasion, and he has an ordinary curveball. Mets officials say in a best-case scenario, Antonini would resemble Mark Buehrle, who has premium command and a cutter, two major separators. Scouts project Antonini as a bullpen/swing pitcher with less-than-overpowering stuff. Regardless, he's proven to be a quick riser. In his first full professional season, Antonini figured he would settle into St. Lucie for the rest of the season after receiving a promotion from low Class A in mid-June. Seven starts later, after posting a 4-0, 1.84 mark, he instead continued his rapid ascent by moving to Double-A. He's scheduled to begin the 2009 season in the Binghamton rotation. He will need to improve his curveball in order to start in the majors.

Year	Club (League)	Class	W	L	ERA	G	GS	CG	SV	IP	H	R	ER	HR	BB	SO	AVG
2007	Kingsport (APP)	R	1	1	3.71	5	3	0	0	17	16	8	7	3	2	18	.239
	Brooklyn (NYP)	SS	0	0	0.46	7	2	0	0	20	13	1	1	0	5	12	.194
2008	Savannah (SAL)	LoA	4	4	2.71	13	13	0	0	73	63	29	22	2	16	61	.227
	St. Lucie (FSL)	HiA	4	0	1.84	7	7	1	0	44	34	10	9	3	7	33	.211
	Binghamton (EL)	AA	1	3	3.74	8	8	0	0	46	43	19	19	10	16	32	.247
MINOR LEAGUE TOTALS			10	8	2.62	40	33	1	0	199	169	67	58	18	46	156	.226

16 RUBEN TEJADA, SS

BORN: Sept. 1, 1989. **B-T:** R-R. **HT.:** 5-11. **WT.:** 165. **SIGNED:** Panama, 2006. **SIGNED BY:** Ismael Cruz/Wilfredo Blanco/Alex Zapata.

Signed out of Panama, Tejada was moved from the Rookie-level Venezuelan Summer League to the Gulf Coast League midway through the 2007 season. That served as a springboard to Tejada producing a hitting exhibition in the 2008 Grapefruit League while being borrowed from minor league camp. Put on the fast track with a two-level promotion to high Class A, Tejada was overmatched at age 18 but handled the challenge. Team officials had Tejada on an extensive weight-training program during the season to build up his strength, which resulted in fatigue later in the year. Despite that, the Mets continued challenging him in Hawaii Winter Baseball, where he impressed more with his grinder mentality than his tools. Tejada has calmness about him and has appeared unfazed by the lack of success. Tejada may hit 10 home runs a season once his skinny frame matures. Hitting line drives, producing a high on-base percentage and using his legs likely will be the keys to his game. He tends to swing for the fences more than he should and needs to focus on making hard, line-drive contact. Solid defensively with a strong arm and excellent lateral range, he's shown the ability to make the spectacular play. Tejada will remain at shortstop for now, though he has experience at second base and ultimately may land there. He's an average baserunner and basestealer, though sound instincts will allow him to swipe some bases. Mets officials laud his heady play and his advanced knowledge of the strike zone. Scouts outside the organization believe he needs another year in high Class A to catch up.

Year	Club (League)	Class	AVG	G	AB	R	H	2B	3B	HR	RBI	BB	SO	SB	OBP	SLG
2007	Mets (VSL)	R	.364	32	121	32	44	5	0	3	25	19	19	16	.466	.479
	Mets (GCL)	R	.283	35	120	13	34	4	3	0	16	19	16	2	.401	.367
2008	St. Lucie (FSL)	HiA	.229	131	497	55	114	19	4	2	37	41	77	8	.293	.296
MINOR LEAGUE TOTALS			.260	198	738	100	192	28	7	5	78	79	112	26	.342	.337

17 DILLON GEE, RHP

BORN: April 28, 1986. **B-T:** R-R. **HT.:** 6-1. **WT.:** 195. **DRAFTED:** Texas-Arlington, 2007 (21st round). **SIGNED BY:** Ray Corbett.

Gee is part of a middle-round college pitching class from the 2007 draft that has Mets officials excited. Mike Antonini (18th round), Dylan Owen (20th round) and Gee (21st round) all finished their first full pro season in Binghamton's rotation. Gee didn't foresee getting picked for the high Class A Florida State League all-star game in 2008, and his subsequent promotion to Double-A was far more than he expected. Gee, who has solid command, asked permission to add a curveball to his repertoire last season, then worked with St. Lucie pitching coach Dan Murray to develop it. He still throws a slider and uses his slow curve more as an early count option. Gee's breaking balls are his current weakness, though that's offset by a solid changeup, sound control and makeup. His fastball generally ranges from 88-90 mph, fringe-average, though he will sneak one in at 91-92 mph now and then and knows how to pitch. His fastball command puts him ahead of Owen and Tobi Stoner in the organization's pecking order. Gee's results are hard to ignore, and the Mets are eager to see how far his pitchability will get him. After pitching well again in Puerto Rico's winter league (on the same Ponce team as Antonini), Gee is expected to open the 2009 season in Binghamton's rotation.

Year	Club (League)	Class	W	L	ERA	G	GS	CG	SV	IP	H	R	ER	HR	BB	SO	AVG
2007	Brooklyn (NYP)	SS	3	1	2.47	14	11	0	0	62	57	17	17	1	9	56	.249
2008	St. Lucie (FSL)	HiA	8	6	3.25	21	21	0	0	127	117	49	46	6	19	94	.245
	Binghamton (EL)	AA	2	0	1.33	4	4	0	0	27	18	4	4	1	5	20	.194
MINOR LEAGUE TOTALS			13	7	2.79	39	36	0	0	216	192	70	67	8	33	170	.240

18 SCOTT SHAW, RHP

BORN: Aug. 3, 1986. **B-T:** R-R. **HT.:** 6-5. **WT.:** 225. **DRAFTED:** Illinois, 2008 (13th round). **SIGNED BY:** Scott Trcka.

Shaw had underwhelming numbers at Illinois, including a 4-4, 7.83 record his final season, dropping his draft stock. But scout Scott Trcka was impressed with Shaw's raw ability, much like the Mets saw potential in Bobby Parnell despite lackluster numbers at Charleston Southern. Shaw did have success in wood-bat summer leagues during college, and Trcka signed him for $30,000. With a superior breaking ball to Dillon Gee, but comparable in terms of being a competitor, Shaw does a solid job mixing what are considered average pitches (fastball, slider, curveball, changeup) and throws strikes. With a big-bodied, strong frame, he may have more left in the tank. His fastball sat at 88-89 mph in Brooklyn, but regularly registered 90 mph in Hawaii Winter Baseball and can reach 92-93 mph. Shaw, who has indicated he overthrew in college trying to impress scouts, has retooled his slider since turning pro and consistently repeats his motion. He used to get college batters to chase the slider by throwing it wide, but professional hitters lay off it, so he's now done a better job of vertically using the strike zone. Scouts in HWB considered him the best of the Mets' contingent in the league, though he'll have to command his fastball better if he doesn't add velocity to it. After he pitched more than 100 innings between Brooklyn and Hawaii, Shaw's arm should be ready for a full season of pro ball. He'll spend 2009 in high Class A.

Year	Club (League)	Class	W	L	ERA	G	GS	CG	SV	IP	H	R	ER	HR	BB	SO	AVG
2008	Brooklyn (NYP)	SS	6	3	2.80	15	14	0	0	74	66	24	23	4	15	79	.238
MINOR LEAGUE TOTALS			6	3	2.80	15	14	0	0	74	66	24	23	4	15	79	.238

19 TOBI STONER, RHP

BORN: Dec. 3, 1984. **B-T:** R-R. **HT.:** 6-2. **WT.:** 190. **DRAFTED:** Davis & Elkins (W.Va.), 2006 (16th round). **SIGNED BY:** Matt Wondolowski.

Born in Landstuhl, Germany, where his father Neil served as an Air Force intelligence officer, Stoner moved to Maryland by the time he turned 6. After two years of junior college, Stoner played NCAA Division II baseball for two seasons at Davis & Elkins (W.Va.). He became the college program's first draft pick since Tim McLoughlin in the 16th round by the Padres 23 years earlier. The Mets stumbled onto Stoner seemingly by accident. Scout Matt Wondolowski attended the Davis & Elkins game in order to watch opponent West Virginia State. Stoner got on the Mets' radar with a 15-strikeout performance, though the game was bittersweet. Stoner surrendered a game-deciding homer at the very game he was handed a Mets questionnaire by Wondolowski. Stoner's four-seam fastball generally sits at 91-92 mph, though he's touched 93. Stoner has a solid slider, which functions as his second pitch, and needs to improve the consistency of his curve and changeup. He has a chance to be a swing guy or set-up man, but needs to improve his changeup to emerge as a starter. Stoner was also part of the Mets' Hawaii contingent and built more stamina and gained experience. He's expected to begin 2009 in Binghamton's rotation with Mike Antonini, Dillon Gee and Dylan Owen.

Year	Club (League)	Class	W	L	ERA	G	GS	CG	SV	IP	H	R	ER	HR	BB	SO	AVG
2006	Brooklyn (NYP)	SS	6	2	2.15	14	14	1	0	84	66	25	20	1	17	62	.219
2007	Savannah (SAL)	LoA	3	5	3.61	11	11	0	0	57	59	32	23	1	17	50	.259
	St. Lucie (FSL)	HiA	4	5	4.90	16	16	0	0	83	90	57	45	9	25	57	.280
2008	St. Lucie (FSL)	HiA	1	5	2.60	9	9	0	0	52	46	17	15	3	9	48	.238
	Binghamton (EL)	AA	4	6	4.33	15	15	0	0	79	80	39	38	7	29	59	.267
MINOR LEAGUE TOTALS			18	23	3.58	65	65	1	0	355	341	170	141	21	97	276	.254

20 LUCAS DUDA, 1B

BORN: Feb. 3, 1986. **B-T:** L-R. **HT.:** 6-4. **WT.:** 225. **DRAFTED:** Southern California, 2007 (7th round). **SIGNED BY:** Steve Leavitt.

Duda shows well above-average power in batting practice and in his 2007 pro debut, when he hit 20 doubles at short-season Brooklyn, but it didn't translate into games in 2008, when the Mets jumped him to high Class A. The first baseman has a long swing and misses too many pitches. Still, his power displays in BP will buy him time, even if he ultimately stalls at Triple-A. In some ways Duda is similar to Ike Davis, as both pitched and hit as prep players. Duda had Tommy John surgery and just hit at Southern California, but both are capable first basemen who could play in the outfield. Another difference is that Davis showed significant improvement as a college junior by better incorporating his lower half into his swing. Last season, Duda fell into a rut of only using his upper body, which the Mets sought to correct when he participated in instructional league. Duda has good strength but hits a lot of balls to the big parts of the field, which the Mets also sought to address. Primarily a first baseman with the Mets with average fielding skills at best, Duda also saw action in seven games in right field and two games in left field in 2008. Duda does not have much speed. His progression should take him to Double-A to open the season.

Year	Club (League)	Class	AVG	G	AB	R	H	2B	3B	HR	RBI	BB	SO	SB	OBP	SLG
2007	Brooklyn (NYP)	SS	.299	67	234	32	70	20	3	4	32	34	45	3	.398	.462
2008	St. Lucie (FSL)	HiA	.263	133	483	58	127	26	3	11	66	66	129	2	.358	.398
MINOR LEAGUE TOTALS			.275	200	717	90	197	46	6	15	98	100	174	5	.371	.418

21 FRANCISCO PENA, C

BORN: Oct, 12, 1989. **B-T:** R-R. **HT.:** 6-2. **WT.:** 230. **SIGNED:** Dominican Republic, 2006. **SIGNED BY:** Ismael Cruz.

The son of five-time all-star Tony Pena, Francisco signed for $750,000 in 2006. He repeated at low Class A Savannah in 2008, and didn't draw rave reviews. Take his throwing arm. He has plus arm strength, and he's been timed as quick as 1.90 to 1.95 seconds on occasion throwing to second base. However, he has widely inconsistent ranges in time and accuracy thanks to an awkward arm action and poor transfers. He threw out just 23 percent of basestealers last season. Pena's weight also has been an issue—scouts estimate he carried at least 250 pounds in 2008—though reports from the instructional league suggested Pena made dramatic improvements in his physical shape. Pena isn't projected to be more than an average hitter or defensive catcher at this point, and is not likely to be moved to another position. He still has youth on his side, as well as raw power and good hands that work behind the plate and can work at the plate. Pena is a pure fastball hitter and needs to learn how to hit the slider, which he chases a lot, in order to advance in the minors. He was exposed in the instructional league by offspeed pitches, which he often waved at. Pena does hit to the opposite field well, so team officials hope it's just a matter of repetition to improve his performance against offspeed pitches. After two seasons in low Class A, Pena should get tested in the Florida State League in 2009.

Year	Club (League)	Class	AVG	G	AB	R	H	2B	3B	HR	RBI	BB	SO	SB	OBP	SLG
2007	Savannah (SAL)	LoA	.210	103	367	26	77	12	0	5	30	24	76	1	.263	.283
2008	Savannah (SAL)	LoA	.264	105	397	34	105	22	3	6	41	25	95	0	.308	.380
MINOR LEAGUE TOTALS			.238	208	764	60	182	34	3	11	71	49	171	1	.286	.334

22 GREG VELOZ, 2B

BORN: June 3, 1988. **B-T:** B-R. **HT.:** 6-1. **WT.:** 175. **SIGNED:** Dominican Republic, 2005. **SIGNED BY:** Ismael Cruz/Sandy Johnson/Eddy Toledo.

An excellent athlete with good makeup, the switch-hitting Veloz doesn't lack confidence. He failed to make adjustments at the plate and rolled over a lot of balls, though he may have been over his head in Class A leagues as a teenager. One scout compared him to a minor league Jose Vidro. Veloz has strength and a line-drive swing but doesn't have significant power potential, and like Vidro in his heyday he does a decent but unspectacular job at second base. After initial struggles, the wiry, athletic Veloz came on at the end of the season. He only began playing second base after signing with the Mets. He had manned third base as a youngster in the Dominican, but his fringy arm strength profiles better for the right side of the diamond. Mets instructors are still teaching Veloz to use his backhand more instead of trying to get in front of everything, and suggest his 19 errors primarily were throwing miscues because he wasn't correctly positioning himself. While his speed is just average, Veloz did record 29 steals. He wore down and didn't impress scouts who saw him in Hawaii Winter Baseball, showing hard hands defensively and poor technique. Veloz is expected to begin 2009 in high Class A, where he played 21 games last season.

Year	Club (League)	Class	AVG	G	AB	R	H	2B	3B	HR	RBI	BB	SO	SB	OBP	SLG
2006	Mets (DSL)	R	.262	63	221	50	58	16	1	4	28	33	57	28	.366	.398
2007	Kingsport (APP)	R	.271	66	258	43	70	13	9	5	28	26	62	18	.344	.450
	Savannah (SAL)	LoA	.171	66	234	20	40	7	1	2	14	23	73	15	.243	.235
2008	Savannah (SAL)	LoA	.286	111	455	68	130	25	5	6	52	32	93	28	.339	.402
	St. Lucie (FSL)	HiA	.234	21	77	8	18	1	0	0	4	7	20	1	.298	.247
MINOR LEAGUE TOTALS			.254	327	1245	189	316	62	16	17	126	121	305	90	.325	.370

23 JOSH THOLE, C

BORN: Oct. 28, 1986. **B-T:** L-R. **HT.:** 6-1. **WT.:** 190. **DRAFTED:** HS—Breese, Ill., 2005 (13th round). **SIGNED BY:** Quincy Boyd.

Thole received limited playing time at St. Lucie to begin 2008, including just three games at catcher during the opening two weeks. But with the team stumbling to a 2-11 start and Sean McCraw struggling at the plate, the door opened for Thole to see more action. He became a Florida State League all-star while hitting .300/.382/.427. Thole caught in high school, but until 2008—when he caught 75 games for St. Lucie—he primarily had played first base as a professional, with just 26 games behind the plate from 2005-07. Working with minor league catching instructor Bob Natal, Thole revamped his catching techniques and did a passable job. At the plate, Thole has a decent swing path and will hit mistakes, but is not projected to hit for much power. His best attribute is his plate discipline, as he gets into hitter's counts and jumps on fastballs. He has a thick lower half and runs poorly, making catcher his best fit. He has plenty of work to do defensively, particularly with his receiving, as he tends to box some pitches. His arm is average but he threw out just 22 percent of basestealers last year. Thole has limited speed. He passed through the Rule 5 draft after being left off the 40-man roster and should report to Double-A in 2009.

Year	Club (League)	Class	AVG	G	AB	R	H	2B	3B	HR	RBI	BB	SO	SB	OBP	SLG
2005	Mets (GCL)	R	.269	35	104	14	28	2	1	1	12	20	11	1	.406	.337
2006	Kingsport (APP)	R	.235	36	98	13	23	4	0	1	12	7	25	1	.300	.306
2007	Savannah (SAL)	LoA	.267	117	389	46	104	17	0	0	36	61	57	4	.372	.311
2008	St. Lucie (FSL)	HiA	.300	111	347	49	104	25	2	5	56	45	38	2	.382	.427
MINOR LEAGUE TOTALS			.276	299	938	122	259	48	3	7	116	133	131	8	.372	.356

24 BRANT RUSTICH, RHP

BORN: Jan. 23, 1985. **B-T:** R-R. **HT.:** 6-6. **WT.:** 230. **DRAFTED:** UCLA, 2007 (2nd round). **SIGNED BY:** Steve Leavitt.

Rustich, a former UCLA closer, had a chance to impress in big league camp in 2008, but arm soreness resulted in him sitting out. The Mets sent him to low Class A to begin the season once he was declared healthy. He pitched poorly in the first half but finally showed improvement after moving to the rotation, posting a 3.03 ERA in that role (4.76 in relief). During the summer Rustich learned that he had been pitching with a broken humerus bone in his arm for mor than a year. Rustich ranges from 91-96 mph with his fastball and has the potential for an above-average slider to go along with a changeup that has flashed plus potential. With Mets special assistant Sandy Johnson watching one game at Savannah, Rustich dominated with five no-hit innings and possessed an unhittable breaking ball. Scouts say that early in the season, that quality of stuff was not there, with a stiff arm action. Mets officials hope he'll grow out of the injury susceptibility, as Johnson once watched Robb Nen and Darren Oliver do in the minors with Texas. Rustich is currently considered a thrower without feel. The Mets haven't yet resolved whether Rustich will be a starter or reliever, but he'll be 24 this year and still will be ticketed for A-ball. He has better stuff than fellow 2007 draftees Mike Antonini, Dillon Gee and Dylan Owen but lacks their durability and feel for pitching.

Year	Club (League)	Class	W	L	ERA	G	GS	CG	SV	IP	H	R	ER	HR	BB	SO	AVG
2007	Kingsport (APP)	R	1	0	0.87	5	2	0	0	10	6	1	1	0	1	10	.158
	Brooklyn (NYP)	SS	2	0	2.13	10	0	0	2	13	4	3	3	2	1	11	.095
2008	Savannah (SAL)	LoA	3	4	3.62	20	8	0	0	50	42	26	20	1	16	48	.231
MINOR LEAGUE TOTALS			6	4	2.97	35	10	0	2	73	52	30	24	3	18	69	.198

25 NATHAN VINEYARD, LHP

BORN: Oct. 3, 1988. **B-T:** L-L. **HT.:** 6-2. **WT.:** 200. **DRAFTED:** HS—Cartersville, Ga., 2007 (1st round supplemental). **SIGNED BY:** Marlin McPhail.

Vineyard made just two starts in low Class A before a shoulder injury led to surgery last May. His recovery is expected to take perhaps longer than a full year, so Vineyard may remain behind in Port St. Lucie, Fla., at the organization's rehab center when the 2009 season begins. Vineyard ranked No. 9 on this list a year ago, and at just 20 years old isn't being written off. The Mets signed Vineyard for $657,000 after he did the summer showcase circuit for Georgia's East Cobb program. Before he got hurt, Vineyard's fastball sat at 88-91 mph with good movement. The Mets projected he would add velocity prior to his injury, and to fulfill that projection he'll have to attack his rehabilitation. His slider was a plus pitch, though he threw too many as an amateur, which may have led to his shoulder injury. He didn't need his changeup much in high school and it needs refinement. Right now, the Mets just hope he'll be healthy enough to log some innings in 2009.

Year	Club (League)	Class	W	L	ERA	G	GS	CG	SV	IP	H	R	ER	HR	BB	SO	AVG
2007	Mets (GCL)	R	0	3	5.27	9	7	0	0	27	30	18	16	4	9	33	.265
2008	Savannah (SAL)	LoA	0	2	14.63	2	2	0	0	8	13	13	13	1	6	3	.382
MINOR LEAGUE TOTALS			0	5	7.39	11	9	0	0	35	43	31	29	5	15	36	.293

26 ELVIN RAMIREZ, RHP

BORN: Oct. 10, 1987. **B-T:** R-R. **HT.:** 6-3. **WT.:** 208. **SIGNED:** Dominican Republic, 2004. **SIGNED BY:** Eddy Toledo/Rafael Bournigal.

Ramirez was just 16 when he signed out of the Dominican Republic and remains fairly raw, but after three years in Rookie ball, the Mets challenged him with a full-season assignment at Savannah. Results were mixed. Ramirez used his plus fastball—which has registered as high as 96-97 mph and sits at 89-94—to pitch well through the first half of the season. His fastball is notable for sink as well as velocity and he got plenty of groundouts (1.77 for every airout) while allowing only one home run. He also showed a hard curveball that has promise and a decent changeup. A muscle strain in his back, injured while exercising, sidelined him, and Ramirez didn't pitch again after July 9. Ramirez returned for instructional league at full strength. Ramirez's rough delivery is hard to repeat, and scouts outside the organization consider Ramirez strictly a reliever in the future. He's inconsistent with getting extension out front in his delivery, and the Mets have worked to lengthen his stride to help him finish off his pitches and gain more velocity. Lean and wiry, he has arm speed and power for a bullpen role. He lacks the command to start anyway. A move to the bullpen could be in the offing as soon as 2009, when Ramirez will head to high Class A.

Year	Club (League)	Class	W	L	ERA	G	GS	CG	SV	IP	H	R	ER	HR	BB	SO	AVG
2005	Mets (DSL)	R	2	6	6.53	16	6	0	0	40	48	38	29	2	23	24	.284
2006	Mets (DSL)	R	0	1	2.63	11	6	0	0	27	16	13	8	0	10	28	.165
2007	Kingsport (APP)	R	1	4	5.52	12	12	0	0	46	52	34	28	5	29	48	.280
2008	Savannah (SAL)	LoA	6	7	3.67	18	18	0	0	81	81	38	33	1	36	62	.257
MINOR LEAGUE TOTALS			9	18	4.55	57	42	0	0	194	197	123	98	8	98	162	.257

27 DARREN O'DAY, RHP

BORN: Oct. 22, 1982. **B-T:** R-R. **HT.:** 6-4. **WT.:** 225. **SIGNED:** Florida, NDFA 2006. **SIGNED BY:** Tom Kotchman (Angels).

Twelve hours after trading sidearm reliever Joe Smith to the Indians in a three-team deal that landed J.J. Putz, the Mets selected the submarine-throwing O'Day in the major league Rule 5 draft to fill Smith's void. O'Day was the closer on Florida's 2005 College World Series team, having created a niche by dropping his arm angle while playing in an adult league in Jacksonville. He earned a spot as a walk-on, pitched four years and signed with the Angels in 2006 as a nondrafted free agent prior to the draft. He surprised observers by making the Angels out of spring training last season. He keeps the ball down and throws strikes, though his fastball registers just 88 mph. In addition to a heavy sinker with a whipping action that's tough on righties, O'Day also throws a sweeping slider. He has a labrum tear but opted to rehab over the winter rather than have surgery and the Mets expect he'll be able to contribute. If he doesn't stick on the big league roster, he has to clear waivers and get offered back to the Angels for half the $50,000 draft price before he can be sent to the minors. New York also took a second big leauge Rule 5 reliever, righthander Rocky Cherry from the Orioles.

Year	Club (League)	Class	W	L	ERA	G	GS	CG	SV	IP	H	R	ER	HR	BB	SO	AVG
2006	Orem (PIO)	R	0	1	2.51	14	0	0	7	14	11	5	4	1	5	15	.208
	Cedar Rapids (MWL)	LoA	3	1	2.70	17	0	0	1	23	20	8	7	1	2	14	.235
2007	R. Cucamonga (CAL)	HiA	4	0	0.75	24	0	0	11	24	10	3	2	1	6	26	.120
	Arkansas (TEX)	AA	3	4	3.99	29	0	0	10	29	27	13	13	3	14	22	.252
2008	Salt Lake (PCL)	AAA	2	2	3.27	21	0	0	7	33	29	13	12	3	7	30	.244
	Los Angeles (AL)	MAJ	0	1	4.57	30	0	0	0	43	49	24	22	2	14	29	.283
MINOR LEAGUE TOTALS			12	8	2.76	105	0	0	36	124	97	42	38	9	34	107	.217
MAJOR LEAGUE TOTALS			0	1	4.57	30	0	0	0	43	49	24	22	2	14	29	.283

28 DYLAN OWEN, RHP

BORN: July, 12, 1986. **B-T:** R-R. **HT.:** 5-11. **WT.:** 203. **DRAFTED:** Francis Marion (S.C.), 2007 (20th round). **SIGNED BY:** Marlin McPhail.

Mets officials consider Owen a strike-throwing machine, and he has had nothing but success the last three years. That includes being a NCAA Division II all-American in 2007, when he led the level with a 1.04 ERA. He set a Peach Belt Conference record with 334 strikeouts in his career. As a pro, he's 22-8, 2.96 despite a short, wide body that lacks projection and modest stuff. While his fastball has hit 93 mph, he sits at 87-90 and has good feel for the pitch, spotting it to all parts of the strike zone. His slider has made progress and can be an above-average pitch at times; he varies the break and velocity on it to get strikeouts or early count groundballs. His curveball and changeup are just playable but he throws them for strikes. Owen was leading the Florida State League in wins and strikeouts and ranked eighth in ERA when he was promoted and got his feet wet in Double-A. He'll return to Binghamton in 2009 with fellow 2007 draftees Dillon Gee and Mike Antonini. His slider is the best breaking ball of the trio, but his fastball ranks third among them and might make him a future relief candidate.

Year	Club (League)	Class	W	L	ERA	G	GS	CG	SV	IP	H	R	ER	HR	BB	SO	AVG
2007	Brooklyn (NYP)	SS	9	1	1.49	14	13	0	0	72	51	13	12	0	12	69	.197
2008	St. Lucie (FSL)	HiA	12	6	3.43	24	24	2	0	134	135	55	51	12	33	116	.265
	Binghamton (EL)	AA	1	1	5.51	3	3	0	0	16	20	10	10	3	9	15	.299
MINOR LEAGUE TOTALS			22	8	2.96	41	40	2	0	222	206	78	73	15	54	200	.247

29 JAVIER RODRIGUEZ, OF

BORN: April 4, 1990. **B-T:** R-R. **HT.:** 6-2. **WT.:** 165. **DRAFTED:** HS—Gurabo, P.R., 2008 (2nd round). **SIGNED BY:** Junior Roman.

Drafted in the second round by the Mets last June out of the Puerto Rico Baseball Academy and signed for $585,000, Rodriguez is a raw player who struggled to make adjustments in the Gulf Coast League. Club officials view Rodriguez as a potential four- or five-tool player, despite his poor debut, and were encouraged by his showing in the instructional league in the Dominican Republic. Rodriguez's best tools are his bat speed and strong arm. He's also an above-average runner, covering 60 yards in 6.7 seconds at a pre-draft workout. Just 18, he's very slim physically but should hit for decent power as he fills out. He has a tendency for a long swing and gets into trouble when he loses his direction with his stride foot and steps in the bucket. He showed major improvement in correcting those flaws in the instructional league, allowing him to stay on pitches longer and use the entire field. Rodriguez needs to improve on his strike-zone discipline. He encouraged club officials by taking charge pre-pitch in instructional league and being a leader among young outfielders. With a strong spring-training performance, Rodriguez could open 2009 in low Class A. If he's still not ready, he'll remain in extended spring training and head to Kingsport.

Year	Club (League)	Class	AVG	G	AB	R	H	2B	3B	HR	RBI	BB	SO	SB	OBP	SLG
2008	Mets (GCL)	R	.193	38	135	17	26	3	0	1	20	10	27	0	.258	.237
MINOR LEAGUE TOTALS			.193	38	135	17	26	3	0	1	20	10	27	0	.258	.237

30 ADERLIN RODRIGUEZ, 3B

BORN: Nov. 18, 1991. **B-T:** R-R. **HT.:** 6-3. **WT.:** 220. **SIGNED:** Dominican Republic, 2008. **SIGNED BY:** Ramon Pena/Ismael Cruz/Franklin Taveras.

The Mets' top international addition in 2008 with a signing bonus of $600,000, Rodriguez is director of international scouting Ismael Cruz's latest find. Rodriguez primarily is a hitter. Third base is a work in progress for the raw fielder, though his showing there was not as bad as had been feared. He has a big frame, having substantially added to his size even from the time the Mets signed him until he began participating in the instructional league. Mets officials are excited about Rodriguez's potential to hit for power, though his swing has a tendency to get a little long and pull-happy—traits attributed to his youth. When he's on, Rodriguez can go to right-center with the best of the Mets' prospects. He has below-average speed, and there's concern he could get too big size-wise for third base. While at this early age the Mets hope Rodriguez can remain there, moving to first base or left field may be in his future. Assuming he follows in the tracks of Jefry Marte and Cesar Puello, the Mets' top Dominican signings from 2007, Rodriguez could find himself in the Gulf Coast League to open 2009.

Year	Club (League)	Class	AVG	G	AB	R	H	2B	3B	HR	RBI	BB	SO	SB	OBP	SLG
2008	Did Not Play—Signed 2009 Contract															

New York Yankees

BY JOHN MANUEL

The last season of Yankee Stadium II figured to end in October. After all, since Major League Baseball added wild cards, there never had been a postseason party that didn't include the Yankees.

Yet when New York played host to the Orioles on Sept. 21, that was it for The House That Ruth Built. In their first season under manager Joe Girardi, the Yankees got within three games of first place in late July, just as they bolstered their roster by acquiring Xavier Nady and Damaso Marte from the Pirates. But New York never got any closer and finished in third place at 89-73, eight games back.

Nothing went as planned, starting with a shoulder injury that limited Jorge Posada to 51 games. Chien-Ming Wang went down with a season-ending foot injury in mid-June, Melky Cabrera and Robinson Cano regressed (with Cabrera optioned to the minors), Joba Chamberlain broke down after moving into the rotation, and Phil Hughes and Ian Kennedy flopped.

The failure of the Yankees' top young players was especially galling as the Rays and Red Sox rode theirs to the postseason. That subject was a focus of the organization's postseason meetings—trying to figure out why its young players haven't translated minor league success to the majors while those on rival teams have.

New York nevertheless re-signed general manager Brian Cashman to a three-year contract shortly after the season ended. The contracts of veterans Bob Abreu, Jason Giambi and Mike Mussina came off the books—they made a combined $48 million in 2008—and the Yankees bolstered their rotation by signing C.C. Sabathia and A.J. Burnett for the staggering combined total cost of $243.5 million. The Yankees already had more resources than any organization, and that will be even more true with the opening of the new $1.3 billion Yankee Stadium.

The Yankees haven't leveraged their financial advantages well this decade, however. They have spent more than $1.3 billion on player salaries since winning the 2000 World Series, and New York's only titles this year came at Triple-A Scranton/Wilkes-Barre and Double-A Trenton. Despite their willingness to spend on draft and international talent, the Yankees have not developed any recent impact players beyond Chamberlain and Cano, and they failed to sign two of their top three picks in the 2008 draft, including first-rounder Gerrit Cole—considered the most electric arm in the

DAVID SCHOFIELD

Phil Hughes continues to struggle to stay healthy and in New York's rotation

TOP 30 PROSPECTS

1. Austin Jackson, of	16. Mike Dunn, lhp
2. Jesus Montero, c	17. Christian Garcia, rhp
3. Andrew Brackman, rhp	18. Arodys Vizcaino, rhp
4. Austin Romine, c	19. Wilkins de la Rossa, lhp
5. Dellin Betances, rhp	20. Juan Miranda, 1b
6. Zach McAllister, rhp	21. Francisco Cervelli, c
7. Alfredo Aceves, rhp	22. Brett Marshall, rhp
8. Phil Coke, lhp	23. George Kontos, rhp
9. Mark Melancon, rhp	24. D.J. Mitchell, rhp
10. Bradley Suttle, 3b	25. Alan Horne, rhp
11. Jeremy Bleich, lhp	26. Anthony Claggett, rhp
12. Jairo Heredia, rhp	27. Kelvin DeLeon, of
13. Brett Gardner, of	28. Carmen Angelini, ss
14. Manny Banuelos, lhp	29. Steven Jackson, rhp
15. David Robertson, rhp	30. Abraham Almonte, of

class of prep pitchers.

The Yankees did see significant progress from high-dollar investments such as Austin Jackson, who could claim their center-field job at some point in 2009, and catcher Jesus Montero, a $1.65 million bonus baby who had an all-star season in low Class A. Righthander Andrew Brackman, who got the largest draft bonus in club history ($3.35 million) as part of a big league contract that could reach $13 million with incentives, finally got on the mound in Hawaii Winter Baseball. He had Tommy John surgery shortly after signing in 2007 and an appendectomy last July.

General Manager: Brian Cashman. **Farm Director:** Mark Newman. **Scouting Director:** Damon Oppenheimer.

Class	Team	League	W	L	PCT	Finish*	Manager	Affiliated
Majors	New York	American	89	73	.549	4th (14)	Joe Girardi	—
Triple-A	Scranton/W-B Yankees	International	88	56	.611	^2nd (14)	Dave Miley	2007
Double-A	Trenton Thunder	Eastern	86	54	.614	^1st (12)	Tony Franklin	2003
High A	Tampa Yankees	Florida State	76	65	.526	6th (12)	Luis Sojo	1994
Low A	Charleston River Dogs	South Atlantic	80	59	.576	3rd (16)	Torre Tyson	2005
Short-season	Staten Island Yankees	New York-Penn	49	26	.653	1st (14)	Pat McMahon	1999
Rookie	GCL Yankees	Gulf Coast	31	27	.534	7th (16)	Jody Reed	1980
Overall 2008 Minor League Record			406	287	.586	1st		

* Finish in overall standings (No. of teams in league). ^League champion.

LAST YEAR'S TOP 30

Rank	Player, Pos.	Status
1.	Joba Chamberlain, rhp	Majors
2.	Austin Jackson, of	No. 1
3.	Jose Tabata, of	(Pirates)
4.	Ian Kennedy, rhp	Majors
5.	Alan Horne, rhp	No. 25
6.	Jesus Montero, c	No. 2
7.	Jeff Marquez, rhp	(White Sox)
8.	Brett Gardner, of	No. 13
9.	Ross Ohlendorf, rhp	(Pirates)
10.	Andrew Brackman, rhp	No. 3
11.	Mark Melancon, rhp	No. 9
12.	Humberto Sanchez, rhp	Dropped out
13.	Dellin Betances, rhp	No. 5
14.	Daniel McCutchen, rhp	(Pirates)
15.	Kevin Whelan, rhp	Dropped out
16.	Carmen Angelini, ss	No. 28
17.	George Kontos, rhp	No. 23
18.	Ivan Nova, rhp	(Padres)
19.	Colin Curtis, of	Dropped out
20.	Jairo Heredia, rhp	No. 12
21.	Juan Miranda, 1b	No. 20
22.	Austin Romine, c	No. 4
23.	Francisco Cervelli, c	No. 21
24.	David Robertson, rhp	No. 15
25.	Mike Dunn, lhp	No. 16
26.	J. Brent Cox, rhp	Dropped out
27.	Mitch Hilligoss, 3b	Dropped out
28.	Scott Patterson, rhp	(Padres)
29.	Edwar Ramirez, rhp	Majors
30.	Zach McAllister, rhp	No. 6

BEST TOOLS

Best Hitter for Average	Bradley Suttle
Best Power Hitter	Jesus Montero
Best Strike-Zone Discipline	Chris Malec
Fastest Baserunner	Brett Gardner
Best Athlete	Austin Jackson
Best Fastball	Andrew Brackman
Best Curveball	Christian Garcia
Best Slider	Anthony Claggett
Best Changeup	Alfredo Aceves
Best Control	Zach McAllister
Best Defensive Catcher	Francisco Cervelli
Best Defensive Infielder	Ramiro Pena
Best Infield Arm	Marcos Vechionacci
Best Defensive Outfielder	Austin Jackson
Best Outfield Arm	Seth Fortenberry

PROJECTED 2012 LINEUP

Catcher	Austin Romine
First Base	Alex Rodriguez
Second Base	Robinson Cano
Third Base	Bradley Suttle
Shortstop	Derek Jeter
Left Field	Xavier Nady
Center Field	Brett Gardner
Right Field	Austin Jackson
Designated Hitter	Jesus Montero
No. 1 Starter	C.C. Sabathia
No. 2 Starter	Joba Chamberlain
No. 3 Starter	A.J. Burnett
No. 4 Starter	Chien-Ming Wang
No. 5 Starter	Andrew Brackman
Closer	Mark Melancon

TOP PROSPECTS OF THE DECADE

Year	Player, Pos.	2008 Org.
1999	Nick Johnson, 1b	Nationals
2000	Nick Johnson, 1b	Nationals
2001	Nick Johnson, 1b	Nationals
2002	Drew Henson, 3b	Out of baseball
2003	Jose Contreras, rhp	White Sox
2004	Dioner Navarro, c	Rays
2005	Eric Duncan, 3b	Yankees
2006	Phil Hughes, rhp	Yankees
2007	Phil Hughes, rhp	Yankees
2008	Joba Chamberlain, rhp	Yankees

TOP DRAFT PICKS OF THE DECADE

Year	Player, Pos.	2008 Org.
1999	David Walling, rhp	Out of baseball
2000	David Parrish, c	Padres
2001	John-Ford Griffin, of	Dodgers
2002	Brandon Weeden, rhp (2nd)	Out of baseball
2003	Eric Duncan, 3b	Yankees
2004	Phil Hughes, rhp	Yankees
2005	C.J. Henry, ss	Yankees
2006	Ian Kennedy, rhp	Yankees
2007	Andrew Brackman, rhp	Yankees
2008	*Gerrit Cole, rhp	None

*Did not sign.

LARGEST BONUSES IN CLUB HISTORY

Hideki Irabu, 1997	$8,500,000
Jose Contreras, 2002	$6,000,000
Andrew Brackman, 2007	$3,350,000
Willy Mo Pena, 1999	$2,440,000
Ian Kennedy, 2006	$2,250,000

NEW YORK YANKEES

TOP 2009 ROOKIE: Alfredo Aceves, rhp. The mature Mexican is ready to contribute in New York's rotation.

BREAKOUT PROSPECT: Manny Banuelos, lhp. Another find from Mexico, the poised southpaw has a chance to move quickly.

SLEEPER: Kevin Russo, 2b/3b. After a fine Arizona Fall League performance, he could bolster the big league bench with his speed.

SOURCE OF TOP 30 TALENT

Homegrown	28	**Acquired**	**2**
College	9	Trades	2
Junior college	0	Rule 5 draft	0
High school	7	Independent leagues	0
Draft-and-follow	2	Free agents/waivers	0
Nondrafted free agents	0		
International	10		

Numbers in parentheses indicate prospect rankings.

LF
Colin Curtis
Justin Christian
Taylor Grote
Austin Krum

CF
Austin Jackson (1)
Brett Gardner (13)
Abraham Almonte (30)
Eduardo Sosa
Ray Kruml
Mike Jones

RF
Kelvin DeLeon (27)
Seth Fortenberry
Dan Brewer

3B
Bradley Suttle (10)
Marcos Vechionacci
Chris Malec
Addison Maruszak

SS
Carmen Angelini (28)
Garrison Lassiter
Eduardo Nunez
Ramiro Pena
Jose Pirela

2B
Kevin Russo
Damon Sublett
Justin Snyder
Corban Joseph
David Adams
Luis Nunez

1B
Juan Miranda (20)
Brandon Laird

C
Jesus Montero (2)
Austin Romine (4)
Francisco Cervelli (21)
Kyle Higashioka
Chase Weems

RHP

Starters	Relievers
Andrew Brackman (3)	Mark Melancon (9)
Dellin Betances (5)	David Robertson (15)
Zach McAllister (6)	Anthony Claggett (26)
Alfredo Aceves (7)	Steven Jackson (29)
Jairo Heredia (12)	Humberto Sanchez
Christian Garcia (17)	Kevin Whelan
Arodys Vizcaino (18)	Kanekoa Texeira
Brett Marshall (22)	J. Brent Cox
George Kontos (23)	Jonathan Albaladejo
D.J. Mitchell (24)	
Alan Horne (25)	
Eric Hacker	
Ryan Pope	
Mikey O'Brien	
Adam Olbrychowski	
Casey Erickson	

LHP

Starters	Relievers
Phil Coke (8)	Mike Dunn (16)
Jeremy Bleich (11)	Wilkins de la Rossa (19)
Manny Banuelos (14)	
Nik Turley	
Chase Wright	

RHP/LHP
Pat Venditte

2008

Best Pure Hitter: 2B Corban Joseph (4) is a batting-cage rat with a pure natural stroke. He also shows pitch recognition and plate discipline.

Best Power Hitter: Power wasn't an emphasis in this draft class, but C Kyle Higashioka (7) and SS Garrison Lassiter (27) both have solid-average pop. Lassiter has a feel for hitting one scout compared to that of Dave Magadan.

Fastest Runner: OF Ray Kruml (11) reminds the Yankees a bit of current farmhand Brett Gardner with his gap-to-gap approach and well-above-average speed.

Best Defensive Player: Higashioka features smooth receiving skills and a slightly above-average arm that plays up because of his accuracy.

Best Fastball: Unsigned RHP Gerrit Cole (1) topped out at 100 mph last spring. RHP Brett Marshall (6) reached 96 mph at times and hit 94 in instructional league.

Best Secondary Pitch: LHP Jeremy Bleich (1s) has a plus curveball and a solid-average changeup.

Best Pro Debut: SS Addison Maruszak (17) hit .317/.372/.503 with six homers at short-season Staten Island and showed solid-average tools across the board except for his below-average speed. Switch-pitcher Pat Venditte (20) converted all 23 save chances for Staten Island, striking out 42 in 33 innings while limiting batters to a .117 average.

Best Athlete: At 6-foot-4 and 203 pounds, OF Mike Jones (29) has a pro body for both baseball and football. He had 10 touchdown catches for Arizona State as a junior and was the Sun Devils' leading receiver as a senior. He had just 93 at-bats in three seasons in college.

Most Intriguing Background: Venditte is trying to become the first fully ambidextrous pitcher in baseball history. He throws a lot of sliders from the left side, where his fastball sits at 76-78 mph. He has better stuff from the right side, but switch-pitching makes him who he is. Joseph's brother Caleb was a seventh-round pick of the Orioles in '08.

Closest To The Majors: Bleich and athletic RHP D.J. Mitchell (10), who has a good sinker/slider mix when he's on, could spend little time in the minors on the way to New York.

Best Late-Round Pick: Lassiter got $675,000 thanks to his offensive potential from the left side and middle-of-the-diamond athleticism. LHP Nik Turley (50) was signed away from Brigham Young for $125,000. The Yankees like his projectable 6-foot-4 frame, solid-average fastball and ability to spin a breaking ball.

The One Who Got Away: The Yankees knew Cole would have a high price tag, but they expected to sign him. The more the summer progressed, though, the more he sold himself on college, and he decided to attend UCLA. The Yankees also failed to land RHP Scott Bittle (2), who returned to Mississippi after a shoulder problem deterred New York from signing him.

Assessment: It's hard for any club to overcome failing to sign two of its first three picks, especially when one is the draft's hardest thrower in Cole. While the Yankees went above slot to sign Marshall ($850,000), Higashioka ($500,000), Mitchell ($450,000) and Lassiter, this draft class still has two holes at the top.

2007

The Yankees guaranteed $4.55 million to RHP Andrew Brackman (1), who has a huge ceiling but has yet to pitch in a minor league game. C Austin Romine (2) and 3B Bradley Suttle (4) are two of the system's few position prospects.

GRADE: C

2006

RHP Joba Chamberlain (1s) was a steal with the 41st overall pick, as medical concerns scared teams off. RHP Ian Kennedy (1) went backward last season, but there's plenty more pitching with RHPs Zach McAllister (3), Dellin Betances (8), Mark Melancon (9) and David Robertson (17).

GRADE: A

2005

SS C.J. Henry (1) was a huge bust, but another basketball star, OF Austin Jackson (8), is now New York's top prospect. OF Brett Gardner (3) may keep the center-field job warm for Jackson in 2009.

GRADE: C+

2004

Though injuries have stalled RHP Phil Hughes (1), he still projects as a No. 3 starter. RHP Jeff Marquez (1s) was used in a deal for Nick Swisher this offseason.

GRADE: C+

Draft analysis by John Manuel (2008) and Jim Callis (2004-07). Numbers in parentheses indicate draft rounds. *Bonuses for 2004-05 are first 10 rounds only.

DAVID SCHOFIELD

PROSPECT

AUSTIN JACKSON, OF

Born: Feb 1, 1987.
Ht.: 6-1. **Wt.:** 185.
Bats: R. **Throws:** R.
Drafted:
HS—Denton, Texas, 2005
(8th round).
Signed by:
Mark Batchko.

Jackson has spent the better part of his career proving he's a baseball player, not just an athlete playing baseball. He had a full ride to play basketball at Georgia Tech when he came out of Ryan High in Denton, Texas, in 2005. The Yankees swayed him to baseball with an $800,000 bonus, an eighth-round record at the time (broken a year later by New York's Dellin Betances). Jackson had halting progress early, striking out too often and seeming a half-step behind in his first full season at low Class A Charleston in 2006. A year later, he broke out at midseason while repeating the level and finished the year with an impressive turn in the Double-A Eastern League playoffs. He returned to Trenton this season and was the Thunder's best player as it repeated as EL champion.

Jackson is a premium athlete who can do a little of everything on the diamond. One EL manager used a football term, calling him a "playmaker." The Yankees' most advanced batting prospect, he's a rhythm hitter who thrives when he's in a groove. He had three hitting streaks of at least 10 games in 2008. He has the bat speed to catch up to the best fastballs, as he showed by crushing a key homer off Clay Buchholz in the EL playoffs, and league managers praised his situational hitting. While Jackson's power comes mostly to the gaps now, scouts and managers agree he'll have average power as he continues to gain experience and strength. He's a smart baserunner with maybe a tick above average speed, though he's not likely to be a big basestealer in the majors. Defensively, Jackson can glide to balls in the gaps with plus range and has a strong, accurate arm that could allow him to move to right field. His strong personality and leadership skills make him a good fit in the clubhouse and for New York.

Reports on Jackson's running ability are mixed. Some scouts say his big hack in the batter's box leads to below-average times from home to first. He may slow down as he matures physically and have to move to an outfield corner, which would be a problem if his power fails to develop. He employs a leg kick and when his timing is off, the rest of his swing falters, leaving him late on good fastballs.

Jackson's greatest weakness may be what he's not: a classic Yankees center fielder. He's no DiMaggio or Mantle, or even Bernie Williams. Jackson lacks a standout tool but earns future grades of solid-average to plus across the board. His all-around ability fits the profile of a center fielder on a championship team, similar to Williams but with less power and better defense. Melky Cabrera's regression and Brett Gardner's lack of power make Jackson New York's best bet for an in-house center fielder, and he began his campaign for the job with a strong stint in the Arizona Fall League. A robust start, either in spring training or at Triple-A Scranton/Wilkes-Barre, could propel Jackson past Cabrera and Gardner for the starting job in New York in 2009.

Year	Club (League)	Class	AVG	G	AB	R	H	2B	3B	HR	RBI	BB	SO	SB	OBP	SLG
2005	Yankees (GCL)	R	.304	40	148	32	45	11	2	0	14	18	26	11	.374	.405
2006	Charleston (SAL)	LoA	.260	134	535	90	139	24	5	4	47	61	151	37	.340	.346
2007	Charleston (SAL)	LoA	.260	60	235	33	61	16	1	3	25	24	59	19	.336	.374
	Tampa (FSL)	HiA	.345	67	258	53	89	15	6	10	34	22	48	13	.398	.566
	Scranton/W-B (IL)	AAA	.333	1	3	2	1	1	0	0	0	2	2	1	.600	.667
2008	Trenton (EL)	AA	.285	131	520	75	148	33	5	9	69	56	113	19	.354	.419
MINOR LEAGUE TOTALS			.284	433	1699	285	483	100	19	26	189	183	399	100	.356	.411

2 JESUS MONTERO, C

BORN: Nov. 28, 1989. **B-T:** R-R. **HT.:** 6-4. **WT.:** 225. **SIGNED:** Venezuela, 2006. **SIGNED BY:** Carlos Rios/Ricardo Finol.

Two years after signing for $1.65 million, Montero broke out, finishing second in the low Class A South Atlantic League in batting (.326) and total bases (258) while leading the league in hits (171). He was an SAL all-star and played at Yankee Stadium in the Futures Game, with his parents flying up from Venezuela to watch him. One club official said Montero has the system's best bat since Derek Jeter, only with much more power. Montero has tremendous strength and generates well-above-average bat speed. He has excellent hands and a feel for hitting balls squarely, and isn't afraid to use the whole field. He also has above-average arm strength and has made significant strides defensively. Offensively, Montero is learning to balance patience with aggressiveness. Defensively, he's so big and inflexible that he has trouble receiving balls down and to his right. His arm strength plays down because he has a slow transfer, and he threw out just 25 percent of basestealers in 2008. Montero has the bat and athleticism to profile as a first baseman or perhaps even a left fielder, but the Yankees see him as another Mike Piazza if he can remain behind the plate. He'll start 2009 at high Class A as a 19-year-old and could jump on an even faster track.

Year	Club (League)	Class	AVG	G	AB	R	H	2B	3B	HR	RBI	BB	SO	SB	OBP	SLG
2007	Yankees (GCL)	R	.280	33	107	13	30	6	0	3	19	12	18	0	.366	.421
2008	Charleston (SAL)	LoA	.326	132	525	86	171	34	1	17	87	37	83	2	.376	.491
MINOR LEAGUE TOTALS			.318	165	632	99	201	40	1	20	106	49	101	2	.374	.479

3 ANDREW BRACKMAN, RHP

BORN: Dec. 4, 1985. **B-T:** R-R. **HT.:** 6-10. **WT.:** 270. **DRAFTED:** North Carolina State, 2007 (1st round). **SIGNED BY:** Steve Swail.

Brackman was a two-sport athlete at North Carolina State for two seasons but dropped basketball to concentrate on baseball as a junior. His 2007 season ended with elbow trouble in May, but the Yankees drafted him in the first round anyway. He had Tommy John surgery shortly after signing a guaranteed $4.55 million major league contract that could pay out as much as $13 million with incentives. Despite not having pitched in a competitive game since May 2007, Brackman opened the 2008 Hawaii Winter Baseball season with a 97 mph fastball. When he's right mechanically, he has two plus pitches—a 91-97 mph heater that has reached 100 in the past and a curveball. He throws two variations of his breaking ball, a conventional curve and a knuckle-curve. His athletic ability separates him from other tall pitchers in terms of aptitude and the ability to repeat his delivery. Brackman remains raw for his age, which wasn't helped by Tommy John surgery or an appendectomy that cost him any chance to pitch in the 2008 regular season. His mechanics can get out of sync easily. He's also just learning a changeup. Brackman has rust to shake off and hasn't really dominated since the Cape Cod League in the summer of 2006. Still, he has more upside than any Yankees farmhand and looks primed to break out when he makes his official pro debut in high Class A.

Year	Club (League)	Class	W	L	ERA	G	GS	CG	SV	IP	H	R	ER	HR	BB	SO	AVG
2007	Did Not Play—Injured																
2008	Did Not Play—Injured																

4 AUSTIN ROMINE, C

BORN: Nov. 22, 1988. **B-T:** R-R. **HT.:** 6-2. **WT.:** 210. **DRAFTED:** HS—Lake Forest, Calif., 2007 (2nd round). **SIGNED BY:** David Keith.

Romine's older brother Andrew, a shortstop in the Angels system, led the Midwest League in steals in 2008, and their father Kevin played seven seasons with the Red Sox as an outfielder. Austin reported to big league camp in spring training, then missed a month with a groin injury before finishing strong in his first full pro season. He hit .359 with four of his 10 home runs in August. Romine combines athletic ability and baseball savvy with impressive raw power and improved hitting ability. He makes consistent hard contact with a simple swing he repeats regularly and projects to hit 20-25 homers annually if it all comes together. As a catcher, he has plus arm strength and made huge strides handling pitchers and calling games. Footwork issues keep Romine from receiving as efficiently as he should or from making quick transfers, and he threw out just 20 percent of basestealers in 2008 despite his arm strength. He was too deferential early in the season but learned how and when to assert himself with teammates. Jesus Montero's bat puts him on a faster track, but Romine looks like the Yankees' catcher of the future. He's expected to move to high Class A, where he'll share catching duties with Montero. Romine should be ready for New York by 2011, the final year of Jorge Posada's contract.

Year	Club (League)	Class	AVG	G	AB	R	H	2B	3B	HR	RBI	BB	SO	SB	OBP	SLG
2007	Yankees (GCL)	R	.500	1	2	2	1	1	0	0	1	1	1	0	.667	1.000
2008	Charleston (SAL)	LoA	.300	104	407	66	122	24	1	10	49	25	56	3	.344	.437
MINOR LEAGUE TOTALS			.301	105	409	68	123	25	1	10	50	26	57	3	.346	.440

STEVE MOORE

5 DELLIN BETANCES, RHP

BORN: March 23, 1988. **B-T:** R-R. **HT.:** 6-8. **WT.:** 245. **DRAFTED:** HS—New York, 2006 (8th round). **SIGNED BY:** Cesar Presbott/Brian Barber.

A $1 million bonus, a record for the eighth round, prompted Betances to spurn Vanderbilt and sign out of high school. He logged just 25 innings in 2007 because he was raw and came down with forearm tightness, but in 2008 he led South Atlantic League starters by averaging 10.5 strikeouts per nine innings. Betances has two plus pitches when he's at his best. His four-seam fastball sits at 94 mph and touches 97, and he uses his height to throw it on a steep downhill plane. His curveball can be a well-above-average hammer. He has improved markedly at quickening his feet, holding runners and fielding his position. Lacking Andrew Brackman's athleticism, Betances loses balance in his delivery and tends to fly open, costing him command and leaving him injury-prone. He missed much of June with a tired shoulder. The Yankees want to smooth out his mechanics before introducing a two-seam sinker to his repertoire, and his changeup remains in its nascent stages. He needs to keep improving his fielding and ability to hold runners. Though he has yet to prove he can stay healthy, Betances has front-of-the-rotation potential. New York would like him to reach 150-160 innings in high Class A in 2009, which would put him on course to pitch in his hometown at some point in 2011.

Year	Club (League)	Class	W	L	ERA	G	GS	CG	SV	IP	H	R	ER	HR	BB	SO	AVG
2006	Yankees (GCL)	R	0	1	1.16	7	7	0	0	23	14	5	3	1	7	27	.173
2007	Staten Island (NYP)	SS	1	2	3.60	6	6	0	0	25	24	11	10	0	17	29	.255
2008	Yankees (GCL)	R	0	1	8.53	3	2	0	0	6	13	7	6	0	3	6	.406
	Charleston (SAL)	LoA	9	4	3.67	22	22	0	0	115	87	57	47	9	59	135	.208
MINOR LEAGUE TOTALS			10	8	3.49	38	37	0	0	170	138	80	66	10	86	197	.220

6 ZACH McALLISTER, RHP

BORN: Dec. 8, 1987. **B-T:** R-R. **HT.:** 6-6. **WT.:** 230. **DRAFTED:** HS—Chillicothe, Ill., 2006 (3rd round). **SIGNED BY:** Steve Lemke.

The Yankees spent two years remaking McAllister, raising his arm slot and having him work with a curveball instead of his natural slider. After struggling with the changes at short-season Staten Island in 2007, McAllister regained his slider in a fall 2007 trip to New York's Dominican Republic instructional league camp. He broke out in 2008, ranking seventh in the minors with a 2.08 ERA, and didn't allow a run in five of his last six outings. Now employing a traditional three-quarters delivery, McAllister works with a 93-94 mph four-seam fastball with modest tail and an 89-91 mph two-seamer with nasty sink and armside run. Command of both pitches stems from his sound mechanics. His slider and changeup are solid offerings that he throws for strikes. A groundball pitcher, McAllister lacks a true strikeout pitch. His command of his secondary stuff is far less consistent than his command of his fastball. He sometimes leaves flat four-seamers up in the strike zone. McAllister has the body, mechanics and repertoire to be a mid-rotation workhorse. After making terrific progress in 2008, he figures to spend most of 2009 in Double-A.

Year	Club (League)	Class	W	L	ERA	G	GS	CG	SV	IP	H	R	ER	HR	BB	SO	AVG
2006	Yankees (GCL)	R	5	2	3.09	11	1	0	0	35	35	14	12	1	12	28	.259
2007	Staten Island (NYP)	SS	4	6	5.17	16	15	0	0	71	80	42	41	3	28	75	.286
2008	Charleston (SAL)	LoA	6	3	2.45	10	10	0	0	62	59	28	17	3	8	53	.245
	Tampa (FSL)	HiA	8	6	1.83	15	14	1	1	89	74	24	18	6	13	62	.225
MINOR LEAGUE TOTALS			23	17	3.08	52	40	1	1	257	248	108	88	13	61	218	.252

7 ALFREDO ACEVES, RHP

BORN: Dec. 8, 1982. **B-T:** R-R. **HT.:** 6-3. **WT.:** 220. **SIGNED:** Mexico, 2001. **SIGNED BY:** Tony Arias (Blue Jays).

Aceves signed with the Blue Jays in 2001, and they sold his contract to Yucatan of the Mexican League the following April. He pitched six seasons in his native country, posting a 34-23, 4.06 record before Yankees scout Lee Sigman recommended and signed him for $450,000 in January 2008. He rose three levels to the majors in his first season in the United States. Aceves throws a variety of average pitches, starting with an 89-91 mph fastball, a curveball and a slider. His changeup creeps into plus territory and rates as the best in the system. He also attacks lefthanded hitters with a split-finger fastball and cutter.

MIKE JANES

He avoids pitch patterns, stays around the plate and misses down when he misses at all. None of Aceves' pitches grades as plus, limiting his ceiling, and he lacks any future projection. He doesn't have one pitch he can go to for a strikeout and needs a quality defense behind him. Aceves resembles Yankees 2006 first-rounder Ian Kennedy but features more command, pitchability and experience. He has a leg up on Kennedy and Phil Hughes for a rotation spot in New York in 2009.

Year	Club (League)	Class	W	L	ERA	G	GS	CG	SV	IP	H	R	ER	HR	BB	SO	AVG
2001	Blue Jays (DSL)	R	2	1	3.10	10	1	0	1	29	29	13	10	1	3	24	.257
2002	Yucatan (MEX)	AAA	1	2	3.00	23	4	0	0	45	42	22	15	0	20	25	.241
2003	Yucatan (MEX)	AAA	1	1	3.35	27	2	0	1	43	49	17	16	3	18	29	.288
2004	Yucatan (MEX)	AAA	4	2	4.55	17	11	0	0	65	64	33	33	4	37	37	.259
2005	Yucatan (MEX)	AAA	9	8	4.32	22	21	3	0	146	155	77	70	12	44	101	.281
2006	Monterrey (MEX)	AAA	8	5	4.50	19	19	3	0	124	126	65	62	15	26	95	.266
2007	Monterrey (MEX)	AAA	11	5	3.64	18	18	1	0	106	96	46	43	6	33	70	.242
2008	Tampa (FSL)	HiA	4	1	2.11	8	8	0	0	47	32	16	11	1	8	37	.188
	Trenton (EL)	AA	2	2	1.80	7	7	1	0	50	37	10	10	3	6	35	.213
	Scranton/W-B (IL)	AAA	2	3	4.12	10	8	0	0	44	42	21	20	6	13	42	.250
	New York (AL)	MAJ	1	0	2.40	6	4	0	0	30	25	8	8	4	10	16	.227
MINOR LEAGUE TOTALS			44	30	3.73	161	99	8	2	699	672	320	290	51	208	495	.242
MAJOR LEAGUE TOTALS			1	0	2.40	6	4	0	0	30	25	8	8	4	10	16	.227

8 PHIL COKE, LHP

DAVID SCHOFIELD

BORN: July 19, 1982. **B-T:** L-L. **HT.:** 6-1. **WT.:** 210. **DRAFTED:** Delta (Calif.) JC, D/F 2002 (26th round). **SIGNED BY:** Tim McIntosh.

Coke failed to rise above high Class A in his first five seasons. He embraced the organization's offseason conditioning program, lost 18 pounds and improved his stuff across the board in 2008. He pitched well as a starter and shined as a reliever, including in September during his first big league callup. As a starter, Coke threw three pitches for strikes, including an 88-92 mph fastball. His slider found the zone much more than his curveball ever had, and his changeup was average. Out of the bullpen, Coke was a different animal. He ran his fastball up to 96 mph and his slider showed signs of becoming a plus pitch with improved tilt. At age 26, Coke most likely is a finished product. His slider remains inconsistent, and as a result, he's often less effective against lefthanded hitters. Coke has earned a spot in the Yankees' plans, probably as a reliever in the short term. He's better in that role anyway, and New York's spending spree in the rotation points him in that direction.

Year	Club (League)	Class	W	L	ERA	G	GS	CG	SV	IP	H	R	ER	HR	BB	SO	AVG
2003	Yankees (GCL)	R	0	0	3.75	10	0	0	0	12	13	7	5	0	3	5	.265
2004	Yankees (GCL)	R	0	1	3.97	7	1	0	0	11	18	7	5	0	3	13	.360
	Staten Island (NYP)	SS	0	0	6.75	3	1	0	0	8	9	6	6	1	3	7	.281
2005	Charelston (SAL)	LoA	8	11	5.42	24	18	0	0	103	122	67	62	11	34	68	.293
2006	Charelston (SAL)	LoA	0	1	0.53	5	2	0	1	17	10	1	1	0	4	19	.169
	Tampa (FSL)	HiA	5	7	3.60	22	18	1	0	110	101	52	44	6	35	88	.239
2007	Tampa (FSL)	HiA	7	3	3.09	17	16	1	0	99	93	36	34	4	37	76	.251
2008	Trenton (EL)	AA	9	4	2.51	23	20	1	0	118	105	39	33	7	39	115	.239
	Scranton/W-B (IL)	AAA	2	2	4.67	14	1	0	0	17	19	11	9	0	5	22	.271
	New York (MAJ)	MAJ	1	0	0.61	12	0	0	0	15	8	1	1	0	2	14	.160
MINOR LEAGUE TOTALS			31	29	3.61	125	77	3	1	496	490	226	199	29	163	413	.257
MAJOR LEAGUE TOTALS			1	0	0.61	12	0	0	0	15	8	1	1	0	2	14	.160

9 MARK MELANCON, RHP

DAVID SCHOFIELD

BORN: March 28, 1985. **B-T:** R-R. **HT.:** 6-2. **WT.:** 215. **DRAFTED:** Arizona, 2006 (9th round). **SIGNED BY:** Andy Stankiewicz.

The Yankees drafted Melancon despite an elbow strain that short-circuited his 2006 college season, and signed him for $600,000. He promptly reinjured his elbow and required Tommy John surgery. After pitching just eight pro innings entering 2008, he stayed healthy and helped Scranton win the Triple-A International League title. Roundly praised for his makeup and work ethic, Melancon responded well to his surgery and rehabilitation, regaining much of his power stuff. His fastball sits at 91-94 mph and touches 95, and he can throw his power curveball for strikes or bury it as a chase pitch. He added a changeup that helped him limit lefties to a .162 average in 2008. Melancon still has just 103 pro innings to his credit and is seeking more consistency with his curveball. He must continue to smooth out his delivery, which had so much effort that it led to his injury. He doesn't hold runners well. The best in-house candidate to eventually replace Mariano Rivera as the Yankees' closer, Melancon has the temperament to handle the role and his stuff is nearly closer-worthy as well. He'll compete for a set-up role in New York in 2009.

Year	Club (League)	Class	W	L	ERA	G	GS	CG	SV	IP	H	R	ER	HR	BB	SO	AVG
2006	Staten Island (NYP)	SS	0	1	3.52	7	0	0	2	8	9	7	3	0	2	8	.281
2007	Did Not Play—Injured																
2008	Tampa (FSL)	HiA	1	0	2.84	13	0	0	0	25	26	9	8	2	6	20	.265
	Trenton (EL)	AA	6	0	1.81	19	0	0	2	50	32	14	10	3	12	47	.183
	Scranton/W-B (IL)	AAA	1	1	2.70	12	0	0	1	20	11	7	6	1	4	22	.162
MINOR LEAGUE TOTALS			8	2	2.37	51	0	0	5	103	78	37	27	6	24	97	.209

10 BRADLEY SUTTLE, 3B

BORN: Jan. 24, 1986. **B-T:** B-R. **HT.:** 6-2. **WT.:** 215. **DRAFTED:** Texas, 2007 (4th round). **SIGNED BY:** Steve Boros.

One of the better pure hitters in the 2007 draft, Suttle batted .359/.450/.603 as a draft-eligible sophomore at Texas. After the Yankees signed him for $1.3 million, he looked lost in Hawaii Winter Baseball that fall, striking out 30 times in 85 at-bats. Undaunted, he made several adjustments at the plate in 2008 and had a successful pro debut despite two stints on the disabled list with hip problems. Suttle has a feel for hitting from both sides of the plate and confidence that leads to excellent strike-zone awareness. He has the strength and enough bat speed to maximize his discipline. After showing an inability to make consistent contact in Hawaii, he was shorter to the ball in 2008. He also improved significantly on defense, showing better range to both sides and coming in on slow rollers. He has good arm strength. Suttle's power may not fit the third-base profile, as his swing from both sides is geared more toward line drives. The Yankees would like him to be more aggressive to exploit pitches he can drive. He's fairly slow and has modest athleticism. Reversing a poor start has Suttle back on track, but with Alex Rodriguez signed through 2017, he's in no rush. He'll start next season in high Class A and could push Rodriguez to a different position in 2011.

Year	Club (League)	Class	AVG	G	AB	R	H	2B	3B	HR	RBI	BB	SO	SB	OBP	SLG
2007	Yankees (GCL)	R	.125	3	8	1	1	0	0	0	1	1	2	0	.222	.125
2008	Charleston (SAL)	LoA	.271	96	377	63	102	23	7	11	44	45	93	2	.348	.456
MINOR LEAGUE TOTALS			.268	99	385	64	103	23	7	11	45	46	95	2	.346	.449

11 JEREMY BLEICH, LHP

BORN: June 18, 1987. **B-T:** L-L. **HT.:** 6-2. **WT.:** 195. **DRAFTED:** Stanford, 2008 (1st round supplemental). **SIGNED BY:** Mike Thurman.

Bleich was part of a loaded 2005 Louisana prep class that included fellow lefthanders Beau Jones and Sean West, who were supplemental first-round picks that year, and Wade Miley, who like Bleich was a supplemental first-rounder in 2008 after three years of college. Bleich went to Stanford and worked primarily as a closer as a freshman before settling into the rotation. He helped lead the Cardinal back to the College World Series in 2008 despite missing nearly two months with what was termed an elbow strain. The Yankees took him 44th overall and signed him late in the summer for a below-slot $700,000, owing to concerns over his elbow. He wound up as their top signee when they failed to sign first-rounder Gerrit Cole. Bleich made two appearances at Staten Island (one in the playoffs) before shining in Hawaii Winter Baseball. He has good control of an 88-91 mph fastball that touches 92, and his curveball grades as above-average. He has a solid-average changeup that has flashed plus potential, particularly in college, but lacks the movement to grade that high for now. Bleich's durability is somewhat of a question, and other clubs wondered whether he'd need Tommy John surgery in the near future. If healthy, his ability to pitch off his fastball, throwing it for strikes to all quadrants, and his quality secondary stuff should allow him to move quickly. He's expected to start 2009 in high Class A.

Year	Club (League)	Class	W	L	ERA	G	GS	CG	SV	IP	H	R	ER	HR	BB	SO	AVG
2008	Staten Island (NYP)	SS	0	0	6.00	1	1	0	0	3	2	2	2	1	0	4	.182
MINOR LEAGUE TOTALS			0	0	6.00	1	1	0	0	3	2	2	2	1	0	4	.182

12 JAIRO HEREDIA, RHP

BORN: Oct. 8, 1989. **B-T:** R-R. **HT.:** 6-1. **WT.:** 190. **SIGNED:** Dominican Republic, 2006. **SIGNED BY:** Victor Mata/Carlos Rios.

The Yankees considered Heredia the top pitcher in their 2006 international signing class, signing him for $350,000, and he has continued to validate their confidence. He missed a month early in 2008 with biceps tendinitis but he came back to pitch well in low Class A as an 18-year-old. Heredia's future depends on one huge factor—fastball development. While his fastball touches 93 mph, he generally sits at 87-89 mph with his four-seamer and hasn't picked up a two-seamer yet. His fastball has decent sink and armside run, but in terms of velocity and command, it's a below-average pitch. Heredia's secondary stuff and feel for his craft are advanced for his age, including an above-average power breaking ball that reaches 83 mph and is his best pitch. The Yankees call it a curve, while scouts outside the organization call it a slider. He made significant progress with a changeup last season that has splitter action. Heredia has a thin, wiry frame and wide shoulders. He averaged fewer than five innings per start and will need time to develop strength and stamina, not to mention his fastball. If he fills out and develops consistent low-90s heat, he'll be a mid-rotation starter. Otherwise, he'll be another back-of-the-rotation starter who has to pitch backwards to survive. Heredia could return to low Class A to start 2009 but is ready to tackle high Class A as a teenager.

Year	Club (League)	Class	W	L	ERA	G	GS	CG	SV	IP	H	R	ER	HR	BB	SO	AVG
2007	Yankees (GCL)	R	2	2	2.72	11	6	0	0	46	39	15	14	4	11	52	.228
2008	Charleston, SC (SAL)	LoA	6	7	3.25	21	21	0	0	102	99	58	37	7	43	95	.249
MINOR LEAGUE TOTALS			8	9	3.09	32	27	0	0	149	138	73	51	11	54	147	.243

13 BRETT GARDNER, OF

BORN: Aug. 24, 1983. **B-T:** L-L. **HT.:** 5-10. **WT.:** 180. **DRAFTED:** Charleston, 2005 (3rd round). **SIGNED BY:** Steve Swail.

Gardner ranked in the Top 10 on this list the previous two seasons and made his big league debut on June 30, going back to the minors in late July before returning for good in mid-August. He got regular playing time in September in an audition to replace Melky Cabrera. Gardner was true to himself in the big leagues, displaying his plus-plus speed but also his usual lack of power and propensity to strike out. He's an excellent baserunner with a unique combination of speed and acceleration. He was caught stealing only once in 14 tries in the majors, when he was picked off by Mark Buehrle, and he also has above-average range in center field, though his arm is below-average. Gardner's power is well-below-average, and pitchers at higher levels have challenged him more, jamming him and keeping him from getting his arms extended. However, Gardner made some adjustments late, hitting safely in his final six big league games. He was too passive in his first major league exposure and has to strike a balance between aggressively looking for pitches to drive and drawing walks to get on base and use his speed. The consensus inside the organization and out sees Gardner as a second-division regular or fourth outfielder. In the best-case scenario, Gardner has a Juan Pierre-type of career with more walks. At worst, he's another Jason Tyner. Depending on what New York does this offseason, Gardner could get a chance to wrest the everyday job from Cabrera in the spring.

Year	Club (League)	Class	AVG	G	AB	R	H	2B	3B	HR	RBI	BB	SO	SB	OBP	SLG
2005	Staten Island (NYP)	SS	.284	73	282	62	80	9	1	5	32	39	49	19	.377	.376
2006	Tampa (FSL)	HiA	.323	63	232	46	75	12	5	0	22	43	51	30	.433	.418
	Trenton (EL)	AA	.272	55	217	41	59	4	3	0	13	27	39	28	.352	.318
2007	Trenton (EL)	AA	.300	54	203	43	61	14	5	0	17	33	32	18	.392	.419
	Scranton/W-B (IL)	AAA	.260	45	181	37	47	4	3	1	9	21	43	21	.343	.331
2008	Scranton/W-B (IL)	AAA	.296	94	341	68	101	12	11	3	32	70	76	37	.414	.422
	New York (AL)	MAJ	.228	42	127	18	29	5	2	0	16	8	30	13	.283	.299
MINOR LEAGUE TOTALS			.291	384	1456	297	423	55	28	9	125	233	290	153	.389	.385
MAJOR LEAGUE TOTALS			.228	42	127	18	29	5	2	0	16	8	30	13	.283	.299

14 MANNY BANUELOS, LHP

BORN: March 13, 1991. **B-T:** L-L. **HT.:** 5-10. **WT.:** 155. **SIGNED:** Mexico, 2008. **SIGNED BY:** Lee Sigman.

The Yankees got a big leaguer out of Mexico in 2008 in Alfredo Aceves, and they also got Banuelos. They're convinced that he has as much potential as any of their young pitchers, and value him for his poise, mound presence and stuff. His arm works well, and despite his modest stature, he already shows an average fastball, at times sitting at 90-92 mph. He doesn't overthrow, using a smooth delivery to produce easy velocity and consistently throw strikes. Banuelos shows an impressive feel for changing speeds on his fastball and has the hand speed to spin a breaking ball, though his curveball needs work. His changeup is in its nascent stages. The Yankees want Banuelos to focus on commanding his four-seamer and curve, and he's expected to do so next season in low Class A. Farm director Mark Newman said he "looks like Whitey Ford out there" in terms of his demeanor and poise, as good an indication as any that Banuelos is on the fast track.

Year	Club (League)	Class	W	L	ERA	G	GS	CG	SV	IP	H	R	ER	HR	BB	SO	AVG
2008	Yankees (GCL)	R	4	1	2.57	12	3	0	0	42	32	14	12	3	13	37	.208
MINOR LEAGUE TOTALS			4	1	2.57	12	3	0	0	42	32	14	12	3	13	37	.208

15 DAVID ROBERTSON, RHP

BORN: April 9, 1985. **B-T:** R-R. **HT.:** 5-11. **WT.:** 180. **DRAFTED:** Alabama, 2006 (17th round). **SIGNED BY:** D.J. Svihlik/Jeff Patterson.

Robertson and his older brother Connor, traded this offseason to the Mets, both have reached the major leagues. David reached New York in just his second pro season after signing following a strong summer in the Cape Cod League in 2006. The Yankees have pushed him and he has responded at every turn, vaulting past higher-drafted relievers such as J. Brent Cox and Mark Melancon. Robertson began 2008 in Double-A and finished it in New York, where he wore down in the second half and surrendered his first homer as a pro July 28, a grand slam by Adam Jones. He gets good sink on his 90-92 mph fastball despite his smallish frame and pitches aggressively with his heater. That sets up his power curveball, a plus pitch he has used to help rack up 12.1 strikeouts per nine innings as a pro. He's working on a changeup to combat lefthanders. Robertson nibbled a bit in the majors and elevated his fastball when he tried to muscle up and do too much. He should be able to hold onto his spot in New York's bullpen this season.

Year	Club (League)	Class	W	L	ERA	G	GS	CG	SV	IP	H	R	ER	HR	BB	SO	AVG
2007	Charelston, SC (SAL)	LoA	5	2	0.77	24	0	0	3	47	25	5	4	0	15	67	.151
	Tampa (FSL)	HiA	3	1	1.08	18	0	0	1	33	18	6	4	0	15	37	.159
	Trenton (EL)	AA	0	0	2.25	2	0	0	0	4	2	1	1	0	2	9	.143
2008	Trenton (EL)	AA	0	0	0.96	9	0	0	2	19	8	2	2	0	6	26	.133
	Scranton/W-B (IL)	AAA	4	0	2.06	21	0	0	1	35	20	11	8	1	17	51	.159
	New York (AL)	MAJ	4	0	5.34	25	0	0	0	30	29	18	18	3	15	36	.257
MINOR LEAGUE TOTALS			12	3	1.24	74	0	0	7	138	73	25	19	1	55	190	.152
MAJOR LEAGUE TOTALS			4	0	5.34	25	0	0	0	30	29	18	18	3	15	36	.257

16 MIKE DUNN, LHP

BORN: May 23, 1985. **B-T:** L-L. **HT.:** 6-1. **WT.:** 185. **DRAFTED:** CC of Southern Nevada, D/F 2004 (33rd round). **SIGNED BY:** Jeff Patterson.

The Yankees' continuing search for homegrown lefthanders has led them to Phil Coke and Jeremy Bleich, while two of their stronger-armed lefties, converted outfielders Dunn and Wilkins de la Rossa, have moved to the bullpen. Dunn is further along and has shown more fastball velocity than de la Rossa, moving him onto the 40-man roster and close to a big league shot. Dunn finished the 2008 season on the upswing, turning in his best month in August and pitching well in the Eastern League playoffs. A two-way player at the CC of Southern Nevada, he moved full-time to the mound in 2006 and to the bullpen at the end of 2008 after nearing his innings limit as a starter. Dunn, who sat at 88-92 mph with his fastball as a starter, jumped to 94-96 in short relief bursts. He also pitched more aggressively, finishing hitters off with his heater or low- to mid-80s slider. While his slider doesn't have two-plane break, it was effective as a power breaking ball. Dunn still fights his command and will have to throw more strikes, particularly on the inner half to righthanders, to be more than a middle reliever. He figures to return to Double-A to start 2009.

Year	Club (League)	Class	W	L	ERA	G	GS	CG	SV	IP	H	R	ER	HR	BB	SO	AVG
2006	Yankees (GCL)	R	3	0	0.73	11	0	0	4	25	13	2	2	0	9	26	.155
	Staten Island (NYP)	SS	0	0	5.68	3	0	0	0	6	3	6	4	0	7	7	.125
2007	Charelston, SC (SAL)	LoA	12	5	3.42	27	27	0	0	145	136	69	55	14	45	138	.253
2008	Tampa (FSL)	HiA	4	7	4.55	30	22	0	1	125	124	70	63	10	58	118	.266
	Trenton (EL)	AA	1	0	0.00	1	0	0	0	2	1	0	0	0	1	2	.167
MINOR LEAGUE TOTALS			20	12	3.70	72	49	0	5	302	277	147	124	24	120	291	.248

17 CHRISTIAN GARCIA, RHP

BORN: Aug. 24, 1985. **B-T:** R-R. **HT.:** 6-4. **WT.:** 220. **DRAFTED:** HS—Miami, 2004 (3rd round). **SIGNED BY:** Dan Radison.

Garcia ranked as high as No. 5 on this list three years ago, before injuries of increasing severity started taking their toll. It began with an elbow strain in 2005 and an oblique strain in 2006. He missed all of 2007, first while recovering from Tommy John surgery and then with a knee problem that required reconstructive surgery as well. Last season, he came down with bursitis in his shoulder during spring training, and then elbow soreness flared up after he made five starts at midseason. Primarily a catcher in high school until his senior season, Garcia needs the development time. He has long had a premium curveball and the pitch still has the same 12-to-6 break it had prior to his elbow surgery, though it hasn't quite regained its power. His fastball also has lost some velocity, now touching 92 mph rather than 96 and sitting at 90-91. He's still rebuilding his arm speed and it's likely he'll regain some velocity in the future if he can stay healthy. In the absence of his power, Garcia has added a changeup that has made surprising progress, and some in the organization consider it a plus pitch and the system's best. After pitching in the Eastern League playoffs, he was shut down for the winter and now must prove he can hold up over a full season. He has been added to the 40-man roster and will try to prove he can make a full complement of starts in 2009, likely starting in the warm weather of Tampa.

Year	Club (League)	Class	W	L	ERA	G	GS	CG	SV	IP	H	R	ER	HR	BB	SO	AVG
2004	Yankees (GCL)	R	3	4	2.84	13	6	0	0	38	26	13	12	1	17	47	.188
2005	Yankees (GCL)	R	0	0	4.50	2	1	0	0	6	4	4	3	0	5	7	.200
	Charelston (SAL)	LoA	5	6	3.91	21	20	0	0	106	102	57	46	3	53	103	.249
2006	Yankees (GCL)	R	0	1	9.53	5	3	0	0	11	15	13	12	1	4	15	.313
	Charelston, SC (SAL)	LoA	2	3	3.46	7	7	0	0	42	37	19	16	2	12	45	.243
2007	Did Not Play—Injured																
2008	Yankees (GCL)	R	0	2	14.73	3	3	0	0	7	19	12	12	3	2	9	.487
	Tampa (FSL)	HiA	4	2	2.90	10	.10	0	0	50	45	20	16	2	17	60	.241
	Trenton (EL)	AA	0	0	3.38	1	0	0	0	5	4	2	2	0	6	5	.211
MINOR LEAGUE TOTALS			14	18	4.04	62	50	0	0	265	252	140	119	12	116	291	.249

18 ARODYS VIZCAINO, RHP

BORN: Nov. 13, 1990. **B-T:** R-R. **HT.:** 6-2. **WT.:** 195. **SIGNED:** Dominican Republic, 2007. **SIGNED BY:** Alfredo Dominquez.

Signed for $800,000 in 2007 out of the Dominican Republic, Vizcaino and 2008 draftee Brett Marshall have the biggest arms among New York's young pitching prospects. Vizcaino was a 6-foot, 189-pounder when he signed and he's already "stretching out," in the words of Yankees pitching coordinator Nardi Contreras. He's close to 6-foot-2 now, and has retained his electric arm speed while adding velocity. Vizcaino sits in the low 90s while touching 95 with his fastball. He also has plenty of hand speed and shows a plus curveball at times, with late break and downer action. The rest of Vizcaino's repertoire still is filling out, with a changeup and two-seam fastball on the horizon. He has a better arm than Manny Banuelos but lacks the command and polish to join him on the fast track at this time. Vizcaino is still quite raw in terms of holding runners, fielding his position and other nuances of the game. He's likely to start 2009 in extended spring training before heading to Staten Island, though if he has a strong spring, he could begin the year in Charleston with Banuelos.

Year	Club (League)	Class	W	L	ERA	G	GS	CG	SV	IP	H	R	ER	HR	BB	SO	AVG
2008	Yankees (GCL)	R	3	2	3.68	12	6	0	0	44	38	22	18	5	13	48	.222
MINOR LEAGUE TOTALS			3	2	3.68	12	6	0	0	44	38	22	18	5	13	48	.222

19 WILKINS DE LA ROSSA, LHP

BORN: Feb. 21, 1985. **B-T:** L-L. **HT.:** 6-1. **WT.:** 185. **SIGNED:** Dominican Republic, 2001. **SIGNED BY:** Carlos Rios.

The Yankees considered de la Rossa a potential pitcher soon after signing him in November 2001, but his athletic ability convinced them to try him as an outfielder for five seasons. He finally moved to the mound in the fall of 2006 after hitting .224 with just three homers in 920 at-bats. He has moved rapidly as a pitcher, finishing 2008 in high Class A and earning a spot on the 40-man roster. De la Rossa projects as a reliever because he lacks a real feel for pitching, but he got needed innings and experience last year and showed a quick, power arm. He grasped his delivery quickly and started throwing strikes with his fastball early in his conversion, and his heater often sits at 93-94 mph. When he needs more velocity, he has shown the ability to reach back and get it. While the Yankees prefer curveballs, De la Rossa's lower arm slot is more suited to sliders, and he also throws a changeup that grades as average. When his slider is on, he's extremely hard to hit. De la Rossa figures to go back to high Class A as a starter to work on throwing more quality strikes.

Year	Club (League)	Class	W	L	ERA	G	GS	CG	SV	IP	H	R	ER	HR	BB	SO	AVG
2007	Yankees (GCL)	R	1	0	2.63	12	0	0	0	24	20	8	7	0	11	32	.235
2008	Charleston (SAL)	LoA	7	3	2.29	29	8	0	0	90	60	31	23	2	39	110	.189
	Tampa (FSL)	HiA	2	1	1.10	3	3	0	0	16	12	4	2	0	5	15	.200
MINOR LEAGUE TOTALS			10	4	2.20	44	'11	0	0	131	92	43	32	2	55	157	.199 ·

20 JUAN MIRANDA, 1B

BORN: April 25, 1983. **B-T:** L-L. **HT.:** 6-0. **WT.:** 220. **SIGNED:** Cuba, 2006. **SIGNED BY:** Ramon Valdivia.

Miranda seemed poised for a breakout season in 2008, his second year after signing for a four-year, $4 million contract. After helping Scranton/Wilkes-Barre to the International League championship—he led the IL with 11 RBIs during the playoffs—he finished the year in the majors and got his first big league hit off A.J. Burnett. But even with Jason Giambi's contract mercifully over, the Yankees aren't handing first base over to Miranda quite yet. He spent two years in limbo after leaving Cuba before becoming a free agent and showed up two years younger than he'd been listed when he played for the Cuban national team. Cuban sources list a 1981 birthdate for Miranda, who will be 28 in 2009 if they're correct. Miranda showed good power potential in the Arizona Fall League in 2007 but didn't carry that over into 2008. While club officials still project him to hit for big home run power in the majors—he puts on raw power displays in batting practice—he has put up modest numbers in the minors and other teams aren't as impressed. He injured his left shoulder in late May trying to field a groundball and wound up missing almost a month. He regained his loose swing swiftly, showing a quick, contact-oriented stroke. Despite that swing, Miranda was helpless against lefthanders, posting a .537 OPS against them in Triple-A (compared to a .973 OPS against righties). He's an average defender at first base, with fair range and decent actions, and a below-average runner. After another fine AFL performance, he's ready for a platoon role in the majors but doesn't project as a championship-caliber regular.

Year	Club (League)	Class	AVG	G	AB	R	H	2B	3B	HR	RBI	BB	SO	SB	OBP	SLG
2007	Tampa (FSL)	HiA	.264	67	250	35	66	17	3	9	50	29	60	1	.348	.464
	Trenton (EL)	AA	.265	55	196	29	52	17	2	7	46	23	46	0	.352	.480
2008	Scranton/W-B (IL)	AAA	.287	99	356	40	102	22	0	12	52	55	79	2	.384	.449
	New York (AL)	MAJ	.400	5	10	2	4	1	0	0	1	2	4	0	.500	.500
MINOR LEAGUE TOTALS			.274	221	802	104	220	56	5	28	148	107	185	3	.365	.461
MAJOR LEAGUE TOTALS			.400	5	10	2	4	1	0	0	1	2	4	0	.500	.500

21 FRANCISCO CERVELLI, C

BORN: March 6, 1986. **B-T:** R-R. **HT.:** 6-1. **WT.:** 210. **SIGNED:** Venezuela, 2003. **SIGNED BY:** Hector Rincones.

Jorge Posada is signed through 2011, and the Yankees' best future options at catcher, Jesus Montero and Austin Romine, spent last season in low Class A. Cervelli has advanced further and is far more polished defensively than either, but he lacks their offensive ceiling. He also lost crucial development time in 2008 when he broke his right wrist in a celebrated home-plate collision with Elliot Johnson during spring training, one that led to a brawl between the Yankees and Rays. Cervelli didn't play until mid-June, and after three games, he went down again with a strained left knee. Cervelli was Trenton's everyday catcher in August and performed well as the team won the Eastern League championship, then got a September callup. Cervelli lacks the bat speed and strength to produce more than below-average power, and while he has shown good plate discipline in the minors, he'll have to earn the respect of pitchers at higher levels. Most scouts expect his bat to be short of a big league regular. His defense is first-rate, however, with a plus arm and above-average receiving and blocking skills. Like most catchers, he's a below-average runner. Set to open 2009 in Double-A, Cervelli will have to pick it up offensively if he wants to establish himself in New York before Montero and Romine arrive.

Year	Club (League)	Class	AVG	G	AB	R	H	2B	3B	HR	RBI	BB	SO	SB	OBP	SLG
2003	Yankees1 (DSL)	R	.239	52	155	14	37	4	1	0	14	24	25	0	.379	.277
2004	Yankees1 (DSL)	R	.216	40	88	14	19	2	0	1	14	19	18	1	.392	.273
2005	Yankees (GCL)	R	.190	24	58	10	11	2	0	1	9	8	13	1	.300	.276
2006	Staten Island (NYP)	SS	.309	42	136	21	42	10	0	2	16	13	30	0	.397	.426
2007	Tampa (FSL)	HiA	.279	89	290	34	81	24	2	2	32	36	59	4	.387	.397
2008	Tampa (FSL)	HiA	.300	3	10	2	3	0	0	0	1	0	3	0	.364	.300
	Yankees (GCL)	R	.250	3	8	0	2	1	0	0	0	0	1	0	.250	.375
	Trenton (EL)	AA	.315	21	73	8	23	5	0	0	8	11	14	0	.432	.384
	New York (AL)	MAJ	.000	3	5	0	0	0	0	0	0	0	3	0	.000	.000
MINOR LEAGUE TOTALS			.267	274	818	103	218	48	3	6	94	111	163	6	.384	.355
MAJOR LEAGUE TOTALS			.000	3	5	0	0	0	0	0	0	0	3	0	.000	.000

22 BRETT MARSHALL, RHP

BORN: March 22, 1990. **B-T:** R-R. **HT.:** 6-0. **WT.:** 195. **DRAFTED:** HS—Baytown, Texas, 2008 (6th round). **SIGNED BY:** Steve Boros.

With first-rounder Gerrit Cole failing to sign and supplemental first-rounder Jeremy Bleich accepting below-slot money, Marshall wound up getting the top bonus of any Yankees draftee in 2008, $850,000 as a sixth-rounder. That's the lowest total for New York's best-paid draftee since 2002, when it didn't have a first-rounder. Marshall rated as the second-best prep righthander in a down year in Texas, and like Carmen Angelini, who got $1 million from the Yankees in 2007, Marshall had committed to Rice. He's a smaller righthander with some effort in his delivery, but pitching coordinator Nardi Contreras considers him one of system's best pitchers in terms of raw arm strength. Marshall touched 96 mph early in the spring to jump up draft boards and topped out at 94 late in the spring and in instructional league. He also has shown the arm speed for a good breaking ball. In high school, he threw a power slider in the mid-80s, but the Yankees tried to get him to use a curveball instead during instructional league. They also introduced him to a changeup. The Charleston rotation looks crowded for 2009, so Marshall likely will open the year in extended spring training.

Year	Club (League)	Class	W	L	ERA	G	GS	CG	SV	IP	H	R	ER	HR	BB	SO	AVG
2008	Yankees (GCL)	R	0	0	0.00	3	3	0	0	6	2	1	0	0	2	8	.087
MINOR LEAGUE TOTALS			0	0	0.00	3	3	0	0	6	2	1	0	0	2	8	.087

23 GEORGE KONTOS, RHP

BORN: June 12, 1985. **B-T:** R-R. **HT.:** 6-3. **WT.:** 215. **DRAFTED:** Northwestern, 2006 (5th round). **SIGNED BY:** Steve Lemke.

Kontos had his most consistent, dependable season as a pro in 2008. He never missed a turn for Trenton, leading the Eastern League champions in innings (152) and ranking third in the EL in strikeouts (152). Kontos never has had a fully dominant season, going 11-19 in three years at Northwestern and 17-20 in three as a pro. He made progress nonetheless in 2008, despite working with less fastball than in the past. Kontos pitched at 88-90 mph, down from 90-93 previously. Kontos' mechanics don't allow him to be consistent, either in terms of velocity or control, as he tends to leak out with his front shoulder and drag his arm. His secondary stuff has improved over his pro career, with his slightly above-average slider remaining his best pitch. He has improved confidence in his changeup, though it's still below-average, and throws a solid-average curveball as well. His effectiveness against righthanders (.602 OPS in 2008), thanks mostly to his slider, should make him an effective reliever, and his four-pitch mix still marks him as at worst a swingman. He's headed to Triple-A for 2009.

Year	Club (League)	Class	W	L	ERA	G	GS	CG	SV	IP	H	R	ER	HR	BB	SO	AVG
2006	Staten Island (NYP)	SS	7	3	2.64	14	14	0	0	78	64	25	23	3	19	82	.227
2007	Tampa (FSL)	HiA	4	6	4.02	19	17	0	0	94	95	51	42	15	30	101	.260
2008	Trenton (EL)	AA	6	11	3.68	27	27	0	0	152	134	76	62	14	57	152	.239
MINOR LEAGUE TOTALS			17	20	3.53	60	58	0	0	324	293	152	127	32	106	335	.243

24 D.J. MITCHELL, RHP

BORN: May 13, 1987. **B-T:** R-R. **HT.:** 6-0. **WT.:** 170. **DRAFTED:** Clemson, 2008 (10th round). **SIGNED BY:** Scott Lovekamp.

Mitchell began his career at Clemson as a speedy outfielder, hitting .289 as a freshman without appearing on the mound. He started pitching as a sophomore and put his bat away for good after a star turn in the Cape Cod League in the summer of 2007. However, Clemson and Mitchell never clicked in 2008, with the team missing regionals for the first time in 22 years and Mitchell falling to the 10th round of the draft. He did sign for $450,000, the equivalent of a third-round bonus. His small stature makes him somewhat unusual for a Yankees big-money draftee, but his athleticism and arm speed were too much to pass up. Mitchell still needs to learn some nuances of pitching and could struggle initially in pro ball, but his potential is obvious. He can touch 93 mph with his fastball, which sits at 89-91 with natural sink and tailing action. He has the hand speed to produce a solid curveball, though he's new to the pitch after throwing a slider in college. He has made progress with a changeup, a potential plus pitch that could be the key to keeping him a starter long-term. His athleticism, makeup and aptitude are huge assets, while his inexperience is his biggest obstacle. Mitchell will compete for a rotation spot in low Class A but could open 2009 in extended spring training.

Year	Club (League)	Class	W	L	ERA	G	GS	CG	SV	IP	H	R	ER	HR	BB	SO	AVG
2008	Did Not Play—Signed Late																

25 ALAN HORNE, RHP

BORN: Jan. 5, 1983. **B-T:** R-R. **HT.:** 6-4. **WT.:** 195. **DRAFTED:** Florida, 2005 (11th round). **SIGNED BY:** Brian Barber.

Horne was left off the Yankees' 40-man roster after a trying season that resulted in August surgery to repair a partially torn rotator cuff. He began throwing again in early December and was expected to be ready for spring training. A healthy Horne would be a boost for the Yankees, whose upper-level starting pitching has thinned with graduations to the majors and attrition. Horne has been on the radar a long time, first coming to national prominence in 2001, when the Indians made him a first-round pick. His college career included three schools—Mississippi, Chipola (Fla.) JC and Florida—one Tommy John surgery and a trip to the 2005 College World Series. He seemed on the cusp of the majors after leading the Eastern League in ERA (3.11) and strikeouts (165 in 153 innings) in 2007, but he left his second start of 2008 with biceps pain. He came back briefly in June before his arm started bothering him again. Horne had shown four plus pitches at times in 2007, including a 92-93 mph fastball that peaked at 95, a power slider, a hard curveball and a surprisingly effective changeup. However, his long arm action in the back of his delivery always has concerned scouts as an injury risk and an obstacle to good command. Now 26, Horne is coming off a lost season and his second major arm surgery as he returns to Triple-A.

Year	Club (League)	Class	W	L	ERA	G	GS	CG	SV	IP	H	R	ER	HR	BB	SO	AVG
2006	Tampa (FSL)	HiA	6	9	4.84	28	26	0	0	123	105	72	66	10	61	122	.230
2007	Trenton (EL)	AA	12	4	3.11	27	27	0	0	153	149	68	53	10	57	165	.256
2008	Scranton/W-B (IL)	AAA	2	3	5.63	8	8	0	0	32	35	25	20	2	22	24	.278
	Tampa (FSL)	HiA	0	1	23.14	3	3	0	0	7	21	18	18	4	5	6	.553
MINOR LEAGUE TOTALS			20	17	4.49	66	64	0	0	315	310	183	157	26	145	317	.258

26 ANTHONY CLAGGETT, RHP

BORN: July 15, 1984. **B-T:** R-R. **HT.:** 6-2. **WT.:** 185. **DRAFTED:** UC Riverside, 2005 (11th round). **SIGNED BY:** Tim McWilliam (Tigers).

Acquired from the Tigers in the Gary Sheffield trade, Claggett has moved past Humberto Sanchez and Kevin Whelan, the other components of the deal who both previously ranked in this Top 10. While Sanchez has had Tommy John surgery and conditioning issues and Whelan has battled injuries and a lack of control, Claggett was added to the 40-man roster this offseason and looks primed to contribute in New York. Though he started for part of 2007, he has had more success in the bullpen. He overcame an early hamstring strain and late shoulder soreness to pitch well in Double-A last season. Claggett's fastball lacks the pure velocity desired of a closer, but he sinks the ball effectively while still sitting at 91-92 mph, and he can reach back for more when he needs to. Better fastball command is essential for him to be more than just a middle reliever. He also needs to pitch inside to set up his calling card—a plus 84-85 mph slider with good depth. He added a changeup when he was starting and it has some fade to it, grading out as average. His starting experience also primed him for longer relief outings, and just five of his 30 outings in 2008 went for one inning or less. He returned from his shoulder problem to pitch effectively in the Eastern League playoffs and should compete for a big league setup job in spring training, though he's more likely to open the season in Triple-A.

Year	Club (League)	Class	W	L	ERA	G	GS	CG	SV	IP	H	R	ER	HR	BB	SO	AVG
2005	Oneonta (NYP)	SS	0	1	4.03	21	0	0	7	22	23	10	10	1	12	25	.271
2006	Toledo (IL)	AAA	0	0	0.00	1	0	0	0	1	1	0	0	0	1	2	.200
	West Michigan (MWL)	LoA	7	2	0.91	51	0	0	14	59	35	7	6	0	20	58	.174
2007	Tampa (FSL)	HiA	9	8	3.69	32	16	0	2	112	119	51	46	7	31	76	.274
	Scranton/W-B (IL)	AAA	0	0	5.40	1	1	0	0	5	5	3	3	1	1	1	.250
2008	Tampa (FSL)	HiA	0	0	3.00	1	0	0	0	3	4	1	1	0	0	3	.400
	Trenton (EL)	AA	4	2	2.15	29	0	0	9	59	52	17	14	1	30	55	.233
MINOR LEAGUE TOTALS			20	13	2.75	136	17	0	32	262	239	89	80	10	95	220	.244

27 KELVIN DeLEON, OF

BORN: Oct. 29, 1990. **B-T:** R-R. **HT.:** 6-2. **WT.:** 180. **SIGNED:** Dominican Republic, 2007. **SIGNED BY:** Carlos Rios/Ramon Valdivia.

The Yankees typically assign their top Latin American prospects—such as Robinson Cano, Jairo Heredia, Jose Tabata, to name a few—to the Rookie-level Gulf Coast League. DeLeon, however, started his career last year in the Rookie-level Dominican Summer League after signing for $1.1 million in 2007. He disclosed in an ESPN.com story that he didn't see his entire bonus, as he had to pay $100,000 to the scouts who signed him, Carlos Rios and Ramon Valdivia. Both scouts were later fired by the Yankees for their role in the Dominican bonus skimming scandal. The Yankees were willing to pay DeLeon a seven-figure bonus because of his raw power. He's exceptionally strong and has a long, powerful swing that helped him hit nine home runs in the DSL, more than a third of his team's total and good for fourth in the league. His game is quite raw, not unexpected for someone who played last season at age 17. His swing can get long and he's prone to strikeouts. The Yankees also didn't think he was ready defensively for the GCL, though he has a strong arm and projects as a right fielder down the line. In other words, despite the $1.1 million bonus, DeLeon is far from a sure thing. He'll make his U.S. debut in 2009, almost certainly in the GCL.

Year	Club (League)	Class	AVG	G	AB	R	H	2B	3B	HR	RBI	BB	SO	SB	OBP	SLG
2008	Yankees2 (DSL)	R	.289	63	235	43	68	16	2	9	43	34	74	8	.399	.489
MINOR LEAGUE TOTALS			.289	63	235	43	68	16	2	9	43	34	74	8	.399	.489

28 CARMEN ANGELINI, SS

BORN: Sept. 22, 1988. **B-T:** R-R. **HT.:** 6-1. **WT.:** 185. **DRAFTED:** HS—Lake Charles, La., 2007 (10th round). **SIGNED BY:** Steve Boros/Tim Kelly.

Angelini was part of New York's $8 million draft class in 2007, as the Yankees signed him away from a Rice commitment with a $1 million bonus. It set a record for a 10th-round pick and raised expectations for a player who earned mixed reviews from area scouts in Louisiana, who liked his scrappiness and defensive abilities but had doubts about his bat. Those fears seemed more legitimate in 2008 as Angelini had a miserable offensive season in low Class A, getting off to a slow start and never quite heating up. Scouts like his swing path and he has good plate coverage. Angelini just lacks the strength to produce good bat speed and consistent hard contact at this stage. He has a strong arm and solid infield actions, though at times the speed of the game got the better of him. He should be able to stay at shortstop but also would make a fine second baseman. His speed is slightly above-average. Angelini learned what it takes to be a pro on and off the field and never quit despite the long season and his poor performance. Projecting him as a big leaguer takes a lot of faith in his bat, but the Yankees will be patient. He's expected to repeat low Class A in 2009.

Year	Club (League)	Class	AVG	G	AB	R	H	2B	3B	HR	RBI	BB	SO	SB	OBP	SLG
2007	Yankees (GCL)	R	.000	1	1	0	0	0	0	0	0	0	1	0	.000	.000
2008	Charleston (SAL)	LoA	.236	134	474	64	112	14	1	4	46	42	99	17	.302	.295
MINOR LEAGUE TOTALS			.236	135	475	64	112	14	1	4	46	42	100	17	.302	.295

29 STEVEN JACKSON, RHP

BORN: March 15, 1982. **B-T:** R-R. **HT.:** 6-5. **WT.:** 215. **DRAFTED:** Clemson, 2004 (10th round). **SIGNED BY:** Howard McCullough (Diamondbacks).

The Yankees added four pitchers to their 40-man roster in the offseason, including Jackson. He's all that's left from the Randy Johnson trade with the Diamondbacks, as the Yankees have dealt off Alberto Gonzalez, Ross Ohlendorf and Luis Vizcaino. Jackson struggled for most of his first two years in the system but finally found a consistent arm slot and started throwing strikes in 2008. He has a low-90s sinker and pounds the bottom of the strike zone. He previously lacked a putaway pitch and was too predictable with his modest slider. With a higher arm angle, he was able to add some tilt to his slider, making it an average pitch. His new slot allows him to elevate his fastball more easily, making his plus splitter more effective. Jackson has a shot at earning a big league job but likely will work with Anthony Claggett at the back of Scranton's 2009 bullpen.

Year	Club (League)	Class	W	L	ERA	G	GS	CG	SV	IP	H	R	ER	HR	BB	SO	AVG
2004	Missoula (PIO)	R	0	1	3.60	7	0	0	0	10	16	9	4	1	2	8	.348
	Yakima (NWL)	SS	1	0	4.56	9	2	0	0	24	24	12	12	4	6	18	.255
2005	South Bend (MWL)	LoA	10	5	5.33	28	28	0	0	159	205	109	94	14	57	89	.321
2006	Tennessee (SL)	AA	8	11	2.65	24	24	1	0	150	131	52	44	6	45	125	.239
2007	Scranton/W-B (IL)	AAA	4	8	5.87	18	11	0	0	69	93	57	45	11	29	50	.317
	Trenton (EL)	AA	0	1	3.86	10	0	0	1	21	20	11	9	1	9	16	.256
2008	Trenton (EL)	AA	1	3	5.74	15	0	0	2	31	28	20	20	2	12	37	.241
	Scranton/W-B (IL)	AAA	3	0	3.17	34	1	0	4	48	44	18	17	2	19	54	.246
MINOR LEAGUE TOTALS			27	29	4.31	145	66	1	7	512	561	288	245	41	179	397	.282

30 ABRAHAM ALMONTE, OF

BORN: June 27, 1989. **B-T:** B-R. **HT.:** 5-9. **WT.:** 205. **SIGNED:** Dominican Republic, 2006. **SIGNED BY:** Hector Luna.

Almonte has tantalized the Yankees with his talent and athleticism, and he continues to add strength to his game. But a second-half swoon in low Class A, where he hit just .191 after the all-star break, has tempered enthusiasm for him. Almonte has added 35 pounds since signing yet remains an athletic, middle-of-the-diamond player. He runs well and has a strong arm, and with time he should become an average or better defender in center field. He's still a bit raw in all phases of the game, especially at the plate. Almonte switch-hits and has a good cut from both sides, giving him potential for both gap power and a speed-based, line-drive game. The key adjustment he must make is better pitch recognition. While he's patient and has a short stroke, he expands his strike zone too easily and swings at pitchers' pitches. Almonte saw a lot of fastballs in the first half of the season and showed the bat speed to catch up—he was a South Atlantic League midseason all-star—then failed to adjust to a steady diet of offspeed stuff in the second half. He also must add polish to bring his plus speed to bear more consistently on the basepaths. Almonte will repeat low Class A to address those issues.

Year	Club (League)	Class	AVG	G	AB	R	H	2B	3B	HR	RBI	BB	SO	SB	OBP	SLG
2006	Yankees1 (DSL)	R	.254	63	209	51	53	11	3	8	26	55	45	36	.409	.450
2007	Yankees (GCL)	R	.288	49	160	29	46	4	3	3	16	21	34	8	.372	.406
2008	Charleston (SAL)	LoA	.228	115	443	61	101	20	7	8	46	47	101	29	.303	.359
MINOR LEAGUE TOTALS			.246	227	812	141	200	35	13	19	88	123	180	73	.346	.392

Oakland Athletics

BY BEN BADLER

After a run of eight consecutive seasons with at least 87 wins, the Athletics have endured back-to-back losing seasons for the first time since 1997-98. But with an influx of talent into the organization from a variety of avenues, another prolonged run of success might not be far away.

With the farm system in disrepair by the end of the 2007 season, Oakland general manager Billy Beane went on a mission to acquire blue-chip prospects. Since then, he has traded veterans Joe Blanton, Rich Harden, Dan Haren and Nick Swisher and acquired building blocks such as lefthanders Brett Anderson and Gio Gonzalez, outfielder Aaron Cunningham, infielder Adrian Cardenas and slugger Chris Carter.

The rebuilding process also afforded the A's the opportunity to give big league playing time to several youngsters. Those deals also netted several players who plugged right into the Oakland roster, including Dana Eveland, Sean Gallagher, Carlos Gonzalez, Greg Smith and Ryan Sweeney.

Brad Ziegler, signed out of an independent league in 2004, was a revelation, setting a major league record with 39 straight scoreless innings to begin his career. Daric Barton (acquired with Haren in a 2004 trade for Mark Mulder) and Travis Buck (a supplemental first-rounder in 2005) weren't as successful but still showed the potential to be mainstays in Oakland's lineup.

The A's might not wait as long to try to contend as originally thought. Beane appeared to shift course with a November blockbuster that shipped Gonzalez, Smith and Street to the Rockies for Matt Holliday, who can become a free agent after the 2009 season. Holliday also could be dealt for more prospects at midseason, or Oakland could recoup two premium draft picks as compensation if he departs.

The A's also were aggressive in the draft and on the international market. They took second baseman Jemile Weeks with the 12th overall pick—their highest since 1999—and also paid dearly for players who slid because of signability, such as righthander Brett Hunter ($1.1 million in the seventh round), outfielder Rashun Dixon ($600,000 in the 10th) and shortstop Dusty Coleman ($675,000 in the 28th). Oakland spent $6.5 million on its draft, up from $4.2 million in 2007 and an industry-low $2.0 million in 2006.

The A's also set a new franchise record for an international signing bonus on July 2 when they signed Dominican righthander Michael Inoa for $4.25 mil-

Former independent leaguer Brad Ziegler took over Oakland's closer job as a rookie

TOP 30 PROSPECTS

1. Brett Anderson, lhp	16. Corey Brown, of
2. Trevor Cahill, rhp	17. Cliff Pennington, ss
3. Michael Inoa, rhp	18. Fautino de los Santos, rhp
4. Aaron Cunningham, of	19. Brett Hunter, rhp
5. Adrian Cardenas, ss/2b	20. Jerry Blevins, lhp
6. Chris Carter, 1b/3b/of	21. Rashun Dixon, of
7. Gio Gonzalez, lhp	22. Dusty Coleman, ss
8. Vin Mazzaro, rhp	23. Andrew Bailey, rhp
9. Jemile Weeks, 2b	24. Craig Italiano, rhp
10. James Simmons, rhp	25. Andrew Carignan, rhp
11. Sean Doolittle, 1b/of	26. Sam Demel, rhp
12. Josh Outman, lhp	27. Jared Lansford, rhp
13. Josh Donaldson, c	28. Matt Sulentic, of
14. Henry Rodriguez, rhp	29. Arnold Leon, rhp
15. Tyson Ross, rhp	30. Grant Desme, of

lion, the largest bonus ever given to a international amateur free agent and the highest bonus of any kind in club history.

Moving into a planned new ballpark in Fremont, Calif., would increase the team's revenue, allowing it to start retaining some of its key free agents while continuing to pay top dollar for amateur talent. The A's hope Cisco Field will be ready for 2011, though the turbulent economy could impede building plans. When they do unveil their new home, they're banking that investing heavily in their farm system will end up paying dividends.

General Manager: Billy Beane. **Farm Director:** Keith Lieppman. **Scouting Director:** Eric Kubota.

Class	Team	League	W	L	PCT	Finish*	Manager	Affiliated
Majors	Oakland	American	75	86	.466	10th (14)	Bob Geren	—
Triple-A	Sacramento River Cats	Pacific Coast	83	61	.576	^3rd (16)	Todd Steverson	2000
Double-A	Midland RockHounds	Texas	75	65	.536	3rd (8)	Webster Garrison	1999
High A	Stockton Ports	California	76	64	.543	^3rd (10)	Darren Bush	2005
Low A	Kane County Cougars	Midwest	72	66	.522	7th (14)	Aaron Nieckula	2003
Short-season	Vancouver Canadians	Northwest	34	42	.447	6th (8)	Rick Magnante	1979
Rookie	AZL Athletics	Arizona	21	35	.375	7th (9)	Ruben Escalera	1988
Overall 2008 Minor League Record			361	333	.520	9th		

* Finish in overall standings (No. of teams in league). ^League champion.

LAST YEAR'S TOP 30

Rank	Player, Pos.	Status
1.	Daric Barton, 1b	Majors
2.	Trevor Cahill, rhp	No. 2
3.	James Simmons, rhp	No. 10
4.	Henry Rodriguez, rhp	No. 14
5.	Andrew Bailey, rhp	No. 23
6.	Corey Brown, of	No. 16
7.	Landon Powell, c	Dropped out
8.	Jermaine Mitchell, of	Dropped out
9.	Javier Herrera, of	Dropped out
10.	Sean Doolittle, 1b	No. 11
11.	Jerry Blevins, lhp	No. 20
12.	Grant Desme, of	No. 30
13.	Gregorio Petit, ss/2b	Dropped out
14.	Justin Sellers, 2b/ss	Dropped out
15.	Richie Robnett, of	Dropped out
16.	Matt Sulentic, of	No. 28
17.	Kevin Melillo, 2b	(Blue Jays)
18.	Vin Mazzaro, rhp	No. 8
19.	Sam Demel, rhp	No. 26
20.	Dan Meyer, lhp	(Marlins)
21.	Jeff Baisley, 3b	Dropped out
22.	Andrew Carignan, rhp	No. 25
23.	Brad Kilby, lhp	Dropped out
24.	Cliff Pennington, ss	No. 17
25.	Travis Banwart, rhp	Dropped out
26.	Josh Horton, ss	Dropped out
27.	Anthony Recker, c	Dropped out
28.	Graham Godfrey, rhp	Dropped out
29.	Fernando Hernandez, rhp	(White Sox)
30.	Craig Italiano, rhp	No. 24

BEST TOOLS

Best Hitter for Average	Adrian Cardenas
Best Power Hitter	Chris Carter
Best Strike-Zone Discipline	Cliff Pennington
Fastest Baserunner	Tyreace House
Best Athlete	Rashun Dixon
Best Fastball	Henry Rodriguez
Best Curveball	Trevor Cahill
Best Slider	Brett Anderson
Best Changeup	James Simmons
Best Control	Brett Anderson
Best Defensive Catcher	Landon Powell
Best Defensive Infielder	Cliff Pennington
Best Infield Arm	Cliff Pennington
Best Defensive Outfielder	Javier Herrera
Best Outfield Arm	Javier Herrera

PROJECTED 2012 LINEUP

Catcher	Kurt Suzuki
First Base	Sean Doolittle
Second Base	Jemile Weeks
Third Base	Adrian Cardenas
Shortstop	Cliff Pennington
Left Field	Matt Holliday
Center Field	Aaron Cunningham
Right Field	Travis Buck
Designated Hitter	Chris Carter
No. 1 Starter	Brett Anderson
No. 2 Starter	Trevor Cahill
No. 3 Starter	Michael Inoa
No. 4 Starter	Sean Gallagher
No. 5 Starter	Gio Gonzalez
Closer	Brad Ziegler

TOP PROSPECTS OF THE DECADE

Year	Player, Pos.	2008 Org.
1999	Eric Chavez, 3b	Athletics
2000	Mark Mulder, lhp	Cardinals
2001	Jose Ortiz, 2b	Chiba Lotte (Japan)
2002	Carlos Pena, 1b	Rays
2003	Rich Harden, rhp	Cubs
2004	Bobby Crosby, ss	Athletics
2005	Nick Swisher, of	White Sox
2006	Daric Barton, 1b	Athletics
2007	Travis Buck, of	Athletics
2008	Daric Barton, 1b	Athletics

TOP DRAFT PICKS OF THE DECADE

Year	Player, Pos.	2008 Org.
1999	Barry Zito, lhp	Giants
2000	Freddie Bynum, ss (2nd round)	Orioles
2001	Bobby Crosby, ss	Athletics
2002	Nick Swisher, of	White Sox
2003	Brad Sullivan, rhp	Out of baseball
2004	Landon Powell, c	Athletics
2005	Cliff Pennington, ss	Athletics
2006	Trevor Cahill, rhp (2nd round)	Athletics
2007	James Simmons, rhp	Athletics
2008	Jemile Weeks, 2b	Athletics

LARGEST BONUSES IN CLUB HISTORY

Michael Inoa, 2008	$4,250,000
Mark Mulder, 1998	$3,200,000
Jemile Weeks, 2008	$1,910,000
Nick Swisher, 2002	$1,780,000
Barry Zito, 1999	$1,625,000

OAKLAND ATHLETICS

TOP 2009 ROOKIE: Gio Gonzalez, lhp. Always among the minor league leaders in strikeouts, he could continue to pile up punchouts in the majors with his nasty curveball.

BREAKOUT PROSPECT: Rashun Dixon, of. Drafted as a 17-year-old, he's raw in all phases of the game but possesses excellent tools and athleticism.

SLEEPER: Robin Rosario, of. The Dominican's $350,000 bonus was a franchise record for an international amateur before Michael Inoa stole that thunder a few months later.

SOURCE OF TOP 30 TALENT			
Homegrown	21	Acquired	9
College	12	Trades	9
Junior college	0	Rule 5 draft	0
High school	6	Independent leagues	0
Draft-and-follow	0	Free agents/waivers	0
Nondrafted free agents	0		
International	3		

Numbers in parentheses indicate prospect rankings.

LF
Aaron Cunningham (4)
Matt Sulentic (28)
Danny Putnam
Richie Robnett

CF
Rashun Dixon (21)
Tyreace House
Javier Herrera
Jermaine Mitchell
Larry Cobb
Mitch LeVier

RF
Corey Brown (16)
Grant Desme (30)
Ben Copeland
Robin Rosario
Jeremy Barfield
Chris Berroa

3B
Jeff Baisley

SS
Cliff Pennington (17)
Dusty Coleman (22)
Jason Christian
Josh Horton
Nino Leyja
Gregorio Petit

2B
Adrian Cardenas (5)
Jemile Weeks (9)
Justin Sellers
Victor Trinidad

1B
Chris Carter (6)
Sean Doolittle (11)
Franklin Hernandez

C
Josh Donaldson (13)
Landon Powell
Anthony Recker

RHP	
Starters	**Relievers**
Trevor Cahill (2)	Henry Rodriguez (14)
Michael Inoa (3)	Brett Hunter (19)
Vin Mazzaro (8)	Andrew Bailey (23)
James Simmons (10)	Andrew Carignan (25)
Tyson Ross (15)	Sam Demel (26)
Fautino de los Santos (18)	Jared Lansford (27)
Craig Italiano (24)	Arnold Leon (29)
Ryan Webb	Daniel Thomas
Travis Banwart	Jay Marshall
Graham Godfrey	Jose Rojas
Jamie Richmond	Lance Sewell
Ronny Morla	Jason Glushon
Ken Smalley	Justin Friend
Shawn Haviland	Chris Farley
Scott Hodsdon	
Scott Mitchinson	

LHP	
Starters	**Relievers**
Brett Anderson (1)	Jerry Blevins (20)
Gio Gonzalez (7)	Brad Kilby
Josh Outman (12)	Ben Hornbeck
Pedro Figueroa	
Anthony Capra	
Carlos Hernandez	

BEST PURE HITTER: 2B Jemile Weeks' (1) quick wrists make him a more potent offensive threat than his 5-foot-9, 180-pound frame might suggest. He batted .297/.422/.405 in 19 games at low Class A before straining a hip flexor.

BEST POWER HITTER: OFs Jeremy Barfield (8) and Rashun Dixon (10) both have considerable raw power. Barfield is more advanced as a hitter at this point, though both will need to make adjustments to handle upper-level pitching.

FASTEST RUNNER: OF Tyreace House (6), who was recruited in football and track coming out of high school, can get from the right side of the plate to first base in less than 4.0 seconds at times. That's 8 speed on the 2-8 scouting scale, while Dixon grades as a 7 runner and Weeks as a 6.

BEST DEFENSIVE PLAYER: SS Dusty Coleman (28) earned a $675,000 bonus in large part because of his offensive showing in the Cape Cod League during the summer. The A's also think he can become a plus defender, thanks to his actions, arm strength and instincts.

BEST FASTBALL: RHP Brett Hunter (7), who signed for $1.1 million, flashed a 100-mph fastball before an elbow injury caused him to slide in the draft. He was back up to 96 mph in instructional league. RHP Daniel Thomas (13) has hit the upper 90s as a reliever.

BEST SECONDARY PITCH: RHP Tyson Ross' (2) slider, though he can fall in love with it too much. Hunter and Thomas have the best curveballs in this crop, while LHP Anthony Capra (4) owns the top changeup.

BEST PRO DEBUT: SS Jason Christian (5) hit .294/.396/.424 with 13 steals while reaching low Class A. He has solid all-around tools for a shortstop.

BEST ATHLETE: Oakland focused on athleticism in this draft, spending $600,000 to sign Dixon away from a football scholarhip from Mississippi State, where his brother Anthony is the starting tailback. Weeks, House and OF Chris Berroa (11) are also quality athletes.

MOST INTRIGUING BACKGROUND: Unsigned OF Brent Warren (27) came back from open-heart surgery in 2007 to re-establish himself as a prospect. Weeks and his brother Rickie are the eighth pair of brothers to be drafted in the first round. Barfield's brother Josh plays for the Indians, and their father Jesse won an American League home run title and two Gold Gloves. RHP Ryan Doolittle's (26) older brother Sean was an A's sandwich pick in 2007.

CLOSEST TO THE MAJORS: Weeks, though Ross and a healthy Hunter could push him.

BEST LATE-ROUND PICK: Nino Leyja (15) is athletic and has a good feel for hitting, giving Oakland a third legitimate shortstop prospect in this draft.

THE ONE WHO GOT AWAY: Warren has the ability to become a first-round pick after three years at Oregon State. LHP Nick Maronde (43) could do the same after attending Florida.

ASSESSMENT: The A's were more aggressive than ever, going well over slot money to sign Hunter, Dixon and Coleman and bolster an already strong system. Weeks was one of the best college athletes in the draft, while Ross could be a second-round steal.

2007   BONUSES: $4.2 MILLION

The A's top three picks—RHP Justin Simmons (1), 1B/OF Sean Doolittle (1s), OF Corey Brown (1s)—all showed promise in their first full pro seasons. Unsigned LHP Daniel Schlereth (8) became a first-rounder a year later.

GRADE: C+

2006   BONUSES: $2.0 MILLION

Oakland didn't own a first-rounder but its top pick, RHP Trevor Cahill (2), sure has performed like one. OF Matt Sulentic (3) got back on track last season and RHP Andrew Bailey (5) continues to be a sleeper.

GRADE: B

2005   BONUSES: $4.8 MILLION*

SS Cliff Pennington (1) and OF Travis Buck (1s) will compete for starting jobs in the majors this season, and RHP Vin Mazzaro (3) isn't far behind. Unsigned 1B Justin Smoak (16) looks like a future star and went 11th overall in the 2008 draft.

GRADE: B

2004   BONUSES: $6.3 MILLION*

The A's had four choices before the second round, but only since-traded RHP Huston Street (1s) looks like he'll be a contributor in the big leagues. C Kurt Suzuki (2) also fits that description, and six others have gotten a cup of coffee.

GRADE: B+

*Draft analysis by Jim Callis. Numbers in parentheses indicate draft rounds. *Bonuses for 2004-05 are first 10 rounds only.*

BILL MITCHELL

BRETT ANDERSON

Born: Feb. 1, 1988.
Ht.: 6-4. **Wt.:** 215.
Bats: L. **Throws:** L.
Drafted: HS—Stillwater, Okla., 2006 (2nd round).
Signed by: Joe Robinson (Diamondbacks).

The exceedingly polished Anderson has had a head start in his development since childhood. He's the son of Oklahoma State coach Frank Anderson, one of college baseball's top pitching coaches before taking over the Cowboys. Brett's feel for his craft has been evident since his amateur days, as he led Team USA's youth and junior teams to silver medals in consecutive summers. He had the stuff to go in the first round of the 2006 draft, but his $1 million asking price dropped him to the Diamondbacks in the second round. He signed late for $950,000, turning down the chance to pitch for his father. Anderson quickly established himself as a premier pitching prospect in 2007, though he and six teammates were involved in a car accident that July, with Anderson sustaining a concussion that effectively ended his season. He and outfielder Carlos Gonzalez were the headline prospects in a six-player package Arizona sent to the Athletics for Dan Haren in December 2007. In his first season in the A's system, Anderson advanced to Double-A Midland and pitched for the U.S. Olympic team. He defeated Japan in the bronze-medal game, allowing four runs in seven innings. After he returned from Beijing, he joined Triple-A Sacramento for the Pacific Coast League playoffs, earning wins in both his starts (including the championship clincher) as well as a save.

Anderson has premium command, averaging 1.9 walks per nine innings in his pro career and frequently locating his fastball on the corners of the plate. He's more proficient working his fastball to his glove side than his arm side. His two-seam fastball sits at 88-92 mph and generates a lot of groundouts. He also can touch 94 mph with his four-seamer. Anderson has above-average secondary pitches across the board, including a mid- to high-70s curveball with two-plane break. His low- to mid-80s slider gives him a second quality breaking ball, and his changeup is often a plus pitch. He used his changeup more frequently once he reached Double-A. Anderson is mechanically solid and repeats his delivery well. He improved his pickoff move after working with fellow lefty Greg Smith, another part of the Haren trade.

The biggest knock on Anderson always has been his lack of athleticism. He got into better shape for the 2008 season, but while he fields his position well if grounders are hit in his vicinity, he's not quick to first base when he needs to cover the bag. He doesn't have overpowering velocity, but he has more than enough zip on his fastball considering his command and deep arsenal.

Anderson and Trevor Cahill teamed up at high Class A Stockton, Midland and the Olympics in 2008. There's debate among scouts about who's the better prospect, with Anderson getting the edge here because he has superior command and a wider array of plus pitches. Both should begin 2009 in Triple-A, with a chance to reach the big leagues by mid-2009. They're the future anchors of Oakland's rotation.

Year	Club (League)	Class	W	L	ERA	G	GS	CG	SV	IP	H	R	ER	HR	BB	SO	AVG
2007	South Bend (MWL)	LoA	8	4	2.21	14	14	0	0	81	76	26	20	3	10	85	.248
	Visalia (CAL)	HiA	3	3	4.85	9	9	0	0	39	50	23	21	6	11	40	.311
2008	Stockton (CAL)	HiA	9	4	4.14	14	13	0	0	74	68	35	34	5	18	80	.238
	Midland (TEX)	AA	2	1	2.61	6	6	0	0	31	27	10	9	3	9	38	.235
MINOR LEAGUE TOTALS			22	12	3.36	43	42	0	0	225	221	94	84	17	48	243	.255

2 TREVOR CAHILL, RHP

STEVE MOORE

BORN: March 1, 1988. **B-T:** R-R. **HT.:** 6-3. **WT.:** 195. **DRAFTED:** HS—Vista, Calif., 2006 (2nd round). **SIGNED BY:** Craig Weissmann.

The A's top pick (second round) in 2006, Cahill teamed with Brett Anderson at two minor league stops and the Olympics, helping Team USA win bronze. Cahill works off an 88-92 mph two-seam fastball with outstanding heavy sink and running life, enabling him to rack up both grounders and swinging strikes. He also can touch 94 mph with his four-seamer. He backs up his fastballs with a nasty 79-81 mph knuckle-curve, a swing-and-miss pitch with hard downward movement. He also has another tough breaking ball in a low-80s slider with cutter-like action at times. He's a good athlete with a simple, compact delivery and good balance over the rubber. Cahill's changeup should become an average pitch, but he'll need to throw it more against higher-caliber competition. Though his mechanics are sound, he sometimes cuts his extension a little short out front, placing more strain on his back and shoulder. He strained his ribcage at the Olympics and didn't pitch afterward, though he threw off flat ground in instructional league and will be ready for 2009. With some slight mechanical tweaks and improved command, Cahill could end up as a top-of-the-rotation starter. He should open 2009 in Triple-A and make his big league debut later in the season.

Year	Club (League)	Class	W	L	ERA	G	GS	CG	SV	IP	H	R	ER	HR	BB	SO	AVG
2006	Athletics (AZL)	R	0	0	3.00	4	4	0	0	9	2	4	3	0	7	11	.071
2007	Kane Country (MWL)	LoA	11	4	2.73	20	19	0	0	105	85	38	32	3	40	117	.220
2008	Stockton (CAL)	HiA	5	4	2.78	14	13	0	0	87	52	29	27	3	31	103	.174
	Midland (TEX)	AA	6	1	2.19	7	6	0	0	37	24	15	9	2	19	33	.190
MINOR LEAGUE TOTALS			22	9	2.68	45	42	0	0	239	163	86	71	8	97	264	.194

3 MICHAEL INOA, RHP

CHRIS KLINE

BORN: Sept. 24, 1991. **B-T:** R-R. **HT.:** 6-7. **WT.:** 205. **SIGNED:** Dominican Republic, 2008. **SIGNED BY:** Raymond Abreu.

Inoa demolished international amateur bonus records when he signed with the A's on July 2 for $4.25 million. His potential was evident at age 13, when he was already 6-foot-4 and reaching 83-84 mph with his fastball. Several scouts have called Inoa one of the best 16-year-old pitchers they've ever seen. He already has a lively low-90s fastball that has touched 94 mph, and with his size and mechanics he projects to throw even harder. He has remarkable athleticism and coordination for his size, allowing him to repeat an effortless delivery and have good command. He has the potential for a plus curveball and also throws a changeup that already grades as fringe average. He also has flashed a splitter, though he didn't use it much leading up to his signing. All the glowing scouting reports are nice, but Inoa has yet to be tested by anything close to professional competition. Though his secondary pitches project as possible plus offerings, they have a ways to go. He needs work on the finer points of the game, such as holding runners. Inoa's ceiling is as high as it gets. Oakland hasn't determined his first assignment yet. He'll likely begin 2009 in extended spring training before reporting to the Rookie-level Arizona League or short-season Vancouver in June.

Year	Club (League)	Class	W	L	ERA	G	GS	CG	SV	IP	H	R	ER	HR	BB	SO	AVG
2008	Did Not Play—Signed 2009 Contract																

4 AARON CUNNINGHAM, OF

STEVE MOORE

BORN: April 24, 1986. **B-T:** R-R. **HT.:** 5-11. **WT.:** 195. **DRAFTED:** Everett (Wash.) CC, 2005 (6th round). **SIGNED BY:** Joe Butler/Adam Virchis (White Sox).

Originally drafted by the White Sox, Cunningham was dealt to Arizona in June 2007 for Danny Richar. He spent just six months with the Diamondbacks before they flipped him to Oakland as part of the package for Dan Haren. Cunningham has hit well everywhere he's been, posting an OPS of at least .852 at each level of full-season ball. He has a good feel for hitting and a knack for squaring up balls with a balanced swing. His bat stays in the hitting zone a long time, generating solid-average power. A good athlete, he runs well and has a solid arm. Cunningham's swing can get a little bit long, and he struggled when he became more pull-conscious during his callup. He doesn't always take direct routes to fly balls, precluding him from being a good defensive center fielder. While his tools are average or better across the board, he doesn't have an outstanding tool that points to star potential. Oakland's trade for Matt Holliday means Cunningham won't be playing left field for the A's in 2009, but he'll compete for a starting job in right. Additional seasoning in Triple-A wouldn't be bad for him, either.

OAKLAND ATHLETICS

Year	Club (League)	Class	AVG	G	AB	R	H	2B	3B	HR	RBI	BB	SO	SB	OBP	SLG
2005	Bristol (APP)	R	.315	56	222	41	70	10	2	5	25	16	45	6	.392	.446
	Kannapolis (SAL)	LoA	.115	10	26	7	3	0	0	0	2	3	7	1	.207	.115
2006	Kannapolis (SAL)	LoA	.305	95	341	58	104	26	3	11	41	34	72	19	.386	.496
2007	Winston-Salem (CAR)	HiA	.294	67	252	51	74	12	5	8	37	34	39	22	.376	.476
	Visalia (CAL)	HiA	.358	29	123	25	44	11	2	3	20	5	23	5	.386	.553
	Mobile (SL)	AA	.288	31	118	25	34	8	3	5	20	12	27	1	.364	.534
2008	Midland (TEX)	AA	.317	87	347	65	110	18	6	12	52	38	92	12	.386	.507
	Sacramento (PCL)	AAA	.382	20	76	21	29	5	0	5	14	11	16	3	.461	.645
	Oakland (AL)	MAJ	.250	22	80	7	20	7	1	1	14	6	24	2	.310	.400
MINOR LEAGUE TOTALS			.311	395	1505	293	468	90	21	49	211	153	321	69	.384	.496
MAJOR LEAGUE TOTALS			.250	22	80	7	20	7	1	1	14	6	24	2	.310	.400

5 ADRIAN CARDENAS, SS/2B

BORN: Oct. 10, 1987. **B-T:** L-R. **HT.:** 5-11. **WT.:** 190. **DRAFTED:** HS—Miami, 2006 (1st round supplemental). **SIGNED BY:** Miguel Machado (Phillies).

Baseball America's 2006 High School Player of the Year, Cardenas made steady progress for two years before Philadelphia used him as the key chip in a mid-July deal for Joe Blanton. Cardenas moved from shortstop to second base in 2007, but Oakland moved him back after the trade. Cardenas has a compact, line-drive stroke and hits the ball to all fields. His swing has drawn comparisons to that of Adrian Gonzalez, and he should develop average power. He recognizes and handles offspeed pitches well, and he shows the ability to handle both lefties and righties. He logged each of his at-bats in a notebook all season and studied his observations of the pitchers he faced. He has solid-average speed and good baserunning instincts. He makes the routine plays in the field and has an accurate arm. After the trade, Cardenas developed a tendency to overswing and lengthen his stroke. His first step, lateral movement and footwork probably won't allow him to stay at shortstop and might be problematic at second base. Cardenas eventually could move to third, where his bat and arm would profile well. He'll return to Double-A and is roughly a year away from the majors.

Year	Club (League)	Class	AVG	G	AB	R	H	2B	3B	HR	RBI	BB	SO	SB	OBP	SLG
2006	Phillies (GCL)	R	.318	41	154	22	49	5	4	2	21	17	28	13	.384	.442
2007	Lakewood (SAL)	LoA	.295	127	499	70	147	30	2	9	79	47	80	20	.354	.417
2008	Clearwater (FSL)	HiA	.307	68	261	44	80	11	6	4	23	28	42	16	.371	.441
	Stockton (CAL)	HiA	.278	15	72	11	20	1	0	1	10	1	14	1	.297	.333
	Midland (TEX)	AA	.279	26	86	12	24	4	0	0	7	15	10	0	.392	.326
MINOR LEAGUE TOTALS			.299	277	1072	159	320	51	12	16	140	108	174	50	.362	.413

6 CHRIS CARTER, 1B/3B/OF

BORN: Dec. 18, 1986. **B-T:** R-R. **HT.:** 6-4. **WT.:** 210. **DRAFTED:** HS—Las Vegas, 2005 (15th round). **SIGNED BY:** George Kachigian/Joe Butler (White Sox).

After leading White Sox farmhands with 25 homers in 2007, Carter was traded twice that December. Chicago traded him to the Diamondbacks for Carlos Quentin before Arizona used him as part of the package to acquire Dan Haren. In 2008, he topped the high Class A California League in runs (101), homers (39), RBIs (104) and slugging percentage (.569) and added five longballs in the playoffs as Stockton won the title. Carter's plus-plus raw power ranks among the best in the minors. He hits the ball deep out of the park to all fields with a fluid swing that generates tremendous loft and natural leverage. He shows the patience to draw walks. He has a strong arm. Carter's outstanding power comes with the tradeoff of a high strikeout rate. He has some holes in his swing and is susceptible to breaking balls. He has some athleticism, but his lack of first-step quickness and range are a liability at third base, where he committed 14 errors in 41 games, and his below-average hands are a handicap at first base, where he made 10 errors in another 41 games. He hasn't been much better as a right fielder. Ticketed for Double-A, Carter should be able to hit his way into Oakland's lineup. The A's will continue to try him at different positions, but he may ultimately wind up as a DH.

BILL MITCHELL

Year	Club (League)	Class	AVG	G	AB	R	H	2B	3B	HR	RBI	BB	SO	SB	OBP	SLG
2005	Bristol (APP)	R	.283	65	233	33	66	17	0	10	37	17	64	2	.350	.485
2006	Kannapolis (SAL)	LoA	.130	13	46	4	6	3	0	1	5	5	17	0	.231	.261
	Great Falls (PIO)	R	.299	69	251	37	75	21	1	15	59	34	70	4	.398	.570
2007	Kannapolis (SAL)	LoA	.291	126	467	84	136	27	3	25	93	67	112	3	.383	.522
2008	Stockton (CAL)	HiA	.259	137	506	101	131	32	4	39	104	77	156	4	.361	.569
MINOR LEAGUE TOTALS			.275	410	1503	259	414	100	8	90	298	200	419	13	.369	.532

7 GIO GONZALEZ, LHP

BORN: Sept. 19, 1985. **B-T:** R-L. **HT.:** 5-11. **WT.:** 185. **DRAFTED:** HS—Miami, 2004 (1st round supplemental). **SIGNED BY:** Jose Ortega (White Sox).

The White Sox drafted Gonzalez in the sandwich round in 2004, sent him to the Phillies for Jim Thome in 2005 and brought him back as part of a package for Freddy Garcia in 2006. After Gonzalez led the minors with 185 strikeouts in 150 innings in 2007, Chicago sent him, Fautino de los Santos and Ryan Sweeney to the A's for Nick Swisher. Gonzalez's best pitch is a 75-78 mph curveball with sharp break and two-plane depth. He throws the curve often, and it has helped him average 10.3 strikeouts per nine innings in the minors. His fastball can touch 93 mph, though it more often sat at 87-91 last season with some run and sink. He has a simple, fluid delivery and throws from a high three-quarters arm slot. Gonzalez has been a prolific strikeout pitcher, but his fastball command is below average and led to an excess of walks in his brief stint with Oakland. He needs to repeat his delivery with more frequency, which in turn will lead to better command. After a long season, he lost velocity early in his big league starts. He'll have to upgrade his 80-84 mph straight changeup to have a legitimate third weapon against major league hitters. Gonzalez should begin 2009 in Oakland's rotation. He could become a frontline starter if he improves his changeup and command.

Year	Club (League)	Class	W	L	ERA	G	GS	CG	SV	IP	H	R	ER	HR	BB	SO	AVG
2004	Bristol (APP)	R	1	2	2.25	7	6	0	0	24	17	8	6	0	8	36	.207
	Kannapolis (SAL)	LoA	1	1	3.03	6	6	0	0	33	30	13	11	1	13	27	.229
2005	Kannapolis (SAL)	LoA	5	3	1.87	11	10	0	0	58	36	16	12	3	22	84	.175
	Winston-Salem (CAR)	HiA	8	3	3.56	13	13	0	0	73	61	33	29	5	25	79	.228
2006	Reading (EL)	AA	7	12	4.66	27	27	0	0	155	140	88	80	24	81	166	.239
2007	Birmingham (SL)	AA	9	7	3.18	27	27	0	0	150	116	57	53	10	57	185	.216
2008	Sacramento (PCL)	AAA	8	7	4.24	23	22	1	0	123	106	65	58	12	61	128	.233
	Oakland (AL)	MAJ	1	4	7.68	10	7	0	0	34	32	34	29	9	25	34	.242
MINOR LEAGUE TOTALS			39	35	3.64	114	111	1	0	615	506	280	249	55	267	705	.223
MAJOR LEAGUE TOTALS			1	4	7.68	10	7	0	0	34	32	34	29	9	25	34	.242

8 VIN MAZZARO, RHP

BORN: Sept. 27, 1986. **B-T:** R-R. **HT.:** 6-2. **WT.:** 190. **DRAFTED:** HS—Rutherford, N.J., 2005 (3rd round). **SIGNED BY:** Jeff Bittiger.

Though he posted a 5.21 ERA over his first two pro seasons, the A's sent Mazzaro to Double-A last season at age 21. He responded by leading the Texas League in ERA (1.90), earning TL pitcher of the year honors and a promotion to Triple-A. Mazzaro's hard sinker sits in the low 90s and touches 95, generating groundballs. He pitches off his fastball, and he shows the ability to sink, run or cut it. His control got significantly better in 2008, allowing him to keep hitters off balance by mixing locations and changing planes. He showed a greater willingness to challenge hitters than he had in the past. His improved slider has tight break and is an average pitch. Mazzaro still is trying to find a reliable offspeed pitch. He didn't throw his changeup much last season, though it took a step forward and could become an average offering. His curveball is more of a show-me pitch. His mechanics are mostly sound, though he does throw slightly across his body. After getting knocked around in Triple-A at the end of last season, he'll return there in 2009. With Brett Anderson and Trevor Cahill nearly ready for the majors, Oakland shouldn't have to rush Mazzaro.

Year	Club (League)	Class	W	L	ERA	G	GS	CG	SV	IP	H	R	ER	HR	BB	SO	AVG
2006	Kane Country (MWL)	LoA	9	9	5.05	24	24	0	0	119	146	81	67	7	42	81	.310
2007	Stockton (CAL)	HiA	9	12	5.33	28	28	0	0	154	159	97	91	13	71	115	.271
2008	Midland (TEX)	AA	12	3	1.90	22	22	0	0	137	115	40	29	3	36	104	.229
	Sacramento (PCL)	AAA	3	3	6.15	6	5	0	0	34	49	26	23	3	9	27	.340
MINOR LEAGUE TOTALS			33	27	4.26	80	79	0	0	444	469	244	210	26	158	327	.275

9 JEMILE WEEKS, 2B

BORN: Jan. 26, 1987. **B-T:** B-R. **HT.:** 5-9. **WT.:** 180. **DRAFTED:** Miami, 2008 (1st round). **SIGNED BY:** Trevor Schaffer.

The A's drafted Weeks with the 12th overall pick in June, their highest selection since they took Barry Zito ninth overall in 1999. That made Weeks and his brother Rickie, the No. 2 overall choice in 2003, the eighth pair of siblings to become first-round picks. An All-American at Miami, he signed for $1.91 million but had his pro debut cut short by a hip flexor injury. Weeks is a quick-twitch athlete with plus speed. A switch-hitter, he has a slashing line-drive stroke, and his strong wrists and plus bat speed help him generate surprising power for a player his size. He has a good feel for the strike zone and profiles as

PAUL GIERHART

a leadoff man. He has the ability to make spectacular defensive plays at second base. Weeks needs to put in more work to make routine plays at second and to turn the double play. He has battled leg injuries the last two years, with repeated hamstring and groin problems hampering his sophomore season. His hip injury kept him out of instructional league. Weeks' bat is advanced enough for him to make his full-season debut in high Class A. He doesn't have his brother's offensive upside, but he's no lightweight as a hitter and is a better defender.

Year	Club (League)	Class	AVG	G	AB	R	H	2B	3B	HR	RBI	BB	SO	SB	OBP	SLG
2008	Kane County (MWL)	LoA	.297	19	74	11	22	3	1	1	8	13	12	6	.422	.405
MINOR LEAGUE TOTALS			.297	19	74	11	22	3	1	1	8	13	12	6	.422	.405

10 JAMES SIMMONS, RHP

JOHN SPEAR

BORN: Sept. 29, 1986. **B-T:** R-R. **HT.:** 6-4. **WT.:** 220. **DRAFTED:** UC Riverside, 2007 (1st round). **SIGNED BY:** Craig Weissmann.

One of the most advanced pitchers in the 2007 draft, Simmons went straight to Double-A after signing for $1,192,000 as the 25th overall pick. He returned to Midland in 2008 and, after a slow start, he went 7-2, 3.00 over the final two months to finish second in the Texas League in strikeouts (120 in 136 innings) and third in ERA (3.51). Simmons has outstanding command of his 88-92 mph fastball, which peaks at 94. He has a two-seamer with some run and mild sink, and he leans heavily on his fastball the first time through the order. His best secondary weapon is his changeup, which has some run and the potential to become a plus pitch. He has a good delivery that he repeats easily. He does a good job fielding his position. Simmons' slider is still a work in progress, and his slow, loopy curveball is just a show-me pitch. He tends to stay a little too upright at the end of his delivery. He went through a brief dead-arm period in May and battled sleep apnea during the season. Simmons will begin the season in Triple-A Sacramento with a chance to crack the big league rotation later in the year. He projects as a solid starter if he can tighten his slider.

Year	Club (League)	Class	W	L	ERA	G	GS	CG	SV	IP	H	R	ER	HR	BB	SO	AVG
2007	Midland (TEX)	AA	0	0	3.94	13	2	0	0	30	36	16	13	2	8	23	.308
2008	Midland (TEX)	AA	9	6	3.51	25	25	0	0	136	150	58	53	11	32	120	.282
MINOR LEAGUE TOTALS			9	6	3.59	38	27	0	0	166	186	74	66	13	40	143	.287

11 SEAN DOOLITTLE, 1B/OF

BORN: Sept. 26, 1986. **B-T:** L-L. **HT.:** 6-3. **WT.:** 190. **DRAFTED:** Virginia, 2007 (1st round supplemental). **SIGNED BY:** Neil Avent.

New Jersey's high school player of the year in 2004, Doolittle turned down the Braves as a 39th-rounder to attend Virginia, where he was a two-way star and the Atlantic Coast Conference player of the year as a sophomore. He signed with the A's for $742,500 as a supplemental first-round pick in 2007 and took up hitting full-time. Without having to split his time between pitching and hitting, Doolittle has bulked up, adding strength and power to his game, a striking difference from his days with the Cavaliers, when he was a disciplined hitter with a contact-oriented approach. Though he still showed patience in his first full season, Doolittle swung and missed enough to strike out 153 times. He uses the opposite field well but he chases pitches out of the strike zone at times. While athletic, he's a below-average runner. The A's gave Doolittle some playing time in the outfield last year, but he fits best at first base, where he's a plus defender with smooth actions. He has the arm strength to play right field but still is learning to make the longer throws after converting from the mound. After a late-season promotion to Double-A, Doolittle should return to Midland to open the 2009 season. Oakland signed his younger brother Ryan, a righthander, as a 26th-round pick out of Cumberland (N.J.) CC in 2008.

Year	Club (League)	Class	AVG	G	AB	R	H	2B	3B	HR	RBI	BB	SO	SB	OBP	SLG
2007	Vancouver (NWL)	SS	.283	13	46	6	13	3	0	0	4	9	10	0	.421	.348
	Kane Country (MWL)	LoA	.233	55	193	23	45	10	0	4	29	24	40	1	.320	.347
2008	Stockton (CAL)	HiA	.305	86	334	64	102	25	3	18	61	46	99	7	.385	.560
	Midland (TEX)	AA	.254	51	201	25	51	15	0	4	30	17	54	1	.311	.388
MINOR LEAGUE TOTALS			.273	205	774	118	211	53	3	26	124	96	203	9	.353	.450

12 JOSH OUTMAN, LHP

BORN: Sept. 14, 1984. **B-T:** L-L. **HT.:** 6-1. **WT.:** 185. **DRAFTED:** Central Missouri State, 2005 (10th round). **SIGNED BY:** Jerry Lafferty (Phillies).

Outman signed with the Phillies as a 10th-round pick in 2005 after leading Central Missouri State to a runner-up finish at the Division II College World Series. Outman pitched for Team USA at the 2007 World Cup in Taiwan, tying for the team high with 10 strikeouts in its gold-medal run. Outman was a starter for his first two full seasons in pro ball, but the Phillies moved him to the bullpen in 2008 with the hopes of quickly moving him into that role for the big league club. Instead, Philadelphia ended up trading Outman along with infielder Adrian Cardenas and outfielder Matt Spencer to the Athletics for righthander Joe Blanton. Oakland used Outman as both a starter and a reliever, and he reached the big leagues in September. A good athlete, Outman saw his velocity spike in the bullpen, with his fastball sitting at 93-96 mph and peaking at 97. As a starter, he worked at 90-94 mph. Outman has an 81-85 mph slider with late bite, a solid 79-83 mph changeup and a curveball that he'll mix in on occasion. His arm action can be a little funky and short in the back, but his delivery also has deception and he generally repeats it well. He battles his control at times, but his mechanics are much more orthodox than they were when he was at St. Louis CC-Forest Park. His father Fritz, who wrote a manual on pitching instruction, had Josh extend his arm straight up, bend it down to nearly touch his opposite shoulder and then take a walking step before throwing. Scouts said it was the most unusual delivery they had ever seen and at the time liked him more as an athletic outfielder. Outman could open 2009 with the big league club, either as a starter or reliever.

Year	Club (League)	Class	W	L	ERA	G	GS	CG	SV	IP	H	R	ER	HR	BB	SO	AVG
2005	Batavia (NYP)	SS	2	1	2.76	11	4	0	0	29	23	14	9	1	14	31	.207
2006	Lakewood (SAL)	LoA	14	6	2.95	27	27	1	0	155	119	61	51	5	75	161	.213
2007	Clearwater (FSL)	HiA	10	4	2.45	20	18	0	0	117	104	35	32	7	54	117	.236
	Reading (EL)	AA	2	3	4.50	7	7	1	0	42	38	25	21	5	23	34	.242
2008	Reading (EL)	AA	5	4	3.20	33	5	0	1	70	68	27	25	3	37	66	.257
	Midland (TEX)	AA	1	0	4.26	4	4	0	0	13	13	7	6	1	3	5	.260
	Sacramento (PCL)	AAA	1	0	1.76	5	2	0	0	15	9	3	3	1	5	15	.167
	Oakland (AL)	MAJ	1	2	4.56	6	4	0	0	26	34	14	13	1	8	19	.327
MINOR LEAGUE TOTALS			35	18	2.99	107	67	2	1	442	374	172	147	23	211	429	.228
MAJOR LEAGUE TOTALS			1	2	4.56	6	4	0	0	26	34	14	13	1	8	19	.327

13 JOSH DONALDSON, C

BORN: Dec. 8, 1985. **B-T:** R-R. **HT.:** 6-1. **WT.:** 215. **DRAFTED:** Auburn, 2007 (1st round supplemental). **SIGNED BY:** Bob Rossi (Cubs).

Donaldson ditched his third baseman's mitt and took up catching as a sophomore at Auburn in 2006, a move that helped propel him up draft boards. The Cubs signed him for $652,500 as the 48th overall pick in 2007, and he began his pro career auspiciously by ranking as the short-season Northwest League's top position prospect. He got off to a horrible start in 2008 in low Class A, though he got his bat going in the hitter-friendly California League following a trade to the A's in which Oakland gave up Rich Harden and Chad Gaudin to acquire him along with Sean Gallagher, Matt Murton and Eric Patterson. He has a good feel for hitting and does a fine job of using the whole field, though some scouts question if he'll hit enough to be a big league regular. He's strong and should produce average power. Donaldson's strength and athleticism are apparent behind the plate, where he has a slightly above-average arm and a quick release that helped him throw out 37 percent of basestealers last season. Still relatively new to the position, he's mastering the finer points of catching, such as blocking after committing 18 passed balls in 94 games. He has close to average speed, unusual for a catcher. Donaldson will advance to Double-A in 2009.

Year	Club (League)	Class	AVG	G	AB	R	H	2B	3B	HR	RBI	BB	SO	SB	OBP	SLG
2007	Cubs (AZL)	R	.182	4	11	1	2	2	0	0	0	2	4	0	.308	.364
	Boise (NWL)	SS	.346	49	162	37	56	11	2	9	35	37	34	6	.470	.605
2008	Peoria (MWL)	LoA	.217	63	235	27	51	13	0	6	23	17	41	7	.276	.349
	Stockton (CAL)	HiA	.330	47	188	37	62	13	2	9	39	17	29	0	.391	.564
MINOR LEAGUE TOTALS			.287	163	596	102	171	39	4	24	97	73	108	13	.370	.487

14 HENRY RODRIGUEZ, RHP

BORN: Feb. 25, 1987. **B-T:** R-R. **HT.:** 6-1. **WT.:** 175. **SIGNED:** Venezuela, 2003. **SIGNED BY:** Julio Franco.

Rodriguez began the year in a prospect-laden Stockton rotation but quickly moved up to Double-A after just three starts. He got rocked in Midland, as Texas League hitters took advantage of his inability to throw enough strikes and get ahead in the count. The A's sent him back down to high Class A in June, put him in the bullpen in August and moved him back up to Double-A for five more relief outings. He still fought his control but he was able to overpower hitters more easily in shorter stints. One of the few Latin American prospects in the organization prior to the Michael Inoa signing, Rodriguez is a good athlete with tremendous arm strength, which he showed by touching 100 mph with his fastball at the Futures Game. As a starter, Rodriguez regularly sits in the low- to mid-90s with some running life, but as a reliever his heater regularly clocks in the upper 90s. His arsenal is hard, hard and harder, as he lacks a reliable off-speed pitch. He has added more pronounced break to his spinning slider, though it remains inconsistent. His changeup has occasional split action, but it's definitely his third pitch. Rodriguez's arm action is short in the back and lacks fluidity. He struggles at times to maintain balance in his delivery and often falls off to the first-base side. Despite his struggles in 2008, he could get the opportunity to open 2009 in the Triple-A bullpen. As soon as he throws strikes on a more consistent basis, he'll be ready for Oakland.

Year	Club (League)	Class	W	L	ERA	G	GS	CG	SV	IP	H	R	ER	HR	BB	SO	AVG
2005	Athletics1 (DSL)	R	0	2	4.03	8	3	0	0	22	14	19	10	1	14	27	.163
2006	Athletics (AZL)	R	5	2	7.42	15	4	0	1	44	46	39	36	1	50	59	.284
2007	Kane Country (MWL)	LoA	6	8	3.07	20	18	1	0	100	75	38	34	2	58	106	.214
2008	Stockton (CAL)	HiA	2	3	3.96	20	13	0	2	75	57	38	33	5	40	104	.208
	Midland (TEX)	AA	2	7	7.46	14	9	0	0	41	51	39	34	1	44	43	.302
MINOR LEAGUE TOTALS			15	22	4.70	77	47	1	3	282	243	173	147	10	206	339	.233

15 TYSON ROSS, RHP

BORN: April 22, 1987. **B-T:** R-R. **HT.:** 6-5. **WT.:** 215. **DRAFTED:** California, 2008 (2nd round). **SIGNED BY:** Jermaine Clark.

After spending the summer of 2007 with Team USA, Ross projected as a possible first-round pick but an inconsistent spring dropped him to the second round last June. The Athletics were thrilled to get him with the 58th overall pick and signed him for $694,000. Ross' fastball sits in the low 90s with hard sink and tops out at 95 mph. His best pitch is his plus slider, which he can throw in the low 80s with two-plane break or add a little velocity and give it shorter, harder break. At times, however, he can rely on his slider too much. A good athlete, Ross throws an average changeup in the low 80s with some tumble, and it could become an above-average offering as well. His unique motion provides deception but also is cause for concern. His arm action is short in the back and he remains upright throughout his delivery. Though he does have good balance, he has an exceptionally short stride to the plate for someone his size, landing on an extremely stiff plant leg and cutting off extension out front, leading to excess stress on his arm and back. He went on the disabled list in July with a strained shoulder, but returned in mid-August to make three more starts for low Class A Kane County. Some scouts think Ross' mechanics eventually will lead him to the bullpen, but Oakland will develop him as a starter. He'll likely start his first full pro season in high Class A. If he stays healthy, he could move quickly through the system, either as a starter or reliever.

Year	Club (League)	Class	W	L	ERA	G	GS	CG	SV	IP	H	R	ER	HR	BB	SO	AVG
2008	Kane County (MWL)	LoA	0	1	4.66	6	4	0	0	19	16	11	10	1	5	16	.219
MINOR LEAGUE TOTALS			0	1	4.66	6	4	0	0	19	16	11	10	1	5	16	.219

16 COREY BROWN, OF

BORN: Nov. 26, 1985. **B-T:** L-L. **HT.:** 6-1. **WT.:** 200. **DRAFTED:** Oklahoma State, 2007 (1st round supplemental). **SIGNED BY:** Blake Davis.

Brown earned attention from college football recruiters as a wide receiver coming out of high school, but he instead chose to play baseball at Oklahoma State. He has performed well since signing for $554,500 as a supplemental first-round pick in 2007, mashing 30 homers between two Class A stops in his first full pro season. His best tool is his plus-plus raw power, which he generates to all fields with a quick bat, leverage and natural loft. Holes in his swing and chasing pitches out of the zone caused him to strike out in 168 times in 2008, however, and he may never hit for a high average. He struggled in Hawaii Winter Baseball, showing the same contact problems that hampered him during the regular season. Brown is a good athlete with solid speed and arm strength, though his throws could be more accurate. He's playable in center field for now, but his range might eventually be better suited for an outfield corner. Though he didn't log much playing time in high Class A, Brown could begin 2009 in Double-A.

Year	Club (League)	Class	AVG	G	AB	R	H	2B	3B	HR	RBI	BB	SO	SB	OBP	SLG
2007	Vancouver (NWL)	SS	.268	59	213	31	57	18	4	11	48	37	77	5	.379	.545
2008	Kane County (MWL)	LoA	.270	85	300	44	81	18	2	14	49	41	96	12	.359	.483
	Stockton (CAL)	HiA	.260	49	196	34	51	9	0	16	34	17	72	4	.322	.551
MINOR LEAGUE TOTALS			.267	193	709	109	189	45	6	41	131	95	245	21	.356	.520

17 CLIFF PENNINGTON, SS

BORN: June 15, 1984. **B-T:** B-R. **HT.:** 5-11. **WT.:** 185. **DRAFTED:** Texas A&M, 2005 (1st round). **SIGNED BY:** Blake Davis.

A first-round pick in 2005, Pennington finally reached the big leagues with a mid-August promotion to Oakland. Nagging hamstring injuries have bothered him in the past, but he put together a healthy season in 2008 after batting a combined .249/.342/.357 in the previous two years. His savvy in all aspects of the game enables him to play above his tools. Pennington always has had a good feel for the strike zone, drawing nearly as many walks as strikeouts throughout his pro career. He worked to maintain a more level swing plane last season, trying to keep the barrel up and online throughout the swing. He still has a tendency to get under the ball too much at times—particularly to the opposite field—rather than driving the ball on a line. His weakest tool is his power, which is well below average, and he has yet to slug better than .368 over a full pro season. Pennington has above-average speed and good baserunning instincts. He excels at taking the extra base and has swiped bags at an 82 percent clip in pro ball. Defensively, he offers plus range, an excellent arm and a quick release at shortstop. Pennington could be a solid big league utility infielder, but additional power could help him earn a starting role.

Year	Club (League)	Class	AVG	G	AB	R	H	2B	3B	HR	RBI	BB	SO	SB	OBP	SLG
2005	Kane Country (MWL)	LoA	.276	69	290	49	80	15	0	3	29	39	47	25	.364	.359
2006	Stockton (CAL)	HiA	.203	46	177	36	36	7	0	2	21	24	35	7	.302	.277
	Athletics (AZL)	R	.464	9	28	3	13	3	1	0	6	4	2	0	.531	.643
2007	Stockton (CAL)	HiA	.255	68	286	50	73	17	3	6	36	43	54	9	.348	.399
	Midland (TEX)	AA	.251	70	271	41	68	13	2	2	21	38	35	8	.343	.336
2008	Midland (TEX)	AA	.260	50	204	42	53	7	2	0	18	39	36	20	.379	.314
	Sacramento (PCL)	AAA	.297	65	236	47	70	9	3	2	16	54	34	11	.426	.386
	Oakland (AL)	MAJ	.242	36	99	14	24	5	0	0	9	13	18	4	.339	.293
MINOR LEAGUE TOTALS			.263	377	1492	268	393	71	11	15	147	241	243	80	.366	.356
MAJOR LEAGUE TOTALS			.242	36	99	14	24	5	0	0	9	13	18	4	.339	.293

18 FAUTINO DE LOS SANTOS, RHP

BORN: Feb. 15, 1986. **B-T:** R-R. **HT.:** 6-2. **WT.:** 190. **SIGNED:** 2005, Dominican Republic. **SIGNED BY:** Denny Gonzalez (White Sox).

De los Santos was an unknown before his spectacular U.S. debut in 2007, when he blew away hitters in Class A and lit up radar guns at the Futures Game. After the season, the White Sox packaged him with Gio Gonzalez and Ryan Sweeney to acquire Nick Swisher from the A's. De los Santos barely pitched for his new organization, however, making just five starts before undergoing Tommy John surgery. Prior to his injury, de los Santos showed a lively fastball. He was capable of pitching down in the zone with a low-90s two-seamer or at the letters with a mid-90s four-seamer that peaked at 97. He also demonstrated the ability to spin both a curveball and a slider, with the latter a plus pitch. He also had a changeup but often threw the pitch too hard. De los Santos has a tendency to get out of control with his delivery, causing him to spin off toward first base. He began a throwing program in November but likely won't begin throwing bullpen sessions until spring training. He could return to regular-season action in June.

Year	Club (League)	Class	W	L	ERA	G	GS	CG	SV	IP	H	R	ER	HR	BB	SO	AVG
2006	White Sox (DSL)	R	3	3	1.86	10	9	0	0	48	44	20	10	0	10	61	.232
2007	Kannapolis (SAL)	LoA	9	4	2.40	21	15	0	0	98	49	33	26	5	36	121	.148
	Winston-Salem (CAR)	HiA	1	1	3.65	5	5	0	0	25	20	12	10	3	7	32	.220
2008	Stockton (CAL)	HiA	2	2	5.87	5	5	0	0	23	29	17	15	3	11	26	.309
MINOR LEAGUE TOTALS			15	10	2.83	41	34	0	0	194	142	82	61	11	64	240	.201

19 BRETT HUNTER, RHP

BORN: June 27, 1987. **B-T:** R-R. **HT.:** 6-4. **WT.:** 215. **DRAFTED:** Pepperdine, 2008 (7th round). **SIGNED BY:** J.T. Stotts.

Hunter was a likely top-10 pick in 2008 before he came down with elbow problems at Pepperdine and saw his peak velocity dip to 92 mph. After watching him with the U.S. college national team during the summer, the A's felt confident enough in his health to sign him for $1.1 million—a record for a seventh-round pick and the equivalent of first-round money. Before he got hurt, Hunter was one of the hardest throwers available in the 2008 draft, having touched 100 mph during fall ball with the Waves. After signing, he spent time focusing on his mechanics and was back up to 94-96 mph in instructional league. Hunter's hard slider can be a knockout pitch when he locates it, though he doesn't do so with enough frequency yet. Scouts' biggest concerns center around his mechanics. His arm action is funky in the back as he drops his arm behind him, making it difficult to repeat his arm slot. He has a head lean in his delivery, a high front leg kick that results in a long stride and doesn't take a direct line to the plate, which leads to below-average command and Hunter getting underneath too many pitches. His stuff, mechanics and medical history profile best in the bullpen, though Oakland may continue developing him as a starter for now.

Year	Club (League)	Class	W	L	ERA	G	GS	CG	SV	IP	H	R	ER	HR	BB	SO	AVG
2008	Athletics (AZL)	R	0	0	0.00	1	1	0	0	1	1	0	0	0	0	2	.250
	Kane County (MWL)	LoA	0	0	5.40	2	0	0	0	2	0	1	1	0	2	1	.000
MINOR LEAGUE TOTALS			0	0	3.38	3	1	0	0	3	1	1	1	0	2	3	.125

20 JERRY BLEVINS, LHP

BORN: Sept. 6, 1983. **B-T:** L-L. **HT.:** 6-6. **WT.:** 190. **DRAFTED:** Dayton, 2004 (17th round). **SIGNED BY:** Brian Williams (Cubs).

A 17th-round pick of the Cubs in 2004, Blevins racked up high strikeout rates up through Double-A in the Cubs system before the A's acquired him and Rob Bowen in a midseason 2007 trade for catcher Jason Kendall. Blevins made his big league debut that September, then won a gold medal pitching with Team USA at the World

Cup in Taiwan. After three months in Triple-A in 2008, he became a regular in the A's bullpen in July. Blevins' fastball sits at 90-92 mph and tops out at 94. His 72-75 mph curveball at times is a swing-and-miss pitch that gives lefthanders trouble. Hitters have difficulty seeing the ball out of Blevins' hand because his delivery provides some deception and he repeats the same arm slot on his fastball and curveball. He's primarily a two-pitch pitcher, though he'll occasionally mix in an 80-83 mph changeup to keep righthanders off balance. His height creates downward angle to the plate, though he's a flyball pitcher. He should continue in his role as a middle reliever in Oakland in 2009.

Year	Club (League)	Class	W	L	ERA	G	GS	CG	SV	IP	H	R	ER	HR	BB	SO	AVG
2004	Boise (NWL)	SS	6	1	1.62	23	0	0	5	33	17	7	6	1	21	42	.145
2005	Peoria (MWL)	LoA	3	7	5.54	48	2	0	14	76	75	51	47	6	38	96	.260
2006	Daytona (FSL)	HiA	0	1	9.00	8	0	0	1	11	18	12	11	0	4	9	.367
	Boise (NWL)	SS	1	2	6.04	16	0	0	0	22	27	22	15	3	8	19	.287
	West Tenn (SL)	AA	0	0	1.42	5	0	0	1	6	5	1	1	0	1	8	.217
2007	Daytona (FSL)	HiA	1	0	0.38	15	0	0	6	24	13	1	1	0	5	32	.159
	Tennessee (SL)	AA	2	2	1.53	23	0	0	3	29	23	5	5	1	8	37	.215
	Midland (TEX)	AA	1	3	3.32	17	0	0	1	22	18	10	8	2	5	29	.234
	Sacramento (PCL)	AAA	1	0	0.00	1	0	0	0	3	1	0	0	0	0	4	.111
	Oakland (AL)	MAJ	0	1	9.64	6	0	0	0	5	8	6	5	1	2	3	.348
2008	Sacramento (PCL)	AAA	2	2	2.78	28	0	0	10	32	31	16	10	3	6	36	.244
	Oakland (AL)	MAJ	1	3	3.11	36	0	0	0	38	32	14	13	2	13	35	.230
MINOR LEAGUE TOTALS			17	18	3.61	184	2	0	41	259	228	125	104	16	96	312	.234
MAJOR LEAGUE TOTALS			1	4	3.83	42	0	0	0	42	40	20	18	3	15	38	.247

21 RASHUN DIXON, OF

BORN: Aug. 27, 1990. **B-T:** R-R. **HT.:** 6-2. **WT.:** 210. **DRAFTED:** HS—Terry, Miss., 2008 (10th round). **SIGNED BY:** Kelcey Mucker.

One of the best athletes and youngest players in the 2008 draft, Dixon dropped to the 10th round because he had committed to play football at Mississippi State, where his brother Anthony is a star running back. Rashun signed quickly for $600,000, the highest bonus in his round. Oddly enough, Dixon was a catcher in high school, but the A's immediately moved him to center field to make the most of his athleticism and plus-plus speed. With good present strength, Dixon has plus raw power to all fields. Oakland helped Dixon set his feet and see the ball better, and to stay back and better leverage his weight transfer, which should help him more easily tap into his power. He led the Arizona League with 10 triples and ranked third with eight homers. While Dixon's upside is considerable, he's still raw in many phases of the game. He has a long swing and chased too many pitches out of the zone, leading the AZL with 68 strikeouts. He made some excellent catches and showed a strong arm in his pro debut, but he also looked lost at times in the outfield and still needs to improve his routes to the ball. He also must learn how to use his quickness on the bases. Dixon could open 2009 in low Class A, but the A's also could play it safe and assign him to short-season Vancouver.

Year	Club (League)	Class	AVG	G	AB	R	H	2B	3B	HR	RBI	BB	SO	SB	OBP	SLG
2008	Athletics (AZL)	R	.263	45	179	32	47	3	10	8	42	18	68	5	.328	.525
MINOR LEAGUE TOTALS			.263	45	179	32	47	3	10	8	42	18	68	5	.328	.525

22 DUSTY COLEMAN, SS

BORN: April 20, 1987. **B-T:** R-R. **HT.:** 6-2. **WT.:** 185. **DRAFTED:** Wichita State, 2008 (28th round). **SIGNED BY:** Yancy Ayres.

Coleman had a decorated athletic career as a high schooler in South Dakota. He was an all-state shortstop his junior and senior seasons; an all-state quarterback for two years, leading his high school to back-to-back state championships; and an all-state basketball player and finalist for the state's Mr. Basketball award as a senior. Undrafted out of high school, Coleman headed to Wichita State and became the team's starting shortstop as a freshman. A draft-eligible sophomore in 2008, he slid to the 28th round because of questionable signability. But when Coleman had an all-star summer in the Cape Cod League, batting .330, the A's anted up $675,000 to sign him. His strength, particularly in his hands, lends itself to above-average bat speed and power to the opposite field. He's an aggressive hitter who chases pitches out of the strike zone. His swing gets long and he needs to do a better job recognizing and handling breaking balls. He's a solid-average runner with good instincts on the basepaths. Coleman's athleticism is evident at shortstop, where he has smooth actions, solid range, a quick first step and a strong arm. He was clocked up to 92 mph when he took the mound at times for Wichita State. Coleman and Jason Christian, a 2008 fifth-rounder, both are ready for low Class A, but to get them both playing time at shortstop, Oakland will try to push one of them to high Class A.

Year	Club (League)	Class	AVG	G	AB	R	H	2B	3B	HR	RBI	BB	SO	SB	OBP	SLG
2008	Athletics (AZL)	R	.222	7	27	4	6	0	0	1	5	2	10	1	.300	.333
	Vancouver (NWL)	SS	.319	19	72	13	23	8	1	0	6	4	26	1	.355	.458
MINOR LEAGUE TOTALS			.293	26	99	17	29	8	1	1	11	6	36	2	.340	.424

23 ANDREW BAILEY, RHP

BORN: May 31, 1984. **B-T:** R-R. **HT.:** 6-3. **WT.:** 220. **DRAFTED:** Wagner, 2006 (6th round). **SIGNED BY:** Jeff Bittiger.

The A's considered drafting Bailey in 2005 until he suffered an elbow injury that required Tommy John surgery. His stuff bounced back the next spring, when Oakland nabbed him in the sixth round. He progressed nicely as a starter until he got to Double-A in 2008, then flourished when he shifted to a relief role in late June. Coming out of the bullpen, he posted a 0.92 ERA (compared to 6.18 in the Midland rotation) and a 41-11 K-BB ratio in 39 innings (compared to a 69-45 K-BB in 71 innings as a starter). He carried over his bullpen success to the Arizona Fall League, where he had a 1.29 ERA and a 16-1 K-BB mark in 14 innings. Bailey now is in position to win a role in the A's bullpen in 2009, perhaps even to start the season. His success comes from the outstanding cutting action he gets on his 88-95 mph fastball, which he throws to both sides of the plate. It eats up both lefthanders and righthanders. Bailey scrapped the two-seamer he had been working with as a starter and focused more on his cutting fastball, which he complements with a hard curveball and an occasional changeup. He throws across his body, which puts some excess strain on his arm but also helps create the natural movement on his fastball.

Year	Club (League)	Class	W	L	ERA	G	GS	CG	SV	IP	H	R	ER	HR	BB	SO	AVG
2006	Vancouver (NWL)	SS	2	5	2.02	13	10	0	0	58	39	20	13	2	20	53	.187
2007	Kane Country (MWL)	LoA	1	4	3.35	11	10	1	0	51	42	25	19	6	22	74	.219
	Stockton (CAL)	HiA	3	4	3.82	11	11	0	0	66	56	31	28	8	31	72	.239
	Sacramento (PCL)	AAA	1	0	1.13	1	1	0	0	8	3	1	1	0	1	4	.115
2008	Midland (TEX)	AA	5	9	4.32	37	15	0	0	110	99	63	53	13	56	110	.240
MINOR LEAGUE TOTALS			12	22	3.50	73	47	1	0	293	239	140	114	29	130	313	.223

24 CRAIG ITALIANO, RHP

BORN: July 22, 1986. **B-T:** R-R. **HT.:** 6-4. **WT.:** 209. **DRAFTED:** HS—Flower Mound, Texas, 2005 (2nd round). **SIGNED BY:** Blake Davis.

Perhaps Italiano's biggest accomplishment in 2008 was that he managed to stay on the field the entire season, though the A's still limited him to 100 innings as he tired down the stretch. In 2006, he appeared in only four games before going down with shoulder problems and having labrum surgery. The following year, he took a line drive off his head and spent three days in a Chicago hospital with a skull fracture, ending his season after six starts. Italiano dominated the low Class A Midwest League in his third try and earned a promotion to high Class A, where Oakland moved him to the bullpen to limit his workload. Italiano has a lively low-90s fastball that tops out at 96 mph. He backs it up with a hard, tight curveball with 12-to-6 break. His changeup is a decent third pitch but not nearly as effective as his fastball and curve. Italiano's control is below average, which along with his mechanics and medical history might lead him to the bullpen. His arm action is a little short in the back and he doesn't pitch downhill as much as one might expect for a pitcher with his size because he collapses his back leg and gets his front shoulder tilted upward. Because of his limited 2008 workload, the A's again will carefully monitor Italiano's innings in 2009, when he'll likely return to Stockton as a starter.

Year	Club (League)	Class	W	L	ERA	G	GS	CG	SV	IP	H	R	ER	HR	BB	SO	AVG
2005	Athletics (AZL)	R	1	2	6.75	8	3	0	0	19	20	17	14	0	8	27	.267
2006	Kane Country (MWL)	LoA	0	1	3.50	4	4	0	0	18	18	12	7	1	9	23	.261
2007	Kane Country (MWL)	LoA	0	3	12.71	6	6	0	0	17	32	25	24	3	16	24	.416
2008	Kane County (MWL)	LoA	7	0	1.16	14	14	0	0	70	43	16	9	2	35	79	.177
	Stockton (CAL)	HiA	1	4	9.90	14	5	0	0	30	44	37	33	7	26	33	.333
MINOR LEAGUE TOTALS			9	10	5.10	46	32	0	0	154	157	107	87	13	94	186	.263

25 ANDREW CARIGNAN, RHP

BORN: July 23, 1986. **B-T:** R-R. **HT.:** 5-11. **WT.:** 215. **DRAFTED:** North Carolina, 2007 (5th round). **SIGNED BY:** Neil Avent.

An all-state baseball and soccer player as a Connecticut high schooler, Carignan was the closer on North Carolina teams that went to back-to-back College World Series finals in 2006 and 2007. His great-grandfather, Augustine "Lefty" Dugas, was a big league outfielder from 1930-34. Carignan is on his way to joining him as a major leaguer, reaching Double-A after just 23 pro innings and posting a 2.01 ERA in his first two years as a pro. His best pitch is a 91-96 mph fastball. He mostly works off his fastball and slider, though he mixed in a curveball last season to give batters another look. His delivery provides some deception, but his fastball doesn't have much movement and at 5-foot-11 he doesn't get much downward plane. He made some progress with his fastball command, but overall he showed below-average control in 2008, walking 6.3 batters per nine innings. Carignan finished the season without allowing a run in 11 of his 12 Arizona Fall League appearances and should begin 2009 in the Triple-A Sacramento bullpen.

Year	Club (League)	Class	W	L	ERA	G	GS	CG	SV	IP	H	R	ER	HR	BB	SO	AVG
2007	Kane Country (MWL)	LoA	1	1	2.03	12	0	0	4	13	6	7	3	0	11	19	.136
2008	Stockton (CAL)	HiA	1	1	0.90	9	0	0	4	10	5	1	1	0	5	17	.147
	Midland (TEX)	AA	3	3	2.22	46	0	0	24	53	36	15	13	4	39	67	.196
MINOR LEAGUE TOTALS			5	5	2.01	67	0	0	32	76	47	23	17	4	55	103	.179

26 SAM DEMEL, RHP

BORN: Oct. 23, 1985. **B-T:** R-R. **HT.:** 6-0. **WT.:** 200. **DRAFTED:** Texas Christian, 2007 (3rd round). **SIGNED BY:** Blake Davis.

A standout pitcher at Spring (Texas) High, Demel set school records with 15 wins and 188 strikeouts (breaking Josh Beckett's mark) as a senior in 2004. He split time between starting and relieving during his first two years at Texas Christian before becoming a full-time closer in 2007 and setting the Horned Frogs' career record for saves (20). In his first full season in pro ball, Demel flourished as a closer in high Class A. His lively 90-93 mph fastball has touched 96 and helped him generate a 2.1-1 groundout-airout ratio last season. His changeup has splitter-like action with downward tumble. His slider at times has good bite but has a tendency to get slurvy. Demel has a max-effort delivery that results in his head coming off line. His herky-jerky motion provides some deception but also impedes his control. He often prefers to throw either his slider or his changeup in three-ball counts because his fastball command is still below average. Demel should open this season closing games in Double-A.

Year	Club (League)	Class	W	L	ERA	G	GS	CG	SV	IP	H	R	ER	HR	BB	SO	AVG
2007	Stockton (CAL)	HiA	0	0	7.07	11	0	0	0	14	16	16	11	2	15	13	.302
	Kane Country (MWL)	LoA	0	1	0.96	9	0	0	4	9	3	2	1	0	4	10	.107
2008	Stockton (CAL)	HiA	5	2	3.36	54	0	0	18	67	61	31	25	5	32	90	.227
MINOR LEAGUE TOTALS			5	3	3.69	74	0	0	22	90	80	49	37	7	51	113	.229

27 JARED LANSFORD, RHP

BORN: Oct. 22, 1986. **B-T:** R-R. **HT.:** 6-0. **WT.:** 190. **DRAFTED:** HS—Mountain View, Calif., 2005 (2nd round). **SIGNED BY:** Scott Kidd.

Lansford is the son of Carney Lansford, who spent 15 years in the big leagues and won a World Series with the A's in 1989. The Lansford baseball lineage is distinguished, as Jared's uncles Phil (Indians, 1978) and Joe (Padres, 1979) were both first-round draft picks and his older brother Josh is a third baseman-turned-pitcher in the Cubs system. Jared is the lone member of his family to sign as a pitcher. After making the Midwest League all-star team in 2006, he pitched just four innings the following season after coming down with shoulder tendinitis. Back on the mound in 2008, Lansford moved from starting to relieving and seemed to find his niche. He works off a 91-94 mph sinker and an 82-84 mph slider that shows quick break after some improvement last year. He also has a curveball, but it's a below-average pitch that he doesn't throw much. The same is true of his changeup, which he doesn't need now that he's in the bullpen. He has some effort in his delivery, though it also creates some deception. He'll move up to Double-A in 2009.

Year	Club (League)	Class	W	L	ERA	G	GS	CG	SV	IP	H	R	ER	HR	BB	SO	AVG
2005	Athletics (AZL)	R	0	1	1.27	7	6	0	0	21	16	4	3	0	5	20	.216
2006	Kane Country (MWL)	LoA	11	6	2.86	18	18	2	0	104	87	40	33	1	42	50	.236
	Stockton (CAL)	HiA	0	1	12.71	3	3	0	0	11	23	19	16	4	5	9	.397
2007	Stockton (CAL)	HiA	0	1	9.00	1	1	0	0	4	5	4	4	0	3	2	.385
2008	Stockton (CAL)	HiA	2	6	4.41	31	2	0	3	63	62	33	31	4	20	75	.258
	Midland (TEX)	AA	3	1	0.70	15	0	0	5	26	20	2	2	0	9	19	.227
MINOR LEAGUE TOTALS			16	16	3.49	75	30	2	8	230	213	102	89	9	84	175	.253

28 MATT SULENTIC, OF

BORN: Oct. 6, 1987. **B-T:** L-L. **HT.:** 5-10. **WT.:** 170. **DRAFTED:** HS—Dallas, 2006 (3rd round). **SIGNED BY:** Blake Davis.

Sulentic ranked fourth on this list after 2006, when he won the Dallas-area high school triple crown by batting .654-20-59, went in the third round of the draft and hit .354/.409/.479 against significantly older competition in the Northwest League. But he followed up in 2007 by hitting .175 in low Class A and showing little willingness to make adjustments, earning a demotion back to the NWL. Despite his struggles, the A's still promoted Sulentic to the California League in 2008, hoping that the league's offensive environment and a lower spot in the batting order would improve his confidence and decrease the pressure on him. He put together a solid season before getting hit by a pitch on July 27, breaking his hand and ending his season. Sulentic has strength, bat speed and good opposite-field power, though he still gets pull-oriented at times and struck out 91 times in 95 games last year. His bat will have to carry him because he's already maxed out physically and has fringy speed to go with below-average arm strength. Oakland tried him at second base in instructional league in 2006, but that experiment didn't work. He'll probably be a left fielder, though he played mainly in right last season. The A's were impressed by the defensive strides he made in 2008. He's on track to move up to Double-A this year.

Year	Club (League)	Class	AVG	G	AB	R	H	2B	3B	HR	RBI	BB	SO	SB	OBP	SLG
2006	Vancouver (NWL)	SS	.354	38	144	24	51	10	1	2	22	14	30	3	.409	.479
	Kane Country (MWL)	LoA	.235	30	98	12	23	4	1	1	13	12	19	1	.327	.327
2007	Kane Country (MWL)	LoA	.175	56	206	14	36	6	0	1	16	13	37	2	.234	.218
	Vancouver (NWL)	SS	.261	71	276	41	72	19	2	4	40	42	79	2	.362	.388
2008	Stockton (CAL)	HiA	.309	95	343	52	106	24	4	9	55	30	91	7	.368	.481
MINOR LEAGUE TOTALS			.270	290	1067	143	288	63	8	17	146	111	256	15	.343	.392

29 ARNOLD LEON, RHP

BORN: Sept. 6, 1988. **B-T:** R-R. **HT.:** 5-11. **WT.:** 190. **SIGNED:** Mexico, 2007. **SIGNED BY:** Randy Johnson/Craig Weissmann.

A's roving infield instructor Juan Navarrete lives in Saltillo, Mexico, where he spotted Leon pitching in the Mexican League. After Navarrete touted him, the A's purchased Leon's contract from the Saltillo Sarape Makers in November 2007. They were allowed to keep him until June 15, then had to return him to Saltillo to finish out the season per the terms of the agreement. He'll be back with the A's full-time in 2009. Leon piled up strikeouts in the California and Mexican leagues by working off a sneaky low-90s fastball that has some sink. Leon's best secondary pitch is a big, slow 68-69 mph curveball, and he also has added a cutter to give him a harder offspeed offering. His changeup is below-average. Leon has a drop-and-drive delivery, which at 5-foot-11 causes his pitches to flatten when he leaves them up in the zone, so he needs to create better downward angle to the plate. Though he was a reliever in his U.S. debut and in Mexico, Oakland may use him as a starter next year.

Year	Club (League)	Class	W	L	ERA	G	GS	CG	SV	IP	H	R	ER	HR	BB	SO	AVG
2006	Saltillo (MEX)	AAA	0	0	2.70	4	0	0	0	3	2	1	1	0	2	2	.167
2007	Saltillo (MEX)	AAA	3	0	1.94	35	0	0	1	42	31	11	9	2	24	38	.217
2008	Stockton (CAL)	HiA	0	0	2.86	20	0	0	2	28	25	12	9	1	9	28	.238
	Saltillo (MEX)	AAA	2	1	4.30	13	0	0	0	15	12	7	7	0	2	21	.235
MINOR LEAGUE TOTALS			5	1	2.66	72	0	0	3	88	70	31	26	3	37	89	.225

30 GRANT DESME, OF

BORN: April 4, 1986. **B-T:** R-R. **HT.:** 6-2. **WT.:** 205. **DRAFTED:** Cal Poly, 2007 (2nd round). **SIGNED BY:** Rick Magnante.

Desme had helium heading into the 2007 draft, but a broken bone in his hand late in his college season curtailed his momentum. The A's were high enough on him to make him a second-round pick, but injuries thus far have limited him to 49 pro at-bats. His wrist flared up again soon after he made his pro debut, leading to offseason surgery. In minor league camp last spring, he separated his left shoulder trying to make a diving catch and got just three at-bats all year. When healthy, Desme generates plus power with good leverage in his swing and excellent bat speed. Though he's a good athlete, his speed is better suited for an outfield corner. He has the arm strength to play right field. The A's hope he'll be healthy enough to return for the start of the 2009, as they've seen little of what he's capable of as a pro.

Year	Club (League)	Class	AVG	G	AB	R	H	2B	3B	HR	RBI	BB	SO	SB	OBP	SLG
2007	Vancouver (NWL)	SS	.261	12	46	6	12	3	0	1	6	6	21	2	.358	.391
2008	Athletics (AZL)	R	.333	2	3	2	1	0	0	1	2	0	0	0	.500	1.333
MINOR LEAGUE TOTALS			.265	14	49	8	13	3	0	2	8	6	21	2	.368	.449

Philadelphia Phillies

BY JOHN MANUEL

For once, the sequel was actually better than the original.

In 2007, the Phillies trailed the Mets by seven games with 17 games to play but overtook New York on the final day of the season to complete the biggest late-season comeback in baseball history. But the Rockies swept Philadelphia in the Division Series, putting a quick end to the feel-good story.

Philadelphia learned from its demise and built on its successes in 2008, stunning the Mets with another September comeback before winning just the second World Series championship in the franchise's long, tortured history. The two championship teams have several similarities that link them in history, providing symmetry that's hard to ignore.

Both clubs built powerful offenses around the major league home run leader. No one's confusing Ryan Howard with Hall of Famer Mike Schmidt, yet Howard remains one of the game's most productive hitters after topping the majors with 48 homers and 146 RBIs. He had more help than Schmidt did, starting with Chase Utley and 2007 MVP Jimmy Rollins.

Lefthanded aces pitched at the front of both rotations. Cole Hamels fills the Steve Carlton role for his generation, with his changeup proving just as unhittable as Lefty's slider. Hamels won the first game of all three postseason series.

Closer Tug McGraw provided the inspiration and the lasting visual images of the Phillies' 1980 title. While Brad Lidge, his 2008 counterpart, can't match McGraw as a quote, he matched him where it mattered, leading a bullpen that was baseball's best.

Philadelphia lost just three games in the postseason, one in each series. Perhaps most gratifying, the Phillies did it with a homegrown core. Rollins (1996), Burrell (1998), Brett Myers (1999), Utley (2000) and Hamels (2002) were first- or second-round picks made good. Howard (fifth round, 2001) and Ryan Madson (ninth, 1998) are also homegrown, the results of drafts orchestrated by Mike Arbuckle and Marti Wolever.

With extra picks in 2008, Wolever fashioned a draft class that could be the best of his tenure. The Phillies gambled on high upsides, taking infielder Anthony Hewitt, outfielders Zach Collier and Anthony Gose, and righthander Jason Knapp with four of the first 71 selections. They mixed in a promising haul of college pitchers led by righties Vance Worley and Mike Stutes.

Down on the farm, Triple-A Lehigh Valley and Double-A Reading finished with the worst records in

Homegrown ace Cole Hamels was MVP of both the NLCS and World Series

TOP 30 PROSPECTS

1. Dominic Brown, of	16. Vance Worley, rhp
2. Carlos Carrasco, rhp	17. Mike Stutes, rhp
3. Lou Marson, c	18. Freddy Galvis, ss
4. Jason Donald, ss	19. Edgar Garcia, rhp
5. Kyle Drabek, rhp	20. Joe Savery, lhp
6. Michael Taylor, of	21. Travis Mattair, 3b
7. Travis d'Arnaud, c	22. Drew Carpenter, rhp
8. Zach Collier, of	23. Jarred Cosart, rhp
9. J.A. Happ, lhp	24. John Mayberry Jr., of
10. Jason Knapp, rhp	25. Quintin Berry, of
11. Antonio Bastardo, lhp	26. Pat Overholt, rhp
12. Julian Sampson, rhp	27. Sergio Escalona, lhp
13. Drew Naylor, rhp	28. Trevor May, rhp
14. Anthony Hewitt, 3b/of	29. Mike Cisco, rhp
15. Anthony Gose, of	30. Colby Shreve, rhp

their leagues, a sign that most of the franchise's minor league talent is collected at lower levels. With the big league team coming off consecutive playoff appearances, the Phillies can afford to be patient.

New general manager Ruben Amaro Jr., promoted from assistant GM when Pat Gillick retired after the World Series, inherits a championship club and a farm system with plenty of high-ceiling talents. He didn't inherit Arbuckle, his fellow assistant GM who took a job with the Royals when he didn't get the GM gig, but other key members of the front office stayed in place.

General Manager: Ruben Amaro Jr. **Farm Director:** Steve Noworyta. **Scouting Director:** Marti Wolever.

Class	Team	League	W	L	PCT	Finish*	Manager	Affiliated
Majors	Philadelphia	National	92	70	.568	^2nd (16)	Charlie Manuel	—
Triple-A	Lehigh Valley Iron Pigs	International	55	89	.382	14th (14)	Dave Huppert	2008
Double-A	Reading Phillies	Eastern	53	89	.373	12th (12)	P.J. Forbes	1967
High A	Clearwater Threshers	Florida State	64	76	.457	9th (12)	Razor Shines	1985
Low A	Lakewood BlueClaws	South Atlantic	80	60	.571	4th (14)	Steve Roadcap	2001
Short-season	Williamsport Crosscutters	New York-Penn	38	37	.507	8th (14)	Dusty Wathan	2007
Rookie	GCL Phillies	Gulf Coast	33	25	.569	^4th (16)	Rolando de Armas	1999
Overall 2008 Minor League Record			323	376	.462	27th		

* Finish in overall standings (No. of teams in league). ^League champion.

LAST YEAR'S TOP 30

Rank	Player, Pos.	Status
1.	Carlos Carrasco, rhp	No. 2
2.	Adrian Cardenas, 2b	(Athletics)
3.	Joe Savery, lhp	No. 20
4.	Josh Outman, lhp	(Athletics)
5.	Kyle Drabek, rhp	No. 5
6.	Dominic Brown, of	No. 1
7.	Greg Golson, of	(Rangers)
8.	Lou Marson, c	No. 3
9.	Drew Carpenter, rhp	No. 22
10.	Jason Jaramillo, c	(Pirates)
11.	J.A. Happ, lhp	No. 9
12.	Scott Mathieson, rhp	Dropped out
13.	Freddy Galvis, ss	No. 18
14.	Edgar Garcia, rhp	No. 19
15.	Jason Donald, ss	No. 4
16.	Travis d'Arnaud, c	No. 7
17.	Heitor Correa, rhp	Dropped out
18.	Travis Mattair, 3b	No. 20
19.	Julian Sampson, rhp	No. 12
20.	Brad Harman, 2b/ss	Dropped out
21.	D'Arby Myers, of	Dropped out
22.	Carlos Monasterios, rhp	Dropped out
23.	Quintin Berry, of	No. 25
24.	Joe Bisenius, rhp	Dropped out
25.	Tyler Mach, 2b	Dropped out
26.	Antonio Bastardo, lhp	No. 11
27.	Mike Zagurski, lhp	Dropped out
28.	Matt Spencer, of	(Athletics)
29.	Drew Naylor, rhp	No. 13
30.	Lincoln Holdzkom, rhp	(Free agent)

BEST TOOLS

Best Hitter for Average	Dominic Brown
Best Power Hitter	Michael Taylor
Best Strike-Zone Discipline	Lou Marson
Fastest Baserunner	Quintin Berry
Best Athlete	Anthony Hewitt
Best Fastball	Carlos Carrasco
Best Curveball	Kyle Drabek
Best Slider	Mike Stutes
Best Changeup	Carlos Carrasco
Best Control	Mike Cisco
Best Defensive Catcher	Lou Marson
Best Defensive Infielder	Freddy Galvis
Best Infield Arm	Freddy Galvis
Best Defensive Outfielder	Anthony Gose
Best Outfield Arm	Dominic Brown

PROJECTED 2012 LINEUP

Catcher	Lou Marson
First Base	Ryan Howard
Second Base	Chase Utley
Third Base	Jason Donald
Shortstop	Jimmy Rollins
Left Field	Michael Taylor
Center Field	Shane Victorino
Right Field	Dominic Brown
No. 1 Starter	Cole Hamels
No. 2 Starter	Carlos Carrasco
No. 3 Starter	Kyle Drabek
No. 4 Starter	Brett Myers
No. 5 Starter	Joe Blanton
Closer	Brad Lidge

TOP PROSPECTS OF THE DECADE

Year	Player, Pos.	2008 Org.
1999	Pat Burrell, 1b	Phillies
2000	Pat Burrell, 1b/of	Phillies
2001	Jimmy Rollins, ss	Phillies
2002	Marlon Byrd, of	Rangers
2003	Gavin Floyd, rhp	White Sox
2004	Cole Hamels, lhp	Phillies
2005	Ryan Howard, 1b	Phillies
2006	Cole Hamels, lhp	Phillies
2007	Carlos Carrasco, rhp	Phillies
2008	Carlos Carrasco, rhp	Phillies

TOP DRAFT PICKS OF THE DECADE

Year	Player, Pos.	2008 Org.
1999	Brett Myers, rhp	Phillies
2000	Chase Utley, 2b	Phillies
2001	Gavin Floyd, rhp	White Sox
2002	Cole Hamels, lhp	Phillies
2003	Tim Moss, 2b (3rd round)	Out of baseball
2004	Greg Golson, of	Phillies
2005	Mike Costanzo, 3b (2nd round)	Orioles
2006	Kyle Drabek, rhp	Phillies
2007	Joe Savery, lhp	Phillies
2008	Anthony Hewitt, 3b/of	Phillies

LARGEST BONUSES IN CLUB HISTORY

Gavin Floyd, 2001	$4,200,000
Pat Burrell, 1998	$3,150,000
Brett Myers, 1999	$2,050,000
Cole Hamels, 2002	$2,000,000
Chase Utley, 2000	$1,780,000

PHILADELPHIA PHILLIES

TOP 2009 ROOKIE: Jason Donald, ss. Injuries open opportunity for Donald at second and third.

BREAKOUT PROSPECT: Julian Sampson, rhp. Athletic Pacific Northwest product should flourish in second full year.

SLEEPER: Justin DeFratus, rhp. Developing arm strength pumps fastball up to 94 mph at times.

SOURCE OF TOP 30 TALENT			
Homegrown	29	Acquired	1
College	10	Trades	1
Junior college	1	Rule 5 draft	0
High school	12	Independent leagues	0
Draft-and-follow	0	Free agents/waivers	0
Nondrafted free agents	0		
International	6		

Numbers in parentheses indicate prospect rankings.

LF
Zach Collier (8)
Steve Susdorf
Jeremy Slayden
Gus Milner
Damarii Saunderson

CF
Anthony Gose (15)
Quintin Berry (25)
D'Arby Myers
Leandro Castro

RF
Dominic Brown (1)
Michael Taylor (6)
John Mayberry Jr. (24)
Brandon Haislet

3B
Jason Donald (4)
Anthony Hewitt (14)
Travis Mattair (21)
Cody Overbeck

SS
Freddy Galvis (18)
Troy Hanzawa
Fidel Hernandez

2B
Brad Harman
Harold Garcia
Derrick Mitchell

1B
Jeremy Hamilton
Michael Durant
Mike Rizzotti

C
Lou Marson (3)
Travis d'Arnaud (7)
Joel Naughton
Jean Carlos Rodriguez
Tuffy Gosewisch

RHP

Starters	Relievers
Carlos Carrasco (2)	Jason Knapp (10)
Kyle Drabek (5)	Pat Overholt (26)
Julian Sampson (12)	B.J. Rosenberg
Drew Naylor (13)	Michael Schwimer
Vance Worley (16)	Chris Kissock
Mike Stutes (17)	Justin De Fratus
Edgar Garcia (19)	Sam Walls
Drew Carpenter (22)	Joe Bisenius
Jarred Cosart (23)	Scott Mathieson
Trevor May (28)	Tyler Cloyd
Mike Cisco (29)	Jordan Ellis
Colby Shreve (30)	
Robert Mosebach	
Tyson Brummett	
Jon Pettibone	
Haitor Correa	
Darren Byrd	
Chance Chapman	

LHP

Starters	Relievers
J.A. Happ (9)	Sergio Escalona (27)
Antonio Bastardo (11)	Mike Zagurski
Joe Savery (20)	Matt German
Jacob Diekman	Sean Grieve
Korey Noles	
Spencer Arroyo	

2008

BONUSES: $6.7 MILLION

BEST PURE HITTER: OF Zach Collier (1s) has a smooth, easy swing and an all-around game that has drawn comparisons to Garret Anderson's.

BEST POWER HITTER: 3B/OF Anthony Hewitt's (1) raw power could produce 30 homers annually if he just hits .250. He'll probably always swing and miss and will require patience, but his raw power is undeniable. 3B Cody Overbeck (9) has more usable power now, with 12 home runs in the short-season New York-Penn League this summer.

FASTEST RUNNER: OF Anthony Gose's (2) 70 speed on the 20-80 scouting scale makes him a little quicker than Hewitt.

BEST DEFENSIVE PLAYER: SS Troy Hanzawa (16) does everything easily, with a strong, accurate arm and premium actions.

BEST FASTBALL: RHP Jason Knapp (2) has premium arm strength, at times sitting at 94-96 mph, a range that RHP Jarred Cosart (38) also reached this summer just before signing for $550,000. The Phillies found several intriguing power arms in the college ranks, as RHPs Vance Worley (3), Mike Stutes (11) and B.J. Rosenberg (13) all can reach 94 mph with their fastballs. So can high school RHP Trevor May (4).

BEST SECONDARY PITCH: May has flashed a power curveball and can throw it for strikes or bury it as a chase pitch when ahead in the count. Stutes' slider also has plus potential, though he threw it too much as an amateur.

BEST PRO DEBUT: Stutes went 7-2, 1.42 with 84 strikeouts in 70 innings between short-season Williamsport and low Class A Lakewood, while RHP Mike Cisco (36) walked none in 35 innings for Lakewood while going 3-1, 0.99 overall.

BEST ATHLETE: Hewitt was the best athlete in the entire draft, with a raw mix of power, speed and explosiveness. Gose, who also was a premium prospect as a hard-throwing lefthander, has five-tool ability in center.

MOST INTRIGUING BACKGROUND: Collier had an operation to improve blood flow to his heart in May 2006, and some teams crossed him off their boards as a result. He has shown no symptoms since the procedure. RHP Colby Shreve (6) was the top junior-college prospect in the country before an elbow injury led to Tommy John surgery in May. The Phillies gave him $400,000 anyway. Cisco's grandfather Galen, the Phillies' pitching coach from 1997-2000, had a seven-year big league career.

CLOSEST TO THE MAJORS: Worley, especially if he takes his fastball/slider mix to the bullpen.

BEST LATE-ROUND PICK: Stutes' strong start grabbed headlines, but Cosart has more upside.

THE ONE WHO GOT AWAY: Athletic OF/3B Johnny Coy (7) will play baseball and basketball at Arizona State. The Phillies also went after RHPs Blaine O'Brien (34) and Joe Pond (39), who wound up at Georgia and Utah, respectively.

ASSESSMENT: The Phillies went after high-upside players in the field and on the mound and came away with depth and impact players. Collier, Worley, Stutes and Overbeck provide polish to complement the raw tools of Hewitt, Gose and Knapp, balancing an impressive class.

2007

BONUSES: $4.2 MILLION

OF Michael Taylor (5) took a huge step forward in 2008, but LHP Joe Savery (1) took a huge step back. C Travis d'Arnaud (2) is a premium defender who's making nice progress with his bat.

GRADE: C

2006

BONUSES: $4.8 MILLION

OF Dominic Brown (20) is the system's best prospect. RHP Kyle Drabek (1) has more upside than any of the Phillies' minor league pitchers and is coming back nicely from Tommy John surgery. 2B/SS Adrian Cardenas (1s) was used in a deal for Joe Blanton, while SS Jason Donald (3) looks like he'll fill in for Chase Utley to start 2009.

GRADE: B+

2005

BONUSES: $1.8 MILLION*

The Phillies didn't have a first-round pick and already have moved their top two choices, 3B Mike Costanzo (2) and LHP Matt Maloney (3), in trades for Brad Lidge and Kyle Lohse. RHP Mike Zagurski (12) may be the only draftee who contributes in Philadelphia.

GRADE: C

2004

BONUSES: $3.4 MILLION*

LHP J.A. Happ (3) and C Lou Marson (4) contributed to the Phillies' stretch drive and will get expanded roles in 2009. The club dealt away its top two picks, OF Greg Golson (1) and C Jason Jaramillo (2), in minor deals this offseason.

GRADE: C

*Draft analysis by John Manuel (2008) and Jim Callis (2004-07). Numbers in parentheses indicate draft rounds. *Bonuses for 2004-05 are first 10 rounds only.*

DAVID SCHOFIELD

DOMINIC BROWN, OF

Born: Sept. 3, 1987.
Ht.: 6-5. **Wt.:** 205.
Bats: L. **Throws:** L.
Drafted:
HS—Redan, Ga., 2006
(20th round).
Signed by:
Chip Lawrence.

Brown had committed to play football (as a wide receiver) and baseball for Miami coming out of Redan (Ga.) High—the alma mater of Brandon Phillips, among others—and his camp threw out some lofty bonus figures during the spring of 2006. That was enough for many scouts to keep their distance, but Phillies area scout Chip Lawrence followed him all spring. When Brown didn't get a qualifying standardized test score to play for the Hurricanes, Philadelphia was able to sign him for $200,000 as a 20th-round pick. Brown has moved slowly, only reaching low Class A Lakewood in his third pro year, and has benefited from the patient approach. He got off to a hot start and had a consistent season while splitting time between center and right field in 2008. He took his game up a notch by winning the batting title in Hawaii Winter Baseball, hitting .389 while drawing more walks (15) than strikeouts (14).

Being tall, wiry strong and black while playing right field earns plenty of Darryl Strawberry comparisons for Brown. He also emulates Strawberry with his swing, a buggy-whip stroke that features a high back elbow and high finish. Like a young Strawberry, Brown shows athleticism, power and speed, yet he's quite different in that his hitting tool is ahead of his power at the early stages of his career. He has good hand-eye coordination and excellent timing, helping him make consistent hard contact. Brown's swing has plenty of leverage, giving him above-average raw power, and he leaves the bat head in the hitting zone a long time. He has above-average pitch recognition and identifies breaking balls out of the pitcher's hand, helping him lay off pitches he wouldn't be able to do much with. An excellent athlete, Brown is a plus runner presently who should become a premium defender in right field. His arm grades as a 70 on the 20-80 scouting scale.

How much power Brown develops will determine his big league value. He still needs to gain strength, and once he does the Phillies believe his hitting ability will result in more homers. His stroke has some length to it, and at his size, he's always going to have some holes in his swing. Some scouts question his long stride at the plate and believe he'll have timing issues as he moves up the ladder. Brown is content for now to simply make contact against lefthanders, batting .268 with just three extra-base hits against them in 2008. He made progress as a basestealer last season, with more improvements necessary in terms of getting better jumps and maximizing his speed.

While club officials try to temper the enthusiasm for him, scouts in other organizations rue missing out on Brown in the draft and consider him the Phillies' top talent. He has yet to break out with a big season and seems poised to do so in 2009 at high Class A Clearwater. It may be too much to expect him to hit 335 career homers like Strawberry. But projecting him to hit 20-25 homers annually while posting above-average on-base percentages and playing stellar right-field defense is reasonable, and would make him an all-star down the line.

Year	Club (League)	Class	AVG	G	AB	R	H	2B	3B	HR	RBI	BB	SO	SB	OBP	SLG
2006	Phillies (GCL)	R	.214	34	117	13	25	3	0	1	7	12	30	13	.292	.265
2007	Clearwater (FSL)	HiA	.444	3	9	2	4	1	0	1	7	2	0	0	.545	.889
	Williamsport (NYP)	SS	.295	74	285	43	84	11	5	3	32	27	49	14	.356	.400
2008	Lakewood (SAL)	LoA	.291	114	444	77	129	23	3	9	54	64	72	22	.382	.417
MINOR LEAGUE TOTALS			.283	225	855	135	242	38	8	14	100	105	151	49	.363	.395

2 CARLOS CARRASCO, RHP

RODGER WOOD

BORN: March 3, 1987. **B-T:** R-R. **HT.:** 6-3. **WT.:** 190. **SIGNED:** Venezuela, 2003. **SIGNED BY:** Sal Agostinelli.

Ever since signing for $300,000 in 2003, Carrasco has ranked among the Phillies' Top 10 Prospects, and he topped this list the previous two years. He repeated Double-A Reading in 2008 and showed better command to earn a late-season promotion to Triple-A Lehigh Valley, where he finished strong. Scouts rave about Carrasco's pure stuff. He'll touch 96 mph with his fastball and sits at 91-94 with late life. His changeup has similar depth and fade, and when he locates it and his fastball, he can cruise through a lineup. His curveball, once a liability, now grades out as average consistently and sometimes gives him a third plus pitch. For all his stuff, he lacks consistency and a killer instinct. Opposing managers and scouts use words such as "fold up" or "soft" to describe Carrasco, who's prone to the big inning. He tends to quicken his delivery, causing his fastball to elevate, and falls in love with his changeup. Inconsistent command and wavering focus land him in tight spots and make it hard for him to work out of trouble. Unsure if he could handle pennant-race pressure, Philadelphia didn't call Carrasco up for September. At the same time, they still consider him a co-No. 1 prospect with Dominic Brown, with a ceiling of a No. 2 starter. He should challenge J.A. Happ and Kyle Kendrick for the last big league rotation spot in spring training. More likely, he'll head back to Triple-A for more seasoning.

Year	Club (League)	Class	W	L	ERA	G	GS	CG	SV	IP	H	R	ER	HR	BB	SO	AVG
2004	Phillies (GCL)	R	5	4	3.56	11	8	0	0	48	53	23	19	2	15	34	.276
2005	Lakewood (SAL)	LoA	1	7	7.04	13	13	1	0	63	78	50	49	11	28	46	.302
	Batavia (NYP)	SS	0	3	13.50	4	4	0	0	15	29	25	23	8	5	12	.392
	Phillies (GCL)	R	0	0	1.80	2	2	0	0	5	3	1	1	0	1	2	.176
2006	Lakewood (SAL)	LoA	12	6	2.26	26	26	2	0	159	103	50	40	6	65	159	.182
2007	Clearwater (FSL)	HiA	6	2	2.84	12	12	1	0	70	49	22	22	8	22	53	.199
	Reading (EL)	AA	6	4	4.86	14	13	1	0	70	65	42	38	9	46	49	.247
2008	Reading (EL)	AA	7	7	4.32	20	19	1	0	115	109	58	55	13	45	109	.254
	Lehigh Valley (IL)	AAA	2	2	1.72	6	6	0	0	37	37	15	7	1	13	46	.250
MINOR LEAGUE TOTALS			39	35	3.93	108	103	6	0	582	526	286	254	58	240	510	.240

3 LOU MARSON, C

BORN: July 26, 1986. **B-T:** R-R. **HT.:** 6-1. **WT.:** 200. **DRAFTED:** HS—Scottsdale, Ariz., 2004 (4th round). **SIGNED BY:** Theron Brockish.

Marson had a breakthrough 2008 season in Double-A and was scheduled to report to the Arizona Fall League, but instead he got a September callup. He made his major league debut in Game 162 by homering off Marco Estrada and throwing out a basestealer. He stuck around Philadelphia as an extra bullpen catcher and possible emergency roster replacement during the playoffs instead of going to the AFL. Marson is the Phillies' most polished minor league hitter, with the system's best plate discipline and a professional approach. He doesn't project to hit for plus power but is learning which balls he can pull with authority. He has used his athletic ability to improve quickly defensively, becoming a solid-average receiver and good leader for a pitching staff. Most big league catchers have better arms than Marson, whose grades out as fringe average. He compensates with accuracy and quick transfers, and he threw out 37 percent of basesteales last season, but he can't afford to lose any arm strength. He needs work calling games and setting up hitters. Phillies starter Carlos Ruiz is a capable defender, but so is Marson, who brings much more to the table offensively. Once he's ready in terms of game-calling and other nuances of catching, Marson will become the regular in Philadelphia, perhaps as soon as the second half of 2009.

Year	Club (League)	Class	AVG	G	AB	R	H	2B	3B	HR	RBI	BB	SO	SB	OBP	SLG
2004	Phillies (GCL)	R	.257	38	113	18	29	3	0	4	8	13	18	4	.333	.389
2005	Batavia (NYP)	SS	.245	60	220	25	54	11	3	5	25	27	52	0	.329	.391
2006	Lakewood (SAL)	LoA	.243	104	350	44	85	16	5	4	39	49	82	4	.343	.351
2007	Clearwater (FSL)	HiA	.288	111	393	68	113	24	1	7	63	52	80	3	.373	.407
2008	Reading (EL)	AA	.314	94	322	55	101	18	0	5	46	68	70	3	.433	.416
	Philadelphia (NL)	MAJ	.500	1	4	2	2	0	0	1	2	0	2	0	.500	1.250
MINOR LEAGUE TOTALS			.273	407	1398	210	382	72	9	25	181	209	302	14	.370	.391
MAJOR LEAGUE TOTALS			.500	1	4	2	2	0	0	1	2	0	2	0	.500	1.250

4 JASON DONALD, SS

RODGER WOOD

BORN: Sept. 8, 1984. **B-T:** R-R. **HT.:** 6-1. **WT.:** 190. **DRAFTED:** Arizona, 2006 (3rd round). **SIGNED BY:** Theron Brockish.

Considered an underachiever in college, Donald has overachieved as a pro. He continued hitting for good power in his first trip to Double-A last year, then was one of Team USA's top players in the Olympics, helping lead the Americans to a bronze medal. He finished up by crushing his way through the Arizona Fall League, ranking second in the league in batting (.407) and extra-base hits (19). Donald is an offensive player with a feel for hitting. He's patient but aggressive, pouncing in hitter's counts and pounding mistakes. He has excellent hands and strong forearms that produce average power to all fields, and he's developing more pop to his pull side. He's a solid, smart runner with an average arm. He prepares well and has excellent work habits. A mechanical fielder, Donald grades out as a below-average shortstop and likely won't be a regular at the position in the majors. He should be average at second base and has enough arm for third, though he needs more work there. At times he can be too hard on himself, taking bad at-bats into the field and vice versa. Both Chase Utley (hip) and Pedro Feliz (back) had offseason surgeries, and Donald played both of their positions in the AFL. He's the Phillies' top in-house option to fill in for Utley at second and to replace Feliz long-term at third. Donald doesn't fit the classic third-base profile and may fit better as a super utility player.

Year	Club (League)	Class	AVG	G	AB	R	H	2B	3B	HR	RBI	BB	SO	SB	OBP	SLG
2006	Batavia (NYP)	SS	.263	63	213	33	56	14	2	1	24	23	42	12	.347	.362
2007	Lakewood (SAL)	LoA	.310	51	197	41	61	9	3	4	30	29	39	2	.409	.447
	Clearwater (FSL)	HiA	.300	83	293	48	88	22	5	8	41	35	70	3	.386	.491
2008	Reading (EL)	AA	.307	92	362	57	111	19	4	14	54	47	86	11	.391	.497
MINOR LEAGUE TOTALS			.297	289	1065	179	316	64	14	27	149	134	237	28	.384	.459

5 KYLE DRABEK, RHP

BORN: Dec. 8, 1987. **B-T:** R-R. **HT.:** 6-1. **WT.:** 190. **DRAFTED:** HS—The Woodlands, Texas, 2006 (1st round). **SIGNED BY:** Steve Cohen.

The son of former Cy Young Award winner Doug Drabek turned a corner in 2008, making the most progress of his pro career while returning from Tommy John surgery. The Phillies used his rehabilitation to tweak his mechanics, removing a hip turn from his delivery, and his stuff returned to pre-injury levels with a strong effort in Hawaii Winter Baseball. The 18th overall pick in the 2006 draft, he signed for $1.55 million. Drabek is on his way to having three average-to-plus pitches. His fastball has reached 95 mph during his comeback and sits in the low 90s, though he hasn't had to carry it deep into games yet. His hard curveball is rounding into above-average shape more consistently. The work he did in instructional league improved both his mechanics and his changeup. Knocked for his immaturity prior to the 2006 draft, Drabek still is no choirboy. One scout said he has baseball makeup, with great competitiveness, but not "take home your daughter" makeup. He needs better arm speed on his changeup after not throwing one in high school, when he used a knuckleball instead. A healthy Drabek could move very quickly. He'll likely start 2009 at high Class A thanks to the warm weather in the Florida State League, but the Phillies expect him to force his way to Double-A sometime during the season.

Year	Club (League)	Class	W	L	ERA	G	GS	CG	SV	IP	H	R	ER	HR	BB	SO	AVG
2006	Phillies (GCL)	R	1	3	7.71	6	6	0	0	23	33	24	20	2	11	14	.333
2007	Lakewood (SAL)	LoA	5	1	4.33	11	10	0	0	54	50	29	26	9	23	46	.239
2008	Phillies (GCL)	R	0	1	2.25	4	4	0	0	12	6	3	3	0	6	6	.150
	Williamsport (NYP)	SS	1	2	2.21	4	4	0	0	20	11	6	5	1	6	10	.159
MINOR LEAGUE TOTALS			7	7	4.43	25	24	0	0	110	100	62	54	12	46	76	.240

6 MICHAEL TAYLOR, OF

BORN: Dec. 19, 1985. **B-T:** R-R. **HT.:** 6-6. **WT.:** 250. **DRAFTED:** Stanford, 2007 (5th round). **SIGNED BY:** Joey Davis.

A highly regarded prospect as a prep player in Florida, Taylor didn't hit enough as a high school senior to overcome a Stanford commitment and juvenile diabetes and get drafted high. He spent two nondescript years with the Cardinal before making huge strides late in his junior season, and he hasn't stopped hitting since. He was named to the low Class A South Atlantic League's midseason all-star game in 2008, then hit for even more power after a promotion. A physical specimen, Taylor has strength, athleticism and explosive power potential. He started using his lower half in his swing, getting the bat head out and producing better bat speed. He has average speed that improves to a tick above average once he gets going, and a plus outfield arm. He uses his intelligence on and off the field, studying the game and learning how to prepare like a pro. Taylor still isn't a natural hitter and likely will struggle to maintain his batting average against better pitching, as he can lose command of the strike zone at times. His swing can get long and he has some holes, especially inside. His route-running in the outfield could stand some improvement. Taylor profiles as the kind of righthanded-hitting corner outfielder the Phillies need and will be a step closer in 2009 at Double-A. If he maintains his 2008 hitting performance, he could reach Philadelphia in 2010.

Year	Club (League)	Class	AVG	G	AB	R	H	2B	3B	HR	RBI	BB	SO	SB	OBP	SLG
2007	Williamsport (NYP)	SS	.227	66	233	30	53	14	0	6	33	23	53	8	.300	.365
2008	Lakewood (SAL)	LoA	.361	67	249	40	90	12	3	10	50	31	43	10	.441	.554
	Clearwater (FSL)	HiA	.329	65	243	36	80	27	1	9	38	19	46	5	.380	.560
MINOR LEAGUE TOTALS			.308	198	725	106	223	53	4	25	121	73	142	23	.376	.495

7 TRAVIS D'ARNAUD, C

BORN: Feb. 10, 1989. **B-T:** R-R. **HT.:** 6-2. **WT.:** 195. **DRAFTED:** HS—Lakewood, Calif., 2007 (1st round supplemental). **SIGNED BY:** Tim Kissner.

D'Arnaud's older brother Chase was a fourth-round pick of the Pirates last year as a shortstop. They would have played together in the short-season New York-Penn League all-star game before the Phillies promoted their d'Arnaud for Lakewood's stretch run. His defense got d'Arnaud drafted 37th overall in 2007. He's athletic with premium catch-and-throw tools, such as soft hands, quick feet and plenty of arm strength. He has made adjustments to get his body more involved in his throws, improving their accuracy. As a bonus, some club officials now believe his offense will be as good as or better than his defense. He has a line-drive swing and gap power with a willingness to use the opposite field. D'Arnaud's swing lacks natural loft, so he's not expected to hit for a lot of power. He threw out just 19 percent of basestealers and committed 16 passed balls in 2008, numbers that don't square with the scouting reports. Phillies officials believe he just needs to gain experience with the speed of the game at the pro level. He runs like a catcher. Lou Marson looks like Philadelphia's catcher of the future, but if he falters, d'Arnaud should be ready soon thereafter. He's on the fast track already and could become trade fodder if he continues his offensive development.

Year	Club (League)	Class	AVG	G	AB	R	H	2B	3B	HR	RBI	BB	SO	SB	OBP	SLG
2007	Phillies (GCL)	R	.241	41	141	18	34	3	0	4	20	4	23	4	.278	.348
2008	Williamsport (NYP)	SS	.309	48	175	21	54	13	1	4	25	18	29	1	.371	.463
	Lakewood (SAL)	LoA	.297	16	64	12	19	5	0	2	5	5	10	0	.357	.469
MINOR LEAGUE TOTALS			.282	105	380	51	107	21	1	10	50	27	62	5	.335	.421

8 ZACH COLLIER, OF

BORN: Sept. 8, 1990. **B-T:** L-L. **HT.:** 6-2. **WT.:** 185. **DRAFTED:** HS—Chino Hills, Calif., 2008 (1st round supplemental). **SIGNED BY:** Darrell Conner.

Collier jumped into first-round consideration after homering off his summer-ball teammate, Twins first-rounder Aaron Hicks, on a 93 mph fastball during an April high school tournament. A surgical procedure on his heart, performed in 2006 to improve blood flow, may have scared some clubs away. The Phillies pounced on Collier with the 34th pick in June and signed him for $1.02 million. With a frame and swing that evoke Garret Anderson, Collier brings a combination of offensive polish and athleticism to the table. He has a projectable frame and present hitting ability thanks to a smooth, strong swing. Some scouts see him developing plus power once he develops physically and learns which pitches he can drive, while others see him as more of a .300 hitter with average pop. He's a plus runner with an average arm. Collier probably will slow down and play either left or right field down the line. He'll have to hit for power or be a steady producer like Anderson to be a regular on a corner. Collier's hitting skills should help him hit the ground running in low Class A in 2009. He's much more polished than fellow 2008 draftees Anthony Hewitt and Anthony Gose, and should be the first hitter from the Phillies' draft class to reach the major leagues.

Year	Club (League)	Class	AVG	G	AB	R	H	2B	3B	HR	RBI	BB	SO	SB	OBP	SLG
2008	Phillies (GCL)	R	.271	37	129	15	35	9	1	0	19	17	28	5	.347	.357
MINOR LEAGUE TOTALS			.271	37	129	15	35	9	1	0	19	17	28	5	.347	.357

9 J.A. HAPP, LHP

BORN: Oct. 19, 1982. **B-T:** L-L. **HT.:** 6-6. **WT.:** 200. **DRAFTED:** Northwestern, 2004 (3rd round). **SIGNED BY:** Bob Szymkowski.

Happ benefited as much as any Phillies farmhand when the organization relocated its Triple-A affiliate from Ottawa to more hospitable Lehigh Valley. He stayed healthy after missing part of 2007 with an elbow strain, led the International League by averaging 9.7 strikeouts per nine innings and made four crucial starts for Philadelphia. He netted his first big league victory with six shutout innings at Atlanta on Sept. 17. Happ's fastball sits at 88-91 mph and gets on top of hitters quickly. He has deception in his delivery and average movement on his heater, and he spotted it better than ever in 2008. His improved changeup is his second-best pitch, and he varies his slider from a true breaking ball to a little cutter that helps him get in on righthanders. Happ lacks a standout pitch and doesn't figure to get all those strikeouts on fastballs as easily in the majors as he did in Triple-A. He's generally a flyball pitcher, a liability in cozy Citizens Bank Park. Happ will compete for Philadelphia's No. 5 starter job in spring training, with the chance to earn a long-relief gig as a fallback. He projects as a fourth starter in the long term.

Year	Club (League)	Class	W	L	ERA	G	GS	CG	SV	IP	H	R	ER	HR	BB	SO	AVG
2004	Batavia (NYP)	SS	1	2	2.02	11	11	0	0	36	22	8	8	1	18	37	.185
2005	Lakewood (SAL)	LoA	4	4	2.36	14	12	0	0	72	57	26	19	3	26	70	.213
	Reading (EL)	AA	1	0	1.50	1	1	0	0	6	3	1	1	0	2	8	.150
2006	Clearwater (FSL)	HiA	3	7	2.81	13	13	0	0	80	63	35	25	9	19	77	.216
	Reading (EL)	AA	6	2	2.65	12	12	0	0	75	58	27	22	2	29	81	.214
	Scranton/W-B (IL)	AAA	1	0	1.50	1	1	0	0	6	3	1	1	1	1	4	.136
2007	Philadelphia (NL)	MAJ	0	1	11.25	1	1	0	0	4	7	5	5	3	2	5	.368
	Ottawa (IL)	AAA	4	6	5.02	24	24	0	0	118	118	74	66	12	62	117	.265
2008	Lehigh Valley (IL)	AAA	8	7	3.60	24	23	0	0	135	116	58	54	14	48	151	.234
	Philadelphia (NL)	MAJ	1	0	3.69	8	4	0	0	32	28	13	13	3	14	26	.233
MINOR LEAGUE TOTALS			28	28	3.34	100	97	0	0	528	440	230	196	42	205	545	.228
MAJOR LEAGUE TOTALS			1	1	4.54	9	5	0	0	36	35	18	18	6	16	31	.252

10 JASON KNAPP, RHP

BORN: Aug. 31, 1990. **B-T:** R-R. **HT.:** 6-5. **WT.:** 215. **DRAFTED:** HS—Annandale, N.J., 2008 (2nd round). **SIGNED BY:** Gene Schall.

Knapp jumped up some teams' draft boards with a boost in velocity during an inconsistent spring. He threw a one-hitter in the New Jersey state playoffs, hitting 97 mph, and had an excellent workout for the Phillies, who took him with their fourth selection in June, 71st overall. He signed for $590,000 and threw well in his debut before a tender elbow kept him out of the Rookie-level Gulf Coast League playoffs. The Phillies are among those who see Knapp potentially throwing 100 mph in short bursts in the future. He has a high-octane delivery that allows him to pump his fastball into the mid-90s when he's right. He has shown the ability to spin a breaking ball, a power slider with some depth. His changeup also has flashes of plus potential. Knapp loses his delivery regularly, dropping his elbow and getting around on his breaking ball frequently. He also loses his arm slot on his fastball, costing him command. He has a lot of work to do and will require patience. It's hard to find pitchers with Knapp's physicality and arm strength, but also difficult to harness that power for a starting pitcher. The Phillies will keep him in the rotation for now, most likely close to his home at Lakewood in 2009, but scouts already are talking about him as a future power bullpen arm, potentially a closer.

Year	Club (League)	Class	W	L	ERA	G	GS	CG	SV	IP	H	R	ER	HR	BB	SO	AVG
2008	Phillies (GCL)	R	3	1	2.61	7	6	0	0	31	26	10	9	1	12	38	.228
MINOR LEAGUE TOTALS			3	1	2.61	7	6	0	0	31	26	10	9	1	12	38	.228

11 ANTONIO BASTARDO, LHP

BORN: Sept. 21, 1985. **B-T:** L-L. **HT.:** 5-11. **WT.:** 168. **SIGNED:** Dominican Republic, 2005. **SIGNED BY:** Sal Agostinelli.

Bastardo hadn't pitched full-season ball until 2007, then nearly reached the majors in 2008. When he got off to a fast start and big leaguers Adam Eaton and Kyle Kendrick struggled into early June, Bastardo had a start cut short and his next start moved up, putting him on the same throwing schedule as Eaton. Primed for a possible promotion, Bastardo instead came down with a tired shoulder and was never the same after coming back about two months later. In fact, he didn't get a win after May 18 until pitching over the winter in the Dominican League. Bastardo has made such rapid progress due to the deception and command he had of his average repertoire. His fastball sits at 87-91 mph and tops out at 93. It gets on top of hitters quickly and has some cut action. He pitches inside, but he's not overly physical or a power pitcher. His changeup is his best pitch but was less consistent than in 2007, while his short slider improved slightly. It still rates as below-average. Bastardo is a flyball pitcher, usually a poor mix for Citizens Bank Park. Yet changeup lefties Cole Hamels and Jamie Moyer thrive for the Phils, and J.A. Happ, far from overpowering, has had some success. Bastardo might have a bit more upside than Happ but isn't as durable, healthy or polished. After making up for some lost time in the Dominican, he's ticketed for his first trip to Triple-A in 2009.

Year	Club (League)	Class	W	L	ERA	G	GS	CG	SV	IP	H	R	ER	HR	BB	SO	AVG
2005	Phillies (DSL)	R	2	2	2.13	11	5	0	1	38	22	14	9	0	22	63	.162
2006	Phillies (GCL)	R	1	2	3.91	9	2	0	0	23	20	16	10	1	14	27	.220
2007	Lakewood (SAL)	LoA	9	0	1.87	15	15	0	0	92	63	23	19	3	42	98	.189
	Clearwater (FSL)	HiA	1	0	7.20	1	1	0	0	5	5	4	4	0	3	12	.250
2008	Clearwater (FSL)	HiA	2	0	1.17	5	5	0	0	31	20	4	4	2	10	47	.183
	Reading (EL)	AA	2	5	3.76	14	14	0	0	67	56	35	28	13	37	62	.223
MINOR LEAGUE TOTALS			17	9	2.61	55	42	0	1	255	186	96	74	19	128	309	.198

12 JULIAN SAMPSON, RHP

BORN: Jan. 21, 1989. **B-T:** R-R. **HT.:** 6-5. **WT.:** 210. **DRAFTED:** HS—Skyline, Wash., 2007 (12th round). **SIGNED BY:** Dave Ryles.

The Phillies play in such a small big league park, they value groundball pitchers in development, and Sampson probably has the best sinker in the system among potential starting pitchers. It's a hard sinker that he uses to consistently get ground balls. Club officials don't worry that opponents hit .285 against him, focusing instead on the fact he gave up just five homers in low Class A. They're also focused on how he kept getting better, posting a 3.83 ERA in his last 14 starts and winning his final five decisions. Sampson also throws a solid slider with plus potential down the line due to its depth. His fastball had average velocity in 2008, getting to 92-93 mph consistently, and he maintained velocity on both pitches throughout the season. Sampson, who signed for a $390,000 bonus, didn't throw much of a changeup in high school, and the pitch made major progress with Lakewood, supplanting his soft curveball as his third pitch. He's shelved the curve in favor of his slider. If it all comes together, Sampson will be throwing 90-94 mph sinkers with a plus slider and average changeup with a big, durable body and clean arm action. He's a potential No. 2 starter ticketed for high Class A this season.

Year	Club (League)	Class	W	L	ERA	G	GS	CG	SV	IP	H	R	ER	HR	BB	SO	AVG
2007	Phillies (GCL)	R	0	0	0.00	1	0	0	0	2	0	0	0	0	0	1	.000
2008	Lakewood (SAL)	LoA	11	4	4.33	25	25	0	0	135	152	73	65	5	52	69	.285
MINOR LEAGUE TOTALS			11	4	4.27	26	25	0	0	137	152	73	65	5	52	70	.281

13 DREW NAYLOR, RHP

BORN: May 31, 1986. **B-T:** R-R. **HT.:** 6-4. **WT.:** 210. **SIGNED:** Australia, 2004. **SIGNED BY:** Sal Agostinelli.

The Phillies have made several forays into Australia of late, with Brad Harman reaching the majors last season. Catcher Joel Naughton and Naylor—teammates back in Queensland in Australia—joined Harman on the 40-man roster this fall. Naylor has asserted himself as the top Aussie prospect, thanks to his combination of size, stuff and accomplishment. Naylor has a big body and ranked 11th in the minors in strikeouts with 156, and projects as a mid-rotation starter. His fastball sits average at 88-92 mph, and he works up in the strike zone with it to set up his true 12-to-6 curveball. Those kind of pitchers tend to be homer prone. He's fairly athletic, though, and does a good job of commanding both pitches as well as his much-improved changeup. He was tougher on lefthanders because he keeps his change down in the zone more effectively than his fastball. Naylor was a bit shellshocked when he first got to high Class A but made adjustments, giving up only one homer in his last six starts. He has a good chance to earn a spot on Australia's World Baseball Classic team in the spring before likely making his Double-A debut.

Year	Club (League)	Class	W	L	ERA	G	GS	CG	SV	IP	H	R	ER	HR	BB	SO	AVG
2006	Phillies (GCL)	R	2	3	4.66	12	2	0	1	37	43	26	19	2	9	22	.297
2007	Williamsport (NYP)	SS	8	6	3.28	14	14	2	0	93	78	39	34	3	28	97	.228
2008	Lakewood (SAL)	LoA	5	3	2.99	14	14	2	0	87	69	32	29	8	21	97	.214
	Clearwater (FSL)	HiA	3	7	4.85	13	13	1	0	78	86	43	42	8	31	59	.282
MINOR LEAGUE TOTALS			18	19	3.78	53	43	5	1	295	276	140	124	21	89	275	.248

14 ANTHONY HEWITT, 3B/OF

BORN: April 27, 1989. **B-T:** R-R. **HT.:** 6-1. **WT.:** 195. **DRAFTED:** HS—Salisbury, Conn., 2008 (1st round). **SIGNED BY:** Gene Schall.

The Phillies had extra draft picks in 2008, with supplemental first- and third-rounders and an extra second-rounder. That allowed Philadelphia to gamble a bit on upside, and no player represents that more than Hewitt, whom it selected 24th overall. A Brooklyn native, Hewitt's academic and athletic pursuits led him to the Salisbury School in Connecticut, where coach Mark Leavitt is a former scout. Scouting directors generally considered Hewitt the 2008 draft class' top athlete thanks to his strength, speed and explosiveness. He wasn't a consensus first-rounder because of his raw status, especially his bat. Undeterred by his lack of experience and Vanderbilt commitment, the Phillies signed Hewitt for $1.38 million. Hewitt has work ethic, charisma, athleticism and intelligence, but right now he has no clue at the plate. He finished the year in a 2-for-38 funk, striking out at least once in 25 of his last 27 games in the Gulf Coast League. Pitch recognition hampered Hewitt, who the Phillies hope was just trying to catch up to tougher competition. He also was shifting from shortstop to third base, though his stiff hands and lack of pure infield actions could force a shift to the outfield. The Phillies consider raw power to be Hewitt's calling card down the line as he gains experience. Scouting director Marti Wolever said Hewitt could hit .250 with 30 home runs in a realistic scenario. He's a long way from that after striking out in nearly half his pro at-bats. Hewitt may repeat the GCL or get a promotion to short-season Williamsport in 2009, and could need 2,000 at-bats to unlock his potential.

Year	Club (League)	Class	AVG	G	AB	R	H	2B	3B	HR	RBI	BB	SO	SB	OBP	SLG
2008	Phillies (GCL)	R	.197	33	117	14	23	7	1	1	9	7	55	2	.256	.299
MINOR LEAGUE TOTALS			.197	33	117	14	23	7	1	1	9	7	55	2	.256	.299

15 ANTHONY GOSE, OF

BORN: Aug. 10, 1990. **B-T:** L-L. **HT.:** 6-1. **WT.:** 190. **DRAFTED:** HS—Bellflower, Calif., 2008 (2nd round). **SIGNED BY:** Tom Kissner.

Many scouts in Southern California thought of Gose as a pitcher first, seeing some Scott Kazmir or Billy Wagner possibilities with his smallish frame and big fastball. He ran it up to 97 mph early in prep games, but shoulder issues that required an MRI in mid-April ended his pitching opportunities. Limited to DH, Gose had a strong spring with the bat and the Phillies took him in the second round as a hitter, giving him a $772,000 bonus. He profiles extremely well as a center fielder. He's one of the organization's best runners and athletes, covering 60 yards in 6.5 seconds and showing plus-plus arm strength when healthy. Wolever and his staff believe in Gose's bat, saying that his hands work, he uses his hips in his swing and has some strength in his hands, with room to grow. The Phillies think Gose will hit for average power, and some in the organization are even more optimistic. They also acknowledge that if Gose's bat doesn't pan out, he can always go back to the mound as a power-armed reliever. Gose will have a chance to earn a spot on the Lakewood roster for 2009 but could join Anthony Hewitt in extended spring and later at Williamsport.

Year	Club (League)	Class	AVG	G	AB	R	H	2B	3B	HR	RBI	BB	SO	SB	OBP	SLG
2008	Phillies (GCL)	R	.256	11	39	4	10	2	1	0	3	1	12	3	.293	.359
MINOR LEAGUE TOTALS			.256	11	39	4	10	2	1	0	3	1	12	3	.293	.359

16 VANCE WORLEY, RHP

BORN: Sept. 25, 1987. **B-T:** R-R. **HT.:** 6-2. **WT.:** 205. **DRAFTED:** Long Beach State, 2008 (3rd round). **SIGNED BY:** Tim Kissner.

Worley was a 20th-round pick in 2005 out of Sacramento's McClatchy High—alma mater of big leaguers such as Larry Bowa, Dion James and Nick Johnson—but turned down the Phillies to attend Long Beach State. He struggled as a freshman but was the Dirtbags' workhorse as a junior and projects as such in pro ball. Philadelphia redrafted him in 2008 and signed him for $355,000 as a third-round pick. He has a clean arm action and easy delivery. While he has hit 94 mph in the past with his four-seamer, Worley generally works at 91-92 mph, mixing in an upper-80s two-seamer. His fastball is his best pitch, and his best attribute is his ability to pitch off it and work to both halves of the plate. His short slider gained a bit of depth after he signed and grades out as average, as does his changeup. Neither is a put-away pitch, however, so Worley doesn't figure to rack up big strikeout numbers and needs to learn to get early-count outs. He runs into trouble when he racks up a succession of deep counts. Worley is at his best when he's getting some ground balls and profiles as a third or fourth starter. He'll front the Clearwater rotation in 2009.

Year	Club (League)	Class	W	L	ERA	G	GS	CG	SV	IP	H	R	ER	HR	BB	SO	AVG
2008	Williamsport (NYP)	SS	0	0	1.13	2	2	0	0	8	3	1	1	0	1	8	.120
	Lakewood (SAL)	LoA	3	2	2.66	11	11	0	0	61	58	25	18	4	7	53	.247
MINOR LEAGUE TOTALS			3	2	2.48	13	13	0	0	69	61	26	19	4	8	61	.235

17 MIKE STUTES, RHP

BORN: Sept. 4, 1986. **B-T:** R-R. **HT.:** 6-1. **WT.:** 185. **DRAFTED:** Oregon State, 2008 (11th round). **SIGNED BY:** Dave Ryles.

Stutes transferred from Santa Clara to Oregon State just in time to play a key role for the 2006 and 2007 College World Series champions. He won eight games for the '06 team as a fourth starter/swing man, then was the ace of the '07 champs, going 12-4, 4.07. The Cardinals drafted him in the ninth round, but he didn't sign and returned for what proved to be a disastrous senior season. Stutes never got into a rhythm and threw too many breaking balls, plummeting to 4-7, 5.32. The Phillies snagged Stutes in the 11th round, signed him for $5,000 and got him to work more off his fastball. The results were staggering. Stutes dominated, averaging 10.9 strikeouts per nine innings while pushing his way to Lakewood. His fastball consistently reached 94 mph and sat around 91-92. His slider can be a plus pitch, and he throws a curveball and changeup. They all played up when he threw his fastball more, and one club official described a late Lakewood outing as "electric," saying Stutes has the highest ceiling of any of the club's 2008 pitching draftees. Stutes has an average feel for pitching and he needs polish on his defense and holding runners. His power, fastball-first approach got him out of his senior-year doldrums, and with him throwing four pitches for strikes, the Phillies see him as a potential mid-rotation starter. He'll join Vance Worley in the high Class A rotation.

Year	Club (League)	Class	W	L	ERA	G	GS	CG	SV	IP	H	R	ER	HR	BB	SO	AVG
2008	Williamsport (NYP)	SS	2	1	1.33	6	6	0	0	27	16	5	4	2	11	31	.172
	Lakewood (SAL)	LoA	5	1	1.48	7	7	0	0	43	20	8	7	1	18	53	.139
MINOR LEAGUE TOTALS			7	2	1.42	13	13	0	0	70	36	13	11	3	29	84	.152

18 FREDDY GALVIS, SS

BORN: Nov. 14, 1989. **B-T:** B-R. **HT.:** 5-10. **WT.:** 154. **SIGNED:** Venezuela, 2006. **SIGNED BY:** Sal Agostinelli.

The Phillies aren't known for their Latin American program, with Carlos Silva their best recent big leaguer and Carlos Carrasco their top prospect from the region. Like those pitchers, Galvis is from Venezuela, and the comparison often thrown around with him is to another Venezuelan, Omar Vizquel. Though Galvis has a chance to be a premium defender, comparing him to a 20-year veteran with more than 2,500 hits is too much. Many big league shortstops put up big error totals in the low minors, trying to make every play. Galvis makes plenty of plays and still led the Sally League with a .968 fielding percentage, making just 21 errors while pacing the league in total chances. Galvis' soft hands, range and arm strength get 70 grades on the 20-80 scouting scale, allowing him to have what one club official called "natural mustard." He makes flashy plays because that's how the play has to be made, not to show off. Galvis' bat will determine whether he's an everyday regular or a 4-A player. His advocates point to his ability to make contact, bunt and handle the bat, saying the body control that makes him a plus defender also helps him avoid strikeouts. He lacks strength and bat speed to hit for power. He's just an average runner. With college draftee Troy Hanzawa, another premium defender, added to the system, Galvis probably will repeat low Class A to give his bat time to develop.

Year	Club (League)	Class	AVG	G	AB	R	H	2B	3B	HR	RBI	BB	SO	SB	OBP	SLG
2007	Williamsport (NYP)	SS	.203	38	143	20	29	5	1	0	7	10	20	9	.255	.252
2008	Lakewood (SAL)	LoA	.238	127	458	59	109	12	1	3	42	39	58	14	.300	.288
MINOR LEAGUE TOTALS			.230	165	601	79	138	17	2	3	49	49	78	23	.289	.280

19 EDGAR GARCIA, RHP

BORN: Sept. 20, 1987. **B-T:** R-R. **HT.:** 6-2. **WT.:** 190. **SIGNED:** Dominican Republic, 2004. **SIGNED BY:** Sal Agostinelli/Will Tejeda.

Garcia signed the same year as Carlos Carrasco and is the top Dominican Republic product in the system, but again took two steps back after taking a step forward in 2008. Garcia began the season with his first trip to high Class A and performed well, winning eight of 10 decisions and throwing strikes with a fastball that at times hit 96 mph. However, Garcia had just two quality starts out of 11 in Double-A, and one club official termed his stay there as "batting practice." Garcia's fastball has good life but he doesn't command it well, as he tends to overthrow. When he gets in trouble, he tries to throw harder, and he threw plenty of 90 mph heaters over the fat part of the plate with Reading. He did make progress with his changeup and has settled on a breaking ball, a hard slurve that should be an average pitch. Garcia will return to Double-A in 2009 as a 21-year-old, and has plenty of time to establish himself, but the influx of pitching talent added in the last two drafts will push Garcia to get better or get out of the way.

Year	Club (League)	Class	W	L	ERA	G	GS	CG	SV	IP	H	R	ER	HR	BB	SO	AVG
2005	Phillies (GCL)	R	4	4	3.56	10	10	0	0	56	63	26	22	4	13	42	.284
2006	Batavia (NYP)	SS	3	5	2.98	12	12	1	0	66	62	28	22	5	10	46	.243
2007	Williamsport (NYP)	SS	1	0	2.16	2	1	0	0	8	6	2	2	0	2	11	.200
	Lakewood (SAL)	LoA	4	9	4.12	20	20	0	0	114	119	61	52	10	32	83	.268
2008	Clearwater (FSL)	HiA	8	2	3.97	14	13	0	0	79	80	36	35	7	20	70	.267
	Reading (EL)	AA	1	7	8.22	11	11	0	0	58	70	56	53	10	29	34	.299
MINOR LEAGUE TOTALS			21	27	4.39	69	67	1	0	381	400	209	186	36	106	286	.269

20 JOE SAVERY, LHP

BORN: Nov. 4, 1985. **B-T:** L-L. **HT.:** 6-3. **WT.:** 215. **DRAFTED:** Rice, 2007 (1st round). **SIGNED BY:** Steve Cohen.

Savery ranked third on this list a year ago, coming off a stellar college career at Rice that included the 2005 Freshman of the Year award and two trips to the College World Series. A two-way player for the Owls, Savery was expected to actually improve a bit as a pitcher once he ditched hitting duties. Instead, the 19th overall pick in the 2007 draft and recipient of a $1,372,500 bonus labored through his first full pro season. On the plus side, Savery led the Florida State League with 150 innings, and his arm works well. He has a big, durable body, and scouts saw flashes of his first-round talent, especially with the sink on his fastball. That said, they were just flashes, and in some outings, Savery wouldn't have been turned in as a prospect if not for his first-round pedigree. His fastball sat at 85-88 mph, and often dropped as low as 82. He got 1.8 groundouts for every airout, and his 76-82 mph slider showed average potential. His breaking ball and changeup both backed up as he lost some arm speed. Savery's critics point to a heavier lower half as the culprit for his decreased arm speed and the resulting loss in velocity. Savery was attacking his conditioning in the offseason. He'll be watched closely in spring training to see what kind of shape he's in. His spring performance will determine whether he earns a move to Double-A.

Year	Club (League)	Class	W	L	ERA	G	GS	CG	SV	IP	H	R	ER	HR	BB	SO	AVG
2007	Williamsport (NYP)	SS	2	3	2.73	7	7	0	0	26	22	9	8	0	13	22	.214
2008	Clearwater (FSL)	HiA	9	10	4.13	27	24	0	0	150	171	84	69	10	60	122	.286
MINOR LEAGUE TOTALS			11	13	3.92	34	31	0	0	177	193	93	77	10	73	144	.276

21 TRAVIS MATTAIR, 3B

BORN: Dec. 21, 1988. **B-T:** R-R. **HT.:** 6-5. **WT.:** 210. **DRAFTED:** HS—Southridge, Wash., 2007 (2nd round). **SIGNED BY:** Dave Ryles.

Mattair was the Phillies' second-round pick in 2007, signing for $395,000. His athleticism and power potential motivated the Phils to lure him away from Oregon State, and he has the leverage in his swing to project above-average power. His inexperience has shown since signing, however. He played basketball in addition to baseball in high school, attracting Division II scholarship offers. His lack of wood-bat experience has led to a long swing and a resulting long adjustment period, but he made progress after a slow start at Lakewood in 2008. He's finding his swing and his athleticism helped him shorten up a bit. He has the bat speed to overcome some holes in his swing caused by his long levers. Defensively, Mattair should be an average third baseman at least, with arm strength and solid range, and could be a plus defender with work. While Mattair made progress as the year went on, he needs to get stronger and add some polish. The Phillies expect him to repeat low Class A in 2009 and turn some of his flashes of power into more consistent production.

Year	Club (League)	Class	AVG	G	AB	R	H	2B	3B	HR	RBI	BB	SO	SB	OBP	SLG
2007	Phillies (GCL)	R	.235	54	200	19	47	10	1	3	21	12	58	3	.297	.340
2008	Lakewood (SAL)	LoA	.254	129	460	59	117	20	1	4	52	36	108	9	.321	.328
MINOR LEAGUE TOTALS			.248	183	660	78	164	30	2	7	73	48	166	12	.314	.332

22 DREW CARPENTER, RHP

BORN: May 18, 1985. **B-T:** R-R. **HT.:** 6-3. **WT.:** 225. **DRAFTED:** Long Beach State, 2006 (2nd round). **SIGNED BY:** Tim Kissner.

Carpenter made it the majors in 2008 after starting the season on a strong note. Carpenter got his first exposure to big league camp and did well in the spotlight, dominating the Yankees in four innings and commanding his plus changeup to all quadrants of the zone. At his best, the former Long Beach workhorse commands his 86-90 mph fastball, gets a good downhill angle and sets up his best pitch—a short, sharp slider that was better prior to 2008. Carpenter has made significant progress with his changeup, throws a get-it-over curveball and will sneak in a split-finger fastball. His conditioning will dictate his future role. Carpenter was just too heavy in 2008, costing him command and stamina. He missed time last year with what was officially turf toe, though the Phillies really wanted him to focus on losing weight during his time on the disabled list. He made some adjustments in the Arizona Fall League and should be ready to be reunited with pitching coach Steve Schrenk, who gets through to him more than most. They'll both be at Reading, at least to start the year.

Year	Club (League)	Class	W	L	ERA	G	GS	CG	SV	IP	H	R	ER	HR	BB	SO	AVG
2006	Phillies (GCL)	R	0	0	0.00	2	1	0	0	3	2	0	0	0	0	4	.200
	Batavia (NYP)	SS	0	0	0.77	3	3	0	0	12	10	1	1	0	5	12	.250
2007	Clearwater (FSL)	HiA	17	6	3.20	27	24	3	1	163	150	65	58	16	53	116	.242
2008	Clearwater (FSL)	HiA	3	3	2.92	8	8	2	0	52	44	17	17	2	9	32	.228
	Reading (EL)	AA	6	8	5.67	16	16	0	0	94	114	68	59	13	30	69	.305
	Philadelphia (NL)	MAJ	0	0	0.00	1	0	0	0	1	1	0	0	0	1	1	.333
	Lehigh Valley (IL)	AAA	0	1	2.57	1	1	0	0	7	6	2	2	1	3	5	.240
MINOR LEAGUE TOTALS			26	18	3.73	57	53	5	1	331	326	153	137	32	100	238	.259
MAJOR LEAGUE TOTALS			0	0	0.00	1	0	0	0	1	1	0	0	0	1	1	.333

23 JARRED COSART, RHP

BORN: May 25, 1990. **B-T:** R-R. **HT.:** 6-3. **WT.:** 180. **DRAFTED:** HS—League City, Texas, 2008 (38th round). **SIGNED BY:** Steve Cohen.

The Phillies gave Cosart more money than any of their pitchers in the 2008 draft other than Knapp, their second-rounder who got $40,000 more than Cosart's $550,000 bonus. Cosart helped make this one of the organization's deepest draft classes in years, as they spent $6.7 million on the group. While he's somewhat slightly built, he has projection in his frame and one of the quickest arms in the organization. He topped out at 92 mph in the spring and was more noted in Texas' high school ranks as a hitter, as he broke Jay Buhner's Clear Creek High record for batting. A two-way Missouri signee, Cosart had Phillies scouts following him the last two summers. They saw him hit 96 last fall, then saw it again this summer as Cosart played American Legion ball. He was at 95-96 with his fastball the day before the signing deadline, and the Phillies liked his arm and live body enough to pay such a lofty bonus. Cosart's delivery includes a pause that the Phillies will work to smooth over, and his breaking ball and changeup are in their early stages, though he has shown the ability to spin a curve at times. His athletic ability and arm strength make him an intriguing project. The Phillies drafted enough depth to take it slow with Cosart, who may not pitch full-season ball until 2010.

Year	Club (League)	Class	W	L	ERA	G	GS	CG	SV	IP	H	R	ER	HR	BB	SO	AVG
2008	Did Not Play—Signed Late																

24 JOHN MAYBERRY JR., OF

BORN: Dec. 21, 1983. **B-T:** R-R. **HT.:** 6-6. **WT.:** 230. **DRAFTED:** Stanford, 2005 (1st round). **SIGNED BY:** Tim Fortugno (Rangers).

Mayberry came to the Phillies in a November trade of first-round picks who haven't worked out. Philadelphia sent toolsy center fielder Greg Golson to the Rangers for Mayberry, and Golson would have ranked higher on this list than Mayberry because he's a superior defensive player. The Phillies, though, were looking for corner bats with power, and Mayberry in some ways is similar to Michael Taylor, his former teammate at Stanford. Taylor runs better, is a bit more athletic and has started incorporating his lower half into his swing better than Mayberry—who continues to get tied up by hard stuff inside. Mayberry has the pedigree to be a big leaguer—his father John was an all-star first baseman with the Royals in the 1970s, and he himself was a first-round pick twice, in 2002 (Mariners), when he didn't sign, and in 2005 out of Stanford. Mayberry has a plus throwing arm in right field and power for the position, with solid athletic ability and running speed. He crushes lefthanders (1.093 OPS in Triple-A) but fails to make adjustments against righties, as he gets worked inside hard, and away with soft stuff. After hitting 30 homers in 2007 and making progress in the Arizona Fall League, Mayberry plummeted to 20 homers in 2008. The Phillies hope a change of scenery unlocks his potential, and he'll anchor the outfield at Lehigh Valley in 2009.

Year	Club (League)	Class	AVG	G	AB	R	H	2B	3B	HR	RBI	BB	SO	SB	OBP	SLG
2005	Spokane (NWL)	SS	.253	71	265	51	67	16	0	11	26	26	71	7	.341	.438
2006	Clinton (MWL)	LoA	.268	126	459	77	123	26	4	21	77	59	117	9	.358	.479
2007	Bakersfield (CAL)	HiA	.230	63	244	47	56	15	1	16	45	28	64	9	.314	.496
	Frisco (TEX)	AA	.241	69	245	35	59	10	0	14	38	20	62	7	.307	.453
2008	Frisco (TEX)	AA	.268	21	82	16	22	8	0	4	13	4	21	4	.322	.512
	Oklahoma (PCL)	AAA	.263	114	437	49	115	30	7	16	58	30	85	6	.316	.474
MINOR LEAGUE TOTALS			.255	464	1732	275	442	105	12	82	257	167	420	42	.330	.472

25 QUINTIN BERRY, OF

BORN: Nov. 21, 1984. **B-T:** L-L. **HT.:** 6-1. **WT.:** 165. **DRAFTED:** San Diego State, 2006 (5th round). **SIGNED BY:** Darrell Conner.

The Phillies used to have a lot of speedsters (Tim Moss, Michael Bourn) in the organization. Through attrition and trades, Berry is the fastest man left standing, with sub-4.0 second times to first base on drag bunts making him a 70 runner. His 51 stolen bases led the Florida State League and the organization. Berry impressed FSL observers with the improvements he made during the course of the season, from running routes to his overall defensive game in center field. He's a slightly above-average center fielder who adds an average arm and excellent range. Berry's offensive ceiling is limited by his lack of power, as his short swing lacks a load and he lacks the strength to drive the ball. He beats out his share of infield hits, puts pressure on defenses with his speed and uses the whole field. He's also not afraid of working deep counts, trying to get walks, and ranked second in the FSL in that category. His combination of speed, aptitude and plate discipline should one day make Berry a second-division regular (after a trade) or key late-inning pinch-runner/defensive replacement.

Year	Club (League)	Class	AVG	G	AB	R	H	2B	3B	HR	RBI	BB	SO	SB	OBP	SLG
2006	Batavia (NYP)	SS	.219	62	210	34	46	2	2	0	13	25	51	19	.314	.248
2007	Lakewood (SAL)	LoA	.312	126	487	86	152	19	4	3	44	61	85	55	.395	.386
2008	Clearwater (FSL)	HiA	.272	134	511	63	139	24	1	3	43	65	103	51	.360	.341
MINOR LEAGUE TOTALS			.279	322	1208	183	337	45	7	6	100	151	239	125	.367	.343

26 PAT OVERHOLT, RHP

BORN: Feb. 8, 1984. **B-T:** R-R. **HT.:** 6-3. **WT.:** 190. **DRAFTED:** Santa Clara, 2005 (22nd round). **SIGNED BY:** Joey Davis.

Overholt was primarily a reliever in college at Santa Clara, where he missed the 2004 season due to Tommy John surgery. The Phillies used him as a starter for most of his pro career as he grew into his body, adding three inches in height since early in his college career. While he lost the closer role during an ugly second half in the Reading bullpen, he made enough progress in 2008 to position himself as a future big league bullpen option. Overholt has a big arm and flashes two plus pitches. His fastball usually sits at 92-93 mph, and his slider is one of the best in the organization, at times coming in at 85-86 mph with late bite. In the second half, he lost his arm slot, lowering his angle. As a result, he elevated his fastball and got around on his slider, causing it to flatten out. He has never had enough command to start but has the stuff to get away with it in relief. He's working on refining a changeup to combat lefthanders, who slugged .504 off him in Double-A. Overholt has spent the last two years in the Arizona Fall League, and the Phils clearly value him as a prospect. However, he wasn't added to the 40-man roster and passed through the Rule 5 draft unpicked. The raw talent is there, and Overholt has to start consistently locating his fastball down in the zone to set up his slider if he wants to avoid another second-half swoon. He's expected to return to Reading but could earn a Triple-A assignment with a strong spring training.

Year	Club (League)	Class	W	L	ERA	G	GS	CG	SV	IP	H	R	ER	HR	BB	SO	AVG
2005	Batavia (NYP)	SS	2	3	2.65	21	0	0	5	34	28	12	10	1	13	51	.224
2006	Lakewood (SAL)	LoA	3	3	3.15	29	0	0	2	46	37	17	16	4	26	52	.223
	Clearwater (FSL)	HiA	5	3	4.10	15	0	0	0	26	20	17	12	5	10	41	.196
2007	Clearwater (FSL)	HiA	4	6	3.82	13	12	0	0	73	67	36	31	10	30	56	.248
	Reading (EL)	AA	6	9	5.90	15	15	0	0	79	92	61	52	10	43	54	.294
2008	Reading (EL)	AA	3	8	5.86	49	1	0	10	78	76	59	51	10	49	73	.245
MINOR LEAGUE TOTALS			23	32	4.60	142	28	0	17	337	320	202	172	40	171	327	.249

27 SERGIO ESCALONA, LHP

BORN: Aug. 3, 1984. **B-T:** L-L. **HT.:** 6-0. **WT.:** 170. **SIGNED:** Venezuela, 2004. **SIGNED BY:** Sal Agostinelli.

Escalona fancied himself an outfielder as an amateur in Venezuela but didn't get anywhere with the bat. He converted to pitching and signed with the Phillies when he was nearly 20 years old. He was a starter in the low minors and a non-factor until 2008, when a move to the bullpen helped him surge through the system. He pitched in both the Arizona Fall League and winter ball in his native Venezuela and earned a spot on the Phillies' 40-man roster. Escalona needs just two pitches, yet has shown three—a fastball with sink at 88-92 mph, a changeup that got better in the AFL, and an inconsistent, raw curveball that he can spin for strikes when he's on. He's shown the hand speed for it to become an average pitch. Club officials use the word "green" to describe Escalona, but he's lefthanded, has shown the ability to get strikeouts and had more than two groundouts for every airout in 2008. It's a good combination of skills for a lefty reliever, and Escalona goes to camp with an outside shot at a big league bullpen spot.

Year	Club (League)	Class	W	L	ERA	G	GS	CG	SV	IP	H	R	ER	HR	BB	SO	AVG
2004	Tronconero 1 (VSL)	R	0	1	1.80	7	0	0	3	10	7	2	2	1	4	7	.226
2005	Phillies (VSL)	R	1	1	2.97	12	8	0	0	36	25	18	12	0	29	34	.203
2006	Phillies (VSL)	R	3	4	2.29	14	12	0	1	71	63	27	18	1	25	71	.239
2007	Clearwater (FSL)	HiA	0	0	2.25	1	1	0	0	4	8	1	1	0	2	4	.444
	Williamsport (NYP)	SS	2	2	7.57	7	7	0	0	27	32	26	23	2	19	26	.302
	Lakewood (SAL)	LoA	1	4	4.15	7	7	0	0	39	51	25	18	4	11	32	.321
2008	Lakewood (SAL)	LoA	5	1	3.43	28	0	0	2	45	36	18	17	1	18	60	.224
	Reading (EL)	AA	0	1	2.22	15	0	0	1	24	27	12	6	3	14	29	.281
MINOR LEAGUE TOTALS			12	14	3.41	91	35	0	7	256	249	129	97	12	122	263	.260

28 TREVOR MAY, RHP

BORN: Sept. 23, 1989. **B-T:** R-R. **HT.:** 6-5. **WT.:** 215. **DRAFTED:** HS—Kelso, Wash., 2008 (4th round). **SIGNED BY:** Dave Ryles.

The Phillies are excited about their pitching class in the 2008 draft, both on the college and high school sides. May ranks ahead of righthander Jon Pettibone, who was taken 26 spots ahead of him, because he's a bit more physical and has a better breaking ball. May follows Julian Sampson in giving the Phillies arguably the top prep pitchers out of Washington the last two years. Other than being righthanded and from the Apple State, though, May has little in common with Sampson. He's a power pitcher with a feel for a good curveball, which plays average but should become a plus pitch as he adds power down the line. May also has shown above-average velocity at times on his fastball, flashing 92-94 mph heat at times but more regularly sitting at 87-90. His arm works well, so he should be able to consistently add velocity. His solid athleticism should allow him to clean up his high-maintenance delivery and develop average control. He will need to work on a changeup as he moves up the ladder, and he made some progress in instructional league. May has a chance to earn a spot in the Lakewood rotation in 2009. His power curve and fastball mark him as a future mid-rotation starter.

Year	Club (League)	Class	W	L	ERA	G	GS	CG	SV	IP	H	R	ER	HR	BB	SO	AVG
2008	Phillies (GCL)	R	1	1	3.75	5	2	0	0	12	11	7	5	0	7	11	.256
MINOR LEAGUE TOTALS			1	1	3.75	5	2	0	0	12	11	7	5	0	7	11	.256

29 MIKE CISCO, RHP

BORN: May 23, 1987. **B-T:** R-R. **HT.:** 5-11. **WT.:** 190. **DRAFTED:** South Carolina, 2008 (36th round). **SIGNED BY:** Roy Tanner.

Cisco's middle name is Galen, hinting at his big league roots. His grandfather Galen pitched parts of seven seasons in the big leagues and was the Phillies' pitching coach from 1997-2000. Mike went 19-10, 4.16 in three seasons at South Carolina, earning a reputation as a soft-tossing strike-thrower. His fastball sat at 84-88 mph, when he threw it. Surprisingly, he signed for $10,000 as a 36th-round pick in June, and then even more surprisingly showed more velocity on his fastball than ever before. South Carolina coach Ray Tanner called Cisco a poor man's Greg Maddux for his ability to command his fastball to all four quadrants, and Cisco did that as a pro. Instead of parking in the mid-80s, however, Cisco's fastball gained velocity as he used it more, peaking at 93-94 mph and usually running from 89-92. He has a feel for pitching and throws strikes with his curveball, changeup and short slider. Cisco's pro debut was a revelation, from his increased stuff to his 30-0 strikeout-walk ratio at Lakewood. He repeats his compact delivery, giving him the best command in the organization. He's likely headed to Clearwater's rotation this year with fellow 2008 draftees Vance Worley and Mike Stutes. He profiles as a middle reliever but could be a fourth or fifth starter if he can maintain his average fastball velocity over a full season.

Year	Club (League)	Class	W	L	ERA	G	GS	CG	SV	IP	H	R	ER	HR	BB	SO	AVG
2008	Williamsport (NYP)	SS	1	0	1.86	9	1	0	0	19	18	5	4	1	5	22	.240
	Lakewood (SAL)	LoA	2	1	0.51	8	6	0	0	35	22	4	2	0	0	30	.173
MINOR LEAGUE TOTALS			3	1	0.99	17	7	0	0	54	40	9	6	1	5	52	.198

30 COLBY SHREVE, RHP

BORN: Jan. 5, 1988. **B-T:** R-R. **HT.:** 6-5. **WT.:** 210. **DRAFTED:** CC of Southern Nevada, 2008 (6th round). **SIGNED BY:** Darrell Conner.

Shreve has yet to even make it through a full season in junior college, and he had Tommy John surgery prior to the 2008 draft. Yet the Phillies took him in the sixth round and paid him an above-slot $400,000 bonus. Shreve has good size, arm strength and fair athleticism. He was a Nevada-Las Vegas recruit, primarily as a third baseman, out of high school but was disappointed when he wasn't drafted and decided to go to junior college instead. He shot up draft boards as a freshman at CC of Southern Nevada, hitting 94-95 mph early in the season, then tumbled as a dead-arm period sapped his velocity. The Braves took him in the eighth round in 2007 but failed to sign him. After entering last season as the nation's top-ranked juco player, he went 5-2, 2.30 and allowed just 23 hits in 47 innings. Yet he broke down in early May and had reconstructive surgery on his elbow. Shreve showed a solid-average slider and life on his fastball prior to his injury. He should be back throwing by midseason and should make his pro debut in the Gulf Coast League, with a chance to jump back on the fast track in 2010.

Year	Club (League)	Class	W	L	ERA	G	GS	CG	SV	IP	H	R	ER	HR	BB	SO	AVG
2008	Did Not Play—Injured																

Pittsburgh Pirates

BY JOHN PERROTTO

The Pirates are likely to set a record for infamy in 2009 as their never-ending rebuilding process continues. Unless they manage to surpass expectations and win 81 games, they'll endure their 17th straight losing season, giving them sole possession of the U.S. major professional sports mark that they currently share with the 1933-48 Phillies.

Pittsburgh went 67-95 last year, its first under a new regime. Frank Coonelly was hired away from his role as Major League Baseball's chief labor lawyer to oversee the franchise as club president. Coonelly installed Indians assistant general manager Neal Huntington as GM. Huntington gave John Russell, manager of the Phillies' Triple-A Ottawa farm club, his first crack as a major league skipper.

The Pirates began another reconstruction under their new administration. Their most visible moves came in late July, when they sent Jason Bay to the Red Sox and Xavier Nady and Damaso Marte to the Yankees in trades that netted eight young players. Craig Hansen, Jeff Karstens, Andy LaRoche, Brandon Moss and Ross Ohlendorf all saw action with the major league club—and no longer qualify for this prospect list—while outfielder Jose Tabata and righthanders Bryan Morris and Daniel McCutchen all rank among the system's top 10 prospects. Following the deals, Pittsburgh went 17-37 while fielding a young lineup over the final two months of the season.

The Pirates showed a new commitment to strengthening their player-development and scouting departments under new leadership in 2008. Huntington named Indians assistant farm director Kyle Stark as farm director and former Tigers scouting director Greg Smith as scouting director.

Pittsburgh began building a new academy in the Dominican Republic that Latin America scouting director Rene Gayo said would be among the nation's top two facilities. The Pirates also spent $9.8 million on draft bonuses, more than any club had ever spent before last summer (albeit the fourth-highest total in 2008).

That total included a $6 million bonus as part of a $6.355 million major league contract for No. 2 overall pick Pedro Alvarez—which included as much drama as it did cash. The Pirates originally announced that Alvarez had agreed to a straight $6 million bonus minutes before the signing deadline on Aug. 15. Twelve days later, agent Scott Boras claimed Alvarez reached his deal two minutes after the midnight deadline, prompting the MLB Players Association to file a griev-

Pittsburgh made trades to bring in more young talent like Andy LaRoche

TOP 30 PROSPECTS

1. Pedro Alvarez, 3b	16. Quinton Miller, rhp
2. Andrew McCutchen, of	17. Chase d'Arnaud, ss
3. Jose Tabata, of	18. Ronald Uviedo, rhp
4. Brad Lincoln, rhp	19. Daniel Moskos, lhp
5. Bryan Morris, rhp	20. Wesley Freeman, of
6. Neil Walker, 3b	21. Steve Lerud, c
7. Jeff Sues, rhp	22. Evan Meek, rhp
8. Shelby Ford, 2b	23. Matt Hague, 3b/1b
9. Daniel McCutchen, rhp	24. Jim Negrych, 3b/2b
10. Robbie Grossman, of	25. Romulo Sanchez, rhp
11. Jamie Romak, of/1b	26. Donald Veal, lhp
12. Jimmy Barthmaier, rhp	27. Brian Bixler, ss/2b
13. Jarek Cunningham, 3b/ss	28. Jason Jaramillo, c
14. Brian Friday, ss	29. Justin Wilson, lhp
15. Jordy Mercer, ss	30. Nelson Pereira, lhp

ance. The two sides eventually settled on Sept. 24 after plenty of rancor between Boras and Coonelly, who conceded afterward that the deal was consummated at 12:02 a.m. on Aug. 16.

In an effort to pump up a woefully thin farm system, the Pirates far exceeded MLB's bonus recommendations to sign a pair of high school seniors: outfielder Robbie Grossman ($1 million in the sixth round) and righthander Quinton Miller ($900,000 in the 20th).

Rule 5 draft selection Donald Veal became the 15th of Pittsburgh's best 30 prospects who joined the organization in 2008.

General Manager: Neal Huntington. **Farm Director:** Kyle Stark. **Scouting Director:** Greg Smith.

Class	Team	League	W	L	PCT	Finish*	Manager	Affiliated
Majors	Pittsburgh	National	67	95	.414	14th (16)	John Russell	—
Triple-A	Indianapolis Indians	International	68	76	.472	9th (14)	Trent Jewett	2005
Double-A	Altoona Curve	Eastern	65	77	.458	9th (12)	Tim Leiper	1999
High A	Lynchburg Hillcats	Carolina	58	80	.420	7th (8)	Jeff Branson	1995
Low A	Hickory Crawdads	South Atlantic	52	87	.374	15th (16)	Gary Green	1999
Short-season	State College Spikes	New York-Penn	18	56	.243	14th (14)	Brad Fischer	1999
Rookie	GCL Pirates	Gulf Coast	37	19	.661	1st (16)	Tom Prince	1967

Overall 2008 Minor League Record 298 395 .430 29th

*Finish in overall standings (No. of teams in league). ^League champion.

LAST YEAR'S TOP 30

Rank	Player, Pos.	Status
1.	Andrew McCutchen, of	No. 2
2.	Neil Walker, 3b	No. 6
3.	Steve Pearce, 1b/of	Majors
4.	Brad Lincoln, rhp	No. 4
5.	Daniel Moskos, lhp	No. 19
6.	Shelby Ford, 2b	No. 8
7.	Jamie Romak, of	No. 11
8.	Brian Bixler, ss/2b	No. 27
9.	Duke Welker, rhp	Dropped out
10.	Brad Corley, of	Dropped out
11.	Tony Watson, lhp	Dropped out
12.	Brian Friday, ss	No. 14
13.	Romulo Sanchez, rhp	No. 25
14.	Bryan Bullington, rhp	(Blue Jays)
15.	Nyjer Morgan, of	Majors
16.	Olivo Astacio, rhp	(Free agent)
17.	Jimmy Barthmaier, rhp	No. 12
18.	Josh Sharpless, rhp	(Giants)
19.	Evan Meek, rhp	No. 22
20.	Andrew Walker, c	Dropped out
21.	Austin McClune, of	Dropped out
22.	Quincy Latimore, of	Dropped out
23.	Dave Davidson, lhp	Dropped out
24.	Pat Bresnehan, rhp	Dropped out
25.	Yoslan Herrera, rhp	Dropped out
26.	Marcus Davis, of	Dropped out
27.	Todd Redmond, rhp	(Braves)
28.	Justin Byler, 1b	Dropped out
29.	Jason Delaney, 1b/of	Dropped out
30.	Luis Munoz, rhp	(Mariners)

BEST TOOLS

Best Hitter for Average	Pedro Alvarez
Best Power Hitter	Pedro Alvarez
Best Strike-Zone Discipline	Jim Negrych
Fastest Baserunner	Jose de los Santos
Best Athlete	Andrew McCutchen
Best Fastball	Jeff Sues
Best Curveball	Brad Lincoln
Best Slider	Daniel Moskos
Best Changeup	Ronald Uviedo
Best Control	Daniel McCutchen
Best Defensive Catcher	Steve Lerud
Best Defensive Infielder	Luis Cruz
Best Infield Arm	Jordy Mercer
Best Defensive Outfielder	Andrew McCutchen
Best Outfield Arm	Austin McClune

PROJECTED 2012 LINEUP

Catcher	Ryan Doumit
First Base	Adam LaRoche
Second Base	Shelby Ford
Third Base	Pedro Alvarez
Shortstop	Jarek Cunningham
Left Field	Nate McLouth
Center Field	Andrew McCutchen
Right Field	Jose Tabata
No. 1 Starter	Brad Lincoln
No. 2 Starter	Ian Snell
No. 3 Starter	Bryan Morris
No. 4 Starter	Paul Maholm
No. 5 Starter	Tom Gorzelanny
Closer	Matt Capps

TOP PROSPECTS OF THE DECADE

Year	Player, Pos.	2008 Org.
1999	Chad Hermansen, of	Mets
2000	Chad Hermansen, of	Mets
2001	J.R. House, c	Astros
2002	J.R. House, c	Astros
2003	John Van Benschoten, rhp	Pirates
2004	John Van Benschoten, rhp	Pirates
2005	Zach Duke, lhp	Pirates
2006	Neil Walker, c	Pirates
2007	Andrew McCutchen, of	Pirates
2008	Andrew McCutchen, of	Pirates

TOP DRAFT PICKS OF THE DECADE

Year	Player, Pos.	2008 Org.
1999	Bobby Bradley, rhp	Out of baseball
2000	Sean Burnett, lhp	Pirates
2001	John Van Benschoten, rhp	Pirates
2002	Bryan Bullington, rhp	Indians
2003	Paul Maholm, lhp	Pirates
2004	Neil Walker, c	Pirates
2005	Andrew McCutchen, of	Pirates
2006	Brad Lincoln, rhp	Pirates
2007	Daniel Moskos, lhp	Pirates
2008	Pedro Alvarez, 3b	Pirates

LARGEST BONUSES IN CLUB HISTORY

Pedro Alvarez, 2008	$6,000,000
Bryan Bullington, 2002	$4,000,000
Brad Lincoln, 2006	$2,750,000
Daniel Moskos, 2007	$2,475,000
John Van Benschoten, 2001	$2,400,000

PITTSBURGH PIRATES

TOP 2009 ROOKIE: Jeff Sues, rhp. Now that he has a healthy shoulder, he should add a needed power arm to the bullpen.

BREAKOUT PROSPECT: Jarek Cunningham, 3b/ss. The Pirates got a steal in the 18th round of the 2008 draft because he had knee issues, but he's healthy and had an outstanding debut.

SLEEPER: Duke Welker, rhp. If he can toughen up his secondary pitches and mound presence, the 2007 second-rounder should rebound from a 4-13, 5.51 disaster in low Class A last season.

SOURCE OF TOP 30 TALENT			
Homegrown	20	Acquired	10
College	12	Trades	5
Junior college	0	Rule 5 draft	2
High school	7	Independent leagues	0
Draft-and-follow	0	Free agents/waivers	3
Nondrafted free agents	0		
International	1		

Numbers in parentheses indicate prospect rankings.

LF
Jared Keel
Eric Huber
Miles Durham

CF
Andrew McCutchen (2)
Robbie Grossman (10)
Wesley Freeman (20)
Austin McClune
Quincy Latimore
Edwin Roman

RF
Jose Tabata (3)
Matt Hague (23)
Brad Corley
Butch Biela

3B
Pedro Alvarez (1)
Neil Walker (6)
Eddie Prasch
Jeremy Farrell

SS
Jarek Cunningham (13)
Brian Friday (14)
Jordy Mercer (15)
Chase D'Arnaud (17)
Luis Cruz
Benji Gonzalez

2B
Shelby Ford (8)
Jim Negrych (24)
Brian Bixler (27)
Matt Cavagnaro

1B
Jamie Romak (11)
Jason Delaney
Calvin Anderson

C
Steve Lerud (21)
Jason Jaramillo (28)
Robinzon Diaz
Andrew Walker

RHP

Starters	Relievers
Brad Lincoln (4)	Jeff Sues (7)
Bryan Morris (5)	Ronald Uviedo (18)
Daniel McCutchen (9)	Evan Meek (22)
Jimmy Barthmaier (12)	Romulo Sanchez (25)
Quinton Miller (16)	Pat Bresnehan
Duke Welker	Eric Krebs
Derek Hankins	Moises Robles
Jared Hughes	Tom Boleska
Mike Crotta	Brent Klinger
Brad Clapp	
Jose Rafael de los Santos	
Matt McSwain	
Jose Diaz	
Kyle McPherson	
Brian Leach	

LHP

Starters	Relievers
Justin Wilson (29)	Daniel Moskos (19)
Nelson Periera (30)	Donald Veal (26)
Tony Watson	Dave Davidson
Zach Oliver	Mike Williams

2008

BEST PURE HITTER: 3B Pedro Alvarez (1) has a polished approach at the plate and repeats his strong, balanced swing well.

BEST POWER HITTER: Alvarez has the strength in his hands and forearms to produce excellent bat speed and could hit 30 or more homers annually. Being able to hit for average and power made him the No. 1 prospect in the 2008 draft class.

FASTEST RUNNER: The fastest member of the Puerto Rico draft class, OF Edwin Roman (27) has run 6.4-second 60-yard dashes and is a 7 runner on the 2-8 scouting scale.

BEST DEFENSIVE PLAYER: The Pirates drafted three shortstops with defensive chops, led by Puerto Rico's Benji Gonzalez (7), who has smooth hands and an above-average arm. Jordy Mercer (3) and Chase d'Arnaud (4) are also strong defenders with athleticism and body control.

BEST FASTBALL: RHP Quinton Miller (20) has reached 95, prompting the Pirates to buy him away from a North Carolina commitment with a $900,000 bonus.

BEST SECONDARY PITCH: Miller's slider has future plus potential. LHP Justin Wilson (4) came on late and helped Fresno State to the national championship after incorporating a solid-average slider into his four-pitch repertoire.

BEST PRO DEBUT: 3B/SS Jarek Cunningham (18) hit .318/.385/.507 to lead the Rookie-level Gulf Coast League Pirates to a playoff berth. 3B/1B Matt Hague (9) showed an advanced bat, hitting .322/.386/.467, mostly with low Class A Hickory.

BEST ATHLETE: OF Wesley Freeman (16) has a prototype body with raw tools, strength and speed. OF Robbie Grossman (6), signed for $1 million, has solid all-around tools and athletic ability.

MOST INTRIGUING BACKGROUND: First baseman Calvin Anderson (12) is the son of former Pittsburgh Steelers defensive lineman Fred Anderson. Anderson was a backup on the Steelers' Super Bowl champions in 1978 and 1979 before becoming a part-time starter with the Seattle Seahawks.

BEST LATE-ROUND PICK: Cunningham dropped off many draft boards because of a spring knee injury but returned for two state playoff games, and the Pirates stayed on him, signing him away from Arizona State. They're also high on Freeman, Miller and RHP Brent Klinger (21), whose fastball reaches 94 mph from a low three-quarters slot.

THE ONE WHO GOT AWAY: RHP Tanner Scheppers (2) would have been a top-10 pick if he hadn't hurt his shoulder, and he still wanted that kind of bonus. The Pirates closely monitored him during the summer but ultimately didn't meet his price. The former Fresno State ace signed with the independent St. Paul Saints (American Association).

ASSESSMENT: The Pirates gambled and tried to get the top bat and one of the top college arms in the same draft. Alvarez will make or break the draft, especially with Scheppers going unsigned. Late-rounders such as Cunningham, Freeman, Miller and Klinger could soften the blow.

2007

The decision to take LHP Daniel Moskos (1) over Matt Wieters with the No. 4 overall pick helped cost former GM Dave Littlefield his job. SS Brian Friday (3) is the best prospect from this disappointing crop.

GRADE: D

2006

RHP Brad Lincoln (1) is bouncing back from Tommy John surgery, while 2B Shelby Ford (3) could be starting for the Pirates in another year. Unsigned SS Lonnie Chisenhall (11) became a first-rounder in 2008.

GRADE: C

2005

OF Andrew McCutchen (1) was by far Pittsburgh's best first-round pick of the decade until Pedro Alvarez came along. SS Brent Lillibridge (4) was an astute choice but was traded to the Braves. RHP Jeff Sues (5) is a sleeper.

GRADE: B

2004

3B Neil Walker (1) has lost value after moving from catcher and slumping in Triple-A. SS/2B Brian Bixler (2) has a chance to become a utilityman.

GRADE: D

---

*Draft analysis by John Manuel (2008) and Jim Callis (2004-07). Numbers in parentheses indicate draft rounds. *Bonuses for 2004-05 are first 10 rounds only.*

BILL MITCHELL

PEDRO ALVAREZ, 3B

Born: Feb. 6, 1987.
Bats: L. **Throws:** R.
Ht.: 6-2. **Wt.:** 225.
Drafted: Vanderbilt,
2008 (1st round).
Signed by: Trevor Haley.

Though his family lived in a two-bedroom apartment and his father drove a delivery cab, Alvarez decided to attend Vanderbilt rather than sign with the Red Sox for sandwich-round money as a 14th-round pick in 2005. He went on to have a storied career with the Commodores, winning Baseball America's 2006 Freshman of the Year award and earning All-America honors in his first two seasons. He entered his junior year rated as the top prospect in the 2008 draft and maintained that distinction despite missing 23 games when an errant pitch broke the hamate bone in his right hand in Vanderbilt's season opener. The Rays passed on Alvarez with the No. 1 overall pick because they already had Evan Longoria. The Pirates, who famously passed on Scott Boras client Matt Wieters in the 2007 draft, didn't hesitate to take Alvarez at No. 2 despite reports Boras was seeking a $9 million major league contract. Pittsburgh announced that Alvarez had agreed to a club-record $6 million bonus shortly before the Aug. 15 signing deadline, but 12 days later Boras claimed Alvarez hadn't signed until 12:02 a.m. After the MLB Players Association filed a grievance, the two sides settled it on Sept. 24, with Alvarez receiving the same bonus as part of a $6.355 million contract. (Club president Frank Coonelly later acknowledged that Alvarez had signed two minutes after the deadline.) He saw his first action with the Pirates in instructional league.

Alvarez's quick hands allow him to let the ball travel deep into the strike zone and enable him to draw comparisons to Albert Pujols. While he doesn't have a lot of loft in his swing, his bat speed and strength allow him to hit with power to all fields. He has an advanced, professional approach at the plate and makes consistent hard contact. Alvarez's best defensive tool is his strong arm and the Pirates believe he'll be a solid third baseman. He shows fairly quick feet for a big man and has worked hard to improve his defense. Despite his contentious negotiations, he has a reputation for outstanding character and leadership.

The biggest question with Alvarez is whether he can stay at third base. He'll have to work hard to maintain his range and agility, which are just decent, and some scouts think he'll be forced to move to an outfield corner or first base. He reported to instructional league overweight, adding fuel to the idea that a position switch could be in his future. He's a below-average runner but moves well enough that he doesn't clog the bases.

Alvarez has the talent and charisma to become the face of a struggling franchise that has lacked star power since Barry Bonds left as a free agent following the 1992 season. Pittsburgh hopes to build a lineup around him that can end a streak of losing seasons that began after Bonds departed. Alvarez likely will start his pro career at high Class A Lynchburg and could make his big league debut by September. He almost certainly will be the Pirates' starting third baseman in 2010.

Year	Club (League)	Class	AVG	G	AB	R	H	2B	3B	HR	RBI	BB	SO	SB	OBP	SLG
2008	Did Not Play—Signed Late															

2 ANDREW McCUTCHEN, OF

BORN: Oct. 10, 1986. **B-T:** R-R. **HT.:** 5-11. **WT.:** 175. **DRAFTED:** HS—Fort Meade, Fla., 2005 (1st round). **SIGNED BY:** Rob Sidwell.

McCutchen ranked No. 1 on this list the past two years, as well as in the Rookie-level Gulf Coast League in 2005 and the low Class A South Atlantic League in 2006. He reached Double-A as a teenager and rated as the No. 2 prospect in the Triple-A International League, where managers tabbed him as the league's most exciting player. McCutchen has quick hands and recognizes pitches extremely well, giving him the ability to wait for the ball to get deeper in the zone while drawing his share of walks. He has outstanding speed that makes him a basestealing threat and a potential Gold Glover. He has outstanding instincts and an average arm in center field. McCutchen is susceptible to breaking pitches, in part because he gets pull-happy, and his power hasn't developed as hoped. He's slow getting out of the batter's box, which prevents him from getting as many infield hits as his speed suggests he should. He still has work to do as a basestealer after leading all Triple-A players by getting caught 19 times in 2008. Though he's the Pirates' center fielder of the near future, McCutchen is slated to return to Indianapolis to start the season. He once looked like a No. 3 hitter but now profiles as a leadoff man.

Year	Club (League)	Class	AVG	G	AB	R	H	2B	3B	HR	RBI	BB	SO	SB	OBP	SLG
2005	Pirates (GCL)	R	.297	45	158	36	47	9	3	2	30	29	24	13	.411	.430
	Williamsport (NYP)	SS	.346	13	52	12	18	3	1	0	5	8	6	4	.443	.442
2006	Hickory (SAL)	LoA	.291	114	453	77	132	20	4	14	62	42	91	22	.356	.446
	Altoona (EL)	AA	.308	20	78	12	24	4	0	3	12	8	20	1	.379	.474
2007	Altoona (EL)	AA	.258	118	446	70	115	20	3	10	48	44	83	17	.327	.383
	Indianapolis (IL)	AAA	.313	17	67	7	21	4	0	1	5	4	11	4	.347	.418
2008	Indianapolis (IL)	AAA	.283	135	512	75	145	26	3	9	50	68	87	34	.372	.398
MINOR LEAGUE TOTALS			.284	462	1766	289	502	86	14	39	212	203	322	95	.362	.415

3 JOSE TABATA, OF

BORN: Aug. 12, 1988. **B-T:** R-R. **HT.:** 5-11. **WT.:** 160. **SIGNED:** Venezuela, 2005. **SIGNED BY:** Ricardo Finol (Yankees).

Once the Yankees' top position prospect, Tabata fell out of favor last April. Upset by a slow start, he left Double-A Trenton in the middle of a game and was suspended for three games. New York traded him along with Jeff Karstens, Ross Ohlendorf and righthander Daniel McCutchen to acquire Xavier Nady and Damaso Marte in July. After recovering from a strained hamstring, Tabata regained his luster with a strong August. Tabata has strong, quick wrists, which make his current gap power likely to turn into home run pop as his body matures. He's an above-average defender who gets good jumps in center field and has the arm strength to play in right. He has average speed. Though Tabata didn't have any issues after the trade, he still has to live down a reputation for having attitude problems and being unreliable. He tends to chase breaking pitches out of the zone. He has slowed down as his body has matured and probably will end up as a below-average runner. The Pirates are leaning toward sending Tabata back to Double-A Altoona to start 2009, but he should reach Triple-A and perhaps the majors by the end of the year. They're convinced he can be a star, and he certainly looked like one after the trade.

Year	Club (League)	Class	AVG	G	AB	R	H	2B	3B	HR	RBI	BB	SO	SB	OBP	SLG
2005	Yankees (GCL)	R	.314	44	156	30	49	5	1	3	25	15	14	22	.382	.417
2006	Charleston (SAL)	LoA	.298	86	319	50	95	22	1	5	51	30	66	15	.377	.420
2007	Tampa (FSL)	HiA	.307	103	411	56	126	16	2	5	54	33	70	15	.371	.392
2008	Trenton (EL)	AA	.248	79	294	40	73	9	0	3	36	26	49	10	.320	.310
	Pirates (GCL)	R	.455	4	11	4	5	1	0	2	7	2	0	0	.538	1.091
	Altoona (EL)	AA	.348	22	89	16	31	6	2	3	13	8	18	8	.402	.562
MINOR LEAGUE TOTALS			.296	338	1280	196	379	59	6	21	186	114	217	70	.366	.401

4 BRAD LINCOLN, RHP

BORN: May 25, 1985. **B-T:** L-R. **HT.:** 6-0. **WT.:** 215. **DRAFTED:** Houston, 2006 (1st round). **SIGNED BY:** Everett Russell.

The fourth overall pick in the 2006 draft, Lincoln signed for $2.75 million. He needed Tommy John surgery the following April, joining a long list of Pirates first-round picks to suffer a major arm injury. After missing the entire 2007 season, he came back last year and made 19 starts without any problems. Lincoln has two plus pitches in a 90-93 mph fastball that touches 95 and a power curveball that he can either bury in the strike zone or make hitters chase. A good athlete who was an excellent hitter in college, he has no problem throwing stirkes. He's an outstanding competitor who relishes challenging hitters. Lincoln isn't very tall and at times he has to fight to keep his arm slot high and throw his pitches on a downhill plane. He tends to catch too much of the strike zone at times, making him susceptible to home runs. His changeup isn't as effective as his other pitches and needs more consistency. The Pirates believe Lincoln is close to major league-ready and will send him to Double-A. He could be in their Opening Day rotation in 2010 and should eventually settle in as a No. 2 or 3 starter.

Year	Club (League)	Class	W	L	ERA	G	GS	CG	SV	IP	H	R	ER	HR	BB	SO	AVG
2006	Pirates (GCL)	R	0	0	0.00	2	2	0	0	8	6	1	0	0	1	9	.222
	Hickory (SAL)	LoA	1	2	6.75	4	4	0	0	16	25	15	12	2	6	10	.368
2007	Did Not Play—Injured																
2008	Hickory (SAL)	LoA	5	5	4.65	11	11	0	0	62	72	34	32	8	6	46	.288
	Lynchburg (CAR)	HiA	1	5	4.75	8	8	1	0	42	42	24	22	5	11	29	.259
MINOR LEAGUE TOTALS			7	12	4.66	25	25	1	0	127	145	74	66	15	24	94	.286

5 BRYAN MORRIS, RHP

BORN: March 28, 1987. **B-T:** L-R. **HT.:** 6-3. **WT.:** 200. **DRAFTED:** Motlow State (Tenn.) CC, 2006 (1st round). **SIGNED BY:** Marty Lamb (Dodgers).

In the three-way trade that sent Jason Bay to the Red Sox and Manny Ramirez to the Dodgers, the Pirates acquired three big leaguers (Andy LaRoche from Los Angeles, Craig Hansen and Brandon Moss from Boston) and Morris. Like Brad Lincoln, Morris was a 2006 first-rounder who missed all of 2007 following Tommy John surgery. The Pirates shut him down late last season when he felt some shoulder pain. Morris' similarities to Lincoln extend to his stuff and his background as a two-way standout in college. He has a live arm and regained full velocity on his fastball after surgery, sitting at 91-93 mph and touching 95. His hard, big-breaking curveball is his money pitch. He scores points for his competitiveness and work ethic. Pittsburgh attributes Morris' shoulder soreness to simple fatigue, but he still will have to prove he can hold up over a full season. As with many young pitchers, his changeup is a work in progress. His mechanics aren't quite ideal, and he sometimes struggles to repeat them and flies open in his delivery. He lacks consistent control and command at this point. One of the few high-ceiling arms in the system, Morris likely will begin 2009 in high Class A. He could move quickly once he starts throwing strikes. He figures to be a fixture in the middle of Pittsburgh's rotation in time, but he'll get a late start to the 2009 season as he recovers from offseason surgery to repair a ligament in his right big toe.

Year	Club (League)	Class	W	L	ERA	G	GS	CG	SV	IP	H	R	ER	HR	BB	SO	AVG
2006	Ogden (PIO)	R	4	5	5.13	14	14	0	0	60	64	44	34	3	40	79	.267
2007	Did Not Play—Injured																
2008	Great Lakes (MWL)	LoA	2	4	3.20	17	17	1	0	82	74	34	29	5	31	72	.247
	Hickory (SAL)	LoA	0	2	5.02	3	3	0	0	14	17	9	8	2	12	11	.288
MINOR LEAGUE TOTALS			6	11	4.10	34	34	1	0	156	155	87	71	10	83	162	.259

6 NEIL WALKER, 3B

BORN: Sept. 10, 1985. **B-T:** B-R. **HT.:** 6-3. **WT.:** 217. **DRAFTED:** HS—Gibsonia, Pa., 2004 (1st round). **SIGNED BY:** Jon Mercurio.

Originally signed as a catcher for $1.95 million with the 12th overall pick in 2004, Walker moved to third base on the first day of spring training in 2007. He has made a smooth transition defensively but has hit the wall offensively in Triple-A. The first-ever Pirates first-rounder from the Pittsburgh area, he's the son of an ex-big leaguer (Tom) and the nephew of another (Chip Lang). A switch-hitter, Walker has pop from both sides of the plate but needs to display it with more consistency. Recruited by college football programs as a wide receiver, he has outstanding athleticism and a strong arm at the hot corner. Managers rated him the International League's best defensive third baseman last season. He's an average runner with good instincts on the bases. He's intelligent and works hard. Walker has been inconsistent throughout his career and has yet to put up a truly big season. His plate discipline never has been strong and fell apart last season. He seemed to panic if he fell behind in the count and chased too many pitches outside the zone. Walker lost some of his value when he moved from behind the plate, and his future at third base is clouded after the Pirates drafted Pedro Alvarez and traded for Andy LaRoche. Ticketed to return to Triple-A, Walker eventually could wind up in right field because of his athletic ability and strong arm.

Year	Club (League)	Class	AVG	G	AB	R	H	2B	3B	HR	RBI	BB	SO	SB	OBP	SLG
2004	Pirates (GCL)	R	.271	52	192	28	52	12	3	4	20	10	33	3	.313	.427
	Williamsport (NYP)	SS	.313	8	32	2	10	3	0	0	7	2	1	1	.343	.406
2005	Hickory (SAL)	LoA	.301	120	485	78	146	33	2	12	68	20	71	7	.332	.452
	Lynchburg (CAR)	HiA	.262	9	42	4	11	2	1	0	12	0	12	0	.244	.357
2006	Lynchburg (CAR)	HiA	.284	72	264	32	75	22	1	3	35	19	41	3	.345	.409
	Altoona (EL)	AA	.161	10	31	5	5	0	0	2	3	1	4	0	.188	.355
2007	Altoona (EL)	AA	.288	117	431	77	124	30	3	13	66	53	73	9	.362	.462

	Club (League)	Class	AVG	G	AB	R	H	2B	3B	HR	RBI	BB	SO	SB	OBP	SLG
	Indianapolis (IL)	AAA	.203	19	64	7	13	3	0	0	0	2	13	1	.261	.250
2008	Indianapolis (IL)	AAA	.242	133	505	69	122	25	7	16	80	29	102	10	.280	.414
MINOR LEAGUE TOTALS			.273	540	2046	302	558	130	17	50	291	136	350	34	.320	.426

7 JEFF SUES, RHP

BORN: June 8, 1983. **B-T:** R-R. **HT.:** 6-4. **WT.:** 228. **DRAFTED:** Vanderbilt, 2005 (5th round). **SIGNED BY:** Jack Powell.

Just before he was scheduled to make his first pro start in 2005, Sues injured his shoulder. Following surgery and a long rehab, he finally made his debut in mid-2007. The Pirates made him a reliever last season and were enthused by the results. Sues throws extremely hard, as his fastball sits at 93-95 mph and tops out at 98. He has added velocity now that he no longer has to pace himself coming out of the bullpen. He also has a power curveball and has the competitive nature to thrive in the late innings. Sues tends to throw first-pitch fastballs a little too often and Pittsburgh would like him to go with his curveball more often early in counts to keep hitters off balance. While he's hard to hit, he's too generous with walks. His changeup is mediocre but rarely comes into play in his new role. Pretty much a finished product, Sues will get the opportunity to win a middle-relief job with Pittsburgh this spring. If he doesn't make the team, he'll go to Triple-A and be groomed as a potential closer. He's more overpowering if not as polished as Pirates incumbent Matt Capps.

Year	Club (League)	Class	W	L	ERA	G	GS	CG	SV	IP	H	R	ER	HR	BB	SO	AVG
2006	Did Not Play—Injured																
2007	Hickory (SAL)	LoA	3	2	7.18	8	8	0	0	31	37	26	25	9	19	26	.294
2008	Lynchburg (CAR)	HiA	1	1	2.11	13	0	0	2	21	11	6	5	3	6	17	.153
	Altoona (EL)	AA	3	1	3.77	24	0	0	1	43	35	19	18	3	20	55	.219
MINOR LEAGUE TOTALS			7	4	4.52	45	8	0	3	96	83	51	48	15	45	98	.232

8 SHELBY FORD, 2B

BORN: Dec. 15, 1984. **B-T:** B-R. **HT.:** 6-3. **WT.:** 190. **DRAFTED:** Oklahoma State, 2006 (3rd round). **SIGNED BY:** Mike Leuzinger.

Ford has been productive as a pro when he's been able to stay healthy. He sat out the final month of 2007 with a strained lower back and missed the first six weeks of 2008 with a strained hip flexor. He went on the disabled list again for two weeks in late July with a high ankle sprain. Ford is an offense-first second baseman with good gap power from both sides of the plate. While he's not a burner, he runs well and uses above-average instincts to steal bases or stretch extra-base hits. He has shown improvement defensively at second base. Ford still is mastering the nuances of second base, such as the double-play pivot, after playing on the left side of the infield in college. He needs to do a better job of turning on fastballs on the inner half of the plate. He makes good contact but doesn't walk enough. Ford will begin this season in Triple-A, one step away if the Pirates decide to trade Freddy Sanchez, who can become a free agent at the end of 2009 if he doesn't trigger playing-time clauses in his contract. Ford is clearly the heir apparent at second base.

Year	Club (League)	Class	AVG	G	AB	R	H	2B	3B	HR	RBI	BB	SO	SB	OBP	SLG
2006	Williamsport (NYP)	SS	.400	7	25	3	10	3	0	0	2	3	3	1	.483	.520
	Hickory (SAL)	LoA	.265	55	223	43	59	16	3	6	27	14	51	4	.329	.444
2007	Lynchburg (CAR)	HiA	.281	94	360	64	101	26	7	5	55	34	68	14	.360	.433
2008	Altoona (EL)	AA	.282	81	319	44	90	22	10	4	32	21	48	19	.335	.451
MINOR LEAGUE TOTALS			.280	237	927	154	260	67	20	15	116	72	170	38	.348	.444

9 DANIEL McCUTCHEN, RHP

BORN: Sept. 26, 1982. **B-T:** R-R. **HT.:** 6-2. **WT.:** 195. **DRAFTED:** Oklahoma, 2006 (13th round). **SIGNED BY:** Mark Batchko (Yankees).

One of four players acquired from the Yankees in the late-July trade for Xavier Nady and Damaso Marte, McCutchen spent part of September with the major league club but didn't get activated. The Pirates didn't want to have to place him on the 40-man roster and wanted him to rest after pitching 171 innings in the minors. McCutchen has good control of a three-pitch arsenal and has averaged a mere 2.0 walks per nine innings as a pro. His best pitch is a fastball that sits at 90-91 mph and occasionally reaches 93. He also has a hard curveball that breaks quickly, almost like a slider. McCutchen still needs to work on his command. He's hittable and prone to giving up homers—he surrendered 12 in 48 innings after the trade—because he sometimes catches too much of the plate with his fastball. His changeup is just serviceable and could use more polish. McCutchen doesn't have a lot left to prove in the minors and will compete for a spot in Pittsburgh's rotation during spring training. He eventually should become a No. 3 or No. 4 starter in the majors.

Year	Club (League)	Class	W	L	ERA	G	GS	CG	SV	IP	H	R	ER	HR	BB	SO	AVG
2006	Staten Island (NYP)	SS	1	0	1.13	2	2	0	0	8	4	1	1	1	1	11	.148
	Charelston, SC (SAL)	LoA	1	0	2.14	7	0	0	1	21	13	5	5	2	5	18	.186
2007	Tampa (FSL)	HiA	11	2	2.50	17	16	0	0	101	86	29	28	7	21	67	.236
	Trenton (EL)	AA	3	2	2.41	7	7	0	0	41	30	11	11	2	12	36	.205
2008	Trenton (EL)	AA	4	3	2.55	9	9	0	0	53	43	16	15	4	18	52	.219
	Scranton/W-B (IL)	AAA	4	6	3.58	11	11	2	0	70	73	32	28	10	11	58	.265
	Indianapolis (IL)	AAA	3	3	4.69	8	8	0	0	48	49	25	25	12	7	41	.261
MINOR LEAGUE TOTALS			27	16	2.97	61	53	2	1	342	298	119	113	38	75	283	.235

10 ROBBIE GROSSMAN, OF

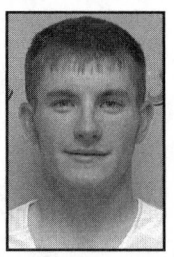

BORN: Sept., 16, 1989. **B-T:** B-L. **HT.:** 6-1. **WT.:** 190. **DRAFTED:** HS—Cypress, Texas, 2008 (6th round). **SIGNED BY:** Mike Leuzinger.

After leading Cy-Fair High to the Texas state 5-A title, topping the U.S. junior national team in hitting (.450) and excelling on the showcase circuit in 2007, Grossman looked like a potential first-round pick. He dropped to the sixth round last June after he committed to Texas and didn't have as strong a senior season. The Pirates loved his athleticism and signed him for $1 million. Grossman has good gap power from both sides of the plate and knows how to turn on a pitch, especially as a lefthanded hitter. He impressed Pirates scouts by homering over the right-field bleachers at PNC Park during a workout last summer. He's also willing to take a walk when he's pitched around. Grossman has good instincts on the bases and in the field and shows enough range to play center field, though he isn't a burner. Whether Grossman can be a long-term center fielder is in question after he lost a step between his junior and senior seasons, with his plus speed becoming average. He has a below-average arm, which means he would have to go to left field if he can't stick in center. With a good showing in spring training, Grossman could begin his first full season at Pittsburgh's new low Class A West Virginia affiliate. He reminds some scouts of center fielder Nate McLouth, who made the all-star team and won a Gold Glove in his first full season as a Pirates starter.

Year	Club (League)	Class	AVG	G	AB	R	H	2B	3B	HR	RBI	BB	SO	SB	OBP	SLG
2008	Pirates (GCL)	R	.188	5	16	3	3	1	0	0	1	4	7	1	.381	.250
MINOR LEAGUE TOTALS			.188	5	16	3	3	1	0	0	1	4	7	1	.381	.250

11 JAMIE ROMAK, OF/1B

BORN: Sept. 30, 1985. **B-T:** R-R. **HT.:** 6-2. **WT.:** 220. **DRAFTED:** HS—London, Ont., 2003 (4th round). **SIGNED BY:** Lonnie Goldberg (Braves).

Romak began his career in the Braves organization and came to the Pirates before the 2007 season with Adam LaRoche in a deal for Mike Gonzalez and Brent Lillibridge. Romak missed the first month of the 2008 season recovering from offseason elbow surgery, but he progressed quickly enough when he returned that he was promoted to Double-A for the final month of the season. He's a three-true-outcomes player, as he hits his fair share of home runs, draws lots of walks and strikes out a ton. His power and patience stand out in a system that lacks hitters with those skills, though he has a tendency to be too passive at the plate, taking hittable pitches. Romak is below-average as a defender and runner. He started off as a third baseman with the Braves and had played primarily left field in recent years. He played solely first base for the first time in his career after moving up to Altoona. He'll return there to start the 2009 season but likely will see time in Triple-A later in the year. He projects as a potential middle-of-the-order hitter in the major leagues if he can find a way to make contact more consistently.

Year	Club (League)	Class	AVG	G	AB	R	H	2B	3B	HR	RBI	BB	SO	SB	OBP	SLG
2003	Braves (GCL)	R	.176	19	51	5	9	2	0	0	4	9	10	0	.300	.216
2004	Danville (APP)	R	.190	48	158	25	30	5	1	5	22	14	56	1	.287	.329
2005	Danville (APP)	R	.274	34	124	25	34	10	1	7	27	14	38	2	.368	.540
2006	Rome (SAL)	LoA	.247	108	348	55	86	26	2	16	68	59	102	3	.369	.471
2007	Hickory (SAL)	LoA	.275	20	69	16	19	4	0	5	15	9	24	0	.393	.551
	Lynchburg (CAR)	HiA	.252	85	294	49	74	21	1	15	45	55	90	2	.380	.483
2008	Lynchburg (CAR)	HiA	.279	77	290	58	81	25	0	18	57	32	95	0	.360	.552
	Altoona (EL)	AA	.208	33	120	15	25	6	0	7	23	17	32	0	.312	.433
MINOR LEAGUE TOTALS			.246	424	1454	248	358	99	5	73	261	209	447	8	.355	.472

12 JIMMY BARTHMAIER, RHP

BORN: Jan. 6, 1984. **B-T:** R-R. **HT.:** 6-5. **WT.:** 240. **DRAFTED:** HS—Roswell, Ga., 2003 (13th round). **SIGNED BY:** Ellis Dungan (Astros).

The Pirates claimed Barthmaier off waivers from the Astros following the 2007 season, and he made his major league debut last June. He's a hard thrower, as his fastball routinely reaches 91-93 mph and can touch 96—though without much movement. Managers rated his hard curve, which usually hovers around 85 mph and drops off the table, as the best breaking ball in the International League last season. He still needs work on his changeup, though it did improve in 2008. Barthmaier is a good athlete who planned to play quarterback at Louisiana State before signing with the Astros for $750,000 as a 13th-rounder in 2003. That bonus still remains the record for that round. He tends to lose confidence at times, and some have questioned his work ethic, though it hasn't been an issue with the Pirates. Barthmaier will be in the mix for a spot in the Pittsburgh rotation in spring training, but he could use more time in Triple-A and won't be expected to reach the majors for good until 2010.

Year	Club (League)	Class	W	L	ERA	G	GS	CG	SV	IP	H	R	ER	HR	BB	SO	AVG
2003	Martinsville (APP)	R	1	1	2.49	8	3	0	0	22	19	9	6	0	7	18	.226
2004	Greeneville (APP)	R	4	3	3.78	13	13	0	0	69	70	32	29	3	22	65	.262
2005	Lexington (SAL)	LoA	11	6	2.27	25	25	0	0	135	108	41	34	3	55	142	.220
	Salem (CAR)	HiA	1	0	1.50	1	0	0	0	6	4	4	1	1	1	6	.167
2006	Salem (CAR)	HiA	11	8	3.62	27	27	0	0	147	137	64	59	6	67	134	.252
2007	Corpus Christi (TEX)	AA	2	9	6.20	24	16	0	0	90	116	73	62	11	44	73	.312
2008	Altoona (EL)	AA	2	4	4.86	10	10	0	0	46	42	27	25	3	21	40	.240
	Indianapolis (IL)	AAA	3	1	3.53	16	16	0	0	79	69	34	31	5	27	71	.235
	Pittsburgh (NL)	MAJ	0	2	10.45	3	3	0	0	10	16	12	12	3	8	6	.364
MINOR LEAGUE TOTALS			35	32	3.75	124	110	0	0	593	565	284	247	32	244	549	.251
MAJOR LEAGUE TOTALS			0	2	10.45	3	3	0	0	10	16	12	12	3	8	6	.364

13 JAREK CUNNINGHAM, 3B/SS

BORN: Dec. 25, 1989. **B-T:** R-R. **HT.:** 6-1. **WT.:** 185. **DRAFTED:** HS—Spokane, Wash., 2008 (18th round). **SIGNED BY:** Greg Hopkins.

Cunningham missed his senior high school season in 2008 because of a knee injury, which caused him to slip to the 18th round of the draft. Doctors originally thought he had torn his anterior cruciate ligament and meniscus, yet when he went in for surgery they found the ACL had reattached itself. The Pirates were thrilled to sign Cunningham away from Arizona State for $100,000. In his debut, they had him play third base in addition to shortstop (his high school position) in order to increase his versatility and reduce strain on his knee, which held up fine. Cunningham has gap power and should hit a fair number of homers as he adds size and strength. He also has a chance to be a plus defender at shortstop because he has good range and an above-average arm. His arm strength makes him a fit at third base if he outgrows shortstop. Cunningham spent part of the offseason at the Athletes Performance Institute in Phoenix, which could give him a head start on winning a spot in low Class A to open 2009. He has the physical ability to move quickly through the system, though a conservative timetable has him making his major league debut in 2012.

Year	Club (League)	Class	AVG	G	AB	R	H	2B	3B	HR	RBI	BB	SO	SB	OBP	SLG
2008	Pirates (GCL)	R	.318	43	148	20	47	11	1	5	22	14	26	2	.385	.507
MINOR LEAGUE TOTALS			.318	43	148	20	47	11	1	5	22	14	26	2	.385	.507

14 BRIAN FRIDAY, SS

BORN: Dec. 16, 1985. **B-T:** R-R. **HT.:** 5-11. **WT.:** 180. **DRAFTED:** Rice, 2007 (3rd round). **SIGNED BY:** Everett Russell.

Friday jumped two levels to high Class A to begin his first full year in the minor leagues, but a promising start was short-circuited by back problems in June. He never was the same and then struggled in Hawaii Winter Baseball as well. A first-team All-American after his sophomore season at Rice, Friday profiles as a top-of-the-order hitter with his ability to work the count and draw walks. He's also an outstanding bunter and is willing to use that skill as a weapon. He doesn't have much power but he knows that isn't his game. He has slightly above-average speed but still is learning how to use it to become a true basestealing threat. Friday is an average defensive shortstop whose strong point is an above-average arm that allows him to make plays from deep in the hole. While he has decent range, he has a tendency to lay back on grounders and allow them to eat him up. The Pirates are giving Friday a mulligan on 2008 because of his strained back. They'll continue to aggressively promote him and he'll begin this season in Double-A, making it a possibility he could reach the major leagues by 2010.

Year	Club (League)	Class	AVG	G	AB	R	H	2B	3B	HR	RBI	BB	SO	SB	OBP	SLG
2007	State College (NYP)	SS	.295	40	156	31	46	10	1	2	13	10	33	6	.371	.410
2008	Pirates (GCL)	R	.182	7	22	2	4	0	1	0	3	2	3	0	.280	.273
	Lynchburg (CAR)	HiA	.287	85	341	59	98	20	4	2	29	34	56	16	.365	.387
MINOR LEAGUE TOTALS			.285	132	519	92	148	30	6	4	45	46	92	22	.363	.389

15 JORDY MERCER, SS

BORN: Aug. 27, 1986. **B-T:** R-R. **HT.:** 6-3. **WT.:** 192. **DRAFTED:** Oklahoma State, 2008 (3rd round). **SIGNED BY:** Matt Bimeal.

The top prospect in Oklahoma for the 2008 draft, Mercer signed for $508,000 as a third-rounder and advanced to low Class A after just a brief stop at short-season State College. He's an offense-first shortstop with pop, a departure from the Pirates' past philosophy of drafting middle infielders who had speed and defensive ability but were often light in the hitting department. Mercer can pull the ball and also go gap-to-gap. However, his plate discipline is severely lacking, and pro pitchers got him to consistently chase high fastballs and breaking balls in the dirt. Mercer is bigger than most shortstops but has good range, above-average instincts and an outstanding arm that prompted Oklahoma State to use him as its closer, with a fastball clocked as high as 95 mph. Yet shortstop is one of the few positions where the Pirates have depth, so Mercer eventually could move to third base or a corner outfield spot. He'll remain at shortstop for now, though, and begin his first full season in high Class A.

Year	Club (League)	Class	AVG	G	AB	R	H	2B	3B	HR	RBI	BB	SO	SB	OBP	SLG
2008	State College (NYP)	SS	.250	6	24	5	6	1	1	1	2	1	3	1	.280	.500
	Hickory (SAL)	LoA	.250	50	192	21	48	7	0	4	18	12	44	4	.300	.349
MINOR LEAGUE TOTALS			.250	56	216	26	54	8	1	5	20	13	47	5	.297	.366

16 QUINTON MILLER, RHP

BORN: Nov. 28, 1989. **B-T:** R-R. **HT.:** 6-1. **WT.:** 185. **DRAFTED:** HS—Medford, N.J., 2008 (20th round). **SIGNED BY:** Buddy Paine.

Miller was regarded as a top-five-rounds talent heading into 2008 but was considered a difficult sign because of his commitment to North Carolina. When he fell to the 20th round, the Pirates took a shot and signed him for $900,000 right before the Aug. 15 deadline. Miller's fastball has been clocked as high as 95 mph, though it was generally in the 86-89 range during his senior high school season. The Pirates expect him to achieve more consistent velocity as his body fills out. His fastball is far ahead of his slider and changeup, but he has a good aptitude for pitching and gets high marks for his competitiveness. Pittsburgh believes his slider will become a plus pitch in time. Some scouts raise red flags, though, because they say Miller is a health risk. He missed part of his junior season with a shoulder impingement and has a high-stress, maximum-effort delivery, something the Pirates are working to tone down. He'll likely begin 2009 in extended spring training because he has yet to throw a pitch as a pro. He's a project, but the Pirates have few power arms in their system and are willing to wait for him to develop.

Year	Club (League)	Class	W	L	ERA	G	GS	CG	SV	IP	H	R	ER	HR	BB	SO	AVG
2008	Did Not Play—Signed Late																

17 CHASE D'ARNAUD, SS

BORN: Jan. 21, 1987. **B-T:** R-R. **HT.:** 6-1. **WT.:** 175. **DRAFTED:** Pepperdine, 2008 (4th round). **SIGNED BY:** Rick Allen.

D'Arnaud, whose younger brother Travis is a Phillies catching prospect, moved to shortstop last season at Pepperdine after spending his first two seasons as a third baseman. He handled the position, which raised his draft stock and earned him a $293,000 bonus as a fourth-rounder. After signing, he missed nearly a month with a sprained foot, but he came back and finished the year on a good note. D'Arnaud has good gap power and puts the bat on the ball consistently. He has a tendency to get overanxious at the plate, which causes problems with offspeed pitches, particularly from righthanders. D'Arnaud is considered an average defender at shortstop at this point but does show good range and a strong arm. He was a standout at third base in college and could end up there because the Pirates have shortstop depth in their system. His speed is a tick above-average, and he makes the most of it by being aggressive on the basepaths. D'Arnaud will make his full-season debut in low Class A and he could see action at second or third base, both to increase his versatility and in deference to Jarek Cunningham, who has better pure shortstop tools.

Year	Club (League)	Class	AVG	G	AB	R	H	2B	3B	HR	RBI	BB	SO	SB	OBP	SLG
2008	State College (NYP)	SS	.286	43	168	26	48	10	5	1	21	11	30	14	.333	.423
MINOR LEAGUE TOTALS			.286	43	168	26	48	10	5	1	21	11	30	14	.333	.423

18 RONALD UVIEDO, RHP

BORN: Oct. 7, 1986. **B-T:** R-R. **HT.:** 6-2. **WT.:** 150. **SIGNED:** Venezuela, 2004. **SIGNED BY:** Luis Martinez (Mariners).

The Pirates signed Uviedo after he was released by the Mariners out of the Rookie-level Venezuelan Summer League in 2005. He made his domestic debut in 2007 as the closer at State College, then had a breakout year in 2008 and won a spot on the 40-man roster. Uviedo is rail-thin, but his fastball reaches 95 mph and sits at 91-93 with good movement. He also has a good, hard slider, though it puts quite a bit of torque on his arm, which is a concern. The Pirates asked him to work on his changeup and it became an average offering by the end of last season. Uviedo is an extreme fly-ball pitcher, working up in the zone with his fastball, so he's susceptible to home runs. Further improving his changeup is imperative because it would give him a pitch to induce more groundballs. He has good control and doesn't beat himself with walks. Uviedo will start 2009 back in high Class A, where he ended 2008, and could get to the majors quickly as a reliever.

Year	Club (League)	Class	W	L	ERA	G	GS	CG	SV	IP	H	R	ER	HR	BB	SO	AVG
2004	Aguirre (VSL)	R	2	1	5.81	11	2	0	0	31	44	23	20	2	13	20	.333
2005	Mariners (VSL)	R	4	3	2.76	12	10	1	0	62	42	22	19	2	17	52	.193
2006	Pirates (VSL)	R	2	0	2.02	25	0	0	11	36	31	13	8	1	10	44	.233
2007	Lynchburg (CAR)	HiA	0	0	4.09	4	0	0	0	11	9	5	5	2	3	7	.225
	State College (NYP)	SS	2	0	3.92	21	0	0	12	21	16	9	9	4	3	26	.216
	Hickory (SAL)	LoA	0	0	9.00	3	0	0	0	3	3	3	3	1	2	7	.250
2008	Hickory (SAL)	LoA	3	1	3.01	33	0	0	5	72	70	31	24	8	15	76	.248
	Lynchburg (CAR)	HiA	0	0	2.25	7	0	0	0	16	5	4	4	1	5	12	.094
MINOR LEAGUE TOTALS			13	5	3.30	116	12	1	28	251	220	110	92	21	68	244	.233

19 DANIEL MOSKOS, LHP

BORN: April 28, 1986. **B-T:** R-L. **HT.:** 6-1. **WT.:** 210. **DRAFTED:** Clemson, 2007 (1st round). **SIGNED BY:** Greg Schilz.

Moskos' pro career couldn't have started much worse. Through no fault of his own, Moskos became a lightning rod for frustrated Pirates fans after the braintrust of former general manager David Littlefield took him instead of Georgia Tech catcher Matt Wieters with the No. 4 overall pick in the 2007 draft. Littlefield thought Wieters would command a $12 million contract, though he settled for $6 million from the Orioles, who took him one pick after Moskos. While Wieters was Baseball America's Minor League Player of the Year in 2008, Moskos has a 5.64 ERA through the first 126 innings of his career. He has lost velocity since college as his fastball rarely has topped 90 mph in pro ball, and the wipeout slider that was his best pitch at Clemson has flattened out. His control was shaky at times, too, which didn't help. Moskos looked like a potential late-inning reliever coming out of college, though he started in high Class A last season in order to get innings. He moved to the bullpen after posting a horrid 11.81 ERA in July and was better in relief, where he didn't have to use his less-effective curveball and changeup as much. If his performance doesn't improve, he'll project as a situational lefthander, which is not what Pittsburgh had in mind when it signed him for $2.475 million.

Year	Club (League)	Class	W	L	ERA	G	GS	CG	SV	IP	H	R	ER	HR	BB	SO	AVG
2007	Pirates (GCL)	R	0	0	0.00	2	0	0	0	3	4	0	0	0	0	3	.333
	State College (NYP)	SS	0	0	4.26	11	0	0	1	13	19	8	6	1	6	13	.328
2008	Lynchburg (CAR)	HiA	7	7	5.95	29	20	0	0	110	124	83	73	8	43	78	.284
MINOR LEAGUE TOTALS			7	7	5.64	42	20	0	1	126	147	91	79	9	49	94	.291

20 WESLEY FREEMAN, OF

BORN: Jan. 29, 1990. **B-T:** R-R. **HT.:** 6-4. **WT.:** 215. **DRAFTED:** HS—Lakeland, Fla., 2008 (16th round). **SIGNED BY:** Joe Salermo.

Freeman was considered a tough sign because of a commitment to play at Central Florida, so he slipped to the 16th round in last year's draft. He had a change of heart when the Golden Knights made a coaching change and signed for $150,000. Freeman could turn out to be a five-tool talent, with an outstanding overall package that includes power potential and good speed. He is raw as a hitter at this point, but the slight lift in his swing and his natural strength portend possible plus power. Freeman has a hitch in his stroke that makes it hard to catch up to good fastballs, though he smoothed it out in instructional league. He chases down fly balls in center field with pure speed now, but is learning the nuances of the position, including taking proper routes. While his strong arm and large frame suggest a right-field profile, his speed could keep him in center and gives him a chance to be an above-average basestealer. Freeman will go back to the Gulf Coast League to start the season, and the Pirates will let him hone his game at his own pace.

Year	Club (League)	Class	AVG	G	AB	R	H	2B	3B	HR	RBI	BB	SO	SB	OBP	SLG
2008	Pirates (GCL)	R	.182	6	22	1	4	1	0	0	2	1	4	0	.250	.227
MINOR LEAGUE TOTALS			.182	6	22	1	4	1	0	0	2	1	4	0	.250	.227

21 STEVE LERUD, C

BORN: Oct. 13, 1984. **B-T:** L-R. **HT.:** 6-1. **WT.:** 215. **DRAFTED:** HS—Reno, Nev., 2003 (4th round). **SIGNED BY:** Jaron Madison.

Lerud finished his high school career as the leading home run hitter in Nevada prep history, breaking Matt Williams' record. His move through the Pirates system was initially slowed by injuries that included a broken foot and broken hand, but he showed enough last year to earn a midseason promotion to Double-A and a spot on the 40-man roster after the season. Because of the scarcity of catchers, Pittsburgh feared losing him in the major league Rule 5 draft. Lerud hasn't hit as well as a pro as he did in high school, but he has pop and has improved his plate discipline. He has worked hard on his defense, showing softer hands and nimbler footwork since being drafted. He has a solid arm and threw out 34 percent of basestealers last season. He has below-average speed and is a station-to-station runner on the bases. Lerud is a bright player with a lot of baseball savvy and could be a manager when his playing days are over. As a lefthanded hitter with power and defensive skills, he has positioned himself to have a major league career as at least a backup.

Year	Club (League)	Class	AVG	G	AB	R	H	2B	3B	HR	RBI	BB	SO	SB	OBP	SLG
2004	Pirates (GCL)	R	.246	48	175	22	43	12	1	5	20	11	38	0	.297	.411
	Williamsport (NYP)	SS	.241	8	29	2	7	0	0	0	2	4	6	0	.353	.241
2005	Hickory (SAL)	LoA	.088	25	80	6	7	2	2	2	13	4	27	0	.149	.238
	Pirates (GCL)	R	.267	18	60	13	16	3	1	2	15	7	13	0	.351	.450
	Williamsport (NYP)	SS	.125	10	32	3	4	0	0	1	2	2	14	0	.176	.219
2006	Hickory (SAL)	LoA	.239	117	393	45	94	28	0	12	57	40	146	4	.330	.402
2007	Lynchburg (CAR)	HiA	.202	84	287	27	58	17	1	4	31	31	63	3	.299	.310
2008	Lynchburg (CAR)	HiA	.256	67	234	36	60	14	0	8	40	26	65	1	.344	.419
	Altoona (EL)	AA	.233	47	146	17	34	7	0	4	18	14	42	1	.302	.363
MINOR LEAGUE TOTALS			.225	424	1436	171	323	83	5	38	198	139	414	9	.308	.369

22 EVAN MEEK, RHP

BORN: May 12, 1983. **B-T:** R-R. **HT.:** 6-0. **WT.:** 220. **DRAFTED:** Bellevue (Wash.) CC, D/F 2002. **SIGNED BY:** Bill Lohr (Twins).

The Pirates selected Meek from the Rays in the major league Rule 5 draft following the 2007 season, and he made their Opening Day roster last season. He struggled to get major league hitters out, but Pittsburgh was able to send him back to the minors and keep him by working out a cash deal with Tampa Bay. Meek is well-traveled, having also spent time in the Twins and Padres organizations, but still has upside. He features a sinking fastball that sits at 91-93 mph and touches 96. It enables him to continually get hitters to beat the ball into the ground. Control long has been Meek's problem, particularly with his slider and splitter, and it hampered him in the majors last season because hitters wouldn't chase his secondary pitches. Meek's delivery has a lot of moving parts, which causes concern because of the stress it puts on his arm. He's also excitable and fights to control his emotions on the mound. Meek showed enough raw ability last season that he'll get another shot at making the Pirates in spring training, and he has a good chance of winning a job as a middle man.

Year	Club (League)	Class	W	L	ERA	G	GS	CG	SV	IP	H	R	ER	HR	BB	SO	AVG
2003	Elizabethton (APP)	R	7	1	2.47	14	8	0	1	51	33	15	14	2	24	47	.178
2004	Quad City (MWL)	LoA	0	0	11.12	3	3	0	0	6	7	7	7	0	15	3	.333
	Elizabethton (APP)	R	1	2	8.06	12	3	0	0	22	18	26	20	1	25	23	.228
2005	Beloit (MWL)	LoA	0	1	10.00	13	0	0	0	18	15	26	20	0	36	11	.231
2006	Lake Elsinore (CAL)	HiA	6	6	4.98	26	25	0	0	119	136	80	66	5	62	113	.288
	Visalia (CAL)	HiA	0	1	9.00	2	0	0	0	5	6	5	5	0	4	7	.300
2007	Montgomery (SL)	AA	2	1	4.30	44	0	0	1	67	74	36	32	2	34	69	.287
2008	Pittsburgh (NL)	MAJ	0	1	6.92	9	0	0	0	13	11	11	10	3	12	7	.239
	Altoona (EL)	AA	1	1	2.81	9	0	0	2	16	14	5	5	0	3	17	.237
	Indianapolis (IL)	AAA	0	0	2.40	23	0	0	2	41	30	12	11	2	14	34	.196
MINOR LEAGUE TOTALS			17	13	4.69	146	39	0	6	346	333	212	180	12	217	324	.254
MAJOR LEAGUE TOTALS			0	1	6.92	9	0	0	0	13	11	11	10	3	12	7	.239

23 MATT HAGUE, 3B/1B

BORN: Aug. 20, 1985. **B-T:** R-R. **HT.:** 6-3. **WT.:** 225. **DRAFTED:** Oklahoma State, 2008 (9th round). **SIGNED BY:** Matt Bimeal.

After playing three years at Washington and turning down the Indians as an 11th-round pick in 2007, Hague transferred to Oklahoma State and went two rounds higher in the 2008 draft, signing for $25,000. He produced with the bat throughout his college career and again in his pro debut, earning a quick promotion to low Class A. Hague has good power potential and the ability to pull the ball over the fence. He has good plate discipline, is willing to take a walk and rarely chases bad pitches. Hague's best defensive attribute is a strong arm at third base—he flashed a 94-mph fastball in relief stints in college—but his lack of first-step quickness and inconsistent footwork make it a strong possibility he could wind up switching positions. A logical move would be to right field, where his arm would play and his feet wouldn't be a problem, and he saw time at first base in his pro debut. He's a below-average runner and athlete, so most of his value is going to come from his bat, no matter where he plays. Hague will open 2009 at third base in high Class A but could find a new defensive home before the end of the year.

Year	Club (League)	Class	AVG	G	AB	R	H	2B	3B	HR	RBI	BB	SO	SB	OBP	SLG
2008	State College (NYP)	SS	.333	7	27	6	9	3	0	0	3	3	5	0	.400	.444
	Hickory (SAL)	LoA	.321	57	215	25	69	14	0	6	29	20	28	1	.384	.470
MINOR LEAGUE TOTALS			.322	64	242	31	78	17	0	6	32	23	33	1	.386	.467

24 JIM NEGRYCH, 3B/2B

BORN: March 2, 1985. **B-T:** L-R. **HT.:** 5-10. **WT.:** 180. **DRAFTED:** Pittsburgh, 2006 (6th round). **SIGNED BY:** Jon Mercurio.

Completely healthy for the first time since being drafted in 2006 from Pittsburgh—where he was the Panthers' first-ever baseball All-American—Negrych was the Pirates' minor league player of the year last season. After missing part of 2006 following thumb surgery and part of 2007 with a strained oblique, he won the high Class A Carolina League batting title with a .370 average and hit well in Double-A in August. Negrych is essentially a one-tool player, but his ability to hit for average is exceptional as he has a knack for putting the bat on the ball. Managers said he had the best strike-zone judgment in the Carolina League last season, and one veteran scout said Negrych reminded him of Wade Boggs at the same stage of his career. He has no more than doubles power, however, and is a below-average runner and poor defender. He has a weak arm and little range at second base, and he wasn't a good fit at third base, which he tried last year to see if he could have a future as a utilityman. Negrych will begin this season back in Altoona and will go as far as his bat takes him.

Year	Club (League)	Class	AVG	G	AB	R	H	2B	3B	HR	RBI	BB	SO	SB	OBP	SLG
2006	Williamsport (NYP)	SS	.267	42	146	12	39	7	2	2	17	13	19	1	.327	.384
2007	Hickory (SAL)	LoA	.282	86	340	57	96	14	4	2	48	27	48	4	.340	.365
2008	Lynchburg (CAR)	HiA	.370	104	386	77	143	36	1	5	62	55	55	7	.448	.508
	Altoona (EL)	AA	.310	25	87	10	27	5	0	0	10	11	14	5	.394	.368
MINOR LEAGUE TOTALS			.318	257	959	156	305	62	7	9	137	106	136	17	.388	.425

25 ROMULO SANCHEZ, RHP

BORN: April 28, 1984. **B-T:** R-R. **HT.:** 6-5. **WT.:** 260. **SIGNED:** Venezuela, 2002. **SIGNED BY:** Camilo Pascual/Doug Carpenter (Dodgers).

The Pirates pulled Sanchez off the scrap heap, signing him in 2004 after the Dodgers released him following two seasons in the Venezuelan Summer League. He reached the major leagues with the Pirates three years later and had another stint in Pittsburgh last season. Sanchez is a big, intimidating presence whose fastball reaches 98 mph, though it usually sits at 92-94. His curveball has improved significantly in recent years, giving him a second quality offering, which is all he needs in relief. He still struggles to command his changeup. While Sanchez throws hard, he also lacks a great feel for pitching and has control lapses that keep him from dominating. He also tends to put on weight, and the Pirates sent him out to minor league camp early in spring training last year because he reported out of shape. Sanchez has the talent to be a big league reliever if he rounds off the rough edges. He'll likely start this season back in Triple-A.

Year	Club (League)	Class	W	L	ERA	G	GS	CG	SV	IP	H	R	ER	HR	BB	SO	AVG
2002	Dodgers E (DSL)	R	1	4	4.44	15	0	0	1	24	24	16	12	4	10	22	.242
2003	Dodgers E (DSL)	R	2	3	4.46	9	9	0	0	38	40	25	19	1	10	21	.255
2004	San Joaquin (VSL)	R	4	2	1.03	21	2	1	6	44	33	9	5	0	7	49	.202
2005	Pirates (GCL)	R	1	0	1.80	2	1	0	0	10	7	2	2	1	4	7	.206
	Altoona (EL)	AA	1	0	3.60	2	2	0	0	10	11	4	4	2	4	5	.282
	Hickory (SAL)	LoA	3	3	4.70	10	10	0	0	54	59	34	28	5	19	24	.292
2006	Hickory (SAL)	LoA	0	3	7.08	21	3	0	4	41	51	36	32	4	18	28	.302
	Lynchburg (CAR)	HiA	0	0	1.04	8	0	0	1	9	7	1	1	0	4	6	.212
	Altoona (EL)	AA	0	0	5.00	8	0	0	0	9	8	5	5	1	8	5	.242
2007	Altoona (EL)	AA	6	3	2.81	40	0	0	1	58	43	24	18	8	17	52	.204
	Pittsburgh (NL)	MAJ	1	0	5.00	16	0	0	0	18	16	10	10	2	8	11	.254
2008	Indianapolis (IL)	AAA	5	1	3.46	33	0	0	4	55	50	27	21	5	19	32	.248
	Pittsburgh (NL)	MAJ	0	0	4.05	10	0	0	1	13	14	6	6	0	6	3	.292
MINOR LEAGUE TOTALS			23	19	3.77	169	27	1	17	351	333	183	147	31	120	251	.248
MAJOR LEAGUE TOTALS			1	0	4.60	26	0	0	1	31	30	16	16	2	14	14	.270

26 DONALD VEAL, LHP

BORN: Sept, 18, 1984. **B-T:** L-L. **HT.:** 6-4. **WT.:** 230. **DRAFTED:** Pima (Ariz.) CC, 2005 (2nd round). **SIGNED BY:** Steve McFarland (Cubs).

Veal was one of the best lefthanded pitching prospects in the game in 2006, when he led all minor league starters with a .175 opponent average. But he since has hit the wall hard in Double-A, struggling so much that the Cubs didn't bother to protect him on their 40-man roster because they didn't think he had any chance to stick with a big league club. The Pirates did take him in the Rule 5 draft, and now they have to keep him on their active big league roster in 2009 or expose him to waivers and offer him back to Chicago. When he was on top of his game, Veal got swings and misses by locating his low-90s fastball to both sides of the plate and confounding hitters with a deceptive delivery that included a big leg kick. He also flashed a plus curveball and a solid changeup. Two years later, he looks like an entirely different pitcher. He'll still touch 94 mph with his heater, but he usually works at 89-90 and doesn't maintain his velocity for more than a couple of innings. His curveball is usually a sweepy pitch with little power and only occasional spin, and he has trouble repeating his changeup.

He can't maintain his mechanics, leading to control and command problems. He has led the Southern League in walks in each of the last two seasons. The Cubs planned on trying him as a reliever, but he got hammered in that role in the Arizona Fall League. On top of all of his pitching problems, Veal also has had to cope with the loss of his mother to cancer in 2004 and his father to a scuba-diving accident three years later. He has had to raise his younger brother Devin, a wide receiver at the University of Arizona. Veal has the raw talent to become a No. 2 starter, but the key word is "raw." He'll be a project for pitching coach Joe Kerrigan in spring training.

Year	Club (League)	Class	W	L	ERA	G	GS	CG	SV	IP	H	R	ER	HR	BB	SO	AVG
2005	Cubs (AZL)	R	0	1	5.06	4	3	0	0	11	8	6	6	2	5	14	.205
	Boise (NWL)	SS	1	2	2.48	7	6	0	0	29	18	11	8	2	15	34	.180
2006	Peoria (MWL)	LoA	5	3	2.69	14	14	0	0	74	45	26	22	4	40	86	.179
	Daytona (FSL)	HiA	6	2	1.67	14	14	0	0	81	46	18	15	3	42	88	.170
2007	Tennessee (SL)	AA	8	10	4.97	28	27	0	0	130	126	80	72	11	73	131	.256
2008	Tennessee (SL)	AA	5	10	4.52	29	29	0	0	145	150	89	73	19	81	123	.276
MINOR LEAGUE TOTALS			25	28	3.76	96	93	0	0	470	393	230	196	41	256	476	.232

27 BRIAN BIXLER, SS/2B

BORN: Oct. 22, 1982. **B-T:** R-R. **HT.:** 6-1. **WT.:** 198. **DRAFTED:** Eastern Michigan, 2004 (2nd round). **SIGNED BY:** Duane Gustavson.

In 2007, Bixler was the International League's all-star shortstop, then helped Team USA win the World Cup in Taiwan following the regular season. He encored with a disappointing 2008, looking overmatched in his major league debut. A lack of plate discipline long has limited Bixler, especially considering his offensive game is predicated on making contact and using his above-average speed. Big league pitchers carved him up by overpowering him with fastballs and getting him to chase offspeed stuff out of the strike zone. Bixler can steal bases but was tentative on the basepaths in the major leagues. He's an average defensive shortstop, though he struggled with routine plays in the majors and could get passed on Pittsburgh's depth chart by better defenders. A telling sign came when Luis Cruz, who had spent eight seasons in the minors, saw more action than Bixler last September when Jack Wilson was out with a broken finger. Bixler also has experience at second base, and scouts say his fringy arm and range are better suited to the position. He now profiles as a utilityman and will compete with Cruz for a backup infield spot on the major league club in spring training.

Year	Club (League)	Class	AVG	G	AB	R	H	2B	3B	HR	RBI	BB	SO	SB	OBP	SLG
2004	Williamsport (NYP)	SS	.276	59	228	40	63	7	4	0	21	15	51	14	.321	.342
2005	Hickory (SAL)	LoA	.281	126	502	74	141	23	2	9	50	38	134	21	.343	.388
2006	Lynchburg (CAR)	HiA	.303	73	267	46	81	16	2	5	33	35	58	18	.402	.434
	Altoona (EL)	AA	.301	60	226	36	68	13	1	3	19	16	57	6	.363	.407
2007	Indianapolis (IL)	AAA	.274	129	475	77	130	23	10	5	51	54	131	28	.368	.396
2008	Indianapolis (IL)	AAA	.280	86	321	44	90	8	5	7	36	27	107	23	.346	.402
	Pittsburgh (NL)	MAJ	.157	50	108	16	17	2	1	0	2	6	36	1	.229	.194
MINOR LEAGUE TOTALS			.284	533	2019	317	573	90	24	29	210	185	538	110	.357	.395
MAJOR LEAGUE TOTALS			.157	50	108	16	17	2	1	0	2	6	36	1	.229	.194

28 JASON JARAMILLO, C

BORN: Oct. 9, 1982. **B-T:** B-R. **HT.:** 6-0. **WT.:** 200. **DRAFTED:** Oklahoma State, 2004 (2nd round). **SIGNED BY:** Paul Scott (Phillies).

Ronny Paulino fell out of favor with the Pirates when he slumped offensively and put on weight after he lost the big league catching job to Ryan Doumit in 2008. After Paulino attracted interest with a strong winter in the Dominican League, Pittsburgh swapped him to the Phillies for Jaramillo. He doesn't have an especially quick bat but he should hit for a decent average while providing gap power from both sides of the plate. He doesn't have much home run power and is a well-below-average runner, though he'll draw a few walks. Jaramillo stands out more with his defense. He has a slightly above-average arm and threw out 36 percent of basestealers last season. He has good receiving skills and moves well behind the plate. Jaramillo, who played for Pirates manager John Russell at Triple-A Ottawa in 2007, profiles as a backup and will compete with Robinzon Diaz for that role in spring training.

Year	Club (League)	Class	AVG	G	AB	R	H	2B	3B	HR	RBI	BB	SO	SB	OBP	SLG
2004	Phillies (GCL)	R	.667	1	3	1	2	0	0	0	1	0	0	0	.667	.667
	Batavia (NYP)	SS	.223	31	112	11	25	5	0	1	14	12	27	0	.299	.295
2005	Lakewood (SAL)	LoA	.304	119	448	46	136	28	4	8	63	44	72	2	.368	.438
2006	Reading (EL)	AA	.248	93	322	35	80	25	1	6	39	32	55	0	.320	.388
	Scranton/W-B (IL)	AAA	.167	2	6	0	1	0	0	0	1	0	1	0	.143	.167
2007	Ottawa (IL)	AAA	.271	118	435	52	118	13	4	6	56	50	79	0	.350	.361
2008	Lehigh Valley (IL)	AAA	.266	115	421	48	112	20	0	8	39	42	82	1	.340	.371
MINOR LEAGUE TOTALS			.271	479	1747	193	474	91	9	29	213	180	316	3	.343	.384

29 JUSTIN WILSON, LHP

BORN: Aug, 18, 1987. **B-T:** L-L. **HT.:** 6-2. **WT.:** 210. **DRAFTED:** Fresno State, 2008 (5th round). **SIGNED BY:** Sean Campbell.

Wilson was one of the heroes of Fresno State's improbable College World Series championship last season, allowing one run and striking out nine in eight innings to beat Georgia in the clincher. He was drafted in the fifth round before the CWS, and he increased his bonus demands after starring in Omaha. He agreed to terms with the Pirates two days before the Aug. 15 signing deadline, getting $195,000—$2,000 below MLB's slot recommendation. Wilson struggled to command his four-pitch repertoire in college and will need to throw more strikes to be successful as a pro. His fastball has good life and has been clocked as high as 93 mph, though it usually sits at 87-89. He also has two breaking pitches, a curveball that breaks sharply and a slider with a shorter break. He has struggled to throw a changeup, and improving it was a point of emphasis during instructional league. Wilson is advanced enough to start this season in low Class A. He could get to the majors quickly if he can dial in his command.

Year	Club (League)	Class	W	L	ERA	G	GS	CG	SV	IP	H	R	ER	HR	BB	SO	AVG
2008	Did Not Play—Signed Late																

30 NELSON PEREIRA, LHP

BORN: Feb. 12, 1989. **B-T:** L-L. **HT.:** 5-11. **WT.:** 180. **SIGNED:** El Salvador, 2006. **SIGNED BY:** Rene Gayo.

Pereira is the only Latin American player originally signed by the Pirates who's on this Top 30, though that could change in coming years if shortstop Andury Acevedo and outfielders Starling Marte and Rogelio Noris continue to progress. Pereira had a successful U.S. debut in 2008, making the transition that so many Pirates international prospects have struggled with in recent years. He has worked both as a starter and in relief, and he has a chance to stick in a rotation thanks to his three-pitch mix. Pereira has a firm fastball in the low-80s, but he gets hitters out with his above-average curveball and changeup. The Pirates think he could add velocity to his fastball as his body matures, though he's undersized and durability could become an issue. Pereira will get a shot at a full-season job with West Virginia in spring training, and he has a chance to make history as the first native of El Salvador to play in the majors.

Year	Club (League)	Class	W	L	ERA	G	GS	CG	SV	IP	H	R	ER	HR	BB	SO	AVG
2006	Pirates (VSL)	R	3	5	2.95	17	9	0	0	58	53	34	19	1	20	39	.244
2007	Pirates (VSL)	R	10	1	2.33	14	12	0	1	66	54	23	17	2	18	59	.220
2008	Pirates (GCL)	R	6	2	1.62	13	6	0	0	50	41	20	9	3	10	46	.219
MINOR LEAGUE TOTALS			19	8	2.33	44	27	0	1	174	148	77	45	6	48	144	.228

St. Louis Cardinals

BY DERRICK GOOLD

Cardinals manager Tony La Russa coaxed 86 wins out of a youth-dotted roster in 2008

The Cardinals had followed a tried and true pattern over the past decade, contending with veteran-laden teams and using their farm system to provide an occasional supplement or, more frequently, to bring back older players in trades.

Since 2005, St. Louis has pledged to restock and lean on its system to do what it long had counted on free agents and trades for. The initiative became more prominent—and more pressing—following the firing of general manager Walt Jocketty and the promotion of assistant GM John Mozeliak to replace him at the end of the 2007 season. At the same time, Jeff Luhnow became the overseer of both scouting and player development.

Mozeliak worked to break down the walls that had developed in the front office and get everyone pulling in the same direction. He determined to clear the way for prospects to get to the majors. If there was a need, a prospect was promoted. The same practice will be in place for 2009, when the Cardinals expect the arrival of outfielder Colby Rasmus and a handful of nearly-ready pitchers.

They went into 2008 viewing it as a transition year and performed slightly better than expected, finishing 86-76, though they missed the playoffs in consecutive years for the first time since 1998-99. More important to the organization's long-term plan, 11 Cardinals made their major league debuts, including the first members of the 2004, 2005 and 2006 draft classes to reach St. Louis.

Righthanders Clayton Mortensen and Jess Todd, two of the team's first four picks in the 2007 draft, also made compelling bids for September callups, personifying the team's plan to push its prospects. What had been an internal suggestion to accelerate the development of prospects became a policy.

"We had to promote players more quickly than planned in 2007 because of injuries and, to be honest, I was surprised at how well our players played when they moved up," Luhnow said. "It gave me and us collectively more confidence that, hey, maybe we can push these guys faster."

Mortensen finished his first full season in Triple-A, as did Todd, who opened in high Class A. Lefthander Jaime Garcia started the year in Double-A and ended it in the major league bullpen (though he had Tommy John surgery after the season). Triple-A third baseman David Freese and 2005 third-round outfielder Daryl Jones both blossomed.

TOP 30 PROSPECTS

1. Colby Rasmus, of	16. Tyler Greene, ss
2. Brett Wallace, 3b	17. P.J. Walters, rhp
3. Chris Perez, rhp	18. Niko Vasquez, ss
4. Jess Todd, rhp	19. Roberto de la Cruz, 3b
5. Bryan Anderson, c	20. Fernando Salas, rhp
6. Clayton Mortensen, rhp	21. Francisco Samuel, rhp
7. Daryl Jones, of	22. Adam Ottavino, rhp
8. Jason Motte, rhp	23. Tyler Herron, rhp
9. David Freese, 3b	24. Richard Castillo, rhp
10. Pete Kozma, ss	25. Steven Hill, 1b/of/c
11. Adam Reifer, rhp	26. Allen Craig, 3b
12. Jon Jay, of	27. Tony Cruz, c/3b
13. Jaime Garcia, lhp	28. Shane Robinson, of
14. Mitchell Boggs, rhp	29. Luke Gregerson, rhp
15. Lance Lynn, rhp	30. Nick Additon, lhp

Throughout the system, the Cardinals' prospect push resulted in their affiliates having among the youngest rosters in their league. And youth still served. Their top six affiliates finished with winning records.

St. Louis' first-round pick in June, Brett Wallace, will be on the fast track, as he's expected to arrive in 2010. The Cardinals also showed a newfound aggression on the international market, handing out the three highest bonuses in franchise history for Latin American outfielders. Those investments were highlighted by a $1.1 million bonus for Dominican infielder Robert de la Cruz.

General Manager: John Mozeliak. **Farm/Scouting Director:** Jeff Luhnow.

Class	Team	League	W	L	PCT	Finish*	Manager	Affiliated
Majors	St. Louis	National	86	76	.531	6th (16)	Tony La Russa	—
Triple-A	Memphis Redbirds	Pacific Coast	75	67	.528	5th (16)	Chris Maloney	1998
Double-A	Springfield Cardinals	Texas	76	64	.543	2nd (8)	Ron Warner	2005
High A	Palm Beach Cardinals	Florida State	75	62	.547	4th (12)	Gaylen Pitts	2003
Low A	Quad Cities River Bandits	Midwest	68	66	.507	9th (14)	Steve Dillard	2005
Short-season	Batavia Muckdogs	New York-Penn	46	28	.662	^2nd (14)	Mark DeJohn	2007
Rookie	Johnson City Cardinals	Appalachian	36	30	.545	3rd (10)	Joe Almaraz	1974
Rookie	GCL Cardinals	Gulf Coast	17	38	.309	15th (16)	Enrique Brito	2007
Overall 2008 Minor League Record			393	355	.525	8th		

* Finish in overall standings (No. of teams in league). ^League champion.

LAST YEAR'S TOP 30

Rank	Player, Pos.	Status
1.	Colby Rasmus, of	No. 1
2.	Chris Perez, rhp	No. 3
3.	Bryan Anderson, c	No. 5
4.	Brian Barton, of	Majors
5.	Jaime Garcia, lhp	No. 13
6.	Adam Ottavino, rhp	No. 22
7.	Pete Kozma, ss	No. 10
8.	Clayton Mortensen, rhp	No. 6
9.	Mitchell Boggs, rhp	No. 14
10.	Tyler Herron, rhp	No. 23
11.	Jon Jay, of	No. 12
12.	Jess Todd, rhp	No. 4
13.	Joe Mather, of/1b	Majors
14.	Kenny Maiques, rhp	Dropped out
15.	Allen Craig, 3b/1b	No. 26
16.	P.J. Walters, rhp	No. 17
17.	Jose Martinez, ss	Dropped out
18.	Brad Furnish, lhp	Dropped out
19.	Kyle McClellan, rhp	Majors
20.	Blake Hawksworth, rhp	Dropped out
21.	Jarrett Hoffpauir, 2b	Dropped out
22.	Mark Worrell, rhp	(Padres)
23.	Mike Parisi, rhp	Dropped out
24.	Jason Motte, rhp	No. 8
25.	Mark McCormick, rhp	Dropped out
26.	Blake King, rhp	Dropped out
27.	Mark Hamilton, 1b	Dropped out
28.	Luke Gregerson, rhp	No. 29
29.	Tyler Greene, ss	No. 16
30.	Luis de la Cruz, c	Dropped out

BEST TOOLS

Best Hitter for Average	Brett Wallace
Best Power Hitter	Colby Rasmus
Best Strike-Zone Discipline	Jarrett Hoffpauir
Fastest Baserunner	Daryl Jones
Best Athlete	Daryl Jones
Best Fastball	Jason Motte
Best Curveball	Jaime Garcia
Best Slider	Chris Perez
Best Changeup	P.J. Walters
Best Control	Fernando Salas
Best Defensive Catcher	Nick Derba
Best Defensive Infielder	Pete Kozma
Best Infield Arm	Tyler Greene
Best Defensive Outfielder	Colby Rasmus
Best Outfield Arm	Jon Edwards

PROJECTED 2012 LINEUP

Catcher	Yadier Molina
First Base	Albert Pujols
Second Base	Pete Kozma
Third Base	Brett Wallace
Shortstop	Khalil Greene
Left Field	Ryan Ludwick
Center Field	Colby Rasmus
Right Field	Rick Ankiel
No. 1 Starter	Adam Wainwright
No. 2 Starter	Jess Todd
No. 3 Starter	Clayton Mortensen
No. 4 Starter	Kyle Lohse
No. 5 Starter	Todd Wellemeyer
Closer	Chris Perez

TOP PROSPECTS OF THE DECADE

Year	Player, Pos.	2008 Org.
1999	J.D. Drew, of	Red Sox
2000	Rick Ankiel, lhp	Cardinals
2001	Bud Smith, lhp	Out of baseball
2002	Jimmy Journell, rhp	Out of baseball
2003	Dan Haren, rhp	Diamondbacks
2004	Blake Hawksworth, rhp	Cardinals
2005	Anthony Reyes, rhp	Indians
2006	Anthony Reyes, rhp	Indians
2007	Colby Rasmus, of	Cardinals
2008	Colby Rasmus, of	Cardinals

TOP DRAFT PICKS OF THE DECADE

Year	Player, Pos.	2008 Org.
1999	Chance Caple, rhp	Out of baseball
2000	Shaun Boyd, of	Camden (Atlantic)
2001	Justin Pope, rhp	Phillies
2002	Calvin Hayes, ss (3rd round)	Out of baseball
2003	Daric Barton, c	Athletics
2004	Chris Lambert, rhp	Tigers
2005	Colby Rasmus, of	Cardinals
2006	Adam Ottavino, rhp	Cardinals
2007	Pete Kozma, ss	Cardinals
2008	Brett Wallace, 3b	Cardinals

LARGEST BONUSES IN CLUB HISTORY

J.D. Drew, 1998	$3,000,000
Rick Ankiel, 1997	$2,500,000
Chad Hutchinson, 1998	$2,300,000
Brett Wallace, 2008	$1,840,000
Shaun Boyd, 2000	$1,750,000

ST. LOUIS CARDINALS

TOP 2009 ROOKIE: Colby Rasmus, of. Three years in the making, the much-hyped arrival of the organization's most celebrated prospect since J.D. Drew is imminent.

BREAKOUT PROSPECT: Niko Vasquez, ss. The 2008 third-rounder packs an offensive punch and is primed for his first full pro season.

SLEEPER: Sam Freeman, lhp. There's an opening for a lefty reliever to soar through the system, and with a fastball that reaches 94 mph, Freeman could take advantage.

SOURCE OF TOP 30 TALENT

Homegrown	29	Acquired	1
College	16	Trades	1
Junior college	1	Rule 5 draft	0
High school	7	Independent leagues	0
Draft-and-follow	1	Free agents/waivers	0
Nondrafted free agents	0		
International	4		

Numbers in parentheses indicate prospect rankings.

LF
Jon Jay (12)
Nick Stavinoha
Amaury Cazana-Marti
Aaron Luna
Chris Swauger

CF
Colby Rasmus (1)
Daryl Jones (7)
Shane Robinson (28)
Jim Rapoport
D'Marcus Ingram
Frederick Parejo
Nathan Southard

RF
Jon Edwards
Tyler Henley
Mark Shorey
Ryde Rodriguez
Shane Peterson
Luke Gorsett
Tommy Pham

3B
Brett Wallace (2)
David Freese (9)
Roberto de la Cruz (19)
Allen Craig (26)
Jermaine Curtis

SS
Pete Kozma (10)
Tyler Greene (16)
Jose Martinez
Donovan Solano
Oliver Marmol
Yunier Castillo

2B
Niko Vasquez (18)
Jarrett Hoffpauir
Daniel Descalso
Isa Garcia
Mike Folli
Colt Sedbrook

1B
Steven Hill (25)
Mark Hamilton
Brandon Buckman
Andrew Brown
Matt Arburr
Curt Smith

C
Bryan Anderson (5)
Tony Cruz (27)
Luis de la Cruz
Nick Derba
Matt Pagnozzi

RHP
Starters	Relievers
Jess Todd (4)	Chris Perez (3)
Clayton Mortensen (6)	Jason Motte (8)
Mitchell Boggs (14)	Adam Reifer (11)
Lance Lynn (15)	Fernando Salas (20)
P.J. Walters (17)	Francisco Samuel (21)
Adam Ottavino (22)	Luke Gregerson (29)
Tyler Herron (23)	Blake King
Richard Castillo (24)	Kenny Maiques
Mike Parisi	Eric Fornataro
Mark Diapoules	
Scott Gorgen	
Mark McCormick	
David Kopp	
Brett Zawacki	

LHP
Starters	Relievers
Jaime Garcia (13)	Justin Fiske
Nick Additon (30)	Sam Freeman
Brad Furnish	Davis Bilardello
Tyler Norrick	Matt Spade
Anthony Ferrara	Ryan Kulik

2008

BEST PURE HITTER: 3B Brett Wallace (1) hit .398 in his three seasons at Arizona State and has a polished approach that resulted in more walks (103) than strikeouts (97).

BEST POWER HITTER: Wallace has raw power and leverage in his swing, giving him above-average present power. OF Chris Swauger (26) used good bat speed and strength to hit a team-high seven homers for short-season Batavia.

FASTEST RUNNER: LHP Sam Freeman (32) gets to first base from the right side in 4.05 seconds. Among position players, 2B Alex Castellanos (10) and OF Michael Swinson (12) are plus runners.

BEST DEFENSIVE PLAYER: SS Niko Vasquez (3) may not have the range to stay at shortstop, but he has excellent hands and enough arm for third base. SS/2B Colt Sedbrook (22) has the utility profile with a strong arm and enough range to play all three infield spots.

BEST FASTBALL: Freeman runs his fastball up to 94 mph and sits at 92-93, though command remains an issue. RHP Eric Fornataro (6) can touch 95 thanks to a quick arm.

BEST SECONDARY PITCH: RHP Scott Gorgen (4) may have had the best changeup in college baseball the last two years, one some scouts have graded a 70 on the 20-80 scouting scale. LHP Ryan Kulik (8) throws a 1-to-7 curveball with good tilt for strikes.

BEST PRO DEBUT: Wallace reached Double-A after mashing his way through the low Class A Midwest League, homered three times in 13 Texas League games and hit .337/.427/.530 overall in 202 at-bats. College senior 1B Curt Smith (39) batted .353/.388/.538 overall and hit eight homers at Rookie-level Johnson City.

BEST ATHLETE: Freeman was a toolsy junior college outfielder who has shown more upside as an athletic pitcher. Nondrafted free agent OF Jarred Bogany, a 12th-round pick out of high school in 2005, went to three colleges in three years and has five-tool ability that remains raw.

MOST INTRIGUING BACKGROUND: Gorgen's twin brother Matt signed as a 16th-round pick of the Rays. Unsigned 2B Shane Boras (35) is the son of agent (and former Cardinals farmhand) Scott.

CLOSEST TO THE MAJORS: Wallace already has reached Double-A. RHP Lance Lynn (1s) has a polished three-pitch mix and a future plus slider that should get him moving as well.

BEST LATE-ROUND PICK: The Cardinals have high hopes for Freeman (who finished the year in the high Class A Florida State League playoffs), Sedbrook and Smith.

THE ONE WHO GOT AWAY: Unsigned RHP Mitch Harris (13) is the best prospect Navy has produced in years but can't start his pro career for five years due to his military commitment. St. Louis tried to sign LHP Danny Jimenez (37), who wound up at John A. Logan (Ill.) CC.

ASSESSMENT: Wallace must stay at third base to make an impact in St. Louis, and early returns are good. Vasquez also shows promise in an otherwise low-upside draft that has few advanced power arms.

2007

SS Pete Kozma (1) is developing slowly but steadily, while RHPs Clayton Mortensen (1s) and Jess Todd (2) have rushed to Triple-A and could pitch in St. Louis by the end of 2009. Another RHP, Adam Reifer (11), touched 99 mph last season.

GRADE: C+

2006

RHP Chris Perez (1s) went 7-for-9 closing games for the Cardinals last summer and is on the verge of taking over the role permanently. OF Jon Jay (2) keeps hitting .300, and RHP P.J. Walters (11) keeps succeeding with finesse. RHP Adam Ottavino (1) went backward last year, however.

GRADE: C+

2005

The Cardinals had four picks before the second round, and only OF Colby Rasmus (1) has lived up to his billing. But he's a future star, and St. Louis hit on later choices such as OF Daryl Jones (3), C Bryan Anderson (4), RHP Mitchell Boggs (5) and LHP Jaime Garcia (22).

GRADE: A

2004

The Redbirds failed to sign a single high school player—and didn't find much talent, either. Since-traded RHP Chris Lambert (1) was a bust, and the only highlight was dealing RHP Mark Worrell (12) for Khalil Greene when the Padres wanted to dump some salary.

GRADE: F

Draft analysis by John Manuel (2008) and Jim Callis (2004-07). Numbers in parentheses indicate draft rounds. *Bonuses for 2004-05 are first 10 rounds only.

PROSPECT

COLBY RASMUS, OF

Born: Aug. 11, 1986.
Ht.: 6-2. **Wt.:** 195.
Bats: L. **Throws:** L.
Drafted:
HS—Phenix City, Ala.,
2005. (1st round).
Signed by:
Scott Nichols.

JOHN WILLIAMSON

The 28th overall pick in the 2005 draft, Rasmus signed for $1 million following a celebrated high school career. He broke Bo Jackson's Alabama state record with 24 homers that spring and led Russell County High to a No. 1 ranking in the final national poll. Rasmus' father Tony coached the team, which also featured Colby's brother Cory (a Braves sandwich pick in 2006) and Kasey Kiker (a Rangers first-rounder in 2006). After a breakout year in the Double-A Texas League in 2007, Rasmus came to spring training last year with an outside chance of making the big league team as a 21-year-old. He impressed the Cardinals, especially with his patience, but he wasn't able to dislodge any of the five outfielders ahead of him on the depth chart. His season quickly eroded into disappointment. He hit .214 in his first two months at Triple-A Memphis, and once he found his stroke he was slowed by a groin injury. Rasmus was starting to catch fire when he sprained his left knee when he checked a swing in late July. The injury all but ended his season and cost him a trip to the Olympics, where he would have started in center field for Team USA. Rasmus ranks No. 1 on this list for the third consecutive year.

Rasmus oozes big league talent and exhibits fluid athleticism at the plate and in the field. He has a balanced, potent swing from the left side and his young frame has filled out with strength, which has begun to turn some of his ropes into the gaps into shots launched over the wall. As he showed in big league camp, Rasmus has the plate discipline to be a leadoff man when he arrives in the majors and the extra-base thump to mature into a middle-of-the-order hitter. The same plus speed and instincts he shows on the bases are even more apparent in center field, where he's a defensive standout. His glove is good enough to keep him in the lineup even when he's scuffling at the plate. A standout pitcher in high school, he owns a strong arm.

Rasmus called the environment at Memphis "weird" and he struggled to get comfortable with the demands and the competition brought on by his proximity to the majors. Slow starts continue to be a signature, and when he slumps, he becomes pull-happy and hastens his swing, prolonging his difficulties. St. Louis would like him to have more structured off-field workouts, and the rehab for his knee forced that upon him. Once his knee was healthy in September, St. Louis strongly urged him to play winter ball but he declined.

The Cardinals will make room for Rasmus the moment he shows he's ready. Since they drafted him, he has been the torchbearer for their initiative to renovate their farm system. He should be the first impact position player signed and developed by St. Louis since Albert Pujols. He will return to Triple-A in 2009 if he doesn't break camp with St. Louis, but isn't far away.

Year	Club (League)	Class	AVG	G	AB	R	H	2B	3B	HR	RBI	BB	SO	SB	OBP	SLG
2005	Johnson City (APP)	R	.296	62	216	47	64	16	5	7	27	21	73	13	.362	.514
2006	Quad Cities (MWL)	LoA	.310	78	303	49	94	22	3	11	50	29	55	17	.373	.512
	Palm Beach (FSL)	HiA	.254	53	193	22	49	4	5	5	35	27	35	11	.351	.404
2007	Springfield (TEX)	AA	.275	128	472	93	130	37	3	29	72	70	108	18	.381	.551
2008	Memphis (PCL)	AAA	.251	90	331	56	83	15	0	11	36	49	72	15	.346	.396
	Cardinals (GCL)	R	.556	3	9	1	5	1	0	1	2	3	2	0	.667	1.000
	Palm Beach (FSL)	HiA	.000	3	9	1	0	0	0	0	0	1	3	0	.182	.000
MINOR LEAGUE TOTALS			.277	417	1533	269	425	95	16	64	222	200	348	74	.366	.485

2 BRETT WALLACE, 3B

BORN: Aug. 26, 1986. **B-T:** L-R. **HT.:** 6-1. **WT.:** 245. **DRAFTED:** Arizona State, 2008 (1st round). **SIGNED BY:** Chuck Fick.

The Cardinals pounced on the chance to draft Wallace, who won the Pacific-10 Conference triple crown in each of the last two seasons, with the 13th overall pick in the 2008 draft—their highest choice since 2000. Less than two months after signing for $1.84 million, he was raking at Double-A Springfield, turning what was supposed to be an injury-replacement cameo into a starting gig. Already one of the best pure hitters in the minors, Wallace has an elegant and refined approach. His balanced, level swing creates consistent line drives, and he isn't easily fooled because of his keen eye and quick adjustments. Plenty of doubles and a fair amount of homers will be the byproduct of his strength and the charge he gets from his methodic, squared-up swings. Think batting champ with the ability to be a big bopper. He has an average arm and surprising footwork at third base. Wallace has a thick lower body and has below-average athleticism, speed and agility. Some scouts say he's too stiff to stay at third base for the long term, while his advocates say he makes the plays he can get to and could become an average defender with more coaching. He'll have to work hard to make sure his body doesn't go south on him. One of two 2008 draft picks to play in the Arizona Fall League, Wallace will spend this season in Triple-A. He should take over at third base for the Cardinals after Troy Glaus' contract expires at the end of 2009. Moving to first base isn't an option with Albert Pujols in St. Louis.

Year	Club (League)	Class	AVG	G	AB	R	H	2B	3B	HR	RBI	BB	SO	SB	OBP	SLG
2008	Quad Cities (MWL)	LoA	.327	41	153	28	50	8	1	5	25	17	32	0	.418	.490
	Springfield (TEX)	AA	.367	13	49	13	18	5	0	3	11	2	7	0	.456	.653
MINOR LEAGUE TOTALS			.337	54	202	41	68	13	1	8	36	19	39	0	.427	.530

3 CHRIS PEREZ, RHP

BORN: July 1, 1985. **B-T:** R-R. **HT.:** 6-4. **WT.:** 225. **DRAFTED:** Miami, 2006 (1st round supplemental). **SIGNED BY:** Steve Turco.

Since signing for $800,000 as a sandwich pick in 2006, Perez has been groomed to be the Cardinals' closer of the future. He got his first taste of the role in August, saving six games in six opportunities. Perez has a wicked fastball that delighted the Busch Stadium radar gun when he arrived. He can throw it consistently at 95 mph and dial up to 97-98 when necessary. His fastball has natural sink and he offsets it with a biting slider that hums in the high-80s. Perez has a gunslinger attitude and was unfazed by his hiccups at the big league level. Command and inexperience continue to block Perez from being dubbed St. Louis' closer. The wipeout slider he could get hitters to fish for in the minors isn't quite as effective in the majors, and he may revisit a curveball to give him a downshift pitch that complements his high-velocity duo. To finish games in the big leagues, he must develop a plus pitch other than his fastball that he can throw for a strike. Manager Tony La Russa refused to anoint Perez his closer in August and won't be doing so to start 2009 either. Perez will open the season as a late-inning reliever, getting his seasoning in the seventh inning with the idea he'll ascend to the ninth once he improves his grip on his repertoire.

Year	Club (League)	Class	W	L	ERA	G	GS	CG	SV	IP	H	R	ER	HR	BB	SO	AVG
2006	Quad Cities (MWL)	LoA	2	0	1.84	25	0	0	12	29	20	9	6	0	19	32	.198
2007	Springfield (TEX)	AA	2	0	2.43	39	0	0	27	41	17	11	11	3	28	62	.126
	Memphis (PCL)	AAA	0	1	4.50	15	0	0	8	14	6	7	7	2	13	15	.143
2008	Memphis (PCL)	AAA	1	1	3.20	26	0	0	11	25	18	9	9	3	12	38	.198
	St. Louis (NL)	MAJ	3	3	3.46	41	0	0	7	42	34	18	16	5	22	42	.227
MINOR LEAGUE TOTALS			5	2	2.72	105	0	0	58	109	61	36	33	8	72	147	.165
MAJOR LEAGUE TOTALS			3	3	3.46	41	0	0	7	42	34	18	16	5	22	42	.227

4 JESS TODD, RHP

BORN: April 20, 1986. **B-T:** R-R. **HT.:** 5-11. **WT.:** 210. **DRAFTED:** Arkansas, 2007 (2nd round). **SIGNED BY:** Roger Smith.

Todd had enough fastball to strike out 128 in 93 innings as a junior at Arkansas, including a Southeastern Conference tournament-record 17 in one start. But before 2008, his first full season in pro ball, a friend suggested he shift his grip and try a cutter. In the first two months of the season, Todd was an all-star at two levels; in the third, he pitched in the Futures Game; and in the fourth, he was in Triple-A. Todd augments an attack-dog mentality with tremendous control of three pitches—the cutter, an 88-91 mph sinker and a tight slider. He also can turn to a four-seamer that reaches 94 mph. He has a feel for when to shoot for a strikeout and when to entice contact. A typical outing for Todd was his seventh at Double-A: He needed 83 pitches to get 22 outs, 44 of his 63 fastballs were for strikes, and 17 of the 20 balls in play were on the ground. To some, Todd profiles as a reliever because there's lingering concern his frame isn't built to handle the grind and innings of the long big league season. His repertoire also may be better suited for the bullpen until he refines a reliable changeup. Skyrocketing to Triple-A last year puts Todd on the radar for the majors in 2009, though he'll start the year in the Memphis rotation. He'll prime his pitches for the moment there's an opening in the rotation or bullpen.

Year	Club (League)	Class	W	L	ERA	G	GS	CG	SV	IP	H	R	ER	HR	BB	SO	AVG
2007	Batavia (NYP)	SS	4	1	2.78	16	7	0	0	58	48	23	18	2	14	69	.223
2008	Palm Beach (FSL)	HiA	3	0	1.65	7	4	0	1	27	18	7	5	0	7	35	.184
	Springfield (TEX)	AA	4	5	2.97	17	16	0	0	103	79	37	34	12	24	81	.216
	Memphis (PCL)	AAA	1	1	3.97	4	4	0	0	23	19	10	10	4	11	20	.232
MINOR LEAGUE TOTALS			12	7	2.85	44	31	0	1	211	164	77	67	18	56	205	.216

5 BRYAN ANDERSON, C

BORN: Dec. 16, 1986. **B-T:** L-R. **HT.:** 6-1. **WT.:** 200. **DRAFTED:** HS—Simi Valley, Calif., 2005 (4th round). **SIGNED BY:** Jay North.

One of the youngest players in every league he's played in during his pro career, Anderson has hit at least .281 at every stop. He figured to spend a second year as an everyday catcher in Double-A, but hit .388 to force a promotion before the end of last April. He has played in the Futures Game and with Team USA. Anderson has a savvy approach at the plate and a fluid lefthanded swing with some elements of an uppercut. He's not flummoxed by southpaws, hitting .308/.384/.415 against them at Triple-A. Scouts still expect him to develop the gap power that hasn't manifested itself as quickly as hoped. Pitchers say he calls a good game. Anderson continues to improve as a catcher, becoming more adept at receiving and blocking balls. His throwing mechanics aren't traditional, costing him accuracy, but he has gotten quicker and caught 38 percent of basestealers in 2008. He tends to snatch at pitches. There's some concern he lacks the size to thrive through a full big league season. If Anderson does shift positions—perhaps to second base?—the Cardinals say it will be because he's blocked by Gold Glove winner Yadier Molina, not his lack of ability. While he offers an intriguing long-term lefthanded complement to Molina, Anderson's immediate future is in Triple-A. He could be the best trade chip St. Louis has.

Year	Club (League)	Class	AVG	G	AB	R	H	2B	3B	HR	RBI	BB	SO	SB	OBP	SLG
2005	Johnson City (APP)	R	.331	51	154	28	51	8	1	6	36	15	29	6	.383	.513
2006	Quad Cities (MWL)	LoA	.302	109	381	50	115	29	3	3	51	42	66	2	.377	.417
2007	Springfield (TEX)	AA	.298	103	389	51	116	15	1	6	53	32	77	0	.350	.388
2008	Springfield (TEX)	AA	.388	19	80	12	31	5	0	2	14	4	12	0	.412	.525
	Memphis (PCL)	AAA	.281	73	235	27	66	13	2	2	27	32	46	2	.367	.379
MINOR LEAGUE TOTALS			.306	355	1239	168	379	70	7	19	181	125	230	10	.369	.420

6 CLAYTON MORTENSEN, RHP

BORN: April 10, 1985. **B-T:** R-R. **HT.:** 6-4. **WT.:** 180. **DRAFTED:** Gonzaga, 2007 (1st round supplemental). **SIGNED BY:** Jay North.

Mortensen became the first Cardinals pitcher to merit an invite to major league spring training the year after being drafted since Braden Looper in 1997. A 2007 sandwich pick who signed for $650,000, he made two spring starts and impressed the big league staff with his diving fastball and his promise. He skipped past high Class A and finished 2008 in the Triple-A rotation. Mortensen operates mainly with a 90-93 mph sinker and a hard slider. His sinker is good enough to induce strikeouts and grounders. He posted a 1.9 groundout/airout ratio in 2008, and righthanders hit .188 against him. He still has room to add more strength to his body and velocity to his body. Propelled to Triple-A in June, Mortensen was too fine around the strike zone and pitched himself into mechanical issues. Control and command troubles cost him late in his college career and returned at Memphis, where he gave up 42 walks and 12 home runs in 80 innings. He needs to improve his changeup to handle lefties, who hit .354 against him last year. Like Jess Todd, Mortensen has been promoted aggressively and will pitch in the Memphis rotation in 2009. The Cardinals believe the kinks in his delivery have been fixed and he'll return to big league camp, this time to leave an impression for a September callup, at least.

Year	Club (League)	Class	W	L	ERA	G	GS	CG	SV	IP	H	R	ER	HR	BB	SO	AVG
2007	Batavia (NYP)	SS	1	1	1.77	6	4	0	0	20	13	4	4	0	11	23	.188
	Quad Cities (MWL)	LoA	0	2	3.12	10	10	0	0	40	44	17	14	2	8	45	.275
2008	Springfield (TEX)	AA	3	4	4.22	11	11	0	0	60	59	31	28	6	22	48	.257
	Memphis (PCL)	AAA	5	6	5.51	15	14	0	0	80	87	50	49	12	42	57	.281
MINOR LEAGUE TOTALS			9	13	4.27	42	39	0	0	200	203	102	95	20	83	173	.264

7 DARYL JONES, OF

BORN: June 24, 1987. **B-T:** L-L. **HT.:** 5-11. **WT.:** 180. **DRAFTED:** HS—Spring, Texas, 2005 (3rd round). **SIGNED BY:** Joe Almaraz.

Dripping with athleticism and tools when he chose pro baseball over college football, Jones hit just .221 in his first three seasons and could not get past low Class A. He regained his prospect status with a breakout 2008, when he was named Cardinals minor league player of the year after batting .316/.407/.483. Jones rivals Colby Rasmus as the finest athlete in system, and he's certainly the speediest. His quickness serves him well at the plate, where he's able to turn line drives into doubles; on the bases, where he's improving as a thief; and in the outfield, where he's adept at all three positions. He had an epiphany at the plate, learning to be aggressive in the right counts instead of overanxiously getting himself out early in at-bats. While he finally has the stats to match his ability, Jones remains raw and his power is only beginning to develop. He's still prone to striking out and needs to emphasize getting on base so he can hit near the top of the order. He's good but not instinctive in the outfield, and his arm is fringy, so he could wind up in left field. Still just 21, Jones will return to Double-A in 2009. A repeat performance could put him in line to compete for a starting job in St. Louis the following season.

Year	Club (League)	Class	AVG	G	AB	R	H	2B	3B	HR	RBI	BB	SO	SB	OBP	SLG
2005	Johnson City (APP)	R	.209	61	182	36	38	6	1	2	10	15	41	10	.311	.286
2006	Johnson City (APP)	R	.265	20	68	15	18	3	1	3	13	8	8	3	.367	.471
	Quad Cities (MWL)	LoA	.235	26	81	15	19	5	1	1	7	6	23	2	.308	.358
2007	Quad Cities (MWL)	LoA	.217	127	419	71	91	15	3	4	31	41	94	22	.304	.296
2008	Palm Beach (FSL)	HiA	.326	87	307	43	100	11	7	7	35	33	67	18	.406	.476
	Springfield (TEX)	AA	.290	36	124	19	36	6	1	6	14	22	30	6	.409	.500
MINOR LEAGUE TOTALS			.256	357	1181	199	302	46	14	23	110	125	263	61	.347	.377

8 JASON MOTTE, RHP

BORN: June 22, 1982. **B-T:** R-R. **HT.:** 6-0. **WT.:** 195. **DRAFTED:** Iona, 2003 (19th round). **SIGNED BY:** Joe Rigoli.

Motte's rapid transformation from light-hitting catcher to lights-out reliever is complete. He was a superb defensive catcher, but a .188 average in his first three pro seasons forced him to the mound. He experienced almost immediate success and has gotten better each year, and he blew away big leaguers last September. Motte has the best fastball in the system, sitting at 95-96 mph with the ability to crank it up to 98 consistently. He's relentlessly aggressive on the mound, usually throwing strikes and daring hitters to catch up to his heat. His past life as a catcher adds deception to his delivery, as he cocks his hand near his ear before firing. He has a fresh, resilient arm. Motte showed no effective second pitch during his big league stint. He has worked on a slider, cutter and splitter but none is reliable yet. His fastball is arrow straight, enhancing the need for something with a lower gear. He battles his command on occasion. Spring training will be a laboratory of sorts for Motte to work on expanding his repertoire so he can be a late-inning reliever in St. Louis. Chris Perez may have the edge in experience, but there are some who see Motte as a viable contender for the long-term closer role.

Year	Club (League)	Class	W	L	ERA	G	GS	CG	SV	IP	H	R	ER	HR	BB	SO	AVG
2006	State College (NYP)	SS	1	2	3.08	21	0	0	8	26	30	12	9	1	4	25	.280
	Quad Cities (MWL)	LoA	1	1	4.97	8	0	0	0	13	16	8	7	1	3	13	.296
2007	Palm Beach (FSL)	HiA	1	0	0.90	9	0	0	3	10	7	2	1	0	1	6	.184
	Springfield (TEX)	AA	3	3	2.20	44	0	0	8	49	36	13	12	3	22	63	.208
2008	Memphis (PCL)	AAA	4	3	3.24	63	0	0	9	67	64	25	24	6	26	110	.245
	St. Louis (NL)	MAJ	0	0	0.82	12	0	0	1	11	5	2	1	0	3	16	.139
MINOR LEAGUE TOTALS			10	9	2.90	145	0	0	28	165	153	60	53	11	56	217	.242
MAJOR LEAGUE TOTALS			0	0	0.82	12	0	0	1	11	5	2	1	0	3	16	.139

9 DAVID FREESE, 3B

BORN: April 28, 1983. **B-T:** R-R. **HT.:** 6-2. **WT.:** 220. **DRAFTED:** South Alabama, 2006 (9th round). **SIGNED BY:** Bob Filotei (Padres).

In the deal that sent icon Jim Edmonds to the Padres last offseason, the Cardinals were willing to cover more of Edmonds' salary if the Padres parted with Freese. At the time, Freese filled a hole on the organization depth chart—a third baseman who could hit—and brought the added virtue of being a native, a graduate of suburban Lafayette High, Ryan Howard's alma mater. St. Louis skipped Freese past Double-A and watched him lead the system in OPS (.911) and RBIs (91). Freese has hit for average throughout the minors and has the ability to drive the ball the opposite way with authority. Of his 26 homers last year, 20 went to center or right field. Billed as nothing special at third base, he impressed the Cardinals with steady play that was more superb than serviceable. Freese can tumble into stretches where he'll get himself out, as he did when striking out 59 times in his first 178 Triple-A at-bats. He's a below-average runner. Though he tried catching in instructional league with the Padres, he offers the most realistic value at third base—a problem with Brett Wallace in the organization. The clock is ticking on Freese, who will be 26 in 2009. Wallace is going to start at third base in Triple-A, so Freese will hope there's room on the big league club for a righthanded bat.

Year	Club (League)	Class	AVG	G	AB	R	H	2B	3B	HR	RBI	BB	SO	SB	OBP	SLG
2006	Eugene (NWL)	SS	.379	18	58	19	22	8	0	5	26	7	12	0	.465	.776
	Fort Wayne (MWL)	LoA	.299	53	204	27	61	13	3	8	44	21	44	1	.374	.510
2007	Lake Elsinore (CAL)	HiA	.302	128	503	104	152	31	6	17	96	69	99	6	.400	.489
2008	Memphis (PCL)	AAA	.306	131	464	83	142	29	3	26	91	39	111	5	.361	.550
MINOR LEAGUE TOTALS			.307	330	1229	233	377	81	12	56	257	136	266	12	.385	.529

10 PETE KOZMA, SS

BORN: April 11, 1988. **B-T:** R-R. **HT.:** 6-0. **WT.:** 170. **DRAFTED:** HS—Owasso, Okla., 2007 (1st round). **SIGNED BY:** Steve Gossett.

Kozma had just led Owasso High to an Oklahoma 6-A state title with a three-homer playoff game when the Cardinals picked him 18th overall in 2007. Signed for $1.395 million, he admits what scouts say about him—he's not a flashy talent. But he's a well-rounded middle infielder who should advance steadily through the system. Kozma has a good feel for hitting and a line-drive swing. The best defensive shortstop in the system, he's a nimble fielder with soft hands and fluid actions. He has an average arm and enhances it with a quick, accurate release. His solid-average speed and fine instincts could allow him to develop into a basestealer. Ideally, Kozma would thrive as a No. 2 hitter, but his bat hasn't progressed as rapidly as hoped. There's no indication he'll generate the bat speed to hit for much power. He struggles to drive the ball to the opposite field and was overmatched following a late-season promotion to high Class A Palm Beach. Kozma will take another crack at high Class A in 2009. How he fares at the plate will dictate how rapidly he makes the next leap.

Year	Club (League)	Class	AVG	G	AB	R	H	2B	3B	HR	RBI	BB	SO	SB	OBP	SLG
2007	Cardinals (GCL)	R	.154	4	13	4	2	0	0	0	2	2	0	.267	.154
	Johnson City (APP)	R	.264	30	106	16	28	8	0	2	9	12	21	3	.350	.396
	Batavia (NYP)	SS	.148	8	27	1	4	0	1	0	2	1	7	1	.179	.222
2008	Quad Cities (MWL)	LoA	.284	99	377	58	107	20	4	5	40	45	69	12	.363	.398
	Palm Beach (FSL)	HiA	.130	24	77	4	10	4	0	0	10	10	27	0	.231	.182
MINOR LEAGUE TOTALS			.252	165	600	83	151	32	5	7	61	70	126	16	.333	.357

11 ADAM REIFER, RHP

BORN: June 3, 1986. **B-T:** R-R. **HT.:** 6-2. **WT.:** 195. **DRAFTED:** UC Riverside, 2007 (11th round). **SIGNED BY:** Jeff Ishii.

The Cardinals felt like they were able to bring in a premium arm when they took Reifer in the 11th round of the 2007 draft, after he had thrown just seven innings during his junior season at UC Riverside. Bone spurs and elbow tendinitis didn't spook the Cardinals, and they signed him for $100,000 and then gave him the rest of the summer off to recover. The investment has returned a high-caliber arm who has back of the bullpen potential. Reifer was rated the top pitching prospect in the short-season New York-Penn League, with the best pure stuff in the league. Radar guns regularly clocked his fastball at 96-97 mph and he touched 99. One scout rated it an 80 pitch on the 20-80 scouting scale and said his slider could be a 70. The slider regularly sits in the low 90s, and he has a developing changeup that sinks in at 86-87 mph. Reifer held lefthanders to a .086 average, and he converted 22 of 24 saves for the championship Batavia club. He's athletic, with a smooth delivery, and he's both aggressive and assertive enough to remain as a closer. One of the biggest arms in the system, Reifer is ticketed for the ninth inning at a full-season club, with a leap to high Class A possible.

Year	Club (League)	Class	W	L	ERA	G	GS	CG	SV	IP	H	R	ER	HR	BB	SO	AVG
2008	Batavia (NYP)	SS	2	1	2.97	32	0	0	22	30	18	14	10	2	15	41	.162
MINOR LEAGUE TOTALS			2	1	2.97	32	0	0	22	30	18	14	10	2	15	41	.162

12 JON JAY, OF

BORN: March 15, 1985. **B-T:** L-L. **HT.:** 5-11. **WT.:** 200. **DRAFTED:** Miami, 2006 (2nd round). **SIGNED BY:** Steve Turco.

After losing 2007 to a string of injuries—two trips to the disabled list for a shoulder injury and one for wrist soreness—Jay recovered and picked up where he left off in 2006, when he was healthy and had the most impressive debut of the anyone in the Cardinals' draft class. The lefthanded-hitting outfielder has an exceptional command of the strike zone and a knack for slashing, driving and even guiding base hits. His swing is built to win a batting title, and early concerns it wouldn't translate at higher levels were allayed by his performance at Triple-A. Jay returned to Double-A to start 2008 but quickly showed he was ready to get back on the fast track, with 114 hits in 96 games, including 11 homers. He has a distinctive hand pump and bat waggle as his timing mechanisms, and while they turn off some scouts, they work for him. What doesn't work for him is the depth chart. Speedy enough to steal a base and cover ample ground in center field, with an average arm, he's hidden behind Rick Ankiel and Colby Rasmus at center and doesn't have the pop for the corners. He'll return to Triple-A to start 2009, where he'll continue to ripen in case there's an opening in St. Louis or elsewhere. His future playing time will be dictated by how high an average he gets with that bat waggle.

Year	Club (League)	Class	AVG	G	AB	R	H	2B	3B	HR	RBI	BB	SO	SB	OBP	SLG
2006	Quad Cities (MWL)	LoA	.342	60	234	42	80	13	3	3	45	28	27	9	.416	.462
2007	Springfield (TEX)	AA	.235	26	102	17	24	4	2	2	11	11	19	4	.333	.373
	Cardinals (GCL)	R	.500	1	2	0	1	0	0	0	0	0	1	0	.500	.500
	Palm Beach (FSL)	HiA	.286	32	126	19	36	8	0	2	10	5	25	5	.321	.397
2008	Springfield (TEX)	AA	.306	96	372	57	114	17	3	11	47	39	46	10	.379	.457
	Memphis (PCL)	AAA	.345	16	58	8	20	4	1	1	10	6	10	0	.406	.500
MINOR LEAGUE TOTALS			.308	231	894	143	275	46	9	19	123	89	128	28	.377	.443

13 JAIME GARCIA, LHP

BORN: June 2, 1986. **B-T:** L-L. **HT.:** 6-2. **WT.:** 200. **DRAFTED:** Mission, Texas, 2005 (22nd round).
SIGNED BY: Joe Almaraz.

Garcia would be the top-ranking starting pitching prospect in the organization—by a good margin—if not for elbow surgery that ended his 2008 season just after he'd found a niche in the Cardinals bullpen. He started the season in the Double-A rotation, had a 4-4, 4.44 turn in Triple-A and finished in the major league bullpen as an apprentice lefty, though he's still viewed as a starter. He had Tommy John surgery and will miss most of the 2009 season. It was the second consecutive season that Garcia has ended with elbow soreness, though the team isn't alarmed by the trend and believes the surgery will correct the soreness that cut short his 2007, too. Garcia has two plus pitches: a fastball that he fires at 88-92 mph and has late bite, and a 12-to-6 curveball that is the best in the system. He has remarkable poise on the mound for his age, but he has had splotches of flighty command, an issue that could be traced to two years of pitching with a tender ligament. The surgery will delay Garcia's shot at being a big league regular, but if his rehab goes well and he returns with the same snap on his pitches, he could find a spot in the rotation waiting for him in 2010.

Year	Club (League)	Class	W	L	ERA	G	GS	CG	SV	IP	H	R	ER	HR	BB	SO	AVG
2006	Quad Cities (MWL)	LoA	5	4	2.90	13	13	1	0	78	67	28	25	1	18	80	.229
	Palm Beach (FSL)	HiA	5	4	3.84	12	12	0	0	77	84	33	33	3	16	51	.282
2007	Springfield (TEX)	AA	5	9	3.75	18	18	0	0	103	93	47	43	14	45	97	.245
2008	Springfield (TEX)	AA	3	2	2.06	6	6	1	0	35	26	10	8	0	16	41	.206
	Memphis (PCL)	AAA	4	4	4.44	13	12	0	0	71	74	41	35	6	26	59	.270
	St. Louis (NL)	MAJ	1	1	5.63	10	1	0	0	16	14	10	10	4	8	8	.233
MINOR LEAGUE TOTALS			22	23	3.56	62	61	2	0	364	344	159	144	24	121	328	.251
MAJOR LEAGUE TOTALS			1	1	5.63	10	1	0	0	16	14	10	10	4	8	8	.233

14 MITCHELL BOGGS, RHP

BORN: Feb. 15, 1984. **B-T:** R-R. **HT.:** 6-3. **WT.:** 215. **DRAFTED:** Georgia, 2005 (5th round).
SIGNED BY: Roger Smith.

Thrust into the major league rotation as an injury replacement, Boggs debuted with a 3-0 start that included a 5⅓-inning gem at Fenway Park on national television. Inexperience and control problems eventually caught up with him, but the brush with the big leagues helped mark him as one of the best pitchers in the Pacific Coast League last year. He won the Pacific Coast League ERA title at 3.45 and made Baseball America's Triple-A postseason all-star team. Boggs features two different fastballs: a four-seam pitch that he can locate and cut and a two-seamer that sinks. He throws in the low 90s and augments his heaters with a put-away slider. Boggs is both consistent and durable, throwing more than 140 innings for the third consecutive season. Observers applaud his smarts and laud his bulldog approach, describing him as an assertive pitcher. Boggs was a two-sport star who tried small-college quarterbacking before transferring to Georgia, where he worked primarily as a reliever. If he can improve his changeup and his command, he has the guile to stay a starter. If not, righthanders' .189 average against him and his fastball/slider combo could return him to those bullpen roots as strong setup righty.

Year	Club (League)	Class	W	L	ERA	G	GS	CG	SV	IP	H	R	ER	HR	BB	SO	AVG
2005	New Jersey (NYP)	SS	4	4	3.89	15	14	0	0	72	77	38	31	5	24	61	.271
2006	Palm Beach (FSL)	HiA	10	6	3.41	27	27	1	0	145	153	69	55	7	51	126	.271
2007	Springfield (TEX)	AA	11	7	3.84	26	26	0	0	152	167	86	65	15	62	117	.279
2008	St. Louis (NL)	MAJ	3	2	7.41	8	6	0	0	34	42	29	28	5	22	13	.304
	Memphis (PCL)	AAA	9	3	3.45	21	21	1	0	125	107	52	48	11	46	81	.235
MINOR LEAGUE TOTALS			34	20	3.62	89	88	2	0	494	504	245	199	38	183	385	.265
MAJOR LEAGUE TOTALS			3	2	7.41	8	6	0	0	34	42	29	28	5	22	13	.304

15 LANCE LYNN, RHP

BORN: May 12, 1987. **B-T:** R-R. **HT.:** 6-5. **WT.:** 250. **DRAFTED:** Mississippi, 2008 (1st round supplemental). **SIGNED BY:** Jay Catalano.

In many ways, Lynn is the prototype pick for a franchise that favors college pitchers, particularly college pitchers with a tangible, steady line of production and a sinking fastball. Lynn fits the Cardinals' mold. He's hulking and has proved his durability in college, and he throws a 90-92 mph fastball that has heavy sink to it. Lynn was drafted in the sixth round in 2005 by the Mariners, but he elected to improve his draft spot and did so with an All-America turn at Mississippi. He has command of four pitches, including a slick slider and a fringy changeup and curve. But he wasn't billed as a first-round pick because his ceiling seems to be as a rotation's innings-eater. The Cardinals put a high value on that and believe he's a safe bet to reach that ceiling, which is why they drafted him 39th overall last June and signed him for $938,000. They expect a bankable prospect whose climb to the majors can almost be plotted by the start. Lynn made eight appearances in his pro debut before missing time with forearm stiffness, but it's not a long-term concern. He pitched as expected in his first pro turns and will likely return to the low Class A Quad Cities rotation to start the year. It will be a short visit.

Year	Club (League)	Class	W	L	ERA	G	GS	CG	SV	IP	H	R	ER	HR	BB	SO	AVG
2008	Batavia (NYP)	SS	1	0	0.96	6	4	0	0	19	12	5	2	0	4	22	.179
	Quad Cities (MWL)	LoA	0	1	2.25	2	2	0	0	8	8	2	2	2	2	7	.258
MINOR LEAGUE TOTALS			1	1	1.35	8	6	0	0	27	20	7	4	2	6	29	.204

16 TYLER GREENE, SS

BORN: Aug. 17, 1983. **B-T:** R-R. **HT.:** 6-2. **WT.:** 185. **DRAFTED:** Georgia Tech, 2005 (1st round). **SIGNED BY:** Roger Smith.

The Cardinals planned to take Greene with the 28th pick of the 2005 draft but caught wind of interest in Colby Rasmus, so they switched their picks and got both players. Greene, a decorated college player, arrived with a $1.1 million bonus and heady expectations. Only in 2008 did he start to reach them, thanks in large measure to regaining trust in his knee. In July 2007, Greene took a swing that ripped his kneecap loose and dislocated it. For a shortstop whose game was based on speed, the injury was a major setback. It took him a year to find his stride again, and he hit .328 after the all-star break in Double-A and left an 18-game hitting steak behind when he was promoted to Triple-A. Overall, he finished four homers shy of a second 20-20 season. The Cardinals added him to the 40-man roster after the season, and he headed to the Arizona Fall League to continue refining a freewheeling approach at the plate. Greene struck out 134 times in 485 at-bats last season, still fighting his habit of chasing pitches. He has the footwork and the arm strength to play short, though he has worked at third and second to give him more versatility. Second base could be the best long-term fit. The Cardinals say Greene has earned an audition for a major league bench job, if not out of spring training then certainly sometime in 2009.

Year	Club (League)	Class	AVG	G	AB	R	H	2B	3B	HR	RBI	BB	SO	SB	OBP	SLG
2005	New Jersey (NYP)	SS	.261	35	138	28	36	12	0	1	18	15	37	13	.352	.370
	Palm Beach (FSL)	HiA	.271	20	85	17	23	4	0	2	5	5	28	6	.326	.388
2006	Palm Beach (FSL)	HiA	.224	71	268	38	60	10	1	5	19	29	90	22	.308	.325
	Quad Cities (MWL)	LoA	.287	59	223	42	64	8	3	15	47	20	65	11	.375	.552
2007	Springfield (TEX)	AA	.244	65	221	41	54	17	2	8	25	16	62	10	.309	.448
2008	Springfield (TEX)	AA	.259	97	374	62	97	15	4	16	41	22	99	14	.307	.449
	Memphis (PCL)	AAA	.234	30	111	17	26	7	0	0	7	11	35	6	.325	.297
MINOR LEAGUE TOTALS			.254	377	1420	245	360	73	10	47	162	118	416	82	.326	.418

17 P.J. WALTERS, RHP

BORN: March 3, 1985. **B-T:** R-R. **HT.:** 6-4. **WT.:** 200. **DRAFTED:** South Alabama, 2006 (11th round). **SIGNED BY:** Scott Nichols.

For the second consecutive season, Walters was among the organization leaders in strikeouts and strikeouts per inning, though he's able to do it by mystifying batters more than overpowering them. He has a workable fastball, one that clocks at 86-89 mph and sometimes touches the low 90s. But his best pitch is so good that people have a hard time describing it. He calls it a changeup, but its rotation and late movement have some scouts and coaches still calling it a screwball. Walters lives in the lower reaches of the strike zone and has impeccable command when he's at his best. His changeup breaks against the grain, and his delivery is deceptive enough that it also makes his fastball look quicker. He has an average breaking ball. He scaled three levels in 2007 and settled in at Triple-A in 2008, but his walks spiked and he allowed 22 homers overall, indicating he needs to throw more quality strikes. Walters was unheralded coming out of college, but now Cardinals officials have no doubt he'll pitch in the majors. After a handful more innings at Memphis, he'll get there as a back-end starter or bullpen arm relying on unerring control and that unnerving changeup.

Year	Club (League)	Class	W	L	ERA	G	GS	CG	SV	IP	H	R	ER	HR	BB	SO	AVG
2006	State College (NYP)	SS	2	1	3.56	26	0	0	8	30	29	15	12	1	9	31	.242
2007	Quad Cities (MWL)	LoA	6	1	2.62	17	10	0	1	69	59	25	20	2	12	73	.229
	Palm Beach (FSL)	HiA	3	1	2.67	5	5	0	0	34	29	10	10	2	6	37	.225
	Springfield (TEX)	AA	3	4	2.37	8	8	0	0	49	42	13	13	4	15	37	.228
2008	Springfield (TEX)	AA	1	2	3.25	6	6	0	0	36	35	17	13	5	8	34	.252
	Memphis (PCL)	AAA	9	4	4.87	23	23	0	0	122	123	71	66	17	62	122	.266
MINOR LEAGUE TOTALS			24	13	3.55	85	52	1	9	340	317	151	134	31	112	334	.245

18 NIKO VASQUEZ, SS

BORN: Feb. 26, 1989. **B-T:** R-R. **HT.:** 5-11. **WT.:** 175. **DRAFTED:** HS—Las Vegas, 2008 (3rd round). **SIGNED BY:** Aaron Krawiec.

Two years after drafting the starting shortstop at Las Vegas' Durango High (Tommy Pham, who played in Class A last year), the Cardinals plucked a Durango shortstop again. This time they think they may have landed a first-round bat with a third-round choice. Vasquez slipped in the draft because of uncertain signability, a commitment to Oregon State and an eyebrow-raising academic suspension. The Cardinals got him with the 91st pick and a $423,000 bonus, and he immediately looked like a steal. He dominated the Rookie-level Appalachian League and finished the year as a 19-year-old in low Class A. Vazquez has the arm to play shortstop, but probably won't have quick enough feet as he matures and fills out his frame, so he's expected to gravitate toward third base or second base. His feel for the middle infield may be enough to keep him at second. While there is no guarantee he'll develop home run pop, Vasquez swings a solid bat and will hit for average. There are hints, however, that as he marches through the organization as a middle infielder and his game and body mature, his sweet-spot contact could erupt into gap power, enough to turn him from a utility glove to an everyday contributor.

Year	Club (League)	Class	AVG	G	AB	R	H	2B	3B	HR	RBI	BB	SO	SB	OBP	SLG
2008	Johnson City (APP)	R	.317	55	208	42	66	16	1	4	25	29	52	8	.416	.462
	Quad Cities (MWL)	LoA	.128	11	39	6	5	1	0	0	3	4	17	0	.205	.154
MINOR LEAGUE TOTALS			.287	66	247	48	71	17	1	4	28	33	69	8	.383	.413

19 ROBERTO DE LA CRUZ, 3B

BORN: Nov. 10, 1991. **B-T:** R-R. **HT.:** 6-2. **WT.:** 180. **SIGNED:** Dominican Republic, 2008. **SIGNED BY:** Domingo Garcia.

Starting with the campus they opened in the Dominican Republic five years ago and continuing with limited spending on free agents in 2007, the Cardinals had been deliberately preparing to make a splash internationally. Farm and scouting director Jeff Luhnow decided 2008 was the right time, and de la Cruz was the right player. Cardinals executives flew to the Dominican to meet with buscones, who act as agents for the players, as a group in January, and lay the groundwork for what became a record outlay of bonuses. A total of three players received more individually than the Cardinals had ever paid before for an international player, and atop that trio was de la Cruz, who received $1.1 million. Also known as Roberto Pina, he was among the best hitters available with speed and quick hands that hint considerable power will develop. The Cardinals were particularly excited by the polish he shows at the plate at a young age. Third base may not fit de la Cruz comfortably in the long term, but that's where he'll start. His bat impressed during instructional league before he returned to the Dominican campus for more work. Just 17, he'll likely get an assignment to Rookie-level Johnson City for 2009.

Year	Club (League)	Class	AVG	G	AB	R	H	2B	3B	HR	RBI	BB	SO	SB	OBP	SLG
2008	Did Not Play—Signed 2009 Contract															

20 FERNANDO SALAS, RHP

BORN: May 30, 1985. **B-T:** R-R. **HT.:** 6-2. **WT.:** 200. **SIGNED:** Mexico, 2007. **SIGNED BY:** Chuck Fick.

The Cardinals sought Salas in February 2007, enticing him to leave the Mexican League for a chance to be a reliever/piggyback starter at Palm Beach. When he struggled, going 2-3, 5.26 in 16 games at high Class A, the Cardinals lent him back to his Mexican team, Saltillo, for the remainder of the 2007 season. A few months into his second try in 2008, Salas represented the Cardinals in the Futures Game. He throws a 91-92 mph fastball and has a serviceable curveball. Yet his most marketable skill is a knack for throwing strikes and working to the four corners of the zone, with movement at every level of the zone. He struck out 100 batters against just 16 walks in 74 innings, and over his final 59 innings he walked just 10 batters. Coaches and scouts called him one of the best in the Texas League at locating his fastball, and he rarely threw behind in the count. When Salas does fall behind in the count, he can be combustible as he allowed 12 homers. Movement at the major league level will dictate his role at Triple-A, but Salas has the ability and moxie to handle a late-inning role, possibly as a setup righthander to begin his major league career.

ST. LOUIS CARDINALS

Year	Club (League)	Class	W	L	ERA	G	GS	CG	SV	IP	H	R	ER	HR	BB	SO	AVG
2005	Saltillo (MEX)	AAA	0	0	2.08	14	1	0	0	17	21	8	4	1	10	12	.304
2006	Saltillo (MEX)	AAA	8	2	3.02	29	1	0	0	48	40	17	16	5	20	38	.231
2007	Palm Beach (FSL)	HiA	2	3	5.26	16	4	0	0	39	39	25	23	12	10	25	.260
	Saltillo (MEX)	AAA	0	0	6.75	3	0	0	0	3	5	2	2	1	2	2	.417
2008	Springfield (TEX)	AA	7	3	3.65	60	0	0	25	74	65	31	30	12	16	100	.236
MINOR LEAGUE TOTALS			17	8	3.73	122	6	0	25	181	170	83	75	31	58	177	.244

21 FRANCISCO SAMUEL, RHP

BORN: Dec. 20, 1986. **B-T:** R-R. **HT.:** 6-1. **WT.:** 150. **SIGNED:** Dominican Republic, 2006. **SIGNED BY:** Rene Rojas.

Samuel is the top candidate to lead the charge for the Cardinals' first generation of players identified and cultivated by their new campus in the Dominican Republic. He also continued a recent trend of dominant closers at Palm Beach. Samuel, a reed-thin reliever, has one of the true power arms in the organization, and one opposing manager last season called his stuff unhittable. He throws consistently from 94-96 mph, and has regularly touched 98 in save situations. He sweetens that pep with a slider that he can throw from 85-90 mph. He rarely throws anything soft because he hasn't needed to at the lower levels. Samuel finished 48 games for Palm Beach last year and ended up with more than twice as many strikeouts as hits allowed. He also had more walks than hits, however. His wildness is intimidating in the lower levels, but control will be the biggest hurdle for him to overcome as he tries to rise through the system. He complicates matters by sometimes allowing his mechanics to fall apart, which makes pitches drift up in the zone. Samuel will inherit the closing job in Springfield, but easily could pitch at multiple levels again in 2009. If his control improves, he will ascend quickly.

Year	Club (League)	Class	W	L	ERA	G	GS	CG	SV	IP	H	R	ER	HR	BB	SO	AVG
2006	Cardinals (DSL)	R	1	3	7.56	11	4	0	0	17	24	19	14	0	19	17	.364
2007	Cardinals (GCL)	R	0	4	9.53	13	6	0	0	34	43	42	36	2	35	40	.309
2008	Quad Cities (MWL)	LoA	2	0	1.23	5	0	0	1	7	4	3	1	0	5	9	.154
	Palm Beach (FSL)	HiA	4	6	3.04	54	0	0	29	56	39	20	19	3	48	85	.196
MINOR LEAGUE TOTALS			7	13	5.51	83	10	0	30	114	110	84	70	5	107	151	.256

22 ADAM OTTAVINO, RHP

BORN: Nov. 22, 1985. **B-T:** R-R. **HT.:** 6-5. **WT.:** 215. **DRAFTED:** Northeastern, 2006 (1st round). **SIGNED BY:** Kobe Perez.

Before the start of major league spring training last year, the Cardinals invited a select group of pitching prospects to what they called a "classic mechanics" mini-camp. Ottavino, the 30th overall pick in the 2006 draft and recipient of a $950,000 bonus, was a willing student. He threw himself into the program, which included scanning tapes of pitching greats and rediscovering what coaches called a "natural rhythm." Yet he may have gotten into it too much, as the power pitcher with the power build got powerfully out of whack and lost confidence. He got hit hard in his first Double-A experience, and the Cardinals shut him down for a couple of stints in May so he could rest a sore shoulder and try to regain confidence in his stuff. He pitched better later in the season, but his mechanics were never consistent all year. Ottavino has a four-seam fastball he can throw at 94 mph, and a two-seamer he has embraced that goes in the 90s. His slurvy breaking ball would be more effective if he used it more, and his changeup still needs work. But teetering mechanics can sabotage all of his pitches. The Cardinals gave him a break to reset and sent him to Arizona Fall League, where his mechanics looked better but he still compiled a 6.17 ERA in 23 innings. He ditched the high hand swing and went to a more compact delivery. He will return to the Springfield rotation in hopes of a bounceback year, and reaching Triple-A would put him back on schedule.

Year	Club (League)	Class	W	L	ERA	G	GS	CG	SV	IP	H	R	ER	HR	BB	SO	AVG
2006	State College (NYP)	SS	2	2	3.14	6	6	0	0	29	23	12	10	1	13	26	.211
	Quad Cities (MWL)	LoA	2	3	3.44	8	8	0	0	37	28	21	14	3	19	38	.211
2007	Palm Beach (FSL)	HiA	12	8	3.08	27	27	1	0	143	130	63	49	10	63	128	.239
2008	Springfield (TEX)	AA	3	7	5.23	24	24	1	0	115	133	75	67	16	52	96	.291
MINOR LEAGUE TOTALS			19	20	3.89	65	65	2	0	324	314	171	140	30	147	288	.253

23 TYLER HERRON, RHP

BORN: Aug. 5, 1986. **B-T:** R-R. **HT.:** 6-3. **WT.:** 190. **DRAFTED:** HS—Wellington, Fla., 2005 (1st round supplemental). **SIGNED BY:** Steve Turco.

Among the youngest starters moving steadily through the Cardinals system, Herron is also usually described as one of the system's most polished players. He was the 46th overall pick back in 2005, taken out of a cradle of pitching, Wellington (Fla.) High and signed for $675,000. His alma mater also spawned first-round picks Bobby Bradley, Sean Burnett and Justin Pope (a Cardinals choice after three years at Central Florida), and big leaguer Mark Brownson. Herron's stint at Palm Beach to open the 2008 season allowed him to live at home, and when he dominated in nine starts he quickly earned a promotion to Double-A. He was knocked around there, however, and returned to Palm Beach to get himself back on track in August. Herron has consistently shown effective control of three average to plus pitches. He throws a sinking fastball at 89-91 mph, and he has a trusty changeup as his second pitch. His curve is good enough to get strikeouts, though he continues to allow both his offspeed pitches to stray too high in the zone. He'll need to sharpen his command to get more advanced hitters out. Herron's smooth, repeatable delivery and access to three quality pitches give the Cardinals faith that he'll be able to advance in spite of his first setback in Double-A. He went to Hawaii Winter Baseball after the season, where he shined as a reliever (0.69 ERA in 13 innings), but he's still viewed as a middle-of-the-rotation starter for now. He'll return to Springfield, where added strength and improved command will curtail the bruising he took there before.

Year	Club (League)	Class	W	L	ERA	G	GS	CG	SV	IP	H	R	ER	HR	BB	SO	AVG
2005	Johnson City (APP)	R	0	3	5.62	13	13	0	0	50	47	35	31	11	27	49	.245
2006	Johnson City (APP)	R	5	6	4.13	13	13	1	0	70	69	41	32	6	22	54	.259
	State College (NYP)	SS	0	1	3.00	1	1	1	0	6	7	2	2	1	1	3	.318
2007	Quad Cities (MWL)	LoA	10	7	3.74	30	22	0	1	137	123	62	57	7	26	130	.240
2008	Springfield (TEX)	AA	5	5	5.20	15	15	0	0	81	101	50	47	9	29	59	.304
	Palm Beach (FSL)	HiA	2	2	2.70	12	9	0	1	57	49	18	17	5	11	43	.234
MINOR LEAGUE TOTALS			22	24	4.18	84	73	2	2	401	396	208	186	39	116	338	.258

24 RICHARD CASTILLO, RHP

BORN: Oct. 11, 1989. **B-T:** R-R. **HT.:** 5-11. **WT.:** 165. **SIGNED:** Venezuela, 2007. **SIGNED BY:** Gregorio Gonzalez.

A byproduct of the Cardinals' aggressive promotion of players was younger players moving quicker and to higher levels. Castillo, a product of the Cardinals' recent initiatives in Venezuela, was 18 when he arrived at Palm Beach because of an injury, and he pitched well above his age. Castillo compiled a 1.13 ERA in 16 innings at Palm Beach as the youngest starter in the league. He has the raw and loose look and live frame of a top-flight prospect, but the combination of his age, his frame and the lack of a track record keeps the Cardinals from getting too high on him. He throws a fastball at 89-90 mph now, and it should gain velocity as he gains strength. His curveball can be an out pitch, but he'll have to become more consistent with it. He also has a changeup that's a work in progress. It's command beyond his years that has helped him to 88 strikeouts in 95 innings against just 28 walks. He struck out 19 of the 65 batters he faced in high Class A. Castillo finished the year as a the headliner of a teen brigade that included center fielder Frederick Parejo, a starter on a championship Batavia team and the New York-Penn League's all-star game MVP. Parejo, too, was just 18. Both could be reunited at Quad Cities, where they'll be full-season starters before they're 20.

Year	Club (League)	Class	W	L	ERA	G	GS	CG	SV	IP	H	R	ER	HR	BB	SO	AVG
2007	Cardinals (VSL)	R	2	2	1.72	17	8	0	2	63	40	20	12	3	22	60	.183
2008	Palm Beach (FSL)	HiA	1	0	1.13	6	2	0	0	16	12	3	2	0	8	19	.222
	Quad Cities (MWL)	LoA	8	4	2.62	13	13	0	0	79	64	26	23	11	20	69	.227
MINOR LEAGUE TOTALS			11	6	2.11	36	23	0	2	158	116	49	37	14	50	148	.209

25 STEVEN HILL, 1B/OF/C

BORN: March 14, 1985. **B-T:** R-R. **HT.:** 5-11. **WT.:** 190. **DRAFTED:** Stephen F. Austin State, 2007 (13th round). **SIGNED BY:** Joe Almaraz.

Hill broke a couple of bones in his left hand when he was hit by a pitch in June, but it did little to slow him down. When he returned to the field to start a rehab assignment, he ripped three home runs in his first game back. Quick starts at the plate are nothing new for Hill. Taken 412th overall in the 2007 draft, he was the Southland Conference player of the year after hitting 24 homers for Stephen F. Austin State. He intrigued the Cardinals because he has a bat for many positions. He played first and had experience in the outfield, and the Cardinals thought he would be willing to catch, too. And while his defensive future is still up in the air, he has been a productive offensive player since signing. Hill has a punchy and forceful swing, with good bat speed and an ability to make solid contact to all fields. He went to the Arizona Fall League as a catcher to work on those skills, and he also hit .304 with three home runs. He's becoming more fluid behind the plate and starting to handle the nuances of the position better. A return to Double-A is likely, with more playing time at catcher this go-round while keeping his other gloves handy. His bat will play in the majors; he just has to find the position that gets him there.

ST. LOUIS CARDINALS

Year	Club (League)	Class	AVG	G	AB	R	H	2B	3B	HR	RBI	BB	SO	SB	OBP	SLG
2007	Batavia (NYP)	SS	.436	10	39	4	17	5	1	1	11	5	5	0	.511	.692
	Quad Cities (MWL)	LoA	.303	62	261	38	79	15	0	11	44	9	58	1	.330	.487
2008	Springfield (TEX)	AA	.303	26	99	13	30	3	1	5	9	3	31	0	.330	.505
	Cardinals (GCL)	R	.313	4	16	4	5	1	0	3	5	0	7	0	.313	.938
	Palm Beach (FSL)	HiA	.285	46	172	28	49	11	2	9	34	15	42	0	.339	.529
MINOR LEAGUE TOTALS			.307	148	587	87	180	35	4	29	103	32	143	1	.345	.528

26 ALLEN CRAIG, 3B

BORN: July 18, 1984. **B-T:** R-R. **HT.:** 6-2. **WT.:** 190. **DRAFTED:** California, 2006 (8th round).
SIGNED BY: Dane Walker.

Craig spent his career at California as a nomadic glove, bouncing from shortstop to left field to first base to third base and back around the horn again. His bat was always the constant, the reason to find him a spot—any spot—in the lineup. It's likely back on positional merry-go-round for Craig as the Cardinals find a spot for the player who was the top slugger on their Double-A team last year. He spent most of the season playing third, though when he missed time with a minor injury he returned to find a new reality: 2008 first-rounder Brett Wallace was at third. Craig is clearly pinched between an on-the-cusp David Freese and the fast-rising Wallace at the hot corner, so his versatility will be helpful. He saw time in the outfield last year and could try first base to get a spot in Triple-A. He has limited range at third and a quirky throwing motion that some thought would prohibit him from advancing at the position anyway. His bat should keep him moving. Craig has great bat speed and can drive the ball to all fields. He's coming off back-to-back, 20-plus home run seasons, so the Cardinals will find a way to get him into the middle of the Memphis lineup.

Year	Club (League)	Class	AVG	G	AB	R	H	2B	3B	HR	RBI	BB	SO	SB	OBP	SLG
2006	State College (NYP)	SS	.257	48	175	21	45	13	0	4	29	13	28	0	.325	.400
2007	Palm Beach (FSL)	HiA	.312	112	423	77	132	25	2	21	77	35	79	8	.370	.530
	Springfield (TEX)	AA	.292	7	24	5	7	2	0	3	3	1	6	0	.320	.750
2008	Springfield (TEX)	AA	.304	129	506	84	154	30	0	22	85	48	87	2	.373	.494
MINOR LEAGUE TOTALS			.300	296	1128	187	338	70	2	50	194	97	200	10	.363	.498

27 TONY CRUZ, C/3B

BORN: Aug. 18, 1986. **B-T:** R-R. **HT.:** 5-11. **WT.:** 205. **DRAFTED:** Palm Beach (Fla.) CC, 2007 (26th round). **SIGNED BY:** Charlie Gonzalez.

Cruz played in the Cardinals' backyard in Florida, showing flashes of the hitter he would become while playing for a junior college team near the team's spring training facility. In the matter of weeks after he was drafted, Cruz blazed through four levels, barely stopping to rake at each. When he topped out at Quad Cities, he hit homers in his first two games and drove in at least a run in his first seven. He followed it up with an all-star season in the high Class A Florida State League. But what could really enhance his value is a change of position. Cruz, a third baseman by trade, came to spring training last year as a catcher, and he went to Hawaii this winter to continue to working at the position. He also hit .323 there. A reliable glove at third, Cruz has proven adept, if not natural, at catcher. His arm is plenty strong for the position, he's a savvy game-caller and his footwork continues to improve. His bat, which hasn't shown more power than consistently ripping doubles, is also a bigger plus at catcher than at third. He has proven that he can turn around even major league-quality fastballs. No matter what position he plays, Cruz will open the season in Double-A.

Year	Club (League)	Class	AVG	G	AB	R	H	2B	3B	HR	RBI	BB	SO	SB	OBP	SLG
2007	Cardinals (GCL)	R	.375	7	32	8	12	5	0	0	4	1	7	1	.382	.531
	Johnson City (APP)	R	.280	6	25	2	7	2	0	2	2	2	2	1	.333	.600
	Batavia (NYP)	SS	.375	4	16	2	6	1	0	0	4	0	5	0	.412	.438
	Quad Cities (MWL)	LoA	.282	49	195	26	55	10	1	5	34	17	25	3	.338	.421
2008	Palm Beach (FSL)	HiA	.279	89	351	41	98	22	3	8	58	19	50	3	.316	.427
MINOR LEAGUE TOTALS			.288	155	619	79	178	40	4	15	102	39	89	8	.329	.438

28 SHANE ROBINSON, OF

BORN: Oct. 30, 1984. **B-T:** R-R. **HT.:** 5-9. **WT.:** 160. **DRAFTED:** Florida State, 2006 (5th round).
SIGNED BY: Steve Turco.

Told often enough that he didn't have the size and strength to play in the majors and certainly didn't have the swing to get there, Robinson raised his hands, changed his stance and started trying to hit like the big bat he believed he had to be. At the start of spring training 2008, Springfield manager Pop Warner offered him an alternate route. Robinson shortened his swing, put his speed to work and let that carry him. Slashing line drives instead of trying to artificially create power with an exaggerated whip, Robinson hit .410/.451/.615 in April and dominated at Springfield to earn a promotion to Memphis. He turned every hit into a track meet. Robinson has plus speed, the kind that turns a single into a double and allows him to score easily from first on an extra-base hit. He has the range and smarts to play center. His numbers slipped after a promotion to Memphis as he lost patience and struck out too much. The Cardinals sent him to the Arizona Fall League to work on his approach and he hit .280 in 107 at-bats, with just 13 strikeouts. His speed could be better utilized with an improved feel for stealing bases. He fits the profile of a spare, speedy outfielder and will play in center field this year at Triple-A.

Year	Club (League)	Class	AVG	G	AB	R	H	2B	3B	HR	RBI	BB	SO	SB	OBP	SLG
2006	Quad Cities (MWL)	LoA	.282	63	252	41	71	9	2	0	21	20	20	13	.346	.333
2007	Cardinals (GCL)	R	.182	4	11	1	2	0	0	0	1	2	1	0	.286	.182
	Palm Beach (FSL)	HiA	.253	43	166	22	42	6	1	3	13	16	16	14	.321	.355
2008	Springfield (TEX)	AA	.352	63	244	46	86	17	3	4	32	17	34	13	.396	.496
	Memphis (PCL)	AAA	.220	42	141	10	31	4	1	1	10	5	24	2	.248	.284
MINOR LEAGUE TOTALS			.285	215	814	120	232	36	7	8	77	60	95	42	.339	.376

29 LUKE GREGERSON, RHP

BORN: May 14, 1984. **B-T:** L-R. **HT.:** 6-3. **WT.:** 200. **DRAFTED:** St. Xavier (Ill.), 2006 (28th round). **SIGNED BY:** Scott Melvin.

The Cardinals are one organization that isn't afraid to use its future relievers as closers in the minor leagues, and Gregerson is a recent graduate from one of the organization's most productive roles: closing for Palm Beach. Like Chris Perez, Mark Worrell (sent to the Padres in the Khalil Greene trade) and Mike Sillman before him, and now Francisco Samuel after him, Gregerson is part of a parade of righthanders who have closed for the team. Gregerson had 10 saves for Springfield last season, pitching more in a setup role, but he continued to riddle opponents with a sinker/slider combination that gets strikeouts as well as ground balls. He has a tall frame, and his delivery adds to the late, boring sink of his fastball. His slider is a plus pitch, and hints of how he could race to the majors became clear in the Double-A bullpen. Gregerson, who has good control overall but whose command sometimes wanders against lefties, held righthanders to a .202 average and struck out 59 of the 217 he faced. Expected to work as a set-up man again this season in Triple-A, his complement of pitches and specialist profile puts him in line for a big league cameo at some time in 2009 and the chance to establish a niche in the majors.

Year	Club (League)	Class	W	L	ERA	G	GS	CG	SV	IP	H	R	ER	HR	BB	SO	AVG
2006	Johnson City (APP)	R	0	1	3.86	15	0	0	5	16	14	10	7	0	6	24	.222
	State College (NYP)	SS	6	1	1.72	12	0	0	4	16	9	5	3	0	9	22	.164
2007	Palm Beach (FSL)	HiA	3	4	1.97	53	0	0	29	64	42	14	14	0	20	69	.188
	Springfield (TEX)	AA	0	0	0.00	1	0	0	0	1	1	0	0	0	0	3	.250
2008	Springfield (TEX)	AA	7	6	3.35	57	0	0	10	75	62	32	28	6	26	78	.221
MINOR LEAGUE TOTALS			16	12	2.72	138	0	0	48	172	128	61	52	6	61	196	.205

30 NICK ADDITON, LHP

BORN: Dec. 16, 1987. **B-T:** L-L. **HT.:** 6-3. **WT.:** 170. **DRAFTED:** Indian River (Fla.) CC, D/F 2006 (46th round). **SIGNED BY:** Charlie Gonzalez.

Additon is a finesse lefty who was a strong candidate for the Cardinals' organization awards last season, primarily for a 31⅔-inning scoreless stretch he pitched at Quad Cities, a streak of shutdown pitching that lasted 41 days and included being part of a combined 13-inning no-hitter. Additon finished the season with more strikeouts (121) than hits allowed (103) and made 19 starts at low Class A before a late-season promotion to Palm Beach. In the bigger parks of the Florida State League, the Florida native was even better, and during the season he had four months when opponents hit .208 or worse against him. Additon works at 84-87 mph and lives off his ability to throw strikes with movement and deception. His breaking ball must be sharper for him to duplicate last year's success at the higher levels, especially when it comes to getting the swings and misses he has in his first two pro seasons. His changeup will also need work. Additon will return to the high Class A rotation and continue to determine if his ceiling is at the back of a big league rotation.

Year	Club (League)	Class	W	L	ERA	G	GS	CG	SV	IP	H	R	ER	HR	BB	SO	AVG
2007	Johnson City (APP)	R	2	1	3.76	14	9	0	1	53	56	23	22	6	11	61	.267
	Batavia (NYP)	SS	1	0	0.00	3	0	0	0	5	2	0	0	0	1	5	.118
2008	Quad Cities (MWL)	LoA	9	5	2.50	25	19	0	1	119	92	41	33	12	35	108	.214
	Palm Beach (FSL)	HiA	2	0	0.50	3	3	1	0	18	11	2	1	1	5	13	.167
MINOR LEAGUE TOTALS			14	6	2.58	45	31	1	2	195	161	66	56	19	52	187	.223

San Diego Padres

BY MATT EDDY

After a tumultuous 2008 season in which the big league club sputtered, several top prospects took steps backwards and another first-round pick was beset by an injury at the onset of his pro career, the Padres seemed much more than a year removed from 2007, when they came within three outs of a third consecutive playoff appearance.

San Diego lost 99 games last season, its most since 1993, and finished in last place in the National League West for the first time since 2003. The future direction of the franchise doesn't look much brighter, as the Padres spent the offseason looking to shed payroll as owner John Moores goes through a divorce. Moores is trying to sell the club as part of the settlement.

The Padres dumped Khalil Greene on the Cardinals in December, but received only righthanded reliever Mark Worrell and a fringe player to be named in return. They unsuccessfully tried to divest themselves of 2007 Cy Young Award winner Jake Peavy because he has $63 million remaining on his contract, but turned down intriguing packages from the Braves (starting with Yunel Escobar and outfield prospect Gorkys Hernandez) and the Cubs (beginning with third baseman Josh Vitters).

With their season going nowhere, the Padres gave auditions to several youngsters. Last year's No. 1 prospect, Chase Headley, played well after a mid-June promotion and took over the left-field job. Likewise, rookie catcher Nick Hundley ascended to the role of regular by season's end. Second baseman Matt Antonelli, righthander Josh Geer, lefty Wade LeBlanc and outfielder Max Venable got the chance to play regularly in September as San Diego searched for potential 2009 contributors.

The farm system produced as many disappointments as it did rookies, however. Antonelli and LeBlanc endured growing pains as they adjusted to Triple-A. Most of the top pitching prospects took a step back, as Mat Latos worked just 25 full-season innings; Drew Miller posted a 6.10 ERA; Steve Garrison had rotator-cuff surgery; and Will Inman saw his control slip.

The Padres' string of draft misfortune continued in 2008. First baseman Allan Dykstra, the 23rd overall pick, had his bonus reduced by $250,000 after a physical raised questions about his right hip. The situation mirrored that of 2003 first-rounder Tim Stauffer, who also signed for a diminished bonus after an MRI revealed weakness in his shoulder.

San Diego has made only one first-round selection in six drafts—Antonelli in 2006—who hasn't been besieged by health concerns. Matt Bush (2004), Cesar

Rookie Chase Headley provided one of the few bright spots in the Padres' lost season

TOP 30 PROSPECTS

1. Kyle Blanks, 1b	16. Wynn Pelzer, rhp
2. Mat Latos, rhp	17. Eric Sogard, 2b
3. Jaff Decker, of	18. Will Inman, rhp
4. Kellen Kulbacki, of	19. Blake Tekotte, of
5. Adys Portillo, rhp	20. Cesar Carrillo, rhp
6. Cedric Hunter, of	21. Nick Schmidt, lhp
7. Will Venable, of	22. Steve Garrison, lhp
8. Allan Dykstra, 1b	23. Chad Huffman, of
9. Matt Antonelli, 2b	24. Everth Cabrera, 2b/ss
10. James Darnell, 3b	25. Mitch Canham, c
11. Logan Forsythe, 3b	26. Drew Miller, rhp
12. Wade LeBlanc, lhp	27. Jeremy Hefner, rhp
13. Josh Geer, rhp	28. Cole Figueroa, ss/2b
14. Simon Castro, rhp	29. Ernesto Frieri, rhp
15. Drew Cumberland, ss	30. Ivan Nova, rhp

Carrillo (2005) and Nick Schmidt (2007) all had Tommy John surgery in 2007.

Perhaps the Padres' most positive development of 2008 occurred on July 2, when international scouting director Randy Smith and his staff signed three premium talents to seven-figure bonuses: Venezuelan righthander Adys Portillo ($2 million), Venezuelan outfielder Luis Domoromo ($1.25 million) and Dominican shortstop Alvaro Aristy ($1 million). The organization also was excited by toolsy Australian rules footballer Corey Adamson ($500,000), whom they envision developing into a slugger.

General Manager: Kevin Towers. **Farm Director:** Grady Fuson. **Scouting Director:** Bill Gayton.

Class	Team	League	W	L	PCT	Finish*	Manager	Affiliated
Majors	San Diego	National	63	99	.389	15th (16)	Bud Black	—
Triple-A	Portland Beavers	Pacific Coast	70	74	.486	9th (16)	Randy Ready	2001
Double-A	San Antonio Missions	Texas	75	65	.536	5th (8)	Bill Masse	2007
High A	Lake Elsinore Storm	California	71	69	.507	4th (10)	Carlos Lezcano	2001
Low A	Fort Wayne Wizards	Midwest	71	69	.507	10th (14)	Doug Dascenzo	1999
Short-season	Eugene Emeralds	Northwest	40	36	.526	3rd (8)	Greg Riddoch	2001
Rookie	AZL Padres	Arizona	33	23	.589	4th (9)	Jose Flores	2004
Overall 2008 Minor League Record			360	336	.517	10th		

* Finish in overall standings (No. of teams in league). ^League champion.

LAST YEAR'S TOP 30

Rank	Player, Pos.	Status
1.	Chase Headley, 3b	Majors
2.	Matt Antonelli, 2b	No. 9
3.	Mat Latos, rhp	No. 2
4.	Wade LeBlanc, lhp	No. 12
5.	Drew Miller, rhp	No. 26
6.	Steve Garrison, lhp	No. 22
7.	Will Inman, rhp	No. 18
8.	Cedric Hunter, of	No. 6
9.	Nick Schmidt, lhp	No. 21
10.	Kyle Blanks, 1b	No. 1
11.	Cesar Carrillo, rhp	No. 20
12.	Cory Luebke, lhp	Dropped out
13.	Yefri Carvajal, of	Dropped out
14.	Kellen Kulbacki, of	No. 4
15.	Will Venable, of	No. 7
16.	Drew Cumberland, ss	No. 15
17.	Mitch Canham, c	No. 25
18.	Cesar Ramos, lhp	Dropped out
19.	Joe Thatcher, lhp	Dropped out
20.	Carlos Guevara, rhp	Dropped out
21.	Matt Buschmann, rhp	Dropped out
22.	Chad Huffman, of	No. 23
23.	Jared Wells, rhp	(Mariners)
24.	Nick Hundley, c	Majors
25.	Jeudy Valdez, ss/2b	Dropped out
26.	Rayner Contreras, 3b/2b	Dropped out
27.	Josh Geer, rhp	No. 13
28.	David Freese, 3b	(Cardinals)
29.	Corey Kluber, rhp	Dropped out
30.	Matt Bush, rhp	Dropped out

BEST TOOLS

Best Hitter for Average	Cedric Hunter
Best Power Hitter	Kyle Blanks
Best Strike-Zone Discipline	Matt Antonelli
Fastest Baserunner	Everth Cabrera
Best Athlete	James Darnell
Best Fastball	Mat Latos
Best Curveball	Ernesto Frieri
Best Slider	Wynn Pelzer
Best Changeup	Wade LeBlanc
Best Control	Nate Culp
Best Defensive Catcher	Jose Lobaton
Best Defensive Infielder	Jesus Lopez
Best Infield Arm	Lance Zawadzki
Best Defensive Outfielder	Brad Chalk
Best Outfield Arm	Yefri Carvajal

PROJECTED 2012 LINEUP

Catcher	Nick Hundley
First Base	Adrian Gonzalez
Second Base	Matt Antonelli
Third Base	Chase Headley
Shortstop	Drew Cumberland
Left Field	Kyle Blanks
Center Field	Cedric Hunter
Right Field	Jaff Decker
No. 1 Starter	Jake Peavy
No. 2 Starter	Chris Young
No. 3 Starter	Mat Latos
No. 4 Starter	Adys Portillo
No. 5 Starter	Wade LeBlanc
Closer	Heath Bell

TOP PROSPECTS OF THE DECADE

Year	Player, Pos.	2008 Org.
1999	Matt Clement, rhp	Cardinals
2000	Sean Burroughs, 3b	Out of baseball
2001	Sean Burroughs, 3b	Out of baseball
2002	Sean Burroughs, 3b	Out of baseball
2003	Xavier Nady, of	Yankees
2004	Josh Barfield, 2b	Indians
2005	Josh Barfield, 2b	Indians
2006	Cesar Carrillo, rhp	Padres
2007	Cedric Hunter, of	Padres
2008	Chase Headley, 3b	Padres

TOP DRAFT PICKS OF THE DECADE

Year	Player, Pos.	2008 Org.
1999	Vince Faison, of	Out of baseball
2000	Mark Phillips, lhp	Out of baseball
2001	Jake Gautreau, 2b	Fort Worth (American Assoc.)
2002	Khalil Greene, ss	Padres
2003	Tim Stauffer, rhp	Padres
2004	Matt Bush, ss	Padres
2005	Cesar Carrillo, rhp	Padres
2006	Matt Antonelli, 3b	Padres
2007	Nick Schmidt, lhp	Padres
2008	Allan Dykstra, 1b	Padres

LARGEST BONUSES IN CLUB HISTORY

Matt Bush, 2004	$3,150,000
Mark Phillips, 2000	$2,200,000
Sean Burroughs, 1998	$2,100,000
Adys Portillo, 2008	$2,000,000
Jake Gautreau, 2001	$1,875,000

SAN DIEGO PADRES

TOP 2009 ROOKIE: Will Venable, of. He's 26, but the former Princeton basketball star made significant improvements with his power and discipline last season.

BREAKOUT PROSPECT: Simon Castro, rhp. He has a power arm and flashes a plus slider, though his command is still a work in progress.

SLEEPER: Lance Zawadzki, ss. His future home may be second base, but the 2007 fourth-rounder has bat control and plus power from both sides of the plate.

SOURCE OF TOP 30 TALENT

Homegrown	26	Acquired	4
College	17	Trades	2
Junior college	0	Rule 5 draft	2
High school	3	Independent leagues	0
Draft-and-follow	3	Free agents/waivers	0
Nondrafted free agents	0		
International	3		

Numbers in parentheses indicate prospect rankings.

LF
Kellen Kulbacki (4)
Will Venable (7)
Chad Huffman (23)
Luis Domoromo
Luis Durango

CF
Cedric Hunter (6)
Blake Tekotte (19)
Danny Payne
Brad Chalk
Drew Macias
Dan Robertson

RF
Jaff Decker (3)
Yefri Carvajal
Sawyer Carroll
Craig Cooper
Mike Baxter
Rymer Liriano

3B
James Darnell (10)
Logan Forsythe (11)
Rayner Contreras
Edinson Rincon

SS
Drew Cumberland (15)
Everth Cabrera (24)
Beamer Weems
Jesus Lopez
Jeudy Valdez
Alavaro Aristy

2B
Matt Antonelli (9)
Eric Sogard (17)
Cole Figueroa (28)
Lance Zawadzki
Jonathan Galvez
Travis Denker

1B
Kyle Blanks (1)
Allan Dykstra (8)
Matt Clark

C
Mitch Canham (25)
Jose Lobaton
Emmanuel Quiles
Adam Zornes

RHP

Starters	Relievers
Mat Latos (2)	Wynn Pelzer (16)
Adys Portillo (5)	Ernesto Frieri (29)
Josh Geer (13)	Mike Ekstrom
Simon Castro (14)	Mark Worrell
Will Inman (18)	Chad Reineke
Cesar Carrillo (20)	Scott Patterson
Drew Miller (26)	Evan Scribner
Jeremy Hefner (27)	Jeremy McBryde
Ivan Nova (30)	Tyson Bagley
Matt Buschmann	Gary Poynter
Corey Kluber	Wilton Lopez
Erik Davis	Greg Burke
Steve Faris	Mike DeMark
	Jackson Quezada
	Anthony Bass
	Matt Bush
	Gabe DeHoyos
	Eduardo Perez

LHP

Starters	Relievers
Wade LeBlanc (12)	Joe Thatcher
Nick Schmidt (21)	Rob Musgrave
Steve Garrison (22)	
Cesar Ramos	
Cory Luebke	
Michael Watt	
Nate Culp	

2008

BEST PURE HITTER: OF Jaff Decker (1s) uses the whole field and has a tremendous approach for a young hitter. He's short to the ball and has a natural feel for hitting.

BEST POWER HITTER: 1B Allan Dykstra (1) had as much raw power as anyone in the draft with tremendous strength, leverage in his swing and the plate discipline to get pitches he can drive. 1B Matt Clark (12) tied for the NCAA Division I lead with 28 homers in 2008 and topped California's juco ranks with 15 in 2007. 3B James Darnell (2) and Decker have above-average power.

FASTEST RUNNER: OF Blake Tekotte (3) is an above-average runner and has good baserunning instincts as well.

BEST DEFENSIVE PLAYER: SS Beamer Weems (8) has prototype hands, range and arm strength, though the switch-hitter didn't answer questions about his offensive ability, batting .207/.355/.299 in 87 at-bats in his pro debut.

BEST FASTBALL: RHP Tyson Bagley (11) can sit at 93-96 mph at his best, though his heater tends to be straight. RHP Gary Poynter (39) has reached the mid-90s with his fastball and sits in the low 90s with heavy sink.

BEST SECONDARY PITCH: LHP Rob Musgrave (14) commands his plus curveball and slightly above-average changeup. RHP Erik Davis (13) also features a plus changeup.

BEST PRO DEBUT: Decker, playing in his hometown of Peoria in the Rookie-level Arizona League, hit .352/.523/.541 and led the league in runs (51) and on-base percentage. OF Dan Robertson (33) was the short-season Northwest League MVP and batting champion, hitting .377/.443/.497 with 20 stolen bases.

BEST ATHLETE: Darnell has a well-muscled, athletic body and surprising agility and speed for his 6-foot-2, 195-pound frame. He may wind up in right field.

MOST INTRIGUING BACKGROUND: Davis nearly lost an eye when he was struck by a batted ball in the Cape Cod League in 2006. He recovered and helped lead Stanford to the 2008 College World Series. 2B Cole Figueroa (6) is the son of Giants minor league manager and ex-big leaguer Bien. Clark's father Terry pitched in the majors and is a pitching coach in the Rangers system.

CLOSEST TO THE MAJORS: Figueroa is a polished hitter who profiles as an offensive second baseman. He had knee surgery during instructional league but shouldn't miss any time next season.

BEST LATE-ROUND PICK: Poynter has big-time stuff, including an erratic power curveball. If he throws strikes, he'll move rapidly.

THE ONE WHO GOT AWAY: LHP Brett Mooneyham (14) could be a first-rounder after three years at Stanford if he throws more strikes with his low-90s fastball and power slider.

ASSESSMENT: The Padres wanted power bats and drafted only one pitcher among their top 10 signees. Dykstra has a chronic hip issue that held up his signing, and Decker's bat could be special enough for him to surpass Dykstra as the top prospect in this class, sooner rather than later.

2007

Early returns are a bit disappointing on a draft class that included six picks before the second round. OF Kellen Kulbacki (1s) is the only one who looks like a future regular, while LHP Nick Schmidt (1) had Tommy John surgery. SS Drew Cumberland (1s) and C Mitch Canham (1s) had so-so first full seasons, while LHP Cory Luebke (1s) and OF Danny Payne (1s) weren't even that good.

GRADE: C

2006

2B Matt Antonelli (1) and LHP Wade LeBlanc (2) got exposed in Triple-A and the majors. RHP Mat Latos (11), a $1.25 million draft-and-follow, showed iffy control, health and makeup. 3B David Freese (9) is on the verge of making the Cardinals after getting traded for Jim Edmonds.

GRADE: C

2005

RHP Cesar Carillo (1) had Tommy John surgery and LHP Cesar Ramos (1s) has stalled, but OF/3B Chase Headley (2) and C Nick Hundley (2) became regulars in San Diego by the end of last season. OF Will Venable (7) could join them in the lineup this year.

GRADE: B

2004

Taking SS Matt Bush (1) with the No. 1 overall pick was a disastrous decision. 1B Kyle Blanks (42) has emerged as the system's top prospect, while SS Sean Kazmar (5) and RHP Mike Ekstrom (12) have played sparingly in the majors.

GRADE: C+

Draft analysis by John Manuel (2008) and Jim Callis (2004-07). Numbers in parentheses indicate draft rounds. *Bonuses for 2004-05 are first 10 rounds only.

JOHN WILLIAMSON

PROSPECT

KYLE BLANKS, 1B

Born: Sept. 11, 1986.
Bats: R. **Throws:** R.
Ht.: 6-6. **Wt.:** 280.
Drafted: Yavapai (Ariz.)
JC, D/F 2004
(42nd round).
Signed by: Jake Wilson.

The Padres had the No. 1 overall pick in the 2004 draft, but their best choice turned out to be their 42nd-rounder. They signed Blanks, a big kid from small Moriarty (N.M.) High, for $260,000 a year later as a draft-and-follow. In his lone season at Yavapai (Ariz.) JC, he led the wood-bat Arizona Community College Athletic Conference in batting (.440), doubles (25) and RBIs (47). Had he not signed, Blanks projected as a top-five-rounds talent for the 2005 draft. He led the Rookie-level Arizona League with seven homers, but a major leg infection knocked him out in mid-July of his 2006 follow-up. He re-established his prospect credentials in 2007, when he became the first righthanded hitter to top 20 homers for high Class A Lake Elsinore since Xavier Nady in 2001. He turned in his second straight 20-homer, 100-RBI campaign in 2008 at Double-A San Antonio, this time in a pitcher's park.

No active player resembles Blanks, not entirely. He's an intimidating 6-foot-6 and 280 pounds and built like a football tight end, yet he exhibits strong bat control instead of always selling out for power. In fact, he takes pride in his ability to hit for average and focuses on taking the ball to center and right field when pitchers work him away—and that's despite having the raw power to rival any player in the system. He has tightened his strike zone and closed holes in his swing each season. Blanks is athletic for his size and an average runner underway. He throws very well and shows surprising agility and hands at first base, where he has average potential as a defender. Blanks' advocates think he has sufficient range and instincts to play an outfield corner, though he has played just two games there as a pro (both in 2005). He has done a good job monitoring his weight since ballooning to nearly 300 pounds after his layoff in 2006.

Despite incorporating a stride and a sense of timing in his swing in 2007, Blanks still has a tendency to hit with dead hands because he uses a minimal load to his swing. That cuts into his home run production, but it does make him less susceptible to hard stuff on the inner half. He hasn't shown much power against lefthanders the last two seasons, as he has struggled to stay back on their backdoor breaking balls. He's much more comfortable facing righthanders, even sidearmers and submariners, because they tend to work him hard inside and he can just react. Blanks will need to continue to make conditioning a priority. He has slowed a bit since signing and isn't quick out of the batter's box.

After refining his batting eye in the Arizona Fall League, where he posted a .430 on-base percentage, Blanks is ticketed for Triple-A Portland. He may learn to play left field, though San Diego has yet to make a final decision. At first base, he's blocked by all-star Adrian Gonzalez. But if Blanks continues to produce like he has the last two seasons, the Padres will find room in their lineup for him. Trading Gonzalez would create an opening and cut costs.

Year	Club (League)	Class	AVG	G	AB	R	H	2B	3B	HR	RBI	BB	SO	SB	OBP	SLG
2005	Padres (AZL)	R	.299	48	164	33	49	10	1	7	30	25	49	3	.420	.500
2006	Fort Wayne (MWL)	LoA	.292	86	308	41	90	20	0	10	52	36	79	2	.382	.455
2007	Lake Elsinore (CAL)	HiA	.301	119	465	94	140	31	4	24	100	44	98	11	.380	.540
2008	San Antonio (TEX)	AA	.325	132	492	75	160	23	5	20	107	51	90	5	.404	.514
MINOR LEAGUE TOTALS			.307	385	1429	243	439	84	10	61	289	156	316	21	.393	.508

2 MAT LATOS, RHP

BORN: Dec. 9, 1987. **B-T:** R-R. **HT.:** 6-5. **WT.:** 210. **DRAFTED:** Broward (Fla.) CC, D/F 2006 (11th round). **SIGNED BY:** Joe Bochy.

Questionable maturity and seven-figure bonus demands pushed Latos to the 11th round of the 2006 draft—even though he featured one of the best pure arms available. He signed for $1.25 million as a draft-and-follow the next spring. Latos ranked as the short-season Northwest League's No. 1 prospect in his 2007 debut, but shoulder, oblique and attitude problems hampered him in 2008. Latos' raw stuff is ridiculously good. His fastball sits at 94-95 mph and touches 97 with tremendous downhill plane by virtue of the leverage created by his 6-foot-5 frame. It's at least a 70 pitch on the 20-80 scouting scale. He cleaned up his hard, late-breaking slider, which features fierce two-plane movement coming out of his high three-quarters arm slot. He came into pro ball with a spike changeup, which he used as a chase pitch, but he took to a straight changeup grip in 2008 and his new pitch shows promise. He showed improved control last season. Though Latos shows strong competitive makeup when pitching, it's a different matter entirely between starts. He tends to reject structure, lacks a commitment to improve and rubs teammates the wrong way with his flippant attitude. His command isn't as good as his control. Latos could pitch at the front of a rotation or in a critical bullpen role, and he could reach the majors as early as 2010. If he stays healthy and focused, he should reach Double-A at some point this year.

Year	Club (League)	Class	W	L	ERA	G	GS	CG	SV	IP	H	R	ER	HR	BB	SO	AVG
2007	Eugene (NWL)	SS	1	4	3.83	16	13	0	0	56	58	30	24	1	22	74	.266
2008	Fort Wayne (MWL)	LoA	0	3	3.28	7	5	0	0	25	24	12	9	3	8	23	.250
	Padres (AZL)	R	1	0	3.21	5	3	0	0	14	12	5	5	0	2	23	.231
	Eugene (NWL)	SS	2	0	1.04	3	3	0	0	17	13	3	2	1	3	23	.197
MINOR LEAGUE TOTALS			4	7	3.20	31	24	0	0	112	107	50	40	5	35	143	.248

3 JAFF DECKER, OF

BORN: Feb. 23, 1990. **B-T:** L-L. **HT.:** 5-10. **WT.:** 190. **DRAFTED:** HS—Peoria, Ariz., 2008 (1st round supplemental). **SIGNED BY:** Dave Lottsfeldt.

Just as Cedric Hunter did in 2006, Decker won Arizona League MVP honors in his pro debut. He led the AZL in runs (51), walks (55) and on-base percentage (.523) while finishing second in the batting race (.352). He played high school ball in Peoria, the same Phoenix suburb where the Padres' training complex is located, and signed for $892,000 as a supplemental first-rounder. Though he has no projection remaining in his 5-foot-10, 190-pound frame, Decker drew San Diego's interest because of his innate hitting ability, strike-zone awareness and plus power potential. He's short and quick to the ball, keeps his hands back and uses the whole field. He threw in the low 90s as a two-way player in high school, so he has a plus arm. Because he hits from an open stance, Decker has a tendency to dive toward the plate. He may need to close his stance somewhat to better stride toward the pitcher. Though he played center field as an amateur, his fringy speed and build will limit him to right field as a pro. He'll need to keep his body in top playing shape to retain his limited athleticism. Decker's debut proved that he was one of the top high school bats in the 2008 draft. He'll advance to the low Class A Midwest League, where the hitting environment and weather is much less hospitable than in the AZL.

Year	Club (League)	Class	AVG	G	AB	R	H	2B	3B	HR	RBI	BB	SO	SB	OBP	SLG
2008	Padres (AZL)	R	.352	49	159	51	56	11	2	5	34	55	36	9	.523	.541
	Eugene (NWL)	SS	.200	3	10	2	2	0	0	0	0	2	5	0	.333	.200
MINOR LEAGUE TOTALS			.343	52	169	53	58	11	2	5	34	57	41	9	.513	.521

4 KELLEN KULBACKI, OF

BORN: Nov. 21, 1985. **B-T:** L-L. **HT.:** 5-11. **WT.:** 185. **DRAFTED:** James Madison, 2007 (1st round supplemental). **SIGNED BY:** Ash Lawson.

Kulbacki led NCAA Division I with 24 homers and a .943 slugging percentage as a James Madison sophomore in 2006. The Padres made him the 40th overall pick a year later and signed him for $765,000. He missed most of spring training last year with a pulled hamstring and consequently started slowly at low Class A Fort Wayne. Promoted to high Class A, he finished fifth in the California League with 20 homers in just 84 games. At his best, Kulbacki employs a short, compact, low-maintenance swing. He took to a mechanical adjustment that helped him keep his head level during his swing, which helped him overcome his struggles early in 2008. Though he possesses just average bat speed, his short arms ensure that he rarely gets tied up inside. With good plate coverage, pitch recognition and a knack for barreling the ball, he projects to hit for average as well as power. With fringy speed and a noncommittal approach to improving his outfield play, Kulbacki profiles best in left field. His arm is average at best. When he gets into ruts, it's usually because he extends his arms too far from his body and doesn't stay through the ball. Kulbacki tore the labrum in his right shoulder after crashing into an outfield wall during the Cal League playoffs, during which he hit two homers in three games. He had surgery and is expected to be ready for spring training, with an assignment to Double-A to follow.

Year	Club (League)	Class	AVG	G	AB	R	H	2B	3B	HR	RBI	BB	SO	SB	OBP	SLG
2007	Eugene (NWL)	SS	.301	61	226	33	68	13	3	8	39	27	56	1	.382	.491
2008	Fort Wayne (MWL)	LoA	.164	18	61	9	10	2	0	2	9	9	19	0	.260	.295
	Lake Elsinore (CAL)	HiA	.332	84	304	62	101	18	0	20	66	47	52	1	.428	.589
MINOR LEAGUE TOTALS			.303	163	591	104	179	33	3	30	114	83	127	2	.393	.521

5 ADYS PORTILLO, RHP

BORN: Dec. 20, 1991. **B-T:** R-R. **HT.:** 6-3. **WT.:** 195. **SIGNED:** Venezuela, 2008. **SIGNED BY:** Yfrain Linares/Felix Feliz/Randy Smith.

The consensus No. 2 pitching prospect during the 2008 international signing period—behind only Athletics righthander Michael Inoa—Portillo signed for $2 million in July. It was the highest bonus ever for a Venezuelan until the Reds signed outfielder Yorman Rodriguez for $2.5 million a month later. A wiry 6-foot-3, Portillo boasts plus arm strength and a classic pitcher's frame and projectability. He already pitches at 90-92 mph and touched 95 in Dominican instructional league. He has shown a feel for a changeup that has above-average potential. The Padres value Portillo's polish, clean mechanics and mound presence. Portillo didn't draw uniformly high marks among international scouts for his command, with the chief criticism being that he was wild in the zone during bullpen sessions. His downer curveball also failed to impress scouts last summer, earning below-average grades, but San Diego is optimistic about its development. Portillo is just 17, so he has plenty of time to develop. The Padres won't rush him, but he's a strong candidate to forego the Rookie-level Dominican Summer League and begin his pro career in the Arizona League.

Year	Club (League)	Class	W	L	ERA	G	GS	CG	SV	IP	H	R	ER	HR	BB	SO	AVG
2008—Did Not Play																	

6 CEDRIC HUNTER, OF

BORN: March 10, 1988. **B-T:** L-L. **HT.:** 6-0. **WT.:** 185. **DRAFTED:** HS—Lithonia, Ga., 2006 (3rd round). **SIGNED BY:** Pete DeYoung.

Hunter won Arizona League MVP honors in his 2006 debut, reaching base in his first 49 games. He appeared much more mortal in the tough hitting environment of the Midwest League in 2007, but he got back to basics last season and led the minors with 186 hits. An aggressive hitter, Hunter has the hand-eye coordination and all-fields approach to hit for a high average. He employs a high leg kick, but he loads his hands well and maintains balance throughout his swing, helping him handle lefties as well as righties. Strong wrists help him generate above-average bat speed. An exceptional contact hitter with plus strike-zone command, Hunter ranked as the fifth most difficult minor leaguer to strike out last year (13.6 plate appearances per whiff). He improved his range in center field by getting better reads on balls. He's a solid runner underway. Hunter can pull the ball for power, but he projects to be below-average in that department because his swing lacks natural loft. He still projects as just a borderline average center fielder because of inconsistent routes and a lack of first-step quickness. His arm is below-average. The Padres noticed an improved disposition from Hunter after he seemed a bit distracted by all his press clippings in 2007. He's ready for Double-A and he could receive a center-field audition in San Diego as early as 2010.

Year	Club (League)	Class	AVG	G	AB	R	H	2B	3B	HR	RBI	BB	SO	SB	OBP	SLG
2006	Padres (AZL)	R	.371	52	213	46	79	13	4	1	44	40	22	17	.467	.484
	Eugene (NWL)	SS	.267	5	15	0	4	0	0	0	0	1	3	0	.313	.267
2007	Fort Wayne (MWL)	LoA	.282	129	496	53	140	20	2	7	58	47	78	8	.344	.373
	Portland (PCL)	AAA	.500	3	4	1	2	0	0	1	3	1	1	0	.600	1.250
2008	Lake Elsinore (CAL)	HiA	.318	134	584	98	186	33	3	11	84	42	47	12	.362	.442
MINOR LEAGUE TOTALS			.313	323	1312	198	411	66	9	20	189	131	151	37	.374	.423

7 WILL VENABLE, OF

BORN: Oct. 29, 1982. **B-T:** L-L. **HT.:** 6-2. **WT.:** 205. **DRAFTED:** Princeton, 2005 (7th round). **SIGNED BY:** Jim Bretz.

An all-Ivy League selection in both basketball and baseball as a senior at Princeton, Venable focused on hoops as an amateur. After a lackluster Double-A season in 2007, he made giant strides in Triple-A last year, hitting for more power while learning to play center field. His father Max, who played 12 years in the majors, served as the hitting coach at Portland. Venable is a strong, live-bodied athlete with the natural aptitude required to pick things up quickly. That's why the Padres view him as a potential 20-25 home run hitter in time. His pure lefthanded stroke and solid bat speed already produce the line drives needed to hit for average. He has average speed and is a smart baserunner who reads pitchers well. He's an average defender in left field. Despite a solid base of skills, Venable lacks the one dominating tool that will guarantee him regular play. He probably lacks the first-step quickness to hold down center field on an everyday basis. His arm is below-average. Though he's already 26, Venable's combination of athleticism and aptitude has won him many admirers in the organization. Those who buy in completely see a potential David Justice, while those who don't see a tweener without enough bat for a corner or range for center. For now, he's in San Diego's center-field mix.

Year	Club (League)	Class	AVG	G	AB	R	H	2B	3B	HR	RBI	BB	SO	SB	OBP	SLG
2005	Padres (AZL)	R	.322	15	59	13	19	4	2	1	12	2	9	4	.385	.508
	Eugene (NWL)	SS	.216	42	139	17	30	5	2	2	14	14	38	2	.295	.324
2006	Fort Wayne (MWL)	LoA	.314	124	472	86	148	34	5	11	91	55	81	18	.389	.477
2007	San Antonio (TEX)	AA	.278	134	515	66	143	19	3	8	68	38	84	21	.337	.373
2008	Portland (PCL)	AAA	.292	120	442	70	129	26	4	14	58	44	103	7	.361	.464
	San Diego (NL)	MAJ	.264	28	110	16	29	4	2	2	10	13	21	1	.339	.391
MINOR LEAGUE TOTALS			.288	435	1627	252	469	88	16	36	243	153	315	52	.357	.428
MAJOR LEAGUE TOTALS			.264	28	110	16	29	4	2	2	10	13	21	1	.339	.391

8 ALLAN DYKSTRA, 1B

BORN: May 21, 1987. **B-T:** L-R. **HT.:** 6-5. **WT.:** 215. **DRAFTED:** Wake Forest, 2008 (1st round). **SIGNED BY:** Ash Lawson.

The Padres drafted Dykstra 23rd overall in 2008 and signed him for $1.15 million, but not before reducing his bonus by $250,000 after a physical raised concerns about his surgically repaired right hip. The San Diego native suffered avascular necrosis in the joint, the result of a fall while playing basketball in high school, and the condition may or may not worsen during his career. For his part, he proved to be durable at Wake Forest, missing just one game in three years. Dykstra features the plus-plus raw power and plate discipline that the Padres covet. He controls the zone and has a true bat path, so he should hit for some average as well. He has an above-average arm, strong enough that he played a bit of third base in college. It's impossible to ignore the degenerative nature of Dykstra's hip ailment. He developed a bad habit of striding toward the plate in college, where pitchers steadily worked him away with offspeed stuff. This resulted in an overly pull-conscious approach and left him vulnerable to good fastballs on the inner third of the plate. He spent time in instructional league simply working on stepping toward the pitcher so that his hands could get to the ball and drive through it. He's a below-average athlete, runner and defender at first base. His power and sound batter's eye should hasten his arrival at Double-A, which could happen at some point in his first full pro season. He's blocked by Adrian Gonzalez and Kyle Blanks ahead of him, and Dykstra can't move to another position.

Year	Club (League)	Class	AVG	G	AB	R	H	2B	3B	HR	RBI	BB	SO	SB	OBP	SLG
2008	Lake Elsinore (CAL)	HiA	.292	7	24	5	7	1	0	1	10	7	7	0	.469	.458
MINOR LEAGUE TOTALS			.292	7	24	5	7	1	0	1	10	7	7	0	.469	.458

9 MATT ANTONELLI, 2B

BORN: April 8, 1985. **B-T:** R-R. **HT.:** 6-0. **WT.:** 200. **DRAFTED:** Wake Forest, 2006 (1st round). **SIGNED BY:** Ash Lawson.

Since signing for $1.575 million as the 2006 draft's 17th overall pick, Antonelli has careened from one extreme to the other—and now back again. He went homerless and slugged .356 in his pro debut, then bashed 21 homers and slugged .491 in 2007. He thudded back to earth last season in Triple-A, then rallied in August to earn a September callup to the majors, where he looked overmatched. Despite his struggles, Antonelli never lost his feel for the strike zone and his 76 walks ranked third in the Pacific Coast League. A quality athlete who's a former Massachusetts high school player of the year in football and hockey, he has average raw power and plus speed underway. His arm is above-average for a second baseman. His outstanding makeup was on full display as he held up mentally while enduring a difficult season. Antonelli never established rhythm at the plate last season, and some wonder if the strength he has added since turning pro has cut into his bat speed and fluidity. He's very rotational in his upper half, as he remains resistant to incorporating a stride and more separation in the load of his swing. As a result, he failed to get carry because he didn't stay through the ball. Added bulk also cost Antonelli a step on defense, where he doesn't get good jumps and struggles with the double-play pivot. Antonelli has much to prove in 2009. He could win San Diego's second-base job, but if his bat doesn't come around, he'll probably see work at third base and center field in an effort to increase his versatility.

Year	Club (League)	Class	AVG	G	AB	R	H	2B	3B	HR	RBI	BB	SO	SB	OBP	SLG
2006	Eugene (NWL)	SS	.286	55	189	38	54	12	1	0	22	46	31	9	.426	.360
	Fort Wayne (MWL)	LoA	.125	5	16	3	2	1	1	0	0	2	6	0	.222	.313
2007	Lake Elsinore (CAL)	HiA	.314	82	347	89	109	14	4	14	54	53	58	18	.409	.499
	San Antonio (TEX)	AA	.294	49	187	34	55	11	1	7	24	30	36	10	.395	.476
2008	Portland (PCL)	AAA	.215	128	451	62	97	19	4	7	39	76	86	6	.335	.322
	San Diego (NL)	MAJ	.193	21	57	6	11	2	0	1	3	5	11	0	.292	.281
MINOR LEAGUE TOTALS			.266	319	1190	226	317	57	11	28	139	207	217	43	.379	.403
MAJOR LEAGUE TOTALS			.193	21	57	6	11	2	0	1	3	5	11	0	.292	.281

10 JAMES DARNELL, 3B

BORN: Jan. 19, 1987. **B-T:** R-R. **HT.:** 6-2. **WT.:** 195. **DRAFTED:** South Carolina, 2008 (2nd round). **SIGNED BY:** Anthony Byrd.

Though he was just the third South Carolina player drafted in June, Darnell offers more athleticism and potential five-tool talent than first-rounders Justin Smoak and Reese Havens. He wowed observers in the Northwest League after signing at the Aug. 15 deadline for $740,000. Darnell generates plus power to all fields with a strong lower half. He consistently has hit for average in college and pro ball. Offering surprising agility for his size, he's a plus runner who has average range and a strong throwing arm at third base. He receives uniformly high marks for his makeup and aptitude, as he worked diligently in instructional league to stay through the ball and add arc to his swing because his homers tend to be of the line-drive variety. Though he recognizes pitches well, Darnell struggles to stay back on offspeed pitches because he rotates early in his swing. While he has flashes of brilliance at the hot corner, his footwork needs refinement, his hands aren't the softest and his arm is erratic at times. He has the tools to play right field if he has to move. Darnell is a classic Padres pick—a high-character college player who controls the strike zone. With his athleticism and power, though, the potential is there for him to develop into a second-round steal. Darnell could begin his first full season in high Class A.

Year	Club (League)	Class	AVG	G	AB	R	H	2B	3B	HR	RBI	BB	SO	SB	OBP	SLG
2008	Eugene (NWL)	SS	.373	16	67	9	25	6	1	2	15	11	12	1	.462	.582
MINOR LEAGUE TOTALS			.373	16	67	9	25	6	1	2	15	11	12	1	.462	.582

11 LOGAN FORSYTHE, 3B

BORN: Jan. 14, 1987. **B-T:** R-R. **HT.:** 6-1. **WT.:** 195. **DRAFTED:** Arkansas, 2008 (1st round supplemental). **SIGNED BY:** Lane Decker.

Forsythe hit .309 for Team USA's college national team after his sophomore season, trailing only 2008 first-rounders Pedro Alvarez and Brett Wallace, and the coaching staff regarded Forsythe as the club's leader. He has dealt with myriad injuries in the past two years. He had surgery to repair a stress fracture in his right foot following the 2007 season, and then pulled a hamstring as a junior. After signing for $835,000 as a supplemental first-round pick, he tore a thumb ligament diving for a ball three games into his pro career, requiring surgery. The lower-body injuries were especially damaging because Forsythe relies on his legs to hit. He has a short, compact swing and hits the ball to all fields, and he handles breaking pitches well because of strong balance. Though he's a physical 6-foot-1 and has good strength, Forsythe has a line-drive swing that doesn't produce natural loft, leading some to project him to have below-average power. He earns high marks for his defense, with good feet and hands to go with an above-average arm at third base. He's also versatile enough to have played second base, shortstop and left field for Team USA. He's a good athlete and a solid-average runner. If healthy, Forsythe will open 2009 in high Class A.

Year	Club (League)	Class	AVG	G	AB	R	H	2B	3B	HR	RBI	BB	SO	SB	OBP	SLG
2008	Eugene (NWL)	SS	.333	3	9	2	3	1	0	0	0	1	3	0	.455	.444
	Padres (AZL)	R	.231	9	26	2	6	0	0	0	0	5	8	0	.429	.231
MINOR LEAGUE TOTALS			.257	12	35	4	9	1	0	0	0	6	11	0	.435	.286

12 WADE LeBLANC, LHP

BORN: Aug. 7, 1984. **B-T:** L-L. **HT.:** 6-3. **WT.:** 200. **DRAFTED:** Alabama, 2006 (2nd round). **SIGNED BY:** Bob Filotei.

In 2007, his first full season, LeBlanc reached Double-A, led the system with 145 strikeouts and finished third with a 2.95 ERA. Last year's results weren't quite as good, as he got thrashed in Triple-A and during his September callup. He did finish strong at Portland, going 7-5, 4.06 in the final three months and ranking second in the Pacific Coast League with 139 strikeouts. LeBlanc handles righthanders with his plus-plus changeup, which he throws with uncanny feel and terrific arm speed. In fact, he has such feel for the pitch that he throws two versions of it—slow and slower. He runs into trouble because he lacks true fastball command, and he doesn't have the velocity or movement to cover mistakes. He sits at 85-86 mph and occasionally scrapes 90, and he's now incorporated a low-80s two-seamer at San Diego's behest. But when LeBlanc misses it's to his arm side, so his fastball tails back over the plate against righthanders. His curveball is an average pitch at times but generally lacks finish or bite, and he would benefit from throwing it more for a surprise strike one. LeBlanc has a smooth, high three-quarters delivery and a competitive makeup, but he'll need better command to make it as a mid-rotation starter, which is his ceiling. He didn't challenge big leaguers enough in September. He's in the running to break camp with San Diego this spring.

Year	Club (League)	Class	W	L	ERA	G	GS	CG	SV	IP	H	R	ER	HR	BB	SO	AVG
2006	Eugene (NWL)	SS	1	0	4.29	7	3	0	0	21	19	10	10	0	6	20	.250
	Fort Wayne (MWL)	LoA	4	1	2.20	7	7	0	0	33	31	8	8	1	10	27	.250
2007	Lake Elsinore (CAL)	HiA	6	5	2.64	16	16	0	0	92	72	32	27	5	17	90	.212
	San Antonio (TEX)	AA	7	3	3.45	12	11	0	0	57	48	22	22	8	19	55	.225
2008	Portland (PCL)	AAA	11	9	5.32	26	25	0	0	139	136	85	82	21	42	139	.259
	San Diego (NL)	MAJ	1	3	8.02	5	4	0	0	21	29	19	19	7	15	14	.330
MINOR LEAGUE TOTALS			29	18	3.92	68	62	0	0	342	306	157	149	35	94	331	.240
MAJOR LEAGUE TOTALS			1	3	8.02	5	4	0	0	21	29	19	19	7	15	14	.330

13 JOSH GEER, RHP

BORN: June 2, 1983. **B-T:** R-R. **HT.:** 6-3. **WT.:** 190. **DRAFTED:** Rice, 2005 (3rd round). **SIGNED BY:** Bob Laurie.

Geer became the staff ace for Rice in 2004, one year after the Owls' big three of Philip Humber, Jeff Niemann and Wade Townsend were drafted in the top eight picks. Though he doesn't have big velocity or stuff, Geer has impressed the Padres with his competitive, strike-throwing nature and steady improvement. His talents were on full display in September, when he made five major league starts and surrendered no more than two runs in any of them. A mild elbow ligament strain forced him to miss his final start, but he'll be ready for spring training. At his best, Geer features pinpoint control of a three-pitch mix, headlined by a sneaky two-seam fastball that he spots at will. He sits at 86-88 mph with good sink and keeps batters off balance with a plus changeup. In the past, he threw a slurvy breaking ball, but he tightened it into an average slider last season. Because he's not overpowering, Geer has to spot all of his pitches down in the zone. With two usable offspeed pitches, he found success last year by pitching backward, helping his modest fastball velocity play up. He has pitched 162, 177 and 194 innings in the last three seasons, so durability never has been a concern. Geer is a strong candidate to nail down a spot in San Diego's rotation in spring training.

Year	Club (League)	Class	W	L	ERA	G	GS	CG	SV	IP	H	R	ER	HR	BB	SO	AVG
2005	Eugene (NWL)	SS	3	1	3.69	7	6	0	0	32	35	13	13	5	4	13	.285
	Fort Wayne (MWL)	LoA	1	1	4.25	5	5	0	0	30	29	16	14	3	9	23	.259
2006	Fort Wayne (MWL)	LoA	6	2	3.10	12	11	1	0	73	72	27	25	3	13	46	.263
	Lake Elsinore (CAL)	HiA	7	4	4.96	15	15	0	0	89	116	60	49	7	16	56	.316
2007	Portland (PCL)	AAA	1	0	3.00	1	1	0	0	6	6	2	2	0	1	6	.286
	San Antonio (TEX)	AA	16	6	3.20	26	26	2	0	171	163	67	61	9	27	102	.252
2008	Portland (PCL)	AAA	8	9	4.54	28	27	0	0	167	187	95	84	22	45	107	.285
	San Diego (NL)	MAJ	2	1	2.67	5	5	0	0	27	29	8	8	2	9	16	.269
MINOR LEAGUE TOTALS			42	23	3.94	94	91	3	0	567	608	280	248	49	115	353	.276
MAJOR LEAGUE TOTALS			2	1	2.67	5	5	0	0	27	29	8	8	2	9	16	.269

14 SIMON CASTRO, RHP

BORN: April 9, 1988. **B-T:** R-R. **HT.:** 6-5. **WT.:** 203. **SIGNED:** Dominican Republic, 2006. **SIGNED BY:** Randy Smith/Felix Francisco.

Castro has been on the Padres' radar since his 2006 debut in the Dominican Summer League. Inconsistent command has held him back, but few San Diego farmhands can match his raw arm strength. The 6-foot-5 Castro, who physically resembles Jose Contreras, began to show results to match his stuff and presence in 2008. He ranked second in the Northwest League in opponent average (.223) and third in strikeouts per nine innings (8.8). Castro throws a 92-95 mph fastball that peaks at 97-98, but his control needs refinement. His arm stroke is long, clean and loose, but he often flies open in his delivery, affecting his arm slot and control. Castro's secondary pitches are works in progress. He'll flash an above-average slider at times, but he lacks confidence in the pitch and often fails to get on top of it. His 84-85 mph changeup shows average potential. Castro has room for even more projection and he takes instruction well, so he could develop into a frontline starter or power reliever if he gets his delivery under control. He's finally ready for a shot at full-season ball in 2009.

Year	Club (League)	Class	W	L	ERA	G	GS	CG	SV	IP	H	R	ER	HR	BB	SO	AVG
2006	Padres (DSL)	R	1	3	4.63	12	12	0	0	47	40	33	24	2	21	58	.219
2007	Padres (AZL)	R	2	6	6.22	14	12	0	0	51	61	48	35	4	30	55	.298
2008	Eugene (NWL)	SS	2	3	3.99	15	15	0	0	65	54	35	29	3	29	64	.223
MINOR LEAGUE TOTALS			5	12	4.87	41	39	0	0	163	155	116	88	9	80	177	.246

15 DREW CUMBERLAND, SS

BORN: Jan. 13, 1989. **B-T:** L-R. **HT.:** 5-10. **WT.:** 175. **DRAFTED:** HS—Pace, Fla., 2007 (1st round supplemental). **SIGNED BY:** Bob Filotei.

Injuries have cost Cumberland valuable developmental time, which he needs after starring as a defensive back and running back in high school diverted his attention from baseball. The brother of Reds outfield prospect Shaun Cumberland, he hurt his hamstring late in his senior high school season. After signing for $661,500 as a supplemental first-round pick in 2007, he missed time with a dislocated finger in his pro debut. A pulled ribcage muscle sidelined him for a couple of weeks last May, and then he jammed the index finger on his throwing hand while turning a double play at the end of June, knocking him out for most of the rest of the year. Cumberland is a plus-plus runner and was one of the more athletic players in the Midwest League last year. With live hands, a quick lefthanded stroke and strong strike-zone awareness, he has the skills to be a plus hitter. He's strong for his size, but his power is strictly of the line-drive variety. Opinions remain mixed on Cumberland's defensive future. He has the range and hands to remain at shortstop, but his average arm strength is sabotaged by a motion that leads to erratic throws. He has 31 errors in 69 pro games at short, and some see him as a future second baseman or center fielder. Cumberland's strong makeup would allow him to handle a jump to high Class A, but the Padres may want him to return to Fort Wayne to begin 2009.

Year	Club (League)	Class	AVG	G	AB	R	H	2B	3B	HR	RBI	BB	SO	SB	OBP	SLG
2007	Padres (AZL)	R	.318	21	85	16	27	2	1	0	7	7	9	6	.389	.365
	Eugene (NWL)	SS	.333	4	18	6	6	1	0	0	0	2	2	0	.429	.389
2008	Fort Wayne (MWL)	LoA	.286	53	206	29	59	8	1	1	17	17	24	16	.348	.350
	Padres (AZL)	R	.500	3	10	3	5	1	2	0	2	0	1	0	.500	1.000
MINOR LEAGUE TOTALS			.304	81	319	54	97	12	4	1	26	26	36	22	.368	.376

16 WYNN PELZER, RHP

BORN: June 23, 1986. **B-T:** R-R. **HT.:** 6-1. **WT.:** 200. **DRAFTED:** South Carolina, 2007 (9th round). **SIGNED BY:** Pete DeYoung.

Pelzer pitched almost exclusively in relief as a junior at South Carolina, and his lack of exposure, 5.22 ERA and choice of agents (Scott Boras) contributed to him dropping to the ninth round of the 2007 draft. He headed to the Cape Cod League after being drafted in an effort to boost his stock, but a line drive broke his kneecap in his third start. He signed with San Diego at the Aug. 15 deadline for $190,000. Pelzer has just one speed: all-out. Illustrating his bulldog mentality, he took a line drive off the head in a May game but returned five days later to throw three strong innings of relief. His fastball sits at 93 mph and touches 95, and his hard slider flashes plus potential. A solid athlete, he has tremendous presence and tempo on the mound and isn't afraid to pitch inside. He holds his velocity late into starts. While Pelzer can intimidate the opposition with his aggressiveness, he has below-average control and lacks a feel for his craft. He has had little success with a changeup after throwing a splitter in college. He gets in trouble when he falls behind and leaves his pitches up in the zone. The Padres held him back from instructional league in 2008 because he had thrown a career-high 118 innings. Pelzer is ready for high Class A, and while he'll continue to start for now, he probably will go back to being a power reliever in the future.

Year	Club (League)	Class	W	L	ERA	G	GS	CG	SV	IP	H	R	ER	HR	BB	SO	AVG
2008	Fort Wayne (MWL)	LoA	9	6	3.19	29	23	0	0	118	114	64	42	9	32	100	.248
	Lake Elsinore (CAL)	HiA	0	0	27.00	1	0	0	0	1	3	4	3	0	1	0	.500
MINOR LEAGUE TOTALS			9	6	3.39	30	23	0	0	119	117	68	45	9	33	100	.251

17 ERIC SOGARD, 2B

BORN: May 22, 1986. **B-T:** L-R. **HT.:** 5-10. **WT.:** 180. **DRAFTED:** Arizona State, 2007 (2nd round). **SIGNED BY:** Dave Lottsfeldt.

Some opponents considered Sogard the key player on Arizona State's 2007 College World Series team, which featured 2008 first-round picks Brett Wallace and Ike Davis. A scrappy player with plus instincts, Sogard led the California League with 42 doubles in his first full season, was the second-toughest batter to strike out (10.0

plate appearances per whiff) and ranked among the leaders in several other categories. The Padres view him as a Todd Walker clone—an offense-oriented, lefthanded-hitting second baseman. While his home run power is below-average, Sogard offers just about everything else a team could want in a hitter. He's quick to the ball, shows gap power, uses the whole field, makes easy contact and controls the strike zone. It's a different story defensively, where Sogard's range is a step short and his hands are just average. He doesn't always read the ball in the hitting zone, affecting his positioning, and struggles with consistency on the double-play pivot. His arm and speed are average. If Sogard cleans up his defense, he could pose a serious challenge to Matt Antonelli's standing as the Padres' second baseman of the future.

Year	Club (League)	Class	AVG	G	AB	R	H	2B	3B	HR	RBI	BB	SO	SB	OBP	SLG
2007	Portland (PCL)	AAA	.000	1	3	0	0	0	0	0	0	0	3	0	.250	.000
	Eugene (NWL)	SS	.256	31	125	20	32	9	0	2	18	19	16	4	.354	.376
	Fort Wayne (MWL)	LoA	.253	22	83	7	21	2	0	2	15	6	13	2	.308	.349
2008	Lake Elsinore (CAL)	HiA	.308	133	536	97	165	42	3	10	87	79	62	16	.394	.453
MINOR LEAGUE TOTALS			.292	187	747	124	218	53	3	14	120	104	94	22	.377	.427

18 WILL INMAN, RHP

BORN: Feb. 6, 1987. **B-T:** R-R. **HT.:** 6-0. **WT.:** 200. **DRAFTED:** HS—Dry Fork, Va., 2005 (3rd round). **SIGNED BY:** Grant Brittain (Brewers).

A product of the Scott Linebrink trade with the Brewers in 2007, Inman has built a distinguished minor league résumé. He compiled the second-lowest ERA (1.71) in the minors in 2006 and followed that with a runner-up finish in strikeouts (180) in 2007. Last year, he led the Double-A Texas League with 140 strikeouts, finished second with a .234 opponent average and appeared in the Futures Game. However, his 71 walks also topped the TL. Inman's funky delivery helps him get by with mediocre stuff. He uses a deep arm action in back while simultaneously sweeping his front arm skyward in exaggerated fashion. It results in a slower tempo, which means he doesn't often get great extension and finish on his pitches. With the Padres' blessing, Inman lowered his arm slot slightly in 2008, and while it boosted his velocity, it took some of the bite out of his fringy curveball and diminished his command. He pitches at 87-90 mph and touches 93, and while his fastball is straight, it gets on batters quickly because of his deception. He does a good job selling his plus changeup. Because he has little room for error, Inman will have to sharpen his command to reach his ceiling as a back-end starter. He's ready for Triple-A.

Year	Club (League)	Class	W	L	ERA	G	GS	CG	SV	IP	H	R	ER	HR	BB	SO	AVG
2005	Brewers (AZL)	R	0	0	0.00	1	0	0	0	2	0	0	0	0	1	1	.000
	Helena (PIO)	R	6	0	2.00	13	5	0	1	45	29	11	10	5	11	58	.182
2006	West Virginia (SAL)	LoA	10	2	1.71	23	20	0	0	111	75	22	21	3	24	134	.190
2007	Brevard County (FSL)	HiA	4	3	1.72	13	13	0	0	79	56	17	15	4	23	98	.198
	Huntsville (SL)	AA	1	5	5.45	8	8	0	0	40	38	24	24	7	16	42	.259
	San Antonio (TEX)	AA	3	3	4.17	7	7	0	0	41	33	19	19	6	19	40	.224
2008	San Antonio (TEX)	AA	9	8	3.52	28	28	2	0	135	119	67	53	10	71	140	.234
MINOR LEAGUE TOTALS			33	21	2.83	93	81	2	1	452	350	160	142	35	165	513	.213

19 BLAKE TEKOTTE, OF

BORN: May 24, 1987. **B-T:** L-R. **HT.:** 6-0. **WT.:** 166. **DRAFTED:** Miami, 2008 (3rd round). **SIGNED BY:** Rob Sidwell.

The fifth Miami player selected in the first three rounds of the 2008 draft, Tekotte served as catalyst for a team that won the Atlantic Coast Conference and finished the regular season ranked No. 1 in the nation. He boosted his draft stock by earning Cape Cod League all-star honors in 2007 and signed for $361,000 last June. An above-average runner with good baserunning instincts, Tekotte plays the small-man's game with aplomb. He puts pressure on defenses with his speed and ability to put the ball in play. He knows how to work the count and seldom chases pitches out of the zone. While he can surprise with his power at times, he figures to be fringe-average at best in that department. He has the hand-eye coordination and all-fields approach to hit for average. Tekotte's speed also plays in center field, where he covers the gaps, shows plus instincts and goes back on the ball well. His arm is just playable. The Padres were pleased with his debut, though he coasted at times by not running out grounders and playing indifferent defense. He also stole just seven bases and needs to improve his reads and jumps. Tekotte addressed the criticism in instructional league, hustling for five weeks and earning MVP honors while doing something to impress the coaching staff every day. He could be a dynamic leadoff man, and he figures to fall in step behind Cedric Hunter and play one level behind him at high Class A this season.

Year	Club (League)	Class	AVG	G	AB	R	H	2B	3B	HR	RBI	BB	SO	SB	OBP	SLG
2008	Eugene (NWL)	SS	.285	47	193	43	55	15	0	6	29	27	45	7	.379	.456
MINOR LEAGUE TOTALS			.285	47	193	43	55	15	0	6	29	27	45	7	.379	.456

20 CESAR CARRILLO, RHP

BORN: April 29, 1984. **B-T:** R-R. **HT.:** 6-3. **WT.:** 175. **DRAFTED:** Miami, 2005 (1st round). **SIGNED BY:** Joe Bochy.

In a distinguished college career at Miami, Carrillo won the first 24 decisions of his career, two shy of the NCAA Division I record. The Padres selected him 18th overall in 2005 and signed him for $1.55 million with the hope he could move quickly. Because of elbow trouble, that hasn't happened. A strained elbow ligament limited him to 10 starts in 2006 and when the condition didn't improve, Carrillo had Tommy John surgery in June 2007. He returned to the hill last June, and his stuff is still recovering. He sat at 85-88 mph during the season before reaching 88-92 by the end of his stint in the Arizona Fall League. He throws his fastball in on righthanders as well as anyone in the system, and the Padres were encouraged that he began hitting his spots away late in the season. Before the surgery, Carrillo showed a 90-94 mph fastball that touched 96 and featured late life and natural sink. His curveball shows tight downward break, and his changeup has average potential. Carrillo profiles as a mid-rotation starter or power reliever, but the Padres won't make that decision until he shows he's fully healthy again.

Year	Club (League)	Class	W	L	ERA	G	GS	CG	SV	IP	H	R	ER	HR	BB	SO	AVG
2005	Mobile (SL)	AA	4	0	3.23	5	5	0	0	31	23	11	11	2	7	35	.204
	Lake Elsinore (CAL)	HiA	1	2	7.01	7	7	0	0	26	30	21	20	3	9	29	.280
2006	Mobile (SL)	AA	1	3	3.02	9	9	0	0	51	45	23	17	5	15	43	.239
	Portland (PCL)	AAA	0	0	6.75	1	1	0	0	3	2	2	2	0	3	1	.222
2007	Portland (PCL)	AAA	0	2	8.62	5	5	0	0	16	22	16	15	2	14	8	.338
2008	Lake Elsinore (CAL)	HiA	3	5	5.97	15	14	0	0	57	69	43	38	6	33	32	.301
MINOR LEAGUE TOTALS			9	12	5.07	42	41	0	0	183	191	116	103	18	81	148	.269

21 NICK SCHMIDT, LHP

BORN: Oct. 10, 1985. **B-T:** L-L. **HT.:** 6-5. **WT.:** 220. **DRAFTED:** Arkansas, 2007 (1st round). **SIGNED BY:** Lane Decker.

Schmidt and Cesar Carrillo remain linked not only as San Diego first-round picks drafted but also as Tommy John surgery alumni. Schmidt went to the operating table in October 2007, four months after Carrillo. Schmidt got back on the mound in instructional league last fall before heading to the Padres' Dominican camp to get in more innings. As an amateur, Schmidt was a polished, durable lefty who had been a Friday starter since he was a freshman at Arkansas. San Diego signed him for $1.26 million as the 23rd overall pick in 2007, but he went down almost immediately. Though he stands 6-foot-5, Schmidt isn't overpowering and lacks a swing-and-miss pitch, but he's adept at using his height to leverage his 86-89 mph fastball down in the zone. He touched 91 in college and showed an above-average curveball and solid-average changeup, and he gets even higher marks for his control and his feel for pitching. His delivery isn't textbook, as he shows the open face of his glove to the batter before he delivers a pitch, but his idiosyncrasies add deception. Schmidt was regarded as a future mid-rotation starter before his surgery, but as with Carrillo, the Padres won't know what they have until he has recovered.

Year	Club (League)	Class	W	L	ERA	G	GS	CG	SV	IP	H	R	ER	HR	BB	SO	AVG
2007	Fort Wayne (MWL)	A	0	1	6.43	3	1	0	0	7	8	5	5	0	6	6	.286
2008	Did Not Play—Injured																
MINOR LEAGUE TOTALS			0	1	6.43	3	1	0	0	7	8	5	5	0	6	6	.286

22 STEVE GARRISON, LHP

BORN: Sept. 12, 1986. **B-T:** B-L. **HT.:** 6-1. **WT.:** 185. **DRAFTED:** HS—Ewing, N.J., 2005 (10th round). **SIGNED BY:** Tony Blengino (Brewers).

Garrison's tumble down the prospect list is not a reflection of his ability, but rather of the shoulder surgery he had in October to clean up his rotator cuff and labrum. He'll miss at least half of the 2009 season, with an optimistic return date set for June. Along with Will Inman and Joe Thatcher, he joined the Padres in the July 2007 trade that sent Scott Linebrink to Milwaukee. A smart and crafty lefty, Garrison pitches above his average stuff by quickly dissecting hitters and attacking their weaknesses. He ranked fourth in the Texas League last season in strikeouts per nine innings (7.5), fewest walks per nine (2.5) and opponent average (.249). The strength of his 88-90 mph fastball is his ability to locate it, even inside on righthanders. Garrison's hard 12-to-6 curveball is his strikeout pitch and he used it to limit Double-A lefties to a .189 average. It's a plus offering at times, as is his changeup. A good athlete, Garrison is an adept fielder with a tough pickoff move. Only 13 runners attempted to steal against him in 24 starts, with nine succeeding.

Year	Club (League)	Class	W	L	ERA	G	GS	CG	SV	IP	H	R	ER	HR	BB	SO	AVG
2005	Brewers (AZL)	R	2	2	2.86	11	4	0	2	35	39	13	11	0	5	28	.300
2006	West Virginia (SAL)	LoA	7	6	3.45	17	16	0	0	89	86	38	34	10	22	77	.253
2007	Brevard County (FSL)	HiA	8	4	3.44	20	20	1	0	105	105	58	40	6	28	74	.253
	Lake Elsinore (CAL)	HiA	2	3	2.79	7	7	0	0	42	32	15	13	2	6	28	.205
2008	San Antonio (TEX)	AA	7	7	3.82	24	24	0	0	130	123	59	55	13	37	108	.249
MINOR LEAGUE TOTALS			26	22	3.45	79	71	1	2	400	385	183	153	31	98	315	.251

23 CHAD HUFFMAN, OF

BORN: April 29, 1985. **B-T:** R-R. **HT.:** 6-1. **WT.:** 200. **DRAFTED:** Texas Christian, 2006 (2nd round). **SIGNED BY:** Tim Holt.

Huffman followed in the footsteps of his brother Royce by playing both baseball and football at Texas Christian. He led the Northwest League with a .439 on-base percentage in his 2006 debut, while also finishing second in batting (.343) and slugging (.576). He clubbed 15 homers in the hitter-friendly California League during the first half of 2007, but just 16 in a year and a half since in Double-A. That's at least partly attributable to San Antonio's Wolff Stadium, a tough park for righthanded hitters. Huffman has above-average raw power and knows the strike zone, but all of his pop is to his pull side because his long stride leaves him out of position to drive offspeed stuff the other way. His plate coverage and bat path are fine most of the time, so he produces enough line drives to hit for a solid average. He's an average runner at best. Despite his high-energy style of play, he shows below-average range and arm strength in left field. He played second base in college. The damage he has done versus Double-A lefties—.350/.434/.538 in 117 at-bats—suggests that Huffman should at least have a future as a platoon outfielder. Look for his home run output to increase in Triple-A this year.

Year	Club (League)	Class	AVG	G	AB	R	H	2B	3B	HR	RBI	BB	SO	SB	OBP	SLG
2006	Eugene (NWL)	SS	.343	54	198	41	68	17	1	9	40	25	34	2	.439	.576
	Fort Wayne (MWL)	LoA	.214	5	14	2	3	0	1	0	0	2	2	0	.313	.357
2007	Lake Elsinore (CAL)	HiA	.307	84	316	63	97	19	2	15	76	42	56	0	.402	.522
	San Antonio (TEX)	AA	.269	49	167	28	45	4	1	7	28	22	44	0	.362	.431
2008	San Antonio (TEX)	AA	.284	119	437	68	124	30	1	9	58	67	83	1	.383	.419
MINOR LEAGUE TOTALS			.298	311	1132	202	337	70	6	40	202	158	219	3	.394	.476

24 EVERTH CABRERA, 2B/SS

BORN: Nov. 17, 1986. **B-T:** B-R. **HT.:** 5-8. **WT.:** 160. **SIGNED:** Nicaragua, 2004. **SIGNED BY:** Rolando Fernandez/Francisco Cartaya (Rockies).

Left off the Rockies' 40-man roster, Cabrera didn't last long in the major league Rule 5 draft. Padres international scout Felix Feliz worked for the Rockies when Cabrera signed, so it was no surprise San Diego grabbed the switch-hitting middle infielder with the third pick. Though he's 22, Cabrera hasn't advanced past low Class A, and spending the entire 2009 season in the majors could harm his development. If he doesn't stay on the Padres' big league roster, they have to place him on waivers and offer him back to Colorado. Cabrera has plus-plus speed and led the minors with 73 steals in 2008. Managers rated him the fastest and best baserunner in the low Class A South Atlantic League. He has shown an ability to work the count, but his 101 strikeouts were too many for a player with his offensive profile. He offers well below-average power. The Asheville coaching staff tried to get him to stay back on the ball and use his hands to hit line drives. Cabrera has played more second base than shortstop in his career, but he seamlessly shifted across the bag during the second half of 2008, showing solid range and arm strength at short. With a dearth of shortstop options, the Padres are committed to giving Cabrera a long look in spring training. However, it's hard to envision him going from low Class A to playing regularly in the big leagues in one year.

Year	Club (League)	Class	AVG	G	AB	R	H	2B	3B	HR	RBI	BB	SO	SB	OBP	SLG
2004	Rockies (DSL)	R	.200	50	170	23	34	2	4	0	11	20	41	8	.292	.259
2005	Rockies (DSL)	R	.309	69	249	51	77	16	3	1	23	39	44	43	.416	.410
2006	Casper (PIO)	R	.254	54	185	30	47	4	2	0	14	37	45	18	.382	.297
2007	Modesto (CAL)	HiA	.267	4	15	3	4	0	1	0	2	2	7	1	.421	.400
	Tri-City (NWL)	SS	.300	42	150	29	45	8	3	1	23	27	24	12	.432	.413
2008	Asheville (SAL)	LoA	.284	121	479	80	136	25	6	6	38	51	101	73	.361	.399
MINOR LEAGUE TOTALS			.275	340	1248	216	343	55	19	8	111	176	262	155	.376	.369

25 MITCH CANHAM, C

BORN: Sept. 25, 1984. **B-T:** L-R. **HT.:** 6-2. **WT.:** 215. **DRAFTED:** Oregon State, 2007 (1st round supplemental). **SIGNED BY:** Josh Boyd.

Canham's offense and leadership helped Oregon State vanquish North Carolina to win College World Series titles in 2006 and 2007. As a polished hitter with incredible makeup, he fits the Padres' player-development mold to a tee. In his first pro summer, he returned to the field just two weeks after having testicular surgery following a foul tip to his protective cup. He played the entire 2008 season with a heavy heart, after his younger brother Dustin, a Marine lance corporal, died in March while serving in Djibouti, Africa. A good athlete, Canham has a smooth, repeatable stroke from the left side and his wrists fly through the hitting zone, attributes that should make him an average hitter. Because he controls the strike zone, he figures to grow into solid-average power. He's a good runner for a catcher. Though Canham takes charge of a pitching staff and calls a good game, his physical tools for the position are fringy. He's also inconsistent in his throwing, blocking and receiving. California League basestealers ran wild on him in 2008, swiping 131 bags in 107 games and getting caught just 17 percent of the time. He doesn't have a great release, transfer or arm strength, and he tends to close off his throwing motion, costing him carry on his throws. He has worked diligently with roving catching instructor Duffy Dyer to improve his technique. Canham's athleticism leaves him fallback options like first base or left field, but his bat doesn't profile for an everyday role at either position. He'll head to Double-A in 2009.

Year	Club (League)	Class	AVG	G	AB	R	H	2B	3B	HR	RBI	BB	SO	SB	OBP	SLG
2007	Eugene (NWL)	SS	.293	28	116	20	34	4	1	2	18	11	35	5	.379	.397
	Lake Elsinore (CAL)	HiA	.000	2	7	0	0	0	0	0	1	0	2	0	.000	.000
2008	Lake Elsinore (CAL)	HiA	.285	113	417	65	119	28	5	8	81	66	73	13	.382	.434
MINOR LEAGUE TOTALS			.283	143	540	85	153	32	6	10	100	77	110	18	.376	.420

26 DREW MILLER, RHP

BORN: Feb. 24, 1986. **B-T:** R-R. **HT.:** 6-4. **WT.:** 190. **DRAFTED:** Seminole State (Okla.) JC, D/F 2005 (37th round). **SIGNED BY:** Lane Decker.

Ranked No. 5 on this list a year ago, Miller slid dramatically because of poor performance and a questionable approach. He signed for $300,000 in May 2006 as a draft-and-follow after posting dominant strikeout totals in junior college, but he hasn't consistently pitched up to his impressive raw stuff as a pro. He posted a 4.69 ERA in the pitcher-friendly Midwest League in 2007, and ranked near the bottom in ERA (6.10) and homers allowed (19) in the California League last season. If there was a silver lining, it was that he stayed healthy and made 26 starts after missing time with shoulder and oblique soreness the year before. Miller has a low-90s heater that touches 94 mph and a plus curveball, which should allow him to succeed. He's trying to find feel for a changeup. Miller's command grades as below-average, and scouts question his composure and competitiveness, as he shows an unwillingness to work inside. Typically, it took batters only a few innings to decode the pattern. With his arm strength, it's impossible to completely write off Miller, who will get another chance to conquer high Class A in 2009.

Year	Club (League)	Class	W	L	ERA	G	GS	CG	SV	IP	H	R	ER	HR	BB	SO	AVG
2006	Padres (AZL)	R	3	0	3.47	7	4	0	0	23	19	15	9	1	10	14	.218
	Eugene (NWL)	SS	2	1	3.62	9	8	0	0	37	39	24	15	0	20	23	.267
2007	Fort Wayne (MWL)	LoA	4	6	4.69	16	16	0	0	81	74	45	42	12	24	87	.244
2008	Lake Elsinore (CAL)	HiA	10	7	6.10	27	26	0	0	134	172	103	91	19	46	100	.313
MINOR LEAGUE TOTALS			19	14	5.13	59	54	0	0	276	304	187	157	32	100	224	.280

27 JEREMY HEFNER, RHP

BORN: March 11, 1986. **B-T:** R-R. **HT.:** 6-4. **WT.:** 215. **DRAFTED:** Oral Roberts, 2007 (5th round). **SIGNED BY:** Lane Decker.

The Mets drafted Hefner out of high school (46th round, 2004) and again out of Seminole State (Okla.) JC (48th round, 2005) but failed to sign him. The Padres had more luck in 2007, signing him for $129,000 as a fifth-rounder. Obscured by teammates Drew Miller and Duke Welker (a Pirates second-rounder in 2007) at Seminole, Hefner went to Oral Roberts for his junior year and thrived. His velocity improved and he learned a two-plane slider, but scouts were more intrigued by his athleticism and arm action. He ranked third in the Midwest League with 144 strikeouts in 2008, though at 22 he was a bit old for the circuit. One Padres official described Hefner's 87-91 mph two-seam fastball as having turbo sink, and because of its movement he sometimes hesitates to throw the pitch when he needed a strike. He lost depth on his slider as a pro, but the reincarnation of his curveball has San Diego excited. He worked in instructional league to relearn the curve he threw in high school. He has a fringy changeup. Because of his sturdy frame, control and great work ethic, Hefner eventually could surface as a back-end starter. He'll head to high Class A in 2009.

Year	Club (League)	Class	W	L	ERA	G	GS	CG	SV	IP	H	R	ER	HR	BB	SO	AVG
2007	Eugene (NWL)	SS	2	5	3.90	17	11	0	0	62	51	33	27	3	20	74	.221
2008	Fort Wayne (MWL)	LoA	10	5	3.33	29	24	0	0	140	117	53	52	12	41	144	.228
	Lake Elsinore (CAL)	HiA	0	0	3.60	1	1	0	0	5	3	2	2	0	2	6	.167
MINOR LEAGUE TOTALS			12	10	3.51	47	36	0	0	208	171	88	81	15	63	224	.224

28 COLE FIGUEROA, SS/2B

BORN: June 30, 1987. **B-T:** L-R. **HT.:** 5-10. **WT.:** 180. **DRAFTED:** Florida, 2008 (6th round). **SIGNED BY:** Rob Sidwell.

A draft-eligible sophomore, Figueroa went in the sixth round last June and used a strong summer in the Cape Cod League to get a $400,000 bonus. He has the instincts and competitive makeup expected from the son of a former big leaguer. His father Bien went 2-for-11 with the 1992 Cardinals and managed Double-A Connecticut in the Giants system in 2008. Cole's physical tools aren't eye-popping, but he gets the most out of them and repeats a sound swing at the plate. He knows the strike zone and he has some gap power, so he projects as a .280 hitter with 10-15 homers per year. Figueroa's biggest limitation is his speed, which rates as a 35 on the 20-80 scouting scale. His savvy makes him an effective baserunner, but his lack of quickness hurts him at shortstop.

Though he played there at Florida and in much of his pro debut, he lacks the range to man the position on a regular basis in the major leagues. His hands and arm are fine, and he projects as an offensive second baseman who offers average to plus defense. Figueroa had minor surgery on his right knee in the fall, but that shouldn't hold him back in 2009, when he could open the season in high Class A.

Year	Club (League)	Class	AVG	G	AB	R	H	2B	3B	HR	RBI	BB	SO	SB	OBP	SLG
2008	Eugene (NWL)	SS	.289	32	114	23	33	6	0	5	16	24	16	7	.410	.474
MINOR LEAGUE TOTALS			.289	32	114	23	33	6	0	5	16	24	16	7	.410	.474

29 ERNESTO FRIERI, RHP

BORN: July 19, 1985. **B-T:** R-R. **HT.:** 6-2. **WT.:** 190. **SIGNED:** Colombia, 2003. **SIGNED BY:** Robert Rowley/Marical DelValle.

The Padres had employed Frieri in a swingman role prior to 2008, but he held up well making a career-high 21 starts last year. San Diego added him to the 40-man roster after the 2007 season, along with another hard thrower in Wilton Lopez. The duo began the year together in high Class A, but Frieri separated himself with better command and results. He features easy 92-94 mph velocity from a high three-quarters arm slot, and he looks like he's playing catch, so the ball gets on batters quickly. He throws a quality changeup. Though Frieri has one of the better curveballs in the organization—it's a hard downer—he struggled in 2008 to get the same peak velocity on the pitch that he had in the past. Continuing to break his hands over the rubber will be key for Frieri to improve his command as he moves up. The Padres like his aptitude and makeup, and he'll probably begin 2009 back in the San Antonio rotation, though his future role may be in the bullpen.

Year	Club (League)	Class	W	L	ERA	G	GS	CG	SV	IP	H	R	ER	HR	BB	SO	AVG
2003	Tronconero 1 (VSL)	R	1	4	4.00	15	4	0	0	36	36	23	16	0	15	49	.265
2004	Padres (DSL)	R	4	0	1.43	21	1	0	1	50	30	14	8	1	24	59	.167
2005	Lake Elsinore (CAL)	HiA	0	0	2.70	2	0	0	0	3	3	1	1	1	1	3	.231
	Padres (AZL)	R	7	1	1.17	17	5	0	0	46	21	7	6	0	29	59	.137
2006	Fort Wayne (MWL)	LoA	0	0	9.00	1	0	0	0	1	1	4	1	0	5	1	.333
	Lake Elsinore (CAL)	HiA	0	0	6.00	2	0	0	0	6	8	4	4	0	3	4	.348
	Eugene (NWL)	SS	3	3	3.82	27	1	0	2	38	31	18	16	3	15	38	.231
2007	Fort Wayne (MWL)	LoA	1	2	2.64	40	0	0	0	65	48	19	19	4	23	65	.209
	Lake Elsinore (CAL)	HiA	1	0	1.25	13	1	0	1	22	11	3	3	1	6	27	.155
2008	Portland (PCL)	AAA	1	0	1.50	1	1	0	0	6	2	1	1	0	2	7	.100
	Lake Elsinore (CAL)	HiA	8	6	4.00	33	18	0	0	124	125	61	55	14	32	108	.262
	San Antonio (TEX)	AA	1	0	4.09	2	2	0	0	11	7	5	5	3	2	10	.184
MINOR LEAGUE TOTALS			27	16	2.98	174	33	0	4	408	323	160	135	27	157	430	.219

30 IVAN NOVA, RHP

BORN: Jan. 12, 1987. **B-T:** R-R. **HT.:** 6-4. **WT.:** 210. **SIGNED:** Dominican Republic, 2005. **SIGNED BY:** Victor Mata/Carlos Rios (Yankees).

The Yankees didn't protect Nova on their 40-man roster, but the Padres found him attractive because of his potential and made him their second selection in the major league Rule 5 draft in December. Nova was regarded as a breakout candidate when he moved up to high Class A last season, but instead he continued to struggle to learn pitch sequences and a feel for the strike zone. Nova can throw strikes with his fastball, curveball and change-up, and all three pitches grade out as above-average when they're on. His fastball reaches 94 mph consistently and his curve can be a hammer, though it's inconsistent. His changeup is at least average most of the time and he throws it with good arm speed. Still, Nova has yet to learn how to set up hitters or get them to chase pitches out of the zone when he's ahead in the count. He also doesn't pitch inside aggressively, which he needs to do to keep lefthanders honest. His delivery lacks deception, making his stuff more hittable. Nova has to stick with the Padres, or else be exposed to waivers and offered back to the Yankees for half his $50,000 draft fee. While he's not ready for the majors, opportunities will be plentiful in San Diego.

Year	Club (League)	Class	W	L	ERA	G	GS	CG	SV	IP	H	R	ER	HR	BB	SO	AVG
2005	Yankees1 (DSL)	R	0	1	2.29	11	7	0	0	39	29	11	10	2	11	38	.200
2006	Yankees (GCL)	R	3	0	2.72	10	5	0	1	43	36	13	13	5	7	36	.229
2007	Charleston (SAL)	LoA	6	8	4.98	21	21	0	0	99	121	64	55	8	31	54	.306
2008	Tampa (FSL)	HiA	8	13	4.36	26	24	0	0	149	168	81	72	6	46	109	.294
MINOR LEAGUE TOTALS			17	22	4.09	68	57	0	1	330	354	169	150	21	95	237	.279

San Francisco Giants

BY ANDY BAGGARLY

The Giants hit just 94 home runs last year, the fewest by a major league club in a non-strike-shortened season since the expansion Marlins in 1993. It was a depressing lack of power for a fan base accustomed to cheering Barry Bonds.

San Francisco took plenty of souvenir baseballs out of play, though. Fifteen players made their major league debuts before Sept. 1, the most by a club since the 1954 Philadelphia Athletics, and seemingly hardly a day went by without someone registering their first hit. After the 162-game experiment ran its course, the Giants identified a few players—Fred Lewis, Sergio Romo, Pablo Sandoval, Brian Wilson—who could be part of their next contender. They also eliminated many others.

Tim Lincecum shined brightest of all. The undersized righthander elevated himself among the game's elite, winning the National League Cy Young Award and becoming the first Giant to lead the majors in strikeouts.

The end result was a 72-90 record and a fourth consecutive losing season, a run of shame San Francisco hadn't experienced since 1974-77.

Yet there's hope deeper in the system and the Giants might not be down for long. First-year scouting director John Barr redirected the club's former pitching-heavy philosophy and took college bats with his top four draft picks. None made a bigger statement than catcher Buster Posey, Baseball America's College Player of the Year and the Golden Spikes Award winner, who signed at the Aug. 15 deadline for $6.2 million.

Posey's signing underscored a sea change that began taking place the previous season under longtime general manager Brian Sabean. Instead of borrowing from the player-development budget to sign veteran free agents, the Giants reduced payroll and spent more on prospects. They also invested in a top-flight international talent, signing 16-year-old Dominican outfielder Rafael Rodriguez for $2.55 million in mid-July.

Though most of the system's top talent is at least a year or two away, 2009 promises to be interesting in San Francisco. Sabean and manager Bruce Bochy have contracts that expire after the season, and new managing partner Bill Neukom doesn't believe in public votes of confidence.

Major League Baseball approved Neukom in August to replace Peter Magowan, whose departure was termed charitably as a retirement. Magowan solidified the Giants' place in San Francisco and his ballpark vision was realized with the construction of

Pablo Sandoval was among 15 players to make their debut in San Francisco last year

TOP 30 PROSPECTS

1. Madison Bumgarner, lhp	16. Jackson Williams, c
2. Buster Posey, c	17. Travis Ishikawa, 1b
3. Angel Villalona, 1b	18. Alex Hinshaw, lhp
4. Tim Alderson, rhp	19. Mike McBryde, of
5. Nick Noonan, 2b	20. Clayton Tanner, lhp
6. Ehire Adrianza, ss	21. Aaron King, lhp
7. Conor Gillaspie, 3b	22. Francisco Peguero, of
8. Rafael Rodriguez, of	23. Thomas Neal, of
9. Scott Barnes, lhp	24. Matt Downs, inf/of
10. Sergio Romo, rhp	25. Edwin Quirarte, rhp
11. Waldis Joaquin, rhp	26. Osiris Matos, rhp
12. Wendell Fairley, of	27. Charlie Culberson, ss
13. Henry Sosa, rhp	28. Luis Perdomo, rhp
14. Roger Kieschnick, of	29. Billy Sadler, rhp
15. Kevin Pucetas, rhp	30. Joey Martinez, rhp

a modern classic on the waterfront. But the Mitchell Report characterized him as a steroids enabler, forever staining his reputation, and there were indications that Magowan's disastrous $126 million signing of Barry Zito made him unpopular with club investors.

Neukom said he expects San Francisco to be competitive in 2009 and contend the following season, all while bringing his "Microsoft meritocracy" to the front office. Even if the Giants show improvement, Neukom could decide he wants a baseball architect with a more modern perspective than Sabean, who isn't known to squint at a laptop screen.

General Manager: Brian Sabean. **Farm Director:** Fred Stanley. **Scouting Director:** John Barr.

Class	Team	League	W	L	PCT	Finish*	Manager	Affiliated
Majors	San Francisco	National	72	90	.444	13th (16)	Bruce Bochy	—
Triple-A	Fresno Grizzlies	Pacific Coast	67	76	.469	11th (16)	Dan Rohn	1998
Double-A	Connecticut Defenders	Eastern	68	73	.482	7th (12)	Bien Figueroa	2003
High A	San Jose Giants	California	85	55	.607	1st (10)	Steve Decker	1988
Low A	Augusta GreenJackets	South Atlantic	88	50	.638	^1st (16)	Andy Skeels	2005
Short-season	Salem-Keizer Volcanoes	Northwest	40	36	.526	4th (8)	Tom Trebelhorn	1997
Rookie	AZL Giants	Arizona	36	20	.643	^2nd (9)	Bert Hunter	2000
Overall 2008 Minor League Record			384	310	.553	3rd		

* Finish in overall standings (No. of teams in league). ^League champion.

LAST YEAR'S TOP 30

Player,	Pos.	Status
1.	Angel Villalona, 3b/1b	No. 3
2.	Tim Alderson, rhp	No. 4
3.	Madison Bumgarner, lhp	No. 1
4.	Nate Schierholtz, of	Majors
5.	Henry Sosa, rhp	No. 13
6.	Nick Noonan, 2b	No. 5
7.	Eugenio Velez, 2b/of	Majors
8.	Wendell Fairley, of	No. 12
9.	John Bowker, of	Majors
10.	Emmanuel Burriss, ss	Majors
11.	Brian Bocock, ss	Dropped out
12.	Clayton Tanner, lhp	No. 20
13.	Mike McBryde, of	No. 19
14.	Charlie Culberson, ss	No. 27
15.	Waldis Joaquin, rhp	No. 11
16.	Nick Pereira, rhp	Dropped out
17.	Osiris Matos, rhp	No. 26
18.	Jackson Williams, c	No. 16
19.	Wilber Bucardo, rhp	Dropped out
20.	Erick Threets, lhp	(Dodgers)
21.	Ben Snyder, rhp	Dropped out
22.	Pat Misch, lhp	Majors
23.	Kelvin Pichardo, rhp	Dropped out
24.	Merkin Valdez, rhp	Dropped out
25.	Brett Pill, 1b	Dropped out
26.	Brian Anderson, rhp	Dropped out
27.	Travis Denker, 2b	(Padres)
28.	Sergio Romo, rhp	No. 10
29.	Brian Horwitz, of	Dropped out
30.	Ben Copeland, of	(Athletics)

BEST TOOLS

Best Hitter for Average	Buster Posey
Best Power Hitter	Angel Villalona
Best Strike-Zone Discipline	Eddy Martinez-Esteve
Fastest Baserunner	Darren Ford
Best Athlete	Wendell Fairley
Best Fastball	Madison Bumgarner
Best Curveball	Tim Alderson
Best Slider	Waldis Joaquin
Best Changeup	Scott Barnes
Best Control	Madison Bumgarner
Best Defensive Catcher	Jackson Williams
Best Defensive Infielder	Brian Bocock
Best Infield Arm	Brian Bocock
Best Defensive Outfielder	Darren Ford
Best Outfield Arm	Mike McBryde

PROJECTED 2012 LINEUP

Catcher	Buster Posey
First Base	Angel Villalona
Second Base	Nick Noonan
Third Base	Conor Gillaspie
Shortstop	Ehire Adrianza
Left Field	Fred Lewis
Center Field	Aaron Rowand
Right Field	Nate Schierholtz
No. 1 Starter	Tim Lincecum
No. 2 Starter	Madison Bumgarner
No. 3 Starter	Matt Cain
No. 4 Starter	Tim Alderson
No. 5 Starter	Barry Zito
Closer	Brian Wilson

TOP PROSPECTS OF THE DECADE

Year	Player, Pos.	2008 Org.
1999	Jason Grilli, rhp	Rockies
2000	Kurt Ainsworth, rhp	Out of baseball
2001	Jerome Williams, rhp	Dodgers
2002	Jerome Williams, rhp	Dodgers
2003	Jesse Foppert, rhp	Giants
2004	Merkin Valdez, rhp	Giants
2005	Matt Cain, rhp	Giants
2006	Matt Cain, rhp	Giants
2007	Tim Lincecum, rhp	Giants
2008	Angel Villalona, 3b/1b	Giants

TOP DRAFT PICKS OF THE DECADE

Year	Player, Pos.	2008 Org.
1998	Tony Torcato, of	Chico (Golden)
1999	Kurt Ainsworth, rhp	Out of baseball
2000	Boof Bonser, rhp	Twins
2001	Brad Hennessey, rhp	Giants
2002	Matt Cain, rhp	Giants
2003	David Aardsma, rhp	Red Sox
2004	Eddy Martinez-Esteve, of (2nd round)	Giants
2005	Ben Copeland, of (4th round)	Giants
2006	Tim Lincecum, rhp	Giants
2007	Madison Bumgarner, lhp	Giants
2008	Buster Posey, c	Giants

LARGEST BONUSES IN CLUB HISTORY

Buster Posey, 2008	$6,200,000
Rafael Rodriguez, 2008	$2,550,000
Angel Villalona, 2006	$2,100,000
Tim Lincecum, 2006	$2,025,000
Madison Bumgarner, 2007	$2,000,000

SAN FRANCISCO GIANTS

TOP 2009 ROOKIE: Sergio Romo, rhp. He became the most trusted set-up man in San Francisco's bullpen by the end of last season.

BREAKOUT PROSPECT: Francisco Peguero, of. Though a bit old at 20 to be playing his first season in the United States, the Giants find his blend of tools and high-energy optimism irresistible.

SLEEPER: Jason Jarvis, rhp. The former Arizona State closer and independent ball refugee touches 97 and could be a huge steal as a 23rd-rounder in the 2008 draft.

SOURCE OF TOP 30 TALENT

Homegrown	29	Acquired	1
College	13	Trades	0
Junior college	1	Rule 5 draft	1
High school	7	Independent leagues	0
Draft-and-follow	1	Free agents/waivers	0
Nondrafted free agents	0		
International	7		

Numbers in parentheses indicate prospect rankings.

LF
Thomas Neal (23)
Eddy Martinez-Esteve
Brian Horwitz

CF
Wendell Fairley (12)
Mike McBryde (19)
Darren Ford
Clay Timpner
Caleb Curry

RF
Rafael Rodriguez (8)
Roger Kieschnick (14)
Francisco Peguero (22)
Juan Carlos Perez
Ryan Mantle

3B
Conor Gillaspie (7)
Matt Downs (24)
Ryan Rohlinger

SS
Ehire Adrianza (6)
Brandon Crawford
Brian Bocock

2B
Nick Noonan (5)
Charlie Culberson (27)
Sharlon Schoop
Marcus Sanders
Brad Boyer

1B
Angel Villalona (3)
Travis Ishikawa (17)
Brett Pill
C.J. Ziegler
Andy D'Alessio

C
Buster Posey (2)
Jackson Williams (16)
Adam Witter
Michael Ambort

RHP

Starters	Relievers
Tim Alderson (4)	Sergio Romo (10)
Henry Sosa (13)	Waldis Joaquin (11)
Kevin Pucetas (15)	Edwin Quirarte (25)
Joey Martinez (30)	Osiris Matos (26)
Ben Snyder	Luis Perdomo (28)
Mike Loree	Billy Sadler (29)
Adam Cowart	Merkin Valdez
Nick Pereira	Jason Jarvis
Kyle Nicholson	Justin Hedrick
Jorge Bucardo	Kelvin Pichardo
Wilber Bucardo	Steve Edlefsen
	Dan Griffin
	Daniel Turpen
	Dan Otero

LHP

Starters	Relievers
Madison Bumgarner (1)	Alex Hinshaw (18)
Scott Barnes (9)	Joe Paterson
Clayton Tanner (20)	Geno Espineli
Aaron King (21)	Wilmin Rodriguez
Eric Surkamp	Paul Oseguera

2008

BEST PURE HITTER: C Buster Posey (1), BA's 2008 College Player of the Year, led NCAA Division I with a .463 average last spring. He has a low-maintenance, short swing. 3B Conor Gillaspie (1s) won the Cape Cod League MVP award and batting title in 2007, hitting .345. He finished the season in San Francisco as part of a predraft arrangement.

BEST POWER HITTER: The ball makes a different sound off the bat of OF Roger Kieschnick (3). He's a streaky hitter who hits 'em as far as anybody. Dominican OF Juan Carlos Perez (13) hit 37 homers in the spring, one shy of the national junior college record. He signed a 2009 contract because of visa issues.

FASTEST RUNNER: OF Caleb Curry (14) is a pure 70 runner on the 20-80 scouting scale, though he was caught on 10 of 23 steal attempts as a pro.

BEST DEFENSIVE PLAYER: Posey has strong catch-and-throw skills, including a plus arm that produced 94-mph fastballs as a pitcher. SS Brandon Crawford (4) has premium arm strength, solid athleticism and the actions to be a plus defender.

BEST FASTBALL: RHPs Jason Jarvis (23) and Aaron King (7) have touched 97 mph in short stints.

BEST SECONDARY PITCH: RHP Edwin Quirarte's (5) splitter is his out pitch, and his slider is also a plus offering. His sinking fastball reaches 92 mph as well.

BEST PRO DEBUT: LHP Scott Barnes (8) went 5-3, 1.91 with 74 strikeouts in 57 innings, including two wins in the low Class A South Atlantic League playoffs. King went 4-2, 2.97 with 45 strikeouts in 33 innings.

BEST ATHLETE: Posey was a shortstop as a freshman at Florida State before moving behind the plate, where his athleticism makes him an elite defender. He also pitched in college and played all nine positions in his last regular season home game.

MOST INTRIGUING BACKGROUND: OF Ryan Mantle (19) is a third cousin of Hall of Famer Mickey. LHP Ari Ronick (12) is a nephew of Los Angeles Lakers coach Phil Jackson. Jarvis left Arizona State in March and was drafted out of the independent American Association.

CLOSEST TO THE MAJORS: Gillaspie already has been there, but Posey should get there to stay sooner.

BEST LATE-ROUND PICK: Perez's power has the Giants eager to see him in a pro uniform. Jarvis turned down six figures from the Angels out of high school in 2006 and was the closer on Arizona State's 2007

College World Series club. He added a changeup in indy ball and signed for $100,000. He needs maturity but has an above-average arm to go with excellent athleticism.

THE ONE WHO GOT AWAY: The Giants wanted RHP Ryan O'Sullivan (10) enough to offer him a chance to be a hitter first as a pro, though they liked him better on the mound. Instead, O'Sullivan will play both ways at San Diego State.

ASSESSMENT: After Posey, San Francisco got players who once projected as first-rounders with its next three picks—Gillaspie, Kieschnick and Crawford—and then a pair of intriguing lefties shortly thereafter with King and Barnes. It adds up to a strong effort for first-year scouting director John Barr.

2007

With three first-rounders, the Giants grabbed a pair of potential aces in LHP Madison Bumgarner (1) and RHP Tim Alderson (1), plus the system's best athlete in OF Wendell Fairley (1). The next choice was sweet-swinging 2B Nick Noonan (1s).

GRADE: A

2006

San Francisco stole RHP Tim Lincecum (1) with the 10th overall choice and saw him win a Cy Young Award just two years later. The rest of this draft is gravy but SSs Emmanuel Burriss (1s) and Brian Bocock (9) also sped to the majors.

GRADE: A

2005

The Giants didn't have picks in the first three rounds and just lost their top choice, OF Ben Copeland (4), in the Rule 5 draft in September. The only highlights were two overachieving relievers, LHP Alex Hinshaw (15) and RHP Sergio Romo (28).

GRADE: D

2004

San Francisco again didn't have a first-rounder but did unearth LHP Jonathan Sanchez (27) late and found some fringe big leaguers in 1B John Bowker (3), OF Clay Timpner (4), INF/OF Kevin Frandsen (12) and LHP Geno Espineli (14).

GRADE: C

*Draft analysis by John Manuel (2008) and Jim Callis (2004-07). Numbers in parentheses indicate draft rounds. *Bonuses for 2004-05 are first 10 rounds only.*

PROSPECT

MADISON BUMGARNER, LHP

Born: Aug, 1, 1989.
Ht.: 6-4. **Wt.:** 215.
Bats: R. **Throws:** L.
Drafted: HS—Hudson, N.C., 2007 (1st round).
Signed by: Pat Portugal.

DAVID SCHOFIELD

S urprise, surprise. For the 13th time in 14 years, the Giants' top prospect is a pitcher. Though teenage slugger Angel Villalona did nothing to diminish his No. 1 status of a year ago, his teammate at low Class A Augusta couldn't be denied. After drafting him 10th overall and signing him for $2 million in 2007, the Giants merely hoped Bumgarner would learn to compete and master simple skills in his first full pro season. Early efforts to smooth out his mechanics were a failure, as he allowed 10 runs over 11⅔ innings in his first three starts. Then the big, strong lefthander went back to his high school delivery and was untouchable, posting a 0.90 ERA in his final 21 regular season outings before allowing just one unearned run in two playoff starts as the GreenJackets won the South Atlantic League title. Bumgarner's overall 1.46 ERA was the lowest in the minors, and he struck out an unreal 7.8 batters for every walk.

There may not be a lefthander with a better fastball than Bumgarner's. He hits 97 mph with minimal effort, consistently pitches at 93-94 and hitters have trouble picking up his heater from his high three-quarters delivery. His fastball has boring action and is a devastating two-strike pitch when he elevates it. He gave up just three homers all season, as his command and control were impeccable. "He has another gear," catcher Jackson Williams said. "He's so long and so loose, the ball just pops—and it pops hard." His breaking ball and changeup showed improvement throughout 2008. Bumgarner, who's from a small town in North Carolina, initially came across as a timid kid when he first reported to instructional league in 2007. But he soon dispelled any concerns about his makeup. "The closer to home plate they get, the more he reaches back and goes after them," Augusta pitching coach Ross Grimsley said. "For 19, he's a very mature, smart kid. He knows he's got some things to work on to make himself a more complete pitcher and not just a thrower." Bumgarner is a physical, durable beast and a good athlete who also makes hard contact as a righthanded hitter.

While Bumgarner's fastball control far exceeded San Francisco's wildest expectations, his secondary pitches remain a work in progress. Coaches worked to replace an erratic curveball with something closer to a true slider that developed depth the more he threw it. He didn't get much practice setting up hitters because his fastball was nearly unhittable. He often threw his changeup in fastball counts just to work on it. "That'll be the biggest thing," Grimsley said. "He'll need the changeup for the higher levels and he understands that."

Bumgarner has all the gifts to be a No. 1 starter, though it's hard to imagine anyone unseating Tim Lincecum in San Francisco in the foreseeable future. The Giants hope to instill a friendly rivalry between Bumgarner and their other first-round prep pitcher from the 2007 draft, Tim Alderson. They're expected to form a supremely talented 1-2 punch at Double-A Connecticut, potentially with 2008 first-rounder Buster Posey as their catcher. If Bumgarner continues to easily dispatch hitters after skipping a level, San Francisco will be tempted to give him a taste of the big leagues in September.

Year	Club (League)	Class	W	L	ERA	G	GS	CG	SV	IP	H	R	ER	HR	BB	SO	AVG
2008	Augusta (SAL)	LoA	15	3	1.46	24	24	1	0	142	111	28	23	3	21	164	.216
MINOR LEAGUE TOTALS			15	3	1.46	24	24	1	0	142	111	28	23	3	21	164	.216

2 BUSTER POSEY, C

BILL MITCHELL

BORN: March 27, 1987. **B-T:** R-R. **HT.:** 6-1. **WT.:** 205. **DRAFTED:** Florida State, 2008 (1st round). **SIGNED BY:** Sean O'Connor.

Posey led NCAA Division I in hitting (.463), on-base percentage (.566), slugging (.879), hits (119), total bases (226) and RBIs (93) in 2008, en route to winning Baseball America's College Player of the Year and the Golden Spikes awards. The Rays considered him with the first overall pick, but he slid to the Giants at No. 5. He received the largest up-front bonus in draft history, $6.2 million. There might have been better pure athletes in the draft, but Posey has few peers when it comes to baseball athleticism. He was drafted out of high school as a pitcher and moved from shortstop to catcher at Florida State, where he once played all nine positions in one game. He profiles as a catcher in the mold of Joe Mauer. Posey has a quick bat and makes consistent contact with gap power to all fields. Arm strength isn't a problem, as he hit 94 mph as an occasional reliever for the Seminoles. He's agile and has soft hands, and he even runs well. He's a captain on the field and wins plaudits for his baseball acumen. Posey is still relatively new to catching and will need time to develop behind the plate, especially his game-calling skills. He had trouble with passed balls in Hawaii Winter Baseball and was sent back to instructional league for a crash course in receiving. Despite his huge power numbers as a college junior, some scouts believe he won't hit more than 10-12 homers annually in the majors. Posey doesn't have to hit for huge power to be an all-star. He's versatile enough to play anywhere on the diamond, but most valuable as a catcher. He's probably headed for Double-A, where he'll catch a talented pitching staff.

Year	Club (League)	Class	AVG	G	AB	R	H	2B	3B	HR	RBI	BB	SO	SB	OBP	SLG
2008	Giants (AZL)	R	.385	7	26	8	10	3	1	1	4	5	4	0	.484	.692
	Salem-Keizer (NWL)	SS	.273	3	11	2	3	2	0	0	2	3	0	0	.429	.455
MINOR LEAGUE TOTALS			.351	10	37	10	13	5	1	1	6	8	4	0	.467	.622

3 ANGEL VILLALONA, 1B

STEVE MOORE

BORN: Aug. 13, 1990. **B-T:** R-R. **HT.:** 6-3. **WT.:** 230. **SIGNED:** Dominican Republic, 2007. **SIGNED BY:** Rick Ragazzo/Pablo Peguero.

The best Giants power-hitting prospect to come along in more than a decade, Villalona signed for a then-club-record $2.1 million in 2007. He had an encouraging first full pro season in 2008, when he was the youngest player in the South Atlantic League. He led a championship Augusta team with 17 homers as a 17-year-old while moving from third base to first base. Villalona's batting practice was a daily fireworks display and he often carried it over to games. He has the ability to hit quality fastballs and hanging breaking balls a long, long way. He has soft hands, a strong, accurate arm and surprising agility for a player his size. He lost almost 40 pounds from spring training to the end of the season and coaches praised his dedication to getting in baseball shape. Villalona lacks patience at the plate, rarely drawing walks and failing to realize when pitchers are trying to pitch around him. It's vital that he continue to take his conditioning seriously. Even after slimming down, he's still a poor runner with no chance of returning to third base. If the Giants promote Villalona a level per year, he'll still reach the majors at age 21, and he might not need that long. His production improved every month at Augusta, and they hope for a similar upswing this season at high Class A San Jose.

Year	Club (League)	Class	AVG	G	AB	R	H	2B	3B	HR	RBI	BB	SO	SB	OBP	SLG
2007	Giants (AZL)	R	.285	52	200	40	57	12	3	5	37	15	42	1	.344	.450
	Salem-Keizer (NWL)	SS	.167	5	12	1	2	0	0	0	1	0	2	1	.231	.167
2008	Augusta (SAL)	LoA	.263	123	464	64	122	29	0	17	64	18	118	1	.312	.435
MINOR LEAGUE TOTALS			.268	180	676	105	181	41	3	22	102	33	162	3	.320	.435

4 TIM ALDERSON, RHP

BILL MITCHELL

BORN: Nov. 3, 1988. **B-T:** R-R. **HT.:** 6-7. **WT.:** 217. **DRAFTED:** HS—Scottsdale, Ariz., 2007 (1st round). **SIGNED BY:** Lee Carballo.

Alderson's advanced command and hard curveball made him the 22nd overall pick and earned him a $1.29 million bonus in 2007. The Giants figured those attributes also prepared him for an aggressive assignment to high Class A in his first full pro season, and he responded by winning the California League ERA title at 2.79. He threw exclusively out of the stretch in high school, but had no problems repeating his delivery from the windup in San Jose. Alderson's curveball is the best in the organization and he works it off an 88-92 mph four-seam fastball with natural cut and late movement. He began throwing a two-seamer to get more grounders, though it's not like he needed to work on pitch efficiency. He's a smart competitor, often throwing curveballs in the first three innings of night games when the conditions were shadowy. He throws strikes and lives at the bottom of the zone. Alderson will develop into a frontline starter if he continues to make steady progress with his changeup. He doesn't have overwhelming velocity, though he still can get outs with his fastball. While he's athletic, like most gangly pitchers he doesn't field his position well. He could be a factor out of a major league bullpen right now, but the Giants have no plans to develop him as anything but a starter. He'll begin 2009 with Madison Bumgarner in Double-A and could finish the season in the big leagues.

Year	Club (League)	Class	W	L	ERA	G	GS	CG	SV	IP	H	R	ER	HR	BB	SO	AVG
2007	Giants (AZL)	R	0	0	0.00	3	2	0	0	5	4	0	0	0	0	12	.211
2008	San Jose (CAL)	HiA	13	4	2.79	26	26	0	0	145	125	48	45	4	34	124	.235
MINOR LEAGUE TOTALS			13	4	2.69	29	28	0	0	150	129	48	45	4	34	136	.234

5 NICK NOONAN, 2B

JOHN SPEAR

BORN: May 4, 1989. **B-T:** L-R. **HT.:** 6-0. **WT.:** 185. **DRAFTED:** HS—San Diego, 2007 (1st round supplemental). **SIGNED BY:** Ray Krawczyk.

After signing for $915,750 as a sandwich pick in 2007, Noonan became a Rookie-level Arizona League all-star and the talk of the Giants' instructional league camp. Last season, he was the most consistent offensive player on a championship Augusta club loaded with teenage talent. Noonan's swing is compact, balanced and direct to the ball, which should allow him to hit for average with gap power. He has outstanding situational hitting skills, bunts well and moves runners. He has above-average speed and an opportunistic nature on the bases, stealing 29 bags in 33 attempts. He made dramatic improvements at second base, especially going to his backhand and turning double plays, after playing shortstop in high school. His game awareness is off the charts. Coaches lauded Noonan's strike-zone awareness before the season began, but he drew just 23 walks and acknowledged that he needs to be more selective. He was so aggressive that he got himself out at times in 2008. He's still learning to play second base and doesn't always take proper angles on grounders. He might not flash enough power to make Chase Utley comparisons hold up, but Noonan is clearly San Francisco's second baseman of the future. While high Class A would be the next logical step, club officials were debating whether he might be ready for a jump to Double-A.

Year	Club (League)	Class	AVG	G	AB	R	H	2B	3B	HR	RBI	BB	SO	SB	OBP	SLG
2007	Giants (AZL)	R	.316	52	206	33	65	11	4	3	40	12	20	18	.357	.451
2008	Augusta (SAL)	LoA	.279	119	499	79	139	27	7	9	68	23	98	29	.315	.415
MINOR LEAGUE TOTALS			.289	171	705	112	204	38	11	12	108	35	118	47	.328	.426

6 EHIRE ADRIANZA, SS

BILL MITCHELL

BORN: Aug. 21, 1989. **B-T:** B-R. **HT.:** 6-1. **WT.:** 155. **SIGNED:** Venezuela, 2006. **SIGNED BY:** Ciro Villalobos.

Despite missing half of the Arizona League season with a broken foot, Adrianza ranked as the circuit's best middle-infield prospect, thanks to his defensive wizardry and ability to make contact from both sides of the plate. When Triple-A Fresno was thin on infielders for a series at Tucson, he was driven over from Scottsdale and promptly collected three hits. Adrianza has excellent range and plays Gold Glove caliber defense up the middle. Even Omar Vizquel, who was in Arizona while rehabbing his knee, commented on Adrianza's soft hands and accurate arm. A natural righthanded hitter, he has a level swing and balanced approach from either side. He has gap power and doesn't try to just slap and dash his way on base. Something of a late bloomer, Adrianza only recently began adding strength to his lanky frame. He's not as fast as most shortstops, though his excellent instincts and first-step quickness make up for that shortcoming in the field. A full season in low Class A at age 19 should be a good test for Adrianza's skills and durability. Though Emmanuel Burriss had his moments as a rookie last season, Adrianza has a higher ceiling offensively and defensively. Free agent pickup Edgar Renteria figures to be gone by the time Adrianza is ready.

Year	Club (League)	Class	AVG	G	AB	R	H	2B	3B	HR	RBI	BB	SO	SB	OBP	SLG
2006	Giants (DSL)	R	.156	44	122	17	19	2	1	0	7	24	31	3	.311	.189
2007	Giants (DSL)	R	.241	66	249	44	60	17	2	0	30	41	31	23	.351	.325
2008	Fresno (PCL)	AAA	.500	2	6	2	3	1	0	0	0	2	1	0	.625	.667
	Giants (AZL)	R	.255	15	55	13	14	4	0	1	6	7	4	0	.349	.382
	Salem-Keizer (NWL)	SS	.400	1	5	3	2	0	0	0	0	0	1	0	.400	.400
MINOR LEAGUE TOTALS			.224	128	437	79	98	24	3	1	43	74	68	26	.344	.300

7 CONOR GILLASPIE, 3B

BORN: July 18, 1987. **B-T:** L-R. **HT.:** 6-1. **WT.:** 200. **DRAFTED:** Wichita State, 2008 (1st round supplemental). **SIGNED BY:** Hugh Walker.

The Cape Cod League MVP and batting champ (.345) in 2007, Gillaspie became the first player from the 2008 draft to reach the majors. He negotiated the callup in return for agreeing to MLB's slot recommendation of $970,000 as the 37th overall pick. He singled off Dan Haren for his first major league hit. Gillaspie has a rare blend of supreme hitting skills and patience at the plate. He wasn't overwhelmed in a handful of big league at-bats, showing good pitch recognition and a confident approach. He has a strong frame, solid speed and an average arm. He gets the most out of his ability and plays the game with a no-nonsense attitude. The Giants aren't convinced Gillaspie will stay at third base, but they will give him every opportunity because they're thin at the position. He tends to hurry in the field and doesn't look smooth. He's more of a doubles hitter than a home run threat, so his power might be a tad light for the hot corner. His intensity can come across as arrogance at times, such as when he annoyed some veterans in September when he said, "I think I can play as good as any of these guys up here." Though he's on the 40-man roster and will be in big league camp, Gillaspie isn't a candidate to be the Opening Day third baseman. He could earn his way back in September after opening the season in high Class A or Double-A.

Year	Club (League)	Class	AVG	G	AB	R	H	2B	3B	HR	RBI	BB	SO	SB	OBP	SLG
2008	Giants (AZL)	R	.273	6	22	2	6	3	0	0	7	3	1	0	.360	.409
	Salem-Keizer (NWL)	SS	.268	18	71	4	19	4	0	0	8	9	13	2	.350	.324
	San Francisco (NL)	MAJ	.200	8	5	1	1	0	0	0	0	2	0	0	.429	.200
MINOR LEAGUE TOTALS			.269	24	93	6	25	7	0	0	15	12	14	2	.352	.344
MAJOR LEAGUE TOTALS			.200	8	5	1	1	0	0	0	0	2	0	0	.429	.200

8 RAFAEL RODRIGUEZ, OF

BORN: July 13, 1992. **B-T:** R-R. **HT.:** 6-5. **WT.:** 198. **SIGNED:** Dominican Republic, 2008. **SIGNED BY:** Felix Peguero/Pablo Peguero.

The Giants sent their entire fleet of top talent evaluators to look at Rodriguez before signing him last July for $2.55 million, a franchise record for an international player. Special assistant Felipe Alou likened Rodriguez's combination of size, strength and speed to a young Vladimir Guerrero. He signed on his 16th birthday, reportedly turning down a higher offer from the Cardinals. Rodriguez has all the tools to be a superstar. Farm director Fred Stanley said Rodriguez reminds him of a young Dave Winfield with a bigger wingspan. Rodriguez profiles perfectly as a right fielder with big-time power potential—"He hits golf balls in B.P.," Alou said—plus speed and a cannon arm. Giants coaches liked his enthusiasm in instructional league and believe he'll take instruction well. Rodriguez hasn't faced quality pitching and other international scouts weren't as sold on his hitting ability. He has a huge strike zone that could prove difficult to cover, and breaking balls figure to be an adventure for a while. Rodriguez will receive daily instruction at the Giants' Dominican complex before he participates in the Rookie-level summer league there. He's not nearly as advanced as fellow Dominican Angel Villalona was at the same stage, and he isn't expected to play for a U.S. affiliate before 2010.

Year	Club (League)	Class	AVG	G	AB	R	H	2B	3B	HR	RBI	BB	SO	SB	OBP	SLG
2008	Did Not Play—Signed 2009 Contract															

9 SCOTT BARNES, LHP

BORN: Sept. 5, 1987. **B-T:** L-L. **HT.:** 6-3. **WT.:** 180. **DRAFTED:** St. John's, 2008 (8th round). **SIGNED BY:** John DiCarlo.

Even when the Giants spend their top four draft picks on college hitters, they manage to unearth a major league arm. Signed for $100,000 as an eighth-rounder, Barnes had a spectacular introduction to pro ball. He posted a 2.06 ERA and 13.0 strikeouts per nine innings, limited opponents to a .155 average, and pitched the clinching game in the South Atlantic League playoffs. Barnes thrives on location and hiding the ball until late in his delivery, but he's more than just a finesse pitcher. He can reach 92 mph when needed and changes speed like a major league veteran. His changeup overwhelmed Sally League hitters down the stretch and his curveball is an effective third pitch. He repeats his fluid delivery well, enabling him to fill the strike zone. He fields his position well and has a good pickoff move. Barnes isn't overpowering, generally pitching in the upper 80s with his fastball, and it remains to be seen how he'll fare against more advanced hitters. Despite having little margin for error, he'll have to continue establishing the inner half against righthanders. Barnes is further along than Noah Lowry at a similar stage and profiles as a possible No. 3 starter.

Because the Giants lack starting depth in the upper levels of their system, they could skip him to Double-A to begin the season.

Year	Club (League)	Class	W	L	ERA	G	GS	CG	SV	IP	H	R	ER	HR	BB	SO	AVG
2008	Giants (AZL)	R	0	1	3.38	3	0	0	0	5	3	2	2	0	4	11	.167
	Salem-Keizer (NWL)	SS	0	0	4.76	2	1	0	0	6	6	3	3	0	1	11	.250
	Augusta (SAL)	LoA	3	2	1.38	6	6	0	0	33	15	6	5	0	7	41	.133
MINOR LEAGUE TOTALS			3	3	2.06	11	7	0	0	44	24	11	10	0	12	63	.155

10 SERGIO ROMO, RHP

BORN: March 4, 1983. **B-T:** R-R. **HT.:** 5-11. **WT.:** 191. **DRAFTED:** Mesa State (Colo.), 2005 (28th round). **SIGNED BY:** Joe Strain.

Romo began 2008 as an occasional name on the travel squad for spring training games and ended it as the most dependable set-up man in San Francisco's bullpen. While he isn't particularly imposing or athletic, there's no downplaying the way he made major league hitters look foolish—including Manny Ramirez, whom he struck out on three pitches. The Giants issued the second-most walks in the National League last year, so Romo's aggressive, strike-throwing approach was a refreshing change. His breaking ball is essentially two different pitches when he changes his arm angle, one of which is a front-door slider that snaps back across the plate against righthanders. He wants the ball and isn't intimidated. He's durable and handled multiple-inning appearances without complaint. Romo's fastball is fringe-average and only touches 90 mph, so he can't get away with mistakes up in the strike zone. Aware that the book will be thicker on him next season, he worked on a changeup while pitching for Mexicali this winter. Romo has had nothing handed to him, yet he has managed to miss bats at every level. He'll hold down a key role in the Giants bullpen in front of closer Brian Wilson.

Year	Club (League)	Class	W	L	ERA	G	GS	CG	SV	IP	H	R	ER	HR	BB	SO	AVG
2005	Salem-Keizer (NWL)	SS	7	1	2.75	15	14	0	0	69	70	24	21	7	9	65	.261
2006	Augusta (SAL)	LoA	10	2	2.53	31	10	0	4	103	78	33	29	9	19	95	.208
2007	San Jose (CAL)	HiA	6	2	1.36	41	0	0	9	66	35	12	10	4	15	106	.155
2008	Connecticut (EL)	AA	1	3	4.15	24	0	0	11	26	22	15	12	1	7	27	.237
	Fresno (PCL)	AAA	0	0	0.00	3	0	0	0	6	3	0	0	0	2	7	.150
	San Francisco (NL)	MAJ	3	1	2.12	29	0	0	0	34	16	13	8	3	8	33	.138
MINOR LEAGUE TOTALS			24	8	2.40	114	24	0	24	270	208	84	72	21	52	300	.212
MAJOR LEAGUE TOTALS			3	1	2.12	29	0	0	0	34	16	13	8	3	8	33	.138

11 WALDIS JOAQUIN, RHP

BORN: Dec. 25, 1986. **B-T:** R-R. **HT.:** 6-2. **WT.:** 190. **SIGNED:** Dominican Republic, 2003. **SIGNED BY:** Rick Ragazzo/Pablo Peguero.

Joaquin had Tommy John surgery in his past, his delivery looks stiff and he takes longer than most pitchers to work himself into shape in the spring. But by the end of each year, he's usually throwing some of the nastiest stuff in the system. Joaquin did it again in 2008, looking uninspired for long stretches in Augusta but throwing gas for San Jose in the California League playoffs. He hit 97 mph in a dominant performance against Stockton, and he can sit at 93-95 when he's at the top of his game. Joaquin's slider is a plus pitch and his changeup is effective enough that club officials haven't ruled out developing him as a starter. He would have to improve his control, though, and his quickest route to the big leagues is in short relief. If he's paired with a catcher who prods him to throw inside, he has a chance to dominate at any level. Joaquin loses focus if he isn't challenged, so the Giants could assign him to Double-A or higher if he shows determination this spring.

Year	Club (League)	Class	W	L	ERA	G	GS	CG	SV	IP	H	R	ER	HR	BB	SO	AVG
2004	Giants (DSL)	R	6	1	1.61	14	13	0	0	61	51	21	11	0	28	44	.229
2005	Giants (AZL)	R	1	1	3.64	10	5	0	1	30	28	17	12	1	10	37	.241
2007	Salem-Keizer (NWL)	SS	3	0	2.84	15	5	0	0	38	24	13	12	2	16	30	.176
2008	Augusta (SAL)	LoA	1	2	4.33	27	3	0	2	52	49	32	25	1	20	49	.247
	San Jose (CAL)	HiA	0	1	4.66	9	4	0	0	19	20	13	10	2	11	23	.274
MINOR LEAGUE TOTALS			11	5	3.14	75	30	0	3	200	172	96	70	6	85	183	.231

12 WENDELL FAIRLEY, OF

BORN: March 17, 1988. **B-T:** L-R. **HT.:** 6-0. **WT.:** 190. **DRAFTED:** HS—Lucedale, Miss., 2007 (1st round). **SIGNED BY:** Andrew Jefferson.

The Giants took Fairley with the third of their first-round picks in the 2007 draft, 29th overall, and they're still not sure exactly what they got with their $1 million investment. A high left ankle sprain late last spring set him back for nearly three months and prevented him from playing in low Class A as hoped. He made his pro debut in the Arizona League, where he hit a triple off a rehabbing Kelvim Escobar. Fairley was one of the top athletes in the 2007 draft but he's quite raw. He has tremendous bat speed and strength that gives him some of the best power potential in the system. He also scored top marks on a vision-tracking test that the Giants gave to their minor leaguers. He's still learning to pick up breaking pitches, however, because he didn't see many quality curveballs from high schoolers in Mississippi. Fairley also is figuring out how to work counts, bunt and steal bases. He has well-above-average speed and plus arm strength. Coaches were happy with the way Fairley competed in instructional league, and they worked him at all three outfield positions. He'll focus on center field in 2009, when he'll head to Augusta a year behind schedule.

Year	Club (League)	Class	AVG	G	AB	R	H	2B	3B	HR	RBI	BB	SO	SB	OBP	SLG
2008	Giants (AZL)	R	.259	52	193	39	50	5	2	2	17	26	37	7	.388	.337
MINOR LEAGUE TOTALS			.259	52	193	39	50	5	2	2	17	26	37	7	.388	.337

13 HENRY SOSA, RHP

BORN: July 28, 1985. **B-T:** R-R. **HT.:** 6-2. **WT.:** 197. **SIGNED:** Dominican Republic, 2004. **SIGNED BY:** Rick Ragazzo/Pablo Peguero.

Sosa took everyone by surprise in 2007 when he established a dominant fastball and represented the Giants at the Futures Game. But he had arthroscopic knee surgery that October and didn't make it out of extended spring until late May last year, then posted mediocre results in 12 high Class A starts. Club officials were disappointed that he never regained his previous form, even when given extra time. He also had a pectoral strain that kept him out for a few weeks. When healthy and repeating his over-the-top delivery, Sosa has a mid-90s fastball. The rest of his game is raw, as he has only a rudimentary grasp of a curveball and changeup, which must continue to develop if he wants to remain a starting pitcher. He did make some strides with his control last year, but his confidence took a jolt and his aggressiveness suffered as a result. Sosa will have to reset himself next season, likely opening back at San Jose. He has all the physical tools to get back on track.

Year	Club (League)	Class	W	L	ERA	G	GS	CG	SV	IP	H	R	ER	HR	BB	SO	AVG
2004	Giants (DSL)	R	0	5	5.30	13	7	0	0	36	40	28	21	2	19	25	.282
2005	Giants (DSL)	R	5	6	3.58	13	12	0	0	55	53	30	22	4	8	46	.250
2006	Giants (AZL)	R	2	1	3.90	9	6	0	0	32	20	15	14	3	12	41	.177
2007	Augusta (SAL)	LoA	6	0	0.73	13	10	0	1	62	30	8	5	2	25	61	.144
	San Jose (CAL)	HiA	5	5	4.38	14	14	0	0	64	66	36	31	8	36	78	.262
2008	San Jose (CAL)	HiA	3	4	4.31	12	12	0	0	56	62	28	27	6	18	58	.283
	Augusta (SAL)	LoA	0	0	0.00	2	0	0	0	1	1	1	0	0	2	0	.250
MINOR LEAGUE TOTALS			21	21	3.52	76	61	0	1	307	272	146	120	25	120	309	.237

14 ROGER KIESCHNICK, OF

BORN: Jan. 21, 1987. **B-T:** L-R. **HT.:** 6-3. **WT.:** 215. **DRAFTED:** Texas Tech, 2008 (3rd round). **SIGNED BY:** Todd Thomas.

Kieschnick has baseball bloodlines, as the first cousin of former two-way major leaguer Brooks Kieschnick. Roger had a chance to join Brooks as a first-round pick, but he slumped last spring, hitting just .305 and chasing enough pitches that he dropped to the third round. Signed two days before the Aug. 15 deadline for a slightly above-slot $525,000, he saw his first pro action in Hawaii Winter Baseball. He's a legitimate power threat who tied Pedro Alvarez (the No. 2 overall pick in 2008) for the team lead with seven homers on Team USA's college squad in 2007. Kieschnick drives the ball to all fields, though he gets himself out by being overly aggressive. A good athlete for his size, he has solid-average speed and arm strength, making him a prototype right fielder if he performs with the bat. He's expected to make his pro debut in high Class A.

Year	Club (League)	Class	AVG	G	AB	R	H	2B	3B	HR	RBI	BB	SO	SB	OBP	SLG
2008	Did Not Play—Signed Late															

15 KEVIN PUCETAS, RHP

BORN: Nov. 27, 1984. **B-T:** R-R. **HT.:** 6-4. **WT.:** 225. **DRAFTED:** Limestone (S.C.), 2006 (17th round). **SIGNED BY:** Pat Portugal.

A year after he led all minor leaguers with a 1.86 ERA, Pucetas would have topped the California League in the same category if not for San Jose rotation-mate Tim Alderson. Pucetas didn't lose a decision until Aug. 17, and his 10-0 start tied Dan Rambo (1990) and Jeff Urban (1998-99) for the longest winning streak in San Jose franchise history. His performance cemented his status as a legitimate pitching prospect, and he has far exceeded expectations as a 17th-round pick out of NCAA Division II Limestone (S.C.). Pucetas earned a trip to the Futures Game in 2008 and was just as impressive in the Arizona Fall League. His fastball won't blow away anyone at 86-88 mph, but he doesn't make many mistakes with it and it plays up because he brings a consistent changeup to the mound every time out. His slider is nearly as dependable, though his curveball comes and goes. It's his feel for the craft and ability to mix and command his pitches that really set him apart. He's strong and durable, and he controls the running game well. As long as he keeps throwing quality strikes, Pucetas could become a back-of-the-rotation starter or long reliever in the majors. San Francisco will give him a chance to fill a rotation slot in spring training, but he's more likely to open the season in Double-A.

Year	Club (League)	Class	W	L	ERA	G	GS	CG	SV	IP	H	R	ER	HR	BB	SO	AVG
2006	Salem-Keizer (NWL)	SS	7	1	2.17	15	15	0	0	71	57	22	17	2	19	60	.222
2007	Augusta (SAL)	LoA	15	4	1.86	27	23	0	1	145	124	40	30	7	21	104	.228
2008	San Jose (CAL)	HiA	10	2	3.02	24	24	0	0	125	115	46	42	6	27	102	.247
MINOR LEAGUE TOTALS			32	7	2.35	66	62	0	1	341	296	108	89	15	67	266	.234

16 JACKSON WILLIAMS, C

BORN: May 14, 1986. **B-T:** R-R. **HT.:** 5-11. **WT.:** 200. **DRAFTED:** Oklahoma, 2007 (1st round supplemental). **SIGNED BY:** Todd Thomas.

You'd imagine the Giants would have been down on Williams after he hit .179 in 47 games in low Class A to start 2008. Instead, they promoted him and he showed improvement at the plate—albeit by batting .231 in the hitter's haven that is the California League. It remains to be seen whether he'll ever hit enough to justify going 43rd overall in the 2007 draft and receiving a $708,750 bonus. But Williams did cut down his stride, shortened up and became more aggressive early in the count. He peaked in instructional league, where club officials insisted he was the best hitter in a camp filled with the organization's elite prospects. Williams originally might have bought into the idea that he's a defensive catcher with limited offensive upside, but coaches disabused him of that notion. There's no doubting his Gold Glove-caliber skills behind the plate. Augusta manager Andy Skeels, who played with Sandy Alomar Jr. and Benito Santiago, said Williams has a quicker release and a more accurate arm than those two former all-stars. He threw out 45 percent of basestealers last season. He blocks balls in the dirt, keeps pitchers focused and calls a good game. If Buster Posey starts 2009 in Double-A, Williams will return to high Class A so both can play every day.

Year	Club (League)	Class	AVG	G	AB	R	H	2B	3B	HR	RBI	BB	SO	SB	OBP	SLG
2007	Salem-Keizer (NWL)	SS	.231	42	130	20	30	3	0	5	20	16	27	0	.338	.369
2008	Augusta (SAL)	LoA	.179	47	156	22	28	7	0	2	13	15	37	0	.275	.263
	San Jose (CAL)	HiA	.231	50	156	11	36	5	0	3	16	15	40	2	.309	.321
MINOR LEAGUE TOTALS			.213	139	442	53	94	15	0	10	49	46	104	2	.306	.314

17 TRAVIS ISHIKAWA, 1B

BORN: Sept. 24, 1983. **B-T:** L-L. **HT.:** 6-3. **WT.:** 225. **DRAFTED:** HS—Federal Way, Wash., 2002 (21st round). **SIGNED BY:** Matt Woodward.

Ishikawa looked like he was falling off the prospect radar in 2007, when he lost his swing and dealt with several nagging injuries. Regarded as the Giants' first baseman of the future when they gave him a $955,000 bonus to steer him away from Oregon State in 2002, he got back on track in 2008. He rescued his career by performing well in a return to Double-A and was even better after a promotion, hitting 16 home runs in 171 Triple-A at-bats. He suddenly found himself with a major league opportunity in mid-August when John Bowker couldn't pull himself out of a prolonged slump. Ishikawa credited his faith with his success, saying belief in a higher power kept him from living and dying with every at-bat. While showing better power last year, he also cut down on his strikeouts considerably and showed good pitch recognition against major league competition, though he remains susceptible to soft stuff away. He's an excellent defensive first baseman with soft hands, above-average range and a terrific feel for the position. He has below-average speed but is decent for a first baseman. He held his own in his big league trial and will be a platoon candidate for the Giants—possibly teaming with switch-hitter Pablo Sandoval—if they don't acquire another first baseman this winter.

Year	Club (League)	Class	AVG	G	AB	R	H	2B	3B	HR	RBI	BB	SO	SB	OBP	SLG
2005	San Jose (CAL)	HiA	.282	127	432	87	122	28	7	22	79	70	129	1	.387	.532
2006	San Francisco (NL)	MAJ	.292	12	24	1	7	3	1	0	4	1	6	0	.320	.500
	Connecticut (EL)	AA	.232	86	298	33	69	13	4	10	42	35	88	0	.316	.403
2007	Connecticut (EL)	AA	.214	48	173	17	37	3	1	3	17	17	48	0	.292	.295
	San Jose (CAL)	HiA	.268	56	198	35	53	15	1	13	34	19	78	0	.342	.551
2008	Connecticut (EL)	AA	.289	64	232	34	67	16	0	8	45	36	45	10	.383	.461
	Fresno (PCL)	AAA	.310	48	171	35	53	19	3	16	46	14	36	0	.370	.737
	San Francisco (NL)	MAJ	.274	33	95	12	26	6	0	3	15	9	27	1	.337	.432
MINOR LEAGUE TOTALS			.267	429	1504	241	401	94	16	72	263	191	424	11	.354	.494
MAJOR LEAGUE TOTALS			.277	45	119	13	33	9	1	3	19	10	33	1	.333	.445

18 ALEX HINSHAW, LHP

BORN: Oct. 31, 1982. **B-T:** L-L. **HT.:** 6-3. **WT.:** 170. **DRAFTED:** San Diego State, 2005 (15th round). **SIGNED BY:** Lee Carballo.

The Giants drafted Hinshaw three times—out of high school in 2000, out of Chaffey (Calif.) JC in 2002 and out of San Diego State in 2005—before he finally signed. In between he was also drafted by the Marlins in 2003 and missed a season following Tommy John surgery. Hinshaw showed what all the fuss was about in an encouraging major league debut season. The wiry lefthander appeared in 48 games, posted a 3.40 ERA and held lefthanders to a .205 average. He remains far from a finished product, often failing to get ahead of hitters and walking his way into trouble. But his low-90s fastball, hard curveball and sweeping slider all can be plus pitches, lending credence to the belief that he'll be more than a lefty specialist. Hinshaw is a fiery competitor who has had his share of dustups, including one ejection for arguing the strike zone. He went to the Arizona Fall League and looked tired there, posting a 6.23 ERA in 17 innings. Hinshaw is even skinnier than teammate Tim Lincecum and probably could stand to gain a few pounds to help increase his stamina. He's a near lock to make San Francisco's Opening Day roster.

Year	Club (League)	Class	W	L	ERA	G	GS	CG	SV	IP	H	R	ER	HR	BB	SO	AVG
2005	Salem-Keizer (NWL)	SS	0	1	3.68	25	0	0	0	22	17	9	9	1	18	33	.227
2006	San Jose (CAL)	HiA	6	3	4.26	30	10	0	0	70	58	48	33	6	60	78	.227
2007	Connecticut (EL)	AA	3	1	1.96	17	5	0	0	41	22	13	9	2	19	50	.155
2008	Fresno (PCL)	AAA	0	0	0.57	13	0	0	7	16	5	1	1	0	4	21	.098
	San Francisco (NL)	MAJ	2	1	3.40	48	0	0	0	40	31	16	15	5	29	47	.220
MINOR LEAGUE TOTALS			9	5	3.15	85	15	0	7	149	102	71	52	9	101	182	.195
MAJOR LEAGUE TOTALS			2	1	3.40	48	0	0	0	40	31	16	15	5	29	47	.220

19 MIKE McBRYDE, OF

BORN: March 22, 1985. **B-T:** R-R. **HT.:** 6-2. **WT.:** 170. **DRAFTED:** Florida Atlantic, 2006 (5th round). **SIGNED BY:** Steve Arnieri.

Scouts weren't sure whether McBryde would make a better hitter or pitcher coming out of Florida Atlantic, as he had served as the Owls' closer at times during his college career. The Giants bet on his plus-plus speed and are encouraged by the results so far. McBryde is a dynamic presence in center field with his speed and arm strength. Physically, he's a stronger version of a young Steve Finley. McBryde improved several aspects of his offensive game last season, cutting down on strikeouts and using his speed to get on base with a flurry of bunt singles and infield hits. He also improved his baserunning skills, stealing 31 bases in 41 attempts after going just 14-for-25 in 2007. The downside was that just 21 of his 124 hits went for extra bases in 2008, and club officials thought he got a little too slap-happy. McBryde hit a few tape-measure home runs, including one at Visalia that went almost 500 feet. But he'll need to drive the ball with more consistency and hit breaking pitches to turn the corner in Double-A this season.

Year	Club (League)	Class	AVG	G	AB	R	H	2B	3B	HR	RBI	BB	SO	SB	OBP	SLG
2006	Salem-Keizer (NWL)	SS	.276	71	225	38	62	9	5	3	34	22	59	16	.344	.400
2007	Augusta (SAL)	LoA	.276	119	417	71	115	17	4	7	61	27	100	14	.328	.386
2008	San Jose (CAL)	HiA	.295	125	420	73	124	10	6	5	46	37	84	31	.368	.383
MINOR LEAGUE TOTALS			.283	315	1062	182	301	36	15	15	141	86	243	61	.348	.388

20 CLAYTON TANNER, LHP

BORN: Dec. 5, 1987. **B-T:** R-L. **HT.:** 6-1. **WT.:** 180. **DRAFTED:** HS—Concord, Calif., 2006 (3rd round). **SIGNED BY:** Keith Snider.

Tanner struggled to stay healthy in 2008, juggled his repertoire and endured a series of frustrations, yet his 3.69 ERA ranked sixth in the California League—and three of the pitchers he trailed were San Jose teammates Tim Alderson, Kevin Pucetas and Jesse English. Tanner also was part of another strong pitching staff at Augusta in 2007, though a heavy workload there may have led to some of Tanner's problems in 2008. He missed nearly a month with a scapular strain and a tight posterior shoulder capsule. He rebounded to pitch well in the second half, due in no small measure to the re-emergence of his curveball. It became such a dependable pitch that he'd work backward, throwing it for first-pitch strikes and using his changeup when behind in the count. Tanner is bright, talkative and studies hitters as well as anyone in the league, and he's not afraid to challenge them even though he doesn't have overpowering stuff. His fastball sat at 88-89 mph last season and he made his share of location mistakes with it, but he has youth and athleticism on his side. He'll get a true test in Double-A this year.

Year	Club (League)	Class	W	L	ERA	G	GS	CG	SV	IP	H	R	ER	HR	BB	SO	AVG
2006	Salem-Keizer (NWL)	SS	2	2	3.46	13	0	0	1	26	17	11	10	1	8	25	.183
2007	Augusta (SAL)	LoA	12	8	3.59	27	23	1	0	135	147	61	54	5	44	104	.282
2008	San Jose (CAL)	HiA	10	8	3.69	24	24	0	0	117	124	61	48	1	39	84	.274
MINOR LEAGUE TOTALS			24	18	3.62	64	47	1	1	278	288	133	112	7	91	213	.270

21 AARON KING, LHP

BORN: April 27, 1989. B-T: L-L. **HT.:** 6-4. **WT.:** 205. **DRAFTED:** Surry (N.C.) CC, 2008 (7th round). **SIGNED BY:** Pat Portugal.

Giants vice president Dick Tidrow saw just a little bit of tape on King heading into the 2008 draft, but he knew immediately that the juco lefthander would be his "priority guy" for the draft. King has a power arm and a big frame that San Francisco projects will get stronger. He has a high leg kick and unleashes a fastball that sits at 93-95 mph and climbs as high as 97 with nice movement. His slider can be a swing-and-miss pitch, too. King doesn't have a feel for his pitches, however, and it will take time for him to develop command and consistency. For now, his fastball is overpowering enough that he'll get away with location mistakes at the lower levels. The Giants regard King as a good gamble for a seventh-round pick and a $110,000 bonus, even if he ends up in a relief role. In addition to throwing a no-hitter at Surry (N.C.) CC, he hit .329 and homered five times in 67 at-bats as a DH. After a strong pro debut in the Arizona League, King likely will jump to low Class A to start his first full season.

Year	Club (League)	Class	W	L	ERA	G	GS	CG	SV	IP	H	R	ER	HR	BB	SO	AVG
2008	Giants (AZL)	R	4	1	2.84	11	6	0	0	32	24	10	10	1	15	41	.216
	Salem-Keizer (NWL)	SS	0	1	5.40	2	0	0	0	2	1	1	1	0	4	4	.200
MINOR LEAGUE TOTALS			4	2	2.97	13	6	0	0	33	25	11	11	1	19	45	.216

22 FRANCISCO PEGUERO, OF

BORN: June 1, 1988. **B-T:** R-R. **HT.:** 6-0. **WT.:** 175. **SIGNED:** Dominican Republic, 2006. **SIGNED BY:** Pablo Peguero.

Few players have a package of tools that excite the Giants more than Peguero. There's no nepotism involved, as he's not directly related to Giants international scout Pablo Peguero, who happened to sign him. When Peguero made his domestic debut last season, officials had the Dominican outfielder jump straight to low Class A. He had a so-so showing there, but really came into his own when he took a step back to short-season Salem-Keizer when the Northwest League season opened in June. He has high upside with four solid tools and emerging power. For now, Giants coaches confidently predict he'll be a 30-doubles guy in the near future. Peguero plays the game with great energy and enthusiasm, running out every grounder like a young Robin Yount. His swing is a little long and he'll need time to learn the strike zone and cope with quality offspeed pitches. He can handle all three outfield positions and will gravitate toward right field because of his above-average arm strength. If he appears ready this spring, the Giants could again challenge Peguero by starting him out in high Class A.

Year	Club (League)	Class	AVG	G	AB	R	H	2B	3B	HR	RBI	BB	SO	SB	OBP	SLG
2006	Giants (DSL)	R	.275	56	182	24	50	10	3	4	16	6	37	3	.307	.429
2007	Giants (DSL)	R	.294	69	235	51	69	12	2	1	17	15	39	25	.341	.374
2008	Augusta (SAL)	LoA	.261	50	180	23	47	2	4	2	15	12	43	15	.309	.350
	Salem-Keizer (NWL)	SS	.307	50	202	33	62	11	4	2	28	9	43	10	.349	.431
MINOR LEAGUE TOTALS			.285	225	799	131	228	35	13	9	76	42	162	53	.328	.395

23 THOMAS NEAL, 1B/OF

BORN: Aug. 17, 1987. **B-T:** R-R. **HT.:** 6-1. **WT.:** 205. **DRAFTED:** Riverside (Calif.) CC, D/F 2005 (36th round). **SIGNED BY:** Lee Carballo.

The Giants signed Neal for a $220,000 bonus as a draft-and-follow in May 2006 after he boosted his stock with a huge season at Riverside (Calif.) CC. His development stalled when he dislocated his shoulder, and reconstructive surgery forced him to miss nearly all of the 2007 season. To make sure he'd get a full season of at-bats in 2008, the Giants had him share first base and DH duties with Angel Villalona at Augusta. Neal responded with a solid year, his 103 strikeouts in 428 at-bats notwithstanding. Despite playing his home games in a cavernous park, Neal hit 15 homers, many of them to center or the opposite field. Only Villalona's power grades out higher among Giants prospects. Neal is still young and his power numbers could explode once he learns to pull the ball with consistency. A below-average runner with a stocky build, he returned to the corner outfield spots in instructional league. His shoulder responded well, though he'll never have more than an average arm. He'll open 2009 as San Jose's left fielder.

Year	Club (League)	Class	AVG	G	AB	R	H	2B	3B	HR	RBI	BB	SO	SB	OBP	SLG
2006	Salem-Keizer (NWL)	SS	.250	50	176	26	44	6	2	4	20	7	44	1	.289	.375
2007	Giants (AZL)	R	.308	10	39	7	12	3	0	1	4	5	7	0	.413	.462
2008	Augusta (SAL)	LoA	.276	117	428	69	118	25	1	15	81	48	103	3	.359	.444
MINOR LEAGUE TOTALS			.271	177	643	102	174	34	3	20	105	60	154	4	.344	.426

24 MATT DOWNS, INF/OF

BORN: March 19, 1984. **B-T:** R-R. **HT.:** 6-2. **WT.:** 190. **DRAFTED:** Alabama, 2006 (36th round). **SIGNED BY:** Lee Elder.

San Francisco general manager Brian Sabean compares Downs to a player from his Yankees days, Shane Spencer. "Wherever you put him, he just hits," Sabean said. Downs was a 36th-round selection in 2006 out of Alabama, where he did anything and everything to help his team win—including a four-inning relief appearance in an NCAA regional game. As a hitter, he's the definition of a tough out. He has a short swing that should continue to work at higher levels, and the ball jumps off his bat, both to the gaps and over the fence. Downs drew

38 walks against 67 strikeouts last season, one of the better ratios in a Giants system that doesn't preach patience especially well. He is an above-average runner and has smarts on the basepaths. Downs shows a plus arm at third base and is equally playable at second, first or either corner outfield spot. He saw action at all those positions in 2008, and his bat also gives him the profile of a utilityman. He doesn't have quite the same feel or softness to his game as Ryan Rohlinger, another utility candidate who got big league time last season. But Downs is a better athlete and is a bit stronger. He's expected to start 2009 in Double-A.

Year	Club (League)	Class	AVG	G	AB	R	H	2B	3B	HR	RBI	BB	SO	SB	OBP	SLG
2006	Giants (AZL)	R	.310	46	168	34	52	16	4	0	29	17	9	6	.373	.452
2007	Salem-Keizer (NWL)	SS	.338	73	287	68	97	33	0	8	48	28	34	16	.410	.537
2008	Fresno (PCL)	AAA	.244	22	86	10	21	5	0	3	7	4	10	1	.298	.407
	San Jose (CAL)	HiA	.304	109	437	74	133	30	1	17	75	34	57	24	.357	.494
MINOR LEAGUE TOTALS			.310	250	978	186	303	84	5	28	159	83	110	47	.371	.492

25 EDWIN QUIRARTE, RHP

BORN: Dec. 20, 1986. **B-T:** R-R. **HT.:** 6-2. **WT.:** 205. **DRAFTED:** Cal State Northridge, 2008 (5th round). **SIGNED BY:** Mike Kendall.

Drafted by the Reds in the 39th round coming out of high school in 2005, Quirarte was a solid contributor at Cal State Northridge in two seasons as a starting pitcher. He jumped up draft lists after the Matadors began using him as a closer in 2008, going in the fifth round and signing for $193,000. Moving to the bullpen added velocity to a fastball that now sits consistently in the low 90s, and a plus splitter became his out pitch. He also commands an above-average slider that has some depth and showed continual improvement last summer. Quirarte is aggressive and pitches with a quick tempo, which works against him at times. He tends to rush his delivery and pitches on adrenaline. He shows an ability to keep the ball down, not yielding a homer in his pro debut and surrendering just two in 56 innings in his final season at Northridge. As a short reliever with some polished weapons, Quirarte could move quickly through the system. He had 14 saves at Salem-Keizer and is a top candidate to close at San Jose this year.

Year	Club (League)	Class	W	L	ERA	G	GS	CG	SV	IP	H	R	ER	HR	BB	SO	AVG
2008	Salem-Keizer (NWL)	SS	3	3	2.12	26	0	0	14	30	23	9	7	0	9	33	.213
MINOR LEAGUE TOTALS			3	3	2.12	26	0	0	14	30	23	9	7	0	9	33	.213

26 OSIRIS MATOS, RHP

BORN: Nov. 6, 1984. **B-T:** R-R. **HT.:** 6-1. **WT.:** 180. **SIGNED:** Dominican Republic, 2002. **SIGNED BY:** Rick Ragazzo.

After spending at least part of the previous three seasons in low Class A, Matos had another statistically dominant season against minor league hitters and broke through with his first big league callup. He failed to make a good first impression in the big leagues, however. In his second career appearance, he couldn't pitch around an error by Fred Lewis and gave up five unearned runs in the sixth inning of a July 4 loss to the Dodgers. A tight lower back caused him to miss two weeks in September, and he got knocked around in the Arizona Fall League. Matos has the fastball to be a major league closer, pitching consistently in the mid-90s, and he fared well against lefties in the minors, which had been a concern in the past. But his lack of a changeup and an inconsistent slider probably limit him to short relief. While Matos has an exciting arm, he'll need to show more consistency with fastball location, especially from the stretch, before he gets an extended chance to pitch in the major league bullpen.

Year	Club (League)	Class	W	L	ERA	G	GS	CG	SV	IP	H	R	ER	HR	BB	SO	AVG
2002	Giants (AZL)	R	4	2	4.65	13	13	0	0	62	63	35	32	3	22	51	.266
2003	Giants (AZL)	R	2	2	4.67	9	6	0	0	35	35	21	18	1	10	28	.261
2004	Giants (AZL)	R	2	0	2.44	11	8	0	1	48	43	23	13	1	20	47	.230
2005	Augusta (SAL)	LoA	8	8	4.99	29	22	0	0	135	162	83	75	12	31	79	.297
2006	Connecticut (EL)	AA	0	0	3.72	6	0	0	2	10	11	4	4	0	2	5	.282
	Augusta (SAL)	LoA	7	3	1.76	44	0	0	13	61	42	13	12	3	12	81	.193
2007	Connecticut (EL)	AA	5	0	2.89	35	0	0	4	56	50	20	18	3	21	43	.239
	Augusta (SAL)	LoA	0	0	0.00	7	0	0	4	9	1	0	0	0	1	9	.036
2008	Connecticut (EL)	AA	0	0	1.23	27	0	0	8	37	25	5	5	0	11	37	.191
	Fresno (PCL)	AAA	1	0	0.00	5	0	0	1	10	5	0	0	0	2	13	.147
	San Francisco (NL)	MAJ	1	2	4.79	20	0	0	0	21	26	17	11	3	9	16	.310
MINOR LEAGUE TOTALS			29	15	3.45	186	49	0	33	462	437	204	177	23	132	393	.248
MAJOR LEAGUE TOTALS			1	2	4.79	20	0	0	0	21	26	17	11	3	9	16	.310

27 CHARLIE CULBERSON, SS

BORN: April 10, 1989. **B-T:** R-R. **HT.:** 6-0. **WT.:** 175. **DRAFTED:** HS—Calhoun, Ga., 2007 (1st round supplemental). **SIGNED BY:** Sean O'Connor.

Culberson teamed in the Augusta middle infield with Nick Noonan last season, but he couldn't match the success of his roommate and fellow 2007 sandwich pick. Culberson, who signed for $607,500 as the 51st overall choice, hit .104 in April. Playing in front of friends and family only increased the pressure on the Georgia native, whose father Charles was the Giants' 16th-round pick in 1984. His baseball bloodlines run deep, as his grandfather Leon played in the majors and he's also related to the Sislers (Hall of Famer George, former all-star Dick and big leaguer Dave). Culberson eventually righted himself, hitting .274 over the rest of the season, though he missed all of August when he hurt his hand punching a paper-towel dispenser in frustration. He did return for instructional league and played well there. Culberson generates a lot of bat speed and has strong hands. He hit a few line-drive homers last season, and the ball jumps off his bat when his swing stays nice and compact. Developing more patience at the plate is a must. He has below-average speed but makes up for it by being aggressive on the bases. Culberson isn't a prototypical shortstop, but he has good feet and gets off strong throws despite an unorthodox release. He let his offensive woes affect him at times and committed 35 errors in 79 games at short, many coming when he tried to make highlight plays instead of eating the ball. He probably would fit better at second base, but Noonan's presence means the Giants will keep Culberson at shortstop for at least a while longer. He consistently comes out for early work and scores points for his attitude. He probably showed enough in the second half to graduate to high Class A.

Year	Club (League)	Class	AVG	G	AB	R	H	2B	3B	HR	RBI	BB	SO	SB	OBP	SLG
2007	Giants (AZL)	R	.286	46	161	32	46	8	5	1	16	19	38	19	.374	.416
2008	Augusta (SAL)	LoA	.234	81	282	31	66	11	2	3	27	18	57	6	.290	.319
MINOR LEAGUE TOTALS			.253	127	443	63	112	19	7	4	43	37	95	25	.322	.354

28 LUIS PERDOMO, RHP

BORN: April 27, 1984. **B-T:** R-R. **HT.:** 6-0. **WT.:** 170. **SIGNED:** Dominican Republic, 2003. **SIGNED BY:** Josue Herrera (Indians).

For the second consecutive year, the Giants used their early position in the Rule 5 draft to take a pitcher from the Dominican Republic. At the 2007 Winter Meetings, they plucked lefthander Jose Capellan from the Red Sox, but he didn't even last through spring training. In 2008, they selected Perdomo from the Cardinals, who had acquired him from the Indians in a July deal for onetime World Series hero Anthony Reyes. Though he stands barely 6 feet, Perdomo owns a consistent 93-95 mph fastball. He has an average-to-plus slider and has shown the ability to throw strikes with his changeup, which should help against lefthanders. He's athletic with good arm speed and the ability to get loose quickly. He needs to improve his command, but he tends to miss down in the zone when he's wild, so he keeps the ball in the park. Perdomo will compete with Pat Misch, Billy Sadler and Keiichi Yabu for a bullpen spot in spring training. Because the Giants remain in rebuilding mode, Perdomo could have the upper hand if he flashes consistency this spring. If he doesn't stick on the active roster, he has to be exposed to waivers and offered back to St. Louis for half the $50,000 draft price.

Year	Club (League)	Class	W	L	ERA	G	GS	CG	SV	IP	H	R	ER	HR	BB	SO	AVG
2003	Indians B (DSL)	R	1	0	4.35	14	0	0	1	21	18	11	10	2	8	10	.222
2004	Indians1 (DSL)	R	4	2	1.35	25	0	0	6	33	21	9	5	1	9	28	.172
2005	Indians1 (DSL)	R	3	2	3.57	23	2	0	7	45	41	22	18	0	14	45	.234
2006	Indians (GCL)	R	0	2	3.60	19	0	0	9	20	11	9	8	1	5	29	.155
2007	Lake County (SAL)	LoA	4	6	3.27	56	0	0	10	66	43	28	24	6	26	81	.181
2008	Kinston (CAR)	HiA	3	1	0.92	31	0	0	18	39	19	6	4	0	17	43	.146
	Akron (EL)	AA	2	0	3.52	9	0	0	1	15	12	6	6	1	7	17	.218
	Springfield (TEX)	AA	2	2	4.50	15	0	0	1	18	18	12	9	2	6	22	.247
MINOR LEAGUE TOTALS			19	15	2.93	192	2	0	53	258	183	103	84	13	92	275	.194

29 BILLY SADLER, RHP

BORN: Sept. 21, 1981. **B-T:** R-R. **HT.:** 6-0. **WT.:** 190. **DRAFTED:** Louisiana State, 2003 (6th round). **SIGNED BY:** Tom Korenek.

Sadler again handled Triple-A hitters in 2008, posting a 1.09 ERA for Fresno and allowing a .165 opponent average, yet he seemed no closer to solving the command problems that have prevented him from becoming an established big league reliever. He shuttled between Triple-A and San Francisco all season, walking 27 in 44 innings for the Giants. Sadler also gave up six homers and learned that 95-mph fastballs at the belt aren't a good idea when facing big league hitters. He has the equipment to be a late-inning force if he can throw strikes, because he backs up his fastball with a hard curveball that misses plenty of bats. Mound presence is a problem for Sadler, who loses his cool while experiencing the highs as well as the lows. He nearly started a bench-clearing brawl with the Dodgers when he celebrated a Manny Ramirez strikeout with a little too much gusto. Like Brian Wilson, Sadler pitched at Louisiana State and had Tommy John surgery while in college, though his elbow reconstruction came while he was at Pensacola (Fla.) JC. If he has a consistent spring, Sadler should break camp with the Giants.

Year	Club (League)	Class	W	L	ERA	G	GS	CG	SV	IP	H	R	ER	HR	BB	SO	AVG
2003	Hagerstown (SAL)	LoA	0	0	4.80	12	0	0	1	15	15	8	8	4	13	10	.263
2004	San Jose (CAL)	HiA	2	2	2.38	30	3	0	0	57	29	17	15	1	40	66	.149
	Norwich (EL)	AA	0	3	3.86	17	0	0	0	30	22	16	13	3	18	24	.195
2005	Norwich (EL)	AA	6	5	3.31	47	0	0	5	84	64	34	31	4	33	81	.208
2006	Connecticut (EL)	AA	4	3	2.56	44	0	0	20	46	23	14	13	1	29	67	.146
	Fresno (PCL)	AAA	2	0	1.80	7	0	0	1	10	5	2	2	1	2	12	.156
	San Francisco (NL)	MAJ	0	0	6.75	5	0	0	0	4	5	3	3	2	2	6	.294
2007	Connecticut (EL)	AA	0	0	0.73	9	0	0	1	12	3	1	1	1	6	18	.083
	Fresno (PCL)	AAA	3	2	5.95	40	0	0	6	42	36	31	28	5	35	59	.229
2008	Fresno (PCL)	AAA	1	0	1.09	22	0	0	1	33	19	7	4	0	21	41	.165
	San Francisco (NL)	MAJ	0	1	4.06	33	0	0	0	44	34	21	20	6	27	42	.215
MINOR LEAGUE TOTALS			18	15	3.14	228	3	0	35	330	216	130	115	20	197	378	.185
MAJOR LEAGUE TOTALS			0	1	4.28	38	0	0	0	48	39	24	23	8	29	48	.223

30 JOEY MARTINEZ, RHP

BORN: Feb. 26, 1983. **B-T:** L-R. **HT.:** 6-2. **WT.:** 193. **DRAFTED:** Boston College, 2005 (12th round). **SIGNED BY:** Glenn Tufts.

Tim Alderson and Madison Bumgarner weren't the only Giants pitching prospects to win ERA titles last year. Martinez quietly put together a sensational season, and his 2.49 ERA edged out Trenton's Phil Coke for the lowest mark in the Double-A Eastern League. While Connecticut's Dodd Stadium is a pitcher-friendly ballpark, Martinez's numbers were actually better on the road. The Boston College product is a ground-ball machine, throwing a sinking 86-88 mph fastball, a true curveball and a plus changeup consistently down in the strike zone. In the past, Martinez would throw 10 good fastballs and follow with five down the middle, but he was consistent with his command throughout 2008. He has been among the system's most durable minor league arms over the past three seasons. The Giants will really begin to get excited about Martinez if he can continue to induce groundouts when he makes the jump to the launching pads of the Pacific Coast League this season.

Year	Club (League)	Class	W	L	ERA	G	GS	CG	SV	IP	H	R	ER	HR	BB	SO	AVG
2005	Salem-Keizer (NWL)	SS	4	3	4.30	15	13	0	0	69	69	33	33	9	15	59	.264
2006	Augusta (SAL)	LoA	15	5	3.01	27	27	1	0	168	156	66	56	9	26	135	.246
2007	San Jose (CAL)	HiA	10	10	4.26	28	28	0	0	163	172	85	77	11	36	151	.276
2008	Connecticut (EL)	AA	10	10	2.49	27	27	0	0	148	131	58	41	6	37	112	.236
MINOR LEAGUE TOTALS			39	28	3.40	97	95	1	0	547	528	242	207	35	114	457	.255

Seattle Mariners

BY MATT EDDY

The 2008 Mariners were a study in dysfunction. They didn't hit, they didn't pitch and they didn't catch the ball, a formula that produced the worst run differential in the American League. In fact, Seattle became the first team to lose 100 games with a $100 million payroll, or $118 million on Opening Day, to be exact.

After the smoke cleared on Seattle's 101-loss disaster—a slip of 27 games from 2007 and the franchise's worst season in 25 years—the road had been paved for a much-needed change in direction.

General manager Bill Bavasi got the ax on June 16, when the Mariners' record stood at 24-45, and manager John McLaren followed him out the door three days later.

After replacing Pat Gillick as GM in November 2003, Bavasi presided over a series of transactions that proved to be devastating to the organization. He traded young players such as Asdrubal Cabrera, Shin-Soo Choo, Carlos Guillen, Rafael Soriano and Matt Thornton for little return. Bavasi also signed mediocre free agents such as Miguel Batista, Richie Sexson, Carlos Silva, Scott Spiezio and Jarrod Washburn to lengthy, expensive contracts. That group cost Seattle $169 million.

Yet his worst move may have been trading five players for Erik Bedard last offseason, as Adam Jones and Chris Tillman now look like future stars for the Orioles and Bedard made just 15 starts before succumbing to shoulder surgery.

In late October, the Mariners settled on former Brewers scouting director Jack Zduriencik as the club's new general manager. Zdurienick, Baseball America's 2007 Executive of the Year, was the catalyst in transforming Milwaukee from a laughingstock into a playoff team almost solely through the draft. Now he'll be asked to do the same in Seattle, where he hired former Athletics bench coach Don Wakamatsu as his manager, named former Brewers crosschecker Tom McNamara his scouting director and promoted Mariners coordinator of instruction Pedro Grifol to farm director.

Despite furnishing the Mariners with big leaguers Jeff Clement, Mark Lowe and Brandon Morrow—not to mention Tillman and other prospects such as outfielder Michael Saunders, righty Phillippe Aumont and catcher Adam Moore—scouting director Bob Fontaine was the first member of the old regime dismissed by Zduriencik. Fontaine's last draft was marred by Seattle's inability to sign its first-round pick, Georgia closer Joshua Fields. As a result, the Mariners have spent less

General manager Jack Zduriencik faces a long road in restoring Seattle's credibility

TOP 30 PROSPECTS

1. Greg Halman, of	16. Maikel Cleto, rhp
2. Michael Saunders, of	17. Mike Carp, 1b
3. Phillippe Aumont, rhp	18. Cesar Jimenez, lhp
4. Carlos Triunfel, ss/2b	19. Gabriel Noriega, ss
5. Juan Ramirez, rhp	20. Tyson Gillies, of
6. Adam Moore, c	21. Gaby Hernandez, rhp
7. Mario Martinez, 3b	22. Denny Almonte, of
8. Jharmidy DeJesus, 3b	23. Justin Thomas, lhp
9. Dennis Raben, of	24. Nathan Adcock, rhp
10. Michael Pineda, rhp	25. Edward Paredes, lhp
11. Carlos Peguero, of	26. Jose Lugo, lhp
12. Julio Morban, of	27. Aaron Pribanic, rhp
13. Rob Johnson, c	28. Brett Lorin, rhp
14. Shawn Kelley, rhp	29. Danny Carroll, of
15. Matt Tuiasosopo, 3b	30. Nolan Gallagher, rhp

on the 2008 draft ($2.5 million) than any other club. A college senior represented by Scott Boras, Fields can continue to negotiate until a week before the 2009 draft. If he doesn't sign, the Mariners would collect the 22nd pick in 2009 as compensation.

Led by international scouting director Bob Engle, the Mariners continued to invest heavily in Latin America. They signed four players to six-figure bonuses in 2008, headlined by Dominican outfielder Julio Morban ($1.1 million) and Nicaraguan righthander Francisco Valdivia ($726,000). Seattle paid out $2.6 million in international six-figure bonuses, ranking seventh among all clubs.

General Manager: Jack Zduriencik. **Farm Director:** Pedro Grifol. **Scouting Director:** Tom McNamara.

Class	Team	League	W	L	PCT	Finish*	Manager	Affiliated
Majors	Seattle	American	61	101	.377	14th (14)	J. McLaren/J. Riggleman	—
Triple-A	Tacoma Rainiers	Pacific Coast	80	64	.556	5th (16)	Darren Brown	1995
Double-A	West Tenn Diamond Jaxx	Southern	70	68	.507	4th (10)	Scott Steinmann	2007
High A	High Desert Mavericks	California	58	82	.414	10th (10)	Jim Horner	2007
Low A	Wisconsin Timber Rattlers	Midwest	56	80	.412	13th (14)	Terry Pollreisz	1993
Short-season	Everett AquaSox	Northwest	32	44	.421	7th (8)	Jose Moreno	1995
Rookie	Pulaski Mariners	Appalachian	40	27	.597	2nd (10)	Rob Mummau	2008
Rookie	AZL Mariners	Arizona	21	35	.375	8th (9)	Andy Bottin	2001
Overall 2008 Minor League Record			357	400	.472	25th		

* Finish in overall standings (No. of teams in league). ^League champion.

LAST YEAR'S TOP 30

Rank	Player, Pos.	Status
1.	Jeff Clement, c	Majors
2.	Phillippe Aumont, rhp	No. 3
3.	Chris Tillman, rhp	(Orioles)
4.	Carlos Triunfel, ss	No. 4
5.	Wladimir Balentien, of	Majors
6.	Michael Saunders, of	No. 2
7.	Juan Ramirez, rhp	No. 5
8.	Mark Lowe, rhp	Majors
9.	Ryan Rowland-Smith, lhp	Majors
10.	Matt Tuiasosopo, 3b	No. 15
11.	Carlos Peguero, dh/of	No. 11
12.	Tony Butler, lhp	(Orioles)
13.	Greg Halman, of	No. 1
14.	Matt Mangini, 3b	Dropped out
15.	Adam Moore, c	No. 6
16.	Jharmidy DeJesus, ss	No. 8
17.	Rob Johnson, c	No. 13
18.	Kam Mickolio, rhp	(Orioles)
19.	Bryan LaHair, 1b	Majors
20.	Yung-Chi Chen, 2b	(Athletics)
21.	Danny Carroll, of	No. 29
22.	Edward Paredes, lhp	No. 25
23.	Mario Martinez, ss/3b	No. 7
24.	Denny Almonte, of	No. 22
25.	Nolan Gallagher, rhp	No. 30
26.	Justin Thomas, lhp	No. 23
27.	Robert Rohrbaugh, lhp	Dropped out
28.	Nick Hill, lhp	Military list (Army)
29.	Alex Liddi, 3b	Dropped out
30.	Anthony Varvaro, rhp	Dropped out

BEST TOOLS

Best Hitter for Average	Carlos Triunfel
Best Power Hitter	Dennis Raben
Best Strike-Zone Discipline	Mike Carp
Fastest Baserunner	Tyson Gillies
Best Athlete	Greg Halman
Best Fastball	Phillippe Aumont
Best Curveball	Nathan Adcock
Best Slider	Shawn Kelley
Best Changeup	Cesar Jimenez
Best Control	Michael Pineda
Best Defensive Catcher	Rob Johnson
Best Defensive Infielder	Gabriel Noriega
Best Infield Arm	Carlos Triunfel
Best Defensive Outfielder	Danny Carroll
Best Outfield Arm	Tyson Gillies

PROJECTED 2012 LINEUP

Catcher	Adam Moore
First Base	Dennis Raben
Second Base	Carlos Triunfel
Third Base	Adrian Beltre
Shortstop	Yuniesky Betancourt
Left Field	Michael Saunders
Center Field	Greg Halman
Right Field	Ichiro Suzuki
Designated Hitter	Jeff Clement
No. 1 Starter	Felix Hernandez
No. 2 Starter	Erik Bedard
No. 3 Starter	Phillippe Aumont
No. 4 Starter	Juan Ramirez
No. 5 Starter	Michael Pineda
Closer	Brandon Morrow

TOP PROSPECTS OF THE DECADE

Year	Player, Pos.	2008 Org.
1999	Ryan Anderson, lhp	Out of baseball
2000	Ryan Anderson, lhp	Out of baseball
2001	Ryan Anderson, lhp	Out of baseball
2002	Ryan Anderson, lhp	Out of baseball
2003	Rafael Soriano, rhp	Braves
2004	Felix Hernandez, rhp	Mariners
2005	Felix Hernandez, rhp	Mariners
2006	Jeff Clement, c	Mariners
2007	Adam Jones, of	Orioles
2008	Jeff Clement, c	Mariners

TOP DRAFT PICKS OF THE DECADE

Year	Player, Pos.	2008 Org.
1999	Ryan Christianson, c	Out of baseball
2000	Sam Hayes, lhp (4th round)	Out of baseball
2001	Michael Garciaparra, ss (1st supp.)	Brewers
2002	*John Mayberry Jr., of	Rangers
2003	Adam Jones, ss/rhp (1st supp.)	Orioles
2004	Matt Tuiasosopo, ss (3rd round)	Mariners
2005	Jeff Clement, c	Mariners
2006	Brandon Morrow, rhp	Mariners
2007	Phillippe Aumont, rhp	Mariners
2008	†Joshua Fields, rhp	None

*Did not sign.
†Has not signed; eligible to sign until June 2, 2009.

LARGEST BONUSES IN CLUB HISTORY

Ichiro Suzuki, 2000	$5,000,000
Jeff Clement, 2005	$3,400,000
Brandon Morrow, 2006	$2,450,000
Matt Tuiasosopo, 2004	$2,290,000
Ryan Anderson, 1997	$2,175,000

SEATTLE MARINERS

TOP 2009 ROOKIE: Shawn Kelley, rhp. A strong showing in the Venezuelan League has the 2007 13th-rounder primed for a role in the Mariners' 2009 bullpen plans.

BREAKOUT PROSPECT: Tyson Gillies, of. One of several Canadian prospects in the system, he's a speedster with leadoff potential and quality center-field defense.

SOURCE OF TOP 30 TALENT			
Homegrown	26	Acquired	4
College	8	Trades	3
Junior college	0	Rule 5 draft	1
High school	5	Independent leagues	0
Draft-and-follow	2	Free agents/waivers	0
Nondrafted free agents	0		
International	11		

SLEEPER: Luke Burnett, rhp. He slid to the 14th round of the 2008 draft after losing his stuff as a starter at Louisiana Tech, but he previously had shown a mid-90s heater and a power slider as a reliever.

Numbers in parentheses indicate prospect rankings.

LF
Dennis Raben (9)
Carlos Peguero (11)
Julio Morban (12)
Michael Wilson
Kuo-Hui Lo

CF
Greg Halman (1)
Tyson Gillies (20)
Denny Almonte (22)
Danny Carroll (29)
Ezequiel Carrera
Jarrett Burgess

RF
Michael Saunders (2)
Efrain Nunez
James McOwen
Jose Rivero
Kalian Sams

3B
Mario Martinez (7)
Jharmidy DeJesus (8)
Matt Tuiasosopo (15)
Alex Liddi
Matt Mangini
Nate Tenbrink

SS
Gabriel Noriega (19)
Oswaldo Navarro
Juan Diaz

2B
Carlos Triunfel (4)
Reegie Corona
Tug Hulett
Edilio Colina

1B
Mike Carp (17)
Joe Dunigan

C
Adam Moore (6)
Rob Johnson (13)
Juan Fuentes
Travis Howell

RHP

Starters	Relievers
Phillippe Aumont (3)	Shawn Kelley (14)
Juan Ramirez (5)	Luke Burnett
Michael Pineda (10)	Marwin Vega
Maikel Cleto (16)	Sean White
Gaby Hernandez (21)	Jared Wells
Nathan Adcock (24)	Joe Woerman
Aaron Pribanic (27)	Stephen Kahn
Brett Lorin (28)	Blake Nation
Nolan Gallagher (30)	
Steven Hensley	
Ricky Orta	
Anthony Varvarro	
Francisco Valvidia	
Brandon Maurer	

LHP

Starters	Relievers
Robert Rohrbaugh	Cesar Jimenez (18)
Donnie Hume	Justin Thomas (23)
Bobby LaFromboise	Edward Paredes (25)
Jose Rios	Jose Lugo (26)
	Fabian Williamson

2008
BONUSES: $2.5 MILLION

BEST PURE HITTER: OF Dennis Raben (2) is best known for his power, but he's also the top hitter in a pitching-focused draft for the Mariners. Unless he makes more consistent contact, he's more of a .275 hitter.

BEST POWER HITTER: Scouts considered Raben the best power hitter in the Cape Cod League in 2007, though back problems slowed him as a Miami junior in 2008. Strong and aggressive, he can drive balls and has adjusted easily to wood bats.

FASTEST RUNNER: OF Jarrett Burgess (6) was bothered by leg injuries as a high school senior, but he has plus-plus speed and stole 17 bases in 21 tries during his debut.

BEST DEFENSIVE PLAYER: C Travis Howell (18) is a good receiver and threw out 42 percent of pro basestealers. 3B Nate Tenbrink (7) has athleticism and arm strength, though his throws can get erratic and he made 17 errors in 46 pro games.

BEST FASTBALL: RHP Joshua Fields (1), who's still negotiating with the Mariners, pitches in the mid-90s and tops out at 98. Among the pitchers under contract, RHP Aaron Pribanic (3) sits at 91-94 mph and peaks at 96.

BEST SECONDARY PITCH: If he signs, it will be Fields, whose power curveball can make hitters look silly. RHP Brett Lorin (5) has a hard three-quarters breaking ball.

BEST PRO DEBUT: Raben hit .275/.411/.560 with five homers in 27 games at short-season Everett despite missing most of August with a finger injury. RHP Blake Nation (22) used his solid stuff to record a 2.74 ERA and 11 saves at Rookie-level Pulaski.

BEST ATHLETE: Burgess has enticing raw power and arm strength to go with his speed.

MOST INTRIGUING BACKGROUND: OF Henry Cotto's (41) father Henry played for the Mariners and was their hitting coach at Everett in 2008. Pribanic's grandfather, Jim Coates, was an all-star pitcher, while OF Ryan Royster's (13) uncle Jerry also played in the majors.

CLOSEST TO THE MAJORS: Even after an extended holdout, Fields could make the Mariners at some point in 2009 if he signs. They showed with 2006 first-rounder Brandon Morrow that they're not afraid to rush pitchers. Seattle could use Raben's power and will put him on the fast track.

BEST LATE-ROUND PICK: RHP Luke Burnett (14) projected as a first-round pick after showing a mid-90s fastball and a nasty slider as a reliever in the Cape Cod League in 2007. But he lost arm speed and his stuff as a starter at Louisiana Tech last spring, causing his stock to plummet. Signed for $200,000, he'll be a bargain if he regains his power arsenal.

THE ONE WHO GOT AWAY: 2B Matt Jensen (11), who elected to attend Cal Poly, has a chance to be an offensive middle infielder.

ASSESSMENT: After taking Fields and Raben with their first two picks, the Mariners didn't get many players with high upsides. They'll recoup the No. 21 pick in 2009 if they can't sign Fields, and as it stands now, they spent less on the draft ($2,545,000) than any club.

2007
BONUSES: $4.5 MILLION

RHP Phillippe Aumont (1) showed first-round stuff in 2008 but also pitched just 56 innings because of a sore elbow. Most of Seattle's other top picks had disappointing first full seasons, with OF Denny Almonte (2) the most promising of that bunch.
GRADE: C

2006
BONUSES: $4.8 MILLION

RHP Brandon Morrow (1) already has two productive big league season as a reliever under his belt, and now he'll try to move into the rotation. RHPs Chris Tillman (2) and Kam Mickolio (18) and C Adam Moore (6) add quality depth, though Tillman and Mickolio went to the Orioles in the ill-conceived Erik Bedard trade.
GRADE: A

2005
BONUSES: $4.1 MILLION*

C Jeff Clement (1) has power but still must prove he can hit big league pitching and stay behind the plate. The Mariners were crippled by not having second- or third-round picks, though LHP Justin Thomas (4) has reached the majors.
GRADE: C+

2004
BONUSES: $3.2 MILLION*

Seattle didn't have picks in the first two rounds, and 3B Matt Tuiasosopo (3) won't live up to his $2.29 million bonus. C/OF Rob Johnson (4) and RHP Mark Lowe (5) should be big league contributors, though, and the real prize is OF Michael Saunders (11).
GRADE: C+

*Draft analysis by Jim Callis. Numbers in parentheses indicate draft rounds. *Bonuses for 2004-05 are first 10 rounds only.*

BILL MITCHELL

PROSPECT

GREG HALMAN, OF

Born: Aug. 26, 1987.
Ht.: 6-4. **Wt.:** 192.
Bats: R. **Throws:** R.
Signed:
Netherlands, 2004.
Signed by:
Wayne Norton/Bob
Engle/Peter Van Dalen.

Halman's father Eduardo played professionally in Holland into his mid-30s, and Greg knew from an early age that he wanted to pursue a career in baseball. He turned pro in 2003 at age 16, when he joined Hoofdklasse Honkbal, or the Dutch Major League. The Twins signed him that year, but the contract later was voided. As a 17-year-old first baseman in 2004, Halman earned MVP honors in the Dutch league while nearly winning its triple crown. He signed with the Mariners for $130,000 that June. After an encouraging U.S. debut in 2005, he played just 28 games in 2006 because he broke his right hand in an on-field brawl. He voiced his displeasure with a 2007 Opening Day assignment to low Class A Wisconsin, but instead of making a case for promotion, he sulked and hit just .182 before earning a demotion to short-season Everett in June. Humbled by experiencing failure for the first time, he led the short-season Northwest League in slugging (.597) while finishing second in homers (16). Halman started putting it all together in 2008, hitting .272/.326/.528 and advancing to Double-A West Tenn, where at age 20 he was the Southern League's youngest regular position player. Halman hit 29 home runs and stole 31 bases, narrowly missing becoming the minors' only 30-30 player since Terry Evans in 2006.

Halman is a physical specimen with the potential for five average or better tools. He has drawn comparisons to Andre Dawson and Alfonso Soriano because he's a long-limbed, high-waisted, quick-twitch athlete. Wiry strong, especially in the wrists and forearms, he figures to add strength as he physically matures. He already has the reflexes and whip-like bat speed to hit for plus-plus power. Seattle believes he has the confidence, hand-eye coordination and ability to make adjustments mid-swing that will enable him to be an above-average hitter in time. Though his speed is just a tick above-average, Halman covers swaths of center field with long, graceful strides. He also thrives as a basestealer because of his first-step quickness and acceleration. He has a plus arm.

For all his upside, Halman presents more risk than most No. 1 prospects. His pitch recognition is below-average, resulting in many swings and misses and mis-hits as he chases pitches out of the zone. He's too aggressive at the plate to execute much of a plan, and as a result he strikes out too much and walks too little. His plate coverage suffers because of his tendency to get pull-happy. Halman shows visible frustration on the field at times and has admitted to having a quick temper. He has improved his maturity by leaps and bounds, however, in part by working with Dr. Jack Curtis, who aids Mariners players with their mental approach.

Halman shows real passion for the game to go with his noteworthy toolset. Because he'll be 21 in 2009 and needs repetitions to get a handle on the strike zone, the new regime in Seattle may opt to slow down his timetable a bit by sending him back to Double-A. He could challenge for a big league job in 2010.

Year	Club (League)	Class	AVG	G	AB	R	H	2B	3B	HR	RBI	BB	SO	SB	OBP	SLG
2005	Mariners (AZL)	R	.258	26	89	17	23	2	3	3	11	10	19	1	.350	.449
2006	Everett (NWL)	SS	.259	28	116	19	30	6	4	5	15	3	32	10	.295	.509
2007	Wisconsin (MWL)	LoA	.182	52	187	26	34	5	0	4	15	8	77	15	.234	.273
	Everett (NWL)	SS	.307	62	238	37	73	19	1	16	37	21	85	16	.371	.597
2008	High Desert (CAL)	HiA	.268	67	257	52	69	15	3	19	53	16	76	23	.320	.572
	West Tenn (SL)	AA	.277	61	235	43	65	14	2	10	30	16	66	8	.332	.481
MINOR LEAGUE TOTALS			.262	296	1122	194	294	61	13	57	161	74	355	73	.319	.492

2 MICHAEL SAUNDERS, OF

RODGER WOOD

BORN: Nov. 19, 1986. **B-T:** L-R. **HT.:** 6-4. **WT.:** 205. **DRAFTED:** Tallahassee (Fla.) CC, D/F 2004 (11th round). **SIGNED BY:** Wayne Norton.

A visa shortage made it impossible for Saunders to play in the United States when he was drafted in 2004, so he spent a year at Tallahassee (Fla.) CC before signing for $237,500 as a draft-and-follow. He followed up on a breakout 2007 with a strong 2008, which included batting .286 and leading Team Canada with two homers at the Beijing Olympics. Saunders' compact lefthanded swing generates leverage, loft and plus power to all fields, and he could develop into a 20-home run hitter as he builds on his 6-foot-4 frame. A good fastball hitter, he already possesses a strong knowledge of the strike zone, and his willingness to use the opposite field suggests he'll be at least an average hitter, too. Saunders has average speed and instincts on the basepaths, and West Tenn manager Scott Steinmann called him the organization's best drag bunter. He has average range for center field, and a plus arm that would fit in right. Saunders strikes out a lot because he still chases offspeed pitches out of the zone. Though added bulk could augment his homer totals, it also stands to detract from his speed and range. Saunders should be ready for spring training after having offseason arthroscopic surgery to repair a torn labrum in his right shoulder. With the Mariners starting a massive rebuilding process, he could make his big league debut at some point in 2009 and figures to man an outfield corner in Seattle for years to come.

Year	Club (League)	Class	AVG	G	AB	R	H	2B	3B	HR	RBI	BB	SO	SB	OBP	SLG
2005	Everett (NWL)	SS	.270	56	196	24	53	13	3	7	39	27	74	2	.361	.474
2006	Wisconsin (MWL)	LoA	.240	104	359	48	86	10	8	4	39	48	103	22	.329	.345
2007	High Desert (CAL)	HiA	.299	108	431	91	129	25	4	14	77	60	116	27	.392	.473
	West Tenn (SL)	AA	.288	15	52	8	15	1	2	1	7	7	20	2	.373	.442
2008	West Tenn (SL)	AA	.290	67	248	46	72	18	3	8	30	30	66	11	.375	.484
	Tacoma (PCL)	AAA	.242	24	95	12	23	4	1	3	16	9	30	1	.308	.400
MINOR LEAGUE TOTALS			.274	374	1381	229	378	71	21	37	208	181	409	65	.362	.436

3 PHILLIPPE AUMONT, RHP

PAUL GIERHART

BORN: Jan. 7, 1989. **B-T:** L-R. **HT.:** 6-7. **WT.:** 220. **DRAFTED:** HS—Gatineau, Quebec, 2007 (1st round). **SIGNED BY:** Wayne Norton.

Aumont's Quebec high school didn't offer baseball, but he impressed scouts so much while pitching for travel teams that the Mariners selected him 11th overall in 2007 and signed him for $1.9 million. He signed late and made his pro debut in 2008, pitching just 56 innings as Seattle took a cautious approach when he developed a sore elbow. Aumont cuts an imposing figure on the mound, and his stuff is just as intimidating. He already throws 90-95 mph with plus-plus sink and boring action, and he may be able to throw even harder as he matures physically. If batters sit on his sinker, he can blow a high-90s four-seam fastball by them. Aumont's crossfire delivery and low three-quarters arm slot can make it tough for batters to pick up his pitches. His low-80s breaking ball has plus potential. For such a high pick, Aumont is quite unpolished, and now he has to prove he can stay healthy. His arm angle makes it hard to stay on top of his breaking ball, and he has a long way to go with a true changeup after using a splitter as an amateur. If he came up with a more balanced delivery, his secondary pitches and his command would benefit. Aumont's physical presence and the natural movement on his pitches suggest that he can fill a role at the front of a rotation. He'll pitch at high Class A High Desert at some point in 2009.

Year	Club (League)	Class	W	L	ERA	G	GS	CG	SV	IP	H	R	ER	HR	BB	SO	AVG
2008	Wisconsin (MWL)	LoA	4	4	2.75	15	8	0	2	56	46	22	17	4	19	50	.224
MINOR LEAGUE TOTALS			4	4	2.75	15	8	0	2	56	46	22	17	4	19	50	.224

4 CARLOS TRIUNFEL, SS/2B

JOHN SPEAR

BORN: Feb. 27, 1990. **B-T:** R-R. **HT.:** 5-11. **WT.:** 175. **SIGNED:** Dominican Republic, 2006. **SIGNED BY:** Patrick Guerrero/Bob Engle.

Triunfel signed for $1.3 million in 2006, the fourth-highest bonus among Latin American free agents that year. He reached high Class A as a 17-year-old in his pro debut and spent the entire season there in 2008, when he was the California League's youngest regular by 15 months. With tremendous hand-eye coordination, vision and barrel awareness, Triunfel has the raw attributes to be an above-average hitter, capable of spraying drives from line to line. His arm rates at least a 70 on the 20-80 scouting scale in terms of both precision and carry. He has solid first-step quickness and strong reactions at third base, his likely position in the future. Triunfel lacks classic shortstop actions and struggles with the angle of the ball off the bat at second base. His smooth swing isn't conducive to generating loft, and he also employs a bat wrap that inhibits his ability to turn on inside pitches. Despite stealing 30 bases in 2008, he's a below-average runner who figures to slow down as he fills out. He drew a 10-game suspension in May for violating team rules, calling into question his attitude and maturity. Triunfel played second base, third base and shortstop in the Arizona Fall League, and the Mariners will keep his options open, as they did with Jose Lopez when he was coming up. Triunfel should advance to Double-A in 2009.

Year	Club (League)	Class	AVG	G	AB	R	H	2B	3B	HR	RBI	BB	SO	SB	OBP	SLG
2007	Wisconsin (MWL)	LoA	.309	43	152	18	47	8	2	0	14	5	23	4	.342	.388
	Mariners (AZL)	R	.273	3	11	1	3	0	0	0	3	0	1	0	.231	.273
	High Desert (CAL)	HiA	.288	50	208	32	60	10	2	0	22	12	31	3	.333	.356
2008	High Desert (CAL)	HiA	.287	108	436	75	125	20	4	8	49	30	52	30	.336	.406
MINOR LEAGUE TOTALS			.291	204	807	126	235	38	8	8	88	47	107	37	.335	.388

5 JUAN RAMIREZ, RHP

BORN: Aug. 16, 1988. **B-T:** R-R. **HT.:** 6-3. **WT.:** 175. **SIGNED:** Nicaragua, 2005. **SIGNED BY:** Luis Molina/Nemesio Porras.

The Mariners have as strong a presence in Nicaragua as any club. They have the nation's top minor league prospect in Ramirez, and signed its top 2008 prospect, righthander Francisco Valdivia, for $726,000 in July. Ramirez handled low Class A well for a teenager last season, showing dominating stuff and improved command. Tall, loose-armed and still projectable, Ramirez fires off easy 92-93 mph heat and can push his four-seam fastball to 97 on occasion. One scout lauded Ramirez for having a heavy ball, and all his pitches feature plus movement as the ball jumps out of his hand from a high three-quarters arm slot. Though he limited Midwest League batters to a .239 average largely on the strength of his fastball, he also throws a hard slider that has plus potential. Like most young flamethrowers, Ramirez lacks feel for his changeup because he's accustomed to blowing the ball past batters. He struggles to stay on top of his secondary pitches on a consistent basis. He needs to do a better job of pacing himself and holding his stuff deep into starts. He also needs to work on controlling the running game. His build and delivery are reminiscent of former Mariner Rafael Soriano. Ramirez has the raw stuff to project as a front-end starter, but he also could follow Soriano into a role as relief ace.

Year	Club (League)	Class	W	L	ERA	G	GS	CG	SV	IP	H	R	ER	HR	BB	SO	AVG
2006	Mariners (VSL)	R	5	1	1.66	14	13	1	0	65	43	16	12	0	35	56	.191
2007	Everett (NWL)	SS	3	7	4.30	15	15	0	0	75	61	49	36	3	43	73	.211
2008	Wisconsin (MWL)	LoA	6	9	4.14	25	22	0	0	124	112	68	57	9	38	113	.239
MINOR LEAGUE TOTALS			14	17	3.58	54	50	1	0	264	216	133	105	12	116	242	.220

6 ADAM MOORE, C

BORN: May 8, 1984. **B-T:** R-R. **HT.:** 6-3. **WT.:** 220. **DRAFTED:** Texas-Arlington, 2006 (6th round). **SIGNED BY:** Mark Lummus.

Moore tore the meniscus in his left knee while at Nebraska, missing the entire 2005 season before transferring to Texas-Arlington. He has been durable and one of Seattle's best minor league hitters since turning pro. After clubbing 22 homers and driving in 102 runs in 2007, he ranked sixth in batting (.319) and third in throwing out basestealers (36 percent) in the Southern League last season. With plus power, a solid arm and natural leadership skills, Moore has all the makings of a starting catcher at the big league level. A career .306 hitter, he has a short swing and good balance at the plate, allowing him to wait on offspeed stuff and to hit with power to all fields. He knows how to work counts and makes steady contact. Moore has improved his blocking and receiving, but some SL observers regarded him as a work in progress defensively, and his 23 passed balls ranked second in the league. A broken hand kept him from honing his defense in the Arizona Fall League. His speed is considerably below-average. Mariners catching instructor Roger Hansen has a strong track record in helping catchers develop—from Dan Wilson to Jeff Clement to Rob Johnson—and Moore could be his next breakthrough. His hand shouldn't hamper him in 2009, when he'll open the year at Triple-A Tacoma.

Year	Club (League)	Class	AVG	G	AB	R	H	2B	3B	HR	RBI	BB	SO	SB	OBP	SLG
2006	Everett (NWL)	SS	.317	16	63	8	20	9	0	0	9	2	10	0	.348	.460
	Wisconsin (MWL)	LoA	.267	44	165	21	44	6	0	7	24	14	38	0	.342	.430
2007	High Desert (CAL)	HiA	.307	115	433	74	133	30	3	22	102	41	84	1	.371	.543
2008	West Tenn (SL)	AA	.319	119	429	60	137	34	2	14	71	40	77	0	.396	.506
MINOR LEAGUE TOTALS			.306	294	1090	163	334	79	5	43	206	97	209	1	.375	.506

7 MARIO MARTINEZ, 3B

BORN: Nov. 13, 1989. **B-T:** R-R. **HT.:** 6-1. **WT.:** 208. **SIGNED:** Venezuela, 2006. **SIGNED BY:** Bob Engle/Emilio Carrasquel.

Carlos Triunfel and Martinez, the headliners from the Mariners' 2006 international haul, have wasted no time in establishing themselves as prospects. Signed as a shortstop for $600,000, Martinez moved to third base full-time in 2008 and ranked eighth in the Rookie-level Appalachian League in hitting (.319). Martinez has an advanced approach for such a young hitter. He stays inside the ball well and looks to use the opposite field with two strikes. His athleticism, strength and body control suggest he'll develop at least average power, and those attributes already have manifested themselves in his defensive game. He has made a smooth transition to third base, where he displays sure hands to go with plus range and a plus throwing arm. The Mariners rave about his makeup, and he learned English during his first instructional league. Now that Martinez has moved to an infield corner, he'll have to prove he can consistently drive the ball. He's already strong and doesn't have a lot of room for projection, despite his youth. As with most young hitters, his swing can get too long at times and he struggles to recognize quality breaking balls. He's a below-average runner. Martinez had little trouble in adjusting to older competition. Look for more of the same in 2009, when he'll move on to Seattle's new low Class A Clinton affiliate.

Year	Club (League)	Class	AVG	G	AB	R	H	2B	3B	HR	RBI	BB	SO	SB	OBP	SLG
2007	Mariners (AZL)	R	.281	53	196	36	55	9	1	1	26	6	31	3	.311	.352
2008	Pulaski (APP)	R	.319	64	251	43	80	15	3	5	32	10	47	2	.344	.462
MINOR LEAGUE TOTALS			.302	117	447	79	135	24	4	6	58	16	78	5	.330	.414

8 JHARMIDY DeJESUS, 3B

BORN: Aug. 30, 1989. **B-T:** R-R. **HT.:** 6-3. **WT.:** 185. **SIGNED:** Dominican Republic, 2007. **SIGNED BY:** Bob Engle/Patrick Guerrero/Franklin Taveras.

DeJesus didn't sign in 2006, his first year of eligibility, because teams failed to meet his asking price. That move paid off in 2007 when the Mariners gave him $1 million, the third-highest international bonus of the summer. He ranked as the No. 3 prospect in the Rookie-level Arizona League and No. 9 in the Northwest League in his 2008 pro debut. As a converted shortstop with present strength and a feel for hitting, he's similar in some ways to Mario Martinez, with more present power and a higher initial trajectory. DeJesus already has demonstrated above-average power and could develop more as he adds to his 185-pound frame. He has taken quickly to third base, where his range and footwork are average and his arm is strong. DeJesus has solid hand-eye coordination, but because he's too pull-conscious and has yet to develop pitch recognition, his ability to hit for average may atrophy as he climbs the ladder. He needs to tighten his strike zone, stop chasing breaking balls and use the entire field. His speed is a tick below-average. If he learns restraint, DeJesus could become a dangerous hitter and his bat could profile at any of the four corner positions. He's ready for low Class A, which could mean a timeshare at third base with Martinez.

Year	Club (League)	Class	AVG	G	AB	R	H	2B	3B	HR	RBI	BB	SO	SB	OBP	SLG
2008	Mariners (AZL)	R	.339	34	127	27	43	12	1	6	18	14	25	4	.417	.591
	Everett (NWL)	SS	.267	28	90	12	24	4	0	4	15	6	28	0	.316	.444
MINOR LEAGUE TOTALS			.309	62	217	39	67	16	1	10	33	20	53	4	.376	.530

9 DENNIS RABEN, OF

BORN: July 31, 1987. **B-T:** L-L. **HT.:** 6-3. **WT.:** 200. **DRAFTED:** Miami, 2008 (2nd round). **SIGNED BY:** Mike Tosar.

The Mariners drafted Raben out of high school in the 49th round in 2005, but he opted to attend Miami, where he led the Hurricanes to the College World Series in 2006 and 2008. He starred in the Cape Cod League as a sophomore, marking him as one of the top college power prospects for 2008, but back problems dropped him to the second round, where Seattle signed him for $616,000. Raben has a patient approach, advanced feel for the strike zone and huge lefthanded power to all fields. He already has demonstrated prowess with wood bats in Cape Cod and in his debut, when he slugged .560 despite a nagging finger injury. He has strong instincts in the outfield, where he's an average defender. His arm is average but quite accurate, as he also pitched in college. The drawback to Raben's power approach is that his long swing leads to frequent swings and misses, which will cut significantly into his average. He hit .275 in his pro debut and topped out at .292 as a junior at Miami. He's a below-average runner, and he may face a move to first base as he slows down. A lefty version of former Hurricane Pat Burrell represents Raben's ultimate upside. He could skip a level and start 2009 in high Class A.

Year	Club (League)	Class	AVG	G	AB	R	H	2B	3B	HR	RBI	BB	SO	SB	OBP	SLG
2008	Everett (NWL)	SS	.275	27	91	24	25	11	0	5	14	19	24	1	.411	.560
MINOR LEAGUE TOTALS			.275	27	91	24	25	11	0	5	14	19	24	1	.411	.560

10 MICHAEL PINEDA

BORN: Jan. 18, 1989. **B-T:** R-R. **HT.:** 6-5. **WT.:** 180. **SIGNED:** Dominican Republic, 2005. **SIGNED BY:** Patrick Guerrero/Franklin Taveras.

Joining Phillippe Aumont and Juan Ramirez, Pineda rounded out the trio of teenage pitching sensations who fronted Wisconsin's 2008 rotation. He spent two seasons in the Rookie-level Dominican Summer League before tearing up the Midwest League in his U.S. debut. He ranked second in the league in ERA (1.95) and opponent average (.216), and he capped his season with a 14-strikeout one-hitter. Pineda spots his 88-92 mph fastball at will and isn't afraid to pitch inside. Batters have a tough time squaring him up because of the life on his pitches. He shows deceptive arm action on an above-average changeup. His durable 6-foot-5 frame and strong control suggest that stamina won't be a problem. Pineda lacks feel for his 77-80 mph slider and could end up in the bullpen as a result. Despite strong fastball command, he has an awkward quality to his arm action and doesn't always repeat his delivery. MWL observers had enough qualms about Pineda's arm action and lack of feel for a breaking ball that they were split on his future role—either No. 3 starter or reliever. His control is so advanced for a 19-year-old, though, that he could move quickly through the system. The Mariners will keep him in the rotation as he advances to high Class A.

Year	Club (League)	Class	W	L	ERA	G	GS	CG	SV	IP	H	R	ER	HR	BB	SO	AVG
2006	Mariners (DSL)	R	2	1	0.44	8	3	0	0	20	14	4	1	0	7	14	.189
2007	Mariners (DSL)	R	6	1	2.29	15	12	0	0	59	70	25	15	2	11	48	.286
2008	Wisconsin (MWL)	LoA	8	6	1.95	26	21	1	0	138	109	38	30	7	35	128	.216
MINOR LEAGUE TOTALS			16	8	1.90	49	36	1	0	218	193	67	46	9	53	190	.235

11 CARLOS PEGUERO, OF

BORN: Feb. 22, 1987. **B-T:** L-L. **HT.:** 6-5. **WT.:** 210. **SIGNED:** Dominican Republic, 2005. **SIGNED BY:** Patrick Guerrero/Bob Engle.

Peguero seemed poised for a huge power year in 2008, but it never materialized. Despite playing in the hitter-happy California League, he slugged .480 and hit 12 homers, just three more than he hit in the pitcher-friendly Midwest League in 2007. Still, Peguero's raw strength (the best in the system), physicality (he's 6-foot-5 and 210 pounds) and past performance suggest he has more power in him. After all, he led the Arizona League in slugging (.649) in 2006 and managed an above-average .465 mark in the MWL the following year. Poor pitch recognition stands in Peguero's way for now, as he likes to swing at the first pitch he can handle, often getting himself out. Pitchers have little reason to feed him pitches in the zone because he has averaged nearly seven strikeouts for every walk during his three seasons in the United States. Though the caveat that he did it in the Cal League applies, he did show an improved feel for hitting last season, batting a career-high .299. A solid athlete for his size, Peguero is a good runner underway, though he's strictly a left fielder in terms of range. His arm is average. His season ended in mid-July with surgery on his left wrist, one year after he was slowed by bone chips in his left elbow. The Mariners still believe Peguero has impact potential as a power hitter, but it's going to take him a few years to deliver. Step one will be improving his command of the strike zone as he repeats high Class A in 2009.

Year	Club (League)	Class	AVG	G	AB	R	H	2B	3B	HR	RBI	BB	SO	SB	OBP	SLG
2005	Mariners (DSL)	R	.251	59	179	31	45	8	4	6	30	22	66	1	.337	.441
2006	Mariners (AZL)	R	.313	34	134	27	42	10	7	7	30	13	49	3	.380	.649
	Everett (NWL)	SS	.204	25	93	7	19	4	1	2	9	2	34	0	.221	.333
2007	Wisconsin (MWL)	LoA	.263	79	297	35	78	21	6	9	50	16	97	4	.315	.465
2008	High Desert (CAL)	HiA	.299	92	371	47	111	25	3	12	74	10	96	6	.317	.480
MINOR LEAGUE TOTALS			.275	289	1074	147	295	68	21	36	193	63	342	14	.320	.478

12 JULIO MORBAN, OF

BORN: Feb. 13, 1992. **B-T:** L-L. **HT.:** 6-1. **WT.:** 190. **SIGNED:** Dominican Republic, 2008. **SIGNED BY:** Patrick Guerrero.

One of the top bats available on the 2008 international market, Morban signed out of the Dominican Republic for $1.1 million, the sixth-highest figure of the signing period. Some scouts even preferred him to the two Latin American outfielders who received the highest bonuses among position players—Dominican Rafael Rodriguez (Giants, $2.55 million) and Venezuelan Yorman Rodriguez (Reds, $2.5 million)—saying that Morban had a more advanced feel for hitting. The Mariners are convinced that he'll hit for average, as one club official extolled him for his practically unparalleled hand-eye coordination and pitch recognition among 16-year-olds. Morban has a clean lefthanded swing and showed a willingness to use the whole field during instructional league. He may not develop into a big-time home run threat, but he has average raw power. An average runner, he'll see time in center field as he begins his pro career, but he's probably best suited for left field because of his fringy arm strength. Morban has a lot to prove in the years to come, but if it all comes together he could be a top-of-the-order presence.

Year	Club (League)	Class	AVG	G	AB	R	H	2B	3B	HR	RBI	BB	SO	SB	OBP	SLG
2008	Did Not Play—Signed 2009 Contract															

13 ROB JOHNSON, C/OF

BORN: July 22, 1983. **B-T:** R-R. **HT.:** 6-1. **WT.:** 210. **DRAFTED:** Houston, 2004 (4th round). **SIGNED BY:** Kyle Van Hook.

The system's best defensive catcher, Johnson finally received a shot as Tacoma's full-time catcher after catching just 143 games in two years as he split the job with Guillermo Quiroz (2006) and Jeff Clement (2007). He responded with his finest offensive season and by throwing out 37 percent of basestealers, the fourth-best figure in the Pacific Coast League. Johnson caught fire in the second half, batting .363/.401/.489 in 135 at-bats. His offense improved when he stopped offering at so many pitches outside the strike zone, and his .363 on-base percentage established a career high. He has solid raw power, but he's better suited by driving the ball into the gaps rather than seeking to hit home runs. His defense, though, is his ticket to the big leagues. Johnson is a solid receiver with a quick, short release on throws to second base. He's a strong game-caller, though he'll have to improve his blocking after leading the PCL with 21 passed balls. An outfielder in college, Johnson played 10 games there for Tacoma in 2008. He has more athleticism and speed than most catchers. With Clement and Adam Moore sandwiching him in the system, Johnson faces an uphill climb to a regular role in Seattle. But because he's so solid defensively and has the versatility to fill in as an outfielder, he could fit nicely as a backup.

Year	Club (League)	Class	AVG	G	AB	R	H	2B	3B	HR	RBI	BB	SO	SB	OBP	SLG
2004	Everett (NWL)	SS	.234	20	77	17	18	3	1	1	7	4	10	6	.286	.338
	Mariners (AZL)	R	.222	8	27	4	6	1	0	0	1	3	7	1	.323	.259
2005	Wisconsin (MWL)	LoA	.272	77	305	41	83	19	1	9	51	20	31	10	.319	.430
	Inland Empire (CAL)	HiA	.314	19	70	15	22	3	0	2	12	10	14	2	.381	.443
2006	Tacoma (PCL)	AAA	.231	97	337	28	78	9	4	4	33	13	74	14	.261	.318
2007	Tacoma (PCL)	AAA	.268	112	422	57	113	26	0	6	40	39	62	7	.331	.372
	Seattle (AL)	MAJ	.333	6	3	1	1	0	0	0	0	0	0	1	.333	.333
2008	Tacoma (PCL)	AAA	.305	112	417	55	127	30	0	9	49	37	61	7	.363	.441
	Seattle (AL)	MAJ	.129	14	31	2	4	0	0	1	2	0	6	0	.129	.226
MINOR LEAGUE TOTALS			.270	445	1655	217	447	91	6	31	193	126	259	47	.323	.389
MAJOR LEAGUE TOTALS			.147	20	34	3	5	0	0	1	2	0	6	1	.147	.235

14 SHAWN KELLEY, RHP

BORN: April 16, 1984. **B-T:** R-R. **HT.:** 6-2. **WT.:** 215. **DRAFTED:** Austin Peay State, 2007 (13th round). **SIGNED BY:** Alvin Rittman.

In the tradition of since-traded scouting find Kam Mickolio (18th round, 2006), Kelley moved quickly from obscurity to the cusp of the big leagues in his first full pro season, reaching Double-A after just 35 pro innings. He had Tommy John surgery as a freshman at Austin Peay State in 2003 but rebounded to pitch four more seasons for the Governors, winning Ohio Valley Conference pitcher of the year honors in 2007, the same year the Mariners drafted him in the 13th round. Kelley pounds the strike zone with a 90-94 mph sinker, while his power slider is his strikeout pitch. He sets them up by mixing in an occasional changeup. With a bulldog mentality and a willingness to throw strikes, Kelley profiles as a setup man. His delivery is a bit unorthodox with a high back elbow, and while it makes his command spotty it does have the benefit of providing natural deception. He's a good athlete who also played third base and the outfield in college. Kelley could see big league time in 2009, especially after spending the winter with Lara of the Venezuelan League.

Year	Club (League)	Class	W	L	ERA	G	GS	CG	SV	IP	H	R	ER	HR	BB	SO	AVG
2007	Everett (NWL)	SS	1	0	3.00	3	0	0	0	3	2	1	1	1	0	4	.200
	Wisconsin (MWL)	LoA	1	1	2.25	9	0	0	0	12	16	4	3	1	4	14	.308
2008	Wisconsin (MWL)	LoA	0	0	3.52	8	0	0	3	8	10	3	3	0	2	12	.323
	High Desert (CAL)	HiA	0	0	0.00	12	0	0	3	12	8	1	0	0	3	12	.186
	West Tenn (SL)	AA	3	1	2.11	29	0	0	9	43	31	12	10	2	17	44	.205
MINOR LEAGUE TOTALS			5	2	1.98	61	0	0	15	77	67	21	17	4	26	86	.233

15 MATT TUIASOSOPO, 3B

BORN: May 10, 1986. **B-T:** R-R. **HT.:** 6-2. **WT.:** 223. **DRAFTED:** HS—Woodinville, Wash., 2004 (3rd round). **SIGNED BY:** Phil Geisler.

The Mariners signed Tuiasosopo for a third round-record $2.29 million in 2004, making his decision to pass on a football scholarship at Washington a relatively easy one. His father Manu and brother Marques both played in the NFL. Tuiasosopo flopped in his first three pro seasons before his bat came alive in Double-A in 2007. He continued hitting in the Arizona Fall League that offseason and in Triple-A last year. In 145 second-half at-bats, he hit .303/.380/.538, earning a September callup to Seattle. Tuiasosopo has no outstanding tool, but he has above-average bat speed to go with solid pitch recognition and plate coverage. His confidence grew as he put together better at-bats with Tacoma, and he began to pull the ball more consistently, establishing a career high with 13 home runs. The ball jumps off his bat at times, though his power still is fringy. He runs well for his size. Drafted as a shortstop, Tuiasosopo has developed into a solid third baseman, with soft hands, above-average arm strength and agility. He had a tough year in terms of throwing accuracy, though, as he led Pacific Coast League third basemen with 27 errors. The Mariners love his makeup and work ethic, but with all the young third baseman in the system and Adrian Beltre in Seattle, Tuiasosopo may not have a wide window to establish himself as a regular.

Year	Club (League)	Class	AVG	G	AB	R	H	2B	3B	HR	RBI	BB	SO	SB	OBP	SLG
2004	Mariners (AZL)	R	.412	20	68	18	28	5	2	4	12	13	14	1	.528	.721
	Everett (NWL)	SS	.248	29	101	18	25	6	1	2	14	10	36	4	.336	.386
2005	Wisconsin (MWL)	LoA	.276	107	409	72	113	21	3	6	45	44	96	8	.359	.386
2006	Inland Empire (CAL)	HiA	.306	59	232	31	71	14	0	1	34	14	58	5	.359	.379
	San Antonio (TEX)	AA	.185	62	216	16	40	4	0	1	10	20	64	2	.259	.218
2007	West Tenn (SL)	AA	.260	129	446	74	116	27	5	9	57	76	113	4	.371	.404
2008	Tacoma (PCL)	AAA	.281	111	437	87	123	32	2	13	73	47	104	4	.364	.453
	Seattle (AL)	MAJ	.159	14	44	1	7	2	1	0	2	2	16	0	.213	.250
MINOR LEAGUE TOTALS			.270	517	1909	316	516	109	13	36	245	224	485	28	.358	.398
MAJOR LEAGUE TOTALS			.159	14	44	1	7	2	1	0	2	2	16	0	.213	.250

16 MAIKEL CLETO, RHP

BORN: May 1, 1989. **B-T:** R-R. **HT.:** 6-3. **WT.:** 218. **SIGNED:** Dominican Republic, 2006. **SIGNED BY:** Ramon Pena (Mets).

Cleto has the highest ceiling of the three prospects the Mariners acquired from the Mets in the three-team, 12-player deal at the Winter Meetings that sent J.J. Putz, Sean Green and Jeremy Reed to New York. Managers rated Cleto's fastball as the best in the low Class A South Atlantic League last year, when he topped out at 100 mph. Unlike many young, hard throwers, he has an idea of where the ball is going. "Anyone who throws 91-98 (mph) and a ton of strikes, you have to pay attention," one scout said. Cleto has a strong body that allowed him to log 141 innings as a teenager in 2008, and Mets officials raved about his work ethic. However, he's far from a finished product. His slurvy breaking ball and changeup need to get a lot better if he's going to keep hitters from sitting on his fastball. His delivery can be a little violent at times, too. He's erratic in terms of results, showing no-hit stuff one day and the inability to get out of the first inning the next. He also led the South Atlantic League with 25 wild pitches. Cleto should start his Mariners career in high Class A.

Year	Club (League)	Class	W	L	ERA	G	GS	CG	SV	IP	H	R	ER	HR	BB	SO	AVG
2007	Mets (GCL)	R	1	2	5.03	11	4	0	1	34	34	21	19	2	25	28	.270
2008	Savannah (SAL)	LoA	5	11	4.25	25	22	1	0	136	140	78	64	8	34	81	.268
	St. Lucie (FSL)	HiA	0	1	9.00	1	1	0	0	5	5	5	5	1	2	1	.278
MINOR LEAGUE TOTALS			6	14	4.53	37	27	1	1	175	179	104	88	11	61	110	.269

17 MIKE CARP, 1B

BORN: June 30, 1986. **B-T:** L-R. **HT.:** 6-2. **WT.:** 215. **DRAFTED:** HS—Lakewood, Calif., 2004 (9th round). **SIGNED BY:** Steve Leavitt (Mets).

Another of the prospects picked up by the Mariners in the three-team, 12-player trade headlined by J.J. Putz going to the Mets, Carp boosted his stock in 2008 by losing weight and turning in a strong performance in Double-A. New York hadn't been thrilled with his conditioning or attitude in 2007, so they snubbed him when they handed out invitations to big league camp last spring. Scouts liken him to Mike Jacobs, another player originally signed by the Mets, in terms of his build and set-up at the plate. Carp hit 17 homers last year, though some scouts wonder whether he'd duplicate that power in the majors when pitchers locate fastballs on the inner half. He does a good job of controlling the strike zone and replaces Luis Valbuena, another piece in the 12-player deal, as the most disciplined hitter in the system. Carp has to avoid stretches of getting pull-happy, because his success comes when he uses the left-center gap. New York experimented with him in left field last season, but his below-average speed, range and arm made him a liability there. He's an average defender at first base, where he should get most of his playing time in Triple-A this season.

Year	Club (League)	Class	AVG	G	AB	R	H	2B	3B	HR	RBI	BB	SO	SB	OBP	SLG
2004	Mets (GCL)	R	.267	57	191	30	51	12	0	4	26	22	51	2	.358	.393
2005	Hagerstown (SAL)	LoA	.249	89	313	49	78	12	1	19	63	35	96	2	.358	.476
2006	St. Lucie (FSL)	HiA	.287	137	491	69	141	27	1	17	88	51	107	2	.379	.450
2007	St. Lucie (FSL)	HiA	.250	1	4	0	1	0	0	0	0	0	0	0	.250	.250
	Binghamton (EL)	AA	.251	97	359	55	90	16	0	11	48	39	75	2	.337	.387
2008	Binghamton (EL)	AA	.299	134	478	67	143	29	1	17	72	79	88	1	.403	.471
MINOR LEAGUE TOTALS			.275	515	1836	270	504	96	3	68	297	226	417	9	.371	.441

18 CESAR JIMENEZ, LHP

BORN: Nov. 12, 1984. **B-T:** L-L. **HT.:** 5-11. **WT.:** 215. **SIGNED:** Venezuela, 2001. **SIGNED BY:** Emilio Carrasquel.

Jimenez's tenure with the Mariners dates all the way back to July 2001, when he signed out of Venezuela at age 16. He has worked as a reliever in most of his eight seasons with the club, receiving just two extended looks as a starter, in 2003 and 2006, and wearing down under the workload both times. In fact, he missed much of 2007 recovering from surgery for a stress fracture in his left elbow. Jimenez was hammered in his big league debut at the end of the 2006 season, but he redeemed himself by pitching effectively in Seattle in 2008. His main weapon is the organization's best changeup, a true equalizer against righthanders, who managed to hit just .203 against him in the big leagues. Jimenez throws his changeup with deceptive arm speed and he consistently gets 10 mph of separation from his fastball, which ranges from 88-93 mph. He's unafraid to throw inside and batters have a tough time picking his pitches up. While Jimenez's slurvy breaking ball remains a work in progress, he showed increased confidence in it last season—though big league lefties hit him for a .317 average. Some club officials believe Jimenez could return to a starting role, but given his durability issues, two-pitch mix and ability to retire righthanders, he seemingly would fit best as a middle reliever.

Year	Club (League)	Class	W	L	ERA	G	GS	CG	SV	IP	H	R	ER	HR	BB	SO	AVG
2002	Aguirre (VSL)	R	7	1	0.83	11	11	2	0	65	37	6	6	0	12	67	.167
	Mariners (AZL)	R	0	0	3.38	1	0	0	0	3	3	2	1	0	0	3	.300
	Everett (NWL)	SS	2	1	2.70	8	0	0	1	20	12	7	6	2	5	25	.174
2003	Wisconsin (MWL)	LoA	8	11	2.94	28	20	0	0	126	134	61	41	7	46	76	.273
2004	Inland Empire (CAL)	HiA	6	7	2.29	43	2	0	6	86	80	28	22	3	19	81	.241
2005	Tacoma (PCL)	AAA	0	0	9.39	4	0	0	0	8	9	8	8	5	1	9	.290
	San Antonio (TEX)	AA	3	5	2.62	45	1	0	4	69	64	21	20	3	24	54	.250
2006	San Antonio (TEX)	AA	0	2	2.76	3	3	0	0	16	10	5	5	0	5	10	.179
	Tacoma (PCL)	AAA	5	10	4.36	24	19	1	3	107	107	54	52	8	55	66	.266
	Seattle (AL)	MAJ	0	0	14.73	4	1	0	0	7	13	12	12	4	4	3	.382
2007	Mariners (AZL)	R	0	0	0.00	3	2	0	0	6	4	0	0	0	0	6	.190
	Tacoma (PCL)	AAA	2	1	3.51	16	0	0	2	26	28	15	10	2	12	23	.269
2008	Tacoma (PCL)	AAA	1	3	3.55	29	0	0	3	38	37	19	15	3	8	47	.239
	Seattle (AL)	MAJ	0	2	3.41	31	2	0	0	34	32	13	13	2	13	26	.258
MINOR LEAGUE TOTALS			34	41	2.94	215	58	3	19	570	525	226	186	33	187	467	.245
MAJOR LEAGUE TOTALS			0	2	5.40	35	3	0	0	42	45	25	25	6	17	29	.285

19 GABRIEL NORIEGA, SS

BORN: Sept. 13, 1990. **B-T:** R-R. **HT.:** 6-2. **WT.:** 170. **SIGNED:** Venezuela, 2007. **SIGNED BY:** Bob Engle/Pedro Avila/Emilio Carrasquel.

Noriega's $800,000 bonus was the fifth-highest in the 2007 international signing period, and the second-highest among Mariners signees behind Jharmidy DeJesus' $1 million. Noriega played his way to the Appalachian League in his pro debut, joining the Mets' Wilmer Flores to give the circuit two premier 17-year-old Venezuelan shortstops. Plus-plus defense is Noriega's ticket to the big leagues, and he's already the best shortstop in the system. Despite no better than average speed, he's a smooth fielder with plus instincts, anticipation and hands at shortstop. He completes his defensive package with a strong arm and excellent footwork. Less accomplished as a hitter, Noriega possesses good hand-eye coordination and stays inside the ball well, lending hope to the idea that he'll hit for average as he matures. He has big hands and broad shoulders, suggesting he may develop fringe-average power for the position. At the moment, his power tool rates much closer to a 20 than to a 45 on the 20-80 scouting scale. Noriega will need to develop his situational hitting ability and feel for the strike zone as he gains experience, but his glove alone will keep him in Seattle's plans.

Year	Club (League)	Class	AVG	G	AB	R	H	2B	3B	HR	RBI	BB	SO	SB	OBP	SLG
2008	Mariners (AZL)	R	.421	9	38	7	16	0	0	0	2	1	6	3	.439	.421
	Pulaski (APP)	R	.238	41	151	11	36	4	2	0	18	6	43	6	.266	.291
MINOR LEAGUE TOTALS			.275	50	189	18	52	4	2	0	20	7	49	9	.302	.317

20 TYSON GILLIES, OF

BORN: Oct. 31, 1988. **B-T:** L-R. **HT.:** 6-2. **WT.:** 190. **DRAFTED:** Iowa Western CC, D/F 2006 (25th round). **SIGNED BY:** Wayne Norton.

A native of Canada like Phillippe Aumont and Michael Saunders, Gillies attended Vancouver's Mountain High and played for Team Canada's youth national team as an amateur. He signed as a draft-and-follow with the Mariners after spending a year at Iowa Western CC, where he helped the Reivers reach the Junior College World Series. With 30 percent hearing in one ear and 60 percent in the other, Gillies wears hearing aids and reads lips, but it hasn't affected his play in the outfield or on the bases. He gets down the first-base line in 3.8 seconds, making him an 80 runner on the 20-80 scouting scale as well as a true stolen-base threat. Gillies puts his top-of-the-scale speed to good use in center field, where he has the plus-plus range to rob hits in the gaps.

He also has a plus arm. Gillies has a chance to be an above-average hitter because of his feel for the strike zone, his all-fields approach and his bunting skills. Though he's sturdily built, he doesn't generate much power with his line-drive stroke. If anything, he relies too much on slapping the ball to the opposite field, and Seattle began stressing the importance of driving the ball into the gaps during instructional league. The Mariners rave about his makeup. If he develops, Gillies has a future as a top-of-the-order batter.

Year	Club (League)	Class	AVG	G	AB	R	H	2B	3B	HR	RBI	BB	SO	SB	OBP	SLG
2007	Mariners (AZL)	R	.221	35	86	20	19	3	2	0	6	6	23	9	.337	.302
	Everett (NWL)	SS	.625	4	8	3	5	0	0	0	2	0	1	2	.625	.625
2008	High Desert (CAL)	HiA	.233	11	30	4	7	0	1	0	1	1	6	1	.281	.300
	Everett (NWL)	SS	.313	61	192	36	60	6	5	2	22	35	46	24	.439	.427
MINOR LEAGUE TOTALS			.288	111	316	63	91	9	8	2	31	42	76	36	.403	.386

21 GABY HERNANDEZ, RHP

BORN: May 21, 1986. **B-T:** R-R. **HT.:** 6-3. **WT.:** 215. **DRAFTED:** HS—Miami, 2004 (3rd round). **SIGNED BY:** Joe Salermo (Mets).

Drafted by the Mets in 2004, Hernandez was sent to the Marlins in a trade for Paul LoDuca in December 2005. Florida, in turn, dealt him to Seattle at the 2008 trade deadline for Arthur Rhodes. Hernandez struggled in six Double-A starts after joining the Mariners organization, and that came on the heels of a first-half thrashing at Triple-A Albuquerque, one of the worst pitching environments on the planet. Hernandez is too critical of himself at times and may have placed undue pressure on himself because a big league callup appeared to be within reach. He's durable and flashes three average or better pitches, but he often tries to be so fine that his stuff plays down. His fastball parks at 88-92 mph and touches 94 with good deception. At his best, he'll show a quality slow curveball and a changeup. He's still quite young and he won't be the last pitcher to be humbled by Isotopes Park, so he can get back on track to become a No. 4 or 5 starter.

Year	Club (League)	Class	W	L	ERA	G	GS	CG	SV	IP	H	R	ER	HR	BB	SO	AVG
2004	Mets (GCL)	R	3	3	1.09	10	9	2	0	50	25	10	6	1	12	58	.151
	Brooklyn (NYP)	SS	1	0	0.00	1	0	0	0	3	2	0	0	0	0	6	.200
2005	Hagerstown (SAL)	LoA	6	1	2.43	18	18	1	0	93	59	29	25	4	30	99	.179
	St. Lucie (FSL)	HiA	2	5	5.74	10	10	0	0	42	48	28	27	1	10	32	.298
2006	Jupiter (FSL)	HiA	9	7	3.68	21	20	0	0	120	120	60	49	7	35	115	.259
2007	Carolina (SL)	AA	9	11	4.22	28	28	1	0	154	144	87	72	14	56	113	.245
2008	Albuquerque (PCL)	AAA	2	8	7.24	13	13	0	0	65	94	59	52	14	26	54	.335
	Carolina (SL)	AA	3	0	4.30	4	4	0	0	23	21	11	11	3	4	17	.236
	West Tenn (SL)	AA	1	1	5.01	6	6	0	0	32	38	19	18	3	15	23	.297
MINOR LEAGUE TOTALS			36	36	4.03	111	108	4	0	581	551	303	260	47	188	517	.249

22 DENNY ALMONTE, OF

BORN: Sept. 24, 1988. **B-T:** B-R. **HT.:** 6-2. **WT.:** 187. **DRAFTED:** HS—Miami, 2007 (2nd round). **SIGNED BY:** Mike Tosar.

Born in the Dominican Republic, Almonte transferred to Miami's Florida Christian High prior to his senior season. Among Mariners prospects, only Greg Halman has a more enticing package of tools. On the other hand, few Mariners prospects are as raw as Almonte. For example, the switch-hitter batted .145 with 37 strikeouts in 76 at-bats during his 2007 pro debut. In 2008, Seattle opted to hold him back in extended spring training until mid-May, though he showed enough once assigned to low Class A to remain there for the rest of the season. While his plus raw power and athleticism are obvious, his swing, especially from the left side, is going to take a lot of repetitions to iron out because he looks as if he's feeling for the ball. Almonte's righthanded swing is more compact and fluid, and he batted .293 from that side last season, compared to .233 as a lefty. He struggled with pitch recognition from both sides, striking out 149 times in 100 games. He's a plus runner, thrower and defender in center field. He hasn't figured out how to use his speed as well on the basepaths, where he was caught 10 times in 24 steal attempts. He would benefit from playing more under control in all phases of the game. Beginning the 2009 season back in low Class A wouldn't be seen as a setback for Almonte, who'll be only 20.

Year	Club (League)	Class	AVG	G	AB	R	H	2B	3B	HR	RBI	BB	SO	SB	OBP	SLG
2007	Mariners (AZL)	R	.161	18	56	11	9	2	1	0	5	6	26	3	.254	.232
	Everett (NWL)	SS	.100	5	20	0	2	0	0	0	1	1	11	1	.143	.100
2008	Wisconsin (MWL)	LoA	.249	100	374	38	93	20	7	10	51	29	149	14	.303	.420
MINOR LEAGUE TOTALS			.231	123	450	49	104	22	8	10	57	36	186	18	.290	.382

23 JUSTIN THOMAS, LHP

BORN: Jan. 18, 1984. **B-T:** L-L. **HT.:** 6-3. **WT.:** 225. **DRAFTED:** Youngstown State, 2005 (4th round). **SIGNED BY:** Ken Madeja.

Thomas handcuffed lefthanders in both Double-A (.224 average) and Triple-A (.136) last year to earn his first big league callup in September. He had spent much of the past two seasons in the Double-A rotation, pitching ineffectively through a bout with bone chips in 2007, but he worked strictly as a reliever in Seattle. Thomas has a fast arm, a short arm swing and as much natural movement on his pitches as any Mariners farmhand. He also has the type of durable frame that should enable him to hold up in any role. He pitches at 88-92 mph with tailing life on his fastball, but he falls in love with his slider, which he throws more than half the time. It arrives in the low 80s with lateral break, and it's effective because when paired with his fastball, it helps him keep the ball on the ground. Thomas mixes in a changeup versus righthanders. He struggles to find the strike zone at times and probably lacks the consistency of his secondary offerings to make it as a starter, but he could develop into an effective left-on-left reliever.

Year	Club (League)	Class	W	L	ERA	G	GS	CG	SV	IP	H	R	ER	HR	BB	SO	AVG
2005	Everett (NWL)	SS	3	3	3.81	18	6	0	0	59	63	31	25	2	20	48	.272
2006	Wisconsin (MWL)	LoA	5	5	3.10	11	11	0	0	61	69	29	21	4	17	51	.286
	Inland Empire (CAL)	HiA	9	4	4.10	17	17	1	0	105	108	58	48	10	45	111	.269
2007	West Tenn (SL)	AA	4	9	5.51	24	24	0	0	119	147	82	73	11	61	100	.308
2008	West Tenn (SL)	AA	7	7	4.32	25	17	1	0	119	116	66	57	11	56	106	.257
	Tacoma (PCL)	AAA	2	1	3.71	7	1	0	1	17	15	7	7	2	9	21	.242
	Seattle (AL)	MAJ	0	1	6.75	8	0	0	0	4	9	3	3	0	2	2	.474
MINOR LEAGUE TOTALS			30	29	4.33	102	76	2	1	480	518	273	231	40	208	437	.278
MAJOR LEAGUE TOTALS			0	1	6.75	8	0	0	0	4	9	3	3	0	2	2	.474

24 NATHAN ADCOCK, RHP

BORN: Feb. 25, 1988. **B-T:** R-R. **HT.:** 6-5. **WT.:** 190. **DRAFTED:** HS—Radcliff, Ky., 2006 (5th round). **SIGNED BY:** Brian Williams.

Seattle focused on physical pitchers with its first five picks in the 2006 draft, selecting Brandon Morrow, Chris Tillman, Tony Butler and Ricky Orta in the first through fourth rounds. They took the big-bodied Adcock, a Kentucky prep product, in the fifth and bought him out of a Louisville commitment for $200,000. He reached high Class A for five starts at the end of his first full season, but headed back to low Class A to begin 2008. He pitched well in the first half before a sprained elbow ended his season after 15 games. The Mariners expect him to be ready for spring training. Adcock's hard, sharp downer curveball ranks as the system's finest breaking ball, but he has to hit his spots with his average 88-92 mph fastball because the pitch is straight. At 6-foot-5 and 190 pounds, he oozes projection and his delivery and arm action both are textbook, so he might gain velocity as he matures. Adcock will flash a quality changeup at times. Because his mound presence has come into question, some questions exist as to whether he'll reach his ceiling as a No. 4 starter.

Year	Club (League)	Class	W	L	ERA	G	GS	CG	SV	IP	H	R	ER	HR	BB	SO	AVG
2006	Mariners (AZL)	R	0	2	3.31	10	6	0	0	35	33	21	13	1	16	31	.243
2007	Wisconsin (MWL)	LoA	2	8	3.70	17	16	0	0	88	85	60	36	7	38	66	.247
	High Desert (CAL)	HiA	1	3	8.84	5	5	0	0	18	20	26	18	0	22	11	.278
2008	Wisconsin (MWL)	LoA	2	5	3.72	15	14	0	0	77	81	45	32	3	29	82	.269
MINOR LEAGUE TOTALS			5	18	4.07	47	41	0	0	219	219	152	99	11	105	190	.257

25 EDWARD PAREDES, LHP

BORN: Sept. 30, 1986. **B-T:** L-L. **HT.:** 6-0. **WT.:** 175. **SIGNED:** Dominican Republic, 2005. **SIGNED BY:** Patrick Guerrero/Bob Engle.

Paredes found mild success as a reliever in the Dominican Summer League in his first two pro seasons, and his first appearance in the United States came as an emergency reliever for Tacoma in June 2007. Immediately thereafter, the Mariners shifted him to the rotation at Everett, where he led the Northwest League in innings (86) and walks (48) as a 20-year-old. He spent most of last season in the Wisconsin rotation, but Seattle envisions him becoming a Felix Heredia-type lefty reliever. The comparison works on a number of levels, from Paredes' smallish stature to his repertoire and bouts of wildness. The lean lefty has a whip-quick arm but struggles to repeat his low three-quarters arm slot, which leads to lapses in control. Paredes throws his fastball at 88-93 mph with natural armside run, and he backs it up with a hard slider featuring 2-to-8 tilt that's murder on lefthanders when he commands it. He shows very little feel for a changeup, which probably means his future is in the bullpen. Though he finished 2008 with a pair of starts in Double-A, including six shutout innings in his final outing, he'll probably open this season in high Class A.

Year	Club (League)	Class	W	L	ERA	G	GS	CG	SV	IP	H	R	ER	HR	BB	SO	AVG
2005	Mariners (DSL)	R	3	0	2.03	12	0	0	1	27	16	11	6	1	13	28	.163
2006	Mariners (DSL)	R	3	3	2.63	24	2	0	14	41	21	18	12	1	19	45	.147
2007	Tacoma (PCL)	AAA	0	0	0.00	1	0	0	0	5	0	0	0	0	1	5	.000
	Everett (NWL)	SS	7	6	3.99	16	15	0	0	86	75	47	38	2	48	61	.235
2008	Wisconsin (MWL)	LoA	7	11	4.63	25	24	0	0	117	121	76	60	10	52	91	.265
	West Tenn (SL)	AA	1	1	7.71	2	2	0	0	9	11	8	8	1	5	10	.314
MINOR LEAGUE TOTALS			21	21	3.92	80	43	0	15	284	244	160	124	15	138	240	.229

26 JOSE LUGO, LHP

BORN: April 10, 1984. **B-T:** L-L. **HT.:** 6-1. **WT.:** 159. **SIGNED:** Dominican Republic, 2002. **SIGNED BY:** Juan Martinez (Athletics).

The Royals selected Lugo with the ninth pick the major league Rule 5 draft in December and then traded him to the Mariners for cash considerations. The lanky lefthander was no stranger to the Rule 5 process. Signed by the Athletics in January 2002, Lugo joined the Twins in 2005 as a Triple-A Rule 5 pick. As with most pitchers taken in the Rule 5 process, he has a terrific arm and very little pitchability. He has pitched mostly in relief since progressing to full-season ball in 2006, his fifth pro season, and can go on extended runs of dominance. One came last July, when he struck out 16 and walked six while allowing one run in 17 relief innings in high Class A. A strong groundball pitcher, Lugo sits in the low 90s with incredible sink while touching 94-95 mph at times. His secondary pitches are much further away, as his changeup is average at best and his slider is fringy. He's too often sabotaged by lapses in command, and he has shown little aptitude for setting up hitters or in identifying the right pitch for the situation. The Mariners must keep Lugo on their 25-man roster all season or place him on waivers before offering him back to the Twins for half his $50,000 purchase price. They face the same situation with infielder Reegie Corona, taken from the Yankees with the second choice in the 2008 Rule 5 draft. Seattle's offseason trade of J.J. Putz and Sean Green to the Mets opens the door a bit wider for Lugo, who will be 25 this season.

Year	Club (League)	Class	W	L	ERA	G	GS	CG	SV	IP	H	R	ER	HR	BB	SO	AVG
2002	Athletics E (DSL)	R	2	0	4.64	9	0	0	1	21	23	16	11	0	9	17	.250
2003	Athletics 2 (DSL)	R	5	2	1.96	14	8	0	2	60	45	21	13	2	23	53	.215
2004	Athletics 1 (DSL)	R	5	1	1.05	13	13	0	0	68	45	14	8	0	25	61	.182
2005	Athletics (AZL)	R	2	3	5.23	15	5	0	0	53	57	42	31	0	18	44	.273
2006	Beloit (MWL)	LoA	1	4	4.45	22	0	0	2	28	30	16	14	1	13	32	.273
	Elizabethton (APP)	R	8	4	3.56	13	13	0	0	73	71	33	29	3	21	70	.253
2007	Beloit (MWL)	LoA	5	6	4.32	40	7	0	2	77	87	43	37	6	39	73	.285
2008	Fort Myers (FSL)	HiA	2	6	4.04	51	0	0	1	69	68	34	31	4	33	76	.254
MINOR LEAGUE TOTALS			30	26	3.48	177	46	0	8	450	426	219	174	16	181	426	.248

27 AARON PRIBANIC, RHP

BORN: Sept. 1, 1986. **B-T:** R-R. **HT.:** 6-4. **WT.:** 200. **DRAFTED:** Nebraska, 2008 (3rd round). **SIGNED BY:** Phil Geisler.

The grandson of former Yankees all-star righthander Jim Coates, Pribanic transferred from Hutchinson (Kan.) CC to Nebraska for his junior year and became one of college baseball's better No. 3 starters. The first Cornhusker drafted in 2008 when the Mariners made him a third-round pick, he signed for $390,000. A physical 6-foot-4 and 200 pounds, Pribanic has plus arm strength, sitting at 91-94 mph and topping out at 96 with his fastball. His arm is fresh, too, because he redshirted during his first year at Hutchinson. Of course, that also means he's rawer than most college pitchers. Pribanic throws both a curveball and a slider, but neither is reliable at the moment. He does have some feel for a splitter he uses as a changeup. He threw just 4⅔ innings in the Arizona League after signing at the end of July. The Mariners worked with Pribanic in instructional league to help him maintain balance over the rubber so that he wouldn't drift and could better incorporate his lower half in his delivery. The adjustments should allow him to get better extension and plane on his pitches. Pribanic could wind up either as a No. 3 or 4 starter or as a power reliever, and he'll pitch in the rotation this year in Class A.

Year	Club (League)	Class	W	L	ERA	G	GS	CG	SV	IP	H	R	ER	HR	BB	SO	AVG
2008	Mariners (AZL)	R	1	2	15.43	3	1	0	0	5	8	8	8	0	5	5	.364
MINOR LEAGUE TOTALS			1	2	15.43	3	1	0	0	5	8	8	8	0	5	5	.364

28 BRETT LORIN, RHP

BORN: March 31, 1987. **B-T:** L-R. **HT.:** 6-7. **WT.:** 245. **DRAFTED:** Long Beach State, 2008 (5th round). **SIGNED BY:** Tim Reynolds.

Lorin may turn out to be the biggest scouting success story from the Mariners' 2008 draft. His collegiate track record coming into the season consisted of 10 relief innings for Arizona, during which he posted a 9.31 ERA while allowing 22 baserunners. After transferring to Long Beach State as a redshirt sophomore, he went 5-3, 2.61 and beat California in regional play. He kept on dealing in pro ball after signing for $170,000, striking out 61 batters in 52 innings and making it to low Class A for eight games. Lorin's best pitch is his hard three-quarters breaking ball, and he also has an 88-92 mph fastball that tops out at 94. His pitches get on batters quickly because he's so tall and naturally deceptive and because he throws on a steep downward plane. He has shown some feel for a changeup. Like fellow college righthander Aaron Pribanic, Seattle's third-round pick last June, Lorin has a fresh arm and room for projection, as well as a similar ceiling as a back-of-the-rotation starter or power reliever.

Year	Club (League)	Class	W	L	ERA	G	GS	CG	SV	IP	H	R	ER	HR	BB	SO	AVG
2008	Everett (NWL)	SS	1	0	2.82	5	5	0	0	22	17	10	7	1	9	29	.207
	Wisconsin (MWL)	LoA	0	2	4.80	8	6	0	0	30	30	17	16	1	16	32	.275
MINOR LEAGUE TOTALS			1	2	3.96	13	11	0	0	52	47	27	23	2	25	61	.246

29 DANNY CARROLL, OF

BORN: Jan. 6, 1989. **B-T:** R-R. **HT.:** 6-1. **WT.:** 175. **DRAFTED:** HS—Moreno Valley, Calif., 2007 (3rd round). **SIGNED BY:** Tim Reynolds.

While many clubs thought Carroll's development would have been better served had he attended college, the Mariners liked him enough to make him a third-round pick in 2007 and gave him a $315,000 bonus so he'd eschew the chance to play for UC Irvine. Carroll finished among the Arizona League leaders in several offensive categories during his pro debut, but he scuffled wildly in his follow-up in 2008. Much of his trouble can be attributed to him playing through two fractured bones in his left wrist, the result of being hit by a pitch. He didn't have surgery and the fracture set itself, though it hampered his ability to swing the bat without pain. Managers, coaches and evaluators share in their admiration for the high-energy Carroll, whom they describe simply as a baseball player. He's a plus runner who led all Seattle farmhands with 38 stolen bases in just 79 games last year. He's also an above-average defender with a strong arm in center field, but he'll go only as far as his bat will take him. Carroll has below-average power, but he has solid hitting instincts and a repeatable swing, lending hope that he can hit for average and draw walks. As such, he profiles as an extra outfielder with a ceiling as a regular in center field.

Year	Club (League)	Class	AVG	G	AB	R	H	2B	3B	HR	RBI	BB	SO	SB	OBP	SLG
2007	Mariners (AZL)	R	.323	53	201	39	65	9	6	0	24	27	56	27	.415	.428
	Everett (NWL)	SS	.176	4	17	0	3	0	0	0	0	0	6	2	.176	.176
2008	Mariners (AZL)	R	.000	2	8	0	0	0	0	0	0	0	5	0	.200	.000
	High Desert (CAL)	HiA	.135	17	74	10	10	2	0	0	5	3	32	7	.210	.162
	Wisconsin (MWL)	LoA	.248	60	238	36	59	7	4	1	17	16	64	31	.325	.324
MINOR LEAGUE TOTALS			.255	136	538	85	137	18	10	1	46	46	163	67	.338	.331

30 NOLAN GALLAGHER, RHP

BORN: Dec. 20, 1985. **B-T:** R-R. **HT.:** 6-3. **WT.:** 190. **DRAFTED:** Stanford, 2007 (4th round). **SIGNED BY:** Stacey Pettis.

A potential supplemental first-round pick heading into his draft year, Gallagher struggled to a 7.39 ERA as a Stanford junior and was moved to the Cardinal's bullpen during Pacific-10 Conference play. He pitched well in the Northwest League during his pro debut, but he also peaked there in 2008. He missed the season's first three months while recovering from surgery to remove loose bodies from his left elbow. If Gallagher ever pieces it together, he could turn out to be a fourth-round steal because he has a clean delivery, a plus breaking ball and a firm fastball. His curveball features tight rotation, and at his best he throws it for strikes. He sits at 88-92 mph with his fastball, though his velocity was down a tick in 2008. A bright kid, Gallagher has only rudimentary command of his changeup and he doesn't always show a feel for disrupting opposing batters. He's 23, so he'll need to show results in high Class A to get his career back on track. He has No. 4 or 5 starter potential.

Year	Club (League)	Class	W	L	ERA	G	GS	CG	SV	IP	H	R	ER	HR	BB	SO	AVG
2007	Everett (NWL)	SS	1	1	0.84	6	6	0	0	32	19	5	3	2	6	24	.167
	Wisconsin (MWL)	LoA	0	2	4.58	4	4	0	0	20	23	13	10	3	14	15	.303
2008	Mariners (AZL)	R	0	0	6.00	3	3	0	0	9	8	7	6	3	5	8	.235
	Everett (NWL)	SS	1	1	2.94	8	6	0	0	34	34	16	11	1	12	23	.258
MINOR LEAGUE TOTALS			2	4	2.86	21	19	0	0	94	84	41	30	9	37	70	.236

Tampa Bay Rays

BY BILL BALLEW

Next up: Pigs fly and hell freezes over. The list of life's impossibilities decreased by one when the Rays went from last place in the American League East to the World Series. They joined the 1991 Braves as the only teams in major league history to reach the playoffs one season after having baseball's worst record.

Sporting the majors' second-lowest Opening Day payroll ($43.8 million) and its third-youngest roster, Tampa Bay entered the campaign never having won more than 70 games in a season and finishing out of last place just once in 10 seasons.

Fittingly, their sudden jump to 97 wins and the AL pennant was accomplished through player development. After some missteps in the franchise's early days, the Rays have built primarily from within. Their World Series roster featured nine first-round picks, including B.J. Upton and AL rookie of the year Evan Longoria, who went in the top three picks, and Matt Garza and Scott Kazmir, acquired in trades for veterans.

The grow-your-own approach isn't expected to end any time soon for an organization that rated No. 1 in our farm system rankings entering 2007 and 2008. Postseason hero David Price, the No. 1 overall pick in 2007, will carve out a significant role for himself in 2009 and headlines the pitching that overflows throughout the system. The position players don't run as deep, with shortstop Reid Brignac topping a thin group at the upper levels. Tampa Bay addressed that by spending six of its first 2008 draft picks on hitters, including shortstop Tim Beckham with the No. 1 overall choice.

Despite the Rays' long-held philosophy of building through the farm system, they never have been more oriented toward developing young players. Tampa Bay has selected several of the youngest players eligible in each of the past two drafts, including righthanders Brad Furdal and Jason McEachern (neither of whom turned 18 until mid-October) in the 2008 draft. Likewise, several of the college players the Rays drafted last June, such as catcher Jake Jefferies and first baseman Mike Sheridan, were 20 during their pro debuts. The organization also is more driven than ever in developing international players after building facilities in the Dominican Republic and Venezuela in the past two years.

The 2008 Organization of the Year has more planning and vision than at any time in its first dozen

Third baseman Evan Longoria was one of several reasons for the Rays' 2008 surge

TOP 30 PROSPECTS

1. David Price, lhp	16. Mitch Talbot, rhp
2. Tim Beckham, ss	17. Alex Cobb, rhp
3. Wade Davis, rhp	18. Jake Jefferies, c
4. Reid Brignac, ss	19. Ryan Royster, of
5. Desmond Jennings, of	20. Reid Fronk, of
6. Matt Moore, lhp	21. Mike Sheridan, 1b
7. Nick Barnese, rhp	22. Chris Luck, rhp
8. Jeremy Hellickson, rhp	23. Joe Cruz, rhp
9. Jake McGee, lhp	24. Alex Colome, rhp
10. Jeff Niemann, rhp	25. Mayo Acosta, c
11. Kyle Lobstein, lhp	26. Mike McCormick, c
12. Albert Suarez, rhp	27. Kyeon Kang, of
13. John Jaso, c	28. Ty Morrison, of
14. Fernando Perez, of	29. Jason McEachern, rhp
15. Heath Rollins, rhp	30. Shawn O'Malley, ss

years. President Matt Silverman and GM Andrew Friedman have displayed a Midas touch with nearly every move they have made, ranging from dropping "Devil" from the team nickname to displaying the proper patience for rising prospects to making the correct decisions in terms of adding major league talent.

Gone are the days when physical ability trumped everything, with strong mental makeup now the most desired trait for any Ray, on the field or off.

The Rays should remain contenders for the foreseeable future. This team was built for the long haul and its sudden surge in 2008 was no fluke.

General Manager: Andrew Friedman. **Farm Director:** Mitch Lukevics. **Scouting Director:** R.J. Harrison.

Class	Team	League	W	L	PCT	Finish*	Manager	Affiliated
Majors	Tampa Bay	American	97	65	.599	^2nd (14)	Joe Maddon	—
Triple-A	Durham Bulls	International	74	70	.514	5th (14)	Charlie Montoyo	1998
Double-A	Montgomery Biscuits	Southern	69	70	.496	6th (10)	Billy Gardner	2004
High A	Vero Beach Devil Rays	Florida State	54	81	.400	11th (12)	Jim Morrison	2007
Low A	Columbus Catfish	South Atlantic	67	69	.493	10th (16)	Matt Quatraro	2007
Short-season	Hudson Valley Renegades	New York-Penn	40	35	.533	6th (14)	Joe Alvarez	1996
Rookie	Princeton Devil Rays	Appalachian	24	38	.387	9th (10)	Joe Szekely	1997
Overall 2008 Minor League Record			328	363	.475	23rd		

* Finish in overall standings (No. of teams in league). ^League champion.

LAST YEAR'S TOP 30

Rank	Player, Pos.	Status
1.	Evan Longoria, 3b	Majors
2.	David Price, lhp	No. 1
3.	Jake McGee, lhp	No. 9
4.	Wade Davis, rhp	No. 3
5.	Reid Brignac, ss	No. 4
6.	Desmond Jennings, of	No. 5
7.	Jeff Niemann, rhp	No. 10
8.	Jeremy Hellickson, rhp	No. 8
9.	Ryan Royster, of	No. 19
10.	Chris Mason, rhp	Dropped out
11.	Glenn Gibson, lhp	Dropped out
12.	Juan Salas, rhp	Majors
13.	John Jaso, c	No. 13
14.	Alex Cobb, rhp	No. 17
15.	Eduardo Morlan, rhp	(Brewers)
16.	Josh Butler, rhp	(Brewers)
17.	Nick Barnese, rhp	No. 7
18.	James Houser, lhp	Dropped out
19.	Heath Rollins, rhp	No. 15
20.	Matt Walker, rhp	Dropped out
21.	Mitch Talbot, rhp	No. 16
22.	Mike McCormick, c	No. 26
23.	Will Kline, rhp	Dropped out
24.	Wade Townsend, rhp	Dropped out
25.	Fernando Perez, of	No. 14
26.	Nevin Ashley, c	Dropped out
27.	Justin Ruggiano, of	Dropped out
28.	Rhyne Hughes, 1b	Dropped out
29.	Joel Guzman, 3b/1b	(Nationals)
30.	D.J. Jones, of	Dropped out

BEST TOOLS

Best Hitter for Average	Tim Beckham
Best Power Hitter	Ryan Royster
Best Strike-Zone Discipline	John Jaso
Fastest Baserunner	Fernando Perez
Best Athlete	Desmond Jennings
Best Fastball	David Price
Best Curveball	Wade Davis
Best Slider	David Price
Best Changeup	Mitch Talbot
Best Control	Jeremy Hellickson
Best Defensive Catcher	Christian Lopez
Best Defensive Infielder	Reid Brignac
Best Infield Arm	Jairo de la Rosa
Best Defensive Outfielder	Fernando Perez
Best Outfield Arm	Justin Ruggiano

PROJECTED 2012 LINEUP

Catcher	Dioner Navarro
First Base	Carlos Pena
Second Base	Akinori Iwamura
Third Base	Evan Longoria
Shortstop	Tim Beckham
Left Field	Carl Crawford
Center Field	Desmond Jennings
Right Field	B.J. Upton
Designated Hitter	John Jaso
No. 1 Starter	David Price
No. 2 Starter	Scott Kazmir
No. 3 Starter	Matt Garza
No. 4 Starter	James Shields
No. 5 Starter	Wade Davis
Closer	Jake McGee

TOP PROSPECTS OF THE DECADE

Year	Player, Pos.	2008 Org.
1999	Matt White, rhp	Out of baseball
2000	Josh Hamilton, of	Rangers
2001	Josh Hamilton, of	Rangers
2002	Josh Hamilton, of	Rangers
2003	Rocco Baldelli, of	Rays
2004	B.J. Upton, ss	Rays
2005	Delmon Young, of	Twins
2006	Delmon Young, of	Twins
2007	Delmon Young, of	Twins
2008	Evan Longoria, 3b	Rays

TOP DRAFT PICKS OF THE DECADE

Year	Player, Pos.	2008 Org.
1999	Josh Hamilton, of	Rangers
2000	Rocco Baldelli, of	Rays
2001	Dewon Brazelton, rhp	Out of baseball
2002	B.J. Upton, ss	Rays
2003	Delmon Young, of	Twins
2004	Jeff Niemann, rhp	Rays
2005	Wade Townsend, rhp	Rays
2006	Evan Longoria, 3b	Rays
2007	David Price, lhp	Rays
2008	Tim Beckham, ss	Rays

LARGEST BONUSES IN CLUB HISTORY

Matt White, 1996	$10,200,000
Rolando Arrojo, 1997	$7,000,000
Tim Beckham, 2008	$6,150,000
David Price, 2007	$5,600,000
B.J. Upton, 2002	$4,600,000

TAMPA BAY RAYS

TOP 2009 ROOKIE: David Price, lhp. The 2007 No. 1 overall pick's spectacular postseason performance should be the launching pad for a brilliant career.

BREAKOUT PROSPECT: Kyle Lobstein, lhp. He's yet to throw a pitch in pro ball, but the Rays spent $1.5 million on their 2008 second-rounder because they think he has a chance to be the total package.

SOURCE OF TOP 30 TALENT			
Homegrown	29	Acquired	1
College	7	Trades	1
Junior college	3	Rule 5 draft	0
High school	15	Independent leagues	0
Draft-and-follow	1	Free agents/waivers	0
Nondrafted free agents	0		
International	3		

SLEEPER: Emeel Salem, of. He was batting .301 and leading the minors with 25 steals when he broke his left elbow on a headfirst slide in mid-May.

Numbers in parentheses indicate prospect rankings.

LF
Ryan Royster (19)
Reid Fronk (20)
Kyeon Kang (27)
Stephen Vogt
D.J. Jones
Pedro Powell
Quinn Stewart

CF
Desmond Jennings (5)
Fernando Perez (14)
Ty Morrison (28)
Emeel Salem
Anthony Scelfo
Brian Bryles

RF
Justin Ruggiano
Sergio Pedroza
Jason Corder

3B
Chris Nowak
Greg Sexton
Burt Reynolds

SS
Tim Beckham (2)
Reid Brignac (4)
Shawn O'Malley (30)
Jairo de la Rosa

2B
Elliot Johnson
Elias Otero
Michael Ross
Chase Fontaine

1B
Mike Sheridan (21)
Rhyne Hughes
Matt Fields

C
John Jaso (13)
Jake Jefferies (18)
Mayo Acosta (25)
Mike McCormick (26)
Matt Spring
Nevin Ashley
Christian Lopez

RHP
Starters	Relievers
Wade Davis (3)	Joe Cruz (23)
Nick Barnese (7)	Alex Colome (24)
Jeremy Hellickson (8)	Matt Gorgen
Jeff Niemann (10)	Neal Frontz
Albert Suarez (12)	Ryan Reid
Heath Rollins (15)	Matt Walker
Mitch Talbot (16)	Jesse Darcy
Alex Cobb (17)	Shane Dyer
Chris Luck (22)	
Jason McEachern (29)	
Will Kline	
Tyree Hayes	
Brad Furdal	

LHP
Starters	Relievers
David Price (1)	Jonathan Barratt
Matt Moore (6)	Neil Schenk
Jake McGee (9)	Josh Satow
Kyle Lobstein (11)	
James Houser	
Glenn Gibson	

2008

BEST PURE HITTER: SS Tim Beckham (1), the No. 1 overall pick, slumped early but batted .275 in the final month and the Rays believe he'll be a five-tool player. They're also enthused about the lefty bats of C Jake Jefferies (3), 1B Mike Sheridan (5) and OF Anthony Scelfo (8).

BEST POWER HITTER: OF Jason Corder (7) has plenty of raw power that was sometimes masked by Long Beach State's Blair Field. Tampa Bay envisions Beckham developing 20-homer power.

FASTEST RUNNER: OFs Ty Morrison (4) and Brian Bryles (12) have plus-plus speed. Bryles was part of an Arkansas high school state champion 400-meter relay team.

BEST DEFENSIVE PLAYER: Unlike B.J. Upton, the last shortstop the Rays took with an early first-round pick, Beckham should be able to stay at the position. He has fluid actions, plenty of range and a strong arm.

BEST FASTBALL: Tampa Bay selected just two pitchers in the first eight rounds and mostly took projectable high schoolers. RHP Matt Gorgen (16) has the best present heater, sitting at 90-92 mph. He could be passed by one of the younger arms, perhaps LHP Kyle Lobstein (2), who's 6-foot-3, 185 pounds and occasionally hits 92 mph. He signed for $1.5 million.

BEST SECONDARY PITCH: RHP Shane Dyer's (6) knuckle-curve. Lobstein and RHP Jason McEachern (13) also have good curveballs, and LHP Josh Satow (25) owns a deceptive changeup.

BEST PRO DEBUT: Gorgen went 1-1, 1.96 with 13 saves and a 35-5 K-BB ratio in 23 innings at short-season Hudson Valley. Opponents hit just .093 against him.

BEST ATHLETE: In terms of pure athleticism, it's Morrison and Bryles, and Bryles also was highly regarded as a pitcher whose fastball peaked in the low 90s. In terms of all-around baseball skills, it's Beckham, who should have four plus tools and solid-average speed when he's a finished product. Scelfo played quarterback at Tulane.

MOST INTRIGUING BACKGROUND: The Rays also signed Beckham's brother, 2B/3B Jeremy (17). The Cardinals signed Gorgen's twin brother Scott as a fourth-rounder. When Scelfo first arrived on campus, his uncle Chris was Tulane's football coach and his father Frank was the offensive coordinator.

CLOSEST TO THE MAJORS: Beckham and Lobstein should move fast for high schoolers. Gorgen may not need much time to get ready for big league bullpen duty.

BEST LATE-ROUND PICK: McEachern or Gorgen. McEachern was throwing just 82-84 mph in the summer before his high school senior year, but he's now up to 88-92 mph and there's more projection remaining with his body and delivery.

THE ONE WHO GOT AWAY: The only players the Rays didn't sign among their first 28 picks were lefty power-hitting 1B Brandon Meredith (15) and 6-foot-5 LHP Ryan Carpenter (21). Meredith is attending San Diego State, while Carpenter is at Gonzaga.

ASSESSMENT: With the last No. 1 overall pick they should have for a while, the Rays went for Beckham over catcher Buster Posey. They also invested heavily in the polished Lobstein, then focused on projectable arms and athletes.

2007

LHP David Price (1) already has justified his No. 1 overall selection with his postseason performance, and that's just the beginning for him. RHP Nick Barnese (3) and LHP Matt Moore (8) are high-ceiling arms just beginning to emerge.

GRADE: A

2006

3B Evan Longoria (1) might have made a run at AL MVP honors as a rookie had he not missed time with a wrist injury. OF Desmond Jennings (10) has all-star potential if he can stay healthy.

GRADE: A

2005

Ownership pushed the scouting department to take RHP Wade Townsend (1), a rare misstep for the Rays with a top-10 pick. RHP Jeremy Hellickson (4) is a solid mid-rotation candidate, but Tampa Bay failed to sign five future first- or sandwich-rounders, most notably 1B Ike Davis (19).

GRADE: C

2004

RHP Jeff Niemann (1) hasn't lived up to the No. 4 overall pick yet, but this is still a strong draft. RHP Andy Sonnastine (13) won 13 games for Tampa Bay last year and OF Fernando Perez (7) was a postseason hero. In the long run, SS Reid Brignac (2), RHP Wade Davis (3) and LHP Jake McGee (5) might be the best of this crop.

GRADE: A

*Draft analysis by Jim Callis. Numbers in parentheses indicate draft rounds. *Bonuses for 2004-05 are first 10 rounds only.*

PROSPECT

DAVID PRICE, LHP
Born: Aug. 26, 1985.
Ht.: 6-6. **Wt.:** 225.
Bats: L. **Throws:** L.
Drafted: Vanderbilt, 2007 (1st round).
Signed by: Brad Matthews.

CARL KLINE

Few players have lived up to the hype, both before and after being the No. 1 overall pick in the draft, better than Price. The Rays targeted the Vanderbilt ace in the fall of 2006 and never had reason to alter their decision to go with the lefthander on draft day in June 2007. He won Baseball America's College Player of the Year and the Golden Spikes awards as a junior after going 11-1, 2.63 and leading NCAA Division I with 194 strikeouts in 133 innings. Price signed at the Aug. 15 deadline, getting an $8.5 million big league contract that included a backloaded $5.6 million bonus, which pushed his pro debut back to 2008. Elbow tenderness in spring training further delayed his first outing until May 22, but he showed no ill effects by going 12-1, 2.30 between three minor league levels. After helping Triple-A Durham reach the International League playoffs, Price joined the Rays in September. He dazzled the Yankees in relief in his first appearance and held the Orioles hitless for five innings in his first start, but the best was yet to come. Added to the playoff roster, he won Game Two and saved Game Seven in the American League Championship Series, then recorded the final seven outs in Tampa Bay's victory in the second game of the World Series.

Price rates off the charts with his stuff, athleticism and disposition, a package that should make him one of the premier pitchers in the majors. He has two plus-plus pitches with a mid-90s fastball and a biting slider. His fastball has outstanding movement with late armside run. His slider is reminiscent of John Smoltz's with its depth and 87-88 mph velocity. He blew away the Red Sox with both pitches in the ALCS clincher, generating several awkward swings. His changeup also can be an above-average offering with impressive deception and fade. Price has the ability to add and subtract velocity from his pitches, and he uses the entire strike zone to his advantage. He receives as much praise for his makeup and humility as he does for his pitching, which is saying a lot. He was unfazed when asked to pitch in pressure situations in the playoffs.

Price lacks full confidence in his changeup. He didn't need that third pitch in college and the minors, but must trust it more and improve its depth to succeed as a big league ace. He never has encountered failure, so he has yet to show he can make the necessary adjustments when the inevitable occurs, but he should be up to the challenge.

Extremely goal-oriented, Price wants to join the Rays rotation to open the 2009 season. He has the talent and work ethic to make that happen. Even if he falls short, it won't be long before he's part of Tampa Bay's rotation for good, and he eventually should become the No. 1 starter on the talented staff. It would be no surprise if he moved to the forefront of the game's elite pitchers at a pace similar to that of Tim Lincecum.

Year	Club (League)	Class	W	L	ERA	G	GS	CG	SV	IP	H	R	ER	HR	BB	SO	AVG
2008	Vero Beach (FSL)	HiA	4	0	1.82	6	6	0	0	35	28	7	7	0	7	37	.220
	Montgomery (SL)	AA	7	0	1.89	9	9	1	0	57	42	13	12	7	16	55	.206
	Durham (IL)	AAA	1	1	4.50	4	4	0	0	18	22	10	9	0	9	17	.301
	Tampa Bay (AL)	MAJ	0	0	1.93	5	1	0	0	14	9	4	3	1	4	12	.176
MINOR LEAGUE TOTALS			12	1	2.30	19	19	1	0	110	92	30	28	7	32	109	.228
MAJOR LEAGUE TOTALS			0	0	1.93	5	1	0	0	14	9	4	3	1	4	12	.176

2 TIM BECKHAM, SS

CLIFF WELCH

BORN: Jan. 27, 1990. **B-T:** R-R. **HT.:** 6-0. **WT.:** 190. **DRAFTED:** HS—Griffin, Ga., 2008 (1st round). **SIGNED BY:** Milt Hill.

Beckham emerged on the showcase circuit during the summer of 2007 and was MVP of the Aflac Classic. He carried that momentum into his senior season of high school and emerged as the No. 1 overall pick in the 2008 draft. After signing quickly for $6.15 million, he rated as the Rookie-level Appalachian League's top prospect while playing alongside his brother Jeremy (a 17th-round pick) in the Princeton infield. An outstanding athlete with easy actions and great instincts, Beckham has all the tools to be a stellar shortstop. He has strong, quick wrists and hands, and good plate discipline. The Rays believe he'll develop 20-homer power with his plus bat speed and the leverage in his swing. Defensively, he has fluid actions, good range, soft hands and a strong arm. His speed is good but not great, though he runs the bases very well. Beckham should make more consistent contact once he irons out some mechanical issues in his swing. His arm slot and footwook need more consistency, particularly so he can get behind the ball on throws. Beckham is a complete package at shortstop, yet has a chance to improve as he smoothes out his rough spots. The Rays' long-term answer at shortstop, Beckham will begin 2009 at their new low Class A Bowling Green affiliate.

Year	Club (League)	Class	AVG	G	AB	R	H	2B	3B	HR	RBI	BB	SO	SB	OBP	SLG
2008	Princeton (APP)	R	.243	46	177	30	43	12	0	2	14	13	43	5	.297	.345
	Hudson Valley (NYP)	SS	.333	2	6	5	2	1	0	0	0	2	1	1	.556	.500
MINOR LEAGUE TOTALS			.246	48	183	35	45	13	0	2	14	15	44	6	.309	.350

3 WADE DAVIS, RHP

CLIFF WELCH

BORN: Sept. 7, 1985. **B-T:** R-R. **HT.:** 6-5. **WT.:** 220. **DRAFTED:** HS—Lake Wales, Fla., 2004 (3rd round). **SIGNED BY:** Kevin Elfering.

The Rays' 2007 minor league pitcher of the year, Davis returned to Double-A Montgomery last spring and was a bit inconsistent before finding his rhythm and earning a promotion in mid-July. He threw seven shutout innings in his first Triple-A start and turned in seven quality starts in nine outings with Durham. Davis is one of the premier power pitching prospects in the game. His four-seam fastball sits in the low- to mid-90s, and he can dial it up to 95-96 mph when needed. He throws his hard 11-to-5 curveball with plus control, and it's filthy when he produces two-plane break. Davis also has a straight changeup and showed an improved cut fastball in Triple-A. Davis simply needs to refine the consistency of his overall feel and his delivery, particularly with his release point. Polishing those two aspects will improve his control and command. He'll need to pitch inside more often in the majors. Davis' stuff and competitiveness have him knocking on the door to the big leagues, though he probably won't bump any of Tampa Bay's established starters out of the rotation in 2009. Another half-season in Triple-A should prove beneficial in his development as a frontline starter.

Year	Club (League)	Class	W	L	ERA	G	GS	CG	SV	IP	H	R	ER	HR	BB	SO	AVG
2004	Princeton (APP)	R	3	5	6.09	13	13	0	0	58	71	46	39	8	19	38	.301
2005	Hudson Valley (NYP)	SS	7	4	2.72	15	15	0	0	86	75	35	26	5	23	97	.234
2006	Southwest Michigan (MWL)	LoA	7	12	3.02	27	27	1	0	146	124	61	49	5	64	165	.234
2007	Vero Beach (FSL)	HiA	3	0	1.84	13	13	1	0	78	54	20	16	5	21	88	.196
	Montgomery (SL)	AA	7	3	3.15	14	14	0	0	80	74	37	28	3	30	81	.249
2008	Montgomery (SL)	AA	9	6	3.85	19	19	0	0	108	104	49	46	7	42	81	.261
	Durham (IL)	AAA	4	2	2.72	9	9	0	0	53	39	16	16	5	24	55	.205
MINOR LEAGUE TOTALS			40	32	3.25	110	110	2	0	609	541	264	220	38	223	605	.240

4 REID BRIGNAC, SS

BORN: Jan. 16, 1986. **B-T:** L-R. **HT.:** 6-3. **WT.:** 180. **DRAFTED:** HS—St. Amant, La., 2004 (2nd round). **SIGNED BY:** Benny Latino.

Brignac has struggled at times with his hitting since winning MVP honors in the California League in 2006. Nevertheless, he received his first big league callup in July and earned International League all-star honors despite missing most of August after an errant pitch broke his wrist. Brignac has made impressive strides with his defense over the past two years. One of the premier glovemen in Triple-A, he has a solid arm and good quickness. He also has shown plus power for a middle infielder and the ability to use the entire field. A good athlete, he possesses above-average speed and an excellent feel for the game. After going 0-for-10 in the big leagues, Brignac hit only .188 the rest of the way because he started trying to do too much at the plate. He has struggled with his patience in the past and needs to improve his approach so he can reduce his high strikeout totals and increase his on-base percentage. He tends not to trust his hands at the plate and becomes pull-happy. His range to his right is fringy. Caught in between big league starter Jason Bartlett and Tim Beckham, Brignac has little opportunity to be the Rays' shortstop of the present or future. Unless he's used as trade bait, he's probably destined to repeat Triple-A in 2009.

Year	Club (League)	Class	AVG	G	AB	R	H	2B	3B	HR	RBI	BB	SO	SB	OBP	SLG
2004	Princeton (APP)	R	.361	25	97	16	35	4	2	1	25	9	10	2	.413	.474
	Charelston, SC (SAL)	LoA	.500	3	14	3	7	1	0	0	5	1	2	0	.533	.571
2005	Southwest Michigan (MWL)	LoA	.264	127	512	77	135	29	2	15	61	40	131	5	.319	.416
2006	Visalia (CAL)	HiA	.326	100	411	82	134	26	3	21	83	35	82	12	.382	.557
	Montgomery (SL)	AA	.300	28	110	18	33	6	2	3	16	7	31	3	.355	.473
2007	Montgomery (SL)	AA	.260	133	527	91	137	30	5	17	81	55	94	15	.328	.433
2008	Tampa Bay (AL)	MAJ	.000	4	10	1	0	0	0	0	0	1	5	0	.091	.000
	Durham (IL)	AAA	.250	97	352	43	88	26	2	9	43	25	93	5	.299	.412
MINOR LEAGUE TOTALS			.281	513	2023	330	569	122	16	66	314	172	443	42	.339	.455
MAJOR LEAGUE TOTALS			.000	4	10	1	0	0	0	0	0	1	5	0	.091	.000

5 DESMOND JENNINGS, OF

BORN: Oct. 30, 1986. **B-T:** R-R. **HT.:** 6-2. **WT.:** 180. **DRAFTED:** Itawamba (Miss.) CC, 2006 (10th round). **SIGNED BY:** Rickey Drexler.

Jennings had a wasted 2008 season after ranking as the top prospect in the South Atlantic League in 2007. The former juco all-America wide receiver homered in his first at-bat after missing the first two months with a back injury, but played just 24 games before needing surgery on his left shoulder that shelved him until the Arizona Fall League. Jennings has the exceptional speed and the discerning eye to become a prototypical leadoff hitter and center fielder. His strike-zone judgment rates among the best in the system. While he has some pop and the ability to drive the ball in the gaps, he knows his role and focuses on getting on base. He covers a wide swath in center and has an average arm. Jennings' biggest need is to stay healthy. In addition to his injury woes in 2008, he missed the final month in 2007 after having arthroscopic knee surgery. He needs game action to improve his reads and jumps in center field. With only a month in high Class A under his belt, Jennings is expected to open 2009 at the Rays' new Charlotte affiliate. A midseason promotion is a strong possibility, and if he can avoid injury, he could be pushing for a role in Tampa Bay at some point in 2010.

Year	Club (League)	Class	AVG	G	AB	R	H	2B	3B	HR	RBI	BB	SO	SB	OBP	SLG
2006	Princeton (APP)	R	.277	56	213	48	59	10	1	4	20	22	39	32	.360	.390
2007	Columbus (SAL)	LoA	.315	99	387	75	122	21	5	9	37	45	53	45	.401	.465
2008	Vero Beach (FSL)	HiA	.259	24	85	17	22	5	1	2	6	14	16	5	.360	.412
MINOR LEAGUE TOTALS			.296	179	685	140	203	36	7	15	63	81	108	82	.383	.435

6 MATT MOORE, LHP

BORN: June 18, 1989. **B-T:** L-L. **HT.:** 6-2. **WT.:** 200. **DRAFTED:** HS—Edgewood, N.M., 2007 (8th round). **SIGNED BY:** Jack Powell.

The Rays have excelled at finding quality arms in the middle rounds, with Moore serving as the latest example. An eighth-round pick in 2007 who signed for $115,000, he repeated the Appalachian League in 2008 and rated as the circuit's top pitching prospect. He fell one-third of an inning shy of qualifying for the league ERA title (1.66) and led all starters in short-season leagues in strikeouts per nine innings (12.8) and opponent batting average (.154). Moore's easy delivery produces a 92-95 mph fastball that has added velocity in the past year. He also throws a tight, late-breaking curveball that was virtually unhittable in the Appy League. Control was an issue in his debut, but he did a much better job of throwing strikes in 2008. His competitiveness gives him another advantage. After Moore improved his control, there isn't much not to like. His changeup has almost a screwball effect in the way it runs away from righthanders, but it still lacks consistency. He still needs to prove himself against much more advanced hitters. The Rays may be loaded with starters in the majors, but Moore has the upside to eventually fit in near the top of the rotation. At least three years away from Tampa Bay, he'll headline a young Bowling Green staff in 2009.

Year	Club (League)	Class	W	L	ERA	G	GS	CG	SV	IP	H	R	ER	HR	BB	SO	AVG
2007	Princeton (APP)	R	0	0	2.66	8	3	0	0	20	12	6	6	1	16	29	.160
2008	Princeton (APP)	R	2	2	1.66	12	12	0	0	54	30	22	10	0	19	77	.154
MINOR LEAGUE TOTALS			2	2	1.93	20	15	0	0	75	42	28	16	1	35	106	.156

7 NICK BARNESE, RHP

RODGER WOOD

BORN: Jan. 11, 1989. **B-T:** R-R. **HT.:** 6-2. **WT.:** 170. **DRAFTED:** HS—Simi Valley, Calif., 2007 (3rd round). **SIGNED BY:** Robbie Moen.

After missing his high school junior season due to a suspension, Barnese emerged as a third-round pick in 2007. Barnese has earned Top 10 Prospect recognition in the Appalachian and short-season New York-Penn leagues in his two pro seasons. At Hudson Valley in 2008, he allowed one earned run or less in nine of his 13 starts while averaging 11.5 strikeouts per nine innings. Barnese pounds the lower half of the strike zone with a low-90s fastball that features excellent late life. His three-quarters breaking ball also has late action with good depth. He has good control and command, and he mixes his pitches well. He has a loose arm and some projection remaining. Barnese competes hard and relishes pitching inside. Barnese worked on his changeup during the summer. It still has a ways to go, but it shows the promise of developing into at least an average pitch. He'll need to throw more strikes against more experienced hitters. Barnese will move up to Bowling Green in 2009 and pitch in a full-season rotation for the first time in his career. While he has the ability to advance quickly, chances are he'll spend the entire year in low Class A. He has a ceiling as a No. 2 starter, though developing into a No. 3 is more realistic.

Year	Club (League)	Class	W	L	ERA	G	GS	CG	SV	IP	H	R	ER	HR	BB	SO	AVG
2007	Princeton (APP)	R	2	2	3.22	9	8	0	0	36	30	19	13	1	4	37	.216
2008	Hudson Valley (NYP)	SS	5	3	2.45	13	13	0	0	66	52	26	18	1	24	84	.212
MINOR LEAGUE TOTALS			7	5	2.73	22	21	0	0	102	82	45	31	2	28	121	.214

8 JEREMY HELLICKSON, RHP

BORN: April 8, 1987. **B-T:** R-R. **HT.:** 6-1. **WT.:** 185. **DRAFTED:** HS—Des Moines, Iowa, 2005 (4th round). **SIGNED BY:** Tom Couston.

The Rays have moved Hellickson slowly because he didn't pitch many innings as an Iowa high schooler. He reported to spring training in great shape in 2008, and proceeded to lead the system in ERA (2.96) and strikeouts (162) while reaching Double-A at age 21. Hellickson has some of the best overall stuff of anyone in the system not named Price. He has a lively low-90s fastball that touches 95 mph, a curveball he'll throw in any count and a solid changeup. He also creates deception by using the same arm angle for his offspeed pitches. He throws inside consistently and rarely gets rattled. Better location, particularly in the strike zone, is Hellickson's greatest need. When his command slips, he's hittable, as evidenced when he surrendered five homers in his first Double-A start. While he's poised, the high Class A Vero Beach coaching staff felt he became a bit lackadaisical prior to his midseason promotion. Though he spent a half-season at Montgomery, Hellickson is likely to open 2009 back in Double-A. In the long term, he's another future candidate for the middle of Tampa Bay's rotation.

Year	Club (League)	Class	W	L	ERA	G	GS	CG	SV	IP	H	R	ER	HR	BB	SO	AVG
2005	Princeton (APP)	R	0	0	6.00	4	0	0	0	6	6	4	4	1	1	11	.240
2006	Hudson Valley (NYP)	SS	4	3	2.43	15	14	0	0	78	55	24	21	3	16	96	.193
2007	Columbus (SAL)	LoA	13	3	2.67	21	21	1	0	111	87	36	33	7	34	106	.214
2008	Vero Beach (FSL)	HiA	7	1	2.00	14	14	0	0	77	64	19	17	7	5	83	.224
	Montgomery (SL)	AA	4	4	3.94	13	13	0	0	75	84	36	33	15	15	79	.292
MINOR LEAGUE TOTALS			28	11	2.80	67	62	1	0	347	296	119	108	33	71	375	.229

9 JAKE McGEE, LHP

STEVE MOORE

BORN: Aug. 6, 1986. **B-T:** L-L. **HT.:** 6-3. **WT.:** 190. **DRAFTED:** HS—Sparks, Nev., 2004 (5th round). **SIGNED BY:** Fred Repke.

After ranking fourth in the minors with 175 strikeouts in 2007, McGee returned to Double-A and was inconsistent prior to tearing the ulnar collateral ligament in his left elbow on June 22. He underwent Tommy John surgery in July and is expected to be sidelined for at least a year. Few lefthanders have better stuff than a healthy McGee, who has a fastball that resides in the mid-90s and touches 98. He also throws a power three-quarters breaking ball with good tilt. He has improved his changeup to where it shows signs of becoming a plus pitch when he trusts it. Aside from getting healthy, McGee must pitch down in the strike zone with more consistency. He struggled with his release point and control early in 2008, and he battles his fastball command when he tries to reach back for something extra. The feel for his changeup comes and goes, which detracts from his confidence in the pitch. McGee isn't expected to be ready to begin pitching until after midseason. The Rays have no need to rush him, though they hope to get him on the mound in 2009 because pitchers usually make their greatest strides in their second year after Tommy John surgery.

Year	Club (League)	Class	W	L	ERA	G	GS	CG	SV	IP	H	R	ER	HR	BB	SO	AVG
2004	Princeton (APP)	R	4	1	3.97	12	12	0	0	57	49	30	25	5	25	53	.244
2005	Hudson Valley (NYP)	SS	5	4	3.64	15	14	0	0	77	64	32	31	4	23	89	.226
2006	Southwest Michigan (MWL)	LoA	7	9	2.96	26	26	0	0	134	103	54	44	7	65	171	.211
2007	Vero Beach (FSL)	HiA	5	4	2.93	21	21	0	0	117	86	45	38	8	39	145	.203
	Montgomery (SL)	AA	3	2	4.24	5	5	0	0	23	19	11	11	2	13	30	.224
2008	Montgomery (SL)	AA	6	4	3.94	15	15	0	0	78	65	38	34	6	37	65	.230
MINOR LEAGUE TOTALS			30	24	3.40	94	93	0	0	485	386	210	183	32	202	553	.219

10 JEFF NIEMANN, RHP

BORN: Feb. 28, 1983. **B-T:** R-R. **HT.:** 6-9. **WT.:** 280. **DRAFTED:** Rice, 2004 (1st round). **SIGNED BY:** Jonathan Bonifay.

The fourth overall pick in the 2004 draft, Niemann has yet to find a role in Tampa Bay but had another solid season in the minors. He limited the Orioles to one run over six innings in his big league debut on April 13, yet was sidelined two weeks with shoulder stiffness upon returning to the minors. He rejoined the Rays as a reliever in September but didn't make the postseason roster. Niemann possesses two above-average pitches, a fastball that sits in the low 90s and tops out at 95 mph and a hard curveball that acts much like a slider on occasion. He has developed a splitter to use as a changeup and looked more comfortable throwing it in 2008. He's an intimidating presence with his size and extended delivery toward the plate. Niemann gets in trouble when he leaves his pitches up in the strike zone. Getting ahead in the count with his fastball and maintaining its command down in the zone would make his secondary stuff play up. He's easy to run on and requires more time than most pitchers to get loose, both of which could preclude using him as a reliever. Niemann will enter the 2009 season with little left to prove in the minors. If the Rays don't have an opening for him, he figures to become a prime trade candidate.

Year	Club (League)	Class	W	L	ERA	G	GS	CG	SV	IP	H	R	ER	HR	BB	SO	AVG
2005	Visalia (CAL)	HiA	0	1	3.98	5	5	0	0	20	12	10	9	3	10	28	.167
	Montgomery (SL)	AA	0	1	4.35	6	3	0	0	10	7	7	5	0	5	14	.184
2006	Montgomery (SL)	AA	5	5	2.68	14	14	0	0	77	56	24	23	6	29	84	.202
2007	Durham (IL)	AAA	12	6	3.98	25	25	0	0	131	144	69	58	13	46	123	.277
2008	Durham (IL)	AAA	9	5	3.59	24	24	3	0	133	101	60	53	15	50	128	.207
	Tampa Bay (AL)	MAJ	2	2	5.06	5	2	0	0	16	18	12	9	3	8	14	.277
MINOR LEAGUE TOTALS			26	18	3.58	74	71	3	0	372	320	170	148	37	140	377	.229
MAJOR LEAGUE TOTALS			2	2	5.06	5	2	0	0	16	18	12	9	3	8	14	.277

11 KYLE LOBSTEIN, LHP

BORN: Aug. 12, 1989. **B-T:** L-L. **HT.:** 6-3. **WT.:** 185. **DRAFTED:** HS—Flagstaff, Ariz., 2008 (2nd round). **SIGNED BY:** Jayson Durocher.

The Rays entered the spring with Lobstein on their short list of potential players for the first overall pick in 2008. His stock dropped when his fastball velocity fell to 87-88 mph in the weeks leading up to the draft, but scouting director R.J. Harrison was thrilled when Lobstein was still on the board with the first pick of the second round. Harrison, who lives in Arizona, had followed Lobstein throughout his high school career and fell in love with his easy delivery, smooth arm action and big league body years ago. He had committed to Arizona as a two-way player but bypassed college for a $1.5 million bonus. Lobstein's fastball has been clocked as high as 92, and his athleticism and projectability give reason to believe that he'll grow into plus velocity. He's not worried about the radar gun, telling area scout Jayson Durocher that he just throws hard enough to get batters out. Lobstein does a good job of mixing his fastball with a promising curveball and a solid-average changeup. He had the best command among high school pitchers in the 2008 draft, a tribute to his feel, mechanics and athleticism. He didn't pitch professionally after signing on the Aug. 15 deadline, but he showed Tampa Bay everything it hoped to see during instructional league. The Rays usually bring their high school pitchers along very slowly, so he'll probably make his pro debut in Rookie ball. At the same time, he's more polished than most prepsters and could move quickly once he gets going.

Year	Club (League)	Class	W	L	ERA	G	GS	CG	SV	IP	H	R	ER	HR	BB	SO	AVG
2008	Did Not Play—Signed Late																

12 ALBERT SUAREZ, RHP

BORN: Oct. 8, 1989. **B-T:** R-R. **HT.:** 6-2. **WT.:** 186. **DRAFTED:** Venezuela, 2006. **SIGNED BY:** Ronnie Blanco.

Signed as a 16-year-old in 2006, Suarez worked out at the Rays' new academy in his native Venezuela before making his pro debut in 2008. He ranked as the No. 9 prospect in the Appalachian League, attracting favorable comparisons to fellow Venezuelan Freddy Garcia. Suarez has a fluid delivery that he repeats very well and easy arm action that produces a 93-94 mph fastball. Though not a giant at 6-foot-2, he throws on a steep downhill plane that causes his plus fastball to jump on hitters. He also has shown promise with his secondary pitches. His curveball has a good break and the potential to be an above-average pitch, but he's still seeking consistency with the offering. He also began working on a changeup during extended spring training but hesitated to throw it at times at Princeton. Both pitches need work, but the Rays believe he has a chance to have three plus pitches. Suarez has shown plus command of his fastball and has good overall control. He also impressed with his overall maturity and the way he adapted to a new culture at the age of 18. He likely will open the 2009 season at Hudson Valley, but could make it to low Class A if he progresses at the same rate as last year.

Year	Club (League)	Class	W	L	ERA	G	GS	CG	SV	IP	H	R	ER	HR	BB	SO	AVG
2008	Princeton (APP)	R	0	2	3.92	11	9	0	0	44	41	28	19	3	7	37	.232
MINOR LEAGUE TOTALS			0	2	3.92	11	9	0	0	44	41	28	19	3	7	37	.232

13 JOHN JASO, C

BORN: Sept. 19, 1983. **B-T:** L-R. **HT.:** 6-2. **WT.:** 205. **DRAFTED:** Southwestern (Calif.) CC, 2003 (12th round). **SIGNED BY:** Craig Weissman.

After earning a spot on Baseball America's year-end Double-A all-star team in 2007, Jaso returned to Montgomery last spring and remained there until mid-July. After finishing second in the Southern League with a .316 average the previous year, he uncharacteristically struggled with the bat at times in the first two months before hitting .298 the rest of the way, including six weeks in Triple-A and his first big league callup. Hitting has been Jaso's calling card despite his rather unconventional swing. He has excellent plate discipline and enough pop to hit 15 homers on an annual basis in the majors. The knock on Jaso early in his career was his inability to stay healthy, but he has overcome a history of shoulder injuries to set career highs in games in each of the last two seasons. His arm strength continues to rank a tick below average and he threw out just 25 percent of basestealers in 2008, though he continues to show better footwork and shorter arm action. His ability to block balls in the dirt also has improved, making him more than serviceable behind the dish. He's no speedster, but he's more athletic and faster than most catchers. A lefthanded-hitting, offensive-minded backstop, Jaso is a leading candidate to serve as Dioner Navarro's backup in Tampa Bay this year.

Year	Club (League)	Class	AVG	G	AB	R	H	2B	3B	HR	RBI	BB	SO	SB	OBP	SLG
2003	Hudson Valley (NYP)	SS	.227	47	154	20	35	7	0	2	20	25	26	2	.344	.312
2004	Hudson Valley (NYP)	SS	.302	57	199	34	60	17	2	2	35	22	32	1	.378	.437
2005	Southwest Michigan (MWL)	LoA	.307	92	332	61	102	25	1	14	50	42	53	3	.383	.515
2006	Visalia (CAL)	HiA	.309	95	366	58	113	22	0	10	55	31	48	1	.362	.451
2007	Montgomery (SL)	AA	.316	109	380	62	120	24	2	12	71	59	49	2	.408	.484
2008	Montgomery (SL)	AA	.271	85	284	51	77	13	2	7	43	62	33	1	.408	.405
	Durham (IL)	AAA	.278	31	108	14	30	7	0	5	24	10	14	1	.339	.481
	Tampa Bay (AL)	MAJ	.200	5	10	2	2	0	0	0	0	0	2	0	.200	.200
MINOR LEAGUE TOTALS			.295	516	1823	300	537	115	7	52	298	251	255	11	.382	.451
MAJOR LEAGUE TOTALS			.200	5	10	2	2	0	0	0	0	0	2	0	.200	.200

14 FERNANDO PEREZ, OF

BORN: April 23, 1983. **B-T:** B-R. **HT.:** 6-1. **WT.:** 195. **DRAFTED:** Columbia, 2004 (7th round). **SIGNED BY:** Brad Matthews.

A September callup, Perez saw considerable activity during the pennant race while B.J. Upton nursed a strained left quadriceps. A member of the Rays' postseason roster in all three series, Perez was a hero in the pivotal Game Two of the American League Championship Series, racing home from third on a short sacrifice fly with the winning run in the bottom of the 11th. One of the fastest players in baseball with incredible first-step explosion, he has game-changing speed on the bases and in center field. He took up switch-hitting in 2006 in order to better utilize his quickness. He has worked diligently on getting better leads, which enabled him to improve his stolen-base success rate to 80 percent last year. Perez, who remains the highest-drafted player ever out of Columbia (seventh round), is on the verge of sticking with Tampa Bay. The key will be how much consistency he can show at the plate. He has quick hands and occasional power, but his strikeout totals (156 in Triple-A) are unacceptable for his profile. He needs to shorten his swing, especially with two strikes, and become a better bunter in order to put more pressure on the defense. If he can't reduce his whiffs, he could resume batting solely righthanded because he makes much more contact from that side of the plate. There's nothing to quibble about Perez defensively, as he has an average arm to go with his exceptional range. Tampa Bay's offseason trade for Matt Joyce means Perez will serve the Rays as a reserve outfielder in 2009.

Year	Club (League)	Class	AVG	G	AB	R	H	2B	3B	HR	RBI	BB	SO	SB	OBP	SLG
2004	Hudson Valley (NYP)	SS	.232	69	267	46	62	8	5	2	20	30	70	24	.314	.322
2005	Southwest Michigan (MWL)	LoA	.289	134	522	93	151	17	13	6	48	58	80	57	.361	.406
2006	Visalia (CAL)	HiA	.307	133	547	123	168	19	9	4	56	78	134	33	.398	.397
2007	Montgomery (SL)	AA	.308	102	393	84	121	24	10	8	33	76	104	32	.423	.481
2008	Durham (IL)	AAA	.288	129	511	86	147	17	11	5	36	58	156	43	.361	.393
	Tampa Bay (AL)	MAJ	.250	23	60	18	15	2	0	3	8	8	16	5	.348	.433
MINOR LEAGUE TOTALS			.290	567	2240	432	649	85	48	25	193	300	544	189	.376	.404
MAJOR LEAGUE TOTALS			.250	23	60	18	15	2	0	3	8	8	16	5	.348	.433

15 HEATH ROLLINS, RHP

BORN: May 25, 1985. **B-T:** L-R. **HT.:** 6-1. **WT.:** 185. **DRAFTED:** Winthrop, 2006 (11th round). **SIGNED BY:** Brad Matthews.

Rollins continued to develop somewhat under the radar in 2008 and is beginning to attract comparisons to Andy Sonnastine from within the organization. After manning the outfield at Winthrop in addition to starting as a pitcher on Fridays and closing on Sundays, Rollins tied for the minor league lead and set a system record with 17 wins in 2007. His record fell to a misleading 6-12 in 2008, but he ranked fifth in the Florida State League in strikeouts (115 in 136 innings) and sixth in ERA (3.30). A focused pitcher with above-average command, Rollins pitches at 89-90 mph and can touch 92 with his fastball. He maintains a good angle on his fastball with his solid mechanics and does an excellent job of mixing in a plus slider and an improving changeup. With his slider and his willingness to pitch inside, Rollins limited righthanders to a .205 average last year. His feel for pitching leads the Rays to believe he'll continue to succeed at higher levels, and he pitched well in four Double-A starts at the end of 2008. His primary weakness is his tendency to give up the longball, as his 15 homers allowed in the FSL were the fifth-most in the league. While he has good athleticism for a pitcher, there's little or no projection remaining in his frame. Rollins probably will open 2009 back in Double-A, but he could be in line for a midseason promotion.

Year	Club (League)	Class	W	L	ERA	G	GS	CG	SV	IP	H	R	ER	HR	BB	SO	AVG
2006	Hudson Valley (NYP)	SS	1	3	4.08	12	10	0	0	46	44	25	21	3	14	48	.249
2007	Columbus (SAL)	LoA	17	4	2.54	27	27	1	0	159	132	57	45	11	38	149	.223
2008	Vero Beach (FSL)	HiA	5	11	3.30	23	21	1	0	136	118	59	50	15	27	115	.228
	Montgomery (SL)	AA	1	1	2.88	4	4	0	0	25	22	9	8	2	6	23	.244
MINOR LEAGUE TOTALS			24	19	3.04	66	62	2	0	367	316	150	124	31	85	335	.230

16 MITCH TALBOT, RHP

BORN: Oct. 17, 1983. **B-T:** R-R. **HT.:** 6-2. **WT.:** 200. **DRAFTED:** HS—Cedar City, Utah, 2002 (2nd round). **SIGNED BY:** Doug Deutsch (Astros).

After an up-and-down 2007 season with Durham, during which he struggled with his control, Talbot was the Bulls' best pitcher last year. He ranked third in the International League in strikeouts (141 in 161 innings) and fifth in wins (13) before receiving his first big league promotion. Acquired with Ben Zobrist from the Astros for Aubrey Huff at the all-star break in 2006, Talbot has an 89-91 mph fastball with good movement, a hard slider with impressive late cutting action and a changeup that continues to show better fade and depth. His control improved immensely compared to 2007, and while his strikeout total was the second-highest in the system, he's not afraid to pitch to contact and let his fielders do their jobs. Talbot has developed a knack for competing without his best stuff. With no foreseen vacancies in the Tampa Bay rotation, his future could be as a middle reliever or as trade bait. A return to Triple-A could be in the offing for 2009, though it's hard to see how that would benefit either Talbot or the organization.

Year	Club (League)	Class	W	L	ERA	G	GS	CG	SV	IP	H	R	ER	HR	BB	SO	AVG
2003	Martinsville (APP)	R	4	4	2.83	12	12	0	0	54	45	26	17	1	11	46	.224
2004	Lexington (SAL)	LoA	10	10	3.83	27	27	1	0	153	145	78	65	16	49	115	.252
2005	Salem (CAR)	HiA	8	11	4.34	27	27	1	0	151	169	90	73	15	46	100	.280
2006	Corpus Christi (TEX)	AA	6	4	3.39	18	17	0	1	90	94	49	34	4	29	96	.269
	Montgomery (SL)	AA	4	3	1.90	10	10	0	0	66	51	16	14	2	18	59	.214
2007	Durham (IL)	AAA	13	9	4.53	29	29	1	0	161	169	89	81	13	59	124	.274
2008	Durham (IL)	AAA	13	9	3.86	28	28	1	0	161	165	79	69	9	35	141	.263
	Tampa Bay (AL)	MAJ	0	0	11.17	3	1	0	0	10	16	12	12	3	11	5	.381
MINOR LEAGUE TOTALS			58	50	3.80	151	150	4	1	837	838	427	353	60	247	681	.261
MAJOR LEAGUE TOTALS			0	0	11.17	3	1	0	0	10	16	12	12	3	11	5	.381

17 ALEX COBB, RHP

BORN: Oct. 7, 1987. **B-T:** R-R. **HT.:** 6-1. **WT.:** 180. **DRAFTED:** HS—Vero Beach, Fla., 2006 (4th round). **SIGNED BY:** Kevin Elfering.

The South Atlantic League was loaded with young prospects in 2008, which led to Cobb flying under the radar. He won nine games and could have easily registered several more, receiving a loss or no decision on seven occasions while yielding one earned run or less. Cobb's best pitch is an 11-to-5 curveball that he throws at any time in the count. His fastball tops out in the low-90s and is sneaky fast with the way it jumps in on hitters at the last instant, thereby limiting the number of hard-hit balls against him. He focused on improving his changeup, which is akin to a splitter, during the 2008 campaign by throwing it more often, and the initial results were promising. He does a nice job of mixing his pitches and keeping hitters off balance. Cobb has excellent control but can be too fine in the strike zone at times. He also tends to depend on his curve too much. A solid athlete who had offers to play quarterback in college, Cobb isn't overpowering but has the pitching know-how and the stuff to become a starter in the back of a major league rotation. His next stop will be high Class A.

Year	Club (League)	Class	W	L	ERA	G	GS	CG	SV	IP	H	R	ER	HR	BB	SO	AVG
2006	Princeton (APP)	R	0	0	5.19	6	1	0	0	9	9	7	5	3	3	8	.265
2007	Hudson Valley (NYP)	SS	5	6	3.54	16	16	0	0	81	78	36	32	4	31	62	.259
2008	Columbus (SAL)	LoA	9	7	3.29	25	25	0	0	140	113	59	51	16	35	97	.224
MINOR LEAGUE TOTALS			14	13	3.45	47	42	0	0	230	200	102	88	23	69	167	.238

18 JAKE JEFFERIES, C

BORN: Oct. 30, 1987. **B-T:** L-R. **HT.:** 6-3. **WT.:** 200. **DRAFTED:** UC Davis, 2008 (3rd round). **SIGNED BY:** Carlos Delgado.

Jefferies wasn't well known in scouting circles prior to his junior season, which coincided with UC Davis' first year with full-fledged NCAA Division I status. He set a school record with 96 hits, was one of college baseball's toughest hitters to strike out (11 whiffs in 248 at-bats) and was named Big West Conference co-player of the year. A third-round pick who signed for $515,000, Jefferies doesn't have an overwhelming tool. But his total package is greater than the sum of his individual parts. He's a contact hitter who bats out of a slight crouch from the left side. He puts the barrel of the bat on the ball with impressive consistency, though he has yet to hit for significant home run power. He uses the entire field and has the frame to drive the ball as he continues to make adjustments to wood bats. Behind the plate, Jefferies has fringe-average arm strength and good accuracy on his throws. He erased just 17 percent of basestealers in his pro debut. He has a quiet set-up and solid footwork, and he receives and blocks the ball well. Jefferies also runs well for a catcher and is a smart baserunner, though his overall speed rates a tick or two below average. With his solid athleticism and plus hand-eye coordination, Jefferies has a chance to be at least a backup catcher at the major league level. He'll open his first full pro season in low Class A.

Year	Club (League)	Class	AVG	G	AB	R	H	2B	3B	HR	RBI	BB	SO	SB	OBP	SLG
2008	Hudson Valley (NYP)	SS	.315	66	238	32	75	16	3	2	41	21	22	1	.379	.433
MINOR LEAGUE TOTALS			.315	66	238	32	75	16	3	2	41	21	22	1	.379	.433

19 RYAN ROYSTER, OF

BORN: July 25, 1986. **B-T:** R-R. **HT.:** 6-2. **WT.:** 210. **DRAFTED:** HS—Eugene, Ore., 2004 (6th round). **SIGNED BY:** Paul Kirsch.

The make-or-break point in a player's career often comes when he has to respond to adversity for the first time. That's what Royster faced during a 2008 campaign after a string of impressive performances earlier in his career. He was Princeton's MVP in 2004 and Hudson Valley's in 2006, then won the Rays' minor league player of the year award in 2007 after leading the South Atlantic League with 30 homers. He did earn Vero Beach's MVP award last season, but that had much to do with the club's overall lack of production. Much of Royster's home run power was compromised by the Florida State League's larger ballparks, and he was hitting just .201 at the end of May. His concentration lapsed at times and he took poor at-bats with him to the field. However, Royster was able to make adjustments at the plate and cope with his frustration with balls dying on the warning track, hitting .307 in the final three months. He has the strength and bat speed to produce at the plate at higher levels, though better plate discipline is a must. He moves well for his size and has good baserunning instincts, though his speed is below-average. Defensively, he struggled with his lateral movement while having to cover more ground in the spacious FSL outfields. His arm strength is average and he fits best in left field. Tampa Bay would like to see Royster make more strides with his mental approach in Double-A this year.

Year	Club (League)	Class	AVG	G	AB	R	H	2B	3B	HR	RBI	BB	SO	SB	OBP	SLG
2004	Princeton (APP)	R	.273	52	176	25	48	10	2	5	26	5	47	3	.297	.438
2005	Princeton (APP)	R	.246	51	187	30	46	8	0	12	37	13	48	6	.300	.481
2006	Hudson Valley (NYP)	SS	.247	63	231	20	57	15	1	8	29	9	65	5	.286	.424
2007	Columbus (SAL)	LoA	.329	125	474	90	156	31	4	30	98	36	121	17	.380	.601
2008	Vero Beach (FSL)	HiA	.265	118	426	50	113	13	3	9	58	32	110	5	.318	.373
MINOR LEAGUE TOTALS			.281	409	1494	215	420	77	10	64	248	95	391	36	.329	.475

20 REID FRONK, OF

BORN: July 21, 1986. **B-T:** L-R. **HT.:** 6-1. **WT.:** 185. **DRAFTED:** North Carolina, 2007 (7th round). **SIGNED BY:** Brad Matthews.

Fronk's first full year in pro ball was a tale of two seasons. He hit .237/.333/.425 during the first half, followed by a .338/.461/.563 performance afterward. His red-hot finish allowed him to rank third in the South Atlantic League in on-base percentage (.398) and sixth in slugging (.492), as well as fourth in the system in RBIs (83), earning Columbus MVP honors. His perseverance was no surprise given his hard-nosed approach. Fronk shows good power and could produce bigger numbers if he added some loft to his swing. He also could hit for a higher average should he flatten his bat's path to the ball. Right now he's a tweener in several aspects of the game, including his defense. A shortstop in high school who played third base at North Carolina, Fronk moved to left field as a junior with the Tar Heels. The Rays gave him a look at both second and third base during instructional league but decided to leave him in left field. He has fringy speed and range to go with average arm strength. His outfield instincts could use some fine-tuning, particularly with his routes on flyballs. Some club officials believe Fronk could excel as a Ryan Freel type, playing a variety of positions in the infield and outfield. Tampa Bay wants him to continue to produce and develop at high Class A in 2009.

Year	Club (League)	Class	AVG	G	AB	R	H	2B	3B	HR	RBI	BB	SO	SB	OBP	SLG
2007	Hudson Valley (NYP)	SS	.311	37	122	28	38	14	1	5	27	15	30	5	.396	.566
2008	Columbus (SAL)	LoA	.287	124	429	76	123	29	4	17	83	74	103	18	.398	.492
MINOR LEAGUE TOTALS			.292	161	551	104	161	43	5	22	110	89	133	23	.398	.508

21 MIKE SHERIDAN, 1B

BORN: Aug. 8, 1987. **B-T:** L-L. **HT.:** 6-2. **WT.:** 205. **DRAFTED:** William & Mary, 2008 (5th round). **SIGNED BY:** Doug Witt.

Sheridan had a monster junior season at William & Mary, leading the Colonial Athletic Association in hitting (.423) while setting school records for runs (76), hits (96), doubles (26) and RBIs (72). The Rays made him a fifth-round pick in June and signed him for $195,000. Sheridan went 4-for-5 in his first pro game but hurt his wrist shortly thereafter and missed five weeks. He possesses a smooth lefthanded swing and solid-average power. Sheridan has an advanced approach and easily makes contact. As a sophomore, he was the toughest batter to strike out in NCAA Division I, fanning just five times in 209 at-bats. Sheridan shows defensive promise as a first baseman but still needs to upgrade his footwork. He's a below-average runner but not a baseclogger. Relatively young for a college draftee, Sheridan didn't turn 21 until August. He'll open 2009 in low Class A but could push for a promotion by midseason.

Year	Club (League)	Class	AVG	G	AB	R	H	2B	3B	HR	RBI	BB	SO	SB	OBP	SLG
2008	Hudson Valley (NYP)	SS	.321	31	78	14	25	5	2	0	5	4	12	1	.354	.436
MINOR LEAGUE TOTALS			.321	31	78	14	25	5	2	0	5	4	12	1	.354	.436

22 CHRIS LUCK, RHP

BORN: July 10, 1989. **B-T:** R-R. **HT.:** 6-4. **WT.:** 190. **DRAFTED:** HS—Raleigh, N.C., 2007 (20th round). **SIGNED BY:** Brad Matthews.

Princeton pitching coach Marty DeMerritt has an excellent track record when it comes to pegging potential major league pitchers, even at the Rookie league level. And DeMerritt, who has coached in the major leagues with the Giants and Cubs, believes that Luck has everything necessary to reach that ultimate destination. He has spent his first two years in pro ball as an Appalachian League reliever, but the Rays believe he has the strength and the stamina to become a starter. He has grown an inch and added 20 pounds since signing, and his fastball has moved up to 90-93 mph. He had a curveball when he signed, but he since has turned his breaking pitch into a hard 81-83 mph slider. He also has made steady progress on a changeup with DeMerritt, and it's possible that Luck one day could own three above-average pitches. He throws strikes with a smooth, easy delivery. He also stands out with his maturity, his willingness to battle and his serious approach to the game. Luck should move into the rotation this year in low Class A.

Year	Club (League)	Class	W	L	ERA	G	GS	CG	SV	IP	H	R	ER	HR	BB	SO	AVG
2007	Princeton (APP)	R	3	1	2.17	13	0	0	0	37	30	15	9	1	12	43	.217
2008	Princeton (APP)	R	6	0	2.25	13	0	0	1	36	30	10	9	3	8	35	.227
MINOR LEAGUE TOTALS			9	1	2.21	26	0	0	1	73	60	25	18	4	20	78	.222

23 JOE CRUZ, RHP

BORN: July 20, 1988. **B-T:** R-R. **HT.:** 6-4. **WT.:** 195. **DRAFTED:** East Los Angeles JC, 2007 (30th round). **SIGNED BY:** Robbie Moen.

The Rays selected Cruz late in the 2007 draft and watched him pitch over the summer before signing him for $100,000 near the Aug. 15 deadline. After making three late-season appearances that summer as a reliever with Princeton, he returned to the Appalachian League in 2008 as a starter and demonstrated a live arm with above-average control. Cruz has an ideal pitcher's body with a smooth delivery and easy arm action. The ball jumps out of his hand, and his fastball sits in the low-90s and reaches 94 mph. He gets good extension out front, making his heater seem even quicker. His secondary pitches also have potential, with his curveball featuring sharp break and his changeup displaying decent depth. He lacks consistency with his curveball, one reason he was more effective against lefties than righties in 2008. Cruz keeps the ball down in the strike zone, generating a lot of groundballs. There's still projectability remaining in his lanky frame, too. Cruz should move up to low Class A to start 2009.

Year	Club (League)	Class	W	L	ERA	G	GS	CG	SV	IP	H	R	ER	HR	BB	SO	AVG
2007	Princeton (APP)	R	2	0	0.00	3	0	0	0	9	5	0	0	0	3	13	.161
2008	Princeton (APP)	R	1	3	3.17	13	13	0	0	54	61	29	19	5	14	62	.270
MINOR LEAGUE TOTALS			3	3	2.71	16	13	0	0	63	66	29	19	5	17	75	.257

24 ALEX COLOME, RHP

BORN: Dec. 31, 1988. **B-T:** R-R. **HT.:** 6-2. **WT.:** 185. **SIGNED:** Dominican Republic, 2007. **SIGNED BY:** Eddy Toledo.

No one on this Top 30 list is more of a project than Colome, whose cousin Jesus pitched six seasons with the Rays. Colome has a 1-11 pro record and was shelled in his U.S. debut last year, but he has an electric arm that just needs to be harnessed. His inconsistency was evident in his last three outings of 2008, in which he surrendered a pair of scoreless four-inning starts around a relief appearance where he was touched for nine runs in 2 ⅓ innings. Colome's fastball has great life and sits at 94-95 mph. He also throws a hard, slurvy breaking ball with plus tilt and a late, sharp bite. Developing a changeup will be imperative for him to remain a starter, though his fastball and breaking ball would be enough to play an important role in a big league bullpen. The key for Colome will be developing his control and command. He walks too many batters and gets hit hard when he takes something off his pitches while trying to find the strike zone. Colome will continue his bid to refine his arsenal at either Hudson Valley or Bowling Green in 2009.

Year	Club (League)	Class	W	L	ERA	G	GS	CG	SV	IP	H	R	ER	HR	BB	SO	AVG
2007	Devil Rays (DSL)	R	1	6	2.97	14	11	0	0	39	30	18	13	1	31	50	.208
2008	Princeton (APP)	R	0	5	6.80	12	11	0	0	46	50	45	35	5	26	52	.272
MINOR LEAGUE TOTALS			1	11	5.04	26	22	0	0	86	80	63	48	6	57	102	.244

25 MAYO ACOSTA, C

BORN: Nov. 20, 1987. **B-T:** R-R. **HT.:** 6-1. **WT.:** 205. **SIGNED:** Dominican Republic, 2006. **SIGNED BY:** Junior Ramirez.

Acosta made one of the biggest jumps of any player in the system last year. Signed out of the Dominican Republic in 2006, he looked more like an organizational player than a prospect in his 2007 pro debut. A logjam at higher levels forced Acosta to return to the Appalachian League last season, and he used the opportunity to improve every facet of his game. Acosta has raw power and makes solid contact, though he needs to refine his approach and turn in quality at-bats on a more consistent basis. He has plus arm strength and threw out 48 percent of basestealers in 2008, ranking second in the Appy League. He also moves well behind the plate and blocks balls well. Acosta showed added maturity last year and has worked hard to become fluent in English, which has improved his ability to work with pitchers. He doesn't run well, which is to be expected of a catcher. The Rays believe Acosta is a sleeper and will promote him to low Class A this year.

Year	Club (League)	Class	AVG	G	AB	R	H	2B	3B	HR	RBI	BB	SO	SB	OBP	SLG
2007	Princeton (APP)	R	.234	38	124	12	29	10	0	1	11	12	33	2	.312	.339
2008	Princeton (APP)	R	.268	43	168	8	45	14	2	2	33	10	25	1	.306	.411
MINOR LEAGUE TOTALS			.253	81	292	20	74	24	2	3	44	22	58	3	.308	.380

26 MIKE McCORMICK, C

BORN: Sept. 6, 1986. **B-T:** R-R. **HT.:** 6-2. **WT.:** 200. **DRAFTED:** HS—Eugene, Ore., 2005 (5th round). **SIGNED BY:** Paul Kirsch.

In his second year after converting from third base, McCormick discovered that a catcher's time commitments honing his skills behind the plate and working with a pitching staff leave little opportunity for him to improve his ability with the lumber. He made significant strides in his catch-and-throw abilities while displaying an above-average arm, good footwork and soft, consistent hands. He threw out 33 percent of basestealers, showed solid athleticism in terms of blocking balls and received raves from Rays coaches for his work ethic. He still needs to improve his game-calling skills and remember not to hurry his throws. All of McCormick's defensive progress came at the expense of his bat. He bottomed out in June, when he hit .131, and struggled to keep his average above the Mendoza Line afterward. He also had surprising difficulty against lefthanders, batting .178/.229/.299 against them. McCormick does have plus bat speed, and scouts believe he will hit for either power or average—if not both—once he makes the adjustments to catching on a full-time basis. While he has below-average speed, he moves better than most catchers. The Rays are confident McCormick will continue to develop because he has the drive to get the most of out of his ability. He should be their everyday catcher in high Class A this year.

Year	Club (League)	Class	AVG	G	AB	R	H	2B	3B	HR	RBI	BB	SO	SB	OBP	SLG
2005	Princeton (APP)	R	.252	32	111	15	28	10	1	3	16	11	31	3	.339	.441
2006	Princeton (APP)	R	.275	62	222	34	61	18	0	10	39	26	64	7	.364	.491
2007	Hudson Valley (NYP)	SS	.276	67	239	35	66	20	1	8	44	27	66	3	.352	.469
2008	Columbus (SAL)	LoA	.216	106	375	37	81	15	1	13	49	31	93	2	.276	.365
MINOR LEAGUE TOTALS			.249	267	947	121	236	63	3	34	148	95	254	15	.324	.430

27 KYEON KANG, OF

BORN: Feb. 6, 1988. **B-T:** L-L. **HT.:** 6-2. **WT.:** 195. **DRAFTED:** Chattahoochee Valley (Ala.) CC, D/F 2006 (15th round). **SIGNED BY:** Milt Hill.

Kang became the first South Korean to enter professional baseball via the amateur draft when the Rays signed him for $75,000 as a draft-and-follow. They took him in the 30th round out of an Atlanta-area high school in 2006 after he had moved to Georgia from his native country two years earlier. He improved in all phases of the game in 2008, earning Hudson Valley's MVP award. Kang is strong and the ball jumps off his bat. While he has above-average power, he's still figuring out nuances of hitting, such as solving lefthanders and tightening his strike zone. He has plus speed and good baserunning instincts, though he's not yet much of a threat to steal. Kang's biggest improvements last year came on defense. He went from a below-average outfielder to one capable of manning center field on occasion for Hudson Valley. His arm strength is fringe-average, and he'll probably wind up in left field. Kang remains raw but is making progress. He'll advance to low Class A in 2009.

Year	Club (League)	Class	AVG	G	AB	R	H	2B	3B	HR	RBI	BB	SO	SB	OBP	SLG
2007	Princeton (APP)	R	.276	55	203	25	56	14	4	3	22	20	44	3	.341	.429
2008	Hudson Valley (NYP)	SS	.278	69	255	38	71	15	7	6	43	20	62	6	.338	.463
MINOR LEAGUE TOTALS			.277	124	458	63	127	29	11	9	65	40	106	9	.339	.448

28 TY MORRISON, OF

BORN: July 22, 1990. **B-T:** L-R. **HT.:** 6-2. **WT.:** 170. **DRAFTED:** HS—Tigard, Ore., 2008 (4th round). **SIGNED BY:** Paul Kirsch.

The Rays spent $500,000 to lure Morrison, a fourth-round pick in 2008, from becoming part of Oregon's born-again baseball program as a member of the Ducks' first recruiting class. He began his high school career in Virginia as a teammate of Justin Upton before moving to Oregon, where he ranked as the state's top prospect last spring. He's a greyhound with impressive tools, though the Rays will need to show patience with his offensive development. Morrison shows some pop during batting practice, but his ability to drive the ball rarely was evident during high school or his brief pro debut. Tampa Bay believes his thin frame possesses raw power, but he needs to add weight and strength in order for that to become a reality. A fast-twitch athlete with plus-plus speed, Morrison can steal bases and has the potential to become a standout defender in center field. He needs work on his jumps and routes on flyballs, though his quickness makes up for a lot of his mistakes. His arm is playable in center. The Rays won't rush Morrison, and he'll almost certainly open 2009 in extended spring training.

Year	Club (League)	Class	AVG	G	AB	R	H	2B	3B	HR	RBI	BB	SO	SB	OBP	SLG
2008	Princeton (APP)	R	.265	10	34	2	9	0	0	0	1	2	12	3	.297	.265
MINOR LEAGUE TOTALS			.265	10	34	2	9	0	0	0	1	2	12	3	.297	.265

29 JASON McEACHERN, RHP

BORN: Oct. 12, 1990. **B-T:** R-R. **HT.:** 6-2. **WT.:** 175. **DRAFTED:** HS—Hickory, N.C., 2008 (13th round). **SIGNED BY:** Brad Matthews.

One of the youngest players drafted in 2008, McEachern is a late bloomer who should continue to get better. He showed excellent pitchability during his high school career, but he didn't attract scouts until his fastball took off from 82-84 mph in the summer before his senior year to 88-92 mph last spring. The Rays drafted him in the 13th round, and a $90,000 bonus enticed him away from a scholarship from Wingate (N.C.), an NCAA Division II program. McEachern's fastball improved as he added 15 pounds to his 6-foot-2 frame, and there's room for him to add more strength and velocity. He had a strong pro debut, limiting opponents to a .193 average while mixing his fastball with a good curveball and a developing changeup. McEachern has a loose arm with a good delivery and command of all his pitches. He has a strong idea of what he's trying to accomplish on the hill, and he refuses to let difficult situations rattle him. The Rays are conservative with promoting high school pitchers early in their careers, so McEachern probably won't move past Hudson Valley in 2009.

Year	Club (League)	Class	W	L	ERA	G	GS	CG	SV	IP	H	R	ER	HR	BB	SO	AVG
2008	Princeton (APP)	R	3	0	1.44	9	2	0	0	25	17	5	4	2	8	16	.193
MINOR LEAGUE TOTALS			3	0	1.44	9	2	0	0	25	17	5	4	2	8	16	.193

30 SHAWN O'MALLEY, SS

BORN: Dec. 28, 1987. **B-T:** B-R. **HT.:** 5-11. **WT.:** 170. **DRAFTED:** HS—Kennewick, Wash., 2006 (5th round). **SIGNED BY:** Paul Kirsch.

O'Malley has developed slowly since being drafted out of a Washington high school in the fifth round in 2006. His biggest assets are his strong arm and relatively soft hands at shortstop, along with his above-average speed, which helped him rank third in the organization last year with 28 steals. Those tools should play in the major leagues . . . provided he hits enough. O'Malley has struggled offensively, never hitting above .242 in any of his three seasons and slugging .298 for his career. He has shown flashes of potential with the bat, particularly with his ability to work the count, but he hasn't displayed any consistency and very little power. His poor performance doesn't come from a lack of effort, as he's a gritty performer who plays the game hard every day. O'Malley has the defensive skills to be an everyday shortstop as well as the athleticism and versatility to become a utilityman. In order for either scenario to become a reality, he must get stronger and make more consistent contact. No. 1 overall pick Tim Beckham is ticketed for low Class A and O'Malley's bat hasn't merited a promotion, leaving his status for 2009 unclear.

Year	Club (League)	Class	AVG	G	AB	R	H	2B	3B	HR	RBI	BB	SO	SB	OBP	SLG
2006	Princeton (APP)	R	.213	50	160	28	34	4	1	1	10	16	38	10	.310	.269
2007	Hudson Valley (NYP)	SS	.242	48	161	21	39	6	4	0	10	20	40	12	.344	.329
2008	Columbus (SAL)	LoA	.237	91	334	48	79	14	3	0	23	34	77	28	.325	.296
MINOR LEAGUE TOTALS			.232	189	655	97	152	24	8	1	43	70	155	50	.326	.298

Texas Rangers

BY AARON FITT

Though the Rangers missed the playoffs for the ninth straight season, 2008 was a success in the broader context of the franchise's long-term vision. Texas remained steadfast in its dedication to rebuilding through scouting and player development, a commitment the organization embraced just before the 2007 trading deadline, when general manager Jon Daniels traded superstar Mark Teixeira and lefthander Ron Mahay to the Braves for a five-player ransom.

That blockbuster looked good for the Rangers at the time, and it looks even better now. Catcher Jarrod Saltalamacchia and lefty Matt Harrison are poised to

become big league regulars after spending large chunks of 2008 in Arlington. Precocious Elvis Andrus performed well beyond his years in Double-A and looks like a franchise shortstop in the making. And best of all, flamethrowing righty Neftali Feliz established himself as one of the best pitching prospects in the minors, rocketing from short-season ball in 2007 to Double-A by the second half of 2008.

Joining Feliz in that ascent to Double-A and to the ranks of elite prospects was lefthander Derek Holland, who saw his velocity spike into the upper 90s by season's end. That duo, combined with the emergence of young Latin American hurlers like Martin Perez, Wilfredo Boscan and Kennil Gomez and the continued steady development of recent first-round picks Michael Main, Blake Beavan and Kasey Kiker gives Texas its deepest stable of high-end pitching prospects ever.

The Rangers also are rich with quality catching, a rare luxury. Saltalamacchia, Taylor Teagarden and Max Ramirez present a catching logjam at the top of the system, while Manuel Pina, Jose Felix, Leonel de los Santos and Tomas Telis offer depth at lower levels. The organization also is stocked with premium athletes (such as outfielders Julio Borbon and Engel Beltre and middle infielders Andrus, Jose Vallejo and Joaquin Arias) and power bats (including first basemen Justin Smoak and Mitch Moreland). Smoak was the first-round pick in Texas' 2008 draft crop, which Baseball America rated No. 1 in the game.

With all that impact talent and depth, it's easy to see why many talent evaluators regard the system as the best in baseball.

Even newly installed team president Nolan Ryan is focused on the farm, instituting new system-wide policies aimed at developing power pitchers. Specifically, Rangers pitching prospects will throw more live batting practice, do more sprinting, and work with

Josh Hamilton gave the Rangers an excellent return for their trade of Edinson Volquez

JOHN WILLIAMSON

TOP 30 PROSPECTS

1. Neftali Feliz, rhp	16. Joe Wieland, rhp
2. Derek Holland, lhp	17. Tommy Hunter, rhp
3. Justin Smoak, 1b	18. Jose Vallejo, 2b
4. Elvis Andrus, ss	19. Kasey Kiker, lhp
5. Martin Perez, lhp	20. Wilmer Font, rhp
6. Taylor Teagarden, c	21. Kennil Gomez, rhp
7. Engel Beltre, of	22. Tim Murphy, lhp
8. Michael Main, rhp	23. Guillermo Moscoso, rhp
9. Julio Borbon, of	24. Omar Poveda, rhp
10. Max Ramirez, c	25. Robbie Ross, lhp
11. Wilfredo Boscan, rhp	26. Greg Golson, of
12. Blake Beavan, rhp	27. Joaquin Arias, 2b/ss
13. Eric Hurley, rhp	28. Thomas Diamond, rhp
14. Warner Madrigal, rhp	29. Clark Murphy, 1b
15. Neil Ramirez, rhp	30. John Bannister, rhp

expanded pitch counts in certain situations.

All the hullaballoo over player development overshadowed the 79-83 major league club, but there were encouraging developments at that level as well. Acquired for Edinson Volquez from the Reds in a trade that was a boon for both teams, Josh Hamilton hit .304 with 32 home runs and an American League-leading 130 RBIs. Rookies Chris Davis and David Murphy combined to slug 32 home runs, and Ian Kinsler turned in an all-star campaign at second base. The Rangers led the majors in scoring (901 runs) but also posted the worst ERA (5.97) in baseball.

General Manager: Jon Daniels. **Farm Director:** Scott Servais. **Scouting Director:** Ron Hopkins.

Class	Team	League	W	L	PCT	Finish*	Manager	Affiliated
Majors	Texas	American	79	83	.488	9th (14)	Ron Washington	—
Triple-A	Oklahoma RedHawks	Pacific Coast	76	68	.528	6th (16)	Bobby Jones	1983
Double-A	Frisco RoughRiders	Texas	84	56	.600	1st (8)	Scott Little	2003
High A	Bakersfield Blaze	California	62	78	.443	9th (10)	Damon Berryhill	2005
Low A	Clinton LumberKings	Midwest	78	59	.569	1st (14)	Mike Micucci	2003
Short-season	Spokane Indians	Northwest	51	25	.671	^1st (8)	Tim Hulett	2003
Rookie	AZL Rangers	Arizona	34	22	.607	3rd (9)	Bill Richardson	2003
Overall 2008 Minor League Record			385	308	.556	2nd		

* Finish in overall standings (No. of teams in league). ^League champion.

LAST YEAR'S TOP 30

Rank	Player, Pos.	Status
1.	Elvis Andrus, ss	No. 4
2.	Chris Davis, 3b	Majors
3.	Eric Hurley, rhp	No. 13
4.	Taylor Teagarden, c	No. 6
5.	Neftali Feliz, rhp	No. 1
6.	Michael Main, rhp	No. 8
7.	Kasey Kiker, lhp	No. 19
8.	Blake Beavan, rhp	No. 12
9.	Julio Borbon, of	No. 9
10.	Engel Beltre, of	No. 7
11.	Omar Poveda, rhp	No. 24
12.	Matt Harrison, lhp	Majors
13.	Neil Ramirez, rhp	No. 15
14.	Fabio Castillo, rhp	Dropped out
15.	Tommy Hunter, rhp	No. 17
16.	German Duran, 2b	Majors
17.	John Mayberry Jr., of	(Phillies)
18.	Wilmer Font, rhp	No. 20
19.	Thomas Diamond, rhp	No. 28
20.	Cristian Santana, c	Dropped out
21.	Johnny Whittleman, 3b	Dropped out
22.	David Murphy, of	Majors
23.	Max Ramirez, c	No. 10
24.	Luis Mendoza, rhp	Majors
25.	Warner Madrigal, rhp	No. 14
26.	Joaquin Arias, ss	No. 27
27.	Zach Phillips, lhp	Dropped out
28.	Jose Vallejo, 2b	No. 18
29.	Brennan Garr, rhp	Dropped out
30.	Armando Galarraga, rhp	(Tigers)

BEST TOOLS

Best Hitter for Average	Max Ramirez
Best Power Hitter	Justin Smoak
Best Strike-Zone Discipline	Justin Smoak
Fastest Baserunner	Greg Golson
Best Athlete	Greg Golson
Best Fastball	Neftali Feliz
Best Curveball	Martin Perez
Best Slider	Warner Madrigal
Best Changeup	Derek Holland
Best Control	Derek Holland
Best Defensive Catcher	Taylor Teagarden
Best Defensive Infielder	Elvis Andrus
Best Infield Arm	Elvis Andrus
Best Defensive Outfielder	David Paisano
Best Outfield Arm	Greg Golson

PROJECTED 2012 LINEUP

Catcher	Taylor Teagarden
First Base	Justin Smoak
Second Base	Ian Kinsler
Third Base	Michael Young
Shortstop	Elvis Andrus
Left Field	Julio Borbon
Center Field	Engel Beltre
Right Field	Josh Hamilton
Designated Hitter	Chris Davis
No. 1 Starter	Neftali Feliz
No. 2 Starter	Derek Holland
No. 3 Starter	Martin Perez
No. 4 Starter	Michael Main
No. 5 Starter	Matt Harrison
Closer	Blake Beavan

TOP PROSPECTS OF THE DECADE

Year	Player, Pos.	2008 Org.
1999	Ruben Mateo, of	Newark (Atlantic)
2000	Ruben Mateo, of	Newark (Atlantic)
2001	Carlos Pena, 1b	Rays
2002	Hank Blalock, 3b	Rangers
2003	Mark Teixeira, 3b	Angels
2004	Adrian Gonzalez, 1b	Padres
2005	Thomas Diamond, rhp	Rangers
2006	Edinson Volquez, rhp	Reds
2007	John Danks, lhp	White Sox
2008	Elvis Andrus, ss	Rangers

TOP DRAFT PICKS OF THE DECADE

Year	Player, Pos.	2008 Org.
1999	Colby Lewis, rhp (1st supp.)	Hiroshima (Japan)
2000	Scott Heard, c	Out of baseball
2001	Mark Teixeira, 3b	Angels
2002	Drew Meyer, ss	Rangers
2003	John Danks, lhp	White Sox
2004	Thomas Diamond, rhp	Rangers
2005	John Mayberry Jr., of	Rangers
2006	Kasey Kiker, lhp	Rangers
2007	Blake Beavan, rhp	Rangers
2008	Justin Smoak, 1b	Rangers

LARGEST BONUSES IN CLUB HISTORY

Mark Teixeira, 2001	$4,500,000
Justin Smoak, 2008	$3,500,000
John Danks, 2003	$2,100,000
Vincent Sinisi, 2003	$2,070,000
Thomas Diamond, 2004	$2,025,000

TEXAS RANGERS

TOP 2009 ROOKIE: Taylor Teagarden, c. After thriving during his first taste of the big leagues late in 2008, he's poised to claim at least a share of the Rangers' catching duties.

BREAKOUT PROSPECT: Joe Wieland, rhp. A projectable strike-thrower with good present stuff, he could emerge as Texas' next blue-chip pitching prospect in 2009.

SLEEPER: Carlos Pimentel, rhp. As an 18-year-old in the Northwest League, the wiry Pimentel came on strong down the stretch, showing a fastball that hit 92 mph, developing offspeed stuff and a fierce desire to succeed.

SOURCE OF TOP 30 TALENT			
Homegrown	22	Acquired	8
College	6	Trades	7
Junior college	0	Rule 5 draft	0
High school	8	Independent leagues	0
Draft-and-follow	1	Free agents/waivers	1
Nondrafted free agents	1		
International	6		

Numbers in parentheses indicate prospect rankings.

LF
Cristian Santana
Mike Bianucci
Tim Smith
Steve Murphy
Jared Bolden

CF
Engel Beltre (7)
Julio Borbon (9)
Greg Golson (26)
David Paisano
Craig Gentry
Hector Martinez
Teodoro Martinez

RF
Esdras Abreu
Ben Harrison
Joey Butler
Guillermo Pimentel

3B
Matt West
Johnny Whittleman

SS
Elvis Andrus (4)
Joaquin Arias (27)
Marcus Lemon
Leury Garcia
Edwin Garcia

2B
Jose Vallejo (18)
Renny Osuna
Edward Martinez

1B
Justin Smoak (3)
Clark Murphy (29)
Mitch Moreland
Chad Tracy
Ian Gac

C
Taylor Teagarden (6)
Max Ramirez (10)
Manuel Pina
Leonel de los Santos
Tomas Telis
Jose Felix
Doug Hogan

RHP		LHP	
Starters	**Relievers**	**Starters**	**Relievers**
Neftali Feliz (1)	Warner Madrigal (14)	Derek Holland (2)	Corey Young
Michael Main (8)	John Bannister (30)	Martin Perez (5)	Geuris Grullon
Wilfredo Boscan (11)	Andrew Laughter	Kasey Kiker (19)	Beau Jones
Blake Beavan (12)	Fabio Castillo	Tim Murphy (22)	Cliff Springston
Eric Hurley (13)	Beau Vaughan	Robbie Ross (25)	
Neil Ramirez (15)	Pedro Strop	Richard Bleier	
Joe Wieland (16)	Brennan Garr	Zach Phillips	
Tommy Hunter (17)	Mark Hamburger	Edwin Escobar	
Wilmer Font (20)	Tanner Roark		
Kennil Gomez (21)	Josh Lueke		
Guillermo Moscoso (23)	Justin Gutsie		
Omar Poveda (24)	Trevor Hurley		
Thomas Diamond (28)			
Carlos Pimentel			
Carlos Melo			
Doug Mathis			

2008

BONUSES: $7.4 MILLION

BEST PURE HITTER: 1B Justin Smoak (1) stands out in a deep crop of Rangers hitters that also includes 1B Clark Murphy (5), OF Mike Bianucci (8), 1B/OF Jared Bolden (9) and OF Joey Butler (15).

BEST POWER HITTER: Smoak offers prodigious power from both sides of the plate. Add in his Gold Glove-caliber defense at first base, and he's reminiscent of former Rangers star Mark Teixeira.

FASTEST RUNNER: Signed as a 24-year-old college senior, OF Rafael Hill (47) is an 8 runner on the 2-8 scouting scale.

BEST DEFENSIVE PLAYER: Smoak. At an up-the-middle position, C Doug Hogan (18) has good catch-and-throw potential. He threw out 37 percent of pro basestealers, though he did have 16 passed balls in 44 games.

BEST FASTBALL: LHPs Robbie Ross (2)—who signed for $1.575 million—and Tim Murphy (3), and RHPs Joe Wieland (4), Matt Thompson (7) and Justin Gutsie (14) all can reach 93-94 mph. Wieland, who's projectable at 6-foot-3 and 175 pounds, could separate himself in the long run.

BEST SECONDARY PITCH: Ross' hard slider or LHP Corey Young's (12) 11-to-5 curveball.

BEST PRO DEBUT: Wieland went 5-1, 1.44 with a 41-8 K-BB ratio in 44 innings in the Rookie-level Arizona League. Clark Murphy hit .358/.435/.526 in the same circuit.

BEST ATHLETE: Butler was a nice senior sign in the 15th round, a 6-foot-2, 210-pounder with solid tools across the board. Hill entered Austin Peay on a football scholarship, and he rushed for 466 yards and five touchdowns as a freshman before deciding to concentrate on baseball.

MOST INTRIGUING BACKGROUND: C Ben Petralli's (33) father Geno and unsigned RHP Jack Armstrong's (36) dad Jack Sr. both played for the Rangers. Petralli's contract was voided in the offseason because he had an elbow injury. Unsigned OF John Ruettiger (35), now at Arizona State) is the nephew of Dan "Rudy" Ruettiger, the Notre Dame walk-on of movie fame.

CLOSEST TO THE MAJORS: Smoak, who batted .304/.355/.518 in a brief stint in low Class A, may not need more than a year in the minors. Young's curveball could take him to the majors quickly as a lefty specialist. Given Texas' constant need for pitching, Tim

Murphy also could move fast as a starter.

BEST LATE-ROUND PICK: Butler and Young.

THE ONE WHO GOT AWAY: The Rangers, who went over slot to sign Smoak, Ross, Clark Murphy, Thompson and Bianucci, also made a serious run at both Armstrong and 3B Harold Martinez (19). After three years at Vanderbilt, Armstrong could join his father as a first-round pick. He's projectable at 6-foot-6 and already touches 93 mph. Martinez projected as a first-rounder entering 2008 but didn't live up to expectations as a high school senior, and he's now at Miami.

ASSESSMENT: Though they cost a combined $5.075 million, getting Smoak at No. 11 and Ross at No. 57 were big scores by the Rangers. Texas also got several other polished hitters and promising arms, adding depth to baseball's best farm system.

2007

BONUSES: $6.6 MILLION

The Rangers had five picks before the second round and are pleased with all of them: RHPs Blake Beavan (1), Michael Main (1), Neil Ramirez (1s) and Tommy Hunter (1s), and OF Julio Borbon (1s).

GRADE: B+

2006

BONUSES: $4.3 MILLION

LHP Kasey Kiker (1) has promise but has been surpassed by two later-round steals: 1B Chris Davis (5), who hit 17 homers in a half-season with Texas, and LHP Derek Holland (25), now one of the game's top lefty pitching prospects.

GRADE: A

2005

BONUSES: $3.9 MILLION*

C Taylor Teagarden (3) may emerge from the Rangers' logjam of catchers to become their starter. OF John Mayberry Jr. (1) didn't develop as quickly as hoped, and Texas traded him in November.

GRADE: C+

2004

BONUSES: $5.0 MILLION*

RHP Eric Hurley (1) made his big league debut in 2008, while RHP Thomas Diamond (1) began his comeback from Tommy John surgery. OF Brandon Boggs (4) was a semi-regular for Texas last year.

GRADE: C

*Draft analysis by Jim Callis. Numbers in parentheses indicate draft rounds. *Bonuses for 2004-05 are first 10 rounds only.*

BRIAN BISSELL

NEFTALI FELIZ, RHP

Born: May 2, 1988.
Ht.: 6-3. **Wt.:** 180.
Bats: R. **Throws:** R.
Signed: Dominican Republic, 2005.
Signed by: Julian Perez/Roberto Aquino (Braves).

Signed by the Braves for $100,000 out of the Dominican Republic, Feliz burst onto the prospect landscape in his U.S. debut in 2006, running his fastball up to 97 mph and striking out 42 in 29 innings as an 18-year-old in the Rookie-level Gulf Coast League. The following summer, he was dealt to the Rangers along with Jarrod Saltalamacchia, Elvis Andrus, Matt Harrison and Beau Jones in exchange for Mark Teixeira and Ron Mahay. He opened his first full season with Texas at low Class A Clinton, where he overpowered Midwest League hitters. The Rangers say they skipped him to Double-A Frisco in July in order to challenge him to command his secondary stuff better against more advanced hitters. He continued to thrive as a 20-year-old against much older players, finishing the year with a minor league-leading 10.8 strikeouts per nine innings between the two levels.

Feliz's fastball might rate as a true 80 pitch on the 20-80 scouting scale. At Clinton, it sat at 94-96 mph and touched 99, and at Frisco it topped out at 101 mph. More impressive, Feliz does it effortlessly, and the ball explodes out of his hand with natural boring life. When he maintains a high three-quarters arm slot, he also gets a good downhill angle on his heater. His secondary pitches both have potential. He throws a power curveball that sometimes reaches 83-84 mph, and it's a plus pitch with 11-to-5 break when he stays on top of it. He shows feel for an 85-87 mph changeup with good fading action. Feliz is a natural athlete who fields his position well. He has a physical, durable frame and an easy arm action, suggesting he should be able to shoulder a significant workload without breaking down. He also has a confident mound presence, and his between-starts routine improved in 2008, demonstrating his continuing maturation.

Sometimes Feliz drops his arm slot, causing his stuff to flatten out. He's still fine-tuning his breaking ball, which can become a slurve. The pitch was suspect early in the season at Clinton, but he made strides with it late in the year. He slows down his arm action at times with his changeup, and the Rangers still have to force him to throw it. He doesn't have pinpoint fastball command—team president Nolan Ryan worked with him during instructional league on locating his fastball down and away—but throwing strikes and pitching to the bottom of the zone come naturally to him. Feliz also worked hard in instructional league on quickening his delivery and varying his times to the plate so he could control the running game better. Opponents stole 32 bases in 38 tries against him last season.

With perhaps the most overpowering fastball in the minors and the makings of two quality offspeed pitches, Feliz has a chance to be a legitimate No. 1 starter. Rather than pitch in winter ball, he worked out at the Rangers' academy in the Dominican Republic, and he'll get a look in big league camp in spring training. He'll probably open 2009 back in the minors, with a callup to Texas possible in the second half.

Year	Club (League)	Class	W	L	ERA	G	GS	CG	SV	IP	H	R	ER	HR	BB	SO	AVG
2005	Braves1 (DSL)	R	0	0	3.60	10	0	0	0	10	7	4	4	0	11	8	.184
2006	Braves (GCL)	R	0	2	4.03	11	5	0	2	29	20	13	13	0	14	42	.192
2007	Danville (APP)	R	2	0	1.98	8	7	0	0	27	18	8	6	0	12	28	.191
	Spokane (NWL)	SS	0	2	3.60	8	1	0	0	15	13	8	6	2	12	27	.228
2008	Clinton (MWL)	LoA	6	3	2.52	17	17	0	0	82	55	25	23	2	28	106	.193
	Frisco (TEX)	AA	4	3	2.98	10	10	0	0	45	34	16	15	1	23	47	.217
MINOR LEAGUE TOTALS			12	10	2.89	64	40	0	2	209	147	74	67	5	100	258	.200

2 DEREK HOLLAND, LHP

BORN: Oct. 9, 1986. **B-T:** B-L. **HT.:** 6-2. **WT.:** 185. **DRAFTED:** Wallace State (Ala.) CC, D/F 2006 (25th round). **SIGNED BY:** Rick Schroeder/Jeff Wood.

Texas took a flier on Holland in the 2006 draft at the recommendation of former area scout Rick Schroeder, who spotted him at the Junior College World Series. Signed for $200,000 as a draft-and-follow, he took off in his first full season, earning Rangers minor league pitcher of the year honors. Holland started the year with an 89-93 mph fastball in Clinton, but his velocity spiked at midseason and he was sitting at 94-95 and touching 97-98 in the Texas League playoffs. His slightly across-the-body delivery and excellent extension give his fastball deception and late life, making it a plus-plus offering. He can blow it by hitters up in the zone or command it down. Holland's second pitch is a slightly above-average 81-83 changeup with good arm speed and fade. He's confident enough to use it in any count. Holland occasionally flashes an average 78-81 mph slider, but it needs to become more consistent and he must learn how and when to use it. It should become a solid third pitch because he shows the ability to throw it for strikes. He's still not overly physical and must prove he can maintain his exceptional fastball over a full season. Holland has a chance to be a frontline starter along the lines of Scott Kazmir. He figures to start 2009 back in Double-A but could reach Texas by season's end.

Year	Club (League)	Class	W	L	ERA	G	GS	CG	SV	IP	H	R	ER	HR	BB	SO	AVG
2007	Spokane (NWL)	SS	4	5	3.22	16	14	0	0	67	57	33	24	7	21	83	.224
2008	Clinton (MWL)	LoA	7	0	2.40	17	17	0	0	94	77	30	25	2	29	91	.228
	Bakersfield (CAL)	HiA	3	1	3.19	5	5	0	0	31	20	12	11	1	5	37	.185
	Frisco (TEX)	AA	3	0	0.69	4	4	0	0	26	14	4	2	0	6	29	.163
MINOR LEAGUE TOTALS			17	6	2.56	42	40	0	0	218	168	79	62	10	61	240	.213

3 JUSTIN SMOAK, 1B

BILL MITCHELL

BORN: Dec. 5, 1986. **B-T:** B-L. **HT.:** 6-3. **WT.:** 200. **DRAFTED:** South Carolina, 2008 (1st round). **SIGNED BY:** Jim Cuthbert.

A high school teammate of Orioles catcher Matt Wieters in Goose Creek, S.C., Smoak started every game during his three-year college career at South Carolina, where he set Gamecocks career records with 62 homers and 207 RBIs. The Rangers were elated to get him with the 11th overall pick in 2008, signing him an hour before the Aug. 15 deadline for $3.5 million. As a switch-hitter with well-above-average power from both sides of the plate and Gold Glove potential at first base, Smoak draws comparisons to former Rangers first baseman Mark Teixeira. Like Teixeira, Smoak is a patient hitter who punishes off-speed stuff as well as fastballs and uses the entire field. He's a hard worker and a good teammate. Smoak has below-average speed and will always be somewhat of a baseclogger, though he's an intelligent runner. Like most switch-hitters, he's better from the left side. Defensively, he still needs to improve his footwork and get used to the speed of the pro game. One of the most advanced hitters in the 2008 draft, Smoak could fly through the Rangers system. He will start his first full season at high Class A Bakersfield and could be entrenched in the big leagues by 2010. He projects as a middle-of-the-order power hitter and has a chance to be a superstar.

Year	Club (League)	Class	AVG	G	AB	R	H	2B	3B	HR	RBI	BB	SO	SB	OBP	SLG
2008	Clinton (MWL)	LoA	.304	14	56	9	17	3	0	3	6	5	10	0	.355	.518
MINOR LEAGUE TOTALS			.304	14	56	9	17	3	0	3	6	5	10	0	.355	.518

4 ELVIS ANDRUS, SS

JOHN SPEAR

BORN: Aug. 26, 1988. **B-T:** R-R. **HT.:** 6-0. **WT.:** 185. **SIGNED:** Venezuela, 2005. **SIGNED BY:** Rolando Petit/Julian Perez (Braves).

A key piece in the Mark Teixeira trade with the Braves, Andrus more than held his own as a teenager in Double-A during his first full season with the Rangers. He tried to play through a broken finger on his right hand early in the year—a major reason for his 11 errors in May—before Texas shut him down for two weeks. He came back strong, hitting .311 over the last three months, then spent the winter playing alongside older brother Erold in the Venezuelan League. With plus range, sure hands, a strong, accurate arm and uncanny instincts, Andrus has all the tools to be a premium defensive shortstop. His above-average speed plays up even more on the bases, where he has learned how to get good jumps, run in breaking ball counts and even steal third base. He has a knack for putting the bat on the ball and getting big hits. His makeup is off the charts. Andrus never will have better than below-average power, but he should be able to drive balls to the gaps if he can get stronger and understand his swing better. He has a tendency to lunge on his front foot at the plate. Andrus sometimes relaxes too much on routine plays, helping account for his 32 errors in 2008. Andrus will be one of the youngest players in the Triple-A Pacific Coast League in 2009, and he seems on schedule for a 2010 arrival in Texas. He profiles as an all-star-caliber shortstop in the Edgar Renteria mold.

Year	Club (League)	Class	AVG	G	AB	R	H	2B	3B	HR	RBI	BB	SO	SB	OBP	SLG
2005	Braves (GCL)	R	.295	46	166	26	49	6	1	3	20	19	28	7	.377	.398
	Danville (APP)	R	.278	6	18	3	5	1	0	0	1	4	4	1	.409	.333
2006	Rome (SAL)	LoA	.265	111	437	67	116	25	4	3	50	36	91	23	.324	.362
2007	Myrtle Beach (CAR)	HiA	.244	99	385	59	94	20	3	3	37	44	88	25	.330	.335
	Bakersfield (CAL)	HiA	.300	27	110	19	33	2	0	2	12	10	19	15	.369	.373
2008	Frisco (TEX)	AA	.295	118	482	82	142	19	2	4	65	38	91	54	.350	.367
MINOR LEAGUE TOTALS			.275	407	1598	256	439	73	10	15	185	151	321	125	.343	.361

5 MARTIN PEREZ, LHP

BORN: April 4, 1991. **B-T:** L-L. **HT.:** 6-0. **WT.:** 165. **SIGNED:** Venezuela, 2007. **SIGNED BY:** Rafic Saab/Manny Batista/Don Welke.

Texas signed Perez for $580,000, with one club official likening him to Ron Guidry and dubbing him "The Venezuelan Gator." During his pro debut he more than held his own against older competition, ranking as the top pitching prospect in the short-season Northwest League. Perez has a compact delivery and a clean arm action that produces 90-94 mph fastballs with life down in the zone. His tight, late-breaking curveball has good depth, giving him a second plus pitch. He has advanced command of both, and he does a good job pitching out of jams. He's fearless on the mound and mature beyond his years. Perez's change-up is a below-average pitch, but he has good feel for it. He's not big or physical, so his long-term durability could be a question. One scout said his arm action, ability to pitch on a downward plane and power repertoire reminded him of Johan Santana. The Rangers, however, would like to temper the enthusiasm about a pitcher so young and far from the majors. He'll probably begin 2009 on a strict pitch count at their new low Class A Hickory affiliate.

Year	Club (League)	Class	W	L	ERA	G	GS	CG	SV	IP	H	R	ER	HR	BB	SO	AVG
2008	Spokane (NWL)	SS	1	2	3.65	15	15	0	0	62	66	32	25	3	28	53	.274
MINOR LEAGUE TOTALS			1	2	3.65	15	15	0	0	62	66	32	25	3	28	53	.274

6 TAYLOR TEAGARDEN, C

BORN: Dec. 21, 1983. **B-T:** R-R. **HT.:** 6-1. **WT.:** 200. **DRAFTED:** Texas, 2005 (3rd round). **SIGNED BY:** Randy Taylor.

Two years removed from Tommy John surgery, Teagarden showed up to major league camp healthy and homered in his first at-bat last spring, only to miss three weeks with a wrist injury. The layoff hurt his offense in the first half of the season, but didn't stop him from earning spots in the Futures Game and on the U.S. Olympic team, as well as his first major league callup. Teagarden's receiving, blocking and throwing all rate as above-average. He has excellent recall and pitchers are comfortable with his game-calling. Offensively, he has solid-average power and a patient approach. Texas was disappointed with Teagarden's bat for most of 2008, and many in the organization doubt he'll ever hit for average. There's length in his stroke and he tends to swing through fastballs. He also strikes out quite a bit, a by-product of the deep counts he often finds himself in. With his defense, leadership and power potential, Teagarden profiles as a solid everyday big league catcher and perhaps an all-star. The Rangers have several candidates, but he could get a shot at their starting job in 2009.

Year	Club (League)	Class	AVG	G	AB	R	H	2B	3B	HR	RBI	BB	SO	SB	OBP	SLG
2005	Spokane (NWL)	SS	.281	31	96	23	27	5	4	7	16	23	32	1	.426	.635
2006	Rangers (AZL)	R	.050	7	20	4	1	0	0	0	1	9	7	1	.345	.050
2007	Bakersfield (CAL)	HiA	.315	81	292	75	92	25	0	20	67	65	89	2	.448	.606
	Frisco (TEX)	AA	.294	29	102	19	30	3	0	7	16	10	39	0	.357	.529
2008	Frisco (TEX)	AA	.169	16	59	6	10	2	0	2	6	8	23	1	.279	.305
	Oklahoma (PCL)	AAA	.225	57	187	26	42	5	3	7	16	28	59	0	.332	.396
	Texas (AL)	MAJ	.319	16	47	10	15	5	0	6	17	5	19	0	.396	.809
MINOR LEAGUE TOTALS			.267	221	756	153	202	40	7	43	122	143	249	5	.390	.509
MAJOR LEAGUE TOTALS			.319	16	47	10	15	5	0	6	17	5	19	0	.396	.809

7 ENGEL BELTRE, OF

BORN: Nov. 1, 1989. **B-T:** L-L. **HT.:** 6-1. **WT.:** 169. **SIGNED:** Dominican Republic, 2006. **SIGNED BY:** Pablo Lantigua (Red Sox).

The Red Sox signed Beltre for $600,000 in 2006 and sent him to Texas along with Kason Gabbard and David Murphy for Eric Gagne at the 2007 trading deadline. In his first full season with the Rangers, Beltre led the Midwest League in runs (87) and hits (160) despite being the circuit's youngest player. He ranked as the league's No. 6 prospect. Beltre's five-tool package has garnered comparisons to big leaguers from Barry Bonds to Kenny Lofton to Andruw Jones. His wiry-strong frame and quick bat easily generate above-average raw power, and his plus speed is an asset on the basepaths and in the outfield. His arm, which rates as a 55 on the 20-80 scouting scale, and his good instincts could make him a premium defender in center. He's a high-energy player and a natural leader. Beltre is aggressive in all phases and sometimes has trouble slowing the game down. He's a free swinger who must improve his patience and pitch selection. While he can punish balls out of the zone at times, he'll have to force more advanced pitchers to throw him strikes. Beltre remains raw but his development is well ahead of schedule and his upside is enormous. Down the road, he could be a five-tool superstar center fielder. He'll advance to high Class A in 2009 and could reach the majors before he turns 22.

Year	Club (League)	Class	AVG	G	AB	R	H	2B	3B	HR	RBI	BB	SO	SB	OBP	SLG
2007	Red Sox (GCL)	R	.208	34	125	20	26	3	3	5	13	12	44	6	.310	.400
	Rangers (AZL)	R	.310	22	84	19	26	3	4	4	15	8	21	3	.388	.583
	Spokane (NWL)	SS	.211	9	38	3	8	0	0	0	1	2	10	2	.250	.211
2008	Clinton (MWL)	LoA	.283	130	566	87	160	26	9	8	47	15	105	31	.308	.403
MINOR LEAGUE TOTALS			.271	195	813	129	220	32	16	17	76	37	180	42	.315	.412

8 MICHAEL MAIN, RHP

BORN: Dec. 14, 1988. **B-T:** R-R. **HT.:** 6-2. **WT.:** 170. **DRAFTED:** HS—DeLand, Fla., 2007 (1st round). **SIGNED BY:** Guy DeMutis.

The 24th overall pick in the 2007 draft, Main signed for $1,237,500. He felt discomfort in his side at the start of spring training in 2008, causing his arm slot to drop and his stuff to suffer, and an X-ray revealed a cracked rib that sidelined him until late June. He returned to pitch well in low Class A in the second half, then stood out in instructional league in the fall. When the Rangers introduced Main to an over-the-head windup to help generate more momentum, his velocity spiked to 92-96 mph in instructional league. He commands his fastball to both halves of the plate, and his tight downer curveball could give him a second plus offering in the future. He's a premium athlete—garnering pro interest as a center fielder—and his athleticism helps him repeat his delivery and throw strikes. He's intelligent and unflappable on the mound. Main still needs to add strength to his slight frame in order to improve his durability. He has good feel for his changeup, which should become an average pitch in time, but right now it lags behind his other two offerings. Main's electric arm could make him a frontline starter after a few years of development. He'll open 2009 with one of Texas' Class A affiliates.

Year	Club (League)	Class	W	L	ERA	G	GS	CG	SV	IP	H	R	ER	HR	BB	SO	AVG
2007	Rangers (AZL)	R	0	1	1.42	5	5	0	0	13	9	2	2	1	6	16	.196
	Spokane (NWL)	SS	2	0	4.70	5	5	0	0	15	14	11	8	1	7	18	.237
2008	Rangers (AZL)	R	1	1	3.38	3	3	0	0	13	9	8	5	1	5	15	.188
	Clinton (MWL)	LoA	2	2	2.58	10	10	0	0	45	38	16	13	4	13	50	.228
MINOR LEAGUE TOTALS			5	4	2.91	23	23	0	0	87	70	37	28	7	31	99	.219

9 JULIO BORBON, OF

BORN: Feb. 20, 1986. **B-T:** L-L. **HT.:** 6-1. **WT.:** 190. **DRAFTED:** Tennessee, 2007 (1st round supplemental). **SIGNED BY:** Jeff Wood.

A 2007 supplemental first-rounder who got a $1.3 million major league contract, Borbon was hampered by a minor leg injury in April. The Rangers liked how he learned to be effective while less than 100 percent, and he hit .321 with 53 steals while reaching Double-A in his first full pro season. Borbon learned to take more advantage of his plus-plus speed in 2008. More pull-oriented in the past, he did a better job using the whole field and keeping the ball on the ground, and he developed a much better feel for bunting. He has strength in his line-drive swing and will hit a few homers. He also worked hard with Rangers outfield instructor Wayne Kirby on improving his jumps and reads in center field, where he can become a plus defender. Though he made progress with his offensive approach, Borbon still needs to work counts better and take more walks. He's learning to pick his spots on the basepaths and how to get good jumps after getting caught 11 times in 28 steal attempts in Double-A. He has a below-average arm, though his accuracy and transfer have improved. Borbon profiles as a slashing leadoff man and solid center fielder in the Johnny Damon mold. He could compete for a big league job by 2010.

Year	Club (League)	Class	AVG	G	AB	R	H	2B	3B	HR	RBI	BB	SO	SB	OBP	SLG
2007	Spokane (NWL)	SS	.172	7	29	1	5	0	0	0	2	2	3	3	.226	.172
	Rangers (AZL)	R	.250	2	8	0	2	1	0	0	0	1	1	0	.333	.375
2008	Bakersfield (CAL)	HiA	.306	66	291	47	89	20	0	2	36	15	30	36	.346	.395
	Frisco (TEX)	AA	.337	60	255	40	86	12	2	5	22	14	32	17	.380	.459
MINOR LEAGUE TOTALS			.312	135	583	88	182	33	2	7	60	32	66	56	.355	.412

10 MAX RAMIREZ, C

BORN: Oct. 11, 1984. **B-T:** R-R. **HT.:** 5-11. **WT.:** 175. **SIGNED:** Venezuela, 2002. **SIGNED BY:** Rolando Petit (Braves).

Ramirez was traded from Atlanta to Cleveland for Bob Wickman in mid-2006, then shipped to Texas for Kenny Lofton a year later. He spent the first half of 2008 in a catcher/DH platoon with Taylor Teagarden before getting his first big league callup when injuries hit the Rangers in late June. Ramirez is a gifted natural hitter who works the count and drives the ball to all fields. His setup has a lot of movement before he gets into hitting position, yet he commands the zone well and is a good two-strike hitter. For the first time in his career, he began unlocking his plus raw power in 2008. Scouts question whether Ramirez can stay behind the plate, where his arm is fringy, his release is slow, his hands are stiff and his agility is below-average. His well-below-average speed could sabotage his chances of being a .300 hitter in the majors. Ramirez played some first base in 2008 to improve his versatility, and his future might be as a first baseman/DH/fill-in catcher. Wherever he plays, Ramirez should hit enough to be a solid big league regular, perhaps as soon as 2009.

Year	Club (League)	Class	AVG	G	AB	R	H	2B	3B	HR	RBI	BB	SO	SB	OBP	SLG
2003	Braves2 (DSL)	R	.305	52	177	27	54	16	1	5	43	20	27	5	.386	.492
2004	Braves (GCL)	R	.275	57	204	20	56	16	1	8	35	19	50	1	.339	.480
2005	Danville (APP)	R	.347	63	239	45	83	19	0	8	47	31	41	1	.424	.527
2006	Rome (SAL)	LoA	.285	80	267	50	76	17	0	9	37	54	72	2	.408	.449
	Lake County (SAL)	LoA	.307	37	127	19	39	6	1	4	26	30	27	0	.435	.465
2007	Kinston (CAR)	HiA	.303	77	277	46	84	20	0	12	62	53	63	1	.418	.505
	Bakersfield (CAL)	HiA	.307	32	114	16	35	10	0	4	20	21	39	1	.420	.500
2008	Frisco (TEX)	AA	.354	69	243	49	86	16	2	17	50	37	56	2	.450	.646
	Rangers (AZL)	R	.800	2	5	4	4	2	0	0	1	2	0	0	.857	1.200
	Oklahoma (PCL)	AAA	.243	10	37	5	9	1	0	2	6	3	13	0	.293	.432
	Texas (AL)	MAJ	.217	17	46	8	10	1	0	2	9	6	15	0	.345	.370
MINOR LEAGUE TOTALS			.311	479	1690	281	526	123	5	69	327	270	388	13	.410	.512
MAJOR LEAGUE TOTALS			.217	17	46	8	10	1	0	2	9	6	15	0	.345	.370

11 WILFREDO BOSCAN, RHP

BORN: Oct. 26, 1989. **B-T:** R-R. **HT.:** 6-2. **WT.:** 160. **SIGNED:** Venezuela, 2007. **SIGNED BY:** Manny Batista.

Boscan was a skinny 17-year-old with an 82-83 mph fastball when he signed in 2007, and his stuff quickly improved. He always has filled up the strike zone—Rangers international scouting director A.J. Preller remembers seeing him throw 60 strikes in a 73-pitch, eight-inning outing in the Rookie-level Dominican Summer League during his debut—and his velocity jumped to 86-92 mph at short-season Spokane in 2008. Boscan has a strong, wiry frame and a loose, easy arm action that suggest he could have a plus fastball in the future. He already shows the ability to touch 93 mph when he needs a big pitch with two strikes. He locates his fastball well to both sides of the plate and can run it back across the outside corner against lefthanders. Boscan also has superb feel for a tumbling, fading changeup that projects as a true plus pitch and already is at times. He throws strikes with his improving curveball, though sometimes his high arm slot drops to three-quarters when he throws it, causing it to get slurvy. Still, it's easy to project his curve as another average pitch, if not a tick better. Boscan's command of all three pitches is advanced for his age. If he adds velocity as he fills out, he could become a frontline starter, and his feel for pitching is good enough that he could succeed in the majors with an average fastball. He should open 2009 in low Class A and could move fairly quickly.

Year	Club (League)	Class	W	L	ERA	G	GS	CG	SV	IP	H	R	ER	HR	BB	SO	AVG
2007	Rangers (DSL)	R	2	1	1.75	13	8	0	0	57	42	14	11	1	13	61	.210
2008	Spokane (NWL)	SS	9	1	3.12	15	12	0	0	69	66	30	24	4	11	70	.251
MINOR LEAGUE TOTALS			11	2	2.50	28	20	0	0	126	108	44	35	5	24	131	.233

12 BLAKE BEAVAN, RHP

BORN: Jan. 17, 1989. **B-T:** R-R. **HT.:** 6-7. **WT.:** 210. **DRAFTED:** HS—Irving, Texas, 2007 (1st round). **SIGNED BY:** Jay Eddings.

Pitching just once a week in high school, Beavan routinely ran his fastball up to 95-96 mph, helping him capture Baseball America's 2006 Youth Player of the Year award and anchor the U.S. junior national team's pitching staff. But after he signed for $1,497,500 as the 17th overall pick in the 2007 draft, his stuff was down for most of his first full pro season in 2008. The good news is that he learned how to succeed without overpowering hitters. He also matured significantly, learning how to deal with the media and be a good teammate. Beavan's fastball sat around 89-91 for most of the year, and he had a tendency to drop his elbow and pitch from a low three-quarters slot, causing his fastball to run but not sink. He worked hard to repeat a higher arm slot and pitch downhill, and to use his height to create more momentum in his delivery. Beavan's velocity climbed back to 93-95 mph in shorter stints during instructional league, and he began filling out his frame, particularly his lower half. He needs to add power to his slider, which tends to break too early out of his hand and often gets slurvy. He flashes an average changeup but is still learning to pitch with it. Beavan never has been afraid to challenge hitters, and perhaps his best asset is his ability to pound the strike zone. With a big, physical frame and the guts to match, Beavan projects as at least an innings-eating sinkerballer or perhaps a late-inning reliever. If his stuff bounces back, his ceiling will be even higher. He'll remain a starter for the foreseeable future and should advance to high Class A in 2009.

Year	Club (League)	Class	W	L	ERA	G	GS	CG	SV	IP	H	R	ER	HR	BB	SO	AVG
2008	Clinton (MWL)	LoA	10	6	2.37	23	23	0	0	122	105	42	32	12	20	73	.234
MINOR LEAGUE TOTALS			10	6	2.37	23	23	0	0	122	105	42	32	12	20	73	.234

13 ERIC HURLEY, RHP

BORN: Sept. 17, 1985. **B-T:** R-R. **HT.:** 6-4. **WT.:** 195. **DRAFTED:** HS—Jacksonville, 2004 (1st round). **SIGNED BY:** Guy DeMutis.

After failing to make the Texas rotation out of spring training, Hurley struggled at Triple-A Oklahoma in April but started to pitch better in May, earning his first career big league callup when injuries struck the Rangers in June. He made four starts, trying to get by with a depleted 88-90 mph fastball before taking two weeks off with shoulder inflammation. He returned to throw 7 1/3 shutout innings in a Double-A rehab start in mid-July, then tweaked his hamstring while running and missed two more weeks. He returned to make one more disastrous start in late July against Oakland, showing an 84-88 mph fastball and a soft spinner of a slider, and the Rangers decided to shut him down for the rest of the year. They made him the 30th overall pick in the 2004 draft, signing him for $1.05 million. Even at full strength, Hurley has a history of pitching around 88-91 early in games, leaving him vulnerable against quality hitters, before dialing his fastball up to 93-95 by the middle innings. At his best, he features a pair of above-average pitches with his sinker and his firm slider with good depth, but he lacked his best stuff in 2008. He did, however, get comfortable with his grip on a split-changeup, finally giving him a solid weapon against lefthanders. After an offseason spent strengthening his shoulder, Hurley will hope he's 100 percent for spring training, when he should vie for a starting rotation spot again. He still has a chance to be a solid mid-rotation starter.

Year	Club (League)	Class	W	L	ERA	G	GS	CG	SV	IP	H	R	ER	HR	BB	SO	AVG
2004	Rangers (AZL)	R	0	1	2.35	6	2	0	0	15	20	8	4	1	4	15	.317
	Spokane (NWL)	SS	0	2	5.40	8	6	0	0	28	31	18	17	6	6	21	.295
2005	Clinton (MWL)	LoA	12	6	3.77	28	28	0	0	155	135	72	65	11	59	152	.234
2006	Bakersfield (CAL)	HiA	5	6	4.11	18	18	1	0	101	92	60	46	12	32	106	.239
	Frisco (TEX)	AA	3	1	1.95	6	6	0	0	37	21	9	8	4	11	31	.168
2007	Frisco (TEX)	AA	7	2	3.25	15	14	1	0	89	71	39	32	13	27	76	.219
	Oklahoma City (PCL)	AAA	4	7	4.91	13	13	0	0	73	65	45	40	13	28	59	.236
2008	Oklahoma (PCL)	AAA	2	5	5.30	13	13	0	0	75	86	51	44	15	29	72	.285
	Frisco (TEX)	AA	1	0	0.00	1	1	0	0	7	4	0	0	0	1	2	.174
	Texas (AL)	MAJ	1	2	5.47	5	5	0	0	25	26	15	15	5	9	13	.268
MINOR LEAGUE TOTALS			34	30	3.97	108	101	2	0	581	525	302	256	75	197	534	.241
MAJOR LEAGUE TOTALS			1	2	5.47	5	5	0	0	25	26	15	15	5	9	13	.268

14 WARNER MADRIGAL, RHP

BORN: March 21, 1984. **B-T:** R-R. **HT.:** 6-0. **WT.:** 200. **SIGNED:** Dominican Republic, 2001. **SIGNED BY:** Leo Perez (Angels).

The Angels converted Madrigal from the outfield to the mound after his disappointing 2006 season with the bat, and the move paid immediate dividends. But after his breakout 2007 season at low Class A, they failed to place him on the 40-man roster before the end of the World Series, inadvertently making him a minor league free agent, and the Rangers pounced on him. He skipped a level and started 2008 in Double-A and spent the entire second half of the season in the majors after injuries hit the Texas bullpen. After posting a 7.94 ERA in July, he compiled a 3.28 mark the rest of the way, and the biggest difference was his secondary stuff. He added velocity to his slider, which often graded as a plus pitch after he boosted it to 84-86 mph. He also got comfortable late in the season with a splitter, an above-average pitch at times with late downer action and fade. His bread-and-butter remains his fastball, which sits at 93-94 mph and touches 95-96. His heater is rather straight and gets hit when he leaves it up in the zone, so the development of his secondary stuff was crucial. Madrigal has an aggressive mentality, a durable frame and a repeatable delivery. He'll stay in the big league bullpen in 2009, probably in a middle-relief or setup role. He has a chance to be a closer at some point if he can keep his fastball down and command his secondary stuff.

Year	Club (League)	Class	W	L	ERA	G	GS	CG	SV	IP	H	R	ER	HR	BB	SO	AVG
2006	Angels (AZL)	R	2	1	3.75	12	0	0	5	12	11	5	5	0	3	13	.250
2007	Cedar Rapids (MWL)	LoA	5	4	2.07	54	0	0	20	61	44	18	14	3	23	75	.202
2008	Frisco (TEX)	AA	1	0	1.72	14	0	0	10	16	11	4	3	1	8	18	.200
	Oklahoma (PCL)	AAA	0	0	3.98	17	0	0	4	20	20	10	9	2	8	25	.247
	Texas (AL)	MAJ	0	2	4.75	31	1	0	1	36	36	22	19	4	14	22	.263
MINOR LEAGUE TOTALS			8	5	2.56	97	0	0	39	109	86	37	31	6	42	131	.216
MAJOR LEAGUE TOTALS			0	2	4.75	31	1	0	1	36	36	22	19	4	14	22	.263

15 NEIL RAMIREZ, RHP

BORN: May 25, 1989. **B-T:** R-R. **HT.:** 6-4. **WT.:** 190. **DRAFTED:** HS—Kempsville, Va., 2007 (1st round supplemental). **SIGNED BY:** Russ Ardolina.

Ramirez accepted a $1 million bonus as a supplemental first-round pick right at the signing deadline in 2007, too late to make his pro debut. The Rangers wanted to challenge him in 2008, so they skipped him over the Rookie-level Arizona League and sent him to Spokane, where he was the Opening Day starter. Though his strict pitch count limited him to fewer than five innings in 11 of his 13 starts, Ramirez mostly overpowered older hitters and ranked as the Northwest League's No. 4 prospect. He has an ultra-projectable frame and an electric arm. He pitches at 91-94 mph and touches 96, and his fastball plays up further because it jumps on hitters. He's capable of buckling hitters' knees with a hard, late-breaking downer curveball that projects as an above-average or better pitch, but it remains inconsistent. While his changeup is improving, he still has limited feel for it. Ramirez sometimes has trouble getting his delivery in sync, as his arm gets deep behind him and he throws across his body. His difficulty repeating his motion negatively affects his fastball command, and he tends to run up high pitch counts. He missed the chance to work on his shortcomings in instructional league because he broke a bone in his hand when he slammed it in a car door. Ramirez has one of the highest ceilings in the system. If everything comes together for him, he could become a true ace with a pair of plus-plus pitches. But concerns over his delivery and command make him far from a safe bet to reach his upside. He'll start 2009 in low Class A.

Year	Club (League)	Class	W	L	ERA	G	GS	CG	SV	IP	H	R	ER	HR	BB	SO	AVG
2008	Spokane (NWL)	SS	1	2	2.66	13	13	0	0	44	25	15	13	5	29	52	.166
MINOR LEAGUE TOTALS			1	2	2.66	13	13	0	0	44	25	15	13	5	29	52	.166

16 JOE WIELAND, RHP

BORN: Jan. 21, 1990. **B-T:** R-R. **HT.:** 6-3. **WT.:** 175. **DRAFTED:** HS—Reno, Nev., 2008 (4th round). **SIGNED BY:** Butch Metzger.

Wieland is the latest quality pitcher to come out of the Reno area, following in the footsteps of the Rays' Jake McGee and the Braves' Cole Rohrbough. Area scouts compared his stuff and command to that of a young Mark Prior. A quality athlete, Wieland had committed to San Diego State as a two-way player but chose instead to sign with the Rangers for $263,000 as a fourth-round pick. His maturity and professional approach stood out during his pro debut in the Rookie-level Arizona League, as he impressed in his side sessions and had no problems during games. His fastball velocity climbed from 88-91 mph in high school to 90-93 in the AZL. His projectable frame, smooth yet deceptive delivery and easy arm action lead the Rangers to believe he will throw harder as he continues to develop. Wieland pounds the bottom of the zone with his fastball, a curveball that projects as a plus pitch and an improving changeup. He made significant strides with both secondary pitches after he was drafted, though both must continue to develop. As a fairly advanced strike-thrower, he could start his first full pro season in low Class A, just as Blake Beavan did in 2008. Wieland has a chance to be a No. 2 or 3 starter down the line.

Year	Club (League)	Class	W	L	ERA	G	GS	CG	SV	IP	H	R	ER	HR	BB	SO	AVG
2008	Rangers (AZL)	R	5	1	1.44	13	7	0	0	44	32	8	7	2	8	41	.200
MINOR LEAGUE TOTALS			5	1	1.44	13	7	0	0	44	32	8	7	2	8	41	.200

17 TOMMY HUNTER, RHP

BORN: July 3, 1986. **B-T:** R-R. **HT.:** 6-3. **WT.:** 255. **DRAFTED:** Alabama, 2007 (1st round supplemental). **SIGNED BY:** Jeff Wood.

One of the most polished pitchers in the 2007 draft, Hunter went 54th overall and signed for $585,000. As expected, he moved quickly during his first full pro season. He jumped a level to high Class A to start 2008, reached Triple-A by early July and received his first big league callup to make three fill-in starts in August. Major leaguers hit him hard, but the experience reinforced to Hunter the need for a third pitch. When he was sent back to the minors, the Rangers asked him whether he wanted to be a starter or a reliever. He chose starter, so he focused on developing his changeup, which he tends to throw too hard. Hunter attacks hitters with a 90-93 mph fastball that has a natural cut action. His 82-84 mph breaking ball can be a power slurve at times and a true downer curveball at others. It's usually a plus pitch, but Hunter struggled to throw his breaking ball for strikes in the majors and was locked into being a one-pitch guy, resulting in his rough debut. On the day before his scheduled start in the Texas League playoffs, Hunter was hit in the forehead with a line drive during batting practice. Despite a big welt on his head, Hunter returned to pitch well four days later, illustrative of his toughness and competitiveness. A good athlete for his size, he fields his position well and is very durable. He profiles as a workhorse in the Joe Blanton mold, and he could reach the big leagues for good sometime in 2009.

Year	Club (League)	Class	W	L	ERA	G	GS	CG	SV	IP	H	R	ER	HR	BB	SO	AVG
2007	Spokane (NWL)	SS	2	3	2.55	10	0	0	1	18	15	7	5	0	1	13	.221
2008	Bakersfield (CAL)	HiA	5	4	3.55	9	9	0	0	58	63	26	23	6	8	50	.279
	Frisco (TEX)	AA	4	2	3.78	8	8	0	0	52	52	24	22	5	17	28	.267
	Texas (AL)	MAJ	0	2	16.36	3	3	0	0	11	23	20	20	4	3	9	.404

Oklahoma (PCL)	AAA	4	2	2.89	8	8	0	0	53	55	18	17	6	9	28	.264
MINOR LEAGUE TOTALS		15	11	3.33	35	25	0	1	181	185	75	67	17	35	119	.265
MAJOR LEAGUE TOTALS		0	2	16.36	3	3	0	0	11	23	20	20	4	3	9	.404

18 JOSE VALLEJO, 2B

BORN: Sept. 11, 1986. **B-T:** B-R. **HT.:** 6-0. **WT.:** 172. **SIGNED:** Dominican Republic, 2004. **SIGNED BY:** Rodolfo Rosario/Manny Batista.

Vallejo has made significant strides during each of his three full seasons in the minors. Since learning how to switch-hit—he was a natural righthander—he has improved his batting average from the left side from .240 in 2006 to .260 in 2007 to .288 last season. He also showed some power for the first time in his career in 2008, prompting some high Class A California League managers to compare him to Jose Reyes. The Rangers originally thought of Vallejo as a leadoff or No. 9 hitter, but after a late June promotion to Double-A, he spent most of his time hitting in No. 3 hole. His best tool is his plus-plus speed, which plays well on the basepaths. Vallejo has stolen 89 bases in 96 attempts over the last two years. Texas still would like Vallejo to make more consistent contact offensively, though he has decreased his strikeout rate from 19 percent of his plate appearances in 2006 to 14.5 percent in 2008. He has very good range and a solid arm at second base, though he has occasional lapses. The Rangers want to increase his versatility, so they planned to work him out at shortstop over the winter. If he can pick up the new position, they envision him becoming a super-utilityman with a chance to be an impact regular, along the lines of Chone Figgins. Added to the 40-man roster in November, Vallejo could return to Double-A to start 2009, with a promotion to Triple-A likely at some point during the year.

Year	Club (League)	Class	AVG	G	AB	R	H	2B	3B	HR	RBI	BB	SO	SB	OBP	SLG
2004	Rangers (DSL)	R	.212	52	170	23	36	4	1	1	19	16	52	9	.302	.265
2005	Rangers (AZL)	R	.291	52	203	28	59	7	2	1	15	19	49	18	.364	.360
2006	Clinton (MWL)	LoA	.234	127	496	62	116	11	4	2	29	32	104	24	.289	.284
2007	Clinton (MWL)	LoA	.269	129	513	68	138	17	5	1	46	44	102	47	.326	.327
2008	Bakersfield (CAL)	HiA	.287	75	310	48	89	14	2	9	50	26	46	27	.349	.432
	Frisco (TEX)	AA	.297	64	259	34	77	15	2	2	31	15	45	15	.341	.394
MINOR LEAGUE TOTALS			.264	499	1951	263	515	68	16	16	190	152	398	140	.324	.340

19 KASEY KIKER, LHP

BORN: Nov. 19, 1987. **B-T:** L-L. **HT.:** 5-10. **WT.:** 170. **DRAFTED:** HS—Seale, Ala., 2006 (1st round). **SIGNED BY:** Jeff Wood.

Shoulder soreness hampered Kiker in camp and caused him to start 2008 in extended spring training. He went to high Class A in late April and struggled to regain his plus fastball velocity for most of the first half, instead working at 88-92 mph. After he threw six shutout innings in front of farm director Scott Servais in early July, the Rangers talked internally about promoting him to Double-A, but Kiker came up sore after the outing and missed three weeks. At times in the second half, he pitched at 90-94 mph with his fastball, but he didn't touch 96-97 like he did in the 2007 Midwest League playoffs. Still, Texas was encouraged that he learned to pitch without his best fastball. Kiker has learned to command his above-average changeup very well and now has the confidence to throw it in any count. More encouraging, he has gotten more consistent with his tight downer curveball, which now rates consistently as a solid-average offering. Kiker has cut his walk rate significantly in each of his three pro seasons, a sign of his improving command and control. The Rangers' biggest concerns with Kiker center around his body. He let his conditioning go during the season, causing team president Nolan Ryan to talk with him during instructional league about staying in better shape. Kiker vowed to work harder this offseason, and Texas hopes he'll be healthy and strong enough to start 2009 in Double-A. With a quality three-pitch mix, Kiker still has a chance to be a mid-rotation starter, but his small frame and competitive demeanor likely will make him a better fit in the bullpen.

Year	Club (League)	Class	W	L	ERA	G	GS	CG	SV	IP	H	R	ER	HR	BB	SO	AVG
2006	Spokane (NWL)	SS	0	7	4.13	16	15	0	0	52	44	34	24	5	35	51	.232
2007	Clinton (MWL)	LoA	7	4	2.90	20	20	0	0	96	84	35	31	10	41	112	.237
2008	Bakersfield (CAL)	HiA	5	5	4.73	23	21	0	0	122	138	72	64	14	37	111	.292
MINOR LEAGUE TOTALS			12	16	3.96	59	56	0	0	270	266	141	119	29	113	274	.261

20 WILMER FONT, RHP

BORN: May 24, 1990. **B-T:** R-R. **HT.:** 6-4. **WT.:** 240. **SIGNED:** Venezuela, 2006. **SIGNED BY:** Manny Batista/Andres Espinosa.

After his solid U.S. debut in 2007, the Rangers hoped to use Font as a closer at Spokane, but he was shut down with shoulder soreness late in spring training. As he tried to work his way back, he developed tendinitis where his knee meets his quadriceps, keeping him out of action until mid-August. He finally took the mound for three outings in the AZL, getting lit up for five runs in a third of an inning in his first game, then pumping 96-98 mph heaters for two perfect innings in his second appearance and working in the 98-100 range during two more perfect innings in his third. He carried his momentum into instructional league, where he regularly threw 97-100 mph. Font throws downhill with his fastball, which projects as a true 80 pitch on the 20-80 scouting scale if he can continue to refine his command. He attacks hitters with the heater and has no problem throwing it for strikes. Texas hasn't wanted him to throw his breaking ball much, so it remains raw, but he can spin it. The pitch is slurvy, however, and probably will end up as a power slider. He shows feel for a changeup, but he tends to throw it too hard, sometimes up to 89 mph. Font's huge frame should make him durable, but he's still working on his coordination. The Rangers figure to develop Font as a starter, but he could take a Jonathan Broxton developmental path and wind up as a flamethrowing closer. He likely will start 2009 at Spokane, with the goal of reaching low Class A during the year.

Year	Club (League)	Class	W	L	ERA	G	GS	CG	SV	IP	H	R	ER	HR	BB	SO	AVG
2007	Rangers (AZL)	R	2	3	4.53	14	10	0	0	46	41	33	23	2	24	61	.238
2008	Rangers (AZL)	R	1	0	10.38	3	0	0	0	4	1	5	5	1	1	6	.071
MINOR LEAGUE TOTALS			3	3	5.04	17	10	0	0	50	42	38	28	3	25	67	.226

21 KENNIL GOMEZ, RHP

BORN: April 8, 1988. **B-T:** R-R. **HT.:** 6-3. **WT.:** 170. **SIGNED:** Dominican Republic, 2006. **SIGNED BY:** Rodolfo Rosario.

Gomez worked mostly in relief during his U.S. debut in 2007, when his velocity climbed as he added weight to his wiry, angular frame. He stood out in instructional league that fall to earn a ticket to low Class A to start 2008. Early in the year, Gomez was the best pitcher on a staff that included Neftali Feliz and Derek Holland, going 8-0, 2.45 through his first nine starts. But the workload proved too much too fast, and the Rangers shut him down for good with a sore shoulder in early July. Gomez's athletic frame and clean, easy arm action evoke Ervin Santana. He has good command of an 88-93 mph fastball with sink and run, and his 75-78 mph three-quarters breaking ball projects as a plus offering. Gomez relies mostly on those two pitches but does show the ability to throw a solid changeup for strikes. He'll need to continue developing his changeup and adding strength to his frame to improve his durability. Club officials rave about his makeup, as he's learning English quickly and is very popular in the clubhouse. Defenders love playing behind him because he works quickly. Down the road, Gomez could be a solid mid-rotation starter. A promotion to high Class A seems likely in 2009.

Year	Club (League)	Class	W	L	ERA	G	GS	CG	SV	IP	H	R	ER	HR	BB	SO	AVG
2006	Rangers (DSL)	R	1	1	3.57	12	0	0	0	18	15	10	7	0	8	18	.208
2007	Rangers (DSL)	R	0	0	0.00	2	0	0	0	3	0	0	0	0	0	4	.000
	Rangers (AZL)	R	2	1	3.15	17	1	0	1	34	30	15	12	0	10	38	.231
2008	Clinton (MWL)	LoA	8	4	2.97	16	15	0	0	88	75	40	29	8	20	70	.232
MINOR LEAGUE TOTALS			11	6	3.02	47	16	0	1	143	120	65	48	8	38	130	.225

22 TIM MURPHY, LHP

BORN: May 7, 1987. **B-T:** L-L. **HT.:** 6-2. **WT.:** 190. **DRAFTED:** UCLA, 2008 (3rd round). **SIGNED BY:** Todd Guggiana.

A physical athlete who played quarterback and safety during his high school football days, Murphy was an 11th-round pick by the Angels in 2005 as an outfielder. He played both ways at UCLA, spending his freshman year as an outfielder before taking over as the Bruins' Saturday starter as a sophomore. He was UCLA's ace as a junior in 2008 before he went in the third round and signed for $436,000. In his pro debut, he worked mostly in relief after a heavy workload in the spring. Murphy's frame is mature and lacks projection, but his present stuff is solid. After pitching around 89-92 mph during much of the summer, he saw his fastball spike back up to 90-94 in instructional league. A fierce competitor, Murphy is not afraid to challenge hitters with his fastball and does a decent job spotting the pitch to all four quadrants. His best pitch is an average-to-plus curveball, that arrives in the mid-70s and has sharp two-plane drop. Murphy's funky delivery is high on the front side, evoking Andy Pettitte, and deep in the back, which gives him deception but also affects his release point and his command. The Rangers want to force him to throw his nascent changeup to see if he can develop a three-pitch repertoire. If so, he can be a solid back-end starter, but otherwise he profiles as a dogged reliever who could eat up lefties. Murphy should move quickly through the system, likely starting 2009 in high Class A and potentially reaching Double-A Frisco by midseason.

Year	Club (League)	Class	W	L	ERA	G	GS	CG	SV	IP	H	R	ER	HR	BB	SO	AVG
2008	Spokane (NWL)	SS	3	1	3.03	13	1	0	2	33	17	12	11	3	15	40	.152
	Clinton (MWL)	LoA	1	0	2.40	3	3	0	0	15	12	4	4	2	3	11	.214
MINOR LEAGUE TOTALS			4	1	2.83	16	4	0	2	48	29	16	15	5	18	51	.173

23 GUILLERMO MOSCOSO, RHP

BORN: Nov. 14, 1983. **B-T:** R-R. **HT.:** 6-1. **WT.:** 160. **SIGNED:** Venezuela, 2003. **SIGNED BY:** Ramon Pena (Tigers).

The Rangers alleviated their catching logjam somewhat by trading big league starter Gerald Laird to the Tigers in December, getting promising righthanders Moscoso and Carlos Melo in return. Moscoso had shoulder surgery in 2005 and missed the first six weeks in 2008 with shoulder soreness. When healthy, he threw a perfect game at short-season Oneonta in 2007 and flourished en route to Double-A last season. Moscoso has a quick arm and a fastball that reaches 91-92 mph with late riding action that makes it a swing-and-miss pitch. He can also use his fastball to handcuff hitters and force easy popouts. His delivery has some deception and hitters have trouble reading his pitches. He's very aggressive in the strike zone and confident on the mound. Moscoso shows a curveball and changeup, but neither is nearly as effective as his fastball. His shoulder problems have limited him to no more than 91 innings in a pro season, which raises the question of whether he would be better suited for the bullpen. It might be easier to keep him healthy as a reliever. If he can stay healthy and develop his secondary pitches, Moscoso could be a No. 3 or 4 starter in the majors. He could reach Texas at some point in 2009.

Year	Club (League)	Class	W	L	ERA	G	GS	CG	SV	IP	H	R	ER	HR	BB	SO	AVG
2003	Tigers (DSL)	R	2	0	1.85	12	2	0	1	39	29	9	8	2	7	44	.200
2004	Tigers (DSL)	R	6	3	1.90	15	11	3	2	90	58	23	19	2	16	102	.181
2005	Oneonta (NYP)	SS	2	2	4.37	11	10	0	0	47	49	27	23	4	11	44	.261
2006	Tigers (GCL)	R	3	2	2.50	13	3	0	0	36	37	14	10	3	8	33	.264
2007	Lakeland (FSL)	HiA	0	0	0.00	1	1	0	0	3	2	0	0	0	1	4	.182
	West Michigan (MWL)	LoA	0	0	1.13	1	1	0	0	8	5	1	1	1	0	7	.185
	Oneonta (NYP)	SS	8	2	2.37	14	14	2	0	80	75	25	21	3	15	68	.248
2008	Lakeland (FSL)	HiA	2	3	2.42	15	6	0	1	52	36	16	14	4	13	72	.196
	Erie (EL)	AA	3	1	3.12	6	6	0	0	35	24	17	12	4	8	50	.190
MINOR LEAGUE TOTALS			26	13	2.49	88	54	5	4	390	315	132	108	23	79	424	.218

24 OMAR POVEDA, RHP

BORN: Sept. 28, 1987. **B-T:** R-R. **HT.:** 6-4. **WT.:** 215. **SIGNED:** Venezuela, 2004. **SIGNED BY:** Andres Espinosa/Manny Batista.

Poveda opened 2008 in high Class A with an eye toward a midseason promotion, but after just three starts, he went down with a shoulder injury that sidelined him until mid-June. He spent his downtime strengthening his shoulder, and when he returned his fastball velocity gradually increased from 88-91 mph to 91-94. He pitched very well in instructional league and made three appearances in the Venezuelan League before the Rangers protected him on their 40-man roster in November. Poveda complements his fastball with an above-average changeup that he can throw in any count against lefties or righties. His curveball has improved every year and is now a solid-average pitch. Sometimes his fastball flattens out and he leaves it up on the strike zone, and he occasionally falls too much in love with his changeup. Poveda is a strike-thrower with a good work ethic. He's still maturing mentally and needs to get a little tougher and learn to trust his ability. He'll advance to Double-A in 2009 and could be a solid back-of-the-rotation starter in Texas in the next couple of years.

Year	Club (League)	Class	W	L	ERA	G	GS	CG	SV	IP	H	R	ER	HR	BB	SO	AVG
2005	Rangers (AZL)	R	2	6	5.71	14	9	0	0	52	64	38	33	1	12	56	.305
2006	Frisco (TEX)	AA	0	1	1.80	1	1	0	0	5	4	2	1	0	5	1	.222
	Clinton (MWL)	LoA	4	13	4.88	26	26	0	0	149	167	92	81	12	37	133	.286
2007	Clinton (MWL)	LoA	11	4	2.79	21	21	0	0	126	94	44	39	10	32	120	.208
	Bakersfield (CAL)	HiA	1	2	5.14	5	5	0	0	28	27	18	16	4	13	33	.250
2008	Bakersfield (CAL)	HiA	4	4	4.47	17	17	0	0	91	82	56	45	10	40	97	.241
MINOR LEAGUE TOTALS			22	30	4.29	84	79	0	0	451	438	250	215	37	139	440	.256

25 ROBBIE ROSS, LHP

BORN: June 24, 1989. **B-T:** L-L. **HT.:** 5-11. **WT.:** 185. **DRAFTED:** HS—Lexington, Ky., 2008 (2nd round). **SIGNED BY:** Jon Poloni.

The top prospect among Kentucky's watershed 2008 high school class, Ross passed up a scholarship from the University of Kentucky to sign with the Rangers for $1.575 million just hours before the Aug. 15 signing deadline. His bonus was the highest in the second round last year and more than double MLB's $705,000 slot recommendation. Ross signed too late to pitch in a minor league game, but club officials got a look at him in instructional league and came away with mixed impressions. Like he did in high school, Ross sat around 90-92 mph with his fastball and touched 93-94. But some Rangers executives were disappointed with his lack of arm speed and fastball life, two of his calling cards in high school. Ross also features a hard slider that he often throws down and in to righthanders, and he has the makings of a good changeup, though it still needs plenty of work. In high school, Ross showed very good command down in the strike zone and a competitive streak. The biggest knock on him is his size, and there's some effort in his delivery. It's tempting to compare him to fellow undersized lefty Kasey Kiker, but Ross has a lower arm slot and a slider, while Kiker uses a curveball and a more advanced changeup. Their ceilings are similar, however. He figures to follow Kiker's developmental path, starting his first full pro season in extended spring training and finishing the year in low Class A.

Year	Club (League)	Class	W	L	ERA	G	GS	CG	SV	IP	H	R	ER	HR	BB	SO	AVG
2008	Did Not Play—Signed Late																

26 GREG GOLSON, OF

BORN: Sept. 17, 1985. **B-T:** R-R. **HT.:** 6-0. **WT.:** 190. **DRAFTED:** HS—Austin, 2004 (1st round).
SIGNED BY: Steve Cohen (Phillies).

The best athlete in the 2004 draft, Golson bypassed a commitment to the University of Texas to sign with the Phillies as the 21st overall pick. He has progressed slowly, showing several premium tools but vexing Philadelphia with his lack of feel for the game. He had his best pro season in 2008 and earned six late at-bats and several pinch-running chances with the eventual World Series champion Phillies. But they ran out of patience with him and swapped him in November for another slow-developing first-round experiment, John Mayberry. Golson immediately became the best athlete in a Rangers system stocked with good athletes. His plus-plus speed plays very well in center field, where he's a plus defender with excellent range and instincts and a strong arm. Golson also has average power despite a poor contact rate. He always has struggled with pitch recognition and making contact against breaking balls, averaging 1.2 whiffs per game during his career. But after whiffing a minor league-leading 173 times while drawing just 23 walks in 2007, he showed some signs of progress by posting a 134-34 K-BB ratio last season. Rated the most exciting player in the Eastern League by managers, Golson draws frequent comparisons to fellow Texas native Ron Gant. In order to become that kind of player, he'll need to continue to improve his bat. At the least, his speed and defense could help him carve out a niche as a reserve in the big leagues, maybe even by season's end.

Year	Club (League)	Class	AVG	G	AB	R	H	2B	3B	HR	RBI	BB	SO	SB	OBP	SLG
2004	Phillies (GCL)	R	.295	47	183	34	54	8	5	1	22	10	54	12	.345	.410
2005	Lakewood (SAL)	LoA	.264	89	375	51	99	19	8	4	27	26	106	25	.322	.389
2006	Lakewood (SAL)	LoA	.220	93	387	56	85	15	4	7	31	19	107	23	.258	.333
	Clearwater (FSL)	HiA	.264	40	159	31	42	11	2	6	17	11	53	7	.324	.472
2007	Clearwater (FSL)	HiA	.285	99	418	66	119	27	3	12	52	21	124	25	.322	.450
	Reading (EL)	AA	.242	37	153	20	37	5	2	3	16	2	49	5	.255	.359
2008	Reading (EL)	AA	.282	106	426	64	120	18	4	13	60	34	130	23	.333	.434
	Philadelphia (NL)	MAJ	.000	6	6	2	0	0	0	0	0	0	4	1	.000	.000
MINOR LEAGUE TOTALS			.265	511	2101	322	556	103	28	46	225	123	623	120	.310	.406
MAJOR LEAGUE TOTALS			.000	6	6	2	0	0	0	0	0	0	4	1	.000	.000

27 JOAQUIN ARIAS, 2B/SS

BORN: Sept. 21, 1984. **B-T:** R-R. **HT.:** 6-1. **WT.:** 165. **SIGNED:** Dominican Republic, 2001.
SIGNED BY: Victor Mata/Carlos Rios/Freddy Tiburcio (Yankees).

Arias had made steady progress since the Rangers acquired him from the Yankees in the 2004 Alex Rodriguez trade, but he was derailed by a shoulder injury in 2007. He played in just five games before season-ending arthroscopic surgery late that summer. Scar tissue in his shoulder continued to affect his range of motion in 2008, relegating him to second base for much of the season. Still, he had a solid bounce-back season in Triple-A and filled in nicely for an injured Ian Kinsler for the final six weeks of the big league season. Arias has a knack for putting the bat on the ball and spraying it around the field, but he never has grown into as much power as the Rangers hoped. He's an aggressive hitter who still strikes out far more than he walks, but he demonstrated improved patience during his stint in the majors. An excellent athlete with a wiry frame, Arias is a plus-plus runner but hasn't shown the instincts to be a true basestealing threat. He has a chance to be a standout defender in the middle of the field, particularly if he can regain his once-outstanding arm strength. It started to return in the fall and Texas hoped to see him play shortstop in the Dominican League over the winter, but he appeared in just one game. Assuming his shoulder is at full strength, Arias should spend 2009 in a utility role at the major league level. Just 24, he still has a shot to become a solid everyday player someday, but that opportunity might not come with the Rangers.

Year	Club (League)	Class	AVG	G	AB	R	H	2B	3B	HR	RBI	BB	SO	SB	OBP	SLG
2002	Yankees (GCL)	R	.300	57	203	29	61	7	6	0	21	12	16	2	.338	.394
2003	Battle Creek (MWL)	LoA	.266	130	481	60	128	12	8	3	48	26	44	12	.306	.343
2004	Stockton (CAL)	HiA	.300	123	500	77	150	20	8	4	62	31	53	30	.344	.396
2005	Frisco (TEX)	AA	.315	120	499	65	157	23	8	5	56	17	46	20	.335	.423
2006	Oklahoma City (PCL)	AAA	.268	124	493	56	132	14	10	4	49	19	64	26	.296	.361
	Texas (AL)	MAJ	.545	6	11	4	6	1	0	0	1	1	0	0	.583	.636
2007	Rangers (AZL)	R	.286	2	7	1	2	1	0	0	1	0	2	0	.250	.429
	Oklahoma City (PCL)	AAA	.182	3	11	3	2	0	0	0	1	0	1	0	.182	.182
2008	Oklahoma (PCL)	AAA	.296	104	432	59	128	15	9	7	49	19	53	23	.329	.421
	Texas (AL)	MAJ	.291	32	110	15	32	7	3	0	9	7	12	4	.345	.409
MINOR LEAGUE TOTALS			.289	663	2626	350	760	92	49	23	287	124	280	114	.322	.388
MAJOR LEAGUE TOTALS			.314	38	121	19	38	8	3	0	10	8	12	4	.366	.430

28 THOMAS DIAMOND, RHP

BORN: April 6, 1983. **B-T:** R-R. **HT.:** 6-3. **WT.:** 245. **DRAFTED:** New Orleans, 2004 (1st round).
SIGNED BY: Randy Taylor.

Diamond ranked as the Rangers' top prospect after his impressive pro debut in 2004, when they made him the 10th overall pick in the draft and signed him for $2,025,000. His climb through the system was slowed by Tommy John surgery in the spring of 2007, causing him to miss the whole season. The primary goal for him in 2008 was to get through the entire year healthy. Texas kept him in extended spring training to start the year, hoping to keep him around 100 innings for the season. While Diamond did not suffer any setbacks with his elbow, he battled fatigue and developed a bone spur in his ankle that ended his season in early August. He had minor surgery to clean up the bone spur and is expected to be 100 percent by spring training. Diamond's fastball velocity was back to 91-95 mph, and he had no problem throwing his quality changeup to lefties or righties. He still runs high pitch counts thanks to his lack of a true putaway breaking ball. He's still trying to add velocity to his curveball to make it less loopy. At full strength, Diamond is a power pitcher with a physical build and a mean streak, but he has yet to prove he has the stuff and command to be a starter against more advanced hitters.

Year	Club (League)	Class	W	L	ERA	G	GS	CG	SV	IP	H	R	ER	HR	BB	SO	AVG
2004	Spokane (NWL)	SS	0	2	2.35	5	3	0	1	15	13	5	4	0	5	26	.220
	Clinton (MWL)	LoA	1	0	2.05	7	7	0	0	31	18	8	7	1	8	42	.175
2005	Bakersfield (CAL)	HiA	8	0	1.99	14	14	1	0	81	53	20	18	3	31	101	.191
	Frisco (TEX)	AA	5	4	5.35	14	14	0	0	69	66	44	41	8	38	68	.249
2006	Frisco (TEX)	AA	12	5	4.24	27	27	1	0	129	104	65	61	14	78	145	.219
2007	Did Not Play—Injured																
2008	Frisco (TEX)	AA	3	3	6.20	12	11	0	0	54	54	39	37	3	37	47	.267
MINOR LEAGUE TOTALS			29	14	3.99	79	76	2	1	379	308	181	168	29	197	429	.223

29 CLARK MURPHY, 1B

BORN: Dec. 18, 1989. **B-T:** L-L. **HT.:** 6-2. **WT.:** 190. **DRAFTED:** HS—Fallbrook, Calif., 2008 (5th round). **SIGNED BY:** Steve Flores.

Murphy opened eyes during the home run contest at the 2007 Aflac Classic, pounding long blasts out of San Diego State's Tony Gwynn Stadium with a wood bat. He struggled in fall and winter showcases and battled a quadriceps injury, causing him to slip to the fifth round of the 2008 draft. It took the Rangers seven weeks to sign him from a UCLA commitment for a slightly above-slot $200,000 bonus. Murphy took a pull-heavy approach into pro ball, but the AZL Rangers coaching staff worked hard to get him to use more of the field and he ended his debut on a 20-for-44 (.455) tear. Murphy has a clean lefthanded swing with a load similar to that of Adam LaRoche. His strong build evokes Ryan Klesko, and he has plus raw power to go along with a sound offensive approach. Defense is more of a question mark. The Rangers worked Murphy out at first base and in the outfield during instructional league, but his below-average speed and mobility figure to tie him to first base. He'll go as far as his bat will carry him, and has a chance to be an impact bat in the big leagues. He should get a crack at low Class A in 2009.

Year	Club (League)	Class	AVG	G	AB	R	H	2B	3B	HR	RBI	BB	SO	SB	OBP	SLG
2008	Rangers (AZL)	R	.358	25	95	13	34	7	3	1	21	12	19	1	.435	.526
MINOR LEAGUE TOTALS			.358	25	95	13	34	7	3	1	21	12	19	1	.435	.526

30 JOHN BANNISTER, RHP

BORN: Jan. 20, 1984. **B-T:** R-R. **HT.:** 6-4. **WT.:** 215. **SIGNED:** HS—Tucson, NDFA 2002. **SIGNED BY:** Dave Birecki.

Though he was a high school teammate of J.J. Hardy, the extra exposure didn't get Bannister drafted. Instead, he signed as a nondrafted free agent for $17,500 and steadily progressed through the system until Tommy John surgery knocked him out for the entire 2007 season. The Rangers moved him to the bullpen when he returned in 2008 and worked to give him more structure and simplify his game. The shift to relief caused his velocity to spike, and by the time he reached the Arizona Fall League, Bannister's fastball was sitting at 93-96 mph and touching 97-98—a jump of 4 mph from his pre-surgery days. That made for an easy decision to add him to the 40-man roster. Before he got hurt, Bannister flashed an excellent curveball, and it now has developed into a hard hammer with 11-to-5 break. He's still working on gaining consistent command of his pitches, but his stuff is better than it ever has been and his feel for pitching is promising. Bannister doesn't always locate his pitches where he needs to in the strike zone, but he does throw the ball over the plate. If he can stay healthy and refine his command, Bannister has the upside of a big league closer. He figures to return to Double-A to start 2009 and could reach the big leagues by season's end.

Year	Club (League)	Class	W	L	ERA	G	GS	CG	SV	IP	H	R	ER	HR	BB	SO	AVG
2003	Rangers (AZL)	R	2	4	4.22	13	7	0	1	43	47	31	20	2	16	28	.283
2004	Spokane (NWL)	SS	2	2	3.51	16	7	0	0	59	49	29	23	3	28	67	.236
	Clinton (MWL)	LoA	0	0	1.80	1	1	0	0	5	5	1	1	0	1	5	.263
2005	Clinton (MWL)	LoA	8	10	4.58	29	28	0	0	157	171	98	80	13	58	127	.275
2006	Rangers (AZL)	R	0	0	4.50	1	0	0	0	2	1	1	1	0	0	6	.143
	Bakersfield (CAL)	HiA	5	8	5.87	18	18	0	0	97	109	69	63	9	53	109	.286
2007	Did Not Play—Injured																
2008	Bakersfield (CAL)	HiA	4	6	4.14	19	9	0	2	63	63	34	29	5	29	51	.265
	Frisco (TEX)	AA	1	0	4.56	11	3	0	1	26	26	14	13	1	22	15	.274
MINOR LEAGUE TOTALS			22	30	4.59	108	73	0	4	451	471	277	230	33	207	408	.271

Toronto Blue Jays

BY MATT EDDY

Despite their strongest showing of the decade, the Blue Jays still couldn't end a playoff drought that dates to their 1993 World Series championship. In general manager J.P. Ricciardi's seventh year at the helm, Toronto had the second-best run differential in the American League and went 86-76, but its reward was a fourth-place finish in the AL East.

Though the Jays' offense again fell flat, their pitching staff led the league with a 3.49 ERA and their defense ranked among the best in the AL. That Toronto's pitching was so strong was a testament to depth, because the club lost young, homegrown righthanders Dustin McGowan (frayed labrum), Shaun Marcum (Tommy John surgery) and Casey Janssen (torn labrum) during the season. Rookie lefthanders David Purcey and Jesse Carlson stepped in and showed enough to warrant consideration for the 2009 staff.

A 2004 first-round pick, Purcey led all Triple-A hurlers with a 2.69 ERA and went 3-6, 5.54 in 12 big league starts as a fill-in for Marcum. Twice signed by the Blue Jays as a minor league free agent, Carlson cleaned up his command and gave Toronto's lefty-dominated bullpen 60 quality innings.

Already accustomed to contending with the Red Sox and Yankees, the Blue Jays were displaced from their usual third-place perch by the surprising Rays. To keep pace in an increasingly rugged division, Toronto will have to rely on its farm system. The good news is that the system is in its best shape since at least 2004, when Alex Rios, McGowan, Gabe Gross, Aaron Hill and David Bush highlighted our Jays Top 10 Prospects list.

Travis Snider, the system's top prospect, spent most of the season in Double-A as a 20-year-old, and when he debuted in the big leagues in September he became the AL's youngest player. The drafting of Snider, a prep product, with the 14th overall pick in 2006 signaled a shift in philosophy for the organization. Toronto used a strictly college-oriented approach in its first four drafts under Ricciardi but since has become more diversified. Just two years ago, our Jays Top 30 featured only one player they had drafted out of high school (Snider), while this year's list has eight.

In the 2007 draft, Toronto held seven of the first 88 picks and spent four of them on high schoolers. Seven players from that draft made the top 10, including prepsters Justin Jackson and Kevin Ahrens.

An increased big league payroll and the addition of a Rookie-level Gulf Coast League affiliate in 2007 have afforded the Blue Jays the patience and the means to

Rookie David Purcey finally delivered on the potential that made him a 2004 first-rounder

BRIAN KUCHEREPA

TOP 30 PROSPECTS

1. Travis Snider, of	16. Eric Eiland, of
2. J.P. Arencibia, c	17. Luis Perez, lhp
3. Brett Cecil, lhp	18. Gustavo Pierre, ss
4. Justin Jackson, ss	19. Mark Sobolewski, 3b
5. David Cooper, 1b	20. Scott Richmond, rhp
6. Kevin Ahrens, 3b	21. Kenny Wilson, of
7. Brad Mills, lhp	22. Andrew Liebel, rhp
8. Ricky Romero, lhp	23. Tyler Pastornicky, ss
9. Marc Rzepczynski, lhp	24. Danny Farquhar, rhp
10. Brad Emaus, 2b/3b	25. Trystan Magnuson, rhp
11. Scott Campbell, 2b	26. Markus Brisker, of
12. Brian Jeroloman, c	27. Curtis Thigpen, c/1b
13. John Tolisano, 2b	28. Balbino Fuenmayor, 3b
14. Alan Farina, rhp	29. Henderson Alvarez, rhp
15. Robert Ray, rhp	30. Tim Collins, lhp

develop less-refined high school and international talents. The younger players they've targeted have generally been more athletic, bolstering depth at key defensive positions. Shortstops Jackson, Gustavo Pierre and Tyler Pastornicky; third baseman Ahrens; second baseman John Tolisano; and center fielders Eric Eiland, Kenny Wilson and Markus Brisker all joined the organization as teenagers in the past two years.

After years of playing it safe on the international market, the Blue Jays signed Pierre, one of the top 16-year-old Dominican talents available, for $700,000 on the first day of the 2008 signing period.

General Manager: J.P. Ricciardi. **Farm Director:** Dick Scott. **Scouting Director:** John Lalonde.

Class	Team	League	W	L	PCT	Finish*	Manager	Affiliated
Majors	Toronto	American	86	76	.531	7th (14)	J. Gibbons/C. Gaston	—
Triple-A	Syracuse Chiefs	International	69	73	.486	8th (14)	Doug Davis	1978
Double-A	New Hampshire Fisher Cats	Eastern	61	81	.430	11th (12)	Gary Cathcart	2003
High A	Dunedin Blue Jays	Florida State	85	53	.616	1st (12)	Omar Malave	1987
Low A	Lansing Lugnuts	Midwest	76	64	.543	3rd (14)	Clayton McCullough	2005
Short-season	Auburn Doubledays	New York-Penn	38	37	.507	7th (14)	Dennis Holmberg	2001
Rookie	GCL Blue Jays	Gulf Coast	26	32	.448	13th (16)	Dave Pano	2007
Overall 2008 Minor League Record			355	340	.511	12th		

*Finish in overall standings (No. of teams in league). ^League champion.

LAST YEAR'S TOP 30

Rank	Player, Pos.	Status
1.	Travis Snider, of	No. 1
2.	Brett Cecil, lhp	No. 3
3.	Kevin Ahrens, 3b/ss	No. 6
4.	J.P. Arencibia, c	No. 2
5.	Ricky Romero, lhp	No. 8
6.	Justin Jackson, ss	No. 4
7.	John Tolisano, 2b	No. 13
8.	Curtis Thigpen, c/1b	No. 27
9.	David Purcey, lhp	Majors
10.	Ryan Patterson, of	Dropped out
11.	Trystan Magnuson, rhp	No. 25
12.	Johermyn Chavez, of	Dropped out
13.	Robinzon Diaz, c	(Pirates)
14.	Eric Eiland, of	No. 16
15.	Alan Farina, rhp	No. 14
16.	Brian Wolfe, rhp	Majors
17.	Kyle Ginley, rhp	Dropped out
18.	Brandon Magee, rhp	Dropped out
19.	Brian Jeroloman, c	No. 12
20.	Brad Mills, lhp	No. 7
21.	Marc Rzepczynski, lhp	No. 9
22.	Randy Wells, rhp	(Cubs)
23.	Buck Coats, of	Dropped out
24.	Balbino Fuenmayor, 3b	No. 28
25.	Josh Banks, rhp	(Padres)
26.	Zach Dials, rhp	Dropped out
27.	Chase Lirette, rhp	Dropped out
28.	Joel Carreno, rhp	Dropped out
29.	Anthony Hatch, 3b/2b	(Dodgers)
30.	Moises Sierra, of	Dropped out

BEST TOOLS

Best Hitter for Average	Travis Snider
Best Power Hitter	Travis Snider
Best Strike-Zone Discipline	Brad Emaus
Fastest Baserunner	Kenny Wilson
Best Athlete	Markus Brisker
Best Fastball	Alan Farina
Best Curveball	Ricky Romero
Best Slider	Brett Cecil
Best Changeup	Brad Mills
Best Control	Andrew Liebel
Best Defensive Catcher	Brian Jeroloman
Best Defensive Infielder	Justin Jackson
Best Infield Arm	Kevin Ahrens
Best Defensive Outfielder	Sean Shoffit
Best Outfield Arm	Moises Sierra

PROJECTED 2012 LINEUP

Catcher	J.P. Arencibia
First Base	David Cooper
Second Base	Aaron Hill
Third Base	Kevin Ahrens
Shortstop	Justin Jackson
Left Field	Travis Snider
Center Field	Vernon Wells
Right Field	Alex Rios
Designated Hitter	Adam Lind
No. 1 Starter	Roy Halladay
No. 2 Starter	Dustin McGowan
No. 3 Starter	Shaun Marcum
No. 4 Starter	Brett Cecil
No. 5 Starter	Jesse Litsch
Closer	B.J. Ryan

TOP PROSPECTS OF THE DECADE

Year	Player, Pos.	2008 Org.
1999	Roy Halladay, rhp	Blue Jays
2000	Vernon Wells, of	Blue Jays
2001	Vernon Wells, of	Blue Jays
2002	Josh Phelps, c	Cardinals
2003	Dustin McGowan, rhp	Blue Jays
2004	Alex Rios, of	Blue Jays
2005	Brandon League, rhp	Blue Jays
2006	Dustin McGowan, rhp	Blue Jays
2007	Adam Lind, of	Blue Jays
2008	Travis Snider, of	Blue Jays

TOP DRAFT PICKS OF THE DECADE

Year	Player, Pos.	2008 Org.
1999	Alex Rios, of	Blue Jays
2000	Miguel Negron, of	White Sox
2001	Gabe Gross, of	Rays
2002	Russ Adams, ss	Blue Jays
2003	Aaron Hill, ss	Blue Jays
2004	David Purcey, lhp	Blue Jays
2005	Ricky Romero, lhp	Blue Jays
2006	Travis Snider, of	Blue Jays
2007	Kevin Ahrens, 3b	Blue Jays
2008	David Cooper, 1b	Blue Jays

LARGEST BONUSES IN CLUB HISTORY

Ricky Romero, 2005	$2,400,000
Felipe Lopez, 1998	$2,000,000
Gabe Gross, 2001	$1,865,000
Russ Adams, 2002	$1,785,000
Travis Snider, 2006	$1,700,000

TORONTO BLUE JAYS

TOP 2009 ROOKIE: Travis Snider, of. Snider is an advanced hitter who has proven he can make adjustments, and he already has an impressive September callup under his belt.

BREAKOUT PROSPECT: Alan Farina, rhp. If his elbow is right, this power reliever could move quickly with his potent fastball and pair of breaking pitches.

SLEEPER: Eric Thames, of. The 2008 seventh-round pick has yet to deliver on his hitting and power potential as a pro because he tore his quad late in the season at Pepperdine.

SOURCE OF TOP 30 TALENT			
Homegrown	29	Acquired	1
College	16	Trades	0
Junior college	0	Rule 5 draft	0
High school	8	Independent leagues	1
Draft-and-follow	0	Free agents/waivers	0
Nondrafted free agents	1		
International	4		

Numbers in parentheses indicate prospect rankings.

LF
Travis Snider (1)
Johermyn Chavez
Eric Thames
Brian Van Kirk
Michael Crouse

CF
Eric Eiland (16)
Kenny Wilson (21)
Markus Brisker (26)
Buck Coats
Sean Shoffit

RF
Moises Sierra
Ryan Patterson

3B
Kevin Ahrens (6)
Mark Sobolewski (19)

SS
Justin Jackson (4)
Gustavo Pierre (18)
Tyler Pastornicky (23)
Luis Sanchez

2B
Brad Emaus (10)
Scott Campbell (11)
John Tolisano (13)

1B
David Cooper (5)
Balbino Fuenmayor (28)
Jon Talley

C
J.P. Arencibia (2)
Brian Jeroloman (12)
Curtis Thigpen (27)
Joel Collins
Antonio Jimenez
Carlos Perez
Jonnathan Valdez

RHP

Starters	Relievers
Robert Ray (15)	Alan Farina (14)
Scott Richmond (20)	Danny Farquhar (24)
Andrew Liebel (22)	Trystan Magnuson (25)
Henderson Alvarez (29)	Zach Dials
Dustin Antolin	Dirk Hayhurst
Marcus Walden	Kyle Ginley
Joel Carreno	Brandon Magee
Castillo Perez	Chad Beck
	Scott Gracey
	Matt Daly
	Chris Holguin

LHP

Starters	Relievers
Brett Cecil (3)	Tim Collins (30)
Brad Mills (7)	Fabio Castro
Ricky Romero (8)	Davis Romero
Marc Rzepczynski (9)	Reid Santos
Luis Perez (17)	Evan Crawford
	Cody Crowell
	Ryan Page
	Joe Wice

2008   BONUSES: $4.4 MILLION

BEST PURE HITTER: 1B David Cooper (1) showed off his sweet lefthanded swing and hand-eye coordination by topping .300 at three different levels, batting a combined .333/.399/.502 and ending the summer in high Class A. The Jays think he'll develop at least average power as he gets stronger.

BEST POWER HITTER: OF Eric Thames (7), who has yet to make his pro debut because he tore a quad muscle late in the college season. 3B Mark Sobolewski (4) and C Jonnathan Valdez (17) also have plus raw power.

FASTEST RUNNER: The Blue Jays have clocked OF Kenny Wilson (2) in 3.7 seconds from the right side to first base on a bunt, and he has recorded sub-4.0 times on full swings. Wilson, who worked on switch-hitting in instructional league, stole 25 bases in 28 tries in the Rookie-level Gulf Coast League.

BEST DEFENSIVE PLAYER: Wilson's speed gives him tremendous range in center field, and he has an average arm. Sobolewski has a strong arm and good range at third base, though he needs to cut down on his throwing errors. Tyler Pastornicky (5) is a rangy shortstop with a plus arm and reliable hands. Toronto likes C Antonio Jimenez's (9) potential behind the plate.

BEST FASTBALL: RHP Chris Holguin (14) has the best pure velocity, maxing out at 96 mph. RHP Danny Farquhar (10) can run his fastball up to 94 and achieves good life while varying his arm angle. RHP Andrew Liebel (3) has excellent command of a heater that tops out at 93, and RHP Dustin Antolin (11) has the same peak velocity and nice sink.

BEST SECONDARY PITCH: Liebel and RHP Bobby Bell (18) have plus changeups. The best breaking ball in this crop is RHP Evan Crawford's (8) curve.

BEST PRO DEBUT: Bell, who had Tommy John surgery at Rice in 2007, had a 0.88 ERA, 11 saves and a 43-0 K-BB ratio in 31 innings while reaching low Class A. Opponents hit just .140 against him.

BEST ATHLETE: Toronto added a fast-twitch athlete in Wilson and two guys with strength and speed in OFs Markus Brisker (6) and Michael Crouse (16).

MOST INTRIGUING BACKGROUND: RHP Jason Roenicke's (19) father Gary, uncle Ron and brother Josh all reached the majors, as did Pastornicky's dad Cliff. Crouse's father Ray was a running back in the NFL and Canadian Football League.

CLOSEST TO THE MAJORS: Cooper has an advanced bat, while Liebel's command and Farquhar's deception help their causes.

BEST LATE-ROUND PICK: Valdez is a lefthanded-hitting catcher with power, average arm strength and raw receiving skills. Antolin intrigues the Jays as well.

THE ONE WHO GOT AWAY: Toronto signed its first 25 draft picks. The highest-ceiling player it missed out on is C Justin Dalles (26), who took his arm strength and power potential to South Carolina.

ASSESSMENT: For the third straight year, the Blue Jays spent most of their early picks on position players. Cooper was one of the 2008 draft's best pure hitters, and Toronto bolstered its stock of power hitters (Sobolewski, Thames, Valdez) and athletes (Wilson, Brisker, Crouse).

2007   BONUSES: $6.6 MILLION

This draft singlehandedly restocked the system, placing seven players on our Toronto Top 10 Prospects list: C J.C. Arencibia (1), LHP Brett Cecil (1s), SS Justin Jackson (1s), 3B Kevin Ahrens (1), LHPs Brad Mills (4) and Mark Rzepczynski (5) and 2B/3B Brad Emaus (11).

GRADE: B+

2006   BONUSES: $3.4 MILLION

For the first time under GM J.P. Ricciardi, the Jays used their first-round pick on a high schooler—OF Travis Snider (1), a savvy choice. The best of the rest of this draft, which didn't include a second- or third-rounder, is 2B Scott Campbell (10).

GRADE: B

2005   BONUSES: $3.6 MILLION*

Passing on Troy Tulowitzki and Jay Bruce, among others, to take LHP Ricky Romero (1) with the sixth overall pick was a mistake. Romero is still the highlight of this crop, which also included unsigned 1B Brett Wallace (42), who developed into one of the best hitters in the 2008 draft.

GRADE: D

2004   BONUSES: $4.6 MILLION*

LHP David Purcey (1) finally reached the majors last season, as have LHP Zach Jackson (1s) and C/1B Curtis Thigpen (2). But the real prizes are OF Adam Lind (3) and RHPs Casey Janssen (4) and Jesse Litsch (24).

GRADE: B

*Draft analysis by Jim Callis. Numbers in parentheses indicate draft rounds. *Bonuses for 2004-05 are first 10 rounds only.*

MIKE JANES

PROSPECT

TRAVIS SNIDER, OF

Born: Feb. 2, 1988.
Ht.: 5-11. **Wt.:** 245.
Bats: L. **Throws:** L.
Drafted:
HS—Mill Creek, Wash.,
2006 (1st round)
Signed by:
Brandon Mozley.

Evan Longoria may be the best hitter taken in the 2006 draft, but Snider has done nothing to diminish his case as the best *high school* hitter from that same draft. After signing for $1.7 million as the 14th overall pick, Snider proceeded to earn Rookie-level Appalachian League MVP and No. 1 prospect honors in his first pro summer. He followed up by leading the low Class A Midwest League with 35 doubles, 58 extra-base hits, 93 RBIs and a .525 slugging percentage in 2007. After hitting .316/.404/.541 as the second-youngest player in the Arizona Fall League, he was expected to begin 2008 at Double-A New Hampshire, but a spring-training right elbow injury relegated him to DH duty with high Class A Dunedin. He started slowly upon a promotion to Double-A in late April, striking out in 42 percent of his at-bats. His ailing elbow negatively affected his swing path, and he developed the bad habit of pulling off the ball as he tried to yank everything to right field. Snider appeared to be fully recovered by mid-May, and in his final 93 minor league games, he batted .293/.368/.499 with 15 homers and 25 doubles. Toronto rewarded Snider with a September callup, during which he batted .301 as the American League's youngest player.

With strength, bat speed and a simple lefthanded swing, Snider projects to hit for average and plus power to all fields in the big leagues. Despite his lofty strikeout totals, he has exceptional control of the bat barrel, showing a knack for hitting balls in any part of the zone with authority. His sound hitting base enhances his balance, and he already uses the opposite field when pitchers try to work him on the outer half. Snider is more athletic than his 5-foot-11, 245-pound frame suggests, and his arm is strong enough for right field. He always puts forth consistent effort on defense. A natural leader, he receives high marks for his competitive makeup.

Because lefthanders threw him a steady diet of offspeed pitches—even in hitter's counts—Snider struggled versus southpaws in the high minors, hitting a mere .233/.295/.310 in 116 Double-A and Triple-A at-bats. Showing a more patient approach could help him overcome this shortcoming, as he showed a tendency toward free swinging as he moved up the ladder. It's not a long-term concern if he refines his approach to the point where he's confident hitting with two strikes. Physically mature with a muscular build and a thick lower half, Snider has below-average running speed and always will need to make conditioning a priority. His outfield range is average at best.

The Matt Stairs trade in August opened a spot for Snider, who took advantage of his opportunity. He figures into the club's 2009 plans, though he may begin the year with the Jays' new Triple-A Las Vegas affiliate. Either way, it shouldn't be long before he takes his place as a middle-of-the-order threat and team leader for Toronto.

Year	Club (League)	Class	AVG	G	AB	R	H	2B	3B	HR	RBI	BB	SO	SB	OBP	SLG
2006	Pulaski (APP)	R	.325	54	194	36	63	12	1	11	41	30	47	6	.412	.567
2007	Lansing (MWL)	LoA	.313	118	457	72	143	35	7	16	93	49	129	3	.377	.525
2008	Dunedin (FSL)	HiA	.279	17	61	15	17	5	0	4	7	5	22	1	.333	.557
	New Hampshire (EL)	AA	.262	98	362	65	95	21	0	17	67	52	116	1	.357	.461
	Syracuse (IL)	AAA	.344	18	64	9	22	5	0	2	17	4	16	1	.386	.516
	Toronto (AL)	MAJ	.301	24	73	9	22	6	0	2	13	5	23	0	.338	.466
MINOR LEAGUE TOTALS			.299	305	1138	197	340	78	8	50	225	140	330	12	.375	.513
MAJOR LEAGUE TOTALS			.301	24	73	9	22	6	0	2	13	5	23	0	.338	.466

2 J.P. ARENCIBIA, C

BORN: Jan. 5, 1986. **B-T:** R-R. **HT.:** 6-1. **WT.:** 215. **DRAFTED:** Tennessee, 2007 (1st round). **SIGNED BY:** Matt Briggs.

The 21st overall pick in 2007, Arencibia signed for $1,327,500 and struggled in his pro debut, in part because he was hit by a pitch on his left wrist. Healthy in 2008, he tied Minor League Player of the Year Matt Wieters for the most homers by a minor league catcher (27) and ranked 10th in the minors with 105 RBIs. Arencibia has impressive power to all fields—especially to center and left field—and rarely gets cheated at the plate. An agile and fundamentally sound receiver who calls a good game, he's bilingual and a natural leader. He threw out 34 percent of basestealers in 2008, and evaluators rave about his easy, accurate and strong throwing arm. He also improved his blocking skills, dramatically reducing his rate of passed balls. Despite batting .298 in his first full pro season, Arencibia projects as an average hitter at best at the big league level. He likes to swing at the first pitch he can handle, leading to few deep counts and even fewer walks, so the Blue Jays challenged him to see more pitches during his stint in the Arizona Fall League. Arencibia's long swing and tendency to uppercut also will cut into his average. As with most catchers, he's a below-average runner. A potential first-division regular, Arencibia is Toronto's catcher of the future. He could be big league-ready by the second half of 2009.

Year	Club (League)	Class	AVG	G	AB	R	H	2B	3B	HR	RBI	BB	SO	SB	OBP	SLG
2007	Auburn (NYP)	SS	.254	63	228	31	58	17	1	3	25	14	56	0	.309	.377
2008	Dunedin (FSL)	HiA	.315	59	248	38	78	22	0	13	62	11	46	0	.344	.560
	New Hampshire (EL)	AA	.282	67	262	32	74	14	0	14	43	7	55	0	.302	.496
MINOR LEAGUE TOTALS			.285	189	738	101	210	53	1	30	130	32	157	0	.318	.481

3 BRETT CECIL, LHP

BORN: July 2, 1986. **B-T:** R-L. **HT.:** 6-3. **WT.:** 220. **DRAFTED:** Maryland, 2007 (1st round supplemental). **SIGNED BY:** Tom Burns.

Cecil served primarily as a reliever in three years at Maryland, but the Blue Jays made him a starter after drafting him 38th overall in 2007. He ranked as the short-season New York-Penn League's No. 1 prospect and pitched Auburn to the league title in his debut, then finished his first full season at Triple-A Syracuse. Cecil attacks batters with two plus pitches and has worked diligently to refine the rest of his repertoire. His two-seam fastball sits at 90-92 mph, while his hard, two-plane slider arrives at 82-84. He generates plenty of swings and misses, not to mention oodles of groundouts. He showed increased confidence in his average curveball as the season wore on. Though Cecil has the raw stuff to succeed in any role, some observers prefer him in relief because his four-seam fastball creeps into the mid-90s in short stints. Stamina will be an issue for Cecil going forward, as he was kept on strict pitch counts in 2008, ranging from 60 in April to 90 in August. He completed six innings in just five starts all season. Because he didn't need it as a reliever, he still struggles with the consistency of his changeup, and his feel for mixing his pitches is unrefined. Toronto has worked with him on keeping his arm stroke more fluid and on hiding the ball better in his delivery. Cecil follows in the footsteps of David Bush and Shaun Marcum as college closers whom the Blue Jays have turned into effective starters. He'll open 2009 back in Triple-A and projects as a No. 3 starter.

Year	Club (League)	Class	W	L	ERA	G	GS	CG	SV	IP	H	R	ER	HR	BB	SO	AVG
2007	Auburn (NYP)	SS	1	0	1.27	14	13	0	0	50	36	10	7	1	11	56	.197
2008	Dunedin (FSL)	HiA	0	0	1.74	4	4	0	0	10	6	2	2	1	2	11	.167
	New Hampshire (EL)	AA	6	2	2.55	18	18	0	0	78	66	24	22	4	23	87	.227
	Syracuse (IL)	AAA	2	3	4.11	6	6	0	0	31	28	17	14	1	16	31	.237
MINOR LEAGUE TOTALS			9	5	2.41	42	41	0	0	168	136	53	45	7	52	185	.217

4 JUSTIN JACKSON, SS

BORN: Dec. 11, 1988. **B-T:** R-R. **HT.:** 6-2. **WT.:** 186. **DRAFTED:** HS—Asheville, N.C., 2007 (1st round supplemental). **SIGNED BY:** Marc Tramuta.

A teammate of Marlins prospect Cameron Maybin in high school, Jackson went 45th overall in the 2007 draft as one of the top shortstops available. He didn't light up the Midwest League in his debut like Maybin did, but Jackson did show a true up-the-middle profile with his wiry athleticism and pure infield actions. Jackson has well above-average range, hands and arm strength at shortstop and the polish not usually associated with such a young player. He consistently fields the ball on the right hop and provides accurate feeds to the second baseman on double plays. Jackson has a simple swing and a good idea of the strike zone, and though his bat speed is just average, he has more than enough power for a middle infielder. He's not afraid to hit with two strikes, allowing him to work deep counts and draw walks. With solid-average speed,

PAUL GIERHART

he should be able to leg out plenty of doubles and triples and kick in 15-20 stolen bases annually. Jackson's 154 strikeouts were fifth-most among low Class A batters. Some MWL scouts criticized Jackson for getting lackadaisical in the field at times and for holding the ball too long in order to show off his arm. Jackson has no peers among shortstops in the system. He'll begin 2009 in high Class A and needs at least a couple more years of seasoning.

Year	Club (League)	Class	AVG	G	AB	R	H	2B	3B	HR	RBI	BB	SO	SB	OBP	SLG
2007	Blue Jays (GCL)	R	.187	42	166	20	31	1	1	2	13	20	44	7	.274	.241
2008	Lansing (MWL)	LoA	.238	121	454	74	108	26	6	7	47	62	154	17	.340	.368
MINOR LEAGUE TOTALS			.224	163	620	94	139	27	7	9	60	82	198	24	.323	.334

5 DAVID COOPER, 1B

PAUL GIERHART

BORN: Feb. 12, 1987. **B-T:** L-L. **HT.:** 6-0. **WT.:** 175. **DRAFTED:** California, 2008 (1st round). **SIGNED BY:** Chris Becerra.

The 17th overall pick in the 2008 draft, Cooper was the first first-rounder to sign, agreeing to a $1.5 million bonus on June 11. Widely regarded as one of the top bats available, he delivered on that promise in his pro debut, finishing in high Class A and batting .333/.399/.502 with 29 doubles in 69 games. A sweet-swinging lefthanded batter, Cooper has tremendous barrel awareness and excellent hand-eye coordination. Factor in his line-drive, all-fields approach and his ability to keep his bat in the hitting zone for a long time, and he should produce high batting averages. As he learns to incorporate his lower half in his swing, he could develop average power and hit 18-20 homers per season. Though he's a natural in the batter's box, Cooper's other tools pale in comparison with his hitting acumen. A below-average athlete and poor runner, he offers limited range and slow reactions at first base. Some evaluators have him pegged as a future DH because he has shown little desire to improve his defensive game. Cooper's bat should be able to carry him to the big leagues. If things go smoothly, he could be established as Toronto's first baseman by 2010. He and Travis Snider figure to form the core of future Blue Jays offenses.

Year	Club (League)	Class	AVG	G	AB	R	H	2B	3B	HR	RBI	BB	SO	SB	OBP	SLG
2008	Auburn (NYP)	SS	.341	21	85	10	29	10	1	2	21	10	16	0	.411	.553
	Lansing (MWL)	LoA	.354	24	96	15	34	10	0	2	17	10	14	0	.415	.521
	Dunedin (FSL)	HiA	.304	24	92	10	28	9	0	1	13	10	16	0	.373	.435
MINOR LEAGUE TOTALS			.333	69	273	35	91	29	1	5	51	30	46	0	.399	.502

6 KEVIN AHRENS, 3B

PAUL GIERHART

BORN: April 26, 1989. **B-T:** B-R. **HT.:** 6-1. **WT.:** 205. **DRAFTED:** HS—Houston, 2007 (1st round). **SIGNED BY:** Andy Beene.

Ahrens began switch-hitting and hitting for power during his junior year in high school, putting him on the path to go 16th overall in the 2007 draft and receive a $1.44 million bonus. He batted just .230/.339/.321 in the Rookie-level Gulf Coast League in his debut and struggled in the tough Midwest League in 2008. Though the results have been underwhelming thus far, Ahrens has an easy swing from both sides of the plate and the patience to wait for his pitch. His all-fields approach is advanced for a young hitter and he figures to hit for a decent average with 20-homer power down the line. His lefty swing has improved to the point where he did more damage from that side in 2008 than from his natural right side. A converted shortstop, he has soft hands, good range to both sides and a plus-plus arm. Some MWL observers regarded Ahrens' bat speed as no more than average, though no obvious mechanical flaw handicaps his upside. While he showed the ability to work counts, he also took a lot of first-pitch fastballs for strikes. Like Justin Jackson, Ahrens tailed off in the second half while adjusting to the physical and mental grind of playing every day for five months. He's a below-average runner but not bad underway. It may take him time to develop, but Ahrens' potential as a hitter and defender place him squarely at the top of the organization's third-base depth chart. He'll move up to high Class A and play alongside Jackson again in 2009.

Year	Club (League)	Class	AVG	G	AB	R	H	2B	3B	HR	RBI	BB	SO	SB	OBP	SLG
2007	Blue Jays (GCL)	R	.230	48	165	19	38	6	0	3	21	25	47	3	.339	.321
2008	Lansing (MWL)	LoA	.259	122	460	54	119	25	5	5	42	45	135	5	.329	.367
MINOR LEAGUE TOTALS			.251	170	625	73	157	31	5	8	63	70	182	8	.331	.355

7 BRAD MILLS, LHP

BORN: March 5, 1985. **B-T:** L-L. **HT.:** 6-0. **WT.:** 185. **DRAFTED:** Arizona, 2007 (4th round). **SIGNED BY:** Dan Cholowsky.

The Blue Jays first drafted Mills in the 22nd round in 2006, but he turned them down so he could complete his civil-engineering degree. Toronto took him 18 rounds higher in 2007 and watched him advance to Double-A in his first full season while ranking fifth in the minors in ERA (1.95) and eighth in strikeouts (159). Despite his strikeout total, Mills doesn't overpower batters in the traditional sense. Instead he relies on a deceptive, herky-jerky delivery and offspeed stuff to put batters away. His well above-average changeup is a true swing-and-miss pitch because his arm speed fools hitters. They also struggle with his average 12-to-6 curveball. He gets high marks for his mound presence and ability to make adjustments. Mills tends to work up in the zone because of his high three-quarters arm slot, which could be a problem against better hitters at the upper levels. Aside from his fastball velocity—he sits at 88-89 mph and touches 91—that's the chief criticism of the lefthander. Success came easily to Mills in 2008, but pitchers who rely on deception usually find it more difficult to fool big league hitters. Evaluators who have seen him pitch believe his stuff will play in the middle or back of a big league rotation.

Year	Club (League)	Class	W	L	ERA	G	GS	CG	SV	IP	H	R	ER	HR	BB	SO	AVG
2007	Auburn (NYP)	SS	2	0	2.00	6	2	0	0	18	9	4	4	0	6	21	.143
2008	Lansing (MWL)	LoA	6	3	2.55	15	15	0	0	81	71	30	23	3	28	92	.233
	New Hampshire (EL)	AA	3	2	1.10	6	6	0	0	33	24	11	4	2	12	32	.205
	Dunedin (FSL)	HiA	4	0	1.35	6	6	0	0	33	25	9	5	2	12	35	.210
MINOR LEAGUE TOTALS			15	5	1.96	33	29	0	0	165	129	54	36	7	58	180	.214

8 RICKY ROMERO, LHP

BORN: Nov. 6, 1984. **B-T:** R-L. **HT.:** 6-1. **WT.:** 200. **DRAFTED:** Cal State Fullerton, 2005 (1st round). **SIGNED BY:** Demerius Pittman.

Late bloomer or bust? That's the question surrounding Romero, whom the Blue Jays selected sixth overall in 2005 and signed for a club-record $2.4 million. He has spent the bulk of the past three seasons in Double-A and been passed by several lefties in the system. Romero may not be ace he was in college, but his stuff still will play in the big leagues if he throws more strikes with it. He pitches at 91-92 mph and touches 94, but he struggles to command his fastball for strikes. His power curveball usually arrives in the high 70s and features sharp downward break, while his power changeup has enough separation and sink to fool batters. Romero is best suited pitching to spots and keeping batters off balance instead of trying to overpower them. He had some success in Triple-A when he emphasized his high-80s two-seamer, a slower version of his curve and a fringy slider, though he still needs to cut down on his walks. He sometimes telegraphs his breaking pitches by altering his arm slot. Romero still needs to show more consistency to reach his ceiling as a No. 3 or 4 starter. Placed on the 40-man roster this offseason, he'll return to Triple-A to begin 2009.

Year	Club (League)	Class	W	L	ERA	G	GS	CG	SV	IP	H	R	ER	HR	BB	SO	AVG
2005	Auburn (NYP)	SS	0	0	0.00	1	1	0	0	2	2	0	0	0	1	2	.250
	Dunedin (FSL)	HiA	1	0	3.82	8	8	0	0	31	36	13	13	2	7	22	.283
2006	Dunedin (FSL)	HiA	2	1	2.47	10	10	1	0	58	48	17	16	5	14	61	.224
	New Hampshire (EL)	AA	2	7	5.08	12	12	0	0	67	65	43	38	7	26	41	.256
2007	Dunedin (FSL)	HiA	0	0	3.86	1	1	0	0	5	4	2	2	0	1	2	.250
	New Hampshire (EL)	AA	3	6	4.89	18	18	1	0	88	98	57	48	9	51	80	.279
2008	New Hampshire (EL)	AA	5	5	4.96	21	21	0	0	122	139	70	67	9	55	78	.294
	Syracuse (IL)	AAA	3	3	3.38	7	7	1	0	43	42	17	16	3	20	38	.263
MINOR LEAGUE TOTALS			16	22	4.33	78	78	3	0	416	434	219	200	35	175	324	.271

9 MARC RZEPCZYNSKI, LHP

BORN: Aug. 29, 1985. **B-T:** L-L. **HT.:** 6-3. **WT.:** 205. **DRAFTED:** UC Riverside, 2007 (5th round). **SIGNED BY:** Demerius Pittman.

In the last three drafts, the Blue Jays have selected four college senior pitchers in the first five rounds (Brandon Magee, Brad Mills, Rzepczynski and Andrew Liebel), believing they could move quickly while simultaneously providing value. Rzepczynski helped pitch Auburn to a league championship in his debut and had a strong 2008 despite missing April with a fracture in his pitching hand. Rzepczynski pounds the bottom of the strike zone with all four of his pitches, as evidenced by his 3.0 groundout/airout ratio in 2008. His sinker sits at 88-90 mph and touches 92 with tremendous tailing life, while his solid-average slider resides at 82-83 and gives him a weapon to the other side of the plate. His sinking changeup grades as an average pitch. Though he got plenty of swings and misses in low Class A, Rzepczynski lacks a true out pitch. His curveball is a tick behind his slider, but he might not need it to be more than a show-me pitch. He's 23 and has yet to pitch above low Class A, so he needs to stay healthy and get going. The Blue Jays will have a better idea of what they have in Rzepczynski if he earns a fast promotion to Double-A in 2009. He's got the stuff to pitch at the back of a big league rotation or as a middle reliever.

Year	Club (League)	Class	W	L	ERA	G	GS	CG	SV	IP	H	R	ER	HR	BB	SO	AVG
2007	Auburn (NYP)	SS	5	0	2.76	11	7	0	0	46	33	21	14	2	17	49	.201
2008	Lansing (MWL)	LoA	7	6	2.83	22	22	0	0	121	100	41	38	2	42	124	.230
MINOR LEAGUE TOTALS			12	6	2.81	33	29	0	0	167	133	62	52	4	59	173	.222

10 BRAD EMAUS, 2B/3B

BORN: March 28, 1986. **B-T:** R-R. **HT.:** 5-11. **WT.:** 200. **DRAFTED:** Tulane, 2007 (11th round). **SIGNED BY:** Matt Briggs.

A Cape Cod League all-star in 2006, Emaus fell to the 11th round of the 2007 draft after an ankle injury slowed him as a junior. He earned an Opening Day assignment to high Class A in 2008 and went on to surprise the Blue Jays with all facets of his game. He ranked sixth in the Florida State League with 49 extra-base hits. A gap hitter with a sturdy build and a short stroke to the ball, Emaus grinds out at-bats and already shows average hitting and power tools. His strong knowledge of the strike zone and his willingness to use all fields should help him refine his offensive potential. He has a strong arm. After playing mostly third base in his debut, Emaus shifted to second base, where he played as a college junior, and proved to be steady on double-play feeds and pivots, but a bit fringy overall in terms of range. He has slightly below-average speed, though he's a smart baserunner who stole 12 bases in 16 attempts in the FSL. Emaus has drawn comparisons with Ty Wigginton for his build, solid righthanded bat and ability to cover second and third base. After the season he headed to Hawaii Winter Baseball, where he played all over the infield while batting .333/.447/.494, and he will advance to Double-A in 2009.

Year	Club (League)	Class	AVG	G	AB	R	H	2B	3B	HR	RBI	BB	SO	SB	OBP	SLG
2007	Auburn (NYP)	SS	.228	39	136	21	31	6	0	2	14	12	26	2	.298	.316
2008	Dunedin (FSL)	HiA	.302	124	473	87	143	34	3	12	71	60	56	12	.380	.463
MINOR LEAGUE TOTALS			.286	163	609	108	174	40	3	14	85	72	82	14	.362	.430

11 SCOTT CAMPBELL, 2B

BORN: Sept. 25, 1984. **B-T:** L-R. **HT.:** 6-0. **WT.:** 200. **DRAFTED:** Gonzaga, 2006 (10th round). **SIGNED BY:** Brandon Mozley.

Born in Auckland, Campbell became only the second New Zealander ever drafted, following catcher Andy Skeels, whom the Padres selected out of Arkansas in the seventh round in 1987. Campbell, who played both soccer and baseball in high school, led Gonzaga with a .388 average as a senior in 2006, showing the same tremendous command of the strike zone that has been an earmark of his pro career. He's a solid-average hitter geared to use all fields, and he rarely chases pitches outside the strike zone. After seamlessly skipping over high Class A to jump to Double-A in 2008, Campbell ranked sixth in the Eastern League in on-base percentage (.398, boosting his career OBP to .395) and 10th in batting (.302). He put up those numbers despite a late-July hand injury that knocked him out for two weeks and affected him after he returned. Campbell has a repeatable lefthanded swing and above-average hand-eye coordination, though he has limited potential as a power hitter and projects to peak at 8-10 homers annually in the majors. He hasn't had a lot of success against lefthanders and Double-A southpaws limited him to a .194 average, albeit with a characteristic 13 walks in 107 plate appearances. A no better than average runner, Campbell has worked hard to smooth out his defensive play at second base, particularly in turning double plays, but he remains below-average at the position. He throws well enough to handle third base. Campbell is ready for Triple-A and could factor in the Blue Jays' plans next season if they need a lefthanded-hitting, offensive-oriented option at second or third base.

Year	Club (League)	Class	AVG	G	AB	R	H	2B	3B	HR	RBI	BB	SO	SB	OBP	SLG
2006	Auburn (NYP)	SS	.292	68	240	39	70	14	0	0	18	33	31	2	.397	.350
2007	Lansing (MWL)	LoA	.279	107	390	68	109	17	4	7	43	68	56	4	.390	.397
2008	New Hampshire (EL)	AA	.302	112	417	70	126	21	2	9	46	66	63	2	.398	.427
MINOR LEAGUE TOTALS			.291	287	1047	177	305	52	6	16	107	167	150	8	.395	.398

12 BRIAN JEROLOMAN, C

BORN: May 10, 1985. **B-T:** L-R. **HT.:** 6-0. **WT.:** 200. **DRAFTED:** Florida, 2006 (6th round). **SIGNED BY:** Joel Grampietro.

Jeroloman entered 2006 as the top catching prospect in college baseball, but he hit just .242 for Florida as a junior and fell to the Blue Jays in the sixth round. As a pro, he has distinguished himself with his plus package of defensive tools and his patient approach at the plate. Like Scott Campbell, he's a lefty batter who rarely goes outside the strike zone—and he has the .392 career on-base percentage to prove it. His bat isn't nearly as refined as Campbell's, though, and he also has below-average power—though he began driving the ball more frequently in Double-A last season. Jeroloman handles the bat well and uses the entire field. But it's on defense that Jeroloman really shines, as he receives well and develops a good rapport with his pitchers because he's locked in on every play. Agility and soft hands enhance his blocking ability, and his pop times on throws to second base consistently register at an excellent 1.9 seconds because of strong footwork and a quick release. He nabbed 37 percent of basestealers in 2008. He's a below-average runner. For now, the Blue Jays will keep Jeroloman and J.P. Arencibia one level apart so that each can play every day. At some point, the duo figures to serve as Toronto's catching tandem, with Arencibia the projected starter.

Year	Club (League)	Class	AVG	G	AB	R	H	2B	3B	HR	RBI	BB	SO	SB	OBP	SLG
2006	Auburn (NYP)	SS	.241	45	141	27	34	10	1	0	21	26	38	0	.363	.326
2007	Dunedin (FSL)	HiA	.259	100	290	32	75	14	0	3	39	85	57	0	.421	.338
2008	New Hampshire (EL)	AA	.270	71	226	30	61	15	0	6	31	47	47	0	.396	.416
	Syracuse (IL)	AAA	.200	25	75	5	15	2	0	0	5	11	17	0	.302	.227
MINOR LEAGUE TOTALS			.253	241	732	94	185	41	1	9	96	169	159	0	.392	.348

13 JOHN TOLISANO, 2B

BORN: Oct. 7, 1988. **B-T:** B-R. **HT.:** 5-11. **WT.:** 190. **DRAFTED:** HS—Estero, Fla., 2007 (1st round supplemental). **SIGNED BY:** Joel Grampietro.

Tolisano made the loudest initial splash of the four high schoolers the Blue Jays took in the first two rounds of the 2007 draft, swatting 10 homers in his debut to pace the Gulf Coast League. But like Justin Jackson and Kevin Ahrens, he struggled with the grind of playing every day in the Midwest League last season and faded in the second half. He hit just .173 in July and .151 in August to finish on a sour note. The Blue Jays believe that adversity was good for Tolisano, who consistently was better than his competition as an underclassman—Baseball America ranked him as the top 14-year-old player in the United States in 2003. A switch-hitter with a mechanically sound swing from both sides, Tolisano has much more hitting ability than he showed in 2008. He's short to the ball and has average bat speed, though his natural strength and the loft in his swing could lead to average power down the road. His lefthanded swing still is ahead of his righty stroke, as he tends to get out on his front side from the right side. Primarily a shortstop as an amateur, Tolisano has played second base exclusively as a pro. While he has made strides there, he still rates as below-average in terms of his hands, positioning and reads on grounders. He made clear improvements in his double-play technique, both in turning the pivot and making feeds to the shortstop. He's an average runner with more than enough arm for second base. Because of their depth at second base, the Blue Jays can afford to be patient with Tolisano. He may require more time in low Class A to get back on track.

Year	Club (League)	Class	AVG	G	AB	R	H	2B	3B	HR	RBI	BB	SO	SB	OBP	SLG
2007	Blue Jays (GCL)	R	.246	49	183	35	45	5	0	10	33	26	40	7	.336	.437
2008	Lansing (MWL)	LoA	.229	120	432	64	99	20	8	6	47	56	110	5	.315	.354
MINOR LEAGUE TOTALS			.234	169	615	99	144	25	8	16	80	82	150	12	.322	.379

14 ALAN FARINA, RHP

BORN: Aug. 9, 1986. **B-T:** R-R. **HT.:** 5-11. **WT.:** 190. **DRAFTED:** Clemson, 2007 (3rd round). **SIGNED BY:** Marc Tramuta.

Farina signed as a third-round pick out of Clemson after improving his velocity and his slider during his junior year by lengthening his stride and getting more extension out front. A turned ankle limited him to 11 innings in his debut, and lingering elbow soreness severely abbreviated his 2008 campaign. Farina went down at the end of May and didn't return until a few days shy of the end of the season. Toronto opted to move him back to the bullpen, where he thrived in college, abandoning plans to convert him into a starter, perhaps permanently. Though he's listed at just 5-foot-11, Farina delivers the ball from a higher three-quarters arm slot and does a good job of generating downhill plane. His four-seam fastball is just filthy, as it sits at 92-93 mph and touches 95 with plus riding action. He can elevate the fastball, too, because he generates such exceptional spin on the ball, making the pitch appear faster. Farina has two quality breaking balls at his disposal, with his two-plane slider ahead of his curveball. He doesn't have much feel for a changeup, nor will he need it in the bullpen. Farina's stuff will play in a big league bullpen, though he'll need to throw more strikes. If healthy, he could reach Double-A in 2009 and be ready for the big leagues not long thereafter.

Year	Club (League)	Class	W	L	ERA	G	GS	CG	SV	IP	H	R	ER	HR	BB	SO	AVG
2007	Auburn (NYP)	SS	0	2	4.91	6	3	0	0	11	10	7	6	1	10	14	.233
2008	Lansing (MWL)	LoA	3	1	3.07	15	0	0	1	29	19	11	10	2	14	37	.179
MINOR LEAGUE TOTALS			3	3	3.57	21	3	0	1	40	29	18	16	3	24	51	.195

15 ROBERT RAY, RHP

BORN: Jan. 21, 1984. **B-T:** R-R. **HT.:** 6-4. **WT.:** 185. **DRAFTED:** Texas A&M, 2005 (7th round). **SIGNED BY:** Andy Beene.

Ray's dominant turn in the 2004 Cape Cod League piqued the interest of the Blue Jays, who took Ray in the seventh round of the 2005 draft despite his inconsistent junior year at Texas A&M. After a promising pro debut, he totaled just 116 innings in 2006-07 as he battled shoulder woes that resulted in labrum surgery. With health restored, Ray made 29 starts in 2008, logging 167 innings and reaching Double-A. Increased emphasis on attacking hitters with his 89-92 mph sinker propelled him to a breakout season. He also did a much better job of throwing strikes with his average slider, which batters struggle to differentiate from his fastball, in part because he works both sides of the plate. He'll also flash an average curveball from time to time. Additionally, Ray made strides with an average splitter that he uses as a changeup. He has two variations of the pitch, one that cuts and one that fades. His arm action isn't textbook, but it works for him. As the top righthanded starting pitching prospect in the system, Ray could surface in Toronto in 2009 if he continues to progress in the minors. He was added to the 40-man roster in the offseason.

Year	Club (League)	Class	W	L	ERA	G	GS	CG	SV	IP	H	R	ER	HR	BB	SO	AVG
2005	Auburn (NYP)	SS	4	3	2.77	15	13	0	0	62	46	22	19	2	20	58	.204
2006	Dunedin (FSL)	HiA	2	4	4.99	14	9	0	0	49	59	34	27	2	13	37	.306
2007	Dunedin (FSL)	HiA	3	3	4.86	18	15	1	1	67	83	40	36	3	24	57	.304
2008	Dunedin (FSL)	HiA	5	3	4.20	13	13	1	0	71	71	37	33	6	18	60	.257
	New Hampshire (EL)	AA	8	6	3.18	16	16	2	0	96	108	43	34	6	27	72	.282
MINOR LEAGUE TOTALS			22	19	3.90	76	66	4	1	344	367	176	149	19	102	284	.272

16 ERIC EILAND, OF

BORN: Sept. 16, 1988. **B-T:** L-L. **HT.:** 6-2. **WT.:** 200. **DRAFTED:** HS—Houston, 2007 (2nd round). **SIGNED BY:** Andy Beene.

Eiland naturally gets lumped in with Toronto's other premium high school draftees from 2007—Kevin Ahrens, Justin Jackson and John Tolisano—but he was different in one key regard: He had much less baseball experience because he was a two-sport star at Houston's Lamar High. An all-state safety, Eiland drew significant interest from college football programs and turned down a Texas A&M baseball scholarship to sign with the Blue Jays. His inexperience meant that he stayed behind in extended spring training until mid-May last year. While he hit just .233 and didn't homer in 74 games in low Class A, he showed a solid array of secondary skills. Most notably, Eiland went 23-for-24 in stolen-base attempts, as he has plus-plus speed and advanced instincts on the basepaths. He puts his speed to good use in center field, where he could develop into a Gold Glove defender. Eiland also showed an uncanny knack for the strike zone, drawing 37 walks in just 249 at-bats, which was good for a .334 on-base percentage, 12 points higher than the Midwest League average. Built like an NFL cornerback, Eiland possesses the raw strength to hit for power, but he needs to make more consistent contact and stay through the ball better to maximize his potential with the bat. Regarded as a potential four-tool center fielder as an amateur, Eiland still grades as a below-average thrower, even with a revamped arm action. It's going to take time for him to attain consistency with his swing, but his upside will buy him some patience.

Year	Club (League)	Class	AVG	G	AB	R	H	2B	3B	HR	RBI	BB	SO	SB	OBP	SLG
2007	Blue Jays (GCL)	R	.216	51	176	22	38	7	1	1	14	22	62	16	.315	.284
2008	Lansing (MWL)	LoA	.233	74	249	32	58	14	2	0	22	37	80	23	.334	.305
MINOR LEAGUE TOTALS			.226	125	425	54	96	21	3	1	36	59	142	39	.327	.296

17 LUIS PEREZ, LHP

BORN: Jan. 20, 1985. **B-T:** L-L. **HT.:** 6-0. **WT.:** 205. **SIGNED:** Dominican Republic, 2003. **SIGNED BY:** Hilario Soriano.

Already 23, Perez has followed a glacially slow developmental path. He completed his first taste of full-season ball with Lansing in 2008—in his fifth professional season. He spent his first three years in the Rookie-level Dominican Summer League and another in the New York-Penn League as he worked to streamline his funky delivery. At his best, Perez flashes three quality pitches. Like fellow lefty Marc Rzepczynski, he racks up high totals of strikeouts and grounders, posting a 3.08 groundout/airout ratio last year. A sturdy 6 feet and 205 pounds, Perez has a unique delivery featuring a long arm action on the back side. His arm is so quick that his timing appears to be off, and as a result, batters struggle to pick the ball up out of his hand. Perez's two-seam fastball sits at 90-91 mph with good downward plane. His curveball and changeup have plus potential, but he often loses his three-quarters arm slot and gets underneath both pitches, flattening them out. For Perez, who was added to the 40-man roster in the offseason, it's all about maintaining his balance over the rubber and staying downhill in his delivery, two keys he'll work to address as he moves to high Class A in 2009. He could surface in the big leagues as a back-end starter or as a left-on-left reliever.

Year	Club (League)	Class	W	L	ERA	G	GS	CG	SV	IP	H	R	ER	HR	BB	SO	AVG
2004	Blue Jays (DSL)	R	0	0	1.69	6	1	0	0	5	13	3	1	0	7	7	.176
2005	Blue Jays (DSL)	R	2	3	4.96	12	11	0	0	53	42	37	29	3	28	68	.206
2006	Blue Jays (DSL)	R	4	0	1.38	14	14	0	0	85	47	19	13	0	23	107	.158
2007	Auburn (NYP)	SS	3	3	3.70	16	16	0	0	75	73	37	31	1	38	71	.252
2008	Lansing (MWL)	LoA	5	12	3.60	28	23	0	0	137	136	68	55	4	51	137	.264
MINOR LEAGUE TOTALS			14	18	3.29	70	64	0	0	350	298	161	128	8	140	383	.228

18 GUSTAVO PIERRE, SS

BORN: Dec. 28, 1991. **B-T:** R-R. **HT.:** 6-2. **WT.:** 183. **SIGNED:** Dominican Republic, 2008. **SIGNED BY:** Miguel Bernard/Hilario Soriano.

The Blue Jays' recent track record in signing international talent is littered with misses, from the Taiwanese duo of lefty Chi-Hung Cheng ($400,000 in 2003) and righty Po-Hsuan Keng ($225,000 in 2004)—both were released in 2008—to Dominican third baseman Lee Soto ($600,000 in 2005), who has batted a miserable .201/.248/.293 in four years of short-season ball. The jury is still out on Venezuelan third baseman Balbino Fuenmayor ($725,000 in 2006) and Cuban righthander Kenny Rodriguez ($240,000 in 2007). Regardless, the organization is excited about the prospects for a pair of 2008 acquisitions from the Dominican, Pierre and 18-year-old catcher Carlos Perez, who signed in January and hit .306/.459/.378 in the Dominican Summer League. Regarded as one of the top international talents available last summer, Pierre signed for $700,000 on July 2, the first day of the signing period. He's a plus athlete and runner with a trim waist and broad shoulders, providing room to project future strength and power. In time, Pierre could outgrow shortstop, where he has average defensive potential, but evaluators disagree on the strength of his arm. Some say it's average and that he could move to third base, while others think he has below-average arm strength and see him as an outfielder. The ball comes off Pierre's bat well, but international scouts dinged him for inconsistent hitting mechanics, which Blue Jays coaches will address in extended spring training and perhaps in the Gulf Coast League in 2009.

Year	Club (League)	Class	AVG	G	AB	R	H	2B	3B	HR	RBI	BB	SO	SB	OBP	SLG
2008	Did Not Play															

19 MARK SOBOLEWSKI, 3B

BORN: Dec. 24, 1986. **B-T:** R-R. **HT.:** 6-0. **WT.:** 190. **DRAFTED:** Miami, 2008 (4th round). **SIGNED BY:** Carlos Rodriguez.

The fifth of five Miami players drafted in the first four rounds in June, Sobolewski signed a month after the draft for $243,000 as a draft-eligible sophomore. Previously drafted by the Astros in the 20th round of the 2006 draft as a high school shortstop, he might have commanded more had he returned to the Hurricanes for his junior year. The early returns on Sobolweski with wood bats haven't been stellar, as he batted .189 without a homer in 39 Cape Cod League games in 2007 and .256 with one homer in 35 games in his pro debut. He was slowed last summer by an injury to an ankle tendon that required surgery and caused him to miss instructional league. A physical hitter, Sobolewski bats from a wide stance and hammers fastballs—especially to his pull side—with above-average bat speed. But because his swing features minimal load, his power output remains inconsistent. His hands are fast and his swing plane is even, so he could develop into an average hitter. His most distinguished defensive tool is a strong throwing arm, and he's adept at charging slow rollers and going to his left. Sobolewski drew criticism as an amateur for dropping down on throws and slinging the ball across the infield, leading to a high error total—and he committed 11 miscues in his debut. He's a below-average runner. Sobolewski is rawer than the typical high pick from a major college program, so he may need additional time to refine his game. If he doesn't clean up his throwing at third, some observers think his arm strength would play well at catcher or right field.

Year	Club (League)	Class	AVG	G	AB	R	H	2B	3B	HR	RBI	BB	SO	SB	OBP	SLG
2008	Auburn (NYP)	SS	.256	35	133	18	34	5	0	1	10	4	32	0	.283	.316
MINOR LEAGUE TOTALS			.256	35	133	18	34	5	0	1	10	4	32	0	.283	.316

20 SCOTT RICHMOND, RHP

BORN: Aug. 30, 1979. **B-T:** R-R. **HT.:** 6-5. **WT.:** 225. **SIGNED:** Edmonton (Northern League), 2007. **SIGNED BY:** Rob Ducey.

Few recent players have faced longer odds of making it to the big leagues than Richmond, whose journey included stops in the Moose Jaw, Sask., amateur ranks and with the independent Edmonton Cracker-Cats. His high school in Aldergrove, B.C., didn't offer baseball, so Richmond instead played summer ball in western Canada. After high school, he worked at various Vancouver shipyards for three years before enrolling at Missouri Valley College, an NAIA program, at age 22. He transferred to Bossier Parish (La.) CC a year later and then to Oklahoma State. An all-Big 12 Conference honorable mention selection as a senior in 2005, he went undrafted because he already was 25. Richmond ultimately signed with Edmonton of the Northern League because securing a work visa to pitch professionally in the United States posed a challenge. After he spent two years as a reliever and a third as a starter with the Cracker-Cats, the Blue Jays signed Richmond out of a Northern League tryout in November 2007, noting his ideal pitcher's build and long, loose delivery. He broke into affiliated ball in April at Double-A New Hampshire and made his big league debut on July 30, vicitimizing Evan Longoria for his first strikeout. Had he not been called up, Richmond was slated to be Team Canada's ace in the Olympics. He attacks batters with a low-90s sinker and a hard cut slider at 85-87 mph, and he's much tougher on righthanders than lefthanders. His changeup is average at times, but his curveball is a bit loopy and rates as below-average. If he can improve his changeup, he'd have a fighting chance against lefties. Richmond picks things up quickly, but he gets in trouble when he elevates his pitches because he doesn't have overpowering stuff. He threw nothing but strikes with the Blue Jays, and he shut out the Orioles for six innings in his final start of 2008 to earn his first big league victory. He could factor into the back of Toronto's rotation in 2009.

Year	Club (League)	Class	W	L	ERA	G	GS	CG	SV	IP	H	R	ER	HR	BB	SO	AVG
2005	Edmonton (NOR)	IND	1	4	6.25	20	7	1	4	59	72	42	41	9	20	42	.305
2006	Edmonton (NOR)	IND	3	6	3.03	39	1	0	8	71	53	26	24	5	17	72	.204
2007	Edmonton (NOR)	IND	10	9	4.26	23	23	2	0	146	147	76	69	7	47	110	.261
2008	New Hampshire (EL)	AA	5	8	4.92	16	16	0	0	90	89	55	49	14	30	84	.251
	Syracuse (IL)	AAA	1	3	3.56	8	8	1	0	48	44	20	19	6	13	40	.244
	Toronto (AL)	MAJ	1	3	4.00	5	5	1	0	27	32	12	12	2	2	20	.296
MINOR LEAGUE TOTALS			6	11	4.45	24	24	1	0	138	133	75	68	20	43	124	.249
MAJOR LEAGUE TOTALS			1	3	4.00	5	5	1	0	27	32	12	12	2	2	20	.296

21 KENNY WILSON, OF

BORN: Jan. 30, 1990. **B-T:** B-R. **HT.:** 6-0. **WT.:** 165. **DRAFTED:** HS—Tampa, 2008 (2nd round). **SIGNED BY:** Joel Grampietro.

An exceptional runner and athlete, Wilson turned down a commitment to Florida to sign for $644,000 as a second-round pick last summer. He gets down the first-base line in 3.9-4.0 seconds on a full swing from the right side of the plate, and he can cut that time to 3.7 seconds on bunts. In fact, Gulf Coast League shortstops struggled to throw him out if the ball bounced more than once on the infield. Wilson uses his legs as a weapon on the basepaths, too, as he stole 25 bases in 28 attempts. His bat isn't nearly so refined, but he has a chance to develop a leadoff batter profile. He could become an above-average hitter, especially when considering infield and bunt hits, but he'll always have below-average power because he emphasizes hitting line drives and hard grounders. Wilson's pitch recognition has a long way to go, but he did finish second on his GCL team with 20 walks. No such concerns exist about his defense, as he's a plus defensive center fielder with an average arm. To get the most out of Wilson's speed and batting potential, the Blue Jays introduced him to switch-hitting during instructional league. He had toyed around with batting lefthanded in batting cages as an amateur, so Wilson was receptive to the plan, though it may dictate that he opens 2009 in extended spring training.

Year	Club (League)	Class	AVG	G	AB	R	H	2B	3B	HR	RBI	BB	SO	SB	OBP	SLG
2008	Blue Jays (GCL)	R	.210	51	162	25	34	6	2	0	12	20	60	25	.319	.272
MINOR LEAGUE TOTALS			.210	51	162	25	34	6	2	0	12	20	60	25	.319	.272

22 ANDREW LIEBEL, RHP

BORN: March 22, 1986. **B-T:** R-R. **HT.:** 6-1. **WT.:** 180. **DRAFTED:** Long Beach State, 2008 (3rd round). **SIGNED BY:** Demerius Pittman.

Liebel worked mostly as a reliever during his first two seasons at Long Beach State before emerging as a consistent starter toward the end of his junior season. He continued to pitch well as a senior in 2008, going 8-4, 2.22 in 15 starts, and represented good value as a polished college righthander with a simple, clean delivery. The Blue Jays signed him for $340,000 as a third-round pick. Liebel covers the plate with four pitches he can throw for strikes in any count, headlined by his 88-90 mph sinker. He touches 93 with his four-seam fastball. Liebel drew pre-draft comparisons to Ian Kennedy as a compact college righty with a wide repertoire. As with Kennedy, his plus changeup consistently rates ahead of his fringe-average breaking pitches, a curveball and a slider. He's mature and knows how to pitch to his strengths, which are locating his fastball and keeping hitters off balance with his changeup. Because of his command and pitchability, Liebel figures to move quickly through the system and probably will begin his first full season in high Class A. He has the makings of a No. 5 starter.

Year	Club (League)	Class	W	L	ERA	G	GS	CG	SV	IP	H	R	ER	HR	BB	SO	AVG
2008	Auburn (NYP)	SS	1	2	3.68	7	1	0	0	15	19	6	6	2	2	19	.311
MINOR LEAGUE TOTALS			1	2	3.68	7	1	0	0	15	19	6	6	2	2	19	.311

23 TYLER PASTORNICKY, SS

BORN: Dec. 13, 1989. **B-T:** R-R. **HT.:** 5-11. **WT.:** 170. **DRAFTED:** HS—Bradenton, Fla., 2008 (5th round). **SIGNED BY:** Joel Grampietro.

The Blue Jays have gone hard after high school talent in the state of Florida in the past two drafts, taking John Tolisano (second round) in 2007 and Kenny Wilson (second), Pastornicky (fifth) and Markus Brisker (sixth) in 2008. Pastornicky signed with the Blue Jays for $175,000, passing on the opportunity to play at Florida State. He has big league bloodlines, as his father Cliff played 10 games at third base for the 1983 Royals and currently scouts for Kansas City. An athletic middle infielder, Pastornicky does a lot of things well but has no standout tool. He's a rangy if unrefined shortstop with good hands and plus arm strength, though he'll need to continue working to handle the defensive demands of the position. A heady player with a feel for the game, he has a chance to be an average hitter with line-drive power. He has good bat speed and uses the whole field, though his swing is too long at times. As he matures, he figures to add muscle to his lean frame. Pastornicky's best attribute is above-average speed, as he runs the 60-yard dash in 6.6 seconds and already is a plus basestealer who expertly cuts the bases while in stride. He led the GCL Blue Jays with 27 stolen bases (in 32 attempts) and 21 walks. Because of his solid all-around game, Pastornicky may develop into a regular, but he also could surface as a utilityman.

Year	Club (League)	Class	AVG	G	AB	R	H	2B	3B	HR	RBI	BB	SO	SB	OBP	SLG
2008	Blue Jays (GCL)	R	.263	50	160	32	42	6	3	1	17	21	21	27	.349	.356
MINOR LEAGUE TOTALS			.263	50	160	32	42	6	3	1	17	21	21	27	.349	.356

24 DANNY FARQUHAR, RHP

BORN: Feb. 17, 1987. **B-T:** R-R. **HT.:** 5-11. **WT.:** 180. **DRAFTED:** Louisiana-Lafayette, 2008 (10th round). **SIGNED BY:** Rob St. Julien.

Farquhar struggled as Louisiana-Lafayette's staff ace and lost velocity in 2008, his junior year, after spending his first two seasons in a swingman role. He dropped to the 10th round in the draft, not only because of his backsliding, but also because he's 5-foot-11, has effort in his delivery and is unconventional. The Blue Jays were rewarded for their $112,500 investment, though, as Farquhar thrived in the Auburn bullpen. His pitching style features two distinct arm slots, from which he can throw strikes with both a quality fastball and breaking ball. He sits at 92 mph and touches 94 from a high three-quarters slot and mixes in an average mid-70s curveball and an occasional cutter. From a below-sidearm angle, Farquhar pitches at 89-90 with incredible life, a product of his long and loose arms. From the lower angle, he also throws a sweeping 78-82 mph Frisbee slider that makes righthanders uncomfortable, and a changeup that serves as a show-me pitch. Farquhar is poised to move quickly now that he's a full-time reliever. He could begin 2009 in high Class A.

Year	Club (League)	Class	W	L	ERA	G	GS	CG	SV	IP	H	R	ER	HR	BB	SO	AVG
2008	Auburn (NYP)	SS	2	2	2.39	12	0	0	0	26	20	10	7	1	6	27	.215
	Lansing (MWL)	LoA	0	0	0.00	3	0	0	0	6	0	1	0	0	2	4	.000
MINOR LEAGUE TOTALS			2	2	1.95	15	0	0	0	32	20	11	7	1	8	31	.180

25 TRYSTAN MAGNUSON, RHP

BORN: June 6, 1985. **B-T:** L-R. **HT.:** 6-8. **WT.:** 205. **DRAFTED:** Louisville, 2007 (1st round supplemental). **SIGNED BY:** Steve Miller.

As a fifth-year senior in 2007, Magnuson would have been free to sign with any club had Louisville not made the College World Series. As it turned it turned out, the Vancouver native signed with the Blue Jays for $462,500 as the 56th overall pick. He signed late, though, and had his pro debut delayed until 2008 by elbow soreness. Magnuson's uncle Keith appeared in two Stanley Cup finals during the 1970s as part of an 11-year career in the NHL. A former walk-on at Louisville, Magnuson thrived when the Cardinals made him their closer in 2007, though Toronto drafted him with designs on developing him as a starter. Because of his limited workloads in college, Magnuson worked on strict pitch counts in 2008, seldom exceeding 65 pitches in an outing. As a result, he completed five innings in a start just four times in 24 tries and still is seeking his first pro victory. Toronto shut him down after his Aug. 11 start because of general fatigue, though he resumed throwing during instructional league. When he starts, Magnuson's fastball sits at 90-92 mph with plus downhill plane—a product of his 6-foot-8 frame—and he still flashes 93-94 mph heat in short stints. His height works against him at times, too, because he doesn't always repeat his mechanics and throw strikes. If Magnuson can harness his 84-87 mph slider, it would give him a second weapon, but it remains inconsistent. He worked on his changeup in a starting role and in regular side sessions, but he lacks feel for the pitch. Because he turns 24 this year and struggled in low Class A, the Blue Jays may be tempted to turn Magnuson loose as a reliever so he can move more quickly.

Year	Club (League)	Class	W	L	ERA	G	GS	CG	SV	IP	H	R	ER	HR	BB	SO	AVG
2008	Lansing (MWL)	LoA	0	9	5.40	24	24	0	0	82	91	57	49	6	35	49	.282
MINOR LEAGUE TOTALS			0	9	5.40	24	24	0	0	82	91	57	49	6	35	49	.282

26 MARKUS BRISKER, OF

BORN: Aug. 21, 1990. **B-T:** R-R. **HT.:** 6-4. **WT.:** 192. **DRAFTED:** HS—Winter Haven, Fla., 2008 (6th round). **SIGNED BY:** Joel Grampietro.

Brisker dropped basketball as a high school senior at Winter Haven (Fla.) High, the alma mater of Braves outfield prospect Jordan Schafer, so he could begin the baseball season on time. The move paid off when the Blue Jays took him in the sixth round of the 2008 draft and signed him for $125,000. To keep his options open, Brisker had committed to Daytona Beach (Fla.) CC. A physical 6-foot-4 and 192 pounds, he offers the best strength and size combination of any of Toronto's 2008 picks. He can cover 60 yards in 6.4 seconds and he can touch 94 mph off the mound, giving him well above-average foot speed and arm strength. In fact, he finished in a dead heat with fleet-footed Jays second-round pick Kenny Wilson at a Florida high school all-star game. Though he's not a traditional power hitter yet, Brisker possesses plus bat speed and projects to add at least average thump to his toolset as he gains strength and at-bats. He was the lone Jays 2008 draftee to top .300 in the Gulf Coast League. Brisker is a steady center fielder, though he may outgrow the position and move to an outfield corner. His stolen-base output also may diminish in time as he fills out. Brisker has a high ceiling but also a long road to travel to reach it. He'll be 18 for most of the 2009 season, so a return engagement in short-season ball wouldn't be viewed as a disappointment.

Year	Club (League)	Class	AVG	G	AB	R	H	2B	3B	HR	RBI	BB	SO	SB	OBP	SLG
2008	Blue Jays (GCL)	R	.306	32	108	16	33	4	0	0	6	11	22	13	.370	.343
MINOR LEAGUE TOTALS			.306	32	108	16	33	4	0	0	6	11	22	13	.370	.343

27 CURTIS THIGPEN, C/1B

BORN: April 19, 1983. **B-T:** R-R. **HT.:** 5-11. **WT.:** 200. **DRAFTED:** Texas, 2004 (2nd round). **SIGNED BY:** Andy Beene.

Thigpen played on three College World Series teams from 2002-04 with Texas, where he served as Taylor Teagarden's backup. Because his catching skills were thought to be less refined, it was a surprise when Thigpen reached Double-A in his first full season and the major leagues in his third. Though he showed a keen eye at the plate and a line-drive stroke as he climbed the ladder, his bat regressed once he reached Triple-A and Toronto. In 593 at-bats for Syracuse from 2006-08, Thigpen batted just .245/.295/.341 with seven home runs and 36 doubles. That might be acceptable if he were an outstanding defensive catcher, but he's merely adequate behind the plate. His receiving skills are strong and he's quite agile, but Thigpen has consistently posted low caught-stealing percentages in the minors. Last season, he nabbed just 16 percent of basestealers. When Brian Jeroloman advanced to Syracuse at the end of July, Thigpen shifted to first base. He also played a handful of games at third base and one at second, and it's as a jack-of-all-trades that he best profiles at the big league level. Because he's so athletic, the Blue Jays have given Thigpen a pass for his poor 2008 campaign and expect him to compete for a backup catcher role until J.P. Arencibia and Jeroloman are ready.

Year	Club (League)	Class	AVG	G	AB	R	H	2B	3B	HR	RBI	BB	SO	SB	OBP	SLG
2004	Auburn (NYP)	SS	.301	45	166	34	50	11	2	7	29	23	32	1	.390	.518
2005	Lansing (MWL)	LoA	.287	79	293	41	84	18	2	5	35	54	34	5	.397	.413
	New Hampshire (EL)	AA	.284	39	141	18	40	8	0	4	15	9	19	0	.340	.426
2006	New Hampshire (EL)	AA	.259	87	309	49	80	25	5	5	36	52	61	5	.370	.421
	Syracuse (IL)	AAA	.264	13	53	3	14	3	0	1	9	2	9	0	.304	.377
2007	Syracuse (IL)	AAA	.285	50	179	20	51	10	0	3	20	17	23	1	.348	.391
	Toronto (AL)	MAJ	.238	47	101	13	24	5	0	0	11	8	17	2	.294	.287
2008	Syracuse (IL)	AAA	.222	96	361	28	80	23	0	3	41	21	58	2	.263	.310
	Toronto (AL)	MAJ	.176	10	17	2	3	0	0	1	1	1	8	0	.263	.353
MINOR LEAGUE TOTALS			.266	409	1502	193	399	98	9	28	185	178	236	14	.347	.399
MAJOR LEAGUE TOTALS			.229	57	118	15	27	5	0	1	12	9	25	2	.289	.297

28 BALBINO FUENMAYOR, 3B

BORN: Nov. 26, 1989. **B-T:** R-R. **HT.:** 6-3. **WT.:** 195. **SIGNED:** Venezuela, 2006. **SIGNED BY:** Rafael Moncada.

Fuenmayor signed with the Blue Jays for $725,000 in August 2006 following an impressive workout at Rogers Centre in front of general manager J.P. Ricciardi. He didn't fare well in his 2007 pro debut as one of the Gulf Coast League's youngest regulars, hitting just .174 and striking out 68 times to pace the league. He performed much better in his repeat of the GCL in 2008, showing a vastly improved hitting approach, including a willingness to go the other way. He still struggled at times with pitch recognition, but his compact swing and solid bat speed portend at least average hitting ability. Fuenmayor may be a late bloomer in terms of power because he still has to learn to turn on pitches consistently. If he does, he could develop average power. Hitting in the GCL is tough, though, because many of the pitchers who throw hard haven't yet refined their control. Already physically mature at age 18, Fuenmayor only will slow down as he ages, and he projects as a below-average runner. He shows below-average lateral movement at third base, too, and likely faces a move to first base or to the corner outfield in the future. His arm is average. Fuenmayor impressed the Blue Jays with his work ethic in 2008 and he has an outside shot at moving up to low Class A in 2009.

Year	Club (League)	Class	AVG	G	AB	R	H	2B	3B	HR	RBI	BB	SO	SB	OBP	SLG
2007	Blue Jays (GCL)	R	.174	48	178	13	31	5	2	1	12	12	68	0	.244	.242
2008	Blue Jays (GCL)	R	.307	50	179	25	55	14	2	3	26	11	48	0	.360	.458
MINOR LEAGUE TOTALS			.241	98	357	38	86	19	4	4	38	23	116	0	.302	.350

29 HENDERSON ALVAREZ, RHP

BORN: April 18, 1990. **B-T:** R-R. **HT.:** 6-1. **WT.:** 175. **SIGNED:** Venezuela, 2006. **SIGNED BY:** Rafael Moncada.

Along with Balbino Fuenmayor and 19-year-old outfielder Johermyn Chavez, Alvarez stands at the forefront of young Venezuelan talent in Toronto's system. Signed in October 2006 at age 16, he has such a live arm that he makes the cut here despite compiling a career 5.63 ERA in his two pro seasons in Rookie ball. He has a chance for three plus pitches, headlined by his dancing 92-93 mph two-seam fastball. Alvarez's four-seamer touches 94 and features natural cutting action. His hard slurve clocks in at 85-87 mph and flashes plus potential, but it's just usable now because he doesn't command it. He also shows hitters a fading changeup that he's still ironing out. Batters just don't seem comfortable facing Alvarez, in part because he lacks reliable fastball command. His control is fine, though, as he has walked just 14 batters in 72 pro innings. Like many teenagers with plus arm strength, Alvarez tries to overthrow everything. He also needs to be mindful of staying on top of his pitches so that they don't flatten out. At times his mound composure breaks down as well. Alvarez has the raw arm strength to profile as either a starter or power reliever, though he's probably still not ready for full-season ball.

Year	Club (League)	Class	W	L	ERA	G	GS	CG	SV	IP	H	R	ER	HR	BB	SO	AVG
2007	Blue Jays (DSL)	R	1	2	5.61	8	7	0	0	26	36	18	16	0	8	20	.324
2008	Blue Jays (GCL)	R	1	4	5.63	12	11	0	0	46	63	41	29	3	6	34	.310
MINOR LEAGUE TOTALS			2	6	5.63	20	18	0	0	72	99	59	45	3	14	54	.315

30 TIM COLLINS, LHP

BORN: Aug. 29, 1989. **B-T:** L-L. **HT.:** 5-7. **WT.:** 155. **SIGNED:** HS—Worcester, Mass., NDFA 2007. **SIGNED BY:** J.P. Ricciardi.

Collins led Worcester (Mass.) Technical High to the state's Division 2 title as a senior in 2007, going 7-0, 0.17 while also leading his league in hitting with a .472 average. To top it off, he pitched a no-hitter in the central Massachusetts title-clincher. He went undrafted that June, though, because he stands at just 5-foot-7 and 155 pounds. Collins was set to attend the CC of Rhode Island before Blue Jays general manager J.P. Ricciardi, who grew up in Worcester and had seen Collins pitch, set up a workout. Toronto signed Collins that July after an impressive bullpen session. He rewarded the organization's faith by converting 14 of 17 saves as Lansing's youngest pitcher, and by leading all minor league relievers by limiting opponents to a .156 average. He also ranked 10th among relievers by averaging 12.9 strikeouts per nine innings. Collins' arm is exceptionally quick and he fires 88-90 mph four-seam fastballs from a high three-quarters arm slot. He gets good spin on the pitch and also on his above-average curveball, which he used to great effect in changing batters' eye levels. A good athlete, he holds runners well and works quickly. Because Collins works up in the zone with his fastball, some observers wonder if his stuff will play at higher levels. He doesn't have much of a changeup. Collins has incredible mental toughness and the bulldog mentality to throw strikes out of the bullpen, but he'll have to keep proving himself at higher levels.

Year	Club (League)	Class	W	L	ERA	G	GS	CG	SV	IP	H	R	ER	HR	BB	SO	AVG
2007	Blue Jays (GCL)	R	0	0	4.50	7	0	0	0	6	6	3	3	0	2	7	.273
2008	Lansing (MWL)	LoA	4	2	1.58	39	0	0	14	68	36	13	12	3	32	98	.156
MINOR LEAGUE TOTALS			4	2	1.82	46	0	0	14	74	42	16	15	3	34	105	.166

Washington Nationals

BY AARON FITT

Washington's first season in brand-new Nationals Park peaked on Opening Day, when franchise player Ryan Zimmerman hit a walkoff home run to beat the Braves. It was all downhill from there, as no Nationals hitter drove in more than 61 runs and no Nats pitcher won more than 10 games while the club posted a major league-worst 59-102 record.

The shoddy on-field product depressed attendance, as Washington drew just 2.3 million fans—the lowest attendance figure for an inaugural year of a ballpark since the modern stadium boom began with Camden Yards in 1992.

There were few bright spots at the major league level. Lastings Milledge, a former überprospect acquired in an offseason trade with the Mets, led the club with 61 RBIs and tied Zimmerman with a team-best 14 homers. Elijah Dukes, another talented outfielder added in an offseason deal, was the Nationals' most dangerous hitter when he wasn't sidelined by knee and calf injuries. Rookies Collin Balester and John Lannan settled into the majors as arms to build around.

It was an up-and-down year for the farm system. Washington's U.S. affiliates won 44 more games than they did a year ago and posted a combined winning record for the first time since 1998. Leading the way was high Class A Potomac, whose Carolina League championship was the first minor league title for a Nats affiliate since the franchise moved in 2005. Several prospects who passed through Potomac took steps forward, headlined by righthander Jordan Zimmermann, who emerged as the clear-cut top prospect in the system.

But last year's No. 1 prospect, first baseman Chris Marrero, suffered a significant setback in June, when he broke his fibula and tore ligaments in his ankle, ending his season. And with the exception of Zimmermann, many of the players from a 2007 draft rated by Baseball America as baseball's best crop that year didn't quite make the impact Washington hoped for last season.

The Nationals' 2008 draft wasn't nearly as productive, as they failed to come to terms with No. 9 overall pick Aaron Crow, who was widely regarded as the best righthander in the draft. In the end, the two sides couldn't bridge the gap between $3.5 million and $4 million, leaving Washington with a compensatory pick (10th overall) in 2009—to go with the No. 1 overall choice it earned with its poor season.

The Nats did get a pair of high-ceiling prep outfielders in second-rounder Destin Hood and 15th-rounder J.P. Ramirez, who both received seven-figure bonuses. Still, Washington spent $3 million less on the draft last year than it did in 2007.

Even the Nationals' progress in Latin America was stunted. They announced their intention to be major players on the international scene by signing infielder Esmailyn Gonzalez for $1.4 million in 2006, but they didn't sign any international player for a six-figure bonus in 2008. Meanwhile, general manager Jim Bowden and special assistant Jose Rijo were questioned by the FBI and Major League Baseball investigators in connection with a Latin America bonus-skimming scandal.

Lastings Milledge showed glimpses of his prodigious talent in Washington's down year

ED WOLFSTEIN

TOP 30 PROSPECTS

1. Jordan Zimmermann, rhp	16. Leonard Davis, of/3b
2. Ross Detwiler, lhp	17. Bill Rhinehart, 1b
3. Chris Marrero, 1b	18. Roger Bernadina, of
4. Michael Burgess, of	19. Ian Desmond, ss
5. Jack McGeary, lhp	20. Craig Stammen, rhp
6. Derek Norris, c	21. Marco Estrada, rhp
7. Destin Hood, of	22. Mike Hinckley, lhp
8. Adrian Nieto, c	23. Stephen King, 3b
9. J.P. Ramirez, of	24. Will Atwood, lhp
10. Esmailyn Gonzalez, ss	25. Josh Smoker, lhp
11. Justin Maxwell, of	26. Colton Willems, rhp
12. Garrett Mock, rhp	27. Luis Atilano, rhp
13. Shairon Martis, rhp	28. Cory Van Allen, lhp
14. Danny Espinosa, ss	29. Luke Montz, c
15. Graham Hicks, lhp	30. Terrell Young, rhp

General Manager: Jim Bowden. **Farm Director:** Bobby Williams. **Scouting Director:** Dana Brown.

Class	Team	League	W	L	PCT	Finish*	Manager	Affiliated
Majors	Washington	National	59	102	.366	16th (16)	Manny Acta	—
Triple-A	Columbus Clippers	International	69	73	.486	7th (14)	Tim Foli	2007
Double-A	Harrisburg Senators	Eastern	73	69	.514	6th (12)	John Stearns	1991
High A	Potomac Nationals	Carolina	79	61	.564	^2nd (8)	Randy Knorr	2005
Low A	Hagerstown Suns	South Atlantic	61	78	.439	13th (16)	Darnell Coles	2007
Short-season	Vermont Lake Monsters	New York-Penn	33	42	.440	11th (14)	Ramon Aviles	1994
Rookie	GCL Nationals	Gulf Coast	33	22	.600	3rd (16)	Bob Henley	1998
Overall 2008 Minor League Record			348	345	.502	17th		

* Finish in overall standings (No. of teams in league). ^League champion.

LAST YEAR'S TOP 30

Rank	Player, Pos.	Status
1.	Chris Marrero, 1b/of	No. 3
2.	Ross Detwiler, lhp	No. 2
3.	Collin Balester, rhp	Majors
4.	Michael Burgess, of	No. 4
5.	Jack McGeary, lhp	No. 5
6.	Josh Smoker, lhp	No. 25
7.	Jordan Zimmermann, rhp	No. 1
8.	Justin Maxwell, of	No. 11
9.	Colton Willems, rhp	No. 26
10.	John Lannan, lhp	Majors
11.	Jake Smolinski, of	(Marlins)
12.	Tyler Clippard, rhp	Dropped out
13.	Adam Carr, rhp	Dropped out
14.	Ian Desmond, ss	No. 19
15.	Garrett Mock, rhp	No. 12
16.	Stephen King, 2b/ss	No. 23
17.	Esmailyn Gonzalez, ss	No. 10
18.	Shairon Martis, rhp	No. 13
19.	Brad Peacock, rhp	Dropped out
20.	Kory Casto, of/3b	Majors
21.	Matt Whitney, 1b	Dropped out
22.	Derek Norris, c	No. 6
23.	Mike Daniel, of	Dropped out
24.	Stephen Englund, of	Dropped out
25.	Jhonny Nunez, rhp	(White Sox)
26.	Hassan Pena, rhp	Dropped out
27.	Martin Beno, rhp	Dropped out
28.	Zech Zinicola, rhp	Dropped out
29.	Roger Bernadina, of	No. 18
30.	P.J. Dean, rhp	(Marlins)

BEST TOOLS

Best Hitter for Average	J.P. Ramirez
Best Power Hitter	Chris Marrero
Best Strike-Zone Discipline	Derek Norris
Fastest Baserunner	Roger Bernadina
Best Athlete	Justin Maxwell
Best Fastball	Jordan Zimmermann
Best Curveball	Jack McGeary
Best Slider	Jordan Zimmermann
Best Changeup	Shairon Martis
Best Control	Jack McGeary
Best Defensive Catcher	Sandy Leon
Best Defensive Infielder	Danny Espinosa
Best Infield Arm	Ian Desmond
Best Defensive Outfielder	Roger Bernadina
Best Outfield Arm	Michael Burgess

PROJECTED 2012 LINEUP

Catcher	Jesus Flores
First Base	Chris Marrero
Second Base	Esmailyn Gonzalez
Third Base	Ryan Zimmerman
Shortstop	Cristian Guzman
Left Field	Elijah Dukes
Center Field	Lastings Milledge
Right Field	Michael Burgess
No. 1 Starter	Jordan Zimmermann
No. 2 Starter	Ross Detwiler
No. 3 Starter	Scott Olsen
No. 4 Starter	Collin Balester
No. 5 Starter	John Lannan
Closer	Garrett Mock

TOP PROSPECTS OF THE DECADE

Year	Player, Pos.	2008 Org.
1999	Michael Barrett, 3b/c	Padres
2000	Tony Armas, rhp	Mets
2001	Donnie Bridges, rhp	Out of baseball
2002	Brandon Phillips, ss	Reds
2003	Clint Everts, rhp	Nationals
2004	Clint Everts, rhp	Nationals
2005	Mike Hinckley, lhp	Nationals
2006	Ryan Zimmerman, 3b	Nationals
2007	Collin Balester, rhp	Nationals
2008	Chris Marrero, 1b/of	Nationals

TOP DRAFT PICKS OF THE DECADE

Year	Player, Pos.	2008 Org.
1998	Josh McKinley, ss	Out of baseball
1999	Josh Girdley, lhp	Out of baseball
2000	Justin Wayne, rhp	Out of baseball
2001	Josh Karp, rhp	Out of baseball
2002	Clint Everts, rhp	Nationals
2003	Chad Cordero, rhp	Nationals
2004	Bill Bray, lhp	Reds
2005	Ryan Zimmerman, 3b	Nationals
2006	Chris Marrero, of	Nationals
2007	Ross Detwiler, lhp	Nationals
2008	*Aaron Crow, rhp	Fort Worth (American Assoc.)

*Did not sign.

LARGEST BONUSES IN CLUB HISTORY

Ryan Zimmerman, 2006	$2,975,000
Justin Wayne, 2000	$2,950,000
Josh Karp, 2001	$2,650,000
Clint Everts, 2002	$2,500,000
Ross Detwiler, 2007	$2,150,000

WASHINGTON NATIONALS

TOP 2009 ROOKIE: Jordan Zimmermann, rhp. Washington's top prospect could start the year in the minors, but his command of a quality four-pitch repertoire should land him in the majors by midseason at the latest.

BREAKOUT PROSPECT: Graham Hicks, lhp. With a loose arm and tall, projectable frame, he has one of the highest ceilings in the organization.

SOURCE OF TOP 30 TALENT			
Homegrown	26	Acquired	4
College	9	Trades	3
Junior college	2	Rule 5 draft	1
High school	13	Independent leagues	0
Draft-and-follow	0	Free agents/waivers	0
Nondrafted free agents	0		
International	2		

SLEEPER: Chris Curran, of. A potential find in the 22nd round of the 2008 draft, the undersized Curran has well above-average speed, excellent defensive skills in center and surprising strength in his swing.

Numbers in parentheses indicate prospect rankings.

LF
Destin Hood (7)
J.P. Ramirez (9)
Leonard Davis (16)
Mike Daniel
Marvin Lowrance
Dee Brown

CF
Justin Maxwell (11)
Rogearvin Bernadina (18)
Chris Curran
Marcus Jones
Stephen Englund
Boomer Whiting

RF
Michael Burgess (4)
J.R. Higley
Edgardo Baez
Aaron Seuss

3B
Stephen King (23)
Steven Souza
Joel Guzman
Ofilio Castro

SS
Danny Espinosa (14)
Ian Desmond (19)
Alberto Gonzalez
Nick Arata

2B
Esmailyn Gonzalez (10)
Seth Bynum
Steve Lombardozzi
Blake Stouffer
Michael Martinez

1B
Chris Marrero (3)
Bill Rhinehart (17)
Matt Whitney

C
Derek Norris (6)
Adrian Nieto (8)
Luke Montz (29)
Danny Killian
Brian Peacock
Sean Rooney
Sandy Leon
Devin Ivany

RHP	
Starters	**Relievers**
Jordan Zimmermann (1)	Luis Atilano (27)
Garrett Mock (12)	Terrell Young (30)
Shairon Martis (13)	Zech Zinicola
Craig Stammen (20)	Adam Carr
Marco Estrada (21)	Juan Jaime
Colton Willems (26)	Martin Beno
Tyler Clippard	Clint Everts
Paul Demny	Cole Kimball
Hassan Pena	Jose Pinales
Brad Peacock	Johan Figuereo
Marcos Frias	Carlos Peralta
Jeff Mandel	Casey Whitmer
Brad Meyers	Josh Wilkie
Adrian Alaniz	Terrence Engles
Patrick Arnold	

LHP	
Starters	**Relievers**
Ross Detwiler (2)	Mike Hinckley (22)
Jack McGeary (5)	Yunior Novoa
Graham Hicks (15)	Ricardo Pecina
Will Atwood (24)	Atahualpa Severino
Josh Smoker (25)	Patrick McCoy
Cory VanAllen (28)	Jack Spradlin
Bobby Hansen	
Justin Jones	
Tommy Milone	

2008

BONUSES: $4.8 MILLION

BEST PURE HITTER: OF J.P. Ramirez (15) used his smooth lefthanded swing to jump right in after signing Aug. 15, going 7-for-16 in the Rookie-level Gulf Coast League playoffs. OF J.R. Higley (9) has a line-drive stroke, while C Adrian Nieto (5) has a good feel from both sides of the plate.

BEST POWER HITTER: OF Destin Hood (2) has electric bat speed and raw power to spare. Nieto has more usable power for now.

FASTEST RUNNER: Five-foot-9 OF Chris Curran (22) is a burner with leadoff skills that earned him all-star honors in the GCL.

BEST DEFENSIVE PLAYER: SS Danny Espinosa (3) has unorthodox actions but a strong arm and instincts that profile well in the middle infield. OF Marcus Jones (11) is a plus defender in center field with a solid-average arm.

BEST FASTBALL: Unsigned RHP Aaron Crow (1) had by far the best fastball in the draft class. Without him, RHP Paul Demny (6) stands out with a heater that touches 94 mph.

BEST SECONDARY PITCH: LHP Will Atwood (12) has command of a solid-average curveball and changeup and plenty of pitchability. LHP Graham Hicks (4) has more upside with a projectable 6-foot-5 frame and a curveball that grades as solid average now.

BEST PRO DEBUT: Atwood allowed 52 baserunners and struck out 60 in 52 innings at short-season Vermont, going 2-1, 2.41. Higley hit .346/.486/.458 while Demny went 4-0, 2.50 with 40 strikeouts in 36 innings to help the Nats win the GCL championship.

BEST ATHLETE: Hood has four average or better raw tools and enough athletic ability to get a football scholarship to Alabama. Only his arm rates below average. A Washington D.C., native, Jones has a lean, athletic frame and needs to add strength to fulfill his projection.

MOST INTRIGUING BACKGROUND: Nieto and his family came to the United States from Cuba when he was 8, and he teamed with No. 3 overall pick Eric Hosmer (Royals) to help American Heritage High win a Florida state championship and Baseball America's final No. 1 ranking in 2008. 2B Steve Lombardozzi (19) is the son of the ex-Twins second baseman of the same name.

CLOSEST TO THE MAJORS: Espinosa has to prove he can hit with wood but has the glove to move quickly. Atwood could do the same, thanks to his polish and secondary stuff.

BEST LATE-ROUND PICK: Ramirez got $1 million at the signing deadline to sway him from a Tulane scholarship.

THE ONE WHO GOT AWAY: The Nationals and the Hendricks brothers (Crow's agents) badly misjudged each other, leaving them too far apart on deadline day, and they weren't able to bridge a $500,000 gap by the deadline.

ASSESSMENT: Not signing Crow leaves the Nats with two of the first 10 picks in 2009 and also without an impact talent in this year's class after Hood. The pitching looks especially thin.

2007

BONUSES: $7.9 MILLION

RHP Jordan Zimmermann (2) has zoomed past the three players the Nationals drafted ahead of him, and LHPs Ross Detwiler (1) and Josh Smoker (1s) and OF Michael Burgess (1s) are solid prospects in their own right. So are C Derek Norris (4) and LHP Jack McGeary (6).

GRADE: B

2006

BONUSES: $5.4 MILLION

An ankle injury ruined 1B Chris Marrero's (1) 2008 season, but he's the still the best position prospect in the system. RHP Colton Willems (1) is moving backward rapidly, however, while RHP Sean Black (2) was the highest unsigned pick in the entire draft.

GRADE: C

2005

BONUSES: $4.0 MILLION*

3B Ryan Zimmerman (1) almost immediately became the face of the franchise. LHP John Lannan (11) was Washington's best starter as a rookie last year, while OF Justin Maxwell (4) offers intriguing upside.

GRADE: A

2004

BONUSES: $3.7 MILLION*

The Nationals found a pair of useful pitchers in LHP Bill Bray (1) and RHP Collin Balester (4), though they traded Bray to the Reds. RHP Brett Campbell (34) appeared briefly in the majors.

GRADE: C+

*Draft analysis by John Manuel (2008) and Jim Callis (2004-07). Numbers in parentheses indicate draft rounds. *Bonuses for 2004-05 are first 10 rounds only.*

KEVIN PATAKY

PROSPECT

JORDAN ZIMMERMANN, RHP

Born: May 23, 1986.
Ht.: 6-1. **Wt.:** 180.
Bats: R. **Throws:** R.
Drafted: Wisconsin-Stevens Point, 2007 (2nd round).
Signed by: Steve Arnieri.

After starring as a two-way player for NCAA Division III Wisconsin-Stevens Point as a sophomore in 2006, Zimmermann exploded onto the prospect landscape that summer in the Northwoods League. He posted a circuit-best 1.01 ERA and 92 strikeouts, boosting his draft stock and ranking as the league's No. 1 prospect. That offseason, he broke his jaw in two places when he was struck by a line drive while throwing live batting practice in a workout. He missed the first three games of the season and lost 10 pounds, then had his wisdom teeth removed during the season. Zimmermann battled through the adversity and earned Most Outstanding Player honors at the Division III College World Series, becoming the first player ever to receive that award without his team reaching the title game. He pitched a complete-game one-hitter with 10 strikeouts against Emory (Ga.), and batted .615 with two homers in four games as a DH. The Nationals signed him for $495,000 after getting him in the second round, and they've said he could have been a top-10 pick had he been healthy and at a higher-profile program. Washington aggressively pushed him to high Class A Potomac to begin his first full pro season, and he needed just five starts to prove he was ready for Double-A Harrisburg, where he ranked as the Eastern League's No. 5 prospect.

Zimmermann is the rare pitcher who projects to have four average or better offerings in the majors. He attacks hitters with a 90-94 mph four-seam fastball that occasionally touches 95. It's a heavy fastball with riding action, and he commands it very well to both sides of the plate, evoking Curt Schilling. Zimmermann also mixes in a sinking two-seamer around 90 mph. He holds his velocity deep into games, works quickly and pounds the strike zone. His slider was his No. 2 pitch in college, but the Nationals wanted him to focus more on tightening his curveball early in his pro career. As a result, he has added power to the curve, which now sits at 75-78 mph and rates as a fringe-average offering, projecting as solid-average or a tick above. His tight, hard-breaking 84-87 slider is mostly average now but has its moments as a plus pitch, and his straight changeup isn't far from being average. Zimmermann has a clean delivery from a high three-quarters slot and a strong, durable frame. His athleticism helps him field his position well, hold runners, handle the bat and bunt well. An intense competitor, he's serious about his craft.

The Nationals forced Zimmermann to throw 15-20 changeups per game in 2008, and while his feel for the pitch is improving, he's still learning how and when to use it. He has good arm speed with the pitch and is effective when he throws it around 82 mph, but he tends to throw it a bit too hard. At times his delivery gets a little too rotational, causing him to get on the side of his slider and turning it into more of a cutter. The slider can be a plus pitch if he can stay on top of it more often. His curveball also lacks consistency.

It's easy to envision Zimmermann refining his command of his secondary stuff quickly and reaching the big leagues by the 2009 all-star break, if not sooner. He figures to start the year at Washington's new Triple-A Syracuse affiliate. He profiles as a frontline starter—probably a solid No. 2 on a first-division club.

Year	Club (League)	Class	W	L	ERA	G	GS	CG	SV	IP	H	R	ER	HR	BB	SO	AVG
2007	Vermont (NYP)	SS	5	2	2.38	13	11	0	0	53	45	14	14	2	18	71	.228
2008	Potomac (CAR)	HiA	3	1	1.65	5	4	0	1	27	15	6	5	1	8	31	.167
	Harrisburg (EL)	AA	7	2	3.21	20	20	0	0	107	89	42	38	9	39	103	.226
MINOR LEAGUE TOTALS			15	5	2.74	38	35	0	1	187	149	62	57	12	65	205	.219

2 ROSS DETWILER, LHP

BORN: March 6, 1986. **B-T:** R-L. **HT.:** 6-5. **WT.:** 185. **DRAFTED:** Missouri State, 2007 (1st round). **SIGNED BY:** Ryan Fox.

Signed for $2.15 million as the No. 6 overall pick in 2007, Detwiler made a big league cameo in just his 10th professional appearance. He spent his first full pro season in 2008 on a strict pitch count in high Class A, where he carried a 5.86 ERA into July before an improved changeup helped him post a 3.84 ERA and a 52-18 strikeout-walk ratio over the final two months. When he's on, as he was during the Carolina League playoffs, Detwiler features two plus pitches and flashes a third. His four-seam fastball can sit between 92-94 mph and touch 96 with explosive life, and his two-seamer has power sink. Detwiler's power curveball has tight 1-to-7 break, and he has the makings of a plus changeup with good arm speed and fade. His deceptive delivery makes his stuff play up even further. Detwiler's mechanics are inconsistent, causing his fastball velocity to dip into the high 80s and affecting his command. Especially in the first half, he threw too far across his body and often struggled to get through his pitches, so the Nationals worked hard on straightening his direction to the plate. It's an ongoing process, but he showed much better alignment in the Arizona Fall League. He's also working on quickening his times to the plate and holding baserunners better. He still must add strength to his wiry frame. Detwiler has the highest ceiling of any pitcher in the system. He'll start 2009 in Double-A, and some club officials believe everything will click and he'll be entrenched in the big leagues by September.

Year	Club (League)	Class	W	L	ERA	G	GS	CG	SV	IP	H	R	ER	HR	BB	SO	AVG
2007	Nationals (GCL)	R	0	0	2.25	4	4	0	0	12	11	3	3	1	3	15	.234
	Potomac (CAR)	HiA	2	2	4.22	5	4	0	0	21	27	11	10	1	9	13	.310
	Washington (NL)	MAJ	0	0	0.00	1	0	0	0	1	0	0	0	0	0	1	.000
2008	Potomac (CAR)	HiA	8	8	4.86	26	26	0	0	124	140	72	67	8	57	114	.289
MINOR LEAGUE TOTALS			10	10	4.58	35	34	0	0	157	178	86	80	10	69	142	.288
MAJOR LEAGUE TOTALS			0	0	0.00	1	0	0	0	1	0	0	0	0	0	1	.000

3 CHRIS MARRERO, 1B

BORN: July 2, 1988. **B-T:** R-R. **HT.:** 6-3. **WT.:** 210. **DRAFTED:** HS—Opa Locka, Fla., 2006 (1ST ROUND). **SIGNED BY:** Tony Arango.

A first-round pick in 2006 who signed for $1.625 million, Marrero entered 2008 as Washington's top prospect but struggled out of the gate, batting .200 with two homers in April. The Nationals noticed he was standing too far off the plate, and he heated up as he improved his plate coverage. But his season was cut short on June 18 when he caught his right cleat in the dirt while sliding into home plate, breaking his fibula and tearing ligaments in his ankle. Marrero has well above-average power from foul pole to foul pole, and his quiet swing has natural leverage. He squares balls up consistently and has a mature offensive approach for his age, projecting as at least an average hitter. He's very driven to succeed and is a tireless worker. After moving from the outfield to first base in 2007, Marrero got bigger and now there's concern he could wind up as a DH, though he dropped a few pounds in the fall of 2008. He's a well below-average runner with below-average range at first, but he does have soft hands and a strong arm. Though his ankle wasn't yet 100 percent, Marrero went to instructional league and had no trouble swinging the bat. He should be healthy by spring training and figures to get a shot at Double-A by midseason, if not out of camp.

Year	Club (League)	Class	AVG	G	AB	R	H	2B	3B	HR	RBI	BB	SO	SB	OBP	SLG
2006	Nationals (GCL)	R	.309	22	81	10	25	9	0	0	16	8	19	0	.374	.420
2007	Hagerstown (SAL)	LoA	.293	57	222	31	65	14	0	14	53	14	39	0	.337	.545
	Potomac (CAR)	HiA	.259	68	255	40	66	11	3	9	35	32	63	0	.338	.431
2008	Potomac (CAR)	HiA	.250	70	256	40	64	15	2	11	38	25	55	0	.325	.453
MINOR LEAGUE TOTALS			.270	217	814	121	220	49	5	34	142	79	176	0	.337	.468

4 MICHAEL BURGESS, OF

BORN: Oct. 20, 1988. **B-T:** L-L. **HT.:** 5-11. **WT.:** 195. **DRAFTED:** HS—Tampa, 2007 (1st round supplemental). **SIGNED BY:** Paul Tinnell.

Burgess ranked as the No. 1 prospect in the Rookie-level Gulf Coast League after the Nationals drafted him in 2007 out of Tampa's Hillsborough High, the same school that produced Dwight Gooden, Gary Sheffield and Elijah Dukes. Washington challenged him in his first full pro season, starting him at low Class A Hagerstown, where he bashed 18 homers in four months and easily won the South Atlantic League home run derby with 16 longballs in 38 swings. After a late promotion to high Class A, his power display continued but his average dipped. Burgess' game is all about strength and aggression. His best tool is his well above-average raw power, which translates to excellent home run production in games, particularly to right field. He also is capable of driving the ball to the opposite field and got better doing so in 2008. His above-average arm helped him lead the minor leagues with 26 outfield assists, and he uses the long hop effectively. His routes in right field have improved, though he sometimes baits runners to take an extra base so he can show off his arm. Burgess generates huge bat speed partly by taking monstrous hacks, and his tendency to overswing leads to very high strikeout totals. He's starting to learn that he doesn't need to swing so hard to drive the ball, but he doesn't ever project to hit for a high average, despite good hand-eye coordination. He's an upright runner with below-average speed who's not particularly fluid in the field or on the basepaths. Assuming Burgess keeps his weight in check and tones down his aggressive approach a bit, he profiles as a power-hitting right fielder who could bat fourth or fifth in a big league lineup. He'll open 2009 back at Potomac and could crack the majors sometime in 2011.

Year	Club (League)	Class	AVG	G	AB	R	H	2B	3B	HR	RBI	BB	SO	SB	OBP	SLG
2007	Nationals (GCL)	R	.336	36	128	22	43	6	3	8	32	25	37	1	.442	.617
	Vermont (NYP)	SS	.286	19	70	10	20	1	1	3	10	10	23	1	.383	.457
2008	Hagerstown (SAL)	LoA	.249	112	401	60	100	26	4	18	60	46	136	5	.335	.469
	Potomac (CAR)	HiA	.225	19	71	12	16	3	0	6	19	9	26	0	.325	.521
MINOR LEAGUE TOTALS			.267	186	670	104	179	36	8	35	121	90	222	7	.360	.501

5 JACK McGEARY, LHP

ED WOLFSTEIN

BORN: March 19, 1989. **B-T:** L-L. **HT.:** 6-3. **WT.:** 195. **DRAFTED:** HS—West Roxbury, Mass., 2007 (6th round). **SIGNED BY:** Mike Alberts.

In order to buy the cerebral McGeary out of a commitment to Stanford, the Nationals not only had to give him a sixth-round-record $1.8 million bonus, but they had to pay for him to attend classes at Stanford from September through early June for the first three years of his career. He didn't report for the 2008 season until mid-June, then led the Gulf Coast League with 64 strikeouts in 60 innings. He spent 10 days in instructional league in the fall, then headed back to college. McGeary is very advanced for his age and experience level. He has superb feel for his above-average curveball, which he can throw in the mid-70s with tight 12-to-6 action, or with more lateral break by dropping his arm angle, or with bigger, slower break for first-pitch strikes. After pitching at 85-87 mph with his fastball during his pro debut, he worked at 88-91 in 2008. He commands his fastball very well. He's an exceptional athlete with a commanding mound presence. McGeary is very dedicated to his offseason workout regimen, but he still needs to add strength, like most young pitchers. He's learning to throw his changeup when behind in the count, and he must improve his command of the pitch. It has good action and projects as an average offering, but it remains inconsistent. McGeary is ready for low Class A once he rejoins the Nationals in June, though he might need a few tuneup outings first. He projects as a mid-rotation starter in the Andy Pettitte mold and could reach the majors by 2011.

Year	Club (League)	Class	W	L	ERA	G	GS	CG	SV	IP	H	R	ER	HR	BB	SO	AVG
2007	Vermont (NYP)	SS	0	1	13.50	2	1	0	0	3	3	5	4	0	5	4	.273
2008	Nationals (GCL)	R	2	2	4.07	12	12	0	0	60	61	34	27	2	13	64	.258
	Vermont (NYP)	SS	0	0	4.50	1	1	0	0	4	6	2	2	0	3	5	.375
MINOR LEAGUE TOTALS			2	3	4.48	15	14	0	0	66	70	41	33	2	21	73	.266

6 DEREK NORRIS, C

RODGER WOOD

BORN: Feb. 14, 1989. **B-T:** R-R. **HT.:** 6-0. **WT.:** 210. **DRAFTED:** HS—Goddard, Kan., 2007 (4th round). **SIGNED BY:** Ryan Fox.

A year after hitting .203 in his pro debut in the Gulf Coast League, Norris took the greatest step forward of any Nats farmhand in 2008. Playing against mostly older competition as a 19-year-old, Norris led the short-season New York-Penn League with 63 walks—22 more than any other hitter in the league—and ranked as its No. 4 prospect. As evidenced by his walk total, Norris has a very patient offensive approach. His strong, sturdy build produces solid-average to plus power, mostly to left field, though he has improved at using the right-center gap. He loves to hit and works hard at his offensive game. He has a strong arm and a quick release, helping him throw out an NY-P-best 47 percent of basestealers in 2008. He runs well for a catcher. Norris didn't start catching until his senior year of high school after spending three years at third base, and his receiving remains very raw, as his 16 passed balls last year attest. He tends to pick balls in the dirt instead of blocking them. The Nationals want him to take more pride in his defense, but some club officials question whether he'll stick behind the plate long-term. If Norris can become just adequate defensively, his bat could make him a star in the big leagues. He'll advance to low Class A in 2009.

Year	Club (League)	Class	AVG	G	AB	R	H	2B	3B	HR	RBI	BB	SO	SB	OBP	SLG
2007	Nationals (GCL)	R	.203	37	123	16	25	6	2	4	15	25	38	2	.344	.382
2008	Vermont (NYP)	SS	.278	70	227	42	63	12	0	10	38	63	56	11	.444	.463
MINOR LEAGUE TOTALS			.251	107	350	58	88	18	2	14	53	88	94	13	.411	.434

7 DESTIN HOOD, OF

BORN: April 30, 1990. **B-T:** R-R. **HT.:** 6-1. **WT.:** 180. **DRAFTED:** HS—Mobile, Ala., 2008 (2nd round). **SIGNED BY:** Eric Robinson.

Hood starred as a shortstop and wide receiver at St. Paul's Episcopal High in Mobile, Ala.—Jake Peavy's alma mater—and committed to play both baseball and football at Alabama. The Nationals took him in the second round and gave him an above-slot $1.1 million bonus to keep him away from the Crimson Tide. They immediately moved him to left field and sent him to the Gulf Coast League, where he raised his average from .175 to .256 over the season's final 13 games. Scouts long have marveled at Hood's electrifying bat speed, which translates into above-average raw power. He swings and misses a lot now, but he keeps the barrel of the bat in the zone for a long time and projects to hit for average as his offensive approach matures. He has a strong, athletic frame and average to plus speed. Underdeveloped as an outfielder, Hood has a long way to go with his reads, jumps and routes. Washington has put him on a long-toss program in an effort to strengthen his below-average arm. He doesn't have a smooth arm action and doesn't use his lower half well when he throws. Offensively, he simply needs experience and refinement. Unless Hood blows the Nationals away in spring training, he'll likely spend 2009 at short-season Vermont, following the same developmental path as 2007 draftee Derek Norris. Down the road, Hood has a chance to be a potent middle-of-the-order bat in the big leagues.

Year	Club (League)	Class	AVG	G	AB	R	H	2B	3B	HR	RBI	BB	SO	SB	OBP	SLG
2008	Nationals (GCL)	R	.256	25	86	18	22	6	1	0	14	8	19	5	.333	.349
MINOR LEAGUE TOTALS			.256	25	86	18	22	6	1	0	14	8	19	5	.333	.349

8 ADRIAN NIETO, C

BORN: Nov. 12, 1989. **B-T:** B-R. **HT.:** 6-0. **WT.:** 200. **DRAFTED:** HS—Plantation, Fla., 2008 (5th round). **SIGNED BY:** Tony Arango.

Nieto and his parents came to the United States from Cuba on a makeshift raft when he was 8. He began catching shortly thereafter and joined a travel team with future No. 3 overall pick Eric Hosmer when he was 11. As high school seniors, they helped lead a loaded American Heritage High team to BA's final No. 1 national ranking, with Nieto blasting two homers in the state championship game. He signed three days before the Aug. 15 signing deadline for a $376,000 bonus, the third-highest in the fifth round. A switch-hitter, Nieto shows solid-average power to all fields from both sides of the plate. Like most young switch-hitters, he's more advanced from the left side, but he has a good feel for hitting from both sides. A natural leader who exudes confidence, Nieto is a student of the game. He knows what pitchers are trying to do to him when he's batting and also knows how to attack other hitters when he's behind the plate. He's surprisingly quick on his feet and good at blocking balls in the dirt. His arm is a tick above average but plays up because of his quick release, accuracy and aggressiveness. Nieto is still working hard on refining his defensive skills, from his receiving to his footwork to fielding bunts and popups. He needs to concentrate on keeping himself in better shape. At the plate, he's still developing his pitch recognition. Nieto has all the tools and intangibles to be a solid regular big league catcher in the Jorge Posada mold.

Year	Club (League)	Class	AVG	G	AB	R	H	2B	3B	HR	RBI	BB	SO	SB	OBP	SLG
2008	Nationals (GCL)	R	.217	8	23	1	5	3	0	0	3	2	7	0	.308	.348
MINOR LEAGUE TOTALS			.217	8	23	1	5	3	0	0	3	2	7	0	.308	.348

9 J.P. RAMIREZ, OF

BORN: Sept. 29, 1989. **B-T:** L-L. **HT.:** 5-10. **WT.:** 185. **DRAFTED:** HS—New Braunfels, Texas, 2008 (15th round). **SIGNED BY:** Tyler Wilt.

Ramirez hit .395 for the U.S. junior national team in 2007 and batted .521 with eight homers as a high school senior to help establish his reputation as the best pure hitter in the Texas draft crop. His bonus demands and commitment to Tulane dropped him to the 15th round, but the Nationals signed him for $1 million in the hours before the Aug. 15 signing deadline as it became apparent they wouldn't sign first-rounder Aaron Crow. Ramirez has a smooth, compact lefthanded stroke and an advanced feel for hitting. He smokes hard line drives from gap to gap and showed at least average power in an impressive instructional league stint. He draws praise from scouts for his mature approach and high-quality makeup. With fringy speed and a below-average arm, Ramirez will be tied to left field in pro ball. Some club officials believe he'll end up with an average arm in time, but he's also got a lot of work to do on his reads and jumps in the outfield. It's unclear if Ramirez will develop enough power to hold down an everyday job in left field at the major league level, and some scouts see him as a tweener. Others, however, see him as a hitting machine in the David Dellucci mold. Ramirez should get a crack at low Class A in 2009.

Year	Club (League)	Class	AVG	G	AB	R	H	2B	3B	HR	RBI	BB	SO	SB	OBP	SLG
2008	Nationals (GCL)	R	.364	5	11	2	4	0	0	0	8	4	0	0	.533	.364
MINOR LEAGUE TOTALS			.364	5	11	2	4	0	0	0	8	4	0	0	.533	.364

10 ESMAILYN GONZALEZ, SS

BORN: Sept. 21, 1989. **B-T:** B-R. **HT.:** 5-11. **WT.:** 175. **SIGNED:** Dominican Republic, 2006. **SIGNED BY:** Jose Rijo.

Though his $1.4 million bonus in 2006 remains controversial, Gonzalez started to give Washington a return on its investment in 2008. After hitting .245 in his 2007 pro debut, he repeated the Gulf Coast League and won the batting title with a .343 average. With a quiet swing and excellent plate discipline for his age, Gonzalez projects to hit for average with gap power and occasional home run pop. The Nationals got on him to improve his conditioning, and he firmed up his body some and added strength, which helped him drive more balls. He also made plenty of progress using the whole field from both sides of the plate. Defensively, he shows smooth actions and soft hands that give him an outside chance to stay at shortstop. Nicknamed "Smiley" in part for his energy and enthusiasm, he showed more vocal on-field leadership in 2008, though he's still far from fluent in English. Gonzalez's substandard range and arm strength are still likely to dictate an eventual move to second base. He's a below-average runner who lacks first-step quickness. If Gonzalez continues to get stronger, he could wind up as a quality all-around second baseman, similar to Jose Vidro but with less power. In the short term, he'll remain at shortstop and advance to low Class A.

Year	Club (League)	Class	AVG	G	AB	R	H	2B	3B	HR	RBI	BB	SO	SB	OBP	SLG
2007	Nationals (GCL)	R	.245	33	106	13	26	3	2	0	11	19	18	4	.382	.311
2008	Nationals (GCL)	R	.343	51	181	42	62	12	3	2	33	23	19	9	.431	.475
MINOR LEAGUE TOTALS			.307	84	287	55	88	15	5	2	44	42	37	13	.412	.415

11 JUSTIN MAXWELL, OF

BORN: Nov. 5, 1983. **B-T:** R-R. **HT.:** 6-5. **WT.:** 245. **DRAFTED:** Maryland, 2005 (4th round). **SIGNED BY:** Alex Smith.

Injuries have dogged Maxwell since his college days at Maryland, but he showed what he could do in a full healthy season in 2007, when he turned in a 25-25 season, earned a late big league callup and delivered a pinch-hit grand slam in his third at-bat. The Nationals expected to see him back in Washington some time in 2008, but he injured his wrist diving for a ball on May 19. He tried to play through the injury over the next week before the Nationals shut him down with what later was discovered to be a small fracture in his wrist. He returned for winter ball in Puerto Rico, where his .162/.330/.446 line in 74 at-bats reflected his patience, power potential and inconsistent contact. A gifted athletic specimen with a big, strong frame, Maxwell has a chance for four average or better tools. He's a patient hitter with average to plus power to all fields. In order to become an average hitter, he needs to stay taller in his stance and avoid collapsing on his back leg. He's a long strider with slightly above-average speed that plays up once he's underway. Maxwell is an intelligent baserunner and has a strong work ethic. He projects as an average defender in center field, but he still takes suspect routes from time to time. His arm is below average and eventually could make him a better fit in left. Maxwell looks more like a solid regular than a star, but he could be ready for an everyday role by the second half of 2010.

Year	Club (League)	Class	AVG	G	AB	R	H	2B	3B	HR	RBI	BB	SO	SB	OBP	SLG
2006	Savannah (SAL)	LoA	.172	17	58	8	10	2	2	1	7	8	23	1	.294	.328
	Vermont (NYP)	SS	.269	74	271	36	73	11	3	4	33	27	61	20	.346	.376
2007	Hagerstown (SAL)	LoA	.301	56	209	51	63	12	2	14	40	26	57	14	.389	.579
	Potomac (CAR)	HiA	.263	58	228	35	60	13	0	13	43	24	65	21	.338	.491
	Washington (NL)	MAJ	.269	15	26	5	7	0	0	2	5	1	8	0	.296	.500
2008	Harrisburg (EL)	AA	.233	43	146	35	34	6	3	7	28	31	28	13	.367	.459
MINOR LEAGUE TOTALS			.263	248	912	165	240	44	10	39	151	116	234	69	.354	.462
MAJOR LEAGUE TOTALS			.269	15	26	5	7	0	0	2	5	1	8	0	.296	.500

12 GARRETT MOCK, RHP

BORN: April 25, 1983. **B-T:** R-R. **HT.:** 6-4. **WT.:** 240. **DRAFTED:** Houston, 2004 (3rd round). **SIGNED BY:** Trip Couch (Diamondbacks).

A favorite of Nationals assistant general manager Mike Rizzo from the days when both were with the Diamondbacks, Mock was acquired as part of the Livan Hernandez trade in 2006, when he struggled while trying to pitch through a knee injury, which limited his workload in 2007. He stayed healthy for all of 2008, pitching well in a starting role in Triple-A before breaking into the big leagues mostly as a reliever. Mock has fought to stay on top of his four-seam fastball by raising his arm slot, so in 2008 he shelved it in favor of a sinking two-seamer that comes more naturally and has better life. He tends to pitch in the high 80s as a starter but works at 90-92 mph out of the bullpen, touching 93-94. He's aggressive with his heater and has improved his command, but it still comes and goes. Mock also features a solid-average slider, a fringe-average curveball and a changeup that can be average at times. He relies mostly on his fastball and slider out of the pen. Some scouts think Mock could follow the development path of Adam Wainwright or Brandon Morrow, breaking into the majors as a reliever before transitioning to a starting role. Others believe he's better suited to a Jon Rauch-type role in the pen, where he can just let it fly and not overthink things. Either way, Mock should stick in the big leagues for good this year.

Year	Club (League)	Class	W	L	ERA	G	GS	CG	SV	IP	H	R	ER	HR	BB	SO	AVG
2004	Yakima (NWL)	SS	2	0	1.54	5	5	0	0	23	18	8	4	1	4	14	.228
	South Bend (MWL)	LoA	3	2	3.00	8	8	1	0	54	49	21	18	2	12	37	.251
2005	Lancaster (CAL)	HiA	14	7	4.18	28	28	0	0	174	202	95	81	19	33	160	.284
2006	Tennessee (SL)	AA	4	8	4.95	23	23	0	0	131	144	81	72	14	50	117	.280
	Harrisburg (EL)	AA	0	4	10.26	4	4	0	0	17	29	21	19	2	5	9	.387
2007	Potomac (CAR)	HiA	1	0	0.00	1	1	0	0	6	3	0	0	0	1	5	.143
	Nationals (GCL)	R	0	2	4.70	3	2	0	0	8	11	7	4	3	1	8	.333
	Harrisburg (EL)	AA	1	5	5.79	11	11	0	0	51	66	41	33	5	28	41	.311
2008	Columbus (IL)	AAA	6	3	3.01	19	17	0	0	105	98	41	35	9	25	96	.249
	Washington (NL)	MAJ	1	3	4.17	26	3	0	0	41	37	20	19	4	23	46	.239
MINOR LEAGUE TOTALS			31	31	4.21	102	99	1	0	569	620	315	266	55	159	487	.278
MAJOR LEAGUE TOTALS			1	3	4.17	26	3	0	0	41	37	20	19	4	23	46	.239

13 SHAIRON MARTIS, RHP

BORN: March 30, 1987. **B-T:** R-R. **HT.:** 6-1. **WT.:** 175. **SIGNED:** Curacao, 2004. **SIGNED BY:** Philip Elhage (Giants).

Acquired from the Giants in the 2006 Mike Stanton trade, Martis has made a name for himself in international competition. He threw a seven-inning no-hitter for the Netherlands against Panama in the 2006 World Baseball Classic, then anchored the Dutch pitching staff in the 2008 Olympics, where he went 0-2, 6.75 and led the team in strikeouts (11) and innings (11). Shortly after returning from Beijing in late August, he was called up to Washington, where he held his own in four starts. Martis is aggressive and throws strikes with an 89-92 mph fastball that tops out at 93. He commands his fastball well in the zone, and it has some life. His best pitch is an above-average changeup with sink and tail at 80-82 mph, and he can throw it in any count. He throws two breaking balls and is inconsistent with both. He occasionally shows an average slider, but he often struggles to finish the pitch, causing it to lack depth and bite. Some prefer his curveball, though he needs to tighten it. Martis gets by more on savvy and competitiveness than on pure stuff, and his upside is limited to back-of-the-rotation starter. He could reach that ceiling sometime in 2009, though he figures to start the season in Triple-A.

Year	Club (League)	Class	W	L	ERA	G	GS	CG	SV	IP	H	R	ER	HR	BB	SO	AVG
2004	Giants (DSL)	R	4	3	1.79	14	12	0	0	70	55	15	14	2	17	63	.221
2005	Giants (AZL)	R	2	1	1.85	11	5	0	1	34	28	10	7	1	9	50	.226
2006	Augusta (SAL)	LoA	6	4	3.64	15	15	0	0	77	76	39	31	3	21	66	.257
	Savannah (SAL)	LoA	1	1	3.80	4	4	0	0	21	23	9	9	2	4	14	.284
	Potomac (CAR)	HiA	0	2	3.00	2	2	0	0	12	9	5	4	0	3	7	.209
	Harrisburg (EL)	AA	0	1	12.60	1	1	0	0	5	8	7	7	4	3	1	.348
2007	Potomac (CAR)	HiA	14	8	4.23	27	26	1	0	151	150	83	71	9	52	108	.258
2008	Harrisburg (EL)	AA	4	4	3.98	14	14	0	0	75	73	35	33	5	28	57	.258
	Columbus (IL)	AAA	1	2	3.02	7	7	0	0	42	42	17	14	2	17	42	.261
	Washington (NL)	MAJ	1	3	5.66	5	4	0	0	21	18	14	13	5	12	23	.228
MINOR LEAGUE TOTALS			32	26	3.51	95	86	1	1	487	464	220	190	28	154	408	.252
MAJOR LEAGUE TOTALS			1	3	5.66	5	4	0	0	21	18	14	13	5	12	23	.228

14 DANNY ESPINOSA, SS

BORN: April 25, 1987. **B-T:** B-R. **HT.:** 6-0. **WT.:** 190. **DRAFTED:** Long Beach State, 2008 (3rd round). **SIGNED BY:** Mark Baca.

A three-year starter and leader at Long Beach State, Espinosa is not surprisingly a throwback dirtbag who plays above his tools. After signing for an above-slot bonus of $525,000 as a third-round pick, he hit .328 at Vermont, though he didn't deliver another extra-base hit after doubling in his first two games. Espinosa's only above-average tool is his strong, accurate arm. He's an aggressive defender whose keen instincts and body control make up for fringy range and unorthodox glove work. Though the switch-hitting Espinosa is regarded as better from his natural right side, he fared much better against righthanders (.353) than lefties (.231) in his debut. He has a knack for squaring balls up and can lace hard line drives to all fields, but many scouts wonder how his bat will play at higher levels, as he's a front-foot hitter who tends to take wicked cuts at anything close. He has a slightly bowlegged running style and average speed at best, though he's a savvy baserunner. One scout likened Espinosa to a young John Valentin, but without as much power potential. He's likely to skip a level and start 2009 at high Class A.

Year	Club (League)	Class	AVG	G	AB	R	H	2B	3B	HR	RBI	BB	SO	SB	OBP	SLG
2008	Vermont (NYP)	SS	.328	19	64	8	21	2	0	0	4	17	17	2	.476	.359
MINOR LEAGUE TOTALS			.328	19	64	8	21	2	0	0	4	17	17	2	.476	.359

15 GRAHAM HICKS, LHP

BORN: Feb. 9, 1990. **B-T:** L-L. **HT.:** 6-5. **WT.:** 170. **DRAFTED:** HS—Lakeland, Fla., 2008 (4th round). **SIGNED BY:** Paul Tinnell.

Hicks made a name for himself at the Florida high school all-star game in Sebring, Fla., last spring, when scouts said he showed first-round talent. After signing for an above-slot $475,000 bonus as a fourth-rounder and making two appearances in his pro debut, Hicks broke his left middle finger fielding a ground ball in instructional league. The Nationals expect him to be back to 100 percent by spring training. With a long, lean frame, Hicks reminds some club officials of Ross Detwiler when he was in high school. He's similarly projectable, but Hicks already reached 92 mph with his fastball in high school, though he worked at 86-89 in his two pro outings. He has good feel for a curveball with tight, downward rotation, and he flashes an average changeup as well. He has a tendency to drift in his delivery, causing his elbow to get a little low, but other than that his arm action is clean and easy. With experience and refinement, Hicks has a chance to be a power lefty with three average or better pitches.

Year	Club (League)	Class	W	L	ERA	G	GS	CG	SV	IP	H	R	ER	HR	BB	SO	AVG
2008	Nationals (GCL)	R	0	0	0.00	1	1	0	0	2	1	0	0	0	0	2	.143
	Vermont (NYP)	SS	0	1	3.00	1	1	0	0	3	3	3	1	0	2	1	.250
MINOR LEAGUE TOTALS			0	1	1.80	2	2	0	0	5	4	3	1	0	2	3	.211

16 LEONARD DAVIS, OF/3B/2B

BORN: Dec. 24, 1983. **B-T:** L-R. **HT.:** 5-10. **WT.:** 195. **DRAFTED:** Fresno, Calif., CC, 2004 (8th round). **SIGNED BY:** Doug McMillan.

Davis's older brothers Marque and Rodney starred as football players for Fresno State, and Davis played one season as a safety at Fresno CC before switching to baseball. A strong, physical athlete, he began tapping into his natural ability in 2008, when he made huge strides refining his offensive approach and rocketed to Triple-A. Though he seemed worn down at the end of the summer, he bounced back in the Arizona Fall League, batting .325/.415/.600 with four homers in 80 at-bats. Davis tried too hard to pull everything when he was younger, but he did a good job utilizing his above-average power to the opposite field in 2008. An average runner with a fringe-average arm, Davis played right field in college and moved to third base in pro ball, and the Nationals have experimented with him at second base and back in the outfield corners in the last two years. He's most comfortable in left but can hold his own at third base and fill in at second. Pitch selection was an issue for Davis in the past, and while he showed more patience in 2008, his 48-5 strikeout-walk ratio in Triple-A is jarring. If he doesn't hit enough for an everyday job in the big leagues, his defensive versatility and power bat still could make him a valuable reserve.

Year	Club (League)	Class	AVG	G	AB	R	H	2B	3B	HR	RBI	BB	SO	SB	OBP	SLG
2004	Expos (GCL)	R	.182	42	143	18	26	6	1	3	14	19	58	2	.295	.301
2005	Vermont (NYP)	SS	.300	67	237	34	71	8	8	7	35	12	64	8	.348	.489
2006	Savannah (SAL)	LoA	.225	83	289	32	65	12	4	8	38	21	87	4	.284	.377
2007	Hagerstown (SAL)	LoA	.290	96	348	47	101	29	4	16	56	25	86	7	.344	.534
	Potomac (CAR)	HiA	.262	23	84	8	22	4	0	4	10	1	22	0	.267	.452
2008	Potomac (CAR)	HiA	.332	63	217	47	72	14	2	14	37	23	47	7	.403	.608
	Harrisburg (EL)	AA	.488	10	41	8	20	1	0	4	10	6	5	2	.553	.805
	Columbus (IL)	AAA	.239	49	180	21	43	13	3	7	29	5	48	1	.266	.461
MINOR LEAGUE TOTALS			.273	433	1539	215	420	87	22	63	229	112	417	31	.330	.481

17 BILL RHINEHART, 1B

BORN: Nov. 22, 1984. **B-T:** L-L. **HT.:** 6-0. **WT.:** 202. **DRAFTED:** Arizona, 2007 (11th round). **SIGNED BY:** Mitch Sokol.

Rhinehart played mostly outfield during his four-year career at Arizona before shifting to first base down the stretch in his breakout senior season. He stayed at first in pro ball and made all-star teams at his first two pro stops in the New York-Penn and South Atlantic leagues. After reaching Double-A in his first full season, Rhinehart finished 2008 on a tear in the Arizona Fall League, going 19-for-39 (.487) in his final nine games. Rhinehart doesn't have huge strength or electric bat speed, but he has a quiet, professional offensive approach and leverage in his swing. He excels at keeping an even keel and making adjustments, which makes him an RBI machine. With an open stance, Rhinehart can drive the ball to the left-center gap or pull a homer to right. He's a below-average runner but not a clogger, and he moves around well at first base, though he's still learning the nuances of the position. His arm is solid for a first baseman. Rhinehart has a chance to be an everyday first baseman in the mold of Lyle Overbay or Nick Johnson, and some Nationals officials expect him to reach the big leagues sometime in 2009.

Year	Club (League)	Class	AVG	G	AB	R	H	2B	3B	HR	RBI	BB	SO	SB	OBP	SLG
2007	Vermont (NYP)	SS	.299	60	214	36	64	18	0	5	43	22	32	5	.377	.453
2008	Hagerstown (SAL)	LoA	.295	65	261	39	77	22	1	9	56	21	36	0	.344	.490
	Potomac (CAR)	HiA	.320	7	25	5	8	2	0	2	4	2	5	1	.370	.640
	Harrisburg (EL)	AA	.233	61	219	23	51	15	0	7	29	27	49	0	.321	.397
MINOR LEAGUE TOTALS			.278	193	719	103	200	57	1	23	132	72	122	6	.348	.456

18 ROGER BERNADINA, OF

BORN: June 12, 1984. **B-T:** L-L. **HT.:** 6-1. **WT.:** 190. **SIGNED:** Netherlands, 2001. **SIGNED BY:** Fred Ferreira.

Bernadina's route to the big leagues has been plodding. He spent three full seasons in low Class A and didn't force his way onto the 40-man roster until his strong performance for the Netherlands in the European Olympic qualifier in 2007. He carried his momentum into 2008, posting by far his best offensive season and earning his first major league callup when Lastings Milledge went on the disabled list in late June. After spending most of July and August in Triple-A, Bernadina returned to Washington for September and struggled to make contact. The fastest runner in the system, he has 65 speed on the 20-80 scouting scale. He stole 41 bases in 52 attempts in the minors in 2008, in line with his career 78 percent success rate. Bernadina's speed translates into excellent range in center field and allows him to compensate for an occasional bad route. His strong, accurate arm completes his outstanding defensive package. Bernadina made much better use of his speed at the plate in 2008, improving his drag bunting and spraying the ball around the field. He has decent raw power and hit the ball with more authority in the past year. Bernadina still has a tendency to cut off his lefthanded swing, pulling the barrel out of the zone too quickly, and despite his offensive progress it's uncertain if he'll ever hit enough to be a big league regular. At the least, he can be a speedy fourth outfielder with strong defensive skills, perhaps as soon as 2009.

Year	Club (League)	Class	AVG	G	AB	R	H	2B	3B	HR	RBI	BB	SO	SB	OBP	SLG
2002	Expos (GCL)	R	.276	57	196	22	54	7	0	3	18	19	25	1	.348	.357
2003	Savannah (SAL)	LoA	.237	77	278	36	66	12	3	4	39	19	53	11	.292	.345
2004	Savannah (SAL)	LoA	.238	129	450	67	107	24	7	7	66	60	113	24	.338	.369
2005	Savannah (SAL)	LoA	.233	122	417	64	97	15	3	12	54	75	92	35	.356	.369
2006	Potomac (CAR)	HiA	.270	123	434	60	117	19	3	6	42	56	98	28	.355	.369
2007	Columbus (IL)	AAA	.167	13	42	6	7	3	0	0	1	9	11	0	.327	.238
	Harrisburg (EL)	AA	.270	97	371	58	100	15	2	6	36	38	80	40	.340	.369
2008	Harrisburg (EL)	AA	.323	73	266	47	86	11	7	5	38	31	64	26	.398	.474
	Columbus (IL)	AAA	.351	47	191	33	67	13	3	4	16	16	37	15	.404	.513
	Washington (NL)	MAJ	.211	26	76	10	16	1	1	0	2	9	21	4	.294	.250
MINOR LEAGUE TOTALS			.265	738	2645	393	701	119	28	47	310	323	573	180	.350	.384
MAJOR LEAGUE TOTALS			.211	26	76	10	16	1	1	0	2	9	21	4	.294	.250

19 IAN DESMOND, SS

BORN: Sept. 20, 1985. **B-T:** R-R. **HT.:** 6-2. **WT.:** 185. **DRAFTED:** HS—Sarasota, Fla., 2004 (3rd round). **SIGNED BY:** Russ Bove.

Early on during Desmond's slow climb through the system, organization officials speculated that he might be the kind of player who needs 2,000 pro at-bats before he's ready for the big leagues. Desmond never has hit better than .264 at any minor league stop, and Washington still is waiting for him to translate his tools into results. After holding his own at Double-A in 2008, he finally took a significant step forward offensively in the Arizona Fall League, batting .267/.364/.525 in 101 at-bats. Desmond generates plenty of bat speed and flashes average power potential. His pitch recognition and selection are starting to improve, but he struggles to maintain a consistent, patient approach. He has average speed and excellent range at shortstop, where his above-average arm allows him to make spectacular plays at times. His error total dropped from 32 in 2007 to 22 in 2008, but he still needs to work on consistently making routine plays. The Nationals hope Desmond is ready to handle Triple-A in 2009. If his bat continues to develop he could compete for Washington's starting shortstop job in 2010.

Year	Club (League)	Class	AVG	G	AB	R	H	2B	3B	HR	RBI	BB	SO	SB	OBP	SLG
2004	Expos (GCL)	R	.227	55	216	28	49	11	0	1	27	10	40	13	.272	.292
	Vermont (NYP)	SS	.250	4	12	2	3	0	0	1	1	0	2	0	.308	.500
2005	Savannah (SAL)	LoA	.247	73	296	37	73	10	2	4	23	13	60	20	.291	.334
	Potomac (CAR)	HiA	.256	55	219	37	56	13	3	3	15	21	53	13	.325	.384
2006	Harrisburg (EL)	AA	.182	37	121	8	22	4	1	0	3	5	35	4	.214	.231
	Potomac (CAR)	HiA	.244	92	365	50	89	20	2	9	45	29	79	14	.313	.384
2007	Potomac (CAR)	HiA	.264	129	458	69	121	30	4	13	45	57	99	27	.357	.432
2008	Nationals (GCL)	R	.385	3	13	1	5	1	0	0	2	0	2	3	.385	.462
	Harrisburg (EL)	AA	.251	93	323	42	81	14	0	12	44	31	78	12	.318	.406
MINOR LEAGUE TOTALS			.247	541	2023	274	499	103	12	43	205	166	448	106	.313	.373

20 CRAIG STAMMEN, RHP

BORN: March 9, 1984. **B-T:** R-R. **HT.:** 6-3. **WT.:** 210. **DRAFTED:** Dayton, 2005 (12th round). **SIGNED BY:** Ben Jones.

Stammen finished his three-year college career as the all-time strikeout leader at Dayton, where he excelled as a closer during his sophomore year and as a starter during his junior campaign. He pitched through a knee injury down the stretch in 2007 and had minor surgery to clean it up after the season. The Nationals started him in the bullpen at Potomac in 2008 until a spot opened up in the rotation. After dominating in high Class A and Double-A, he finished the season in Triple-A, where he took his lumps but still showed good stuff. Stammen pitches at 90-94 mph with his four-seam fastball, but the pitch is rather straight, so he began throwing more 89-92 mph two-seamers in 2008. He commands his fastball well and it plays up out of the bullpen. His short, tight curveball is an average pitch that flashes plus at times, and his changeup is another average offering. He sometimes drifts in his delivery, causing his fastball to lose power. Despite his physical, workhorse frame, Stammen needs to incorporate his lower half more into his delivery to make better use of his leverage. He also needs to finish his delivery better. His solid three-pitch mix gives him a chance to be a No. 4 or 5 starter, but some Nats officials see him as a strike-throwing bulldog out of the pen. He'll likely start 2009 in Triple-A but could see significant action in the majors.

Year	Club (League)	Class	W	L	ERA	G	GS	CG	SV	IP	H	R	ER	HR	BB	SO	AVG
2005	Vermont (NYP)	SS	4	5	4.06	13	7	0	0	51	62	36	23	2	12	32	.297
2006	Savannah (SAL)	LoA	6	9	3.58	21	21	0	0	113	110	55	45	10	29	93	.251
	Potomac (CAR)	HiA	0	2	5.76	7	6	0	0	30	34	20	19	5	7	16	.288
2007	Potomac (CAR)	HiA	8	6	4.18	28	22	0	0	125	156	79	58	9	54	96	.311
	Columbus (IL)	AAA	0	1	12.27	1	1	0	0	4	4	5	5	1	3	2	.267
2008	Potomac (CAR)	HiA	4	2	2.21	15	9	0	1	69	59	24	17	6	17	62	.227
	Harrisburg (EL)	AA	3	1	1.64	6	6	0	0	38	22	8	7	1	11	31	.171
	Columbus (IL)	AAA	1	4	7.33	9	8	0	0	43	62	35	35	3	16	35	.354
MINOR LEAGUE TOTALS			26	30	3.98	100	80	0	1	473	509	262	209	37	149	367	.276

21 MARCO ESTRADA, RHP

BORN: July 5, 1983. **B-T:** R-R. **HT.:** 6-0. **WT.:** 180. **DRAFTED:** Long Beach State, 2005 (6th round). **SIGNED BY:** Brian Hunter/Brian Parker.

Estrada pitched for two years at Glendale (Calif.) CC before transferring to Long Beach State for his junior year, when he went 8-3, 2.43 and climbed to the sixth round of the draft. A broken collarbone delayed the start of his season in 2006, but he finished strong as the No. 10 prospect in Hawaii Winter Baseball that offseason. After a disappointing 2007, he excelled in the upper minors last year and finished the season in a big league relief role, where his stuff was down due to fatigue. Estrada is a less physical version of Craig Stammen, and his three-pitch repertoire is similar. Despite his smallish build, Estrada holds the 90-92 mph velocity on his fastball into the sixth or seventh inning as a starter, regularly touching 93-94. His best pitch is a plus changeup with good arm speed and tumbling action. He also features two different curveballs: an average 78-81 offering with some sharpness to it, and a slower pitch that he uses as a change of pace. He tried to overthrow in his big league stint and flew open in his delivery, but he ordinarily has good command and fine mechanics. Estrada is a strike-thrower who works quickly and holds runners well, giving him the ingredients to be a successful reliever if he can't stick as a starter. His quality three-pitch mix gives him a chance to be a back-end starter, but his size limits his ceiling.

Year	Club (League)	Class	W	L	ERA	G	GS	CG	SV	IP	H	R	ER	HR	BB	SO	AVG
2005	Vermont (NYP)	SS	1	3	5.08	9	6	0	1	34	31	21	19	4	16	37	.231
2006	Nationals (GCL)	R	2	0	1.52	5	4	0	0	24	14	4	4	1	6	27	.165
	Savannah (SAL)	LoA	1	4	5.59	8	8	0	0	37	44	23	23	6	14	29	.301
2007	Hagerstown (SAL)	LoA	1	5	5.25	8	8	0	0	36	39	24	21	4	17	35	.279
	Nationals (GCL)	R	0	0	3.18	4	4	0	0	11	19	6	4	1	3	13	.365
	Potomac (CAR)	HiA	5	3	4.94	11	11	0	0	58	67	32	32	7	17	54	.291
2008	Harrisburg (EL)	AA	6	3	2.66	13	13	1	0	74	62	27	22	5	32	67	.223
	Columbus (IL)	AAA	3	3	3.58	12	12	0	0	65	73	28	26	3	21	52	.287
	Washington (NL)	MAJ	0	0	7.82	11	0	0	0	13	17	13	11	4	5	10	.304
MINOR LEAGUE TOTALS			19	21	4.00	70	66	1	1	340	349	165	151	31	126	314	.265
MAJOR LEAGUE TOTALS			0	0	7.82	11	0	0	0	13	17	13	11	4	5	10	.304

22 MIKE HINCKLEY, LHP

BORN: Oct. 5, 1982. **B-T:** L-L. **HT.:** 6-3. **WT.:** 170. **DRAFTED:** HS—Moore, Okla., 2001 (3rd round). **SIGNED BY:** Darrell Brown.

Hinckley ranked as the Nationals' No. 1 prospect after his stellar 2004 campaign, but he hurt his shoulder in big league camp the following spring and spent the next three years wandering through the prospect wilderness. He re-signed with the Nationals as a minor league free agent before the 2008 season, and the organization decided to move him to the bullpen. He responded with a bounce-back season that landed him in the big leagues, where he didn't allow an earned run in his first 14 innings. A few mechanical adjustments helped Hinckley regain his fastball velocity, as he worked at 88-91 mph and bumped 92 occasionally. The Nationals focused on getting him to keep his upper body back longer in his delivery and gave him a slight shoulder tilt that helps him drive the ball down in the zone, reminiscent of Andy Pettitte's motion. He works mostly with his fastball and a good curveball with tight 1-to-7 break, which he commanded much better in 2008 than he had in recent years. He can throw a 78 mph changeup with some sink but seldom uses it in a relief role. Hinckley should be a key lefthander in Washington's bullpen out of spring training. He can be more than a left-on-left specialist, but he'll never be more than a middle reliever.

Year	Club (League)	Class	W	L	ERA	G	GS	CG	SV	IP	H	R	ER	HR	BB	SO	AVG
2001	Expos (GCL)	R	2	2	5.24	8	5	0	0	34	46	23	20	1	12	28	.329

Year	Club (League)	Class	W	L	ERA	G	GS	CG	SV	IP	H	R	ER	HR	BB	SO	AVG
2002	Vermont (NYP)	SS	6	2	1.37	16	16	0	0	92	60	19	14	4	30	66	.188
2003	Savannah (SAL)	LoA	9	5	3.64	23	23	2	0	121	124	54	49	4	41	111	.271
	Brevard County (FSL)	HiA	4	0	0.72	4	4	1	0	25	14	2	2	1	1	23	.159
2004	Brevard County (FSL)	HiA	6	2	2.61	10	10	0	0	62	47	23	18	6	18	51	.211
	Harrisburg (EL)	AA	5	2	2.87	16	16	0	0	94	83	34	30	5	23	80	.250
2005	Potomac (CAR)	HiA	3	9	4.93	22	21	1	0	128	151	90	70	10	51	80	.293
2006	Potomac (CAR)	HiA	6	8	5.52	28	28	0	0	148	178	102	91	18	63	79	.303
2007	Harrisburg (EL)	AA	9	10	5.83	25	23	0	0	117	145	85	76	15	59	70	.304
2008	Harrisburg (EL)	AA	5	3	5.12	23	6	0	0	65	79	40	37	6	40	53	.307
	Columbus (IL)	AAA	0	2	3.16	20	1	0	1	26	27	11	9	0	15	20	.278
	Washington (NL)	MAJ	0	0	0.00	14	0	0	0	14	8	1	0	0	3	9	.178
MINOR LEAGUE TOTALS			55	45	4.11	195	153	4	1	912	954	483	416	70	353	661	.273
MAJOR LEAGUE TOTALS			0	0	0.00	14	0	0	0	14	8	1	0	0	3	9	.178

23 STEPHEN KING, 3B

BORN: Oct. 2, 1987. **B-T:** R-R. **HT.:** 6-2. **WT.:** 195. **DRAFTED:** HS—Winter Park, Fla., 2006 (3rd round). **SIGNED BY:** Tony Arango.

King signed late for a $750,000 bonus in 2006, then split his 2007 pro debut between shortstop and second base while struggling offensively in the lower minors. He found a home at third base in 2008 and fared much better with the bat in his second go-round at low Class A, then was overmatched against older competition at high Class A in August. The Nationals say King made huge strides with his maturity and his all-around game. He has quick wrists and a swing that evokes Travis Fryman. With a strong, physical frame, King projects for average power, though he's more of a gap-to-gap hitter at this stage of his development. He's an average runner with good range, a strong arm and decent actions at third base, though he's still learning the position. Offensively, King must improve his pitch selection, as he has a tendency to chase breaking pitches down and out of the zone. He has a quality all-around package that gives him a chance to be a solid everyday big leaguer down the road, but he has plenty of work to do in all phases before he can be regarded as anything close to a safe bet. King will return to high Class A in 2009.

Year	Club (League)	Class	AVG	G	AB	R	H	2B	3B	HR	RBI	BB	SO	SB	OBP	SLG
2007	Hagerstown (SAL)	LoA	.180	35	128	16	23	4	0	2	9	13	51	5	.261	.258
	Nationals (GCL)	R	.248	42	161	20	40	6	1	9	30	12	47	1	.315	.466
	Vermont (NYP)	SS	.333	6	24	3	8	2	0	0	2	1	7	0	.360	.417
2008	Hagerstown (SAL)	LoA	.284	87	335	39	95	21	1	6	33	22	75	4	.336	.406
	Potomac (CAR)	HiA	.214	19	70	4	15	2	1	0	7	5	11	1	.267	.271
MINOR LEAGUE TOTALS			.252	189	718	82	181	35	3	17	81	53	191	11	.312	.380

24 WILL ATWOOD, LHP

BORN: Jan. 13, 1987. **B-T:** L-L. **HT.:** 6-2. **WT.:** 180. **DRAFTED:** South Carolina, 2008 (12th round). **SIGNED BY:** Bob Hamelin.

Atwood worked as a starter and reliever in three years at South Carolina but never quite figured out the Southeastern Conference, posting a 5.21 career ERA. He had some success against wood bats in his two summers in the Cape Cod League, however, and he had a dominant pro debut. Atwood throws strikes with a quality three-pitch mix. His fastball sat at 86-89 mph last summer but reached 90-91 in instructional league, when he was one of Washington's top pitchers. He uses a slow curveball in the high 60s to low 70s, but he worked hard to tighten it up in the fall, throwing more of a mid-70s slider with 2-to-8 break. He has good feel for the breaking ball, which he can throw for strikes or bury. His changeup is a third average offering. Atwood has a skinny frame and whippy arm action that leads the Nationals to believe he could add velocity to his fastball as he matures. He reminds some of John Lannan and has a similar ceiling as a back-of-the-rotation starter. Atwood should move quickly through the system and could skip a level to high Class A in 2009.

Year	Club (League)	Class	W	L	ERA	G	GS	CG	SV	IP	H	R	ER	HR	BB	SO	AVG
2008	Vermont (NYP)	SS	2	1	2.41	12	12	0	0	52	40	17	14	2	9	60	.205
MINOR LEAGUE TOTALS			2	1	2.41	12	12	0	0	52	40	17	14	2	9	60	.205

25 JOSH SMOKER, LHP

BORN: Nov. 26, 1988. **B-T:** L-L. **HT.:** 6-2. **WT.:** 195. **DRAFTED:** HS—Calhoun, Ga., 2007 (1st round supplemental). **SIGNED BY:** Eric Robinson.

Smoker turned down a scholarship from Clemson to sign with the Nationals for $1 million, but he arrived at his first spring training with a sore shoulder that got worse as he tried too hard to make an impression in big league camp. The Nationals started him slowly in extended spring training, then sent him to low Class A when he started to pitch better. His shoulder discomfort lingered, affecting his range of motion and causing him to work in the mid-80s with his fastball, instead of his former 90-94 range. He pitched better after a demotion to the Gulf Coast League, but his velocity didn't return and he had surgery in November to remove a bone spur from his shoulder. At his best, Smoker's repertoire includes a curveball that can be plus at times and a promising changeup.

He's a fierce competitor with a good feel for pitching, but he needs to do a better job commanding his curveball. Not only was Smoker's fastball velocity down in 2008, but the pitch also lacked life. The Nationals hope he'll be back to 100 percent by the spring and regain his former stuff, but there are no guarantees with shoulder injuries. Smoker is coming off a lost year, but he still has a chance to be a solid mid-rotation starter down the road.

Year	Club (League)	Class	W	L	ERA	G	GS	CG	SV	IP	H	R	ER	HR	BB	SO	AVG
2007	Vermont (NYP)	SS	0	0	4.50	2	2	0	0	4	2	2	2	0	3	5	.167
2008	Hagerstown (SAL)	LoA	0	4	11.50	5	5	0	0	18	31	27	23	5	9	21	.360
	Nationals (GCL)	R	2	1	1.37	6	6	0	0	26	20	11	4	0	13	16	.213
MINOR LEAGUE TOTALS			2	5	5.40	13	13	0	0	48	53	40	29	5	25	42	.276

26 COLTON WILLEMS, RHP

BORN: July 30, 1988. **B-T:** R-R. **HT.:** 6-3. **WT.:** 175. **DRAFTED:** HS—Fort Pierce, Fla., 2006 (1st round). **SIGNED BY:** Tony Arango.

Willems never has shown the overpowering stuff in pro ball that made him a first-round pick worth a $1.425 million bonus coming out of high school. He hasn't missed many bats in his first three pro seasons, though he did stay healthy for a full season in 2008 and posted decent results thanks to his competitiveness. Far from the 93-97 mph fastball he showed in high school, Willems' heater sat at 87-90 and topped out at 91 in 2008. He threw a slider in his prep days, but the Nationals made him switch to a curveball shortly after he joined the system. He raised his arm slot in order to throw the curve, and it affected his velocity. Washington let him go back to the slider in 2008, and he showed an improved ability to power through the pitch. He also threw some promising curves in instructional league. Willems has made progress over the last two years with his changeup, which is now close to an average pitch. He tends to cut his fastball a bit, which might be another reason his velocity has dropped. The Nationals want Willems to work on just throwing the ball instead of placing it. If he ever can regain his former stuff, Willems still has plenty of upside, but it's hard to imagine him succeeding at higher levels with what he showed in 2008.

Year	Club (League)	Class	W	L	ERA	G	GS	CG	SV	IP	H	R	ER	HR	BB	SO	AVG
2006	Nationals (GCL)	R	0	1	3.38	5	5	0	0	16	23	8	6	1	3	8	.338
2007	Vermont (NYP)	SS	3	2	1.84	12	12	0	0	59	55	25	12	2	26	31	.251
2008	Hagerstown (SAL)	LoA	5	9	3.70	20	20	0	0	109	103	58	45	7	31	60	.254
MINOR LEAGUE TOTALS			8	12	3.08	37	37	0	0	184	181	91	63	10	60	99	.261

27 LUIS ATILANO, RHP

BORN: May 10, 1985. **B-T:** R-R. **HT.:** 6-3. **WT.:** 215. **DRAFTED:** HS—San Juan, P.R., 2003 (1st round supplemental). **SIGNED BY:** Julian Perez (Braves).

Atilano signed for $950,000 as the 35th overall pick in 2003 and gradually climbed through the Braves system before he was derailed by Tommy John surgery in August 2006. Atlanta dealt him to Washington for Daryle Ward that same month. He returned to make one appearance in 2007 before the Nationals shut him down with a strained forearm muscle, but he bounced back in 2008 to help Potomac to the Carolina League title and land on Washington's 40-man roster. Atilano's solid three-pitch mix is highlighted by an average-to-plus changeup with good arm speed, and a heavy 89-91 mph fastball that tops out at 92-93. His mid- to upper-70s curveball has some depth and projects as an average pitch, but he needs to improve his command of it. Atilano was rail-thin out of high school, but he let his body go during his downtime. He got into better shape in 2008 but still must improve his conditioning. Though Atilano has a live arm and a clean arm action, he doesn't throw as hard as he could because he doesn't use his legs well, and he doesn't repeat his delivery. With physical and mechanical fine-tuning, Atilano could add velocity and become a mid-rotation starter, but some see him strictly as a bullpen arm down the road.

Year	Club (League)	Class	W	L	ERA	G	GS	CG	SV	IP	H	R	ER	HR	BB	SO	AVG
2003	Braves (GCL)	R	3	2	3.83	12	12	1	0	54	61	25	23	5	7	24	.288
2004	Danville (APP)	R	5	1	4.20	13	13	0	0	64	64	32	30	7	10	54	.260
2005	Rome (SAL)	LoA	8	9	4.17	24	24	1	0	136	138	77	63	17	32	66	.261
2006	Myrtle Beach (CAR)	HiA	6	7	4.50	19	18	2	0	116	134	63	58	16	27	45	.298
2007	Nationals (GCL)	R	0	0	6.75	1	0	0	0	1	1	1	1	0	1	2	.200
2008	Hagerstown (SAL)	LoA	0	0	3.16	7	3	0	1	26	29	14	9	1	7	13	.276
	Harrisburg (EL)	AA	0	1	1.50	2	1	0	0	6	6	3	1	0	2	3	.300
	Potomac (CAR)	HiA	5	2	2.32	15	11	0	0	62	50	21	16	5	14	39	.229
MINOR LEAGUE TOTALS			27	22	3.89	93	82	4	1	465	483	236	201	51	100	246	.271

28 CORY VAN ALLEN, LHP

BORN: Dec. 24, 1984. **B-T:** L-L. **HT.:** 6-3. **WT.:** 180. **DRAFTED:** Baylor, 2006 (5th round). **SIGNED BY:** Bob Laurie.

An unsigned third-round pick by the Dodgers out of high school in 2003, Van Allen had a decent three-year career at Baylor but never became the staff ace the Bears envisioned. Since the Nationals took him in the fifth round in 2006, he has been hampered by nagging injuries, from toe and chest problems in 2007 to forearm tendinitis that caused him to miss nearly all of June and July in 2008. He finished the year with a 2-1, 5.84 stint in the Arizona Fall League, and he showed good stuff there. Van Allen has an athletic frame, loose arm action and decent command of a three-pitch mix. He does a good job pitching off his 90-91 mph fastball, which touched 92-93 in the AFL. He has been caught between a curveball and a slider for much of his career, but he settled on a slider with good depth in 2008. He ordinarily can throw his average changeup for strikes, but he has trouble commanding all three of his pitches at the same time. If he can put it all together, Van Allen can be a strike-throwing No. 4 starter in the big leagues. He's likely to return to Double-A in 2009 and could arrive in the big leagues in the second half.

Year	Club (League)	Class	W	L	ERA	G	GS	CG	SV	IP	H	R	ER	HR	BB	SO	AVG
2006	Vermont (NYP)	SS	1	4	4.06	13	9	0	0	58	53	29	26	5	16	41	.248
2007	Hagerstown (SAL)	LoA	1	3	3.62	11	11	0	0	55	67	37	22	5	6	51	.291
	Potomac (CAR)	HiA	3	7	5.49	13	13	0	0	59	78	43	36	3	23	54	.325
2008	Potomac (CAR)	HiA	3	0	0.66	5	4	0	0	27	18	6	2	1	7	19	.186
	Nationals (GCL)	R	0	0	0.00	1	1	0	0	4	3	1	0	0	0	2	.231
	Harrisburg (EL)	AA	3	3	5.13	10	10	0	0	47	64	30	27	4	11	36	.318
MINOR LEAGUE TOTALS			11	17	4.07	53	48	0	0	250	283	146	113	18	63	203	.284

29 LUKE MONTZ, C

BORN: July 7, 1983. **B-T:** R-R. **HT.:** 6-2. **WT.:** 205. **DRAFTED:** Hill (Texas) CC, 2003 (17th round). **SIGNED BY:** Ray Corbett.

Montz has worked hard to make himself into a legitimate prospect. He had a reputation as a horrible defensive catcher early in his career, a label that gained traction when he hit Collin Balester in the head while trying to throw a ball to second base in 2005. Montz split time between catcher and first base until 2007, when he became a full-time catcher and started making big strides on his defense. He had a breakout year at Double-A in 2008 and finished the season in the big leagues, where he appeared somewhat intimidated and overmatched at the plate. Montz has above-average power but it's almost exclusively to the pull side. He started using the opposite field better at Harrisburg and adopted a more patient approach. Montz has a strong arm and threw out 37 percent of basestealers last season. Working with former catchers Bobby Henley, John Stearns, Randy Knorr and Bob Boone over the last two years has helped his defense, but Montz still needs plenty of work on his blocking and receiving. He may never catch well enough to be an everyday player, but he can be a valuable backup catcher with a power bat off the bench.

Year	Club (League)	Class	AVG	G	AB	R	H	2B	3B	HR	RBI	BB	SO	SB	OBP	SLG
2003	Expos (GCL)	R	.223	32	103	8	23	0	0	2	9	9	21	1	.286	.282
2004	Brevard County (FSL)	HiA	.500	1	2	0	1	1	0	0	0	2	1	0	.750	1.000
	Vermont (NYP)	SS	.250	62	204	31	51	11	0	10	34	33	42	2	.361	.451
2005	Savannah (SAL)	LoA	.224	100	343	66	77	24	1	19	68	50	95	1	.324	.466
2006	Potomac (CAR)	HiA	.229	131	449	59	103	27	3	16	76	51	91	3	.313	.410
2007	Potomac (CAR)	HiA	.269	60	201	43	54	15	1	7	39	45	54	3	.406	.458
	Harrisburg (EL)	AA	.233	40	146	22	34	5	1	5	19	8	50	0	.274	.384
2008	Harrisburg (EL)	AA	.282	63	220	30	62	14	0	14	53	31	46	0	.368	.536
	Columbus (IL)	AAA	.256	48	168	18	43	8	1	2	18	13	37	1	.309	.351
	Washington (NL)	MAJ	.143	10	21	2	3	0	0	1	3	5	9	0	.308	.286
MINOR LEAGUE TOTALS			.244	537	1836	277	448	105	7	75	316	242	437	11	.334	.431
MAJOR LEAGUE TOTALS			.143	10	21	2	3	0	0	1	3	5	9	0	.308	.286

30 TERRELL YOUNG, RHP

BORN: Aug. 7, 1985. **B-T:** R-R. **HT.:** 6-3. **WT.:** 175. **DRAFTED:** HS—Grenada, Miss., 2004 (10th round). **SIGNED BY:** Jerry Flowers (Reds).

Young dropped to the 10th round of the 2004 draft because of concerns about his makeup, and there's reason to question his aptitude after it took him five years to reach high Class A in the Reds system. But Young had a breakout year in 2008, and the Nationals took him with the first pick in the major league Rule 5 draft. He has an electric arm and will have a chance to stay in the big leagues as a reliever in the patchwork Washington bullpen. Young's best pitch is a 93-95 mph fastball that touches 98. It can be an above-average or better pitch if he can improve his command of it. He has made strides with his secondary stuff, but it's still lacking. His changeup is a fringy and merely adequate No. 2 pitch, and he struggles to locate his below-average slider. The Nats believe Young has matured and can absorb instruction, but the jury is still out. He'll never be more than a middle reliever or setup man, but his power arm gives him a chance to stay on Washington's big league roster in 2008.

Year	Club (League)	Class	W	L	ERA	G	GS	CG	SV	IP	H	R	ER	HR	BB	SO	AVG
2004	Reds (GCL)	R	0	1	3.86	10	0	0	0	14	12	6	6	3	9	8	.240
2005	Reds (GCL)	R	2	0	6.75	3	0	0	0	4	4	3	3	0	2	6	.267
2006	Dayton (MWL)	LoA	0	1	8.10	4	0	0	0	7	6	7	6	0	6	5	.231
	Billings (PIO)	R	3	1	2.70	25	0	0	9	23	11	10	7	2	20	32	.145
2007	Dayton (MWL)	LoA	1	4	4.08	23	0	0	0	35	27	16	16	2	22	33	.216
2008	Dayton (MWL)	LoA	1	3	3.51	18	0	0	1	26	25	11	10	1	15	21	.266
	Sarasota (FSL)	HiA	1	2	2.41	25	0	0	2	34	31	13	9	0	13	26	.237
MINOR LEAGUE TOTALS			8	12	3.60	108	0	0	12	143	116	66	57	8	87	131	.224

Major League Baseball's signing deadline for draft picks is Aug. 15—with one exception. College seniors who have completed their eligibility may continue negotiating up until a week before the next year's draft. That's the situation Georgia righthander Joshua Fields, the No. 20 overall pick in the 2008 draft, found himself in with the Mariners as the Prospect Handbook went to press.

Complicating matters further, both the general manager (Bill Bavasi) and scouting director (Bob Fontaine) who drafted Fields since have been fired, with former Brewers scouting director Jack Zduriencik taking over as GM. Zduriencik said during the Winter Meetings that if a deal is worked out, it would before spring training so Fields won't miss any more development time. If he doesn't sign by then, Fields likely will sign with an independent league team and prepare to re-enter the 2009 draft. If that happens, Seattle would receive the No. 21 choice as compensation.

We present Fields' scouting report below. He would have ranked No. 6 on our Mariners prospect list had he signed in time to be included.

JOSHUA FIELDS, RHP

BORN: Aug. **19, 1985. B-T:** R-R. **HT.:** 6-0. **WT.:** 178. **DRAFTED:** Georgia, 2008 (1st round).

Fields has now been through three drafts and has yet to turn pro. As a high school senior, he entered 2004 as a potential third- to fifth-round pick, but told scouts he wanted a seven-figure bonus to sway him away from a commitment to Georgia. He went undrafted and served as the Bulldogs' closer for the better part of four years, setting a Southeastern Conference record with 41 career saves. Fields put himself in position to be an early first-round pick in 2007 by tearing up the Cape Cod League the previous summer, but he slumped and dropped to the Braves in the second round. Atlanta thought it had met Fields' asking price, but he ultimately decided to return to Georgia for his senior year. Fields bounced back in a big way, leading NCAA Division I with 18 saves, earning SEC pitcher of the year honors and pitching the Bulldogs to a runner-up finish at the College World Series. The Mariners drafted him 20th overall, making him the first pure reliever drafted. Fields is slightly built but has lightning in his arm, regularly pumping mid-90s fastballs and touching 98. He has a second plus pitch in his hard downer curveball, which freezes righthanders when it's on. He throws it in the low 80s, but tends to hang it when he's not right mechanically. He'll miss up with his fastball as well when he doesn't finish his delivery. Fields' slight frame leads to durability concerns, and he rarely worked more than an inning at a time for Georgia. In four college seasons, he pitched just 154 innings. One of Fields' biggest selling points is that he's nearly ready for the big leagues. Despite his extended holdout, he could pitch in Seattle at some point in 2009 if he does come to terms. The Mariners have no obvious closer after trading J.J. Putz and moving Brandon Morrow into the rotation, and Fields might fill that role within a year of signing.

2008 DRAFT

FIRST FIVE ROUNDS

Bonuses and estimated slot recommendations by Major League Baseball for the first five rounds of the 2008 draft. MLB established guidelines for every pick through the first five rounds, and set a $150,000 ceiling (roughly equivalent to the final choice in the fifth round) for subsequent rounds. An asterisk indicates the bonus was part of a major league contract and a cross signifies a two-sport contract (allowing the club to spread the bonus over as many as five years).

FIRST ROUND

Pick. Team: Player, Pos.	Bonus	Slot
1. TB: Tim Beckham, ss	+$6,150,000	$4,000,000
2. Pit: Pedro Alvarez, 3b	*$6,000,000	$3,500,000
3. KC: Eric Hosmer, 1b	$6,000,000	$3,000,000
4. Bal: Brian Matusz, lhp	*$3,200,000	$2,750,000
5. SF: Buster Posey, c	$6,200,000	$2,500,000
6. Fla: Kyle Skipworth, c	$2,300,000	$2,400,000
7. Cin: Yonder Alonso, 1b	*$2,000,000	$2,310,000
8. CWS: Gordon Beckham, ss	$2,600,000	$2,230,000
9. Was: Aaron Crow, rhp	Did Not Sign	$2,150,000
10. Hou: Jason Castro, c	$2,070,000	$2,070,000
11. Tex: Justin Smoak, 1b	$3,500,000	$2,000,000
12. Oak: Jemile Weeks, 2b	$1,910,000	$1,910,000
13. StL: Brett Wallace, 3b/1b	$1,840,000	$1,840,000
14. Min: Aaron Hicks, of	$1,780,000	$1,780,000
15. LAD: Ethan Martin, rhp	$1,730,000	$1,730,000
16. Mil: Brett Lawrie, c/3b	$1,700,000	$1,680,000
17. Tor: David Cooper, 1b	$1,500,000	$1,630,000
18. NYM: Ike Davis, 1b	$1,575,000	$1,580,000
19. ChC: Andrew Cashner, rhp	$1,540,000	$1,540,000
20. Sea: Joshua Fields, rhp	Unsigned	$1,500,000
21. Det: Ryan Perry, rhp	$1,480,000	$1,480,000
22. NYM: Reese Havens, ss	$1,419,000	$1,430,000
23. SD: Allan Dykstra, 1b	$1,150,000	$1,400,000
24. Phi: Anthony Hewitt, 3b	$1,380,000	$1,380,000
25. Col: Christian Friedrich, lhp	$1,350,000	$1,350,000
26. Ari: Daniel Schlereth, lhp	$1,330,000	$1,330,000
27. Min: Carlos Gutierrez, rhp	$1,290,000	$1,290,000
28. NYY: Gerrit Cole, rhp	Did Not Sign	$1,260,000
29. Cle: Lonnie Chisenhall, ss	$1,100,000	$1,230,000
30. Bos: Casey Kelly, rhp/ss	+$3,000,000	$1,200,000

SUPPLEMENTAL FIRST ROUND

Pick. Team: Player, Pos.	Bonus	Slot
31. Min: Shooter Hunt, rhp	$1,080,000	$1,080,000
32. Mil: Jake Odorizzi, rhp	$1,060,000	$1,060,000
33. NYM: Brad Holt, rhp	$1,040,000	$1,040,000
34. Phi: Zach Collier, of	$1,020,000	$1,020,000
35. Mil: Evan Frederickson, lhp	$1,010,000	$1,010,000
36. KC: Mike Montgomery, lhp	$988,000	$988,000
37. SF: Conor Gillaspie, 3b	$970,000	$970,000
38. Hou: Jordan Lyles, rhp	$930,000	$954,000
39. StL: Lance Lynn, rhp	$938,000	$938,000
40. Atl: Brett DeVall, lhp	$1,000,000	$922,000
41. ChC: Ryan Flaherty, ss	$906,000	$906,000
42. SD: Jaff Decker, of	$892,000	$892,000
43. Ari: Wade Miley, lhp	$877,000	$877,000
44. NYY: Jeremy Bleich, lhp	$700,000	$863,000
45. Bos: Bryan Price, rhp	$849,000	$849,000
46. SD: Logan Forsythe, 3b	$835,000	$835,000

SECOND ROUND

Pick. Team: Player, Pos.	Bonus	Slot
47. TB: Kyle Lobstein, lhp	$1,500,000	$822,000
48. Pit: Tanner Scheppers, rhp	Did Not Sign	$809,000
49. KC: Johnny Giavotella, 2b	$787,000	$796,000
50. Bal: Xavier Avery, of	+$900,000	$784,000
51. Phi: Anthony Gose, of	$772,000	$772,000
52. Fla: Brad Hand, lhp	$760,000	$760,000
53. Mil: Seth Lintz, rhp	$900,000	$748,000
54. Mil: Cutter Dykstra, of	$737,000	$737,000
55. Was: Destin Hood, of	+$1,100,000	$726,000
56. Hou: Jay Austin, of	$715,000	$715,000
57. Tex: Robbie Ross, lhp	$1,575,000	$705,000
58. Oak: Tyson Ross, rhp	$694,000	$694,000
59. StL: Shane Peterson, of	$683,000	$683,000
60. Min: Tyler Ladendorf, ss	$673,000	$673,000
61. LAD: Josh Lindblom, rhp	$663,000	$663,000
62. Mil: Cody Adams, rhp	$653,000	$653,000
63. Tor: Kenny Wilson, of	$644,000	$644,000
64. Atl: Tyler Stovall, lhp	$750,000	$634,000
65. ChC: Aaron Shafer, rhp	$625,000	$625,000
66. Sea: Dennis Raben, of	$616,000	$616,000
67. Det: Cody Satterwhite, rhp	$606,000	$606,000
68. NYM: Javier Rodriguez, of	$585,000	$597,000
69. SD: James Darnell, 3b	$740,000	$589,000
70. Atl: Zeke Spruill, rhp	$600,000	$580,000
71. Phi: Jason Knapp, rhp	$590,000	$572,000
72. Col: Charlie Blackmon, of	$563,000	$563,000
73. Ari: Bryan Shaw, rhp	$553,000	$553,000
74. LAA: Tyler Chatwood, rhp	$547,000	$547,000
75. NYY: Scott Bittle, rhp	Did Not Sign	$539,000
76. Cle: Trey Haley, rhp	$1,250,000	$531,000
77. Bos: Derrik Gibson, ss	$600,000	$523,000

THIRD ROUND

Pick. Team: Player, Pos.	Bonus	Slot
78. TB: Jake Jefferies, c	$515,000	$515,000
79. Pit: Jordy Mercer, ss	$508,000	$508,000
80. KC: Tyler Sample, rhp	$500,000	$500,000
81. Bal: L.J. Hoes, 2b	$490,000	$492,000
82. SF: Roger Kieschnick, of	$525,000	$485,000
83. Fla: Edgar Olmos, lhp	$478,000	$478,000
84. Cin: Zach Stewart, rhp	$450,000	$471,000
85. Bos: Stephen Fife, rhp	$464,000	$464,000
86. CWS: Brent Morel, 3b	$440,000	$457,000
87. Was: Danny Espinosa, ss	$525,000	$450,000
88. Hou: Chase Davidson, 1b	Did Not Sign	$443,000
89. Tex: Tim Murphy, lhp	$436,000	$436,000
90. Oak: Petey Paramore, c	$430,000	$430,000
91. StL: Niko Vasquez, ss	$423,000	$423,000
92. Min: Bobby Lanigan, rhp	$417,000	$417,000
93. LAD: Kyle Russell, of	$410,000	$410,000
94. Mil: Logan Schafer, of	$404,000	$404,000
95. Tor: Andrew Liebel, rhp	$340,000	$397,000
96. Atl: Craig Kimbrel, rhp	$391,000	$391,000
97. ChC: Chris Carpenter, rhp	$385,000	$385,000
98. Sea: Aaron Pribanic, rhp	$390,000	$379,000
99. Det: Scott Green, rhp	$373,000	$373,000
100. NYM: Kirk Nieuwenhuis, of	$360,000	$367,000
101. SD: Blake Tekotte, of	$361,000	$361,000
102. Phi: Vance Worley, rhp	$355,000	$355,000
103. Col: Aaron Weatherford, rhp	$350,000	$350,000

104. Ari: Kevin Eichhorn, rhp	$500,000	$344,000
105. LAA: Ryan Chaffee, rhp	$338,000	$338,000
106. NYY: David Adams, 2b	$333,000	$333,000
107. Cle: Cord Phelps, 2b	$327,000	$327,000
108. Bos: Kyle Weiland, rhp	$322,000	$322,000

SUPPLEMENTAL THIRD ROUND

Pick. Team: Player, Pos.	Bonus	Slot
109. Hou: Ross Seaton, rhp	$700,000	$316,000
110. Phi: Jon Pettibone, rhp	$500,000	$311,000
111. SD: Sawyer Carroll, of	$125,000	$305,000
112. LAA: Zach Cone, of	Did Not Sign	$300,000

FOURTH ROUND

Pick. Team: Player, Pos.	Bonus	Slot
113. TB: Ty Morrison, of	+$500,000	$297,000
114. Pit: Chase d'Arnaud, ss	$293,000	$293,000
115. KC: Tim Melville, rhp	$1,250,000	$290,000
116. Bal: Kyle Hudson, of	$287,000	$287,000
117. SF: Brandon Crawford, ss	$375,000	$283,000
118. Fla: Curtis Petersen, rhp	$350,000	$280,000
119. Cin: Tyler Cline, rhp	$240,000	$277,000
120. CWS: Drew O'Neil, rhp	$260,000	$273,000
121. Was: Graham Hicks, lhp	$475,000	$270,000
122. Hou: T.J. Steele, of	$267,000	$267,000
123. Tex: Joe Wieland, rhp	$263,000	$263,000
124. Oak: Anthony Capra, lhp	$260,000	$260,000
125. StL: Scott Gorgen, rhp	$250,000	$257,000
126. Min: Danny Ortiz, of	$253,000	$253,000
127. LAD: Devaris Gordon, ss	$250,000	$250,000
128. Mil: Josh Romanski, lhp	$247,000	$247,000
129. Tor: Mark Sobolewski, 3b	$243,000	$243,000
130. Atl: Braeden Schlehuber, c	$240,000	$240,000
131. ChC: Matt Cerda, ss/c	$500,000	$237,000
132. Sea: Steven Hensley, rhp	$233,000	$233,000
133. Det: Brett Jacobson, rhp	$230,000	$230,000
134. NYM: Sean Ratliff, of	$225,000	$227,000
135. SD: Jason Kipnis, of	Did Not Sign	$223,000
136. Phi: Trevor May, rhp	$375,000	$220,000
137. Col: Ethan Hollingsworth, rhp	$215,000	$217,000
138. Ari: Ryne White, 1b	$213,000	$213,000
139. LAA: Buddy Boshiers, lhp	$210,000	$210,000
140. NYY: Corban Joseph, ss	$207,000	$207,000
141. Cle: David Roberts, rhp	$200,000	$203,000
142. Bos: Pete Hissey, of	$1,000,000	$200,000

FIFTH ROUND

Pick. Team: Player, Pos.	Bonus	Slot
143. TB: Mike Sheridan, 1b	$195,000	$199,000
144. Pit: Justin Wilson, lhp	$195,000	$197,000
145. KC: John Lamb, lhp	$165,000	$196,000
146. Bal: Greg Miclat, ss	$225,000	$194,000
147. SF: Edwin Quirarte, rhp	$193,000	$193,000
148. Fla: Pete Andrelczyk, rhp	$185,000	$191,000
149. Cin: Clayton Shunick, rhp	$175,000	$190,000
150. CWS: Dan Hudson, rhp	$180,000	$188,000
151. Was: Adrian Nieto, c	$376,000	$187,000
152. Hou: David Duncan, lhp	$185,000	$185,000
153. Tex: Clark Murphy, 1b	$200,000	$184,000
154. Oak: Jason Christian, ss	$182,000	$182,000
155. StL: Jermaine Curtis, 3b	$181,000	$181,000
156. Min: Nick Romero, 3b	$179,000	$179,000
157. LAD: Jon Michael Redding, rhp	$178,000	$178,000
158. Mil: Maverick Lasker, rhp	$176,000	$176,000
159. Tor: Tyler Pastornicky, ss	$175,000	$175,000
160. Atl: Jacob Thompson, rhp	$190,000	$173,000
161. ChC: Justin Bristow, rhp	$172,000	$172,000
162. Sea: Brett Lorin, rhp	$170,000	$170,000
163. Det: Alex Avila, c	$169,000	$169,000
164. NYM: Dock Doyle, c	$167,000	$167,000
165. SD: Anthony Bass, rhp	$166,000	$166,000
166. Phi: Jeremy Hamilton, 1b	$164,000	$164,000
167. Col: Chris Dominguez, 3b	Did Not Sign	$163,000
168. Ari: Colin Cowgill, of	$155,000	$161,000
169. LAA: Khiry Cooper, of	Did Not Sign	$160,000
170. NYY: Chris Smith, of	$158,000	$158,000
171. Cle: Zach Putnam, rhp	$600,000	$157,000
172. Bos: Ryan Westmoreland, of	+$2,000,000	$155,000

SIGNING BONUSES

2007 DRAFT

FIRST ROUND

Pick. Team: Player, Pos.	Bonus	Slot
1. TB: David Price, lhp	*$5,600,000	$3,600,000
2. KC: Mike Moustakas, ss/3b	$4,000,000	$3,150,000
3. CHC: Josh Vitters, 3b	$3,200,000	$2,700,000
4. Pit: Daniel Moskos, lhp	$2,475,000	$2,475,000
5. Bal: Matt Wieters, c	$6,000,000	$2,250,000
6. Was: Ross Detwiler, lhp	$2,150,000	$2,160,000
7. Mil: Matt LaPorta, of/1b	$2,000,000	$2,070,000
8. Col: Casey Weathers, rhp	$1,800,000	$1,980,000
9. Ari: Jarrod Parker, rhp	$2,100,000	$1,890,000
10. SF: Madison Bumgarner, lhp	$2,000,000	$1,800,000
11. Sea: Phillippe Aumont, rhp	$1,900,000	$1,710,000
12. Fla: Matt Dominguez, 3b	$1,800,000	$1,620,000
13. Cle: Beau Mills, 3b/1b	$1,575,000	$1,575,000
14. Atl: Jason Heyward, of	$1,700,000	$1,530,000
15. Cin: Devin Mesoraco, c	$1,400,000	$1,485,000
16. Tor: Kevin Ahrens, ss/3b	$1,440,000	$1,440,000
17. Tex: Blake Beavan, rhp	$1,497,500	$1,417,500
18. StL: Pete Kozma, ss	$1,395,000	$1,395,000
19. Phi: Joe Savery, lhp	$1,372,500	$1,372,500
20. LAD: Chris Withrow, rhp	$1,350,000	$1,350,000
21. Tor: J.P. Arencibia, c	$1,327,500	$1,327,500
22. SF: Tim Alderson, rhp	$1,290,000	$1,282,500
23. SD: Nick Schmidt, lhp	$1,260,000	$1,260,000
24. Tex: Michael Main, rhp	$1,237,500	$1,237,500
25. CWS: Aaron Poreda, lhp	$1,200,000	$1,215,000
26. Oak: James Simmons, rhp	$1,192,500	$1,192,500
27. Det: Rick Porcello, rhp	*$3,580,000	$1,170,000
28. Mil: Ben Revere, of	$750,000	$1,080,000
29. SF: Wendell Fairley, of	$1,000,000	$990,000
30. NYY: Andrew Brackman, rhp	*$3,350,000	$945,000

SUPPLEMENTAL FIRST ROUND

Pick. Team: Player, Pos.	Bonus	Slot
31. Was: Josh Smoker, lhp	$1,000,000	$922,500
32. SF: Nick Noonan, ss/2b	$915,750	$915,750
33. Atl: Jon Gilmore, 3b	$900,000	$900,000
34. Cin: Todd Frazier, ss	$825,000	$877,500
35. Tex: Julio Borbon, of	*$800,000	$855,000
36. StL: Clayton Mortensen, rhp	$650,000	$855,000
37. Phi: Travis d'Arnaud, c	$832,500	$832,500
38. Tor: Brett Cecil, lhp	$810,000	$810,000
39. LAD: James Adkins, lhp	$787,500	$787,500
40. SD: Kellen Kulbacki, of	$765,000	$765,000
41. Oak: Sean Doolittle, 1b	$742,500	$742,500
42. NYM: Eddie Kunz, rhp	$720,000	$720,000
43. SF: Jackson Williams, c	$708,750	$708,750
44. Tex: Neil Ramirez, rhp	$1,000,000	$697,500
45. Tor: Justin Jackson, ss	$675,000	$675,000
46. SD: Drew Cumberland, ss	$661,500	$661,500
47. NYM: Nathan Vineyard, lhp	$657,000	$657,000
48. CHC: Josh Donaldson, c	$652,500	$652,500
49. Was: Michael Burgess, of	$630,000	$630,000
50. Ari: Wes Roemer, rhp	$620,000	$621,000
51. SF: Charlie Culberson, ss	$607,500	$607,500

Pick. Team: Player, Pos.	Bonus	Slot
52. Sea: Matt Mangini, 3b	$603,000	$603,000
53. Cin: Kyle Lotzkar, rhp	$594,000	$594,000
54. Tex: Tommy Hunter, rhp	$585,000	$585,000
55. Bos: Nick Hagadone, lhp	$571,500	$571,500
56. Tor: Trystan Magnuson, rhp	$462,500	$567,000
57. SD: Mitch Canham, c	$552,500	$562,500
58. LAA: Jon Bachanov, rhp	$553,300	$553,500
59. Oak: Corey Brown, of	$544,500	$544,500
60. Det: Brandon Hamilton, rhp	$540,000	$540,000
61. Ari: Ed Easley, c	$531,000	$531,000
62. Bos: Ryan Dent, ss	$571,000	$526,500
63. SD: Cory Luebke, lhp	$515,000	$522,000
64. SD: Danny Payne, of	$517,500	$517,500

SECOND ROUND

Pick. Team: Player, Pos.	Bonus	Slot
65. TB: Will Kline, rhp	$513,000	$513,000
66. KC: Sam Runion, rhp	$504,000	$504,000
67. Was: Jordan Zimmermann, rhp	$495,000	$495,000
68. Pit: Duke Welker, rhp	$477,000	$477,000
69. Atl: Joshua Fields, rhp	Did Not Sign	$472,500
70. Was: Jake Smolinski, 3b	$452,500	$463,500
71. StL: David Kopp, rhp	$459,000	$459,000
72. Col: Brian Rike, of	$450,000	$450,000
73. Ari: Barry Enright, rhp	$441,000	$441,000
74. Oak: Grant Desme, of	$432,000	$432,000
75. Sea: Denny Almonte, of	$427,500	$427,500
76. Fla: Mike Stanton, of	+$475,000	$418,500
77. NYM: Scott Moviel, rhp	$414,000	$414,000
78. Atl: Freddie Freeman, 1b	$409,500	$409,500
79. Cin: Zack Cozart, ss	$407,250	$407,250
80. Tex: Matt West, inf	$405,000	$405,000
81. SD: Eric Sogard, 2b	$400,000	$400,500
82. StL: Jess Todd, rhp	$400,000	$400,500
83. Phi: Travis Mattair, 3b	$395,000	$396,000
84. Bos: Hunter Morris, 3b	Did Not Sign	$393,750
85. Tor: John Tolisano, 2b	$391,500	$391,500
86. LAD: Michael Watt, lhp	$389,000	$389,250
87. SD: Brad Chalk, of	$300,000	$387,000
88. Tor: Eric Eiland, of	$384,750	$384,750
89. CWS: Nevin Griffith, rhp	$382,500	$382,500
90. Oak: Josh Horton, ss	$380,250	$380,250
91. Det: Danny Worth, ss	$378,000	$378,000
92. Mil: Danny Rams, c	$375,000	$375,750
93. NYM: Brant Rustich, rhp	$373,500	$373,500
94. NYY: Austin Romine, c	$500,000	$369,000

THIRD ROUND

Pick. Team: Player, Pos.	Bonus	Slot
95. TB: Nick Barnese, rhp	$366,000	$366,750
96. KC: Danny Duffy, lhp	$365,000	$364,500
97. CHC: Tony Thomas, 2b	$360,000	$360,000
98. Pit: Brian Friday, ss	$355,500	$355,500
99. NYM: Eric Niesen, lhp	$351,000	$351,000
100. Was: Steven Souza, 3b	$346,000	$346,500

2006 DRAFT

FIRST ROUND

No. Team. Player, Pos.	Bonus
1. KC: Luke Hochevar, rhp	*$3,500,000
2. Col: Greg Reynolds, rhp	$3,250,000
3. TB: Evan Longoria, 3b	$3,000,000
4. Pit: Brad Lincoln, rhp	$2,750,000
5. Sea: Brandon Morrow, rhp	$2,450,000
6. Det: Andrew Miller, lhp	*$3,550,000
7. LAD: Clayton Kershaw, lhp	$2,300,000
8. Cin: Drew Stubbs, of	$2,000,000
9. Bal: Bill Rowell, 3b	$2,100,000
10. SF: Tim Lincecum, rhp	$2,025,000
11. Ari: Max Scherzer, rhp	*$3,000,000
12. Tex: Kasey Kiker, lhp	$1,600,000
13. CHC: Tyler Colvin, of	$1,475,000
14. Tor: Travis Snider, of	$1,700,000
15. Was: Chris Marrero, of	$1,625,000
16. Mil: Jeremy Jeffress, rhp	$1,550,000
17. SD: Matt Antonelli, 3b	$1,575,000
18. Phi: Kyle Drabek, rhp/ss	$1,550,000
19. Fla: Brett Sinkbeil, rhp	$1,525,000
20. Min: Chris Parmelee, of/1b	$1,500,000
21. NYY: Ian Kennedy, rhp	$2,250,000
22. Was: Colton Willems, rhp	$1,425,000
23. Hou: Max Sapp, c	$1,400,000
24. Atl: Cody Johnson, 1b	$1,375,000
25. LAA: Hank Conger, c	$1,350,000
26. LAD: Bryan Morris, rhp	$1,325,000
27. Bos: Jason Place, of	$1,300,000
28. Bos: Daniel Bard, rhp	$1,550,000
29. CWS: Kyle McCulloch, rhp	$1,050,000
30. StL: Adam Ottavino, rhp	$950,000

SUPPLEMENTAL FIRST ROUND

No. Team. Player, Pos.	Bonus
31. LAD: Preston Mattingly, ss	$1,000,000
32. Bal: Pedro Beato, rhp	$1,000,000
33. SF: Emmanuel Burriss, ss	$1,000,000
34. Ari: Brooks Brown, rhp	$900,000
35. SD: Kyler Burke, of	$950,000
36. Fla: Chris Coghlan, 3b	$950,000
37. Phi: Adrian Cardenas, ss	$925,000
38. Atl: Cory Rasmus, rhp	$900,000
39. Cle: David Huff, lhp	$900,000
40. Bos: Kris Johnson, lhp	$850,000
41. NYY: Joba Chamberlain, rhp	$1,150,000
42. StL: Chris Perez, rhp	$800,000
43. Atl: Steve Evarts, lhp	$800,000
44. Bos: Caleb Clay, rhp	$775,000

SECOND ROUND

No. Team. Player, Pos.	Bonus
45. KC: Jason Taylor, of	$762,500
46. Col: David Christensen, of	$750,000
47. TB: Josh Butler, rhp	$725,000
48. Pit: Mike Felix, lhp	$725,000
49. Sea: Chris Tillman, rhp	$680,000
50. Det: Ronnie Bourquin, 3b	$690,000
51. Atl: Jeff Locke, lhp	$675,000
52. Cin: Sean Watson, rhp	$670,000
53. SD: Chad Huffman, of	$660,000
54. StL: Brad Furnish, lhp	$600,000
55. Ari: Brett Anderson, lhp	$950,000
56. Cle: Steven Wright, rhp	$630,000
57. Cle: Josh Rodriguez, ss	$625,000
58. Bal: Ryan Adams, 2b	$675,000
59. Was: Sean Black, rhp	Did Not Sign
60. Mil: Brent Brewer, ss	+$600,000
61. SD: Wade LeBlanc, lhp	$590,000
62. NYM. Kevin Mulvey, rhp	$585,000
63. Fla: Tom Hickman, of	$575,000
64. Min: Joe Benson, of	$575,000
65. Phi: Drew Carpenter, rhp	$570,000
66. Oak: Trevor Cahill, rhp	$560,000
67. Hou: Sergio Perez, rhp	$550,000
68. Atl: Dustin Evans, rhp	$530,000
69. Cle: Wes Hodges, 3b	$1,000,000
70. Was: Stephen Englund, of	$515,000
71. Bos: Justin Masterson, rhp	$510,000
72. Atl: Chase Fontaine, ss	$500,000
73. CWS: Matt Long, rhp	$330,000
74. StL: Jon Jay, of	$480,000

SUPPLEMENTAL SECOND ROUND

No. Team. Player, Pos.	Bonus
75. Cle: Matt McBride, c	$445,000
76. StL: Mark Hamilton, 1b	$465,000

THIRD ROUND

No. Team. Player, Pos.	Bonus
77. KC: Blake Wood, rhp	$460,000
78. Col: Keith Weiser, lhp	$455,000
79. TB: Nick Fuller, rhp	Did Not Sign
80. Pit: Shelby Ford, 2b	$450,000
81. Sea: Tony Butler, lhp	$445,000
82. Det: Brennan Boesch, of	$445,000
83. Bos: Aaron Bates, 1b	$440,000
84. Cin: Chris Valaika, ss	$437,500
85. Bal: Zach Britton, lhp	$435,000
86. Ari: Dallas Buck, rhp	$250,000
87. Ari: Cyle Hankerd, of	$430,000
88. Tex: Chad Tracy, c	$427,500
89. SF: Clayton Tanner, lhp	$425,000
90. Fla: Torre Langley, c	$422,500
91. Was: Stephen King, ss	$750,000
92. Mil: Cole Gillespie, of	$417,500
93. SD: Cedric Hunter, of	$415,000
94. NYM. Joe Smith, rhp	$410,000
95. Fla: Scott Cousins, of	$407,500
96. Min: Tyler Robertson, lhp	$405,000
97. Phi: Jason Donald, ss	$400,000
98. Oak: Matt Sulentic, of	$395,000
99. Hou: Nick Moresi, of	$390,000
100. Atl: Chad Rodgers, lhp	$385,000

COLLEGE TOP 100

Rank	Player	Pos.	Class	B-T	Ht.	Wt.	School
1.	Stephen Strasburg	rhp	Jr.	R-R	6-5	225	San Diego State
2.	Alex White	rhp	Jr.	R-R	6-3	193	North Carolina
3.	Grant Green	ss	Jr.	R-R	6-3	180	Southern California
4.	Dustin Ackley	1b/of	Jr.	L-R	6-1	184	North Carolina
5.	Mike Minor	lhp	Jr.	L-L	6-4	210	Vanderbilt
6.	Kendal Volz	rhp	Jr.	R-R	6-4	220	Baylor
7.	Kyle Gibson	rhp	Jr.	R-R	6-6	195	Missouri
8.	Andrew Oliver	lhp	Jr.	L-L	6-3	209	Oklahoma State
9.	Kentrail Davis	of	So.	L-R	5-9	200	Tennessee
10.	Blake Smith	of/rhp	Jr.	L-R	6-2	220	California
11.	Mike Leake	rhp/if	Jr.	R-R	6-0	170	Arizona State
12.	Jason Stoffel	rhp	Jr.	R-R	6-2	215	Arizona
13.	Ryan Jackson	ss	Jr.	R-R	6-3	180	Miami
14.	Ben Tootle	rhp	Jr.	R-R	6-0	170	Jacksonville State
15.	D.J. LeMahieu	ss	So.	R-R	6-4	190	Louisiana State
16.	A.J. Pollock	2b/of	Jr.	R-R	6-1	200	Notre Dame
17.	Brett Jackson	of	Jr.	L-R	6-2	210	California
18.	Matt den Dekker	of	Jr.	L-L	6-1	205	Florida
19.	Tyler Lyons	lhp	Jr.	B-L	6-2	195	Oklahoma State
20.	Jeff Inman	rhp	Jr.	R-R	6-2	185	Stanford
21.	Brad Stillings	rhp	Jr.	R-L	6-3	200	Kent State
22.	Shawn Tolleson	rhp	So.	R-R	6-2	220	Baylor
23.	Robbie Shields	ss/2b	Jr.	R-R	6-1	195	Florida Southern
24.	Ben Paulsen	1b	Jr.	L-R	6-3	195	Clemson
25.	Alex Wilson	rhp	Jr.	R-R	6-1	215	Texas A&M
26.	Alex McRee	lhp	Jr.	L-L	6-6	230	Georgia
27.	Kyle Heckathorn	rhp	Jr.	R-R	6-6	235	Kennesaw State
28.	Matt Thomson	rhp	Jr.	R-R	6-4	195	San Diego
29.	Mike Nesseth	rhp	So.	R-R	6-5	213	Nebraska
30.	James Jones	lhp	Jr.	L-L	6-3	185	Long Island
31.	Jared Mitchell	of	Jr.	L-L	6-0	185	Louisiana State
32.	Josh Phegley	c	Jr.	R-R	5-11	215	Indiana
33.	Rich Poythress	1b	Jr.	R-R	6-4	235	Georgia
34.	Joe Kelly	rhp	Jr.	R-R	6-1	165	UC Riverside
35.	Bryan Morgado	lhp	So.	L-L	6-3	203	Tennessee
36.	Brad Boxberger	rhp	Jr.	R-R	6-2	195	Southern California
37.	Craig Fritsch	rhp	So.	R-R	6-4	185	Baylor
38.	Tim Wheeler	of	Jr.	L-R	6-4	195	Sacramento State
39.	Scott Bittle	rhp	Sr.	R-R	6-2	195	Mississippi
40.	Sean Black	rhp	Jr.	R-R	6-5	195	Seton Hall
41.	Del Howell	lhp	Jr.	L-L	6-3	200	Alabama
42.	Trevor Coleman	c	Jr.	B-R	6-1	214	Missouri
43.	Nick Hernandez	lhp	Jr.	L-L	6-4	200	Tennessee
44.	Marc Krauss	of	Jr.	L-R	6-3	225	Ohio
45.	Matt Bashore	lhp	Jr.	L-L	6-3	200	Indiana
46.	Ryan Wheeler	1b/3b	Jr.	L-R	6-4	220	Loyola Marymount
47.	Chris Dominguez	3b	Jr.	R-R	6-4	240	Louisville
48.	Zach Von Tersch	rhp	Jr.	R-R	6-5	202	Georgia Tech
49.	Drew Storen	rhp	So.	B-R	6-2	175	Stanford
50.	Ryan Jones	of	Jr.	L-L	6-0	185	Wichita State

COLLEGE TOP 100

Rank	Player	Pos.	Class	B-T	Ht.	Wt.	School
51.	Steve Fischback	rhp	Jr.	R-R	6-3	200	Cal Poly
52.	Tommy Mendonca	3b	Jr.	L-R	6-1	200	Fresno State
53.	Kyle Seager	2b	Jr.	L-R	6-1	187	North Carolina
54.	Josh Fellhauer	of	Jr.	L-L	5-11	180	Cal State Fullerton
55.	Kyle Smith	rhp	Jr.	R-R	6-6	195	Kent State
56.	Aaron Barrett	rhp	Jr.	R-R	6-4	205	Mississippi
57.	Jason Kipnis	of	Jr.	L-R	6-0	180	Arizona State
58.	Graham Stoneburner	rhp	So.	R-R	6-0	185	Clemson
59.	Ryan Berry	rhp	Jr.	R-R	6-1	195	Rice
60.	Tony Sanchez	c	Jr.	R-R	6-0	220	Boston College
61.	Tommy Medica	c	Jr.	R-R	6-1	190	Santa Clara
62.	Aaron Miller	of/lhp	Jr.	L-L	6-3	220	Baylor
63.	Sam Dyson	rhp	So.	R-R	6-2	195	South Carolina
64.	Nathan Karns	rhp	Jr.	R-R	6-3	210	Texas Tech
65.	Jerry Sullivan	rhp	Jr.	R-R	6-4	200	Oral Roberts
66.	Garrett Richards	rhp	Jr.	R-R	6-2	217	Oklahoma
67.	A.J. Griffin	rhp	Jr.	R-R	6-5	215	San Diego
68.	Angelo Songco	of	Jr.	L-R	6-0	175	Loyola Marymount
69.	Blake Dean	of	Jr.	L-L	6-0	179	Louisiana State
70.	Justin Marks	lhp	Jr.	L-L	6-3	195	Louisville
71.	Dustin Dickerson	1b	Jr.	L-R	6-4	220	Baylor
72.	Rex Brothers	lhp	Jr.	L-L	6-1	205	Lipscomb
73.	Wes Musick	lhp	Jr.	L-L	6-0	190	Houston
74.	Michael Morrison	rhp	Jr.	R-R	6-1	195	Cal State Fullerton
75.	Kevin Landry	rhp	Jr.	R-R	6-4	195	William & Mary
76.	Jorge Reyes	rhp	Jr.	R-R	6-2	175	Oregon State
77.	Connor Powers	3b	Jr.	R-R	6-2	230	Mississippi State
78.	Victor Black	rhp	Jr.	R-R	6-4	204	Dallas Baptist
79.	Joseph Sanders	2b	Jr.	R-R	6-1	205	Auburn
80.	Brooks Raley	lhp/of	So.	L-L	6-0	170	Texas A&M
81.	Aaron Senne	of	Jr.	L-L	6-2	201	Missouri
82.	Christopher Manno	lhp	Jr.	L-L	6-2	160	Duke
83.	Jordan Henry	of	Jr.	L-R	6-0	164	Mississippi
84.	Eric Erickson	lhp	Jr.	R-L	6-0	190	Miami
85.	Dean Weaver	rhp	Jr.	R-R	6-4	207	Georgia
86.	Ryan Ortiz	c	Jr.	R-R	6-3	185	Oregon Sate
87.	Kyle Thebeau	rhp	Sr.	R-R	6-1	195	Texas A&M
88.	Mario Hollands	lhp	So.	L-L	6-5	205	UC Santa Barbara
89.	David Hale	rhp	Jr.	R-R	6-2	195	Princeton
90.	Jeff Kobernus	3b	Jr.	R-R	6-2	195	California
91.	Eric Decker	of	Jr.	L-L	6-2	215	Minnesota
92.	Trevor Holder	rhp	Sr.	R-R	6-3	195	Georgia
93.	Preston Guilmet	rhp	Sr.	R-R	6-2	200	Arizona
94.	Neil Medchill	of	Jr.	L-R	6-4	200	Oklahoma State
95.	Gavin Brooks	lhp	Jr.	L-L	6-3	210	UCLA
96.	Greg Peavey	rhp	So.	R-R	6-2	185	Oregon State
97.	Robert Stock	c/rhp	Jr.	L-R	6-1	190	Southern California
98.	Steven Sultzbaugh	of	Jr.	R-R	6-3	200	Rice
99.	Andrew Carraway	rhp	Sr.	R-R	6-2	200	Virginia
100.	Diego Seastrunk	c/3b	Jr.	B-R	5-10	180	Rice

HIGH SCHOOL TOP 100

Rank	Player	Pos.	B-T	Ht.	Wt.	School
1.	Tyler Matzek	LHP	L-L	6-3	185	Capistrano Valley HS, Mission Viejo, Calif.
2.	Donavan Tate	OF	R-R	6-3	200	Cartersville (Ga.) HS
3.	Matt Purke	LHP	L-L	6-3	180	Klein (Texas) HS
4.	Shelby Miller	RHP	R-R	6-3	195	Brownwood (Texas) HS
5.	Jacob Turner	RHP	R-R	6-4	205	Westminster Christian Academy, St. Louis
6.	Zack Wheeler	RHP	S-R	6-4	170	East Paulding HS, Dallas, Ga.
7.	Luke Bailey	C	R-R	6-0	175	Troup HS, LaGrange, Ga.
8.	Tyler Skaggs	LHP	L-L	6-5	175	Santa Monica (Calif.) HS
9.	Mychal Givens	RHP/SS	R-R	6-1	180	Plant HS, Tampa
10.	Brian Goodwin	OF	L-R	6-1	185	Rocky Mount (N.C.) HS
11.	Scott Griggs	RHP	R-R	6-2	180	San Ramon Valley HS, Danville, Calif.
12.	Bobby Borchering	1B/3B	B-R	6-3	180	Bishop Verot HS, Fort Myers, Fla.
13.	Jiovanni Mier	SS	R-R	6-2	170	Bonita HS, La Verne, Calif.
14.	Wil Myers	C/3B	R-R	6-3	190	Weseleyan Christian Academy, High Point, N.C.
15.	Max Stassi	C	R-R	5-10	190	Yuba City (Calif.) HS
16.	Matt Davidson	3B	R-R	6-3	216	Yucaipa (Calif.) HS
17.	Chad James	LHP	L-L	6-3	185	Yukon (Okla.) HS
18.	Austin Maddox	C	R-R	6-2	220	Eagle's View Academy, Jacksonville
19.	Madison Younginer	RHP	R-R	6-3	185	Mauldin (S.C.), HS
20.	LeVon Washington	2B	L-R	5-10	170	Gainesville (Fla.) HS
21.	Jacob Marisnick	OF	R-R	6-4	200	Riverside (Calif.) Poly HS
22.	Matt Hobgood	RHP	R-R	6-4	245	Norco (Calif.) HS
23.	Chad Thompson	RHP	R-R	6-8	195	El Toro HS, Lake Forest, Calif.
24.	Keyvius Sampson	RHP	R-R	6-1	180	Forest HS, Ocala, Fla.
25.	Stephen Perez	SS	B-R	5-10	165	Gulliver Prep, Miami
26.	Slade Heathcott	OF	L-L	6-0	192	Texas HS, Texarkana, Texas
27.	Ian Krol	LHP	L-L	6-1	175	Neuqua Valley HS, Naperville, Ill.
28.	Richie Shaffer	3B	R-R	6-2	180	Providence HS, Charlotte
29.	Deven Marrero	SS	R-R	6-1	180	American Heritage HS, Plantation, Fla.
30.	Beau Wright	LHP	L-L	6-2	200	Los Alamitos (Calif.) HS
31.	Geno Escalante	C	R-R	5-10	185	Fairfield (Calif.) HS
32.	Nick Franklin	SS	B-R	6-1	170	Lake Brantley HS, Altamonte Springs, Fla.
33.	Brody Colvin	RHP	R-R	6-4	190	St. Thomas More HS, Lafayette, La.
34.	Jonathan Walsh	C	B-R	6-3	215	Coppell (Texas) HS
35.	Scooter Gennett	2B	L-R	5-10	165	Sarasota (Fla.) HS
36.	Zach Von Rosenberg	RHP	R-R	6-5	196	Zachary (La.) HS
37.	Mark Appel	RHP	R-R	6-4	185	Monte Vista HS, Danville, Calif.
38.	Everett Williams	OF	L-R	5-10	200	McCallum HS, Austin
39.	Michael Dedrick	RHP	R-R	6-3	185	Canyon View HS, Cedar City, Utah
40.	Andrew Susac	C	R-R	6-1	190	Jesuit HS, Carmichael, Calif.
41.	Drew Steckenrider	OF	B-R	6-3	190	Greater Atlanta Christian HS
42.	Patrick Schuster	LHP	L-L	6-3	175	Mitchell HS, New Port Richey, Fla.
43.	David Renfroe	RHP	R-R	6-3	195	South Panola HS, Batesville, Miss.
44.	Colton Cain	1B	L-L	6-3	225	Waxahachie (Texas) HS
45.	Michael Heller	RHP	R-R	6-2	190	Cardinal Mooney HS, Sarasota, Fla.
46.	David Nick	SS/2B	R-R	6-1	165	Cypress (Calif.) HS
47.	Daniel Tuttle	RHP	R-R	6-2	190	Randleman (N.C.) HS
48.	Matt Graham	RHP	R-R	6-4	215	Oak Ridge HS, Conroe, Texas
49.	Michael Revell	SS	L-R	6-2	196	Florida State University HS, Tallahassee, Fla.
50.	Michael Zunino	C	R-R	6-0	185	Mariner HS, Cape Coral, Fla.

HIGH SCHOOL TOP 100

Rank	Player	Pos.	B-T	Ht.	Wt.	School
51.	David Holmberg	LHP	R-L	6-4	210	Port Charlotte (Fla.) HS
52.	Matt Moynihan	OF	L-R	6-2	205	Cathedral Catholic HS, San Diego
53.	Jeff Malm	1B	L-L	6-3	225	Bishop Gorman HS, Las Vegas
54.	Jake Barrett	RHP	R-R	6-4	225	Desert Ridge, Mesa, Ariz.
55.	Todd Glaesmann	OF	R-R	6-4	199	Midway HS, Waco, Texas
56.	Dylan Floro	RHP	L-R	6-1	170	Buhach Colony HS, Atwater, Calif.
57.	Garrett Gould	RHP	R-R	6-4	195	Maize HS, Wichita
58.	Jacob Morris	OF	B-R	6-3	195	Coppell (Texas) HS
59.	Kyrell Hudson	OF	R-R	6-2	185	Evergreen HS, Vancouver, Wash.
60.	Richard Stock	C	L-R	6-1	170	Agoura HS, Agoura Hills, Calif.
61.	Christopher Jenkins	RHP	R-R	6-7	230	Westfield (N.J.) HS
62.	Brooks Hall	3B	R-R	6-5	190	T.L. Hanna HS, Anderson, S.C.
63.	Cameron Garfield	C	R-R	6-1	195	Murrieta (Calif.) Valley HS
64.	Daniel Fields	SS	L-R	6-2	195	University of Detroit Jesuit HS
65.	Kris Hobson	1B	L-L	6-3	210	Stockdale HS, Bakersfield, Calif.
66.	Brooks Pounders	RHP	R-R	6-5	240	Temecula (Calif.) Valley HS
67.	Jason Thompson	SS	R-R	6-0	185	Germantown (Tenn.) HS
68.	James Needy	RHP	R-R	6-6	195	Santana HS, Santee, Calif.
69.	Randal Grichuk	OF	R-R	6-0	177	Lamar HS, Houston
70.	Telvin Nash	1B	R-R	6-2	225	Griffin (Ga.) HS
71.	Justin Bellez	RHP	R-R	6-1	180	Mira Mesa HS, San Diego
72.	Mitch Haniger	OF	R-R	6-2	180	Archbishop Mitty HS, San Jose, Calif.
73.	Jacob Lamb	3B	L-R	6-3	190	Bishop Blanchete HS, Seattle
74.	Chad Kettler	RHP	B-R	6-1	190	Coppell (Texas) HS
75.	Keifer Nuncio	RHP	R-R	6-2	195	Katy (Texas) HS
76.	Jerad Grundy	LHP	L-L	6-0	185	Johnsburg (Ill.) HS
77.	Victor Roache	OF	R-R	6-1	201	Lincoln HS, Ypsilanti, Mich.
78.	Jonathan Singleton	1B	L-L	6-2	216	Millikan HS, Long Beach
79.	Reggie Williams	OF	B-R	6-4	190	Brooks-DeBartolo Collegiate HS, Tampa
80.	Mike Trout	RHP	R-R	6-1	190	Millville (N.J.) HS
81.	Jordan Cooper	RHP	B-R	6-3	185	Shelbyville (Tenn.) Central HS
82.	Cody Stiles	OF	R-R	6-1	175	Taravella HS, Coral Springs, Fla.
83.	Kenny Diekroger	SS	R-R	6-2	185	Menlo HS, Atherton, Calif.
84.	Brian Johnson	LHP	L-L	6-4	220	Cocoa Beach (Fla.) HS
85.	Tarran Senay	OF	L-R	6-1	205	South Park (Pa.) HS
86.	Zach Dotson	LHP	L-L	6-3	185	Effingham County HS, Springfield, Ga.
87.	Forrest Garrett	LHP	L-L	6-3	170	Norcross (Ga.) HS
88.	Matt Nadolski	LHP	L-L	6-2	192	Casa Grande HS, Petaluma, Calif.
89.	Matt Koch	RHP	R-R	6-3	185	Washington HS, Cherokee, Iowa
90.	Nolan Arenado	3B/1B	R-R	6-2	196	El Toro HS, Lake Forest, Calif.
91.	Rudy Flores	1B	L-R	6-3	203	Moody (Texas) HS
92.	Chris Velez	SS/2B	R-R	6-4	185	Sickles HS, Tampa
93.	Brett Lee	LHP	L-L	6-5	185	West Florida HS, Pensacola, Fla.
94.	Cade Kreuter	3B/1B	R-R	6-6	185	Valencia (Calif.) HS
95.	Anthony Gomez	SS	R-R	6-0	180	Don Bosco Preparatory HS, Ramsey, N.J.
96.	Marcus Stroman	SS	R-R	5-9	175	Patchogue-Medford HS, Medford, N.Y.
97.	Billy Hamilton	OF/SS	B-R	6-0	150	Taylorsville (Miss.) HS
98.	Felix Roque	RHP	R-R	6-5	195	Gulliver Prep, Miami
99.	Tucker Barnhart	C	B-R	5-9	170	Brownsburg (Ind.) HS
100.	Raul Rivera	RHP	R-R	6-2	170	Colegio San Vicente de Paul, Santurce, P.R.

FROM EVERY MINOR LEAGUE

As a complement to our organizational prospect lists, Baseball America also ranks prospects in each minor league. Like the organization lists, they place more weight on potential than performance and should not be regarded as all-star teams. Unlike the organization lists, which are from more of a scouting perspective and look at what a player might eventually do, the minor league lists reflect the views of minor league managers, who give more weight to what a player does on the field. We think both perspectives are useful, so we give you both, even though they don't always match up. For a player to qualify for a league prospect list, he must have spent at least one-third of the season in a league.

TRIPLE-A

INTERNATIONAL LEAGUE

1 Jay Bruce, of, Louisville (Reds)
2 Andrew McCutchen, of, Indianapolis (Pirates)
3 Wade Davis, rhp, Durham (Rays)
4 Reid Brignac, ss, Durham (Rays)
5 Jed Lowrie, ss, Pawtucket (Red Sox)
6 David Huff, lhp, Buffalo (Indians)
7 Neil Walker, 3b, Indianapolis (Pirates)
8 Denard Span, of, Rochester (Twins)
9 Charlie Morton, rhp, Richmond (Braves)
10 Homer Bailey, rhp, Louisville (Reds)
11 David Purcey, lhp, Syracuse (Blue Jays)
12 Kevin Mulvey, rhp, Rochester (Twins)
13 Matt Joyce, of, Toledo (Tigers)
14 Brandon Moss, of/1b, Pawtucket (Red Sox)
15 J.A. Happ, lhp, Lehigh Valley (Phillies)
16 Jeff Niemann, rhp, Durham (Rays)
17 Brandon Jones, of, Richmond (Braves)
18 Collin Balester, rhp, Columbus (Nationals)
19 Brett Gardner, of, Scranton/Wilkes-Barre (Yankees)
20 Chris Getz, ss/2b, Charlotte (White Sox)

PACIFIC COAST LEAGUE

1 Colby Rasmus, of, Memphis (Cardinals)
2 Chase Headley, of/3b, Portland (Padres)
3 Max Scherzer, rhp, Tucson (Diamondbacks)
4 Brandon Wood, ss/3b, Salt Lake (Angels)
5 Carlos Gonzalez, of, Sacramento (Athletics)
6 Jeff Clement, c, Tacoma (Mariners)
7 Ian Stewart, 3b, Colorado Springs (Rockies)
8 Gio Gonzalez, lhp, Sacramento (Athletics)
9 Andy LaRoche, 3b, Las Vegas (Dodgers)
10 Wladimir Balentien, of, Tacoma (Mariners)
11 Sean Rodriguez, 2b, Salt Lake (Angels)
12 Chris Perez, rhp, Memphis (Cardinals)
13 Nate Schierholtz, of, Fresno (Giants)
14 Bryan Anderson, c, Memphis (Cardinals)
15 Franklin Morales, lhp, Colorado Springs (Rockies)
16 Jaime Garcia, lhp, Memphis (Cardinals)
17 Mitchell Boggs, rhp, Memphis (Cardinals)
18 Carlos Rosa, rhp, Omaha (Royals)
19 Nick Adenhart, rhp, Salt Lake (Angels)
20 Greg Reynolds, rhp, Colorado Springs (Rockies)

DOUBLE-A

EASTERN LEAGUE

1 Matt Wieters, c, Bowie (Orioles)
2 Chris Tillman, rhp, Bowie (Orioles)
3 Travis Snider, of, New Hampshire (Blue Jays)
4 Lars Anderson, 1b, Portland (Red Sox)
5 Jordan Zimmermann, rhp, Harrisburg (Nationals)
6 Carlos Carrasco, rhp, Reading (Phillies)
7 Fernando Martinez, of, Binghamton (Mets)
8 J.P. Arencibia, c, New Hampshire (Blue Jays)
9 Daniel Bard, rhp, Portland (Red Sox)
10 Austin Jackson, of, Trenton (Yankees)
11 David Huff, lhp, Akron (Indians)
12 Jose Tabata, of, Trenton (Yankees)/Altoona (Pirates)
13 Daniel Murphy, 3b/of, Binghamton (Mets)
14 Lou Marson, c, Reading (Phillies)
15 Michael Bowden, rhp, Portland (Red Sox)
16 Wes Hodges, 3b, Akron (Indians)
17 Brett Cecil, lhp, New Hampshire (Blue Jays)
18 Jonathon Niese, lhp, Binghamton (Mets)
19 Pablo Sandoval, c/1b, Connecticut (Giants)
20 Greg Golson, of, Reading (Phillies)

SOUTHERN LEAGUE

1 Clayton Kershaw, lhp, Jacksonville (Dodgers)
2 David Price, lhp, Montgomery (Rays)
3 Cameron Maybin, of, Carolina (Marlins)
4 Matt LaPorta, of, Huntsville (Brewers)
5 Alcides Escobar, ss, Huntsville (Brewers)
6 Chris Volstad, rhp, Carolina (Marlins)
7 Mat Gamel, 3b, Huntsville (Brewers)
8 Michael Saunders, of, West Tenn (Mariners)
9 Tommy Hanson, rhp, Mississippi (Braves)
10 Wade Davis, rhp, Montgomery (Rays)
11 Chris Coghlan, 2b, Carolina (Marlins)
12 Jeremy Hellickson, rhp, Montgomery (Rays)
13 Jordan Schafer, of, Mississippi (Braves)
14 James McDonald, rhp, Jacksonville (Dodgers)
15 Ivan DeJesus Jr., ss, Jacksonville (Dodgers)
16 Jake McGee, lhp, Montgomery (Rays)
17 Angel Salome, c, Huntsville (Brewers)
18 Michael Brantley, of, Huntsville (Brewers)
19 Adam Moore, c, West Tenn (Mariners)
20 Luis Valbuena, 2b, West Tenn (Mariners)

TEXAS LEAGUE

1 Dexter Fowler, of, Tulsa (Rockies)
2 Chris Davis, 1b, Frisco (Rangers)
3 Kyle Blanks, 1b, San Antonio (Padres)
4 Vin Mazzaro, rhp, Midland (Athletics)
5 Elvis Andrus, ss, Frisco (Rangers)
6 Daniel Cortes, rhp, Northwest Arkansas (Royals)
7 Jess Todd, rhp, Springfield (Cardinals)
8 Julio Borbon, of, Frisco (Rangers)
9 Max Ramirez, c, Frisco (Rangers)
10 James Simmons, rhp, Midland (Athletics)
11 Aaron Cunningham, of, Midland (Athletics)
12 Kila Ka'aihue, 1b, Northwest Arkansas (Royals)

13 Daryl Jones, of, Springfield (Cardinals)
14 Steve Garrison, lhp, San Antonio (Padres)
15 Will Inman, rhp, San Antonio (Padres)
16 Jon Jay, of, Springfield (Cardinals)
17 Kevin Jepsen, rhp, Arkansas (Angels)
18 Fernando Salas, rhp, Springfield (Cardinals)
19 Casey Weathers, rhp, Tulsa (Rockies)
20 Chris Johnson, 3b, Corpus Christi (Astros)

13 Chris Valaika, ss, Sarasota (Reds)
14 Jose Ceda, rhp, Daytona (Cubs)
15 Juan Francisco, 3b, Sarasota (Reds)
16 Taylor Green, 3b, Brevard County (Brewers)
17 Cale Iorg, ss, Lakeland (Tigers)
18 Francisco Samuel, rhp, Palm Beach (Cardinals)
19 Jonathan Lucroy, c, Brevard County (Brewers)
20 Zach McAllister, rhp, Tampa (Yankees)

HIGH CLASS A

CALIFORNIA LEAGUE

1   Trevor Cahill, rhp, Stockton (Athletics)
2   Carlos Santana, c, Inland Empire (Dodgers)
3   Lars Anderson, 1b, Lancaster (Red Sox)
4   Brett Anderson, lhp, Stockton (Athletics)
5   Jhoulys Chacin, rhp, Modesto (Rockies)
6   Tim Alderson, rhp, San Jose (Giants)
7   Pablo Sandoval, c, San Jose (Giants)
8   Josh Reddick, of, Lancaster (Red Sox)
9   Henry Rodriguez, rhp, Stockton (Athletics)
10 Cedric Hunter, of, Lake Elsinore (Padres)
11 Julio Borbon, of, Bakersfield (Rangers)
12 Jordan Walden, rhp, Rancho Cucamonga (Angels)
13 Greg Halman, of, High Desert (Mariners)
14 Chris Carter, 1b/3b/of, Stockton (Athletics)
15 Carlos Triunfel, ss, High Desert (Mariners)
16 Sean Doolittle, 1b, Stockton (Athletics)
17 Peter Bourjos, of, Rancho Cucamonga (Angels)
18 Sean O'Sullivan, rhp, Rancho Cucamonga (Angels)
19 Josh Donaldson, c, Stockton (Athletics)
20 Kellen Kulbacki, of, Lake Elsinore (Padres)

CAROLINA LEAGUE

1   Matt Wieters, c, Frederick (Orioles)
2   Jake Arrieta, rhp, Frederick (Orioles)
3   Gorkys Hernandez, of, Myrtle Beach (Braves)
4   Nick Weglarz, of, Kinston (Indians)
5   Beau Mills, 1b, Kinston (Indians)
6   Aaron Poreda, lhp, Winston-Salem (White Sox)
7   Blake Wood, rhp, Wilmington (Royals)
8   Brandon Erbe, rhp, Frederick (Orioles)
9   Hector Rondon, rhp, Kinston (Indians)
10 Chris Marrero, 1b, Potomac (Nationals)
11 Ross Detwiler, lhp, Potomac (Nationals)
12 Tyler Flowers, c, Myrtle Beach (Braves)
13 Brandon Hicks, ss, Myrtle Beach (Braves)
14 Brandon Allen, 1b, Winston-Salem (White Sox)
15 Carlos Rivero, ss, Kinston (Indians)
16 Brandon Snyder, 1b, Frederick (Orioles)
17 John Ely, rhp, Winston-Salem (White Sox)
18 Josh Tomlin, rhp, Kinston (Indians)
19 Kanekoa Texeira, rhp, Winston-Salem (White Sox)
20 Bill Rowell, 3b, Frederick (Orioles)

FLORIDA STATE LEAGUE

1   Rick Porcello, rhp, Lakeland (Tigers)
2   J.P. Arencibia, c, Dunedin (Blue Jays)
3   Logan Morrison, 1b, Jupiter (Marlins)
4   Jeremy Jeffress, rhp, Brevard County (Brewers)
5   Adrian Cardenas, 2b, Clearwater (Phillies)
6   Jeremy Hellickson, rhp, Vero Beach (Rays)
7   Sean West, lhp, Jupiter (Marlins)
8   Wilson Ramos, c, Fort Myers (Twins)
9   Scott Cousins, of, Jupiter (Marlins)
10 Michael Taylor, of, Clearwater (Phillies)
11 Todd Frazier, ss/3b, Sarasota (Reds)
12 Drew Stubbs, of, Sarasota (Reds)

LOW CLASS A

MIDWEST LEAGUE

1   Mike Moustakas, 3b/ss, Burlington (Royals)
2   Neftali Feliz, rhp, Clinton (Rangers)
3   Jarrod Parker, rhp, South Bend (Diamondbacks)
4   Ben Revere, of, Beloit (Twins)
5   Brett Wallace, 3b, Quad Cities (Cardinals)
6   Engel Beltre, of, Clinton (Rangers)
7   Andrew Lambo, of, Great Lakes (Dodgers)
8   Philippe Aumont, rhp, Wisconsin (Mariners)
9   Derek Holland, lhp, Clinton (Rangers)
10 Neftali Soto, 3b, Dayton (Reds)
11 Danny Duffy, lhp, Burlington (Royals)
12 Craig Italiano, rhp, Kane County (Athletics)
13 Jordan Walden, rhp, Cedar Rapids (Angels)
14 Justin Jackson, ss, Lansing (Blue Jays)
15 Pete Kozma, ss, Quad Cities (Cardinals)
16 Corey Brown, of, Kane County (Athletics)
17 Juan Ramirez, rhp, Wisconsin (Mariners)
18 Danny Gutierrez, rhp, Burlington (Royals)
19 Kevin Ahrens, 3b, Lansing (Blue Jays)
20 Trevor Reckling, lhp, Cedar Rapids (Angels)

SOUTH ATLANTIC LEAGUE

1   Madison Bumgarner, lhp, Augusta (Giants)
2   Jason Heyward, of, Rome (Braves)
3   Mike Stanton, of, Greensboro (Marlins)
4   Jhoulys Chacin, rhp, Asheville (Rockies)
5   Matt Dominguez, 3b, Greensboro (Marlins)
6   Angel Villalona, 1b, Augusta (Giants)
7   Jesus Montero, c, Charleston (Yankees)
8   Austin Romine, c, Charleston (Yankees)
9   Nick Noonan, 2b, Augusta (Giants)
10 Freddie Freeman, 1b, Rome (Braves)
11 Michael Burgess, of, Hagerstown (Nationals)
12 Che-Hsuan Lin, of, Greenville (Red Sox)
13 Cole Rohrbough, lhp, Rome (Braves)
14 Jeff Locke, lhp, Rome (Braves)
15 Michael Taylor, of, Lakewood (Phillies)
16 Alex Cobb, rhp, Columbus (Rays)
17 Darin Holcomb, 3b, Asheville (Rockies)
18 Caleb Gindl, of, West Virginia (Brewers)
19 Ryan Kalish, of, Greenville (Red Sox)
20 Cody Johnson, of, Rome (Braves)

SHORT-SEASON

NEW YORK-PENN LEAGUE

1   Jason Castro, c, Tri-City (Astros)
2   David Cooper, 1b, Auburn (Blue Jays)
3   Adam Reifer, rhp, Batavia (Cardinals)
4   Derek Norris, c, Vermont (Nationals)
5   Travis d'Arnaud, c, Williamsport (Phillies)
6   Lonnie Chisenhall, ss, Mahoning Valley (Indians)
7   Brad Holt, rhp, Brooklyn (Mets)
8   Nick Barnese, rhp, Hudson Valley (Rays)
9   Jenrry Mejia, rhp, Brooklyn (Mets)
10 P.J. Dean, rhp, Vermont (Nationals)

11 Reese Havens, ss, Brooklyn (Mets)
12 Bryan Price, rhp, Lowell (Red Sox)
13 Brock Huntzinger, rhp, Lowell (Red Sox)
14 Danny Espinosa, ss, Vermont (Nationals)
15 Kyle Weiland, rhp, Lowell (Red Sox)
16 Tim Fedroff, of, Mahoning Valley (Indians)
17 Ike Davis, 1b, Brooklyn (Mets)
18 Chase d'Arnaud, ss, State College (Pirates)
19 Cord Phelps, 2b, Mahoning Valley (Indians)
20 Danny Farquhar, rhp, Auburn (Blue Jays)

NORTHWEST LEAGUE

1 Josh Vitters, 3b, Boise (Cubs)
2 Martin Perez, lhp, Spokane (Rangers)
3 Christian Friedrich, lhp, Tri-City (Rockies)
4 Neil Ramirez, rhp, Spokane (Rangers)
5 Conor Gillaspie, 3b, Salem-Keizer (Giants)
6 Wilfredo Boscan, rhp, Spokane (Rangers)
7 James Darnell, 3b, Eugene (Padres)
8 Tim Murphy, lhp, Spokane (Rangers)
9 Jharmidy DeJesus, 3b, Everett (Mariners)
10 Charlie Blackmon, of, Tri-City (Rockies)
11 Blake Tekotte, of, Eugene (Padres)
12 Ryan Flaherty, ss, Boise (Cubs)
13 Dennis Raben, of, Everett (Mariners)
14 Simon Castro, rhp, Eugene (Padres)
15 Tyson Gillies, of, Everett (Mariners)
16 Matt West, 3b, Spokane (Rangers)
17 Jason Christian, ss, Vancouver (Athletics)
18 Dusty Coleman, ss, Vancouver (Athletics)
19 Cole Figueroa, 2b/ss, Eugene (Padres)
20 Collin Cowgill, of, Yakima (Diamondbacks)

ROOKIE

APPALACHIAN LEAGUE

1 Tim Beckham, ss, Princeton Devil Rays
2 Wilmer Flores, ss, Kingsport Mets
3 Matt Moore, lhp, Princeton Devil Rays
4 Gabriel Noriega, ss, Pulaski Mariners
5 Mario Martinez, 3b, Pulaski Mariners
6 Randall Delgado, rhp, Danville Braves
7 Jordan Lyles, rhp, Greeneville Astros
8 Angel Morales, of, Elizabethton Twins
9 Albert Suarez, rhp, Princeton Devil Rays
10 Kelvin Herrera, rhp, Burlington Royals
11 Jon Gilmore, 3b, Danville Braves
12 Jay Austin, of, Greeneville Astros
13 Niko Vasquez, ss, Johnson City Cardinals
14 Craig Kimbrel, rhp, Danville Braves
15 Paul Clemens, rhp, Danville Braves
16 Gregory Infante, rhp, Bristol Sox
17 Sam Runion, rhp, Burlington Royals
18 Federico Hernandez, c, Greeneville Astros
19 Juan Silverio, ss, Bristol Sox
20 Fernando Cruz, 3b, Burlington Royals

PIONEER LEAGUE

1 Wilin Rosario, c, Casper (Rockies)
2 Cutter Dykstra, of, Helena (Brewers)
3 Will Smith, lhp, Orem (Angels)
4 Devaris Gordon, ss, Ogden (Dodgers)
5 Luis Jimenez, 3b, Orem (Angels)
6 Delta Cleary, of, Casper (Rockies)
7 Bryan Shaw, rhp, Missoula (Diamondbacks)
8 Trevor Harden, rhp, Missoula (Diamondbacks)
9 Dexter Carter, rhp, Great Falls (White Sox)
10 Kyle Russell, of, Ogden (Dodgers)

11 Pedro Baez, 3b, Ogden (Dodgers)
12 Jose Perez, rhp, Orem (Angels)
13 Efrain Nieves, lhp, Helena (Brewers)
14 Rossmel Perez, c, Missoula (Diamondbacks)
15 Angel Castillo, of, Orem (Angels)
16 Wily Peralta, rhp, Helena (Brewers)
17 Erik Komatsu, of, Helena (Brewers)
18 Dan Hudson, rhp, Great Falls (White Sox)
19 Tony Delmonico, 2b, Ogden (Dodgers)
20 Michael Kohn, rhp, Orem (Angels)

ARIZONA LEAGUE

1 Mike Montgomery, lhp, Royals
2 Jaff Decker, of, Padres
3 Jharmidy DeJesus, 3b, Mariners
4 Ehire Adrianza, ss, Giants
5 Manuarys Correa, rhp, Angels
6 Rashun Dixon, of, Athletics
7 Jake Odorizzi, rhp, Brewers
8 Tyler Sample, rhp, Royals
9 Jose Casilla, rhp, Giants
10 Yowill Espinal, ss/2b, Royals
11 Joe Wieland, rhp, Rangers
12 Tyler Chatwood, rhp, Angels
13 Jose Bonilla, c, Royals
14 Starlin Castro, ss/2b, Cubs
15 Seth Lintz, rhp, Brewers
16 Junior Lake, ss, Cubs
17 Kyle Nicholson, rhp, Giants
18 Clark Murphy, 1b, Rangers
19 Terrell Alliman, of/3b, Angels
20 Wendell Fairley, of, Giants

GULF COAST LEAGUE

1 Aaron Hicks, of, Twins
2 Kyle Skipworth, c, Marlins
3 Jefry Marte, 3b, Mets
4 Jason Knapp, rhp, Phillies
5 Michael Almanzar, 3b, Red Sox
6 Casey Kelly, ss/rhp, Red Sox
7 Sebastian Valle, c, Phillies
8 Zach Collier, of, Phillies
9 Jack McGeary, lhp, Nationals
10 Abner Abreu, 3b, Indians
11 Arodys Vizcaino, rhp, Yankees
12 Cesar Puello, of, Mets
13 Anthony Hewitt, 3b, Phillies
14 Esmailyn Gonzalez, ss, Nationals
15 L.J. Hoes, 2b, Orioles
16 Isaac Galloway, of, Marlins
17 Zeke Spruill, rhp, Braves
18 Destin Hood, of, Nationals
19 Derrik Gibson, 3b, Red Sox
20 Jarek Cunningham, 3b/ss, Pirates

FALL LEAGUES

ARIZONA FALL LEAGUE

1 Matt Wieters, c, Rafters (Orioles)
2 Tommy Hanson, rhp, Solar Sox (Braves)
3 Brian Matusz, lhp, Rafters (Orioles)
4 Logan Morrison, 1b, Solar Sox (Marlins)
5 Carlos Triunfel, ss/3b, Javelinas (Mariners)
6 Bud Norris, rhp, Scorpions (Astros)
7 Gordon Beckham, ss, Saguaros (White Sox)
8 J.P. Arencibia, c, Desert Dogs (Blue Jays)
9 Justin Smoak, 1b, Javelinas (Rangers)
10 Brett Wallace, 3b, Saguaros (Cardinals)

11 Daniel Cortes, rhp, Rafters (Royals)
12 Sean West, lhp, Solar Sox (Marlins)
13 Julio Borbon, of, Rafters (Rangers)
14 Sean Doolittle, of/1b, Desert Dogs (Athletics)
15 Tyler Flowers, c, Solar Sox (Braves)
16 Aaron Poreda, lhp, Saguaros (White Sox)
17 Jason Donald, ss, Solar Sox (Phillies)
18 Scott Cousins, of, Solar Sox (Marlins)
19 Jeff Manship, rhp, Desert Dogs (Twins)
20 Eric Young Jr., of, Desert Dogs (Rockies)

HAWAII WINTER BASEBALL

1 Buster Posey, c, Waikiki (Giants)
2 Andrew Brackman, rhp, Waikiki (Yankees)
3 Yonder Alonso, 1b, Waikiki (Reds)
4 Dominic Brown, of, Honolulu (Phillies)

5   Kyle Drabek, rhp, Honolulu (Phillies)
6   Jason Castro, c, North Shore (Astros)
7   Todd Frazier, ss/of, Waikiki (Reds)
8   Jeremy Bleich, lhp, Waikiki (Yankees)
9   Michael Taylor, of, Honolulu (Phillies)
10 Roger Kieschnick, of, Waikiki (Giants)
11 Chris Carter, 1b, North Shore (Athletics)
12 Caleb Gindl, of, West Oahu (Brewers)
13 Brad Emaus, 2b/3b, Honolulu (Blue Jays)
14 Jonny Venters, lhp, Honolulu (Braves)
15 Kyle Martin, ss/3b, North Shore (Royals)
16 Ryan Kalish, of, North Shore (Red Sox)
17 Mark Hallberg, 2b, West Oahu (Diamondbacks)
18 Javy Guerra, rhp, Waikiki (Dodgers)
19 Kyle Bloom, lhp, West Oahu (Pirates)
20 Andy Graham, rhp, Honolulu (Rockies)

INDEX

Clevenger, Steve (Cubs) 86
Cobb, Alex (Rays) 440
Coghlan, Chris (Marlins) 181
Coke, Phil (Yankees) 309
Coleman, Dusty (Athletics) 330
Collier, Zach (Phillies) 341
Collins, Tim (Blue Jays) 477
Colome, Alex (Rays) 443
Colonel, Christian (Rockies) 156
Colvin, Tyler (Cubs) 88
Conger, Hank (Angels) 229
Cooney, Brandon (Orioles) 59
Cooper, David (Blue Jays) 468
Correa, Hector (Marlins) 186
Correa, Manuarys (Angels) 233
Cortes, Daniel (Royals) 211
Cosart, Jarred (Phillies) 347
Cousins, Scott (Marlins) 183
Cowgill, Collin (Diamondbacks) 22
Cozart, Zach (Reds) 121
Craig, Allen (Cardinals) 380
Crosby, Casey (Tigers) 163
Crowe, Trevor (Indians) 134
Cruz, Joe (Rays) 443
Cruz, Luis (Astros) 205
Cruz, Tony (Cardinals) 380
Culberson, Charlie (Giants) 412
Cumberland, Drew (Padres) 392
Cunningham, Aaron (Athletics) 323
Cunningham, Jarek (Pirates) 359

D

Daeges, Zach (Red Sox) 75
Danks, Jordan (White Sox) 101
D'Arnaud, Chase (Pirates) 360
D'Arnaud, Travis (Phillies) 341
Darnell, James (Padres) 390
Darrow, Rudy (Tigers) 167
Davis, Ike (Mets) 294
Davis, Leonard (Nationals) 488
Davis, Wade (Rays) 435
De la Cruz, Eulogio (Marlins) 186
De la Cruz, Kelvin (Indians) 131
De la Cruz, Roberto (Cardinals) 377
De la Rossa, Wilkins (Yankees) 313
De la Vara, Gilbert (Astros) 202
De los Santos, Fautino (Athletics) 329
Dean, P.J. (Marlins) 185
Decker, Jaff (Padres) 387
DeJesus Jr., Ivan (Dodgers) 244
DeJesus, Jharmidy (Mariners) 421
Delaney, Rob (Twins) 283
DeLeon, Kelvin (Yankees) 316
Delgado, Jesus (Marlins) 186
Delgado, Randall (Braves) 39
Delmonico, Tony (Dodgers) 249
DeLome, Collin (Astros) 198
Demel, Sam (Athletics) 332
Dening, Mitch (Red Sox) 75
Desme, Grant (Athletics) 333
Desmond, Ian (Nationals) 489
Detwiler, Ross (Nationals) 483
DeVall, Brett (Braves) 39
Diamond, Scott (Braves) 43
Diamond, Thomas (Rangers) 460
Diaz, Argenis (Red Sox) 72
Dickerson, Chris (Reds) 118
Dickerson, Joe (Royals) 219
Dillard, Tim (Brewers) 269
Disher, Phil (Astros) 204
Dixon, Rashun (Athletics) 330
Dolsi, Freddy (Tigers) 168
Dominguez, Matt (Marlins) 180

Donald, Jason (Phillies) 340
Donaldson, Josh (Athletics) 327
Doolittle, Sean (Athletics) 326
Dorn, Danny (Reds) 123
Doubront, Felix (Red Sox) 76
Douglas, Brandon (Tigers) 171
Downs, Matt (Giants) 410
Drabek, Kyle (Phillies) 340
Duda, Lucas (Mets) 297
Duensing, Brian (Twins) 280
Duffy, Danny (Royals) 212
Duncan, David (Astros) 200
Dunn, Mike (Yankees) 312
Duran, Juan (Reds) 117
Dydalewicz, Brad (Astros) 199
Dykstra, Allan (Padres) 389
Dykstra, Cutter (Brewers) 261

E

Easley, Ed (Diamondbacks) 29
Eichhorn, Kevin (Diamondbacks) 20
Eiland, Eric (Blue Jays) 472
Elbert, Scott (Dodgers) 244
Ely, John (White Sox) 102
Emaus, Brad (Blue Jays) 470
Enright, Barry (Diamondbacks) 22
Eovaldi, Nathan (Dodgers) 246
Erbe, Brandon (Orioles) 52
Escalona, Sergio (Phillies) 348
Escobar, Alcides (Brewers) 258
Escobar, Eduardo (White Sox) 103
Espinal, Yowill (Royals) 221
Espinosa, Danny (Nationals) 487
Estrada, Marco (Nationals) 490
Evans, Nick (Mets) 293
Exposito, Luis (Red Sox) 72

F

Fairley, Wendell (Giants) 406
Farina, Alan (Blue Jays) 471
Farquhar, Danny (Blue Jays) 475
Farris, Eric (Brewers) 268
Fedroff, Tim (Indians) 137
Feliz, Neftali (Rangers) 450
Fien, Casey (Tigers) 166
Fife, Stephen (Red Sox) 76
Figaro, Alfredo (Tigers) 168
Figueroa, Cole (Padres) 396
Fish, Robert (Angels) 233
Fisher, Carlos (Reds) 123
Flaherty, Ryan (Cubs) 85
Flores, Josh (Astros) 200
Flores, Wilmer (Mets) 291
Flowers, Tyler (White Sox) 99
Font, Wilmer (Rangers) 457
Ford, Shelby (Pirates) 357
Forsythe, Logan (Padres) 390
Fortuna, Carlos (Royals) 217
Fowler, Dexter (Rockies) 146
Fox, Jake (Cubs) 91
Francisco, Juan (Reds) 117
Frazier, Parker (Rockies) 151
Frazier, Todd (Reds) 115
Frederickson, Evan (Brewers) 267
Freeman, Freddie (Braves) 36
Freeman, Wesley (Pirates) 361
Freese, David (Cardinals) 373
Frey, Evan (Diamondbacks) 24
Friday, Brian (Pirates) 359
Friedrich, Christian (Rockies) 147
Frieri, Ernesto (Padres) 397
Fronk, Reid (Rays) 442

Fuenmayor, Balbino (Blue Jays) 476
Fuller, Clay (Angels) 232

G

Gallagher, Austin (Dodgers) 246
Gallagher, Nolan (Mariners) 429
Galloway, Isaac (Marlins) 184
Galvis, Freddy (Phillies) 345
Gamel, Mat (Brewers) 259
Garate, Victor (Dodgers) 251
Garcia, Christian (Yankees) 312
Garcia, Edgar (Phillies) 345
Garcia, Jaime (Cardinals) 375
Gardner, Brett (Yankees) 311
Garrison, Steve (Padres) 394
Gaub, John (Indians) 139
Gee, Dillon (Mets) 296
Geer, Josh (Padres) 391
Gervacio, Samuel (Astros) 201
Getz, Chris (White Sox) 102
Giavotella, Johnny (Royals) 214
Gibson, Derrik (Red Sox) 74
Gillaspie, Conor (Giants) 405
Gillespie, Cole (Brewers) 262
Gillies, Tyson (Mariners) 425
Gilmore, Jon (White Sox) 106
Gindl, Caleb (Brewers) 263
Golson, Greg (Rangers) 460
Gomez, Hector (Rockies) 148
Gomez, Kennil (Rangers) 458
Gomez, Rolando (Angels) 234
Gonzalez, Esmailyn (Nationals) 486
Gonzalez, Gio (Athletics) 325
Gordon, Devaris (Dodgers) 245
Gose, Anthony (Phillies) 344
Graham, Connor (Rockies) 150
Green, Nick (Angels) 236
Green, Scott (Tigers) 169
Green, Taylor (Brewers) 261
Greene, Tyler (Cardinals) 376
Gregerson, Luke (Cardinals) 381
Grossman, Robbie (Pirates) 358
Guerra, Deolis (Twins) 282
Guerra, Javy (Dodgers) 251
Gutierrez, Carlos (Twins) 277
Gutierrez, Daniel (Royals) 212
Guyer, Brandon (Cubs) 87

H

Hagadone, Nick (Red Sox) 67
Hague, Matt (Pirates) 362
Haley, Trey (Indians) 135
Hallberg, Mark (Diamondbacks) 19
Halman, Greg (Mariners) 418
Hamilton, Brandon (Tigers) 172
Hand, Brad (Marlins) 185
Hanigan, Ryan (Reds) 120
Hankerd, Cyle (Diamondbacks) 26
Hanson, Tommy (Braves) 34
Happ, J.A. (Phillies) 342
Harden, Trevor (Diamondbacks) 23
Hart, Kevin (Cubs) 84
Havens, Reese (Mets) 293
Haydel, Lee (Brewers) 264
Hayenga, Keaton (Royals) 221
Hayes, Brett (Marlins) 188
Hefner, Jeremy (Padres) 396
Heisey, Chris (Reds) 122
Hellickson, Jeremy (Rays) 437
Henson, Tyler (Orioles) 57
Heredia, Jairo (Yankees) 310
Hernandez, David (Orioles) 56

Hernandez, Federico (Astros)	202	Johnson, Kris (Red Sox)	72	Manship, Jeff (Twins)	278
Hernandez, Gaby (Mariners)	426	Johnson, Rob (Mariners)	423	Manuel, Robert (Reds)	124
Hernandez, Gorkys (Braves)	35	Johnson, Steven (Dodgers)	247	Manzella, Tommy (Astros)	198
Herndon, David (Angels)	236	Jones, Daryl (Cardinals)	373	Marek, Stephen (Braves)	42
Herrera, Jonathan (Rockies)	155	Joseph, Caleb (Orioles)	61	Marquez, Jeff (White Sox)	106
Herrera, Kelvin (Royals)	214	Jung, Su-Min (Cubs)	93	Marrero, Chris (Nationals)	483
Herron, Tyler (Cardinals)	378			Marshall, Brett (Yankees)	314
Hewitt, Anthony (Phillies)	343	**K**		Marson, Lou (Phillies)	339
Heyward, Jason (Braves)	35			Marte, Jefry (Mets)	292
Hicks, Aaron (Twins)	274	Ka'aihue, Kila (Royals)	213	Marte, Luis (Tigers)	168
Hicks, Brandon (Braves)	38	Kalish, Ryan (Red Sox)	71	Martin, Ethan (Dodgers)	243
Hicks, Chris (Astros)	201	Kang, Kyeong (Rays)	444	Martin, Kyle (Royals)	220
Hicks, Graham (Nationals)	488	Kelley, Shawn (Mariners)	423	Martinez, Carlos (Rockies)	157
Hill, Steven (Cardinals)	379	Kelly, Casey (Red Sox)	68	Martinez, Fernando (Mets)	290
Hinckley, Mike (Nationals)	490	Kennelly, Matt (Braves)	41	Martinez, Joey (Giants)	413
Hinshaw, Alex (Giants)	408	Kibler, Jonathan (Tigers)	169	Martinez, Jose (White Sox)	104
Hissey, Pete (Red Sox)	73	Kieschnick, Roger (Giants)	407	Martinez, Mario (Mariners)	421
Hodges, Wes (Indians)	133	Kiker, Kasey (Rangers)	457	Martis, Shairon (Nationals)	487
Hoes, L.J. (Orioles)	55	Kimbrel, Craig (Braves)	38	Massey, Tyler (Rockies)	151
Hoffmann, Jamie (Dodgers)	250	King, Aaron (Giants)	409	Mateo, Marcos (Cubs)	88
Hoffpauir, Micah (Cubs)	86	King, Stephen (Nationals)	491	Matos, Osiris (Giants)	411
Holcomb, Darin (Rockies)	153	Knapp, Jason (Phillies)	342	Mattair, Travis (Phillies)	346
Holland, Derek (Rangers)	451	Kontos, George (Yankees)	315	Mattheus, Ryan (Rockies)	153
Hollimon, Michael (Tigers)	171	Koshansky, Joe (Rockies)	156	Matusz, Brian (Orioles)	51
Holloway, Jarrod (Astros)	204	Kozma, Pete (Cardinals)	374	Maxwell, Justin (Nationals)	486
Holt, Brad (Mets)	292	Kulbacki, Kellen (Padres)	387	May, Lucas (Dodgers)	252
Hood, Destin (Nationals)	485	Kunz, Eddie (Mets)	294	May, Trevor (Phillies)	348
Hoover, J.J. (Braves)	43			Mayberry Jr., John (Phillies)	347
Horne, Alan (Yankees)	315	**L**		Maybin, Cameron (Marlins)	178
Hosmer, Eric (Royals)	211			Mazzaro, Vin (Athletics)	325
House, T.J. (Indians)	133	Lake, Junior (Cubs)	87	McAllister, Zach (Yankees)	308
Hudson, Dan (White Sox)	107	Lambo, Andrew (Dodgers)	242	McBryde, Mike (Giants)	409
Huff, David (Indians)	131	Lansford, Jared (Athletics)	332	McCardell, Michael (Twins)	284
Huffman, Chad (Padres)	395	LaPorta, Matt (Indians)	129	McCormick, Mike (Rays)	444
Hughes, Luke (Twins)	280	Larish, Jeff (Tigers)	164	McCrory, Bob (Orioles)	58
Humber, Philip (Twins)	284	Latos, Mat (Padres)	387	McCutchen, Andrew (Pirates)	355
Hunt, Shooter (Twins)	277	Lawrie, Brett (Brewers)	259	McCutchen, Daniel (Pirates)	357
Hunter, Brett (Athletics)	329	Leach, Brent (Dodgers)	249	McDonald, James (Dodgers)	243
Hunter, Cedric (Padres)	388	LeBlanc, Wade (Padres)	391	McEachern, Jason (Rays)	445
Hunter, Tommy (Rangers)	456	Lee, Hak-Ju (Cubs)	86	McGeary, Jack (Nationals)	484
Huntzinger, Brock (Red Sox)	77	Lentz, Richie (Red Sox)	75	McGee, Jake (Rays)	437
Hurley, Eric (Rangers)	455	Leon, Arnold (Athletics)	333	McKenry, Michael (Rockies)	149
Hynick, Brandon (Rockies)	154	Leroux, Chris (Marlins)	184	Medlen, Kris (Braves)	37
		Lerud, Steve (Pirates)	361	Meek, Evan (Pirates)	362
I		Lewis, Scott (Indians)	136	Mejia, Jenrry (Mets)	293
		Liebel, Andrew (Blue Jays)	474	Melancon, Mark (Yankees)	309
Infante, Gregory (White Sox)	109	Lillibridge, Brent (White Sox)	101	Meloan, John (Indians)	135
Inman, Will (Padres)	393	Lin, Che-Hsuan (Red Sox)	71	Melville, Tim (Royals)	212
Inoa, Michael (Athletics)	323	Lincoln, Brad (Pirates)	355	Mercer, Jordy (Pirates)	359
Iorg, Cale (Tigers)	163	Lindblom, Josh (Dodgers)	243	Mesoraco, Devin (Reds)	118
Iorg, Eli (Astros)	203	Lindsay, Shane (Rockies)	152	Meyer, Dan (Marlins)	188
Ishikawa, Travis (Giants)	408	Link, Jon (White Sox)	106	Mickolio, Kam (Orioles)	54
Italiano, Craig (Athletics)	331	Lintz, Seth (Brewers)	265	Miclat, Greg (Orioles)	58
		Lo, Chia-Jen (Astros)	199	Middlebrooks, Will (Red Sox)	73
J		Lobstein, Kyle (Rays)	438	Mijares, Jose (Twins)	275
		Locke, Jeff (Braves)	37	Miley, Wade (Diamondbacks)	20
Jackson, Austin (Yankees)	306	Lorin, Brett (Mariners)	428	Miller, Adam (Indians)	129
Jackson, Jay (Cubs)	85	Lotzkar, Kyle (Reds)	116	Miller, Drew (Padres)	396
Jackson, Justin (Blue Jays)	467	Lough, David (Royals)	215	Miller, Justin (Dodgers)	249
Jackson, Steven (Yankees)	317	Luck, Chris (Rays)	442	Miller, Quinton (Pirates)	360
Jacobson, Brett (Tigers)	166	Lucroy, Jonathan (Brewers)	262	Mills, Beau (Indians)	130
James, Brad (Astros)	200	Lugo, Jose (Mariners)	428	Mills, Brad (Blue Jays)	469
Jaramillo, Jason (Pirates)	364	Lutz, Zach (Mets)	295	Miranda, Juan (Yankees)	313
Jaso, John (Rays)	439	Lyles, Jordan (Astros)	196	Mitchell, D.J. (Yankees)	315
Jay, Jon (Cardinals)	374	Lynn, Lance (Cardinals)	376	Mitchell, Matt (Royals)	218
Jefferies, Jake (Rays)	441			Mock, Garrett (Nationals)	486
Jeffress, Jeremy (Brewers)	259	**M**		Montanez, Lou (Orioles)	61
Jennings, Desmond (Rays)	436			Montero, Jesus (Yankees)	307
Jepsen, Kevin (Angels)	228	Madrigal, Warner (Rangers)	455	Montgomery, Mike (Royals)	211
Jeroloman, Brian (Blue Jays)	470	Maestri, Alex (Cubs)	93	Montz, Luke (Nationals)	493
Jimenez, Cesar (Mariners)	425	Magnuson, Trystan (Blue Jays)	475	Moore, Adam (Mariners)	420
Jimenez, Luis (Angels)	235	Maier, Mitch (Royals)	218	Moore, Matt (Rays)	436
Johnson, Chris (Astros)	196	Main, Michael (Rangers)	453	Morales, Angel (Twins)	278
Johnson, Cody (Braves)	39	Maloney, Matt (Reds)	121	Morban, Julio (Mariners)	422

Morel, Brent (White Sox) 105
Morillo, Juan (Rockies) 154
Morlan, Eduardo (Brewers) 265
Morris, Bryan (Pirates) 356
Morrison, Logan (Marlins) 179
Morrison, Ty (Rays) 444
Mortensen, Clayton (Cardinals) 372
Moscoso, Guillermo (Rangers) 458
Moskos, Daniel (Pirates) 361
Motte, Jason (Cardinals) 373
Mount, Ryan (Angels) 231
Moustakas, Mike (Royals) 210
Moviel, Scott (Mets) 295
Mulvey, Kevin (Twins) 277
Murphy, Clark (Rangers) 461
Murphy, Tim (Rangers) 458

N

Navarro, Reynaldo (Diamondbacks) 22
Navarro, Yamaico (Red Sox) 70
Naylor, Drew (Phillies) 343
Neal, Thomas (Giants) 410
Negrych, Jim (Pirates) 363
Nelson, Chris (Rockies) 151
Newby, Kyler (Diamondbacks) 27
Niemann, Jeff (Rays) 438
Niese, Jonathon (Mets) 291
Nieto, Adrian (Nationals) 485
Nieves, Efrain (Brewers) 266
Nix, Jayson (White Sox) 108
Noonan, Nick (Giants) 404
Noriega, Gabriel (Mariners) 425
Norris, Bud (Astros) 195
Norris, Derek (Nationals) 484
Nova, Ivan (Padres) 397
Nunez, Jhonny (White Sox) 104

O

O'Day, Darren (Mets) 300
Odorizzi, Jake (Brewers) 262
Olmos, Edgar (Marlins) 187
O'Malley, Shawn (Rays) 445
Omogrosso, Brian (White Sox) 105
Ortega, Anthony (Angels) 229
Ortiz, Adrian (Royals) 218
O'Sullivan, Sean (Angels) 228
Osuna, Edgar (Braves) 40
Ottavino, Adam (Cardinals) 378
Outman, Josh (Athletics) 326
Overholt, Pat (Phillies) 348
Owen, Dylan (Mets) 300
Ozoria, Jose (Indians) 139

P

Palmisano, Lou (Astros) 205
Paredes, Edward (Mariners) 427
Parker, Blake (Cubs) 92
Parker, Jarrod (Diamondbacks) 18
Parmelee, Chris (Twins) 279
Parnell, Bobby (Mets) 292
Parr, James (Braves) 44
Parra, Gerardo (Diamondbacks) 19
Pastornicky, Tyler (Blue Jays) 475
Patton, Troy (Orioles) 53
Paul, Xavier (Dodgers) 248
Paulino, Felipe (Astros) 197
Peguero, Carlos (Mariners) 422
Peguero, Francisco (Giants) 410
Pelzer, Wynn (Padres) 392
Pena, Francisco (Mets) 298
Pena, Luis (Brewers) 267

Pennington, Cliff (Athletics) 328
Peralta, Wily (Brewers) 266
Perdomo, Luis (Giants) 412
Pereira, Nelson (Pirates) 365
Perez, Chris (Cardinals) 371
Perez, Fernando (Rays) 439
Perez, Luis (Blue Jays) 472
Perez, Martin (Rangers) 452
Perez, Rossmel (Diamondbacks) 24
Perez, Salvador (Royals) 217
Perez, Sergio (Astros) 199
Periard, Alexandre (Brewers) 263
Perry, Ryan (Tigers) 163
Petersen, Bryan (Marlins) 185
Pettit, Chris (Angels) 232
Phelps, Cord (Indians) 137
Pierre, Gustavo (Blue Jays) 473
Pimentel, Julio (Royals) 217
Pimentel, Stolmy (Red Sox) 70
Pineda, Michael (Mariners) 422
Plouffe, Trevor (Twins) 279
Porcello, Rick (Tigers) 162
Poreda, Aaron (White Sox) 99
Portillo, Adys (Padres) 388
Posey, Buster (Giants) 403
Poveda, Omar (Rangers) 459
Pratt, Jordan (Dodgers) 253
Pribanic, Aaron (Mariners) 428
Price, Bryan (Red Sox) 73
Price, David (Rays) 434
Pucetas, Kevin (Giants) 407
Puello, Cesar (Mets) 295
Putnam, Zach (Indians) 136

Q

Quirarte, Edwin (Giants) 411

R

Raben, Dennis (Mariners) 421
Ramirez, Elvin (Mets) 299
Ramirez, J.P. (Nationals) 485
Ramirez, Juan (Mariners) 420
Ramirez, Max (Rangers) 454
Ramirez, Neil (Rangers) 456
Ramirez, Ramon (Reds) 120
Ramirez, Wilkin (Tigers) 164
Ramos, Wilson (Twins) 275
Rasmus, Colby (Cardinals) 370
Ray, Robert (Blue Jays) 472
Raynor, John (Marlins) 182
Reckling, Trevor (Angels) 227
Reddick, Josh (Red Sox) 68
Redding, Jon Michael (Dodgers) 248
Redmond, Todd (Braves) 45
Reifer, Adam (Cardinals) 374
Reimold, Nolan (Orioles) 52
Retherford, C.J. (White Sox) 109
Revere, Ben (Twins) 275
Rhee, Dae-Eun (Cubs) 83
Rhinehart, Bill (Nationals) 488
Rhymes, Will (Tigers) 173
Richard, Clayton (White Sox) 100
Richmond, Scott (Blue Jays) 473
Riordan, Cory (Rockies) 154
Rivas, Amaury (Brewers) 267
Rivero, Carlos (Indians) 132
Rizzo, Anthony (Red Sox) 74
Robertson, David (Yankees) 311
Robertson, Tyler (Twins) 278
Robinson, Derrick (Royals) 216
Robinson, Shane (Cardinals) 380
Robles, Mauricio (Tigers) 171

Rodgers, Chad (Braves) 43
Rodriguez, Aderlin (Mets) 301
Rodriguez, Aneury (Rockies) 152
Rodriguez, Henry (Athletics) 327
Rodriguez, Javier (Mets) 301
Rodriguez, Rafael (Angels) 232
Rodriguez, Rafael (Giants) 405
Rodriguez, Santos (White Sox) 105
Rodriguez, Yorman (Reds) 116
Roe, Chaz (Rockies) 155
Roemer, Wes (Diamondbacks) 26
Roenicke, Josh (Reds) 119
Rogers, Esmil (Rockies) 148
Rohrbough, Cole (Braves) 36
Rollins, Heath (Rays) 440
Romak, Jamie (Pirates) 358
Romero, Deibinson (Twins) 282
Romero, Ricky (Blue Jays) 469
Romine, Andrew (Angels) 234
Romine, Austin (Yankees) 307
Romo, Sergio (Giants) 406
Rondon, Daigoro (Dodgers) 250
Rondon, Hector (Indians) 133
Rosa, Carlos (Royals) 213
Rosa, Jovan (Cubs) 88
Rosales, Adam (Reds) 125
Rosario, Wilin (Rockies) 147
Ross, Robbie (Rangers) 459
Ross, Tyson (Athletics) 328
Rowell, Billy (Orioles) 53
Royster, Ryan (Rays) 441
Runion, Sam (Royals) 220
Russell, Adam (White Sox) 108
Russell, Kyle (Dodgers) 248
Rustich, Brant (Mets) 299
Ryan, Dusty (Tigers) 165
Rzepczynski, Marc (Blue Jays) 469

S

Sadler, Billy (Giants) 413
Salas, Fernando (Cardinals) 377
Salome, Angel (Brewers) 260
Samardzija, Jeff (Cubs) 83
Sample, Tyler (Royals) 215
Sampson, Julian (Phillies) 343
Samuel, Francisco (Cardinals) 378
Sanchez, Gaby (Marlins) 181
Sanchez, Romulo (Pirates) 363
Santana, Carlos (Indians) 128
Santeliz, Clevan (White Sox) 103
Satterwhite, Cody (Tigers) 165
Saunders, Michael (Mariners) 419
Savery, Joe (Phillies) 345
Scarpetta, Cody (Brewers) 264
Schafer, Jordan (Braves) 35
Schafer, Logan (Brewers) 268
Schlehuber, Braeden (Braves) 41
Schlereth, Daniel (Diamondbacks) 19
Schlichting, Travis (Dodgers) 247
Schmidt, Nick (Padres) 394
Seaton, Ross (Astros) 195
Seidel, R.J. (Brewers) 265
Septimo, Leyson (Diamondbacks) 28
Shaw, Bryan (Diamondbacks) 24
Shaw, Scott (Mets) 297
Shelby, John (White Sox) 102
Sheridan, Mike (Rays) 442
Shreve, Colby (Phillies) 349
Silverio, Alfredo (Dodgers) 252
Simmons, James (Athletics) 326
Simons, Zach (Tigers) 172
Sinkbeil, Brett (Marlins) 183
Sipp, Tony (Indians) 134

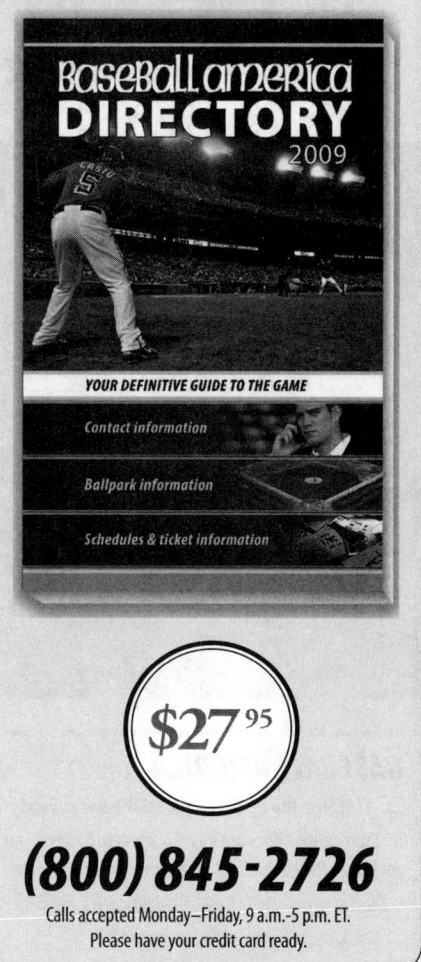